Written by
Kevin Sullivan, Steve Pantaleo, & Keith Elliot Greenberg

ENCYCLOPEDIA

UPDATED & EXPANDED

THE DEFINITIVE GUIDE TO WWE

3RD EDITION

TO THE WWE UNIVERSE:

It is with tremendous pride that we present to you this latest edition of the *WWE Encyclopedia*. The vibrant collection of images and information in your hands represents our most ambitious project to date, as we have delved into the archives of sports-entertainment further than we ever thought possible. The history of our industry features a cast of characters as diverse as the global audience that enjoys them today. Throughout this book, we document the thrills and the excitement they have delivered as well as those who carry on their legacy in today's WWE.

No matter how you choose to enjoy it—as a reference guide, an impressive display piece, a WWE Network viewing companion, or a home for your autograph collection—we hope you find the experience as rewarding as we did creating it.

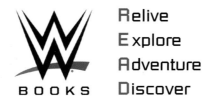

Relive
Explore
Adventure
Discover

BOOKS

LONDON, NEW YORK,
MELBOURNE, AND DELHI

CREDITS

Development Editor
Matt Buchanan

Senior Development Editor
Jennifer Sims

Book Designer
Tim Amrhein

Senior Production Designer
Areva

Production
Beth Guzman

PRIMA GAMES STAFF

VP & Publisher
Mike Degler

Editorial Manager
Tim Fitzpatrick

Design and Layout Manager
Tracy Wehmeyer

Licensing
Christian Sumner
Paul Giacomotto

Marketing
Katie Hemlock

Digital Publishing
Julie Asbury
Tim Cox
Shaida Boroumand

Operations Manager
Stacey Ginther

2016 DK/Prima Games, a division of Penguin Random House LLC. Prima Games® is a registered trademark of Penguin Random House LLC. All rights reserved, including the right of reproduction in whole or in part in any form.

The Prima Games logo and Primagames.com are registered trademarks of Penguin Random House LLC, registered in the United States. Prima Games is an imprint of DK, a division of Penguin Random House LLC, New York.

DK/Prima Games, a division of Penguin Random House LLC
6081 East 82nd Street, Suite #400
Indianapolis, IN 46250

ISBN: 978-1-4654-5313-6

Printing Code: The rightmost double-digit number is the year of the book's printing; the rightmost single-digit number is the number of the book's printing. For example, 16-1 shows that the first printing of the book occurred in 2016.

19 18 17 16   4 3 2 1

001-294686-August/2016

Printed in China.

CONSUMER PRODUCTS

Global Publishing Manager
Steve Pantaleo

Vice President, North American Licensing
Jess Richardson

Executive Vice President, Consumer Products
Casey Collins

PHOTO DEPARTMENT

Josh Tottenham, Frank Vitucci, Georgiana Dallas, Jamie Nelson, Melissa Halladay, Mike Moran, and JD Sestito

ARCHIVES

Archivist
Ben Brown

LEGAL

Vice President, Intellectual Property
Lauren Dienes-Middlen

CREATIVE SERVICES

Senior Vice President, Creative Services
Stan Stanski

Creative Director
John Jones

Senior Art Director
Carla Leighton

Project Managers
Sara Vazquez
Tim Carroll

Cover Designer
Adam McGinnis

CREATIVE WRITING

Michael Kirshenbaum
John Swikata
Chris Scoville
Fernando Acevedo
Johnny Russo
Andrew Lewis
Nick Manfredini
Dave Kapoor
Tom Casiello
Ben Mayer

ABOUT THE AUTHORS

KEVIN SULLIVAN

A graduate of Fairfield University, Kevin Sullivan began his sports-entertainment career in 1998 when he accepted a position within WWE. Over the course of the next decade, he played an integral role in *WWE.com*'s content creation process, most recently as the site's Content Director. He also served as managing editor of WWE's *Raw Magazine*.

Sullivan left WWE on a full-time basis in 2008, but continues to work closely with the company's publishing department. His first book, the *WWE Encyclopedia*, became an instant hit and peaked at No. 8 on the *New York Times* best sellers list. From there, Sullivan teamed with Simon & Schuster to put out *The WWE Championship: A Look Back at the Rich History of the WWE Championship*. The 320-page narrative tracks sports-entertainment's most prestigious prize from its first days in 1963 all the way up to today.

Sullivan also wrote the *New York Times* best-selling *WWE 50* book and co-authored the second edition of the best-selling *WWE Encyclopedia*. Additionally, Sullivan has penned seven children's books for WWE, including biographies on Undertaker, John Cena, and Big Show.

Follow Sullivan on Twitter: @SullivanBooks

STEVE PANTALEO

Steve Pantaleo has worked at WWE for twelve years and currently manages its global publishing business. Not content to leave his literary adventures behind at five o'clock, he moonlights as the author of select WWE Books, drawing from historical knowledge gained as a lifelong fan and honed in over a decade of bringing the WWE brand to shelves in various Consumer Products. Steve is also the author of the *WWE Ultimate Superstar Guide*, *Hustle, Loyalty, and Respect: The World of John Cena*, and three DK Readers. He lives in Seymour, Connecticut, with his wife, Lisa, and energetic two daughters, Samantha and Jillian. In his limited free time, he enjoys a high-tempo exercise routine and watching his beloved New York Mets with stubborn optimism.

KEITH ELLIOT GREENBERG

Keith Elliot Greenberg wrote for WWE's publications for more than 20 years, and co-authored the autobiographies of "Classy" Freddie Blassie and Superstar Billy Graham, as well as the *New York Times* bestselling life story of "Nature Boy" Ric Flair. His work has been seen in *Men's Journal*, the *Village Voice*, *Huffington Post*, *Playboy*, *Maxim*, *Bleacher Report*, *USA Today*, and others. Away from sports-entertainment, his wide list of books includes *December 8, 1980: The Day John Lennon Died* and *Too Fast to Live, Too Young to Die: James Dean's Final Hours*. Greenberg is also a television producer whose stories have appeared on PBS, MSNBC, the History Channel, Discovery ID, TLC, Lifetime and Fox News Channel. He and his family live in Brooklyn, New York.

LEGEND

Articles in this edition of the *WWE Encyclopedia* include height, weight, billed place of origin and signature move(s) for many profiled Superstars. For WWE Hall of Famers and those with Championship resumes, we have also added the below emblems to their profile headers in recognition of these achievements. As you read about your favorite sports-entertainment Superstars, use the below guide for reference.

Among the Championships included are current and defunct WWE titles, the classic World Heavyweight Championship extending through the history of WCW and the NWA, as well as the World Championships of ECW and the AWA. For performers known for celebrated reigns with other titles from sports-entertainment lore, we have done our best to recognize these accomplishments within the body of their profiles.

 WWE Hall of Famer

 WWE World Heavyweight Championship
1963-

 WWE Women's Championship
2016-

 World Heavyweight Championship
NWA World Championship (prior to 1991)
WCW Championship (1991-2001)
World Heavyweight Championship (2002-2013)

 Intercontinental Championship
1979-

 United States Championship
1975-

 WWE Tag Team Championship
2002-

 Women's Championship
1956-2010

 WWE Divas Championship
2008-2016

 NXT Championship
2012-

 NXT Women's Championship
2013-

 NXT Tag Team Championship
2013-

 ECW Championship
1994-2010

 AWA World Championship

 Cruiserweight Championship
1991-2007

 European Championship
1997-2002

 Hardcore Championship
1998-2002

 International Tag Team Championship
1969-1971, 1985

 Junior Heavyweight Championship
1978-1985

 US Tag Team Championship
1963-1967

 World Tag Team Championship
1971-2010

 WWE Light Heavyweight Championship
1997-2001

 WWE Women's Tag Team Championship
1983-1988

3MB

| **MEMBERS** | Heath Slater, Jinder Mahal, & Drew McIntyre | **COMBINED WT** | 692 lbs. |

When Heath Slater's One-Man Band act failed to keep his good times rolling in 2012, the former Tag Team Champion decided to try again with a little help from his friends. With air guitars shredding and the power of 1000 imaginary Marshall stacks behind them, 3MB rocked forward. Jinder Mahal and Drew McIntyre completed the newly formed trio with Slater as its leather-clad front man.

3MB spent nearly two years as a consistent presence in tag team competition, the extra member at ringside serving to pester their opponents. The musical misfits could not capture gold in the form of records or WWE Titles, but their unabashed rock and roll swagger never wavered in rivalries with Los Matadores, The Prime Time Players, and several others.

In 2014, Hornswoggle ditched his leprechaun garb for denim and leather, rocking out as a pseudo-member of 3MB. The eclectic group ultimately disbanded in June of that year when Mahal and McIntyre were released by WWE.

3-MINUTE WARNING

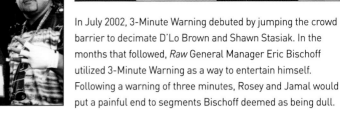

| **MEMBERS** | Rosey & Jamal | **COMBINED WT** | 939 lbs. |

In July 2002, 3-Minute Warning debuted by jumping the crowd barrier to decimate D'Lo Brown and Shawn Stasiak. In the months that followed, *Raw* General Manager Eric Bischoff utilized 3-Minute Warning as a way to entertain himself. Following a warning of three minutes, Rosey and Jamal would put a painful end to segments Bischoff deemed as being dull.

The most memorable moment of 3-Minute Warning's brief WWE career was Billy and Chuck's highly publicized commitment ceremony. Shortly after crashing the festivities, Rosey and Jamal (with Rico) were defeated in a high-profile Elimination Tables Match at *Survivor Series*. The duo never bounced back from the loss and went their separate ways shortly after.

ABE "KNUCKLEBALL" SCHWARTZ

| **HT** | 6'0" | **WT** | 240 lbs. |
| **FROM** | Brooklyn, New York | | |

During the Major League Baseball strike of 1994, WWE did their part in bringing the national pastime to fans when they introduced Abe "Knuckleball" Schwartz (sometimes referred to as MVP). With a baseball painted on his face and sporting a double-zero numbered uniform, Schwartz gave fans a piece of the baseball action they were missing.

Accompanied to the ring by a slightly demonic version of "Take Me Out to the Ball Game," Schwartz had big-league aspirations. Unfortunately for him, however, he struck out when it came to WWE. The closest Schwartz came to fame was competing in a Battle Royal where the two Superstars left standing would battle for the Intercontinental Championship. Schwartz made it halfway through before being eliminated by Owen Hart.

50TH STATE WRESTLING

Because of Hawaii's blend of cultures—western, Polynesian, and Asian—and location between the United States and Japan, the 50th State Wrestling promotion was unlike any other.

The territory was started in 1936 by the "Russian Lion" Al Karasick, who featured stars like Tosh Togo, Oki Shikina, and Ed Francis. Francis took the reins in 1962, running weekly, sold-out shows at the Honolulu Civic Auditorium, as well as Kona, Hilo, and Kauai.

Along with mainstays like Don Muraco, Sam Steamboat, Ripper Collins, and King Curtis Iaukea, cards featured Killer Kowalski, Dick the Bruiser, Dusty Rhodes, Nick Bockwinkel, Freddie Blassie, Bruiser Brody, and Superstar Billy Graham—many of whom were stopping off en route to Japan.

Hawaii's Japanese fans often booed the Americans when they tangled with Nipponese legends like Rikidozan, Shohei Baba, and Antonio Inoki.

High Chief Peter Maivia took charge in 1979, and the name was eventually changed to Pacific Polynesian Wrestling. When Maivia died in 1982, his widow, Lia, took over, highlighting Polynesians like Siva Afi, Superfly Tui, and Farmer Boy Ipo.

ABRAHAM WASHINGTON

| **HT** | 6'2" | **WT** | 220 lbs. |

He may not have matched the thirty-year run of Johnny Carson, but over the course of his seven months on the air, Abraham Washington certainly managed to create a buzz with his late-night talk show. Unfortunately for Washington, the buzz wasn't always positive.

As host of *The Abraham Washington Show* on *ECW*, Washington's self-centered approach to creating compelling conversations continually rubbed audiences the wrong way. And much of what the arrogant host had to say was drowned out by boos, despite Washington's pleading for applause on the show's big screen.

With Tony Atlas as his trusty sidekick, Washington welcomed many of ECW's biggest names to his show, including Tommy Dreamer, Sheamus, and Christian. On nearly every episode, Washington's words successfully irritated his guest. But much to the disdain of the Superstars and fans, the big mouth never backed it up in the ring.

After ECW went off the air in February 2010, Washington briefly managed the teams of Primo & Epico and The Prime Time Players before parting ways with WWE in 2012.

ADAM BOMB

HT	6'6"	**WT**	290 lbs.
FROM	Three Mile Island		
SIGNATURE MOVE	The Meltdown		

WWE faced a nuclear threat starting in May 1993. Introduced to fans by manager Johnny Polo, Adam Bomb was a powerhouse intent on capturing the coveted WWE Championship. But when he failed to win the Title, Adam Bomb relieved Polo of his managerial duties, replacing him with the ever-slippery Harvey Wippleman.

Eventually, Adam Bomb's relationship with Wippleman also soured, much to the delight of the WWE Universe. With the fans firmly in his corner, Adam Bomb battled such villains as King Kong Bundy and Bam Bam Bigelow.

By August 1995, WWE's apocalyptic threat was diffused and Adam Bomb disappeared from the scene. Though he only spent a few years with the organization, he will always be remembered as an unrelenting force in the ring.

ADAM ROSE

HT	6'1"	**WT**	218 lbs.
FROM	Musha Cay, Bahamas		
SIGNATURE MOVE	Party Foul		

When Adam Rose debuted in WWE, he was not just the life of the party—he was the party! Wherever Rose went, fun followed. The flamboyant Superstar brought his signature brand of revelry to WWE arenas proclaiming, "It's party time, all the time."

With his like-minded pack of "Rosebuds" forming a jubilant conga line in his wake, consecutive victories left many believing there were no stops on The Exotic Express. As his psychedelic festivities raged on, no one expected the token party pooper to be Rose himself. Enter The Bunny.

Rose's furry friend once faded into the background with his fellow costume-clad carousers until his bumbling distractions started crimping Rose's style. With momentum fading and his spotlight hijacked by a six-foot tall Peter Cottontail, Rose lashed out. Not even the services of the spicy Rosa Mendes could refuel his fiesta.

"The Radical Mongoose" soon turned toward fellow eccentrics Heath Slater, Bo Dallas, and Curtis Axel. As The Social Outcasts, they plan to turn their collective frustrations around as a cohesive unit.

"ADORABLE" ADRIAN ADONIS

HT	5'11"	**WT**	298 lbs.	**FROM**	New York City, New York
SIGNATURE MOVE	Sleeper Hold				

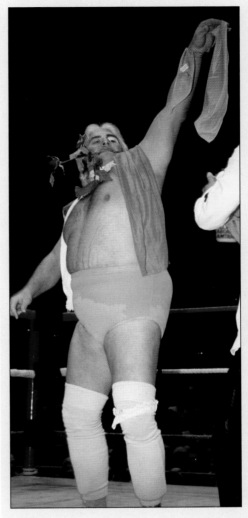

With a nickname of "Adorable," some might expect Adrian Adonis to be a bit soft in the ring. But those people would be dead wrong. Despite displaying an overtly feminine persona later in his career, Adonis was one of the toughest men of his time.

Adonis arrived in WWE in the early 1980s, alongside his Tag Team partner, Jesse "The Body" Ventura. When injuries prevented Ventura from competing regularly, Adonis joined forces with fellow tough man Dick Murdoch. Together, Adonis and Murdoch captured the World Tag Team Championship when they defeated Tony Atlas and Rocky Johnson in April 1984. They held the Titles for nine months before losing to the U.S. Express: Mike Rotundo and Barry Windham.

Following the loss, Adonis's rugged biker persona gave way to a more flamboyant appearance. Despite the effeminate makeover, Adonis remained a force in the ring, as evidenced by his convincing victory over Uncle Elmer at *WrestleMania 2*.

In addition to excelling in the ring, the "Adorable One" also hosted his own interview segment dubbed *The Flower Shop*. Adonis's supposed copycat tactics infuriated *Piper's Pit* host "Rowdy" Roddy Piper, causing the two Superstars to engage in a memorable rivalry. Their conflict culminated in a Hair vs. Hair Match at *WrestleMania III*, which saw Piper get the win and Adonis get a haircut.

AGUILA

HT	5'10"	**WT**	184 lbs.	**FROM**	Guadalajara, Mexico
SIGNATURE MOVE	Moonsault				

Some men spend countless years honing their skills with the hope of one day earning a WWE contract. Not Aguila. In November 1997, the masked man from Mexico made his WWE debut at just 19 years of age. Competing in the first round of the Light Heavyweight Championship tournament, the youngster defeated Super Loco after hitting him with a gravity-defying Moonsault.

Aguila's early success earned him a coveted spot on the *WrestleMania XIV* card, where he challenged Taka Michinoku for the Light Heavyweight Title. Despite coming up short in his quest to claim the gold that night, Aguila and his in-ring aerial expertise successfully won over the imaginations of the capacity crowd in Boston and fans watching worldwide on pay-per-view.

Unfortunately for Aguila, he failed to meet the fans' expectations of him following his *WrestleMania* thriller. He competed in a few more *Raw* matches before finally retiring his mask for good in the spring of 1998.

AHMED JOHNSON

| HT | 6'2" | WT | 305 lbs. | FROM | Pearl River, Michigan |

| SIGNATURE MOVE | Pearl River Plunge |

A powerhouse from the streets of Pearl River, Michigan, Ahmed Johnson proved his worth right from the start when he bodyslammed the mighty Yokozuna during his *Monday Night Raw* debut in October 1995. The success continued for Johnson when he defeated Buddy Landell a few months later at *In Your House: Season's Beatings* in a match that lasted just under 45 seconds.

At the 1996 *King of the Ring*, Johnson made history when he defeated Goldust to become the first African-American Intercontinental Champion. He also formed an alliance with Shawn Michaels to help in HBK's battle against Camp Cornette.

Unfortunately, a serious kidney injury at the hands of Ron "Faarooq" Simmons forced Johnson to vacate the Intercontinental Championship. When he returned, the Pearl River powerhouse engaged in an on-and-off relationship with the Nation of Domination.

Johnson's WWE career ended in 1998. He resurfaced for a brief run in WCW starting in late 1999. Johnson also appeared in the 2001 movie *Too Legit: The MC Hammer Story*.

AJ LEE

| HT | 5'2" | FROM | Union City, New Jersey |

| SIGNATURE MOVE | Black Widow, Shining Wizard |

Dangerous, devious, and devilish, AJ Lee was the type of Diva that would stomp on your heart with a smile on her face and then have you beggingher to do it again.

First seen in WWE on the all-Divas third season of *NXT*, AJ captivated audiences with her spunk and unabashed fandom of geek culture. A ComicCon patron's dream, AJ quickly developed a following in WWE. Though she was eliminated from *NXT* one week before the season finale, fans were delighted to see her back in WWE in the Spring of 2011.

AJ's first infamous moment came at *WrestleMania XXVIII* at the expense of her then love interest, Daniel Bryan. Her unwitting distraction led to Bryan's eighteen-second defeat and the demise of their relationship. An emotional wreck, AJ became romantically linked to several top Superstars in a short time span. Her fractured psyche and fluctuating moods gave her an air of mystery, and soon it was AJ tugging on the heartstrings of others.

Mr. McMahon offered AJ the position of *Raw* General Manager, and after a brief but memorable stint in charge, she was back to her manipulative ways. This time she spurned John Cena's friendship in favor of Dolph Ziggler, and supported the Showoff as he cashed in his Money in the Bank contract the night after *WrestleMania 29*.

Having gained notoriety by the side of several male Superstars, AJ quickly proved that the only person she needed to lean on for success was herself. She struck out on her own, developing an edge and honing her ring skills. On June 16, 2013, AJ topped former friend Kaitlyn to become the fifteenth Divas Champion of all-time. With her deadly Black Widow finishing move, she kept the Title in her clutches for 296 days, breaking the previous record of 212 days. During her historic reign, she instigated a fierce rivalry with the stars of *Total Divas*, sharing some harsh opinions of the reality TV starlets.

AJ Lee retired during her prime in April of 2015, inspiring the hash tag #thankyouaj, which soon trended worldwide.

AJ STYLES

| HT | 5'11" | WT | 218 lbs. | FROM | Gainesville, Georgia | SIGNATURE MOVE | Styles Clash |

When AJ Styles entered the 2016 Royal Rumble, spectators who'd been following his international exploits erupted.

The celebrated high flier had held the prestigious IWGP Heavyweight Championship in Japan, and been a star in Mexico and the North American independent scene. Steve Austin, Bret Hart, and Mick Foley were among the WWE Hall of Famers who applauded the acquisition.

Chris Jericho was also purported to be a fan, but wanted to test Styles in the ring. The pair engaged in a series of matches, and tried teaming up. But when they couldn't win on *Raw*, Jericho attacked his partner.

On the night after *WrestleMania 32*, Styles pinned his bitter rival in a Fatal 4-Way match on *Raw*, declaring that a new era was officially beginning.

AKSANA

HT	5'6"	FROM	Alytus, Lithuania
SIGNATURE MOVE		Spinebuster	

A former bodybuilder and model, this Lithuanian beauty broke into WWE by way of *NXT* Season 3. Facing immigration issues, she baited a love-struck Goldust into marriage to finalize her passage into the United States. The cold-hearted play was a sign of things to come.

Aksana used her raven hair, impossible curves, and flirtatious nature to render Theodore Long smitten. Her seductive power over the *SmackDown* GM helped to advance her career. Once he served his purpose, she promptly dumped him for the younger Antonio Cesaro.

Determined to prove she was more than just a leather-clad temptress, Aksana excelled in the Divas division. She boasts victories over several former Divas Champions including Layla, Kaitlyn, Natalya, and both Bella Twins. In 2013, she supported AJ Lee's anti-*Total Divas* crusade, then months later competed for the Divas Championship at *WrestleMania 30*. Allied with Alicia Fox as one half of the formidable "Foxsana," she continued to clash with WWE's top Divas. After Fox severed the partnership, Aksana left WWE.

AL PEREZ

HT	6'1"	WT	245 lbs.	FROM	Tampa, Florida
SIGNATURE MOVE		German Suplex			

Al Perez began wrestling as an amateur in high school and became one of the top athletes in the state of Florida. Trained by the famed Boris Malenko, he made his pro debut in 1982 and established himself in the mid-1980s as "The Latin Heartthrob" in World Class Championship Wrestling. In 1989, Perez arrived in WWE with hopes of becoming a major championship contender.

Perez's WWE tenure saw him battle the likes of the Brooklyn Brawler, Koko B. Ware, and Bret Hart. Unfortunately for Perez, he was unable to gain any true momentum, and in the beginning of 1990, he left WWE. Perez spent the rest of the decade competing in independent promotions throughout the United States before retiring in 2002.

AL SNOW

HT	6'1"	WT	235 lbs.	FROM	Lima, Ohio
SIGNATURE MOVE		Snowplow			

Al Snow's quirky persona made him stand out and brought him success. Despite owning impressive in-ring skills, the delusional Superstar's actions oftentimes made fans scratch their heads, especially when he would talk to his "Head," the mannequin cranium he would keep at ringside for inspiration.

While competing in ECW, Snow developed a close relationship with Head. He'd found him close to the ECW Arena during Philadelphia's famed Mummers Parade, and adopted him as his own. The popularity of Snow and Head eventually caught the attention of WWE. With Head in tow, Snow moved to WWE in 1998, where he became an immediate fixture in the budding hardcore division.

Using the experience he gained while competing in ECW, Snow went on to capture WWE's Hardcore Championship six times. In November 1999, Snow teamed with the equally deranged Mankind to capture the World Tag Team Championship. While the reign only lasted four days, it remains one of the brightest moments of Snow's WWE career.

ALBERT

HT	6'7"	WT	331 lbs.	FROM	Boston, Massachusetts
SIGNATURE MOVE		Baldo Bomb			

When Albert first stepped foot in a WWE arena in April 1999, fans couldn't help but be taken by the big man's multiple piercings and wealth of body hair. But once the bell rang, Albert's unique appearance was soon overshadowed by his incredible domination in the ring.

After a brief union with Test as part of the T&A tag team, Albert joined forces with Justin Credible and X-Pac to form X-Factor. It was as a member of the outlandish faction that Albert arguably enjoyed his greatest success. And in June 2001, he defeated Kane to capture the Intercontinental Championship.

Following X-Factor's disbanding, Albert linked up with Scotty 2 Hotty and Paul Heyman before ultimately leaving WWE in November 2004. He briefly returned to WWE rings eight years later and, while dominant, his greatest contributions upon returning actually came after retiring from active competition. Albert (now known as Matt Bloom) went on to become a NXT announcer and the Head Coach to the Superstars of tomorrow at the WWE Performance Center.

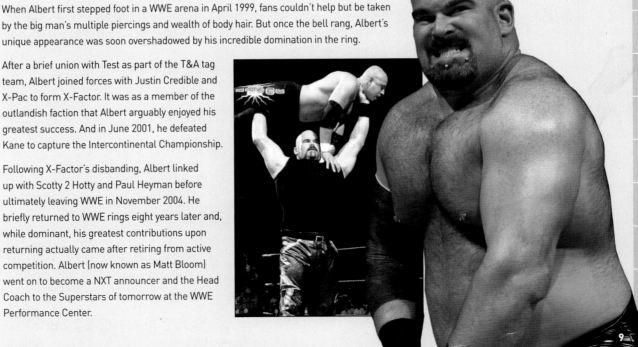

ALBERTO DEL RIO

HT	6'5"	**WT**	239 lbs.	**FROM** San Luis Potosi, Mexico
SIGNATURE MOVE		Cross Armbreaker		

His name is Alberto Del Rio...but you already knew that. As the son of Mexican legend Dos Caras and nephew of WWE Hall of Famer Mil Mascaras, this "Man of Destiny" arrived in 2010 flaunting an endless supply of resources. With the temerity to employ a personal ring announcer, Ricardo Rodriguez, Del Rio was easy to loathe.

The elitist quickly shelved top stars such as Rey Mysterio and Christian with his debilitating Cross Armbreaker. With an increasing sense of entitlement, Del Rio backed up his boasts by winning the largest Royal Rumble Match in WWE history in 2011 by outlasting thirty-nine other WWE Superstars. That July, Alberto took another step toward fulfilling his destiny by capturing the WWE Championship Money in the Bank briefcase. He then cashed in his WWE Title opportunity and defeated an exhausted CM Punk at *SummerSlam 2011*. After losing to John Cena at *Night of Champions*, the "Essence of Excellence" regained the Title in the first-ever Triple Threat Hell in a Cell Match, proving he was no fluke.

In 2012, Del Rio pursued the World Heavyweight Championship. Despite several close calls, the aristocrat fell short of his goal. Then in January 2013, his persistence paid off when he toppled reigning Champion Big Show in a Last Man Standing Match. This valiant climb to the top and subsequent Title reign altered perceptions of Del Rio. His efforts embodied the American Dream, an ideal he defended successfully against Jack Swagger at *WrestleMania 29*.

These warm feelings, however, soon faded. His dastardly actions against Dolph Ziggler at *Payback 2013* and callous dismissal of Ricardo Rodriguez revealed Del Rio's true colors. Fans clamored for someone to rip the gold from his waist. That someone was John Cena at *Hell in a Cell 2013*. The following summer, Alberto's WWE career went on hiatus, but the four-time World Champion would be back.

At *Hell in a Cell 2015*, during John Cena's United States Championship Open Challenge, Alberto Del Rio revealed himself as Cena's shocking mystery opponent. As dangerous as ever, alongside his former enemy Zeb Colter, Del Rio stunned the Los Angeles crowd as well as Cena. Since this triumphant return, the privileged one has formed the League of Nations with Sheamus, Rusev, and King Barrett, while trading U.S. gold in thrilling encounters with Kalisto. Alberto and the League of Nations bested The New Day in a Six-Man Tag Team Match at *WrestleMania 32*.

ALDO MONTOYA

HT	6'1"	**WT**	225 lbs.	**FROM** Portugal

Clad in his country's colors of green, red, and yellow, Aldo Montoya arrived in WWE to much fanfare in 1994. Dubbed the "Portuguese Man O' War," the proud Superstar from Portugal used his quickness to baffle foes.

Eventually, Superstars were able to scout Montoya's speed and counter his offense. As a result, it wasn't long before the Portuguese Superstar found himself getting tossed around the ring by larger, more skilled opponents like Vader and Goldust.

As the losses began to mount, people began to tease Montoya, saying the mask he wore resembled an athletic supporter. Montoya was never able to attain the level of success many expected from him; by 1997, he began to compete in fewer matches before disappearing from WWE completely.

ALEXA BLISS

HT	5'1"	**FROM**	Columbus, Ohio
SIGNATURE MOVE		Sparkle Splash	

As the self-professed "glitter queen" of NXT, Alexa Bliss taught foes that behind her scintillating exterior was a volcanic drive for perfection.

A fan of WWE legends Trish Stratus and Rey Mysterio, Bliss became a competitive athlete at age five, participating in kickboxing, gymnastics, softball, competitive bodybuilding, and Division I cheerleading.

In 2014, her taste for bling drew her toward NXT gold when she defeated then-Women's Champion Sasha Banks in a non-Title match. She'd later pursue Bayley for the Championship, as well. Aligning herself with Blake and Murphy, she helped the tandem hold onto their NXT Tag Team Championship on several occasions during their nearly seven-month reign in 2015. But her ultimate goal, according to Bliss, is ornamenting herself in WWE gold.

ALEX RILEY

HT	6'3"	**WT**	236 lbs.	**FROM** Washington, D.C.
SIGNATURE MOVE		Implant DDT		

Alex Riley began as an aspiring Superstar on season two of *NXT*. Today he is one of WWE's most well rounded Superstars. Riley's charismatic personality and communications background served him well in a transition from competing to commentating, earning him the nickname "The Analyst."

Riley's true passion, however, lies within the WWE ropes. The former college jock assisted The Miz as he defended the WWE Championship against John Cena at *WrestleMania XXVII*. When Cena eventually secured the gold from Miz, Riley became an easy scapegoat for his former *NXT* mentor.

Rather than sitting back and accepting Miz's verbal assault, Riley struck back, much to the delight of the WWE Universe. Free of Miz's demeaning leadership, Riley picked up several huge victories, including a feel-good win over The Miz at *Capitol Punishment 2011*.

For a while, Riley seemed relegated to microphone duty, but the determined Superstar thrilled the WWE Universe once again in 2015 by returning to the ring on *NXT*.

ALEXIS SMIRNOFF

HT	6'3"	**WT**	255 lbs.	**FROM** Russia
SIGNATURE MOVE		Heart Punch		

Entering WWE in the early 1980s, Alexis Smirnoff used his "Mad Russian" persona to strike fear into audiences nationwide, while his paralyzing Heart Punch instilled terror through WWE locker rooms.

Though his WWE legacy will never equal that of fellow Russians Ivan Koloff and Nikolai Volkoff, Smirnoff is remembered for setting lofty goals for himself. Upon entering the promotion, Smirnoff immediately sought out the top stars, which resulted in memorable matches with WWE Hall of Famers Andre the Giant, Pedro Morales, Rocky Johnson, and Ivan Putski.

Smirnoff left WWE in 1986. He went on to compete in Japan and for the AWA before ultimately retiring from full-time competition in 1988.

ALICIA FOX

| HT | 5'9" | FROM | Ponte Vedra Beach, Florida |
| SIGNATURE MOVE | Scissors Kick |

Since her WWE debut in 2008 as the wedding planner for Edge and Vickie Guerrero, Alicia Fox has turned heads and opened eyes. Her versatile in-ring arsenal has served her well, highlighted by her signature Scissors Kick that cuts opponents down to size.

In the summer of 2010, "Foxy" bested three of WWE's top female Superstars to become the first-ever African-American woman to become Divas champion. After a two-month reign, Alicia remained a top competitor in the Diva's division but grew frustrated after enduring consecutive years without the gold.

Her fuse burned out after the Divas Invitational at *WrestleMania 30* and subsequent losses to Paige. Fox's post-match meltdowns inspired anyone within arm's reach to run for cover. Despite this emotional maelstrom, Fox has had no shortage of allies. Paige, Aksana, and The Bellas have all benefited by befriending the feisty Superstar. As one-third of Team Bella, Alicia and her twin allies outfoxed several formidable competitors. On the *WrestleMania 32* pre-show, Fox and her *Total Divas* castmates prevailed over B.A.D. and Blonde in a 10-Superstar Tag Team Match.

THE ALLIANCE

This menagerie came together in July 2001 as members of Shane McMahon's newly acquired WCW joined forces with Paul Heyman and ECW in the hopes of eliminating WWE. Shane broke a pact he made with his father to keep ECW out of WWE, leading to the violent unison of two one-time corporate rivals with WWE serving as their common enemy. As ECW and WCW stood tall together in the ring, Shane dropped another bombshell when he introduced the new owner of ECW, his sister Stephanie McMahon-Helmsley.

Despite Mr. McMahon's son and daughter turning their backs on WWE, the conflict's most shocking moment was arguably at the *Invasion* pay-per-view when Stone Cold Steve Austin betrayed WWE and became the Alliance leader. The callous trio of Shane, Stephanie, and Paul Heyman devised plans for Austin and his followers to carry out. At *Survivor Series 2001*, this war was finally settled as Team WWE defeated Team Alliance in a Winner Take-all 10-man Tag Team Elimination Match. With the victory, WWE survived yet another hostile takeover attempt from its most threatening competition.

ALLIED POWERS

| MEMBERS | British Bulldog & Lex Luger | COMBINED WT | 525 lbs. |

Fate brought these two pillars of strength together during a January 1995 episode of *Monday Night Raw*. History repeated itself as England's British Bulldog and America's Lex Luger combined forces and battled Ted DiBiase's Million Dollar Corporation. The duo became World Tag Team Title contenders after an impressive win at *WrestleMania XI* over Jacob and Eli Blu.

Despite heated bouts with then-World Tag Team Champions Owen Hart and Yokozuna, British Bulldog and Lex Luger were unable to win the Tag Titles. That August saw a sad turn of events take place during *Monday Night Raw*. When Luger couldn't compete due to a sudden family emergency, Bulldog recruited Diesel to be his partner. After the make-shift duo lost in a valiant effort, British Bulldog turned on Diesel. Unaware of his partner's actions, Luger returned days before *SummerSlam* expecting to reconnect with his partner. To the disappointment of WWE fans all over the world, the Allied Powers were no more. The British Bulldog joined the ranks of Camp Cornette.

ALL-STAR WRESTLING VANCOUVER

With its prominence on satellite TV, Vancouver-based All-Star Wrestling was seen all over Canada. This meant that viewers as far away as Ontario were familiar with announcer Ed Karl reading postcards from fans, a group of cheerleaders in the stands who called themselves the Vancouver Pacesetters, and promoter and main eventer Al Tomko showcasing his strength by tearing phone books and license plates. In one unforgettable interview, Roddy Piper demonstrated his toughness by breaking a beer bottle on his head.

Gene Kiniski and Sandor Kovac purchased the promotion in 1968, and engaged in regular talent exchanges with Portland promoter Don Owen. Tomko, a former Winnipeg promoter for the AWA, bought out Kovac in 1977.

Among the stars seen in towns all over British Columbia—including Kerrisdale, Cologne and Abbotsford—were Don Leo Jonathan, John Tolos, Dutch Savage, and Whipper Billy Watson in the 1960s, and Seigfried Steinke, Tiger Jeet Singh, Iron Sheik, and Dean Higuchi (a.k.a. Dean Ho) in the 1970s.

Eventually, fans tired of seeing Tomko in high-profile matches, and the territory closed in 1989.

ALUNDRA BLAYZE

HT	5'10"
FROM	Tampa, Florida
SIGNATURE MOVE	Bridging German Suplex

Alundra Blayze's dangerous combination of athleticism and sex appeal made her the ultimate female force in WWE's women's division, as evidenced by her December 1993 victory over Heidi Lee Morgan to crown a new Women's Champion. With the newly-reintroduced Title in tow, the buxom blonde went on to dominate the division for nearly one year before being toppled by Bull Nakano in November 1994.

Early the next year, Blayze gained revenge when she upended Nakano on *Monday Night Raw* to regain the Women's Championship. Unfortunately, however, she was derailed by yet another colossal competitor when Bertha Faye defeated Blayze at *SummerSlam 1995*. The loss to Faye proved to be just a blip on the screen, as Blayze recaptured the gold less than two months later.

Blayze held the Women's Championship until December 1995 when she defected to WCW. In one of the most infamous moments in the history of the Monday Night War, Blayze's WCW debut saw her throw the WWE Women's Championship in a garbage can on *Monday Nitro*.

While with WCW, Blayze (then known as Madusa) went on to capture the Cruiserweight Championship when she defeated Evan Karagias at *Starrcade 1999*.

Blayze's impact on women's wrestling was recognized in March 2015 when she was inducted into the WWE Hall of Fame.

AMERICAN ALPHA

MEMBERS	Jason Jordan & Chad Gable	COMBINED WT	447 lbs.

Evoking memories of the Varsity Club in WCW and World's Greatest Tag Team in WWE, Jason Jordan and Chad Gable are a blue chip combination channeling amateur triumphs toward professional eminence.

Jordan was offered the opportunity to play professional baseball, but chose instead to wrestle at Indiana University, where he was a three-time NCAA Division I qualifier. Gable represented the United States in the 2012 Olympics.

It was Gable who decided to merge forces with Jordan in NXT. Although initially standoffish, Jordan became fully convinced following a win over The Ascension, after the hulking duo had been elevated to the WWE roster. When Jordan and Gable toppled former NXT Tag Team Champions, the Vaudevillians, in 2016, they adopted the moniker "American Alpha." At *NXT Takeover: Dallas* American Alpha defeated The Revival to capture their 1st NXT Tag Team Championships.

AMY WEBER

FROM	Mapleton, Illinois

In November 2004, a few months after falling short in the *Raw* Diva Search, Amy Weber was hired as the image consultant for WWE Champion JBL. Realizing that image is everything, JBL turned to Amy, who played the scorching hot babe in Toby Keith's "Whiskey Girl" video, to make him look good at all times.

Amy excelled at her job until February 2005 when she accidentally shot JBL in the face with a tranquilizer gun. The mishap was too much for her to overcome. The following week, JBL fired her and she was never heard from again. While Amy's stay in WWE was brief, she was undefeated in the ring. She won her only match by forfeit because JBL kidnapped her opponent before the match.

ANDRE THE GIANT

see page 14

ANGELO "KING KONG" MOSCA

HT	6'4"	WT	319 lbs.	FROM	Toronto, Ontario, Canada
SIGNATURE MOVE	Sleeper				

Before his career in the ring, Angelo Mosca played fourteen seasons as a defensive tackle in the Canadian Football League and was a five-time Grey Cup winner. A regular in the Stampede and Montreal territories, "King Kong" debuted in WWE in 1970.

Through the 1970s, Mosca toured the NWA and AWA, winning several singles and tag team Titles. "King Kong" returned to WWE in 1981 and immediately became a top contender for Bob Backlund's WWE Championship.

As the mid-1980s approached, Mosca traded in his boots for a microphone and became part of the WWE announce team. The foray into announcing proved to be a short one, as in 1985, Mosca shifted his focus to managing the ring career of his son, Angelo Mosca, Jr.

ANGELO MOSCA, JR.

WT	230 lbs.	FROM	Boston, Massachusetts
SIGNATURE MOVE		Flying Cross Body	

Trained and managed by his legendary father, Angelo Mosca, Angelo Mosca, Jr. certainly had big shoes to fill upon entering the sports-entertainment industry in the early 1980s, and he didn't disappoint. The younger Mosca caught the attention of the entire industry when he defeated "The Russian Bear" Ivan Koloff for the Mid-Atlantic Heavyweight Championship on two separate occasions in 1984.

Mosca made his WWE debut in late 1984. His father served as his manager, but was unable to bring the young Mosca much success. He left WWE in April 1985 and went on to compete mainly in Canada, where he once again defeated Ivan Koloff for gold, this time the NWA Canadian Heavyweight Championship, in June 1984.

ANGELO SAVOLDI

FROM Hoboken, New Jersey

Spending the majority of his career competing at approximately 210 pounds, Angelo Savoldi was a true trailblazer for today's cruiserweights. Savoldi made his professional debut in New York in 1937. Over the next several decades, he competed in main events in Puerto Rico and Boston, but it was in Oklahoma where he attained his greatest notoriety, capturing the National Wrestling Alliance World Junior Heavyweight Championship on three occasions.

Savoldi didn't enter WWE until the 1970s, which was well after his prime. However, that didn't stop him from being a force within the promotion. Realizing his competitive days were behind him, Savoldi began training many of WWE's younger Superstars. He even became a minority partner in the company, which was owned by Vincent J. McMahon at the time.

In 1984, Savoldi and his sons Mario, Joe, and Tom formed the Boston-based International Championship Wrestling. The promotion boasted an impressive roster of future WWE Superstars, including Mick Foley, Chris Candido, and Tazz.

ANONYMOUS RAW GENERAL MANAGER

Over the course of *Monday Night Raw*'s record-breaking history, some of sports-entertainment's greatest names have steered the ship, including Ric Flair, Eric Bischoff, and Stephanie McMahon.

On June 21, 2010, another authority figure was added to the list of *Raw* leaders. However, that person would remain nameless for over two years as he chose to run the show anonymously.

Ruling from afar, the mysterious GM sent instructions to the show via e-mail. Messages were then relayed to the audience via Michael Cole, prompting a resounding chorus of boos from the WWE Universe. It was never clear, however, whether the animosity was meant solely for Cole or the Anonymous *Raw* General Manger's rulings.

The GM's erratic and controversial decisions left Superstars and spectators befuddled. Then on *Raw*'s 1000th episode, it was revealed to be Hornswoggle behind the shenanigans the entire time. The shocking revelation eased the mass confusion—temporarily. On *Raw*'s "Cyber Monday" in 2014, the Anonymous GM returned for one night and the identity of this individual is still unknown.

ANTONINO ROCCA

see page 16

ANTONIO INOKI

HoF

HT	6'2"	**WT**	240 lbs.
FROM	Yokohama, Japan		

Antonio Inoki is an iconic figure in Japan's professional wrestling and martial arts scene. But what many fans may not realize is that he also competed in some of WWE's most controversial Title matches. While on tour of Japan in 1979, WWE Champion Bob Backlund lost to Inoki in a shocking upset. The following night, Backlund cashed in his rematch clause and regained the WWE Championship. However, to further complicate matters, outside interference in the rematch caused then-WWE President Hisashi Shinma to return the Title to Inoki. The Japanese legend refused to accept the Title in such a manner, resulting in the WWE Championship being briefly vacated. Back in the United States, Backlund won a match to reclaim the vacated WWE Championship. As a result of the controversies surrounding the series of matches, WWE later chose not to recognize the Title changes.

A few years prior to the controversial Championship matches, the Japanese star gained worldwide exposure when he battled Muhammad Ali in a Boxer vs. Wrestler Match. The restricting rules of the encounter heavily diminished Inoki's offensive arsenal. After fifteen rounds of action (or inaction), the match ended in a draw. Over the next twenty-two years, Inoki remained a dominant force in sports-entertainment as the head of New Japan Pro Wrestling. In March 2010, Inoki celebrated the 50th anniversary of his first match and took his place in the WWE Hall of Fame.

THE APA

MEMBERS	Faarooq & Bradshaw
COMBINED WT	574 lbs.

These Superstars first came together as members of Hell's Henchmen, but then fell under the spell of Undertaker's Ministry of Darkness. The Acolytes won their first World Tag Team Championship from Kane and X-Pac in May 1999. After they went on their own, they formed the Acolytes Protection Agency, or APA for short. JBL's enterprising mind concocted the idea after the Mean Street Posse paid them in return for protection.

As the roughnecks' reputation grew, so did their business. They operated from a backstage "office," which was secluded by a standing doorframe and not much else, and could often be found puffing on cigars, playing cards, and downing beers. If you had the money, they had the time to keep you protected. The bruising brawlers also continued their success in the ring. In total, they won three World Tag Team Championships. The APA lived by a simple company motto, "Drink and Fight," which was taken literally at *Vengeance 2003* when they hosted a Bar Room Brawl.

When Bradshaw became immersed in Wall Street, the APA separated but has reformed on occasion. At the *Raw 15th Anniversary*, they beat Carlito and Jonathan Coachman for Hornswoggle. They rushed to Lita's aid at *Raw 1000* and in 2015, sided with the nWo and DX against The Ascension. Faarooq and JBL are still close buddies, and for the right price, can always reunite to provide their protection services.

ANDRE THE GIANT

HT	7'4"
WT	540 lbs.
FROM	Grenoble, France

SIGNATURE MOVE
Sitdown Splash

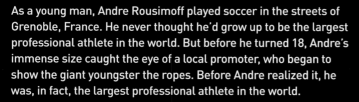

As a young man, Andre Rousimoff played soccer in the streets of Grenoble, France. He never thought he'd grow up to be the largest professional athlete in the world. But before he turned 18, Andre's immense size caught the eye of a local promoter, who began to show the giant youngster the ropes. Before Andre realized it, he was, in fact, the largest professional athlete in the world.

Audiences awed at Andre's amazing size, remarkable agility, and immeasurable strength. And unlike most big men, he could even throw dropkicks and leap from the top rope. Since most of his singles matches were lopsided affairs, he was often showcased in Handicap Matches against two, three, or even four opponents. Soon his fame reached the lights of Paris and he adopted the name "Monster" Eiffel Tower.

Andre traveled to Japan in 1969 where he frightened everyone as "Monster" Rousimoff. While there, doctors diagnosed him with Acromegaly, commonly known as "Giantism," an endocrinological disease that causes one to grow at an accelerated rate beyond the age of physical maturity.

WORLDWIDE FAME

After a successful Asian tour, Andre began competing in Canada. Though wrestling was broken down into regional territories at the time, the Canadian fans knew exactly who the 500-pound newcomer was. Andre was quickly becoming the world's most popular attraction and had earned the nickname "The Eighth Wonder of the World," a moniker that stayed with him his entire career.

In 1971, Andre met with Vince McMahon Sr., and was contracted to work in WWE. On March 26, 1973, he debuted in Madison Square Garden and for the first time was called Andre the Giant. During the 1970s, Andre broke into the mainstream. In 1974, he turned down a lucrative contract offer from the National Football League's Washington Redskins to remain in the squared circle. Soon Hollywood knocked on his door and he appeared on television programs including *The Tonight Show*, *The Merv Griffin Show*, and in 1975 he made his acting debut as Bigfoot on *The Six Million Dollar Man*.

At the 1976 *Showdown at Shea*, Andre fought the 6'5" "Bayonne Bleeder" Chuck Wepner in a Boxer vs. Wrestler Match. Wepner looked like a mere toddler next to Andre and ended up being launched into the third-row seats. In 1980 Andre returned to Shea for another epic showdown. This time, he defeated Hulk Hogan, who at the time wore a cape and retained the services of manager "Classy" Freddie Blassie.

Andre continued to travel the world and briefly appeared in the territories of the National Wrestling Alliance, where he held several regional tag team Championships. When he returned to WWE, the feared Killer Kahn was waiting for him. During their May 1981 match, Kahn jumped from the top rope and broke Andre's ankle, putting him out of action. Andre recovered and got retribution when he defeated his attacker in a Mongolian Stretcher Match in November 1981.

By the mid '80s, Andre was embroiled in a bitter rivalry with the Heenan Family. In an attempt to strip Andre of his dignity, Big John Studd, Ken Patera, and Bobby Heenan ganged up on the giant, beating him unconscious then cutting his hair.

Fueled by revenge, Andre first took out The Olympic Strongman before turning his attention toward Big John Studd. The two towering Superstars fought over which was sports-entertainment's true giant. Their rivalry culminated at the first-ever *WrestleMania* when Andre defeated Big John Studd in a $15,000 Body Slam Challenge. Unfortunately for Andre, the victory was somewhat bittersweet, as an outraged Heenan jumped into the ring and took the bag of money from Andre.

At *WrestleMania 2*, Andre added another victory to his record-setting number of Battle Royal wins when he last eliminated The Hart Foundation from the 20-man WWE/NFL Battle Royal. Outlasting the likes of Bruno Sammartino, Iron Sheik, and Pedro Morales, as well as the NFL's William "The Refrigerator" Perry, Jimbo Covert, and Ernie Holmes served as a reminder that Andre truly was the entire sports world's most dominant figure.

In 1986, Andre was suspended by then-President Jack Tunney for uncharacteristically not appearing at matches. While he served his suspension under strong protest, a three-man team from Japan called The Machines debuted. Their largest member, Giant Machine, became the target of a witch hunt conceived by Bobby Heenan, who was convinced the massive masked newcomer was actually Andre the Giant. After battling with the Heenan Family, the Machines left WWE and their identities were never discovered.

WINNING A TITLE BY ANY MEANS NECESSARY

After co-starring in the 1987 hit movie *The Princess Bride*, Andre returned to WWE with a new attitude foreign to longtime fans. No longer was he the lovable giant with the contagious smile. Instead, Andre adopted a dark demeanor and began employing the managerial services of the loathed Bobby Heenan. With "The Brain" by his side, Andre appeared on *Piper's Pit* to issue a challenge to supposed friend Hulk Hogan for a WWE Championship Match at *WrestleMania III*.

In front of a record-breaking 93,173 fans at the Pontiac Silverdome, Andre attempted to end the more than three-year reign of Hogan. But in the end, the power of Hulkamania bested Andre, who saw his fifteen-year undefeated streak shattered.

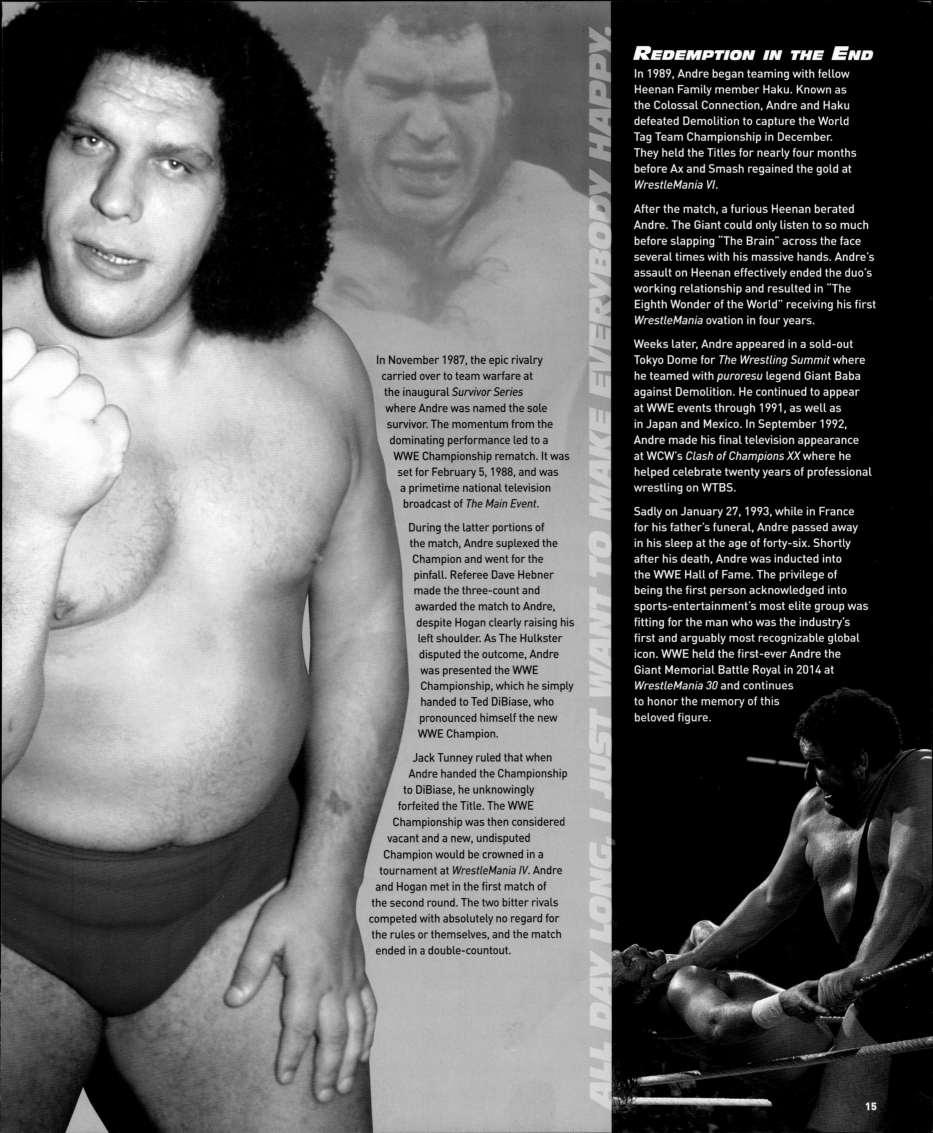

In November 1987, the epic rivalry carried over to team warfare at the inaugural *Survivor Series* where Andre was named the sole survivor. The momentum from the dominating performance led to a WWE Championship rematch. It was set for February 5, 1988, and was a primetime national television broadcast of *The Main Event*.

During the latter portions of the match, Andre suplexed the Champion and went for the pinfall. Referee Dave Hebner made the three-count and awarded the match to Andre, despite Hogan clearly raising his left shoulder. As The Hulkster disputed the outcome, Andre was presented the WWE Championship, which he simply handed to Ted DiBiase, who pronounced himself the new WWE Champion.

Jack Tunney ruled that when Andre handed the Championship to DiBiase, he unknowingly forfeited the Title. The WWE Championship was then considered vacant and a new, undisputed Champion would be crowned in a tournament at *WrestleMania IV*. Andre and Hogan met in the first match of the second round. The two bitter rivals competed with absolutely no regard for the rules or themselves, and the match ended in a double-countout.

REDEMPTION IN THE END

In 1989, Andre began teaming with fellow Heenan Family member Haku. Known as the Colossal Connection, Andre and Haku defeated Demolition to capture the World Tag Team Championship in December. They held the Titles for nearly four months before Ax and Smash regained the gold at *WrestleMania VI*.

After the match, a furious Heenan berated Andre. The Giant could only listen to so much before slapping "The Brain" across the face several times with his massive hands. Andre's assault on Heenan effectively ended the duo's working relationship and resulted in "The Eighth Wonder of the World" receiving his first *WrestleMania* ovation in four years.

Weeks later, Andre appeared in a sold-out Tokyo Dome for *The Wrestling Summit* where he teamed with *puroresu* legend Giant Baba against Demolition. He continued to appear at WWE events through 1991, as well as in Japan and Mexico. In September 1992, Andre made his final television appearance at WCW's *Clash of Champions XX* where he helped celebrate twenty years of professional wrestling on WTBS.

Sadly on January 27, 1993, while in France for his father's funeral, Andre passed away in his sleep at the age of forty-six. Shortly after his death, Andre was inducted into the WWE Hall of Fame. The privilege of being the first person acknowledged into sports-entertainment's most elite group was fitting for the man who was the industry's first and arguably most recognizable global icon. WWE held the first-ever Andre the Giant Memorial Battle Royal in 2014 at *WrestleMania 30* and continues to honor the memory of this beloved figure.

HT	6'0"
WT	224 lbs.
FROM	Buenos Aires, Argentina

SIGNATURE MOVE
The Argentine Backbreaker

Antonino Rocca was one of the most beloved heroes of all-time. His amazing array of maneuvers astounded millions around the world, and his signature repertoire has proven to be timeless. His influence has transcended generations and cultures, which is a testament to the quality of man and the limitless scope of his vision. Rocca is credited with bringing past fans back to sports-entertainment and welcoming new ones, as well as being one of the greatest innovators in the history of the art form. He was one of the biggest stars responsible for the sport's first "Golden Age." His fearless nature in the ring ushered in a new style that high-flyers of the squared circle will surely study forever.

Born in Trevino, Italy, this trailblazer grew up in Argentina and started his career in professional sports as a soccer player. When a leg injury ended his career, he yearned for another outlet to showcase his charisma, heart, and unparalleled athleticism. Trained by Stanislaus Zbyszko, Rocca received the lessons he needed to succeed in the ultra-competitive world of sports-entertainment.

He debuted in South America in 1942 and competed as he felt most comfortable—barefoot. Unlike anything ever seen before in the ring, Antonino was in constant motion and beautifully executed exciting maneuvers both in the air and on the mat.

THE UNITED STATES AND THE NWA

In the late 1940s, Rocca arrived in the United States and started competing in Texas, where he was a main event star as the NWA Texas Heavyweight Champion. It was then that promoter Kola Kwariani introduced Antonino to former wrestler and Goldust Trio member Joseph Raymond "Toots" Mondt, the kingpin of wrestling in the Big Apple. Rocca was brought to Manhattan and shared with other promoters in the region, including a newcomer from Washington, D.C., Vincent J. McMahon.

The barefoot boy of Argentina was a breath of fresh air. With his elegant balance, showmanship, and energetic poise, he put Madison Square Garden back on the map as the ultimate venue for sports-entertainment. Hurricanranas, flying dropkicks from any angle, victory rolls, and flying body presses dazzled audiences who were accustomed to athletes who never left their feet. His finishing move, the Argentine Backbreaker, brought crowds to a frenzy and dastardly foes to submission as they yelled in incredible pain. From the Empire State Building in New York City to the Grand Olympic Auditorium in Los Angeles and all places in between, "The Amazing Rocca" was king. He was the most dynamic performer the industry had seen to that point and a legitimate phenomenon.

ANTONINO ROCCA

ARGENTINA

Shows at Madison Square Garden that hosted the NWA Champion saw the Argentine acrobat in the main event. During this period only Gorgeous George was a bigger star. Rocca's ethnicity played a role in his following as well. He was of Italian heritage and hailed from Latin America, which made him a huge attraction for two of the New York area's largest immigrant populations. His fans were so devoted to him, that when Dick The Bruiser split him open during their match in Madison Square Garden, a violent riot ensued. Soon after, an image from the melee taken by a brave photographer was featured on the cover of *LIFE*.

GREATER SUCCESS AND FAME

As time went on and Rocca's popularity grew, McMahon convinced him to join his outfit full-time. In 1956 Antonino created a team with Puerto Rican Superstar Miguel Perez, and on March 30, 1957, the duo became the first holders of the United States Tag Team Championship when they defeated Don and Jackie Fargo. During this era, the Argentine Superstar competed with the likes of Hans Schmidt, The Kangaroos, Éduard Carpentier, Johnny Valentine, Don Leo Jonathan, and Lou Thesz. He also took on Gene Kiniski, Skull Murphy, Pampero Firpo, Dr. Jerry Graham, and future WWE Hall of Famers Eddie Graham, Killer Kowalski, Verne Gagne, and "Classy" Freddie Blassie. In July 1959 Argentina bested future WWE Hall of Famer "Nature Boy" Buddy Rogers in the tournament finals for the International Heavyweight Championship, which he turned into the longest reign of any International Heavyweight Champion.

Rocca's fame carried him into the early 1960s as his number of fans continued to grow. After he graced countless magazine covers, in August 1962 DC Comics featured him on the cover of *Superman* #155 throwing The Man of Steel out of the ring. On television, Rocca even grappled with the "King of Late Night" Johnny Carson on *The Tonight Show*. A Latin music LP by famous artist Billy Mure was released on MGM Records titled, *In This Corner, the Musical World of Argentina Rocca* and showed the Superstar performing a dropkick on the album cover.

To frustrate opponents and delight fans, Antonino used to slap his opposition in the face with his feet.

CHANGING OF THE GUARD

By the time WWE was independent from the National Wrestling Alliance, Rocca relinquished his title as the company's top Superstar to Bruno Sammartino. In one of his last bouts with WWE, he once again stood across the ring from "Nature Boy" Buddy Rogers in a tournament final. This time, it was in Rio de Janeiro, Brazil, for the newly created WWE Championship.

On that evening it was Rogers' turn to lift the gold into the air in victory. For the remainder of the decade Argentina wrestled and officiated for the Japanese Pro Wrestling Association. In the early 1970s, he worked for New Japan Pro Wrestling and officiated the classic bout between Antonio Inoki and Karl Gotch. Rocca returned to North America in 1976 and in November of that year he made his silver screen debut in *Alice, Sweet Alice* starring Brooke Shields.

Over a decade since his last appearance, Antonino Rocca returned to WWE as an announcer. Each week he called the action with Vincent K. McMahon, the legendary promoter's son and future Chairman of WWE. On February 25, 1977, he donned the referee's shirt and was the man in the middle of a boxing match that featured future WWE Hall of Famers Gorilla Monsoon and Andre the Giant at Madison Square Garden. Tragically, on March 15, 1977, this uniquely gifted individual suddenly passed.

The greatest honor Antonino Rocca would receive came in 1995, when then-WWE Champion, Diesel posthumously inducted the father of aerial assault into the WWE Hall of Fame, permanently marking his place among sports-entertainment's elite figures.

I was poor. I didn't have enough money to buy shoes...By being barefoot, I get a better grip on an opponent and have better balance.

I WAS POOR. I DIDN'T HAVE ENOUGH MONEY TO BUY SHOES...

APOLLO CREWS

HT	6'1"	WT	240 lbs.
FROM	Stone Mountain, Georgia		
SIGNATURE MOVE	Spinout Powerbomb		

In 2015, NXT General Manager William Regal announced that a new era was beginning, as Apollo Crews signed a contract with the group.

If a scientist could have designed a modern day Superstar, Crews would be the finished product. Despite his muscularity, Crews exhibits both unworldly speed and agility, punishing foes with his spin-out powerbomb, as well as a gorilla press followed by a standing moonsault.

Inspired by former WWE greats Kurt Angle, Stone Cold Steve Austin, and The Rock, Crews was trained by Curtis "Mr." Hughes, becoming a star on the American indie circuit and Japan. After his NXT debut, he warred with Tye Dillinger, Baron Corbin, and Finn Bálor, proving with each successive battle that he's capable to living up to, and exceeding, all expectations.

ARGENTINA APOLLO

 | **FROM** | Buenos Aires, Argentina |

Argentina Apollo's approach to wrestling was unmistakable. Not only did he compete barefoot, but the high-flying Superstar also confused opponents with his dizzying arsenal of moves. The agile Superstar also appeared on the east coast under the name Vittorio Apollo.

Most of Apollo's success came in the tag team ranks. He formed a popular union with legend Bruno Sammartino, but it was with Don McClarity that he captured his only WWE Title. In February 1964, Apollo and McClarity defeated the famed Tolos Brothers for the United States Tag Team Championship. They successfully defended the Titles for four months before finally falling to Dr. Jerry Graham and Luke Graham in Washington, D.C.

Apollo continued to excel in tag team competition after leaving WWE. In April 1970, he teamed with Jose Lothario to claim the National Wrestling Alliance Florida Tag Team Championship. Two years later, he captured the Georgia version of the NWA Tag Team Championship with partner Dick Steinborn.

ARIEL

With her jet-black hair, blood-red eye shadow, and fanged teeth, Ariel possessed a terrifying vampire-like quality. However, her fishnet stockings, knee-high boots, and uncanny ability to hang upside down also made her more than a little sexy.

As Kevin Thorn's bloodthirsty valet in ECW, Ariel could always be found by the side of her man, who she oftentimes kissed mid-match. At *December to Dismember* in 2006, she and Thorn defeated another ECW couple, Kelly Kelly and Mike Knox, in a Mixed Tag Match. Unfortunately, Ariel's signature tarot cards did not hold any further fortunes in WWE. Ariel accompanied Thorn and the New Breed at *WrestleMania 23* only to witness the extreme upstarts fall short to the ECW Originals. A month later, Ariel left WWE.

ARMANDO ESTRADA

HT	6'2"	WT	230 lbs.	FROM	Havana, Cuba

His name is Armando Alejandro Estrrrrrada!!

This Cuban businessman came to WWE in April 2006 as the manager of the savage Umaga. Under Estrada's shrewd leadership, the "Samoan Bulldozer" became one of the fiercest competitors in WWE.

After leading Umaga to the Intercontinental Championship and the famous Battle of the Billionaires at *WrestleMania 23*, Estrada left his protégé's side in May 2007. He resurfaced as ECW's General Manager and ruled like a powerful dictator. Estrada made life hell for many ECW stars, especially Colin Delaney.

After Theodore Long relieved Estrada of his GM duties, Estrada embarked on a career in the ring. Ironically, he earned his ECW contract by defeating Tommy Dreamer with help from Delaney. That November, Armando left WWE. Though only seen on WWE programming once since then, this industrialist has undoubtedly found new, successful business opportunities.

ARNOLD SKAALAND

HoF	TT USA	HT	6'0"	WT	240 lbs.
		FROM	White Plains, New York		

There was nothing Arnold Skaaland couldn't do. He was an accomplished wrestler, legendary manager, brilliant promoter, and cherished friend to countless names within the wrestling industry. This rare combination of greatness led Skaaland to one of the finest careers in sports-entertainment history.

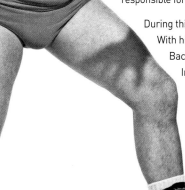

After representing the U.S. Marines in World War II, Skaaland kept in shape by competing as an amateur boxer. He proved to be a force within the ropes, but never believed he could make a living in the sport. Instead, he focused his efforts on wrestling, an up-and-coming profession that was gaining popularity thanks to television.

Skaaland made his professional debut in 1946, competing mainly in the Northeast. His speed, toughness, and overall intelligence quickly earned him the nickname "The Golden Boy." By the early 1960s, he had earned several opportunities at what was then considered the industry's leading Title, the National Wrestling Alliance (NWA) Championship.

In 1963, Skaaland began working for Vincent J. McMahon's newly-created WWE. It was here that he gained his greatest success. Not only did Skaaland enjoy a reign as one-half of the United States Tag Team Champions (with Spiros Arion), but he also became a shareholder in McMahon's company. As part owner, Skaaland was responsible for handling a great deal of the company's finances.

During this time, Skaaland also made a successful transition into the managerial ranks. With his supreme level of wrestling knowledge, he guided Bruno Sammartino and Bob Backlund to three of the most remarkable WWE Championship reigns in history. In fact, aside from ten months in the late 1970s, Skaaland's men held the WWE Championship uninterrupted from December 1973 to December 1983.

Skaaland's managerial career came to an end shortly after he threw in the towel on Backlund's reign in his loss to Iron Sheik in December 1983. From there, he assumed several backstage responsibilities until his retirement in the early 1990s. In 1994, Skaaland's tireless efforts in the sports-entertainment industry were recognized when he was inducted into the WWE Hall of Fame.

THE ASCENSION

MEMBERS	Konnor & Viktor
COMBINED WT	487 lbs.

Shrouded in mystery and consumed by a dark purpose only they can understand, The Ascension rose from the ranks of NXT, where they pummeled the tag team division to ruins for over two years. After a dominating and record-setting 344-day reign as NXT Tag Team Champions, this forceful pair that was "born and bred to rip and shred" promised to dine on destruction and feast upon fear as they embarked on their next merciless quest.

Those who failed to heed their warnings saw firsthand the devastation they were capable of causing. Weeks after their December 2014 debut, Konnor and Viktor ravaged through three sets of former Tag Team Champions. Later in 2015, The Ascension began dishing out punishment on behalf of the demented Stardust, forming an ungodly triad called The Cosmic Wasteland.

ASHLEY

HT 5'5" **FROM**	New York, New York
SIGNATURE MOVE	Starstruck

A bad girl from the Big Apple, this punk chick entered WWE after winning the 2005 *Raw* Diva Search contest. She soon fought off Divas Candice Michelle, Melina, and Torrie Wilson and aligned herself with Trish Stratus.

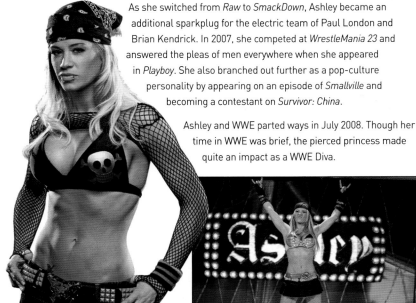

As she switched from *Raw* to *SmackDown*, Ashley became an additional sparkplug for the electric team of Paul London and Brian Kendrick. In 2007, she competed at *WrestleMania 23* and answered the pleas of men everywhere when she appeared in *Playboy*. She also branched out further as a pop-culture personality by appearing on an episode of *Smallville* and becoming a contestant on *Survivor: China*.

Ashley and WWE parted ways in July 2008. Though her time in WWE was brief, the pierced princess made quite an impact as a WWE Diva.

ASUKA

HT 5'3" **FROM**	Osaka, Japan
SIGNATURE MOVE	Asuka Tock

Asuka's ring name is an homage to Lioness Asuka, a member of Japan's most celebrated women's duo, the Crush Girls of the 1980s. Three decades later, Asuka hopes to become the face of female combat not only in Japan, but worldwide.

While training as a competitor, the Osaka native designed video game graphics, a fitting sideline since she's often described as a real-life avatar, with her multi-colored hair, face paint, and staggering arsenal. Because of her lightning fast spin kicks, Asuka often has the advantage over larger opponents. In ten years of competition in Asia, she mastered a number of deadly submissions.

Asuka first appeared in NXT in late 2015, but rose to prominence quickly, sometimes laughing out loud while rallying to victory. At *NXT Takeover: Dallas* Asuka defeated Bayley to capture her first NXT Women's Championship.

ATLANTIC GRAND PRIX WRESTLING

In the Maritimes—the eastern Canadian provinces that comprise New Brunswick, Nova Scotia, and Prince Edward Island—winters are long, and summers are for wrestling. Although far smaller than in times past, one of the premier warm weather Maritime events is Atlantic Grand Prix Wrestling.

In 1977, New Brunswick native Emille Dupree launched the seasonal territory, running a schedule that included towns like St. John and Moncton in New Brunswick, Halifax and Sydney, Nova Scotia, and Summerside, Prince Edward Island.

Some wrestlers returned every year, including Killer Karl Krupp, Stephen Pettipas, Leo Burke, "No Class" Bobby Bass, and the Cuban Assassin. But Sweet Daddy Siki, Randy "Macho Man" Savage, Andre the Giant, Bulldog Bob Brown, and The Spoiler all cycled through.

The territory closed in 2008. But in 2013, Atlantic Grand Prix Wrestling reopened, with much of the action centered around Emille Dupree's son, Rene, a former WWE Tag Team Champion. The Great Muta and other Japanese talent have also appeared.

AUSTIN ARIES

HT 5'9"	**WT** 202 lbs.	**FROM**	Milwaukee, Wisconsin
SIGNATURE MOVE	Rolling Elbow		

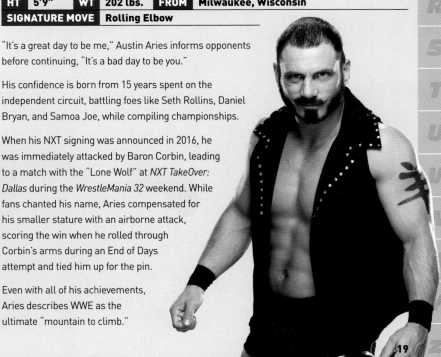

"It's a great day to be me," Austin Aries informs opponents before continuing, "It's a bad day to be you."

His confidence is born from 15 years spent on the independent circuit, battling foes like Seth Rollins, Daniel Bryan, and Samoa Joe, while compiling championships.

When his NXT signing was announced in 2016, he was immediately attacked by Baron Corbin, leading to a match with the "Lone Wolf" at *NXT TakeOver: Dallas* during the *WrestleMania 32* weekend. While fans chanted his name, Aries compensated for his smaller stature with an airborne attack, scoring the win when he rolled through Corbin's arms during an End of Days attempt and tied him up for the pin.

Even with all of his achievements, Aries describes WWE as the ultimate "mountain to climb."

THE AUTHORITY

MEMBERS Triple H and Stephanie McMahon (leaders), Corporate Kane, Seth Rollins, J&J Security, Randy Orton, New Age Outlaws, The Shield, Batista, & Big Show

It was only a matter of time. Stephanie McMahon has been WWE royalty since she was the size of a turnbuckle pad. Triple H has ascended to the sports-entertainment throne by systematically conquering all realms of the WWE kingdom, seizing fourteen World Championships and the imperious title of WWE COO. Together, this husband-and-wife team's ascension to power was inevitable and, in 2013, the era of The Authority began with a Pedigree.

Since Triple H's surprise ambush of Daniel Bryan at *SummerSlam 2013*, the ruthless power couple has molded WWE into their own image. With an eye toward what they decree is "best for business," they do what is necessary to produce their desired results, paying little heed to such trivial matters as compassion or popular opinion. The Authority used every page in its corporate playbook in an attempt to silence the "Yes!" Movement. They have also made life miserable for the Rhodes family, Big Show, John Cena, Roman Reigns, and countless other fan-favorites.

Many Superstars are willing to endure the fans' scorn and play ball with The Authority, swayed by the allure of deep pockets. One of the first to buy in was Kane, who traded his infernal mask for a suit in 2013. "Corporate Kane" championed the bigwigs' various agendas for two years, at one point working with the tandem of J&J Security to protect the interests of The Authority's most notorious defection, Seth Rollins.

After turning his back on The Shield, Rollins supplanted The Authority's golden child, Randy Orton, and was christened as the handpicked future of WWE. Rollins repaid his benefactors in December 2014 when his heinous attack on Edge led to The Authority's reinstatement after John Cena's team drove them from power at *Survivor Series*.

Since this brief respite, the brass has wielded their iron fist with an even greater fury. When Roman Reigns defied an offer to fall under The Authority's influence, Triple H ensured Roman's downfall as WWE World Heavyweight Champion. Then at *Royal Rumble 2016*, Triple H seized the Title for himself, reminding all who defy him and Stephanie that their monarchy extends across all of WWE, from the ring to the office.

AVATAR

HT	6'0"	WT	235 lbs.	FROM	Parts Unknown
SIGNATURE MOVE	Frog Splash				

This enigmatic competitor combined martial arts with high-flying moves, and made his debut on *Raw* in October 1995. Unlike most masked Superstars, he didn't put on a mask until he was in the ring, and removed it after a victory. His version of the Frog Splash was also a bit different. To begin, he'd stand on the sternum of his fallen opponent, jump from their body and land on them with a body splash.

Avatar became a fan-favorite as he battled Sycho Sid, Isaac Yankem DDS, Brooklyn Brawler, and Bradshaw. He also formed an exciting tag team with fellow aerialist Aldo Montoya. By March 1997, Avatar vanished from WWE. Though his stay was brief, Avatar showcased talents that only a select few possess.

AWA
see page 22

BAD NEWS BROWN

HT	6'2"	WT	271 lbs.	FROM	Harlem, New York
SIGNATURE MOVE	Ghetto Blaster				

An Olympic bronze medalist in Judo, Bad News Brown transferred his combat skills to the wrestling ring in 1977 after being trained by the legendary Antonio Inoki. His early days were spent in Japan and Canada, though he later moved to WWE where he proved to be one of the meanest Superstars of his time.

In addition to an unmatched viciousness, Brown was also a persuasive swindler. In 1988, he led Bret Hart to believe the two Superstars would be declared co-winners of the *WrestleMania IV* Battle Royal. But when Hart's guard was down, Brown attacked him from behind to claim the victory on his own.

Continuing to prove he could not be trusted, Brown repeatedly walked out on his teammates during *Survivor Series* elimination matches. On his own, however, he was as good as it got and proved to be a serious threat to the reign of then-WWE Champion Randy Savage.

In 1990, Bad News vanished from WWE after accosting then-WWE President Jack Tunney. He spent the rest of the decade competing primarily in Mexico, Japan, and Canada. A chronic knee injury forced Brown into retirement in 1999. After hanging up the boots, he briefly owned and operated his own training facility in his adopted home of Calgary, Alberta, Canada.

Sadly, Bad News Brown passed away in March 2007. Though gone, he continues to be regarded as one of the toughest men to ever compete.

BAD NEWS BARRETT

	HT	6'7"	WT	246 lbs.	FROM	Preston, England
	SIGNATURE MOVE	Bull Hammer Elbow				

From the day he broke in to WWE as the winner of *NXT* Season One, Wade Barrett's presence has meant one thing—Bad News. Whether leading the ruthless Nexus, running with The Corre, or inflicting his "Barrett Barrage" himself, the former bare-knuckle brawler has taken his place in WWE by force.

His first Intercontinental Championship came in 2011 on his native soil as the ornery Brit topped Kofi Kingston in Manchester, England. Over the next four years, Barrett held the revered Title another four times. Beyond tangible accolades, Barrett has been outspoken in his desire to decimate everything in his path. Even his words pack the same blunt force as his Bull Hammer Elbow.

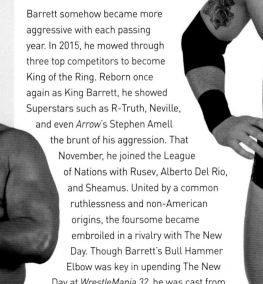

In late 2013, Barrett traded in the name "Wade" to reflect his new role as WWE's official bearer of bad news. Armed with a gavel, Bad News Barrett hurled insults in all directions. The sight of his ostentatious podium elicited a hailstorm of boos from the WWE Universe, who could not drown out Barrett's unflattering barbs.

Barrett somehow became more aggressive with each passing year. In 2015, he mowed through three top competitors to become King of the Ring. Reborn once again as King Barrett, he showed Superstars such as R-Truth, Neville, and even *Arrow*'s Stephen Amell the brunt of his aggression. That November, he joined the League of Nations with Rusev, Alberto Del Rio, and Sheamus. United by a common ruthlessness and non-American origins, the foursome became embroiled in a rivalry with The New Day. Though Barrett's Bull Hammer Elbow was key in upending The New Day at *WrestleMania 32*, he was cast from the group the next day.

BALLS MAHONEY

HT	6'2"	WT	305 lbs.	FROM	Nutley, New Jersey

SIGNATURE MOVE Nutcracker Suite

Upon kicking off his sports-entertainment career in 1987, Balls Mahoney began touring the United States, Canada, and Puerto Rico. He won numerous singles and tag team Championships on the independent circuit, catching the eye of ECW boss Paul Heyman. Heyman welcomed Mahoney into the fold in 1996 and the promotion's demanding fans quickly embraced his quirky yet extreme persona.

While in ECW, Mahoney formed a tag team with fellow purveyor of pain Axl Rotten, collectively known as the Chair Swingin' Freaks. When the original ECW went out of business in early 2001, Mahoney returned to the independent scenes of the United States and Asia.

In 2005, Mahoney surprised fans everywhere when he brawled with the Blue World Order at ECW's *One Night Stand*. He stayed with WWE's ECW brand until April 2008 when he was released from his contract. In addition to being an ECW original Mahoney was also an advisor on the Sci-Fi Channel's reality show *Who Wants to Be a Superhero?*

BAM BAM BIGELOW

	HT	6'4"	WT	390 lbs.	FROM	Asbury Park, New Jersey

SIGNATURE MOVE Slingshot Splash, Greeting from Asbury Park

Unlike most heavyweights, Bam Bam Bigelow moved around the ring with the grace and agility of a gazelle, while also packing the raw power of a buffalo. And to further accentuate his uniqueness, the "Beast from the East" topped off his colorful ring attire with a fireball tattoo that covered his entire skull.

When Bigelow arrived in WWE in 1987, nearly every WWE manager competed for his services. In the end, Bigelow selected the great Sir Oliver Humperdink to guide his career. Together, they ravaged WWE's locker room, most notably Nikolai Volkoff, Harley Race, and Lanny Poffo.

Bigelow was selected as a member of Hulk Hogan's team at the first *Survivor Series*. The latter portions of the match saw the "Beast from the East" outnumbered three-to-one; but despite the numbers disadvantage, he still managed to eliminate King Kong Bundy and One Man Gang before finally being eliminated by Andre The Giant. Bigelow's last appearance of the decade was in the *WrestleMania IV* WWE Championship tournament where he lost to One Man Gang via countout in just under three minutes.

Bigelow returned to WWE in 1992 and later became a member of Ted DiBiase's Million-Dollar Corporation. In 1995, he had the elite honor of competing in a *WrestleMania* main event when he squared off against football Hall of Famer Lawrence Taylor in the main event of *WrestleMania XI*. Though he came up short against L.T., Bigelow's performance in the match made headline news all over the globe.

After a stint in Japan, Bigelow surfaced in ECW where he captured both the promotion's World Television and World Heavyweight Championships. Bigelow later used his experience in the Land of the Extreme to capture the WCW Hardcore Championship in 2000. After WCW closed its doors in 2001, Bigelow returned to the independent scene where he stayed until 2006.

Bam Bam Bigelow passed away in January 2007. He will forever be remembered as a physical phenomenon and one of the greatest big men to ever compete.

BAM NEELY

HT	6'7"	WT	275 lbs.
FROM	Robbinsdale, Minnesota		

Bam Neely comes from a town rich in ring tradition. Hailing from Robbinsdale, Minnesota, the former border patrol agent shares the same zip code as the late, great WWE Legends Rick Rude and Curt Hennig. In the ring, however, Neely shares no likenesses with his renowned predecessors. Instead, he substitutes pure power for their technical ability. His overwhelming strength caught the eye of Chavo Guerrero, who hired Neely as his bodyguard in April 2008. This led to Bam's inclusion in the insidious alliance led by Edge, known as La Familia. Since he departed from WWE in January 2009, Neely has been in rings on the American independent scene and on the island of Puerto Rico.

BARBARA BUSH

Barbara Bush first appeared as an EMT tending to injured Superstars during the fall of 1999. Often referred to simply as B.B., the buxom blonde transferred from the medical community to the ring in November 1999 after Ivory tossed her into a giant bowl of gravy.

B.B. challenged Ivory for her Women's Championship in a Four-Way Evening Gown Match at *Armageddon 1999* that also included Jacqueline and eventual winner Miss Kitty. She then went on to be in Val Venis's corner during his Holiday Topless Top-Rope Match against Hardcore Holly. Unfortunately for B.B., her man was tossed over the top twice, meaning she was forced to disrobe.

B.B. disappeared from the scene after being viciously tossed through a table in 2000.

AWA

AMERICAN WRESTLING ASSOCIATION

For three decades, the Minneapolis-based AWA was seen in such far-flung locations as Omaha, Denver, Winnipeg, Salt Lake City, Phoenix, and San Francisco. Its most influential star, Verne Gagne, purchased the territory in 1959 with promoter Wally Karbo. In 1960, they named the NWA Titlist, Pat O'Connor, its inaugural Champion. When O'Connor ignored a challenge to defend the crown within 90 days, Gagne was awarded the prize.

Gagne held the AWA Championship ten times. Among the other greats to wear the gold were Dick the Bruiser, The Crusher, Mad Dog Vachon, the masked Dr. X (known elsewhere as The Destroyer), the erudite Nick Bockwinkel, Curt Hennig, and Jerry Lawler. In addition, Austria's Otto Wanz and Japan's Jumbo Tsuruta brought the Title back to their respective countries.

The AWA was where Hulk Hogan and The Rockers (Shawn Michaels and Marty Jannetty) first gained hero status. Ric Flair, Ricky Steamboat, Sergeant Slaughter, Iron Sheik, and Vader all started in the AWA. In 1991, after the final Champion, Larry Zbyszko, departed for WCW, the AWA officially closed down.

VERNE GAGNE

HT	5'11"
WT	215 lbs.
FROM	Minneapolis, Minnesota

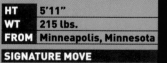

SIGNATURE MOVE
Sleeper

For more than three decades, Verne Gagne personified both scientific wrestling and the promotion he founded, the American Wrestling Association (AWA), a Minneapolis-based operation whose Champions were recognized as far away as Germany and Japan.

While attending the University of Minnesota, Gagne captured two NCAA and AAU Titles apiece, and was an alternate on the 1948 United States Olympic team. Although recruited by the NFL, by the early 1950s, he was nationally known from his appearances defending the NWA United States Championship on the Dumont television network.

In 1960, frustrated over his inability to snare the NWA Championship, Gagne and promotional partner Wally Karbo named NWA Champion Pat O'Connor the kingpin of the new AWA. When O'Connor refused to defend the fledgling Title against Gagne, the Minnesotan was crowned. Early on, there were two branches of the AWA, in Minneapolis and Omaha, but the Championship was unified in 1963.

Gagne held the Title ten times, warring with the likes of Gene Kiniski, Larry "The Axe" Hennig, Ray Stevens, Mad Doug Vachon, and Nick Bockwinkel—even appearing on WWE shows at Madison Square Garden. He also starred in the 1974 movie, *The Wrestler*, later colliding with his on-screen opponent, Billy Robinson.

Gagne favored athletics over showmanship, and trained some of the most capable wrestlers in the industry, including Ric Flair, Iron Sheik, Ricky Steamboat, Dick the Bruiser, Ken Patera, Sgt. Slaughter, Baron Von Raschke, and the Blackjacks.

But the AWA faltered when its most popular star at the time, Hulk Hogan, defected to WWE in 1983, where he was joined by such former AWA personalities as Jesse "The Body" Ventura, Bobby "The Brain" Heenan, Rick Martel, Jumping Jim Brunzell, and announcer "Mean" Gene Okerlund.

A warrior at heart, Gagne continued fighting, promoting new talent like The Rockers, Vader, Col. DeBeers, and Curt Hennig, as well as former WWE Superstars Bob Backlund, Jimmy "Superfly" Snuka, and Sgt. Slaughter.

For his dedication to the sport he loved, Gagne was inducted into the WWE Hall of Fame in 2006. He passed away in 2015.

OTTO WANZ

HT	6'2"
WT	375 lbs.
FROM	Graz, Austria
SIGNATURE MOVE	
Steamroller	

Otto Wanz was virtually unknown in the United States when he achieved what appeared to be the impossible: dethroning the crafty Nick Bockwinkel for the AWA Championship in 1982.

Wanz was a rotund powerhouse who'd literally roll over opponents—somersaulting onto their mid-sections—around Europe, Africa, and Asia, defending his Austria-based Catch Wrestling Association (CWA) Title. But when he came to the St. Paul Civic Center on August 29, 1982, few fans were familiar with his track record.

Like Verne Gagne, he also owned the promotion where he became famous. After establishing himself as an amateur boxer, he began wrestling in 1969, intimidating rivals by tearing telephone books in half. He founded the CWA and won its first Championship in 1973. Over the years, he battled a dazzling array of rivals from all continents, including Andre the Giant, Terry Funk, Antonio Inoki, and Vader.

Wanz and Bockwinkel had fought to a draw in 1981 in Bremen, Germany, and agreed to a rematch on American soil, with both Titles at stake. Wanz prevailed when he turned a belly-to-belly suplex effort into a backdrop, falling on top of the Champion for the stunning pinfall. He held the AWA Championship for 41 days before losing it to Bockwinkel.

As a promoter, Wanz was best-known for his twice-annual tournament in Germany and Austria, attracting Superstars like Yokozuna, Owen Hart, Scott Hall, JBL, Lance Storm, and Ultimate Warrior.

THE CRUSHER

"The Man Who Made Milwaukee Famous" was one of the toughest and most entertaining wrestlers of his time. Reggie "The Crusher" Lisowski loved to brawl against rugged adversaries like Mad Dog Vachon, Blackjack Lanza, and Jerry "Crusher" Blackwell. He claimed to have a very unorthodox training routine: running along the Milwaukee waterfront with a beer barrel on each shoulder. By the time his run was finished, it was alleged, the beer was often drained. The cigar-chomping, barrel-chested headliner also attributed his endurance in the ring to dancing all night with corpulent barmaids he referred to as his "dollies."

HT	6'0"
WT	251 lbs.
FROM	Milwaukee, Wisconsin
SIGNATURE MOVE	
Bolo Punch	

The Crusher made his mat debut in 1949, but the response was initially lackluster and he was forced to supplement his income by bricklaying and working in a meat-packing plant. In 1954, his matches were broadcast nationally on the Dumont network, and he was transformed into a star.

In February, 1963, he held a version of the AWA Championship recognized solely in Nebraska, while Verne Gagne was considered the kingpin in Minnesota, but Crusher unified the Title by defeating Gagne in July.

Of all his varied tag team partners, Crusher is best remembered for his colorful affiliation with his cousin, Dick the Bruiser. If their opponents weren't inflicting enough harm, the pair would pummel each other for amusement.

At age 75, Lisowski could still bench press 350 pounds. He died four years later in 2005.

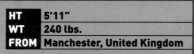

BILLY ROBINSON

HT	5'11"
WT	240 lbs.
FROM	Manchester, United Kingdom

SIGNATURE MOVE
Suplex

Descended from a family of boxers, Billy Robinson learned to fight at age four and never stopped. Long after he'd retired from active combat, he taught the brutal "catch" style of wrestling to new generations of fighters. Were it not for Robinson passing on his secrets of submission wrestling, the art may have been lost.

As an amateur, Robinson was both a British National and European Open Wrestling Champion. After training for eight years at England's notorious Snake Pit—where Karl Gotch and the British Bulldogs also learned their craft—he debuted in the AWA, where he nearly wrested the promotion's Title away from Verne Gagne in a celebrated match at Chicago's Comiskey Park. He was also Gagne's on-screen opponent in the 1974 movie, *The Wrestler*. In 1982, Robinson battled WWE Champion Bob Backlund to a 60-minute draw in Montreal.

Behind the scenes, Robinson worked as a trainer for Gagne, testing out blue chip talent like Ric Flair, Ken Patera, and Iron Sheik before their AWA debuts. He was unforgiving during these sessions, showing no tolerance for physical or mental weakness.

His reputation extended around the world. In Japan, where his 1975 match with Antonio Inoki was headline news, he was considered a godlike trainer. In the UK, he taught greats like Marty Jones and Johnny Saint. He also coached MMA Champion Josh Barnett.

The lifetime warrior died in 2014.

  # NICK BOCKWINKEL

Nick Bockwinkel frequently bragged, "I am the smartest wrestler alive." Even fans who took issue with his arrogance conceded that he might have been correct. Not only was Bockwinkel one of the most absorbing speakers in sports-entertainment, he was also a supreme technician and ring psychologist who could out-wrestle and out-think opponents.

HT	5"10"
WT	240 lbs.
FROM	St. Paul, Minnesota

SIGNATURE MOVE
Piledriver, Sleeper

In the AWA, Bockwinkel was a four-time Champion, as well as a three-time Tag Team Titlist. After Verne Gagne, no other competitor was as closely associated with the AWA.

A second-generation Superstar, Bockwinkel was trained by his father, Warren, as well as the iconic Lou Thesz. By the time he debuted at age 16, he was worlds ahead of much older rivals. Because of his charisma and ability to turn a phrase, he became a crossover personality, exhibiting his wit on the *Hollywood Squares* game show, and playing a wrestler on *The Monkees*.

He thrived wherever he traveled, but once Bockwinkel arrived in the AWA in 1970, he made the league his own. With Bobby "The Brain" Heenan advising him, Bockwinkel achieved every goal he set.

Although he periodically teamed with Pat Patterson, he and Ray Stevens formed a near-unbeatable tandem, winning the AWA Tag Team Title three times. In 1975, he ended Gagne's seven-year tenure as AWA kingpin, the first of four reigns.

Bockwinkel's ambitions were so large that he attempted to unify the AWA Championship with the WWE Title, wrestling Bob Backlund to a double count-out in Toronto in 1979. One of his most controversial defenses involved Hulk Hogan, who appeared to beat Bockwinkel for the AWA Championship in 1983, only to have the decision overruled because the Hulkster had tossed the Champion over the ropes before the pinfall. Frustrated, Hogan soon left for WWE where he ushered in a new era. In between AWA reigns, Bockwinkel attempted to wrest the NWA Championship from Ric Flair in 1986.

After retirement, Bockwinkel worked as a commentator for WWE, providing scholarly advice to a new generation of Superstars. He also served as WCW Commissioner. A 2007 WWE Hall of Famer, he died in 2015.

HT	6'2"
WT	235 lbs.
FROM	Van Nuys, California
SIGNATURE MOVE	
Abdominal Stretch	

Known as "the world's most scientific wrestler," Wilbur Snyder is often credited with inventing the abdominal stretch. Although others likely employed the move before, few applied it as effectively.

The Californian with a crew-cut initially aspired for a career in professional football, but while playing for the Edmonton Eskimos of the Canadian Football League (CFL), teammates Gene Kiniski and Joe Blanchard convinced Snyder of wrestling's money-making potential.

Trained by former Champion Sandor Szabo and Warren Bockwinkel, father of future AWA kingpin Nick Bockwinkel, Snyder gained fame quickly, executing high arm drags, head scissors, and maneuvers based on his football background. In 1954, the "California Comet" battled NWA Champion Lou Thesz to a draw on national television.

Before the AWA unified its two versions of its World Title, Snyder held the Omaha Championship twice, defeating Verne Gagne in 1958 and Dick the Bruiser a year later. He and Bruiser later formed both a tag team and promotional partnership. In 1984, Snyder was an AWA co-promoter in Indianapolis. He died in 1991.

CHRIS TAYLOR

HT	6'5"
WT	412 lbs.
FROM	Dowagiac, Michigan
SIGNATURE MOVE	
Bearhug	

The debut of Chris Taylor after his bronze medal showing in the 1972 Olympics was one of the most anticipated events among AWA international sports observers. Tipping the scales at more than 400 pounds, Taylor had been the heaviest athlete in Olympic history at that point. While competing at Iowa State University, he'd often draw out his matches until the cheerleaders signaled for him to pin his mismatched opponents.

Unbeaten in college, Taylor was a two-time NCAA freestyle heavyweight Champion. This intrigued AWA boss Verne Gagne, who preferred featuring combatants with prior sports credentials.

After scoring a win in his first match in December 1973 against a brown-haired Ric Flair, Taylor battled a range of adversaries, including Nick Bockwinkel, Baron Von Raschke, Ox Baker, and "Cowboy" Bob Orton. In 1974, he won a two-ring battle royal that received national exposure, but not before he was bloodied by Mad Dog Vachon.

Unfortunately, Taylor's weight continued to increase and his health problems escalated. He retired in 1977 and died two years later.

BRAD RHEINGANS

HT	5'10"
WT	248 lbs.
FROM	Appleton, Minnesota
SIGNATURE MOVE	
Bridging Cradle Suplex	

From an athletic perspective, Brad Rheingans was in the same elite category as Bob Backlund and Jack Brisco. While hailed in Japan for his skills, Rheingans remains underrated in North America. However, in the WWE dressing room, Rheingans is held in the proper regard. Brock Lesnar, JBL, Curtis Axel, Vader, and the Nasty Boys have all been Rheingans trainees.

An NCAA Division II Champion for North Dakota State, Rheingans placed fourth in the 1976 Olympics. He was recruited for the AWA, and made his debut in 1983.

That year, he stunned AWA fans by wrestling Champion Nick Bockwinkel to a draw in a televised match. After Rick Martel captured the Title in 1984, Rheingans battled him to a time-limit draw.

In 1986, Rheingans briefly competed in WWE, but returned to the AWA and won tag team gold with fellow Olympian Ken Patera. After retirement, he devoted himself to coaching.

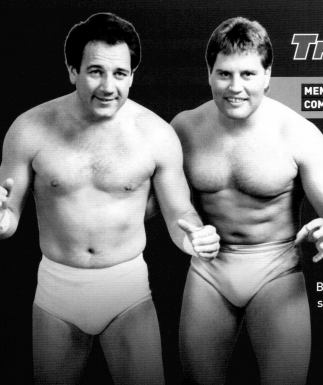

THE HIGH FLYERS

MEMBERS	Greg Gagne & Jumpin' Jim Brunzell
COMBINED WT	455 lbs.

As one of the AWA's most synchronized tag teams, the High Flyers flourished against both fellow speedsters and powerhouse tandems. Greg Gagne and Jim Brunzell met at the University of Minnesota. Knowing that his father, Verne, was about to run a training camp in 1972, Gagne convinced his friend to participate. In 1974, they merged forces. The High Flyers name seemed natural given their repertoire: Gagne's flying head scissors and Brunzell's soaring dropkicks.

Because of his family background, Gagne expected to be tested in the ring and had developed a toughness that belied his lanky frame. Brunzell was endowed with the same attitude and, together, they toppled the dangerous duo of Blackjack Lanza and Bobby Duncum for the AWA Tag Team Championship in 1977.

They won their second Title from Jesse Ventura and Adrian Adonis in 1981. Other rivals included Nick Bockwinkel and Ray Stevens, Crusher Blackwell and Ken Patera, and Tito Santana and Rick Martel. They split in 1985 when Brunzell left for WWE, but, after retirement rekindled their partnership as trainers.

COLONEL DeBEERS

In 1985, as Nelson Mandela was imprisoned in South Africa for fighting to end the country's system of apartheid, a bizarre character arrived in the AWA. Marching across the ring in camouflage fatigues and waving the South African flag, Colonel DeBeers raised the fury of fans with proclamations that couldn't be considered anything other than racist.

HT	6'4"
WT	270 lbs.
FROM	Cape Town, South Africa
SIGNATURE MOVE	
Front-Face Piledriver	

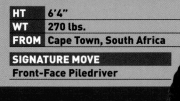

Many of the statements are too offensive to reprint. DeBeers claimed descent from a diamond-mining family and pledged to use his wealth to conquer the AWA. He boasted that he wasn't satisfied unless his foe left on a stretcher.

The Colonel's most notorious rivalry was sparked when he interfered in one of Jimmy "Superfly" Snuka's matches, knocking him off the top rope onto the arena floor and piledriving the future WWE Hall of Famer's face into the floor. Snuka gained revenge in a series of clashes, and others lined up to tear into DeBeers, including Scott Hall, Sgt. Slaughter, and Wahoo McDaniel. With the closure of the AWA, DeBeers lost his main platform.

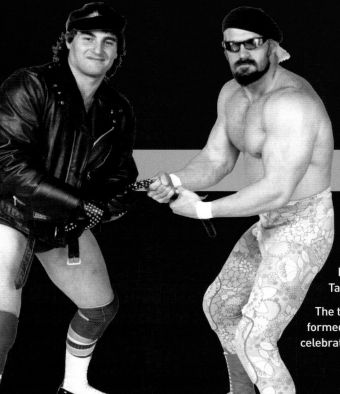

THE EAST-WEST CONNECTION

MEMBERS	Adrian Adonis & Jesse "The Body" Ventura
COMBINED WT	512 lbs.

According to Adrian Adonis and Jesse "The Body" Ventura, there was a cultural divide between the east and west coasts of the United States, and it was their mission to unite the country.

As the East-West Connection, New Yorker Adonis aligned with the future governor, then billing himself as a California blond. AWA rivals included Mad Dog Vachon and Verne Gagne, The Crusher and Dick the Bruiser, Ray Stevens and Pat Patterson, and the High Flyers. In July 1980, they became AWA Tag Team Champions, holding the gold for more than a year.

The two briefly reunited in WWE, where they were managed by "Classy" Freddie Blassie. Adonis later formed a similar team, the North-South Connection, with Dick Murdoch, while Ventura became a celebrated announcer.

Steve Regal

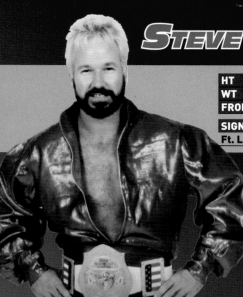

HT	6'1"
WT	220 lbs.
FROM	Indianapolis, Indiana
SIGNATURE MOVE	
Ft. Lauderdale Leglock	

Known as "Mr. Electricity," Steve Regal was featured on every major AWA show in the mid-1980s, frequently with some form of gold strapped around his waist.

Regal was fortunate to learn the sport from his father-in-law, former AWA kingpin Wilbur Snyder. In 1984, he won the Light Heavyweight crown from Buck "Rock'n'Roll" Zumhofe, trading the Title back to him a year later.

In one of the AWA's strangest incidents, Regal and partner Jimmy Garvin were battling the mighty Road Warriors, the current Tag Team Title holders, in 1985 when the Fabulous Freebirds interfered and went after the Legion of Doom. In the skirmish, the overmatched duo of Regal and Garvin emerged as Champions, shocking observers.

Regal left the AWA in 1986, and briefly wrestled in WWE.

Kenny Jay

HT	6'3"
WT	226 lbs.
FROM	Cleveland, Ohio
SIGNATURE MOVE	
Backdrop	

When Harley Race was asked about the best opponent that he ever had, the eight-time NWA Champion cited Kenny Jay, a competitor who lost practically every week on AWA television.

Still, every opponent conceded, Jay always gave them a fight. Because of this, AWA ring announcer Al DeRusha called the competitor "the very capable Kenny Jay." Others referred to him as "Sodbuster," due to his day job as a landscaper.

Jay lost so often that his wins stand out, particularly a 1965 battle in which he teamed with Verne Gagne and The Crusher to topple Race, Larry Hennig, and Chris Markoff.

In 1976, he fought Muhammad Ali in a boxer vs. wrestler clash. Ali won via knockout, but, as always, Kenny tried his hardest.

George "Scrap Iron" Gadaski

HT	6'0"
WT	224 lbs.
FROM	Great Fall, Minnesota
SIGNATURE MOVE	
Armdrag	

To a generation of AWA fans, George "Scrap Iron" Gadaski was a constant presence. While his victories were few, Gadaski tangled with every star, from Verne Gagne to Jesse "The Body" Ventura. Behind the scenes, he played an indispensible role, driving the ring from town to town and personally putting it up.

Gadaski developed his toughness working in Canadian lumber camps, where he rarely lost a fight. Trained by Stu Hart, he arrived in the AWA in 1967, ready to take on anyone. He was Ric Flair's first opponent in 1972, wrestling the "Nature Boy" to a draw. In 1977, The Crusher picked Gadaski to be his partner in a war against the Super Destroyer and Lord Al Hayes. He died in 1982.

See Also:

JESSE VENTURA

LARRY "THE AX" HENNIG

MAD DOG VACHON

BARON VON RASCHKE

BARBARIAN

HT	6'2"	WT	300 lbs.	FROM	The Isle of Tonga
SIGNATURE MOVE	Kick of Fear				

After years of competing in the intimidating Powers of Pain tag team, The Barbarian washed the paint from his face and went in search of singles success in 1990.

The Barbarian's solo quest began when his manager, Mr. Fuji, sold his contract to Bobby Heenan. Under The Brain's tutelage, The Barbarian altered his image, trading in his leather and chains for a skull-and-antler headdress and warrior-like fur robes. The makeover paid early dividends, as the new-look Barbarian got off to an impressive start, defeating Tito Santana at *WrestleMania VI*.

Unfortunately for The Barbarian, *WrestleMania VI* is where the winning stopped. He spent most of the following year coming up short against the likes of Big Boss Man and Bret Hart. Realizing a solo career wasn't yielding benefits, Heenan paired The Barbarian with Haku in hopes of recreating some of the strong man's earlier tag success.

The Barbarian's return to the tag scene proved just as futile. After his team lost to The Rockers at *WrestleMania VII*, The Barbarian struggled to get back on track. By mid-1992, he left WWE.

BARON CORBIN

HT	6'8"	WT	275 lbs.	FROM	Kansas City
SIGNATURE MOVE	End of Days				

A man of Baron Corbin's imposing size and power can compete in just about anything he desires. A former Golden Gloves boxing champion and NFL offensive lineman, Corbin's latest conquest is WWE.

In 2013, Corbin promised to "hand out a great deal of punishment to all competition." Several unfortunate NXT competitors soon found out first-hand what the tattooed powerhouse meant. Corbin found rivalries in fellow brute Bull Dempsey and WWE veteran Rhyno. Though nicknamed "The Lone Wolf," tag team competition seemed to suit Corbin when he allied with Rhyno to reach the finals of the Dusty Rhodes Tag Team Classic.

Corbin remained a feared NXT competitor until *WrestleMania 32*, when he debuted under the WWE spotlight in a major way. "The Lone Wolf" won the 3rd Annual Andre the Giant Memorial Battle Royal in front of over 101,000 spectators. The following night, he decimated Dolph Ziggler, putting the WWE locker room on notice.

BARON MIKEL SCICLUNA

HT	6'3"	WT	256 lbs.	FROM	Isle of Malta
SIGNATURE MOVE	Use of Foreign Objects				

For Baron Mikel Scicluna, a win's a win, regardless of how you attain it. The WWE Hall of Famer made a career out of cheating to gain victory, usually by thumping opponents with a roll of coins he kept concealed in his boots.

Upon entering WWE, Scicluna was thrust into a rivalry with the legendary Bruno Sammartino. Scicluna failed to pry the WWE Championship from Sammartino, but that didn't stop him from eyeing other golden opportunities. In late 1966, Scicluna enjoyed a three-month reign as United States Tag Team Champion with partner Smasher Sloan. Six years later, he teamed with King Curtis Iaukea to claim the most prestigious prize in tag team wrestling: the World Tag Team Championship.

Scicluna continued to wrestle for WWE until his retirement in 1984. Twelve years after hanging up his coin-filled boots, Scicluna was awarded the ultimate honor when he was inducted into the WWE Hall of Fame by longtime nemesis, Gorilla Monsoon.

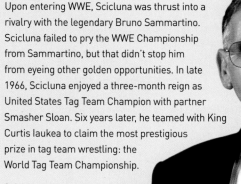

BARON VON RASCHKE

HT	6'3"	WT	280 lbs.	FROM	Germany
SIGNATURE MOVE	Brain Claw				

"That is all the people need to know," Baron Von Raschke was known to say in heavily accented English at the conclusion of his interviews, generally after predicting the destruction of an opponent.

Despite his bluster and colorful persona, "The Baron" knew how to make good on a promise. As an amateur, he was a Greco-Roman medalist who'd qualified for the Olympics. In 1966, he made his debut in the AWA.

Soon, the bald grappler was using the brain claw as a finisher, sometimes gripping his wrist and goose-stepping across the ring before applying the move. He'd also occasionally load the black glove that he wore on his right hand.

In 1970, after battling fellow German Fritz Von Erich in Dallas, Von Raschke captured the old World Wrestling Association (WWA) Heavyweight Championship from Dick the Bruiser. For the next three years, he'd trade the title with Bruiser, "Sailor" Art Thomas, and Cowboy Bob Ellis, often relying on manager "Pretty Boy" Bobby Heenan's machinations to win.

As a tag team performer, Von Raschke won the AWA title with Horst Hoffman, and NWA honors with Greg Valentine and Paul Jones. He later became a fan favorite, and, in 1988, managed the Powers of Pain in WWE, billed simply as "The Baron."

After his 1995 retirement, Von Raschke was the subject of a play presented at the Minnesota History Theatre.

BARRY HOROWITZ

HT	6'0"	WT	221 lbs.	FROM	St. Petersburg, Florida
SIGNATURE MOVE		The Cloverleaf			

Barry Horowitz was a touted high school amateur wrestler, who went on to compete collegiately at Florida State University. Trained by the legendary Boris Malenko, he made a brief WWE stop in 1983 before making a more extended stay in 1987. Upon his return, Horowitz appeared on programs such as *Prime Time Wrestling, All-Star Wrestling, Superstars of Wrestling,* and *Wrestling Challenge.*

After recovering from a serious neck injury, Horowitz's shining moment came when he defeated Bodydonna Skip at *SummerSlam 1995.* That year, he also won *Pro Wrestling Illustrated*'s "Most Inspirational Wrestler of The Year" Award. He maintained a place on WWE cards through 1997, when he moved to WCW, where he stayed until 2000.

One of the most well-traveled ring veterans ever, Barry Horowitz has appeared in promotions all over the world, patting himself on the back each step of the way. In a career that spanned twenty-one years, Barry is considered by ring aficionados to be one of the most technically-sound competitors to ever step inside the ring.

BARRY O

HT	6'1"	WT	235 lbs.
FROM	Las Vegas, Nevada		

With legendary Bob Orton, Sr. as his father, Barry O was pegged for greatness by many sports-entertainment insiders. Unfortunately for the younger Orton, those predictions never turned into reality.

Unlike his brother, Bob Orton, Barry O had difficulty getting his WWE career off the ground. While brother Bob was competing in main events, Barry O struggled against opponents like Outback Jack and Paul Roma.

Despite his WWE troubles, Barry O did manage to gain some success while in Stu Hart's Stampede Wrestling. Competing under a mask, Barry O called himself The Zodiac, which was a tribute to his father, who wrestled under the same name during the 1970s. While today's WWE fans may not recognize the name Barry O, they certainly know his nephew, Randy Orton.

BARRY WINDHAM

HT	6'6"	WT	275 lbs.	FROM	Sweetwater, Texas
SIGNATURE MOVE		Superplex			

WWE fans were first introduced to the son of Blackjack Mulligan in 1984 when he debuted as one-half of the incredibly popular U.S. Express tag team. Along with partner Mike Rotundo, Barry Windham defended the World Tag Team Championship against Iron Sheik and Nikolai Volkoff at the first-ever *WrestleMania.* The U.S. Express came up short at the inaugural extravaganza, and Windham left WWE soon after. He remained active in the NWA for most of the next five years, at one point shocking the wrestling world by joining the Four Horsemen.

In June 1989, Windham returned to WWE as a man who lived by his own laws. Dressed in black and calling himself the Widowmaker, he stalked WWE Superstars, taking his time to extract what he wanted from them. As the Widowmaker, Windham clashed with Superstars such as Koko B. Ware, Paul Roma, Sam Houston, the Red Rooster, and Tito Santana. He also appeared alongside Marc Mero, Jake Roberts, and a debuting Rocky Maivia to take on Jerry Lawler, Hunter Hearst-Helmsley, Crush, and Goldust at *Survivor Series 1996.*

Windham went on to form The New Blackjacks tag team with partner Blackjack Bradshaw. He left WWE in 1998 and went on to briefly appear in WCW. In 2012, Windham was inducted into the WWE Hall of Fame for his work in the legendary Four Horsemen.

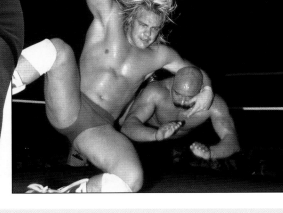

BART GUNN

HT	6'4"	WT	275 lbs.
FROM	Austin, Texas		

Beside his brother Billy, Bart Gunn wrangled up three World Tag Team Championship reigns. As a solo Superstar, Bart was not as memorable, save for the mainstream attention he garnered in 1999.

After tearing through four Superstars to win WWE's Brawl for All Tournament, Bart legitimized himself as one of WWE's toughest Superstars. The victory led to Gunn facing heavyweight boxer Butterbean in a similarly-styled contest at *WrestleMania XV.* Just seconds into the match, Butterbean flattened Bart with a devastating right hand. Miraculously, Bart climbed to his feet only to be dropped yet again by a powerful right. The wince-inducing punch was featured on ESPN's *SportsCenter* and its force knocked Bart straight out of WWE. Bart made a cameo appearance at *Raw*'s 15th Anniversary special in 2007 and received a warm ovation from the WWE fans.

BASHAM BROTHERS

| MEMBERS | Danny Basham & Doug Basham | COMBINED WT | 495 lbs. |
| FROM | Columbus, Ohio | | |

Danny and Doug Basham played rough both in the ring and out. Just ask their muscular manager, Shaniqua. Introduced to WWE audiences in May 2003, the Basham Brothers utilized their similar looks to confound opponents. The successful form of trickery eventually led them to a WWE Tag Team Championship opportunity against Los Guerreros, who they defeated for the Titles in October 2003. The brothers held the gold until February 2004.

The Bashams struggled to find their way after losing the Titles, but in November 2004, their careers took a positive turn when they joined forces with WWE Champion JBL. As his "Secretaries of Defense," the Bashams enjoyed another reign atop *SmackDown*'s tag team division. Despite their success, their main job description was to shield JBL from any apparent danger, even if it meant causing harm to themselves. In June 2005, the brothers were forced to go their separate ways when Danny was traded to *Raw*. Neither Superstar was able to duplicate the success they achieved as a team. They both left WWE shortly after.

BASTION BOOGER

| HT | 6'1" | WT | 401 lbs. |
| FROM | Parts Unknown | | |

Upon arriving in WWE in 1994, Bastion Booger immediately started making those around him physically ill with his repulsive appearance and disgusting behavior. In fact, he was so gross that many recognized him as the only Superstar to use his nose as a snack dispenser.

After a relatively uneventful singles career, Booger entered into a short-lived alliance with Bam Bam Bigelow, which eventually dissolved on an episode of *Raw* when he planted a passionate kiss on Bigelow's valet, Luna Vachon. In early 1995, Booger left WWE and returned to parts unknown. Though some thought he would be dormant forever, Booger shocked the world when he arrived at the *Raw* 15th Anniversary show in 2007.

BATISTA

| HT | 6'6" | WT | 290 lbs. | FROM | Washington, D.C. |
| SIGNATURE MOVE | Batista Bomb | | | | |

To think, WCW officials once told Batista he'd never make it in sports-entertainment! Nicknamed "The Animal," Batista's tenacity following his 2002 debut impressed Ric Flair and Triple H, who brought him aboard as part of their Evolution faction.

Batista earned his first championship alongside "The Nature Boy" when the duo captured the WWE Tag Team Championships in December 2003. As Evolution dominated WWE, Batista became hungry to step out of Triple H's shadows. After winning the 2005 Royal Rumble Match and ending The Game's World Heavyweight Championship reign at *WrestleMania 21*, Batista was officially unleashed.

Batista's insatiable appetite and otherworldly physique kept him in the championship hunt for the rest of his career. As *SmackDown*'s top attraction, he claimed the World Heavyweight Championship again at *Survivor Series 2006* and nearly broke Undertaker's undefeated streak at *WrestleMania 23*. At *Cyber Sunday 2008*, Batista silenced the egotistical Chris Jericho to claim the top prize once again.

Content with nothing less than the apex of the food chain, Batista attacked Rey Mysterio after a loss to Undertaker, blaming Rey for costing him the Title. The callous betrayal shocked the WWE Universe and the ensuing rivalry among former friends revealed Batista's vicious side. Soon after, Batista brutalized John Cena at the conclusion of *Elimination Chamber 2010*. His inner rage over Cena's top billing in WWE had boiled over, fueling a fierce rivalry.

After a four-year hiatus, Batista returned to WWE and instantly won his second Royal Rumble Match. This leaner, meaner version of The Animal struck intimidation into a new generation of Superstars. He fell short in the main event of *WrestleMania 30*, but his comeback was just getting started. He reunited with Evolution under the group's new mantra, "Adapt or perish," and set his sights on dismantling The Shield.

Batista left WWE after a string of heated 3-on-3 brawls with the Hounds of Justice, admitting to some frustration over his ill-fated Title opportunity.

BATTLE KAT

HT	5'10"	WT	225 lbs.	FROM	Parts Unknown
SIGNATURE MOVE	Moonsault				

In October 1990, WWE was introduced to a talented competitor with the martial-arts skills of a ninja, high-flying acrobatics of a gymnast, and technical wrestling skills of a world-class athlete. His identity hidden behind a feline-like mask, Battle Kat displayed his amazing abilities against such Superstars as the Barbarian, Boris Zhukov, Pez Whatley, and "Playboy" Buddy Rose.

The mysterious Battle Kat ran away from WWE soon after his debut. Reports at the time speculated that he traveled to Japan, where he resumed his in-ring career. Today, despite being a bit of a cult favorite, Battle Kat's true identity remains unknown.

BATTMAN

HT	5'10"	WT	240 lbs.	FROM	Gotham City
SIGNATURE MOVE	Abdominal Stretch				

Battman made his debut in Buffalo in 1966, much to the joy of fans and dismay of villains everywhere. Opponents were immediately taken aback by his physical conditioning, wrestling skill, intellect, and acts of escape artistry.

The masked superhero-like Superstar quickly amassed an impressive win-loss record, and would go on to co-hold the prestigious International Tag Team Championship with then-WWE Champion Bruno Sammartino.

Though he never gained long-term national success, Battman was well recognized in the Pittsburgh territory. He'll also forever be remembered for maintaining law and order across WWE during the turbulent late 1960s and into the next decade.

BAYLEY

HT	5'6"	FROM	San Jose, California
SIGNATURE MOVE	Bayley-to-Belly Suplex		

Bayley was first seen as a bashful and over-excited trainee at the WWE Performance Center. Living out her childhood dream, Bayley has proven that her genuine enthusiasm is matched only by her talent. Outside the ring, she is full of hugs and sweet sentiments. Inside, she is as dangerous as any Superstar, possessing a full arsenal highlighted by her crowd-pleasing Bayley-to-Belly Suplex.

Bayley came within a whisker of the NXT Women's Championship several times. Then at the sold-out *NXT TakeOver: Brooklyn*, Bayley dethroned Sasha Banks in an exhilarating battle. Her emotional journey continued as she valiantly defended her Title for 224 days, proving to the WWE Universe that Bayley's future in WWE is a bright one.

THE BEAST

HT	5'10"	WT	255 lbs.	FROM	Dorchester, New Brunswick, Canada

With a big, bushy beard and wild hair, The Beast certainly appeared to be well-named. He even played the role with his savage in-ring approach. However, behind the wild exterior was a man with close familial ties. Believe it or not, the untamed Superstar is the oldest of four wrestling brothers. His younger, more-refined siblings, Rudy Kay, Bobby Kay, and Leo Burke all made a living inside the ring as well.

The Beast toured the globe seven times during his nearly 40-year career. His undomesticated style attracted huge crowds in Australia and even landed him in a match against the legendary Giant Baba in front of 45,000 rabid fans in Japan.

It was in Canada that The Beast gained his greatest notoriety. In 1966, he defeated Dave Ruhl for Calgary's National Wrestling Alliance Canadian Heavyweight Championship. He also held Toronto's version of the NWA United States Heavyweight Championship for five months after defeating Johnny Valentine in October 1963.

"BEAUTIFUL" BOBBY HARMON

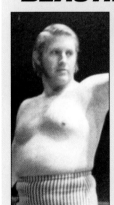

FROM	Cincinnati, Ohio
SIGNATURE MOVE	The Bobby Lock

Known for his flamboyant personality, "Beautiful" Bobby Harmon would oftentimes strut to the ring wearing dark sunglasses and over-the-top satin robes. His glitz and gaudiness was only matched by that of his manager, The Grand Wizard.

Over the course of his career, Harmon formed several successful tag teams. His partners included the effeminate Magnificent Maurice, Blackjack Mulligan, and Jimmy Valiant. In 1971, Harmon and Valiant began using entrance music. Like many of that era past, the duo claimed to be the first to do so. True or not, one thing remains certain: Harmon was a competitor ahead of his time.

BEAVER CLEAVAGE

HT	6'0"
WT	243 lbs.

Despite having a shelf life of less than one month, Beaver Cleavage successfully created a controversy that is still being talked about today.

In the summer of 1999, Beaver debuted alongside the sexy Mrs. Cleavage in several black-and-white vignettes filled with double entendres. Many thought the controversy surrounding Beaver's sexual innuendos would ultimately prevent him from ever entering the ring. But in June 1999, he defeated Christian in his first in-ring appearance. Despite the victory, Cleavage was canceled from WWE television a few weeks later. Perhaps his brand of entertainment was too hot for TV.

BECKY LYNCH

HT	5'6"	FROM	Dublin, Ireland	SIGNATURE MOVE	Dis-Arm-Her

Burning down the entrance ramp like some incendiary enchantress, Becky Lynch possesses a mystical quality to match her finely honed athleticism.

A lifetime wrestling fan, the indomitable lass from the Emerald Isle grew up playing basketball, swimming, and horseback riding. But, at a young age, she showed a propensity for submission competition—a characteristic she's channeled into her painful armbar variation.

Working as an actress and a flight attendant, Lynch never let go of her dream. She was trained by future NXT Champion, Finn Bálor, and once managed fellow Superstar, Paige, in the UK.

Initially a shining light in the Divas Revolution with partners Sasha Banks and Charlotte, Lynch had a falling out with both, leading to a Triple Threat clash at *WrestleMania 32*.

Although Becky fell short in her goal of winning the newly-branded WWE Women's Championship, she performed at her usual high standard, and highlights of the heralded match were shown all over the world, inspiring her to continue striving for the premier prize in women's competition.

BERTHA FAYE

HT	5'8"	FROM	Walls, Mississippi
SIGNATURE MOVE		Sit-Out Powerbomb	

Bertha Faye may not have been the most attractive woman to set foot in the ring, but she might just have been the most loved. Despite the fact that she dwarfed him, Harvey Wippleman adored Bertha with all his heart.

Wippleman first introduced fans to Bertha in April 1995 when she attacked Alundra Blayze on *Raw*. As a result of the assault, Blayze suffered a broken nose, which ultimately ignited an intense rivalry between the two. At *SummerSlam 1995*, Bertha flattened her rival with a Sit-Out Powerbomb, enabling her to capture her first-and-only Women's Championship. Two months after winning the Title, Bertha found herself on the losing end of a *Raw* rematch with Blayze. Shortly after she left WWE for good.

THE BERZERKER

HT	6'8"	WT	323 lbs.	FROM	Parts Unknown
SIGNATURE MOVE		Big Boot			

Unleashed on WWE by Mr. Fuji in 1991, The Berzerker immediately caught the eyes of fans by continually throwing opponents over the top rope, leaving them on the arena floor unable to return to the ring. A consistent Championship contender, The Berzerker regularly faced off against the likes of Tito Santana, Jimmy "Superfly" Snuka, Bret "Hit Man" Hart, and Greg Valentine.

In early 1993, The Berzerker left WWE and has not been seen since. Today, fans' curiosity is still piqued when archived footage is shown of his matches and interviews. He'll always be remembered as one of the most unique and dangerous personas in WWE history.

BELLA TWINS

MEMBERS	Brie & Nikki	HT	5'6"
FROM	Scottsdale, Arizona		

In August 2008, the Bella Twins dazzled the WWE Universe with a dose of "Twin Magic," and have not looked back since. For years, the identical sisters have been double trouble for all in their path, whether switching places during a match right under the referee's nose or simply leaning on each other for support.

With Divas Championships on both their resumes, the Bellas have crushed any notions that they are just two (extremely) pretty faces. Still, not a moment goes by without the eyes of smitten fans or the lenses of several cameras tracing their every move. In 2013, the Bellas became the centerpiece of the smash hit E! reality show *Total Divas*. Along with their castmates, Brie and Nikki give viewers an eye-opening look into their lives behind the scenes. From backstage drama to personal conquests and various trials and tribulations, the program has given the Bellas and the women of WWE the notoriety they richly deserve.

A sisterly bond is never complete without a sibling rivalry, and the Bellas have had their share of dust ups. Nikki's cold betrayal of Brie during her *SummerSlam 2014* match against Stephanie McMahon left their relationship fractured. After months of bitterness, however, they were able to patch things up and become more cohesive than ever.

With "Twin Magic" revived, jealousy over the Bellas success began to permeate the locker room. Paige, one of Nikki's chief rivals during her historic Divas Championship reign, attempted to rally the entire Divas roster against the two starlets. Nikki and Brie watched each other's backs through the animosity. Nikki's Title reign eventually came to an end at the hands of Charlotte, but not before eclipsing AJ Lee's mark for the longest Divas Championship reign of all time.

In 2015, the Bellas received reinforcements when Alicia Fox took their side in squabbles with up-and-coming Superstars such as Charlotte, Sasha Banks, and Becky Lynch. As Team Bella gained numbers, the one-two punch of "Fearless Nikki" and the indomitable "Brie Mode" became even more unstoppable. As Nikki fearlessly began to battle back from an injury, Brie took her sister's inspiration into the *WrestleMania 32* pre-show. In a 10-Superstar Tag Team Match, Brie led the cast of *Total Divas* to an emotional victory. A proud Nikki emerged wearing an ear-to-ear smile to join the celebration.

BETH PHOENIX

HT	5'7"	FROM	Buffalo, New York
SIGNATURE MOVE			Glam Slam

Beth Phoenix was dominant long before her exceptional career in WWE. She became the first female amateur wrestler in her high school's history to compete on its varsity team. After extensive training, she made the leap to sports-entertainment.

In May 2006, Phoenix debuted on *Raw* looking to settle a longstanding beef with Mickie James. After a forceful introduction to the WWE Universe, Phoenix suffered a fractured mandible that sidelined her for over one year.

Fully healed with lost time to make up for, "The Glamazon" hunted for Women's Championship gold. She defeated Candice Michelle for the Title at *No Mercy 2007* and ruled for five months. In 2008, she won her first *WrestleMania* match and grabbed her second Title in a "Winner Take All Match" at *SummerSlam 2008*. During this time, an unexpected romance with Santino Marella earned the odd couple the endearing nickname of "Glamorella."

The 2008 "Diva of the Year" continued to amaze for the next several years. At the 2010 *Royal Rumble*, she not only became the second woman to ever compete in the battle royal, she eliminated the Great Khali from the match! Later that year, she and Natalya won the first-ever Divas Tables Match in WWE history. On October 2, 2011 Phoenix craftily captured her first Divas Championship, joining a small handful of names in Women's and Divas Championship lineage.

With enough accomplishments to assure her a permanent spot among the great Divas in history, "The Glamazon" left WWE in October of 2012.

BIG BOSS MAN

HT	6'7"	WT	330 lbs.	FROM	Cobb County, Georgia
SIGNATURE MOVE					Side Slam

Managed by the "Doctor of Style," Slick, Big Boss Man gave new meaning to the term "Protect and Serve." Wielding a nightstick and a loose definition of justice, the domineering cop was soon paired with Akeem to form the Twin Towers, one of the largest teams in WWE history. Big Boss Man became a threat to Hulkamania, and on October 1989, battled the Hulkster in a Steel Cage Match on *Saturday Night's Main Event*.

After he showed "Million Dollar Man" Ted DiBiase he couldn't be bought, the former prison guard became a fan favorite. He taught Bobby "The Brain" Heenan some manners and entered into an ideological dispute over law and order with The Mountie. After Big Boss Man won their Jailhouse Match at *SummerSlam 1991*, Mountie spent a night in a New York City lockup. Boss Man protected WWE from one of his former inmates, Nailz, defeating the ex-con in a Nightstick Match at *Survivor Series 1992*.

In October 1998, after time in WCW, Big Boss Man returned to WWE as the head of personal security for Mr. McMahon. Wearing S.W.A.T.-like attire, he displayed an updated attitude suitable for the era, rivaling with Undertaker and committing unspeakable atrocities following the passing of Big Show's father. Boss Man formed brief alliances with Bull Buchanan, Booker T, and Mr. Perfect before leaving WWE in 2003. Sadly, Big Boss Man passed away in September 2004. One of the most agile big men and toughest Superstars to ever enter the ring, his memory was honored at the 2016 WWE Hall of Fame Ceremony. Boss Man's loving family accepted his induction by his former manager, Slick.

BEVERLY BROTHERS

MEMBERS	Beau & Blake
COMBINED WT	514 lbs.

When the Beverly Brothers debuted in May 1991, they arrogantly proclaimed, "The Bevs want it all and we'll get it all." And after getting off to a hot start, Beau and Blake looked as though they would back up their lofty claims, especially considering the incredible impact of their Shaker Heights Spike signature move.

After a series of impressive showings, the brothers battled the Natural Disasters for the World Tag Team Championship, but were ultimately unsuccessful in defeating Typhoon and Earthquake. The team disbanded in early 1993 after Blake left WWE. Beau stayed with the company for a short period afterward, but could never replicate the success he had as part of the Beverly Brothers.

BIG BULLY BUSICK

HT	6'0"	WT	265 lbs.	FROM	Weirton, West Virginia

Managed by Harvey Wippleman, Big Bully Busick arrived in WWE in the early 1990s with grand plans of pushing around his fellow Superstars. Ironically, however, when it came to his in-ring action, the only Superstar getting bullied was him. He even lost to perennial loser Brooklyn Brawler.

Realizing he wasn't going to push around the Superstars of WWE, Busick turned his attention to much smaller targets. It wasn't uncommon to see him bullying ring announcers and kids in the audience. He once went so far as to steal a youngster's balloon. The mean-spirited act turned heartbreaking when he popped the colorful balloon right in front of the little girl.

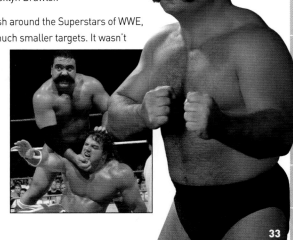

BIG DADDY V

HT	6'9"	WT	487 lbs.	FROM	Harlem, New York
SIGNATURE MOVE		Big Daddy V Drop			

Covered in curious tattoos, Big Daddy V was brought to ECW to protect Matt Striker from The Boogeyman. After ridding Striker of his worm-eating nemesis, Big Daddy V focused much of his devastation on bigger Superstars including Undertaker and Kane. By the end of 2007, he was embroiled in battles with the Brothers of Destruction, and managed to defeat Kane in an Extreme Rules Match. In his final WWE appearance in 2008, he faced CM Punk in a Money in the Bank qualifying match. Sadly, Big Daddy V passed away in 2014, and is remembered by fans as one of the most imposing Superstars of all time.

BIG DICK JOHNSON

"Lock up your daughters, lock up your wives. Lock up the back door and run for your lives..."

Those words came from the revolting exhibitions brought to WWE courtesy of Big Dick Johnson. Appearing when fans least expected it, Big Dick loved prancing around WWE events showing off his finest features. He appeared on *ECW* with the Sandman, wished everyone a Merry Christmas at *Armageddon 2006*, and at one point was even considered among the possibilities of being Mr. McMahon's illegitimate son.

No matter where you are in the world, if you hear the beat to his familiar theme music, it might be Big Dick Johnson coming through to add a little something special to the festivities!

BIG E

HT	5'11"	WT	285 lbs	FROM	Tampa, Florida
SIGNATURE MOVE		Big Ending			

If you could bench-press nearly 600 pounds and deadlift 800 pounds, you would think positively too. These days, the human bulldozer known as Big E can be seen clapping and gyrating with gleeful exuberance alongside New Day cohorts Kofi Kingston and Xavier Woods. The trio's upbeat attitude has sparked them to an amazing run that has seen them dominate the WWE Tag Team Division carrying and defending the WWE Tag Team Championships for several months. The sight of the trio "Freebirding" around with the Titles was maddening to the WWE Universe at first. Over time, however, New Day's infectious optimism turned jeers into jubilant claps. But before this new lease on life, Big E's pulverizing strength established him as one of WWE's most feared Superstars.

The former champion power lifter caught the eye of Dolph Ziggler and at the end 2012 Big E made a huge impact by dropping John Cena. After proving to be a force on his own, Big E ditched the Showoff and pursued the Intercontinental Championship. He defeated Curtis Axel for the prize in November 2013 and held it for an impressive 167 days.

Big E's first Title reign ended, but through the power of positivity (and several healthy servings of Booty-O's), Big E is stronger and faster than ever and is a force to be reckoned with in WWE. It will take one colossal effort to wipe the smile off his face. So don't you dare be sour! Clap for your world famous Tag Team Champion and Feel the Power!

BIG JOHN STUDD

HT	6'10"	WT	364 lbs.
FROM		Los Angeles, California	

During WWE's magical mainstream renaissance of the 1980s, Big John Studd proved himself as a larger-than-life villain. With an awe-inspiring frame that stood nearly seven-feet tall, Studd thwarted countless attempts to chop him down to size. With each passing conquest, he further cemented his legacy as one of sports-entertainment's greatest giants.

After being trained by WWE Hall of Famer Killer Kowalski, Studd joined WWE in the early 1980s. Upon entering the company, he was managed by Freddie Blassie, but quickly switched to Bobby "The Brain" Heenan.

By 1983, Studd began promoting himself as WWE's only true giant. The claim didn't sit well with Andre the Giant. And over the course of the next several years, the two Superstars engaged in a bitter battle designed to crown WWE's elite giant.

Studd gained a favorable advantage over Andre when he cut his foe's hair in December 1984. The stunt eventually led to a $15,000 Bodyslam Challenge at *WrestleMania*. In the end, Andre lifted Studd over his head and slammed him to the mat for the win. Afterward, Andre attempted to share his $15,000 with the fans, but a lightning-quick Heenan swooped in to steal the giant's winnings.

The following year, Studd was considered by many as the favorite heading into the *WrestleMania 2* WWE/NFL Battle Royal. But after tossing out William Perry, Studd was eliminated as well when "The Refrigerator" pulled him out under the guise of a handshake.

When not dominating the singles circuit, Studd oftentimes teamed with fellow Heenan Family member King Kong Bundy. Together, the formidable duo made life miserable for many tag teams until they were eventually derailed by Giant Machine, who was actually Andre the Giant under a mask.

After a brief hiatus, Studd returned to WWE in late 1988. This time, however, the fans cheered the big man after he turned his back on Heenan. Studd's second WWE stint was highlighted by a victory in the 1989 Royal Rumble Match.

Big John Studd, one of the greatest giants sports-entertainment has ever seen, was honored with induction into the WWE Hall of Fame in 2004.

BIG MAN STEEL

HT	6'3"	WT	384 lbs.
SIGNATURE MOVE		Bearhug	

A protégé of the "Doctor of Style" Slick, Big Man Steel arrived in WWE in June 1989. A villain of the most brutal kind, the monstrous Superstar shook the very foundation of the Convention Center in Niagara Falls upon his entrance. And when he set foot in the ring during the episode of *Wrestling Challenge*, everyone in attendance watched in awe as he manhandled rugged veteran Tom Horner.

Big Man Steel and his manager had a falling out following the match and what was supposed to be the beginning of an era of dominance turned out to be simply a one-time experiment.

BIG SHOW

HT	7'0"
WT	450 lbs.
FROM	Tampa, Florida

SIGNATURE MOVE
Chokeslam, KO Punch, Colossal Clutch

Just like Andre The Giant and Big John Studd before him, Big Show can inspire fear at first sight. He is the World's Largest Athlete, with measurements that are astounding: 450 pounds, 7 feet tall, size 22 EEEEE shoes, 22 1/2 ring size, and a 64-inch chest. This man can go wherever he pleases, and do whatever he pleases. If you think you can stop him, just have a look at his astounding 20-year track record. Many have crossed this legendary big man, and most often, the outcome is not pretty.

A GIANT AMONG BIG BOYS

Big Show first emerged in WCW in 1995, known simply as The Giant. Within six months of his debut, the mammoth rookie defeated Hulk Hogan to become WCW Champion, the youngest in the company's history. The Giant went on to claim his second WCW Title the following year by toppling another legend, "Nature Boy" Ric Flair.

Weeks after a newly villainous Hogan ended his reign, The Giant did the unthinkable. Rather than fight Hogan and the nWo, he joined them! This shocking defection made the venomous faction more threatening than ever, but it was short-lived. By year's end, The Giant was back at odds with the white and black. Over the next two years, he enjoyed two tag team reigns and one more dominant stint in the nWo as part of its splintered Hollywood stable.

THE SHOW MOVES ON

As sports-entertainment exploded, Paul Wight (soon-to-be dubbed Big Show) knew WWE was the place to be. In 1999, he debuted by tossing Stone Cold through a cage wall. Crossing over in the thick of the Attitude Era, Big Show fit right in. He rivaled The Rock, Mankind, Triple H, and several others. At *Survivor Series 1999*, he won his first WWE Championship and months later, headlined *WrestleMania 2000*.

As the '90s gave way to a new millennium, Big Show began to forge his legacy as one the era's definitive stars. In addition to collecting nearly every available Title, his fabled feats of strength added to his allure. On an episode of *SmackDown*, he overturned a Jeep with his bare hands! Big Show solidified his place in history when he defeated Rob Van Dam in 2006 to become the only individual to ever hold the WWE, WCW, and ECW Championships.

FRIEND OR FOE?

After a year hiatus, Big Show made a stunning return at *No Way Out 2008*. Leaner and meaner, Show stepped outside of his traditional opponent pool at *WrestleMania XXIV* when he faced boxing great Floyd "Money" Mayweather. Big Show added a new finishing move to his expansive list, a devastating right-handed knockout punch that could bring a locomotive to a dead stop.

Since unveiling this deadly maneuver, Big Show has been one of WWE's biggest wildcards, often transforming from affable giant to callous mercenary seemingly on a whim.

At *Backlash 2009*, Big Show's long-standing conflict with John Cena was brought to new levels when he interfered in Cena's Last Man Standing Match with Edge. Show hurled The Champ through a ringside spotlight, the impact causing a frightening explosion with The Champ engulfed in the flames. Despite Big Show's dangerous disposition, he soon became a valuable tag team partner. He captured Championships with two of WWE's most contemptuous characters, first forming "Jeri-Show" with Chris Jericho, then "Sho-Miz" with The Miz.

The WWE Universe again cheered for Big Show as he took on the Straight Edge Society, Nexus, and the Corre. In the process, Show reunited with Kane to win another WWE Tag Team Championship, and also found time to play the starring role in the WWE Studios film *Knucklehead*. At *WrestleMania XXVIII*, Big Show finally found that elusive *WrestleMania* moment when he defeated Cody Rhodes for the Intercontinental Championship.

In recent years, his dreaded mean streak always seems to resurface just when the WWE Universe lets their guard down. At *Over the Limit 2012*, he KO'd an unsuspecting John Cena to earn an "iron clad" contract from the smarmy John Laurinaitis. This newfound job security gave him the confidence to grab another World Heavyweight Championship at *Hell in a Cell 2012*, but did not save him from heavy-handed corporate influence. When The Authority usurped control over WWE, the domineering bosses used Big Show as a reluctant enforcer. Often torn between his pride and his pockets, Big Show has swung his cannonball-sized fist both for and against the sinister suits.

In a 20-year career that has included more than 20 Championships, Big Show's expansive footprint has become embedded in the foundation of sports-entertainment. At *WrestleMania 31*, he won the Andre the Giant Memorial Battle Royal, a fitting accolade for the Modern Era's preeminent giant. At the following year's Battle Royal, he shared a tense stare down with NBA legend, Shaq, rekindling an old rivalry. No matter what comes next, his towering shadow will linger over WWE for generations to follow.

IF YOU STEP IN THE RING WITH ME, I'M GONNA HURT YOU.

BIG TIME WRESTLING DETROIT

Although this territory existed since the 1920s, most ring historians associate Detroit with the blood-inducing, fire-throwing antics of the "most feared man in sport," the original Sheik.

What fans never knew was that "the wild man from Syria" also owned the promotion where he traded the United States Title with a roster that included Bobo Brazil, Johnny Valentine, Pampero Firpo, Adbullah the Butcher, Mark Lewin, Terry Funk, and Chief Jay Strongbow.

Harry Light was the Detroit promoter when he helped found the NWA in 1948, but sold it to Johnny Doyle and Jim Barnett ten years later. Verne Gagne, Wilbur Snyder, Hans Schmidt, Dick the Bruiser, and Angelo Poffo were among the early United States Champions.

In 1964, The Sheik and Francis Flescher purchased the territory, which promoted in Michigan, Ohio, Kentucky, and West Virginia.

In December 1980 The Sheik closed up shop in the Motor City, although he continued promoting for a short period in Flint, Michigan. He also held onto the United States Title and periodically defended it in unrestrained contests around the world.

BIG TIME WRESTLING SAN FRANCISCO

In 1961, longtime wrestler Roy Shire went to war with established San Francisco promoter Joe Malcewicz, procuring television coverage six weeks before the upstart's premier card at the celebrated Cow Palace.

Some believed that Shire was overreaching, but he had a weapon: "Blond Bomber" Ray Stevens. The Blond Bomber debuted at the Palace as the United States Titlist, enabling the company to eclipse Malcewicz.

Originally called the American Wrestling Alliance (AWA), this group had no ties to Verne Gagne's organization, and was soon rebranded as Big Time Wrestling. The territory's cities included Oakland, San Jose, Sacramento, and Fresno, among other places.

Known for its annual battle royal, the territory was largely built around Stevens, along with stars Pepper Gomez, Kenji Shibuya, Peter Maivia, Paul DeMarco, and manager Dr. Ken Ramey. Pat Patterson was another sensation—first as Steven's partner, then as his bitter rival.

In 1968, the company joined the NWA. But in 1978, United States Champ Moondog Mayne died in a car accident, and the company declined from there. In 1981, Gagne's AWA moved in to replace Shire.

BILL DEMOTT

| HT | 6'2" | WT | 280 lbs. | FROM | Trenton, New Jersey |
| SIGNATURE MOVE | No Laughing Matter |

For years, fans only knew Bill DeMott as WCW's fun-but-dangerous Hugh Morrus. In 2002, the former United States Champion's career took a serious turn when he began training the Superstars of tomorrow on *Tough Enough*. Under his given name, DeMott used fear as his chief teaching technique. His most noteworthy pupils were Matt Cappotelli and John Morrison.

As Hugh Morrus in WWE, DeMott competed on *SmackDown* and *Velocity* before settling into the *Velocity* announcers' booth. DeMott called the action alongside *Tough Enough* alum Josh Matthews. When *Tough Enough 4* completed, DeMott became a full-time trainer in WWE's developmental system. After a four-year hiatus, he returned in 2011 as the head trainer for the revival of *Tough Enough* alongside WWE Hall of Famer Stone Cold Steve Austin. Soon after, WWE opened its famed Performance Center in Orlando, Florida, where DeMott served as head coach for two years.

BILL MILLER

| HT | 6'6" | WT | 290 lbs. | FROM | Fremont, Ohio |
| SIGNATURE MOVE | Backbreaker |

A licensed veterinarian and member of the United States Navy, Dr. Bill Miller started his rounds in 1952, competing mainly in the AWA and NWA promotions.

In 1964, the doctor debuted in WWE and tested his skills against the world's fiercest ring animals. He and his brother, Dan, won the United States Tag Team Championship in August 1965 when they beat Cowboy Bill Watts and Gorilla Monsoon.

Miller retired from wrestling in 1973, but continued working as a veterinarian. The Navy veteran passed away in 1997. That same year, he was inducted into the Hall of Fame of his alma mater, Ohio State.

BILL WATTS

HT	6'3"	WT	290 lbs.	FROM	Oklahoma
SIGNATURE MOVE		Oklahoma Stampede			

"Cowboy" Bill Watts is one of the few sports-entertainment personalities that can confidently say he was a winner both in the ring and behind the scenes. After debuting in 1963, Watts briefly travelled the territories before settling into a successful WWE pairing with Gorilla Monsoon. In April 1965, the oversized duo defeated Gene Kiniski and Waldo Von Erich for the WWE United States Tag Team Championship. They held the Titles for four months before falling to Dan Miller and Dr. Bill Miller. Watts later challenged Bruno Sammartino for the WWE Championship on several occasions. Each time, Sammartino miraculously managed to walk away victorious.

When it came time to hang up the boots, Watts embarked on an impressive career as a promoter. As the leading force behind Mid South Wrestling, the "Cowboy" helped launch the careers of many Hall of Famers, including Junkyard Dog and Ted DiBiase. He later went on to become a WCW executive in the early 1990s. Watts' excellence was recognized in 2009 when he was inducted into the WWE Hall of Fame.

BILLY AND CHUCK

MEMBERS	Billy Gunn & Chuck Palumbo
COMBINED WT	535 lbs.

With their matching headbands, boy-band entrance theme, and touchy-feely affection for one another, the relationship between Billy and Chuck seemed to exceed that of simple tag team partners.

In September 2002, Chuck presented Billy with a gorgeous ring and asked Billy to be his partner for life. Billy excitedly agreed and the story began to dominate national news.

By the time the commitment ceremony rolled around, Billy developed a case of cold feet. Just moments before the actual ceremony took place, the duo put a halt to it and claimed their entire union was nothing but a publicity stunt. Following the shocking revelation, Billy and Chuck went their separate ways

BILLY GUNN

HT	6'3"	WT	260 lbs.	FROM	Orlando, Florida
SIGNATURE MOVE		The Fame-asser			

Few Superstars have undergone more fascinating evolutions in one career than Billy Gunn. He and his brother Bart came out shooting in 1993 as the Smokin' Gunns. The Wild West inspired wranglers held the World Tag Team Championship three times.

Billy would become a magnet for tag team gold, but first he traded in his six-shooter for a six string and became Rockabilly, a 1950's rocker managed by—who else?—The Honky Tonk Man. However, when the WWE Universe tuned out this throwback persona, Gunn and rival Jesse James agreed to change course and form the New Age Outlaws. With a brash, defiant new attitude, the Outlaws began to embody the cocky swagger of the Attitude Era.

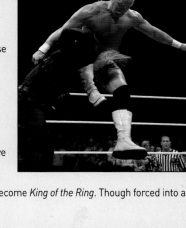

One of the most boisterous duos of all time, Gunn and the newly reinvented Road Dogg became a perfect fit for D-Generation X. Triple H made the alliance official after *WrestleMania XIV*. During this time, the Outlaws etched their names among the greatest duos of all time, topping several legendary tandems. After five Tag Team Championships and endless debauchery, Billy's new focus was two-fold: singles gold and his rear end.

Known as "Mr. Ass," he became a Hardcore Champion for the first time in 1999. Three months later, he defeated X-Pac to become *King of the Ring*. Though forced into a more censor-friendly persona called "The One," Gunn still became Intercontinental Champion in November 2000.

After briefly reforming the New Age Outlaws, Billy tasted tag team success once again with Chuck Palumbo. Billy and Chuck's persona was controversial at the time, but it didn't stop the close buddies from becoming WWE Tag Team Champions. In 2003, Billy went solo and drove female fans wild as the ever-popular "Mr. Ass."

Gunn departed WWE in 2004, but was not done. At *Royal Rumble 2014*, the reunited New Age Outlaws won their sixth Tag Team Titles nearly fourteen years removed from their fifth Title reign, a storybook comeback.

BILLY JACK HAYNES

HT	6'3"	WT	246 lbs.	FROM	Portland, Oregon
SIGNATURE MOVE		Full Nelson			

The pride of Portland, Billy Jack Haynes began his in-ring career in 1982. Over the next few years, he developed a fan following in the Portland, Florida, Mid-Atlantic, and World Class territories. Haynes possessed immense power and an impressive array of mat wrestling moves.

Haynes debuted in WWE in 1986 and was an immediate hit with audiences around the country. His impressive start made him a contender for the Intercontinental Championship, and his matches with Randy Savage got the attention of the WWE Championship Committee. He is most remembered for a vicious *WrestleMania III* confrontation with a fellow user of the Full Nelson, Hercules.

BILLY KIDMAN

HT	5'10"	WT	195 lbs.	FROM	Allentown, Pennsylvania
SIGNATURE MOVE	Shooting Star Press				

The multi-skilled Billy Kidman came to WWE following the promotion's acquisition of WCW in 2001. He made a strong first impression, upending Gregory Helms to claim the Cruiserweight Championship in his debut match. The win served as a sign of things to come for Kidman, who went on to capture the Title three more times while in WWE.

In July 2004, Kidman teamed with Paul London to defeat The Dudley Boyz for the WWE Tag Team Championship. It appeared as though things couldn't be going any better for the high-flying Superstar. However, when his signature Shooting Star Press nearly ended the career of Chavo Guerrero, feelings of extreme guilt began to set in on Kidman. It wasn't long before he couldn't bring himself to execute his most powerful weapon. A dejected Kidman even walked away from a September 2004 title defense, leaving his partner to fend for himself.

Kidman later blamed the fans for his emotional turmoil, and grew more vicious in the ring. The following year, Kidman left WWE. This time away from sports-entertainment served him well. In 2006 he returned as a trainer in WWE's development territory, Florida Championship Wrestling, a forerunner of NXT. In his capacity as a trainer, Kidman trained future Superstars like Sheamus, Koi Kingston, and Justin Gabriel, and became adept at television production. He soon combined his ring knowledge with his technical acumen, serving as a producer for *Raw* and *SmackDown*.

BILLY THE KID

Named after the infamous American outlaw, Billy the Kid was one of the South's most renowned dwarf wrestlers of the 1970s. Clad in a 10-gallon hat and scruffy beard, his cowboy persona helped solidify his status as one of the division's premier attractions.

For much of 1972, Billy the Kid formed a popular tag team with Wee Wee Wilson. In December, they teamed with Darling Dagmar to turn back Little Bruiser, Diamond Lil, and Johnny Reb in a memorable six-man tag team match. The bout proved to be one of the last times Billy the Kid and Wee Wee Wilson worked as a team, as they soon found themselves engaged in a bitter rivalry.

BILLY WHITE WOLF

HT	6'0"	WT	245 lbs.	FROM	Oklahoma
SIGNATURE MOVE	The Indian Deathlock				

Chief Billy White Wolf made his WWE debut in the late 1960s. A master of Indian Death Matches, he famously battled the likes of Bruiser Brody, The Executioners, Crusher Blackwell, and future WWE Hall of Famers Stan Hansen and Baron Mikel Scicluna. White Wolf's great combination of agility, classic mat wrestling, and spirit made him a favorite with fans all over the world.

White Wolf's virtuous path brought him together with another ring great, future WWE Hall of Famer and fellow native Oklahoman Chief Jay Strongbow. On December 7, 1976, White Wolf and Strongbow defeated The Executioners, and the duo of Nikolai Volkoff and Tor Kamata in a three-team tournament for the then-vacant World Tag Team Championship. The Native Americans held the ultimate tag team prize for eight months until White Wolf suffered a debilitating injury. While his career ended prematurely, Chief Billy White Wolf will always be remembered as a hero and a pioneer in the sport by fans all over the world.

BLACK BART

HT	6'4"	WT	350 lbs.	FROM	Pampa, Texas
SIGNATURE MOVE	Flying Leg Drop				

A tough-as-nails Texan, Black Bart literally left a lasting impression on his opposition, as it wasn't uncommon to see him mark his opponents using his trademark "BB" branding iron. Prior to his brief WWE stint in 1989, Black Bart gained notoriety competing in the southern territories of the United States with his tag team partner, Ron Bass. The duo carried their successful union from state to state before ultimately going their separate ways in 1985.

As a singles competitor, perhaps Black Bart's biggest victory came in September 1986 when he defeated Chris Adams for the World Class Championship Wrestling Title. Unfortunately for Bart, however, he lost the Title one month later to Kevin Von Erich.

BLACK GORDMAN

HT	5'10"	WT	233 lbs.	FROM	New Mexico
SIGNATURE MOVE	Abdominal Stretch				

When Black Gordman and his partner, the Great Goliath, were introduced at Los Angeles' Olympic Auditorium, they antagonized Latino fans by insisting that they weren't Mexican. Instead, they claimed they hailed from New Mexico.

The truth was that Gordman was a member of one of Mexico's most celebrated families, a brother-in-law of sometime opponent Mil Mascaras, and uncle of Alberto Del Rio. With Goliath, he held the NWA Americas Tag Team Championship 18 times. He won the Americas single's title on five occasions.

Although he also competed in San Antonio, Georgia, and other territories, Gordman was best known in southern California, where he won NWA Hollywood's famed battle royal in 1974. He fought both Pedro Morales and Victor Rivera in Madison Square Garden.

BLACK TIGER

HT	5'8"	WT	220 lbs.
FROM	England		

As the name suggests, Black Tiger concealed his identity by wearing a dark tiger mask. However, his in-ring skills were easily recognizable. Despite being a native of England, Black Tiger competed mainly in Japan where he was lauded for his hard-hitting aerial style. While competing in Fukuoka, the high-flyer defeated Gran Hamada for the now-defunct WWE Junior Heavyweight Championship. This was Black Tiger's first-and-only taste of WWE gold.

Twenty days after topping Hamada, Black Tiger lost the Junior Heavyweight Championship to his chief rival, Tiger Mask. Black Tiger's ties to the growing U.S. promotion began to fade following the loss. For the remainder of the decade, the masked Superstar continued to compete in Japan, depriving fans in the States of his jaw-dropping skills.

THE BLACKJACKS

MEMBERS	Blackjack Mulligan & Blackjack Lanza
COMBINED WT	585 lbs.

A couple of rough and tumble Texans, Blackjack Mulligan and Blackjack Lanza broke nearly every rule in the book on their way to the WWE Hall of Fame.

The Blackjacks first began teaming in the early 1970s. Clad in their signature cowboy hats, leather vests, and black gloves, Mulligan and Lanza captured tag team championships in the World Wrestling Association and National Wrestling Alliance before bringing their game to WWE in the mid-1970s.

Individually, both Blackjacks enjoyed stellar careers. In WWE, Mulligan was a top contender, while Lanza is often associated with the AWA and manager Bobby Heenan.

The Blackjacks enjoyed a nearly three-month World Tag Team Championship reign in 1975. After losing the Titles in November, Mulligan and Lanza failed to reach the same heights, but their amazing legacy would be recreated two decades later.

In 1996, Barry Windham, the son of Blackjack Mulligan, teamed with Blackjack Lanza's nephew, Justin "Hawk" Bradshaw, to form The New Blackjacks. In appearance, the tag team looked identical to the original tandem. Unfortunately, that's where the similarities stopped. After failing to properly represent the legend of the original Blackjacks, Windham and Bradshaw parted company.

In 2006, Blackjack Mulligan and Blackjack Lanza received the ultimate honor when their efforts in the tag team ranks landed them in the WWE Hall of Fame.

BLAKE AND MURPHY

MEMBERS	Wesley Blake & Buddy Murphy	COMBINED WT	467 lbs.

Blake and Murphy came from different disciplines before fusing their styles to transform into one of NXT's most prolific tag teams.

A native of San Antonio, Texas, Blake competes in a fiery, but methodical, manner that would have made him a headliner in the southern wrestling territories of old. By contrast, Australian-bred Murphy is a daredevil who enjoys bungee jumping and swimming with whales—and overwhelming foes with an unpredictable arsenal.

In 2015, the pair won the NXT Tag Team Championship and held it for close to seven months. Their wily valet, Alexa Bliss, serves as an extra weapon, as evidenced during the duo's rivalry with Enzo Amore and Colin Cassady. In those contests, Bliss regularly undermined the presence of Amore and Cassady's valet, Carmella.

THE BLU BROTHERS

MEMBERS	Jacob & Eli
COMBINED WT	640 lbs.

Identical twins from the Appalachian Mountains, Jacob and Eli Blu were led to WWE by their Uncle Zebekiah in January 1995. Their long hair and bushy beards provided for an unorthodox appearance, but when the bell rang, the Blu Brothers proved to possess a traditional powerhouse approach to competition.

Jacob and Eli often used their identical appearances to confuse opponents, officials, and onlookers. Their sly tricks, coupled with their immense power, guided them to many victories. After months of impressing WWE officials, Jacob and Eli earned a spot on *WrestleMania XI*, where they unsuccessfully battled Lex Luger and British Bulldog.

The brothers cooled following their *WrestleMania* loss. After failing to defeat The Smokin' Gunns at *SummerSlam 1995*, Jacob and Eli made a quiet exit from WWE.

BLUE MEANIE

HT	6'1"	WT	323 lbs.
FROM	Atlantic City, New Jersey		
SIGNATURE MOVE	Meaniesault		

Following a comedic ECW career, Blue Meanie made his WWE debut in late 1998. Originally a member of Al Snow's JOB Squad, the blue-haired Superstar proved to be equally entertaining inside WWE rings.

In early 1999, Meanie resumed the impersonations that made him so popular in ECW. As Bluedust, he battled Goldust at *St. Valentine's Day Massacre*, losing the match but winning the crowd.

In June 2005, Blue Meanie returned at the *ECW One Night Stand* pay-per-view with the rest of the Blue World Order. After a few more appearances, including a win over JBL following assists from Stevie Richards and Batista, Meanie left WWE. He currently competes on the independent circuit and trains aspiring Superstars at New Jersey's famous Monster Factory.

BLUE PANTS

HT	5'2"	FROM	The Clearance Rack
SIGNATURE MOVE	Superkick		

What started as a taunt ended up transforming an unknown into a cult figure.

In 2014, Carmella was in the ring at NXT, accompanied by her ever-present contingent, Enzo Amore and Colin Cassady. Before the action started, Enzo grabbed the microphone to introduce Carmella's opponent. Noticing the woman's ring outfit, Amore mockingly declared, "Coming from the clearance rack...Blue Pants."

He unwittingly created a legend.

From that point forward, fans cheered wildly whenever Blue Pants was announced. She even helped the Vaudevillians win the NXT Tag Team Title at *NXT Takeover: Brooklyn* by neutralizing Blake and Murphy's valet, Alexa Bliss.

Despite her erratic NXT appearances, the mention of "Blue Pants" generally has fans roaring in approval.

BO DALLAS

HT	6'1"	WT	234 lbs.

FROM Brooksville, Florida

SIGNATURE MOVE Running Bo-Dog

Bo Dallas was once the longest reigning Champion in NXT history, holding the Title for 261 days. Such a feat would give anyone confidence, but to truly shoot for the stars, one must Bo-lieve!

Dallas began spreading this Bo-tivational message in 2014 through a series of inspirational self-help vignettes. With an ear-to-ear grin plastered across his face, he emerged in WWE beaming with positivity and an indomitable spirit. A hot start only added to his fervor, his pep talks and victory laps getting more emphatic as his win-loss record climbed to "17 & Bo."

Bo's winning streak may have stopped but his mouth never lost a beat. This trait has earned the grinning grappler beatings from stars such as Ryback, Sting, and Brock Lesnar. However, not everyone is infuriated by Dallas. He found common ground with Heath Slater, Curtis Axel, and Adam Rose in 2015. With his fellow Social Outcasts, Dallas continues to show his un-Bo-lievable athletic ability. If he has taken his own moving messages to heart, all he has to do is BO-LIEVE!

BOBBY DUNCUM

HT	6'7"	WT	285 lbs.	FROM	Amarillo, Texas

SIGNATURE MOVE Sleeper

"Cowboy" Bobby Duncum made his ring debut in 1971 following a stint in the NFL. He was known to do things his way, and if someone didn't like it, they'd usually get a fist straight to the jaw.

In his first year of competition, Duncum captured an amazing five championships, including Florida's NWA Southern Heavyweight Championship. In 1974, Duncum arrived in WWE and immediately made his presence known when he won a 20-man over-the-top-rope Battle Royal. He then moved on to a series of memorable contests against Bruno Sammartino, including a Texas Death Match at the Boston Garden with Gorilla Monsoon as special guest referee. After leaving the company in 1975, Duncum won several regional territory titles in the NWA.

In 1979, Duncum, alongside manager The Grand Wizard, returned to WWE with the hopes of dominating then-WWE Champion Bob Backlund. In 1982, the Cowboy from Austin left WWE for good. In later years, Duncum's son, Bobby Duncum Jr., competed globally, most notably in ECW and WCW.

BOB BACKLUND

see page 41

BOBBY HEENAN

see page 42

BOB ORTON SR.

HT	6'2"	WT	235 lbs.

FROM Kansas City, Kansas

Today's fans recognize Randy Orton as a truly elite Superstar; and they recall Randy's father, Bob Orton, with great respect and admiration. But before these two Ortons ruled WWE rings, there was the original Orton: Bob Orton Sr.

As the patriarch of the Orton family, Bob Sr. competed mainly in the Florida and Central States territories, where he captured more than fifteen regional titles, including the NWA Florida Tag Team Championship with his son, Bob Jr. Orton briefly competed in WWE as Rocky Fitzpatrick. Under the new name, Orton formed a formidable union with Buddy Rogers.

After nearly fifty years, "The Big O" finally hung up his boots at the turn of the century, leaving behind an amazing legacy and a foundation for future Orton family success.

BOBBY DAVIS

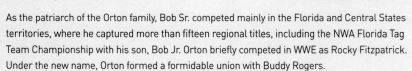

When a serious neck injury ended his in-ring dreams, Bobby Davis didn't walk away from wrestling completely. Instead, the persistent youngster shifted his focus from competing in the ring to managing the ring's competitors.

As a manager, the charismatic Davis compiled an impressive stable that included such top names as Johnny Valentine, Dr. Bill Miller, the Graham brothers, and Magnificent Maurice. Perhaps his most notable client was the first-ever WWE Champion, Buddy Rogers.

Together, the arrogant pairing of Rogers and Davis verbally tore down the Champ's opposition on a routine basis. Of course, if Rogers ever found himself in trouble at any point during the match, Davis was not above employing some underhanded tactics to ensure his client picked up the win.

BOBBY LASHLEY

Bobby Lashley's time in WWE was fleeting, but during that time he dominated the land of extreme and even forcefully shaved the Chairman of WWE bald!

A U.S. Army product, Lashley was a decorated amateur wrestling champion in both the college and military ranks. In September 2005, Bobby debuted in WWE. His immediate dominance led to a United States Championship and World Championship opportunities within his rookie year. In 2006, he became ECW Champion after surviving WWE's first-ever Extreme Elimination Chamber. Bobby's crowning achievement came at *WrestleMania 23* when he represented Donald Trump in "The Battle of The Billionaires." Fans saw Mr. McMahon lose his famed hairdo when Bobby Lashley defeated the Chairman's representative, Umaga. Lashley beat the Chairman himself at *One Night Stand* in a Street Fight to become a two-time ECW Champion.

Lashley aimed for the WWE Championship in 2007 but was defeated by John Cena in a tense match at *The Great American Bash*. In early 2008, Lashley left WWE to pursue a career in MMA.

BOB BACKLUND

HT	6'1"
WT	234 lbs.
FROM	Princeton, Minnesota

SIGNATURE MOVE
Crossface Chickenwing

It was always easy to cheer for Bob Backlund during the late 1970s and early 1980s. His boy-next-door looks made him impossible to dislike, while his superior athleticism solidified his lofty in-ring status. Backlund's second stint with WWE, however, was a completely different story. With age, he became more maniacal. And by the mid 1990s, he was borderline insane, which makes the Bob Backlund story even more fascinating.

Backlund first made a name for himself within wrestling circles while competing at North Dakota State University, where he captured the NCAA Division II heavyweight wrestling championship. Shortly after college, the successful amateur wrestler took his game to the pro ranks, debuting for his home state's American Wrestling Association (AWA) in 1974. For the next several years, Backlund bounced between various wrestling regions.

WWE COMES CALLING

In the spring of 1977, Backlund received the opportunity of a lifetime when Vincent J. McMahon called to offer him a spot with WWE. He quickly accepted, packed his bags and left his small-town life in Minnesota for the bright lights of New York City. With Arnold Skaaland as his manager, Backlund became an instant hit with WWE fans. His All-American persona gave audiences somebody they could look up to; within months of his arrival, he was catapulted to the top of the card.

After several unsuccessful attempts to capture the WWE Championship, Backlund finally dethroned "Superstar" Billy Graham in February 1978, despite the Champion's leg being on the ropes during the pinfall. His reign will forever go down in history as one of the greatest of all time, lasting nearly six years (second only to Bruno Sammartino's nearly eight-year reign).

In search of more gold, Backlund teamed with Pedro Morales to defeat the Wild Samoans for the World Tag Team Championship at Shea Stadium in August 1980. Unfortunately for Backlund, he was forced to vacate the Title due to a WWE rule at the time that prohibited a Superstar from holding more than one Championship at any given time.

Backlund's epic WWE Championship reign came to a controversial end in December 1983. While defending against Iron Sheik, Backlund found himself locked in the challenger's dreaded Camel Clutch. Refusing to submit, he suffered in the submission move for an extended period of time.

Finally, in an attempt to prevent permanent damage, Arnold Skaaland threw in the towel for Backlund. The popular former Champion later suggested that his reign should never have ceased, due to the fact that he didn't give up. The protest proved ineffective and Backlund quickly left WWE soon after.

THAT'S 'MISTER' BACKLUND!

A NEW ERA, AND A NEW ATTITUDE

Nearly one decade after vanishing from the sports-entertainment world, Mr. Backlund made a shocking return to WWE in 1992. In his early 40s at the time, WWE fans didn't expect much success from the aging Superstar. They were soon proven wrong.

The 1990s version of Bob Backlund proved to be much different than the boy-next-door champion everybody loved in the 1970s and 1980s. This Bob Backlund was a rage-filled, middle-aged maniac who quickly drew the ire of fans with his endless rants and overly verbose vocabulary. Inside the ring, however, he was just as dangerous as ever.

In November 1994, the aging Backlund defied the odds when he defeated Bret Hart for the WWE Championship at *Survivor Series*. Ironically, his second reign began the same way his first one ended when Hart's mother threw in the towel, signifying the end of her son's reign.

Backlund's second run as WWE Champion failed to mirror the success of his first. A mere three days after capturing the Title, he was defeated by Diesel in a match that lasted only eight seconds.

The WWE record books will forever recognize Backlund's second reign as one of the shortest of all time. Despite the loss to Diesel, however, his brief time atop WWE capped off one of the most successful returns in sports-entertainment history.

In 2013, Backlund's greatness was recognized with induction into the WWE Hall of Fame. The honor put a fitting exclamation point on a career that will be remembered as one of the brightest of all time.

BOBBY THE BRAIN HEENAN

HT	5'10"
WT	242 lbs.
FROM	Beverly Hills, California

Bobby Heenan is inarguably one of the most gifted minds in sports-entertainment history. In addition to being perhaps the greatest manager of all time, "The Brain" was also a fearless broadcast journalist, who, along with Gorilla Monsoon, made up one of the industry's most revered commentary teams.

Forced to leave school in the seventh grade to care for his family, Heenan took a job selling programs at local wrestling events in Indianapolis. It wasn't long before his charisma caught the eye of the competitors, who soon welcomed him into their fraternity. The likable youngster made his debut in 1965 as a wrestler/manager known as "Pretty Boy" Bobby Heenan. Later while managing the duo of Ray Stevens and Nick Bockwinkel in the AWA, he announced that he should be referred to as "The Brain."

THE HEENAN FAMILY

While wreaking havoc through Minneapolis, Heenan accumulated a collection of outlaws known as "The Heenan Family." The founding members consisted of Stevens, Bockwinkel, Bobby Duncum Sr., Dick Warren, and Blackjack Lanza. In 1984, the manager took his talents to the nationally-expanding WWE and immediately began his quest to topple its most beloved heroes, most notably Andre the Giant and Hulk Hogan.

Heenan's first client, Big John Studd, served as The Heenan Family cornerstone. Standing nearly 7-foot tall, Studd set his sights on Andre the Giant. The two behemoths battled in a Body Slam Match at the first-ever WrestleMania, where Andre won after slamming Studd to the mat. With the victory, the Giant claimed $15,000 in prize money, which he chose to share with the crowd. Before he could spread the wealth, Heenan swooped in and stole the bag full of cash.

As Heenan expanded his strategic assembly of WWE's most feared figures, he welcomed the likes of King Kong Bundy, Ken Patera, and Paul Orndorff into the fold. But if he was to succeed in conquering Hulkamania, The Brain knew he had to come up with something big. That's when he turned to former foe Andre the Giant.

Heenan's conniving ways amazingly persuaded the Giant to turn his back on friend Hulk Hogan and challenge him to a WWE Championship match at WrestleMania III. In the end, Heenan's man was unable to dethrone The Hulkster, but the Andre-Hogan match will forever go down as one of sports-entertainment's most historic matches.

Heenan claimed his first taste of WWE gold in 1989 when Rick Rude defeated Ultimate Warrior for the Intercontinental Championship at WrestleMania V. Though the victory was not without controversy. In typical Heenan fashion, the manager interfered when he held Warrior's legs down, making it easier for Rude to score the pin.

Later that same year, Heenan collected even more gold when he managed both the Brain Busters and Colossal Connection to the World Tag Team Championship. As the new decade emerged, Heenan continued his magic touch, leading Mr. Perfect to the Intercontinental Championship.

Perhaps Heenan's greatest success as a manager came in 1991 when he played an instrumental role in bringing multiple-time NWA and WCW Champion Ric Flair to WWE. Though he didn't always accompany the "Nature Boy" to the ring, he successfully advised his WWE career, en route to the legend capturing two WWE Championship reigns.

THE BRAIN PICKS UP THE MIC

Heenan's amazing gift for gab eventually led him to a career behind the microphone. In addition to hosting the cult favorite Bobby Heenan Show, The Brain also became one of the most entertaining color commentators in sports-entertainment history. And as fledgling Monday Night Raw began to take shape, Heenan hoped to continue his career at the announce table. Unfortunately for The Brain, however, it was not to be. In December 1993, Heenan was given his WWE exit when Gorilla Monsoon tossed him and his belongings into the cold for good.

Heenan's contributions to the sports-entertainment industry continued following his WWE departure. As a member of WCW, he called the action during Monday Nitro's rise to prominence in the Monday Night War. Following WCW's sale in 2001, Heenan returned to WWE alongside "Mean" Gene Okerlund to call the action at WrestleMania X-Seven's Gimmick Battle Royal.

In March 2004, Bobby Heenan's unparalleled career was honored when he was inducted into the WWE Hall of Fame the night before WrestleMania XX.

YOU LISTEN TO ME, YOU GO TO THE TOP!

BOBO BRAZIL

HT	6'6"	WT	270 lbs.	FROM	Benton Harbor, Michigan
SIGNATURE MOVE			Coco Butt		

The legend of Bobo Brazil goes well beyond wins and losses. As a black man competing during a turbulent time in America, Brazil showed amazing grace while overcoming racial stereotypes and barriers. Along the way, he became recognized as sports-entertainment's Jackie Robinson and one of the industry's most influential figures.

Originally named Boo Boo Brazil, the Michigan native made his professional debut in 1951 and competed in the Detroit area. It wasn't until a printing error billed him as Bobo that fans began to recognize Brazil under his now-famous name.

It was common practice during this time for African-American competitors to be booked against each other. Because of that, Brazil spent much of his career battling the likes of Ernie Ladd and Thunderbolt Patterson. However, his in-ring arsenal, highlighted by the "Coco Butt" head butt, eventually proved to be too valuable for promoters to limit. As a result, he finally battled such legendary opponents as Killer Kowalski and Freddie Blassie. Brazil's fans eventually demanded to see more and more of their hero. His popularity initially forced many promoters to book him in dream matches against several other popular Superstars of the time, such as Andre the Giant and Bruno Sammartino.

After leaving WWE in the late 1960s, Brazil went on to compete throughout Los Angeles, Detroit, and Japan among other locales. During this time, he engaged in a bloody rivalry with The Sheik that saw Brazil capture a version of the United States Championship (not the current WWE title). When Brazil returned to WWE in 1976, the promotion actually announced him as the U.S. Champion, despite the fact that it was not a WWE-recognized Title. The act was an enormous sign of respect for the sports-entertainment pioneer.

Bobo Brazil's remarkable career was honored with induction into the WWE Hall of Fame in 1994. The ceremony recognized his amazing in-ring conquests, as well as his tireless civil rights efforts that helped pave the way for those who followed.

THE BODYDONNAS

MEMBERS	Skip & Zip
COMBINED WT	455 lbs.

While accomplished competitors, fitness gurus Skip and Zip are perhaps best known for nauseating the WWE Universe with their constant pushups and jumping jacks. When they weren't showing off their incredible endurance, The Bodydonnas were often seen challenging fans to get off their butts and get into shape.

With some help from manager Sunny, Skip and Zip reached their pinnacle when they won the World Tag Team Championship at *WrestleMania XII*'s Free for All. Unfortunately for the exercise fiends, they lost the Titles to the Godwinns less than two months later. Adding insult to injury, Sunny followed the gold and started managing the Godwinns.

Skip and Zip tried to fill the empty position with a new manager, Kloudy. But the union was short-lived. The Bodydonnas disbanded in 1996, but will forever be remembered for their fitness as much as for their seamless teamwork in the ring. The message from their former manager, Sunny, summed it up well: "You've seen the rest; now see the best."

BOLO MONGOL

HT	6'3"	WT	291 lbs.	FROM	Mongolia

In the late 1960s and early 1970s, Geto and Bepo Mongol terrorized the tag team ranks of WWE. Collectively known as The Mongol Brothers, their unorthodox style led them to countless victories, including a reign as WWE's International Tag Team Champions. After more than a year with the Titles, The Mongols lost the gold to Bruno Sammartino and Dominic DeNucci in June 1971.

The loss failed to set The Mongols back, as they quickly resumed their habit of pulverizing opponents. Then, suddenly, their plans seemed to go awry when a freak injury sidelined Bepo. Many thought that the injury meant the end of The Mongols, but Geto quickly replaced his partner with the equally unorthodox Bolo Mongol.

Bolo had the signature Mongol look, complete with horns of hair on an otherwise bald head. Together, Bolo and Geto briefly kept the legend of The Mongols alive in the Pittsburgh territory, as well as Japan and the short-lived renegade promotion, the IWA. However, after this run, Bolo broke away from Geto, and the Mongols were nevermore.

THE BOLSHEVIKS

MEMBERS	Nikolai Volkoff & Boris Zhukov
COMBINED WT	604 lbs.

Two powerful Russian Superstars, Nikolai Volkoff and Boris Zhukov, joined forces in the spring of 1988. To the disgust of fans and opponents all over the globe, The Bolsheviks waived Soviet flags en route to the ring and sang the Russian National Anthem before each match.

Once the bell rang, Volkoff and Zhukov specialized in crushing double-team moves and underhanded tactics. Their success eventually earned them a spot on the inaugural *SummerSlam* card, where they fell to the mighty Powers of Pain. Volkoff and Zhukov rebounded nicely from the loss and were granted a match at *WrestleMania VI* against the Hart Foundation. Unfortunately for the Soviets, they were defeated in less than twenty seconds in front of a capacity SkyDome crowd.

Soon after the loss, the bond that held The Bolsheviks together was irrevocably broken. Volkoff and Zhukov battled across the United States and, for the first time in his career, Volkoff was cheered for his efforts. Zhukov remained one of WWE's most hated villains until his departure in 1991.

BOOGEYMAN

HT	6'2"	WT	260 lbs.	FROM	The Bottomless Pit
SIGNATURE MOVE	Boogeyslam

WWE Superstars are among the toughest men to walk the planet, but when the lights go out, you wouldn't blame them if they feared the Boogeyman. Hailing from The Bottomless Pit, Boogeyman first started spooking WWE in October 2005, when he began frightening Superstars with disturbing renditions of classic nursery rhymes.

After pummeling Simon Dean in his December 2005 in-ring debut, Boogeyman set his sights on former WWE Champion John "Bradshaw" Layfield. And at the 2006 *Royal Rumble*, Boogeyman made quick work of JBL, finishing him off with his patented pump-handle slam. After the match, Boogeyman celebrated his first pay-per-view victory with a mouthful of live worms.

Boogeyman then focused his sinister sights on yet another past Titleholder, defeating King Booker on the grand stage of *WrestleMania 22*, but not before planting a worm-filled kiss on Queen Sharmell.

The Boogeyman slipped back into the darkness in 2009, only to rear his face-painted head on select occasions. Given the unpredictability of when he'll appear next, it's safe to say that several WWE Superstars probably sleep with the lights on.

BOOKER T

see page 45

BORIS MALENKO

HT	5'10"	WT	220 lbs.	FROM	Moscow, Russia
SIGNATURE MOVE	Russian Sickle

With the "Red Scare" still lingering in the United States, Boris Malenko used his Russian ancestry to strike fear into both opponents and fans. A master antagonist, Malenko could draw more hatred from audiences than any other Superstar of his time.

Malenko was much more than an ire-inspiring Russian; he was also a brilliant competitor inside the ring. In fact, his amazing abilities earned him the nicknames, "The Great Malenko" and "Professor Malenko." Despite possessing superior skills, Malenko was not above cheating to earn a victory. It wasn't uncommon to see him biting or jabbing the eyes of an opponent to gain the upper hand.

In May 1967, Malenko defeated Wahoo McDaniel to capture the National Wrestling Alliance Florida Heavyweight Championship. It was his first of eleven NWA Titles, including seven reigns as the Florida Brass Knuckles Champion. Malenko passed away in 1994, but he left behind an amazing legacy, which includes two sons who also competed in the ring, Joe and Dean Malenko.

BORIS ZHUKOV

HT	6'2"	WT	275 lbs.	FROM	Siberia, Russia
SIGNATURE MOVE	Flying Clothesline

Boris Zhukov first appeared in World Class Championship Wrestling in the early 1980s and later toured the Southeastern United States before moving to the AWA in 1985. While in the Minnesota territory, Zhukov made a name for himself battling foes such as Sgt. Slaughter and Jimmy Snuka.

In 1987, the formidable Russian traveled to WWE and immediately teamed with Nikolai Volkoff to form the Bolsheviks. Managed by Slick, the powerhouses were initially seen as serious threats to the World Tag Team Championship, but their credibility soon faded following a loss to the Hart Foundation in less than twenty seconds at *WrestleMania VI*.

The mighty Russians went their separate ways shortly after the *WrestleMania* loss. Zhukov competed on his own until he left WWE in 1991.

BRAD MADDOX

HT	5'11"	WT	207 lbs.	FROM	Charlotte, North Carolina

Some people will do anything to gain notoriety in WWE, but clock Ryback in the family jewels? That is insane! But that is exactly what Brad Maddox did at *Hell in a Cell 2012*. As a result, Maddox lost all credibility as a ref but earned himself a series of WWE tryout matches.

After falling short in the ring, Maddox shifted gears. He politicked himself into Mr. McMahon's good graces and eventually became *Raw* General Manager. The self-dubbed "Braditude Era" on *Raw* lasted nearly a year. Maddox's leadership, however, was overshadowed by more domineering personalities on the corporate ladder. Failing to please The Authority, Maddox was fired by Stephanie McMahon and subsequently flattened by Kane. Maddox was released by WWE in late 2015, but not before donning a turkey suit and getting Tombstoned by Undertaker on Jimmy Fallon's Thanksgiving episode.

BOOKER T

HT	6'3"
WT	253 lbs.
FROM	Houston, Texas

SIGNATURE MOVE
Book End, Scissor Kick

After a difficult and troublesome early life, Booker T turned to sports-entertainment to overcome his past and carve himself a promising future. Stepping out from his job at a storage company and into a pair of boots, the Houston native never could have imagined becoming sports-entertainment royalty.

HEATING UP

Booker and his brother Stevie Ray joined WCW as Harlem Heat in August of 1993. After signing Sherri Martel as their manager, the duo went on to dominate the WCW tag team scene in the 1990s. They defeated stalwarts such as the Steiner Brothers, Nasty Boys, Public Enemy, and more on their way to becoming WCW World Tag Team Champions a record ten times.

An injury to Stevie Ray in 1997 gave Booker the opportunity to prove his worth as a solo competitor. He took advantage by claiming the WCW World Television Title, an accolade he would claim six times to again set a WCW record. As the calendar turned to a new millennium, it was clear Booker was destined for WCW's top prize.

5-TIME! 5-TIME! 5-TIME! 5-TIME! 5-TIME!

As an impromptu stand-in at *Bash at the Beach 2000*, Booker capitalized on the opportunity and defeated Jeff Jarrett for his first WCW Championship. He held the coveted gold three times in the year 2000 and in 2001, Booker ended the historic last episode of *WCW Monday Nitro* by becoming WCW Champion again. His now-famous tally of five WCW Title reigns was eventually book-ended by a win over Kurt Angle when the WCW gold was contested on WWE programming.

In the weeks that followed WWE's purchase of its one-time rival, Booker T invaded WWE and attacked Stone Cold Steve Austin at *King of the Ring*. Booker then participated in the first-ever WCW match to be held on WWE programming when he defended his WCW Championship on *Monday Night Raw* against Buff Bagwell. Booker became a key member of The Alliance as they attempted to overthrow WWE. He won the World Tag Team Championship in November of 2001 when he and Test defeated The Rock and Chris Jericho on *SmackDown*.

A BIZARRE BROTHERHOOD

In 2002, "The Bizarre One" Goldust convinced a skeptical Booker that their two divergent personalities could form a great duo. They were able to blend their different ring styles into one to create an indescribable chemistry. They also provided some of the funniest segments in *Raw* history as hosts of "Booker T & Goldust At The Movies."

At *Armageddon 2002*, they won a Fatal-Four Way Elimination Match for the World Tag Team Championship but lost the Titles to Lance Storm and William Regal weeks later on *Raw*. After failed attempts to win back the gold, the team split, but the two Superstars remained allies.

Booker spent subsequent years scissor-kicking his way through the tag team and singles ranks. His rivalry with a young John Cena over the United States Championship became one of *SmackDown's* key attractions.

ALL HAIL!

Perhaps Booker's crowning achievement came in 2006. As winner of the King of the Ring tournament, Booker embraced the WWE monarchy like no other. Speaking in a faux-accent worthy of Elizabethan England, he and his Queen Sharmell ruled with an iron fist. With cape and scepter in tow, Booker conquered Rey Mysterio for the World Heavyweight Championship at *The Great American Bash 2006*. His imperial reign reached its apex when he won a Champion of Champions Match at *Cyber Sunday 2006*, defeating both the reigning WWE and ECW Champions.

After a three-year hiatus, the master of the Spin-A-Rooni returned as a participant in the *2011 Royal Rumble*. He has since brought his signature sounds to the *SmackDown* announce team, served as *SmackDown* General Manager, and drilled WWE hopefuls as a hardnosed trainer on *Tough Enough*. Whether in the ring, behind the microphone, or training potential Superstars, Booker T is truly in a class by himself. That is why in 2013, WWE honored him with induction into its Hall of Fame. Now can you dig that, sucka?

NOW CAN YOU DIG THAT, SUCKA?

BRADEN WALKER

HT	6'4"	WT	262 lbs.
FROM	Ft. Wright, Kentucky		

"Knock, knock." "Who's there?"

"Braden Walker, and I'm gonna knock your brains out."

A confident Braden Walker had the above exchange with Armando Estrada during his *ECW* debut in July 2008. And just as he prophetically forecasted, the new Superstar defeated Estrada after connecting with a top rope flying crossbody.

As a member of General Manager Theodore Long's New Superstar Initiative, the future was looking bright for Walker. The big Kentuckian followed up on his debut victory with a win over James Curtis. But with two wins in his back pocket, Walker mysteriously vanished in August 2008, never to be seen again. Despite his quick disappearance, Walker's debut knock-knock joke is still referenced by the WWE Universe as one of the oddest comments ever uttered.

BRADY BOONE

HT	5'10"	WT	220 lbs.
FROM	Oregon City, Oregon		
SIGNATURE MOVE	Moonsault		

Hailing from the state of Oregon, Brady Boone was recognized as one of the top high school gymnasts in the country before embarking on a sports-entertainment career. He debuted in WWE in the late 1980s and quickly awed audiences with his high-flying style. Among the Superstars who couldn't solve Boone's amazing aerial skills include Steve Lombardi and Barry Horowitz.

As his in-ring career came to a close, Boone was hired by WCW to serve as a referee. Sadly, in December 1998, Brady Boone's was killed in an automobile accident in Orlando, FL. His high-flying legacy will always be remembered and admired by true mat fans all over the globe.

BRAIN BUSTERS

MEMBERS	Arn Anderson & Tully Blanchard
COMBINED WT	475 lbs.

As founding members of the legendary Four Horsemen, Arn Anderson and Tully Blanchard created historic reputations that preceded their WWE debut. Once they arrived in WWE, their impressive teamwork went a long way in proving they were just as good as everybody said.

Trading in manager J.J. Dillon for Bobby "The Brain" Heenan, the two-time NWA Tag Team Champions made their way to WWE in 1988. Billed as the Brain Busters (playing off their manager's nickname), Anderson and Blanchard made quick work of WWE's top teams, including The Rockers on *Saturday Night's Main Event* and Strike Force at *WrestleMania V*. Despite their impressive record, it took the team more than seven months to receive their first high-profile World Tag Team Championship opportunity.

In May 1989, the Brain Busters challenged Demolition for the tag Titles on *Saturday Night's Main Event*. Anderson and Blanchard walked away with the disqualification victory, but not the Championship. Two months later, they finished the job when they beat Demolition in a two-out-of-three falls match. With the Titles in their possession, the Brain Busters were finally considered a part of WWE's upper echelon of Superstars.

The Brain Busters left WWE in late 1989. While their stay in the promotion was brief, Anderson and Blanchard used the time to successfully prove to a national audience that they were one of the most intelligent and technically sound tag teams of the 1980s.

BRAKKUS

HT	6'0"	WT	275 lbs.	FROM	Germany	SIGNATURE MOVE	Powerslam

If physiques alone equated to success in sports-entertainment, Brakkus would be a first-ballot Hall of Famer. A former professional bodybuilder, the mighty German made his WWE debut in 1996 and quickly learned that a Superstar needed more than enormous muscles to be successful.

Shortly after being introduced, WWE shipped Brakkus off to the USWA and ECW where he could gain some much-needed experience. In February 1998, he challenged Tazz for the ECW World Television Championship at *CyberSlam*, but was unable to wrest the Title away.

Later that year, Brakkus returned to WWE and competed in the Brawl For All tournament, where he lost in disappointing fashion to Savio Vega. Afterward, Brakkus returned to Europe and has not been seen in WWE since.

BRAUN STROWMAN

HT	6'8"	WT	385 lbs.

With his mammoth proportions, unnerving stare and bulging tree trunks for arms, Braun Strowman would be terrifying even without the influence of backwoods madman, Bray Wyatt. Forget following the buzzards, this man is huge enough to reach up and swat them out of the sky. Nevertheless, Strowman arrived beside the Wyatt clan in August 2015 as the family's black sheep, both in stature and face decor. As the Wyatt's newest weapon, many have already fallen victim to his might, including Dean Ambrose, Chris Jericho, and the Dudleys.

Strowman delivered a scary statement in the 2016 *Royal Rumble Match* when he outmuscled *Rumble* legend Kane and the 480-pound Big Show upon entering the match. With this sinister spawn on the loose, there is no predicting the wreckage in store.

BRAY WYATT

HT	6'3"	WT	285 lbs.
SIGNATURE MOVE			Sister Abigail

Perched in a creaky old rocking chair and illuminated by the glow of an ominous lantern, Bray Wyatt offered his first eerie warnings to WWE in 2013. That summer, a "New Face of Fear" was born as Wyatt's every move added to the dread and mystique that surrounded him. Flanked by two oversized goons willing to cater to his every sinister whim, Wyatt began his dark pursuit by punishing all who refused to "follow the buzzards."

After Daniel Bryan rebuffed Wyatt's horrifying recruiting attempts, the Eater of Worlds and his flock targeted John Cena. Though Cena debunked Wyatt's accusations that his gallant reputation was a façade, a disturbing development unfolded that saw some of Cenation's most impressionable minds become spellbound by Wyatt's cryptic prose. Soon, darkened arenas were speckled with flickering lights that became known as Wyatt's "fireflies." As his demonic influence seduced fragile psyches, Wyatt cast his original followers, Harper and Rowan, off to inflict their own brand of chaos.

In the ring, Wyatt's victories over Cena, Dean Ambrose, and Chris Jericho highlighted his growing resume, and he soon became fixated on becoming WWE's most dreaded force. Wyatt's twisted mind games to resurrect Undertaker did not lead to a defining *WrestleMania* victory but still proved the lengths Wyatt would go to fulfill his vision. In the summer of 2015, Wyatt reunited his family and resumed his quest, promising doom for all who stand in his way, especially Roman Reigns.

Despite Wyatt's threats at *WrestleMania 32*, The Rock paid him the ultimate compliment, pointing out his in-ring talent and charisma. The following night, Wyatt and company thrashed the League of Nations.

If you take one word of advice from this silver-tongued lunatic, let it be this—"Run!"

BRET HART

see page 48

THE BRIAN KENDRICK

HT	5'8"	WT	170 lbs.	**FROM**	Venice, California
SIGNATURE MOVE			The Kendrick		

A graduate of the Shawn Michaels Wrestling Academy, Brian Kendrick entered WWE with the technique, toughness, and flare that only HBK could teach. In 2003, Brian debuted in WWE and wowed crowds with his aerial moves and speed. He soon found a tag team partner in fellow high-flyer Paul London. In early 2004, Kendrick left WWE to hone his skills overseas.

In September 2005, he returned stronger, faster, and tougher. Reunited with London, the two thrilled audiences en route to the WWE Tag Team Championship in May 2006. Kendrick and London held the Titles for an unprecedented 334 days. During a tour of South Africa in 2007, they defeated Lance Cade and Trevor Murdoch to capture the World Tag Team Championship. Though they lost the prizes three days later, they are one of few teams to hold both Championships.

In 2008, Kendrick unveiled a new attitude, an updated wardrobe, and a bodyguard named Ezekiel. Rechristened as "The" Brian Kendrick, the suddenly sneaky rule-breaker unveiled some body rockin' dance moves. He focused on a singles career until his departure from WWE in 2009.

Kendrick has recently reappeared sporadically on *NXT* competing against the Superstars of tomorrow. He has also been training WWE Diva Eva Marie, who is adopting The Kendrick as her own finisher.

BRIAN PILLMAN

HT	6'0"	WT	227 lbs.
FROM			Cincinnati, Ohio

Brian Pillman made a name for himself as the "Loose Cannon," an unpredictable force who blazed through WCW, ECW, and WWE. Were it not for his untimely death, many believe that Brian Pillman would have been one of the leaders of WWE's Attitude Era.

A former football player for the Cincinnati Bengals, Pillman journeyed north to play for the Canadian Football League's Calgary Stampeders in 1986. In Calgary, he began training in Stu Hart's legendary "dungeon." No longer restricted by the shoulder pads and helmet, the wild Superstar was able to unleash his true self in the ring.

Alongside Bruce Hart, Pillman formed the duo, Bad Company, winning Stampede Wrestling's International Tag Team Championship, and establishing himself as one of the industry's premier high flyers.

In 1989, he arrived as "Flyin' Brian" Pillman in WCW, mounting a devastating aerial assault, procuring two Light Heavyweight Championships and the WCW Tag Team Championship alongside Barry Windham. Although he and Steve Austin teamed in WCW as the Hollywood Blonds, they had a falling out that would extend into WWE. In the interim, he competed in ECW, becoming as notorious for his outrageous commentary about fans and officials as his actions between the ropes.

It wasn't until Pillman made his way to WWE in 1996 that the wider world learned about the real "Loose Cannon." Despite being sidelined with a severe ankle injury for much of his WWE tenure, Pillman managed to shock audiences with his erratically entertaining antics.

His crazed confrontations with Austin included an infamous encounter in which Stone Cold Steve Austin burst into the Pillman family home. When Austin began warring with the Hart Foundation in a war pitting American values against Canadian values, the "Loose Cannon" sided with his old friends from Calgary.

Perhaps seeing a part of himself in the "Bizarre One," Goldust, a sight that was too close for comfort, Pillman engaged in a memorable rivalry with the flamboyant performer. Unfortunately, just prior to a pay-per-view, Pillman unexpectedly passed away. His tragic death robbed sports-entertainment of one of its most colorful personalities.

BRET *Hit Man* HART

HT	6'0"
WT	235 lbs.
FROM	Calgary, Alberta, Canada

SIGNATURE MOVE
Sharpshooter

Born into wrestling royalty, Bret Hart was destined to make his living inside the ring. His father, Stu, was a well-known competitor and promoter, as well as one of the greatest trainers of his time. Some of Bret's earliest memories include sitting in the family basement, watching his father physically dissect men half his age.

It wasn't long before Bret started building his own reputation while competing in his father's Stampede Wrestling. He quickly became one of Calgary's top draws and caught the eye of Vince McMahon. In 1984, rather than trying to lure Bret to WWE, McMahon simply bought Stampede Wrestling and the rights to its competitors, including Bret.

THE HART FOUNDATION AND WORLD CHAMPIONSHIPS

In WWE, Bret teamed with Jim Neidhart to form the Hart Foundation. Together, they possessed the perfect combination of technical ability and pure power. With Jimmy Hart as their manager, the Hart Foundation earned two World Tag Team Championship reigns.

After losing the Titles to the Nasty Boys at *WrestleMania VII*, Bret leapt into singles competition. It didn't surprise many when, in a matter of mere months, he won his first singles Title, defeating Mr. Perfect for the Intercontinental Championship at *SummerSlam 1991*. Bret would go on to capture the Intercontinental Title once more before setting his sights on the WWE Championship.

On October 12, 1992, Bret won his first of five WWE Championships when he defeated Ric Flair in his home country of Canada. Unfortunately for Bret, his Title reign was derailed by Yokozuna at *WrestleMania IX*. In typical Bret Hart fashion, he refused to let the loss get him off track. More determined than ever, he turned back Razor Ramon, Mr. Perfect, and Bam Bam Bigelow to be crowned the 1993 King of the Ring.

Now the owner of a highly-decorated résumé, Bret had little left to prove. However, he refused to rest on his legendary reputation. Intent on regaining sports-entertainment's ultimate prize, Bret was declared co-winner of the 1994 Royal Rumble Match. The victory earned him another opportunity at the WWE Championship, which he capitalized on at *WrestleMania X*, defeating Yokozuna to reclaim the Title.

TROUBLE IN THE FAMILY

Bret will always be remembered as one of the greatest champions in WWE history, but one of his most memorable rivalries revolved around so much more than gold. In 1994, the Harts became a family in crisis when Bret's brother, Owen, attacked the "Hit Man" in a jealous rage.

The rivalry resulted in some of WWE's most emotionally-charged encounters. Owen was never able to wrest the WWE Championship away, but his *WrestleMania X* victory over his older brother went a long way toward his jumping out from under Bret's shadow.

Unfortunately, Bret's final WWE match in the 1990s was widely recognized as one of the most infamous moments in sports-entertainment history. While defending the WWE Championship against Shawn Michaels at *Survivor Series 1997*, Bret found himself locked in an HBK Sharpshooter. While in the hold, the referee called for the bell and awarded the Title to Michaels, despite the "Hit Man" never submitting.

Known as the "Montreal Screwjob," the controversial event marred the final days of what was otherwise one of the greatest careers in WWE history. Hart then moved to rival WCW, where he spent three forgettable years, despite being in the ring with such legendary names as Sting, Goldberg, and Lex Luger. Along the way, though, he did manage to capture the promotion's World Heavyweight, Tag Team, and United States Championship.

Proving time heals all wounds, Hart and WWE rekindled their working relationship in 2005 when the "Hit Man" helped produce a WWE Home Video release. The following year, Hart's amazing career was honored with induction into the WWE Hall of Fame.

Hart returned to *Raw* in January 2010, marking his first live appearance on WWE television in more than a decade. Upon arriving, the "Hit Man" engaged in an epic moment of reconciliation with his greatest rival, Shawn Michaels. He also presumably reconciled with Mr. McMahon, though a low-blow from the Chairman confirmed otherwise. This set the stage for the longtime rivals' *WrestleMania XXVI* showdown, which the "Hit Man" won. Two months later, Hart even captured the U.S. Championship when he forced The Miz to submit to the Sharpshooter. Hart also went on to briefly serve as the *Raw* General Manager in the spring of 2010.

Today, the "Hit Man" continues to surprise the WWE Universe with sporadic appearances on *Raw*, *SmackDown*, pay-per-views, and live events all over the world.

I'M THE BEST THERE IS, THE BEST THERE WAS, AND THE BEST THERE EVER WILL BE.

BRIE BELLA

HT	5'6"
FROM	Scottsdale, Arizona

Brie Bella debuted in 2008 and quickly racked up victories with her identical sister, Nikki, popping up in the nick of time to score the winning pinfall. Brie was an instant target of affection and valuable ally. She supported the Colon brothers as they unified the WWE and World Tag Team Championships. In 2010, Brie began to fancy her future husband, Daniel Bryan. Ironically, she and Nikki jockeyed for Bryan's attention long before the first follicles of his famous beard revealed themselves.

2011 was Brie's breakout year. On an April *Raw*, she used "Twin Magic" to capture her first Divas Championship. Brie held onto the prize for two months. The following year, it appeared the Bellas were done with WWE, but their brief hiatus was merely a prelude to greater success. The Bellas returned and became the lead fixtures on E!'s *Total Divas*. It was here that "Brie Mode" became a household term. Their revitalized fame earned the Bellas Diva of the Year honors in 2013.

Brie stood up to Stephanie McMahon in 2014, having WWE's domineering Principle Owner arrested and then facing her at *SummerSlam*. Though a shocking betrayal by her own sister cost her the match, Brie managed to forgive Nikki. When not fighting by her sister's side, Brie kicks into "Brie Mode" and takes on WWE's top female Superstars herself with a "Yes!" Movement-inspired offense.

The Road to *WrestleMania 32* encapsulated the reasons Brie is one of WWE's most popular and inspiring Superstars. She competed through a rocky course of events that included her husband's emotional retirement and a scary injury to her sister, Nikki. Brie endured these hardships into the Show of Shows, where she cinched on the winning "Yes!" Lock to win a 10-Superstar Pre-Show Tag Team Match for her *Total Divas* teammates.

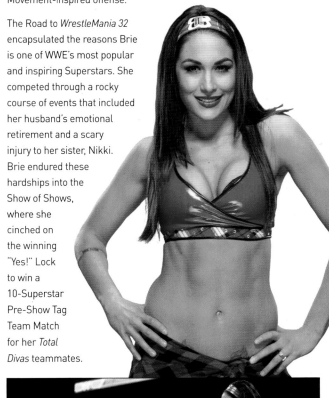

BRISCO BROTHERS

MEMBERS	Jack & Gerald
COMBINED WT	461 lbs.

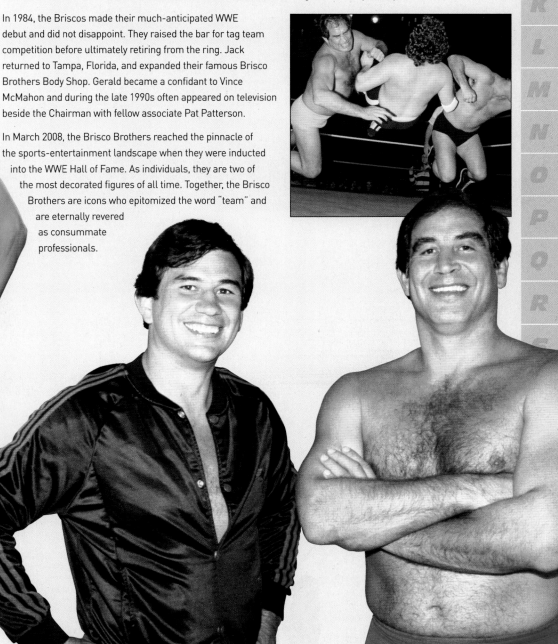

Throughout sports-entertainment's rich history, there have been several famous brother tag team combinations. While they are all exceptional in their own right, Jack and Gerald Brisco are a cut above the rest.

The elder brother, Jack, was a stand-out amateur wrestler at Oklahoma State and is one of only three men to hold the NCAA Wrestling and NWA World Heavyweight Championships. He made his pro debut in 1965 and went on to worldwide stardom, defeating such legendary names as Harley Race, Terry Funk, Giant Baba, Bob Backlund, and "Rowdy" Roddy Piper, among many others.

Gerald, like his brother Jack, knew success in the amateur ranks and won several AAU Tournaments. He was also a stand-out at Oklahoma State. Trained by Jack, Gerald debuted in 1968 and went on to hold many Titles throughout the NWA, including the World Junior Heavyweight, Southern Heavyweight, and Southeastern Heavyweight Championships.

As a team during the 1970s, Jack and Gerald displayed poetic continuity and superior ring strategy. Their dominance was shown in the ring as well as in their standing offer to any misguided challengers, "C'mon down! You know where the gold is!" And they were right. Together, the Brisco Brothers held dozens of tag team Championships.

In 1984, the Briscos made their much-anticipated WWE debut and did not disappoint. They raised the bar for tag team competition before ultimately retiring from the ring. Jack returned to Tampa, Florida, and expanded their famous Brisco Brothers Body Shop. Gerald became a confidant to Vince McMahon and during the late 1990s often appeared on television beside the Chairman with fellow associate Pat Patterson.

In March 2008, the Brisco Brothers reached the pinnacle of the sports-entertainment landscape when they were inducted into the WWE Hall of Fame. As individuals, they are two of the most decorated figures of all time. Together, the Brisco Brothers are icons who epitomized the word "team" and are eternally revered as consummate professionals.

"THE BRITISH BULLDOG" DAVEY BOY SMITH

HT	5'11"	WT	260 lbs.	FROM	Manchester, England
SIGNATURE MOVE		Powerslam			

WWE audiences first saw Davey Boy Smith in 1985 as a member of the British Bulldogs, alongside Dynamite Kid. Together, they amazed audiences with their in-ring acrobatics and fluid teamwork. At *WrestleMania 2*, the Bulldogs defeated Brutus Beefcake and Greg Valentine to capture the World Tag Team Championship. After a nine-month Title reign, they lost the gold in controversial fashion to the Hart Foundation.

In 1990, the protégé of mat legend Stu Hart broke out on his own and began referring to himself as simply "The British Bulldog." Sporting the Union Jack, his blend of power, agility, and aerial moves made him a top attraction worldwide.

Perhaps the Bulldog's greatest moment came in August 1992 when he battled his brother-in-law, Bret "Hit Man" Hart, in the main event of *SummerSlam*. In front of more than 80,000 fans at Wembley Stadium, the powerhouse emerged victorious in a thrilling contest, capturing the Intercontinental Championship in the process.

The Bulldog left WWE after a disappointing loss to Shawn Michaels on an October 1992 episode of *Saturday Night's Main Event*. He would soon return to form the popular Allied Powers tag team with Lex Luger.

Despite the fans' approval, the Bulldog turned his back on Luger to join the hated Camp Cornette. While teamed with another brother-in-law, Owen Hart, the duo won the World Tag Team Championship from the Smokin' Guns at *In Your House: Mind Games* in 1996. The Bulldog then took a bite out of the history books in February 1997, when he defeated Owen to become the first European Champion.

In late 1997, the Bulldog joined Bret, Owen, Jim Neidhart, and Brian Pillman in the ever-dangerous Hart Foundation. After the infamous "Montreal Screwjob" where HBK defeated Bret Hart amid high controversy at *Survivor Series 1997*, Bulldog followed the "Hit Man" and Neidhart to WCW. He wouldn't stay long, though, as he returned to WWE in August 1999 and tangled with main event Superstars The Rock, Triple H, Mankind, and Big Show.

Sadly, Davey Boy Smith passed away in 2002. An incredible performer, Smith is fondly remembered as a true champion.

BRITISH BULLDOGS

MEMBERS	Davey Boy Smith & Dynamite Kid		
COMBINED WT	471 lbs.	FROM	England

Behind the perfect combination of speed and power, the British Bulldogs became one of the most popular tag teams of their time. Originally competing in promotions throughout Canada and Japan, Dynamite Kid and Davey Boy Smith jumped to WWE in the mid-1980s and quickly gained tag-team success, as well as the hearts of the fans.

Shortly after making their WWE debut, the British Bulldogs, with the tutelage of Capt. Lou Albano and rocker Ozzy Osbourne, defeated the Dream Team (Greg Valentine and Brutus Beefcake) for the World Tag Team Championship at *WrestleMania 2*. The popular duo maintained a strong hold of the Titles for nearly ten months before losing to the Hart Foundation in January 1987. The match proved very costly, as some questionable officiating by Danny Davis also led to Dynamite Kid suffering serious injury.

Following the loss, the Bulldogs took some time off to rehab Dynamite Kid's injuries. When they returned, they immediately set their sights on gaining revenge on Davis. Teaming with Tito Santana, The Bulldogs sought vengeance at *WrestleMania III* when they battled Davis and the Hart Foundation. Unfortunately, the match didn't go in their favor, as the dastardly Davis weaseled his way to a win.

The Bulldogs' popularity reached new heights when they added mascot Matilda to the team. The lovable bulldog accompanied Dynamite Kid and Davey Boy Smith to ringside for all their matches and quickly became a fan favorite. Her popularity eventually drew the ire of The Islanders, who dognapped the adorable pooch.

The Islanders' distasteful act lead the Bulldogs to another Six-Man Tag Team Match when they partnered with fellow animal lover Koko B. Ware to battle the dognappers and their manager, Bobby Heenan, at *WrestleMania IV*. Much like their *WrestleMania III* match, the Bulldogs were unable to secure victory.

The Bulldogs struggled to get back on track following the *WrestleMania IV* loss, and disappeared from WWE by 1989. Despite the woes they experienced late in their tenure, Dynamite Kid and Davey Boy Smith used a unique blend of quickness and strength to build an impressive legacy that is still admired today.

BROCK LESNAR

HT	6'3"
WT	286 lbs.
FROM	Minneapolis, Minnesota

SIGNATURE MOVE
F-5, Kimura Lock

What Brock Lesnar sees, he conquers. Plain and simple. A genetic anomaly, Lesnar possesses a combination of size, power, agility, and skill that is typically reserved for mutants. Infuse these qualities with a beastlike disposition devoid of remorse, and you have the most dangerous specimen in the history of any combat-based profession.

HERE COMES THE PAIN

Even before Paul Heyman unleashed his prized client on WWE in 2002, "The Next Big Thing" was dominating the collegiate ranks. At the University of Minnesota, Lesnar was known to toss 260-pound men like ragdolls with cruiserweight finesse despite being heavier than your average college heavyweight. He won the 2000 NCAA Division 1 Heavyweight Championship. Two years later, he debuted in WWE.

As quickly as Lesnar arrived, he destroyed everything in his path. For a company with a glorious history of awe-inspiring behemoths, no one had seen anything like him. He won the King of the Ring tournament, outlasted 29 Superstars in the Royal Rumble and defeated Undertaker, The Rock, and Hulk Hogan in his rookie year. And, oh, by the way, he became the youngest WWE Champion in history. The Beast headlined his first *WrestleMania*, where he overcame another amateur wrestling extraordinaire, Kurt Angle, to seize his second WWE Championship.

NEW CONQUESTS

It was clear no one could stop Lesnar's all-out blitz through the WWE record books. No one but Lesnar himself, that is. After a sophomore campaign highlighted by an imploded *SmackDown* ring and an epic Iron Man Match victory over Angle, Lesnar decided to split from WWE. At *WrestleMania XX*, an ornery crowd voiced their disappointment during what was to be his final match. The Beast would be back, but the WWE Universe would have to wait.

After a brief stint with the NFL's Minnesota Vikings and New Japan Pro Wrestling, Lesnar set his sights on MMA. In just his fourth professional fight, Lesnar won the UFC Heavyweight Championship to become the only competitor to complete the Championship trifecta of MMA, NCAA, and WWE.

"WE WANT LESNAR!"

The night after *WrestleMania XXVIII*, the aftermath of the Show of Shows was permeated with whispers of a Lesnar return. As John Cena stood in the *Raw* ring, familiar and ominous thumps blared through the loudspeakers to confirm the rumors. Lesnar declared his intentions by planting Cena with a monstrous F-5.

It had been eight years since his previous WWE match but Lesnar had somehow become even scarier. His confrontations with John Cena left many cringing at his sick brutality and the pleasure with which he inflicted pain. He followed this up by igniting a personal rivalry with The King of Kings, Triple H. During these bruising encounters, a seemingly amplified "Beast Incarnate" unveiled the deadly Kimura Lock and used the submission move to break the arms of both Triple H and Shawn Michaels.

I WAS PUT ON THIS EARTH TO SEEK AND DESTROY AND TO HURT PEOPLE.

EAT, SLEEP, CONQUER, REPEAT

Lesnar sent shockwaves through the WWE Universe at *WrestleMania 30* when he did what twenty-one other challengers before him could not—break Undertaker's revered winning streak. The unthinkable feat propelled Lesnar to the WWE World Heavyweight Championship. The Conqueror claimed the gold by dismantling John Cena with an unfathomable sixteen German Suplexes, the most lopsided loss in The Champ's career.

Both Cena and Seth Rollins made valiant attempts to dethrone Lesnar, but The Beast survived heading into the Road to *WrestleMania*. His challenger at the Show of Shows, an up-and-coming Roman Reigns, gave him all he could handle but it was Rollins who snuck away with the Title. The Money in the Bank holder swooped in mid-match to pin Reigns, not Lesnar, to end his reign.

An infuriated Beast took Rollins to "Suplex City" in his rematch but his chance for Championship vengeance was thwarted by another vengeful soul, Undertaker. Their *WrestleMania 30* bombshell still lingering in the air, the bitter rivals clashed at *SummerSlam 2015* and *Hell in a Cell 2015*. In their brutal final bout, Lesnar dropped The Deadman inside "The Devil's Playground" to once again gain the upper hand in the vicious vendetta.

Lesnar once again turned his attention toward the WWE World Heavyweight Championship. Eyeing a Title opportunity at *WrestleMania 32*, his efforts were thwarted thanks in part to Dean Ambrose. Amidst a sea of wreckage, Lesnar dropped a persistent Ambrose at the Show of Shows, uncorking thirteen German Suplexes in front a rowdy AT&T Stadium crowd.

Since his 2012 return, Lesnar, along with his boastful advocate Paul Heyman, has delivered on his promise to unleash "utter freakin' chaos" on the WWE landscape. Whatever he has planned next, be glad you are not standing in his path.

BRODUS CLAY

HT	6'7"	WT	375 lbs.	FROM	Planet Funk
SIGNATURE MOVE	Fall of Humanity				

As the only living, breathing, rompin', stompin', Funkasaurus in captivity, Brodus Clay possessed a dangerous combination of domination and funk. And with the beautiful Funkadactyls by his side, it was nearly impossible not to dance when his music played.

At nearly 400 pounds, the Funkasaurus was both an irresistible force and an immovable object rolled into one mass of humanity. Making matters worse for his opposition, Clay coupled his jaw-dropping girth with an agility rarely found in men his size.

After a notable singles career, Clay formed a partnership with the equally-imposing Tensai in early 2013. Known as Tons of Funk, the duo defeated several top teams, en route to what appeared to be a promising union. But later that year, Clay began to display a dishonorable side, which caused an irreconcilable rift between the two mammoths.

Eying singles success, Clay broke out on his own. He unsuccessfully competed in the *WrestleMania 30* Andre the Giant Memorial Battle Royal before briefly heading to NXT. Clay was then released by WWE in the summer of 2014.

THE BROOD

MEMBERS	David Heath (formerly known as Gangrel), Edge & Christian, & Matt & Jeff Hardy

In 1998, a mystical force appeared in WWE. Led by David Heath, a.k.a. Gangrel, Edge and Christian rose to the entrance ramp surrounded by a circle of flames. Then, they crept to the ring as their leader sipped blood from his chalice and ejected it toward the crowd.

The Brood were known for their infamous "Bloodbath," wherein during the course of a match, the lights in the arena would darken, while a red light appeared. When the lights came back on, the Brood's opponents would be found prone and drenched in blood. In early 1999, the rogue Brood joined forces with Undertaker's Ministry of Darkness.

The Brood soon left Undertaker's faction and battled the Hardy Boyz. During one match, the brothers and their manager, Michael P.S. Hayes were doused in red gore. As Edge and Christian grew as a tag team, they distanced themselves from their leader's influence. As a form of revenge, the Superstar known as Gangrel managed to recruit the Hardyz, forming the New Brood. But the combination didn't last long, as the Hardyz renounced Gangrel's teachings and adopted Terri Runnels as their manager.

Soon after The Brood was in their pasts, both Edge & Christian and the Hardy Boyz went on the become two of WWE's most successful tag teams.

BROOKE

HT	5'4"	FROM	Houston, Texas

Brooke saw the 2006 WWE Diva Search as her ticket to the big time. WWE, on the other hand, did not. She was cut from the competition just prior to the final eight hopefuls being announced.

Despite being eliminated, the aspiring Diva made a solid impression on WWE officials, who offered her a spot in their developmental system. After just a few months of training, the beautiful brunette made it to the big time when she debuted on *ECW* in January 2007. As a member of Extreme Exposé, Brooke performed seductive dance routines alongside Kelly Kelly and Layla. The threesome electrified male audiences and caught the eye of recording artist Timbaland, who placed the girls in his music video, "Throw it on Me."

BROOKLYN BRAWLER

HT	6'0".	WT	248 lbs.	FROM	Brooklyn, New York
SIGNATURE MOVE	Sidewalk Smash				

From the rough streets of Brooklyn, New York, this Superstar was brought into WWE by Bobby "The Brain" Heenan. During a 1989 episode of *Prime Time Wrestling*, the Brooklyn Brawler made his presence felt when he handed the Red Rooster a five boroughs beat-down.

The man from the County of Kings had a short-lived partnership with another New York City native, Bad News Brown. Brawler also battled Koko B. Ware after the fans voted for the two Superstars to lock up for a Coliseum Home Video special.

The Brooklyn Brawler continued his street-fighting ways into the 1990s, developing a reputation for showing up at random for some old fashioned fisticuffs. Brawler is infamous for his regrettable win-loss record, but at *TLC 2012* he finally earned himself the winner's spoils. In his home borough, he applied the winning submission on 3MB as the surprise tag team partner for The Miz and Alberto Del Rio. Brawler's Big Apple neighbors roared with approval.

BROTHER LOVE

Dressed in a white suit, the red-faced Brother Love claimed to preach the good word of love to WWE audiences of the late 1980s and early 1990s. The sight of him invoked thoughts of scandalous televangelists. Despite nearly being booed out of every arena, he constantly used his annoying catchphrase to tell people how he felt: "I love you!"

Brother Love is best known for hosting a weekly interview segment appropriately named *The Brother Love Show*. He used the segment to verbally attack popular Superstars of the time. His long list of dissatisfied guests includes Hulk Hogan, Brutus Beefcake, and Dusty Rhodes.

While Brother Love's antics on *The Brother Love Show* are widely chronicled by WWE historians, it's a lesser-known fact that might just be the preacher's ultimate career highlight. Amazingly, it was Brother Love, not Paul Bearer, who first introduced WWE audiences to Undertaker at *Survivor Series 1990*. He went on to manage The Deadman through February 1991, at which time he sold the future WWE Hall of Famer's contract to Bearer.

THE BROTHERS OF DESTRUCTION

MEMBERS	Undertaker & Kane
COMBINED WT	628 lbs.

When Undertaker's half-brother, Kane, first emerged in WWE, it appeared the rivalry between them would smolder until hell froze over. However, through common enemies and a hereditary knack for destruction, the sinister siblings have managed to bond over the broken bodies of many top tag teams over the years.

Early signs of what they could be as a united force were first seen at the *2001 Royal Rumble*. Soon it was clear that their forces combined were too powerful to keep apart. With their immense power, they crushed anyone who got in their way. Their fiery path of destruction led them to their first World Tag Team Championship in April 2001, when they defeated Edge and Christian. During WWE's battles with The Alliance, The Brothers of Destruction became the first team ever to unify the WWE and WCW Tag Team Championships in a Steel Cage Match at *SummerSlam 2001*.

Families fight but these two take it to hellish extremes. Over the years, Undertaker has set Kane on fire while Kane has buried Undertaker alive and in 2010, put him in a vegetative state. However, history and stretchers have shown the worst beatings in WWE happen when The Brothers of Destruction join forces. Most recently, they reunited against The Wyatt Family after The Wyatts attempted to eliminate them by taking their powers. Unfortunately for The Wyatt Family, The Brothers of Destruction showed why they are a force to be reckoned with, especially during the 25 Year Anniversary of Undertaker at *Survivor Series 2015*.

When you face The Brothers of Destruction, winning becomes a secondary concern to survival.

BRUISER BRODY

HT	6'8"	WT	283 lbs.	FROM	Santa Fe, New Mexico
SIGNATURE MOVE	Knee Drop				

Known for his wild hair, big bushy beard, and bulging eyes, Bruiser Brody was a madman in the truest sense of the word. After fifteen unpredictable years in the ring, the brawler earned the reputation as one of the toughest of his time and a cult hero, whose legacy still shines bright today.

After making his professional debut in Texas in 1973, Brody became known as a bit of a nomad. Bouncing around from promotion to promotion, he never stayed in one place for very long. During his brief stints in WWE, WCCW, AWA, and the NWA, among other places, Brody took part in memorable battles against such legendary names as Andre the Giant, Abdullah the Butcher, Dick the Bruiser, and the Von Erichs. And each match was more vicious than the next.

Brody was equally respected internationally. In Japan, he captured numerous titles, including tag team gold with partner Stan Hansen. And in Puerto Rico, Brody's name was nothing short of legendary. Unfortunately, however, Puerto Rican rings would be the last in which he would ever compete. In July 1988, Frank "Bruiser Brody" Goodish was stabbed to death in a locker room shower. Brody's impact and frenetic ring style live on in the memories of all who witnessed his mayhem.

BRUNO SAMMARTINO

HT	5'10"
WT	265 lbs.
FROM	Pizzoferrato, Italy

SIGNATURE MOVE
Bearhug

Bruno Sammartino graced the covers of countless magazines, was a mainstream cultural icon, and holds the record of 211 consecutive Madison Square Garden sell-outs. Over the course of his heralded career, he was WWE Champion a combined 13 years. In his day, Sammartino was WWE's cultural ambassador, as popular as Stone Cold Steve Austin, The Rock, and John Cena.

Born in October 1935, Bruno Sammartino grew up as one of seven siblings in the Abruzzi section of Italy. As a boy, he played soccer and excelled in both Greco-Roman and freestyle wrestling. After surviving the horrors of World War II, 16-year-old Bruno arrived at Ellis Island, weighing barely 90 pounds. In his adopted city of Pittsburgh, he was often bullied at school and heckled for not speaking English properly. Determined to put an end to the harassment, Bruno began an exhausting weightlifting regimen at a nearby Young Men's Hebrew Association gym. The regimen worked; by 18, he weighed 257 lbs. In 1959, Sammartino set world records by bench pressing 569 lbs., squatting 715 lbs., and deadlifting 700 lbs. He was ready for the ring.

Within six months of his debut, Sammartino was in the main event at Madison Square Garden, where he teamed with Antonino "Argentina" Rocca. Despite early success, Bruno was frustrated with certain aspects of the business and took a break from the ring.

A NEW CHAMPION GAINS GOLDEN GUIDANCE

In February 1963, Bruno returned to Vince J. McMahon. After Bruno's impressive showings, new Champion "Nature Boy" Buddy Rogers and the "Italian Strongman" were on a collision course. On May 17, 1963, the two met in front of a sold-out Madison Square Garden crowd. In an unbelievable turn of events, Sammartino hoisted Rogers into a backbreaker, forcing him to submit in just 48 seconds.

With the most prestigious Championship in the world around his waist, Bruno needed a trusted advisor to assist in the guidance of his career. "Golden Boy" Arnold Skaaland answered the call and remained with Sammartino for almost 20 years. Along the way, Bruno amassed an amazing following that eclipsed all who came before him. In fact, Bruno hosted his own radio show in New York City, where he played opera songs from his prized personal record collection.

Bruno traveled tirelessly, carrying the WWE Championship with pride. In August 1968, he ventured to Japan for a series of "Champion vs. Champion" best Two-Out-Of-Three Falls Matches against puroresu legend, Shohei "Giant" Baba. Bruno also teamed with former foe Skull Murphy and took on Baba with fellow Rikidozan protégé Antonio Inoki.

Of all his challengers during the late 1960s, no one was more vicious, and physically capable, than Killer Kowalski. The bouts between these men were not showcases of technical ring skill or displays of power; they were epic, blood-soaked battles. In 1969, the two combatants had a match that ended in pure bedlam in the main event of the only wrestling card in the history of Boston's Fenway Park.

Even though he was known as a singles Superstar, Bruno was also an excellent tag team competitor. On July 26, 1967, he teamed with Spiros Arion to defeat The Sicilians for the United States Tag Team Championship. Unfortunately, due to Sammartino's responsibilities as WWE Champion, he was forced to relinquish the Title.

A RECORD REIGN ENDS

On January 18, 1971, "The Russian Bear" Ivan Koloff shocked the world when he defeated Sammartino at Madison Square Garden to win the WWE Championship. Bruno's record-setting reign of seven years, eight months, and one day was over. His return to the ring in 1972 began in Los Angeles, where he made a special appearance and won a 22-man Battle Royal. On September 30, 1972, at the original *Showdown at Shea*, Sammartino met friend and then-champion Pedro Morales in a classic one-hour, 18-minute match, which was made even more incredible because it was contested on a rain-slicked mat. Despite the treacherous conditions, the curfew time limit draw is considered one of the most technically sound wrestling matches of its time.

In 1973, Bruno returned to WWE to standing ovations throughout the region. On December 10, he became the first two-time WWE Champion when he defeated Stan "The Man" Stasiak. Due to the prestige Sammartino brought to WWE's richest prize, rule-breakers from far and wide traveled to WWE in search of fame and fortune. The treacherous managerial trio of The Grand Wizard, Captain Lou Albano, and "Classy" Freddie Blassie recruited contenders from all corners of the Earth to dethrone Sammartino. As the dishonorable threesome learned time and time again, the power and heart of Sammartino was too much for the wretched henchmen they employed.

A new crop of opponents now targeted Sammartino. In 1976, former Olympian Ken Patera arrived in WWE, one of the few contenders who matched the Champion's strength. Blassie brought in Stan Hansen. During their Championship match on April 26, Hansen broke Sammartino's neck with his dreaded Lariat clothesline. Driven by revenge, Bruno returned weeks later, against doctor's orders, to defeat Hansen at the second *Showdown at Shea* event—on a card that featured a closed circuit telecast of Muhammad Ali battling Inoki in a rare boxer vs. wrestler confrontation.

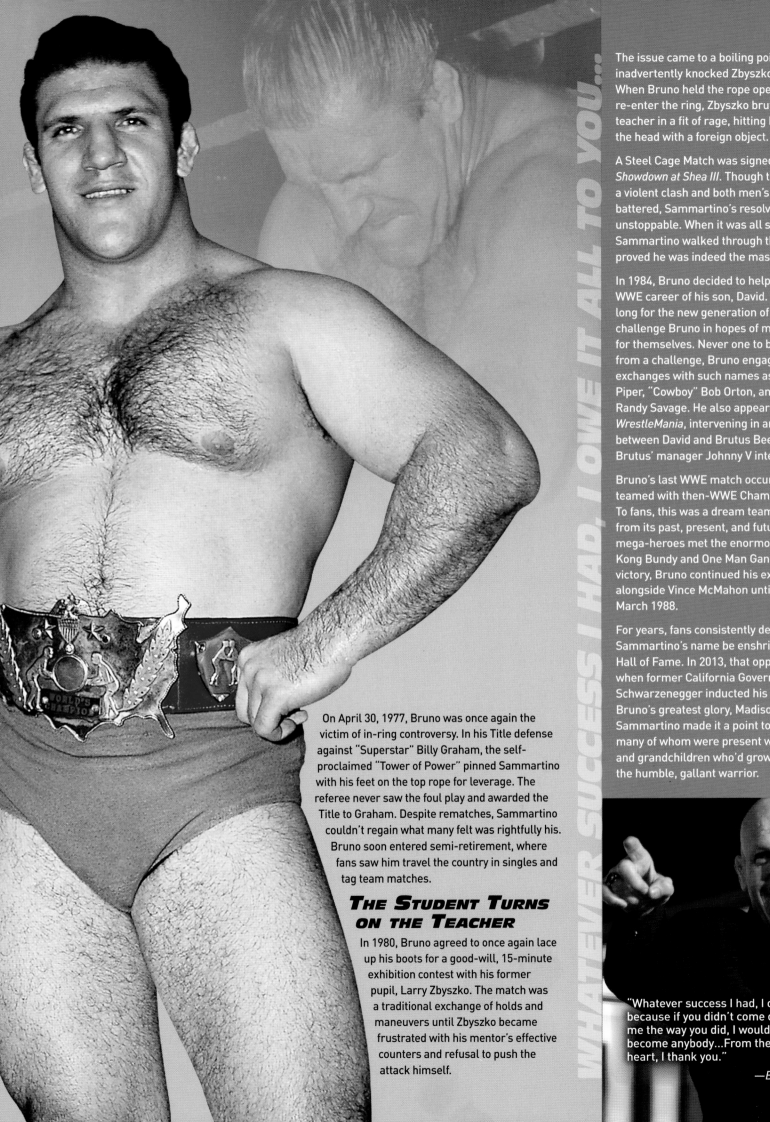

The issue came to a boiling point as Sammartino inadvertently knocked Zbyszko out of the ring. When Bruno held the rope open for Larry to re-enter the ring, Zbyszko brutally attacked his teacher in a fit of rage, hitting him three times in the head with a foreign object.

A Steel Cage Match was signed for the historic *Showdown at Shea III*. Though the match was a violent clash and both men's bodies were battered, Sammartino's resolve made him unstoppable. When it was all said and done, Sammartino walked through the cage door and proved he was indeed the master.

In 1984, Bruno decided to help guide the WWE career of his son, David. It didn't take long for the new generation of Superstars to challenge Bruno in hopes of making a name for themselves. Never one to back down from a challenge, Bruno engaged in heated exchanges with such names as "Rowdy" Roddy Piper, "Cowboy" Bob Orton, and "Macho Man" Randy Savage. He also appeared at the first *WrestleMania*, intervening in an exchange between David and Brutus Beefcake, after Brutus' manager Johnny V interfered.

Bruno's last WWE match occurred when he teamed with then-WWE Champion Hulk Hogan. To fans, this was a dream team of WWE's best from its past, present, and future, as the two mega-heroes met the enormous pair of King Kong Bundy and One Man Gang. After their victory, Bruno continued his expert commentary alongside Vince McMahon until he left WWE in March 1988.

For years, fans consistently demanded that Sammartino's name be enshrined in the WWE Hall of Fame. In 2013, that opportunity came when former California Governor Arnold Schwarzenegger inducted his hero at the site of Bruno's greatest glory, Madison Square Garden. Sammartino made it a point to thank his fans— many of whom were present with their children and grandchildren who'd grown up on stories of the humble, gallant warrior.

On April 30, 1977, Bruno was once again the victim of in-ring controversy. In his Title defense against "Superstar" Billy Graham, the self-proclaimed "Tower of Power" pinned Sammartino with his feet on the top rope for leverage. The referee never saw the foul play and awarded the Title to Graham. Despite rematches, Sammartino couldn't regain what many felt was rightfully his. Bruno soon entered semi-retirement, where fans saw him travel the country in singles and tag team matches.

THE STUDENT TURNS ON THE TEACHER

In 1980, Bruno agreed to once again lace up his boots for a good-will, 15-minute exhibition contest with his former pupil, Larry Zbyszko. The match was a traditional exchange of holds and maneuvers until Zbyszko became frustrated with his mentor's effective counters and refusal to push the attack himself.

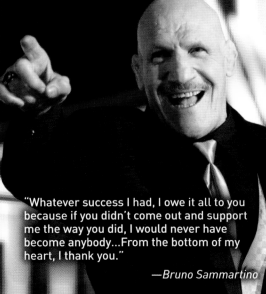

"Whatever success I had, I owe it all to you because if you didn't come out and support me the way you did, I would never have become anybody...From the bottom of my heart, I thank you."

—*Bruno Sammartino*

BRUTE BERNARD

HT	6'2"	WT	250 lbs.
FROM	Montreal, Quebec, Canada		

A true Canadian wild man, Brute Bernard featured an uncontrollable, untamed ring style, sometimes focusing his ire on referees as well as opponents. Despite his unruly attitude, he always managed to find a tag team partner. In fact, many consider him to be one of the finest tag team wrestlers of his time.

The biggest win of Bernard's WWE career came in May 1963 when he teamed with Skull Murphy to defeat The Great Scott and "Killer" Buddy Austin for the United States Tag Team Championship, the predecessor to today's World Tag Team Championship. The duo held the Titles for six long months before finally being upended by Hall of Famers Gorilla Monsoon and Killer Kowalski.

In 1966, the chrome-headed tandem journeyed to Australia, where they also captured tag team gold, tussling with teams like George and Sandy Scott, and Mark Lewin and Bearcat Wright.

In addition to his union with Murphy, Bernard also formed successful tag teams with Larry Hamilton, The Angel, Jay York, and Mike Paidousis. Brute Bernard passed away in 1984.

BRUTUS BEEFCAKE

HT	6'4"	WT	272 lbs.	FROM	San Francisco, California
SIGNATURE MOVE	Sleeper				

Managed by "Luscious" Johnny Valiant, Brutus Beefcake made his WWE debut in 1984. A hated rule breaker, he often strutted his stuff in the ring while fans chanted "Fruitcake." And much to the fans' dismay, the barbs only made him strut more.

Beefcake formed the vaunted Dream Team with Greg Valentine in 1985. The arrogant pair captured the World Tag Team Championship by defeating the U.S. Express in August 1985. They held the Titles until *WrestleMania 2* when they were defeated by the British Bulldogs.

Valentine eventually turned on Beefcake after the Dream Team's match against the Rougeaus at *WrestleMania III*. The act of betrayal failed to slow Beefcake, who instead reinvented himself as "The Barber" and went on to achieve even greater success.

Armed with grooming sheers, "The Barber" went cuttin' and struttin' on the hair of any opponent he knocked out via his dreaded sleeper. His newfound success eventually led to an intense rivalry with Intercontinental Champion, The Honky Tonk Man, who Beefcake was scheduled to battle at the inaugural *SummerSlam*. Sadly, Beefcake never made the match, as Ron Bass viciously attacked him days before the event.

"The Barber" eventually returned, coming to the aid of Hulk Hogan in his longtime friend's battle against Randy Savage and Zeus. The union resulted in great success for Beefcake, including a victory in the *SummerSlam 1989* main event. But again, before Beefcake could capitalize on his success, he suffered a major setback when he was seriously injured in a parasailing accident.

Beefcake was rushed into emergency surgery that lasted over seven hours. Eight titanium plates, thirty-two screws, and one hundred feet of steel wire were used to reconstruct his skull. While the surgery was considered a success, Beefcake was told he'd never walk again. But after months of rehabilitation, he returned to WWE and launched his talk show, *The Barber Shop*. When he was back at full strength, he formed the Mega-Maniacs with Hogan.

Beefcake's life is one of courage, commitment, and desire. A beloved hero, he has left an undeniable mark on the heads of opponents and in the hearts of fans.

BUDDY AUSTIN

HT	6'2"	WT	240 lbs.	FROM	Lovejoy, Georgia
SIGNATURE MOVE	Piledriver				

Buddy Austin was a satanic Superstar who loved to be hated. And luckily for him, everybody hated him. After debuting in 1956, Austin became known as the competitor with a lethal piledriver. Stories quickly began to spread about the up-and-comer with the career-ending maneuver. As time passed, Austin's hit list was highlighted by top names, including Bobo Brazil and Pedro Morales. He beat both men for the WWA World Heavyweight Championship on separate occasions in 1966.

While in WWE, Austin briefly teamed with Great Scott to capture the United States Tag Team Championship from Buddy Rogers and Johnny Barend. Austin also formed several successful tag teams outside of WWE, including one with Freddie Blassie, which culminated in a WWA World Tag Team Championship reign in 1967.

BUDDY LANDEL

HT	6'0"	WT	220 lbs.	FROM	Knoxville, Tennessee
SIGNATURE MOVE	Figure-Four Leglock				

After making his 1979 debut in Bill Watts's Mid-South Wrestling, Buddy Landel traveled throughout the United States, en route to becoming one of the ring's toughest veterans. In the mid-1980s, he became notorious throughout Tennessee and Jim Crockett Promotions, where he famously battled Ric Flair. Landel continued to appear on independent cards through the early 1990s, and saw success in Smoky Mountain Wrestling.

In December 1995, Landel battled Ahmed Johnson in a losing effort at WWE's *In Your House* pay-per-view. Over the next six years, Landel appeared sporadically for WWE in matches against Bob Holly, Matt Hardy, Bret "Hit Man" Hart, and Edge, among others.

BUDDY ROGERS

see page 58

BUDDY ROSE

| HT | 6'1" | WT | 271 lbs. | FROM | Las Vegas, Nevada |

| SIGNATURE MOVE | Las Vegas Jackpot |

Shortly after his 1973 debut, "Playboy" Buddy Rose was seen as one of the brightest up-and-coming stars of his time. Fast-forward two decades and he was still competing, but by this time, Rose was universally scoffed for letting his figure grow to unhealthy proportions.

The young Rose was never short on arrogance. Born with a platinum spoon in his mouth, Rose was afforded the finest things in life, including limousines and private jets. In the ring, however, he was anything but a preppy snob. In fact, his brutality made him one of the most feared Superstars of the early 1980s, and eventually led to a series of WWE Championship opportunities against Bob Backlund.

Over time, Rose began to gain a considerable amount of weight. With each pound he packed on, the less intimidating he became. By the end of his career, Rose was relegated to comedy sketches. His most infamous scene portrayed him as the star of an infomercial for the Blow Away diet. According to Blow Away, losing weight was a breeze. Rose's figure told another story.

BUDDY WOLFE

| HT | 6'1" | WT | 260 lbs. | FROM | St. Cloud, Minnesota |

| SIGNATURE MOVE | Reverse Neck Breaker |

A former professional football player in the Continental Football League, Buddy Wolfe hung up his cleats in 1968 to tackle a career in sports-entertainment. After training with Verne Gagne, Wolfe spent his early years competing in the Carolinas and Dallas, where he squared off against the likes of Fritz Von Erich, Wahoo McDaniel, and Ole Anderson.

In 1972, Wolfe travelled north to begin competing for WWE. His earliest matches were against Blackjack Slade, El Olympico, and Sonny King. Wolfe won them all and quickly earned an opportunity at Pedro Morales's coveted WWE Championship. Over the course of the next year, Wolfe and Morales battled over the WWE Title several times. Each time, though, Morales managed to walk away unscathed. The closest Wolfe came was in April 1973, but the match was forced to end prematurely when Wolfe began bleeding profusely from the forehead.

Wolfe is also known for facing Andre the Giant in the Hall of Famer's 1973 Madison Square Garden debut. Additionally, he fought boxing legend Muhammad Ali in an exhibition match in 1976.

BUFF BAGWELL

| HT | 6'1" | WT | 245 lbs. | FROM | Marietta, Georgia |

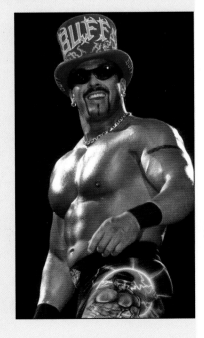

While competing in WCW, Buff Bagwell certainly could make a case for being "The Stuff." While in WWE, however, not so much. The entirety of Bagwell's WWE career essentially consisted of one *Raw* match against Booker T in July 2001. Recognized as one of the most awkward matches in sports-entertainment history, the contest was panned by many fans and insiders.

Who was at fault for the poorly-received match is up for debate, but one-half of its combatants revealed his opinion years later.

"[Buff] wasn't capable of putting on a good enough match to impress anybody that night," said Bagwell's opponent, Booker T.

Days later, Buff Bagwell was released from his WWE contract.

BUGSY MCGRAW

| HT | 6'3" | WT | 301 lbs. | FROM | Lafayette, Indiana |

| SIGNATURE MOVE | Splash |

Bugsy McGraw certainly was odd, even among his oftentimes off-color cohorts. If he wasn't wearing swimming goggles en route to the ring, he probably had on a big top hat or colorful scarves or maybe even all three. When it came to Bugsy McGraw, fans never really knew what to expect.

The words that came out of McGraw's mouth were equally incomprehensible. Much like the Ultimate Warrior years later, McGraw liked to break into rants that made sense only to him. When he was done, he'd usually sprint around the ring with no true purpose.

While fans looked at McGraw quizzically, his opposition knew he was no laughing matter. Once the bell rang, the bearded behemoth was all business. Utilizing his signature splash, McGraw captured more than twenty NWA regional titles, including the Florida Heavyweight Championship, which he won from Don Muraco in 1980.

Later in his career, McGraw teamed with the evenly offbeat Jimmy Valiant. Together, the "Boogie Woogie Man" and McGraw electrified the Carolinas with their flamboyant approach to wrestling.

BUDDY ROGERS

HT	6'0"
WT	235 lbs.
FROM	Camden, New Jersey

SIGNATURE MOVE
Figure-Four Leglock

Being a WWE Superstar is an honor reserved for the world's most amazing athletes. Of these esteemed men, only a select few ever gain entry into the prestigious fraternity of WWE Champions. The select few boast such great names as Triple H, Ric Flair, Hulk Hogan, and John Cena. While these men earned immortality, there was one man who blazed the trail they rode to greatness: "Nature Boy" Buddy Rogers.

Rogers' first career choice was that of a police officer. While enforcing the law proved to be an honorable profession, he yearned for the spotlight. With no professional experience to his credit, Rogers confronted New Jersey promoters Ray and Frank Hanley and demanded an opportunity to prove himself in the ring. Impressed by the youngster's aggressive behavior, they offered him twenty dollars and a match on the following evening's show. On July 4, 1939, Rogers made his debut with an easy victory.

"NATURE BOY" EARNS GOLD

Rogers' early years in the ring were spent competing under several names, but in Texas in 1944 he settled on the name, Buddy Rogers, and added the nickname, "Nature Boy." With the new name came a new look and attitude, which included an arrogant air, blond hair, tanned muscles, and a deliberately cocky strut. Decades later, the legendary Ric Flair patterned his entire persona after Rogers, right down to the signature figure-four leglock.

At one point, future WWE Women's Champion, the Fabulous Moolah, then partial to form-fitting leopard skin, was Rogers' valet.

The new Rogers turned heads as he began to compile an impressive record. Shortly after becoming "Nature Boy," he carried his newfound success straight to the National Wrestling Alliance Texas Heavyweight Championship.

On January 1, 1950, "The Nature Boy" added to his legacy when he defeated Johnny Valentine in the finals of a tournament to crown the first-ever NWA United States Champion. He went on to hold the Title for an unprecedented 11 years.

TERRITORIAL CONFLICT

As was normally the case in those days, Rogers bounced around from territory to territory, mainly working in the United States' Midwestern region. When he made trips to the Northeast, however, Rogers worked for Jack Pfeffer until the promoter left the territory. With Pfeffer out of the New York scene, Rogers was left without a Northeast promoter. The powerhouse promoting tandem of Vincent J. McMahon and Toots Mondt moved quickly to sign Rogers to Capitol Wrestling Corporation.

Shortly after aligning with Capitol Wrestling, Rogers captured the NWA Championship when he defeated Pat O'Connor in front of a record crowd at Chicago's Comiskey Park on June 30, 1961. After the victory, the cocky Rogers grabbed the microphone and proclaimed, "To a nicer guy, it couldn't happen." It was this type of egotistical display that made the "Nature Boy" one of the most despised Superstars by both the fans and his fellow competitors.

Despite his conceited persona, Rogers had an amazing ability to fill arenas, especially after winning the NWA Championship. This proved to be huge for Capitol Wrestling, which controlled Rogers' schedule. Over the next two years, McMahon and Mondt sold out arenas behind Rogers' star power.

Among his notable challengers: Édouard Carpentier, Cowboy Bob Ellis, Antonino Rocca, Valentine, The Crusher, and future NWA World Heavyweight Champions Gene Kiniski and Shohei "Giant" Baba.

During this period, Rogers was the biggest box office hit in North America. But that wasn't necessarily good news for everybody. His lack of Title defenses outside the Northeast didn't sit well with the other NWA promoters. Eventually, the NWA collectively decided that having Rogers defend the Title almost exclusively in the Northeast was bad for business.

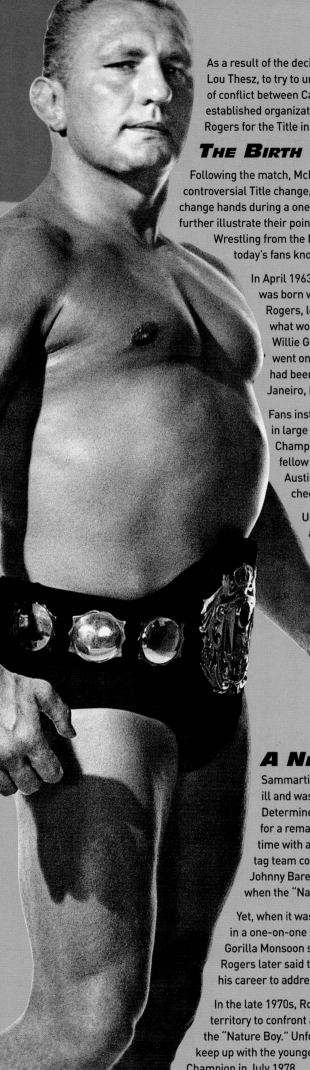

As a result of the decision, they contacted multi-time Champion, Lou Thesz, to try to unseat Rogers. This caused a certain degree of conflict between Capitol Wrestling and the NWA. Yet, the established organization got their way when Thesz toppled Rogers for the Title in Toronto on January 14, 1963.

THE BIRTH OF WWE

Following the match, McMahon and Mondt refused to recognize the controversial Title change, claiming that a Championship could not change hands during a one-fall match (a common rule at the time). To further illustrate their point, McMahon and Mondt withdrew Capitol Wrestling from the NWA to form their own promotion, which today's fans know as WWE.

In April 1963, McMahon and Mondt's new promotion was born with their hand-picked Superstar, Buddy Rogers, leading the way as Champion. Addressing, what would later become the WWE Universe, Willie Gilzenberg, the company's first president, went on television and announced that Rogers had been crowned during a tournament in Rio de Janeiro, Brazil.

Fans instantly took to the new promotion, thanks in large part to the credibility Rogers brought as Champion. When he defended the Title against fellow villains, Killer Kowalski and "Killer" Buddy Austin, fans were split—with a sizeable share cheering the charismatic Rogers.

Unfortunately, Rogers claimed that soon after his Title win, he was beset by health problems. In May 1963, he was reportedly pulled out of the hospital by Mondt and forced to step into the ring with Bruno Sammartino at Madison Square Garden. Although Bruno won in less than a minute, the "Nature Boy" truly blazed the trail for the WWE Champions that followed.

A NEW GENERATION

Sammartino always claimed that Rogers was never ill and was just feigning illness to avoid the inevitable. Determined to prove Bruno wrong, Rogers prepared for a rematch, topping tough Hans Mortier in record time with a figure four in Madison Square Garden. In a tag team confrontation, Rogers teamed with Handsome Johnny Barend to beat Sammartino and Bobo Brazil, when the "Nature Boy" pinned the WWE Champion.

Yet, when it was time for Rogers and Sammartino to collide in a one-on-one match at Roosevelt Stadium in New Jersey, Gorilla Monsoon stepped in as a substitute challenger. Rogers later said that he was forced to take a step back from his career to address his various health issues.

In the late 1970s, Rogers reemerged in the Mid-Atlantic territory to confront a young Ric Flair, who also claimed to be the "Nature Boy." Unfortunately for Rogers, he was unable to keep up with the younger Flair. He fell to the future 16-time World Champion in July 1978.

THERE'S ONLY ONE DIAMOND IN THIS BUSINESS, AND YOU'RE LOOKING AT HIM.

Still, Rogers maintained his confidence. "There's only one diamond in this business," he boasted to Flair in a private moment, "and you're looking at him."

While in the Charlotte territory, Rogers also worked as a manager, handling the careers of talent like Ken Patera, Big John Studd, and Jimmy "Superfly" Snuka.

In the early-1980s, Rogers made a brief return to WWE to manage his old charge, Snuka. On rare occasions, he would even lace up his boots to compete alongside Snuka in tag action. However, after suffering a broken hip in a match against Captain Lou Albano and Ray Stevens, it seemed as if the original "Nature Boy's" days between the ropes were finally behind him.

Yet, the intensely competitive Rogers still believed that he could not only contribute to the industry, but sell out arenas. In 1992, the 71-year-old former Champion proclaimed that he was ready to step in the ring one last time at a show in Philadelphia. His motive: silencing yet one more claimant to the name "Nature Boy," Buddy Landel. The impending contest generated a great deal of excitement, but before the two could compete, Rogers' old health issues resurfaced.

The great Buddy Rogers passed away on July 6, 1992, due to complications from a heart attack and multiple strokes. Rogers received the ultimate honor when he was posthumously inducted into the WWE Hall of Fame by then-WWE Champion, Bret Hart, in June of 1994. The induction was a fitting honor for the man who was first to hold the prestigious Title known today as the WWE Championship.

BULL BUCHANAN

| HT | 6'7" | WT | 296 lbs. | FROM | Cobb County, Georgia |
| SIGNATURE MOVE | Scissors Kick |

A former prison guard, Bull Buchanan built his tough exterior while maintaining order in Georgia's most notorious penitentiaries. When pushing around hardened criminals became mundane, he turned to the rough rings of WWE in 2000.

Originally the tag team partner of fellow prison guard Big Boss Man, Buchanan finally found the challenge he was looking for. The duo's brief time together featured many highlights, including a victory over The Godfather & D-Lo Brown at *WrestleMania 2000*.

Shortly after *WrestleMania*, Buchanan joined Steven Richards' Right to Censor campaign. Trading in his nightstick for a shirt and tie, the massive Superstar became a force in the tag ranks with partner, The Goodfather. The converted tandem held the World Tag Team Championship for one a month in late 2000.

After Right to Censor disbanded, Buchanan vanished from WWE. When he returned in late 2002, he became B² and began sporting some serious bling-bling as John Cena's heavy. However, after shouldering the blame for a loss to Los Guerreros, Cena ditched him for a new partner in Thuganomics.

BULL DEMPSEY

| HT | 6'2" | WT | 300 lbs. | FROM | Brooklyn, New York | SIGNATURE MOVE | The Bulldozer |

Perhaps no one has been able to turn a deficiency into an asset as seamlessly as Bull Dempsey. When the Brooklyn native was criticized for being out of shape, he became obsessive with training, even doing jumping jacks between leg dives and hip tosses during his NXT matches. In the process, he developed thousands of new followers—all dedicated to his goal of becoming "Bull-Fit."

While Dempsey received most of his attention in 2015, he'd been competing on the indie circuit for the previous decade, after being trained by Matt Borne and Tazz. In 2013, he debuted in NXT, forming a tandem with Mojo Rawley that never quite clicked.

His high profile "Bull-Fit" regimen notwithstanding, he departed from NXT in 2016.

BULL NAKANO

| HT | 5'7" | FROM | Kawaguchi, Japan |
| SIGNATURE MOVE | Guillotine Legdrop |

Bull Nakano began her professional career competing for All Japan Women's Pro-Wrestling at the age of 15. While there, she captured the Women's Junior Championship and began to catch the attention of fans and promoters worldwide. In March 1986, while still a teenager, Nakano teamed with the legendary Dump Matsumoto to make her WWE debut against Dawn Marie Johnston and Velvet McIntyre.

In 1994, Nakano returned to WWE to compete for the only Title that eluded her for her entire career, the WWE Women's Championship. In front of more than 45,000 fans at Tokyo's Egg Dome, Nakano defeated Alundra Blayze in November 1994 to accomplish her goal of attaining the top prize in WWE's women's division. Nakano held the Title for more than four months before losing it back to Blayze on *Monday Night Raw*.

Nakano left WWE in 1995, but surfaced in WCW the following year. While there, she resumed her rivalry with Blayze (now known as Madusa), most notably in a Battle of the Bikes Match at *Hog Wild*, which Nakano lost. As a result of the loss, pre-match stipulations allowed Madusa to trash Nakano's motorcycle.

Bull Nakano retired from active competition in 1997 and will forever be remembered as one of the greatest female competitors of all time.

BULL ORTEGA

| HT | 5'11" | WT | 300 lbs. |

A pillar of power, Bull Ortega caught the eye of fan and foe alike upon making his WWE debut in 1966. His offense was built around power and submission moves, but Ortega also possessed deceptive speed. After emerging victorious in a series of handicap matches, he was considered a serious WWE Championship contender.

When circumstances called for it, Ortega joined forces with fellow rule-breakers of the era, including Luke Graham, Bulldog Brower, Tank Morgan, and future WWE Hall of Famer Baron Mikel Scicluna. Ortega's toughest challenge came in the form of then-WWE Champion Bruno Sammartino. Though he tried often, Ortega was never able to defeat Sammartino for the Title.

BULL RAMOS

| HT | 6'0" | WT | 350 lbs. | FROM | Houston, Texas |

"Apache" Bull Ramos was a tough Native American who displayed his skills all over the world. In addition to finding great success in America, Ramos used his massive girth to dominate opponents in Korea, Australia, and Japan.

As a member of WWE, Ramos earned the unique distinction of competing in the old Madison Square Garden's final show, as well as the new Garden's first show. He successfully turned back Antonio Pugliese in the old Garden, but came up short in the new arena, losing to WWE Champion Bruno Sammartino.

After failing in several attempts to dethrone Sammartino, Ramos headed west where he was able to capture the NWA Pacific Northwest Tag Team Championship with WWE Hall of Famer Jesse Ventura.

BULLDOG BROWER

HT	5'8"	WT	270 lbs.	FROM	Hamilton, Ontario, Canada
SIGNATURE MOVE	The Brower Lock				

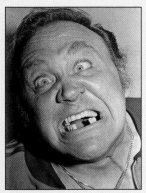

Bulldog Brower, a former chiropractic student who started in Stampede Wrestling, was infamous all over the world as the "One Man Riot Squad." At one point, he even tangled with Terrible Ted, The Wrestling Bear, and body slammed the gargantuan Haystacks Calhoun!

Often led to the ring by future WWE Hall of Famer Capt. Lou Albano, Brower challenged WWE Champions Bruno Sammartino, Pedro Morales, and Bob Backlund.

Brower retired from active competition in 1988. On September 15, 1997, he passed away from complications following hip surgery. Both fans and fellow Superstars fondly remember his classic battles, terrorizing presence, and chilling interviews.

THE BUNNY

Back in Adam Rose's party days, the Bahamian Superstar was known to keep some pretty peculiar company. Perhaps no member of his famed Rosebuds posse was more unique than The Bunny.

Blessed with superior athletic skills not normally found in a rabbit, The Bunny began teaming with Rose in September 2014. The interspecies tandem gained early success, defeating Slater-Gator on several occasions. But just when it looked like they would make waves in the tag division, dissention set in when the conductor of the Exotic Express became jealous over his furry friend's fame.

The Bunny and Rose tried to work through their issues. But in the end, The Bunny's popularity was too much for Rose, who viciously attacked his party animal friend in December 2015. Since the attack we haven't seen or heard from The Bunny.

BUSHWHACKERS

(HoF)	MEMBERS	Butch & Luke	COMBINED WT	498 lbs.
	FROM	New Zealand		

Luke and Butch traveled to WWE by way of New Zealand in 1989. Known for licking fans' heads and affectionately yelling in their ears, The Bushwhackers quickly proved they were more than just a quirky duo, scoring victories over the likes of the Brain Busters and Powers of Pain.

The Bushwhackers' unorthodox ring style combined primitive roughhousing with sophisticated tag team tactics. Among their most devastating double-team moves was the Double Gutbuster, which neutralized many top teams over the years, including the Rougeaus and Bolsheviks.

Luke and Butch's unique lifestyle eventually proved to be contagious and even caught the interest of "Mean" Gene Okerlund, who traveled to New Zealand to conduct a special profile on the tandem. The team's meager accommodations in the outback initially caught Okerlund off guard, but once he had their fresh grilled Bushwhacker Buzzard, he felt right at home, complete with black tank-top and camouflage pants.

Prior to joining WWE, Luke and Butch spent more than two decades solidifying themselves as one of sports-entertainment's greatest teams, capturing 26 tag team Championships all over the globe. They even earned the reputation for being hardcore before ECW made hardcore vogue. In 2015, The Bushwhackers were recognized for their decades of excellence with induction into the WWE Hall of Fame.

BUTCH REED

HT	6'2"	WT	255 lbs.	FROM	Kansas City, Missouri

Originally a football player by trade, Butch Reed jumped to wrestling in 1978. While most football players find it difficult to make the transition, Reed picked up his new craft quickly, resulting in many claiming he was a "natural."

Reed's early days were spent competing in Mid-South, but when he came up short in a Loser Leaves Town Match, the athletic Superstar was forced to find a new home. It didn't take long for Reed to land on his feet, as WWE officials had been watching him from afar and jumped at the opportunity to bring him in.

With manager Slick by his side, Reed debuted in WWE in 1986 with a new look. He dyed his hair blonde, adopted "The Natural" nickname, and developed an arrogant attitude. In the ring, though, he was still the same dominant force.

Reed's first big WWE win came at the expense of Koko B. Ware at *WrestleMania III*. The victory eventually landed Reed a series of Intercontinental Championship matches against Ricky Steamboat. Reed was ultimately unsuccessful in capturing the title, but didn't let that deter him from being a force in WWE. Later that year, he teamed with One Man Gang to sneak attack "Superstar" Billy Graham. The savage beating forced Graham into permanent retirement.

Reed left WWE in 1988, but resurfaced in WCW as Ron Simmons's partner in the powerful tag team Doom.

BUTCHER BRANNIGAN

HT	6'3"	WT	290 lbs.	FROM	Ireland

SIGNATURE MOVE	Bearhug

In the 1970s, Butcher Brannigan literally wandered the world. Wherever he landed, he took on the top attraction: Steve Rickard in New Zealand, Otto Wanz in Germany, Big Daddy in England, Jan Wilkens in South Africa.

His win-loss record is spotty. He enjoyed his greatest fame in New Zealand and Australia and, in 1974, won America's Tag Team gold in the Los Angeles territory with Man Mountain Mike.

The same year, he competed for WWE in Madison Square Garden, crunching Mike Pappas. What fans didn't realize is that he'd previously passed through the northeast, using the name Joe Nova and tangling with foes like Spiros Arion, "Flyin'" Fred Curry, and Jimmy Valiant.

After retirement, he taught fine arts to prisoners, and died in 2009.

BUTCHER VACHON

HT	6'2"	WT	282 lbs.

FROM	Montreal, Quebec, Canada

Paul Vachon made his professional wrestling debut in 1957. Known as "Butcher," the crazed Canadian hoped to equal the success enjoyed by his older brother, Maurice "Mad Dog" Vachon.

After a few years of competing on his own, Butcher united with his brother to form one of history's most unorthodox tandems. Known for their hardcore style, the Vachons terrorized their way to tag team Titles across North America. Perhaps their most impressive reign came when they topped Dick the Bruiser and The Crusher for the AWA World Tag Team Championship in August, 1969. Butcher and Mad Dog went on to hold the gold for an amazing 623 days.

In WWE, Butcher Vachon went toe-to-toe with many legendary names, including Sgt. Slaughter, Jimmy Snuka, and Bob Backlund. Despite these battles, it was his 1984 in-ring wedding for which he is often remembered. With many of WWE's top Superstars serving as witnesses, Vachon and his bride tied the knot in a ceremony marred by David Schultz' physical interference.

Butcher's step-daughter, Luna Vachon, was also a force in WWE.

BUTTERBEAN

HT	5'11"	WT	316 lbs.	FROM	Jasper, Alabama

A famous Toughman contest winner, boxer, and mixed martial artist, Eric "Butterbean" Esch began boxing professionally in 1994. As his loyal fan following grew, the famed heavyweight caught the eye of WWE officials. And in 1997, Butterbean made his first WWE appearance, defeating Marc Mero via disqualification at *In Your House: D-Generation X*.

Butterbean returned to WWE in 1999 to battle Bart Gunn in a Brawl For All Match at *WrestleMania XV*. The contest will forever be remembered as one of the most lopsided matches in *WrestleMania* history, as Butterbean destroyed Gunn in just over thirty seconds. Years later, the sight of Butterbean's right hand flooring Gunn remains a WWE highlight reel staple.

BUZZ SAWYER

HT	5'9"	WT	240 lbs.

FROM	St. Petersburg, Florida

Buzz Sawyer's WWE career only consisted of a handful of matches, but outside of WWE, the man known as "Mad Dog" attained great success in almost every territory where he appeared.

Despite an intimate understanding of technical wrestling, Sawyer always preferred a brawl. In 1983, Sawyer was an original member of the Legion of Doom, along with the Road Warriors, the Spoiler, and King Kong Bundy. That distinction is often overlooked because of another incident that occurred that year.

For months, Sawyer had been engaged in a bloody war with Tommy Rich that frequently spilled all over the arena and outside of buildings. As a result, the two were paired in an enclosed cage at an event called the "Last Battle of Atlanta." Sawyer's manager, Precious Paul Ellering, was suspended from a second cage 20 feet above the ring. Later, this encounter would be the inspiration for WWE's Hell in a Cell matches.

Upon entering WWE in 1984, Sawyer was called "Bulldog" rather than "Mad Dog" because of the presence of Mad Dog Vachon in the company. A protégé of Lou Albano's, Sawyer was led to the ring by a chain and literally barked at fans.

He also appeared in the Portland, Mid-South, and World Class promotions, where he fought Brian Adias, the Von Erichs, and the Dingo Warrior (later known as Ultimate Warrior). He died in 1992.

bWo (BLUE WORLD ORDER)

MEMBERS	Big Stevie Cool, The Blue Guy, & Hollywood Nova

During the height of the New World Order's popularity, a band of ECW misfits joined forces to parody the powerful WCW faction. Known as the Blue World Order, each Superstar assumed the identity of an nWo member. As expected, the bWo garnered more laughs than victories, but that didn't stop them from mocking the nWo each week while brashly declaring, "We're taking over!"

Eight years after the bWo disbanded, the faction made an unexpected return at *ECW One Night Stand 2005*, disrupting the main event between The Dudley Boyz versus Tommy Dreamer and The Sandman. The bWo had a final match the following month at *The Great American Bash* before leaving WWE.

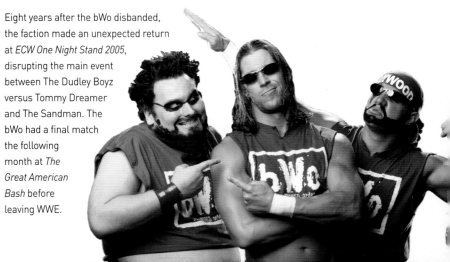

BYRON SAXTON

HT	6'1"	WT	212 lbs.
FROM	Burke, Virginia		

In recent years, Byron Saxton has proven himself as a trusted voice on WWE's top television shows. His route to becoming a commentator, however, was somewhat unorthodox.

Originally seeking a career in news, Saxton worked for WJXT in Jacksonville, Florida, but it wasn't long before the bright lights of WWE came calling. Starting in 2007, Saxton found himself competing, managing, and commentating for WWE's then-developmental system, Florida Championship Wrestling.

Though he had successfully proven to be a jack of all trades, Saxton's future appeared to be as a competitor when he was selected to be a Rookie on seasons four and five of the original *NXT* series.

Unable to capture the prize on either season, Saxton later dedicated himself to becoming a respected commentator. And when NXT rebranded in 2012, Saxton was tapped to be the voice of the brand. Saxton's work behind the mic impressed WWE executives, who quickly promoted the young announcer to the main roster in 2014. Since then, Saxton has called the action for several shows, including *Superstars*, *SmackDown*, and *Monday Night Raw*.

CAMACHO

HT	6'2"	WT	230 lbs.	FROM	Juarez, Mexico

Camacho credits longtime friend Hunico with saving his life back in the barrio where the two Superstars grew up. Years later, Camacho returned the favor. With Hunico standing on pegs on the back of his lowrider bicycle, Camacho slowly rolled to the ring with his signature scowl on his face, a silent warning to anyone looking to rough up his vato. The street-tough Superstar's lowrider bicycle was an expression of his culture, built from scratch with the finest materials.

Camacho fought his own battles as well, taking his intimidating presence back and forth from WWE to NXT rings until his departure in 2014.

CANADIAN HEAVYWEIGHT CHAMPIONSHIP

The WWE Canadian Heavyweight Championship was introduced in the summer of 1985 as WWE expanded its global reach into the provinces of Canada. The Championship was awarded to Dino Bravo on August 1, 1985. However, this was not a random selection of the champion that would represent Canada. Bravo had arguably been the most successful competitor in Lutte International, a Montreal-based promotion that had a relationship with WWE in the 1980s, holding the organization's Canadian International Heavyweight Title after defeating capable rivals like King Tonga, Rick Martel, and Billy Robinson. In WWE, Bravo defended his Canadian Heavyweight Championship against Nikolai Volkoff, Randy Savage, Jim Neidhart, Moondog Spot, and others. But, within less than a year, WWE discontinued the Title, as Bravo decided to concentrate on pursuing the WWE World Heavyweight Championship instead.

CAMERON

HT	5'4"	FROM	Northridge, California	SIGNATURE MOVE	Girl Bye

Once a contestant on *Tough Enough*, Cameron laced up her dancing shoes for her first steps into WWE. As one half of the Funkadactyls, she boogied down to Brodus Clay's funky beats alongside her partner in funk, Naomi. The delectable duo continued to back the big man until the dissolution of Tons of Funk in 2013 put them on separate paths.

After Cameron said "Girl Bye" to Tons of Funk, it allowed her to focus on competing in the Divas division. At *Elimination Chamber 2014*, she battled AJ Lee in the midst of AJ's historic Divas Championship reign and nearly pulled off an incredible upset. As an original cast member of *Total Divas*, Cameron's continued clashes with other Divas were put on full display, including her unpleasant final split with Naomi.

Cameron brought a blend of sass and spunk to WWE rings for over three years before her departure in May 2016.

THE CAN-AM CONNECTION

MEMBERS	Rick Martel & Tom Zenk	COMBINED WT	471 lbs.

Take a Canadian top grappler and add one of Minnesota's best athletes and you get the high-flying Can-Am Connection. Rick Martel and Tom Zenk debuted in 1987 and became almost instant Championship contenders after defeating Magnificent Muraco and Bob Orton at *WrestleMania III*.

The Can-Am Connection eventually earned an opportunity at the World Tag Team Championship. However, then-Champions the Hart Foundation took out Zenk before the match started. Zenk never fully recovered from his injuries and disappeared from WWE. Martel, seeking revenge for the heinous action, recruited Tito Santana, and the pair competed under the name Strike Force.

The Can-Am Connection enjoyed incredible success during their brief time together. Fans to this day wonder what might have been had the duo remained together.

CAMP CORNETTE

MEMBERS	Vader, Owen Hart, & British Bulldog

Jim Cornette's quest to dominate WWE during the mid-to-late 1990s largely depended on the success of three men: Vader, Owen Hart, and British Bulldog. Collectively known as Camp Cornette, the trio was assembled with hopes of catapulting the manager's career to the WWE Championship, a status he formerly held while working with Yokozuna.

As the largest Superstar in the stable, Vader seemed the logical choice to capture the Title. Unfortunately for Camp Cornette, however, a WWE Championship reign was not in the cards, as Shawn Michaels defeated Vader at *SummerSlam 1996*. Both Hart and Bulldog also competed on the *SummerSlam* card; but Cornette was too busy working with Vader to pay much attention to them, which eventually led to the demise of Camp Cornette.

CANDICE MICHELLE

| HT | 5'7" | FROM | Milwaukee, Wisconsin |
| SIGNATURE MOVE | | | Candywrapper |

Candice's WWE career nearly ended before it ever began. After failing to win the 2004 Diva Search, it appeared as though the beautiful brunette was at a career crossroads. Fortunately, WWE officials saw something they liked in her and offered a contract. While she enjoyed the attention she was garnering in non-competitive roles, Candice wanted more than to be regarded as eye candy.

With countless hours of training from former Four Horsemen enforcer Arn Anderson, Candice became a legitimate threat in the Women's Division. On June 24, 2007, she proved her worth when she defeated Melina for the coveted Women's Championship at *Vengeance*.

The win capped off Candice's amazing evolution into a dominant female force in the ring. All the while, she maintained her unmatched sensuality that landed her in controversial Go Daddy ads and even on the cover of *Playboy*. She remained a top contender for the prestigious Women's Championship until injuries forced her to leave sports-entertainment sooner than expected.

CARLITO

| HT | 5'10" | WT | 220 lbs. | FROM | The Caribbean |
| SIGNATURE MOVE | | | The Backstabber | | |

This brash second-generation Superstar made an unbelievable debut in October 2004 when he beat John Cena for the United States Championship on *SmackDown*. Carlito warned everyone that he spits in the face of people who don't want to be "cool," a quality that he rarely saw in anyone. On his talk segment, "Carlito's Cabana," he disrespected guests and fans on a frequent basis.

Carlito was drafted to *Raw* and again made an incredible debut, beating Shelton Benjamin for the Intercontinental Championship. Though he lost it later in the year to "Nature Boy" Ric Flair, this bad apple remained a serious threat to any WWE Champion. He also lucked out with the ladies as he developed a romance with Torrie Wilson.

In 2008, he formed a Championship combination with his brother, Primo. The brothers won a historic match to unify the WWE and World Tag Team Championships at *WrestleMania 25*. After losing the Titles, Carlito turned on his brother and temporarily took on Rosa Mendes as a manager. Before his departure from WWE in 2010, Carlito served as a pro on the first season of *WWE NXT* and reunited with Primo.

In 2014, Carlito appeared to induct his father, Carlos Colon Sr., into the WWE Hall of Fame.

CARLOS COLON

| HT | 5'10" | WT | 246 lbs. | FROM | Santa Isabel, Puerto Rico |

Puerto Rican fans recognize Carlos Colon as the founder and star of the World Wrestling Council promotion. While his in-ring dominance certainly leaves an impressive legacy, the legend of Carlos Colon continued to grow well after his prime, every time his two sons entered a WWE ring.

After spending the late 1960s competing in the northeast territories of the United States, Colon returned to his native Puerto Rico, where he became an iconic figure. Colon briefly competed in WWE during the early 1990s. The only high-profile account of his tenure was his participation in the 1993 Royal Rumble Match. Colon managed to eliminate Damian Damento from the contest before being tossed out by the mighty Yokozuna. Colon's greatest contributions to WWE would come more than ten years later when his son Carlito made his WWE debut, followed by another son, Primo.

In 2014, Colon's contributions to the sports-entertainment industry were recognized with induction into the WWE Hall of Fame.

CARMELLA

| HT | 5'5" | FROM | Staten Island, New York |

Despite calling herself "The Princess of Staten Island," Carmella possesses enough New York grit for all five boroughs. Which is why it is no surprise the former NFL and NBA dancer clicked instantaneously with Enzo Amore and Colin Cassady. Following an ill-fated hairdressing incident, Enzo and Big Cass prepared Carmella for the *NXT* ring. Her fabulous debut in October 2014 put the entire *NXT* women's locker room on notice, as Carmella displayed a potent submission move in a decisive win over Blue Pants.

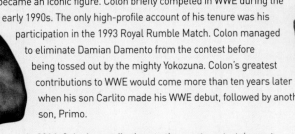

Carmella gained valuable experience in 2015, competing in physical encounters with Alexa Bliss, Emma, and Eva Marie. Eva defeated Carmella at *NXT Takeover: Brooklyn* but Carmella scored revenge when she last eliminated her crimson clad rival in a January 2016 #1 Contender's Battle Royal.

CAYLEN CROFT

| HT | 6'0" | WT | 220 lbs. | FROM | Akron, Ohio |

After *ECW*'s New Superstar Initiative brought the colorful Caylen Croft to WWE in December 2009, Croft and his longtime best friend Trent Barreta racked up several impressive victories as a tag team. Unfortunately for Croft, however, *ECW* ceased existing shortly after his debut; with it went the new Superstar's success.

Croft and Barreta ultimately signed with *SmackDown*, where they struggled mightily. Teams such as Cryme Tyme, The Hart Dynasty and many others padded their win-loss records courtesy of Croft and Barreta. Hoping a change in identity would help, the buddies christened themselves "The Dudebusters" in April 2010. The new name did little to improve their luck. The Dudebusters did not pick up their first win as *SmackDown* stars until later that summer, defeating Curt Hawkins and Vance Archer.

CHAMPIONSHIP WRESTLING FROM FLORIDA

see page 66

CHARLIE FULTON

| HT | 6'2" | WT | 246 lbs. | FROM | Marion, Ohio |
| SIGNATURE MOVE | Piledriver |

Charlie Fulton kicked off his career in March 1968. But shortly after his debut, the military draft forced him into the army. Fulton served his country for several years before returning to the ring.

Fulton spent the majority of the 1970s and early 1980s travelling the territories. Texas, Montreal, Florida, Charlotte, Detroit, Tennessee—he competed in them all. Along the way, he stood across the ring from the greats, including Lou Thesz and Bruno Sammartino.

One of Fulton's few tastes of gold came when he teamed with Bobby Mayne to defeat Ron Gibson and Stan Pulaski for the NWA Southern Tag Team Championship in June 1974. Fulton ventured to WWE in the early '80s where he battled the likes of Tony Atlas, Rocky Johnson, and S.D. Jones.

CESARO

| HT | 6'5" | WT | 232 lbs. | FROM | Lucerne, Switzerland |
| SIGNATURE MOVE | The Neutralizer, Cesaro Swing |

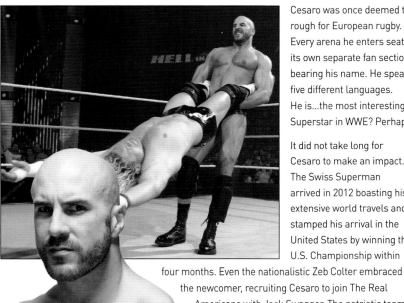

Cesaro was once deemed too rough for European rugby. Every arena he enters seats its own separate fan section bearing his name. He speaks five different languages. He is...the most interesting Superstar in WWE? Perhaps.

It did not take long for Cesaro to make an impact. The Swiss Superman arrived in 2012 boasting his extensive world travels and stamped his arrival in the United States by winning the U.S. Championship within four months. Even the nationalistic Zeb Colter embraced the newcomer, recruiting Cesaro to join The Real Americans with Jack Swagger. The patriotic team was successful, but Cesaro wanted more. At *WrestleMania 30*, fans got their first real taste of his herculean strength when he heaved the 480-pound Big Show over the top rope to win the Andre the Giant Memorial Battle Royal.

After a fleeting stint under Paul Heyman's guidance, Cesaro joined the tag team ranks once again, this time with Tyson Kidd. The old-school grappler and the Hart Dungeon alumnus found immediate chemistry. They enjoyed a Tag Team Championship reign and with Kidd rehabbing a severe injury, the best days might be forthcoming for this duo. In the meantime, Cesaro continues to impress on his own. His crowd-pleasing Cesaro Swing highlights an eclectic and dangerous arsenal.

CHARLIE HAAS

| HT | 6'2" | WT | 242 lbs. | FROM | Edmond, Oklahoma |
| SIGNATURE MOVE | Haas of Pain |

As a former two-time Big East amateur wrestling Champion at Seton Hall University, Charlie Haas parlayed his grappling mastery into a successful WWE career. Haas made his debut on Dec. 26, 2002, as a member of Team Angle along with his partner, Shelton Benjamin. While protecting Kurt Angle's WWE Championship reign, Haas and Benjamin won some gold of their own, defeating Los Guerreros for the WWE Tag Team Championship in February 2003.

The self-dubbed "World's Greatest Tag Team," low on creativity but high on ability, stayed together until March 2004 when Benjamin was drafted to *Raw*. Despite the separation, Haas sought another WWE Tag Team Championship and got one alongside the eccentric Rico in April 2004. Miss Jackie helped guide the odd pairing past Rikishi and Scotty 2 Hotty. Later that year, Haas ditched both Jackie and Dawn Marie in the ring to squash a burgeoning love triangle.

Haas departed WWE in July 2005 only to return in April 2006, shocking his former partner, Shelton Benjamin. The duo would reunite, but not before Haas injured Lilian Garcia inadvertently, sparking a rivalry with Viscera. In the summer of 2008, Haas took his career in an unexpected direction. He began to perform dead-ringer impersonations of WWE Legends and Superstars in the ring, earning a 2008 Slammy Award.

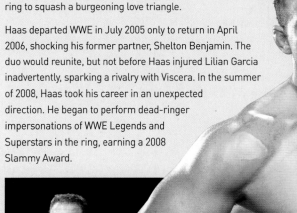

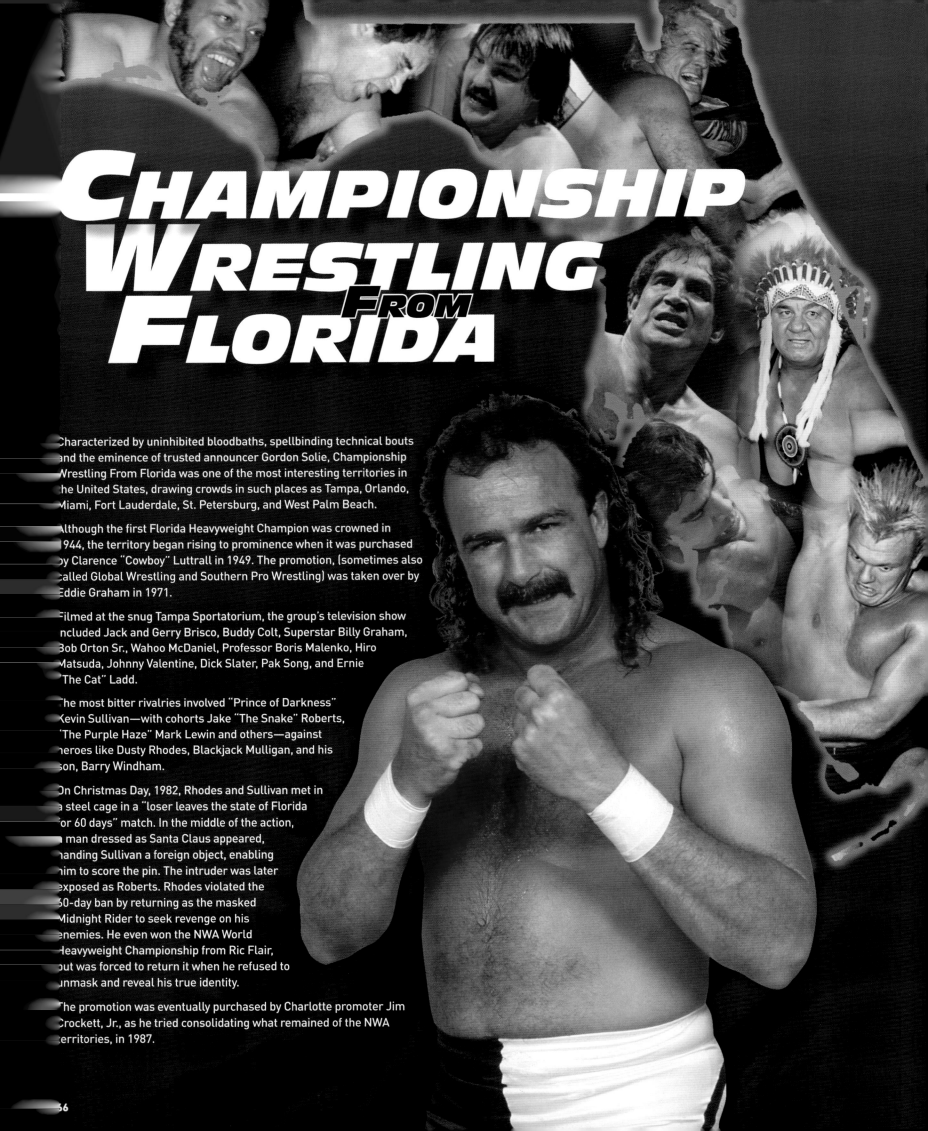

CHAMPIONSHIP WRESTLING FROM FLORIDA

Characterized by uninhibited bloodbaths, spellbinding technical bouts and the eminence of trusted announcer Gordon Solie, Championship Wrestling From Florida was one of the most interesting territories in the United States, drawing crowds in such places as Tampa, Orlando, Miami, Fort Lauderdale, St. Petersburg, and West Palm Beach.

Although the first Florida Heavyweight Champion was crowned in 1944, the territory began rising to prominence when it was purchased by Clarence "Cowboy" Luttrall in 1949. The promotion, (sometimes also called Global Wrestling and Southern Pro Wrestling) was taken over by Eddie Graham in 1971.

Filmed at the snug Tampa Sportatorium, the group's television show included Jack and Gerry Brisco, Buddy Colt, Superstar Billy Graham, Bob Orton Sr., Wahoo McDaniel, Professor Boris Malenko, Hiro Matsuda, Johnny Valentine, Dick Slater, Pak Song, and Ernie "The Cat" Ladd.

The most bitter rivalries involved "Prince of Darkness" Kevin Sullivan—with cohorts Jake "The Snake" Roberts, "The Purple Haze" Mark Lewin and others—against heroes like Dusty Rhodes, Blackjack Mulligan, and his son, Barry Windham.

On Christmas Day, 1982, Rhodes and Sullivan met in a steel cage in a "loser leaves the state of Florida for 60 days" match. In the middle of the action, a man dressed as Santa Claus appeared, handing Sullivan a foreign object, enabling him to score the pin. The intruder was later exposed as Roberts. Rhodes violated the 60-day ban by returning as the masked Midnight Rider to seek revenge on his enemies. He even won the NWA World Heavyweight Championship from Ric Flair, but was forced to return it when he refused to unmask and reveal his true identity.

The promotion was eventually purchased by Charlotte promoter Jim Crockett, Jr., as he tried consolidating what remained of the NWA territories, in 1987.

CHARLIE MINN

His tenure with WWE only lasted a few months, but Charlie Minn will always be remembered by longtime fans as the overly-excited announcer on *WWE Action Zone*.

Minn also brought a never-before-seen level of energy to WWE's Live Event News updates. As the segment's anchor, Minn enthusiastically alerted the WWE Universe to upcoming events in their area, complete with information on how to purchase tickets.

When he wasn't pushing ticket sales, Minn could also be seen interviewing Superstars. Unlike WWE Hall of Famer "Mean" Gene Okerlund, who conducted his interviews with a great deal of professionalism, Minn often appeared in awe of the Superstars he was interviewing.

Minn's WWE career came to a quick close in early 1995.

CHARLOTTE

HT	5'10"	FROM	The Queen City
SIGNATURE MOVE			Figure Eight, Natural Selection

If you're gonna do it, do it with Flair. And that's exactly what Charlotte has done since her NXT debut in 2013. As the daughter of the legendary Ric Flair, Charlotte wasted little time creating her own Championship legacy when she defeated Natalya in a tournament final to claim the NXT Women's Title in May 2014.

As Champion, Charlotte helped establish the strength of the women's division with thrilling victories over the likes of Bayley, Becky Lynch, and Sasha Banks.

After 258 days with the Championship, Charlotte was called up to the main WWE roster. Upon her arrival, she teamed with Paige and Becky Lynch to form Team PCB. Together, the trio battled Team Bella and Team B.A.D., en route to establishing the great Divas Revolution in WWE.

Charlotte added more gold to her trophy case when she forced Divas Champion Nikki Bella to tap to the Figure Eight Leg Lock at *Night of Champions 2015*. With the victory, Charlotte ended Nikki's record 301-day reign and proved herself as a force for years to come. At *WrestleMania 32*, Charlotte cemented her name in WWE lore by winning a Triple Threat Match to be crowned the inaugural WWE Women's Champion.

CHAVO GUERRERO

HT	5'9"	WT	215 lbs.	FROM	El Paso, Texas
SIGNATURE MOVE		Frog Splash			

As a member of the famed Guerrero family, Chavo Guerrero was born with sports-entertainment running through his veins. He spent his childhood honing his skills in the family ring and began his career competing across Mexico and Japan. Guerrero was introduced to American audiences in 1996, when he debuted in WCW. Though his own uncle, Eddie Guerrero, deemed him too loony for his Latino World Order stable, Chavo kept it together enough to win two Cruiserweight Titles. Of course, it was Eddie who drove him crazy in the first place!

In WWE, the Guerreros gelled much better, capturing two WWE Tag Team Titles with their everlasting mantra "Lie, Cheat & Steal." Chavo continued to make his family proud over the next few years, winning the Cruiserweight Championship three times. Still, Chavo somehow believed his Hispanic heritage was holding him back, inspiring a bizarre decision to change his name to Kerwin White.

Chavo reclaimed the Guerrero name in November 2005, following the passing of his uncle, Eddie. Adopting the famed Frog Splash as his own, Guerrero went on to capture his fourth WWE Cruiserweight Championship and later, the ECW Championship.

The proud warrior also supported his aunt Vickie Guerrero and had several run-ins with the mischievous Hornswoggle before leaving WWE in June 2011.

CHAVO GUERRERO, SR.

HT	5'11"	WT	229 lbs.
FROM	El Paso, Texas		

Chavo Guerrero, Sr. came from wrestling royalty on both sides of his family. His mother's brother was Mexican star Enrique Llanes, while his father was the legendary Gory Guerrero. As the oldest son of the next generation of Guerreros, Chavo ushered in a new breed of Superstars, including Mando, Hector, and Eddie Guerrero.

A hero to Mexican-Americans in Los Angeles, Chavo captured the territory's Americas Heavyweight Championship 15 times during the 1970s and early 1980s. His record breaking number of Title reigns came at the expense of such greats as Ernie Ladd, Dory Funk Jr., and Pat Patterson. But his rivalry with "Rowdy" Roddy Piper (a series of emotional battles waged as far away as Mexico) may have been what kept the territory alive during its final days. He also claimed tag team gold with his father, brother Hector, Butcher Vachon, John Tolos, and others.

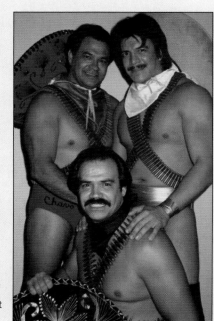

In 2004, Chavo arrived in WWE alongside his son, Chavo Guerrero. Referring to himself as "Chavo Classic" during this time, he mainly served as a mentor to his son. However, in May of 2004, the elder Guerrero was uncharacteristically placed in a Triple Threat Match against his boy and Spike Dudley. In a shocking turn of events, Chavo Classic capitalized on a bizarre set of circumstances to defeat the younger Guerrero for the Cruiserweight Championship. He lost the Title to Rey Mysterio one month later.

CHIEF BIG HEART

FROM	Oklahoma
SIGNATURE MOVE	The Bow & Arrow

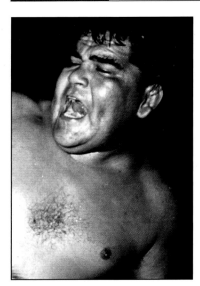

Adorned in a Native American headdress and long leather robe, Chief Big Heart made his way to the ring with a huge smile on his face. Once the bell rang, however, the Oklahoman concealed his jolly side and became all business.

Chief Big Heart formed several successful tag teams with partners Suni War Cloud, Red McIntyre, and Chief Little Eagle. He captured NWA tag team gold in Georgia with McIntyre and Little Eagle. He also paired with Little Eagle to win the Texas version of the NWA tag titles in April 1959.

Chief Big Heart briefly held the NWA Southern Heavyweight Championship when he defeated Jerry Graham in January 1957. One week later, he lost the Title back to Graham, ending his only taste of singles gold.

CHIEF WHITE OWL

HT	5'10"	WT	230 lbs.	FROM	Cherokee, North Carolina
SIGNATURE MOVE	Tomahawk Chop				

Chief White Owl, a proud Native American from the Cherokee Tribe, started his in-ring career in the mid-1950s. Utilizing a Tomahawk Chop as a finisher, his early career was highlighted by runs in several different territories, including Montreal, Florida, Pittsburgh, and even the Bahamas.

After making a name for himself in promotions worldwide, Chief White Owl briefly joined WWE, where he gained notoriety teaming with fellow Native Americans Wahoo McDaniel and Chief Big Heart. Madison Square Garden was the site of his greatest WWE victory, as he teamed with Big Heart to defeat Smasher Sloan and Waldo Von Erich in May 1965.

After leaving WWE, Chief White Owl went on to compete in Detroit before eventually landing with the Buffalo-based National Wrestling Federation.

CHIEF JAY STRONGBOW
see page 69

CHRIS BENOIT

HT	5'11"	WT	229 lbs.	FROM	Edmonton, Alberta, Canada
SIGNATURE MOVE	Crippler Crossface				

Inspired by the Dynamite Kid, Chris Benoit knew he wanted to be a sports-entertainer at age twelve. After graduating high school in 1985, Chris drove almost two-hundred miles to train every week in Stu Hart's famous Dungeon. Following this tireless training, Benoit debuted in Calgary's Stampede Wrestling and in Japan.

By the early 1990s Benoit had a reputation as one of the world's greatest technical competitors. After he won Japan's prestigious Super J-Cup Tournament in 1994, he arrived in ECW where he held the ECW World Tag Team Championship with Dean Malenko. In October 1995 Benoit signed with WCW and was quickly recruited by "Nature Boy" Ric Flair for a revival of The Four Horsemen. While Chris eventually held every championship WCW had to offer, he felt he could achieve more.

In January 2000, he made a radical debut alongside future WWE Hall of Famer Eddie Guerrero, Dean Malenko, and Perry Saturn. In WWE, Benoit competed against many of the best, including Stone Cold Steve Austin, The Rock, Undertaker, and Chris Jericho. He defied the odds when he bested twenty-nine other Superstars to win the 2004 Royal Rumble. This monumental accomplishment led him to *WrestleMania XX*, where he captured the World Heavyweight Championship in a Triple Threat Match. Benoit held the prestigious prize for nine months. After losing it to Randy Orton at *SummerSlam*, he remained a top contender for many of WWE's renowned Championships.

CHRIS JERICHO
see page 70

CHRIS MASTERS

HT	6'4"	WT	265 lbs.	FROM	Los Angeles, California
SIGNATURE MOVE	Master Lock				

Chris Masters was introduced in January 2005, flaunting a physique that resembled ancient statues chiseled from stone. Masters was so confident in his debilitating full nelson, the Master Lock, he instituted the "Master Lock Challenge." He offered $1,000 to anyone who could break the hold. The dollar amount grew each week and, at its height, reached $20,000.

Between these ballyhooed strength exhibitions, Masters was also a fierce competitor. He vied for the WWE Championship inside the Elimination Chamber and battled Shawn Michaels on pay-per-view. The Master Lock stayed unbroken for two years until Bobby Lashley finally matched Masters' strength in 2007.

After spending a few years abroad, "The Masterpiece" returned to WWE in July 2009 with the same bouncing pectorals and an even deadlier Master Lock. In a new, unfamiliar role as fan favorite, he battled stars such as Chavo Guerrero and Jack Swagger. While he was released in August 2011, history has shown "The Masterpiece" could become a fixture in WWE again.

CHIEF JAY STRONGBOW

HT	6'2"
WT	247 lbs.
FROM	Pawhuska, Oklahoma

SIGNATURE MOVE
Tomahawk Chop

This future WWE Hall of Famer's career began in 1947. Throughout the 1950s and 1960s, he was one of the brightest stars in the NWA and held several singles and tag team Titles around the southeastern United States. In 1970, Chief Jay Strongbow debuted in WWE and became an instant hero with his colorful Native American ring attire and high-flying attacks. The Chief fought rule-breakers such as Professor Toru Tanaka, Waldo Von Erich, Ivan Koloff, Pampero Firpo, Tarzan Tyler, Crusher Verdu, and future WWE Hall of Famers George "The Animal" Steele, Killer Kowalski, The Sheik, Johnny Rodz, and Blackjack Mulligan.

In the ring, Strongbow could endure an inordinate amount of punishment, then summon up his ancestral spirits and mete out revenge, doing a war dance between the ropes. Opponents would frequently try to halt his momentum by pounding on Strongbow during this ritual, but it seemed like he couldn't feel the blows.

With each Tomahawk Chop, Strongbow's popularity rose. In May 1972, he won his first of four WWE World Tag Team Championships as he and Sonny King defeated future WWE Hall of Famer Baron Mikel Scicluna and King Curtis Iaukea. Although Strongbow and King only held the Title for one month, Chief established himself as a fierce competitor and some argued that he should be given a WWE World Heavyweight Title opportunity.

Yet, his main focus remained tag team competition. He captured his second tag team Championship in 1976 when he formed an alliance with fellow Native American warrior Chief Billy White Wolf. Their Title reign was suddenly cut short when White Wolf suffered a career-ending neck injury at the hands of Ken Patera. Strongbow sought to avenge this heartless attack on his partner.

STRIVING FOR GOLD

At the time, WWE had a policy that generally prevented fan favorites from battling other fan-favorites. That meant that during the Bruno Sammartino and Pedro Morales eras, Strongbow was excluded from world Title contention. But when Superstar Billy Graham became WWE Champion in 1977, the Chief's fortunes changed. In a number of main events, Strongbow came close to procuring the gold from Graham, and was consistently the sentimental favorite.

Other high profile single's rivals from this period included Stan "The Man" Stasiak, Tor Kamata, Baron Von Raschke, and future WWE Hall of Famers Mr. Fuji and The Valiant Brothers. When Spiros Arion humiliated Strongbow by tearing his headdress and shoving his feathers in his mouth, the Greek combatant absorbed the proud Native's full fury.

The Chief's violent battles against WWE's most vicious villains continued, and in 1979, he waged war on future WWE Hall of Famer Greg "The Hammer" Valentine. After Valentine broke Strongbow's leg, the Chief came back with a vengeance and settled their score in an Indian Strap Match at Madison Square Garden.

In 1980, Strongbow took a brief hiatus from WWE and toured Puerto Rico. He was then brought into Georgia Championship Wrestling and joined another Native American great, Chief Wahoo McDaniel.

THICKER THAN WATER

Strongbow returned to WWE in 1982 and formed another strong tag team. This time, the men were bonded by blood, as he was joined by his brother, Jules. The pair from Pawhuska, Oklahoma, defeated Mr. Fuji and Mr. Saito for the Titles on June 28th. The Strongbows lost and regained the Titles from Fuji and Saito later that year before they finally succumbed to future WWE Hall of Famers, The Wild Samoans, in 1983.

Strongbow's remarkable popularity brought him to Hollywood, where he appeared in 1984's *Micki & Maude*, starring Dudley Moore.

In 1985, the Chief retired from full-time action and became a high-ranking member of the WWE front-office. Fans saw him return to television in 1994 when he mentored newcomer Tatanka in the young Native American's rivalry against Irwin R. Schyster. The relationship between the two Native Americans was so strong that Chief gave Tatanka a sacred headdress in recognition of his WWE success. That June, Strongbow's unbelievable six-decade career was honored as Tatanka inducted him into the WWE Hall of Fame.

Chief Jay Strongbow is warmly remembered as one of the most beloved figures in WWE history. Sadly, this legendary Superstar passed away on April 3, 2012.

> "We lost face at home. We thought we did a disservice to our people. We were a little ashamed of going home. Now, we're going home."
> — *Chief Jay Strongbow on regaining the WWE Tag Team Championship with brother, Jules, in 1982*

NOW WE'RE GOING HOME

CHRIS JERICHO

HT	6'0"
WT	227 lbs.
FROM	Winnipeg, Manitoba, Canada

SIGNATURE MOVE
Codebreaker, Walls of Jericho, Lionsault

Chris Jericho never fails to make a memorable first impression. His 1999 WWE debut following the mysterious countdown of the millennium clock remains one of the most brilliant entrances of all time. Years later, Jericho managed to out-do himself when he returned as the savior behind a cryptic binary code and again with the apocalyptic warnings that preceded his 2012 return. But there is a lot more to Chris Jericho than his flashy arrivals. This multi-platform Superstar boasts, "I am the best in the world at what I do," and he does a lot!

LIONHEART

Prior to amazing WWE audiences, the Canadian competitor gained a cult-like following while competing in ECW and WCW. His stint in Paul Heyman's "Land of Extreme" was brief, but his Television Championship battles and other extreme exploits grabbed the attention of the WCW brass.

Typecast as a cruiserweight competitor, Jericho showcased his eclectic grappling style on the way to multiple Cruiserweight Titles. So wide-ranging was his repertoire of maneuvers that he proclaimed his total to be 1004—four more than rival Dean Malenko. This amusing boast was an early preview of the magnetic personality he would possess. His charisma and talent forced WCW to elevate his positioning but Bischoff and company were too late. Jericho had his heart set on WWE.

"WELCOME TO RAW IS JERICHO!"

Moments after interrupting The Rock in his ballyhooed August 1999 debut, Jericho found himself clashing with sports-entertainment's biggest names. He won the Intercontinental Championship in December 1999. The victory marked the first of a record nine Intercontinental Title reigns in his career. In April 2000, Jericho flirted with the WWE Championship until Triple H used his stroke to get Y2J's Title-clinching victory reversed.

Jericho was undeterred following the controversy. He went on to claim a bevy of Championships in subsequent months and knew it was only a matter of time before his chance at immortality would come.

UNDISPUTED

That chance came at *Vengeance 2001*. With both The Rock and Stone Cold Steve Austin standing in his way, Jericho defeated both icons in one night to become the first-ever Undisputed WWE Champion. This crowning achievement gave Jericho eternal bragging rights, which the "Ayatollah of Rock n' Rolla" has taken full advantage of over the years. Proving his victory wasn't a fluke, Jericho once again defeated Rock and Austin in the weeks that followed. He defended the Title until the main event of *WrestleMania X8*, where he lost to Triple H.

Jericho remained a prominent part of WWE's most high-profile matches, including an epic encounter against his longtime idol, Shawn Michaels, at *WrestleMania XIX*. Two years later, he proved to be a mastermind when he pioneered the groundbreaking Money in the Bank Ladder Match at *WrestleMania 21*. Despite his laundry list of accomplishments, however, his failure to regain the WWE Championship in a "You're Fired" Match against John Cena in August 2005 cost him his job.

BREAKING THE CODE

In November 2007, Jericho finally returned to WWE in an attempt to "save us" from Randy Orton. Slowly, Jericho's savior persona evolved into a trancelike paranoia. With delusions of bias and persecution, a self-righteous Y2J set about saving himself. Now reviled and refocused, Jericho produced arguably the most successful stretch of his career. The apex was his victory in *Unforgiven 2008*'s World Heavyweight Championship Scramble Match and his gruesome renewed rivalry with Shawn Michaels. All told, Jericho claimed three World Heavyweight Title reigns from 2008-2010. He also combined with Big Show to form Jeri-Show, one of the modern era's most dominant twosomes.

SIMPLY THE BEST?

After an extended hiatus, Jericho's flashing neon jacket lit up the WWE arena once again in January 2012. At first, Y2J was uncharacteristically speechless, but soon turned his trademark vocal torrents on CM Punk. The two battled over the "Best in the World" moniker at *WrestleMania XXVIII* and deeper into 2012. After an athletic series of encounters with fellow showoff Dolph Ziggler, Jericho again took time away from the ring.

This time, Y2J was not gone for long. He was entrant #2 in the 2013 Royal Rumble. Then he irked Fandango by butchering the fleet-footed Superstar's name. The dancing Superstar is one of many contemporary stars to clash with the veteran icon. He has recently battled Ryback, the sadistic Bray Wyatt, Kevin Owens, and a surprise newcomer to WWE, AJ Styles.

Following Styles' 2016 debut, Jericho took the popular competitor to task in a series of competitive matches. A mutual respect developed, which united the friendly rivals into the moniker "Y2AJ." However, feeling upstaged by "AJ Styles" chants, Jericho severed the partnership. At *WrestleMania 32*, Jericho scored a narrow victory over AJ in a bout that was hailed as wrestling clinic.

Away from WWE, Jericho fronts the heavy metal band Fozzy, has hosted numerous TV shows, written three books, and is an all-around media megastar. Nearly twenty-five years from his first match, he is still breaking down the walls.

I AM THE BEST IN THE WORLD AT WHAT I DO.

CHRIS TOLOS

HT	6'0"	WT	220 lbs.
FROM	Hamilton, Ontario, Canada		

Decades after dominating the tag team scene in the 1950s and 1960s, Chris and John Tolos are still considered one of the greatest duos to ever come out of Canada. Known as The Canadian Wrecking Crew, the brothers captured Titles all over North American wrestling territories, including Florida, Detroit, and Toronto.

While in the WWE, Chris, the older of the two Tolos brothers, helped lead the team to the United States Tag Team Championship in December 1963. They defeated future WWE Hall of Famers Gorilla Monsoon and Killer Kowalski for the titles in Teaneck, New Jersey. The brothers went on to hold the gold for over one month before eventually being upended by Vittorio Apollo and Don McClarty in New Haven, Connecticut.

Though primarily a tag team competitor, Chris, who adopted the nickname "The Body," had a memorable 1968 rivalry with Mike DiBiase, father of WWE Hall of Famer "Million Dollar Man" Ted DiBiase.

CHRIS WALKER

FROM	Atlanta, Georgia

Chris Walker certainly had the look of a championship-caliber contender. His physique appeared as if it were carved out of granite, and he sported a long, curly, blonde mullet that was fitting for a competitor of the early 1990s. But after picking up two quick wins over Brooklyn Brawler and Kato, the muscular newcomer struggled to keep his career on track. Walker eventually disappeared from WWE in early 1992 after falling to The Warlord and Sid Justice.

Prior to WWE, Walker gained recognition in the Texas-based Global Wrestling Federation. While there, he teamed with Steve Simpson to defeat Scotty Anthony and Rip Rogers in a tournament finals match to crown the first-ever GWF Tag Team Champions in July 1991. They held the Titles for four months before losing to the California Connection, John Tatum and Rod Price.

Walker briefly competed for Southern States Wrestling in the late 1990s. In March 1999, he defeated Heinrich Franz Keller to capture the now-defunct SSW International Cup.

CHRISTIAN

HT	6'1"	WT	212 lbs.	FROM	Toronto, Ontario, Canada
SIGNATURE MOVE	Killswitch				

With nearly two decades of in-ring WWE service to his credit, Christian literally grew up in front of the WWE Universe. And while his earliest days were spent as a brooding introvert, fans watched as the Canadian Superstar eventually grew into one of the most charismatic and highly-decorated competitors ever.

Success came quickly for Christian, who captured the Light Heavyweight Championship in his debut match in October 1998. From there, the young Superstar partnered with longtime friend Edge to form what would become one of history's most revolutionary teams. Over the course of their pairing, Edge and Christian captured an amazing seven World Tag Team Championships.

The legacy of Edge and Christian isn't just about Titles; the awe-inspiring duo is also credited for their part in creating the popular TLC Match. Together, "E&C" turned back the Dudleys and Hardys in Triple Threat TLC Matches at both *SummerSlam 2000* and *WrestleMania X-Seven*.

Christian's singles career was equally successful. In addition to capturing the Intercontinental Championship, Captain Charisma also proudly held the ECW and European Titles, among others. His greatest success, however, came in 2011 when he finally reached WWE's pinnacle.

After injury forced Edge to relinquish the World Heavyweight Championship in April 2011, Christian earned his opportunity at greatness when he battled Albert Del Rio at *Extreme Rules*. Competing in a Ladder Match, Christian scaled to the top of sports-entertainment when he grabbed the gold and became World Heavyweight Champion.

Christian celebrated the momentous win with Edge in the center of the ring. Unfortunately, however, the party didn't last long. Only a few days later, Randy Orton upended the new Champ. The loss sent Christian's "Peeps" into an uproar. They took their frustration to Twitter, where they flooded people's timelines with their displeasure.

Luckily for Christian's followers, the World Heavyweight Championship soon found its way back around the waist of Captain Charisma when Christian defeated Orton to regain the gold at *Money in the Bank 2011*.

While Christian's in-ring days are now behind him, his Peeps still hold hope that they might see Captain Charisma in "one more match."

CHRISTOPHER NOWINSKI

HT	6'5"	WT	270 lbs.	FROM	Watertown, Massachusetts
SIGNATURE MOVE	Honor Roll				

Christopher Nowinski is brilliant, and he's not afraid to remind you of it, either. The self-absorbed Harvard graduate first began annoying fans in 2001 as a *Tough Enough* cast member. He failed to win the competition, but impressed officials enough to earn a WWE contract. As a WWE Superstar, Nowinski's holier-than-thou attitude made him tough to like, but his in-ring abilities were undeniable.

By the end of his rookie campaign, Nowinski had scored victories over his trainer, Al Snow, and *Tough Enough* champion Maven. Unfortunately, however, his promising career came to an abrupt halt due to post-concussion syndrome.

Since hanging up the boots, Nowinski has become a major player in concussion advocacy. He is currently the co-founder and executive director for the Concussion Legacy Foundation.

CHRISTY HEMME

HT	5'5"	FROM	Los Angeles, California
SIGNATURE MOVE	Standing Split-Legged Leg Drop		

Christy Hemme's life changed forever in 2004 when she outlasted over 7,000 women to win the first *Raw* Diva Search. The redheaded firecracker wasted no time spicing things up in Lingerie Pillow Fights, limbo contests, dodge ball games and more. But behind the cover girl was a competitor, and Hemme began to channel her undying spunk into her training.

While serving as a special guest ring announcer and timekeeper for some of WWE's biggest matches, she learned the ropes from a future WWE Hall of Famer, Lita. In April 2005, Christy landed on the cover of *Playboy*, creating some friction in the Divas locker room. She soon stood across the ring from her most vocal critic, Trish Stratus, at *WrestleMania 21*. Christy lost to the Women's Champion that night, but her training led to success later in 2005. She ran with legendary Tag Team LOD and even hit the winning Doomsday Device on MNM at *No Mercy 2005*. What a rush!

CHUCK PALUMBO

HT	6'7"	WT	280 lbs.	FROM	San Diego, California
SIGNATURE MOVE	Full Throttle				

Chuck Palumbo's WWE career is the story of two completely different Superstars. After Palumbo and Sean O'Haire lost the WCW Tag Team Championship in 2001, he found his career going nowhere fast. With nothing to lose, Palumbo formed a union with tag team specialist Billy Gunn. The result was the most controversial pairing in sports-entertainment history.

Billy and Chuck enjoyed two World Tag Team Championship reigns, but it was the flamboyant tandem's commitment ceremony that attracted the highest levels of national attention. Moments before officially becoming partners for life, though, Billy and Chuck revealed that the entire event was a hoax. The team split up soon after.

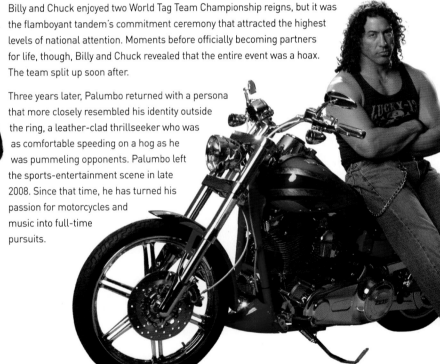

Three years later, Palumbo returned with a persona that more closely resembled his identity outside the ring, a leather-clad thrillseeker who was as comfortable speeding on a hog as he was pummeling opponents. Palumbo left the sports-entertainment scene in late 2008. Since that time, he has turned his passion for motorcycles and music into full-time pursuits.

CHUCK RICHARDS

HT	5'11"	WT	246 lbs.	FROM	Cartaret, New Jersey
SIGNATURE MOVE	Forearm Smash				

Chuck Richards was the kind of guy who'd fight anybody. And often, it seemed like he didn't mind if he won or lost.

The grandfather of future WWE World Tag Team Champion Chris Candido, aka Skip of the Bodydonnas, was nicknamed "Popeye" because of his resemblance to the cartoon character. With his wide jaw and sailor tattoos, he appeared pre-destined for trouble. In 1970, he flared at referee Lou Super during a match, sparking a series of clashes.

In 1967, Arnold Skaaland asked Richards to help defend the United States Tag Team Championship when Co-Titlist Spiros Arion was unavailable. The duo promptly lost the gold to The Sicilians. Even when Richards wore a mask, as the Red Demon, his fortunes failed to improve. He died in 1995.

CHUCK TANNER

Chuck Tanner's tattoo-covered arms certainly helped him look the part of a successful Superstar. The truth is, however, the only thing Tanner was good at in the ring was making his competition look impressive.

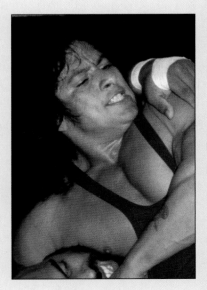

During the early 1980s, despite failing to garner any success, Tanner continually stepped into the ring to challenge the likes of Iron Sheik, Don Muraco, and "Mr. Wonderful" Paul Orndorff. Each time, he was met with the same fate: Defeat. Today, Tanner's unimpressive win-loss record puts him alongside some of history's most unsuccessful Superstars, including Brooklyn Brawler, Frankie Williams, and Barry Horowitz.

CHYNA

HT	5'10"
FROM	Londonderry, New Hampshire

After her days in the Peace Corps, Chyna undertook grueling days of training at Killer Kowalski's Pro Wrestling School. At the time, no one thought they were witnessing the development of one of the most ground-breaking figures in sports-entertainment history. She was first seen in WWE coming from the crowd to assist Hunter Hearst-Helmsley and became the famous enforcer for D-Generation X. Even while handcuffed to Sgt. Slaughter for Triple H's match at *WrestleMania XIV*, Chyna was still able to be the difference maker at ringside after she blinded "Sarge" with a mysterious white powder.

As Chyna broke away from the notorious faction she began to fight her own battles; as she did, her star grew brighter. Chyna became the first-ever female competitor in the Royal Rumble Match. In the ring, Chyna became known as "The 9th Wonder of The World." She made history at *No Mercy 1999* when she beat Jeff Jarrett to be crowned the first female Intercontinental Champion in WWE history! Chris Jericho soon became Chyna's chief rival for the prestigious Title. After one controversial match ended with no clear winner, the two competitors were briefly recognized as "co-Champions." Despite the rivalry, Jericho and Chyna became allies.

The spotlight on Chyna grew as she was a presenter at *The MTV Movie Awards*, released her own fitness video, and appeared on the television show *3rd Rock From The Sun*. On WWE programming, she became Eddie Guerrero's "mamacita" and shortly after graced the cover of *Playboy*. Months later, Chyna's life story *If They Only Knew* attacked the New York Times Best Seller list. At *WrestleMania X-Seven*, Chyna fulfilled another dream when she beat Ivory for the Women's Championship. Shortly thereafter, she was the host of *Robot Wars: Extreme Warriors*.

After parting ways with WWE in November of 2001, she remained in the public eye. Sadly, Chyna passed away in 2016. The world will never forget her contributions to sports-entertainment as a Superstar, pop-culture figure, and a pioneer for women. In her prime, she was an unstoppable force who opened a new realm for WWE's female Superstars.

CLARENCE MASON

One of the most litigious men to ever practice law, Clarence Mason debuted in WWE as the attorney for James E. Cornette. Upon arriving, Mason made an immediate impact when he used a technicality to preserve Owen Hart and British Bulldog's World Tag Team Championship reign, despite losing a Title defense at an *In Your House* pay-per-view.

After his tenure with Camp Cornette, Mason focused on the career of Crush. He soon guided the Nation of Domination until the group disbanded in the late 1990s. The loudmouth lawyer then left WWE to open his own law practice in South Florida.

CM PUNK

HT	6'2"	WT	218 lbs.	FROM	Chicago, Illinois
SIGNATURE MOVE		G.T.S. (Go to Sleep), Anaconda Vise			

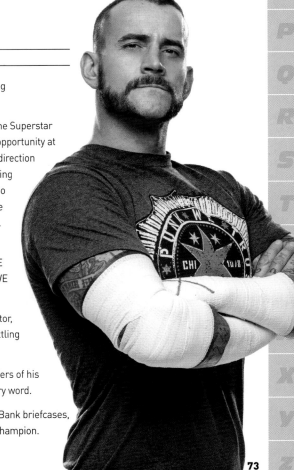

From his debut in the summer of 2006, there was always one constant surrounding CM Punk: controversy.

Punk's controversial demeanor turned scandalous in the summer of 2011 when the Superstar threatened to leave the company with the WWE Championship following his Title opportunity at *Money in the Bank*. Prior to the match, Punk's verbal "pipe bomb" exploded in the direction of WWE management. The now-famous tirade accused Mr. McMahon of surrounding himself with "glad-handing, nonsensical yes-men like John Laurinaitis." Punk also took personal shots at Stephanie McMahon and Triple H. This bold move may have infuriated the brass, but it certainly boosted his profile to astonishing new heights.

As promised, Punk won the WWE Championship at *Money in the Bank* and immediately left the company, marking one of the most uncertain periods in WWE history. Punk later re-signed with WWE, stating he wanted to be a beacon of change. He captured his third WWE Championship at *Survivor Series 2011* and for over a year backed up his famous boast that he was the "Best in the World." His 434-day WWE Championship reign was the longest since Hulk Hogan's first reign ended in 1988.

Equally loved and loathed, Punk defeated a litany of top challengers as Champion, both on his own and with the services of long time mentor, Paul Heyman. Upon losing the gold he continued to compete at the highest level, challenging Undertaker's Streak at *WrestleMania* and battling The Beast Incarnate, Brock Lesnar.

Prior to the controversial summer of 2011, Punk used his power of persuasion and intelligence to become one of the most influential leaders of his time. First guiding the sanctimonious Straight Edge Society and later New Nexus, Punk had Superstars and fans alike hanging on his every word.

Punk's skills in the ring were equally impressive. In addition to being a multiple-time WWE Champion, he also captured two Money in the Bank briefcases, both times cashing in to claim the World Heavyweight Championship. Punk is also a former ECW, Intercontinental, and World Tag Team Champion.

THE COACH

After a making a career of bringing professional athletes across all sports to unprecedented heights, The Coach brought his combination of intellect and training techniques to WWE in 1991. The core of his belief system was simple: Win! Win! Win! However, his desire for victory also extended to rule breaking and getting involved in the action behind the referee's back. Through it all, Coach barked from ringside, "Discipline! Break their legs, smash their faces. The only people I want with me are winners!"

On an episode of "The Funeral Parlor," Bobby Heenan introduced Coach as his replacement to manage then-Intercontinental Champion, Mr. Perfect. Under new management, Perfect thrived and gave credibility to Coach's strategies. Coach expanded his talent pool and brought the Beverly Brothers into WWE, only to hang up his whistle later that same year. Coach is remembered as one of the most intense and physical managers ever.

THE COBRA

HT	5'10"	WT	224 lbs.
FROM	Japan		

Like many other masked Superstars of the 1980s, The Cobra was lightning quick with a strong aerial assault. Unlike his veiled counterparts, however, The Cobra was quite a sharp-dressed man. The custom-made sports coat he often wore to the ring went a long way in setting him apart from his masked colleagues.

One of The Cobra's first tastes of championship gold came in November 1983 when he defeated Davey Boy Smith for the National Wrestling Alliance Junior Heavyweight Championship. When the Dynamite Kid, Smith's future British Bulldogs tag team partner, vacated the WWE Junior Heavyweight Championship one year later, The Cobra defeated Black Tiger in New York City to claim the Title.

The masked Superstar held the WWE Junior Heavyweight Championship for five months before losing to Hiro Saito in Hiroshima, Japan. The Cobra eventually regained the Title two months later, but was forced to vacate it when WWE discontinued recognizing the Championship in October 1985.

COLIN DELANEY

HT	5'9"	WT	172 lbs.	FROM	Rochester, New York

Perhaps the most persistent Superstar in WWE history, Colin Delaney continually climbed in the ring despite suffering devastating beatings from bigger foes such as Mark Henry and Kane. The punishment he received would have crippled a lesser man, but Delaney's heart would not let him quit. He finally picked up his first win when he teamed with his mentor, Tommy Dreamer, to defeat The Miz and John Morrison in February 2008.

Delaney finally earned a full-time contract in May after defeating ECW general manager Armando Estrada. With job security in his back pocket, Delaney revealed his true colors by turning on Dreamer at The Great American Bash. Dreamer's revenge came in August when he defeated his protégé in an Extreme Rules Match. Delaney left ECW a few days later.

CODY RHODES

HT	6'1"	WT	219 lbs.	FROM	Marietta, Georgia
SIGNATURE MOVE	Cross Rhodes				

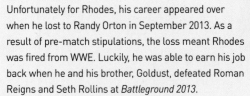

The career of Cody Rhodes is among the most curious of any competitor. Once a promising upstart, Rhodes would eventually go on to seemingly snap, en route to becoming one of sports-entertainment's most eccentric personalities.

As the son of the legendary Dusty Rhodes, Cody was brought up to respect sports-entertainment's unwritten rules of conduct. Despite the valuable education, Rhodes spit in the face of tradition when he turned his back on mentor Hardcore Holly, claiming, "When you're this good, you don't pay dues."

Following the betrayal, Rhodes aligned himself with Ted DiBiase Jr. The heirs of WWE Hall of Famers dominated the tag team scene during the second half of 2008. Success eventually led the duo to another multi-generational Superstar, Randy Orton. Collectively, they became known as Legacy.

Following Legacy's 2010 breakup, Rhodes travelled to *SmackDown* where he became incredibly arrogant. After being named "Most Handsome Superstar," Rhodes proudly added "Dashing" to his name and went on to offer fans grooming advice.

In September 2010, Rhodes teamed with Drew McIntyre to defeat The Hart Dynasty for the WWE Tag Team Championship. The following year, the second-generation Superstar captured his first Intercontinental Championship when he defeated Ezekiel Jackson on *SmackDown*.

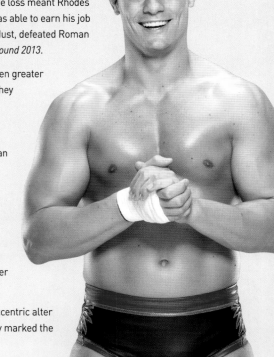

Unfortunately for Rhodes, his career appeared over when he lost to Randy Orton in September 2013. As a result of pre-match stipulations, the loss meant Rhodes was fired from WWE. Luckily, he was able to earn his job back when he and his brother, Goldust, defeated Roman Reigns and Seth Rollins at *Battleground 2013*.

The brothers went on to achieve even greater success the following week when they defeated Reigns and Rollins again, this time to capture the WWE Tag Team Championship. Rhodes and Goldust held the Titles for more than three months before losing to the New Age Outlaws.

The loss sent the brothers into a terrible tailspin, and Rhodes eventually determined he wasn't worthy of teaming with Goldust. Instead, Rhodes found a new partner for his brother: Stardust.

In reality, Stardust was Rhodes's eccentric alter ego. And his introduction effectively marked the end of Cody Rhodes.

COLONEL MUSTAFA

HT	6'0"	WT	263 lbs.	FROM	Iraq
SIGNATURE MOVE	Camel Clutch				

While the United States was in the midst of the Gulf War in 1991, WWE found itself under attack by one-time hero Sgt. Slaughter. And unfortunately for WWE's fan favorites, Slaughter was not alone. Joining him in his assault were General Adnan and Colonel Mustafa.

During his offensive on WWE, Mustafa targeted Superstars such as Undertaker, Big Boss Man, Koko B. Ware, "Hacksaw" Jim Duggan, and Bret "Hit Man" Hart. The mighty Iraqi was also a part of the famous "Match Made In Hell" at *SummerSlam 1991* where he teamed with Adnan and Slaughter to battle Hulk Hogan and Ultimate Warrior. By May 1992, Mustafa returned to the Middle East.

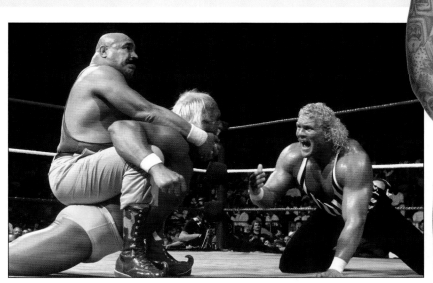

COREY GRAVES

HT	6'1"	WT	208 lbs.	FROM	Pittsburgh, Pennsylvania
SIGNATURE MOVE	Lucky 13				

When Corey Graves signed a WWE developmental deal in August 2011, it was evident that he would one day make a name for himself in the sports-entertainment industry. And while he has achieved the success many predicted, his route to superstardom didn't go quite as planned.

With wins over established stars such as Alex Riley and Yoshi Tatsu, Graves was considered one of NXT's can't-miss stars. He even added gold to his resume when he teamed with Neville to defeat Luke Harper and Erick Rowan for the NXT Tag Team Titles in July 2013. Unfortunately for Graves, however, his in-ring days were unknowingly coming to an end.

Graves's future became uncertain when serious injuries sidelined him in the spring of 2014. Realizing his health was of utmost importance, Graves retired from the ring in December 2014, but transitioned quickly into a role as an *NXT* announcer.

Now working behind the microphone, Graves has established himself as a fresh, young, and edgy personality that has forever changed the look and dynamic of *NXT* and the WWE Network.

THE COLOSSAL CONNECTION

MEMBERS	Andre The Giant & Haku
COMBINED WT	852 lbs.

At the 1989 *Survivor Series*, future WWE Hall of Famer Bobby "The Brain" Heenan unveiled his Colossal Connection, Haku and Andre the Giant. They manhandled their opponents, and just weeks later, conquered Demolition to earn the World Tag Team Championship during a period when it was unheard of for Ax and Smash to be dominated in that fashion.

As Champions, the Colossal Connection seemed unstoppable. As the Connection entered a new decade, their stranglehold on the Titles appeared to have no boundary. However, after a botched double-team move led to Demolition regaining the tag titles at *WrestleMania VI*, "The Brain" lost his wits. After a slap in the face from his manager, Andre cleared the ring of his former allies, and the Colossal Connection ceased to exist.

CORPORAL KIRCHNER

HT	6'2"	WT	263 lbs.	FROM	Fort Bragg, North Carolina
SIGNATURE MOVE	Corporal Clutch				

A former member of the 82nd Airborne division of the U.S. Army, Corporal Kirchner fought for the American way in and out of the ring. When he debuted in 1985, the American hero targeted many of WWE's most foreign menaces, most notably Nikolai Volkoff. In fact, it was against the Russian powerhouse that Kirchner picked up his biggest win, besting Volkoff in a Flag Match at *WrestleMania 2*.

Unfortunately for Kirchner, victories were few and far between following *WrestleMania 2*. After only moderate success against the likes of Iron Sheik and Adrian Adonis, the Corporal turned his sights to the tag scene, teaming up with Danny Spivey. The duo, however, failed to make waves in the tag team division. Kirchner left WWE shortly after. Despite Kirchner's short stay in WWE, longtime fans will always look back at his tenure with great fondness, as it was difficult not to cheer for the tough serviceman who carried Old Glory to the ring.

THE CORPORATION

MEMBERS Mr. McMahon, Shane McMahon, The Rock, Big Show, Big Boss Man, Ken Shamrock, Kane, Triple H, Chyna, Test, Shawn Michaels, Gerald Brisco, Pat Patterson, Sgt. Slaughter, Pete Gas, Rodney, & Joey Abs

Leading up to *Survivor Series 1998*, Mr. McMahon began to surround himself with his own entourage of former Superstars, which consisted of Sgt. Slaughter, Gerald Brisco, and Pat Patterson. The group had some influence, largely due to McMahon's influence within WWE, but lacked any real Superstar power. That all changed at *Survivor Series* when Mr. McMahon and his son Shane helped The Rock capture the WWE Championship, marking the official start of The Corporation.

With The Rock in the fold, The Corporation became an enticing destination for WWE Superstars. They knew that with Mr. McMahon making the calls, they'd be set up for instant greatness. Just as many predicted, The Corporation owned all the major Titles by year's end (The Rock was WWE Champion, Ken Shamrock was Intercontinental Champion, and Big Boss Man and Shamrock were World Tag Team Champions).

Though dominant in their rivalries with Stone Cold Steve Austin, Mankind, and D-Generation X, The Corporation enjoyed only a brief existence. The beginning of the end came in April 1999 when Shane assumed leadership after claiming his father had misaligned priorities. According to the younger McMahon, Vince cared more about combating Undertaker's obsession with Stephanie than he did The Corporation. From that point, the male McMahons engaged in a bitter rivalry that eventually resulted in Shane merging his Corporation with Undertaker's Ministry of Darkness. The result was one super faction called The Corporate Ministry.

THE CORRE

MEMBERS Wade Barrett, Justin Gabriel, Heath Slater, & Ezekiel Jackson

When CM Punk replaced Wade Barrett as Nexus leader in January 2011, original Nexus members Justin Gabriel and Heath Slater jumped the *Raw* ship and joined Barrett on *SmackDown*.

Billing themselves as a leaderless group of equals, the former Nexus members soon welcomed Ezekiel Jackson into their pack and immediately became a force on *SmackDown*. Collectively known as The Corre, they quickly claimed gold when Gabriel and Slater defeated Santino Marella and Vladimir Kozlov for the Tag Titles in February 2011. The following month, Barrett brought the Intercontinental Title into the fold when he topped Kofi Kingston.

Despite their terrifying reign over much of *SmackDown*'s roster, The Corre started to become their own worst enemy following a *WrestleMania* loss to Big Show, Kane, Kingston, and Marella. Soon Barrett and Jackson evolved into bitter enemies, battling over the Intercontinental Championship. Later, the group quietly disbanded after Barrett abandoned Gabriel and Slater during a *SmackDown* tag match.

"COWBOY" BOB ORTON

	HT	6'1"	WT	242 lbs.	FROM	Kansas City, Kansas
HoF	**SIGNATURE MOVE**		Superplex			

Managed by The Grand Wizard, "Cowboy" Bob Orton first appeared in WWE in 1982 with the goal of dethroning then-WWE Champion Bob Backlund. When he failed to wrest the Title away from Backlund, Orton headed to the NWA where he made headlines when he and Dick Slater accepted $25,000 from Harley Race to end the career of "Nature Boy" Ric Flair.

The man credited with inventing the Superplex returned to WWE in the spring of 1984. Upon arriving, Orton unfortunately broke his left forearm while competing in a match. This was often the subject of great controversy, as "Cowboy" was often accused of using his cast as a weapon well after the injury had presumably healed.

In addition to continuing his impressive in-ring career, Orton famously became bodyguard to "Rowdy" Roddy Piper. As Hot Rod's heavy, "Cowboy" played a major role in the outcome of the first-ever *WrestleMania* main event when he attempted to nail Mr. T with his cast. Instead of hitting his intended target, however, Orton flattened Piper's partner, Paul Orndorff, allowing Hulk Hogan and Mr. T to pick up the win.

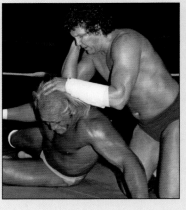

Orton continued to back Piper through his *WrestleMania 2* boxing match against Mr. T. But when Piper changed his rule-breaking ways, Orton swore his allegiance to "Adorable" Adrian Adonis. The "Ace" also formed a successful tag team with Magnificent Muraco, managed by Mr. Fuji.

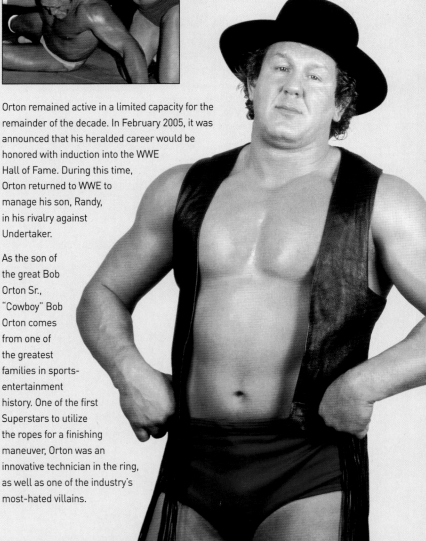

Orton remained active in a limited capacity for the remainder of the decade. In February 2005, it was announced that his heralded career would be honored with induction into the WWE Hall of Fame. During this time, Orton returned to WWE to manage his son, Randy, in his rivalry against Undertaker.

As the son of the great Bob Orton Sr., "Cowboy" Bob Orton comes from one of the greatest families in sports-entertainment history. One of the first Superstars to utilize the ropes for a finishing maneuver, Orton was an innovative technician in the ring, as well as one of the industry's most-hated villains.

COWBOY LANG

For more than 30 years, Cowboy Lang was considered one of the world's premier dwarf wrestlers. Debuting in the mid-1960s at just 16 years old, Lang charged to the ring in his signature cowboy hat and boots.

Over the course of his successful career, Lang performed on some of the biggest cards of his time, including the AWA's *WrestleRock* in April 1986. On this night, Lang teamed with Little Mr. T to defeat Lord Littlebrook and Little Tokyo.

Throughout Lang's career, Little Tokyo proved to be one of his most bitter rivals. The foes spent much of the early 1980s battling over the NWA World Midget Championship, which they traded on two separate occasions.

CRAIG DEGEORGE

Craig DeGeorge grew up watching Pedro Morales and "Superstar" Billy Graham, hoping one day he could rub shoulders with the larger-than-life personalities he saw on television.

With aspirations of calling action from behind the microphone, DeGeorge enrolled in Syracuse University, where he earned a broadcast journalism degree. After graduating in 1985, DeGeorge was brought into WWE as an announcer. While his stay was brief, DeGeorge did manage to leave a lasting impression. Fans today still talk about his rhythmically-challenged do-si-do with Hillbilly Jim.

After leaving WWE in the late 1980s, DeGeorge briefly called the action for the California-based Universal Wrestling Federation. He later moved on to the XFL, United Football League, and FOX Sports Florida where he covers the Marlins and Panthers (as Craig Minervini).

CRASH HOLLY

HT	5'10"	WT	Over 400 lbs. (alleged)	FROM	Mobile, Alabama
SIGNATURE MOVE		The Crash Course			

Despite his diminutive size, Crash Holly could not be deterred from joining his cousin, Hardcore Holly, in WWE. He was also adamant about competing among sports-entertainment's greatest heavyweights. In 1999, Holly debuted on *Raw* and became known for bringing a scale with him to the ring and forcing opponents to step on and prove they measured up.

While he and his cousin often argued, the Hollys proved to be a formidable team. This was no more evident than when they won the World Tag Team Championship from the Rock 'N' Sock Connection in October 1999.

In 2000, Holly joined the Hardcore Division, and over the next three years became known as the Houdini of Hardcore. Crash captured the Hardcore Championship on more than 20 occasions. Later in the year, he was accompanied to the ring by his cousin, Molly, and occasionally reformed his team with Hardcore Holly.

Holly later added more trophies to his mantle when he won the European Championship in December 2000 and the Light Heavyweight Championship in March 2001.

The incredibly-confident Holly continued to get in the face of all challengers no matter their size or reputation until he left the company in June 2003. Sadly, Crash Holly passed away in November 2003. He entertained millions with his performances in the ring and touched even more with his heart.

CRUISERWEIGHT CHAMPIONSHIP
see page 78

CRUSH

HT	6'6"	WT	315 lbs.	FROM	Kona, Hawaii
SIGNATURE MOVE		The Skull Crush			

Crush burst onto the scene as the third member of the World Tag Team Championship team of Demolition in the summer of 1990. The trio defended the gold under the "Freebird Rule" through August when they were defeated by The Hart Foundation. Shortly after the loss, Demolition disbanded and Crush temporarily disappeared.

Crush returned to WWE in 1992 as the happy Hawaiian with bright tights and a big smile. Upon his return, he famously squared off against Doink at *WrestleMania IX*. Unfortunately for Crush, he fell to the clown thanks in large part to an interfering Doink doppelganger.

The *WrestleMania* loss put an attitude change in motion for Crush, who soon fell under the dangerous influence of Mr. Fuji. Using the heart punch to finish opponents, he attacked former friend Randy "Macho Man" Savage. The battles between the two raged on until their Falls Count Anywhere Match at *WrestleMania X*.

Crush joined The Nation of Domination in 1996, and later formed the Disciples of the Apocalypse faction with Chainz, Skull, and 8-Ball.

After leaving WWE in late 1997, Crush competed in WCW and Japan before a spinal injury forced him into retirement. Sadly, Crush passed away in August 2007. Whether he was beloved or booed, the powerhouse was undeniably one of WWE's biggest Superstars of the 1990s.

CRUISERWEIGHT CHAMPIONSHIP

The WWE Cruiserweight Championship originated in World Championship Wrestling (WCW) in 1991. Held by such acclaimed high-flyers as Brian Pillman, Chris Jericho, and Rey Mysterio, the Title was brought to WWE after Shane McMahon purchased WCW in 2001.

Throughout its WWE existence, the Cruiserweight Championship brought some of the most athletic Superstars in the world together for the right to continue its lineage. In 2006-2007, Gregory Helms shattered the record for longest reign with Cruiserweight gold. The ex-Hurricane held the Title for 385 days. Months later, Hornswoggle became the final Cruiserweight Champ as the Title was retired.

1991

October 27 • Chattanooga, TN
In the finals of a tournament to crown the first-ever Cruiserweight Champion, **Brian Pillman** def. **Richard Morton**.

December 25 • Atlanta, GA
Jushin Liger def. **Brian Pillman**

1992

February 29 • Milwaukee, WI
Brian Pillman def. **Jushin Liger**

June 20 • Augusta, GA
Scotty Flamingo def. **Brian Pillman**

July 5 • Atlanta, GA
Brad Armstrong def. **Scotty Flamingo**
An injury forced Brad Armstrong to vacate the Cruiserweight Championship in September 1992.

1996

March 20 • Nagoya, Japan
Shinjiro Otani def. **Chris Benoit** in the finals of a tournament to crown a new Cruiserweight Champion.

May 2 • Orlando, FL
Dean Malenko def. **Shinjiro Otani**

July 8 • Orlando, FL
Rey Mysterio def. **Dean Malenko**

October 27 • Las Vegas, NV
Dean Malenko def. **Rey Mysterio**

December 29 • Nashville, TN
Ultimo Dragon def. **Dean Malenko**

1997

January 22 • Milwaukee, WI
Dean Malenko def. **Ultimo Dragon**

February 24 • San Francisco, CA
Syxx def. **Dean Malenko**

June 28 • Los Angeles, CA
Chris Jericho def. **Syxx**

July 28 • Charleston, WV
Alex Wright def. **Chris Jericho**

August 16 • Colorado Springs, CO
Chris Jericho def. **Alex Wright**

September 14 • Winston-Salem, NC
Eddie Guerrero def. **Chris Jericho**

October 26 • Las Vegas, NV
Rey Mysterio def. **Eddie Guerrero**

November 10 • Memphis, TN
Eddie Guerrero def. **Rey Mysterio**

December 29 • Baltimore, MD
Ultimo Dragon def. **Eddie Guerrero**

1998

January 8 • Daytona Beach, FL
Juventud Guerrera def. **Ultimo Dragon**

January 15 • Lakeland, FL
Rey Mysterio def. **Juventud Guerrera**

May 17 • Worcester, MA
Dean Malenko def. **Chris Jericho**
Dean Malenko was forced to vacate the Championship because he wore a mask to the ring when he won the right to face Chris Jericho for the Title.

June 14 • Baltimore, MD
Chris Jericho def. **Dean Malenko**

August 8 • Sturgis, SD
Juventud Guerrera def. **Chris Jericho**

September 14 • Greenville, SC
Billy Kidman def. **Juventud Guerrera**

November 16 • Wichita, KS
Juventud Guerrera def. **Billy Kidman**

November 22 • Auburn Hills, MI
Billy Kidman def. **Juventud Guerrera**

1999

March 15 • Cincinnati, OH
Rey Mysterio def. **Billy Kidman**

April 19 • Gainesville, FL
Psicosis won a Fatal Four Way Match that also included **Blitzkreig**, **Juventud Guerrera**, and then-Champion **Rey Mysterio**.

August 19 • Lubbock, TX
Lenny Lane def. **Rey Mysterio**
WCW stripped Lenny Lane of the Cruiserweight Championship.

October 4 • Kansas City, MO
Psicosis was awarded the Cruiserweight Championship

October 4 • Kansas City, MO
Disco Inferno def. **Psicosis**

November 21 • Toronto, Ontario
Evan Karagias def. **Disco Inferno**

December 19 • Washington, D.C.
Madusa def. **Evan Karagias**

2000

January 16 • Cincinnati, OH
Oklahoma def. **Madusa**
Oklahoma was forced to vacate the Cruiserweight Championship after exceeding the weight limit.

February 20 • San Francisco, CA
The Artist def. **Lash LeRoux** in the finals of a tournament to crown a new Cruiserweight Champion.

March 30 • Baltimore, MD
Billy Kidman def. **The Artist**

March 31 • Pittsburgh, PA
The Artist def. **Billy Kidman**

April 16 • Chicago, IL
Chris Candido def. **Juventud Guerrera**, **Shannon Moore**, **Crowbar**, **Lash LeRoux**, and **The Artist** to become the new titleholder.

May 15 • Biloxi, MS
Crowbar and **Daffney** beat **Chris Candido** and **Tammy Sytch** in a Mixed Tag Team Match to become co-holders of the Cruiserweight Championship.

May 22 • Grand Rapids, MI
Daffney def. **Crowbar**

June 6 • Knoxville, TN
Lt. Loco won a Triple Threat Match that included **Disco Inferno** and then-Champion **Daffney**.

July 31 • Cincinnati, OH
Lance Storm def. **Lt. Loco**

August 14 • Kelowna, B.C.
Elix Skipper awarded Cruiserweight Championship by **Lance Storm**.

October 2 • San Francisco, CA
Mike Sanders def. **Elix Skipper**
Mike Sanders and **Kevin Nash** beat **Elix Skipper** in a Handicap Match.

December 4 • Lincoln, NE
Chavo Guerrero def. **Mike Sanders**

2001

March 18 • Jacksonville, FL
Shane Helms def. **Chavo Guerrero**

July 5 • Tacoma, WA
Billy Kidman def. **Shane Helms**

July 30 • Philadelphia, PA
X-Pac def. **Billy Kidman** to unify the Light Heavyweight and Cruiserweight Championships.

October 11 • Moline, IL
Billy Kidman def. **X-Pac**

October 22 • Kansas City, MO
Tajiri def. **Billy Kidman**

2002

April 4 • Rochester, NY
Billy Kidman def. **Tajiri**

April 21 • Kansas City, MO
Tajiri def. **Billy Kidman**

May 16 • Montreal, Quebec
The Hurricane pinned **Tajiri** in a Triple Threat Match that also included **Billy Kidman**.

June 23 • Columbus, OH
Jamie Noble def. **The Hurricane**

November 17 • New York, NY
Billy Kidman def. **Jamie Noble**

2003

February 23 • Montreal, Quebec
Matt Hardy def. **Billy Kidman**

June 5 • Anaheim, CA
Rey Mysterio def. **Matt Hardy**

September 25 • Philadelphia, PA
Tajiri def. **Rey Mysterio**

2004

January 1 • Washington, D.C.
Rey Mysterio def. **Tajiri**

February 15 • San Francisco, CA
Chavo Guerrero def. **Rey Mysterio**

May 6 • Tucson, AZ
Jacqueline def. **Chavo Guerrero**

May 16 • Los Angeles, CA
Chavo Guerrero def. **Jacqueline**

May 20 • Las Vegas, NV
Chavo Classic pinned **Chavo Guerrero** in a Triple Threat Match that also included **Spike Dudley**.

June 17 • Chicago, IL
Rey Mysterio def. **Chavo Classic**

July 29 • Cincinnati, OH
Spike Dudley def. **Rey Mysterio**

December 12 • Atlanta, GA
Funaki def. **Spike Dudley**

2005

February 20 • Pittsburgh, PA
Chavo Guerrero last eliminated **Paul London** from an Elimination Match that also included **Akio**, **Spike Dudley**, **Shannon Moore**, and then-Champion **Funaki**.

March 31 • Houston, TX
Paul London last eliminated **Billy Kidman** from an 8-man Battle Royal that also included **Funaki**, **Scotty 2 Hotty**, **Akio**, **Nunzio**, **Spike Dudley**, and then-Champion **Chavo Guerrero**.

August 6 • Bridgeport, CT
Nunzio def. **Paul London**

October 9 • Houston, TX
Juventud def. **Nunzio**

November 15 • Rome, Italy
Nunzio def. **Juventud**

November 25 • Sheffield, England
Juventud def. **Nunzio**

December 18 • Providence, RI
Kid Kash def. **Juventud**

2006

January 29 • Miami, FL
Gregory Helms pinned **Funaki** in a Cruiserweight Championship Invitational Match that also included **Paul London**, **Jamie Noble**, **Nunzio**, and then-Champion **Kid Kash**.

2007

February 18 • Los Angeles, CA
Chavo Guerrero pinned **Jimmy Wang Yang** in a Cruiserweight Open that also included **Daivari**, **Funaki**, **Shannon Moore**, **Scotty 2 Hotty**, **Jamie Noble**, and then-Champion **Gregory Helms**.

July 22 • San Jose, CA
Hornswoggle pinned **Jamie Noble** in a Cruiserweight Open that included **Shannon Moore**, **Jimmy Wang Yang**, **Funaki**, and then-Champion **Chavo Guerrero**.

"CRUSHER" JERRY BLACKWELL

HT	5'9"	WT	473 lbs.	FROM	Stone Mountain, Georgia
SIGNATURE MOVE	**Big Splash**				

At nearly 500 pounds, Jerry Blackwell earned his nickname "The Mountain from Stone Mountain." But he wasn't just big. Blackwell also moved around the ring with the quickness of a cat, often employing maneuvers only seen by men half his size.

Blackwell's WWE days in the 1970s were fleeting, but painful for those who got in his way, including Dominic DeNucci, Ivan Putski, Andre the Giant, and the WWE World Heavyweight Champion, Bob Backlund.

After leaving the Northeast territory, the man known as "Crusher" competed in the 1979 World's Strongest Man competition before finally settling into a memorable AWA career.

Blackwell was showered with boos during the early part of his AWA tenure. But when Hulk Hogan left the territory in 1983, the AWA fans were left searching for somebody to cheer. As the fans' oversized hero, it was Blackwell's job to thwart former allies like Abdullah the Butcher and King Kong Brody. He challenged both Stan Hansen and Curt Hennig for the promotion's title.

He died in 1995.

CRYME TYME

MEMBERS	Shad & JTG	COMBINED WT	530 lbs.	FROM	Brooklyn, New York

Cryme Tyme's over-the-top persona parodied societal stereotypes they encountered during their lives. Vignettes showed the duo stealing cars, televisions, wallets, and more, all for "that money, money... yea yea!!"

Shad and JTG brought their larger than life personalities to the ring as well. With JTG's speed and Shad's power, many of WWE's best teams were leery about throwing down with Cryme Tyme. In their first pay-per-view match at *Cyber Sunday*, they stole a win from the Highlanders, Lance Cade and Trevor Murdoch, and Charlie Haas and Viscera.

In 2008, Cryme Tyme proved too much to handle for several top teams. They even backed up John Cena during his war against JBL. Moving to *SmackDown*, the Brooklyn boys became #1 contenders for the WWE Unified Tag Team Championship. After several unsuccessful attempts to win the gold, Shad brutally attacked his life-long friend. With their bond broken, Cryme Tyme disbanded in 2010. JTG scored his revenge by beating Shad in a brutal Strap Match.

CRUSHER VERDU

HT	5'10"	WT	275 lbs.	FROM	Columbus, Ohio
SIGNATURE MOVE	**Bear Hug**				

Known as "The Spanish Hercules", Crusher Verdu was an amateur wrestling champion and regarded as a powerhouse across Europe and the territories of the National Wrestling Alliance. When he entered WWE, Superstars were placed on alert. Verdu, it was said, had never been knocked off his feet.

Managed by the likes of Tony Angelo and Capt. Lou Albano, he stopped at nothing to reach the top. Although he was an almost instant contender for the WWE Championship, Verdu was driven to dethrone Champion Bruno Sammartino. Yet, he never managed to beat the Italian Strongman.

Crusher Verdu retired in the early 1980s, yet To this day, his name is still invoked when experts talk about all-time strongmen.

CRYBABY CANNON

FROM	Montreal, Quebec, Canada

At 360 pounds, George "Crybaby" Cannon was a mountain of a man. Prior to his days inside the ring, Cannon parlayed his massive size into a successful football career, playing for the Canadian Football League's Regina Roughriders.

While his massive frame helped him earn many wins as a sports-entertainer, Cannon gained most of his notoriety from being a manager. In addition to guiding the careers of the Mongols, he managed the famed tag team, The Fabulous Kangaroos. In 1983, Cannon struck a deal with Vince McMahon to help bring WWE to Detroit.

CURT HAWKINS

	HT	6'1"	WT	223 lbs.	FROM	Queens, New York
	SIGNATURE MOVE	**Hangman's Facebuster**				

Curt Hawkins first showed what he was capable of when he, along with Zack Ryder, helped Edge capture the World Heavyweight Championship at *Armageddon 2007*. Hawkins and Ryder stayed by Edge's side, ensuring he kept a firm grasp on the gold. But it wasn't long before these "Edgeheads" had gold of their own.

Hawkins and Ryder captured the WWE Tag Team Championship in a Fatal 4-Way Match in July 2008. However, when their reign ended a few months later, Hawkins disappeared for more than a year.

Hawkins returned to *SmackDown* in May 2010 with Vance Archer as his partner. The new tandem, known as the Gatecrashers, made an impact. However, as the year wore on their momentum faded and their union ended on a sour note. Hawkins teamed with Tyler Reks in 2012 until Reks left WWE that August. He finished his WWE career as a solo competitor, competing mainly on *NXT* against stars such as Neville, Sami Zayn, and Bo Dallas.

CURTIS AXEL

HT	6'3"	WT	228 lbs.
FROM	Champlin, Minnesota		

Given Curtis Axel's legacy, many fans wondered why he wasn't immediately thrust into main events. In May 2013, Paul Heyman answered that query by claiming a legacy in WWE is nothing but an albatross. And being the son of Mr. Perfect and grandson of Larry Hennig, few had a legacy as rich as Axel.

Alongside Heyman, Axel bucked the supposed trend by beating the likes of Triple H and John Cena, albeit somewhat controversially. Axel then achieved greatness by defeating The Miz and Wade Barrett at *Payback* to capture the Intercontinental Championship, the same Title his father famously held decades earlier.

After splitting with Heyman in late 2013, Axel formed a partnership with Ryback. Known as RybAxel, the duo eyed the WWE Tag Team Championship, which Axel previously held with David Otunga. Unfortunately for RybAxel, they were unable to capture the Titles and soon went their separate ways.

Hoping to regain top singles status, Axel was scheduled to compete in the 2015 Royal Rumble Match. But before entering, Axel was attacked by Erick Rowan, rendering him unable to compete. Axel later claimed he had never been eliminated from the match and deserved a WWE World Heavyweight Championship opportunity. While he spoke with great conviction, the WWE Universe largely saw Axel as delusional. Despite his sometimes inflated sense of self-worth, one thing you cannot take away from Curtis Axel is his superior in-ring skill, which makes him one of WWE's most dangerous Superstars.

DAMIEN SANDOW

HT	6'4"	WT	247 lbs.	FROM	Palo Alto, California
SIGNATURE MOVE	Terminus				

Normally an identity crisis would be reason for concern. Unless of course, you're Damien Sandow, in which case pretending to be somebody else has resulted in great success.

The holier-than-thou Sandow arrived in WWE in the spring of 2012. And despite being relentlessly booed, the Intellectual Savior managed to win several high-profile matches, including the 2013 World Heavyweight Championship Money in the Bank Ladder Match.

Sandow cashed in his Championship opportunity in October, when he battled John Cena for the gold. Unfortunately for Sandow, Cena was able to thwart the challenge. Almost immediately following the loss, Sandow's career was sent into a terrible tailspin.

Hoping to break from his funk, Sandow shelved his haughty persona and began mimicking historic figures from the past. The change slowly began to turn Sandow's career around. He then started associating with The Miz, serving as the A-Lister's stunt double. Changing his name to Damien Mizdow and copying The Miz's every move, Sandow became more popular than ever. The duo even captured the WWE Tag Team Championship from Gold and Stardust in November 2014.

Jealousy over Mizdow's popularity eventually resulted in The Miz continually disrespecting his partner. Sandow finally grew tired of the abuse and eliminated The Miz from the Andre the Giant Memorial Battle Royal at *WrestleMania 31*.

Free from The Miz's incivility, Sandow continued to entertain audiences worldwide with his impersonations, most notably his version of Randy Savage he affectionately calls Macho Mandow. He parted ways with WWE in May 2016.

DAIVARI

HT	5'10"	WT	206 lbs.	FROM	Detroit, Michigan

Detroit native Daivari accused his fellow countrymen of racist activity toward him and other Arab-Americans. Clearly, his sentiments did not sit well with the melting pot of WWE fans, but that didn't stop him from continually spewing his unpopular opinions.

In the ring, Daivari's early days looked bright, especially after defeating Shawn Michaels in his singles debut in April 2005. When his partner, Muhammad Hassan, left WWE later that summer, Daivari's career was knocked off track and never fully recovered. Daivari later shifted his focus toward managing. His list of clients included Kurt Angle, Mark Henry, and The Great Khali.

DAMIAN DEMENTO

HT	6'3"	WT	269 lbs.	FROM	The Outer Reaches Of Your Mind
SIGNATURE MOVE	Jumping Knee Drop				

Damian Demento and his odd forms of behavior inhabited WWE for the first time in October 1992. Upon arriving, he would often be seen prowling the rings and speaking aloud to the voices he heard in his head. Among the Superstars he disturbed included Virgil, Bob Backlund, and Tito Santana.

Perhaps Demento's greatest claim to fame came in January 1993 when he stood across the ring from Undertaker in the first-ever *Monday Night Raw* main event. Unfortunately for Demento, he couldn't solve The Deadman in the historic match. The peculiar Superstar returned to The Outer Reaches Of Your Mind months later, never to be seen again.

DAN MILLER

HT	6'1"	WT	245 lbs.	FROM	Columbus, Ohio
SIGNATURE MOVE	Alligator Clutch				

When Dr. Bill Miller arrived in WWE in 1965, he had a new weapon in his arsenal, his brother, Dan. The younger Miller followed his older sibling into sports-entertainment ten years earlier, establishing a successful duo with Nelson Royal. But when a third brother, Ed Miller, broke his ankle in 1957, Bill asked Dan to be his partner.

In WWE, Dan and Bill snared the United States Tag Team Championship, upending Gorilla Monsoon and Bill Watts. They also competed under masks in Japan.

On his own, Dan held tag titles with Fritz Von Erich in Texas and Jose Lothario in Florida. He expanded his skills as a manager in Australia. When his 22 year in-ring career ended, Dan worked backstage for the Charlotte and Florida territories.

DAN SEVERN

HT 6'2" **WT** 250 lbs. **FROM** Coldwater, Michigan

Walking to the ring in a plain grey T-shirt, Dan Severn gave the impression of being the ultimate no-frills Superstar. And when the bell rang, he did little to change people's perception. His no-nonsense offense was simple, and certainly made him deserving of the nickname "The Beast."

Upon entering WWE, Severn's résumé already included 85 wrestling Titles, including the NWA Championship. His long list of accolades, coupled with his mixed martial arts submission style, made Severn a multi-faceted threat to the entire roster.

Following a fallout with manager Jim Cornette, Severn chose to find his own competition. The choice proved wise, as his wars against Owen Hart will forever be remembered as some of his greatest WWE action. Unfortunately for Severn, however, a piledriver delivered by Hart caused a severe injury to his neck.

Severn's career never got back on track after the neck injury. As a result, some say his WWE days never lived up to their expectations. The Beast's success outside WWE, however, is something he can hang his hat on proudly.

DANIEL BRYAN

see page 82

DANNY DAVIS

HT 6'0" **WT** 180 lbs. **FROM** Dover, New Hampshire
SIGNATURE MOVE Boston Crab

WWE audiences were introduced to Davis in the early 1980s as a referee. However, a disturbing trend was soon uncovered as Davis seemingly became tolerant of rule-breaking tactics. Alleged offenses included making fast counts, not enforcing basic rules, and turning a blind eye to questionable activities.

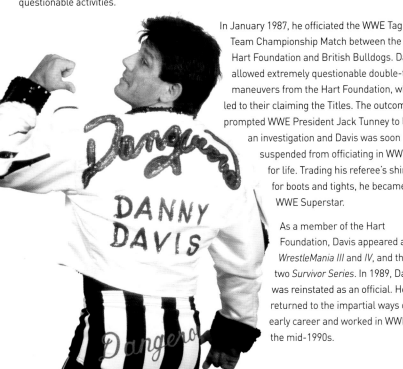

In January 1987, he officiated the WWE Tag Team Championship Match between the Hart Foundation and British Bulldogs. Davis allowed extremely questionable double-team maneuvers from the Hart Foundation, which led to their claiming the Titles. The outcome prompted WWE President Jack Tunney to launch an investigation and Davis was soon suspended from officiating in WWE for life. Trading his referee's shirt for boots and tights, he became a WWE Superstar.

As a member of the Hart Foundation, Davis appeared at *WrestleMania III* and *IV*, and the first two *Survivor Series*. In 1989, Davis was reinstated as an official. He returned to the impartial ways of his early career and worked in WWE until the mid-1990s.

DANNY DORING

HT 5'10" **WT** 219 lbs. **FROM** Wildwood, New Jersey

Alongside partner Roadkill, Danny Doring has the honor of being one-half of the last-ever ECW Tag Team Champions. Unfortunately for Doring, however, that accolade failed to result in any WWE success. In fact, his entire WWE career only amounted to a handful of matches, none of which he won.

During 2004 and 2005, Doring made a few unsuccessful appearances on *Heat* and *Velocity*. Despite his losing record, he was awarded a contract to compete on WWE's reborn ECW brand. After disappointing losses to Mike Knox, Rob Van Dam, and CM Punk, Doring was released from his contract in December 2006.

DANNY SPIVEY

HT 6'8" **WT** 280 lbs. **FROM** Tampa, Florida
SIGNATURE MOVE Bulldog

Trained primarily by Dusty Rhodes, alongside Scott Hall, "Golden Boy" Danny Spivey made his WWE debut in 1985 after appearances in the Charlotte and Kansas City territories. When Barry Windham left WWE, Spivey took his place in the popular tag team known as the U.S. Express. With Mike Rotundo, he came to the ring proudly waving the Stars and Stripes. In 1988, Spivey left the company to tour with All-Japan Pro Wrestling and the World Wrestling Council in Puerto Rico.

Spivey spent the early 1990s in WCW, All-Japan Pro Wrestling, and the independent circuit, where he was often billed as "Dangerous" Danny Spivey. He was forced to retire from the ring in the mid-1990s following a back injury.

DARREN YOUNG

HT 6'1" **WT** 239 lbs.
FROM Miami, Florida
SIGNATURE MOVE Gut Check

After impressing on *NXT* season one, Darren Young became a founding member of the renegade Nexus. However, a disheartening loss to John Cena left him exiled from the pack, putting the heavy-hitter back at square one. A tough task...unless your nickname is "Mr. No Days Off."

Young rediscovered his swagger with another *NXT* alum, Titus O'Neil. As the Prime Time Players, Young and O'Neil talked the talk, proclaiming to be worth "millions of dollars." Gone was the scowl Young wore in Nexus, but not his tenacity. PTP snagged victories over many top teams until a Championship-starved Titus brutally assaulted Young in January 2014, severing their bond and igniting a fierce rivalry.

After a year rehabbing a gruesome injury, The Ascension attacked, looking to sideline Young once again. That's when Titus O'Neil rushed in to save the day. Reunited and closer than ever, the duo worth "millions of dollars" finally captured those elusive Titles, appropriately enough, at *Money in the Bank 2015*.

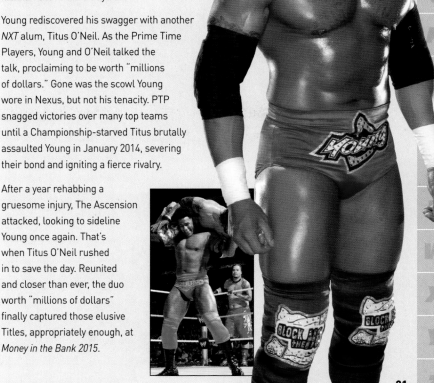

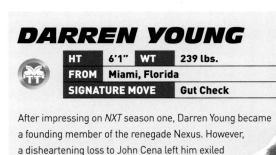

DANIEL BRYAN

HT	5'10"
WT	210 lbs.
FROM	Aberdeen, Washington

SIGNATURE MOVE
"Yes!" Lock

Since 1963, no Superstar has defied WWE's time-honored archetype for a headlining Superstar quite like Daniel Bryan. From a humble logging town in the Pacific Northwest, Bryan lacks the musculature of a comic book hero. His size is on par with the average adult male, his appearance does not have GQ photographers banging on his door, and his persona is as down-to-earth as the plants he favors over a juicy steak. Yet for a period, this scruffy Superstar once dismissed as an "Internet darling" took over sports-entertainment.

A LOOSE DEFINITION OF "ROOKIE"

Daniel Bryan was first introduced to WWE as The Miz's unassuming rookie on *NXT* Season 1. This arrangement drove educated fans mad. Though Bryan was new to WWE, many argued that he was qualified to mentor The Miz. Bryan was trained by Shawn Michaels and had spent ten years sharpening his eclectic arsenal across the globe. Once known as "The American Dragon," Bryan was a feared submissions master in Japan and several other promotions. The Miz finally learned this the hard way at *Night of Champions 2010* when he submitted to Bryan's signature LeBell Lock, giving Bryan the United States Championship. This revenge victory was also validation for Daniel. Months earlier, WWE fired him hours after his debut as a member of Nexus.

The following year, Bryan won the coveted Money in the Bank Contract. At *TLC 2011*, he used the opportunity to topple Big Show, a Superstar more than twice his size, for the World Heavyweight Championship. His unlikely reign brought out his cocky side, and this newfound boastfulness drew the ire of crowds.

ANGER MANAGEMENT

Bryan carried his self-assured swagger all the way to *WrestleMania XXVIII*. But when he was given a good luck kiss from AJ Lee, Bryan lost focus and was defeated by Sheamus in a record eighteen seconds. The loss sent Bryan into a mental tailspin that eventually landed him in anger management class. While there, he formed an unlikely bond with the Demon Kane.

Despite their forced partnership and endless bickering, the duo channeled their anger into pummeling WWE's top tag teams. The duo was given the name Team Hell No by the WWE Universe and the odd couple held Tag Team gold for 245 days.

THE YES! MOVEMENT

In 2013, Bryan's game and popularity were at an all-time high. The WWE Universe was now chanting "Yes! Yes! Yes!" as a rallying cry. Fans clamored for "The Beard" to get his big break and WWE Champion John Cena acquiesced by handpicking Bryan as his challenger at *SummerSlam*. In a rare clash of fan-favorites, Bryan pulled off the miraculous Championship victory!

However, with confetti still falling, Triple H leveled Bryan with a Pedigree to allow Randy Orton to swoop in and steal the Title by cashing in his Money in the Bank Contract.

I AM NOT THE BIGGEST, I AM NOT THE STRONGEST, BUT I AM DAMN SURE THE TOUGHEST!

As The Authority, Triple H and Stephanie McMahon flexed their corporate muscles to keep Bryan safely under WWE's glass ceiling. Bryan was determined to shatter it. "Yes!" evolved from a chant to an anti-establishment movement.

Bryan continued his pursuit enduring corrupt officiating, untimely interference, and The Authority's power plays. The sadistic Bray Wyatt appeared to lure him to the dark side, but "Daniel Wyatt" was merely masquerading to infiltrate the Wyatt clan. After defeating Bray at *Royal Rumble 2014*, Bryan was withheld from the Royal Rumble Match. Frustrated fans became fed up.

The "Yes!" Movement hijacked an episode of *Raw*, forcing Triple H into action at *WrestleMania 30*. Bryan finally earned his opportunity to compete for the WWE World Heavyweight Championship in the main event by defeating The Game in the extravaganza's opening match. Later that night, as the added ingredient in a Triple Threat Match, Bryan completed his improbable journey by submitting Batista with a Yes! Lock to claim the WWE World Heavyweight Championship. Days later, he married Brie Bella, capping perhaps the greatest week in human male history.

A NEW JOURNEY BEGINS

Bryan recounted his unbelievable climb to WWE's apex in his bestselling 2015 book, *YES*. He was unable to reach the main event of *WrestleMania 31* but still added a new accolade to his name. Bryan outlasted six Superstars to capture the Intercontinental Championship in a Ladder Match. Unfortunately, injury forced him to relinquish the prize in May. In February 2016, Daniel confirmed what millions feared. On an emotional *Raw* in his home city of Seattle, Bryan revealed that mounting injuries had taken their toll and that his sixteen-year career in the ring was over. Despite being cut short sooner than anyone desired, Daniel Bryan's tenure in WWE is among the most inspiring of all time.

Though Bryan's future remains uncharted, one thing is for certain. No matter what new challenges await in his post-WWE life, Bryan will tackle them Beard-first with a loud, emphatic "YES!"

DAVE TAYLOR

HT	6'3"	WT	256 lbs.
FROM	Yorkshire, England		

Ten years after teaming with William Regal as the Blue Bloods in WCW, Dave Taylor reunited with his longtime friend on *SmackDown* in October 2006. The brawling Brits made an instant impact, defeating Scotty 2 Hotty and Funaki in their debut, then toppled the mighty Bobby Lashley and Tatanka in their second match. The team's momentum eventually carried them to a Ladder Match for the WWE Tag Team Championship against Paul London and Brian Kendrick at *Armageddon 2006*. Taylor and Regal failed to capture the Titles that night, but solidified their status in the tag ranks.

After the 2007 WWE Draft forced the successful British tandem to go their separate ways, Taylor briefly teamed with Paul Burchill before serving as Drew McIntyre's mentor.

DAVID HART SMITH

HT	6'5"	WT	250 lbs.
FROM	Calgary, Alberta, Canada		
SIGNATURE MOVE	Running Powerslam		

David Hart Smith was raised around some of the greatest figures to set foot in the ring. His father was the British Bulldog while his uncles included Bret "Hit Man" Hart, Owen Hart, and Jim "The Anvil" Neidhart. DH idolized his legendary relatives and decided to carry on the Hart legacy forged by his grandfather, Stu Hart. In WWE, his powerful offensive arsenal was the spitting image of his renowned father.

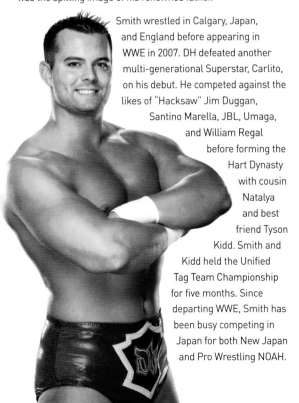

Smith wrestled in Calgary, Japan, and England before appearing in WWE in 2007. DH defeated another multi-generational Superstar, Carlito, on his debut. He competed against the likes of "Hacksaw" Jim Duggan, Santino Marella, JBL, Umaga, and William Regal before forming the Hart Dynasty with cousin Natalya and best friend Tyson Kidd. Smith and Kidd held the Unified Tag Team Championship for five months. Since departing WWE, Smith has been busy competing in Japan for both New Japan and Pro Wrestling NOAH.

DAVID OTUNGA

HT	6'0"	WT	229 lbs.	FROM	Hollywood, California
SIGNATURE MOVE	Spinebuster				

David Otunga has it all: a chiseled physique, a beautiful fiancé in the Oscar-winning Jennifer Hudson, an A-list Hollywood lifestyle, a successful career and a powerful intelligence, evidenced by his Harvard Law School degree. When put together, these characteristics equate to a major force in WWE.

Originally *NXT*'s runner-up from season one, it wasn't until after the show's completion that Otunga truly started to shine. As a member of the controversial Nexus faction, the newcomer teamed with the rest of the *NXT* roster to strike fear into the WWE locker room. He also used his alliance with Wade Barrett and company to strongarm his way to two WWE Tag Team Title reigns, one with reluctant partner John Cena and later, with Michael McGillicutty. With help from their Nexus cohorts, the duo held the Titles for three months.

Outside of the ring, Otunga was a valuable legal eagle for John Laurinaitis during his reign of power in WWE. Fueled by a constant coffee fix, Otunga has also lended council to Ricardo Rodriguez, Curtis Axel, and others looking for alternate means to settle their scores.

Otunga is always keeping busy. In 2013, he portrayed a police officer in the Halle Berry film *The Call*. Most recently, he has provided insightful analysis on WWE Network pre-shows.

DAVID SAMMARTINO

HT	5'8"	WT	252 lbs.	FROM	Pittsburg, Pennsylvania
SIGNATURE MOVE	Figure-Four Leg Lock				

The son of former WWE Champion and all-time great Bruno Sammartino, young David dreamed about creating his own path to stardom in the sports-entertainment industry. He began his career under the name Bruno Sammartino Jr., but soon opted to compete under his birth name. In 1984, David entered WWE and pinned Jerry Valiant during his television debut. He used the momentum from the win to earn a spot on the first-ever *WrestleMania* card, where he battled Brutus Beefcake to a no-contest.

David left WWE in the summer of 1986 and briefly appeared in the AWA, where he challenged Stan Hansen for the promotion's World Heavyweight Championship. For the remainder of the 1980s, David traveled to various independent promotions throughout the United States. In 1990, he was part of the short-lived UWF, and later went on to compete in WCW's cruiserweight division. Upon arriving in WCW, he was immediately granted an opportunity at Dean Malenko's Cruiserweight Championship. Unfortunately for David, Malenko won the match in convincing fashion.

DAWN MARIE

HT 5'7" **FROM** Rahway, New Jersey

Sports-entertainment has seen its share of seductive women; but never before has a Diva used sex as a weapon as effectively, or lethally, as Dawn Marie.

Perhaps Dawn Marie's greatest romantic exploit came in October 2002 when she fell for Al Wilson, the father of fellow Diva Torrie Wilson. Despite being half Wilson's age, Dawn Marie engaged in a passionate relationship with Mr. Wilson. And after just weeks together, the two lovebirds agreed to marry.

Dressed in nothing but their very revealing underwear, the couple was married in January 2003. Unfortunately, the wedding was one of the last times anybody would see Al Wilson alive, as Dawn Marie proved to be too much woman for him. His heart eventually gave out and he died on their honeymoon.

Proving a leopard never changes her spots, Dawn Marie was back at it the following year when her affair with Charlie Haas effectively ended his engagement to Miss Jackie. Luckily for all the WWE Superstars (and their fathers), the seductive Diva left WWE shortly thereafter.

DEAN AMBROSE

HT 6'4" **WT** 225 lbs. **FROM** Cincinnati, Ohio
SIGNATURE MOVE Dirty Deeds

It's tough to tell what makes a man like Dean Ambrose tick. At times, this unstable Superstar seems to derive equal satisfaction from the pain he absorbs and the pain he inflicts. So long as there is chaos involved, Ambrose is game. Though no mental institutions have come forward (so far) to claim Ambrose as their escapee, his mentality has inspired the nickname "Lunatic Fringe."

In 2012, Ambrose debuted in WWE not in a straightjacket but a flak jacket. As the maniacal mouthpiece of The Shield beside Seth Rollins and Roman Reigns, he upset the balance of power in WWE. While fighting injustice with the notorious trio, he also managed an impressive, yearlong reign with the United States Championship. After The Shield dissolved, no one doubted Dean's ability to make an impact on his own.

Ambrose showed zero fear in several brawls with members of the Wyatt Family that left both contestants bruised and battered. The scrappy competitor remained in the mix for various singles Titles. His closest brush with immortality came at *Survivor Series 2015*, when he was narrowly defeated by his former Shield-mate, Reigns, for the WWE World Heavyweight Championship.

At *TLC 2015*, Ambrose defeated celebrated prizefighter Kevin Owens for the Intercontinental Championship. His victory led to a gutsy series of matches that nearly saw Ambrose grab WWE's ultimate prize. After withstanding Brock Lesnar's worst at *WrestleMania 32*, the Lunatic Fringe is ready for whatever danger lies ahead.

DEAN DOUGLAS

HT 6'1" **WT** 234 lbs. **FROM** The University of Knowledge
SIGNATURE MOVE Final Exam

No other Superstar in WWE history had an easier route to the Intercontinental Championship than Dean Douglas. When injuries prevented Shawn Michaels from defending the Title, it was simply handed to Douglas in October 1995. Without even breaking a sweat, Douglas celebrated becoming the new Intercontinental Champion, much to the chagrin of the WWE Universe.

Luckily for fans everywhere, the celebration didn't last long. Within moments of being awarded the Intercontinental Championship, Douglas was forced to defend against Razor Ramon, who promptly defeated him and took the Title.

Despite owning one of the least impressive Intercontinental Championship reigns in WWE history, the arrogant Douglas believed he had something he could teach all his fellow Superstars. Watching from his satellite classroom, he would often grade the action he saw in the ring. Douglas proved to be a tough man to impress, as he never gave a favorable review. Some of the more notable Superstars Douglas offered failing grades to include The 1-2-3 Kid, Barry Horowitz, and Shawn Michaels.

DEAN HO

HT	6'0"	WT	264 lbs.	FROM	Honolulu, Hawaii
SIGNATURE MOVE		The Full Nelson			

This happy Hawaiian was a bodybuilder who won the "Mr. Hawaiian Islands" Championship in 1956. The next year, he opened a Honolulu gym that was popular with many wrestlers.

In 1962, Dean Ho made his ring debut in the Pacific Northwest Wrestling territory. For the next decade, Ho appeared all over Oregon, Washington, Hawaii, and British Columbia, boasting an in-ring style that combined martial arts, technical grappling, and aerial moves.

After arriving in WWE in 1973, he formed a popular tag team with Tony Garea, and the duo went on to hold the World Tag Team Championship for close to six months. Dean continued to appear in WWE until 1976. He then traveled to Georgia and San Francisco, and returned to Vancouver and Portland. He decided to hang up his boots in December 1983.

After retirement, the happy Hawaiian lived in Vancouver, B.C. and opened a highly touted gourmet catering business. Dean Ho is recognized for his in-ring accomplishments and versatility, as well as a disposition that brightened the hearts of fans.

DEBRA

HT	5'5"
FROM	Tuscaloosa, Alabama

A former beauty queen, Debra brought her award-winning looks to WCW in 1996. Alongside then-husband Steve McMichael, the curvy blonde was originally seen as nothing more than eye candy. By the end of her career, however, she was seen as an incredibly powerful female figure.

Debra jumped to WWE in 1998. At first glance, she gave the impression of a no-nonsense businesswoman, but later revealed herself as quite an exhibitionist. It wasn't uncommon to see Debra remove her suits in an attempt to help her man, Jeff Jarrett, pick up wins.

As a competitor, Debra didn't have the skills of a Fabulous Moolah, but that didn't stop her from capturing the Women's Championship, albeit on a technicality. In May 1999, Sable disrobed Debra in an Evening Gown Match, thus presumably winning the encounter. But Commissioner Shawn Michaels liked what he saw from the uncovered Debra and actually awarded her the Women's Championship instead.

Debra later went on to become HBK's Lieutenant Commissioner, thus proving herself as one of sports-entertainment's most powerful women.

DEAN MALENKO

HT	5'10"	WT	212 lbs.	FROM	Tampa, Florida
SIGNATURE MOVE		Texas Cloverleaf			

Trained by his famous father, "Professor" Boris Malenko, Dean was refereeing matches in his teens, using the unique vantage point to learn from the competitors.

By the early 1990s, Dean and his brother, Joe, were regulars in Mexico and Japan, and quickly earned the respect of more seasoned athletes by adapting to a variety of styles. He gained his first national exposure in the United States in ECW, taking on equally proficient opponents like 2 Cold Scorpio and Eddie Guerrero. It was in ECW where Malenko earned two monikers: the "Iceman," for his cold, calculating approach, and "The Man Of 1,000 Holds."

In 1995, Malenko was recruited by WCW. There, he won both the Cruiserweight and United States Championships, battling skilled tacticians like Guerrero, Chris Jericho, and Ultimo Dragon. He made such an impressive showing that he was accepted into the elite faction known as the Four Horsemen. After the Horsemen split in 1999, he joined Shane Douglas' group, The Revolution.

WCW was a chaotic place at the time, and Malenko had been raised to be in an environment where the in-ring product took precedence over everything else. Unhappy with the direction of the company, Malenko, Guerrero, Chris Benoit, and Perry Saturn collectively left for WWE in January 2000, and formed a faction called the Radicalz. Immediately, Malenko made an impact in the Light Heavyweight Division, defeating Essa Rios in March to become Light Heavyweight Champion, a Title he held for most of the following year.

However, he seemed to lose focus when he became obsessed with future WWE Hall of Famer, Lita. The two engaged in several skirmishes, and Malenko also found himself in entanglements with Ivory and Jacqueline. In 2001, after a series of intergender matches, he retired from the ring to work behind the scenes as a member of WWE's front office.

Going back to his roots, Malenko became one of WWE's most respected coaches, passing on the lessons he learned from his father.

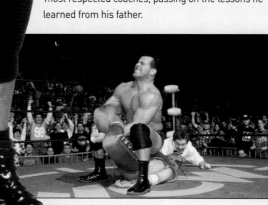

DEMOLITION

MEMBERS	Ax, Smash, & Crush		
COMBINED WT	978 lbs.	FROM	Parts Unknown

Originally derided by many as a cheap Road Warriors rip off, Demolition could have very easily folded under the weight of the naysayers. Instead, they combined their intimidating appearance with their aggressive in-ring abilities to dominate the WWE tag team scene for five years.

Clad in studded leather and colorful face paint, Ax & Smash made their WWE debut in 1987. The intimidating duo soon dismissed their original manager, Luscious Johnny Valiant, in favor of the conniving Mr. Fuji. With Fuji as their manager, Demolition destroyed their early competition, which consisted of some of the most popular tag teams of the era, including the British Bulldogs, Young Stallions, and Killer Bees.

The following year, Demolition carried their dominance into *WrestleMania IV*, where they defeated Strike Force for the World Tag Team Championship. Behind the devastation of their Decapitation finisher, Ax and Smash held the Titles for a record-breaking sixteen months.

In the midst of Demolition's epic World Tag Team Championship reign, the conniving Mr. Fuji turned his back on his clients to join forces with the Powers of Pain. Sympathetic fans everywhere began to see Ax & Smash in a new light. Almost overnight, Demolition was transformed into the most popular tag team in WWE.

Demolition's dominance grew throughout 1990 when they added Crush as the team's third member. Younger and stronger, Crush served as the muscle for the already-forceful tag team. On several occasions, he also stepped in to help Smash through the team's third reign as World Tag Team Champions.

By 1991, the trio began to fade, making way for such tag teams as The Nasty Boys and Road Warriors. Their final high-profile match came in a losing effort when they fell to international sensations Genichiro Tenryu & Koji Kitao at *WrestleMania VII*.

To this day, fans look back at Demolition's dominance over WWE as one of the most impressive displays in the history of tag team wrestling. Not bad for a team who were originally thought of as copycats.

DESIREE PETERSON

HT	5'9"	FROM	Copenhagen, Denmark

Desiree Peterson made her professional debut against Velvet McIntyre in January 1983. Ironically, the two women would soon cross paths again; this time as partners. When McIntyre's tag-team partner, Princess Victoria, suffered a career-ending injury in late 1984, it was Peterson who filled in as her partner. For Peterson, it was like winning the lottery, as teaming with McIntyre also meant she assumed Victoria's role as one-half of the Women's Tag Team Champions.

When she wasn't defending the tag Titles with McIntyre, Peterson made a name for herself competing in the women's singles division. There she battled many of sports-entertainment's most legendary female combatants, including Fabulous Moolah, Leilani Kai, and Donna Christanello.

Peterson and McIntyre eventually lost their gold to The Glamour Girls in a rare match contested in Egypt in August 1985. The Denmark native left WWE immediately after the loss. She later returned in 1988 to challenge Sherri Martel for the Women's Championship. After failing to wrestle the gold away from the now Hall of Famer, Peterson left WWE for good.

THE DESTROYER

HT	5'10"	WT	246 lbs.	FROM	Parts Unknown
SIGNATURE MOVE	Figure-Four Leglock				

Eloquent, educated, and energetic, the man who called himself "the Intelligent, Sensational Destroyer" was one of the most accomplished masked headliners ever, dictating the rules of the game wherever he traveled.

In 1962, he defeated future WWE Hall of Famer "Classy" Freddie Blassie to win the first of his three Worldwide Wrestling Associates (WWA) World Heavyweight Championships. After dropping the title in 1963, he toured Japan, achieving mythic status in that country by becoming the last wrestler to beat national icon Rikidozan.

In the AWA, he called himself Dr. X, but had similar success, capturing the group's World Heavyweight crown in 1968. Revered in the United States, the Destroyer became a crossover star in Japan, whose rigorous fitness regimen inspired generations of competitors.

DEUCE AND DOMINO WITH CHERRY

MEMBERS	Deuce & Domino	COMBINED WT	730 lbs.
FROM	The Other Side of The Tracks		

Deuce and Domino made their WWE debut in 2007, looking like the Fonze's long lost cousins. Led to the ring by Domino's sister, Cherry, the 1950s inspired duo considered themselves God's gift to women.

Deuce and Domino shocked the world when they beat Brian Kendrick and Paul London for the WWE Tag Team Championship. They held the Titles for four months, eventually losing to MVP and Matt Hardy. Cracks in the team began to show when Cherry started to run around with Michelle McCool. Deuce and Domino kicked her to the curb in favor of Maryse. Unfortunately for fans of these throwbacks, a lost match prompted a brawl between the pair, ending their partnership. In August 2008, Domino left WWE and Deuce tried his hand at singles competition.

D-GENERATION X

MEMBERS
Triple H, Shawn Michaels, Chyna, Road Dogg and Billy Gunn (The New Age Outlaws), X-Pac, & Rick Rude

Throughout the storied history of sports-entertainment, no faction has ruffled more feathers than D-Generation X. Catalysts of the Attitude Era, DX's defiant antics became an instant sensation in late 1997. Fans could not help but rally behind their anti-establishment message.

It all started with the notorious bond between Shawn Michaels and Triple H. The former Kliq buddies brought their sophomoric locker room humor to the fore, prompting Bret Hart to publicly deride them as "a couple of degenerates." Alongside bodyguard Chyna and "insurance policy" Rick Rude, the faction quickly became a thorn in the side of authority.

AT ODDS WITH AUTHORITY

DX's brand of humor infuriated WWE Commissioner Sgt. Slaughter, but the more Slaughter tried to silence them, the louder they got. It wasn't long before they were mooning audiences and telling people to "Suck it!"

The crude behavior only increased their popularity. When Michaels defeated Bret Hart for the WWE Championship at *Survivor Series 1997*, the highly controversial victory stirred even more arrogance and anarchy from the group. Slaughter attempted to sideline DX's chaotic behavior by forcing Michaels and Triple H to face each other for HBK's European Championship, but ultimately the joke was on Slaughter. Michaels simply laid down and allowed his partner to pin him, once again sticking it to the rule makers.

The lawlessness of D-Generation X continued following HBK's temporary retirement in 1998. Triple H saw an opportunity to pick up the ball and run with it. He replaced Michaels in DX with three equally immature Superstars: Road Dogg, Billy Gunn, and longtime friend, X-Pac.

The new DX never skipped a beat. Within weeks of their reformation, the faction invaded rival WCW's *Monday Nitro* telecast and corporate headquarters in Atlanta. The jaw-dropping stunts helped turn the tide of the Monday Night War to WWE's side.

With the chaos at full tilt at *WrestleMania XV*, a shocking turn of events saw DX crumble to the ground. Triple H appeared headed to the ring to help X-Pac battle Shane McMahon. Instead, he clobbered his DX partner, signifying the end of the popular faction.

THE REBIRTH OF REBELLION

Eight years and countless accolades later, Triple H and Shawn Michaels began to hint at a possible reunion. At *WrestleMania 22*, both Superstars revived the faction's signature crotch chop. Seeds were planted for months, stirring cautious excitement among fans. DX's founding fathers finally put the speculation to rest when they reformed in June 2006. Triple H made the reunion official by mooning Mr. McMahon.

Fueled by the sole goal of embarrassing the Chairman, Triple H and HBK used every childish trick in the book. The more immature the gag, the louder the cheers became. They were still crude like the early days, but with an added level of creativity. Mr. McMahon nearly had a nervous breakdown seeing his limousine, his private jet, and even the WWE Tower tagged with lime green DX spray paint.

DX's rivalry with Mr. McMahon culminated at *Unforgiven,* the lasting image of the Hell in a Cell Match being Mr. McMahon's head shoved into Big Show's gigantic bare behind.

After the victory, D-Generation X changed targets and focused on Rated-RKO. The factional rivalry culminated in a *Survivor Series* match where Triple H and Shawn Michaels formed a team that swept Rated-RKO's side 5-0. An injury to Triple H forced the duo to focus on individual career goals, but in 2009, circumstances brought the beloved rebels back together once again.

ONE LAST STAND

With Shawn Michaels on hiatus from WWE, Triple H decided to search for his best friend to aid in his battles with the Legacy. He found him, of all the random places, serving blue-plate specials as a short-order cook. The entertaining segments culminated with Triple H convincing HBK to rediscover his edge. At *SummerSlam,* DX emerged atop a tank and capped the night by standing in triumph over Legacy.

DX's final invasion tour continued into late 2009, when their friendship survived a Triple Threat Match for the WWE Championship that pitted D-Generation X against each other and John Cena. Triple H and HBK remained close allies up to their last televised match on March 1, 2010.

AND IF YOU'RE NOT DOWN WITH THAT...

HBK has honored his vow to remain retired from competition after his *WrestleMania XXVI* loss to Undertaker. That does not mean he cannot dust off the old Superkick from time to time. At *WrestleMania 31*, "old HB-shizzle," as he has playfully called himself, and the rest of the DX cohorts rushed to the aid of Triple H as he battled Sting. When the nWo emerged, sports-entertainment fans finally witnessed the collision they always dreamed of, pitting the Monday Night War's most notorious factions against each other.

This battle in the Bay Area proved that at any time the music can still hit, the green glow sticks can still fly, and DX can still creep out of the cracks to once again break it down.

87

DIAMOND DALLAS PAGE

HT	6'5"	WT	248 lbs.	FROM	The Jersey Shore
SIGNATURE MOVE		Diamond Cutter			

Diamond Dallas Page was thirty-five years old when he competed in his first professional wrestling match. At an age when many professional athletes contemplate retirement, the New Jersey native was a rookie. That didn't matter for Page, whose magnetic charisma and unparalleled dedication eventually made him a Champion and all-time WCW great.

With a popular finishing maneuver, the Diamond Cutter, Page won the WCW Television Championship and United States Championship. His success caught the eye of NBA legend Karl Malone, who joined Page in the ring to aid in his rivalry with the villainous nWo. DDP's valiant stand against the dangerous faction caused his popularity to skyrocket. He earned a long-awaited WCW Championship opportunity at *Spring Stampede* and won by hitting "Nature Boy" Ric Flair with his trademark move.

Page won the WCW Championship twice more before the promotion closed its doors in 2001. Making the leap to WWE, he chose to make a statement by stalking Undertaker's wife, Sara. For weeks, DDP sat outside the couple's ranch and videotaped her most intimate moments. In the end, this decision proved ill-advised. An infuriated Undertaker and Kane seized the World Tag Team Championship from Page and his partner, Kanyon.

Despite his unsuccessful rivalry against Undertaker, DDP developed an overly optimistic attitude in 2002. With a new, cheerful catchphrase, "that's not a bad thing, that's a good thing," the positive Page captured the European Championship from Christian in January.

A few months after winning the European Championship, injury forced DDP to walk away from the ring, leaving behind a decorated career worthy of a "Self High Five." Today, DDP has reinvented himself as the practitioner of his own successful yoga program. DDP Yoga was designed for regular guys and over the years has even helped Superstars such as Chris Jericho, Scott Hall, and Jake "The Snake" Roberts improve their health. Roberts has even credited DDP for helping to repair his personal life. Page also reaps the benefits of his program. At age sixty, he remained in tremendous shape, which he displayed at *WrestleMania 32* as a surprise entrant in the Andre the Giant Memorial Battle Royal.

DICK MURDOCH

HT	6'2"	WT	288 lbs.	FROM	Waxahachie, Texas
SIGNATURE MOVE		Brainbuster			

The son of grappler Frankie Hill Murdoch, Dick Murdoch grew up hanging out at arenas, and sometimes brawling, with Terry and Dory Funk, Jr. After learning his perilous finishing move from the masterful "Killer" Karl Kox, Murdoch formed a partnership with Dusty Rhodes in 1968, calling themselves The Texas Outlaws. From time to time, the pair broke up and tore buildings apart, only to reunite against common foes.

In 1983, the ruffian from the Lone Star State and partner Adrian Adonis brought their blend of chaos to WWE. As the North-South Connection, they broke every rule in existence. In April, 1984, they defeated Rocky Johnson and Tony Atlas for the World Tag Team Championship.

In 1985, Murdoch left WWE, returned to the NWA as "Captain Redneck" and toured independent promotions in North America and Japan. In 1995, Murdoch made a surprise return appearance in WWE at the *Royal Rumble*, and was one of the last Superstars in the ring before he was eliminated by Henry Godwinn. Sadly, Murdoch passed away the next year.

DICK SLATER

HT	6'0"	WT	233 lbs.
FROM	Richmond, Virginia		

Success followed Dick Slater everywhere he went, except to WWE. Known as "The Rebel" during his brief WWE run, Slater never seemed to get his career out of first gear. Elsewhere, however, the man known as "Dirty" Dick Slater cheated his way to an impressive win-loss record.

While competing for the National Wrestling Alliance, Slater captured many Titles, including the Florida, Missouri, Georgia, Mid-Atlantic, and Southeastern Heavyweight Championships, but it was the tag team Title earned in WCW that gained him the most national exposure. In June 1992, Slater and his partner, The Barbarian, defeated the Fabulous Freebirds for the WCW United States Tag Team Championship. Three years later, he teamed with the rugged Bunkhouse Buck to take the WCW Tag Team Championship from Harlem Heat.

DICK THE BRUISER

HT	6'1"	WT	261 lbs.	FROM	Reno, Nevada
SIGNATURE MOVE		Top Rope Knee Drop			

After spending the early 1950s as a member of the Green Bay Packers, Dick the Bruiser made the jump to wrestling in 1954. His affinity for breaking bones immediately earned him the reputation as "The World's Most Dangerous Wrestler." The lofty status went straight to his head, as the egotistical tough guy was often heard saying, "There isn't a man alive I can't lick."

Dick the Bruiser is most recognized for his efforts as a wrestler and promoter of the Indianapolis-based World Wrestling Association. While there, he became one of the industry's greatest tag team competitors, capturing the promotion's tag Titles fourteen times with the likes of The Crusher, Bill Miller, and the legendary Bruno Sammartino.

In 1971, Dick the Bruiser found himself on the wrong side of one of history's most significant matches. With The Sheik as his partner, he came up short against Tarzan Tyler and Luke Graham in a match to declare the first-ever World Tag Team Champions in WWE history. Undeterred by the loss, The Bruiser went on to capture eight more tag team Championships over the next fifteen years.

While Dick the Bruiser is best remembered for being a noted tough man, many fail to credit him with one of the wittiest comments of all time. According to legend, The Bruiser is the first person to call Bobby Heenan "The Weasel." Decades later, Heenan still gets taunted by the derogatory nickname.

THE DICKS

MEMBERS	Chad Dick & James Dick	COMBINED WT	430 lbs.

Clad in Chippendales outfits and carrying mirrors to the ring, Chad and James Dicks' pre-match ritual saw them strip down to their ring attire to what they believed was the delight of female fans.

Upon their debut in late 2005, the egotistical tandem scored a few big victories. It wasn't long before the WWE caught up to them, which resulted in a series of losses. In February 2006, the Dicks came up short in handicap action against Boogeyman. They were released from WWE immediately after.

DIESEL/KEVIN NASH

see page 90

DINK THE CLOWN

HT	4'0"	WT	95 lbs.
FROM	Parts Unknown		
SIGNATURE MOVE		Cannonball	

Presented as a gift to Doink the Clown, Dink packed quite a punch when called upon. He rarely left the side of Doink during the clown's days in WWE and gave splitting headaches to referees and opposing Superstars alike.

In search of his *WrestleMania* moment, Dink joined Doink to battle Bam Bam Bigelow and Luna Vachon at *WrestleMania X*. Unfortunately for the pint-sized Superstar, there was nothing to laugh about on this night, as Bigelow and Vachon walked away with the win. From there, the mischievous clowns took their act to *Survivor Series 1994*, where they teamed with Pink and Wink in a losing effort to take on Jerry Lawler and his vertically-challenged partners, Queazy, Sleazy, and Cheezy. Dink left WWE a few months later.

DINO BRAVO

HT	6'0"	WT	248 lbs.	FROM	Montreal, Quebec, Canada
SIGNATURE MOVE		Side Suplex			

Trained by Canadian legend Gino Brito, Dino Bravo began his in-ring career in 1970. His earliest days were spent as a tag team specialist, forming successful pairings with Brito, Mr. Wrestling, and Victor Rivera, among others.

In 1978, Bravo debuted in WWE and soon won the World Tag Team Championship with partner Dominic DeNucci. The duo held the Titles for more than three months before losing to the Yukon Lumberjacks in June 1978. Following the loss, Bravo competed in singles competition before leaving WWE in 1979.

After a seven-year absence, Bravo returned to WWE as the bleached-blond associate of the Dream Team. Later, he became one-half of the New Dream Team when Brutus Beefcake was exiled from the group. Bravo also formed a feared alliance with the mighty Earthquake.

In the spring of 1992, Bravo retired from active competition and opened a training school. Sadly, the Canadian legend died at his Montreal home in March 1993. Bravo will forever be remembered as one of the most powerful men in WWE history.

DIESEL/ KEVIN NASH

HT	6'10"
WT	328 lbs.
FROM	Detroit, Michigan

SIGNATURE MOVE
Jackknife Powerbomb

With the strength of a Mack truck and a swagger second to none, Kevin Nash spent more than two decades cementing his legacy as one of the elite big men in sports-entertainment history. Along the way, he collected more than 15 Championships between WWE and WCW, and was one of the driving forces that helped change the industry forever during the Monday Night War.

While the WWE Universe rightfully recognizes Nash as one of the best in the business, his initial path to greatness was paved with some less-than-great personas. Upon debuting in WCW in 1990, Nash became known as Steel of the Master Blasters tag team. When Steel failed to take off, Nash portrayed the equally unpopular Oz and Vinnie Vegas personas. Luckily for Nash, Shawn Michaels was watching from a distance and requested the big man become his bodyguard.

DIESEL POWER

Nash jumped at the opportunity to leave WCW and in 1993, began serving as HBK's heavy in WWE. Known as Diesel, his job responsibilities consisted solely of watching Michaels's back. But it wasn't long before Big Daddy Cool's immense size and brute strength catapulted him to an in-ring career.

Mere months into his WWE career, Diesel dominated much of the 1994 Royal Rumble Match, eliminating seven Superstars, including Owen Hart, Billy Gunn, and Bob Backlund. The impressive performance served as the launching point for what would become one of the most remarkable years any Superstar has ever had.

A few short months later, Diesel won his first of many Titles when he defeated Razor Ramon for the Intercontinental Championship in April 1994. While still Champion, Big Daddy Cool then teamed up with HBK to capture the World Tag Team Titles from The Headshrinkers. And later that same year, Diesel reached the pinnacle of the sports-entertainment world when he defeated Bob Backlund for the WWE Championship in November. With the victory, Diesel successfully captured all three major WWE Titles in the same calendar year.

Diesel went on to hold the Championship for nearly one full year, giving WWE the stability at the top of the roster that it hadn't seen since the days of Hulk Hogan and Randy Savage.

DEFECTION TO WCW

Following a loss to Undertaker at *WrestleMania XII*, Diesel fled WWE in favor of rival WCW. The defection was a massive hit to the WWE roster and would go down as a move that changed the sports-entertainment landscape both in and out of the ring. From a business standpoint, Nash, along with close friend Scott Hall, was given a contract that guaranteed a large base salary. At the time, WWE was not offering the same type of deals, but would soon be forced to change the way it structured agreements, thanks in large part to Nash's WCW contract.

In front of the camera, Nash's performance was equally landscape-altering. As a founding member of the New World Order, he had become partly responsible for ushering in an attitude in sports-entertainment that was wholly unlike WWE's New Generation.

After a brief hiatus following WCW's closure, Nash once again teamed with Hall and Hogan to reform the nWo in WWE in February 2002. Their reunion, however, was short-lived as Nash and Hall soon turned their back on The Hulkster after Hogan's *WrestleMania X8* encounter with The Rock.

DIESEL VS. THE GAME

After recovering from a series of injuries, Nash returned in April 2003 to save Shawn Michaels from a beating at the hands of Triple H. This led to many battles with The Game, including a Hell In A Cell Match at *Bad Blood*. Nash disappeared from the scene shortly after his rivalry with Triple H, though the two former friends would square off again in the future.

Competing once again as Diesel, Nash returned to WWE at the 2011 *Royal Rumble* to a deafening ovation. Though he didn't win the match, Nash's participation remains one of the biggest surprises in Rumble history. Months later, Nash controversially raided the *SummerSlam* main event, which set off an explosive series of encounters with Triple H, highlighted by their Sledgehammer Ladder Match at *WWE TLC* in December 2011.

In March 2015, Nash received the ultimate honor when he was inducted into the WWE Hall of Fame.

I'VE GOT THE WWE RUNNING ON DIESEL POWER!

THE DISCIPLES OF APOCALYPSE

MEMBERS Crush, Chainz, Skull, & 8-Ball

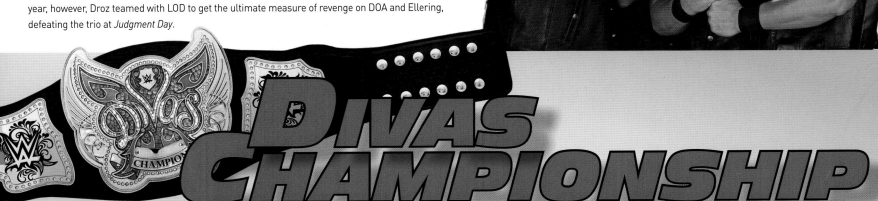

After being fired from the Nation of Domination, Crush formed a biker gang of Superstars he called the Disciples of Apocalypse. According to the former Nation member, DOA was a true brotherhood of Superstars who lived, rode, and fought together. Fans expected greatness from Crush, Chainz, Skull, and 8-Ball after they made their debut in June 1997, but by the end of the year, Crush had left WWE and Chainz went on to pursue a singles career, leaving Skull and 8-Ball as the sole members of the faction.

As a tag team, Skull and 8-Ball engaged in an intense rivalry against the Legion of Doom. During this time, longtime LOD manager Paul Ellering shockingly turned on his team to join forces with DOA.

With Ellering by their side, Skull and 8-Ball were able to turn back LOD at *Fully Loaded 1998*. Later that year, however, Droz teamed with LOD to get the ultimate measure of revenge on DOA and Ellering, defeating the trio at *Judgment Day*.

DIVAS CHAMPIONSHIP

At *The Great American Bash 2008*, Michelle McCool etched her name in history by becoming the first-ever Divas Champion, defeating Natalya in a tournament final. Michelle later unified the butterfly with its counterpart, the WWE Women's Championship, establishing the Diva's Title as the ultimate accolade among WWE's feisty female competitors.

Many talented women held the prize in its eight-year history including Eve, AJ Lee, and Charlotte. Among all these illustrious names, Nikki Bella emerged from the pack in 2015 with a record run of 301 days as Champion. At *WrestleMania 32*, the Divas Revolution in WWE came full circle when WWE Hall of Famer Lita introduced the new WWE Women's Championship, officially ending the era of the Divas Championship.

2008

July 20 • Uniondale, NY
Michelle McCool def. **Natalya** in the finals of a tournament to crown the inaugural Divas Champion

December 26 • Toronto, Ontario
Maryse def. **Michelle McCool**

2009

July 26 • Philadelphia, PA
Mickie James def. **Maryse**

October 12 • Indianapolis, IN
Jillian def. **Mickie James**

October 12 • Indianapolis, IN
Melina def. **Jillian**
Melina was forced to vacate the Title due to injury.

2010

February 22 • Indianapolis, IN
Maryse def. **Gail Kim** in the finals of a tournament to crown a new Champion

April 12 • London, England
Eve def. **Maryse**

June 20 • Uniondale, NY
Alicia Fox def. Eve, Maryse and Gail Kim in a Fatal 4-Way Match

August 15 • Los Angeles, CA
Melina def. **Alicia Fox**

September 19 • Chicago, IL
Michelle McCool def. **Melina**
Michelle McCool's victory unified the Divas and Women's Championships. In addition, Layla was named co-Champion meaning the Title could be defended by either Michelle McCool or Layla

November 21 • Miami, FL
Natalya def. **Michelle McCool** and **Layla** in a Handicap Match

2011

January 30 • Boston, MA
Eve def. **Natalya**, **Michelle McCool**, and **Layla** in a Fatal 4-Way Match

April 11 • Bridgeport, CT
Brie Bella def. **Eve**

2012

April 23 • Detroit, MI
Nikki Bella def. **Beth Phoenix** in a Lumberjill Match

June 20 • Baltimore, MD
Kelly Kelly def. **Brie Bella**

October 2 • New Orleans, LA
Beth Phoenix def. **Kelly Kelly**

2013

January 14 • Houston, TX
Kaitlyn def. **Eve**

June 16 • Rosemont, IL
AJ Lee def. **Kaitlyn**

2014

April 7, 2014 • New Orleans, LA
Paige def. **AJ Lee** in her WWE debut

April 29 • Rosemont, IL
Layla def. **Nikki Bella**

September 16 • Boston, MA
Eve def. **Layla**

June 30 • Hartford, CT
AJ Lee def. **Paige**

August 17 • Los Angeles, CA
Paige def. **AJ Lee**

September 21 • Nashville, TN
AJ Lee def. **Paige** and **Nikki Bella** in a Triple Threat Match

November 23 • St. Louis, MO
Nikki Bella def. **AJ Lee**

2015

September 20 • Houston, TX
Charlotte def. **Nikki Bella**

The Divas Championship was retired on April 3, 2016.

DJ GABRIEL

| HT | 6'2" | WT | 252 lbs. | FROM | Wokingham, England |
| SIGNATURE MOVE | Flying European Uppercut |

In November 2008, *ECW* was introduced to sports-entertainment's most questionable dancer since "Das Wunderkind" Alex Wright when DJ Gabriel debuted. Displaying fancy footwork, the new Superstar easily emerged victorious from his first-ever *ECW* match. Gabriel's future was looking bright, perhaps justifying the shades he wore to the ring.

With the beautiful Alicia Fox by his side, Gabriel went undefeated for the remainder of 2008. In 2009, Gabriel's competition started to pick up, first with fellow countryman Paul Burchill, then with the massive Mark Henry. The World's Strongest Man dealt Gabriel his first loss. Then when his dance partner Fox was drafted to *SmackDown*, Gabriel soon faded away from WWE.

D'LO BROWN

HT	6'3"	**WT**	268 lbs.
FROM	Chicago, Illinois		

D'Lo Brown made his WWE debut to very little fanfare in 1997. As a supporting member of the Nation of Domination, he did little more than accompany leader Faarooq to the ring. But it wasn't long before the Nation realized his talents and started utilizing him in competition.

Brown captured his first title in WWE in July 1998 when he defeated Triple H for the European Championship on *Monday Night Raw*. He would go on to capture the Title on three more occasions. During his third reign, Brown made history when he defeated Jeff Jarrett in July 1999 to also capture the Intercontinental Championship. With the win, Brown became the first Superstar to hold the European and Intercontinental Titles concurrently.

After a brief partnership with the Godfather, Brown partnered with former Headbanger Chaz to form Lo-Down. Later in 2002, he acquired the managerial services of Theodore Long and became part of Thuggin' and Buggin' Enterprises, a group formed to fight oppression within WWE. Soon after, Brown and WWE went their separate ways.

For the next four years, Brown competed on the independent scene and in Japan. In June 2008, he briefly returned to WWE to remind those who crossed his path that, "Chumps better recognize and become down with the Brown!"

DOINK

HT	5'10"	**WT**	243 lbs.	**FROM**	Parts Unknown
SIGNATURE MOVE	The Whoopie Cushion, The Stump Puller				

In late 1992, this clown brought his circus act to WWE. His mean-spirited pranks both in and out of the ring made him a prime target of competitors and audiences alike. At *WrestleMania IX*, he attacked Crush with the aid of an imposter, adding confusion to his cruel antics. Doink could not contain the joy he received by making others miserable.

After an incident with Jerry "The King" Lawler, fans began to embrace Doink, who displayed a softer side. His pranks brought out laughter from audiences and he introduced a sidekick, named Dink. The two battled Bam Bam Bigelow and Luna Vachon at *WrestleMania X*. At that year's *Survivor Series*, he assembled a crew of Dink, Wink, and Pink to battle Lawler's team of Queazy, Cheesy, and Sleazy.

Over the years, Doink has continued to bring his one-man circus back to town for some nostalgic hijinks. He participated in the Gimmick Battle Royal at *WrestleMania X-7*. In 2012, he resurfaced on *Raw* to battle Heath Slater. Though Doink's brand of humor has not always tickled the funny bone, he has always kept his opponents in stitches.

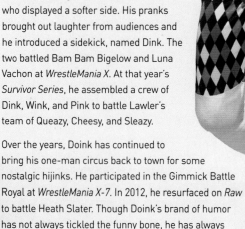

DOK HENDRIX

Put a microphone in front of Dok Hendrix and he could talk for hours. In fact, the only thing that was louder than the boisterous announcer was his neon-colored suits.

The energetic Hendrix began his WWE announcing career in 1995. His high-octane style propelled him to become a regular on such weekly WWE shows as *Superstars* and *Action Zone*. Hendrix even assumed color commentator duties for several pay-per-view matches.

In addition to sitting at the announce table, Hendrix also served as WWE's main interviewer, a role made famous years earlier by WWE Hall of Famer "Mean" Gene Okerlund. Hendrix's most famous interview occurred at the 1996 *King of the Ring* when he held the microphone for Stone Cold Steve Austin's now famous "Austin 3:16" rant.

DOLPH ZIGGLER

HT	6'0"	WT	218 lbs.	FROM	Hollywood, Florida
SIGNATURE MOVE		Zig Zag			

Dolph Ziggler might just be the perfect WWE Superstar, at least that's what he wants you to believe. Blessed with amazing athleticism and an unmatched arrogance, the Florida native isn't afraid to show off his superiority.

Ziggler took great steps toward solidifying his cocky claims when he defeated Kofi Kingston in August 2010 for his first of many Intercontinental Championship reigns. One year later, Ziggler added United States Champion to his resume when he again defeated Kingston at *Capitol Punishment*.

As many predicted, Ziggler reached the top of the sports-entertainment industry when he became World Heavyweight Champion in February 2011. But it wasn't his athleticism that carried him to the Title. Instead, Ziggler was simply handed the gold from then-Acting *SmackDown* General Manager Vickie Guerrero.

Unfortunately for Ziggler, his reign only lasted a few fleeting moments. Shortly after The Showoff was awarded the Title, Theodore Long returned to his post atop *SmackDown* and demanded the new Champ defend against Edge, who speared his way to victory.

Ziggler would eventually go on to win the World Heavyweight Championship in a more legitimate fashion when he successfully cashed in his Money in the Bank contract against Alberto Del Rio the night after *WrestleMania 29*. During his reign, Ziggler unfortunately suffered an injury. He eventually worked his way back from the sidelines, but Alberto Del Rio sensed that he was still weakened. The man of privilege viciously targeted Ziggler's injury during their match at *Payback 2013*.

Ziggler fought valiantly, which won him the respect of the WWE Universe. Unfortunately, however, he wasn't able to win the match, as Del Rio walked away with the victory and Title.

Ziggler's popularity reached an all-time high at *Survivor Series 2014*. As a member of Team Cena, Ziggler raised eyebrows when he fended off Seth Rollins, Luke Harper, Kane, Rusev, and Mark Henry—with the surprising help of "The Vigilante" Sting who made his first appearance in WWE to help Ziggler become the match's sole survivor. As a result of the victory, The Authority was ousted from power and Ziggler reminded fans why he is considered among the best in the business.

DOMINIC DENUCCI

HT	6'3"	WT	245 lbs.	FROM	Pittsburgh, Pennsylvania
SIGNATURE MOVE		Airplane Spin			

Dominic DeNucci made his WWE debut in 1965 and fans were instantly in awe of his superior mat skills and amazing strength. DeNucci won his first major Title in 1971 when he teamed with Bruno Sammartino to defeat the Mongols for the International Tag Team Championship. In 1975, he teamed with Victor Rivera to win the World Tag Team Championship. DeNucci earned a third tag team championship in 1978, partnering with Dino Bravo.

DeNucci retired from the ring in the mid-1980s. After hanging up his boots, he opened a wrestling school in Freedom, Pennsylvania, and trained the likes of hardcore legend Mick Foley, former ECW Champion Shane Douglas, and former WCW referee Brian Hildebrand.

DON CURTIS

HT	5'11"	WT	220 lbs.	FROM	Buffalo, New York
SIGNATURE MOVE		Sleeper Hold			

During the late 1950s, Don Curtis and partner Mark Lewin were one of the most popular tag teams appearing on shows promoted by Capitol Wrestling, trading the United States Tag Team Championship with the "Golden Grahams," Eddie and Jerry, twice in 1958.

Curtis was the veteran of the squad, having been trained by the great Lou Thesz after the multiple-time NWA Champion spotted him wrestling for the University of Buffalo in 1951. Curtis received much of his early seasoning while competing in Australia. After their run in the northeast, Curtis and Lewin reunited in Florida, where Curtis moved in 1962.

Later, Curtis offered expert commentary on the Florida territory's broadcasts, and managed the Jacksonville Coliseum. He died in 2008.

DON KERNODLE

HT	6'1"	WT	290 lbs.	FROM	Burlington, North Carolina

As part of Sgt. Slaughter's Cobra Corps, Don Kernodle's early years were filled with a great education and many victories. Known then as Pvt. Don Kernodle, the North Carolinian used what he learned from Slaughter to rise to the top of the NWA tag team ranks with partner Pvt. Jim Nelson.

In 1983, Kernodle began a successful union with "Cowboy" Bob Orton, before ultimately turning his back on the United States to align himself with hated Russian Ivan Koloff. In May 1984, Kernodle and Koloff captured the NWA Mid-Atlantic Tag Team Championship.

In addition to wrestling, Kernodle's resume features a role in the 1978 motion picture *Paradise Alley*. He appropriately played a wrestler, alongside other Superstars such as Dick Murdoch, Ted DiBiase, and Ray Stevens.

DON LEO JONATHAN

HT	6'6"	WT	300 lbs.	FROM	Salt Lake City, Utah

Decades before high-flying action became the rage in sports-entertainment; Don Leo Jonathan was mesmerizing opponents with standing dropkicks, backflips, and even lofty leaps over the top rope. What made Jonathan's cat-like agility even more jaw-dropping was the fact that he was the size of a small tree at 6'6" and 300 pounds.

Over the course of his thirty-year career, Jonathan competed all over the globe, including Europe, Canada, South Africa, Australia, and Japan. Known as "The Mormon Giant," Jonathan enjoyed his greatest notoriety in the early 1970s while battling another colossal figure, Andre the Giant. In addition, Jonathan found great success competing in the tag team division with such partners as Jimmy Snuka, Haystacks Calhoun, and Rocky Johnson.

DON MCCLARTY

| HT | 6'4" | WT | 260 lbs | FROM | New York | SIGNATURE MOVE | Kneelift |

In the 1960s, "Irish" Don McClarty was a solid WWE journeyman, occasionally teaming with future WWE Hall of Famer Bruno Sammartino and Bill Watts, and competing against rivals like Waldo Von Erich and Gorilla Monsoon.

After debuting in 1959, McClarty acquired quite a few road miles, sometimes alongside his brother, Roy McClarty. In 1963, he arrived in the AWA, where he partnered with Verne Gagne and once went to a time limit draw with The Crusher. His most notable accomplishment was snaring the United States Tag Team Championship with partner Argentina Apollo in WWE in 1964.

After his time in WWE he ventured to Amarillo, taking on future NWA World Heavyweight Champion Dory Funk Jr. and Jose Lothario, among other headliners, and to Vancouver, where he teamed with future WWE Hall of Famer Rocky Johnson.

DON MURACO

| | | HT | 6'3" | WT | 275 lbs. |
| FROM | Sunset Beach, Hawaii | | | | |

One of the most hated Superstars of the 1980s, Don Muraco was often showered with chants of "beach bum." Once the bell rang, however, he proved to be anything but a bum. His technical mastery carried him to a Hall of Fame career, which was highlighted by two lengthy reigns as Intercontinental Champion.

Managed by The Grand Wizard, Muraco entered WWE in 1980. Dubbed "The Magnificent One," the cocky Superstar drew the fans' rage when he defeated the immensely popular Pedro Morales for the Intercontinental Championship in June 1981. Coincidentally, Morales was also the victim of Muraco's second Intercontinental Championship win in January 1983.

Muraco's second reign will forever be highlighted by a historic Title defense that saw Jimmy Snuka execute his Superfly Splash from the top of the towering cage. Despite Snuka's inspirational leap, it was Muraco who walked out of Madison Square Garden as Champion. When he finally lost his Title in February 1984, his reign had lasted over a year.

A proven Champion, Muraco employed Mr. Fuji as his manager and challenged Hulk Hogan for the WWE Championship on several occasions. He never captured the ultimate prize but still etched his name into WWE lore. In July 1985, Muraco won the first-ever King of the Ring tournament. Later that year, he and Fuji unveiled *Fuji Vice*, the first of several amusing TV show parodies.

After a reviled alliance with "Cowboy" Bob Orton, Muraco took on the managerial services of another future Hall of Famer, "Superstar" Billy Graham. With a newly chiseled physique, Muraco worked his way into the good graces of the fans and became the first Superstar to be called "The Rock."

The new-look Muraco competed in the main event of the first-ever *Survivor Series* before disappearing from WWE in 1988. In 2004, he returned to the WWE scene to be recognized with induction into the WWE Hall of Fame. Three years later, Muraco was back at the podium to bestow the same honor on his former manager, Mr. Fuji.

DORY DIXON

| HT | 5'9" | WT | 209 lbs. | FROM | Jamaica | SIGNATURE MOVE | Flying Bodyblock |

Dory Dixon spent the early 1950s working as a teacher. He never planned to wrestle, but a chance meeting with Mexican promoter Salvador Lutteroth changed everything.

Lutteroth persuaded Dixon to compete, and in 1955, the former schoolteacher made his professional debut. Dixon spent most of his career in Mexico, where he captured the NWA World Light Heavyweight Championship in February 1958.

In the early 1960s, Dixon travelled to the United States, where he teamed with such partners as Pepper Gomez and Rito Romero. But it was his union with Bobo Brazil that is remembered most.

While in the Northeast, Dixon battled Buddy Rogers to draws on two separate occasions. He also competed on the same 1963 card that saw Bruno Sammartino defeat Rogers for the WWE Championship.

DORY FUNK, JR.

HT	6'2"	WT	240 lbs.
FROM	The Double Cross Ranch		
SIGNATURE MOVE	Spinning Toe Hold		

A second-generation competitor, Dory Funk, Jr. made his professional debut in 1963. His earliest days were spent in his legendary father's promotion in Amarillo, Texas. Funk also plied his trade internationally in Canada and Japan.

Funk permanently etched his name in the record books as one of the all-time greats when he defeated Gene Kiniski to capture the NWA World Heavyweight Championship in February 1969. He went on to hold the Title for more than four years, defeating the likes of Pat O'Connor, Dick the Bruiser, and Jack Brisco. Only Lou Thesz could boast a longer reign.

In 1986, Funk ventured to WWE where he competed as Hoss. While there, he and brother Terry became notorious for branding the logo from their famed Double Cross Ranch into the flesh of their beaten opponents. Perhaps the Funks' biggest WWE match came at *WrestleMania 2* when they teamed up to defeat the Junkyard Dog and Tito Santana.

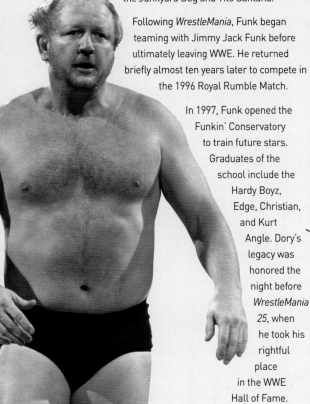

Following *WrestleMania*, Funk began teaming with Jimmy Jack Funk before ultimately leaving WWE. He returned briefly almost ten years later to compete in the 1996 Royal Rumble Match.

In 1997, Funk opened the Funkin' Conservatory to train future stars. Graduates of the school include the Hardy Boyz, Edge, Christian, and Kurt Angle. Dory's legacy was honored the night before *WrestleMania 25*, when he took his rightful place in the WWE Hall of Fame.

DOUG FURNAS AND PHIL LAFON

MEMBERS	Doug Furnas & Phil Lafon	COMBINED WT	484 lbs.

Years before making their WWE debut in 1996, Doug Furnas and Phil Lafon made a name for themselves in Japan and Mexico. While in Japan, the duo captured the AJPW All Asia Tag Team Championship five times. Over the course of their battles, they crossed paths with many names familiar to the WWE Universe, including Dynamite Kid and Johnny Ace (John Laurinaitis). Following Japan, Furnas and Lafon made a brief stop in Mexico, where they captured the UWA World Tag Team Championship twice.

The highly-decorated duo traveled to the United States in 1996. They made a quick stop in ECW before debuting in WWE later in the year. At *Survivor Series 1996*, Furnas and Lafon outlasted British Bulldog, Owen Hart, and the New Rockers to be their team's sole survivors.

Furnas and Lafon spent the early part of 1997 chasing the World Tag Team Championship. When they were unsuccessful in claiming the gold, they moved on to a brief rivalry with the Legion of Doom before leaving WWE in the summer of 1997.

DOUG "GASHOUSE" GILBERT

FROM	Omaha, Nebraska	SIGNATURE MOVE	Top-Rope Backflip

Doug Gilbert was a barrel-chested brute of a man who first made a name for himself in the AWA during the early 1960s. Nicknamed "Gashouse," Gilbert's early AWA days were highlighted by three Midwest Tag Team Championship reigns with partner Reggie Parks. Over the course of their stints with the Gold, Gilbert and Parks mainly clashed with future WWE Hall of Famers Bob Orton Sr. and Mad Dog Vachon.

Gilbert jumped to the NWA in the late 1960s. During this period, it wasn't uncommon to see the cocky competitor sit on his fallen opponent's chest, stroking his mustache while the referee counted to three. Overall, Gilbert staked claim to fourteen regional NWA championships, including three Georgia Heavyweight Title victories (competing as The Professional).

When Gilbert made his way to WWE in the mid-1970s, his best years were already behind him. But that didn't stop him from competing in some thrilling matches against such luminaries as Bobo Brazil and Tony Garea.

DOUG GILBERT

HT	6'0"	WT	240 lbs.	FROM	Lexington, Tennessee
SIGNATURE MOVE	Piledriver				

Following in the footsteps of his father, Tommy, and brother, Eddie, "Dangerous" Doug Gilbert made his professional debut in 1986. Throughout the late 1980s and early 1990s, he competed mainly in the southeast United States and Puerto Rico.

As Gilbert's travels continued, he became increasingly well-versed in the hardcore style, which he would go on to employ in ECW and the USWA. In January 1996, Gilbert won a *Royal Rumble*-style match in Memphis, which earned him the right to compete in WWE's Royal Rumble Match weeks later. Unfortunately for Gilbert, he lasted fewer than three minutes before being eliminated by Vader.

Following the *Royal Rumble*, Gilbert went on to compete in independent promotions all over the globe.

"DR. D" DAVID SHULTZ

| **HT** 6'6" | **WT** 267 lbs. | **FROM** Nashville, Tennessee | **SIGNATURE MOVE** Flying Corkscrew Elbow |

Before launching an all-out assault on WWE, David Schultz was one of the most feared men in sports-entertainment territories across North America. To Dr. D, matches were not contests to determine which opponent was the better man; they were personal wars where everything was on the line and no tactic was off limits.

In 1984, Dr. D prescribed his form of pain on WWE Superstars, while also aligning himself with "Rowdy" Roddy Piper, "Mr. Wonderful" Paul Orndorff, and "Cowboy" Bob Orton. As his reputation for being one of the most dangerous WWE Superstars grew, Shultz was rewarded with an opportunity at Hulk Hogan's WWE Championship.

Unfortunately for Shultz, he was unable to unseat The Hulkster. But the loss only proved to be a minor setback, as he continued to be viewed as an imposing figure that should be feared. One person who learned this the hard way was *20/20* reporter John Stossel, who was victimized by Dr. D's rage in late 1984. Shultz's WWE tenure ended shortly after the incident.

THE DREAM TEAM

| **MEMBERS** | Greg Valentine & Brutus Beefcake |
| **COMBINED WT** | 520 lbs. |

The Dream Team consisted of an established, rugged second-generation Superstar and two-time Intercontinental Champion in Greg "The Hammer" Valentine, and a brash, powerful competitor in Brutus Beefcake whose strength was only second to his vanity.

Managed by "Luscious" Johnny Valiant, the pair were considered Championship contenders after impressive showings against the likes of The Killer Bees, Junkyard Dog and Jimmy "Superfly" Snuka, and Tito Santana and Pedro Morales. As many forecasted, Beefcake and Valentine reached the top of the tag team mountain when they defeated the U.S. Express for the World Tag Team Championship in August 1985 at the Philadelphia Spectrum.

The Dream Team broke every rule in the book to maintain their stranglehold on the Titles. They enjoyed an almost seven-month reign before being upended by The British Bulldogs at *WrestleMania 2*. While they continued to be threats within the tag team division, an associate was soon added in Canadian strongman Dino Bravo. Despite a win at *WrestleMania III* against the Rougeau Brothers, dissention within the Dream Team ranks overflowed and Beefcake became the odd man out. As Bravo became the new member of group, they were appropriately renamed the New Dream Team. Later that night Beefcake officially became a fan favorite when the "Barber" in him came out.

DREW MCINTYRE

| **HT** 6'5" | **WT** 254 lbs. | **FROM** Ayre, Scotland |
| **SIGNATURE MOVE** Future Shock DDT | | |

WWE Chairman Mr. McMahon personally signed Drew McIntyre in September 2009, earning the Scottish Superstar the nickname of "The Chosen One." With this invaluable backing, McIntyre became Intercontinental Champion by the end of the year, defeating John Morrison at *WWE TLC*. As Champion, McIntyre acted as if he ran *SmackDown*, routinely having unfavorable decisions reversed by the Chairman.

After a five-month reign, McIntyre earned tag team gold with Cody Rhodes. When this short-lived alliance disolved, McIntyre struggled, prompting *SmackDown* GM Teddy Long to dismiss him. At *WrestleMania XXVIII*, he helped John Laurinaitis oust Long from power, a satisfying revenge.

Later in 2012, McIntyre teamed up with Jinder Mahal and Heath Slater to form 3MB. With attire seemingly stolen from Axl Rose's closet, the new formed "band" rocked WWE rings with spirited air guitar riffs. With 3MB's backing, McIntyre maintained a showmanlike stage presence until his departure from WWE in June of 2014.

DROZ

| **HT** 6'4" | **WT** 270 lbs. | **FROM** Mays Landing, New Jersey |
| **SIGNATURE MOVE** New Jersey Naptime | | |

Darren Drozdov was one of the top NCAA football players of the early 1990s. After graduation, he played for the NFL's Denver Broncos before training for a career in the ring. His earliest days saw him compete in ECW, before ultimately debuting in WWE in 1998.

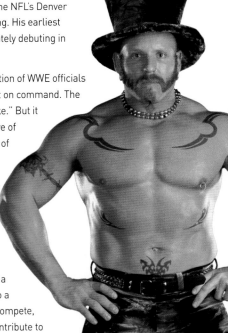

Upon arriving in WWE, Droz caught the attention of WWE officials and fans when it was revealed he could vomit on command. The peculiar trick earned him the nickname "Puke." But it was Droz's in-ring abilities that caught the eye of the WWE Superstars, particularly the Legion of Doom, who welcomed the young competitor into their legendary fold in the spring of 1998.

When the LOD went their separate ways in 1999, Droz formed an alliance with fellow pierced Superstar, Albert. Tragically, before this latest phase of his career could gain momentum, Droz suffered a career-ending injury that has confined him to a wheelchair. Despite no longer being able to compete, the eternally-optimistic Droz continued to contribute to WWE through his commentaries on *WWE.com* and in print.

THE DUDLEY BOYZ

MEMBERS	D-Von & Bubba Ray
COMBINED WT	565 lbs.

Few teams revolutionized tag team competition more than The Dudley Boyz, and none have achieved more success. In fact, D-Von and Bubba Ray are the only tandem in sports-entertainment history to capture the ECW, WCW, and WWE World Tag Team Titles.

The brutish half-brothers first made a name for themselves competing in ECW during the late 1990s. While there, they earned a reputation as hardcore powerhouses, as well as a record eight reigns with the promotion's tag team Titles. That's twice as many reigns as the next closest team, The Public Enemy, who had four runs with the gold.

THE DUDLEYS COME TO WWE

In 1999, The Dudleys took their success to WWE where they gained instant national recognition. Within months of their arrival, D-Von and Bubba Ray defeated the legendary New Age Outlaws at *No Way Out* to claim their first of a record eight World Tag Team Championship reigns. Subsequent tag team Championship runs came at the expense of such great tag teams as Edge and Christian, the Hardy Boyz, and the Brothers of Destruction.

In addition to being WWE's most decorated pairing, D-Von and Bubba Ray Dudley painfully introduced a new brand of hardcore competition to WWE's tag team division. The Dudleys' penchant for driving opponents through wooden tables via the Dudley Death Drop paved the way for several groundbreaking matches. At the 2000 *Royal Rumble*, D-Von and Bubba Ray battled the Hardy Boyz in the first-ever Tag Team Tables Match. The Dudleys fell to the brothers from North Carolina, but the match was successful in raising the stakes for even more dangerous encounters. Later that year, Bubba Ray and D-Von took part in the first-ever Tables, Ladders and Chairs Match against Edge and Christian and the Hardy Boyz at *SummerSlam*. The same three teams battled in an epic TLC encore at *WrestleMania X-Seven*. Both matches, which were won by Edge and Christian, helped revitalize the tag team division as some of the most exciting competition of its era.

D-Von and Bubba Ray added to their already-historic resume when they defeated Matt and Jeff Hardy for the WCW Tag Team Championship in October 2001. With the victory, The Dudley Boyz permanently stamped their names alongside The Minnesota Wrecking Crew, The Fabulous Freebirds, The Rock 'n' Roll Express, and all the other the great tandems of Jim Crocket Promotions, a territory known for tag team competition. D-Von and Bubba Ray would later unify the WCW and WWE World Tag Team Championships when they defeated the Hardy Boyz again at *Survivor Series*.

The unthinkable occurred in 2002 when the WWE Draft separated D-Von and Bubba Ray. On their own, the half-brothers struggled to replicate the success they gained as a team. Luckily, their solo efforts only lasted eight months before the duo shockingly reunited at *Survivor Series*.

Together again, The Dudleys picked up right where they left off, dominating the tag team scene. In June 2004, D-Von and Bubba Ray defeated Charlie Haas and Rico on *SmackDown* to claim their first WWE Tag Team Championship. They held the Titles for three weeks before being dethroned by Billy Kidman and Paul London.

THE BOYZ ARE BACK

The Dudleys' WWE careers seemingly ended forever when they left the promotion in 2005. But a decade later, Bubba Ray made a shocking return at the 2015 *Royal Rumble*. The appearance fueled the imaginations of fans, who wondered if D-Von couldn't be far behind. He wasn't.

In August 2015, D-Von and Bubba Ray made their collective WWE return and immediately targeted The New Day. Over the next several months, the hardcore duo taught the arrogant threesome what being true tag team legends is all about, particularly Xavier Woods, who found himself driven through a table on numerous occasions.

Nearly two decades after their WWE debut, The Dudleys continue to prove their excellence in the ring. And when they finally decide to return to Dudleyville, D-Von and Bubba Ray will undoubtedly leave behind a legacy second to none.

D-VON! GET THE TABLES!

DUKE "THE DUMPSTER" DROESE

HT 6'6" **WT** 305 lbs. **FROM** Mount Trashmore, Florida

When it comes to taking out the trash, few Superstars did it with as much enthusiasm as Duke "The Dumpster" Droese. Originally a sanitation engineer, Droese made the transition from garbage route to squared circle with one goal in mind: ridding WWE of its trash.

According to Droese, the Superstar with the most stink on him was Hunter Hearst-Helmsley, and it was against Helmsley that Droese picked up the biggest victory of his career. With the coveted No. 30 spot in the 1996 Royal Rumble Match on the line, Droese defeated the Greenwich blue blood via reverse decision.

Unfortunately for Droese, Helmsley went on to have one of the greatest careers of all time, while the sanitation engineer soon found himself back on his garbage route. Droese did, however, manage to make a brief but memorable return to the ring in 2001 when he competed in *WrestleMania X-Seven*'s Gimmick Battle Royal, which was ultimately won by former WWE Champion, Iron Sheik.

DYNAMITE KID

  HT 5'9" **WT** 225 lbs. **FROM** Manchester, England
SIGNATURE MOVE Flying Headbutt

Faster than lighting and as technically sound as anybody to ever lace a pair of boots, Dynamite Kid is among the most emulated Superstars of all time. In the decades since his debut, Kid's influence can be found in the work of countless greats, including Bret Hart and Chris Jericho.

After dominating Europe, Canada, and Japan, Dynamite Kid became a top contender for the WWE Junior Heavyweight Championship in the mid-1980s. He eventually captured the Title when he defeated The Cobra in a tournament finals match in February 1984.

Later that same year, Dynamite Kid joined Davey Boy Smith to form the British Bulldogs. Managed by Capt. Lou Albano, the duo claimed the World Tag Team Championship from The Dream Team at *WrestleMania 2*. After losing the Titles to the Hart Foundation, the Bulldogs left WWE in November 1988.

Dynamite Kid retired from active competition in 1991. He will forever be remembered as possibly the greatest pound-for-pound Superstar of all-time.

DUSTY RHODES

see page 99

DUSTY WOLFE

HT 5'11" **WT** 215 lbs. **FROM** San Antonio, Texas
SIGNATURE MOVE Spinning Toe Hold

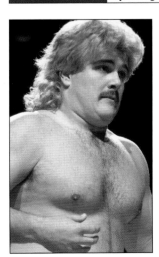

Dusty Wolfe started his career in his hometown of San Antonio. In 1984, he decided it was time to travel to territories in Kansas City, Memphis, Florida, and the Von Erich's World Class region. From there, Wolfe went to Puerto Rico and Hawaii, becoming skilled in various ring styles.

Dusty Wolfe debuted in WWE in 1987 and quickly became a staple on its televised programs. He traded blows with the likes of Jake "The Snake" Roberts, "Ravishing" Rick Rude, "Hacksaw" Jim Duggan, The Blue Blazer, and Junkyard Dog. In 1993, Wolfe departed WWE and traveled to South Africa, Japan, and WCW. When asked to summarize his career, Wolfe was once quoted as saying, "Getting in the ring was a privilege."

EARL MAYNARD

HT 5'11" **WT** 240 lbs. **FROM** Barbados
SIGNATURE MOVE Headbutt

As a boy growing up in Barbados, Earl Maynard had visions of greatness. Already a top bodybuilder and member of the British Air Force, he competed as a means of staying in peak physical condition.

For two decades, Maynard pulled double-duty as a competitor in both sports-entertainment and bodybuilding. While in WWE, he collided with the likes of future WWE Hall of Famers Baron Mikel Scicluna, Johnny Rodz, and Gorilla Monsoon.

In 1968, Maynard added another element to his already versatile persona when he made his silver screen debut in the feature film *Melinda*. He continued to appear in movies for many years, and went on to become an accomplished producer and director.

DUSTY RHODES
THE AMERICAN DREAM

HT	6'2"
WT	275 lbs.
FROM	Austin, Texas

SIGNATURE MOVE
Bionic Elbow

Born the son of a plumber, Dusty Rhodes captured the essence of "the everyman" perhaps better than any other Superstar in history. Behind his blue-collar work ethic and undeniable charisma, "The American Dream" became one of the biggest stars of his era. And when his in-ring days concluded, Rhodes's influence on the industry intensified, as he became recognized as one of the most respected mentors to the stars of tomorrow.

WWE fans were forced to stand up and take notice of Rhodes in September 1977 when "The American Dream" waged war on then-WWE Champion "Superstar" Billy Graham. Selling out Madison Square Garden on multiple occasions, Rhodes and Graham competed in a series of historic encounters, culminating in a Texas Bullrope Match that "The American Dream" won in August 1978.

HARD TIMES

Following his victory over Graham, Rhodes went on to achieve great success in Florida and the Carolinas, capturing the NWA World Heavyweight Championship on three separate occasions, twice from Harley Race and once from Ric Flair. During his rivalry with Flair, Rhodes gave what is now recognized as one of the greatest interviews sports-entertainment has ever seen. Known as the "Hard Times" interview, Rhodes used his uncanny ability to connect with the viewer by putting his hand to the camera and telling them that his hand was touching theirs and saying that they've all experienced hard times together. Years later, The Rock would pay homage to "The American Dream" by delivering his own version of Rhodes's "Hard Times" interview at the 2013 *Royal Rumble*.

While in the Carolinas, in addition to cementing his legacy as one of sports-entertainment's best in-ring competitors, Rhodes also established himself as a powerful figure behind the scenes. As an executive in Jim Crockett Promotions, Rhodes was credited with being a major influence on many revolutionary ideas, including *Starrcade* and *The Great American Bash*.

I HAVE WINED AND DINED WITH KINGS AND QUEENS AND I'VE SLEPT IN ALLEYS AND DINED ON PORK N' BEANS

Rhodes returned to WWE in 1990 as the polka-dot wearing common man that arenas loved to cheer. With his valet, Sapphire, by his side, Rhodes's popularity reached amazing heights, as he engaged in bitter rivalries with the likes of the Big Boss Man, "Million Dollar Man" Ted DiBiase, and "Macho King" Randy Savage, who famously teamed with Queen Sherri in a losing effort against Rhodes and Sapphire at *WrestleMania VI*.

Following his stay in WWE, Rhodes returned to WCW in the early 1990s, working mainly as an announcer. Though he spent most of his time behind the microphone, Rhodes did manage to step into the ring from time to time, most notably when he teamed with his son, Dustin, to defeat Terry Funk and Bunkhouse Buck at *Clash of the Champions* in August 1994. Rhodes also joined the New World Order after turning on Larry Zbyszko at *Souled Out* in January 1998.

A LEGEND RECOGNIZED

Rhodes's years of excellence were recognized when his sons, Dustin and Cody, inducted him into the WWE Hall of Fame in 2007. In the years that followed, Rhodes would serve as the inductor for many names from his past, including Eddie Graham, the Funks, and the Four Horsemen.

Most recently, Rhodes worked behind the scenes in WWE's developmental system, NXT. While there, he not only became a mentor to the next generation of WWE Superstars, but also a respected father figure and beloved friend. Sadly, the sports-entertainment world lost one of its greatest legends when Rhodes passed away in June 2015 at the age of 69.

Though gone, Dusty Rhodes will never be forgotten. And to ensure his memory will live on forever, NXT has created the Dusty Rhodes Tag Team Classic. After winning the inaugural tournament in October 2015, Finn Bálor and Samoa Joe were presented with a giant trophy by members of Rhodes's family during an emotional ceremony. And as the capacity crowd chanted his name, it became even more evident that Dusty Rhodes undoubtedly lived life at the end of a lightning bolt.

EARTHQUAKE

HT	6'7"	WT	468 lbs.	FROM	Vancouver, British Columbia, Canada
SIGNATURE MOVE	Earthquake Splash				

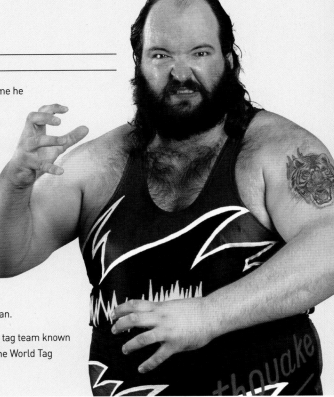

With more than 450 pounds tacked to his enormous frame, Earthquake made arenas shake and Superstars tremble every time he walked the aisle. Behind the threat of his ring-rattling Earthquake Splash finisher, the massive Superstar was a perennial contender for every WWE Title.

Disguised as a fan, Earthquake made his WWE debut in November 1989 when Jimmy Hart pulled him out of the audience to sit on Ultimate Warrior's back as the Superstar attempted pushups. Once in the ring, Earthquake revealed his allegiance to Hart by squashing the unexpected Warrior like a grape. From that point on, the oversized Superstar proved himself as one of WWE's most dangerous competitors. His assaults were so severe, in fact, that many of his opponents were forced to leave the ring on a stretcher.

Earthquake quickly reached main event status after attacking Hulk Hogan on an edition of *The Brother Love Show*. The assault left The Hulkster's ribs severely injured and made Earthquake the target of the fans' hatred worldwide. Their rivalry culminated at *SummerSlam 1990* where Hogan earned a countout victory over the big man.

The following year, Earthquake teamed with Typhoon to form the colossal tag team known as the Natural Disasters. Together, they defeated Money, Inc. to capture the World Tag Team Championship in July 1992.

THE EAST-WEST CONNECTION

MEMBERS	Adrian Adonis & Jesse "The Body" Ventura	COMBINED WT	580 lbs.

This team first formed in the late 1970s in the AWA. Noticed by manager "Classy" Freddie Blassie, Adonis and Ventura were brought to WWE in 1981. With Blassie in their corner, they became prime-time players in WWE, both as contenders for WWE Tag Team gold and individual singles competitors.

A combination of injuries and different goals led to The East-West Connection's separation, though they remained close allies. Ventura went on to become one of the great color commentators and a 2004 WWE Hall of Famer. Adonis transformed into one of WWE's most versatile and gifted performers. The legendary East-West Connection should always be included in a discussion of influential tag teams. Whether fans approved of their practices or not, no one ever denied their contributions.

ECW

see page 102

ECW ZOMBIE

When ECW re-launched in 2006, longtime fans of the extreme brand eagerly tuned into Syfy hoping to see the in-your-face style to which they had become accustomed. Instead, they got The Zombie.

Unlike anything ever seen in ECW, The Zombie slowly marched to the ring, while commentator Tazz asked if the unusual competitor's presence was a rib. Once in the ring, The Zombie unintelligibly groaned into the microphone.

"I can assure everyone watching the world premiere of *ECW on Syfy* The Zombie is not an offering of ECW," said a seemingly embarrassed Joey Styles. Luckily, the embarrassment didn't last long, as The Sandman quickly made his way to the ring and mercilessly caned The Zombie.

That was the last anybody ever saw of The Zombie.

EDDIE GILBERT

HT	5'10"	WT	222 lbs.	FROM	Lexington, Kentucky
SIGNATURE MOVE	Hot Shot				

Proudly nicknamed "Hot Stuff," Eddie Gilbert certainly had a high opinion of his in-ring abilities. Coming from the popular Gilbert wrestling family, he had every right to be a little cocky. Growing up, Eddie and brother Doug learned the business firsthand from their father, Tennessee wrestling great Tommy Gilbert.

Despite being remembered as one of the South's greatest competitors, Gilbert's brief WWE career never really took off. He gained some notoriety as a protégé to WWE Champion Bob Backlund. The relationship, however, was short-lived and Gilbert soon returned to the South.

Gilbert owns the distinction of being involved in the first-ever NWA pay-per-view match. Teaming with Larry Zbyszko and Rick Steiner, he battled Sting, Michael Hayes, and Jimmy Garvin at *Starrcade 1987*. Over the next several years, Gilbert gained the reputation of coming up big when it counted, including several times against Jerry "The King" Lawler when the United States Wrestling Association Unified World Heavyweight Championship was on the line.

EDDIE GRAHAM

HT	5'11"	WT	215 lbs.
FROM	Tampa, Florida		

WWE's national spotlight never shined on Eddie Graham. But that doesn't mean he wasn't one of the most influential personalities of his time. Over the course of his thirty-year career, Graham became known as a skilled competitor and brilliant promoter.

Early in his career, Graham teamed with his brother, Jerry, to capture the United States Tag Team Championship four times while competing in Vincent J. McMahon's Capitol Wrestling. The success led to great notoriety in the Northeast, but it wasn't until he moved to Florida in 1960 that Graham really began to come into his own.

By 1968, Graham had become a legend in Florida, but when a locker room window fell on his head, he was unfortunately sidelined for fifteen months. Unable to compete, Graham still managed to make waves when he took over responsibilities of Championship Wrestling from Florida. As a promoter, Graham built an impressive roster, which included such legends as Dusty Rhodes, Dory Funk Jr., and Bruiser Brody.

Graham's power continued to grow in 1976 when he was elected NWA president. While in office, he helped create the first-ever World Title unification match, which pit NWA Champion Harley Race against WWE Champion "Superstar" Billy Graham. Health reasons forced Graham to step down from his post in 1978, officially marking the end of one of the industry's most influential careers. In 2008, Graham's excellence was recognized with induction into the WWE Hall of Fame.

EDDIE GUERRERO
see page 106

EDGE
see page 108

EDEN

HT	5'5"	FROM	Canton, Michigan

With her seductive eyes, gorgeous smile, and curvaceous frame, Eden's beauty is undeniable. The WWE announcer turns heads everywhere she goes.

Naturally, Eden's pre-WWE days were spent modeling, where she became the focus of countless cameras, including those of *Maxim* magazine. She also competed in many pageants, such as the popular Hawaiian Tropic competition. But being a lifelong athlete, Eden was naturally drawn to the competition found in WWE. And in 2011, the Michigan native took her first step toward WWE superstardom when she began training at the former developmental system Florida Championship Wrestling.

After only a few months honing her skills, Eden was called up to the big stage when she debuted as the ring announcer for *WWE Superstars*. Her run on the globally-televised program was brief, however, as Eden soon embarked on a two-year hiatus from the sports-entertainment world.

Upon returning to WWE, Eden resumed her ring announcing responsibilities on such shows as *NXT*, *SmackDown*, and *Raw* until she parted ways with WWE in May 2016.

EDGE AND CHRISTIAN
see page 110

ÉDOUARD CARPENTIER

HT	5'10"	WT	228 lbs.	FROM	Montreal, Quebec, Canada
SIGNATURE MOVE	Flying Head Scissors				

More recent fans recognize Édouard Carpentier as the former host of WWE's French programming during the 1980s. But it was his awe-inspiring arsenal of high-flying ring action that endeared him to sports-entertainment fans decades prior.

Dubbed "The Flying Frenchman," Carpentier's aerial assault left opponents' heads spinning. His acrobatic style eventually led him to a reign as National Wrestling Alliance World Heavyweight Champion. He gained the accolade by defeating the legendary Lou Thesz in June 1957; but his reign was marred by controversy when the NWA governing body later failed to recognize the victory after Carpentier's manager left the promotion. The incident will forever be remembered as one of the most controversial moments in NWA history.

In the northeast, Carpentier formed a successful pairing with future WWE Hall of Famer Bobo Brazil. Together, the duo headlined the famed Madison Square Garden on several occasions.

With more than twenty Championships to his credit, Carpentier retired in the early 1980s. He will be remembered for his innovative offense, which employed a healthy dose of somersaults and cartwheels.

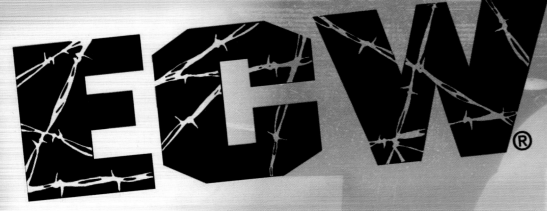

ECW®

From a converted bingo hall in industrial South Philadelphia, Extreme Championship Wrestling (ECW) challenged societal and sports-entertainment standards. Between 1992 and 2001, ECW confronted everything that came before—until the very promotions they defied began to tolerate the group's exuberant lawlessness, and then adopted it as their own.

Paul Heyman, the man most closely associated with ECW never ceased praising the virtues of the promotion to which he dedicated his life. "ECW was a lifestyle," he proclaimed during a 2005 altercation with former WCW head Eric Bischoff on *Raw*. "It was anti-establishment. It was counterculture. It was up and in your face."

And years after the final ECW match was fought, its fans remain as devoted to its memory, and its influence on the rest of the industry, as its former owner. They view the ECW Arena—a onetime freight warehouse and bingo hall wedged below a highway—as a shrine, expressing a fervor about the ECW era that can only be categorized as religious.

Rules, cultivated in the bygone days of William Muldoon, the Civil War veteran and Greco Roman champion who once battled a man for seven straight hours, were all but disregarded. The sole purpose of referees appeared to be separating the competitors from the ropes, counting pinfalls, and acknowledging submissions. The Texas Death and "Lights Out" matches from the recent past seemed quaint compared to ECW's offerings: Barbed Wire brawls, Flaming Tables matches, Singapore Cane clashes, and other vicious confrontations. Fans brought pots and pans, stop signs, and cheese graters for their favorite brawlers to wield as weapons.

Yet, ECW also boasted some of the most exhilarating technical matches of its time. Combatants considered too small or too rooted in wrestling's fundamentals to thrive elsewhere found a welcome home at the ECW Arena. In addition to featuring some of the best scientific artisans in North America, the promotion exposed its audiences to styles previously confined to Latin America and the Far East.

Originally called Eastern Championship Wrestling, the company was started in 1992 by pawnbroker and jewelry store owner Tod Gordon. The first show took place in front of 100 fans. In the main event, future WWE competitor Stevie Richards battled to a 20-minute draw with an opponent named Jimmy Janetty. Among the early names seen on Gordon's cards were a number of former WWE Superstars: Jim "The Anvil" Neidhart, "The Magnificent" Don Muraco, and the first ECW Champion, Jimmy "Superfly" Snuka.

Gordon knew that ECW would only succeed if he had somebody with an astute wrestling mind beside him. He believed that he found that person in "Hot Stuff" Eddie Gilbert, who was known as much for his creativity as his abilities between the ropes. Gilbert fancied himself as an outsider, and hired the ultimate agitator, Paul Heyman, as an assistant.

That's when everything changed.

Since age 13, Heyman had been talking himself into WWE events at New York's Madison Square Garden, where he photographed the Superstars for various magazines. Eventually, he turned his talents to announcing for a number of promotions, including WCW. Around the business, he had a reputation as a mad genius.

He began scanning the independent circuit for talent, drawing attention to ECW when he signed Sabu, aka the "homicidal, suicidal, genocidal man," whose specialties included ramming people through tables and bashing them with barbed-wire-covered baseball bats. Heyman also merged Rocco Rock and Johnny Grunge, creating the enduring tag team Public Enemy.

Eddie Gilbert's tenure in ECW was short, and soon Heyman was the main creative force. Although he'd been a WWE fan his entire life, Heyman was proud that ECW was nothing like the "big two" promotions at the time, WWE and WCW. Whenever a WWE veteran attempted to compete at the ECW Arena, he was generally matched up against six-foot-eight-inch 911, and Chokeslammed into the canvas.

At one point in 1994, WCW and ECW attempted a co-promotion. Long before he was the loveable character who dressed as Santa Claus, Mick Foley, then known as Cactus Jack, was more hardcore than anyone in sports-entertainment. To prove his credentials, Foley, the WCW Tag Team Co-Titlist with Kevin Sullivan at the time, delighted the ECW crowd by spitting on the Championship.

If Foley had a hardcore mentor, it was Terry Funk. The former NWA Champion was in his fifties when he became a staple in ECW, and set the bar for unbridled combat, elevating adversaries like Sabu, Tommy Dreamer, and the Sandman.

On August 13, 1994, Funk and Cactus Jack had just finished battling Public Enemy when Terry asked a fan to toss him a chair. Feeling inspired, he dared the audience to throw him some more. In the carnage that followed, chairs were hurled into the ring from every direction, piling up on the mat and knocking out the Texan. But Terry wasn't angry. He was proud of doing his part to establish ECW's renegade status.

And it was about to get wilder.

Although the storied NWA Championship had largely lost its allure with the emergence of WCW, the organization attempted to revive itself with a tournament, comprised of representatives from a number of smaller promotions, to crown a new Titlist. On August 27, 1994, Shane Douglas—known as "The Franchise" in ECW, and notorious for brutally honest on-camera rants—ended up in the finals against the gifted 2 Cold Scorpio. When Douglas emerged victorious, he shocked attendees by throwing down the NWA Title, proclaiming the ECW version the only real championship.

"I am not the man who accepts the torch to be handed down to me from an organization that died," he said after listing a number of great NWA Champions, then announcing that they could kiss his derriere.

From that point forward, Eastern Championship Wrestling would be known as Extreme Championship Wrestling. And it always lived up to its name. Outside events had their impact on ECW.

After an American teenager convicted of vandalism in Singapore was sentenced to be lashed with a cane,

Sandman began carrying the weapon to the ring. Up until this point, his rival, Tommy Dreamer, was seen as a little too "nice" for ECW.

But when Sandman repeatedly battered him in an "I Quit" match, the lacerated grappler refused to give up, instead demanding, "Please, sir, may I have another?" In that instant, Dreamer became the new face of extreme.

The news was transmitted by phone, newsletter, and the new medium called the Internet. Soon, visitors began coming to the ECW Arena from as far away as Japan. But a sizeable number of attendees were there for every show, boldly chanting the organization's letters, "He's Hardcore" and "We Want Blood," along with numerous unprintable slogans.

Some of the emerging stars had been fans a few short years earlier. Like Dreamer, Mikey Whipwreck appeared no different than a guy in the crowd, except he was capable of weathering enormous amounts of abuse. In one confrontation, he and Cactus Jack won the ECW Tag Team Championship from Public Enemy after Rocco Rock tripped over Whipwreck, who happened to be unconscious.

The chaos was complemented by the thrilling clinics performed by world class athletes like Dean Malenko, Eddie Guerrero, Chis Benoit, Rey Mysterio, Juventud Guerrera and Psicosis. As a result, fans developed eclectic tastes, screaming during a table-splitting brawl, and then respectfully applauding the two next competitors for a sequence of chain wrestling that could have occurred in an NCAA tournament.

By 1995, Paul Heyman and ECW were considered one and the same. Therefore, it surprised no one when Heyman purchased the company. Although Tod Gordon remained as a commissioner for a period of time, all of the promotion's triumphs and follies from this point forward can be directly attributed to Heyman.

After Steve Austin was fired from WCW while injured, Heyman brought him into ECW and turned him loose on the microphone. Fans who'd known "Stunning" Steve Austin as a blond hunk were not prepared for his anger

or his wit, as he parodied Hulk Hogan, Eric Bischoff, and others. Austin's microphone skills forced WWE to take notice, and served as the genesis of the character that became Stone Cold.

Similarly, the competitor initially called The Tazmaniac was viewed as a powerhouse in the ring, but an inexperienced talker. In ECW, he shorted his name to Taz (he'd add an extra "z" in WWE) and channeled his intensity into his interviews, a quality that later enabled the "Human Suplex Machine" to become one of WWE's most respected announcers.

As WCW planned to create its own Monday night show, *Nitro*, to contest the dominance of *Raw*, the Atlanta-based promotion decided to complement its roster with agile cruiserweights, and began cherry picking some of the brightest talents in ECW. On the night before their departure, Dean Malenko and Eddie Guerrero demonstrated their appreciation to fans by putting on a thrilling Two-out-of-Three Falls Match incorporating Mexican, Japanese, and other moves rarely seen in the United States. Generally, when one of the "big two" promotions snagged ECW stars, devotees chanted, "You sold out!" On this night, they yelled, "Please don't go!"

Heyman's goal was to fill every void with someone just as exceptional, so fans never felt like ECW was declining. In came the Dudley Boyz (D-Von Dudley was the first graduate of ECW's House of Hardcore training school), Rob Van Dam, Chris Jericho, the Eliminators (Perry Saturn and John Kronus), the Gangstas, and the Blue World Order, or bWo. A knockoff of the nWo. in WCW, bWo centered around the eminently entertaining Blue Meanie, Stevie Richards, and Nova.

And the raids went in the other direction, as well. Sabu returned from WCW. Shane Douglas, who'd been floundering in WWE as Dean Douglas, became "The Franchise" again. Longtime WCW manager Missy Hyatt stirred up passions on and off camera.

The quality of the on-camera intrigue never faltered. Peaches, the Sandman's former wife, became a follower of Raven's cult—along with the Hardcore Icon's ten-year-old son, Tyler. On one occasion, Sandman attempted to spank his child, but Raven intercepted. As Sandman lay beaten on the ground, Tyler stood over him, arms raised in Raven's signature pose.

For two years, Raven and Dreamer fought voraciously, continuing hostilities that apparently emerged when the two attended the same summer camp as teenagers. In 1997, the rivalry ended with a "Loser Leaves ECW" contest. Dreamer won; he'd be the only competitor to remain in the "Land of Extreme" from its beginning to end. Raven went to WCW, where he quickly snared the United States Championship.

By this point, both WWE and WCW were being influenced by ECW. Many enthusiasts claim that WWE's "Attitude Era" was instigated by what transpired at the ECW Arena, as well as its satellite facility, Lost Batallion Hall in Queens, New York, and other venues where the excitement had spread. Nonetheless, the Monday Night Wars had a debilitating impact on ECW, with the larger groups constantly helping themselves to the rebel organization's stars. Still, ECW fought back, bringing in names like former WWE Superstar Bam Bam Bigelow, Ballz Mahoney, aka "the guy who gets powerbombed through flaming tables," Tazz's cousin, Chris Chetti, Lance Storm, Angelica (the future Lita in WWE), and Justin Credible.

Al Snow appeared with "Head" a mannequin cranium that seemed to send him deranged messages.

The unthinkable occurred when Paul Heyman and several ECW standouts raided a broadcast of *Raw*, electrifying fans of both groups. The highlight was Sabu leaping off the towering letters spelling out *Raw*.

By Heyman's own admission, he was a terrible businessman, and had difficulties keeping ECW afloat. In 1999, the company appeared to receive a lifeline when TNN, the cable network later known as Spike, began broadcasting ECW. More stars continued to shine, including Rhyno and Steve Corino, who tangled with the immortal Dusty Rhodes.

The relationship with WWE deepened. When ECW Champion Mike Awesome signed with WCW, he made one last Title defense and was defeated by Tazz, who was then in WWE. One week later, the new ECW Champion battled Triple H, the WWE Champion, on *Smackdown*.

Despite all this, TNN executives were uncomfortable with the havoc common on ECW's programs, and frustrated that the promotion wasn't drawing WWE-caliber ratings. In 2000, the show was cancelled.

The next year, after its final pay-per-view, *Guilty as Charged,* the company declared bankruptcy. By then, though, Paul Heyman had appeared as an announcer on *Raw*, and was plotting an ECW revival.

ECW IN WWE

ECW was the promotion that refused to die. After it officially folded in 2001, it was revived by WWE in 2006, blending its old stars with new ones for the next four years.

Months after ECW's last officially-sanctioned match in 2001, its owner, Paul Heyman made a startling announcement. He was affiliating himself with Shane and Stephanie McMahon to wrest power away from their father, Vince, and WWE. And he would do it under the ECW banner.

The declaration occurred during a pivotal period in sports-entertainment. The same year that ECW closed, WWE purchased its chief rival, WCW. The insurrection threatened WWE's position as the most dominant promotion in the world.

Raven, Lance Storm, the Dudley Boyz, Rob Van Dam, and Tazz were among the former ECW stars who participated in Heyman's scheme, alongside several ex-WCW standouts. Although WWE eventually prevailed, it was clear that fans craved anything associated with ECW.

ECW merchandise continued to sell briskly. In 2004, WWE produced a DVD set called *The Rise and Fall of ECW,* featuring a three-hour documentary, along with the promotion's most titillating matches. While producers viewed the project as a post-mortem, fans refused to accept that ECW was part of the past.

The roster also included the runt of the Dudley litter, Spike, a remarkable performer who could be tossed long distances into the crowd, surface unscathed, and storm the ring again.

So in 2005, WWE, after purchasing ECW's assets two years earlier, acquiesced to popular demand, presenting the *One Night Stand* pay-per-view, a rambunctious ECW reunion. With ECW announcer Joey Styles shouting his familiar, "Oh my God," fans were transported into the past, watching Mexican gladiator Super Crazy perform a moonsault from the balcony, Sabu propel himself over the ropes from a folding chair onto Rhyno, and Tommy Dreamer and his valet, Beula McGillicutty, deliver dual DDTs to Bubba and D-Von Dudley.

It was supposed to be ECW's epilogue. But the fans *still* wanted more.

In 2006, WWE added ECW as a brand, complete with its own television program on Syfy. Heyman, now acting as ECW's official representative, was given options on one draft pick apiece from *Raw* and *SmackDown*, and selected Rob Van Dam and Kurt Angle respectively.

The first telecast of the ECW relaunch was a pay-per-view, the second *One Night Stand*. Van Dam represented ECW in the main event against WWE Champion John Cena, winning with a Five-Star Frog Splash after accomplice Edge speared the Titlist through a table. Two referees were also knocked out in the fracas. It was Heyman who rushed down the aisle and counted the pinfall himself.

The next night on *Raw*, Heyman stated that, since the clash had been fought under very lenient ECW rules, Van Dam's win allowed him to claim the newly-instated ECW Championship.

As time went on, ECW matches frequently fell under standard WWE guidelines, allowing referees to disqualify or count out a competitor. But many other contests were determined by unrestrained "Extreme Rules."

Male performers were classified as "Extremists" rather than "Superstars," while females were called "Vixens" instead of "Divas." However, matches took place in larger buildings, in contrast to the small venues of the prior era.

Heyman also did not remain with this incarnation the entire time. Armando Estrada, Theodore Long, and Tiffany were all ECW General Managers.

At *WrestleMania 23* in 2007, a team called the ECW Originals—Van Dam, Dreamer, The Sandman, and Sabu—won an eight-man tag contest in front of 80,000 spectators, bringing a slice of the tattered ECW Arena to the world's largest stage.

The next year, at *WrestleMania XXIV*, another historic moment occurred when Kane captured the ECW Championship from Chavo Guerrero in eight seconds, the shortest match in *WrestleMania* history.

A far more compelling victory occurred in 2009 at the *Extreme Rules* pay-per-view. This was not an official ECW event—the only pay-per-view ever presented by WWE's ECW brand, *December to Dismember*, occurred in 2006—but the renegade organization fostered the concept.

In a Triple Threat Match, Dreamer outlasted Christian and Jack Swagger to capture the ECW Title, becoming the only Superstar to hold the gold in both the original and WWE versions of the promotion.

Soon, though, it would all end for good.

In the final ECW program on Syfy in 2010, Ezekiel Jackson, spurred on by his mentor, William Regal, became the last ECW Titleholder by smashing the reigning Champion, Christian, through a table.

Although CM Punk never won the brand's Title, many argue that, as with Steve Austin so many years before him, his time in ECW enabled him to harness his skills and directed him toward WWE glory later on.

The brand also became a showplace for talent emerging from WWE's developmental ranks. In fact, the ECW program on Syfy was replaced with *WWE NXT*, providing a critical link between the Superstars of the future and the fabled Land of Extreme.

EDDIE GUERRERO

HT	5'8"
WT	220 lbs.
FROM	El Paso, Texas

SIGNATURE MOVE
Frog Splash, Lasso from
El Paso, Three Amigos

The story of Eddie Guerrero is one of inspiration and heartbreak. After personal demons cost the second-generation Superstar his career and family, he dedicated himself to becoming clean and returning to society. The inspirational Guerrero eventually defeated his demons and returned to greatness. Tragically, however, Eddie Guerrero was taken from this world shortly after clawing his way back to the top of sports-entertainment.

SECOND GENERATION SUPERSTAR

As the son of influential Mexican wrestler Gory Guerrero, Eddie grew up in and around the business. From an early age, it was clear his passion was sports-entertainment. He spent most of his time in the family's wrestling ring, which was situated in the backyard. Before his fifth birthday, he was already delivering dropkicks to his older brothers.

Guerrero started his career in Mexico and Japan. It wasn't until he began working for Extreme Championship Wrestling in 1995 that he gained any true exposure in the United States. While in ECW, Guerrero captured the Television Championship twice and produced classic matches against Dean Malenko that caught the eye of WCW officials.

After joining WCW, Guerrero won the United States Championship, then became an instant fixture in the promotion's lauded cruiserweight division. Fighting from the shadows of their larger contemporaries, Guerrero, Malenko, Chris Jericho, and several others provided jaw-dropping displays of athleticism. It was here that Eddie's now-famous rivalry with close friend Rey Mysterio took root. He and the masked Superstar traded the WCW Cruiserweight Championship in an epic trilogy of matches at *Halloween Havoc 1998*, an episode of *Nitro*, and *World War 3*.

While things were going great for Guerrero inside the ring, his personal life was in severe jeopardy. In 1999, an impaired Guerrero nearly killed himself in a violent car wreck. Fortunately, Guerrero lived, but he failed to address the demons that were invading his life. In 2000, Guerrero moved to WWE where he gained instant notoriety as Chyna's fun-loving boyfriend. Affectionately referred to as "Latino Heat," Guerrero won the European and Intercontinental Championships within his first year with the company. However, Guerrero's in-ring success couldn't help fend off his personal demons. Addiction again caught up with him. This time, it cost him his wife and his job. He had hit rock bottom.

TURNING AROUND HIS LIFE

Rather than slipping further into addiction, Guerrero used his recent woes to help drive him. He eventually crushed his demons, won back his wife, and was given a second chance with WWE. The WWE Universe welcomed back the new Eddie Guerrero with open arms. Much like his first stint with the company, he compiled an impressive list of Championships. In addition to becoming a four-time WWE Tag Team Champion, Guerrero had the honor of bringing the United States Championship back to prominence in 2003.

Guerrero's greatest in-ring conquest came in February 2004 when he defeated Brock Lesnar for the WWE Championship at *No Way Out*. The victory brought Guerrero full circle and completed his quest for redemption. As WWE Champion, Guerrero earned the ultimate opportunity of defending his Title at *WrestleMania XX* at the famed Madison Square Garden. In the world of sports-entertainment, there is no greater honor. Guerrero seized the opportunity, defeating Kurt Angle to retain the Title.

Guerrero's inspirational WWE Championship reign came to an end when John "Bradshaw" Layfield defeated him in a Texas Bull Rope Match at *The Great American Bash* in June 2004. Undeterred by the loss, Guerrero, as he had done so many times before, fought to regain his lofty status. By late 2005, he had solidified himself as a legitimate threat for the World Heavyweight Championship.

A TRAGIC END

On November 13, 2005, Eddie Guerrero was found dead in his hotel room in Minneapolis. He was thirty-eight. In the days that followed, the entire wrestling world publicly mourned the tragic loss of an inspirational human being. In 2006, Guerrero took his rightful place in wrestling history when he was posthumously inducted into the WWE Hall of Fame. The night's celebration was proof that the great memories of Eddie Guerrero will live on forever.

IF YOU'RE NOT CHEATING, YOU'RE NOT TRYING

EL OLYMPICO

HT	5'9"	WT	234 lbs.	FROM	Mexico City, Mexico
SIGNATURE MOVE	Flying Cross Body				

This high-flying masked man began his career in his homeland of Mexico and arrived in WWE in 1972. He became an instant fan favorite with his mixture of high-flying maneuvers and submission holds. El Olympico showcased his skills in front of a packed Shea Stadium at the 1972 *Showdown At Shea*, as he defeated Chuck O'Connor.

Throughout his career, the man from south of the border stood on the opposite side of the ring from a number of future WWE Hall of Famers including Terry Funk, Greg "The Hammer" Valentine, and Mr. Fuji. Interestingly, New York state had a "no mask" rule at the time, and El Olympico was forced to compete in Madison Square Garden with a hole cut into his disguise.

ELIJAH BURKE

HT	6'1"	WT	235 lbs.	FROM	Jacksonville, Florida
SIGNATURE MOVE	The Elijah Express				

Elijah Burke was a naturally gifted athlete who won several tough man contests across the Eastern United States prior to entering WWE. He also earned an amateur boxing record of 103-1, with 102 knockouts.

Burke first appeared on *SmackDown* in July 2006. In November, he joined the ranks of *ECW*, where he regularly disrespected the original ECW establishment, particularly Rob Van Dam, Sabu, Tommy Dreamer, and The Sandman. The "Paragon of Virtue" formed a faction called the New Breed to battle the ECW Originals at *WrestleMania 23*. Burke also appeared in a battle royal at *WrestleMania XXIV* before leaving WWE in 2008.

ELIZABETH

FROM	Louisville, Kentucky

Decades after making her WWE debut, Elizabeth's impact is still felt today. Appropriately nicknamed the "First Lady of Wrestling," her gentle-yet-influential contributions helped pave the way for generations of female performers.

In 1985, WWE newcomer Randy "Macho Man" Savage set out on a search to find a manager. In the end, the sought-after Superstar unveiled the beautiful Miss Elizabeth as his choice. Over the next seven years, Savage and Elizabeth's very public rollercoaster relationship provided fans with a soap-opera type romance never before seen in WWE.

Fans and Superstars were instantly smitten by her innocent smile and impeccable style. The admiration she received, however, didn't sit well with Savage. The jealous Superstar continually took his frustrations out on his harmless manager even though she never acted on anybody's advances.

The always-classy Elizabeth took Savage's verbal attacks in stride. Instead of simply walking away, she stood by her man and helped guide him to greatness. In 1988, Elizabeth achieved the ultimate goal when she managed Savage to the WWE Championship at *WrestleMania IV*. The win made Elizabeth the first woman to manage a WWE Champion.

Elizabeth's relationship with Savage reached its boiling point in 1989 when her friendship with Hulk Hogan sent Macho Man into a jealous rage. The couple split soon after, sending Elizabeth into a more private lifestyle and Savage into a working relationship with Sensational Sherri.

In 1991, after Savage lost a Retirement Match to Ultimate Warrior at *WrestleMania VII*, Elizabeth reemerged to save Savage from an attacking Sherri. Following the save, the reunited couple shared a loving embrace that drew tears of happiness from nearly everybody watching. At *SummerSlam 1991*, Savage and Elizabeth were married in what was dubbed the "Match Made in Heaven."

As sweet as Elizabeth was, that did not stop her from joining the nWo in 1996, once again supporting "Macho Man" and Hulk Hogan. She finished her career in WCW, where she also spent time aligning with Ric Flair and the Four Horsemen. Through it all, she never lost the pure elegance that first captured the heart of the sports-entertainment world.

EMMA

HT	5'5"	FROM	Melbourne, Australia	SIGNATURE MOVE	Emma Lock

Once a loveably quirky Diva whose dance moves captured the hearts of the WWE Universe, Emma has since traded in her whacky side for a more edgy attitude. And the new look certainly seems to fit her.

Before adopting the brash attitude, Emma became known as the can't-miss beauty walking around WWE arenas holding #EMMAism signs in early 2014. After weeks of being amongst the crowd, Emma finally got her big break when Santino Marella invited her into the ring to compete in a dance competition against Summer Rae.

Proving she was so much more than a supposedly good dancer, Emma followed up her exhibition against Summer Rae with big wins over the likes of Layla, Alicia Fox, and Cameron. Despite the victories, however, Emma went down to NXT in January 2015, claiming her WWE career didn't go quite as planned.

With the move to NXT came an overbearing arrogance that has turned off even the biggest of Emma fans. But regardless of her unpopularity, nobody can deny Emma's incredible athleticism.

EDGE

HT	6'5"
WT	241 lbs.
FROM	Toronto, Canada

SIGNATURE MOVE
Spear

WWE has been home to sports-entertainment's greatest Superstars, including Shawn Michaels, Ric Flair, and The Rock. None of these men, however, have accumulated as many accolades as Edge. With more than 30 WWE Titles to his credit, the "Rated-R Superstar" is the most decorated competitor of all time.

Edge's journey to greatness can be tracked all the way back to 1990. As a 16-year old, the future Hall of Famer sat in the crowd at Toronto's SkyDome to witness Ultimate Warrior challenge Hulk Hogan at *WrestleMania VI*. Surrounded by the pageantry of sports-entertainment's crown jewel, Edge vowed that night that he would one day headline *WrestleMania*.

YOU THINK YOU KNOW ME

Eight long years later, which included an extended stay on the independent wrestling scene, Edge came one step closer to realizing his dream when he debuted in WWE. Shortly after his initial appearance, he teamed with longtime friend Christian to form one of the most successful pairings in tag-team history. Together, Edge and Christian captured seven World Tag Team Championships, while also revolutionizing the division with such innovations as the TLC Match.

As 2001 unfolded, the tag-team division proved unable to contain Edge's Superstardom.

Starting with his King of the Ring crowning in June, the Toronto native began to show signs of being a main-event player. All the success, however, came at a price. A jealous Christian soon turned on Edge, marking the end of the popular pairing.

As a singles star, Edge quickly claimed the coveted Intercontinental Championship, a Title he held proudly on five separate occasions. He also defeated Kurt Angle to capture the United States Championship in November 2001.

After proving himself as a legitimate Intercontinental Championship threat, Edge turned his attention to capturing sports-entertainment's richest prize. At *WrestleMania 21*, he moved one step closer when he won the first ever Money in the Bank Ladder Match.

Edge toted his guaranteed Title opportunity for nine long months before cashing in at *New Year's Revolution 2006*. At the event, John Cena retained the WWE Championship against five other Superstars in a grueling Elimination Chamber Match. Realizing Cena was at his weakest following the match, Edge wisely demanded his opportunity and defeated Cena to claim his first WWE Championship. The victory forever etched Edge's name next to the elite few that have owned the WWE Title, including his boyhood idol, Hulk Hogan.

THE ULTIMATE OPPORTUNIST

Edge and Lita tried to commemorate the victory by engaging in a live sex celebration the next night on *Raw*. Thankfully, John Cena arrived to spoil their night before Edge's "Rated-R" nickname became too literal, but not before the segment registered an amazing 5.2 rating. As a result of its popularity, Edge began touting himself as the most-watched WWE Champion of all time.

Edge added the World Heavyweight Championship to his résumé when he defeated Undertaker in May 2007. Like his first WWE Championship victory, the "Rated-R Superstar" took advantage of a beaten and battered Deadman to claim the Title. As a result of his continued shrewd maneuvering, Edge was appropriately tagged with the "Ultimate Opportunist" moniker.

Undertaker later gained retribution for the loss when he defeated Edge for the gold at *WrestleMania XXIV*. For Edge, the loss was bittersweet. It clearly marked the end of his Title reign, but the match was also the culmination of a nearly 20-year old dream to main event *WrestleMania*.

Edge was back on top soon enough. For the next year he traded World Heavyweight Championship victories with Undertaker, CM Punk, Triple H, and others. During this time, the master manipulator used his questionable relationship with *SmackDown* General Manager Vickie Guerrero to his advantage. Waiting in the wings was also a team of Edge lookalikes, Curt Hawkins and Zack Ryder, ready to do his bidding. The faction, known as La Familia, slowly dissolved but Edge remained at his villainous best. He defeated his nemesis John Cena for the gold in a Last Man Standing Match at *Backlash 2009* after Big Show hurled Cena through a spotlight. When Vickie lost her authority and Edge lost the Title, Edge divorced Vickie, claiming she was no longer of any use to him.

In January 2010, Edge bolstered his historic legacy when he last eliminated John Cena to win the Royal Rumble Match. With the victory, Edge became the only Superstar in history to have won the King of the Ring tournament, Money in the Bank contract, and Royal Rumble Match.

AFTER WATCHING THAT, I GOTTA ADMIT, I AM AWESOME!

Edge captured his eleventh and final World Title when he defeated Dolph Ziggler for the World Heavyweight Championship in February 2011 on *SmackDown*. He carried the Title into *WrestleMania XXVII* where he defeated Alberto Del Rio. At the time, the win appeared to be the latest in what many anticipated to be a lengthy reign. In reality, however, it proved to be Edge's final stand.

Shortly after *WrestleMania*, the "Rated-R Superstar" announced that injuries to his spine would prevent him from ever being medically cleared to compete again. As a result, Edge was forced into early retirement. On March 30, 2012, Edge's awesome career was capped off when he was inducted into the WWE Hall of Fame by his best friend, Christian.

Edge continued to entertain with his reoccurring role on the SyFy series *Haven* and other acting endeavors, but never left WWE fully behind. He has brought back his popular "Cutting Edge" talk show on occasion, where he has hosted John Cena, Seth Rollins, Team Hell No, and others. In February 2016, *Edge & Christian's Show That Totally Reeks of Awesomeness* debuted on the WWE Network. Edge shares his memories of WWE past, including some of the countless amazing moments that belong to him.

EDGE AND CHRISTIAN

COMBINED WT 470 lbs.

"For the benefit of those with flash photography," Edge and Christian would oftentimes strike a pre-match pose, allowing fans to snap a photograph of the seven-time World Tag Team Champions. With their oversized sunglasses and corny catchphrases, the charismatic combination always managed to get a reluctant laugh out of the fans who loved to hate them. In the ring, however, their offensive onslaught was no joke.

Edge and Christian first began to open eyes as a unit when they competed against Matt and Jeff Hardy in the Terri Invitational Tournament in 1999. The best-of-five series culminated in a *No Mercy* Ladder Match, which proved to be a precursor for the innovative action the proud Canadians would display in the years that followed.

Following the success of *No Mercy*, Edge and Christian paired again to take on the Hardys and World Tag Team Champions, the Dudley Boyz, at *WrestleMania 2000*. The bout was billed as a Triangle Ladder Match, but it wasn't long before other dangerous elements also found their way into the battlefield. Looking back, the historic *WrestleMania 2000* contest can be credited for the creation of the wildly popular TLC Match. And more importantly for Edge and Christian, it also marked their first World Tag Team Championship victory.

Thanks in large part to two successful TLC Matches against the Dudleys and Hardys at *SummerSlam* and *WrestleMania X-Seven*, Edge and Christian cemented themselves as one of the greatest tag teams of all time. But as Edge began to breakout as a singles star, animosity found its way into the team. Jealousy eventually overtook Christian, who turned on his longtime partner in September 2001.

It took 10 long years, but in March 2011, Edge and Christian finally repaired their severed relationship when they teamed to defeat Alberto Del Rio and Brodus Clay. The two Superstars were inseparable over the next few weeks, but then injury pushed the Rated-R Superstar into early retirement. The pair was forced to close the book on their historic partnership in the ring but not outside of it. Today, their collective wit can be enjoyed weekly on a WWE Network program appropriately titled *The Edge & Christian Show That Totally Reeks of Awesomeness*.

WE'VE BROUGHT A LITTLE HIGH OCTANE COOLOSITY WITH US!

ENZO AMORE AND COLIN CASSADY

| MEMBERS | Enzo Amore & Colin Cassady | COMBINED WT | 476 lbs. |

"We're stars," Enzo Amore has boasted of his partnership with Colin Cassady. "We take meteor showers."

Even before the bell rings, the two know how to entertain a crowd. Enzo claims to represent his home state of New Jersey "like 225 on a barbell, ten pounds of hair gel, steadily working on his swell."

He met Queens native Cassady during a pickup basketball game in Manhattan as a teen. At six-foot-ten, "Big Cass" is partial to compressing opponents with his East River Crossing.

With "The Princess of Staten Island," Carmella at their side, Amore and Cassady were voted top tag team of 2015 by the NXT Universe. Fans couldn't help but chant along with Amore as he proclaimed, "And you can't teach that!"

EPICO

| HT | 6'2" | WT | 217 lbs. | FROM | San Juan, Puerto Rico |
| SIGNATURE MOVE | Backstabber |

As the nephew of Puerto Rican wrestling legend Carlos Colon, Epico had to live up to high expectations upon breaking into WWE. His first order of business in November 2011 was to help Hunico in his ongoing conflict with Sin Cara.

Shortly after, Epico teamed with his cousin, Primo. As a unit, Epico and Primo enjoyed immediate success, defeating the Usos on an episode of *WWE Superstars*. When the tandem teamed up with the stunning Rosa Mendes they realized their true potential. In January 2012, Epico and Primo defeated Air Boom to claim the coveted WWE Tag Team Championship and held the gold for over three months.

ERIC BISCHOFF

see page 112

ERIC ESCOBAR

| HT | 6'3" | WT | 246 lbs. | FROM | San Juan, Puerto Rico |
| SIGNATURE MOVE | Pure Escobar |

Introduced in 2009 as Vickie Guerrero's love interest, Eric Escobar assumed being romantically linked to such a powerful figure would help him reach the top of the *SmackDown* mountain. Unfortunately for him, however, he soon learned that Guerrero's stroke could only get him so far.

After earning only a handful of victories, Escobar was curiously granted an opportunity at the Intercontinental Championship. But when he was unable to dethrone John Morrison, Escobar soon felt the wrath of his lady.

Disgusted by her man's inability to beat Morrison, Guerrero berated Escobar in the middle of the ring before slapping him and running off. Coincidentally, Escobar didn't last very long in WWE after his public breakup up with Guerrero.

ERICK ROWAN

| HT | 6'8" | WT | 315 lbs. |
| SIGNATURE MOVE | The Way |

In 2012, Bray Wyatt announced on NXT that his "first son" Luke Harper now had a sibling—eerily silent, red-bearded Erick Rowan, who'd shamble to the ring with a bizarre sheep mask obscuring his features.

With Bray shouting incantations in their ears, Rowan and Harper won the NXT Tag Team Championship from Neville and Bo Dallas.

In 2013, the backwoods trio emerged in WWE, staging a gang attack on "The Devil's Favorite Demon," Kane.

For much of the next year, Rowan listened to the instructions implanted by Wyatt, assisting him in rivalries again John Cena and The Shield. Then, in 2014, inexplicably, Wyatt set his "sons" free. For a brief period, Rowan waged war against Harper and Wyatt. But by 2015, he'd not only rejoined the family but found a new "brother" in Braun Strowman.

Since then, he's engaged in a number of acts that defy reason, including participating in a shocking assault on Brock Lesnar, a decision that can only be attributed to an individual incapable of thinking for himself.

ERNEST "THE CAT" MILLER

| HT | 6'2" | WT | 235 lbs. | FROM | Atlanta, Georgia |

Fans who witnessed Ernest Miller's brief WWE in-ring career probably assume "The Cat" was a loudmouthed Superstar who was more concerned with dancing than actually competing. And they'd be right. In fact, at the 2004 *Royal Rumble*, Miller spent more time showing off his moves than he did competing. As a result, he was easily eliminated by Randy Orton mid-dance.

Miller's brief appearance accurately sums up much of his WWE tenure. It makes up the majority of his WCW career, as well. Unlike the WWE Universe, however, WCW crowds ate up Miller's act. They jumped to their feet each time "The Cat" donned his patented ruby-red slippers and broke into dance. Even the original Godfather

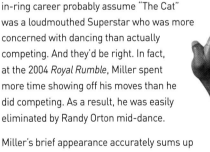

of Soul, James Brown, became a fan of Miller's moves, and at *SuperBrawl 2000*, the legendary singer/songwriter showed up to dance with "The Cat."

If sports-entertainment was a dance contest, Miller would be a first-ballot Hall of Famer. Instead, "The Cat" was put out of his misery in 2004, never to be seen again.

ERIC BISCHOFF

5'10"
195 lbs.
Detroit, Michigan

Years after the Monday Night War, Eric Bischoff is still recognized as the controversial sports-entertainment executive responsible for launching much of the legendary era's success. Credited with creating *Monday Nitro*, the New World Order, and free pay-per-view quality matches on weekly television, his impact on the industry is still being felt today.

While Bischoff has become one of sports-entertainment's most recognizable faces, he actually never sought out a career in front of the camera. Bischoff began his journey in August 1987 in the syndication and sales department for Verne Gagne's American Wrestling Association. It wasn't until years later when Gagne was left scrambling for an announcer on short notice that Bischoff was given an opportunity.

Stricken by the announcing bug, Bischoff looked to advance his career by auditioning for WWE in June 1990. During the process, he was asked to interview a broom, which he did. He did not, however, get the job. In retrospect, Bischoff not landing the WWE gig turned out to be a blessing in disguise, as big things were just around the corner.

In 1991, Bischoff moved to World Championship Wrestling, where he continued his career as an announcer. But when Bill Watts left the company just a few short years later, Bischoff applied for and was given the Executive Producer position in WCW. It was the beginning of Bischoff's climb to the top of the sports-entertainment ladder.

As Bischoff's responsibilities increased over the following few years, so did WCW's level of success. It wasn't long before such legendary names like Hulk Hogan and Randy Savage were lured into Bischoff's fold. Armed with an increasingly impressive roster of competitors, Bischoff took the bold step of challenging Vince McMahon when he launched WCW *Monday Nitro* to go head to head with WWE's *Monday Night Raw* in 1995.

Unlike most *Raw* episodes at the time, *Nitro* was broadcast live on a weekly basis and presented high-profile matches usually reserved for pay-per-view. Before long, the Bischoff-led WCW went from a perennial loss-leader to a more than $300 million sports-entertainment and broadcasting juggernaut.

Naturally, *Nitro*'s success caught the eye of WWE's locker room, and it wasn't long before even more Superstars were making the jump to WCW. Among the biggest defections were Scott Hall and Kevin Nash.

Dubbed The Outsiders, Hall and Nash teamed with Hogan to form the nWo. The rebellious faction captured the imagination of viewers, leading WCW to defeat WWE in the ratings for more than eighty straight weeks.

Eventually, the power of WWE was too much to keep at bay. By the end of the decade, *Raw* had regained ratings supremacy and Bischoff found himself in and out of power at various times. Finally, despite attempting to purchase WCW, Bischoff was again out of power prior to the company closing its doors in 2001.

Feeling he still had plenty to offer the sports-entertainment industry, Bischoff shocked fans worldwide when Mr. McMahon introduced him as the new *Raw* General Manager in the summer of 2002. Upon the introduction, Bischoff and McMahon shared an on-stage embrace that remains one of the most surreal moments in the history of the industry.

With Bischoff at the helm, *Raw* regularly competed against Stephanie McMahon's *SmackDown* brand, creating the next generation of Bischoff versus McMahon. The Bischoff Era also saw the creation of the Elimination Chamber Match and *Raw* Roulette.

Despite being one of the longest-running GMs in WWE history, Bischoff was fired from his post in December 2005. Upon being relieved of his duties, Mr. McMahon scooped Bischoff up and tossed him into the back of a garbage truck. That was the last anyone ever saw of Bischoff on live WWE television.

While no longer a permanent fixture on WWE TV, Bischoff still manages to make waves with the WWE Universe. In 2006, his autobiography, *Controversy Creates Cash*, was released and sky-rocketed to The New York Times Best Seller List. Bischoff was also the focus of WWE Network's first episodes of *Legends with JBL* in 2015.

What the future holds for Eric Bischoff is anybody's guess. But you can guarantee that whatever he decides to do will be met with incredible controversy and amazing success.

CONTROVERSY CREATES CASH.

ERNIE LADD

HT	6'9"	WT	320 lbs.
FROM	New Orleans, Louisiana		

Ernie "The Big Cat" Ladd was a two-sport athlete before being a two-sport athlete was vogue. After being selected by the San Diego Chargers in the 1961 American Football League draft, Ladd called the gridiron home for eight grueling seasons. During this time, he played in three AFL Championship Games, winning titles in 1963 with the Chargers and in 1967 with the Kansas City Chiefs.

While still an active member of the AFL, Ladd took part in a publicity stunt that saw him answer the challenge of several Los Angeles wrestlers. He went into the encounter assuming he would mop the floor with the smaller competition. Instead, they proved their dominance over Ladd, which eventually fueled the fire within "The Big Cat" to learn the craft of wrestling.

In the early 1960s, Ladd began competing in the Los Angeles area during AFL off-seasons. Behind the name he already built for himself on the football field, he became an instant hit, as fans loved to hate the arrogant footballer-turned-wrestler.

Ladd landed in WWE in 1968. Guided by legendary manager The Grand Wizard, he became a perennial challenger for the promotion's top prize. And when he wasn't trying to claim the WWE Championship from Bruno Sammartino, he was engaging in memorable rivalries with fellow big men Andre the Giant, Gorilla Monsoon, and Haystacks Calhoun.

Ladd's latter years were spent competing in the Mid-South territory. When his in-ring career came to a close in the mid-1980s, Ladd remained a part of the sports-entertainment community as a manager and color commentator. His most notable time behind the mic saw him call a portion of the action at *WrestleMania 2*.

In 1981, the San Diego Chargers recognized Ladd as a gridiron great when they inducted him into their Hall of Fame. His in-ring accomplishments were later honored when he took his rightful spot in the WCW Hall of Fame in 1994 and WWE Hall of Fame in 1995.

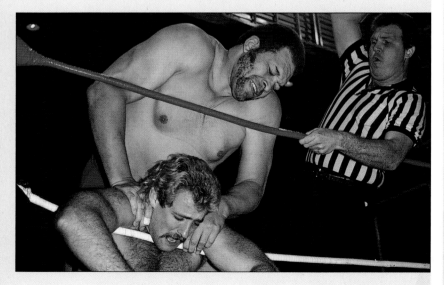

ESSA RIOS

HT	5'10"	WT	215 lbs.	FROM	Guadalajara, Mexico
SIGNATURE MOVE	Moonsault				

Accompanied by valet Lita, Essa Rios made his WWE debut on a February 2000 edition of *Heat*. It didn't take long for the newcomer to make his mark, as he quickly defeated Gillberg to capture the Light Heavyweight Championship.

Many pegged Rios as the future of the light heavyweight division; but after losing the Title to Dean Malenko one month later, the high-flyer's stock began to nosedive. Rios struggled to regain momentum, and became increasingly angered by mounting losses. Eventually, he took his frustration out on Lita, which did not sit well with the Hardy Boyz, who quickly came to her rescue.

Rios left WWE in 2001. Since then, he has appeared in various promotions throughout his homeland of Mexico and the United States.

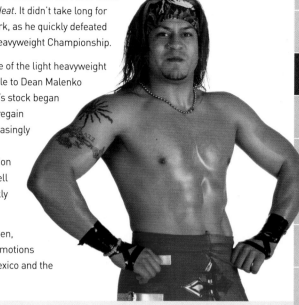

EUGENE

HT	6'1"	WT	225 lbs.	FROM	Louisville, Kentucky
SIGNATURE MOVE	Special versions of other Superstars' moves				

When Eugene first arrived on the WWE scene in April 2004, nobody could have predicted he'd become a future World Tag Team Champion. As the special-needs nephew of *Raw* General Manager Eric Bischoff, Eugene was seen by many as a non-threat. When the bell rang, Eugene proved to be a wrestling savant.

Using moves he learned while watching his favorite Superstars years earlier, Eugene was able to catch opponents off guard en route to an impressive early career. In addition to his expansive repertoire of moves, Eugene also possessed incredible strength.

Despite being a special Superstar, Eugene managed to earn major pay-per-view matches against the industry's greatest stars, including contests against Triple H and Kurt Angle on back-to-back *SummerSlams*. However, it was his teaming with William Regal that garnered the most success. In November 2004, the duo defeated La Resistance and Tajiri and Rhyno to capture the coveted World Tag Team Championship.

EUROPEAN CHAMPIONSHIP

Introduced to WWE audiences in February 1997, the European Championship was widely recognized as a stepping-stone to greatness, as many of its holders went on to capture World Championships later in their careers, including Triple H, Kurt Angle, and Eddie Guerrero.

After defeating Owen Hart in a tournament final, the British Bulldog was recognized as the first-ever European Champion. His reign lasted more than 200 days, longer than any other European Champion in history. The Title was eventually vacated in July 2002 when Rob Van Dam defeated Jeff Hardy to unify the European and Intercontinental Championships.

 1997

February 26 • Berlin, Germany
British Bulldog def. **Owen Hart**
In the finals of a tournament to crown the first-ever European Champion, British Bulldog defeated Owen Hart.

September 20 • Birmingham, England
Shawn Michaels def. **British Bulldog**

December 22 • Lowell, MA
Triple H def. **Shawn Michaels**

 1998

January 22 • Davis, CA
Owen Hart def. **Goldust**
Owen Hart beat Goldust, who was dressed as then-champion Triple H, to win the European Championship. Despite Triple H not officially being involved in the match, Commissioner Sgt. Slaughter allowed the decision to stand.

March 16 • Phoenix, AZ
Triple H def. **Owen Hart**

July 20 • Binghamton, NY
D-Lo Brown def. **Triple H**

September 21 • Sacramento, CA
X-Pac def. **D-Lo Brown**

October 5 • East Lansing, MI
D-Lo Brown def. **X-Pac**

October 18 • Chicago, IL
X-Pac def. **D-Lo Brown**

 **1999**

February 15 • Birmingham, AL
Shane McMahon def. **X-Pac**
Shane McMahon and Kane defeated X-Pac and Triple H when McMahon pinned X-Pac. Pre-match stipulations stated that if anybody pinned X-Pac, that man would be awarded the European Championship.

June 21 • Memphis, TN
Mideon became European Champion
Mideon was declared European Champion after he found the Title in Shane McMahon's bag.

July 25 • Buffalo, NY
D-Lo Brown def. **Mideon**

August 22 • Minneapolis, MN
Jeff Jarrett def. **D-Lo Brown**

August 23 • Ames, IA
Mark Henry became European Champion
Jeff Jarrett awarded the European Championship to Mark Henry after he helped Jarrett defeat D-Lo Brown one night earlier.

September 26 • Charlotte, NC
D-Lo Brown def. **Mark Henry**

October 28 • Springfield, MA
British Bulldog def. **D-Lo Brown**

December 12 • Fort Lauderdale, FL
Val Venis def. **British Bulldog**
Val Venis pinned British Bulldog to win the European Championship in a Triple Threat Match that also included D'Lo Brown.

2000

February 10 • Austin, TX
Kurt Angle def. **Val Venis**

April 2 • Anaheim, CA
Chris Jericho def. **Chris Benoit**
Chris Jericho pinned Chris Benoit to win the European Championship in a Triple Threat Match that also included then-champion Kurt Angle.

April 3 • Los Angeles, CA
Eddie Guerrero def. **Chris Jericho**

July 23 • Dallas, TX
Perry Saturn def. **Eddie Guerrero**

August 31 • Fayetteville, NC
Al Snow def. **Perry Saturn**

October 16 • Detroit, MI
William Regal def. **Al Snow**

December 2 • Sheffield, England
Crash Holly def. **William Regal**

December 4 • East Rutherford, NJ
William Regal def. **Crash Holly**

2001

January 22 • Lafayette, LA
Test def. **William Regal**

April 1 • Houston, TX
Eddie Guerrero def. **Test**

April 26 • Denver, CO
Matt Hardy def. **Eddie Guerrero**

August 27 • Grand Rapids, MI
The Hurricane def. **Matt Hardy**

October 22 • Kansas City, MO
Bradshaw def. **The Hurricane**

November 1 • Cincinnati, OH
Christian def. **Bradshaw**

 **2002**

January 31 • Norfolk, VA
Diamond Dallas Page def. **Christian**

March 21 • Ottawa, Ontario
William Regal def. **Diamond Dallas Page**

April 8 • Phoenix, AZ
Spike Dudley def. **William Regal**

May 6 • Hartford, CT
William Regal def. **Spike Dudley**

July 8 • Philadelphia, PA
Jeff Hardy def. **William Regal**
Rob Van Dam defeated Jeff Hardy on July 21, 2002 to unify the European and Intercontinental Championships.

EVA MARIE

HT 5'8" **FROM** Concord, California   **SIGNATURE MOVE** Sliced Red No. 2

Whether you love her or love to boo her, you cannot deny that Eva Marie is one of WWE's fastest rising Divas.

A model-turned-Diva, Eva Marie first opened eyes in July 2013 as part of the E! hit reality series *Total Divas*, where cameras followed the stunning newcomer on her path to WWE. Once she finally arrived in front of a live audience, Eva Marie wasted no time making an impression when she slapped Jerry Lawler across the face.

After nearly two years competing on WWE's main roster, Eva Marie showed up at NXT in June 2015. Wanting to be part of the buzz surrounding NXT women's division, Eva Marie rededicated herself to becoming the best competitor possible. Despite her hard work, however, most of the NXT Universe failed to recognize her improving skills. The criticism spurred Eva Marie to work even harder. And in the weeks that followed, her impressive win-loss record told the story of a Diva who was on top of her game. With victories over Carmella, Cassie, and Billie Kay, Eva Marie effectively proved all her naysayers wrong.

Despite her successes, Eva Marie remains one of the most polarizing Divas in WWE history. But she knows if given the chance, she has what it takes to make fans out of the entire WWE Universe.

"Open your eyes," Eva Marie says, "because you're going to like what you see."

EVAN BOURNE

 HT 5'9" **WT** 165 lbs. **FROM** St. Louis, Missouri
SIGNATURE MOVE Air Bourne

Evan Bourne forged his sports-entertainment career determined to become a unique blend of the high-flying cruiserweights and hardnosed ECW originals that he idolized. In June 2008, he joined WWE's reincarnation of ECW and instantly amazed. His array of gravity defying maneuvers, including a mind-boggling version of the Shooting Star Press, helped redefine "extreme."

With a disciplined formula—positive attitude, technical brilliance, and aerial magic—the Bourne Combination thrived in WWE for six years. The compact Superstar showed enough firepower to compete on *Raw* against larger peers such as Randy Orton and Jack Swagger. In two Money In the Bank matches, he thrilled crowds and nearly grabbed the sought after briefcase. Joining forces with another explosive high-flyer, Kofi Kingston, Bourne became a WWE Tag Team Champion and enjoyed his greatest success in WWE. Known as Air Boom, the friendly-yet-fiery tandem held the gold for nearly five months.

EVE TORRES

HT 5'8" **FROM** Denver, Colorado

This vision of beauty first showed WWE audiences her desire when she won the 2007 WWE Diva Search. Already experienced in several entertainment mediums, the former Los Angeles Clipper's spirit dancer debuted on *SmackDown* in February 2008 as an interviewer. Her beauty was obvious, but WWE had no idea the blend of power, brains, and ruthlessness that was coming.

Trained in Gracie Jiu-Jitsu with a *Muscle & Fitness* physique, Eve was a top-notch competitor in the Divas division. Competing against Natalya, Beth Phoenix, and several others, Eve proved worthy of a Divas Championship opportunity. In April 2010, she collected her first of three career Titles by defeating Maryse. Her second came in a controversial Fatal 4-Way Match in 2011, highlighted by Eve's breathtaking moonsault.

Later that year, Eve began using her sex appeal to manipulate her way to the top. She feigned romantic feelings for both Zack Ryder and John Cena, straining their friendship for the sake of boosting her profile. The devious Diva fully revealed her true colors when she clocked Ryder in the groin at *WrestleMania XXVIII*, helping John Laurinaitis usurp full control over the Superstar roster. "Big Johnny" rewarded Eve with a corporate position where she helped propagate his "People Power" agenda.

When her third Divas Championship reign was cut short by Kaitlyn in January 2013, Eve quit WWE in a post-match tirade.

EXECUTIONER

FROM Parts Unknown

After several grueling months of trying, Undertaker was finally on the verge of ridding WWE of his arch nemesis, Mankind, at *In Your House: Buried Alive*. However, before The Phenom could complete the daunting task, a mysterious masked man viciously attacked him from behind with a steel shovel. The masked monster, who was later revealed to be Paul Bearer's hired assassin known as The Executioner, then proceeded to bury The Deadman under six feet of soil.

Miraculously, Undertaker survived the chilling burial and challenged The Executioner to a match at *In Your House: It's Time* in December 1996. Under "Armageddon Rules," The Phenom Tombstoned his way to victory over his masked foe.

Following the loss, The Executioner struggled to remain relevant. He later came up short again when he battled Goldust on a January 1997 edition of *WWE Superstars*. The loss infuriated Bearer, who nailed the mysterious competitor with his urn. The Executioner was gone from WWE soon after.

EVOLUTION

MEMBERS "Nature Boy" Ric Flair, Triple H, Batista, & Randy Orton

In 2003, Triple H formed a group that represented the evolution of sports-entertainment. As leader of the villainous faction and foremost Superstar of modern times, Triple H aligned with the greatest of sports-entertainment past, Ric Flair. The Championship-laden pair then recruited two bright, future Superstars to fall under their wing, Batista and Randy Orton. The arrangement assured The Game a numbers advantage in all situations while the budding stars soaked up valuable knowledge and wisdom. During its existence, this group butted heads with Superstars of all types including Shawn Michaels, Goldberg, Rob Van Dam, Mick Foley, Edge, and the Dudley Boyz.

Evolution reached its apex when all four members held WWE Championships. Triple H was the World Heavyweight Champion, Flair and Batista were World Tag Team Champions and Orton was the Intercontinental Champion. Deep down, Triple H's lone objective was protecting his own interests in the gold. So when Randy Orton won the World Heavyweight Championship in August 2004, he was unceremoniously removed from the group. Batista later freed himself from Triple H's influence after winning the 2005 Royal Rumble and successfully challenging for Triple H's Title at *WrestleMania 21*. At WWE Homecoming, Triple H turned on Flair, cutting all Evolution ties.

At *Raw's* 15th Anniversary, Triple H, Ric Flair, and Batista teamed up for a six-man match. When Randy Orton refused to rejoin his former team, he opposed them with Edge and Umaga.

Evolution was about success, domination, and the spoils of victory. After the group dissolved, Triple H maintained his imperial reign over WWE and continues to wear a king's crown today. Batista and Randy Orton went on to become multi-time World Champions and perennial *WrestleMania* fixtures.

Nearly a decade after disbanding, Evolution reformed hoping to prove their superiority in the annals of great WWE factions. Determined to destroy The Shield, the reunited stable mates (sans Flair) unleashed their signature brutality on their younger counterparts like it was 2004. The Shield was up to the task, and after successive defeats, a frustrated Batista quit WWE, ending the reunion.

THE EXECUTIONERS

MEMBERS	Executioner No. 1, Executioner No. 2, & Executioner No. 3
COMBINED WT	758 lbs.	FROM	Parts Unknown

Very little is known about The Executioners other than they were complete terrors in the ring. Hiding their faces with masks and replacing their names with numbers, Executioner No. 1 and Executioner No. 2 instilled the fear of the unknown into the WWE locker room during the mid-1970s.

In May 1976, The Executioners, who were managed by Capt. Lou Albano, reached the top of the tag division when they defeated Louis Cerdan and Tony Parisi for the World Tag Team Championship in Philadelphia. The mysterious duo held the Titles for seven months before controversy caused them to lose the gold.

By this time, the tag team had welcomed a third member into the fold, appropriately named Executioner No. 3. The new member participated in a Title defense against Billy White Wolf and Chief Jay Strongbow. More recent tag teams like The New Day and Spirit Squad regularly employ the tactic now known as the "Freebird Rule." During the 1970s, however, this was an illegal practice, resulting in The Executioners being stripped of the Titles.

EXTREME EXPOSÉ

MEMBERS	Kelly Kelly, Layla, & Brooke

Kelly Kelly laid the groundwork for this extreme dance group when she started her WWE career in 2006. In January 2007, Kelly brought her Exposé back to *ECW* with friends Layla and Brooke. The trio danced in the ring with moves so hot the ring almost melted during their performances.

That August, the three Divas brought the extreme to *FHM* and appeared in an exclusive online pictorial that drove web traffic off the charts. Unfortunately for its devout followers, dissention amongst the Exposé members set in when chick magnet, The Miz, appeared on the *ECW* scene. In November, the group dissolved for good after Brooke parted ways with WWE while Kelly Kelly and Layla settled their differences in the ring.

EZEKIEL JACKSON

HT	6'3"	WT	280 lbs.	FROM	Guyana, South America
SIGNATURE MOVE	The Book of Ezekiel

A monstrous competitor with pulverizing strength, Ezekiel Jackson made his WWE debut in July 2008 as the advisor to The Brian Kendrick. "The Personification of Domination" easily transitioned from advisor to competitor. As a solo Superstar in *ECW*, Jackson was a dominant force and became a permanent piece of historical trivia as the last-ever ECW champion.

On *SmackDown*, Jackson enlisted in Wade Barrett's insidious faction, The Corre. After several months of service, his former cohorts attacked him and nearly ended his career. Jackson returned stronger and, before parting with WWE, got revenge on Barrett by claiming his Intercontinental Title at *Capitol Punishment 2011*.

THE FABULOUS FREEBIRDS

see page 117

THE FABULOUS KANGAROOS

MEMBERS	Al Costello, Roy Heffernan, & Don Kent

Many historians consider the original Fabulous Kangaroos, Al Costello and Roy Heffernan, to be the duo responsible for putting tag team competition on the map. Managed by Wild Red Berry, The Fabulous Kangaroos made their debut in the late 1950s. The Australian tandem quickly endeared themselves to New York City crowds by tossing boomerangs into the audience.

Costello and Heffernan enjoyed three runs as NWA United States Tag Team Champions before WWE claimed the Titles as their own starting in 1963. Their final reign proved to be their most successful, as the Kangaroos maintained a firm grip on the Titles for more than one year before finally losing to Johnny Valentine and Bob Ellis in January 1962. Shortly after the loss, Costello and Heffernan left WWE to work in various other United States territories, as well as Canada. The Fabulous Kangaroos did make a brief return in the early 1970s. This time, however, Heffernan was replaced by Don Kent.

FABULOUS MOOLAH

see page 119

FABULOUS FREEBIRDS

MEMBERS	Michael Hayes, Terry Gordy, Buddy Roberts, Jimmy Garvin, & Badstreet
FROM	Badstreet, USA

The Fabulous Freebirds lived by one simple rule: Live hard, play hard. And that's exactly what they did for fifteen years, en route to establishing themselves as perhaps the most revolutionary team of all time.

Formed in 1979, the original Freebirds comprised of three wholly distinct personalities that combined to create one singular force that craved attention, competition, and partying. A showman by nature, the group's leader, Michael P.S. Hayes, was known to walk the walk while also talking the seemingly never-ending talk. Terry "Bam Bam" Gordy was the Freebirds' heavy. Hovering at around 300 pounds, the powerhouse was known as one of the toughest competitors in the industry, while also being one of the craziest. And finally, Buddy "Jack" Roberts was a technician in the ring, who could also get down and dirty with any grappler in any territory.

Within months, The Freebirds became Tag Team Champions in both the Mid-South and Georgia territories. It was during this time that they revolutionized the sports-entertainment industry with their now-famous "Freebird Rule," which stated any two members of the three-man group could defend their Titles at any time. Over the years, some of the industry's greatest tag teams went on to employ the "Freebird Rule" while defending their Titles, including Demolition, New World Order, and The New Day.

Further cementing themselves as visionaries, The Freebirds forced the entire industry to stand up and take notice when they began entering the ring to "Badstreet USA," a song performed by Hayes himself. While many competitors over the years have claimed to be the first to utilize entrance music, The Freebirds can stake claim to performing their own theme years before it became vogue. Shawn Michaels, John Cena, Tyler Breeze, and a whole host of others followed The Freebirds' lead in the years that followed.

RIVALRY FOR THE AGES

While competing in World Class Championship Wrestling, The Freebirds engaged in one of the greatest rivalries of all time when they squared off against the beloved Von Erichs. At first it appeared the trio would befriend the famous family from Dallas, Texas. But The Freebirds' true colors were revealed at WCCW *Christmas Star Wars* in 1982. While serving as the Guest Referee for the NWA World Heavyweight Championship Steel Cage Match between Ric Flair and Kerry Von Erich, Hayes got into a physical altercation with the combatants that ultimately led to Gordy slamming the cage door on Von Erich's head.

The heinous act solidified The Freebirds as the most despised team in Texas. For the next several years, fans packed the famed Dallas Sportatorium hoping to see their all-American, whole milk-drinking Von Erichs topple the whiskey-chugging Freebirds.

The Freebirds made a very quick stop in WWE before heading to the AWA. While in the Minnesota-based promotion, the trio battled with the legendary Road Warriors over the AWA World Tag Team Championship. At *SuperClash 1985*, Hayes and Gordy seemingly dethroned Hawk and Animal to become Champions, but the decision was later reversed when it was learned that The Freebirds used illegal tactics to earn the victory. Though they were unsuccessful in unseating their rivals, The Freebirds later played a big role in the Road Warriors eventually losing the gold when they helped longtime associate Jimmy Garvin and Steve Regal defeat Hawk and Animal for the Titles.

Coincidentally, Garvin would later become an official member of The Freebirds when the famous faction moved to WCW in the late-1980s. With Jimmy "Jam" in the fold, The Freebirds continued to cement their legacy when Garvin and Hayes captured both the WCW World Tag Team and United States Tag Team Championships on two separate occasions. Garvin and Hayes also staked claim to the Six-Man Tag Team Championship when they teamed with fleeting Freebird member Badstreet to defeat Junkyard Dog, Tommy Rich, and Ricky Morton in June 1991.

A LASTING LEGACY

With fifteen years of success across multiple territories, The Freebirds are undoubtedly one of the most celebrated teams of all time. And while many factions have since replicated their approach, none will ever be able to duplicate the impact The Fabulous Freebirds had on the sports-entertainment industry. The Fabulous Freebirds' legacy was honored when they were inducted into the WWE Hall of Fame Class of 2016.

BADSTREET USA: THE FURTHER DOWN THE BLOCK YOU WENT, THE BADDER IT GOT AND WE LIVED IN THE LAST HOUSE ON THE RIGHT.

FABULOUS MOOLAH

HT 5'5"
FROM Columbia, South Carolina

SIGNATURE MOVE
The Backbreaker

Greatness in women's wrestling is measured by the success of one legendary competitor: The Fabulous Moolah. Over the course of her more than fifty-year career, she became recognized and admired as the ultimate measuring stick by which generations of Divas measure their own success.

Moolah's sports-entertainment career kicked off in the late-1940s. Her earliest days saw her turn heads as the leopard-skirt wearing Slave Girl Moolah. At the time, her main responsibility was escorting the likes of Buddy Rogers and The Elephant Boy to the ring. But it wasn't long before Moolah became her own force in the ring and began to revolutionize the women's wrestling scene.

Rechristened as the Fabulous Moolah, the young competitor outlasted twelve other ladies to capture the vacant Women's Championship in 1956. When she raised her arms in triumph, Moolah took the first step toward an unprecedented Championship dynasty that lasted nearly thirty years. Never before or after has an individual or team held a Championship longer. Over the decades that followed, Moolah's fame became immeasurable, and it wasn't uncommon to see close friends Elvis Presley and Jerry Lee Lewis in attendance at her matches.

In 1972, Moolah's legend grew when she and Vincent J. McMahon successfully lifted the ban that prohibited women from wrestling at Madison Square Garden. That September, she continued to conquer New York when she successfully defended her Title against Debbie Johnson at the first-ever *Showdown At Shea* event.

DECADES OF DOMINATION

As The Fabulous Moolah entered her fourth decade in the ring, a new era was beginning to dawn, one that was built on the foundation she laid decades prior. In 1983, Moolah signed an exclusive agreement with Vincent K. McMahon and her Women's Championship became a key component to WWE's national expansion.

Unfortunately for Moolah, her historic Title reign ended in July 1984, when she fell to sensation Wendi Richter on MTV's *The Brawl To End It All*. Defeating the great Moolah gave Richter the credibility she needed to take the Women's Championship into the next generation.

Given Moolah's advanced age at the time of the loss, many assumed her Championship days were firmly behind her. In reality, though, she was far from ready to give up her throne. In February 1985, Moolah managed protégé, Lelani Kai to the Title. Later that same year, she reclaimed the Women's Championship herself when she defeated Richter at MSG. The match remains one of the most talked-about contests, as a masked Moolah competed in the contest as Spider Lady. It wasn't until after she won the Title, that the legend was unmasked and revealed to be Moolah.

Moolah earned her third Championship reign when she defeated Velvet McIntyre in Australia in July 1986. She held the Title for just over one year before losing to Sherri Martel. Moolah then left WWE by decade's end.

In 1995, Moolah took her rightful place among the immortals as the first woman inducted into the WWE Hall of Fame. Unlike most Hall of Famers, though, she wasn't ready to give up on her in-ring career. And in October 1999, the nearly eighty-year-old Moolah actually captured her fourth Women's Championship when she defeated Ivory at *No Mercy*. The shocking victory came forty-three years after her first Women's Title victory.

The spotlight continued to follow Moolah into the new century. In 2002 she authored her autobiography, *The Fabulous Moolah: First Goddess of the Squared Circle*. And in September 2003, Moolah became the first octogenarian to compete in a WWE ring when she defeated Victoria on her 80th birthday during *Monday Night Raw*.

The Fabulous Moolah passed away on November 2, 2007. She will forever be regarded as the undisputed icon of women's wrestling. A true pioneer of sports-entertainment, Moolah's dominance is unmatched by any figure in any sport, male or female.

I AM THE WORLD CHAMPION, AND I INTEND TO STAY THERE.

THE FABULOUS ROUGEAU BROTHERS

MEMBERS	Jacques Rougeau & Raymond Rougeau		
COMBINED WT	472 lbs.	FROM	Montreal, Quebec, Canada

Trained by their legendary father Jacques Rougeau Sr., Jacques and Raymond were fixtures on the Montreal wrestling scene in the 1970s. While there, they captured Lutte Internationale's Canadian International Tag Team Championship on three separate occasions.

The Fabulous Rougeau Brothers jumped to WWE in 1986. They immediately gained the fans' favor with their quick tags and smooth double-team moves. But the cheers soon turned to jeers when the Rougeaus resorted to cheating in a victory over the Killer Bees.

Following the controversial victory, the once-honorable Rougeaus became condescending and smarmy, as they mocked the United States on a regular basis. To make matters worse, their new manager, Jimmy Hart, still had the Hart Foundation's contract and gave a percentage of their earnings to the Rougeaus as performance bonuses.

In 1989, the Rougeaus engaged in a series of memorable matches against the Rockers, which lead to a six-man clash at *SummerSlam*. With Rick Martel as their partner, Jacques and Raymond successfully turned back Shawn Michaels, Marty Jannetty, and Tito Santana.

In 1990, Raymond was forced to retire due to injuries, but found a second career as a broadcaster on WWE French television. After his brother's career-ending injury, Jacques went on to gain great success as The Mountie, and later as one-half of the Quebecers tag team.

FANDANGO

HT	6'4"	WT	244 lbs.
SIGNATURE MOVE	Last Dance		

Graceful both in and out of the ring, Fandango made the successful transition from ballroom dance floors to WWE rings in 2012. Despite the heavy fanfare accompanying his debut, many wondered if the elegant, yet dangerous, Superstar would ever compete.

Following months of hype, Fandango finally made his first live appearance in March, but refused to compete when his name was not pronounced to his liking (according to him, it's FAHN-DAHN-GO). Realizing he could have some fun with the newcomer, Chris Jericho began intentionally mispronouncing Fandango's name, leading to a showdown at *WrestleMania 29*, which Fandango won via pinfall.

Following his *WrestleMania* victory over Y2J, Fandango became a pop culture phenomenon when dancing to his theme song became a global craze. Known as "Fandangoing," fans, celebrities, and athletes alike all joined in the rhythmic revolution.

The Fandangoing craze eventually caught the eye of Summer Rae, who jumped at the opportunity to become the dashing Superstar's dance partner. The two made beautiful music together until Fandango ditched Summer Rae in favor of Layla, and later Rosa Mendes.

FARMER PETE

With his torn jeans, ragged hat, and lucky horseshoe placed around his neck, Farmer Pete certainly looked as though he spent plenty of time in the fields, which is surprising as he dedicated much of his life to the ring.

A legend in Canada, the dwarf wrestler spent decades competing in the Ontario territory. When he competed in the United States, Farmer Pete worked in numerous regions, most notably Georgia. During the early 1950s, the Peach State was the site of Pete's memorable rivalries with Sky Low Low and Irish Jackie.

Farmer Pete journeyed to New York in the 1960s where he often teamed with the likes of Tiny Tim and Sonny Boy Cassidy at the famed Madison Square Garden.

FATU

HT	6'1"	WT	282 lbs.	FROM	The Isle of Samoa
SIGNATURE MOVE	Monster Splash				

First seen by devotees in Puerto Rico, Fatu was one half of the Samoan Swat Team with cousin Samu. The barefoot pair then migrated to the World Class territory in Texas before appearing in WCW, and battling teams like the Midnight Express, Doom, the Road Warriors, and the Steiner Brothers.

Samu and Fatu debuted in WWE in August, 1992 as the feared Headshrinkers. The cousins reached the top of the mountain in April 1994 when they became World Tag Team Champions, upending the Quebecers. They also occasionally assisted another relative, Yokozuna. After the team disbanded in early 1995, Fatu became a singles competitor, earning the fans' approval and making a difference before leaving WWE a year later.

FBI (FULL BLOODED ITALIANS)

MEMBERS	Nunzio, Chuck Palumbo, Johnny Stanboli, Tony Mamaluke, & Trinity

A former member of ECW's Full Blooded Italians, Nunzio resurrected the group in WWE in 2003. With Chuck Palumbo and Johnny Stamboli also in the fold, the FBI, complete with every Italian stereotype, got off to a brilliant start when they whacked Nathan Jones just minutes before *WrestleMania XIX*. Unfortunately for the FBI, that's where their highlights stopped.

In the following months, Nunzio, Palumbo, and Stamboli fell to the likes of Billy Kidman, Booker T, and an up-and-coming John Cena. By the end of 2004, the Italian trio quietly went their separate ways but left behind a legacy WWE fans would rather "fuhgetabout." When ECW was revived by WWE in 2006, Nunzio briefly teamed again with Tony Mamaluke, with Trinity at their side.

FINLAY

HT	6'2"	WT	233 lbs.	FROM	Belfast, Northern Ireland

SIGNATURE MOVE Celtic Cross

For over 20 years, this third-generation bruiser from Belfast was known throughout Europe and Asia as one of the ring's most brutal competitors. He held 16 major Championships before coming to the United States in 1996 as a member of WCW. The Irishman's goal was to settle an old grudge between his countrymen and their British neighbors. Blackpool, England's William Regal became his bitter enemy. The legendary brawlers even took matters outside for a Parking Lot Brawl that resulted in Finlay suffering an eye injury from broken glass. Despite the injury, he continued to compete wearing an eye-patch.

Then known as Fit Finlay, the tough-as-nails bruiser found his footing in WCW in the late 1990s. He defeated Booker T for the WCW Television Title in May 1998 and defended it successfully against Eddie Guerrero, Chris Benoit, and Psicosis before losing it back to Booker at *The Great American Bash*. Despite the loss, Finlay continued to cement his reputation, giving some of WCW's top names a lesson in hardcore until he departed the United States in 2000.

In January 2006, Finlay debuted in WWE and put everyone on notice that he loved to fight. With the help of his shillelagh, Finlay quickly established himself as the most vicious Superstar on *SmackDown*.

During his first year in WWE, Finlay managed to capture the United States Championship with an assist from Hornswoggle and his shillelagh. The mystery of Finlay's parental ties to Hornswoggle put him at odds with Mr. McMahon and JBL in 2007. The events led to a brutal Belfast Brawl at *WrestleMania XXIV*. Finlay and Hornswoggle were soon drafted to *ECW* and immediately felt at home in the Land of Extreme. The Irish bruiser battled top Superstars like Tommy Dreamer, Christian, The Miz, and Jack Swagger.

Since hanging up his shillelagh, Finlay has been a producer behind the scenes for WWE. One of the most respected personalities backstage, Superstars turn to him for advice for fighting their own battles in today's WWE. He also emerges from behind the curtain on occasion to help restore order when chaos breaks out on *Raw*.

FINN BÁLOR

HT	5'11"	WT	190 lbs.	FROM	Bray, County Wicklow, Ireland

SIGNATURE MOVE Coup de Grace, 1916

Where Finn Bálor goes, people pay attention. From his native Ireland to the UK, the merciless dojos of Japan and now NXT, Bálor has captivated all who have witnessed him. In 2014, this international sensation finally touched down on United States soil and adopted a name derived from Irish mythology. With the looks of a prince, the spirit of a warrior, and a seemingly supernatural alter ego, Bálor instantly had the NXT Universe in the palm of his hand.

When circumstances demand it, Bálor unleashes his demonic other self with breathtaking body paint designs. One such instance was the WWE Network special on July 4, 2015 held in Tokyo. Returning to the land where he held the IWGP Junior Heavyweight Championship for over 1000 combined days, Bálor won his first NXT Championship by defeating Kevin Owens. Later, he teamed with Samoa Joe to win the inaugural Dusty Rhodes Tag Team Classic Cup. After winning the prestigious tournament, Finn's longtime friend turned on him. Joe and Finn would battle over the NXT Championship in classic matches in which Finn retained the NXT Title at *NXT Takeover: London* and *NXT Takeover: Dallas*. The future is now for Finn Bálor, and many believe that for WWE, the future is Finn Bálor.

FISHMAN

HT	5'8"	WT	220 lbs.	FROM	Torreon, Coahuila, Mexico

Fans in the United States may not recognize the name Fishman, but the successful Mexican grappler has a history that traces all the way back to the early days of the Light Heavyweight Championship.

In 1981, WWE entered into a lengthy partnership with the Mexican-based Universal Wrestling Association. As part of the agreement, the UWA was entitled to defend the WWE Light Heavyweight Championship on its cards. In September 1981, the masked Fishman became the second competitor to ever hold the Title when he defeated Perro Aguayo.

Fishman held the Title for less than a month before losing it back to Aguayo. Five years later, Fishman captured the prestigious Championship again, this time from Villano III. Ironically, his second reign was also ended by Aguayo.

FLASH FUNK

HT	5'11"	WT	243 lbs.	FROM	Philadelphia, Pennsylvania

SIGNATURE MOVE Funky Flash Splash

Prior to discovering his funky side in WWE, this accomplished Superstar gained notoriety as 2 Cold Scorpio in WCW and ECW. In the "Land of Extreme," he collected multiple ECW Television Titles before making his WWE debut at *Survivor Series 1996* as a member of Team Yokozuna. Flanked by female dancers dubbed the Funkettes, it was clear this Superstar was unique. His aerial attacks were felt by many top Superstars until he left WWE in the spring of 1998. Flash Funk returned briefly in 2006 and again during the *Raw 15th Anniversary* special.

The funk phenomenon and his flawlessly executed 450 Splash, known as the Funky Flash Splash, are fondly remembered. Flash Funk was so funky, he showed the WWE Universe how to get up and boogie down!

"FLYIN'" FRED CURRY

HT	5'11"	**WT**	232 lbs.	**FROM**	Hartford, Connecticut
SIGNATURE MOVE	Dropkick				

Trained by his father, "Wild Bull" Curry, "Flyin'" Fred Curry began his in-ring career in the early 1960s. Despite being considerably more mild mannered than his famous father, Fred spent much of his early years teaming with the elder Curry, who was known for his vicious attitude and wildly bushy eyebrows.

Curry's first taste of gold came with his dad as his tag team partner. In July 1964, the father-son combination topped Kurt and Karl von Stroheim to capture the NWA Texas International Tag Team Championship. They held the Titles for two years before losing them back to the von Stroheims.

Over the course of his career, Curry claimed several other regional NWA tag Titles with many notable partners, including Bobo Brazil and Fritz Von Erich. The high-flyer was also successful as a singles star. He won both the NWA Texas Junior Heavyweight Championship, as well as the NWA Hawaii Heavyweight Championship, which he claimed from the legendary Gene Kiniski.

FLYING NUNS

MEMBERS	Sister Angelica & Mother Smucker
COMBINED WT	488 lbs.
FROM	A Tibetan order in the Himalayas

Looking to push the envelope in January 1997, WWE made the controversial decision to promote a male vs. female tag match. The Godwinns fit the bill for the male duo. The females, however, were a little suspect. When Sister Angelica and Mother Smucker, collectively known as the Flying Nuns, made their way to the ring, people couldn't help but notice their goatees. Nevertheless, Angelica and Smucker competed in the match and defeated the Godwinns. With the win, many assumed a blessed career was in the their future. But Angelica and Smucker later ran afoul of the law and were arrested.

Incidentally, the Headbangers filled in for the Nuns while they were incarcerated. Mosh and Thrasher went on to achieve great success in the tag division.

THE FOUR HORSEMEN
see page 122

FRANCINE

HT	5'7"	
FROM	Philadelphia, Pennsylvania	
SIGNATURE MOVE	DDT	

Just one look at Francine and it's clear why ECW competitors absolutely fawned over her. She had it all—beauty, brains, and most importantly, the cunning needed to take her men to the top.

Francine first made an impact as Stevie Richards' obsessed girlfriend. But when Richards eventually turned on her, the sultry manager began guiding The Pitbulls, whom she led to the ECW World Tag Team Championship.

Perhaps Francine's greatest accomplishments came alongside Shane Douglas. Known as the head cheerleader of his Triple Threat, Francine helped Douglas capture two ECW World Heavyweight Championships.

Francine also managed Tommy Dreamer, Raven, and Justin Credible before ECW closed in 2001. She also appeared at *ECW One Night Stand 2005*, and briefly participated in WWE's re-launch of ECW in 2006.

FRANK "SPACEMAN" HICKEY

HT	5'10"	**WT**	258 lbs.
FROM	Albany, Kentucky		
SIGNATURE MOVE	Bearhug		

Wearing leather head gear reminiscent of a World War I pilot, a blaring red singlet, purple tights, and a white cape splotched with a design resembling a target, Frank Hickey had the aura of a man who came from another world.

That was the whole idea. Hickey called himself "Spaceman," and posed for photos in a bubble-like astronaut's helmet.

As early as 1948, Hickey, sometimes known as "Bozo Brown," was traversing the wrestling world, earning bizarre distinctions everywhere. He was the last wrestling opponent former boxing champion Joe Louis ever fought, and competed in mixed matches beside Mae Young. His WWE visits, between 1964 and 1974, generally resulted in losses.

In 2003, months before his death, Hickey, 78, still threatened to "grind" his rivals.

FRANK "THE MOOSE" MONROE

WT	295 lbs.	**FROM**	Canada

When you're a nearly 300-pound Canadian, you have every right to call yourself "The Moose," which is what Frank Monroe did while competing in WWE in the 1970s and '80s.

Unfortunately, unlike most moose, Monroe failed to strike fear in his opponents. And rather than use his immense size to his advantage, Monroe gained a reputation for being more of a brawler, whose offense was comprised mainly of punches and kicks.

Monroe's opposition usually had the big man well scouted. They would wait for him to miss an ill-timed punch, and then attack when his weight forced him off balance. Because of this, many of Monroe's matches lasted less than three minutes. In fact, in 1979, Tony Atlas beat "The Moose" in less than one minute.

FRANKIE KAZARIAN

HT	6'1"	**WT**	210 lbs.	**FROM**	Anaheim, California

Frankie Kazarian was arrogant, abrasive, and obnoxious. But most of all, he was confident. In fact, Kazarian was so confident that he billed himself as "The Future" of WWE after only his first match.

With his debut win over Nunzio in his back pocket, the conceited Kazarian looked to make good on his prediction. After wins over Scotty 2 Hotty, Funaki, and Danny Doring, fans were forced to take notice of the talented newcomer.

In August 2005, Kazarian carried his undefeated record into *Velocity* for perhaps his toughest challenge: Paul London. Kazarian was able to beat London, and fans started to think the cocky Superstar might actually be the future of WWE. Mysteriously, though, the undefeated Kazarian disappeared from WWE following his win over London.

FRANKIE WILLIAMS

HT	5'9"	**WT**	239 lbs.	**FROM**	Columbus, Ohio

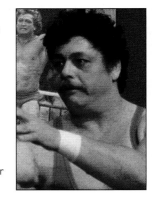

This rugged competitor from the midwestern United States came to WWE in 1976. In one of his first matches, he took on "Nature Boy" Ric Flair at Madison Square Garden. For the next decade, Williams made it tough on opponents like Ken Patera, Ivan Koloff, Nikolai Volkoff, Greg "The Hammer" Valentine, and other WWE legends.

Williams' highest profile battle came in March 1984 when he was a guest on *Piper's Pit* and was attacked by the "Hot Rod," who proceeded to drop his famous line, "Just when they think they got the answers, I change the questions!" In 1991, Frankie Williams passed away. He is warmly remembered as a fan favorite who fought with the heart of a lion.

THE FOUR HORSEMEN

MEMBERS

Ric Flair, Arn Anderson, Tully Blanchard, Ole Anderson, James J. Dillon, Lex Luger, Barry Windham, Sting, Sid Vicious, Paul Roma, Brian Pillman, Chris Benoit, Steve McMichael, Jeff Jarrett, Curt Hennig, & Dean Malenko

Before the New World Order or D-Generation X, there was the Four Horsemen. Originally comprised of Ric Flair, Tully Blanchard, Arn Anderson, Ole Anderson, and manager James J. Dillon, the Horsemen dominated the sports-entertainment scene of the 1980s and '90s, en route to becoming arguably the most influential faction of all time.

In their earliest days, the Horsemen targeted Jim Crockett Promotions's greatest heroes, most notably Magnum TA and Dusty Rhodes. Along the way, the faction's jet flying and limousine riding lifestyle made them tough to dislike, despite their penchant for playing dirty. But when the Horsemen decimated Rhodes's leg in Atlanta's Omni Coliseum in the fall of 1985, fans finally had enough of their reprehensible actions. In fact, a riot nearly broke out after they attacked The American Dream inside a locked steel cage. As a result of the mayhem, it took a half hour for the group to navigate through the crowd and get back to the safety of the locker room.

As the son of a plumber, Rhodes represented everything that the Horsemen were not. He was a common man, while the Horsemen were known for their $700 shoes, nice cars, and big houses. The juxtaposition of the two styles resulted in one of the greatest rivalries of all time.

CHANGING OF THE GUARD

By 1987, Ole Anderson had become increasingly unreliable. He often missed shows in favor of attending his son's amateur wrestling events, which rubbed the other Horsemen the wrong way. Eventually, Anderson's unreliability became too much and he was replaced by Lex Luger in March 1987.

Luger gave the Horsemen an element of raw power they didn't previously have. But despite filling a hole, he didn't quite fit the part of a Horseman, and the two sides went through an ugly split resulting in a bitter rivalry. Joining Luger in his war against the Horsemen was Barry Windham, though he proved to be of little help. In April 1988, Windham turned on Luger and revealed himself to be the newest member of the Horsemen.

Decades later, the Flair-Anderson-Blanchard-Windham-Dillon incarnation of the Four Horsemen is widely regarded as the most successful.

En route to dominating the industry, the foursome claimed every major Championship in the territory.

Flair was World Heavyweight Champion; Windham was United States Champion; and Anderson and Blanchard were World Tag Team Champions.

Perhaps the greatest threat to the Horsemen's reign came at *The Great American Bash* in 1988 when all their Titles were on the line. But by night's end, they once again proved their worth when Anderson and Blanchard fended off Sting and Nikita Koloff, Windham defeated Rhodes, and Flair beat Luger.

COMING AND GOING

To the fans, the Horsemen appeared to be firing on all cylinders. Behind the scenes, however, internal politics began to take its toll on the powerful faction. Among the most impacted by the games played were Anderson and Blanchard, who were reportedly given only $1,000 for their part in *The Great American Bash*. Their manager, Dillon, took home three times that number.

Irate over being underpaid and underappreciated, Anderson and Blanchard defected to WWE. The shocking move effectively destroyed the Four Horsemen, and marked the end of an era that has never been replicated since, despite continued attempts.

After a successful year in WWE, Anderson returned to WCW and played a central part in recreating the legendary faction. This time, however, the Horsemen welcomed Sting in as their fourth member. While popular at first, bringing Sting into the fold quickly proved to be a mistake, as he and longtime rival Flair butted heads over the World Heavyweight Championship.

THE LATER YEARS

Sting was ousted from the Horsemen in early 1990. Following his banishment, such names as Sid Vicious, Brian Pillman, and Curt Hennig all held up the legendary four fingers. And while their versions of the faction never mirrored the success of earlier incarnations, they still managed to leave an indelible mark on WCW.

Nearly two decades after disbanding, the Four Horsemen are still regarded as one of the most notorious groups ever assembled. And in 2012, they took their rightful place among the greats when they were inducted into the WWE Hall of Fame.

IT'S AN ALL NIGHT RIDE!

FREDDIE BLASSIE

HT	5'10"
WT	220 lbs.
FROM	St. Louis, Missouri

Freddie Blassie was a trusted member of the WWE family for more than thirty years. While the fans loved to hate him, everybody who knew him simply loved him.

Born in February 1918, Blassie grew up in St. Louis, where he initially developed his love for wrestling. After getting his feet wet competing in carnivals, he started working for several Midwest and Northeast promoters. While in the Northeast, he briefly competed for Jess McMahon, grandfather of WWE Chairman and CEO Vince McMahon.

THE CLASSY VETERAN

Blassie's budding wrestling career was temporarily derailed when the United States Navy called him to serve in World War II. After the war, in an attempt to capitalize on his Naval experience, he returned to the ring as "Sailor" Fred Blassie. The sailor persona didn't take off the way Blassie had hoped, as he seemed to garner more boos from the fans than his rule-breaking opponents. In what would prove to be a wise move, Blassie embraced their hatred. He ditched his sailor's cap, dyed his hair blonde, and began insulting the fans. The result: "Classy" Freddie Blassie, one of the most hated Superstars of all time.

The ire Blassie drew from the fans is legendary and may never be duplicated. After being stabbed by angry fans more than twenty times and having acid thrown on him, Blassie was eventually forced to travel with full security forces at all times.

WORLDWIDE NOTORIETY

Throughout the 1950s, Blassie captured numerous Championships while competing in the country's Southeast territories. He moved to Los Angeles in 1960, where he duplicated his success by capturing the World Wrestling Association Heavyweight Championship on four occasions. During this time, Blassie competed in a legendary battle with Japanese wrestler Rikidozan. According to legend, Blassie bloodied Rikidozan so badly that it caused several elderly Japanese fans to suffer heart attacks.

The popularity of the bloodbath earned Blassie an opportunity at Bruno Sammartino's WWE Championship in 1964.

Unfortunately, Blassie's penchant for breaking the rules cost him the match. Several years later, he unsuccessfully challenged Pedro Morales for the WWE Championship, as well.

Blassie's in-ring career began to slow down by the mid-1970s. Despite not being able to compete in the ring, he yearned to remain a part of the wrestling community. That's when Vincent J. McMahon hired Blassie to be a manager. He spent the next thirteen years developing one of the most successful managerial careers in sports-entertainment history.

In September 1977, Blassie guided Mr. Fuji and Professor Tanaka to the World Tag Team Championship. A few years later, he had the distinction of introducing a young Hulk Hogan to WWE audiences. But Blassie's greatest success came while managing Iron Sheik. In December 1983, he was in Sheik's corner when the Iranian Superstar ended Bob Backlund's nearly six-year WWE Championship reign. The victory proved to be the biggest of any Blassie protégé.

In March 1985, Blassie became a part of history when he led Nikolai Volkoff and Iron Sheik to the first-ever Title change in *WrestleMania* history. In traditional Blassie fashion, he used his cane to help his duo turn back Barry Windham and Mike Rotundo for the World Tag Team Championship at the inaugural *WrestleMania*.

The following year, Blassie sold half interest in his stable of Superstars to managing newcomer, Slick. Shortly after that, he decided to retire, awarding the "Doctor of Style" full control of his men.

In 1994, Blassie assumed his rightful spot in history when he was inducted into the WWE Hall of Fame. Nearly a decade later, he returned to WWE television when he famously instructed D-Von Dudley to get his signature tables.

The wrestling world lost one of its greatest entertainers when Freddie Blassie passed away in June 2003. Despite their dislike for his underhanded tactics, fans everywhere will forever remember with great fondness when he would call them "pencil-neck geeks!"

LISTEN, YOU PENCIL-NECKED GEEK!

FREDDY JOE FLOYD

| HT | 6'1" | WT | 235 lbs. | FROM | Bowlegs, Oklahoma |

Freddy Joe Floyd was a Southern boy trying to make good in the world of sports-entertainment. When he finally broke into WWE in the mid-1990s, he became an overnight sensation in his small hometown of Bowlegs, Oklahoma. Unfortunately for Floyd, however, the admiration of his hometown did not equate to wins in the ring. Week after week, Bowlegs residents would huddle around a small television only to watch their hero continually fall to the likes of Vader, Billy Gunn, and the deranged Mankind.

The unrelenting Floyd kept battling, despite his unimpressive record. His perseverance finally paid off when he scored a count-out victory over Triple H, thanks in large part to interference by Mr. Perfect. When Floyd's singles career failed to take off, he tried his hand at tag team competition. With fellow journeyman Barry Horowitz by his side, the Southerner suffered a similar fate. By mid-1997, he had left WWE to return to his humble home in Bowlegs.

FRENCHY MARTIN

| HT | 6'2" | WT | 240 lbs. | FROM | Quebec City, Quebec |
| SIGNATURE MOVE | Knee Drop |

Frenchy Martin started his in-ring career in 1971 in Quebec and soon traveled west to Stu Hart's Stampede Wrestling. From there, he found success in Puerto Rico and Japan in both singles and tag team action. In 1986, Frenchy moved south to WWE.

After success as a competitor, Martin decided to share his wealth of knowledge as a manager, beginning in 1987 with Dino Bravo. Martin guided Bravo to Championship contention, while also launching an anti-American campaign that revolved around the slogan, "USA Is Not Okay." Frenchy was also known to assist his client with a punch or kick whenever necessary. As he entered his third decade in sports-entertainment, Martin became a color commentator for WWE's French programming.

FRIAR FERGUSON

| HT | 6'1" | WT | 385 lbs. |

Unlike most men of the cloth, Friar Ferguson enjoyed inflicting pain on people. He loved it so much, in fact, that he oftentimes broke out into dance whenever he felled an opponent. Ferguson's love for brutality wasn't the only characteristic that set him apart from his fellow religious servants. Unlike most friars, Ferguson completely ignored his vow of poverty, spending staggering amounts of money at the buffet line. At nearly four-hundred pounds, he was one of the largest Superstars of his time.

After only a few weeks, Ferguson disappeared from WWE, presumably to return to a life of preaching the good word.

FUNAKI

| HT | 5'7" | WT | 180 lbs. | FROM | Japan |
| SIGNATURE MOVE | Rising Sun |

Funaki made his WWE debut in 1998 as part of the "evil" Japanese faction, Kaientai. Over time, fans had no choice but to cheer for Funaki, as he brought entire arenas to laughter with just one word—INDEED!

With the fans by his side, Funaki's career began to build steam. At *WrestleMania 2000*, he managed to pin the monstrous Viscera to capture the Hardcore Championship. Despite barely understanding a word of English, Funaki was tapped by Stephanie McMahon to become a backstage interviewer in 2002. The Japanese Superstar happily accepted the position and amazingly nicknamed himself "*SmackDown*'s No. 1 Announcer."

Funaki silenced his microphone in late 2004 in an attempt to gain more Championship gold. He accomplished his goal when he toppled Spike Dudley at *Armageddon* to capture the Cruiserweight Championship. Later in his WWE career, he became Kung Fu Naki and showed off a special set of martial arts strikes and holds.

THE FUNK BROTHERS

| MEMBERS | Terry, Dory/Hoss, & Jimmy Jack | COMBINED WT | 587 lbs. |

When it comes to being the roughest, toughest, meanest, and most technically gifted Superstars to ever compete in the ring, you'll be hard pressed to find many greater than the legendary Funk Brothers.

After cementing their legacies with NWA World Heavyweight Championship reigns, Dory (rechristened "Hoss") and Terry Funk entered WWE in the mid-1980s. Under the tutelage of Jimmy "The Mouth of the South" Hart, The Amarillo ruffians administered beatings to dozens of Superstars, branding their fallen foes with the Double-Cross Ranch logo along the way.

While the Funk Brothers clashed with the likes of Ricky Steamboat, the British Bulldogs, Hulk Hogan, Pedro Morales, and Paul Orndorff, their battles against Junkyard Dog remain some of the most vicious times in WWE history. Their rivalry culminated in a tag team match at *WrestleMania 2*, which saw the Funks defeat JYD and partner Tito Santana after Terry nailed the Dog with Hart's signature megaphone.

By summer of 1986, Terry left WWE, while Dory continued to appear briefly alongside mysterious younger brother Jimmy Jack. In the early 1990s, Terry and Dory appeared in ECW and cemented their iconic status throughout Asia. After more than forty years captivating audiences, Terry and Dory's magnificent contributions were celebrated when they entered the WWE Hall of Fame in 2009.

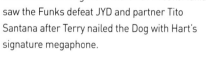

FUZZY CUPID

| HT | 4'0" | WT | 86 lbs. | FROM | Newport, Rhode Island |

When he was a young adult, Leon Stap took a trip to Texas that would forever change his life. While there, he attended a wrestling event and became awed by the athleticism of the dwarf competitors. He sought out the show's promoter, who sent Stap to Detroit for training. The rest is sports-entertainment history.

After training, Stap debuted in 1952 as Fuzzy Cupid. He quickly became one of the most unpopular Superstars in his division, as there wasn't a rule he wouldn't break.

Cupid earned his greatest success competing as a tag team with Sky Low Low. Together, they ruled the Canadian dwarf scene of the mid-1960s. Cupid and Low Low also engaged in a brief WWE rivalry with Tiny Tim and Pancho Lopez.

GAIL KIM

| HT | 5'4" | FROM | Toronto, Ontario, Canada |
| SIGNATURE MOVE | | Top-Rope Hurricanrana |

Gail Kim walked to the ring in sleek, long leather coats and sunglasses. Inside the ring, she used a mix of lucha libre, Japanese, and Canadian grappling styles, along with a variety of unique submission holds that left opponents broken and battered.

This Maple-Leaf minx burst on the WWE scene and made history winning the Women's Championship in her debut in June 2003. Kim bested seven other Divas in an over-the-top rope Battle Royal. She lost the Title to the persistent Molly Holly one month later and spent the majority of the next year trying unsuccessfully to get it back.

Gail left WWE but returned in 2009 to become an immediate contender for the Divas Championship. During that time she grew close with Daniel Bryan. Their relationship did not sit well with the Bella Twins, which resulted in frequent confrontations. Despite her best efforts, Gail never attained her Championship goals before parting with the company again in 2011.

GAMA SINGH

| HT | 5'10" | WT | 225 lbs. | FROM | Punjabi, India |
| SIGNATURE MOVE | | Camel Clutch |

Born in India, Gama Singh never fully achieved a solid reputation in the United States. He did, however, become a major draw for WWE during the promotion's international tours of the early-to-mid 1980s. Fans in such places as Australia, Kuwait, and Dubai came out in droves every time Singh was advertised to compete. His chief competition during this time was future WWE Hall of Famer "Rowdy" Roddy Piper.

Singh also had many memorable battles with legends Don Muraco and "Cowboy" Bob Orton. When not competing in WWE, Singh was very successful competing in Stu Hart's Stampede Wrestling in Calgary, Alberta, Canada.

DAVID HEATH
(KNOWN IN WWE AS GANGREL)

| HT | 6'1" | WT | 250 lbs. | FROM | The Other Side of Darkness |
| SIGNATURE MOVE | | Blood Bath |

Being elevated through a ring of fire, David Heath, known as Gangrel in WWE, had one of the most ominous entrances ever. Once he hit the ring, the fang-toothed Superstar would sip from his medieval goblet and spew a blood-colored liquid into the crowd.

Despite targeting many of WWE's fan favorites, Gangrel's vampire-like appearance actually became appealing to many fans. Within weeks of his 1998 debut, he had acquired a strong cult following. His popularity grew even greater after forming an alliance with Edge and Christian.

Known as The Brood, the goth trio vandalized the WWE roster, oftentimes soaking them with a blood-like substance. The event, which became known as a Blood Bath, struck fear into many. It wasn't long before their demonic behavior caught the eye of Undertaker, who recruited them into his Ministry of Darkness.

In August 1999, David Heath, formerly known as Gangrel, betrayed Edge and Christian and formed The New Brood with the Hardy Boyz. Despite the Hardys' talents, the new union quickly fizzled. With Luna Vachon, he then set out on a singles career where he often appeared on *Heat* and *Jakked*.

Heath's Gangrel persona made vampires cool before they exploded in modern pop culture. WWE fans were teeming with excitement when he appeared at *Raw's* 15th Anniversary.

GARY MICHAEL CAPPETTA

Longtime fan Gary Michael Cappetta began his WWE career in 1974 when he volunteered to be a ring announcer on a northeastern card. Once his voice traveled through the arena, WWE knew they had their man for events in the New Jersey, Delaware, and Pennsylvania areas.

The advent of cable television and home video resulted in Cappetta being the first ring announcer to enjoy an international following. He continued to announce the world's biggest matches until his departure from WWE in 1985.

In 1989, Cappetta accepted an offer from WCW and appeared at all of the promotion's major events. Since he was fluent in Spanish, Cappetta also commentated on WCW's Spanish telecasts before retiring in May 1995.

GAVIN SPEARS

HT	6'3"	WT	225 lbs.
FROM	Niagara Falls, Ontario, Canada		
SIGNATURE MOVE	Running Death Valley Driver		

From a long line of distinguished grapplers from the Great White North, Gavin Spears is accustomed to being the best at whatever endeavor he pursues. A top hockey player for over a decade, Spears decided to leave the rink and enter the ring following boyhood idols like "Ravishing" Rick Rude, Rick Martel, Mr. Perfect, and "Nature Boy" Ric Flair.

In August 2008, Spears debuted and announced he was the "Crown jewel of ECW's New Superstar Initiative." Spears encouraged others to study him to learn what wrestling was really about. While his claims were great, and the matches he had with the likes of Tommy Dreamer, Finlay, and Super Crazy were solid efforts, Spears' time in ECW did not pan out the way he had expected.

GENE AND STEVE STANLEE

COMBINED WT	435 lbs.

Gene and Steve Stanlee were known as the "Mr. Americas of Wrestling," two supremely fit athletes who added a much-needed flourish to the sport in television's early years.

Both brothers had served in the US Navy in World War II. While deployed in the South Pacific, Gene wrestled for the other sailors. Steve became an expert at both judo and karate.

The "Stanlee Steamers" began teaming together in 1951. Gene was a true showman who strutted down the aisle, and wore ring jackets—a rarity for the time—as well as monogrammed towels.

After Gene left the industry to promote his regimen of yoga and vegetarianism to Hollywood stars, Steve appeared on WWE cards in the mid-1960s, scoring wins over Baron Mikel Scicluna and Arnold Skaaland.

GENE DUBOIS

HT	5'11"	WT	235 lbs.
FROM	North Bay, Ontario		
SIGNATURE MOVE	Bearhug		

When Ivan Koloff shocked the world in 1971 by defeating WWE World Heavyweight Champion Bruno Sammartino, most of wrestling's major names lined up for a title opportunity. The majority missed their chance, since Koloff was dethroned by Pedro Morales after 21 days. Gene DuBois was a notable exception. Although that effort failed, DuBois spent the rest of his career satisfied with having taken advantage of the opportunity.

DuBois had come up rough, sometimes wrestling a bear when no other opponents were available. From 1969 to 1972, he made regular appearances in WWE, trying his hand against Blackjack Mulligan, Tarzan Tyler, Professor Toru Tanaka, and other foes, while teaming with fan favorites like Gorilla Monsoon and Dominic DeNucci. He passed away in 1988.

GENE KINISKI

HT	6'4"	WT	270 lbs.	FROM	Edmonton, Alberta, Canada
SIGNATURE MOVE	Backbreaker				

One of the greatest athletes to ever come out of Canada, Gene Kiniski excelled in the Canadian Football League before turning down National Football League offers to embark on a career in the ring. Armed with the training he received from Tony Morelli and the legendary Dory Funk Sr., Kiniski debuted in 1953. Within two years, he was challenging Lou Thesz for the NWA Championship. Still relatively inexperienced, Kiniski failed to wrest the Title away from Thesz, but the two Superstars would meet again more than ten years later.

In 1961, Kiniski defeated Verne Gagne to capture the AWA Championship. The victory gave him his first World Title and opened the doors to several WWE Championship opportunities against Bruno Sammartino. At one point in 1964, Kiniski actually believed he defeated Sammartino for the Title and left Madison Square Garden with the WWE Championship. Kiniski, though not the rightful Champion, kept the Title in his possession for nearly one month before losing to Sammartino in a rematch.

More than a decade after failing in his initial attempts to gain the NWA Championship, Kiniski beat the legendary Thesz for the Title in January 1966. He held the Championship for more than three years before being upended by Dory Funk Jr. At the time of his defeat, Kiniski owned the second longest reign in NWA history, thus proving himself as one of the greatest competitors of all time.

GENE OKERLUND

"Mean" Gene Okerlund is arguably the most recognizable interviewer in the history of the ring. Over the course of his 40 years in wrestling, his pull-no-punches approach has coaxed revealing answers from the game's greatest, including Andre the Giant, Ric Flair, and Hulk Hogan.

Okerlund's first big break came in the early 1970s, when he was tapped to serve as a temporary interviewer in the AWA. His line of questioning, however, was so impressive that he soon earned a full-time role. While there, he interviewed many future WWE stars, such as Hulk Hogan and Bobby Heenan. It was during this period when Jesse Ventura gave him the moniker, "Mean" Gene, which took root and lasts to this day.

In 1984, Okerlund made the jump to WWE. It's here that he proved his esteemed place in ring lore. No pre- or post-match interview was complete without "Mean Gene" interjecting with his insightful wit, which also served him well as a host of several WWE programs. On one occasion, Okerlund even competed in a tag team match where he and Hulk Hogan defeated Mr. Fuji and George "The Animal" Steele. He also proved to be quite the vocalist, as he sang the national anthem at the inaugural *WrestleMania*. Outside the ring, Okerlund's adventures alongside personalities like Heenan and The Bushwhackers provided timeless laughter for fans.

After nine years of asking WWE Superstars the tough questions, Okerlund headed to WCW in 1993. As a member of WCW's announce team, he served as the promotion's backstage interviewer during the height of the Monday Night War. He chided Hulk Hogan for joining the nWo at *Bash at the Beach 1996*. However by April 2006, all was forgiven when Okerlund's longtime friend inducted him into the WWE Hall of Fame.

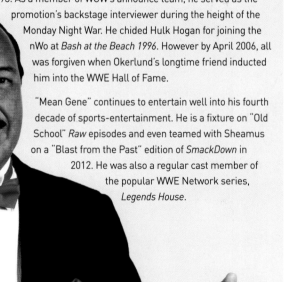

"Mean Gene" continues to entertain well into his fourth decade of sports-entertainment. He is a fixture on "Old School" *Raw* episodes and even teamed with Sheamus on a "Blast from the Past" edition of *SmackDown* in 2012. He was also a regular cast member of the popular WWE Network series, *Legends House*.

GENERAL ADNAN

HT	6'0"	WT	245 lbs.	FROM	Iraq

With the Gulf War foremost in Americans' minds, Iraqi sympathizer Sgt. Slaughter introduced WWE audiences to General Adnan in 1991. Striking an eerie resemblance to Saddam Hussein, Adnan was brought in to serve as Slaughter's commanding officer. According to Slaughter, Adnan was a great military mind from a great military power, Iraq.

The defining moment of Adnan's WWE career saw the Iraqi holding a Hulk Hogan T-shirt while Slaughter set it ablaze. The fire incited fans, who at the time recognized The Hulkster as the definitive American hero. In the ultimate sign of disrespect, Adnan simply laughed as the shirt went up in flames.

In addition to acting as manager, Adnan also competed in the ring alongside Col. Mustafa and Slaughter. Known as The Triangle of Terror, Adnan, Mustafa, and Slaughter headlined *SummerSlam 1991* when they battled Hogan and Ultimate Warrior. Dubbed "A Match Made in Hell," Hogan and Warrior turned back The Triangle in a thrilling encounter. Afterward, Adnan and Mustafa publicly blamed Slaughter for the loss, marking the official end of The Triangle.

GENICHIRO TENRYU

HT	6'1"	WT	260 lbs.	FROM	Katsuyama City, Japan
SIGNATURE MOVE		**Northern Lights Bomb**			

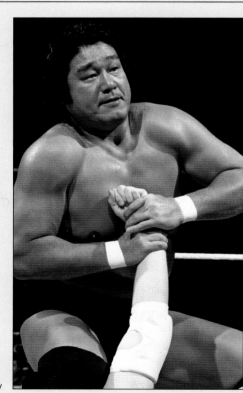

During the 1960s and '70s, Genichiro Tenryu excelled as a renowned sumo wrestler before switching gears and embarking on what would become a storied career in sports-entertainment.

Tenryu made several WWE appearances in the early-1990s. His first official showing was at *WrestleMania VII* when he and partner Koji Katao demolished Demolition in less than five minutes. The next battle was in his homeland of Japan during the SWS/WWE series of co-promoted supershows. On the first night, Tenryu pinned Randy "Macho Man" Savage in front of a capacity Tokyo Dome crowd. One week later, he joined forces with Hulk Hogan in a battle against The Legion of Doom.

Tenryu competed in the 1993 and 1994 Royal Rumble Matches before returning to his homeland. With nearly forty years of experience, Genichiro Tenryu is regarded as one of the best competitors to emerge from Japan and is among a small group of men in the history of puroresu to hold pinfall victories over both Antonio Inoki and Shohei "Giant" Baba.

"GENTLEMAN" JERRY VALIANT

HT	6'0"	FROM	New York, New York
SIGNATURE MOVE		Sleeper	

In 1979, while "Handsome" Jimmy and "Luscious" Johnny Valiant were at the peak of their fame, Jimmy suddenly fell ill. Rather than disband, the pair contacted their third brother, "Gentleman" Jerry Valiant and asked him to join them in WWE.

Although Jerry and Johnny Valiant were managed by Captain Lou Albano, Jimmy was also a presence in their corner, carefully grooming Jerry until he came into his own. The lessons worked quickly. On March 24, 1979, Jerry and Johnny bested Tony Garea and Larry Zbyszko to etch the family name in the annals of WWE as World Tag Team Champions. They held the Titles for more than seven months before losing them to Tito Santana and Ivan Putski. When Jimmy recovered, the three Valiant siblings also appeared in six-man clashes.

In 1980, the Valiants went their separate ways. However, Jerry returned to WWE in single's action in 1983, where he remained for the next three years. In 2005, fans gathered to celebrate the three Valiants at a reunion in New Jersey.

GEORGE SOUTH

HT	6'2"	WT	240 lbs.	FROM	Atlanta, Georgia
SIGNATURE MOVE		The Claw Hold			

A fixture of Jim Crockett Promotions in the early and mid-1980s, George South is remembered for a thrilling televised challenge he gave NWA Champion Ric Flair.

Later, he plied his trade in WWE and continued his rule-breaking ways against opponents like Ricky "The Dragon" Steamboat, The British Bulldogs, Koko B. Ware, Jake "The Snake" Roberts, and future WWE Hall of Famers including Tito Santana and the Junkyard Dog.

Today, George continues to bring his opponents to the limit all around the world, and owns his own school, training the prospective stars of tomorrow.

GEORGE "THE ANIMAL" STEELE
see page 129

GEORGE WELLS

HT	6'3"	WT	243 lbs.	FROM	Oakland, California

An accomplished linebacker for New Mexico State University, George Wells was drafted by the San Francisco 49ers in the fifth round of the 1971 NFL Draft. He then went on to play eight seasons in the Canadian Football League before shifting his focus to WWE, where he would become known for his run-in with Jake Roberts's famous snake.

After Roberts soundly defeated Wells at *WrestleMania 2*, Jake's snake aggressively wrapped itself around the former football player's neck. The force of the attack caused Wells to foam from the mouth and fans worldwide to hide their eyes in fear. Wells's brief stay in WWE ended quickly after.

GEORGIA CHAMPIONSHIP WRESTLING

With its national outlet on Ted Turner's TBS Superstation, Georgia Championship Wrestling was one of the most visible territories of the 1980s—and the center point of several promotional wars.

Started in 1944 by promoter Paul Jones, the territory's main spot was Atlanta's Municipal Auditorium, where Freddie Blassie and Don McIntyre competed for the NWA Southern Heavyweight Championship in the 1950s. In 1972, after promoter Ray Gunkel died following a match in Savannah, his widow, Ann, started a rival group, All-South Wrestling. Both Georgia promotions ran on TBS until All-South folded in 1974.

In 1982, promoter Jim Barnett changed the name "Georgia Championship Wrestling" to "World Championship Wrestling" (WCW), a moniker he'd used when he promoted in Australia, and took advantage of TBS's national exposure to promote in Ohio and Michigan. Then, in 1984, WWE secured the company's time slot on TBS, prompting a short-lived group headed by Ole Anderson to also run a show on the network. In 1985, WWE sold its slot to Charlotte promoter, Jim Crockett Jr., who eventually absorbed the territory.

GIANT GONZALES

HT	8'0"	WT	460 lbs.
FROM	Argentina		
SIGNATURE MOVE		Chokeslam	

Towering at 8-feet, Giant Gonzales was the tallest Superstar in WWE history. Beginning his career as El Gigante (Spanish for The Giant) in WCW, he battled the likes of Sid Vicious and Ric Flair before coming to WWE. At *Royal Rumble 1993*, he debuted by eliminating Undertaker from the 30-Man Royal Rumble Match. The move laid the foundation for a rivalry that lasted the entire length of Gonzales' WWE career.

At *WrestleMania IX*, Gonzales attacked Undertaker with a cloth soaked in chloroform. With Undertaker rendered motionless, many onlookers began to fear the worst. Miraculously, however, Undertaker rose to his feet and cleared the ring of his nemesis.

Following this savage attack, Gonzales tried to finish the job at *SummerSlam 1993* in a Rest in Peace Match. Like *WrestleMania*, however, the result favored Undertaker. After the match, a frustrated Gonzales hit his smarmy manager, Harvey Wippleman, with his signature Chokeslam. Though the move delighted fans, Gonzales was gone from WWE soon thereafter.

GEORGE
THE ANIMAL
STEELE (HoF)

HT	6'1"
WT	275 lbs.
FROM	Detroit, Michigan

SIGNATURE MOVE
The Flying Hammerlock

Since its inception in 1963, WWE has been home to some of the most bizarre individuals to walk the earth. However, no one has proved to be more peculiar than WWE Hall of Famer, George "The Animal" Steele. With his bushy body, green tongue, and voracious appetite for turnbuckles, Steele's eccentric behavior made him one of sports-entertainment's most curious figures.

Seen as an uncontrollable maniac, Steele debuted in WWE during the summer of 1968. To the horror of audiences, he regularly attacked heroes such as Édouard Carpentier, "Golden Boy" Arnold Skaaland, "High Chief" Peter Maivia, and Chief Jay Strongbow. The Animal also engaged in a vicious rivalry with WWE Champion Bruno Sammartino. Steele stopped at nothing to maim the Champion, which appeared to be his main goal, followed by claiming the prized Title. Over the course of their rivalry, the two competitors collided in Lumberjack, Stretcher, and Steel Cage Matches. Despite their continued conflicts, nothing seemed to settle their score. Furthermore, their Texas Death Match had to be officiated by boxing legend Joe Louis.

In the years that followed, The Animal was one of the most serious threats to the Championship reigns of Pedro Morales and Bob Backlund. Though his unorthodox behavior and bizarre outbursts frightened fans, it was his flying hammerlock that caused fear within WWE. If allowed, Steele could use the submission hold to break an opponent's arm or separate a shoulder within seconds.

The Animal's multitude of illegal tactics included unending biting fits, blatant chokes, scratching, clawing, and eye-raking. In keeping with the rule-breaking theme, Steele was also dubbed, "The Master of the Foreign Object," as he had a propensity of hiding weapons on his person. Over the course of his terror-filled time in the ring, Steele was guided by "Classy" Freddie Blassie, The Grand Wizard, Mr. Fuji, and "Luscious" Johnny Valiant, though none could truly control The Animal's irrepressible rage.

The notoriously-vicious Steele had a surprising change of ways in the 1980s. The longtime antagonist actually became one of sports-entertainment's most beloved figures after he was abandoned by partners Iron Sheik and Nikolai Volkoff on *Saturday Night's Main Event*. Sympathizing with Steele, fans began to cheer every unpredictable move The Animal made.

GREEN TONGUE-TIED IN LOVE

In 1986 The Animal found himself in the middle of an intense, yet puzzling love triangle with then-Intercontinental Champion, Randy "Macho Man" Savage, and his manager, the lovely Miss Elizabeth. While fans adored the "Beauty and the Beast" aspect to Steele's interest in Elizabeth, Savage was incensed by The Animal's actions toward her. The rivalry culminated at *WrestleMania 2* where Savage successfully defended his Title against Steele.

While *WrestleMania 2* failed to give "The Animal" the storybook ending he had hoped, Steele continued to be a nuisance to the "Macho Man." And at *WrestleMania III*, he gained his revenge by helping Ricky Steamboat defeat Savage for the coveted Intercontinental Championship.

The Animal continued to rip turnbuckles and destroy opponents into the latter part of the 1980s. To add to his already perplexing persona, Steele also began walking to the ring with new friend, "Mine," a huggable stuffed bear that bore an unusual resemblance to The Animal. By decade's end, Steele temporarily disappeared from the WWE.

In 1994, "The Animal" invaded Hollywood when he debuted in acclaimed director, Tim Burton's Oscar-winning film, *Ed Wood*. The following year, he took his rightful place in the WWE Hall of Fame. Then, in typical fashion, Steele astonished fans when he returned to WWE during the "Attitude Era" as a member of the lovable Oddities.

The lore of George Steele becomes greater as time goes on. He is one of the most adored characters in the history of sports-entertainment and an individual who entertained legions of fans wherever he went.

HEY I'M NOT AN ANIMAL I'M A PEOPLE I'M A PEOPLE I'M A PEOPLE

MINE

GILLBERG

| HT | 6'0" | WT | 227 lbs. | FROM | Atlanta, Georgia |

| SIGNATURE MOVE | The Jackhammer |

The thunderous music, blinding pyrotechnics, tribal body art, and sports-entertainment's most incredible streak must mean only one Superstar is on the way to the ring: Gillberg!

A parody of WCW's Goldberg, Gillberg exploded onto WWE during the height of the Monday Night War. While he started as a playful poke at the then-WCW Champion, Gillberg soon shocked the world when he defeated Christian for the WWE Light Heavyweight Championship, a Title he held for nearly fifteen months. Along the way, Gillberg joined forces with the vaunted J.O.B. Squad, who also doubled as his pyro-technicians.

Though Gillberg never achieved the success of his WCW counterpart, he still remains one of the most revered Superstars of the Attitude Era.

GINO BRITO

| HT | 5'10" | WT | 240 lbs. | FROM | Montreal, Quebec, Canada |

Prior to becoming an accomplished in-ring competitor, Gino Brito worked for his father, promoter Jack Britton, in Montreal. His chief responsibility was escorting his family's famous faction of pocket-sized Superstars from town to town. Once he became old enough, the fiery Italian Superstar hit the ring, teaming with best friend Tony Parisi.

Brito also competed under the name Louis Cerdan in the WWE. With Parisi as his partner, Cerdan defeated The Blackjacks for the World Tag Team Championship in November 1975. They held the Titles for more than six months before being dethroned by The Executioners.

GLAMOUR GIRLS

| MEMBERS | Judy Martin & Leilani Kai |

With long blonde hair and glittery gold tights, Judy Martin and Leilani Kai claimed to bring glamour to WWE's women's division in the mid-to-late 1980s. The egotistical duo, appropriately named the Glamour Girls, are remembered as the only two-time WWE Women's Tag Team Champions.

Martin and Kai earned their first reign in August 1985 at the expense of Velvet McIntyre and Desiree Peterson. With manager Jimmy Hart leading the way, the Glamour Girls held a firm grasp on the gold until January 1988 when the Jumping Bomb Angels upset them at the inaugural *Royal Rumble*.

After reclaiming the Titles from the Jumping Bomb Angels in Japan, Martin and Kai returned to the United States, where they successfully defended the gold until the Titles became defunct in 1989.

In addition to being the most decorated women's tag team in WWE history, the Glamour Girls were also famously a part of Sensational Sherri Martel's team that fell to the Fabulous Moolah's squad at the first-ever *Survivor Series*.

THE GOBBLEDY GOOKER

At *Survivor Series 1990*, a giant egg sat outside the arena. "Mean" Gene Okerlund was determined to find out what was waiting inside. The weeks of speculation ended when the egg hatched and the Gobbledy Gooker emerged. Once in the ring, this agile cross between a human and a turkey shook a leg with dance moves, forward rolls, and flips over the ropes.

The Gobbledy Gooker quietly vanished after its initial appearance, but just when the world thought it was safe from this avian anomaly, Gooker's feathered fury appeared at *WrestleMania X-Seven*'s Gimmick Battle Royal. Unfortunately, it was eliminated in short order.

In recent years, new Gooker misadventures have been seen on a *WWE.com* video playlist called "Gobbledy Gooker Goes to Work." The New Day's Xavier Woods also wore the infamous suit for a Thanksgiving Pot Luck dinner in 2015.

THE GODFATHER

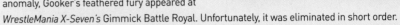

| HT | 6'6" | WT | 330 lbs. | FROM | Las Vegas, Nevada |

| SIGNATURE MOVE | Pimp Drop & Ho Train |

WWE's popular Attitude Era was defined by Superstars who pushed the bounds of decency. During this controversial period, no Superstar ruffled more feathers than The Godfather.

As the Nation of Domination dissolved, the former member became consumed by his pimp persona. Each night, he was led to the ring by a long line of scantily clad women he affectionately referred to as his "Ho Train." Despite being surrounded by miles of shapely curves, he somehow was under the impression that "pimpin' ain't easy."

In the ring, the normally fun-loving Superstar was all business. He defeated Faarooq, Marc Mero, Viscera, and others on his way to the Intercontinental Championship, which he captured from Goldust in April 1999. He went on to defend the Title for six weeks before Jeff Jarrett upended him on an episode of *Raw*.

The Godfather's "Ho Train" was briefly derailed when he joined Steven Richards' Right to Censor crusade in 2000. While he did manage to claim the World Tag Team Championship under the RTC banner, fans couldn't come to grips with a WWE sans their favorite pimp. Luckily for everybody, The Godfather came to his senses and once again began keeping company with his lovely ladies in 2002.

Though his train left the WWE station over a decade ago, he still takes an easygoing stroll down the ramp on occasion, most recently at *Royal Rumble 2013*. In 2016, he dazzled at the podium during the Hall of Fame Induction Ceremony, as he accepted WWE's most prestigious honor.

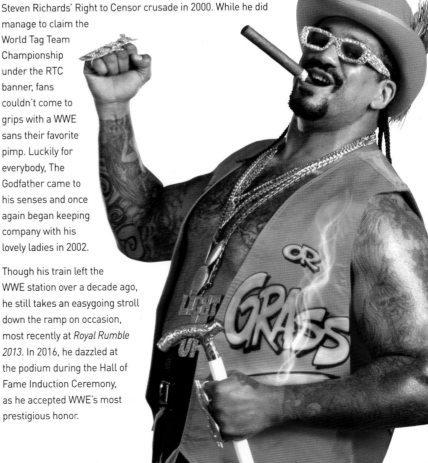

THE GODWINNS

MEMBERS	Phineas I. & Henry O.		
COMBINED WT	576 lbs.	FROM	Bitters, Arkansas

These hog farmers brought their bucket of slop to WWE from Arkansas in the mid-1990s. Managed by Hillbilly Jim, Phineas and Henry brought the fighting style from the back of the barn into the ring. The "good ol' boys" scuffled with the likes of the Bodydonnas, the Smokin' Gunns, and the New Rockers, often finishing off opponents with the Slop Drop.

In May 1996, they became World Tag Team Champions, but their reign lasted only a single week. During a match against the Legion of Doom, Henry was hit with a Doomsday Device, which resulted in a serious injury. That incident sparked a new attitude in the Godwinns. They dismissed Hillbilly Jim and attacked opponents with slop buckets. At *In Your House: Badd Blood* they defeated the Headbangers for a second run with the World Tag Team Championship, but lost their Titles two days later to Hawk and Animal.

Despite two Title reigns that were among the shortest in WWE history, the Godwinns are remembered fondly for bringing their unique style to sports-entertainment.

GOLDBERG

HT	6'4"	WT	285 lbs.	FROM	Atlanta, Georgia
SIGNATURE MOVE	Jackhammer				

A former member of the NFL's Atlanta Falcons, Goldberg turned to sports-entertainment in 1997. What followed was the single most impressive rookie campaign in history. With no experience, Goldberg used his immense size to rack up an improbable 173-0 record. With each passing victory, the newcomer confidently questioned, "Who's next?"

Goldberg's early WCW days saw him pick up wins over seasoned veterans such as Raven and Perry Saturn. It wasn't long before his impressive spear and Jackhammer started shooting him up the rankings. By the end of his first year, the undefeated Goldberg had captured the prestigious United States Championship.

Goldberg put his unbelievable streak on the line against Hollywood Hogan's WCW Championship on a July 1998 edition of *Monday Nitro*. The dream continued for Goldberg that night, as he defeated the legendary Hulkster for the biggest prize in WCW. He went on to defend the Championship for five months before losing both the Title and his undefeated streak to Kevin Nash at *Starrcade 1998*.

WWE fans finally got their first glimpse of Goldberg when he made his highly-anticipated debut in March 2003. Much like his early days in WCW, Goldberg's impact was immediately felt. The Rock, Chris Jericho, and Christian were just a few of the high-profile names that fell to the mighty newcomer.

By July, Goldberg had his sights set on claiming the World Heavyweight Championship. Unlike his first WCW Championship victory, however, then-Champion Triple H wasn't going to go down easy. To ensure he would continue to hold the gold, "The Game" had Evolution watching his back.

After a few failed attempts at getting through Evolution, Goldberg put his career on the line against Triple H's Title at *Unforgiven 2003*. In the end, it was Goldberg who walked away with the gold. Unfortunately for the new Champion, he failed to recreate the same magic he made while holding the WCW Championship.

In his final match, Goldberg defeated Brock Lesnar at *WrestleMania XX*. Afterward, Special Guest Referee Stone Cold Steve Austin delivered Stunners to both Goldberg and Lesnar.

THE GOLDEN TERROR

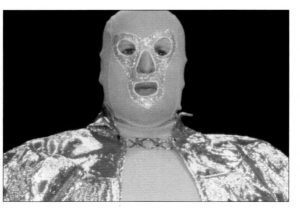

Despite the mystery surrounding The Golden Terror's career, records can accurately prove that he competed during the 1960s. He had a brief WWE stay that saw him fall to WWE Champion Bruno Sammartino on several different occasions. In addition to Sammartino, The Golden Terror's unimpressive win-loss record was also marred by Arnold Skaaland, Bobo Brazil, and Chief Wahoo McDaniel, among others.

After competing in WWE, The Golden Terror moved his mysterious mat game to Georgia where he formed regular tag teams with Butcher Vachon and George Harris. According to record books, The Golden Terror's time in Georgia was equally unsuccessful as his WWE days.

GOLDUST

HT	6'6"	WT	260 lbs.	FROM	Hollywood, California
SIGNATURE MOVE		Curtain Call			

Dressed in gold from head to toe, Goldust made his WWE debut in 1995 and resembled more of an award statue than a WWE Superstar. His appearance was fitting considering his fondness for quoting classic movies, but it was also a bit peculiar when you take into account that underneath all that gold garb was Dustin Rhodes, the son of the legendary Dusty Rhodes, and the same all-American boy who achieved great success while competing in WCW in the early-to-mid 1990s.

Upon adopting the bizarre Goldust persona, Rhodes began complementing his superior in-ring skills with a brand of psychological warfare never before seen in WWE. Playing off the presumed homophobic fears of his opponents, Goldust oftentimes made suggestive advances toward his foes, leaving them vulnerable for him to land his signature Curtain Call.

Within months of his debut, Goldust coupled his natural ability and unparalleled mind games to defeat Razor Ramon for the Intercontinental Championship. It was The Bizarre One's first of three reigns with the prestigious Title. In subsequent years, Goldust defeated both Savio Vega and Road Dogg to claim the Championship.

In late 1997, a confused Goldust left his "director," Marlena, to become an even more bizarre Superstar referred to as The Artist Formerly Known as Goldust. With Luna Vachon by his side, he engaged in a brief rivalry with Marc Mero and Sable before finally coming to his senses and returning to the Goldust persona.

Goldust left WWE in 1999, only to return again two years later. Upon his return, he became a force in the hardcore division, capturing the Hardcore Championship nine times. Goldust also became a World Tag Team Champion when he teamed with Booker T to win a Fatal 4-Way Match at *Armageddon 2002*.

Goldust continued to prove his worth as a tag team competitor in more recent years when he joined forces with his brother, Cody Rhodes. Together, the duo defeated The Shield for the WWE Tag Team Championship in October 2013. And when Cody later transformed into the inter-dimensional oddity known as Stardust, the brothers captured more gold when they defeated The Usos in September 2014.

More than two decades after his controversial WWE debut, Goldust continues to be a major force in WWE.

THE GOON

HT	6'1"	WT	250 lbs.	FROM	Duluth, Minnesota

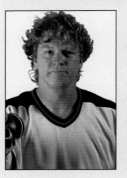

Extended stays in the penalty box for slashing and high-sticking deemed The Goon too rough for hockey. After getting kicked off every team he played for, he finally took his brutal style of competition to the one place that welcomed rough-housing: WWE.

Clad in a complete hockey uniform, including skate-like boots, The Goon used hockey-style checks to put his opponents on ice. At *WrestleMania X-Seven*, he competed in the biggest match of his career when he participated in the famed Gimmick Battle Royal. Six years later, The Goon returned to WWE to take part in the 15th Anniversary Battle Royal at *Raw*'s 15th Anniversary Special.

GORILLA MONSOON

see page 133

GRAN HAMADA

HT	5'6"	WT	202 lbs.	FROM	Maebashi, Gunma, Japan

Gran Hamada has the honor of being one-half of the only WWE Intercontinental Tag Team Champions. While competing in the Japanese-based Universal Wrestling Federation, Hamada and partner Perro Aguayo were awarded the Titles in January 1991. As part of a working agreement with WWE, the UWF was empowered to defend the Titles on its shows. Unfortunately for Hamada and Aguayo, WWE and the UWF ended their relationship shortly after the Titles were created.

Hamada's tag Title reign was not the first time he benefitted from a WWE international working agreement. In 1982, while competing for Mexico's Universal Wrestling Association, Hamada defeated Aguayo for the now-defunct WWE Light Heavyweight Championship. He repeated the act two years later to become a two-time Light Heavyweight Champion.

GRAND MASTER SEXAY

HT	5'10"	WT	222 lbs.	FROM	Memphis, Tennessee
SIGNATURE MOVE		Hip Hop Drop			

Grand Master Sexay and Scotty Too Hotty were one of WWE's most popular tag teams of the late 1990s and early 2000s. Collectively known as "Too Cool," the over-the-top tandem proved there was more to them than just whacky dance routines when they defeated Edge and Christian for the World Tag Team Championship in May 2000. That same year, they also competed at *WrestleMania 2000*, where they teamed with Chyna to defeat The Radicalz in a Six-Person Intergender Tag Team Match.

Prior to teaming with Scotty Too Hotty, Grand Master Sexay was known as Brian Christopher. Competing as Christopher, the dynamic Superstar reached the finals of the 1997 Light Heavyweight Championship tournament, where he ultimately fell to Taka Michinoku.

Since leaving WWE in 2001, Christopher has made a handful of surprise returns. In March 2011, he verbally humiliated his father, Jerry "The King" Lawler, heading into the Hall of Famer's *WrestleMania* match with Michael Cole. In January 2014, Too Cool and Rikishi reunited to defeat 3MB in a Six-Man Tag Team Match on *Raw*.

GORILLA MONSOON

HT 6'7"
WT 401 lbs.

More recent fans may only recognize Gorilla Monsoon by the legendary words he spoke while announcing WWE action during the 1980s and '90s. Lines such as "he's unloading the heavy artillery" and "the irresistible force meeting the immovable object" made him a lovable legend, but it was his brute force in the ring decades prior that made him one of the most hated Superstars of his time.

Before entering the pro ranks, Monsoon excelled as an amateur wrestler at Ithaca University. In fact, his accomplishments landed him induction into the school's Athletic Hall of Fame in 1973. After a successful collegiate career, Monsoon made the leap to the pros, defeating Pauncho Lopez in his 1959 debut. From that moment, it was clear the oversized athlete would be a force to be reckoned with in the ring.

CHAMPIONSHIP DOMINATION

In November 1963, Monsoon claimed his first WWE Title when he teamed with Killer Kowalski to wrest the United States Tag Team Championship from Skull Murphy and Brute Bernard. Just days after the victory, Monsoon challenged Bruno Sammartino for the WWE Championship at Madison Square Garden. The now-famous encounter went to a ninety-minute draw. Both Superstars later cited the match as the toughest of their respective careers.

The rule-breaking tandem of Monsoon and Kowalski lost their tag Titles to the Tolos Brothers in December 1963. Monsoon eventually reclaimed gold when he teamed with Bill Watts to defeat Gene Kiniski and Waldo Von Erich in April 1965.

On a fateful night in 1969, Monsoon made the unlikely transition to one of sports-entertainment's most-beloved figures when he found himself on the receiving end of a brutal attack at the hands of the despised Sheik. Former rival Bruno Sammartino ran to Monsoon's aid, signifying to the crowd that it was acceptable to cheer the big man. As a fan favorite, Monsoon spent the rest of his legendary career battling the likes of "Superstar" Billy Graham and Ernie Ladd.

The most highly publicized event of Monsoon's career took place in 1976 when an arrogant Muhammad Ali tried to steal the spotlight from the action in the ring. Upset with the antics, Monsoon lifted Ali up into his signature airplane spin and dropped him to the ground. The move was front-page news across the nation.

A NEW LIFE JUST OUTSIDE THE RING

After more than twenty years in the ring, Monsoon's competitive career came to an end when he lost a Retirement Match to Ken Patera in 1980. While the loss marked the end of a successful in-ring career for Monsoon, it also sparked the beginning of the next chapter in the big man's legendary story.

In 1982, WWE's new owner, Vince McMahon, who actually bought a fraction of the company from Monsoon, among others, put the retired Superstar behind the announcers' table. In the years that followed, Monsoon's voice became synonymous with WWE's biggest matches. In addition to calling the action at the first-ever *WrestleMania*, Monsoon and his partner, Jesse "The Body" Ventura, were behind the desk for the epic *WrestleMania III* encounter between Andre the Giant and Hulk Hogan.

In 1994, Monsoon received the ultimate honor when he was inducted into the WWE Hall of Fame. However, unlike most Hall of Famers, he didn't retreat back into retirement. Monsoon stayed active behind the microphone before finally elevating his status to WWE President, a role he held for two years.

Monsoon made his final WWE appearance in 1999 when he served as a ringside judge for the Butterbean versus Bart Gunn Brawl For All Match at *WrestleMania XV*. The emotional ovation he received by the WWE fans in Philadelphia capped off an amazing career that may never be duplicated.

Robert "Gorilla Monsoon" Marella passed away later that year at the age of 62. He will forever be remembered as a true gentle giant who did it all in the world of sports-entertainment.

THE IRRESISTIBLE FORCE MEETING THE IMMOVABLE OBJECT!

GRAND WIZARD

As a radio disc jockey in the 1960s, the Grand Wizard flipped phrases with the speed of an auctioneer and the eloquence of a beat poet. This led to a sports-entertainment career. Using a number of aliases—including Mr. Clean and J. Wellington Radcliffe—he managed such stars as Ray Stevens, Magnificent Maurice, and Handsome Johnny Barend.

But his career truly took off in Detroit's "Big Time Wrestling" promotion, where he managed The Sheik. Despite his diminutive size, he occasionally inserted himself into contests on his client's behalf—to the point where he was once confined to a small cage suspended above the ring.

Clad in a mish-mash of spangled attire, including a turban and wrap-around sunglasses, the Grand Wizard ominously walked to the ring with the presence of a giant. The mere sight of this man incited near riots throughout the northeastern United States. He possessed a vocabulary like no other and frightened all who listened to him. He could weave words into images of destruction, punctuated by the pain delivered by the ruthless men in his employ.

He made an eternal impact on WWE when his protégé, Stan "The Man" Stasiak ended the historic WWE Championship reign of Pedro Morales in 1973. The Wizard put sports-entertainment's richest prize around the waist of another one of his henchman in 1977 when "Superstar" Billy Graham defeated Bruno Sammartino. He also managed greats such as Pat Patterson, Ken Patera, and the Magnificent Muraco to the Intercontinental Championship.

He guided other notable figures, including Killer Kowalski, Mr. Fuji, "Big Cat" Ernie Ladd, Greg "The Hammer" Valentine, and "Cowboy" Bob Orton. He often conspired with "Classy" Freddie Blassie and Capt. Lou Albano to rid WWE of its greatest heroes. The Grand Wizard was always quick to remind the public, "It's hard to be humble when you're great!"

Sadly, on Oct. 12, 1983, this innovative sports-entertainment figure passed away. The Grand Wizard's immeasurable influence was recognized when he was posthumously inducted in the WWE Hall of Fame in 1995.

THE GREAT GOLIATH

HT	6'0"	WT	240 lbs.	FROM	New Mexico
SIGNATURE MOVE		Mexican Stretch			

On both sides of the border, the Great Goliath was a major force, winning the Mexican National Heavyweight Championship in 1967, and titles in the Los Angeles, San Francisco, Central States, and other territories.

He's best remembered for his 18 Americas Heavyweight Tag Team Championship reigns with Black Gordman in southern California. The team, which denied their Mexican heritage to enflame Latino fans, were sometimes called the "Red Devils."

The powerful Goliath was discovered by a Mexican promoter while driving a taxi. Among his notable opponents were future WWE Hall of Famers "Classy" Freddie Blassie, Mil Mascaras, Rocky Johnson, Tatsumi Fujinami, and Roddy Piper.

Before his death in 2004, he ran a wrestling school and promoted small shows in the San Bernardino, California, area.

GREAT HOSSEIN ARAB

HT	6'0"	WT	258 lbs.	FROM	Tehran, Iran

The Great Hossein Arab didn't compete for WWE very long, but he certainly managed to leave a lasting impression. Alongside manager "Classy" Freddie Blassie, the proud Iranian arrived in 1979 and immediately pronounced his disdain for the United States and its people. He then focused his attention on destroying WWE's American Superstars.

Utilizing a healthy repertoire of suplexes and an impressive Greco-Roman style offense, Arab regularly made short work of his opponents, which included Larry Zbyszko, Ted DiBiase, and Chief Jay Strongbow. On the rare occasion he found himself in trouble, Arab would resort to using one of his controversial toe-curled boots as a weapon.

Arab's greatest WWE moment came at the famed Madison Square Garden when he won a Battle Royal to earn an opportunity at Bob Backlund's WWE Championship. With all of Iran rooting for him, Arab fell short of his goal to dethrone the Champ.

THE GREAT KABUKI

HT	5'10"	WT	240 lbs.	FROM	Singapore
SIGNATURE MOVE	Thrust Kick				

This martial-arts expert arrived in the United States in the 1970s. Long black hair and paint in the design of an ancient Japanese warrior combined to shroud the scarred features of his face, disfigured from hot coals in his youth. During his time in America, he appeared throughout the NWA and was the first to spit a secret green mist at his opponents.

In the early 1990s, Kabuki appeared on the famed co-promoted SWS/WWE supershows throughout Japan. At the behest of Mr. Fuji, the legendary mercenary made his sole WWE appearance at the 1994 Royal Rumble Match to take out Lex Luger. Despite his attacks, Kabuki was eventually eliminated by Luger, the eventual co-winner of the event with Bret Hart. He soon returned to Japan and retired from the ring in 1998 after more than 30 years in sports-entertainment.

The Great Kabuki set a standard that changed the face of sports-entertainment. His merciless attacks and style were influential in the development of future Superstars Killer Kahn and Tajiri.

THE GREAT KHALI

HT	7'1"	WT	347 lbs.	FROM	India
SIGNATURE MOVE	Punjabi Plunge, Khali Vise Grip				

Rumor has it if you stand on the Great Khali's shoulders, you can see all the way from Hollywood to Bollywood. The first WWE Superstar to call India home, "The Punjabi Nightmare" has made a name in both film hubs but is best known for his near decade of towering over WWE's roster.

Khali put an immediate scare into audiences when he felled Undertaker with one mighty chop in his April 2006 debut, an unprecedented feat. Within weeks, he used the devastating Punjabi Plunge and skull-crushing Vise Grip to defeat some of WWE's elite. In the summer of 2007, the menacing Superstar realized his full potential. With the World Heavyweight Championship vacated, Khali dominated a 20-man *SmackDown* Battle Royal to claim the Title.

Over time Khali transformed from "nightmare" to Casanova and was dubbed "The Punjabi Playboy." This called for a weekly "Khali Kiss Cam" where women enjoyed an in-ring smooch from Khali. His fun-loving attitude attracted new allies such as Santino Marella, Hornswoggle, and Natalya, who stood by the giant as he out-stepped Fandango in a *Raw* dance contest.

This imposing presence with a heart of gold continued his dominance in Battle Royals, winning at *WrestleMania XXVII* and on a December 2012 episode of *Main Event* to contend for the U.S. Championship. Khali continued to delight the WWE Universe until he parted from WWE in 2014.

THE GREAT SASUKE

HT	5'8"	WT	198 lbs.	FROM	Iwate, Japan
SIGNATURE MOVE	The Thunder Firebomb				

Trained in Japan by the original Tiger Mask, the Great Sasuke developed a stellar reputation throughout Japan in the early 1990s. The black-masked man impressed audiences throughout his native land with his lethal mixture of martial arts, counterattacks, and aerial maneuvers.

In July 1997, the Great Sasuke traveled to the United States where he defeated Taka Michinoku in a thrilling match at WWE's *In Your House: Canadian Stampede*. Sasuke went on to defeat Michinoku a few more times before ending his WWE tenure by year's end. Following his departure, Sasuke returned to Japan where he continued his in-ring career.

In 2003, Sasuke became the first masked sports-entertainer elected to political office. While fulfilling his public duties, he also continued to compete in Japan.

The Great Sasuke is a highly-decorated competitor with dozens of Championships in light heavyweight, cruiserweight, and welterweight divisions all over the world. Though his WWE time was fleeting, Sasuke is recognized as a pioneer, whose innovations will undoubtedly inspire future Superstars.

THE GREAT SCOTT

WT	225 lbs.
FROM	St. Andrews, Scotland

During the 1950s and '60s, The Great Scott regularly travelled the United States' roughest territories looking for a fight. And behind the power of his pulverizing piledriver and dizzying Highland Fling, he usually won those fights.

The Great Scott defeated Johnny Valentine in May 1953 to claim the West Virginia Heavyweight Championship, the first of many Titles for the Scottish competitor. He then moved to Ohio, where he teamed with future WWE Champion Buddy Rogers to win the Midwest Wrestling Association American Tag Team Titles three times. He also captured several Tag Team Championships in the NWA with such partners as Bob Orton Sr. and Buddy Austin.

GREG "THE HAMMER" VALENTINE

| **HT** | 6'0" | **WT** | 243 lbs. | **FROM** | Seattle, Washington |
| **SIGNATURE MOVE** | | | Figure Four Leglock | | |

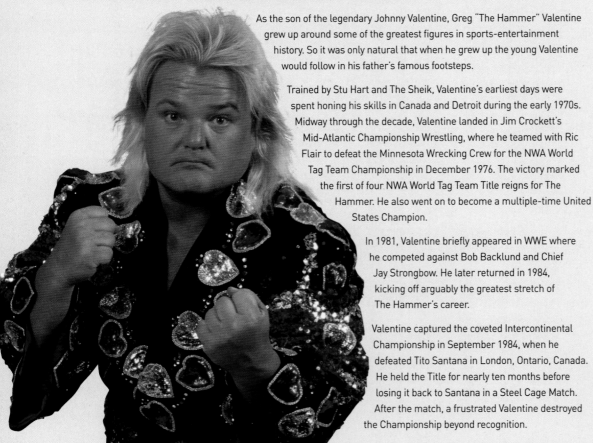

As the son of the legendary Johnny Valentine, Greg "The Hammer" Valentine grew up around some of the greatest figures in sports-entertainment history. So it was only natural that when he grew up the young Valentine would follow in his father's famous footsteps.

Trained by Stu Hart and The Sheik, Valentine's earliest days were spent honing his skills in Canada and Detroit during the early 1970s. Midway through the decade, Valentine landed in Jim Crockett's Mid-Atlantic Championship Wrestling, where he teamed with Ric Flair to defeat the Minnesota Wrecking Crew for the NWA World Tag Team Championship in December 1976. The victory marked the first of four NWA World Tag Team Title reigns for The Hammer. He also went on to become a multiple-time United States Champion.

In 1981, Valentine briefly appeared in WWE where he competed against Bob Backlund and Chief Jay Strongbow. He later returned in 1984, kicking off arguably the greatest stretch of The Hammer's career.

Valentine captured the coveted Intercontinental Championship in September 1984, when he defeated Tito Santana in London, Ontario, Canada. He held the Title for nearly ten months before losing it back to Santana in a Steel Cage Match. After the match, a frustrated Valentine destroyed the Championship beyond recognition.

The Hammer then formed the Dream Team tag team with WWE up-and-comer Brutus Beefcake. Managed by "Luscious" Johnny Valiant, the duo reached the top of the tag team mountain when they defeated the U.S. Express for the World Tag Team Championship in August 1985. Their seven-month Title reign ended with a loss to the British Bulldogs at *WrestleMania 2*.

After the duo split, Valentine went on to create teams with both Dino Bravo and the Honky Tonk Man. Though neither tandem was able to replicate the success of The Dream Team.

Valentine remained a contender for both WWE's major Championships throughout the 1990s. In March 2004, The Hammer's famed career was celebrated with an induction to the WWE Hall of Fame. Upon accepting, Valentine dedicated the amazing honor to his late father, Johnny.

GUILLOTINE GORDON

| **HT** | 6'0" | **WT** | 260 lbs. |
| **SIGNATURE MOVE** | | | Piledriver |

Through the early to mid-1960s, this man received attention for taking rule-breaking to all-new lows in Georgia. In 1965, Guillotine Gordon brought his cut-and-slash style to WWE and made it difficult for anyone to prosper while he was in the ring.

A famous powerhouse and brawler, he battled the top Superstars of the era, including Angelo Savoldi, Smasher Sloan, Bulldog Brower, Spiros Arion, and Carlos Colon. As his reputation grew and his regard for rules lessened, Gordon earned a shot at then-WWE Champion Bruno Sammartino in brawls throughout the Northeast.

In 1969, Guillotine Gordon left WWE and returned to the territories of the National Wrestling Alliance (NWA). Though it's been almost 40 years since he brutalized opponents in a WWE ring, his rule-breaking ways inspired new Superstars looking to take the quick and easy path to cheap victories.

GULF COAST/ CONTINENTAL CHAMPIONSHIP WRESTLING

Known as the "lost promotion," Gulf Coast Championship Wrestling thrived in cities like Mobile and Dothan, Alabama; Hattisburg, Mississippi; and Pensacola and Panama City, Florida. But few outsiders knew about the phenomenon because promoters discouraged the media from covering events.

To fans, though, Gulf Coast was a secret treasure, featuring stars like Cowboy Bob Kelly, "Bullet" Bob Armstrong, the Dirty Daltons, Billy Wicks, Don Carson, Ox Baker, "Dangerous" Danny McShain, the Interns and Ken Lucas.

At the center of the territory was a complex family network. Roy Welch and his son, Buddy Fuller, founded Gulf Coast in 1954. Among the draws were Buddy's cousins, Lee, Don, and Bobby Fields—as well as their father, Virgil "Speedy" Hatfield. Lee took over the territory in 1959.

In 1978, he sold the group to another cousin, Ron Fuller—Buddy's son—who'd been running Knoxville-based Southeastern Championship Wrestling.

In 1988, television executive David Woods took over and changed the name to Continental Championship Wrestling, hoping to finally attract outside interest. But the promotion closed in late 1989.

GUNNER SCOTT

HT	6'0"	WT	230 lbs.	FROM	Tulsa, Oklahoma
SIGNATURE MOVE		The Crowbar			

In April 2006, Gunner Scott shocked the sports-entertainment world when he defeated Booker T in his *SmackDown* debut. Gunner continued to taste success in bouts against Simon Dean, Finlay, Orlando Jordan, Gregory Helms, and Sylvester Terkay. His version of the dangerous Fujiwara armbar known as the Crowbar showed he could mix it up in any situation versus virtually any opponent.

As Gunner's star was on the rise it suddenly burned out that June. After a match with Mr. Kennedy, The Great Khali planted Scott with a double choke throw and Daivari stuffed the young hopeful inside a body bag. That was the last anyone ever saw of Gunner Scott.

THE GYMINI

MEMBERS	Jesse & Jake	COMBINED WT	608 lbs.

In January 2006, fitness guru Simon Dean introduced the world to two massive twins collectively known as The Gymini. For months, the only thing known about the tandem was their colossal size. After several victories on *SmackDown* and *Velocity*, the identical duo finally revealed themselves as Jesse and Jake. Despite the revelation, opponents and commentators still couldn't tell the two Superstars apart.

Luckily, confused onlookers didn't need to struggle with their identity for long. In May, just four months after their debut, The Gymini made their final televised WWE appearance.

"HACKSAW" JIM DUGGAN

HT	6'3"	WT	240 lbs.	FROM	Glen Falls, New York
SIGNATURE MOVE		Three Point Stance Clothesline			

Above all else, "Hacksaw" Jim Duggan certainly knows how to withstand the test of time. The patriotic Superstar has competed in each of the past five decades, en route to becoming one of the most recognizable Superstars of all time.

After nearly ten years of competing in various smaller promotions, Duggan debuted in WWE in January 1987. He made his first major statement at *WrestleMania III*, attacking Iron Sheik and Nikolai Volkoff during the singing of the Russian National Anthem. The act solidified Duggan's status as one of America's most patriotic Superstars. He even taped a small American flag to his signature 2x4.

The following year, Duggan made history when he eliminated One Man Gang to win the first-ever Royal Rumble Match. The popularity of the event led WWE to create an entire pay-per-view around the match the following January. One year later, Duggan claimed the King of the Ring crown from Haku. Again, the popular event would later become an annual pay-per-view extravaganza.

Behind the power of his devastating three-point stance clothesline, Duggan earned an opportunity at American turncoat Sgt. Slaughter's WWE Championship in 1991. Despite having Hulk Hogan in his corner, Duggan was unable to unseat the Champion, but he did earn a disqualification victory.

In 1994, Duggan jumped to WCW where he enjoyed a measure of success. Perhaps his greatest victory during his WCW stay came in 1998 when he overcame kidney cancer. The brave Duggan credits early detection, the grace of God, and a superior medical team for saving his life.

With a new outlook on life, Duggan returned to WWE in 2005 where he had many memorable battles with Edge, the Spirit Squad, and Eugene, among others. And in 2011, "Hacksaw" took his rightful place in the WWE Hall of Fame on the eve of *WrestleMania XXVII*. Following his induction, Duggan revealed a never-before-seen side of himself as a cast member on WWE Network's reality show, *WWE Legends' House*. Decades after breaking into the sports-entertainment industry, Jim Duggan continues to prove he is a tough guy, "Hooooooo!"

HAITI KID

FROM	Haiti

Haiti Kid's contributions to mini wrestling earned him great respect from Superstars of all sizes. In fact, many of the larger Superstars from the 1980s considered him a close friend, including Hillbilly Jim and Mr. T.

Prior to *WrestleMania 2*, Kid's alliance with Mr. T caused him great humiliation. Attempting to get under Mr. T's skin, Roddy Piper abducted Kid and proceeded to cut his hair. Afterward, Mr. T demanded Kid be in his corner at *WrestleMania 2* when he gained revenge on Piper.

The following year, Kid found himself in the center of one of history's most infamous *WrestleMania* moments. With Hillbilly Jim and Little Beaver as his partners, he battled King Kong Bundy, Lord Littlebrook, and Little Tokyo. Unfortunately, when things started going poorly for Bundy, the big man took out his aggression on the smaller Beaver. Kid, along with the two other minis and Hillbilly Jim, came to Beaver's aid. The image of friends and foes banding together to help Beaver will forever be remembered as an amazing *WrestleMania* memory.

A B C D E F G H I J K L M N O P Q R S T U V W X Y Z

HAKU

HT	6'1"	WT	275 lbs.
FROM	Isle of Tonga		
SIGNATURE MOVE	Savate Kick		

Skilled in the art of sumo wrestling and various martial arts styles, Haku first appeared on the scene in the mid-1980s as King Tonga. After slamming Big John Studd during the $15,000 Body Slam Challenge in June 1986, the Polynesian powerhouse became known as Haku and joined forces with Tama to form The Islanders. The duo was originally cheered, but eventually garnered jeers after viciously attacking the Can-Am Connection and falling under the influence of Bobby "The Brain" Heenan.

Following The Islanders' disbanding in 1988, Haku set out on a very successful singles career. Within months, he proved his worth by succeeding the legendary Harley Race in becoming King of WWE. Haku later returned to tag team action when he paired up with Andre the Giant to form the Colossal Connection. Together, Haku and Andre dominated the tag team division, as evidenced by their World Tag Team Championship victory over Demolition in December 1989.

After losing the Titles at *WrestleMania VI*, Haku began teaming with the Barbarian before leaving WWE in late 1992. Haku and Barbarian would later reform their partnership in WCW during the mid-1990s. Haku returned to WWE in 2001 when he competed in the Royal Rumble Match. In early 2002, he left WWE and returned to the independent scene of the United States and Japan.

HAKUSHI

HT	5'11"	WT	238 lbs.	FROM	Japan

Well respected in his homeland of Japan for his innovative offense, Hakushi unleashed his unique in-ring style on WWE in 1995. With his entire body covered in Japanese script, he certainly drew the attention of fans. But it was his combination of superior martial arts skills and amazing agility that caught the eyes of his competition.

After impressive showings against then-unknown rookie Matt Hardy and Ricky Santana, Hakushi was catapulted into a high-profile rivalry with Bret Hart. Against one of WWE's best, Hakushi certainly impressed many, despite coming up short at *In Your House* in May 1995.

Undeterred by the loss, Hakushi used his lightning-quick speed to upend the equally fast 1-2-3 Kid at *SummerSlam* 1995. Initially, the win looked like the launching pad he needed to rise through the WWE ranks. Inexplicably, however, he soon found himself involved with perennial loser Barry Horowitz. Hakushi's career never recovered.

In 1996, Hakushi became victimized by Justin "Hawk" Bradshaw's branding iron. Greatly embarrassed by the situation, the Japanese Superstar never showed his face in WWE again.

THE HANGMAN

HT	6'3"	WT	292 lbs.	FROM	Matane, Quebec, Canada
SIGNATURE MOVE	Bearhug				

Dressed head to toe in black, The Hangman was known for his unmatched viciousness that carried over into his gross post-match mistreatment of defeated foes.

The Hangman debuted in WWE in 1980 with manager Freddie Blassie in his corner. Upon arriving, he made short work of Rick McGraw, Frank Williams, and Baron Mikel Scicluna, among others. When he defeated Rene Goulet at *Showdown at Shea* in August, The Hangman became a serious contender for the WWE Championship, then held by Bob Backlund.

By 1982, The Hangman left WWE to spread terror through promotions all over the world. In 1986, he hung up his boots and returned to his homeland of Canada.

HANS MORTIER

HT	5'11"	WT	250 lbs.	FROM	Nuremberg, Germany
SIGNATURE MOVE	The Full Nelson				

Prior to becoming a force in the ring, Hans Mortier excelled as a world-class bodybuilder. Behind the force of his unbreakable Full Nelson, Mortier made the transition from the weight room to the squared circle in the mid-1940s.

Led to the ring by "Wild" Red Berry, Mortier debuted in WWE in the 1960s and immediately became a threat to then-WWE Champion Bruno Sammartino. Their matches over sports-entertainment's richest prize were so physical that the rivalry had to be settled in a Texas Death Match in Philadelphia.

In addition to being one of sports-entertainment's most despised villains and a legitimate threat to Sammartino's WWE Championship, Mortier also teamed with his brother, Max, to wreak havoc on opposing tandems.

HANS SCHMIDT

HT	6'4"	WT	250 lbs.	FROM	Munich, Germany

Few competitors elicited more contempt from the fans than Hans Schmidt. Known as the Teuton Terror, he stepped to the ring wearing a German World War II helmet, which enraged American audiences. Schmidt's brute, powerhouse style struck instant fear into his opponents. And his complete disregard for the rules made it nearly impossible for referees to maintain order in his matches.

Schmidt captured several Titles while competing for the National Wrestling Alliance. However, the mighty German was never able to score the big one, as his continued attempts to topple NWA World Heavyweight Champion Lou Thesz fell short.

HARDCORE CHAMPIONSHIP
see page 140

HARDCORE HOLLY

HT	6'0"	WT	235 lbs.	FROM	Mobile, Alabama
SIGNATURE MOVE	Alabama Slam				

Few Superstars can boast as lengthy a WWE career as Bob "Hardcore" Holly. During his fifteen years he saw it all, from the New Generation to the Attitude Era to the WCW Invasion. But while the scenery often changed over the course of his career, there was always one constant: Bob Holly equaled Hardcore. He was one of the leanest, meanest, roughest, and toughest Superstars to ever enter the ring.

The tough-as-nails Superstar earned his "Hardcore" moniker during the height of the hardcore division's popularity. Known for having no mercy in the ring, Holly brutalized his opponents on his way to six Hardcore Championship reigns. After the Title became dormant, the "Alabama Slammer" still competed like the prize was on the line.

Over the years, Holly's hard-hitting ring style also translated to success in the tag team ranks. A three-time World Tag Team Champion, he captured the gold with partners 1-2-3 Kid, Crash Holly, and Cody Rhodes.

In 2001, the normally gruff Holly took a hiatus from the ring to teach WWE hopefuls on *WWE Tough Enough*. Using tough love as his primary teaching tool, Holly molded several future Superstars, including Matt Morgan and Jackie Gayda. He remained true to his name throughout the decade before retiring in 2009.

THE HARDY BOYZ

MEMBERS	Matt Hardy & Jeff Hardy
COMBINED WT	461 lbs.

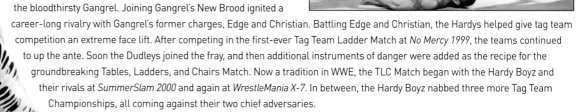

Matt and Jeff Hardy fell in love with sports-entertainment at a young age. Known for their trampoline wrestling exploits and self-promoted local shows, it is a fitting twist of fate that the two brothers would one day help revolutionize tag team competition in WWE. The sibling duo was first seen by WWE cameras in the mid-1990s playing menial roles, such as court jesters at *King of the Ring*. WWE soon began taking them seriously, however, when their raw talent and chemistry became obvious.

The Carolinians first big break came in 1999 when they fell under the guidance of legendary tag team competitor Michael "P.S." Hayes. With Hayes, they enjoyed their first World Tag Team Championship reign. Still not satisfied, The Hardys turned their backs on Hayes in favor of the bloodthirsty Gangrel. Joining Gangrel's New Brood ignited a career-long rivalry with Gangrel's former charges, Edge and Christian. Battling Edge and Christian, the Hardys helped give tag team competition an extreme face lift. After competing in the first-ever Tag Team Ladder Match at *No Mercy 1999*, the teams continued to up the ante. Soon the Dudleys joined the fray, and then additional instruments of danger were added as the recipe for the groundbreaking Tables, Ladders, and Chairs Match. Now a tradition in WWE, the TLC Match began with the Hardy Boyz and their rivals at *SummerSlam 2000* and again at *WrestleMania X-7*. In between, the Hardy Boyz nabbed three more Tag Team Championships, all coming against their two chief adversaries.

With Lita providing an exciting third element, the risk-taking group became known as Team Extreme. Lita helped the team defeat Booker T and Test for their fifth Tag Titles. The trio seemed unstoppable until jealousy drove them apart in 2002.

After pursuing singles accolades, Matt and Jeff reunited in 2006 to join Team DX at *Survivor Series*. The duo did not miss a beat and became Tag Team Champions again in April 2007. Still, a sibling rivalry was unavoidable. The brothers turned their innovative offense against each other in an Extreme Rules Match at *WrestleMania 25*. The rivalry extended to Stretcher and "I Quit" Matches before they reconciled. The Hardys faded from WWE after Jeff lost a "Loser Leaves WWE" Steel Cage Match to CM Punk, and Matt parted with the company in October 2010.

HARDCORE CHAMPIONSHIP

The Hardcore Championship not only broke all the rules, it took the rules and smashed them into thousands of little pieces. Ironically, that was the same concept behind the Hardcore Championship belt—an old WWE Championship that was broken into little pieces and then taped back together.

In a Hardcore Championship Title defense, anything and everything was legal, including the use of weapons and competing in locations outside the traditional arena. As the Title started to take on a life of its own, so did its lack of rules. It wasn't long before the Hardcore Championship was being defended under 24/7 rules, meaning any Superstar could challenge the Champion at any time of the day, as long as he or she had a referee with him or her. The 24/7 rules resulted in an exorbitant amount of Title changes. In fact, over its lifespan, which lasted less than four years, the Hardcore Championship changed hands more than 200 times!

The Hardcore Championship became defunct in August 2002, when Rob Van Dam defeated Tommy Dreamer to unify it with the Intercontinental Championship. Following their brutal match at *WrestleMania 22*, Edge and Mick Foley declared themselves "co-holders of the Hardcore Title" but their reign was never officially recognized.

1998

November 2 • Houston, TX
Mr. McMahon awarded **Mankind** the Hardcore Championship, crowning him the first-ever titleholder.

November 30 • Baltimore, MD
Big Boss Man def. **Mankind**

December 15 • Spokane, WA
Road Dogg def. **Big Boss Man**
Injury forced Road Dogg to vacate the Hardcore Championship in February 1999.

1999

February 14 • Memphis, TN
Hardcore Holly def. **Al Snow**

March 15 • San Jose, CA
Billy Gunn def. **Hardcore Holly**

March 28 • Philadelphia, PA
Hardcore Holly def. **Billy Gunn**

April 25 • Providence, RI
Al Snow def. **Hardcore Holly**

July 25 • Buffalo, NY
Big Boss Man def. **Al Snow**

August 22 • Minneapolis, MN
Al Snow def. **Big Boss Man**

August 24 • Kansas City, MO
Big Boss Man def. **Al Snow**

September 9 • Albany, NY
British Bulldog def. **Big Boss Man**
After defeating Big Boss Man for the Hardcore Championship, British Bulldog gave the Title to Al Snow.

October 14 • Birmingham, AL
Big Boss Man def. **Al Snow**

2000

January 17 • New Haven, CT
Test def. **Big Boss Man**

February 24 • Nashville, TN
Crash Holly def. **Test**

March 13 • Newark, NJ
Pete Gas def. **Crash Holly**
Crash Holly def. **Pete Gas**

April 2 • Anaheim, CA
Tazz def. **Crash Holly**
Viscera def. **Tazz**
Funaki def. **Viscera**
Rodney def. **Funaki**
Joey Abs def. **Rodney**
Thrasher def. **Joey Abs**
Pete Gas def. **Thrasher**
Tazz def. **Pete Gas**
Crash Holly def. **Tazz**
Hardcore Holly def. **Crash Holly**

April 3 • Los Angeles, CA
Crash Holly def. **Hardcore Holly**

April 13 • Tampa, FL
Perry Saturn def. **Crash Holly**
Tazz def. **Perry Saturn**
Crash Holly def. **Tazz**

April 24 • Raleigh, NC
Matt Hardy def. **Crash Holly**

April 27 • Charlotte, NC
Crash Holly def. **Matt Hardy**

May 6 • London, England
British Bulldog def. **Crash Holly**

May 11 • New Haven, CT
Crash Holly def. **British Bulldog**

May 15 • Cleveland, OH
Godfather's Ho def. **Crash Holly**
Crash Holly def. **Godfather's Ho**

May 18 • Detroit, MI
Gerald Brisco def. **Crash Holly**

June 12 • St. Louis, MO
Crash Holly def. **Gerald Brisco**

June 19 • Nashville, TN
Gerald Brisco def. **Crash Holly**
Pat Patterson def. **Gerald Brisco**

June 25 • Boston, MA
Crash Holly def. **Pat Patterson**

June 29 • Hartford, CT
Steve Blackman def. **Crash Holly**

July 2 • Tampa, FL
Crash Holly def. **Steve Blackman**
Steve Blackman def. **Crash Holly**

August 21 • Lafayette, LA
Shane McMahon def. **Steve Blackman**

August 27 • Raleigh, NC
Steve Blackman def. **Shane McMahon**

September 24 • Philadelphia, PA
Crash Holly def. **Steve Blackman**
Perry Saturn def. **Crash Holly**

December 22 • Chattanooga, TN
Raven def. **Steve Blackman**

2001

January 22 • Lafayette, LA
Al Snow def. **Raven**
Raven def. **Al Snow**

February 3 • Greensboro, NC
K-Kwick def. **Raven**
Crash Holly def. **K-Kwick**
Raven def. **Crash Holly**

February 4 • Columbia, SC
K-Kwick def. **Raven**
Crash Holly def. **K-Kwick**
Raven def. **Crash Holly**

February 8 • North Charleston, SC
Hardcore Holly def. **Raven**
Raven def. **Hardcore Holly**

February 10 • St. Paul, MN
Hardcore Holly def. **Raven**
Raven def. **Hardcore Holly**

February 11 • Boston, MA
Hardcore Holly def. **Raven**
Al Snow def. **Hardcore Holly**
Raven def. **Al Snow**

February 17 • Cedar Falls, IA
Steve Blackman def. **Raven**
Raven def. **Steve Blackman**

February 18 • Cape Girardeau, MO
Steve Blackman def. **Raven**
Raven def. **Steve Blackman**

February 25 • Las Vegas, NV
Billy Gunn def. **Raven**
Raven def. **Billy Gunn**
Big Show def. **Raven**

March 19 • Albany, NY
Raven def. **Big Show**

April 1 • Houston, TX
Kane def. **Raven**

April 19 • Nashville, TN
Rhyno def. **Kane**

May 21 • San Jose, CA
Big Show def. **Rhyno**

May 28 • Calgary, Alberta
Chris Jericho def. **Big Show**
Rhyno def. **Chris Jericho**

June 16 • Baltimore, MD
Test def. **Rhyno**

June 25 • New York, NY
Rhyno def. **Test**
Mike Awesome def. **Rhyno**

July 12 • Birmingham, AL
Jeff Hardy def. **Mike Awesome**

July 22 • Cleveland, OH
Rob Van Dam def. **Jeff Hardy**

August 13 • Chicago, IL
Jeff Hardy def. **Rob Van Dam**

August 19 • San Jose, CA
Rob Van Dam def. **Jeff Hardy**

September 10 • San Antonio, TX
Kurt Angle def. **Rob Van Dam**
Rob Van Dam def. **Kurt Angle**

December 9 • San Diego, CA
Undertaker def. **Rob Van Dam**

2002

February 7 • Los Angeles, CA
Maven def. **Undertaker**

February 28 • Boston, MA
Goldust def. **Maven**

March 11 • Detroit, MI
Al Snow def. **Goldust**

March 14 • Cleveland, OH
Maven def. **Al Snow**

March 17 • Toronto, Ontario
Spike Dudley def. **Maven**
The Hurricane def. **Spike Dudley**
Mighty Molly def. **The Hurricane**
Christian def. **Mighty Molly**
Maven def. **Christian**

March 28 • Philadelphia, PA
Raven def. Maven

April 1 • Albany, NY
Bubba Ray Dudley def. Raven

April 7 • Denver, CO
William Regal def. Bubba Ray Dudley
Goldust def. William Regal
Raven def. Goldust
Bubba Ray Dudley def. Raven

April 13 • Odessa, TX
William Regal def. Bubba Ray Dudley
Spike Dudley def. William Regal
Goldust def. Spike Dudley
Bubba Ray Dudley def. Goldust

April 14 • Abilene, TX
William Regal def. Bubba Ray Dudley
Spike Dudley def. William Regal
Goldust def. Spike Dudley
Bubba Ray Dudley def. Goldust

April 15 • College Station, TX
Raven def. Bubba Ray Dudley
Tommy Dreamer def. Raven
Stevie Richards def. Tommy Dreamer
Bubba Ray Dudley def. Stevie Richards

April 19 • Uniondale, NY
Goldust def. Bubba Ray Dudley
Raven def. Goldust
Bubba Ray Dudley def. Raven

April 20 • Des Moines, IA
Goldust def. Bubba Ray Dudley
Raven def. Goldust
Bubba Ray Dudley def. Raven

April 29 • Buffalo, NY
Stevie Richards def. Bubba Ray Dudley

May 1 • Cologne, Germany
Tommy Dreamer def. Stevie Richards
Goldust def. Tommy Dreamer
Stevie Richards def. Goldust

May 2 • Glasgow, Scotland
Shawn Stasiak def. Stevie Richards
Justin Credible def. Shawn Stasiak
Crash Holly def. Justin Credible
Stevie Richards def. Crash Holly
Shawn Stasiak def. Stevie Richards
Stevie Richards def. Shawn Stasiak

May 3 • Birmingham, England
Crash Holly def. Stevie Richards
Stevie Richards def. Crash Holly

May 4 • London, England
Booker T def. Stevie Richards
Crash Holly def. Booker T
Booker T def. Crash Holly
Stevie Richards def. Booker T

May 6 • Hartford, CT
Bubba Ray Dudley def. Stevie Richards
Raven def. Bubba Ray Dudley
Justin Credible def. Raven
Crash Holly def. Justin Credible
Trish Stratus def. Crash Holly
Stevie Richards def. Trish Stratus

May 25 • Winnipeg, Manitoba
Tommy Dreamer def. Stevie Richards
Raven def. Tommy Dreamer
Stevie Richards def. Raven

May 26 • Red Deer, Saskatchewan
Tommy Dreamer def. Stevie Richards
Raven def. Tommy Dreamer
Stevie Richards def. Raven

May 27 • Edmonton, Alberta
Terri def. Stevie Richards
Stevie Richard def. Terri

June 2 • New Orleans, LA
Tommy Dreamer def. Stevie Richards
Raven def. Tommy Dreamer
Stevie Richards def. Raven

June 3 • Dallas, TX
Bradshaw def. Stevie Richards

June 22 • Cincinnati, OH
Raven def. Bradshaw
Spike Dudley def. Raven
Shawn Stasiak def. Spike Dudley
Bradshaw def. Shawn Stasiak

June 28 • Washington, DC
Shawn Stasiak def. Bradshaw
Spike Dudley def. Shawn Stasiak
Stevie Richards def. Spike Dudley
Bradshaw def. Stevie Richards

June 29 • New York, NY
Shawn Stasiak def. Bradshaw
Spike Dudley def. Shawn Stasiak
Stevie Richards def. Spike Dudley
Bradshaw def. Stevie Richards

June 30 • Uncasville, CT
Raven def. Bradshaw
Crash Holly def. Raven
Stevie Richards def. Crash Holly
Bradshaw def. Stevie Richards

July 6 • Frederick, MD
Stevie Richards def. Bradshaw
Crash Holly def. Stevie Richards
Christopher Nowinski def. Crash Holly
Bradshaw def. Christopher Nowinski

July 7 • Wildwood, NJ
Stevie Richards def. Bradshaw
Crash Holly def. Stevie Richards
Christopher Nowinski def. Crash Holly
Bradshaw def. Christopher Nowinski

July 12 • Lakeland, FL
Justin Credible def. Bradshaw
Spike Dudley def. Justin Credible
Big Show def. Spike Dudley
Bradshaw def. Big Show

July 13 • Daytona Beach, FL
Justin Credible def. Bradshaw
Shawn Stasiak def. Justin Credible
Bradshaw def. Shawn Stasiak

July 14 • Bethlehem, PA
Justin Credible def. Bradshaw
Shawn Stasiak def. def. Shawn Stasiak

July 15 • East Rutherford, NJ
Johnny Stamboli def. Bradshaw
Bradshaw def. Johnny Stamboli

July 26 • Houston, TX
Raven def. Bradshaw
Justin Credible def. Raven
Shawn Stasiak def. Justin Credible
Bradshaw def. Shawn Stasiak

July 27 • San Antonio, TX
Raven def. Bradshaw
Justin Credible def. Raven
Shawn Stasiak def. Justin Credible
Bradshaw def. Shawn Stasiak

July 28 • Columbia, SC
Raven def. Bradshaw
Justin Credible def. Raven
Shawn Stasiak def. Justin Credible
Bradshaw def. Shawn Stasiak

July 29 • Greensboro, NC
Jeff Hardy def. Bradshaw
Johnny Stamboli def. Jeff Hardy
Tommy Dreamer def. Johnny Stamboli

August 3 • Miami, FL
Bradshaw def. Tommy Dreamer
Tommy Dreamer def. Bradshaw

August 4 • Pittsburgh, PA
Bradshaw def. Tommy Dreamer
Tommy Dreamer def. Bradshaw

August 9 • Kelowna, British Columbia
Shawn Stasiak def. Tommy Dreamer
Stevie Richards def. Shawn Stasiak
Tommy Dreamer def. Stevie Richards

August 10 • Kamloops, British Columbia
Shawn Stasiak def. Tommy Dreamer
Stevie Richards def. Shawn Stasiak
Tommy Dreamer def. Stevie Richards

August 11 • Vancouver, British Columbia
Shawn Stasiak def. Tommy Dreamer
Stevie Richards def. Shawn Stasiak
Tommy Dreamer def. Stevie Richards

August 17 • Terre Haute, IN
Raven def. Tommy Dreamer
Shawn Stasiak def. Raven
Tommy Dreamer def. Shawn Stasiak

August 18 • Evansville, IN
Shawn Stasiak def. Tommy Dreamer
Stevie Richards def. Shawn Stasiak
Tommy Dreamer def. Stevie Richards

August 19 • Norfolk, VA
Bradshaw def. Tommy Dreamer
Crash Holly def. Bradshaw
Tommy Dreamer def. Crash Holly

August 26 • New York, NY
Rob Van Dam def. Tommy Dreamer
Rob Van Dam beat Tommy Dreamer to unify the Hardcore and Intercontinental Championships.

HARLEY RACE

HT	6'1"
WT	253 lbs.
FROM	Kansas City, Missouri

SIGNATURE MOVE
Fisherman Suplex

In a profession where only the tough succeed, Harley Race proved to be among the absolute toughest to ever lace a pair of boots. Along the way, he amassed near countless accolades, including eight NWA World Heavyweight Championships, the United States Championship, and a reign as WWE's prestigious King of the Ring.

Race's career kicked off in 1960 when he was a teenager. His earliest days were spent in several southern territories, most notably Nashville and Amarillo. While in Amarillo, Race formed a tag team with Larry "The Axe" Hennig. Before the two could make waves in Texas, however, they moved to Minnesota, where they captured the AWA World Tag Team Championship on three separate occasions.

Though successful in the tag team ranks, Race yearned for singles success. And in the early 1970s, he competed in various NWA territories with the goal of claiming the NWA World Heavyweight Championship. In May 1973, Race accomplished his goal when he defeated Dory Funk Jr. for the Title in Kansas City, Missouri. He held the Title for nearly two months before losing it to Jack Brisco.

Race waited nearly four years before he was able to once again climb to the top of the NWA mountain. But when he did, he unequivocally proved that he was among the absolute elite in the industry. After defeating Terry Funk in February 1977, Race went on to hold the Championship for an amazing 926 days. Only four men can boast longer NWA World Heavyweight Championship reigns.

In subsequent years, Race's NWA World Heavyweight Championship résumé was bolstered at the expense of Dusty Rhodes, Giant Baba, Tommy Rich, and Ric Flair. Only Flair can claim more reigns with the prestigious Championship. In all, Race's eight reigns lasted 1,799 days. Only Flair and Lou Thesz have longer combined reigns.

In addition to being recognized as one of the greatest World Champions of all time, Race also owns the distinct pleasure of being the first-ever United States Champion. He won the Title by defeating Johnny Weaver in a tournament finals match in January 1975. With Race as Champion, the U.S. Title was given the foundation needed to establish itself as a major prize in the industry. In the years that followed, sports-entertainment's greatest names have held the Championship, including Bobo Brazil, Steve Austin, and John Cena.

I PROVED TO EVERYBODY IN WRESTLING WHETHER THEY LIKED ME OR THEY DISLIKED ME, THAT I AM MADE OF CHAMPIONSHIP CALIBER.

KING OF THE RING

Already considered one of sports-entertainment's most successful competitors, Race jumped to WWE in 1986 and cemented his already impressive legacy by defeating Pedro Morales in the finals of the King of the Ring tournament. With the crown in his possession and manager Bobby "The Brain" Heenan leading the way, Race squared off against WWE's best, including Ricky "The Dragon" Steamboat, Hillbilly Jim, Tito Santana, and Junkyard Dog, who he defeated in a "Loser Must Bow" Match at *WrestleMania III.*

Race also famously battled Hulk Hogan on a March 1988 edition of *Saturday Night's Main Event.* During the match, he leapt off the ring apron in an attempt to nail a head-butt on The Hulkster, who was laid out on a ringside table. But Hogan moved at the last moment and Race went bowling through the table. As a result of the mistimed move, Race suffered a serious injury that ultimately marked the end of his kingship.

Following his WWE career, Race became an influential manager in WCW. During his tenure, he led both Lex Luger and Vader to the WCW World Heavyweight Championship before retiring in 1995.

In 2004, Race's iconic career was immortalized with induction into the WWE Hall of Fame on the eve of *WrestleMania XX.* With his tough-as-nails presence in the ring and stellar championship pedigree, Harley Race will go down in history as one of the greatest competitors in the storied history of sports-entertainment.

THE HART DYNASTY

MEMBERS	Tyson Kidd, David Hart Smith, & Natalya
FROM	Calgary, Alberta, Canada

Nearly 100 years after his birth, Stu Hart's amazing legacy lived on in the form of The Hart Dynasty. Featuring Hart's grandchildren David Hart Smith and Natalya, as well as close family friend Tyson Kidd, The Hart Dynasty picked up where the Hart Foundation left off: ruling the tag-team division.

In April 2010, Smith and Kidd defeated Big Show and The Miz to claim the Unified Tag Team Championship. The victory etched their names next to so many other Harts that carried tag team gold, including Smith's father, the British Bulldog, and Natalya's father, Jim "The Anvil" Neidhart.

The Hart Dynasty's five-month reign represented a high watermark for the group. They also restored some family pride by helping their uncle, Bret Hart, exact a therapeutic revenge on Mr. McMahon at *WrestleMania XXVI*. Their union eventually fractured when a frustrated Kidd turned his back on Smith during a match on *Raw*.

HARVEY WIPPLEMAN

FROM	Walls, Mississippi

Despite being short in stature, Harvey Wippleman guided some of sports-entertainment's biggest Superstars. His list of oversized clients included Sid Justice, Giant Gonzales, Kamala, Adam Bomb, and Bertha Faye.

Wippleman's managerial prowess led his protégés to many high-profile encounters, including major *WrestleMania* matches. In the main event of *WrestleMania VIII*, he guided Sid Justice to a controversial disqualification loss to Hulk Hogan. One year later at *WrestleMania IX*, Wippleman led the nearly 8-foot Giant Gonzales into battle against Undertaker.

Despite building a stable with the biggest horses in the game, Wippleman always had trouble winning Titles for his clients. Then he met love interest Bertha Faye. Wippleman guided his girlfriend's career from the trailer park all the way to the Women's Championship in 1995. The Title was the only one Wippleman ever captured during his days as a WWE manager.

Five years after managing a Women's Champion, Wippleman actually won the Title himself. Disguised as a female named Hervina, he defeated The Kat in a Lumberjill Snow Bunny Match to capture the Title.

THE HART FOUNDATION

MEMBERS	Bret "Hit Man" Hart, Jim "The Anvil" Neidhart, Owen Hart, Davey Boy Smith, & Brian Pillman

To fully appreciate The Hart Foundation's impact on sports-entertainment, you must travel through two decades of WWE action to examine the legendary faction's different incarnations.

Originally a tag team, The Hart Foundation debuted as a rule-breaking tandem in the mid-1980s. Bret "Hit Man" Hart provided the team's quickness and technical skill, while Jim "The Anvil" Neidhart served as the muscle. The duo, which was managed by Jimmy "Mouth of the South" Hart, enjoyed two World Tag Team Championship reigns. In January 1987, they defeated the British Bulldogs to claim their first. Three years later, Hart and Neidhart downed Demolition to reclaim the Titles.

By the end of 1990, it was becoming evident that the "Hit Man" was destined for singles success. Following a loss to The Nasty Boys at *WrestleMania VII*, The Hart Foundation split and Bret went on to achieve legendary status as a singles competitor. Seven years later, Hart and Neidhart reunited to wage war against the United States. This time, however, they welcomed Owen Hart, Davey Boy Smith, and Brian Pillman into the fold, bringing The Hart Foundation's membership up to five.

The new Hart Foundation, which was led by then-WWE Champion Bret Hart, arrogantly waved Canadian and British flags, while denouncing the supposed immoral values of the United States. Their actions clearly infuriated American fans but made The Hart Foundation heroes in Canada, which was the site of their greatest victory.

In front of a capacity crowd in Calgary's Saddledome at *In Your House: Canadian Stampede*, The Hart Foundation defeated Stone Cold Steve Austin, The Legion of Doom, Goldust, and Ken Shamrock. The Canadian crowd enthusiastically cheered their heroes, as numerous members of the Hart family celebrated in the ring, including future WWE Superstars Tyson Kidd, David Hart Smith, and Natalya, who would go on to become The Hart Dynasty years later.

HAYSTACKS CALHOUN

 HT 6'4" **WT** 601 lbs. **FROM** Morgan's Corner, Arkansas
SIGNATURE MOVE Big Splash

Recognized by many as sports-entertainment's first giant, Haystacks Calhoun made his professional debut in the 1950s. Originally called "Country Boy" Calhoun, he is said to have gained the "Haystacks" moniker when promoter Vincent James McMahon—father of WWE boss Vincent Kennedy McMahon—remarked, "He's as big as Haystacks."

His battles with fellow colossus, the over 700 pound Happy Humphrey, gave new meaning to the term "when worlds collide."

Crushing his way into the 1960s Calhoun was revered as a legend of the ring with his trademark beard, overalls, and horse shoe around his neck. Indeed, when an adversary attempted to overcome the size deficiency in the ring and bend the rules, Haystacks was not beyond reaching for his lucky horseshoe and wielding it as a weapon.

Early in his career, Calhoun formed a tandem with 600-plus pound Man Mountain Mike, the heftiest team in history at that point. During Bruno Sammartino's rise to greatness, he showcased his strength by hoisting up Calhoun and rattling the rafters by slamming him.

In 1964, this jolly behemoth began a memorable run in WWE and became one of the most popular figures throughout the Northeast. Calhoun promised all, "There are going to be a lot of pancakes around here before I get finished."

"Stacks" formed a formidable team with Bobo Brazil, and the duo were top contenders for the U.S. Tag Team Championship. By August, 1965, Calhoun left the company looking for a new challenge.

Like Andre the Giant, Haystacks was an international attraction, whose specialty was the Battle Royal. He had a reputation for winning most of these encounters until 1972 when nine Superstars ganged up on him at the Annual Battle Royal at the Olympic Auditorium in Los Angeles. Unable to pin Haystacks, they piled on top of him until his shoulders were down.

In May 1973, Calhoun and Tony Garea defeated Mr. Fuji and Professor Toru Tanaka and became WWE World Tag Team Champions.

Haystacks continued to amaze WWE audiences through 1979. He passed away in December 1989.

THE HEADBANGERS

 MEMBERS Mosh & Thrasher **COMBINED WT** 492 lbs.
FROM Mosh Pits Across America

Real men wear skirts. At least that's what the kilt-wearing Mosh and Thrasher claimed upon making their WWE debut in 1997. Collectively known as The Headbangers, the duo blended speed and power to soften up their opponents, then finished them off with their signature Stage Dive.

The Headbangers' career reached its peak in September 1997 when Mosh and Thrasher outlasted the Godwinns, Legion of Doom, and Owen Hart and the British Bulldog at *In Your House: Ground Zero* to claim the World Tag Team Championship. They held the Titles for close to one month before a disappointing loss to the Godwinns at *In Your House: Badd Blood*.

By 2000, the metalheads parted ways to pursue individual careers within WWE. Both Mosh and Thrasher competed in *WrestleMania 2000*'s Hardcore Battle Royal where Thrasher claimed the Hardcore Championship for less than one minute. In subsequent months, The Headbangers formed temporary partnerships, but couldn't duplicate past successes. By 2001, both had left WWE to compete around the United States.

THE HEADSHRINKERS

 MEMBERS Samu, Fatu, & Sionne

Samu and Fatu are proud members of a long line of Samoan Superstars to have terrorized WWE. Collectively known as The Headshrinkers, the duo displayed a dangerous combination of size, agility, and ferocity on their way to becoming one of the most feared teams of the mid-1990s.

Originally managed solely by Afa, The Headshrinkers eventually also employed the services of Capt. Lou Albano. With the "Manager of Champions" leading the way, The Headshrinkers quickly became top contenders for the tag Titles. In April 1994, they shot to the top when they defeated The Quebecers for the World Tag Team Championship. Over the course of the next four months, Samu and Fatu turned back all comers, including the Smokin' Gunns and Yokozuna and Crush. Unfortunately for The Headshrinkers, their impressive reign was derailed when Shawn Michaels and Diesel defeated them in August.

Following the loss, a frustrated Samu left WWE. The massive Sionne briefly filled the vacancy, but the new version of The Headshrinkers simply couldn't recreate the magic. Fatu and Sionne split soon after.

THE HEART THROBS

MEMBERS Antonio & Romeo

These heartbreakers entered WWE in 2005 and were so sexy they almost didn't know what to do with themselves. Antonio and Romeo wrapped up the attention of the ladies in the audience with their charisma, and placed feathered boas around choice females to dance in the ring with them after victories.

The Heart Throbs battled for tag team gold against the likes of William Regal and Tajiri, The Hurricane and Rosey, Lance Cade and Trevor Murdoch, Big Show and Kane, and Snitsky and Tomko. They also teamed with Victoria in intense mixed tag matches. In February 2006, the two self-proclaimed Don Juans left WWE.

THE HEAVENLY BODIES

MEMBERS Jimmy Del Ray & Tom Prichard **COMBINED WT** 460 lbs.

Smooth operators "Gigolo" Jimmy Del Ray and Dr. Tom Prichard came to WWE by way of Smoky Mountain Wrestling in the summer of 1993. With manager, James E. Cornette, in their corner, the duo was a well-oiled machine with an innate mean streak.

Upon arriving, Del Ray and Prichard racked up several impressive victories, en route to earning an opportunity at The Steiner Brothers' World Tag Team Championship at SummerSlam. While the encounter with Rick and Scott Steiner ended in defeat, the Heavenly Bodies were quickly able to get back to their winning ways, including a big victory over the Smokin' Gunns in September.

In November 1993, the Heavenly Bodies captured the Smoky Mountain Tag Team Championship when they defeated the Rock 'n' Roll Express at Survivor Series. Del Ray and Prichard carried the Titles into the new year, while regularly flaunting the SMW gold on WWE television.

The Heavenly Bodies ventured to ECW in 1995, but eventually went their separate ways when SMW ceased operations in December.

HEATH SLATER

HT 6'2"	**WT** 216 lbs.	**FROM** Pineville, West Virginia
SIGNATURE MOVE Sweetness		

Some dance to the beat of their own drum, and then there is Heath Slater. A self-proclaimed "One Man Band," Slater is always making noise whether on his own or surrounded by equally talented Superstars. Slater formed Nexus with his fellow *NXT* Season one graduates and then jumped to The Corre where he formed a successful tag team with Justin Gabriel. Slater and Gabriel became three-time WWE Tag Team Champions.

Slater severed ties with Gabriel in July 2011. Determined to rock forward as a solo act, his disrespect toward the WWE Legends left no one screaming for an encore. Slater found back-up in Jinder Mahal and Drew McIntyre and formed 3MB. Together this offbeat trio enjoyed spirited air guitar sessions and interfering in each other's matches.

When 3MB dissolved, Slater was not a solo act for long. He formed Slator Gator with Florida football alum, Titus O'Neil. In 2015, Slater lobbied to challenge U.S. Champion John Cena but was routinely shelved by other challengers. Fed up with this type of treatment, Slater found common ground with other frustrated Superstars Bo Dallas, Adam Rose, and Curtis Axel to form the Social Outcasts. The newfound allies targeted Dolph Ziggler in January 2016 as their first step toward gaining the respect they deserve.

THE HEENAN FAMILY

MEMBERS Andre the Giant, Big John Studd, King Kong Bundy, Ken Patera, The Missing Link, Adrian Adonis, Paul Orndorff, Harley Race, Hercules, The Barbarian, Rick Rude, Haku, Tama, Brooklyn Brawler, Mr. Perfect, Red Rooster, Arn Anderson, & Tully Blanchard

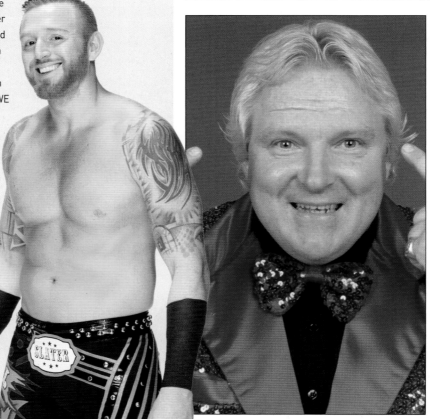

Bobby "The Brain" Heenan believed a "stable" was for horses. His roster of Superstars would be his family, The Heenan Family. This impressive ensemble traces its roots back to the early 1970s and the Minneapolis-based AWA promotion, where Heenan guided the careers of Nick Bockwinkel, "Cowboy" Bob Orton, and other top Superstars.

In 1984, Heenan moved to WWE, where his new family approach paid instant dividends. New client Big John Studd's sudden main-event status convinced many other Superstars to knock on Heenan's door. Before long, Heenan's family multiplied faster than rabbits. Superstars such as King Kong Bundy and Harley Race joined the fold, but the Family's biggest acquisition came in 1987 when Andre the Giant joined. Landing the massive Superstar proved to be a major coup for Heenan and a major headache for his nemesis, Hulk Hogan.

Heenan later guided Andre and Haku as well as the Brain Busters to the World Tag Team Championship. He also managed Rick Rude and Mr. Perfect to the Intercontinental Championship.

HEIDENREICH

HT	6'7"	WT	285 lbs.	FROM	New Orleans, Louisiana
SIGNATURE MOVE			Cobra Clutch		

Heidenreich's size certainly intimidated opponents, but it was his patently crazed head that truly scared Superstars. With tattoos spread over his chiseled frame, Heidenreich was known for reciting cryptic poetry before attacking. Even more unnerving was the fact that nobody was safe from him, as Heidenreich was known to assault Superstars, announcers, and even fans.

In October 2004, Heidenreich cost Undertaker an opportunity to reclaim the WWE Championship. This was a mistake. Undertaker introduced the raging lunatic to his one severe phobia by shutting him inside a casket at *Royal Rumble 2005*.

After falling to Undertaker multiple times, Heidenreich took a more friendly approach to life. His poems, which he called "disasterpieces," softened in content, and he even began making friends with young WWE fans. The new-and-improved Heidenreich also began forming friendships with fellow Superstars, including "Road Warrior" Animal. Together, the duo defeated MNM to capture the WWE Tag Team Championship in July 2005.

HEIDI LEE MORGAN

FROM	New Jersey

Despite her father, Lester Morgan, being a sports-entertainer, Heidi Lee Morgan never dreamed of an in-ring career. Instead, her passion was in bodybuilding. But after a chance meeting with Vince McMahon, she soon changed her mind.

After meeting McMahon, Morgan traveled to South Carolina where she trained with the legendary Fabulous Moolah. She made her debut in 1987 and immediately caught the attention of fans with her high-flying offense and equally-high blonde hair.

Success came early for Morgan, as she was immediately thrust into matches with former WWE Women's Champion Wendi Richter. Their rivalry was highlighted by a May 1987 Steel Cage Match, one of the first-ever cage matches featuring women in the United States.

Morgan turned her attention to the WWE Women's Championship in late 1993. In a tournament designed to crown a new Champion, she advanced to the finals before losing to eventual winner Alundra Blayze. After a few unsuccessful rematches, Morgan joined forces with Blayze to battle Luna Vachon and Bull Nakano before leaving WWE in 1994.

HERCULES

HT	6'1"	WT	270 lbs.	FROM	Tampa, Florida
SIGNATURE MOVE			The Human Torture Rack		

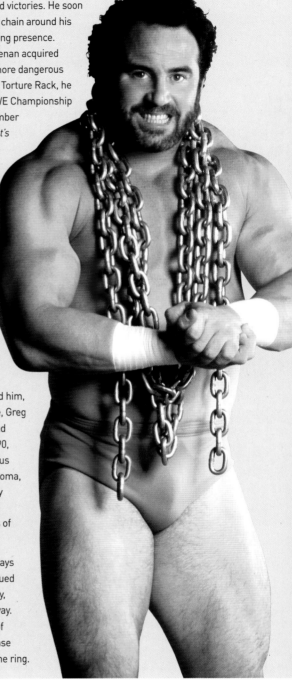

This stoic pillar of power came to WWE in 1986 managed by "Classy" Freddie Blassie. The strength of Hercules led him to numerous lopsided victories. He soon came to the ring with a steel chain around his neck, adding to his intimidating presence. When Bobby "The Brain" Heenan acquired his contract, Hercules was more dangerous than ever. With his signature Torture Rack, he nearly strong-armed the WWE Championship from Hulk Hogan on a November 1986 edition of *Saturday Night's Main Event*.

He battled Billy Jack Haynes in a violent "Full Nelson Challenge" at *WrestleMania III*. At *WrestleMania IV*, Hercules was pitted against Ultimate Warrior, culminating a power vs. power rivalry with the Warrior. Hercules became victim of a plot in 1988 when Heenan tried to sell him to "Million-Dollar Man" Ted DiBiase. With the fans behind him, Hercules battled Earthquake, Greg "The Hammer" Valentine, and Mr. Perfect. At the end of 1990, Hercules formed the villainous Power and Glory with Paul Roma, managed by Slick. While they made for a formidable team, they separated after a series of disappointing defeats.

Hercules and WWE parted ways in 1991 but his career continued through the mid-1990s. Sadly, in March 2004, he passed away. This WWE Legend was one of the strongest and most intense competitors to ever step in the ring.

HERCULES AYALA

HT	6'1"	WT	265 lbs.	FROM	Puerto Rico

Growing up in Puerto Rico, Hercules Ayala idolized island star Hurricane Castillo. Ayala later relocated to Boston where he met Angelo Savoldi while working out at a gym. The two formed a bond and Savoldi soon began training Ayala for a career in the ring.

Shortly after his 1970 debut, Ayala made a few appearances in WWE, but he made his biggest splash internationally. Still only a few years into his career, Ayala returned to Puerto Rico where he became one of the World Wrestling Council's most despised villains. Ayala also excelled in Canada, where he was known as "The Strongest Man in Wrestling." Along the way, he regularly tangled with Dynamite Kid, Harley Race, Bret Hart, and others from Stu Hart's Stampede Wrestling promotion.

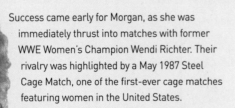

HIDEO ITAMI

| **HT** | 5'9" | **WT** | 182 lbs. | **FROM** | Tokyo, Japan | **SIGNATURE MOVE** | Shotgun Kick |

Hideo Itami's dizzying array of lightning fast kicks has been thrilling Japanese fans of sports-entertainment since the year 2000. So when WWE signed this celebrated athlete in the summer of 2014, the only people not excited from Orlando to Tokyo were those having to face his lethal offense inside NXT's yellow ropes. The Ascension were the first to experience Itami firsthand, with the result not going the way the painted pair had hoped. Itami and another prized free agent, Finn Bálor, teamed up to defeat one of the most dominant tag teams in NXT history at *NXT Takeover: R Evolution*. Itami gained another impressive victory at *NXT Takeover: Rival* against Tyler Breeze and later earned a spot in the Andre the Giant Memorial Battle Royal at *WrestleMania 31*. A mysterious parking lot attack sidelined Hideo for the rest of 2015, but this proud Superstar is hungry to return and show all of WWE exactly why he is one of the world's most respected competitors.

HIGH ENERGY

| **MEMBERS** | Owen Hart & Koko B. Ware | **COMBINED WT** | 456 lbs. |

Owen Hart and Koko B. Ware joined forces while also throwing fashion sense out the window in 1992. Collectively known as High Energy, the duo used their fluorescent pants and checkered suspenders to dizzy opponents before finishing them off with their amazing speed and superior athleticism.

Unfortunately for High Energy, Hart was sidelined with a serious knee injury just as they were taking off. By the time he returned, Koko B. Ware was off spreading his wings in other promotions. Fans of the colorful tandem certainly wish their partnership could've lasted longer, as the excitement High Energy brought to WWE was electric.

THE HIGHLANDERS

| **MEMBERS** | Rory McAllister & Robbie McAllister | **COMBINED WT** | 470 lbs. |
| **FROM** | Oban, Scotland | | |

Rory and Robbie McAllister left their homes in the rugged Scottish Highlands in search of tag team gold in July 2006. They did not have the easiest time adjusting to the American way of life, however.

When not struggling with such technological advancements as televisions or cell phones, The Highlanders were found roughhousing WWE's top teams. Utilizing the Scot Drop, the fighting cousins scored victories over The Spirit Squad, Cade and Murdoch, and others.

Much like WWE Hall of Famer and fellow Scotsman, "Rowdy" Roddy Piper, The Highlanders sported traditional plaid kilts to the ring. Their opponents may scoff at the pleated skirt-like garment, but The Highlanders proved their grit in WWE.

THE HILLBILLIES

| **MEMBERS** | Hillbilly Jim, Uncle Elmer, Cousin Luke, & Cousin Junior |

Don't go messin' with these country boys! The Hillbillies came to WWE in 1985 to help Hillbilly Jim even the score in his battles against sports-entertainment's most reviled villains, including the Heenan Family, Jesse Ventura, Roddy Piper, and Mr. Fuji, among others. Jim's relatives were a huge hit with audiences, as Elmer, Luke, and Junior brought a unique country flavor to both singles and tag team action.

In one of the most touching moments in WWE history, Uncle Elmer married the lovely Joyce on an October 1985 edition of *Saturday Night's Main Event*. Despite crude attempts by Piper to interrupt the ceremony, the event was a star-studded extravaganza that included a poem by "Leapin'" Lanny Poffo and a surprise appearance from Tiny Tim.

By 1986, the cousins went back to the farm, while Hillbilly Jim stayed behind to tackle WWE's no-good vermin. Decades later, the Hillbillies are still remembered for putting smiles on the faces of fans worldwide.

HILLBILLY JIM

| **HT** | 6'7" | **WT** | 285 lbs. | **FROM** | Mudlick, Kentucky | **SIGNATURE MOVE** | Bear Hug |

At six-foot-seven, it's hard not to notice Hillbilly Jim, especially when he's sitting in the front row. In late 1984, "Rowdy" Roddy Piper spotted the towering fan at a WWE Live Event and asked him to come on *Piper's Pit*. The arrogant "Hot Rod" mocked Jim's big bushy beard and denim overalls, but eventually offered to train him for a WWE career. Jim, despite wanting to start his career, declined the offer and chose to learn from Hulk Hogan instead.

After several weeks of training, the Kentucky native made his in-ring debut, defeating veteran Terry Gibbs with an impressive bear hug. The win marked the beginning of a long love affair between the fans and Hillbilly Jim. Audiences loved the country boy so much, in fact, that they began demanding more of him. Unable to keep up with the lofty demands, Hillbilly Jim introduced his equally lovable family members Uncle Elmer, Cousin Luke, and Cousin Junior.

At *WrestleMania III*, Hillbilly Jim competed in the biggest match of his career when he teamed with pocket-sized Superstars, Little Beaver and Haiti Kid, to battle King Kong Bundy and his pint-sized pals, Lord Littlebrook and Little Tokyo. The match was marred by controversy when the gigantic Bundy attacked Little Beaver. The sight of Hillbilly Jim carrying his limp little friend from the ring that night remains one of *WrestleMania*'s most memorable images.

HIRO SAITO

| HT | 5'9" | WT | 240 lbs. | FROM | Kawasaki, Japan |

Known for his buck-the-system attitude, Japanese Superstar Hiro Saito proved to be the perfect fit for the New World Order during the expansion into Asia. Known as nWo Japan, the group was led by Masahiro Chono and featured such members as Buff Bagwell, Scott Norton, and Hiroyoshi Tenzan.

Years before Saito joined nWo Japan, he gained notoriety for his lengthy rivalry with The Cobra. In May 1985, Saito defeated The Cobra to claim the WWE Junior Heavyweight Championship. Two months later, he lost the Title back to The Cobra in Osaka, Japan.

Saito was also an accomplished tag-team competitor. With Super Strong Machine as his partner, he won the International Wrestling Grand Prix Tag Team Championship in December 1990.

HIROKO

| FROM | The Land of the Rising Sun |

Clad in a Japanese kimono and sporting traditional white face makeup and red lipstick, Hiroko gave the impression of an unassuming geisha. In reality, though, she was a dangerous Diva with an unmatched temper.

She and Kenzo Suzuki came to WWE in 2004. Serving as Suzuki's translator, Hiroko oftentimes stepped outside her job description to help her man achieve victory. The devious geisha tossed exotic powders into the eyes of Suzuki's opponents. Hiroko also proved to have a jealous side. When Suzuki's eyes wandered toward the direction of another Diva, Hiroko was overcome with rage. Both Michelle McCool and Torrie Wilson felt Hiroko's jealous wrath before she and Suzuki were released from WWE in July 2005.

HISASHI SHINMA

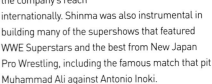

Assuming the role of WWE President in 1978, Hisashi Shinma set a tone of no nonsense leadership, while also making important strides toward expanding the company's reach internationally. Shinma was also instrumental in building many of the supershows that featured WWE Superstars and the best from New Japan Pro Wrestling, including the famous match that pit Muhammad Ali against Antonio Inoki.

Shinma honored the position with his wisdom, dignity, and respect until 1984, when he was succeeded by Jack Tunney. He will always be heralded as the man who upheld the standards of WWE at all costs, regardless of the circumstances or existing public pressures.

THE HOLLY COUSINS

| MEMBERS | Crash, Hardcore, & Molly |
| COMBINED WT | Over 800 lbs. (allegedly) |

Though family and partners, Crash and Hardcore Holly constantly bickered about who was tougher. Calling themselves the "Superheavyweights," they claimed a combined weight of allegedly over 800 pounds and insisted on competing with WWE's giants. Crash brought a scale to the ring to ensure that opponents measured up to the Superheavyweights' lofty standards.

In October 1999, Crash and Hardcore Holly defeated the dysfunctional Rock 'N' Sock Connection to win the World Tag Team Championship. In 2000, the beautiful and talented Molly Holly entered WWE and stepped right into the family business. At WrestleMania 2000, Crash and Hardcore took part in a Hardcore Battle Royal.

The three cousins all enjoyed success on their own, but many fans argue that this trio made the most magic as a family.

HONKY TONK MAN

| | HT | 6'1" | WT | 243 lbs. | FROM | Memphis, Tennessee |
| | SIGNATURE MOVE | Shake, Rattle, and Roll |

Many consider the Honky Tonk Man to be among the greatest Superstars of the 1980s, including the Honky Tonk Man himself. Taking arrogance to a whole new level, it wasn't uncommon to hear the guitar-wielding competitor remind audiences, "I'm cool, I'm cocky, I'm bad." Unfortunately for all the Honky Tonk Man detractors, of which there were plenty, he was everything he claimed to be.

With long sideburns and slicked-back hair, Honky Tonk Man rode into WWE in a pink Cadillac in 1986. Upon arriving, the Elvis lookalike expected to be showered with admiration. Instead, fans vehemently despised the cocky newcomer. The boos, however, never deterred the Honky Tonk Man from succeeding in the ring. Alongside his manager "Colonel" Jimmy Hart, he set out on an impressive string of victories over WWE's most-noted Superstars, including his first big-name victim, Jake "The Snake" Roberts at WrestleMania III.

Shortly after WrestleMania, the Honky Tonk Man defeated Ricky "The Dragon" Steamboat for the Intercontinental Championship in Buffalo, New York. The win proved historic, as he went on to hold the Title for nearly fifteen months, longer than any other Superstar in history.

The Honky Tonk Man's record-breaking Intercontinental Championship reign came to an abrupt halt when Ultimate Warrior dethroned the Champion at SummerSlam 1988 in a match that lasted a mere thirty seconds. Despite the humiliating loss, the length of Honky Tonk Man's reign gave the cocky Superstar ammunition to claim he was the greatest Intercontinental Champion of all time, which he did ad nauseam.

Following his record-breaking reign, the Honky Tonk Man set out to create another record—a musical record. He teamed with Greg Valentine to form the singing duo known as Rhythm & Blues. At WrestleMania VI, much to the disgust of the sold-out SkyDome, they performed their single "Hunka, Hunka, Hunka Honky Love."

The twilight of the Honky Tonk Man's legendary career saw the singing Superstar contribute in several different capacities, including manager and commentator. Despite achieving moderate success in these new roles, however, fans everywhere will always remember him as the longest reigning Intercontinental Champion of all time.

HORNSWOGGLE

HT	4'5"	WT	142 lbs.
SIGNATURE MOVE		Tadpole Splash	

For a man so small in stature, Hornswoggle can sure cause a commotion. Once thought to be Mr. McMahon's illegitimate son, the miniature Superstar had the entire WWE Universe buzzing over his newfound power, only for JBL to reveal he was actually Finlay's son. To this day, Hornswoggle's true parentage and origins remain a mystery. Nothing is simple with Hornswoggle. He likes it that way.

This pint-sized pack of concentrated chaos was first seen in 2006. First wreaking havoc on Finlay's behalf, he soon began stirring trouble up on his own. In July 2007, he used his Tadpole Splash to become the lightest (and the last) Cruiserweight Champion in history. The little guy fulfilled another dream in 2009 when he became the official mascot of D-Generation X, a settlement brokered in a miniature courtroom-based segment dubbed—you guessed it—"Little People's Court."

Hornswoggle continued living large in 2011 when he helped John Cena eliminate several Superstars from the Royal Rumble Match. He later bookended the year by being granted the ability to speak, a Holiday miracle aided by Santa enthusiast Mick Foley. Little did anyone know, Hornswoggle had been communicating just fine via email, shrouded in secrecy as the Anonymous *Raw* General Manager! Hornswoggle became an unofficial member of 3MB in 2014, and also starred in the WWE Studios film *Leprechaun: Origins*.

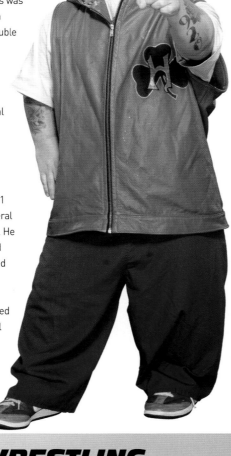

HOUSTON WRESTLING

When the words "Houston Wrestling" are invoked, one man's name comes to mind: Paul Boesch. The longtime promoter worked with territories all over the country, enabling WWE Champions like Superstar Billy Graham and Bob Backlund to defend their Titles in front of Texas crowds.

Boesch had previously been a competitor in Houston, on shows presented by Morris Sigel. Sigel began promoting in 1929, replacing his brother, Julius, who'd staged irregular shows since 1915.

In 1947, an accident forced Boesch to end his career, and he became the promotion's radio announcer. When television started in the city in 1949, Boesch switched to the new medium, even though he'd never seen a television show himself.

Following Sigel's death in 1967, Boesch bought the company, showcasing stars like Mil Mascaras, Wahoo McDaniel, Johnny Valentine, Nick Kozak, Al Madril, Fritz Von Erich, and the Junkyard Dog. Ernie Ladd was a Houston favorite, mainly because he'd played football there. He was jeered virtually everywhere else.

Shortly before his 1987 retirement, Boesch formed a working arrangement with WWE.

HOWARD FINKEL

FROM Stamford, Connecticut

Howard Finkel began his career in the early 1970s as an usher at the New Haven Coliseum. After he persuaded his boss to contact WWE about holding events there, he met Vince McMahon, and by 1976, he was the ring announcer during WWE events at the venue. In 1980, Finkel became a full-time WWE employee and the first staff member of Titan Sports, hired by Vince and Linda McMahon.

As the company entered its critical phase of national expansion, Finkel was selected as the lead ring announcer during a time when WWE needed its own voice. Howard Finkel was heard everywhere on television programs such as *Championship Wrestling*, *Tuesday Night Titans*, *Superstars of Wrestling*, and *Saturday Night's Main Event*.

Finkel also appeared at untelevised stadium shows and pay-per-view events, and provided voice-overs for live event advertisements. WWE was a global entity and Howard Finkel's distinctive delivery was recognized by fans. Into the 1990s, fans and colleagues bestowed him the nickname "The Fink," and at *WrestleMania IX*, he was introduced as "Finkus Maximus." From 1993 to 1997, he was the ring announcer for the company's flagship show, *Monday Night Raw*.

Toward the late 1990s, Howard took on a lighter schedule and announced for live events while branching out to co-host *WWE Byte This*. In August, 2002, he entered into a dispute with up-and-coming ring announcer Lilian Garcia, which turned physical. Unfortunately for "The Fink," he came up on the short end of the stick in an Evening Gown/Tuxedo Match for the right to be the *Raw* ring announcer.

Today, Finkel works behind the scenes, contributes his historic knowledge for the company's television shows, WWE.com, and the WWE Network, and announces the Hall of Fame inductees at *WrestleMania*. In 2009, it was his turn to be announced, as the night before *WrestleMania XXV*, he was inducted into the WWE Hall of Fame.

Howard is the only person to appear on camera at every *WrestleMania*. He also appeared in the WWE Network reality show, *WWE Legends' House*.

HULK HOGAN

see page 152

HUNICO

HT	5'10"	WT	205 lbs.	FROM	Mexico City, Mexico
SIGNATURE MOVE		Senton Bomb			

The WWE Universe caught Sin Cara fever when the masked Superstar made his jaw-dropping debut in 2011. But after several months, fans questioned their allegiance to Sin Cara when he started displaying unbecoming characteristics. But it wasn't really Sin Cara under the mask! Instead, the Superstar who was turning fans off was a disguised Hunico.

Following the revelation, Hunico and Sin Cara squared off in a Mask vs. Mask Match, which Hunico lost. As a result, the Mexican Superstar was forced to no longer compete as Sin Cara.

With Sin Cara behind him, the unmasked Hunico was unable to catch steam in WWE and soon disappeared. His signature senton bomb, however, is still being used by Sin Cara, perhaps as a dig to his former foe.

THE HURRICANE

HT	6'0"	WT	215 lbs.	FROM	Raleigh, North Carolina
SIGNATURE MOVE		Shining Wizard, Eye of the Hurricane			

Gregory Helms initially garnered attention in WCW, first as part of millennial boy band, 3 Count, and later as a top Cruiserweight. In fact, Helms was the Cruiserweight Champion when WWE purchased WCW in 2001.

After WCW's Invasion, WWE audiences saw the mild-mannered Helms transform into The Hurricane, a masked superhero who protected truth, justice, and the WWE way. In times of peril, his warning beckoned, "Stand back, there's a Hurricane coming through!"

In 2002, The Hurricane captured the Cruiserweight Championship and found an unlikely, yet successful, masked allegiance with Kane. During his righteous run in WWE, super-sidekicks such as "Mighty Molly," "Superhero-in-Training" Rosey, and Stacy Keibler also aided his noble cause. He and Rosey even won the World Tag Team Championships. Fearless and bold as any Superstar, The Hurricane shocked the WWE Universe on the March 10, 2003, edition of *Raw* when he pinned The Rock.

The Hurricane ditched his crime-fighting persona in 2006, competing with a new attitude under his real name, Gregory Helms. He immediately captured the Cruiserweight Championship and held it for thirteen months, a WWE record. Helms finished his WWE career on *ECW* where he conducted backstage interviews and mysteriously disappeared whenever The Hurricane made a surprise return.

HUSKY HARRIS

HT	6'3"	WT	300 lbs.
FROM	Brooksville, Florida		
SIGNATURE MOVE		Swinging Reverse STO	

First appearing on WWE television as a part of *NXT* Season 2, Husky Harris was as big as a tank and as fast as a Ferrari. With an unorthodox style to complete the package, it was clear Harris was a budding star. Following his time on *NXT*, Harris helped Wade Barrett defeat John Cena at *Hell in a Cell 2010*. This paved the way for Harris to be inducted into Nexus, where he remained until the end of the year. Then in January 2011, he was punted by Randy Orton. The impact of the blow was so great that Harris never returned to WWE.

INTERCONTINENTAL CHAMPIONSHIP

see page 154

INTERNATIONAL WRESTLING MONTREAL

International Wrestling—also known by its French name, *Lutte Internationale*—was a Montreal-based territory that continued the city's rich traditions that started in 1939 when Eddie Quinn began promoting shows at the Montreal Forum.

In the 1970s, two rival promotions competed for fan loyalties: Grand Prix, run by the Vachon family, and the Rougeau clan's All-Star Wrestling. By 1975, they'd cancelled each other out.

International Wrestling, formed in 1980 by a consortium of Gino Brito, Andre the Giant, and his manager, Frank Valois, attempted to fill the void. Other partners included Rick Martel, who defended his AWA Championship in his hometown of Quebec City, and Canadian Heavyweight Champion, Dino Bravo.

Crowds tended to cheer Quebec-raised Superstars against outsiders often managed by Lord Alfred Hayes and Eddie Creatchman, both of whom were bilingual and could taunt crowds in French.

During its seven year history, International Wrestling had talent-trading agreements with the AWA, WWE, and Puerto Rico's WWC. When the promotion closed in 1987, stars like Haku, the Fabulous Rougeaus, Martel, and Bravo were in WWE.

THE INVADERS

In 1983, an exotic, masked team arrived in WWE, enlivening fans with a fast-paced, Latin-accented style, while clashing with tandems like the Wild Samoans, Roddy Piper and Paul Orndorff, and Mr. Fuji and Tiger Chung Lee.

Like the Lucha Dragons three decades later, the Invaders assailed their adversaries from the air. But the duo exuded a toughness born in their native Puerto Rico.

Invader #1 had been a mainstay on the island since 1973, colliding with such rivals as Ivan Koloff, Dick Murdoch, and Abdullah the Butcher. His most successful tag team was with the man who accompanied him to WWE, Invader #2. However, in Puerto Rico, there was also an Invader #3 and Invader #4.

Invader #1 retired in 2006.

IRISH JACKIE

Prior to entering WWE, the diminutive Superstar, Irish Jackie, struggled to make it big while competing in Southern territories. For much of the 1950s, Irish Jackie fell short against the likes of Little Beaver and Pee Wee James.

After moving north to WWE in the 1960s, Irish Jackie began to find his winning ways. He wowed northern audiences alongside his new partner, the Jamaica Kid. The famed Boston Garden was the scene of many of the team's victories over rivals Sky Low Low and Little Brutus. Irish Jackie also had many remarkable battles against Sonny Boy Cassidy in the late 1960s.

IRISH PAT BARRETT

HT	6'0"	WT	250 lbs.	FROM	Dublin, Ireland
SIGNATURE MOVE	The Killarney				

For "Irish" Pat Barrett, Victor Rivera's loss was his gain. In May, 1975, Rivera teamed with Dominic DeNucci to win the World Tag Team Championship. But only four weeks into the reign, Rivera abruptly left WWE, leaving his half of the coveted Titles behind.

After an extensive search, DeNucci chose internationally acclaimed Barrett as his new partner. As a result, the Irish Superstar stepped into the tag team Title picture.

During a prior WWE run, announcer Ray Morgan asked fans to name Pat's favorite move, which involved jumping and driving his head into an opponent's chin. The maneuver was dubbed the "Killarney Kiss." When provoked, Barrett would hit foes with his ever-present shillelagh.

After his 1985 retirement, Barrett became a trainer.

IRON SHEIK

see page 156

"IRON" MIKE SHARPE

HT	6'4"	WT	283 lbs.	FROM	Hamilton, Ontario, Canada
SIGNATURE MOVE	Forearm Smash				

A second-generation Superstar, "Iron" Mike Sharpe was a seemingly rough and tough customer who often cockily proclaimed himself "Canada's Greatest Athlete." His WWE win-loss record, however, failed to back his lofty claims.

Regularly falling to the likes of Tugboat, Hercules, and Tito Santana, Sharpe rarely walked away from a match victorious, despite sporting a mysterious black arm pad that many assumed concealed a foreign object.

Despite his lack of WWE victories, Sharpe did achieve a level of success in the NWA, where he claimed more than 10 Championships, including the Calgary version of the International Tag Team Titles with partner, Jim Wright.

IRWIN R. SCHYSTER

see page 157

ISAAC YANKEM DDS

HT	6'10"	WT	300 lbs.	FROM	Decatur, Illinois
SIGNATURE MOVE	DDS				

According to Isaac Yankem, he let his teeth deteriorate to show "rotten-teethed idiots" the dangers of bad oral hygiene. Jerry Lawler introduced this evil dentist to WWE in the summer of 1995. As "The King's" personal dentist, Yankem's sole purpose was to extract pain (and teeth) from Lawler's chief rival, Bret Hart.

When Yankem and Hart finally competed at *SummerSlam 1995*, a victory was not the dentist's prime objective. Instead, Yankem set out to permanently end Hart's career. Despite some sadistic tactics, the "Hit Man" was still standing tall after *SummerSlam*. Months later, Hart beat him in a Steel Cage Match with Lawler suspended from a cage above the ring. Finding wins was like pulling teeth for Yankem after that and he soon disappeared.

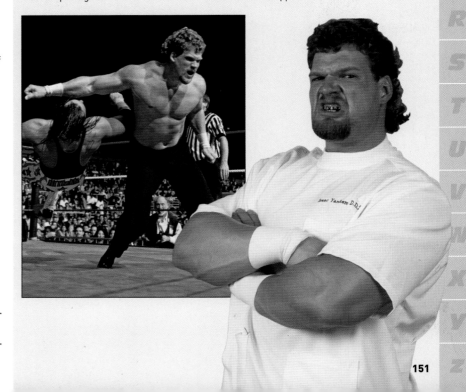

HULK HOGAN

HT	6'7"
WT	302 lbs.
FROM	Venice Beach, California

SIGNATURE MOVE
Leg Drop

As one of the most recognizable figures in sports-entertainment history, Hulk Hogan has arguably impacted the industry more than any Superstar of his era. Along the way, he became a major force in WWE's booming popularity of the 1980s, while also proudly carrying the WWE Championship on six separate occasions.

Hogan's success can be traced back to a chance meeting with Jack and Gerald Brisco. After being taken aback by his size, the brothers convinced Hogan to pursue a career in sports-entertainment. He heeded their advice and began training with Hiro Matsuda before kicking off his career in the Florida, Alabama, and Memphis territories.

Hogan made his WWE debut in November 1979, defeating Harry Valdez with an overhead backbreaker. The up-and-comer gained victories over such established stars as Gorilla Monsoon, Dominic DeNucci, and Tito Santana. Hogan even defeated then-WWE Champion Bob Backlund via countout on several occasions.

Hogan's success led to a high profile encounter with Andre the Giant at *Showdown at Shea* in August 1980. Despite coming up short against the Giant, Hogan was seen by many as a rising star. But before he could continue to climb the ladder, Hogan took time off to film *Rocky III*.

Hogan's decision to pursue Hollywood was against Vincent J. McMahon's wishes and ultimately resulted in his departure. No longer a member of WWE, he drifted to the AWA where he became a top contender for the AWA Championship. In fact, Hogan defeated Nick Bockwinkel for the AWA Championship in April 1983. However, the decision was later overturned and Hogan's victory was never recognized by the AWA.

HULKAMANIA RUNS WILD

After nearly a three-year absence, Hogan returned to WWE in December 1983, defeating Bill Dixon with a Leg Drop. Unlike his earlier WWE days, Hogan used his unmatched charisma and amazing physique to lure the fans into his corner. With the crowd firmly behind him, Hogan was ready to catapult to the top.

Hogan's time came in January 1984, when he defeated Iron Sheik for the WWE Championship. With the win came the birth of the most powerful force in sports-entertainment, Hulkamania! Hogan soon became the voice of an entire generation.

He professed the importance of training, prayers, and vitamins. And by 1985, The Hulkster was splashed all over mainstream media, including appearances on *The A-Team* and *Saturday Night Live*, as well as landing on the cover of *Sports Illustrated*.

Coinciding with Hogan's success, WWE's merchandising soon took off as well. Backed by the power of The Hulkster's red and yellow, WWE couldn't keep store shelves stocked with their action figures, apparel, and workout sets. Hogan even landed his own animated series, *Hulk Hogan's Rock 'n' Wrestling*.

With Hogan cemented firmly as the top star in sports-entertainment, WWE took the calculated risk of promoting its largest ever show, *WrestleMania*, in March 1985. In the main event, Hogan and Mr. T defeated Roddy Piper and Paul Orndorff. As a result of the inaugural show's success, *WrestleMania* has gone on to become one of the biggest brands in all of entertainment, generating hundreds of millions of dollars for host cities.

WHEN IT COMES CRASHING DOWN

A gigantic threat to Hogan's career came in an unexpected form when Andre the Giant challenged The Hulkster to a WWE Championship Match at *WrestleMania III*. Never one to sidestep a challenge, Hogan accepted and the two former friends faced each other in front of more than 93,000 fans at the Pontiac Silverdome. Regularly regarded as one of the most historic matches ever, Hogan wowed the crowd when he hoisted the colossal Giant for a bodyslam. The Hulkster then dropped the big leg on his friend-turned-opponent, en route to one of the greatest victories of his career.

Despite the victory, Hogan wasn't done with Andre, as the two met again in February 1988. Heading into the match, Andre had formed an alliance with Ted DiBiase, who went to great lengths to assure Hogan would lose the gold. Late in the contest, Andre pinned the Champ after a rather pedestrian suplex, despite The Hulkster getting his shoulder up well in advance of the three-count. It was later revealed that DiBiase had planted the devious referee in the match. But the damage was done; Hogan's epic Title reign had come to an end.

THE RISE AND FALL OF THE MEGA POWERS

No longer the Champion, Hogan went on to help Randy Savage defeat DiBiase to claim the Title at *WrestleMania IV*. Following the event, the two Superstars became inseparable and soon formed an all-star tag team known as the Mega Powers. Together, Hogan and Savage bested DiBiase and Andre at the first-ever *SummerSlam*.

Unfortunately, a series of misunderstandings between Hogan and Savage led to the "Macho Man" thinking "The Hulkster" had eyes for Miss Elizabeth. Savage's jealousy eventually caused him to attack Hogan, marking the end of the Mega Powers and the beginning of a bitter rivalry. With the WWE Championship on the line, the former friends competed at *WrestleMania V*, where Hogan defeated Savage to reclaim the gold.

THE ULTIMATE CHALLENGE

With the WWE Championship back around his waist, Hogan went on to enjoy one of the brightest years in WWE history. In addition to starring in the movie, *No Holds Barred*, The Hulkster successfully fended off threats from Mr. Perfect, Big Boss Man, and Bad News Brown, among others. He even won his first of two consecutive Royal Rumble Matches. But at *WrestleMania VI*, he would compete against a force that would prove to be unstoppable.

In a Title vs. Title Match, Hogan defended his WWE Championship against Ultimate Warrior's Intercontinental Championship. In front of more than 67,000 fans in Toronto's SkyDome, Warrior defeated The Hulkster to capture the WWE Title. Despite the loss, Hogan left the stadium with the grace of a Champion, holding Warrior's arm high before handing over the spotlight.

A REAL AMERICAN

In typical Hogan fashion, he refused to stay down for long. And when his fans and country needed him most, The Hulkster responded with perhaps the most emotionally-charged victory of his career.

While the United States was reeling from the ongoing conflict in the Middle East, American hero Sgt. Slaughter did the unthinkable when he turned his back on his country to become an Iraqi sympathizer. Making matters worse, he even defeated Ultimate Warrior to claim the WWE Championship in January 1991.

Unable to sit back and allow Slaughter's reign of terror to continue, Hogan challenged the turncoat to a match at *WrestleMania VII*. To the delight of an entire nation, The Hulkster defeated Slaughter to kick off his third WWE Championship reign.

In subsequent years, Hogan added to his WWE Championship résumé with victories over Undertaker and Yokozuna before shifting his focus to acting.

WCW AND THE nWo

Hogan was lured back to sports-entertainment by WCW in the summer of 1994. Within weeks of returning, The Hulkster defeated Ric Flair to capture his first of six WCW Championships. But despite his multiple reigns, Hogan's WCW tenure is most remembered for his shocking actions at *Bash at the Beach 1996* when he turned his back on the fans to join forces with The Outsiders, Scott Hall and Kevin Nash.

Collectively known as the New World Order, Hogan and company went on to run roughshod over WCW for years. And when WCW closed its doors, the nWo simply picked up where they left off and began wreaking havoc in WWE in 2002.

After nearly a decade away, the returning Hogan found himself back in the WWE spotlight when he faced The Rock at *WrestleMania X8*. Unfortunately for The Hulkster, after losing to The Great One, he became the target of an attack at the hands of Hall and Nash.

RETURN TO THE RED AND YELLOW

No longer a member of the nWo, Hogan dusted off his red and yellow ring gear and returned to being one of the fans' favorite Superstars. The return to his roots also helped reinvigorate his career, as The Hulkster was able to reclaim the WWE Championship when he defeated Triple H at *Backlash 2002*. He later defeated Mr. McMahon in a Street Fight at *WrestleMania XIX*, as well as Shawn Michaels at *SummerSlam 2005*.

Hulk Hogan's sports-entertainment excellence was honored in April 2005 when he was inducted into the WWE Hall of Fame. Nearly a decade later, Hogan served as the host of *WrestleMania 30*, where he shared a historic in-ring toast with The Rock and Stone Cold Steve Austin.

WHATCHA GONNA DO WHEN HULKAMANIA RUNS WILD ON YOU?

INTERCONTINENTAL CHAMPIONSHIP

After unifying the North and South American Championships in September 1979, Pat Patterson was recognized as the first-ever Intercontinental Champion. Patterson's impressive resumé prior to becoming Intercontinental Champion gave the Title instant credibility. However, nobody could have predicted that the Intercontinental Championship would eventually become one of the most prestigious Titles in sports-entertainment history.

Over the next several decades, many future Hall of Famers went on to prove their greatness with the Intercontinental Championship strapped around their waist, including Greg "The Hammer" Valentine, Mr. Perfect, and "Rowdy" Roddy Piper. Several others used the Title to propel themselves to eventual main event status, including Shawn Michaels, Stone Cold Steve Austin, and The Rock.

1979

September 1 • Rio de Janeiro
Pat Patterson becomes Intercontinental Champion
After winning a tournament in Rio de Janeiro, Pat Patterson unified the North and South American Championships to become the first-ever Intercontinental Champion.

1980

April 21 • New York, NY
Ken Patera def. **Pat Patterson**

December 8 • New York, NY
Pedro Morales def. **Ken Patera**

1981

June 20 • Philadelphia, PA
Don Muraco def. **Pedro Morales**

November 23 • New York, NY
Pedro Morales def. **Don Muraco**

1983

January 22 • New York, NY
Don Muraco def. **Pedro Morales**

1984

February 11 • Boston, MA
Tito Santana def. **Don Muraco**

September 24 • London, Ontario
Greg Valentine def. **Tito Santana**

1985

July 6 • Baltimore, MD
Tito Santana def. **Greg Valentine**

1986

February 8 • Boston, MA
Randy Savage def. **Tito Santana**

1987

March 29 • Pontiac, MI
Ricky Steamboat def. **Randy Savage**

June 2 • Buffalo, NY
Honky Tonk Man def. **Ricky Steamboat**

1988

August 29 • New York, NY
Ultimate Warrior def. **Honky Tonk Man**

1989

April 2 • Atlantic City, NJ
Rick Rude def. **Ultimate Warrior**

August 28 • East Rutherford, NJ
Ultimate Warrior def. **Rick Rude**
Ultimate Warrior vacated the Intercontinental Championship shortly after defeating Hulk Hogan for the WWE Championship in April 1990.

1990

April 23 • Austin, TX
Mr. Perfect def. **Tito Santana** in the finals of a tournament to crown a new Intercontinental Champion.

August 27 • Philadelphia, PA
Texas Tornado def. **Mr. Perfect**

November 19 • Rochester, NY
Mr. Perfect def. **Texas Tornado**

1991

August 26 • New York, NY
Bret Hart def. **Mr. Perfect**

1992

January 17 • Springfield, MA
The Mountie def. **Bret Hart**

January 19 • Albany, NY
Roddy Piper def. **The Mountie**

April 5 • Indianapolis, IN
Bret Hart def. **Roddy Piper**

August 29 • London, England
British Bulldog def. **Bret Hart**

October 27 • Terre Haute, IN
Shawn Michaels def. **British Bulldog**

1993

May 17 • New York, NY
Marty Jannetty def. **Shawn Michaels**

June 6 • Albany, NY
Shawn Michaels def. **Marty Jannetty**
After failing to defend the Intercontinental Championship for 30 days, Shawn Michaels was stripped of the Title.

September 27 • New Haven, CT
Razor Ramon def. **Rick Martel**
After being the last two Superstars standing in a Battle Royal, Razor Ramon and Rick Martel squared off to crown a new Intercontinental Champion.

1994

April 13 • Rochester, NY
Diesel def. **Razor Ramon**

August 29 • Chicago, IL
Razor Ramon def. **Diesel**

1995

January 22 • Tampa, FL
Jeff Jarrett def. **Razor Ramon**
Jeff Jarrett was stripped of the Intercontinental Championship on April 26 after a Title defense against Bob Holly ended in controversy.

April 26 • Moline, IL
Jeff Jarrett def. **Bob Holly** to reclaim the vacated Title

May 19 • Montreal, Quebec
Razor Ramon def. **Jeff Jarrett**

May 22 • Trios-Rivieres, Quebec
Jeff Jarrett def. **Razor Ramon**

July 23 • Nashville, TN
Shawn Michaels def. **Jeff Jarrett**
Injuries forced Shawn Michaels to relinquish the Intercontinental Championship on October 22.

October 22 • Winnipeg, Manitoba
Dean Douglas is awarded Intercontinental Championship

October 22 • Winnipeg, Manitoba
Razor Ramon def. **Dean Douglas**

1996

January 21 • Fresno, CA
Goldust def. **Razor Ramon**
Goldust was stripped of the Intercontinental Championship after a Title defense against Savio Vega ended in controversy.

April 1 • San Bernardino, CA
Goldust def. **Savio Vega**

June 23 • Milwaukee, WI
Ahmed Johnson def. **Goldust**
Injuries forced Ahmed Johnson to relinquish the Intercontinental Championship on August 12.

September 23 • Hershey, PA
Marc Mero def. **Faarooq** in the finals of a tournament to crown a new Intercontinental Champion

October 21 • Fort Wayne, IN
Hunter Hearst Helmsley def. **Marc Mero**

1997

February 13 • Lowell, MA
Rocky Maivia def. **Hunter Hearst Helmsley**

April 28 • Omaha, NE
Owen Hart def. **Rocky Maivia**

August 3 • East Rutherford, NJ
Stone Cold Steve Austin def. **Owen Hart**
Shortly after winning the Intercontinental Championship, injuries forced Stone Cold Steve Austin to relinquish the Title.

October 5 • St. Louis, MO
Owen Hart def. **Faarooq** in the finals of a tournament to crown a new Intercontinental Champion

November 9 • Montreal, Quebec
Stone Cold Steve Austin def. **Owen Hart**
Stone Cold Steve Austin vacated the Championship by throwing the Title into a river.

December 8 • Portland, ME
The Rock was awarded the Intercontinental Championship

1998

August 30 • New York, NY
Triple H def. **The Rock**
Injuries forced Triple H to relinquish the Intercontinental Championship on October 9.

October 12 • Uniondale, NY
Ken Shamrock def. **X-Pac** in the finals of a tournament to crown a new Intercontinental Champion

1999

February 14 • Memphis, TN
Val Venis def. **Ken Shamrock**

March 15 • San Jose, CA
Road Dogg def. **Val Venis**

March 29 • East Rutherford, NJ
Goldust def. **Road Dogg**

April 12 • Detroit, MI
The Godfather def. **Goldust**

May 31 • Moline, IL
Jeff Jarrett def. **The Godfather**

July 24 • Toronto, Ontario
Edge def. **Jeff Jarrett**

July 25 • Buffalo, NY
Jeff Jarrett def. **Edge**

July 26 • Dayton, OH
D'Lo Brown def. **Jeff Jarrett**

August 22 • Minneapolis, MN
Jeff Jarrett def. **D'Lo Brown**

October 17 • Cleveland, OH
Chyna def. **Jeff Jarrett**

December 12 • Sunrise, FL
Chris Jericho def. **Chyna**
Chris Jericho and Chyna were declared co-Intercontinental Champions on January 3, after a match between the two ended in a double pinfall.

2000

January 23 • New York, NY
Chris Jericho def. **Chyna** and **Hardcore Holly** in a Triple Threat Match

February 27 • Hartford, CT
Kurt Angle def. **Chris Jericho**

April 2 • Anaheim, CA
Chris Benoit def. **Chris Jericho** and **Kurt Angle** in a Triple Threat Match

May 4 • Richmond, VA
Chris Jericho def. **Chris Benoit**

May 8 • Uniondale, NY
Chris Benoit def. **Chris Jericho**

June 22 • Memphis, TN
Rikishi def. **Chris Benoit**

July 6 • Ft. Lauderdale, FL
Val Venis def. **Rikishi**

August 27 • Raleigh, NC
Chyna and **Eddie Guerrero** def. **Val Venis** and **Trish Stratus** in a Mixed-Tag Team Match where the winner of the match would be declared Intercontinental Champion; **Chyna** pinned **Trish Stratus** to win the Title

September 3 • Knoxville, TN
Eddie Guerrero def. **Chyna** and **Kurt Angle** in a Triple Threat Match

November 23 • Sunrise, FL
Billy Gunn def. **Eddie Guerrero**

December 10 • Birmingham, AL
Chris Benoit def. **Billy Gunn**

2001

January 21 • New Orleans, LA
Chris Jericho def. **Chris Benoit**

April 5 • Oklahoma City, OK
Triple H def. **Chris Jericho**

April 12 • Philadelphia, PA
Jeff Hardy def. **Triple H**

April 16 • Knoxville, TN
Triple H def. **Jeff Hardy**

May 20 • Sacramento, CA
Kane def. **Triple H**

June 28 • New York, NY
Albert def. **Kane**

July 23 • Buffalo, NY
Lance Storm def. **Albert**

August 19 • San Jose, CA
Edge def. **Lance Storm**

September 23 • Pittsburgh, PA
Christian def. **Edge**

October 21 • St. Louis, MO
Edge def. **Christian**

November 5 • Uniondale, NY
Test def. **Edge**

November 18 • Greensboro, NC
Edge def. **Test**
Edge unified the Intercontinental and United States Championships.

2002

January 20 • Atlanta, GA
William Regal def. **Edge**

March 17 • Toronto, Ontario
Rob Van Dam def. **William Regal**

April 21 • Kansas City, MO
Eddie Guerrero def. **Rob Van Dam**

May 27 • Edmonton, Alberta
Rob Van Dam def. **Eddie Guerrero**

July 29 • Greensboro, NC
Chris Benoit def. **Rob Van Dam**

August 25 • Uniondale, NY
Rob Van Dam def. **Chris Benoit**

September 16 • Denver, CO
Chris Jericho def. **Rob Van Dam**

September 30 • Houston, TX
Kane def. **Chris Jericho**

October 20 • Little Rock, AR
Triple H def. **Kane**
Triple H unified the World Heavyweight Championship with the Intercontinental Championship; the Intercontinental Title remained inactive until May 2003.

2003

May 18 • Charlotte, NC
Christian last eliminated **Booker T** in a Battle Royal to crown the new Intercontinental Champion

July 7 • Montreal, Quebec
Booker T def. **Christian**

August 10 • Des Moines, IA
Christian def. **Booker T**

Septemberr 29 • Chicago, IL
Rob Van Dam def. **Christian**

October 27 • Fayetteville, NC
Chris Jericho def. **Rob Van Dam**

October 27 • Fayetteville, NC
Rob Van Dam def. **Chris Jericho**

December 14 • Orlando, FL
Randy Orton def. **Rob Van Dam**

2004

July 11 • Hartford, CT
Edge def. **Randy Orton**
Injuries forced Edge to relinquish the Intercontinental Championship in September 2004.

September 12 • Portland, OR
Chris Jericho def. **Christian** in a Ladder Match to crown a new Intercontinental Champion.

October 19 • Milwaukee, WI
Shelton Benjamin def. **Chris Jericho**

2005

June 21 • Phoenix, AZ
Carlito def. **Shelton Benjamin**

September 19 Oklahoma, City, OK
Ric Flair def. **Carlito**

2006

February 20 • Trenton, NJ
Shelton Benjamin def. **Ric Flair**

April 30 • Lexington, KY
Rob Van Dam def. **Shelton Benjamin**

May 15 • Lubbock, TX
Shelton Benjamin, **Chris Masters**, and **Triple H** battled **John Cena** and **Rob Van Dam** in a 3-on-2 Handicap Texas Tornado Match. Pre-match stipulations stated that if any member of Benjamin's team def. John Cena or Rob Van Dam, they would win that Superstar's Championship; Benjamin pinned Rob Van Dam to win the Intercontinental Championship.

June 25 • Charlotte, NC
Johnny Nitro def. **Shelton Benjamin** and **Carlito** in a Triple Threat Match

October 2 • Topeka, KS
Jeff Hardy def. **Johnny Nitro**

November 6 • Columbus, OH
Johnny Nitro def. **Jeff Hardy**

November 13 • Manchester, England
Jeff Hardy def. **Johnny Nitro**

2007

February 19 • Bakersfield, CA
Umaga def. **Jeff Hardy**

April 16 • Milan, Italy
Santino Marella def. **Umaga**

July 2 • Dallas, TX
Umaga def. **Santino Marella**

September 3 • Columbus, OH
Jeff Hardy def. **Umaga**

2008

March 10 • Milwaukee, WI
Chris Jericho def. **Jeff Hardy**

June 29 • Dallas, TX
Kofi Kingston def. **Chris Jericho**

August 17 • Indianapolis, IN
Santino Marella and **Beth Phoenix** def. **Kofi Kingston** and **Mickie James** in an Intergender Winners-Take-All Tag Team Match

November 10 • Manchester, England
William Regal def. **Santino Marella**

2009

January 19 • Chicago, IL
CM Punk def. **William Regal**

March 9 • Jacksonville, FL
JBL def. **CM Punk**

April 5 • Houston, TX
Rey Mysterio def. **JBL**

June 7 • New Orleans, LA
Chris Jericho def. **Rey Mysterio**

June 28 • Sacramento, CA
Rey Mysterio def. **Chris Jericho**

September 4 • Cleveland, OH
John Morrison def. **Rey Mysterio**

December 13 • San Antonio, TX
Drew McIntyre def. **John Morrison**

2010

May 23 • Detroit, MI
Kofi Kingston def. **Drew McIntyre**

August 6 • Laredo, TX
Dolph Ziggler def. **Kofi Kingston**

2011

January 7 • Tucson, AZ
Kofi Kingston def. **Dolph Ziggler**

March 25 • Columbus, OH
Wade Barrett def. **Kofi Kingston**

June 19 • Washington, D.C.
Ezekiel Jackson def. **Wade Barrett**

August 12 • Sacramento, CA
Cody Rhodes def. **Ezekiel Jackson**

2012

April 1 • Miami, FL
Big Show def. **Cody Rhodes**

April 29 • Chicago, IL
Cody Rhodes def. **Big Show**

May 20 • Raleigh, NC
Christian def. **Cody Rhodes**

July 23 • St. Louis, MO
The Miz def. **Christian**

October 16 • Memphis, TN
Kofi Kingston def. **The Miz**

Dec.r 29 • Washington, DC
Wade Barrett def. **Kofi Kingston**

2013

April 7 • East Rutherford, NJ
The Miz def. **Wade Barrett**

April 8 • East Rutherford, NJ
Wade Barrett def. **The Miz**

June 16 • Chicago IL
Curtis Axel def. **Wade Barrett** and **The Miz** in a Triple Threat Match

November 18 • Nashville, TN
Big E def. **Curtis Axel**

2014

May 4 • East Rutherford, NJ
Bad News Barrett def. **Big E**
A shoulder injury forced Bad News Barrett to vacate the Intercontinental Championship in June 2014.

July 20 • Tampa, FL
The Miz won a Battle Royal to crown a new Intercontinental Champion

August 17 • Los Angeles, CA
Dolph Ziggler def. **The Miz**

September 21 • Nashville, TN
The Miz def. **Dolph Ziggler**

September 22 • Memphis, TN
Dolph Ziggler def. **The Miz**

November 17 • Roanoke, VA
Luke Harper def. **Dolph Ziggler**

December 14 • Cleveland, OH
Dolph Ziggler def. **Luke Harper**

2015

January 5 • Corpus Christi, TX
Bad News Barrett def. **Dolph Ziggler**

March 29 • Santa Clara, CA
Daniel Bryan def. **Bad News Barrett**, **Dolph Ziggler**, **Dean Ambrose**, **Stardust**, **R-Truth**, and **Luke Harper** in a Ladder Match
Injuries forced Daniel Bryan to vacate the Intercontinental Championship in May 2015.

May 31 • Corpus Christi, TX
Ryback def. **R-Truth**, **Sheamus**, **King Barrett**, **Dolph Ziggler**, and **Mark Henry** in an Elimination Chamber Match to crown a new Intercontinental Champion

September 20 • Houston, TX
Kevin Owens def. **Ryback**

December 13 • Boston, MA
Dean Ambrose def. **Kevin Owens**

2016

February 15 • Anaheim, CA
Kevin Owens won a Fatal 5-Way Match against **Dean Ambrose**, **Dolph Ziggler**, **Tyler Breeze** and **Stardust**

April 3 • Arlington, TX
Zack Ryder defeated **Kevin Owens**, **The Miz**, **Stardust**, **Dolph Ziggler**, **Sami Zayn**, and **Sin Cara**

April 4 • Dallas, TX
The Miz defeated **Zack Ryder**

IRON SHEIK

HT	6'0"
WT	258 lbs.
FROM	Tehran, Iran

SIGNATURE MOVE
Camel Clutch

Iron Sheik will forever be remembered as one of the most loathed villains in sports-entertainment history. At a time when America was still reeling from the Iran hostage crisis, Sheik used his Iranian nationalism to strike fear into WWE audiences. But it was his amazing athleticism and superior technical skills that terrorized WWE locker rooms.

Prior to competing in WWE, Sheik was a member of the Iranian Army, a national amateur wrestling Champion, and the bodyguard for Mohammed Reza Pahlavi, the Shah of Iran. He was also an alternate on the 1968 Iranian Olympic amateur wrestling team and a two-time Asian freestyle Champion.

In 1970, Sheik risked his life when he defected to the United States. While in America, he won several AAU Championships before joining the coaching staff of the 1972 U.S. Olympic team. It was during this time that Sheik also began training for a professional career. Under the tutelage of Verne Gagne, Sheik's earliest days were spent competing in the AWA.

Iron Sheik made his first of several WWE stops in 1979. He immediately impressed the northeast audience by winning a Battle Royal at the famed Madison Square Garden. With the win, Sheik was awarded an opportunity at Bob Backlund's WWE Championship. Unfortunately, he wasn't able to dethrone Backlund, but it would not be the last time the two Superstars squared off for the richest prize in the industry.

WWE CHAMPION

Sheik left WWE in 1980 and spent the next few years competing in the NWA's southeastern territories. When he returned in 1983, he had his sights set on the WWE Championship, which was still being held by old foe, Bob Backlund. In December 1983, Sheik finished what he started years earlier when he used his feared Camel Clutch to defeat Backlund at MSG to claim the Title.

With the victory, Sheik brought to an end one of the longest reigns in WWE history. Unfortunately for him, however, his time atop WWE was fleeting. Less than a month after capturing the Championship, Sheik fell victim to Hulkamania, as Hulk Hogan defeated him to embark on an epic reign of his own.

Following the loss, Iron Sheik targeted another American hero, Sgt. Slaughter. The two Superstars engaged in destructive battles across America. Perhaps their most memorable encounter came in June 1984, when Sheik and Slaughter used MSG as their battlefield in a legendary Boot Camp Match.

RUSSIA NO. 1, IRAN NO. 1, USA PHOOEY

Eyeing more gold for his trophy case, Iron Sheik began teaming with Nikolai Volkoff in 1984. Managed by "Classy" Freddie Blassie, the duo instantly became recognized as one of WWE's most dangerous tag teams.

At the inaugural *WrestleMania* in 1985, Sheik and Volkoff used some help from their manager's infamous cane to defeat the U.S. Express for the World Tag Team Championship. The victory marked the first-ever Title change in *WrestleMania* history. The duo went on to hold the Titles for nearly three months before Mike Rotundo and Barry Windham reclaimed the gold in Poughkeepsie, New York.

No longer Champions, the duo temporarily set out on singles careers, which were highlighted by Sheik making it to the finals of the first-ever King Of The Ring tournament in 1985. At *WrestleMania III*, Sheik and Volkoff reunited with new manager, Slick, to battle The Killer Bees in a melee that was ultimately interrupted by "Hacksaw" Jim Duggan.

After competing in various promotions throughout the late-1980s and early-1990s, Sheik briefly returned to WWE in 1996 to manage The Sultan. In 2001, he returned yet again to win *WrestleMania X-Seven*'s Gimmick Battle Royal.

Iron Sheik's excellence in the ring was ultimately honored in 2005 when he was inducted into the WWE Hall of Fame. It was a fitting honor for a Superstar who will forever be remembered as one of sports-entertainment's most terrorizing forces.

I'M THE BEST OF PROFESSIONAL WRESTLING, TOUGHEST, ROUGHEST SPORT IN THE WORLD.

IRWIN R. SCHYSTER

HT	6'3"	WT	248 lbs.	FROM	Washington, D.C.
SIGNATURE MOVE	The Write-Off				

In 1991, WWE was antagonized by a man with the most dreaded initials in the United States—I.R.S. He accused everyone of being worthless tax cheats and reminded everyone of their duty to pay their taxes to Uncle Sam. While his lengthy diatribes upheld U.S. tax laws, he had no problem whatsoever breaking the rules of WWE during his matches.

This technically sound competitor was not afraid to wallop opponents with his trusty briefcase, which he insisted on having with him at all times. Schyster made it to the finals of the 1991 *King of the Ring*, where he met Bret "Hit Man" Hart. Soon after, he joined forces with another Superstar who was infatuated with money, "Million Dollar Man" Ted DiBiase. As a tag team, they were known as Money, Inc. They took out an insurance policy and acquired the managerial services of "Mouth of the South" Jimmy Hart. As one of the most cunning duos in history, Money, Inc., soon had their first taste of WWE gold after winning the World Tag Team Championship on February 7, 1992.

When the team parted ways, I.R.S. returned to singles competition and was one of the early fixtures of *Monday Night Raw*. With every match, he proved why he was a top contender for the WWE Championship. In 1994, he joined the ranks of the Million Dollar Corporation. Schyster knew no boundaries as he interfered in Undertaker's matches and repossessed sacred gravesites until their match at the 1995 *Royal Rumble*.

During his WWE tenure, this suspender-clad Superstar was one of the most talented and versatile in the entire company. Just like your tax filing deadline, he is always looming. He finished as the runner up in a Legends' Battle Royal at *Raw*'s 15th Anniversary when his old partner DiBiase paid him to eliminate himself. He also appeared on Bob Barker's, "The Price is *Raw*," and is often spotted lingering backstage. No matter what time of year it is, or how much money you have in the bank, you're never safe from the taxman.

THE ISLANDERS

MEMBERS	Haku & Tama	**COMBINED WT**	501 lbs.

Upon arriving in WWE in the mid-1980s, Haku and Tama were an upstanding duo who regularly fought to the letter of the law. Unfortunately for them, however, following the rules didn't get them very far.

Tired of losing to the likes of Demolition and the Hart Foundation, The Islanders employed the services of Bobby "The Brain" Heenan and viciously attacked fan favorites, the Can-Am Connection.

With a newfound aggression, Haku and Tama ruthlessly took aim at WWE's most popular tag teams, particularly the British Bulldogs. In December 1987, they did the unthinkable when they dog-napped the Bulldogs' mascot, Matilda. The heartless act led to a showdown at *WrestleMania IV*, where The Islanders and Heenan defeated Davey Boy Smith, Dynamite Kid, and Koko B. Ware.

The Islanders soon went their separate ways. Tama left WWE in April 1988, while Haku went on to achieve great success as "King" Haku. He also captured the World Tag Team Championhip as a part of the Colossal Connection with Andre the Giant.

THE ITALIAN STALLION

HT	6'3"	WT	260 lbs.	FROM	Naples, Italy
SIGNATURE MOVE	Powerslam				

An accomplished amateur athlete, the Italian Stallion immigrated to the United States from Naples, Italy, with the dream of becoming a star in the sports-entertainment industry. He kicked off his career in 1983 and spent his formative years in Jim Crockett Promotions. During his time there, the Italian Stallion competed in the "Jim Crockett Sr. Memorial Cup Tag Team Tournament" on several occasions. He also battled "Dr. Death" Steve Williams in a losing effort at *Clash of Champions IV*.

The Stallion began testing his mettle against WWE's Superstars during the 1990s. He appeared on broadcasts of *Superstars of Wrestling* and *Wrestling Challenge*, unsuccessfully facing the Honky Tonk Man, Shawn Michaels, and Greg "The Hammer" Valentine, among others.

Upon leaving WWE, the Stallion spent time competing throughout the southeastern United States. After returning to his adopted home in North Carolina, the Stallion opened a training school with George South. Noted alumni from their academy include R-Truth, and Jeff and Matt Hardy.

IVAN KOLOFF

HT	6'1"	WT	298 lbs.	FROM	Moscow, Russia
SIGNATURE MOVE			Bear Hug		

At a time when tension between the United States and Soviet Union was at its height, Russian powerhouse Ivan Koloff proved to be the ultimate threat to American fans' in-ring heroes. Known as "The Russian Bear," Koloff joined WWE in 1970, under the tutelage of manager Capt. Lou Albano. The sight of him struck communistic fears into American fans everywhere, but it was his dreaded bear hug and knee drop that frightened WWE Superstars.

Within months of Koloff's debut, fans had their greatest fear realized when "The Russian Bear" handily defeated their Champion of nearly eight years, Bruno Sammartino. A stunned Madison Square Garden crowd watched in disbelief as their hero's shoulders were pinned to the mat for seemingly the longest three seconds in sports-entertainment history. After the match, the ring announcer refused to announce Koloff as the winner and new WWE Champion, fearing a riot might ensue.

A mere three weeks into his shocking WWE Championship reign, Koloff crossed paths with a hungry Pedro Morales. Much to the fans' delight, Morales beat Koloff for the Championship, marking the end of the most terrifying Title reign to date.

Shortly after the loss, Koloff disappeared from the WWE scene, only to return periodically during the 1970s and 1980s to challenge Sammartino and Bob Backlund. When he wasn't making rare WWE appearances, "The Russian Bear" was gaining tag team notoriety in the Mid-Atlantic territory. His impressive list of tag partners includes Ray Stevens, Krusher Khruschev, Dick Murdoch, and nephew Nikita Koloff. Along the way, he captured the coveted NWA World Tag Team Championship on five separate occasions.

At age fifty, Koloff took his game to the budding Eastern Championship Wrestling promotion in Philadelphia. His popular past and memorable matches with Jimmy "Superfly" Snuka and The Sandman helped the promotion build the foundation for what would later be recognized as the hardcore powerhouse Extreme Championship Wrestling.

IVAN PUTSKI

HT	5'10"	WT	245 lbs.	FROM	Krakow, Poland
SIGNATURE MOVE			The Polish Hammer		

In 1976, WWE was introduced to the phenomenon known as "Polish Power." Ivan Putski had an interesting back story; his family was on one of the last ships to dock at Ellis Island. Although he grew to embrace his new homeland, he remained fiercely proud of his Polish ancestry. In fact, "Polish Power" became a rallying cry not just for his fellow Poles, but fans of all ethnic persuasions who related to his pursuit of the American Dream.

As a former professional body builder, Ivan Putski possessed great strength and a fire that burned to rid WWE of its questionable elements. He was the first Polish immigrant Superstar and, with his success and charisma, became one of the top names in WWE.

He took the fight to individuals such as Crusher Blackwell, Bruiser Brody, Stan Hansen, Ivan Koloff, Spiros Arion, and Baron Mikel Scicluna. Putski's feats of strength continued to garner attention, and he competed in the 1978 World's Strongest Man Competition. As his following grew, Putski began to speak more English to his legion of fans, sang his favorite Polish songs, and professed the importance of "Polish Power" after his matches.

On October 22, 1979, Putski teamed with Tito Santana to defeat Johnny and Jerry Valiant to win the WWE World Tag Team Championship. The duo complemented each other perfectly, and held the Titles for months before losing to the Wild Samoans. As "Polish Power" entered the 1980s, he remained a huge star, not just in WWE, but in Southwest Championship Wrestling in his adopted city of San Antonio.

In 1995, Ivan took his rightful place among sports-entertainment's elite when he was enshrined in the WWE Hall of Fame. "Polish Power" made his triumphant return to WWE television in 1997 when he appeared alongside his son, Scott, on *Monday Night Raw*, and tangled with another father-son duo, Jerry "The King" Lawler and Brian Christopher.

Ivan Putski is one of sports-entertainment's most admired individuals whose fame transcended ethnicities and broke down geographic barriers. For this, everyone loves "Polish Power!"

IVORY

 | **HT** 5'5" | **FROM** Seattle, Washington

Blessed with a fabulous physique, infectious smile, and a never-ending supply of energy, Ivory will forever be remembered as one of the most accomplished Divas of her generation.

Originally a Valentine's Day gift from D'Lo Brown to tag team partner Mark Henry, Ivory quickly proved she was so much more than an attractive valet. Within months of her debut, she defeated Debra for the Women's Championship on a June 1999 episode of *Raw*. For more than four months, she successfully defended the Title before being upended by the legendary Fabulous Moolah at *No Mercy*.

Luckily for Ivory, she was able to reclaim the Title merely one week later. The charismatic Diva held the Championship through mid-December when Miss Kitty claimed the Title by winning a Four Corners Evening Gown Pool Match.

In September 2000, Ivory traded in her suggestive ring gear in favor of a more conservative look. As a member of the Right To Censor, ankle-length skirts and button-down white shirts became her fashion of choice. Despite the change in appearance, Ivory's excellence in the ring remained the same. And in November 2000, she won a Fatal 4-Way Match to claim her third Women's Championship.

After the Right to Censor disbanded, Ivory became a trainer on the second season of *WWE Tough Enough*. She then traded in her ring gear for a microphone as the co-host of the now-defunct *WWE Experience*.

J&J SECURITY

MEMBERS	Jamie Noble & Joey Mercury
COMBINED WT	393 lbs.

As The Authority groomed Seth Rollins to be the Undisputed Future of WWE in 2014, they protected their asset by hiring J&J Security. With the seven-foot Corporate Kane already at their disposal, Triple H and Stephanie McMahon now had a former Cruiserweight Champion, Noble, and a former Tag Team Champion, Mercury, to do their bidding.

Wearing black suits and yellow ties to match Rollins' hair, the duo served Rollins at the direction of the The Authority. Oftentimes, The Authority's unpopular decisions put J&J in the crosshairs of WWE's most volatile Superstars. In July 2015, an enraged Brock Lesnar destroyed a Cadillac that Rollins had gifted J&J. The Beast then turned his rage on J&J Security, the resulting damage sidelining both Superstars indefinitely.

JACK SWAGGER

  | **HT** 6'7" | **WT** 275 lbs. | **FROM** Perry, Oklahoma
SIGNATURE MOVE Patriot Lock, Swagger Bomb

Jack Swagger's stellar amateur background and signature mean streak established him as one of WWE's most dangerous Superstars. At times, the former Oklahoma Sooner has been tough to cheer for. He is as cocky as his surname suggests and the company he's kept has been questionable. Still, "we the people" can often identify with his patriotic pride and old-fashioned American grit.

Swagger's charisma caught the eye of ECW general manager Theodore Long in September 2008. The self-proclaimed "All American American" became a part of Teddy's New Superstar Initiative. This was just the break Swagger needed. Within his rookie year, Swagger defeated Matt Hardy to win the ECW Championship. Soon, his rising stock shot through the roof when he won the Money in the Bank Ladder Match at *WrestleMania XXVI*. Swagger carefully chose his time to cash-in his World Heavyweight Championship opportunity. Only five days removed from his *WrestleMania* victory, he defeated a weakened Chris Jericho.

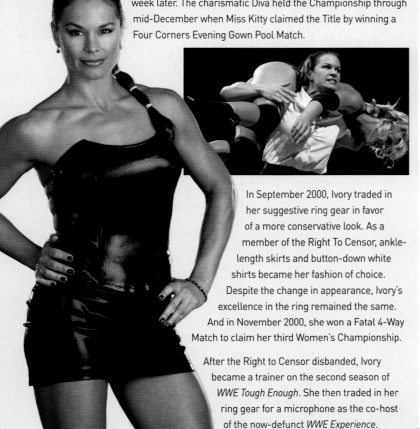

Swagger became an insufferable villain, flaunting his trophies like an arrogant jock, applying his Ankle Lock in uncalled-for situations, and even appointing an Eagle as his All-American mascot. Though he became part of both Michael Cole's and Team Johnny's wins at consecutive *WrestleMania*s, Swagger soon found himself in a rut. So, he turned to Zeb Colter.

Under Zeb's maniacal leadership, Swagger was reborn as a self-described "Real American." Meaner than ever, Swagger ripped through the WWE locker room like a man possessed. He won the namesake match at *Elimination Chamber 2013* for the right to challenge Alberto Del Rio for the World Heavyweight Championship at *WrestleMania 29*. Though unsuccessful, Swagger continued to champion Colter's radical ideals on U.S. foreign policy. Ironically, he found an ally in the Swiss-born Cesaro to help spread his message. As "The Real Americans," Swagger and Cesaro saw uneven results.

Following their 2014 split, Swagger began to win the trust of the WWE Universe. After repeatedly standing up to the Russian menace Rusev, he became a fan-favorite. With hand over heart, his pledge is to make America and its allies proud each time he steps in the ring.

JACK TUNNEY

As WWE President, Jack Tunney was one of the most respected authoritative figures of his time. Usually governing from afar, unlike many of today's leaders, he only showed up when matters were at their most dire. And when he did appear, fans knew he'd be ruling with an iron fist.

Many of Tunney's decisions are looked back upon with great fondness. In 1986, he made the difficult decision to suspend Andre the Giant after the popular Superstar skipped several contracted appearances. A few months later, Tunney made a similar ruling when he suspended rogue official, Danny Davis, for life, following the referee's blatant bias toward rule breakers.

Perhaps Tunney's toughest decision came when a series of controversial matches between Hulk Hogan and Undertaker forced him to vacate the WWE Championship in 1991. The ruling eventually led to the WWE Championship being on the line at the 1992 Royal Rumble Match.

Decades later, Tunney is still remembered as a no-nonsense leader who stewarded WWE's ship during an incredibly popular period in sports-entertainment history.

JACKSON ANDREWS

HT 6'11" **WT** 320 lbs. **FROM** Houston, Texas

At almost 7-feet tall and weighing in at well over 300 pounds, Jackson Andrews certainly looked the part, which is probably why Tyson Kidd tapped him to be his bodyguard in late 2010. But after only a few weeks on the job, Andrews found himself on the receiving end of a devastating World's Strongest Slam at the hands of Mark Henry, causing the bodyguard to rethink his choice of occupation. Andrews was gone from WWE shortly thereafter.

Prior to debuting alongside Kidd, Andrews spent approximately one year competing in WWE's former developmental system, Florida Championship Wrestling.

JACQUELINE

HT 5'3" **FROM** Dallas, Texas
SIGNATURE MOVE Tornado DDT

Over the course of her amazing WWE career, Jacqueline had the unique distinction of being equally successful against both male and female competitors. In fact, her impressive record against the men of WWE actually carried her to the male-dominated Cruiserweight Championship. The bombshell from Dallas defeated Chavo Guerrero in May 2004 to become the only woman in WWE history to ever hold the gold.

Jacqueline's Cruiserweight Championship proved to be the final highlight of her brilliant six-year WWE run. It also served as a golden bookend to a career that took off after capturing the Women's Championship mere months after making her debut. The victory came in September 1998 when Jacqueline defeated Sable to become WWE's first Women's Champion in nearly three years. Jacqueline's second reign came at the expense of Hervina in February 2000.

The period between Jacqueline's high-profile debut and ground-breaking finale was filled with one memorable moment after another. The feisty Diva will forever be remembered for her involvement in the all-female faction Pretty Mean Sisters. Affectionately referred to as P.M.S., Jacqueline, alongside Terri and Ryan Shamrock, preyed on the male Superstars of WWE, usually making them their love slaves. A list of their ultimate conquests includes D'Lo Brown, Mark Henry, and Meat.

In 2016, Jacqueline took her well-deserved place among other trailblazers in sports-entertainment history when she was inducted into the WWE Hall of Fame in her hometown of Dallas, Texas.

JACKIE GAYDA

HT 5'7" **FROM** Cleveland, Ohio
SIGNATURE MOVE Neckbreaker

Jackie Gayda's determination, strength, and in-ring ability led to her becoming the co-winner of the second season of *WWE Tough Enough*. Before she knew it, Miss Jackie was strutting her stuff on *Raw* and *SmackDown* with the most beautiful and dangerous women in all of sports-entertainment.

In 2003, she added manager to her resumé when she began to accompany Rico to the ring. Later in her career, she managed Rico and Charlie Haas to the WWE Tag Team Championship. Fond of interfering on her team's behalf, Jackie found herself competing alongside her team in Mixed Tag Team Matches. On her own, Jackie competed against Trish Stratus and Lita and became a contender for the Women's Championship. At *WrestleMania XX*, she partnered with Stacy Keibler against Torrie Wilson and Sable in a Playboy Evening Gown Match. Jackie left WWE in June 2005 and spent a brief time showcasing her talents across the United States before retiring from the ring.

JAKE THE SNAKE ROBERTS

HoF

HT	6'6"
WT	249 lbs.
FROM	Stone Mountain, Georgia

SIGNATURE MOVE
DDT

The son of the legendary Grizzly Smith, Jake Roberts' career in sports-entertainment began in Louisiana as a referee. He traveled throughout the Southeastern United States and Calgary's Stampede Wrestling, gaining the reputation of being a superior technician and ring psychologist. Along the way, he invented one of the most lethal moves in the history of sports-entertainment, the DDT, named after a potent poison known for stopping pests in their tracks.

SLITHERING INTO WWE

Jake "The Snake" Roberts debuted in WWE in 1986 alongside his python, Damien, who was often restless inside his burlap sack during Jake's matches. After a DDT, Jake often brought out Damien and dropped the snake on his fallen opponents. Roberts sustained a psychological edge over his foes like no one before him. If his actions in the ring were not freaky enough, the mind games continued on his eerie talk show, The Snake Pit.

From the start of his WWE career, Jake was often at the center of intense rivalries. In one of his first matches, Jake delivered a DDT to Ricky "The Dragon" Steamboat on concrete during Saturday Night's Main Event. The attack left Steamboat unconscious and sparked a bitter rivalry that led to a Snake Pit Match at The Big Event in Toronto.

Jake Roberts quickly became known for cryptic interviews that sent chills down the spines of all who saw them. During an episode of The Snake Pit, the Honky Tonk Man tried to silence Roberts by attacking him with his signature guitar. The instrument shattered on impact. This heinous action lead to a match at WrestleMania III. Jake's rivalry with Honky Tonk changed the attitude of fans, and suddenly capacity crowds were calling for Jake's signature DDT.

Jake was featured at WrestleMania for the next several years, including a match against Andre the Giant at WrestleMania V, and a Blindfold Match against Rick "The Model" Martel at WrestleMania VII after Roberts was blinded by Martel's signature cologne, Arrogance.

GETTING PERSONAL

The intensity of those rivalries could not compare to the emotions generated by personal attacks against those closest to Jake. "Ravishing" Rick Rude would often select a female fan from the audience for a post-match kiss. One night, he picked Jake's wife, who refused to participate. After a slap and a shove, Jake arrived to defend his wife. Roberts and Rude engaged in a brutal war that lasted several months and was exacerbated each time Rude's attire bore a likeness of Roberts' wife.

Damien was the target of another Superstar who tried to attack Jake by proxy. The behemoth Earthquake crushed Damien while a tangled Jake watched helplessly. After the loss of his snake, Roberts went back home to Stone Mountain, Georgia. When Roberts finally returned, he unveiled a monstrous python he called Lucifer.

NEVER TRUST A SNAKE

After revealing that Lucifer was Damien's older brother, a demonic-looking Roberts boldly claimed his new snake was the devil himself. Coincidentally, Roberts began to display a darker persona after the debut of Lucifer. When Ultimate Warrior made the mistake of trusting the forked tongued Superstar, Roberts imprisoned him in a snake pit packed from floor-to-ceiling with slithering serpentines.

Months later, Roberts injected his brand of poison into the nuptials of "Macho Man" Randy Savage and Miss Elizabeth. He planted a poisonous cobra inside the happy couple's wedding gifts. Then, in one of the most horrific scenes in WWE history, Roberts allowed his pet king cobra to sink its teeth into Macho Man's exposed arm. This terrifying return to the dark side led Jake into the path of Undertaker, who defeated him at WrestleMania VIII. Jake mysteriously disappeared from WWE shortly after.

ROAD TO REDEMPTION

"The Snake" spent the next few years in seclusion, but returned at the 1996 Royal Rumble Match. While Jake struck fear into the hearts of a new generation, he met his match in Stone Cold Steve Austin at the King Of The Ring finals.

Jake once again made an incredible return in March 2005 to warn "Legend Killer" Randy Orton about the fear one feels when facing Undertaker at WrestleMania. Over the next several years, Jake would find healing power in DDP Yoga. The well-known exercise program helped Roberts repair his life outside the ring, and in 2014, a triumphant Snake stood at the WWE Hall of Fame podium to accept WWE's highest honor.

THE SNAKE WILL ALWAYS BITE BACK.

JAMAICA KID

| **HT** 4'4" | **WT** 94 lbs. | **FROM** Jamaica | **SIGNATURE MOVE** Jumping Headbutt |

An outstanding export from the island of the Greater Antilles, Jamaica Kid arrived in WWE in 1964. For over a decade he was a mainstay with a jumping headbutt that stopped foes dead in their tracks. His matches were filled with action and entertained audiences wherever he appeared.

Jamaica's battles with the likes of Sky Low Low, Fuzzy Cupid, Billy the Kid, Farmer Pete, Little Brutus, Frenchy Lamont, Pee Wee Adams, and Dirty Morgan helped put the miniature division on the map. He had a steady array of tag team partners that included Little Beaver, Tiny Tim, Irish Jackie, Sonny Boy Cassidy, Pancho Lopez, Cowboy Bradley, and Little Louie. These bouts were as unpredictable and exciting as anything ever seen in the ring.

JAMES DUDLEY

"Had there been no James Dudley, the WWE possibly wouldn't exist as it does today," said Vincent K. McMahon regarding the massive influence Dudley had on the industry.

Before playing an integral role behind the scenes in WWE, Dudley played for the Baltimore Elite Giants of the Negro League. When his playing days ended in the 1940s, he became an employee of Jess McMahon, and ultimately a trusted associate of Vincent J. McMahon. It was during this time that Dudley became manager of Turner Arena in Washington, D.C., making him the first African-American to run a major venue in the United States.

As WWE's reach expanded, Dudley's job responsibilities also continued to grow. It wasn't long before he became one of the industry's most influential figures. Following his retirement, Dudley became a valued consultant to Vincent K. McMahon. In 1994, he was honored with induction into the WWE Hall of Fame.

Dudley passed away in June 2004 at the age of 93. He will forever be remembered as a cherished friend and brilliant businessman.

JAMIE NOBLE

| **HT** 5'9" | **WT** 202 lbs. | **FROM** Hanover, West Virginia |
| **SIGNATURE MOVE** | Modified Dragon Sleeper | |

From masked high-flyer to corporate henchmen, Jamie Noble is not your stereotypical bumpkin from West Virginia. First seen in WCW, Noble donned a Japanese mask and joined the Jung Dragons. After some entertaining battles with 3-Count, Noble split and tagged with a 3-Count castoff, Evan Karagias, until WCW closed up shop in 2001.

In WWE, Noble embraced his down home roots. With fellow trailer park product, Nidia, as his other half, Noble won the Cruiserweight Championship from The Hurricane at the 2002 *King of the Ring* and enjoyed a nearly five-month reign. Noble and Nidia would strike it rich by getting an unexpected inheritance, but after things went sour, Noble left WWE. When he returned, the tenacious competitor was part of a short-lived team called The Pitbulls before competing solo against both Cruiserweights and big men alike.

In November 2009, an attack by Sheamus ended Noble's nearly 15-year career in the ring. Still scrappy as ever, Noble continued his career as a coach and then as part of J&J Security, protecting the interests of The Authority.

JAMISON

Jamison told everybody he was an "everyday, ordinary kind of guy." But in reality, the socially challenged boy of a man was a nerd.

Redeeming qualities were lost on Jamison. He didn't have a job, girlfriend, or even a place to live. Despite all his shortcomings, though, Jamison found his way onto WWE television during the late 1980s and early 1990s.

During his WWE stay, Jamison managed to consistently irritate Bobby "The Brain" Heenan. Each time, "The Brain" responded by tossing insults the nerdy uber-fan's way.

Jamison also became the target of a Viking ritual that saw The Berzerker attempt to burn him at the stake. Luckily for him, the lighter outsmarted Berzerker. Jamison eventually latched on to an equally odd pairing when he briefly managed the Bushwhackers.

JAZZ

| **HT** 5'4" |
| **FROM** New Orleans, Louisiana |

With washboard abs and muscles on top of muscles, Jazz was one of WWE's most-feared Divas between 2001 and 2004. The tattooed powerhouse debuted on one of WWE's biggest stages when she competed in a Six-Pack Challenge at the 2001 *Survivor Series*. The encounter whet her appetite for Championship glory, and in February 2002, she defeated Trish Stratus for the Women's Championship.

After a successful Championship stint, Jazz took on Theodore Long as her manager. With Long leading her career, Jazz was able to upend Stratus a second time for the Title at *Backlash 2003*. She held the Championship for more than two months before losing it to Gail Kim in a Seven-Diva Battle Royal on *Raw*. Jazz left WWE a few months later.

Jazz returned in June 2006 when she represented *ECW* in a match against Women's Champion Mickie James. Jazz came up short in her attempt to topple James, and was never seen on WWE television again.

JEAN PIERRE LAFITTE

HT 6'1" **WT** 235 lbs. **FROM** New Orleans, Louisiana

A descendant of the infamous LaFitte family of pirates, Jean Pierre LaFitte made his WWE debut in 1995. His goal was to exact revenge on the United States, starting with WWE Superstars, for the Embargo Act of 1807 that forced his family out of New Orleans, Louisiana.

With a patch over his right eye, LaFitte showed all the characteristics of an evil pirate, including thievery. His most-noted victim was Bret "Hit Man" Hart, from whom he stole his signature leather jacket and sunglasses. Unfortunately for LaFitte, Hart gained revenge when he defeated him at the third installment of *In Your House* in September 1995.

Aside from the loss to Hart, LaFitte looked impressive in his wins over the likes of Man Mountain Rock, Duke "The Dumpster" Droese, and Duane Gill. The victories eventually catapulted him to a match against then-WWE Champion, Diesel. But when LaFitte was unable to take the Title from Big Daddy Cool, he packed his bags and left WWE.

JEFF HARDY

HT 6'1" **WT** 225 lbs. **FROM** Cameron, North Carolina
SIGNATURE MOVE Swanton Bomb, Whisper in the Wind, Twist of Fate

Jeff and Matt Hardy spent much of the late 1990s and early 2000s redefining the art of tag team competition as The Hardy Boyz. Their battles against The Dudley Boyz and Edge and Christian, particularly their Tables, Ladders, and Chairs Matches, featured truly groundbreaking action that today's tag teams strive to recreate.

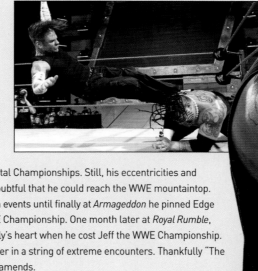

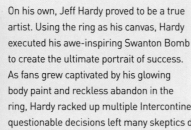

On his own, Jeff Hardy proved to be a true artist. Using the ring as his canvas, Hardy executed his awe-inspiring Swanton Bomb to create the ultimate portrait of success. As fans grew captivated by his glowing body paint and reckless abandon in the ring, Hardy racked up multiple Intercontinental Championships. Still, his eccentricities and questionable decisions left many skeptics doubtful that he could reach the WWE mountaintop. Through much of 2008, he competed in main events until finally at *Armageddon* he pinned Edge during a Triple Threat Match to win the WWE Championship. One month later at *Royal Rumble*, Jeff's brother, Matt, drove a stake in his family's heart when he cost Jeff the WWE Championship. Left with no alternative, Jeff fought his brother in a string of extreme encounters. Thankfully "The Charismatic Enigma" and his brother made amends.

Jeff enjoyed two more World Championship reigns in 2009. Then on August 28, Jeff lost a "Loser Leaves WWE" Steel Cage Match to CM Punk. The defeat ended his lengthy tenure in WWE, but this daring Superstar left an endless reel of highlights for the WWE Universe to enjoy for generations.

JEFF JARRETT

HT 6'0" **WT** 230 lbs. **FROM** Nashville, Tennessee
SIGNATURE MOVE Figure-Four Leglock

Jarrett debuted in WWE as a flashy country music star in 1994. While "Double J" didn't quite make it to the top of Nashville charts with his single, "With My Baby Tonight," he did become Intercontinental Champion for the first time at the 1995 Royal Rumble. He held that Title twice more before he left WWE in 1996.

Jarrett then appeared in WCW and became a United States Champion as well as member of the famed Four Horsemen. In 1997, he returned to WWE where he ditched his country-western aspirations and developed an angrier persona. With his manager Debra's considerable assets added to his formidable arsenal, Jeff then formed a well-known tandem with Owen Hart.

Hart and Jarrett won the WWE World Tag Team Championship in 1999. After Owen died later that year, Jarrett never forgot his friend, shouting Hart's name following an Intercontinental Title win. In total, Jarrett held the Intercontinental honors six times.

He also had memorable battles against Chyna, who defeated him in a rare male-female matchup to claim the Intercontinental prize. Jarrett parted ways with WWE again and returned to WCW where he proclaimed himself "The Chosen One." He remained with the organization, where he became WCW Champion, until it closed in March, 2001.

Jarrett has since competed in Mexico and Japan, among other locations, and worked as a promoter.

JERRY GRAHAM

HT	5'10"	WT	245 lbs.
FROM	Phoenix, Arizona		

A member of the famed Graham family, Dr. Jerry Graham was a noted troublemaker in and out of the ring. When the madman wasn't wreaking havoc with brothers Crazy Luke, Eddie, and "Superstar" Billy Graham in the ring, he was known for butting heads with law enforcement all over the nation.

Graham won Tag Team Titles in six different promotions over the course of his career. His first taste of success came in 1955 when he teamed with Don McIntyre to topple Bill and Fred Blassie for the Georgia version of the NWA Tag Team Championship. Over the next twenty years, Graham formed Championship teams with Abdullah the Butcher, Jim Wright, and brother Eddie. He even captured the WWE United States Tag Team Titles with brother Luke in June 1964.

While Graham's main source of fame came from his action in between the ropes, his run-ins with the law are nothing short of legendary. Following the passing of his mother, Graham reportedly broke into the morgue to steal her corpse. In doing so, he attacked several morgue workers and security. A few years later, the police picked him up after he was seen shooting the lights out at a Utah house of worship. According to legend, Graham maintained his outlaw-like attitude all the way through his final days in 1997.

JERRY LAWLER
see page 165

JERRY LYNN

	HT	5'11"	WT	212 lbs.	FROM	Minneapolis, Minnesota
SIGNATURE MOVE	Cradle Piledriver					

Jerry Lynn began his career in the late 1980s. As his reputation began to grow, he made appearances in WCW and WWE, where he attempted to capture the Light Heavyweight Championship. Lynn's next stop was ECW, leading to a series of matches with Rob Van Dam that were considered classics among the promotion's zealous supporters. He also won the ECW World Heavyweight Championship from Justin Credible.

In the weeks and months that followed ECW's 2001 closure, Jerry explored his options and concluded that he needed to prove himself where the world would be watching.

In April, 2001, Lynn came back to WWE. In his first match, the former ECW Champion pinned Crash Holly and won the prized Light Heavyweight Championship that had eluded him four years prior.

Unfortunately, Lynn lost the Title a little over one month later to a determined Jeff Hardy. Lynn renewed his rivalry against Rob Van Dam, but he suffered a torn patella and ultimately parted ways with the company in February 2002.

After 25 years in the industry, he retired in 2013.

JESS MCMAHON

Without the imagination, innovation and raw ambition of Jess McMahon, WWE would not exist today.

Roderick James McMahon, better known as Jess, was born in New York in 1882 to immigrants from Ireland's County Galway. Possessing the type of drive common to new Americans, Jess and his brother, Edward, were endowed with both business acumen and a showman's flair. By 1909, they were promoting boxing in New York's Harlem neighborhood. Although many sports contests were segregated at the time, the McMahons overlooked ethnicity, and featured bouts between blacks and whites on a regular basis.

In 1911, the McMahon brothers expanded their sports enterprises to include an all-black baseball team, the New York Lincoln Giants. The pair would also field an all-black basketball team at a time when the races rarely mixed.

The McMahon siblings' greatest achievement occurred in 1915 when Jack Johnson, the controversial African-American boxing champion, dropped his title to Jess Willard in 45 rounds in Havana, Cuba.

The same year, Jess began promoting wrestling in the New York metropolitan area, highlighting performers like Jim Browning and Everett Marshall, both of whom were later recognized as world champions.

He eventually became the official wrestling matchmaker at Madison Square Garden. Jess died in 1954, paving the way for his son, Vincent J. McMahon, father of current WWE mogul Vincent K. McMahon, to pick up where the originator left off.

JERRY THE KING LAWLER

HoF **AWA**

HT	6'0"
WT	243 lbs.
FROM	Memphis, Tennessee

SIGNATURE MOVE
Piledriver

Few personalities can boast as successful a career as Jerry Lawler. Having left an indelible stamp on each of the past five decades, "The King" has proven that his reign is among the most influential in the history of sports-entertainment.

Trained by the legendary "Fabulous" Jackie Fargo, Lawler began his career in the early 1970s and quickly became a dominant force in the Mid-South and Memphis territories. Along the way, he captured literally hundreds of championships, including the Memphis Wrestling Southern Heavyweight Title an astounding fifty-two times.

Despite establishing himself as a legend inside the ring, perhaps Lawler's greatest rivalry began outside the arena. In the early 1980s, The King and Andy Kaufman became mainstream news when Lawler slapped the Hollywood star out of his chair while on the set of *Late Night with David Letterman*, sending Kaufman into an obscenity-laced tirade. The assault came fresh off the heels of an earlier altercation between the two that famously saw "The King" send Kaufman to the hospital following two piledrivers delivered during a match in Memphis.

The Lawler-Kaufman rivalry was later recreated by Hollywood in the 1999 major motion picture *Man on the Moon*. The movie also marked "The King's" silver-screen debut.

Nearly two decades after his debut, Lawler achieved World Championship status when he defeated Curt Hennig for the AWA Championship in May 1988. Later that year, he beat WCWA World Heavyweight Champion Kerry Von Erich at *SuperClash III* to unify the Titles. Lawler carried the Championship into the new year, but was eventually stripped of the gold following a reported falling out with AWA boss Verne Gagne.

WWE DOUBLE DUTY

Lawler jumped to WWE in the early 1990s and quickly became both an irritating, yet-trusted, voice at the announce table, and a legitimate threat in the ring. Among his earliest and most famous WWE rivalries began in 1993 when Lawler took exception to Bret Hart winning the prestigious WWE King of the Ring. The two kings spent the next several years competing in many memorable matches, including a Kiss My Foot Match at *King of the Ring 1995*, which Hart won. Following the loss, Lawler enlisted his dentist, Isaac Yankem, D.D.S., to take out the "Hit Man." Unfortunately for Lawler, his guy came up short against Hart at *SummerSlam 1995*.

Lawler shifted his ire toward an entire promotion in 1997, when he began to publicly criticize ECW, calling it "Extremely Crappy Wrestling." Lawler's disdain for the Philadelphia-based promotion led to several encounters with ECW's most hardcore competitors, most notably Tommy Dreamer, who defeated Lawler at ECW *Hardcore Heaven* in August 1997.

Aside from occasional in-ring appearances, Lawler began to focus much of his efforts toward announcing in the late 1990s. The result was one of the most brilliant commentating careers in all of sports-entertainment. Throughout the Attitude Era and beyond, his pairing with Jim Ross on *Monday Night Raw* cemented itself as one of the most entertaining and informative tandems to ever call sports-entertainment.

Lawler's brilliance was recognized in 2007 when his longtime friend, William Shatner, inducted him into the *WWE Hall of Fame* on the eve of *WrestleMania 23*. The honor symbolically capped off one of the greatest careers in sports-entertainment history. Though, unlike most Hall of Famers, "The King" wasn't quite ready to hang up the boots. In his mind, he still had more to accomplish, including finally competing in his first-ever *WrestleMania* match.

Lawler achieved his goal four years later when he competed against Michael Cole at *WrestleMania XXVII*. Unfortunately for "The King," the record books will forever show Cole besting Lawler via disqualification. In reality, though, "The King" dominated Cole throughout the match and only lost due to a controversial technicality.

In September 2012, Lawler suffered a heart attack while commentating on *Raw*. The scare resulted in "The King" being clinically dead before medical personnel were able to revive and stabilize him. Miraculously, Lawler returned to the announce table two months later and has since continued to cement his legacy as one of sports-entertainment's greatest personalities. Long live "The King!"

IT'S GOOD TO BE THE KING.

165

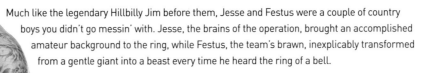

JESSE AND FESTUS

| MEMBERS | Jesse & Festus | COMBINED WT | 501 lbs. |

Much like the legendary Hillbilly Jim before them, Jesse and Festus were a couple of country boys you didn't go messin' with. Jesse, the brains of the operation, brought an accomplished amateur background to the ring, while Festus, the team's brawn, inexplicably transformed from a gentle giant into a beast every time he heard the ring of a bell.

After making their WWE debut in October 2007, Jesse and Festus made short work of many top tag teams. They even defeated then-WWE Tag Team Champions The Miz and John Morrison in non-Title action in early 2008. The duo remained Championship contenders through the year but tag team gold was ultimately not meant to be. The team disbanded soon after when Festus was drafted to *Raw*.

JESSE "THE BODY" VENTURA

| HT | 6'2" | WT | 245 lbs. |
| FROM | Brooklyn Park, Minnesota | | |

"Win if you can. Lose if you must. But always cheat."

Luckily for residents of Minnesota, Jesse Ventura didn't employ his famous phrase while serving as their governor. He did, however, live by the motto during his days in the ring.

After a successful stint with the AWA, Ventura, whose impressive build earned him the nickname "The Body," entered WWE in the early-1980s. As a member of the East-West Connection with Adrian Adonis, he nearly claimed the World Tag Team Championship on several occasions.

Ventura's singles career mirrored his tag days, as he came close to claiming the WWE Championship from Bob Backlund, but was never able to seal the deal. Another opportunity came Ventura's way when he was scheduled to challenge Hulk Hogan in 1984. Unfortunately, health issues prevented "The Body" from taking part in the match. He later retired to the broadcast booth.

As a commentator, Ventura sat ringside for some of WWE's biggest matches, including the *WrestleMania III* encounter between Hogan and Andre the Giant. Just like his days in the ring, Ventura pulled no punches when it came to voicing his opinions. This bold attitude served as the perfect complement to his legendary partner, Gorilla Monsoon's, more direct approach to announcing.

Ventura left WWE in favor of WCW in 1992. As was the case during his WWE days, "The Body" was behind the mic for some of WCW's most-noted matches, including Sting versus Jake Roberts in a Coal Miner's Glove Match at *Halloween Havoc* 1992 and the White Castle of Fear Strap Match between Sting and Vader at *SuperBrawl III*.

Blessed with a magnetic personality, Ventura made the natural progression into Hollywood in 1987. His long-list of credits include box-office hits such as: *Predator*, *The Running Man*, and *Demolition Man*.

Ventura's career took an unexpected turn in 1990 when he became mayor of Brooklyn Park, Minnesota. Eight years later, he rose to the office of governor, where he was affectionately known as "The Governing Body."

In 2004, Ventura's accomplishments in and out of the ring were honored when he was inducted into the WWE Hall of Fame.

JESÚS

| HT | 6'3" | WT | 262 lbs. |

The latter portions of 2004 were rough for John Cena, thanks in part to Jesús. Serving as Carlito's bodyguard, the ruthless Superstar made an instant impact by allegedly attacking Cena in a Boston nightclub. The severity of the attack sidelined Cena for over a month.

When Cena returned, Jesús picked up where he left off. He attacked Cena's kidney then proudly paraded about with Cena's signature chain around his neck. Big mistake.

Cena exacted his revenge at *Armageddon 2004* in a Street Fight for the United States Championship. Jesús tried to exploit Cena's injured kidney but The Champ was up to task—and angry. Cena brutalized Jesús in a one-sided match, proving his superiority. Jesús was never heard from again.

JILLIAN

HT	5'6"	FROM	Louisville, Kentucky
SIGNATURE MOVE			The High Note

This Diva first appeared in late 2005 as a "fixer" for MNM. She was later seen at the side of business mogul, John "Bradshaw" Layfield. Within a short period, Jillian made it clear that if she were at ringside, she would make her presence felt and her voice heard.

In the ring, she became a top contender for the Women's Championship. But at *No Way Out* in 2007, Jillian proudly made her WWE singing debut and, though her lead vocals were greeted by a chorus of boos, she was motivated to become the greatest pop recording artist on the planet. In December 2007, she released her debut album titled, *A Jingle with Jillian*. This collection of her favorite Christmas tunes was a hit with fans.

In October of 2009, Jillian reached the crescendo of her career when she defeated Mickie James for the Divas Championship. Though the tone-deaf Diva lost the Title to Melina immediately afterwards, being a Champion for even just a few moments is more than most will ever accomplish in their career.

JIM "THE ANVIL" NEIDHART

HT	6'2"	WT	281 lbs.	FROM	Reno, Nevada
SIGNATURE MOVE		Anvil Flattener			

His menacing laugh, barrel chest, and pointy goatee made Jim Neidhart one of the most recognizable Superstars of the 1980s and 1990s. As a member of the Hart Foundation, "The Anvil" was one of the most feared competitors of his time.

A product of Stu Hart's legendary Dungeon, Neidhart began in Calgary's Stampede Wrestling. It was here that he earned his famous moniker. After Stu Hart paid him $500 to enter and win a local anvil-throwing contest, Helen Hart started calling him "The Anvil." The nickname has stuck with him ever since.

In the early 1980s, Neidhart moved to WWE after Vince McMahon purchased Stampede Wrestling. It was not long before he teamed with Bret Hart, and manager Jimmy Hart, to form the Hart Foundation. With Bret's technical artistry and Neidhart's bruising bulk, they became two-time Tag Team Champions and one of history's most successful teams before splitting up in 1991.

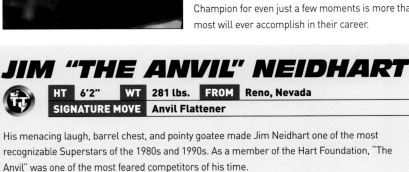

Neidhart turned to Bret's brother, Owen, and aided the younger Hart against his older sibling in the mid-1990s. The family quarrel was eventually resolved, however, and "The Anvil" later reunited with both brothers to form the New Hart Foundation. Today, WWE's spotlight has drifted to "The Anvil's" daughter, Natalya. While Jim makes rare WWE appearances, "Natty" carries his legacy, displaying her dad's dungeon-born intensity when she competes. The father-daughter combo has been seen together outside the ring on E!'s *Total Divas*.

JIM CORNETTE

FROM	Louisville, Kentucky

One of the most controversial and outspoken men in sports-entertainment history, James E. Cornette first rose to prominence as the manager of the Midnight Express in the NWA. With his always-present tennis racket in tow, he managed both iterations of the Midnight Express to the NWA Tag Team Championship and United States Tag Team Championship.

Perhaps Cornette's most infamous moment as manager of the Midnight Express came at *Starrcade 1986* when he and his team competed against The Road Warriors and Paul Ellering in a Skywalkers Match. During the unique contest, Cornette severely injured his knee when he fell from a scaffold erected high above the ring.

Following his stay in the NWA/WCW, Cornette started his own regional promotion in 1991. Known as Smoky Mountain Wrestling, the promotion lasted more than four years and famously played home to such competitors as Chris Jericho, Lance Storm, and Chris Candido.

While still promoting Smoky Mountain Wrestling, Cornette debuted for WWE in 1993 and quickly became known as the American spokesperson for then-WWE Champion Yokozuna. In 1996, he created Camp Cornette featuring the British Bulldog, Owen Hart, and Vader. He led his trio to victory over Shawn Michaels, Sycho Sid, and Ahmed Johnson in the main event of *In Your House: International Incident* in July 1996.

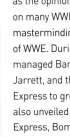

In later years, Cornette would serve as the opinionated color commentator on many WWE broadcasts before masterminding the 1998 NWA invasion of WWE. During this time, he managed Barry Windham, Jeff Jarrett, and the Rock 'n' Roll Express to great success. He also unveiled the New Midnight Express, Bombastic Bob, and Bodacious Bart.

Cornette made one of his final WWE appearances at *WrestleMania X-Seven* when he competed in the Gimmick Battle Royal. He managed to oust Bushwhacker Luke from the match before ultimately being eliminated by Hillbilly Jim.

Cornette and WWE ended their 12-year relationship in 2005. Over the course of his decade-plus with the company, he successfully cemented his legacy as one of the greatest managers of all time.

JIM POWERS

| HT | 6'1" | WT | 235 lbs. | FROM | New York City |

| SIGNATURE MOVE | Powerslam |

After training with the legendary Big John Studd, Jim Powers made his WWE debut in 1984. Given his good looks and impressive physique, Powers was an instant hit with the women of the WWE Universe. Attractiveness aside, he was also recognized as an outstanding in-ring competitor who excited crowds all over the world.

After initially competing as a singles competitor, Powers started a search for a tag team partner toward the end of 1986. Shortly after the New Year, he aligned with Paul Roma to form The Young Stallions. Entering the ring to their "Crank It Up" theme song, the gutsy duo utilized a high-flying style, thrilling double-team maneuvers, and quick tags to dizzy their opponents.

Unfortunately for The Young Stallions, their inability to capture the World Tag Team Championship resulted in a bitter split. Powers resumed his singles career and appeared at WWE events through 1994 before leaving for WCW, where he wrapped up his career in sports-entertainment.

JIM ROSS

see page 169

JIM YOUNG

| HT | 6'1" | WT | 254 lbs. | FROM | Miami, Florida |

With a big, burly moustache and long curly brown hair, Jim Young reminded many wrestling fans of Magnum T.A. Unfortunately for Young, however, his appearance was the only characteristic that reminded fans of the legendary NWA competitor.

During his WWE tenure from the early-to-mid 1980s, Young lost more often than not. The WWE Superstars who regularly bettered their record against him included Don Muraco, Big John Studd, The Missing Link, and "Dr. D" David Schultz.

Though he was the owner of an unimpressive win-loss record, Young did manage to score a victory over Rusty Brooks in his home state of Florida in November 1985.

JIMMY "SUPERFLY" SNUKA

| HT | 5'10" | WT | 235 lbs. | FROM | The Fiji Islands |

| SIGNATURE MOVE | Superfly Splash |

No nickname in sports-entertainment history has been more fitting than "Superfly." Gliding through the sky, Jimmy Snuka used his aerial theatrics to amaze audiences and inspire countless future Superstars.

The journey from his native Fiji took Snuka through Hawaii, the Pacific Northwest, and the Mid-Atlantic territory before the Superfly Splash landed in WWE in 1982. Managed by Capt. Lou Albano, the newcomer faced Bob Backlund for the WWE Championship at Madison Square Garden. Snuka climbed to the top of the 15-foot steel cage and dove straight down toward Backlund's body, only to narrowly miss the Champion. The stunt cost Snuka the match, but remains a memorable moment in WWE lore.

After "Superfly" discovered Albano was stealing from him, he immediately fired Albano in favor of Buddy Rogers. Looking for revenge, Albano sent his new protégé, Ray Stevens, after Snuka. The two Superstars shared an intense rivalry.

In 1983, Snuka focused his attention on Don Muraco's Intercontinental Championship. Once again, Snuka's road to glory went through a Steel Cage Match. This time, "Superfly" landed his breath-taking leap from the cage's apex; however, Muraco had already won the match. Snuka failed to pry the Intercontinental Championship away that night but he did successfully inspire a young Mick Foley, who was looking on from the third row.

Snuka's rising popularity made him the target of the era's biggest scourge, "Rowdy" Roddy Piper. In 1984, the loudmouth Scot blasted Snuka with a coconut, sending Snuka and the *Piper's Pit* set crashing to the ground. Piper's assault is considered one of WWE's most infamous moments.

Following the incident, Snuka was in the corner of Hulk Hogan and Mr. T when they battled Piper and Paul Orndorff in the main event of the first-ever *WrestleMania*. After the event, "Superfly" made appearances in other territories and became the first-ever recognized ECW Champion.

"Superfly" donned his leopard-print trunks sporadically since his retirement. At *WrestleMania 25*, Snuka aided his old rival, Roddy Piper, and Ricky Steamboat in a battle against Chris Jericho.

JIMMY HART

see page 170

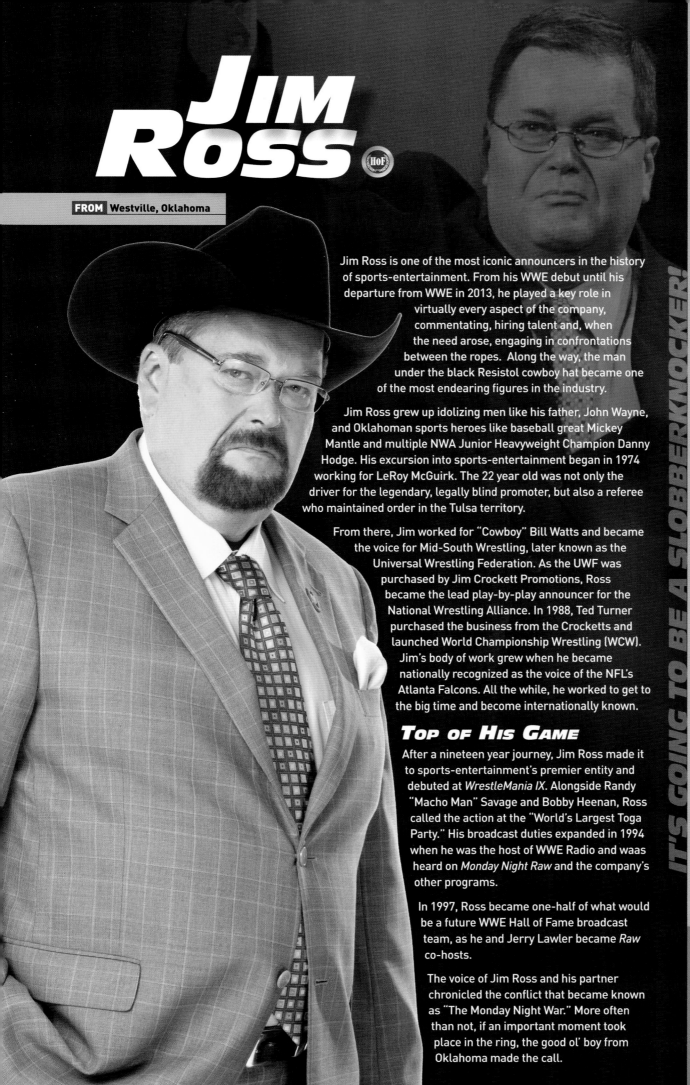

JIM ROSS

FROM Westville, Oklahoma

Jim Ross is one of the most iconic announcers in the history of sports-entertainment. From his WWE debut until his departure from WWE in 2013, he played a key role in virtually every aspect of the company, commentating, hiring talent and, when the need arose, engaging in confrontations between the ropes. Along the way, the man under the black Resistol cowboy hat became one of the most endearing figures in the industry.

Jim Ross grew up idolizing men like his father, John Wayne, and Oklahoman sports heroes like baseball great Mickey Mantle and multiple NWA Junior Heavyweight Champion Danny Hodge. His excursion into sports-entertainment began in 1974 working for LeRoy McGuirk. The 22 year old was not only the driver for the legendary, legally blind promoter, but also a referee who maintained order in the Tulsa territory.

From there, Jim worked for "Cowboy" Bill Watts and became the voice for Mid-South Wrestling, later known as the Universal Wrestling Federation. As the UWF was purchased by Jim Crockett Promotions, Ross became the lead play-by-play announcer for the National Wrestling Alliance. In 1988, Ted Turner purchased the business from the Crocketts and launched World Championship Wrestling (WCW). Jim's body of work grew when he became nationally recognized as the voice of the NFL's Atlanta Falcons. All the while, he worked to get to the big time and become internationally known.

TOP OF HIS GAME

After a nineteen year journey, Jim Ross made it to sports-entertainment's premier entity and debuted at *WrestleMania IX*. Alongside Randy "Macho Man" Savage and Bobby Heenan, Ross called the action at the "World's Largest Toga Party." His broadcast duties expanded in 1994 when he was the host of WWE Radio and waas heard on *Monday Night Raw* and the company's other programs.

In 1997, Ross became one-half of what would be a future WWE Hall of Fame broadcast team, as he and Jerry Lawler became *Raw* co-hosts.

The voice of Jim Ross and his partner chronicled the conflict that became known as "The Monday Night War." More often than not, if an important moment took place in the ring, the good ol' boy from Oklahoma made the call.

IT'S GOING TO BE A SLOBBERKNOCKER!

In 1999, J.R.'s fame led him to the silver screen when he appeared in the critically acclaimed *Man on the Moon*. As J.R. continued to broaden the scope of announcing, he also brought his many talents to the world of publishing. In 2003 he penned his top-selling cookbook, *J.R.'s Cookbook: True Ringside Tales, BBQ, and Down-Home Recipes*. He also began marketing his popular barbeque sauce and eventually opened JR's Family Bar-BQ in Norman, Oklahoma.

EXPERT AND LEGEND

But at his core, Jim Ross will be perennially considered an esteemed authority on the history of sports-entertainment and one of the most inventive broadcast personalities to ever hold the microphone. In 2007, Ross traveled to the world of higher learning and gave lectures at MIT about the global phenomenon of sports-entertainment. Days later, Ross entered the chamber of immortals as he was inducted into the WWE Hall of Fame.

After the 2008 Draft, Ross brought his Hall of Fame voice to *SmackDown*. Regardless of the WWE outlet, some of the most prominent figures in sports-entertainment gave "Good Ol' J.R." their universal endorsement. Triple H said, "There is no else I'd rather have call my match than Jim Ross." WWE Hall of Famer "Nature Boy" Ric Flair added, "A lot of people are good, few are great. Jim Ross is great." Perhaps no words rang truer than those of Stone Cold Steve Austin, who proclaimed, "Jim Ross is the best ever, end of story."

Although Jim Ross was a WWE institution and soundtrack to the greatest moments in sports-entertainment history, he parted ways with the company in 2013. But his voice did not grow silent. Sports organizations around the world have coveted his services, based on the rich, verbal murals he painted while in WWE.

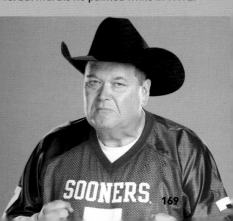

JIMMY HART

When it comes to managers in sports-entertainment, few can outshine the accomplishments of "Mouth of the South," Jimmy Hart. In addition to his sheer longevity in the industry, Hart has also been a creative influence, using his early career as a recording artist to add an essence to the mat action that was missing in previous generations.

Hart attended Treadwell High School in Memphis, an institution that includes Elvis Presley and Jerry "The King" Lawler among its alumni. While still a student, Jimmy and his band, The Gentrys, had a hit song, "Keep On Dancing" in 1965. When his principal urged Hart to get a haircut or risk not receiving his diploma on stage, he coolly replied, "I'm on stage every weekend anyway."

MEMPHIS MADNESS

Lawler and Hart should have been natural allies. But Hart was determined to become the city's most famous man since Elvis, and formed a unit known as The First Family to battle Lawler. Among the members were future WWE Superstars Randy "Macho Man" Savage, "The Genius" Lanny Poffo, "Ravishing" Rick Rude, King Kong Bundy, and Iron Sheik. But he gained national notoriety for being the manager of the comedian Andy Kaufman in his battles with the King of Memphis.

Jimmy Hart arrived in WWE in 1985 just prior to the groundbreaking first *WrestleMania*. This was the "Rock 'n' Wrestling" age, and no one was more rock 'n' roll than the "Mouth of the South." Coming to the ring in shades and specially airbrushed jackets, Hart brandished a multi-colored megaphone, broadcasting his charges' virtues during their matches. This had a dual effect: instilling his protégés with positive reinforcement and more importantly, distracting their opponents and referees.

MEGAPHONE MAN

The first of his many WWE clients included the massive Bundy and then-Intercontinental Champion, Greg "The Hammer" Valentine. Hart became known as a manager who quickly changed the fortunes of a given Superstar, causing chaotic scenes with the greatest of ease. With megaphone in hand, Hart's amplified voice was so piercing that during televised broadcasts, "The Mouth" could be heard by the audience watching at home. This communication piece also came in handy as a weapon to change the outcome of many matches.

Giants, technical standouts, brawlers, monsters, law enforcers, tag teams— "The Mouth" managed them all. He handled dangerous but athletically proficient teams like Terry and Dory Funk Jr., (both former NWA World Heavyweight Champions) and led the Hart Foundation, Nasty Boys, Natural Disasters, and Money, Inc., to the WWE World Tag Team Championship. In addition to the "The Hammer," Jimmy also managed the Honky Tonk Man and The Mountie to the Intercontinental Championship. Jimmy's managerial genius extended to the Women's ranks, as he managed the Glamour Girls to the WWE Women's Tag Team Championship. He capped off his WWE career in style in 1993 when he managed Hulk Hogan to his fifth WWE Championship.

BACK TO DIXIE

In 1994, Jimmy took his megaphone south. When Hulk Hogan announced that he'd decided to make the switch to WCW, it was Hart who was beside him, receiving the public accolades. At the *Bash at the Beach* pay-per-view that year, Hart was in Hogan's corner when he won his first WCW World Heavyweight Championship, the first manager to advise both a WWE and WCW Champion. Yet, before Hogan became a central component in the nWo, fans were stunned to witness the "Mouth of the South" going over to the dark side first, forsaking the Hulkster for The Giant, later known to the WWE Universe as Big Show. He also managed "Nature Boy" Ric Flair during this period.

What spectators never realized was that Hart had other tasks in the company, such as writing entrance themes for WCW performers and using his artistic ingenuity backstage to help the overall presentation run smoothly.

In 2005, the "Mouth of the South's" exceptional career was honored as he was inducted into the WWE Hall of Fame. By now, the imagery of fans booing Hart was a distant memory. Everywhere he appeared, he was wildly cheered, and WWE began using him as a goodwill ambassador. In 2014, the world learned about the complex man behind the megaphone when he was included in the WWE Network reality series, *Legends House*.

JIMMY JACK FUNK

| HT | 6'0" | WT | 242 lbs. | FROM | Amarillo, Texas |

| SIGNATURE MOVE | Bulldog |

Jimmy Jack Funk was crazy, even by Funk standards.

For decades, fans feared the wild Funk brothers. Hailing from Amarillo, Texas, Terry and Hoss made a career out of their maniacal in-ring actions. Little did anybody know, however, that there was a younger Funk back home at the Double Cross Ranch who was even crazier. In 1986, Terry and Hoss finally introduced WWE audiences to Jimmy Jack, their uncontrollable and unpredictable brother.

Managed by Jimmy Hart, Jimmy Jack kept with the Funk ways by wearing a cowboy hat and boots to the ring. In addition to the classic Funk garb, he also sported a mask over his eyes and rope around his neck.

According to the Funks, Jimmy Jack was an amazing amateur wrestler who only missed competing in the Olympics because of the American boycott of the Moscow Games in 1980. Unfortunately for Jimmy Jack, his supposed amateur success never equated to wins in a WWE ring, as he frequently fell short in matches against the likes of Blackjack Mulligan and Hillbilly Jim.

JIMMY WANG YANG

| HT | 5'9" | WT | 206 lbs. | FROM | Austell, Georgia |

| SIGNATURE MOVE | Corkscrew 450 Splash |

In August 2006, this newcomer appeared on *SmackDown* and showed he's not the one to ask where to find good Chinese food. Jimmy Wang Yang could not be more proud of his affinity for anything country. With a fusion of martial arts and good old-fashioned Southern roughhousing, Jimmy Wang Yang became one of the premier Cruiserweights in the world.

The black cowboy hat-wearing Superstar was a favorite of the WWE Universe. As country tunes filled arenas, his entrance to the ring got crowds on their feet as he took on challengers of all shapes and sizes. Jimmy was not the stereotypical redneck, and brought a style all his own to WWE.

JINDER MAHAL

| HT | 6'5" | WT | 222 lbs. | FROM | Punjab, India |

| SIGNATURE MOVE | Camel Clutch |

After gaining success as a movie studio executive in India, Jinder Mahal came to WWE in 2011 demanding respect, particularly from The Great Khali. Mahal began playing mind games with Khali, twisting his emotions to the breaking point and convincing the oversized Superstar to turn on his brother, Ranjin Singh.

Together, Mahal and Khali seemed unstoppable but after only a few months, Khali realized he was being used by Mahal. The former World Heavyweight Champion soon turned on Mahal, delighting the WWE Universe.

The arrogant newcomer brushed off Khali's betrayal, claiming he didn't need the big man to gain notoriety. He targeted Superstars such as Ted DiBiase and Sheamus, but struggled to gain momentum as a solo act.

In 2012, Mahal began dancing to the beat of a different tune when he joined 3MB, a hair metal-inspired trio consisting of Heath Slater and Drew McIntyre. The new persona gave Mahal a boost in confidence, which showed in the ring until he parted from WWE in 2014.

J.O.B. SQUAD

| MEMBERS | Al Snow, Hardcore Holly, Scorpio, Gillberg, & The Blue Meanie |

Headed by Al Snow, the J.O.B. Squad banded together in 1998 after coming to the realization that they weren't getting what they believed was the proper exposure. Rather than complain, they accepted their place on the roster, even developing the catchphrase "pin me, pay me," which meant they would put up with losing as long as they were paid.

Ironically, shortly after coming together, each member of the J.O.B. Squad began to experience greater success. In fact, during their brief stay together, the J.O.B. Squad captured three Championships. Gillberg became Light Heavyweight Champion, while both Al Snow and Hardcore Holly individually captured the Hardcore Championship.

JOE MCHUGH

Over the years, it has become commonplace to hear ring announcers put their own spin on Superstar introductions. But perhaps no announcer in history put as big of a personalized stamp on introductions as Joe McHugh.

As an announcer in the 1970s, McHugh introduced the likes of Pat Patterson, Pedro Morales, and Jimmy Snuka. But because McHugh's style incorporated an overemphasis on enunciating (as well as adding extra syllables), the names normally sounded a bit different. For example, he would introduce Snuka as "Jim-eee Super-Fa-Ly Sanooka."

McHugh's style usually resulted in elongated introductions. But fans didn't mind; they found his distinct vocals entertaining and worthy of imitation.

McHugh also announced more than 10,000 boxing matches. He passed away in 1993 at the age of 88.

JOE TURCO

WT 237 lbs. **FROM** Catania, Sicily

With his unruly hair, bushy goatee, and dark hooded cape, Joe Turco was one of the most fearsome-looking opponents of all time. Then the bell rang. Unfortunately for Turco, his in-ring abilities failed to match his terrifying appearance.

Nicknamed the "Continental Nobleman," Turco competed for WWE in the late 1960s and early 1970s. Fans loved to boo the unsuccessful Superstar; each time that they did, he responded with several rude hand gestures. Eventually, Turco started to gain more notoriety for the entertaining way in which he responded to fans than his actual athleticism.

Turco often teamed with the equally unsuccessful Pancho Valdez. They hoped that through a combined effort they could rise up the card. They didn't.

In 1975, Turco received the opportunity of his career when he challenged future WWE Hall of Famer Mil Mascaras for the now-defunct IWA International Championship. As expected, Mascaras proved superior and Turco submitted to a modified abdominal stretch.

JOEY ABS

HT 6'3" **WT** 277 lbs. **FROM** Greenwich, Connecticut

When the Mean Street Posse walked the affluent streets of Greenwich, Connecticut, they made their fellow sweater-vest-wearing neighbors tremble in fear. When they appeared in WWE in 1999, however, they failed to induce the same trepidation. Instead, WWE Superstars simply looked down upon them as Shane McMahon's bratty friends. At least that's how they saw Pete Gas and Rodney. Joey Abs was a different story.

As the biggest and baddest member of the Mean Street Posse, Abs picked up significantly more victories than his stablemates. He also managed to permanently etch his name into the WWE record books when he captured the Hardcore Championship at *WrestleMania 2000*. Though, in typical Mean Street Posse fashion, he lost the gold only seconds after capturing it.

JOEY MAGGS

HT 6'0" **WT** 235 lbs. **FROM** Baltimore, Maryland

Joey Maggs was never the biggest Superstar on the card, but what he lacked in size, he made up for in agility. Dubbed "Jumping" Joey Maggs, the Superstar from Baltimore used his speed to bounce around the ring and dizzy his opponents.

People began to take notice of Maggs while he was competing in the United States Wrestling Association in the early 1990s. He soon left for the bright lights of WCW, where he battled the likes of Steve Austin and Sid Vicious.

Maggs made sporadic appearances in WWE throughout the 1990s. His most notable matches saw him come up short against Yokozuna and Ric Flair in 1992 and Shawn Michaels and Lex Luger in 1993.

JOEY MERCURY

 HT 5'9" **WT** 191 lbs. **FROM** Los Angeles, California

Only a handful of Superstars can say they won WWE gold in their first-ever WWE match. Joey Mercury is one of those elite few. In April 2005, Mercury debuted alongside Johnny Nitro to defeat the reigning WWE Tag Team Champions, Eddie Guerrero and Rey Mysterio. The win shocked the WWE Universe, but for the cocky newcomers, known as MNM, the win was a mere formality.

With Melina as their manager, MNM went on to enjoy three WWE Tag Team Championship reigns. But despite their success as Champions, one of Mercury's most memorable moments was one he'd rather forget. While competing in a Fatal 4-Way Ladder Match at *Armageddon 2006*, the arrogant Superstar was nailed in the face with a ladder, which shattered his nose. Shortly after, Mercury left WWE for several years.

More recently, Mercury reemerged alongside Jamie Noble as one half of J&J Security. As trusted members of The Authority, Mercury and Noble were assigned the task of protecting Seth Rollins at all costs.

JOEY STYLES

FROM Stamford, Connecticut

With a nearly-unrivaled knowledge of the industry and his trademark call, "Oh My God," Joey Styles will be forever associated with the rise of ECW. During an internship at *Pro Wrestling Illustrated*, he met Paul Heyman, who soon took over Eastern Championship Wrestling. Joey Styles was Heyman's choice to serve as its television commentator, where his insight and distinctive voice provided the perfect accompaniment as the promotion transitioned to Extreme Championship Wrestling.

Styles made history during ECW's *Barely Legal* as he became the first announcer to call a live pay-per-view broadcast by himself. From June 1993 until the bitter end of the original ECW, Styles provided the soundtrack, articulating both heinous carnage and the complexities of lucha libre and puroresu with equal precision.

It was only natural that Styles resurfaced in June 2005 when ECW was revived at *One Night Stand*. His performance exceeded expectations and earned him a spot on *Monday Night Raw*. He also fulfilled a lifelong dream, calling a Hardcore Match at *WrestleMania 22*. However, after his announcing style clashed with the WWE mold, a frustrated Styles quit *Raw* on the air, sending some controversial barbs over the airwaves in the process. Despite this, he returned to WWE television when WWE re-launched *ECW* as a brand in 2006.

In 2008, Styles retired from announcing. He began working for WWE.com, now serving as WWE's Vice President of Digital Media Content. Fans can still catch the voice of ECW on WWE Network specials and the web feature, "WWE Warehouse."

JOHN "BRADSHAW" LAYFIELD

HT	6'6"
WT	290 lbs.
FROM	New York, New York

SIGNATURE MOVE
Clothesline From Hell

Whether it's on Wall Street or in a Street Fight, John "Bradshaw" Layfield is a dangerous man. The self-made millionaire's investing acumen has earned him a reputation as a stock market genius, while his devastating Clothesline From Hell propelled him to the top of WWE.

TAG TEAM TITAN

Following a brief professional football career, JBL turned his attention to entering sports-entertainment. After making the leap to WWE, the burly Texan competed first as Justin "Hawk" Bradshaw and then alongside Barry Windham as The New Blackjacks, yet his dominance was not put on full display until he joined forces with Faarooq, becoming The Acolytes.

As part of Undertaker's Ministry of Darkness, Faarooq and Bradshaw served The Deadman's evil agenda. As the Ministry began to dissolve, so did the Acolytes taste for the dark side. The duo soon developed a new preference for pilsner and cigars. From a makeshift backstage "office," the rechristened APA (Acolytes Protection Agency) played cards and waited to be called upon to inflict their bruising brand of "protection." All told, Bradshaw claimed three Tag Team Championships with Faarooq and proved himself as one of WWE's toughest Superstars.

BARROOM TO BOARDROOM

After eight years in WWE, Bradshaw began to publicize his impressive portfolio in March 2004. His self-made financial success came at the expense of his partnership, as Paul Heyman helped convince him that he no longer needed Faarooq. Bradshaw walked out on his partner and the following week, unveiled a swagger more befitting of a financial tycoon.

Claiming to be a great American, the new JBL focused his energies on many of the United States' political matters. His bold statements drew the attention of then-WWE Champion Eddie Guerrero. The two Superstars quickly engaged in a memorable rivalry that saw JBL claim the WWE Championship from Guerrero in June 2004.

As WWE Champion, JBL sought complete control over *SmackDown*. He formed The Cabinet with Chief of Staff, Orlando Jordan, and Secretaries of Defense, Danny and Doug Basham. He went on to become the longest-reigning WWE Champion in *SmackDown* history.

I HAVE ALWAYS BEEN SMARTER. I HAVE ALWAYS BEEN BETTER AND I HAVE ALWAYS WORKED HARDER THAN ANYONE ELSE AROUND ME.

RETURN OF A "WRESTLING GOD"

In May 2006, a defeat at the hands of Rey Mysterio forced him into early retirement. Instead of retreating back to Wall Street, he donned a headset and became *SmackDown's* color commentator alongside play-by-play man Michael Cole. JBL remained a fixture at the announce booth until Chris Jericho lured him out of retirement in December 2007.

Back in the ring, the self-proclaimed "Wrestling God" picked up right where he left off. Frustrated with seeing other Superstars claiming accolades that were once his, he promised a ruthless new era of JBL on *Raw*. He defeated Jericho at *Royal Rumble*, and then went on to top Finlay at *WrestleMania XXIV* in the Irishman's signature match, a Belfast Brawl.

JBL even managed to gain a level of retribution from the man who took his WWE Championship from him, John Cena. He won a New York City Parking Lot Brawl against The Champ at *The Great American Bash 2008*, backing up his claim that he owned The Big Apple.

Nothing exhibited JBL's shrewd business practices like when he forced Shawn Michaels to work for him after HBK lost his family savings during America's financial crisis. After Michaels won back his freedom, Layfield enjoyed one last taste of WWE gold. He defeated CM Punk for the Intercontinental Championship in March 2009. At *WrestleMania 25*, JBL quit WWE in a fit of rage after losing the Intercontinental Title in embarrassing fashion. JBL stormed up the ramp warning fans, "You'll miss JBL!" But the WWE Universe would not miss him for long.

NO HOLDS BARRED COMMENTARY

In 2012, JBL returned to the announcers' table, where his hard-hitting commentary was like a verbal Clothesline from Hell on the WWE action. Though he often bickered with Michael Cole, the odd pairing found enough common ground to form a likeable chemistry working together. Their web show series, *The JBL and Cole Show* was one of WWE's most popular shows on YouTube. Though JBL occasionally gets the itch to step back in the ring, these days, he is content maintaining his many career ventures outside the ropes.

JOHN CENA
see page 176

JOHN LAURINAITIS

FROM Philadelphia, Pennsylvania

CM Punk once dismissed John Laurinaitis as a glad-handing, nonsensical, yes man (among other things). Laurinaitis, however, had a considerably higher view of his position within WWE. With a bowed chest and an arrogant smirk, "Big Johnny" threw his executive weight around with cold, corporate savvy.

Prior to being bestowed with the most obnoxiously long job title since the Industrial Revolution, Laurinaitis was an accomplished competitor. Throughout the 1980s and 1990s, he competed in the United States and Japan, where he claimed several Tag Team Championship reigns.

After retiring from the ring in 2000, Laurinaitis joined WCW's front office. He then landed in Mr. McMahon's company and soared up the corporate ladder. While content with his behind-the-scenes success, Punk's tirade lured him into the public spotlight in 2011. Soon, he usurped control over both *Raw* and *SmackDown*, with his team besting *SmackDown* GM Teddy Long's crew at *WrestleMania XXVIII*.

Aided by David Otunga's legal counsel and the conniving Eve, Laurinaitis trumpeted a new era of "People Power," but his propaganda was not fooling anyone. He abused his authority on a weekly basis, firing Big Show in humiliating fashion only to use the giant to personally gain a tainted victory over John Cena at *Over the Limit 2012*. Cena gained his revenge by winning a match with Laurinaitis' career on the line. While Mr. McMahon sent the raspy voiced exec on to his future endeavors, Laurinaitis' impact is still felt today.

JOHN MORRISON

HT	6'0"	WT	215 lbs.	FROM	Los Angeles, California
SIGNATURE MOVE		Moonlight Drive, Starship Pain			

For much of his WWE career, John Morrison's arrogant attitude made him tough to like. You just couldn't tell him that; his warped impression of himself had him believing the earth is covered with Morrison Followers, "MoFos," as he called them, who eagerly awaited the weekly installments of *The Dirt Sheet*.

Ever since Morrison's *SmackDown* debut in April 2005 (as Johnny Nitro), gold gravitated to his waist. A multiple-time Intercontinental and WWE Tag Team Champion, it wasn't until he was drafted to ECW in June 2007 that Morrison truly took his game to the next level. Within one week of his arrival on the extreme brand, the self-appointed "Tuesday Night Delight" defeated CM Punk for the vacant ECW Championship. Over the next several months, Morrison defeated Punk time and time again before the challenger finally defeated him in September to become the ECW Champion for the first time.

In typical Morrison fashion, he wasn't without gold for long. In November, he teamed with then-rival, The Miz, to capture the WWE Tag Team Championship from Matt Hardy and MVP. After the victory, the two conceited Superstars realized they had more in common than originally thought and went on to enjoy a lengthy eight-month reign.

The partnership ended when The Miz moved to *Raw*, and Morrison took to the air on *SmackDown*. On September 4th, Morrison won the Intercontinental Championship from Rey Mysterio. The Shaman of Sexy then fist-pumped his way to top pop-culture status when he joined WWE legend Trish Stratus and Jersey Shore star Snooki in a mixed tag match at *WrestleMania XXVII* against Lay-Cool and Dolph Ziggler.

The last time he was seen in WWE, Morrison fell victim to a ghastly attack from former partner, The Miz. As a capacity crowd sat in silence, Morrison was carried out on a stretcher by emergency medical technicians. Fans hold hope that the Guru of Greatness will one day return to WWE.

JOHN MORRISON & THE MIZ

MEMBERS	John Morrison & The Miz
COMBINED WT	439 lbs.

John Morrison and The Miz might just be the most self-centered tag team in sports-entertainment history. Respectively known as "The Shaman of Sexy" and "The Chick Magnet," Morrison and Miz's larger-than-life egos drew instant ire from audiences. Unfortunately for the fans who loved to hate them, the arrogant duo backed up their narcissism with in-ring success.

In November 2007, the egotistical Superstars took full advantage of the *SmackDown/ECW* working agreement, which allowed talent to cross from brand to brand. They jumped to the Friday night show to upend Matt Hardy and MVP for the WWE Tag Team Championship. After the win, Morrison and Miz successfully defended the Titles against Jesse and Festus, CM Punk and Kane, the father-son duo of Finlay and Hornswoggle, and others. This impressive run earned them the 2008 Slammy Award for Tag Team of the Year, just another reason to remind others to "be jealous." As if they needed more bragging material, they claimed World Tag Team gold the following week.

While they saw incredible success in the ring, they also became media sensations outside of it for their award-winning WWE.com webcast, *The Dirt Sheet*. This weekly program saw both Superstars mock their most recent challengers as well as pop-culture figures. This team fell apart when The Miz was drafted to *Raw* in 2009. In a show of his awesomeness and underlying selfishness, The Miz attacked Morrison once the move was official.

JOHN TOLOS

HT	6'2"	WT	240 lbs.	FROM	Hamilton, Ontario, Canada
SIGNATURE MOVE	Knuckle Corkscrew				

"Golden Greek" John Tolos was one of the biggest stars in all of sports-entertainment. At one time, he held five territory Championships simultaneously and was known for appearing on television wearing all the Titles simultaneously. He and his brother Chris, known as the Canadian Wrecking Crew, dissected opponents and won Tag Team Championships wherever they traveled. On December 28, 1963, they defeated future WWE Hall of Famers Killer Kowalski and Gorilla Monsoon for the United States Tag Team Championship. Tolos was also a major contender to the WWE Championship, held at the time by Bruno Sammartino.

Whether appearing in tag team matches with his brother Chris or in singles competition, the "Golden Greek" helped change the face of wrestling. His villainous ways continue to influence rule-breakers all over the world. His famous proclamation can still be heard today: "The only way to spell wrestling is T-O-L-O-S!" The world of sports-entertainment suffered a tremendous loss when John Tolos passed away on May 21, 2009.

JOHNNY BAREND

HT	6'1"	WT	230 lbs.	FROM	Rochester, New York
SIGNATURE MOVE	Atomic Drop				

Johnny Barend began his in-ring career after wrestling in the U.S. Navy during World War II. His earliest matches emanated from the New York territory, mainly Buffalo, with a few stops at the famed Madison Square Garden. He later moved to California, where he gained great success as a tag team specialist. He and Enrique Torres defeated Gene Kiniski and James Blears for the San Francisco NWA World Tag Team Championship in July 1955. The win marked the first of many tag Title reigns for Barend with nine separate partners.

Despite his success in California, Barend took his game to Hawaii in the 1960s. The decision proved to be wise as Barend became a true legend in Hawaii. Each week, more than half the island would turn on their televisions just to see the charismatic and crazy Barend compete. Equally entertaining were his wild interview segments, which he conducted from a casket inside a smoke-filled room. Few actually understood what the wild man was saying, but that simply helped add to his allure.

JOHNNY CURTIS

HT	6'4"	WT	244 lbs.	FROM	Westbrook, Maine

Longtime fan Johnny Curtis achieved his dream of becoming a WWE Superstar when he won season four of *NXT*. As a result of his victory, he and his Pro, R-Truth, were awarded an opportunity at the WWE Tag Team Championship. Unfortunately for Curtis, though, R-Truth refused to participate in the match.

The unpredictable Superstar had a knack for words. In anticipation of his *SmackDown* debut, he sarcastically told the WWE Universe he'd be able to "cut the mustard" before also declaring that he'd "take the cake."

Curtis' clever forecasting proved incorrect. The Maine native lost his debut match to Mark Henry in less than one minute and only appeared sparingly following the loss. This resulted in Curtis developing "a chip on his shoulder" before fading from the scene. Curtis resurfaced in NXT. He and his girlfriend, Maxine, caused a lot of drama before going their separate ways.

JOHN CENA

HT	6'1"
WT	251 lbs.
FROM	West Newbury, Massachusetts

SIGNATURE MOVE
Attitude Adjustment, STF

John Cena's unprecedented accolades in WWE are overshadowed only by The Champ's near-superhuman desire to achieve more. One of the most in-demand professional athletes in the world, Cena continues to build on a fourteen year-long career that includes fifteen World Championships, five United States Championships, over 500 wishes granted for the Make-a-Wish Foundation, and unparalleled (if polarizing) popularity.

Before becoming a worldwide megastar, Cena excelled as an All-American offensive lineman at Springfield College, where he also earned a degree in Exercise Physiology. Following graduation, Cena worked at a Gold's Gym before choosing to pursue a career in sports-entertainment. The chiseled, charismatic youngster soon became The Prototype in WWE's then-developmental system, OVW.

RUTHLESS AGGRESSION

Cena graduated to the main WWE roster under his own name in June 2002. From the start, his brazen slap to Kurt Angle showed that he possessed the "ruthless aggression" needed to succeed in WWE. He also had a way with words. As the "Doctor of Thuganomics," Cena wore a thick steel chain around his neck and baggy jean shorts, while he dissed other Superstars with his freestyle rapping skills. First seen as cocky, his street-tough persona became popular and eventually earned him a United States Championship Match against Big Show at *WrestleMania XX*. Cena chopped the giant down to size for the first of his career's many victorious *WrestleMania* moments.

By 2005, there was no denying that Cena's time to shine was now. At *WrestleMania 21*, a sold-out Staples Center witnessed Cena etch his name in the annals of sports-entertainment history when he dropped JBL with an Attitude Adjustment to claim his first WWE Championship. To prove his reign was no fluke, the new Champ followed up his *WrestleMania* victory with another win over JBL in a gruesome "I Quit" Match at *Judgment Day*.

As WWE Champion, Cena's star shot higher and faster than any other Superstar in recent memory. When not competing in the ring, he was fulfilling countless personal appearances on top of training and exhausting travel. Somehow, he found time to record his debut rap album, *You Can't See Me*, which hit No. 15 on the Billboard charts.

Cena also redesigned the WWE Championship, giving the Title a flashy, spinning WWE logo. Many traditionalists gasped at the transformation of the elite Championship but Cena simply shrugged off the naysayers, astutely pointing to the evolutionary nature of WWE.

During his amazing nine-month maiden voyage with the prize, a growing sentiment developed among many fans who resented Cena's unique style. To this day, Cena draws a mixed, if equally passionate, reaction of both cheers and boos, a fascinating dynamic that he has long embraced.

At *New Year's Revolution 2006*, Cena survived a grueling half-hour Elimination Chamber Match, only to find himself forced to defend his Title yet again when Edge emerged to cash in his Money in the Bank briefcase. The exhausted Champ was no match for the well-rested Rated-R Superstar and his lethal Spear. While the loss marked the end of his first reign atop WWE, Cena only had to wait three weeks before gaining revenge on Edge, reclaiming his Title at *Royal Rumble*. This was only the beginning of a years-long grudge between Cena and his bitter rival, Edge.

Cena suffered a discouraging loss to Rob Van Dam at *One Night Stand 2006* but it failed to derail him. By year's end, he reclaimed the WWE Title for a third time and held it for over 380 days, the longest reign since Hulk Hogan first held the Title from 1984-1988. Unfortunately, a torn pectoral tendon put a premature end to his epic Title reign. The injury required surgery and a six-month rehabilitation period. But after only three months, a determined Cena made a shocking return to win the 2008 *Royal Rumble*.

Though Cena was unable to regain the WWE Championship at *WrestleMania XXIV*, he would not be out of the title picture for long. After overcoming another injury, Cena returned at *Survivor Series 2008* to win the World Heavyweight Championship by defeating Chris Jericho. Cena topped Edge and Big Show at *WrestleMania XXV* to tack a second World Heavyweight Championship reign to his credit before turning his attention back to the WWE Championship. In September 2009—three years after last losing the WWE Championship—Cena overcame Randy Orton in a thrilling "I Quit" Match to finally regain the Title. The victory gave Cena his fourth reign with the WWE Championship. Reign Number 5 also came at Orton's expense, while a victory over Sheamus awarded Cena his sixth run at the top. *WrestleMania XXVI* was the historic backdrop for Cena's thrilling victory over Batista and with it came his seventh WWE Title reign.

Cena challenged The Miz for his record-tying eighth WWE Title at *WrestleMania XXVII* but the event's host, The Rock, had other plans. Toward the end of the match, The Rock flattened Cena with a Rock Bottom, allowing The Miz to pick up the win. Rock's controversial actions set the wheels in motion for the epic year-long rivalry which culminated in a "Once in a Lifetime" match at *WrestleMania XXVIII*.

During the unprecedented build-up to the encounter, Cena finally wrested the Title away from The Miz in May 2011. He also topped Rey Mysterio to claim his record-breaking ninth WWE Title, then padded his record to ten reigns at the expense of Alberto Del Rio. Despite all his Championship success, Cena's sole focus became defeating The Rock in an inter-generational showdown for the ages. Unfortunately for Cena, The Rock got the best of him on the Grandest Stage of Them All. The devastating loss kicked off the most taxing year in Cena's career.

THE CHAMP PREVAILS

With a menacing old foe, Brock Lesnar, back in WWE and the vile John Laurinaitis in control of the WWE roster, Cena endured devastating setbacks in 2012. Though he won the Money in the Bank briefcase for the first time in June, a surprise attack by Big Show spoiled his cash-in attempt. At the year's final pay-per-view, Cena vied for WWE's other Money in the Bank briefcase held by Dolph Ziggler. In the final moments of the tense Ladder Match, his supposed friend AJ Lee knocked him off the ladder and aligned herself with Ziggler. The disheartening loss brought a year of tough breaks to a crescendo.

Cena vowed to turn things around and within the month, won his second career Royal Rumble Match. The victory earned him an unexpected chance at the ultimate redemption, as it aligned him once again with newly-crowned Champion, The Rock in the main event of *WrestleMania*, this time with the WWE Championship on the line. On a breezy night in New Jersey's MetLife Stadium, Cena overcame three Rock Bottoms, only to drop his rival with a final AA for the three count. After a respectful handshake, The Rock raised Cena's hand while Cena raised his eleventh WWE Title.

With a year of misfortune behind him, the rejuvenated Cena surged forward. He held the Title for 133 days, his longest reign since 2006, until his hand-picked challenger Daniel Bryan defeated him at *SummerSlam 2013*. Always resilient, Cena was forced to have his troublesome triceps fixed, but was back on top just two months after surgery. He defeated Alberto Del Rio for the World Heavyweight Championship.

Though John Cena fell short in a historic TLC Match with Randy Orton to unify WWE's two World Championships, the WWE Universe knew Cena's legacy was unparalleled. So did Bray Wyatt. The sadistic backwoods preacher tried to exterminate "the lie" he claimed John Cena to be, but ultimately failed to overcome Cena at *Wrestlemania 30*. His legacy still intact, Cena outlasted Wyatt and six other Superstars at *Money in the Bank 2014* to claim the unified WWE World Heavyweight Championship. The win put him one shy of Ric Flair for the all-time record for combined World Championship reigns.

At *SummerSlam 2014*, Cena suffered the most lopsided defeat in his career, sustaining sixteen heinous German suplexes from Brock Lesnar. Some questioned the sanity of Cena's "Never Give Up" mentality as he did not hesitate to get back in the ring with Lesnar. But if not for the added ingredient of a pesky Seth Rollins, Cena's valiant bid to conquer The Conqueror perhaps would have been successful. His newfound bad blood with The Authority's golden child, Rollins, put him at odds with the WWE brass but Cena paid little heed to Triple H's warnings not to "fight the future."

In 2015, Cena turned his attention to the Championship that first put him on the map, the United States Championship. After he freed the patriotic prize from Rusev's clutches at *WrestleMania 31*, he hosted a weekly "US Open Challenge" in which several young, hungry challengers emerged. As promised, Cena restored pride in the U.S. Championship. Along the way, he and the newly-debuted NXT Champion Kevin Owens stole the show in an epic trilogy of matches. Cena also nearly usurped Seth Rollins at *SummerSlam* to tie Flair's record and become a dual Champion until, of all people, TV personality Jon Stewart intervened to spoil his opportunity.

John Cena has recently appeared in the blockbuster comedy film *Trainwreck* and in 2016, became the host of the TV series *American Grit*. His home, however, will always be in the ring. For over a dozen years, Cena has built an unmatched legacy in WWE. No matter what lies ahead for The Champ, he has cemented a permanent place among the most elite Superstars in WWE history.

JOHNNY DEFAZIO

FROM Pittsburgh, Pennsylvania

A native of Pittsburgh, "Jumpin'" Johnny DeFazio started his career competing for his hometown's Studio Wrestling promotion in the 1960s. While he enjoyed great success there, DeFazio will forever be remembered for being WWE's first-ever Junior Heavyweight Champion. He went on to win the now-defunct Title a record four times.

In addition to his Junior Heavyweight Championship reigns, DeFazio went on to form several winning tag teams, including unions with Ace Freeman and Geto Mongol. But it was his alliance with Bepo Mongol that garnered the most success. DeFazio and Bepo defeated Luke Graham and Tarzan Tyler for the International Tag Team Championship in November 1971.

Before retiring in the mid-1980s, DeFazio engaged in many brutal battles with Sgt. Slaughter and Bobby Duncum.

JOHNNY PARISI

HT 5'10" **WT** 247 lbs. **FROM** Long Island, New York

According to second-generation Superstar Johnny Parisi, "it ain't easy being Parisi."

The frustrated Parisi made the declaration after an embarrassing losing streak resulted in the WWE Universe booing him wildly. Rather than silence them with his work in the ring, he grabbed a microphone and demanded their respect. He didn't get it. But what he did get was a battle with Kane, who batted Parisi around like a cat playing with a defeated mouse.

Kane's assault was just one example of what had become commonplace toward the end of Parisi's WWE stint. Other Superstars who bolstered their records at Parisi's expense include Chavo Guerrero, Ron Simmons, and The Hurricane. Unable to turn his luck around, Parisi was released from WWE after less than one year of service in June 2006.

JOHNNY POLO

Seen by many as a preppy and pompous brat, Johnny Polo joined WWE as the manager of the mighty Adam Bomb in May 1993. With his trusty polo mallet by his side, the overly-enthusiastic manager led Bomb to victories over several established Superstars, including Owen Hart and El Matador.

Perhaps Polo's greatest managerial exploits came while guiding The Quebecers, whom he led to three World Tag Team Championship reigns, starting with a victory over Rick and Scott Steiner in September 1993. Subsequent Championship victories came at the expense of 1-2-3 Kid and Marty Jannetty and Men on a Mission.

Polo also spent some time in the ring facing such stars as Lex Luger, Virgil, and Doink. In 1994, he even unsuccessfully squared off against his one-time client, Adam Bomb.

Polo's motor mouth eventually led him to the broadcast booth, where he served as color commentator for many WWE shows, including *Monday Night Raw*, before leaving the company in October 1994.

JOHNNY POWERS

HT 6'4" **WT** 265 lbs. **FROM** Hamilton, Ontario, Canada
SIGNATURE MOVE Powerlock

On more than one occasion, Johnny Powers came within a millisecond of dethroning longtime WWE Champion Bruno Sammartino. Had things played out just a little differently, fans today could have been looking back at Powers's career as one of the greatest in WWE history. Instead, Powers now has little to show for his brief WWE stay, aside from a handful of victories over Gino Brito.

Powers used a modified version of the figure four leglock known as the Powerlock to turn back opponents in many Northern wrestling territories. Along the way, he defeated Waldo Von Erich, Johnny Valentine, and Ernie Ladd, among others to become a twelve-time NWF North American Champion.

JOHNNY RODZ

HT 5'8" **WT** 239 lbs. **FROM** New York, New York
SIGNATURE MOVE Falling Headbutt

Widely recognized as the hardest working man in sports-entertainment, "The Unpredictable" Johnny Rodz used his undying passion for competition to earn the respect of his peers in the locker room. Unfortunately for Rodz, his hard work rarely resulted in victories, as the New York City native lost more matches than he won. Though, one of his greatest accomplishments in the ring was a February 1982 victory over the great Baron Mikel Scicluna.

Despite his unenviable win-loss record, Rodz earned the ultimate honor of being inducted into the WWE Hall of Fame in 1996. Arnold Skaaland, a fellow New Yorker and Hall of Famer, inducted Rodz during an emotional ceremony in the Big Apple.

After retiring from the ring in the mid-1980s, Rodz began training the Superstars of tomorrow. Using the gritty Gleason's Gym as a training facility, Rodz harnessed his unorthodox style to teach aspiring competitors respect for the game. Many of his pupils went on to enjoy high-profile WWE careers, including Tommy Dreamer, Tazz, and Colin Cassady.

JOHNNY VALENTINE

HT 6'4" **WT** 255 lbs. **FROM** Maple Valley, Washington
SIGNATURE MOVE Atomic Skull Crusher

With his tanned skin, sculpted frame and bleached-blonde hair, Johnny Valentine certainly had the look of a successful professional wrestler. And once the bell rang, he backed up his imposing appearance with his superior in-ring arsenal. Much to the ire of his detractors, Valentine was well aware of his greatness. Calling himself "Handsome," his arrogant attitude made him one of the most hated men in wrestling for close to three decades.

Valentine started his career by competing in Argentina in 1947, but soon afterwards, he was back in the United States where he began to build one of the game's greatest legacies. With more than fifty different National Wrestling Alliance Titles to his credit, few can match Valetine's success in the ring.

In July 1975, Valentine defeated Harley Race for the United States Championship. Well into his third decade of competition, the victory proved Valentine to be a timeless talent with plenty of fight left in him. Unfortunately, a mere three months after capturing the Title, Valentine's life would tragically change forever when he was involved in a plane crash. The impact from the accident, which also involved Ric Flair, David Crockett, Tim Woods, and Bob Bruggers, left Valentine partially paralyzed.

No longer able to compete in the ring, Valentine watched from the sidelines with great pride as his son, Greg "The Hammer" Valentine, carried on the family legacy throughout his Hall of Fame career.

JOHNNY VALIANT

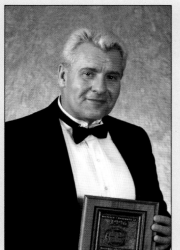

HT 6'4" **WT** 245 lbs.
FROM New York City, New York

One of the most colorful Superstars of his time, "Luscious" Johnny Valiant drew the attention of fans everywhere with his outrageous outfits and boisterous personality. However, what really caught the eye of his competition was his rugged in-ring skills, particularly in the tag team ranks.

After heeding the advice of the legendary Bruno Sammartino, Valiant embarked on his Hall of Fame career in 1967. He spent a few years bouncing around as a singles competitor before finally deciding to try his hand in the tag team division with his brother "Handsome" Jimmy Valiant. Together, the Valiants found their niche and over the next decade, the duo cemented their legacy as one of the greatest brotherly duos to ever compete.

In May 1974, the Valiant Brothers defeated Tony Garea and Dean Ho to capture the coveted World Tag Team Championship. For more than a year, the flamboyant combination successfully defended the Titles until they were finally upended by Victor Rivera and Dominic DeNucci. At the time, their reign was recognized as the longest in WWE tag team history.

Following his in-ring career, Valiant turned his efforts toward managing. After a brief stint guiding the career of a young Hulk Hogan in the AWA, "Luscious" Johnny jumped back to WWE, where he led Brutus Beefcake and Greg Valentine to the World Tag Team Championship.

JOJO

Introduced as a WWE newbie on *Total Divas* season one, Jojo is out to prove to the WWE Universe that big things come in small packages. What Jojo lacks in stature, she makes up for in talent. Viewers of *SummerSlam 2013* were dazzled by her rendition of the national anthem and her dance moves have stacked up to the Funkadactyls.

Jojo strives to do it all in WWE. So following *Total Divas*, she packed for NXT where she could refine her skills to do just that. The spunky newcomer assumed a regular role as NXT ring announcer and in 2015, started to find opportunities on *Raw* and *SmackDown*. In addition to announcing matches, Jojo has been tasked with interviewing some of WWE biggest stars.

JOINT PROMOTIONS UK

From 1964 to 1985, Britain's *World of Sport* television show created fans from all levels of society fixated by such stars as Mick McManus, Tony St. Clair, Johnny Saint, Giant Haystacks, Jim Breaks, and Jackie "Mr. TV" Pallo.

Although sports-entertainment had been an entertainment option in England since the early 20th Century, the modern age started in 1947 with the creation of the Admiral-Lord Mountevans Rules. Among the regulations was that British wrestling would be fought in rounds.

In 1952, promoters around the country created an organization much like the NWA to trade talent and rally against competitors. The most prominent member of the group, Joint Promotions, was Dale Martin in London, but there were representatives in Yorkshire, Liverpool, Manchester, and other locations. Joint Promotions merged into one company in 1969.

In the 1970s, promoter Max Crabtree's brother, jolly Shirley "Big Daddy" Crabtree became England's biggest star, often teaming with more athletic newcomers like Chris Adams, Dynamite Kid, Davey Boy Smith, and William Regal.

By the 1990s, most British fans had shifted their allegiance to WWE.

JONATHAN COACHMAN

FROM Wichita, Kansas

In 2000, Jonathan Coachman became a regular member of the WWE broadcast team as he conducted backstage interviews and wrap-up segments. Coachman was an energetic young reporter who often entertained WWE fans with his antics during interviews. His segments with The Rock became immensely popular as the "Brahma Bull" often forced him to sing, dance, and smile for the camera after multiple insults.

Coachman worked his way into announcing duties on *Sunday Night Heat* with Al Snow and then onto *Raw* alongside Jim Ross and Jerry Lawler. He also co-hosted the first-ever WWE Diva Search and *CoachCast* on WWE.com. Coachman also found time to compete in the ring, including appearances at *Backlash 2004*, *Taboo Tuesday 2005* and two *Royal Rumble* matches.

After first acting as an Executive Assistant to the McMahon family, Coachman traded General Manager duties with William Regal from August to October of 2007. Coach's final role with WWE was as part of the *SmackDown* announce team with Michael Cole.

Jonathan Coachman departed WWE on amicable terms in the spring of 2008, but it wasn't long before sports and entertainment fans heard The Coach's voice on their televisions once again. He soon joined ESPN as an anchor on *SportsCenter*, fulfilling his dream of becoming a sports broadcaster. Today, he can often be seen interviewing current WWE Superstars for ESPN's regular WWE segments, his previous career providing a natural connection with his subjects.

JOS LEDUC

HT 6'1" **WT** 280 lbs. **FROM** Godbout, Quebec, Canada
SIGNATURE MOVE One-Armed Backbreaker

During an interview, Jos LeDuc once said, "When I'm breathing, I make things happen..." This was a concise summation of what turned into a storied four decade career. Trained in Judo, Jos LeDuc received his degree in ring arts from Calgary's Stu Hart. In the early 1970s the lumberjack appeared on WWE cards in singles action, and in tag team matches with brother, Paul, among other partners. During this time, LeDuc also sparked a bloody rivalry against Bruno Sammartino over the WWE Championship.

In 1988, he re-emerged in WWE under the guidance of Frenchy Martin, and continued to destroy opponents until his retirement in 1995. While visiting family in 1999, this wrestling legend passed away.

JOSE ESTRADA

 FROM Brooklyn, New York

From Brooklyn, New York, via Puerto Rico, Jose Estrada entered WWE in the late 1970s. His first few years in the promotion were somewhat rough, regularly losing to the likes of Bob Backlund, SD Jones, and Ivan Putski. But his luck turned around in January 1978 when he defeated Tony Garea in the finals of a tournament to crown a new Junior Heavyweight Champion.

Unfortunately for Estrada, his reign was fleeting. Three days after becoming Champion, he lost the Title to Japanese star Tatsumi Fujinami in New York City. Estrada was never able to reclaim the prize.

Back in his native Puerto Rico, Estrada honed his craft competing for the World Wrestling Council. His legacy continued through his son, former WWE Superstar Jose Estrada Jr.

JOSE LOTHARIO

HT 5'7" **WT** 245 lbs. **FROM** San Antonio, Texas

Jose "El Gran" Lothario was already winning regional titles as early as 1960. Lothario quickly became a hero to millions throughout the southern United States in the territories of the NWA and in Mexico. He also spent time in successful tag teams with Dory Funk Jr., Mil Mascaras, Chief Wahoo McDaniel, Eddie Graham, Ivan Putski, and Rocky Johnson.

Many WWE fans saw him for the first time in August 1987 at the retirement show for legendary promoter Paul Boesch. Jose was in the corner of Tito Santana and Mil Mascaras. In 1996, he appeared in WWE as the manager of the man he trained, Shawn Michaels, in his quest for the WWE Championship. Lothario also teamed with his star pupil against members of Camp Cornette. He even stepped into the ring with James E. Cornette at *In Your House: Mind Games*.

By early 1997, Jose returned to San Antonio and shared his love of the action in the ring with students. Lothario will always be remembered as both a mat hero and an excellent teacher.

JOSE LUIS RIVERA

HT 6'3" **WT** 231 lbs. **FROM** Puerto Rico
SIGNATURE MOVE Boston Crab

Jose Luis Rivera, coming from a long line of Latin grapplers, graced WWE from 1984 until 1990. With a background including boxing, Jose rarely hesitated to resort to fisticuffs when necessary. During a 1986 episode of *Piper's Pit*, Roddy Piper expressed doubt in Rivera's abilities in the ring while mocking his Spanish accent. Although Jose was unable to best the loudmouth and his bodyguard in the end, both found out that Jose Luis Rivera had an unwavering will and an excess of courage.

During his career in WWE, Jose Luis Rivera's actions in the ring left everyone from Puerto Rico with a feeling of pride due to his toughness and fighting spirit.

JOSEPH RAYMOND "TOOTS" MONDT

A young Joe Mondt subscribed to a wrestling correspondence course, offered by the renowned "Farmer" Burns, to hone his "hooking," the ability to apply crippling submission holds. Mondt became part of a traveling show and was discovered by the man whose correspondence course led him to the sport.

Mondt had developed his strength working on his family's Colorado farm, but his ruthlessness on the mat was something that was inborn. Burns, a tough former Champion, recognized this, and took Mondt on as his protégé. The young man was called "Toots" because of his youth; at the time, he was the youngest student in Burns' Omaha school.

Sports-entertainment changed forever in 1919 when Mondt met promoter Billy Sandow and legendary grappler Ed "Strangler" Lewis. This triumvirate became a business force known as the Gold Dust Trio.

"Toots" had a vision to change the way sports-entertainment, as a product, was presented to the public. To make it more entertaining, he introduced "Slam Bang Western Wrestling" which was a style that mixed kicking, strikes, and various forms of contact to generate more excitement. He developed the concept of time limit matches, and a packaged show that featured programs with rivalries between "good guys" and "bad guys."

By the end of the 1940s, "Toots" had positioned himself as the undisputed czar of sports-entertainment in the Northeastern United States. In the 1950s, Mondt's stranglehold in this region was contested by a promoter with strong ties to the television industry, Vincent J. McMahon. At the same time, McMahon courted Mondt's top attraction, Antonino "Argentina" Rocca.

The two former rivals soon became allies. While Mondt had experience, McMahon offered innovation. Together, they broke away from the NWA to form WWE in 1963, acquiring so much authority that even rival promoters wanted to remain in their good graces.

In 1965, McMahon replaced his partner as the promoter at Madison Square Garden. Four years later, a number of health issues forced "Toots" to retire to St. Louis, where he stayed close to the industry until he passed away on June 11, 1976.

JOSH MATHEWS

After nearly winning the first season of *Tough Enough* in 2001, Josh Mathews traded in his ring gear for a microphone. While the move ended his dream of becoming a Superstar, it kickstarted what eventually became an impressive career as a WWE personality. His initial responsibilities included backstage interviews for *SmackDown* and hosting *WWE.com*'s *Byte This!* webcast.

As WWE evolved, Mathews expanded into more diverse and high-profile positions, most notably commentating on both *Raw* and *SmackDown*. He even called the action at *WrestleMania XXVII* before Stone Cold Steve Austin ended his night prematurely with a jaw-rattling Stunner. Over the years, Mathews endured several hard knocks as a result of his close encounters with volatile Superstars.

Though best known for his wit and polished wardrobe, Mathews did reach deep into his bag of *Tough Enough* tricks in 2004. First, he teamed with Booker T to defeat JBL and Orlando Jordan, and later defeated Jordan in a solo match. When Booker and JBL eventually became Mathews' announcing colleagues, Josh's impressive 2-0 record was often a fun subject for banter.

JOY GIOVANNI

HT	5'4"	**FROM**	Boston, Massachusetts

Joy Giovanni's curvaceous frame first caught the attention of the WWE Universe in 2004 when she finished in the top three of the *Raw* Diva Search. WWE hired her to be a massage therapist later that year. She quickly became friends with Big Show and engaged in a rivalry with fellow Diva Search contestant Amy Weber.

Things turned disturbing for Giovanni when Weber and JBL kidnapped her and kept her in the trunk of a limo. The traumatizing incident failed to derail Joy. The following month, at *No Way Out*, she won the 2005 Rookie Diva of the Year contest, turning back Michelle McCool, Rochelle, and Lauren. Joy left WWE only a few months later and was not seen again until a brief appearance in the Miss WrestleMania Battle Royal at *WrestleMania 25*.

JTG

HT	6'2"	**WT**	232 lbs.	**FROM**	Brooklyn, New York
SIGNATURE MOVE	The Shout Out				

Hold on to your valuables, it's JTG. During his WWE career, the street-tough Brooklyn brawler wasn't above stealing anybody's belongings and selling them for "money, money, yeah, yeah."

Alongside partner Shad Gaspard, JTG enjoyed success as a member of Cryme Tyme starting in 2006. But as the years passed and tag team gold continued to elude them, a frustrated Gaspard attacked JTG in 2010, putting an end to the popular union.

JTG eventually gained retribution, defeating Gaspard in a Strap Match at *Extreme Rules 2010*. Unfortunately for JTG, the victory over Gaspard was among his final WWE highlights. Afterwards, he regularly found himself on the wrong side of decisions against the likes of Santino Marella and Justin Gabriel. JTG was ultimately released from his WWE contract in June 2014.

JUDY GRABLE

HT	5'4"	FROM	Bremerton, Washington
SIGNATURE MOVE			Dropkick

Judy Grable was one of sports-entertainment's first sex symbols. Debuting in 1938, the fair-haired femme excited male audiences decades before blonde bombshells in sports-entertainment were in vogue. Despite her beauty, rooting for Grable proved difficult, as she established herself as one of her generation's strongest rule breakers.

Grable's greatest rivalry came against the Fabulous Moolah, whom she battled for nearly a decade. Their most memorable encounter came in 1956 when Moolah defeated Grable in the finals of a tournament to crown the first-ever WWE Women's Champion. Moolah went on to hold the Title for nearly thirty years.

Grable retired shortly after her 1956 loss to Moolah. Despite never capturing the Women's Championship, she will forever be remembered as a true trailblazer of women in sports-entertainment.

JUDY MARTIN

HT	5'6"
SIGNATURE MOVE	Powerbomb

Platinum-haired Judy Martin first appeared in WWE in 1979, becoming regular partners with Leilani Kai, and battling the likes of Donna Christianello, Joyce Grable, Desiree Peterson, and Fabulous Moolah.

During the mid-1980s, Martin became a threat to the reign of then-Women's Champion, Wendi Richter. In 1987, she reunited with Kai to form the Glamour Girls and, with Jimmy Hart in their corner, the team traded the WWE Women's Tag Team Championship back and forth with the Jumping Bomb Angels in both the United States and Japan.

She challenged Rockin' Robin for the WWE Women's Championship at the 1989 Royal Rumble before departing the company later that year. She later worked in law enforcement.

THE JUMPING BOMB ANGELS

MEMBERS	Noriyo Tateno & Itsuki Yamazaki
FROM	Tokyo, Japan

Just as the Summer of 1987 got underway, Noriyo Tateno and Itsuki Yamazaki came to WWE, instantly heating up the Women's Division. The Jumping Bomb Angels had already made a name for themselves in Japan with their fast tags, quick countermoves, and impressive acrobatics, all of which translated into a high-power offense.

As members of Fabulous Moolah's team at the first *Survivor Series*, they emerged the sole survivors. At the 1988 *Royal Rumble*, they captured tag team gold in a thrilling two-out-of-three falls match with Leilani Kai and Judy Martin, aka the Glamour Girls. As they proudly defended the Titles, Tateno and Yamazaki became heroes to female fans across the United States and the WWE Universe. Soon after their Title reign came to an end, the duo moved on from WWE.

During their time together, the Jumping Bomb Angels lifted fans to their feet and dropped opponents to the canvas in all four corners of the Earth. In the process, they changed the face of women's wrestling forever.

JUNIOR HEAVYWEIGHT CHAMPIONSHIP

The now-defunct WWE Junior Heavyweight Championship was a precursor to the more recent WWE Cruiserweight Championship. Designed to recognize the achievements of Superstars 220 pounds and under, names like Black Tiger, Tiger Mask, and Dynamite Kid all enjoyed reigns as Junior Heavyweight Champion. The lighter Superstars thrilled audiences with their quick-paced action until 1985 when the Title was vacated.

Early records of the Championship offer conflicting reports, but between 1967 and 1972 the Title was traded multiple times between "Jumpin'" Johnny De Fazio and Jackie Nichols. The Championship was inactive from De Fazio's retirement in 1972 until 1978, when journeyman Jose Estrada had a brief run. Later, the Title was exclusively defended in the New Japan promotion.

1978

January 20 • Uniondale, NY
Carlos Estrada def. **Tony Garea**

January 23 • New York, NY
Tatsumi Fujinami def. **Jose Estrada**

1979

October 2 • Osaka, Japan
Ryuma Go def. **Tatsumi Fujinami**

October 4 • Tokyo, Japan
Tatsumi Fujinami def. **Ryuma Go**
Tatsumi Fujinami vacated the Junior Heavyweight Championship in December 1981 after entering the heavyweight division.

1982

January 1 • Tokyo, Japan
Tiger Mask def. **Dynamite Kid** in a match to crown a new Junior Heavyweight Champion.
Injury forced Tiger Mask to vacate the Title in April 1982.

May 6 • Fukuoka, Japan
Black Tiger def. **Gran Hamada** in a match to crown a new Junior Heavyweight Champion.

May 26 • Osaka, Japan
Tiger Mask def. **Black Tiger**
Injury forced Tiger Mask to vacate the Junior Heavyweight Championship on April 3, 1983.

1983

June 13 • Mexico City, Mexico
Tiger Mask def. **Fishman** in a match to crown a new Junior Heavyweight Champion.
Tiger Mask vacated the Title after retiring in August 1983.

1984

February 7 • Tokyo, Japan
Dynamite Kid def. **The Cobra** in a match to crown a new Junior Heavyweight Champion.
Dynamite Kid vacated the Title in November 1984.

December 28 • New York, NY
The Cobra def. **Black Tiger** in a match to crown a new Junior Heavyweight Champion.

1985

May 20 • Hiroshima, Japan
Hiro Saito def. **The Cobra**

July 20 • Osaka, Japan
The Cobra def. **Hiro Saito**

JUNKYARD DOG
see page 183

JUST JOE

HT	6'4"	WT	252 lbs.
FROM	Toronto, Ontario, Canada		

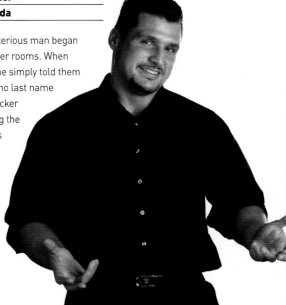

During the latter half of 2000, a mysterious man began to sporadically show up in WWE locker rooms. When Superstars asked him who he was, he simply told them he was Joe, Just Joe. The man with no last name was an unpopular presence in the locker room area. He was known for stirring the pot, always telling people that others were talking trash about them. On the rare occasion that Joe stepped into the ring, he proved to be just as unsuccessful as he was unpopular. He routinely lost to the likes of Essa Rios, Steve Blackman, and even Brooklyn Brawler. By 2001, Joe had quietly disappeared from WWE.

JUNKYARD DOG

HT	6'3"
WT	280 lbs.
FROM	Charlotte, North Carolina

SIGNATURE MOVE
Powerslam

Today, the WWE Universe recognizes Junkyard Dog as the nearly 300-pound powerhouse who used his incomparable charisma and amazing athleticism to achieve Hall of Fame greatness. Decades after his time in the spotlight, it's hard to imagine JYD being anything but the accomplished Superstar he became, but in reality, it once seemed the mighty North Carolinian was destined for a career on the football field.

A two-time Honorable Mention All-American at Fayetteville State University, JYD went on to have ties with both the Green Bay Packers and Houston Oilers following graduation. Luckily for sports-entertainment fans, he ultimately ended his football career to focus on a career in the ring. Dog's earliest days were spent mainly in Tennessee and Calgary, where he claimed Stampede Wrestling's North American Heavyweight Championship on two occasions. But it wasn't until he debuted in the Mid-South territory in the early 1980s that he truly started to turn heads as a main event player.

JYD's popularity at the time rivaled that of any other competitor in the United States. But while fans loved to cheer him, the Fabulous Freebirds couldn't stand the Dog. And to prove their disdain, the Freebirds eventually threw hair products in his face, leaving JYD temporarily blinded. As a result of the attack, Junkyard Dog was unable to see the earliest days of his baby daughter's life. But the disability didn't stop JYD from exacting revenge on the Freebirds when he defeated Michael Hayes in a Dog Collar Match inside the Superdome in Louisiana. In subsequent years, the dog collar would go on to become synonymous with Junkyard Dog, who wore the chain around his neck each time he entered the ring.

WWE STARDOM

Seeking the national spotlight, Junkyard Dog jumped to WWE in 1984 and became an instant star. He had his own action figures, T-shirts, and posters. He even sang his own popular entrance theme, "Grab Them Cakes." More importantly, however, he continued to prove himself as a force inside the ring. With his rolling headbutt and patented powerslam, fans and opponents alike knew that JYD's bite was just as bad as his bark.

among the first WWE Superstars to experience the wrath of the Dog. In fact, JYD's prowess was so great that when Valentine defended his Intercontinental Championship against him at the first-ever *WrestleMania*, The Hammer chose to take the countout loss rather than stay in the ring and continue to battle the Dog.

One of Junkyard Dog's brightest moments came in November 1985, when he defeated Randy "Macho Man" Savage in the finals of a 16-Superstar tournament at *The Wrestling Classic* pay-per-view event. In previous rounds, JYD defeated Iron Sheik and Moondog Spot before receiving a bye in the semi-finals.

Following the tournament, Junkyard Dog teamed with Tito Santana to unsuccessfully challenge Terry and Hoss Funk at *WrestleMania 2*. He later went on to engage in a bitter rivalry with "King" Harley Race, who took exception to JYD's refusal to bow to him. Their conflict culminated at *WrestleMania III*, when Race used a distraction from Bobby Heenan to overcome the Dog. Pre-match stipulations required JYD to bow to Race, which he reluctantly did. But afterward, the Dog attacked the King before leaving the ring with his royal robe.

WWE and Junkyard Dog parted ways in late 1988. In subsequent years, he went on to compete for rival WCW where he regularly battled the likes of Ric Flair, Arn Anderson, and Iron Sheik. He also captured the short-lived WCW World Six-Man Tag Team Championship, teaming with Ricky Morton and Tommy Rich to defeat Dutch Mantel, Buddy Landel, and Dr. X in February 1991.

Junkyard Dog's years of excellence were ultimately recognized on the eve of *WrestleMania XX* when he was inducted into the WWE Hall of Fame.

Tragically, while travelling from his daughter's high school graduation in June 1998, Junkyard Dog was involved in a single-car accident that claimed his life at the age of 45. Though gone, he will forever be remembered as the charismatic competitor that continually captured the imaginations of fans of all ages, races, and religions.

I'M LIVE AND IN SURE ENOUGH LIVING COLOR.

JUSTIN "HAWK" BRADSHAW

HT	6'6"	WT	309 lbs.	FROM	Roscoe, Texas
SIGNATURE MOVE	Lariat Clothesline				

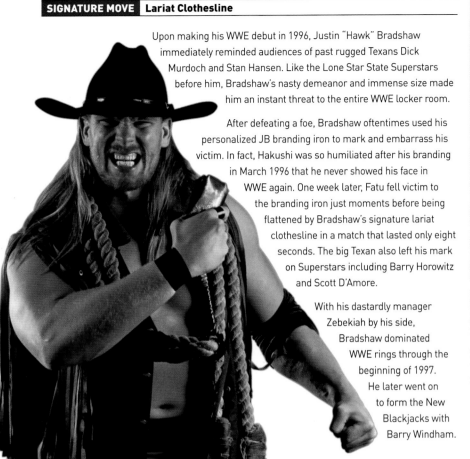

Upon making his WWE debut in 1996, Justin "Hawk" Bradshaw immediately reminded audiences of past rugged Texans Dick Murdoch and Stan Hansen. Like the Lone Star State Superstars before him, Bradshaw's nasty demeanor and immense size made him an instant threat to the entire WWE locker room.

After defeating a foe, Bradshaw oftentimes used his personalized JB branding iron to mark and embarrass his victim. In fact, Hakushi was so humiliated after his branding in March 1996 that he never showed his face in WWE again. One week later, Fatu fell victim to the branding iron just moments before being flattened by Bradshaw's signature lariat clothesline in a match that lasted only eight seconds. The big Texan also left his mark on Superstars including Barry Horowitz and Scott D'Amore.

With his dastardly manager Zebekiah by his side, Bradshaw dominated WWE rings through the beginning of 1997. He later went on to form the New Blackjacks with Barry Windham.

JUSTIN GABRIEL

HT	6'1"	WT	213 lbs.	FROM	Cape Town, South Africa
SIGNATURE MOVE	450 Splash				

Handsome yet deceptively dangerous, Justin Gabriel used a repertoire in WWE that blended lightning-fast speed with amazing aerial skills.

The South African Superstar was an original member of Nexus along with his fellow *NXT* season one classmates. His amazing 450 Splash often served as the final death knell for targets of the renegade faction's attacks. Gabriel, Wade Barrett, and Heath Slater later formed a splinter faction called The Corre. As members of the new group, Gabriel and Slater won the latter two of their three WWE Tag Titles.

In 2012, Gabriel paired with another former Tag Team Champion, Tyson Kidd. The two athletic dynamos brought energy and technical prowess to the tag ranks but failed to capture gold. In 2014, Kidd and Gabriel reunited on *NXT*. Showing a new villainous side, they handed Sami Zayn a post-match beat down. After several battles against Zayn, Rusev and others, Justin Gabriel was released from WWE.

JUSTIN CREDIBLE

HT	6'0"	WT	225 lbs.	FROM	Ozone Park, New York
SIGNATURE MOVE	That's Incredible				

This ego-maniac came to the original ECW with a chip on his shoulder and a Singapore cane in his hand. His finishing maneuver, "That's Incredible" was a spinning Tombstone Piledriver that planted his opponent's head on the mat and brought him much success in sports-entertainment. He formed "The Impact Players" with Lance Storm and proceeded to hold multiple titles in ECW.

His most incredible achievement came at *Cyberslam 2000*. After ECW heart and soul Tommy Dreamer finally won his first ECW Championship, Dreamer accepted Justin's challenge to defend the Title right there on the spot. Like a Money in the Bank cash-in moment, Credible spoiled Dreamer's glory and won the gold for himself.

After joining WWE, Justin Credible became a member of X-Factor, then joined the ECW/WCW Alliance. Before he left the company in 2003, he was able to capture the Hardcore Championship on several, albeit brief, occasions. Justin returned to WWE in 2006 as part of the new ECW and tangled with CM Punk before parting ways with the company that September.

JUSTIN ROBERTS

As a child growing up in the Windy City, Justin Roberts loved watching WWE and dreamed of one day being under those bright lights himself. When he was 16, Justin started working for local wrestling events and became comfortable in front of various size crowds. After graduating from the University of Arizona, Roberts auditioned for WWE and began his sports-entertainment career in 2002, filling in during *Raw* and *SmackDown* events. Two years later, he became a full-time member of WWE.

Roberts developed an impressive body of work during his time with WWE, heralding the returns of both The Rock and Bret "Hit Man" Hart to WWE. His resilience was tested in June 2010 when he fell victim to a vicious Nexus attack. Roberts dusted himself off and continued to live his dream, earning the nod to introduce the action at *WrestleMania XXVII*. Justin has tied his voice to several watershed moments in WWE history including Brock Lesnar's conquering of Undertaker's Streak at *WrestleMania 30*. Roberts left WWE in October of 2014.

KAIENTAI

MEMBERS	Taka Michinoku, Funaki, Mens Teioh, Dick Togo, & Yamaguchi-San
FROM	Japan

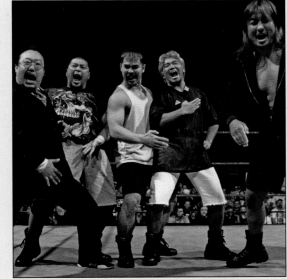

Funaki, Mens Teioh, and Dick Togo were first introduced to American audiences when they attacked Taka Michinoku in March 1998. Managed by Yamaguchi-San, the group known as Kaientai wowed fans with their rapid-fire offensive onslaught.

Shortly after Kaientai's debut, it was revealed that Yamaguchi-San's wife was having an affair with Val Venis. This lead to one of the most infamous moments in WWE history, as Yamaguchi-San violently threatened Venis' livelihood with a sword.

The following week, Venis tagged with Michinoku to battle Kaientai. During the match, however, Michinoku turned on his partner and helped Yamaguchi attempt to make good on his promise. Luckily for Venis, Yamaguchi-San's aim wasn't very good.

With Michinoku in the fold, Kaientai became even more dangerous. Unfortunately, the promising Japanese faction didn't last long as Teioh, Togo, and Yamaguchi-San left WWE in late 1998.

As the sole remaining members, Michinoku and Funaki remained a tag team, wasting little time showing WWE audiences the true meaning of "EEEEEVVIIIL." With a sloppy English translation blaring over the loudspeakers, the duo's diatribes were reminiscent of Japanese monster movies. The WWE Universe caught on and soon their signature sign off, "INDEED!" became one of WWE's popular catchphrases. With newfound crowd support, the pared down version of Kaientai lasted until 2001. Michinoku went back to Japan, where he now runs a wrestling school. Funaki became *SmackDown's* #1 Announcer and later won the WWE Cruiserweight Championship.

KAITLYN

HT	5'6"	**FROM**	Houston, Texas
SIGNATURE MOVE	Spear		

Despite being a last-minute replacement, the stunning and spunky Kaitlyn shined on *NXT* season three. After three months of grueling competition, the beautiful Texas native was announced as WWE's next breakout Diva.

Signed to a *SmackDown* contract by Theodore Long, Kaitlyn partnered with AJ Lee to form a popular tag team called The Chickbusters. After their friendship soured, Kaitlyn turned her sights on becoming Divas Champion.

Building a reputation as a "Hybrid Diva," a combination of strength and glamour, Kaitlyn appeared to be headed toward her goal when a backstage attacked derailed her momemtum. Undettered, Kaityn recuperated and topped Eve on *Raw*'s 20th Anniversary to claim the WWE Diva's Championship gold in front of her hometown. She enjoyed a five month reign until her former friend AJ got the best of her at *Payback 2013*.

Kaitlyn held her head high despite the defeat and AJ's heartless personal attacks, earning the adoration of the WWE Universe. Though she is now pursuing other interests, Kaitlyn's quirky personality and in-ring prowess are fondly remembered.

KALISTO

HT	5'6"	**WT**	170 lbs.	**FROM**	Mexico City
SIGNATURE MOVE	Salida Del Sol				

That neon streak of light blazing through the night air is Kalisto. An accomplished lucha libre star in his native Mexico, this speedster first began wowing the WWE Universe as part of NXT. While there, he formed the Lucha Dragons with veteran high-flyer Sin Cara. This daring duo was responsible for ending the dominant NXT Tag Team Championship reign of The Ascension.

"The King of Flight" soon soared to WWE's main roster, where his blistering pace continues to baffle the competition. Careening from rope to rope like a pinball with legs and contorting himself at impossible angles, this masked wonder has proven dangerous in both tag team and singles ranks. In 2016, he felled his countryman Alberto Del Rio twice for the United States Championship and showed the 290-pound Ryback that "Big Guys" come in all sizes.

KAMA MUSTAFA

HT	6'6"	**WT**	320 lbs.
SIGNATURE MOVE	Turning Side Slam		

Originally known as the "Supreme Fighting Machine," Kama was an enforcer for Ted DiBiase's Million Dollar Corporation. His most infamous act came at *WrestleMania XI* where Kama stole The Deadman's mystical urn and later had it melted down into a necklace. Undertaker reaped his revenge in a Casket Match at *SummerSlam 1995*. In early 1997, Kama became a member of the Nation of Domination where his vicious fighting style aided the Nation in their battles against the Legion of Doom, Ken Shamrock, Ahmed Johnson, Disciples of the Apocalypse, Los Boriquas, and D-Generation X.

During 1998, the Nation of Domination dissolved while Kama became consumed with his new persona. Kama parted ways with the militant faction and eventually mastered the fine art of pimpin' as The Godfather.

KAMALA

| HT | 6'7" | WT | 380 lbs. | FROM | Uganda |

| SIGNATURE MOVE | Big Splash |

Hailing from the Ugandan jungle and tipping the scales at nearly 400 pounds, Kamala is regularly recognized as one of history's most frightening Superstars. But, believe it or not, his overwhelming size may not have been his scariest trait. Some Superstars are on record saying they feared not knowing what his simple mind was thinking more than anything else.

Kamala's pre-WWE days saw him terrorize the Memphis, Mid-South, and Dallas territories. His limited intellect prevented him from properly communicating with those around him. Instead, the Ugandan Giant let his savage beatings do the talking for him. This was something many of the all-time best competitors painfully experienced firsthand, including Jerry Lawler, Bruiser Brody, and the Von Erichs.

With an impressive list of victims to his credit, Kamala entered WWE in 1984, spending the next few years making short work of the likes of Steve Lombardi, Lanny Poffo, and Tony Garea. His dominance eventually led to a series of WWE Championship opportunities against Hulk Hogan in 1986 and 1987.

After failing to capture the gold, Kamala traveled back to the dark jungles of Uganda, only to return to WWE in 1992. With handler Kim Chee and manager Harvey Wippleman leading the way, Kamala set out to take down Undertaker. The two giants squared off in a memorable series of matches, most notably WWE's first-ever Casket Match (known then as a Coffin Match) at *Survivor Series 1992*.

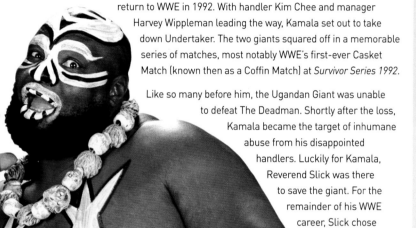

Like so many before him, the Ugandan Giant was unable to defeat The Deadman. Shortly after the loss, Kamala became the target of inhumane abuse from his disappointed handlers. Luckily for Kamala, Reverend Slick was there to save the giant. For the remainder of his WWE career, Slick chose to treat Kamala as more man than savage. Unfortunately, the new approach didn't result in many wins. Among those who defeated Kamala in 1993 include Doink, Yokozuna, and Shawn Michaels.

KARL ANDERSON

| HT | 6' 0.5" | WT | 241 lbs. |

| SIGNATURE MOVE | Magic Killer |

Known throughout the world as "The Machine Gun," Karl Anderson arrived in WWE in April of 2016 alongside his bruising tag team partner, Luke Gallows. Anderson is best known for his time in Japan where he was a feared competitor in the country's largest sports-entertainment promotion, New Japan.

Anderson and Gallows attacked The Usos as an opening salvo to the WWE tag team division. Since then, they have competed as "The Club," hoping to build on the success they saw in The Land of the Rising Sun, where they held the IWGP Tag Team Championship. Anderson and The Club have already orchestrated attacks on The New Day, John Cena, and other top stars in their short WWE tenure, proving to be one of the most dangerous additions to WWE in a long time.

KANE

see page 188

KANYON

| HT | 6'4" | WT | 245 lbs. | FROM | Queens, New York |

| SIGNATURE MOVE | The Flatliner |

"Who's better than Kanyon?"

Don't answer that. It's the rhetorical question that the confident Kanyon often asked before his matches. Of course, his arrogance rubbed many fans the wrong way. But in Kanyon's mind, he had every right to brag.

Kanyon won the WCW World Tag Team Championship with fellow Jersey Triad members, Diamond Dallas Page and Bam Bam Bigelow, in June 1999, defending the titles using the "Freebird Rule." He was also known for helping celebrities such as Dennis Rodman and Karl Malone prepare themselves for the ring. After his successful WCW career, Kanyon helped his fellow WCW alums invade WWE in 2001 as a member of The Alliance. Shortly after his debut, Kanyon was handed the United States Championship by then-champ and fellow Alliance member, Booker T. Despite not winning the Title in an athletic contest, Kanyon quickly anointed himself the "Alliance MVP."

Kanyon added more gold to his trophy case when he reunited with DDP to defeat the APA for the World Tag Team Championship in August 2001.

After The Alliance was turned aside, Kanyon competed mainly on *Velocity* before being released in early 2004.

KARL GOTCH

| HT | 6'1" | WT | 245 lbs. |

| FROM | Hamburg, Germany |

In Japan, Karl Gotch is known as "Kamisama," or "God of Wrestling," a tribute to his time not only competing there, but teaching submissions to some of the country's most heralded grapplers.

Born in Belgium but raised in Germany, Gotch was in a concentration camp during World War II. By 1948, he had recovered from the ordeal and represented Belgium in the Olympics. He spent his early pro years competing in Europe. In India, he learned native martial arts, enabling him to coach future students on Hindu squats and other training techniques.

In 1959, Gotch began competing in the United States, where he's credited with popularizing the German suplex. Although he and multiple-time NWA Champion Lou Thesz were adversaries in the ring, they greatly respected one another.

Gotch's WWE career was fleeting, but did result in a Championship reign. In December 1971, he teamed with Rene Goulet to snare the WWE World Tag Team Championship from "Crazy" Luke Graham and Tarzan Tyler.

He died in his adopted city of Tampa in 2007.

KARL VON HESS

HT	5'10"	WT	220 lbs.	FROM	Germany
SIGNATURE MOVE	The Claw				

During the mid-1950s, this vile Nazi sympathizer nearly caused riots wherever he appeared in Vincent J. McMahon's Capitol Wrestling territory. This incredible physical specimen was resoundingly booed as he battled the best Superstars of the era, including "Golden Boy" Arnold Skaaland and Antonino "Argentina" Rocca.

Von Hess quickly became known as the worst type of villain and reminded audiences of a darker period of the world's history. By the late 1960s he left the world of sports-entertainment to the joy of all who saw him compete, or fell victim to his brutal attacks.

He then settled in New Jersey, where he renounced his past and embraced the American way of life. He died in 2009.

KATIE LEA BURCHILL

FROM	Chelsea, England

As the little sister to Paul Burchill, Katie Lea loved nothing more than to see her "most brutal, most vicious, most beautiful" brother destroy his competition. In fact, the sinister sibling became inexplicably happy when her brother Paul inflicted pain on opponents.

In the ring, Katie Lea was no stranger to handing out her own form of punishment, battling both men and women. During her WWE career, "The Beautiful Nightmare" faced off against opponents like The Bellas, Eve Torres, Mickie James, and Kelly Kelly.

Katie Lea's closest brush with the Women's Championship came in a match against Mickie James at Night of Champions 2008. After making some scandalous insinuations about Mickie's path to success, she was ultimately unsuccessful in challenging James for the Title. She left WWE in April 2010.

KAVAL

HT	5'8"	WT	174 lbs.	FROM	Brooklyn, New York
SIGNATURE MOVE	The Warrior's Way				

Known as Low Ki throughout the world, this no-nonsense Superstar competed for twelve years before coming to WWE under the name Kaval in 2010. His all-business demeanor could not have clashed more with Lay-Cool, his outspoken WWE mentors, but that did not stop the Internet sensation from winning NXT Season 2.

Following NXT, Kaval began his quest to become WWE's next breakout star while competing on SmackDown. It took over two months for Kaval to pick up that elusive first victory in a November match with Dolph Ziggler. Looking to maintain the momentum, he decided to cash in the Title opportunity he earned by winning NXT. At Survivor Series 2010, he challenged Ziggler for the Intercontinental Championship but came up short. Soon after failing to capitalize on his momentum, Kaval left WWE.

KC JAMES AND IDOL STEVENS

MEMBERS	KC James & Idol Stevens	COMBINED WT	470 lbs.

For a few months in 2006, KC James & Idol Stevens were the hottest tag team on SmackDown. Managed by Michelle McCool, the young tandem defeated Scotty 2 Hotty and Funaki in their August debut. The momentum of their initial victory carried James and Stevens to a shocking non-title win over WWE Tag Team Champions Paul London and Brian Kendrick a few days later.

With this impressive victory to their credit, James and Stevens became an overnight success. Over the next few weeks, their wins started to mount up and at No Mercy 2006, James and Stevens were awarded an opportunity at London and Kendrick's Titles. After coming up short in their attempt to claim the gold, the duo disappeared just as quickly as they had exploded onto the scene.

KELLY KELLY

	DIVAS	HT	5'5"	FROM	Jacksonville, Florida

Kelly Kelly gained instant popularity in 2006 with her risqué "Kelly's Exposé" segments, much to the chagrin of her short-lived boyfriend, Mike Knox. The beautiful blonde's exhibitions soon blossomed into Extreme Exposé, a dancing trio that also included Layla and Brooke.

Determined to prove she was equal parts guts and glamour, Kelly broke out as a competitor in 2011. On June 20th she defeated Brie Bella for her first WWE Divas Championship, That same year, she was voted #82 in Maxim's Top 100 list and graced the cover of Maxim's December issue. With looks and momentum approaching maximum hotness, she aligned with NBC Extra host Maria Menounos to topple Beth Phoenix and Eve at WrestleMania XXVIII. Months later, Kelly Kelly broke hearts by departing WWE.

Kelly was one of the most adored Divas of her generation, and her WWE accomplishments were achieved before the age of 26. Wherever she chooses to go next, Kelly Kelly is sure to be "so nice you have to say it twice."

KANE

HT	7'0"
WT	323 lbs.
FROM	Parts Unknown

SIGNATURE MOVE
Chokeslam, Tombstone Piledriver

No Superstar's road through WWE has been wrought with as many dark twists and turns as Kane's. "The Big Red Monster" had to overcome physical deformity, emotional scarring, and the inability to speak just to reach WWE. Twenty years later, his actions still jump from heroic to villainous as his tortured psyche struggles to keep his inner demons at bay.

BIG RED DEBUT

Throughout 1997, Paul Bearer provided frightening descriptions and dire predictions that Undertaker's half-brother, long thought dead, was on his way to exact his revenge. For years, "The Phenom" thought Kane had perished in a fire that also claimed the lives of Undertaker's mother and father. Audiences first laid eyes on the masked Kane at *Badd Blood 1997* where he tore off the Hell in a Cell door to confront Undertaker. After a brief standoff, Kane used a crushing Tombstone Piledriver and left Undertaker unconscious in the ring.

While Undertaker initially refused to fight his own flesh and blood, the brothers met at *WrestleMania XIV*. The match marked the first sordid chapter of their endlessly reoccurring sibling rivalry. Among the many grisly stipulations attached to many of their encounters, the Inferno Match hit closest to home, as Kane was set ablaze and forced to relive the horrors of his childhood.

NEWFOUND ALLIES AND THE BROTHERS OF DESTRUCTION

Kane is one of the most prolific tag team competitors in WWE history beginning with his WWE Tag Team Championhip run with Mankind. He has also won Titles with X-Pac, Big Show, The Hurricane, Rob Van Dam, Daniel Bryan, and of course, Undertaker. While successful, most of Kane's partnerships fell into one of two categories— volatile or bizarre.

X-Pac took Kane down an unfamiliar path in 1999, that of a fan favorite. He even found his first love in Tori, and the world heard him speak without the aid of a voicebox. The duo held the World Tag Team Championship twice, but the partnership dissolved when X-Pac and Tori turned on Kane. Kane managed to get a measure of revenge at *WrestleMania 2000*.

For Undertaker and Kane, time has both healed the wounds of their past and also ripped them open again fresh again. The warring brothers occasionally find it within themselves to operate together when they aren't trying to destroy each other.

Teaming up as The Brothers of Destruction, they captured the World Tag Team Championship twice. They even jointly held the WWE and WCW tag team crowns during the 2001 Alliance Invasion and are nearly unstoppable when the wounds of the past don't drive them apart.

THE MASK OF KANE

The horrific fire from Kane's childhood caused him to hide behind a mysterious red and black mask. Kane used the mask as a psychological crutch, suppressing his pain, and hiding from the ridicule of others. However, after losing a World Championship vs. Mask match against Triple H, the "Big Red Monster" was forced to remove his mask and face the world. No longer hiding behind the mask, Kane proved to be more emotionally unstable. The troubled Superstar went on a rampage, highlighted by setting Jim Ross on fire, delivering a Tombstone Piledriver to then-WWE CEO Linda McMahon, electrocuting Shane McMahon, and rekindling his violent rivalry with Undertaker by burying his brother alive at *Survivor Series 2003*. The act only served to resurrect The Deadman, but a second *WrestleMania* defeat at Undertaker's hands did nothing to quell Kane's appetite for atrocities. That summer, he forced Lita to join him in unholy matrimony.

In the ring, Kane remained equally destructive while fighting off the challenge of an imposter in 2006, spreading fear and darkness on *SmackDown*, and winning the ECW Championship in record time at *WrestleMania XXIV*. Kane has competed in a few Money in the Bank Ladder Matches, but his victory at the 2010 edition allowed him to defeat Rey Mysterio later that same night to claim the World Heavyweight Championship.

During this time, mystery swirled as to the culprit of an attack that left Undertaker in a vegetative state. After weeks of casting false accusations, it was revealed that Kane himself was responsible. The brothers' rekindled animosity brought Paul Bearer to the fore. After Bearer sided with Kane, he made a second attempt to end his brother at *Bragging Rights 2010*.

Late in 2011, chilling vignettes aired around the world, heralding the return of a masked Kane. Now known as "The Devil's Favorite Demon," Kane made sadistic attempts to provoke an inner demon inside John Cena's psyche. When this proved futile, he targeted Randy Orton and beat "The Apex Predator" at *WrestleMania XXVIII*.

TEAM HELL NO

Remasked and revitalized, Kane fiery swath of wreckage burned at scorching new levels. In an attempt to harness his rage, *Raw* General Manager AJ Lee enrolled him in anger management classes alongside his most recent foil, Daniel Bryan. Through an unwilling partnership prescribed by their therapist, Dr. Shelby, not only did the temperamental tandem manage to "hug it out," they won the WWE Tag Team Championships at *Night of Champions 2012*.

I AM THE NIGHTMARE THAT YOU WILL NEVER WAKE UP FROM.

While their bickering only intensified, it failed to divide them. Instead, they unleashed their combined fury on WWE's tag team division. They held the gold for 245 days, which included a win at *WrestleMania 29*.

BEST FOR BUSINESS

After being carried away from a Ring of Fire Match by the spooky Wyatt Family at *SummerSlam 2013*, Kane began to undergo a change. When he returned months later, he handed over his demonic mask to Stephanie McMahon and became part of The Authority. Though clad in his signature colors, a black office suit and red tie hardly resembled the monster fans had grown accustomed to. Corporate Kane was something worse than a monster—an executive.

As WWE's Director of Operations, the now buttoned up Kane carried out the decisions of the WWE brass, no matter how unscrupulous. He helped protect The Authority's valuable assets such as Randy Orton and Seth Rollins while terrorizing several fan favorites, including former partner Daniel Bryan.

Later in 2015, as Seth Rollins petulance and his overbearing bosses began to wear on his nerves, an interesting phenomenon began. One moment, fans witnessed Corporate Kane towing the company line. Then the next, his classic Demon Kane persona emerged seemingly transported from the pits of hell. Despite his suited doppelganger's denial of any involvement, his visage dragging Rollins to his doom under the ring and doling out Tombstones was unmistakable.

This return to the dark side allowed Kane to once again find common ground with Undertaker. He stood by his brother to battle The Wyatt Family at *Survivor Series 2015* and still endeavors to rid WWE of this troublesome flock. Demon Kane was the last Superstar eliminated from the 2016 Andre the Giant Memorial Battle Royal, proving his fire is still as scalding as it was twenty years ago.

Whether in the boardroom or standing next to the devil himself, Kane is the most frightening figure in the room. There is no telling what type of carnage he has in store as he approaches his third decade in sports-entertainment.

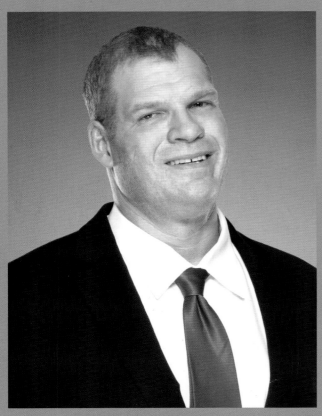

KEN PATERA

HT	6'1"	WT	267 lbs.	FROM	Portland, Oregon
SIGNATURE MOVE		**Full Nelson**			

Ken Patera was a world-class powerlifter who won four gold medals at the 1971 Pan-Am Games and a bronze medal at the 1972 Olympics. After training with Verne Gagne, Patera debuted for the AWA in 1973 and quickly became one of its most dangerous rule-breakers.

Patera came to WWE in 1977 and stalked then-Champion Bruno Sammartino. That year, he also competed in several of the World's Strongest Man Competitions, and ended the career of Chief Billy White Wolf with his swinging neckbreaker. As a result, Patera was voted "Most Hated Wrestler" by *Pro Wrestling Illustrated*.

But nothing seemed to deter his success. In 1980, he defeated Pat Patterson to become the second Intercontinental Champion—at the same time that he held the prestigious Missouri Title in the NWA.

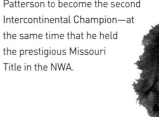

After a hiatus from WWE, he returned in 1987 with a new attitude, determined to rid WWE of his former manager, Bobby Heenan. In response, Heenan unleashed his charges, Harley Race, Hercules, King Kong Bundy, and Paul Orndorff. Patera held his own, but left WWE shortly afterward.

Ken Patera will always be remembered as one of sports-entertainment's most decorated and powerful performers. Whether a dastardly rule-breaker or determined American hero, he entertained fans everywhere.

KEN RESNICK

While doing local sports for a Minnesota television station, Ken Resnick conducted countless interviews. But there was one in late 1983 that would change his life forever.

While working a celebrity golf tournament, Ken Resnick interviewed AWA owner Verne Gagne. The timing couldn't have been more perfect. With Mean Gene Okerlund leaving the AWA for WWE, Gagne was looking for a new announcer. And shortly after meeting Resnick, Gagne offered him the job.

Resnick spent the next two years interviewing AWA's best and brightest, including The Crusher, Sgt. Slaughter, and Curt Hennig.

Following AWA's *WrestleRock* in April 1986, Resnick took his interviewing skills to WWE, where he asked his hard-hitting questions to the likes of Hulk Hogan, Iron Sheik, and Junkyard Dog.

KEN SHAMROCK

HT	6'1"	WT	243 lbs.	FROM	Sacramento, California
SIGNATURE MOVE	Ankle Lock				

Competing in the world of mixed martial arts does not always translate to success in WWE. However, "The World's Most Dangerous Man," Ken Shamrock proved that it could be done.

Having established himself as a pioneer and legend in UFC, Shamrock joined WWE in 1997, seeking a new challenge. Shamrock's first role in WWE was that of special guest referee for Stone Cold Steve Austin's epic "I Quit" Match against Bret "Hit Man" Hart at *WrestleMania 13*. Following *WrestleMania*, Shamrock made his own in-ring debut, destroying Vernon White. The convincing victory showed the WWE Universe that the MMA legend was a legitimate threat in WWE.

In June 1998, Shamrock achieved his first major WWE accolade when he defeated The Rock to win the prestigious King of the Ring tournament. Later that year, he used the Ankle Lock to breeze through yet another tournament. This time, the prize was the coveted Intercontinental Championship. Shamrock later teamed with fellow Corporation member Big Boss Man to claim the World Tag Team Championships.

After less than three years in WWE, Shamrock left to restart his MMA career. While his sports-entertainment tenure was brief, it proved memorable. His temper instilled fear in his opponents and was often uncontrollable. So intense was Shamrock that he inspired WWE to introduce the Lion's Den Match, Iron Circle Match, and other fierce stipulations into their repertoire.

KENNY DYKSTRA

HT	6'4"	WT	240 lbs.
FROM	Worcester, Massachusetts		
SIGNATURE MOVE	Guillotine Leg Drop		

This gifted Superstar first appeared in WWE in 2005 as a member of the golden quintet known as the Spirit Squad. Brazen on the mic and versatile in the ring, Kenny wasted no time making his mark against Ric Flair, Jeff Hardy, Rey Mysterio, and others. The night after *WrestleMania 22*, Kenny and Mikey shocked the sports-entertainment world when they beat Big Show and Kane and became World Tag Team Champions. After a lengthy seven-month reign, they ultimately lost to the legendary team of "Nature Boy" Ric Flair and "Rowdy" Roddy Piper.

During the 2007 Supplemental Draft, Kenny was sent to *SmackDown* and gave the program one of WWE's brashest young Superstars. He competed on the blue brand until he parted ways with WWE in late 2008.

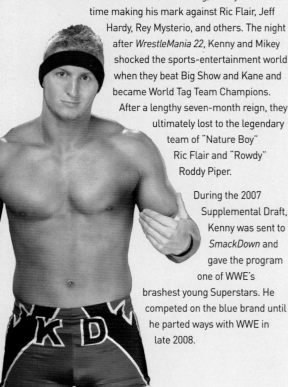

THE KENTUCKIANS

MEMBERS	Grizzly Smith & Luke Brown
COMBINED WT	620 lbs.

These good old boys from Kentucky brought a different style to WWE when they arrived in 1964. Grizzly Smith and Luke Brown were a colorful pair who inspired fans to jump to their feet in battles with Eddie and "The Good Doctor" Jerry Graham, Hans and Max Mortier, Magnificent Maurice and Professor Boris Malenko, and Killer Kowalski and Gorilla

Monsoon. The team from the Blue Grass State went on to hold numerous championships in NWA territories around the United States.

The Kentuckians are remembered as one of the most beloved tag teams in sports-entertainment history. Despite the cultural difference between Appalachia and the northeastern United States, Grizzly Smith and Luke Brown were popular figures in the early days of WWE.

KENZO SUZUKI

HT	6'3"	WT	250 lbs.
FROM	The Land of the Rising Sun		
SIGNATURE MOVE	Claw Leg Sweep		

Alongside his geisha valet, Hiroko, Kenzo Suzuki debuted in June 2004. Claiming to be fueled by hate and a hunger for redemption, the new Superstar from the "Land of the Rising Sun" debuted with impressive wins over Scotty 2 Hotty, Billy Gunn, and Spike Dudley.

Teaming with Rene Dupree, Suzuki's serious side faded, but his aggression did not. The duo captured the WWE Tag Team Championship in September 2004.

Suzuki tried to make amends with fans by claiming he loved the United States. He even loved its women, particularly Torrie Wilson. However, this love affair with America was short-lived as Suzuki left WWE in 2005.

KERRY VON ERICH

HT 6'2"	**WT** 254 lbs. **FROM** Denton, Texas
SIGNATURE MOVE	The Claw, Discus Punch

Years before ever competing in his first WWE match, the "Texas Tornado" Kerry Von Erich was an international icon, holding more than 30 titles in various promotions.

For much of his childhood, Kerry travelled with his family, watching his father, Fritz Von Erich, compete. In 1979, Kerry made his debut, competing against Paul Perschmann, later known as "Playboy" Buddy Rose. Because of his granite physique, Kerry was labeled the "Modern Day Warrior," facing a range of opponents including Ernie "The Cat" Ladd, King Kong Bundy, Gino Hernandez, the Masked Superstar, and the NWA Champion at the time, Harley Race. Within two years of his first match, Kerry, alongside brothers David and Kevin, was the main draw of World Class Championship Wrestling.

In 1982, "Nature Boy" Ric Flair came to World Class to put up his NWA World Heavyweight Championship against the sensation. In a thrilling match at the Reunion Arena, the pair fought to a two-out-of-three fall double disqualification and Flair escaped with his Championship. Due to popular demand, Flair returned to World Class on Christmas night to again defend his Title against Kerry in a steel cage. Kerry wanted a referee who could rule with authority, and asked the fans to vote on a candidate. Overwhelmingly, Kerry's supporters chose future WWE Hall of Famer Michael Hayes of the Fabulous Freebirds. When the battle intensified, Hayes inserted himself on Kerry's behalf, flooring the "Nature Boy." Kerry was not willing to win the prestigious Title by cheating, and reprimanded Hayes for his lack of sportsmanship. This prompted Gordy, to slam the cage door on Kerry's head, costing him the Championship. For the next five years, the Freebirds and Von Erichs engaged in a bitter rivalry.

After David Von Erich died, Kerry proclaimed that he wanted to win the NWA Title to honor his late brother. On May 6, 1984, Kerry accomplished his dream in the main event of the *David Von Erich Memorial Parade of Champions*, besting Flair. The reign only lasted 18 days before Flair reclaimed the Championship. For much of the next year, Kerry attempted to win back the gold, frequently leaving the World Class territory in pursuit of Flair, but Von Erich was unable to repeat history.

In 1986, Fritz Von Erich reclassified the World Class Title as a world championship. Kerry shifted much of his focus to pursuing the crown, toppling "Iceman" King Parsons for the prize in 1988. The World Class Heavyweight Championship was not held in the same regard as the WWE or NWA Titles. In an effort to alter this perception, Kerry challenged AWA World Heavyweight Champion Jerry "The King" Lawler in a winner-take-all battle. At the AWA's *Superclash III* pay-per-view, Lawler bloodied Kerry, but the Modern Day Warrior fought back and trapped "The King" in the Iron Claw. Just as Lawler was about to submit, the referee examined Kerry's cuts and stopped the match. Lawler was awarded both Titles.

When he made his WWE debut in July 1990, Von Erich's powerful past earning him the moniker the "Texas Tornado." Interestingly, his first WWE adversary was "Playboy" Buddy Rose, the man he'd faced in his professional debut. He used his family's famed claw, coupled with a devastating discus punch, to tear through the WWE roster. His impact earned him an Intercontinental Championship opportunity less than one month into his WWE tenure. He capitalized on this chance, defeating Mr. Perfect for the Title at *SummerSlam*.

That November, Kerry and the Ultimate Warrior joined with the Legion of Doom to form arguably the most potent *Survivor Series* team ever. Although the squad triumphed, Kerry's elimination by Mr. Perfect was a bad omen. Three months after winning the Intercontinental Championship, Von Erich lost the Title to the former Champion. The defeat didn't deter him though, as he spent the next two years competing on some of the biggest cards of the time, including *WrestleMania VII*.

Sadly, Kerry had a complicated life outside of the ring, dealing with the grief of losing three of his brothers and enormous pain from a motorcycle crash. His ability to compete after the accident was a testament to his innate toughness. He died in 1993. On April 4, 2009, the Von Erich family's amazing accomplishments were celebrated when their old rival, Michael Hayes, inducted them into the WWE Hall of Fame.

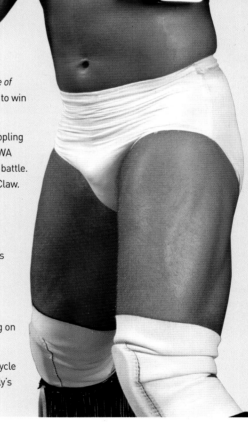

KEVIN KELLY

After earning a degree in communications from Florida State University, longtime fan Kevin Kelly began his journey to WWE by working as a disc jockey and broadcasting independent wrestling. By 1996, he was brought into the WWE fold.

Over the course of his seven-year stay with the company, Kelly held numerous job responsibilities, both in front of and behind the camera. Most fans remember him for his humorous exchanges with The Rock, in which "The Great One" not-so-affectionately dubbed the announcer "Hermie."

In addition to sitting alongside Michael Cole to call the action on Monday nights, Kelly served as a backstage interviewer for *Raw* and *SmackDown*, and worked in talent relations and for WWE's publications.

He departed WWE in 2003, and remains active in sports-entertainment.

KEVIN OWENS

HT	6'0"	WT	266 lbs.	FROM	Marieville, Quebec, Canada

SIGNATURE MOVE	Pop-Up Powerbomb

A prizefighter with years of experience, Kevin Owens established himself as a tough-as-nails competitor while battling the likes of Seth Rollins, Daniel Bryan, and Sami Zayn on the independent scene. In the case of Zayn, their ongoing saga continued when both men made it to the big stage of WWE.

Following Zayn's NXT Championship victory at *NXT TakeOver: R Evolution*, the same night Owens made his NXT debut, Owens emerged to seemingly celebrate with his friend. Though Owens' true intentions were revealed when he viciously assaulted the new Champ.

Owens' attack proved he was less interested in friendship and more concerned with providing for his family and winning championships. It didn't take long for him to do the latter, as Owens claimed the NXT Championship from Zayn just two months later.

Owens' fast-track continued when he defeated John Cena at *Elimination Chamber 2015* after hitting Cena with a Pop-Up Powerbomb. With a win over the Cenation leader, Owens immediately became recognized as one of WWE's top Superstars. Owens' 2015 trilogy with John Cena will go down as one of the best trilogies in WWE history.

Momentum carried Owens into *Night of Champions*, where he defeated Ryback for his first of multiple Intercontinental Championship reigns. Months later, The Prizefighter made headline news when he eliminated AJ Styles from the Royal Rumble Match. The elimination continued to prove that Owens isn't motivated by popularity contests. He just wants to fight!

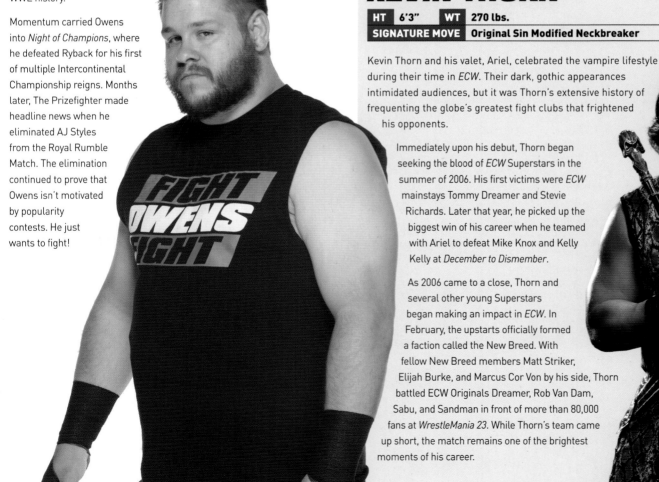

KEVIN SULLIVAN

HT	5'11"	WT	235 lbs.	FROM	Boston, Massachusetts

SIGNATURE MOVE	Spinning Toe Hold

This controversial athlete began his career as a respectable sportsman. In 1972, Kevin Sullivan and Mike Graham won the tag team title in Florida. Two years later, Sullivan migrated to WWE, drawing particularly enthusiastic crowds in his hometown of Boston. Within the next few years, Sullivan would move on to the Georgia, San Francisco, and Memphis territories, then double back to Florida.

Somewhere along the line, he'd undergone a drastic change and become one of the darkest villains to ever grace the mats of the Sunshine State. His opponents, including old partner Mike Graham, Dusty Rhodes, and Barry Windham, described Sullivan as evil incarnate. And they weren't alone. "Purple Haze" Mark Lewin, Bob Roop, and the Fallen Angel were among the members of Sullivan's "Army of Darkness," and claimed to take orders from a mystic being called Abudadeen. Sometimes known as "The Taskmaster," he later appeared in ECW, where he won tag team gold with Tazz. In 1997, he lost a Retirement Match to Chris Benoit in WCW.

KEVIN THORN

HT	6'3"	WT	270 lbs.

SIGNATURE MOVE	Original Sin Modified Neckbreaker

Kevin Thorn and his valet, Ariel, celebrated the vampire lifestyle during their time in *ECW*. Their dark, gothic appearances intimidated audiences, but it was Thorn's extensive history of frequenting the globe's greatest fight clubs that frightened his opponents.

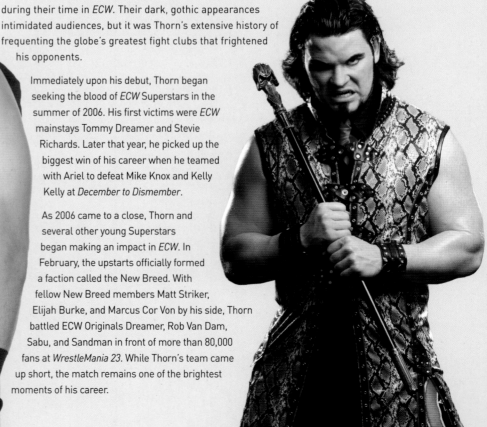

Immediately upon his debut, Thorn began seeking the blood of *ECW* Superstars in the summer of 2006. His first victims were *ECW* mainstays Tommy Dreamer and Stevie Richards. Later that year, he picked up the biggest win of his career when he teamed with Ariel to defeat Mike Knox and Kelly Kelly at *December to Dismember*.

As 2006 came to a close, Thorn and several other young Superstars began making an impact in *ECW*. In February, the upstarts officially formed a faction called the New Breed. With fellow New Breed members Matt Striker, Elijah Burke, and Marcus Cor Von by his side, Thorn battled ECW Originals Dreamer, Rob Van Dam, Sabu, and Sandman in front of more than 80,000 fans at *WrestleMania 23*. While Thorn's team came up short, the match remains one of the brightest moments of his career.

KEY

| HT | 6'4" | WT | 315 lbs. |

Aside from his massive size and all white ring attire, which announcers noted "made him look like an ice cream salesman," very little was known about Key. He debuted in the summer of 1999, aiding Prince Albert and Droz in their *Monday Night Raw* encounter with Val Venis and The Godfather. From there, the threesome formed a mysterious union that some claimed was based on Key pushing Albert and Droz to live an unsavory lifestyle.

Key's stay in WWE was very brief. Prior to leaving the company, he scored a handful of victories, most notably when he teamed with Albert and Droz to topple Anthony McMurphy, Cody Hawk, and Brett Keene in an August 1999 *Shotgun Saturday Night* match.

KHARMA

| HT | 5'11" |

Kharma was not your typical Diva. At nearly 300 pounds, she was a mountain of a woman who provided a terrifying presence in the ring. Once told during a *Tough Enough* audition she was "too fat" to succeed in WWE, Kharma made it her goal to prove her detractors wrong.

She first appeared on WWE television in April 2011. In the lead up to her debut, mysterious videos depicted her sinister laughter as she dismembered pretty little dolls. Without stepping foot in a ring, Kharma sent a chilling message.

Kharma finally debuted at *Extreme Rules 2011* when she brutally attacked Michelle McCool. For the next several weeks, she decimated Maryse, Eve, Layla, and others. While Kharma's reign of terror seemed unstoppable, the Divas locker room breathed a collective sigh of relief when Kharma abruptly left WWE.

KID KASH

| HT | 5'9" | WT | 200 lbs. | FROM | Johnson City, Tennessee |
| SIGNATURE MOVE | Dead Level |

A former ECW Television Champion, Kid Kash jumped to WWE in June 2005. In his debut match, the cruiserweight came up short against the lightning-quick Tajiri. The loss proved costly, as Kash failed to see any more time on WWE television for several months.

Shortly after reemerging, a refocused Kash began to make quick work of *SmackDown's* top cruiserweights, including Paul London and Super Crazy. He found his way to capturing the WWE Cruiserweight Championship when he defeated Juventud at *Armageddon 2005*.

Kash also formed a brief but successful paring with Jamie Noble. Collectively known as The Pitbulls, the duo displayed an unorthodox style that oftentimes saw them bite their opponents. The Pitbulls remained threats to the WWE Tag Team Championship until Kash's departure from WWE in 2006.

THE KILLER BEES

| MEMBERS | B. Brian Blair & Jumpin' Jim Brunzell |
| COMBINED WT | 465 lbs. |

The Killer Bees buzzed into WWE in 1985 to take the tag team division on an exciting ride. Both members were incredibly gifted. B. Brian Blair had been trained by the same man who prepared Hulk Hogan for ring combat, Hiro Matsuda. "Jumpin'" Jim Brunzell was the product of a rigorous training camp overseen by perennial AWA World Heavyweight Champion Verne Gagne, and was a two-time AWA Tag Team Co-Titlist. Each was adept at both singles and tag team competition.

The Bees used outstanding teamwork and high-flying maneuvers to establish themselves as one of the top teams in WWE. When opponents would come at the duo with underhanded tricks, the Killer Bees would often resort to "masked confusion," donning matching masks and switching places in the ring without making tags. Although the Bees never held a Championship in WWE, they gained notoriety during confrontations with the Hart Foundation, Demolition, and Nikolai Volkoff and Iron Sheik.

The team split up when B. Brian Blair left the company in 1988, with Brunzell departing shortly thereafter.

KILLER KHAN

| HT | 6'5" | WT | 310 lbs. | FROM | Upper Mongolia |
| SIGNATURE MOVE | Top Rope Knee Drop |

This Superstar debuted in the 1970s, frightening audiences and opponents wherever he appeared. In 1980, Khan debuted in WWE with "Classy" Freddie Blassie at his side. Khan also teamed with George "The Animal" Steele from time to time.

Most WWE fans remember him for his infamous actions in May 1981, breaking the ankle of Andre the Giant. After Andre returned, their matches were intense, culminating in their infamous Mongolian Stretcher Match, which is still referred to with awe to this day.

Khan left WWE in 1982, but returned in 1987 with Mr. Fuji leading him into battle, determined to wrest the WWE Championship away from Hulk Hogan. Killer Khan went barefoot, utilized a sumo-inspired pre-match ritual and spewed green mist into the eyes of his opponents. But by 1988, his attempt to best Hogan unsuccessful, he returned to Mongolia. He later moved to Tokyo, where he opened a successful restaurant.

Memories of Killer Kahn and his violent acts in the ring will continue to haunt fans and Superstars for decades to come.

KILLER KOWALSKI

see page 195

KIM CHEE

An expert handler of wild animals, this masked man's identity has been a topic of debate since he arrived in WWE in 1986. As part of the contingent that came with Kamala "the Ugandan Giant" to the ring, Kim Chee was the only individual that could communicate with Kamala and curtail his behavior. Given his unique talents, he was an invaluable asset to managers who wanted the giant as part of their stable of WWE Superstars.

Kim Chee was also willing to interfere in a match on Kamala's behalf if he deemed it necessary. However, when he began to mistreat Kamala in 1993, Slick took over handling duties for the massive Superstar. Not to be deterred and ever the opportunist, Kim Chee would find his way back to Kamala's side throughout the years.

KING CURTIS IAUKEA

HT	6'3"	WT	290 lbs.	FROM	Honolulu, Hawaii
SIGNATURE MOVE		Splash			

King Curtis Iaukea began his illustrious career in the early 1960s, competing mainly for promotions in Australia and his home state of Hawaii. Despite a blatant disregard for the rules and his unkempt appearance, audiences in both locales accepted him with great fondness.

The mighty Hawaiian didn't spend much time in WWE, but during his brief stint, he did manage to gain great success in the promotion. In February 1972, Iaukea teamed with Baron Mikel Scicluna to defeat Karl Gotch and Rene Goulet for the World Tag Team Championship. With Lou Albano as their manager, Iaukea and Scicluna held the gold for more than three months before being dethroned by Chief Jay Strongbow and Sonny King.

Using a patented, crushing splash to finish off his foes, Iaukea eventually compiled enough victories to earn an opportunity at the coveted WWE Championship, held at the time by Pedro Morales. Unfortunately for the King, he was unable to unseat Morales. He left WWE soon after.

KING KONG BUNDY

HT	6'4"	WT	485 lbs.
FROM	Atlantic City, New Jersey		
SIGNATURE MOVE	Avalanche Splash		

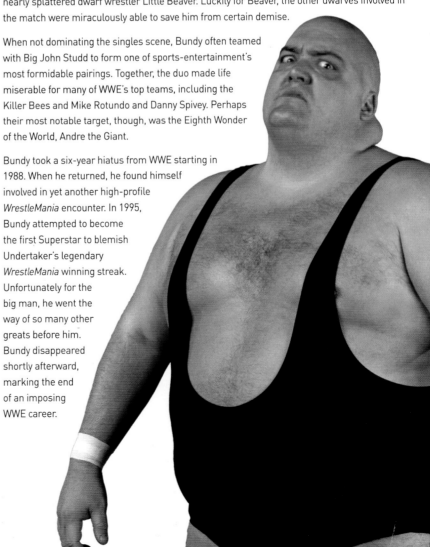

The rules of the ring are simple. To defeat your opponent via pinfall, you must keep his shoulders on the mat for three seconds. Unless of course, you're King Kong Bundy. The massive man appropriately dubbed "The Walking Condominium" demanded referees count to five while he arrogantly covered his pummeled foes.

Originally managed by Jimmy Hart, Bundy used the inaugural *WrestleMania* as the site of his first commanding victory when he crushed S.D. Jones in just nine seconds. The victory opened the eyes of everybody associated with WWE, including Bobby Heenan, who acquired Bundy from Hart shortly after *WrestleMania*.

Under Heenan's tutelage, Bundy set his sights on destroying Hulk Hogan. He nearly accomplished his goal when he ambushed The Hulkster on *Saturday Night's Main Event* in December 1985. With help from Don Muraco, Bundy delivered several rib-crushing splashes that almost ended Hogan's career.

The Hulkster eventually recovered and put his WWE Championship on the line against Bundy in a Steel Cage Match at *WrestleMania 2*. The match, which Hogan won, is still *WrestleMania*'s only steel cage main event.

Bundy's string of memorable *WrestleMania* moments continued the following year when he nearly splattered dwarf wrestler Little Beaver. Luckily for Beaver, the other dwarves involved in the match were miraculously able to save him from certain demise.

When not dominating the singles scene, Bundy often teamed with Big John Studd to form one of sports-entertainment's most formidable pairings. Together, the duo made life miserable for many of WWE's top teams, including the Killer Bees and Mike Rotundo and Danny Spivey. Perhaps their most notable target, though, was the Eighth Wonder of the World, Andre the Giant.

Bundy took a six-year hiatus from WWE starting in 1988. When he returned, he found himself involved in yet another high-profile *WrestleMania* encounter. In 1995, Bundy attempted to become the first Superstar to blemish Undertaker's legendary *WrestleMania* winning streak. Unfortunately for the big man, he went the way of so many other greats before him. Bundy disappeared shortly afterward, marking the end of an imposing WWE career.

KILLER KOWALSKI

HT	6'7"
WT	280 lbs.
FROM	Windsor, Ontario, Canada

SIGNATURE MOVE
Stomach Claw

When Killer Kowalski would bring his nephew to the matches, the celebrated villain dropped off the boy outside the arena and met him in a safe spot after the show. The routine confused the young man—until he realized that Kowalski was so universally despised that he had to fight his way in and out of buildings.

In a 2007 interview, Kowalski recalled meeting a female spectator after a match who told him, "I'm glad you didn't get hurt." A moment later, she thrust a knife in his back. By that point of his career, he was used to the abuse. He patched up the wound, and went on to his next booking.

Wladek Kowalski was the son of Polish immigrants to Canada. While vigorously working out at a local YMCA, he was also laboring in a Windsor, Ontario auto plant, hoping to become an electrical engineer. But when a scout spotted his impressive physique, Kowalski was recruited for a career in the ring.

He made his in-ring debut in 1947 as Tarzan Kowalski. Over the next seven years, he captured several regional singles and tag team Titles in multiple NWA territories. In 1950, he defeated the Texas Tag Team Champions in a handicap match by himself!

The pivotal moment of his career involved a freak accident. In October, 1952, he was wrestling Yukon Eric at the Montreal Forum, and delivering a knee drop from the ropes. Suddenly, Eric moved his head, and Kowalski's knee caught his rival's cauliflower ear, severing it. Kowalski watched in disbelief as the ear rolled across the ring.

The promoter demanded that Kowalski apologize. But when he arrived at the hospital, and saw the 6-foot-five, 280-pound Eric wrapped up "like a mummy," Kowalski started to laugh.

A headline the next day announced, "Kowalski Visits Yukon in Hospital and Laughs." Word spread and the next time that he competed, fans peppered Kowalski with chants of "Killer!"

The name stuck. As his reputation grew, fan anger became so intense that he required police escorts to and from the ring to ensure his safety.

In January 1953, Kowalski and Eric met again at the Montreal Forum. The grudge match was the first wrestling skirmish ever shown on Canadian television.

KILLER COMES TO WWE

In 1957, he arrived in Vincent J. McMahon's Capitol Wrestling Corporation and displayed his bloodthirsty tendencies. Kowalski returned in 1963 and began a relentless pursuit of the WWE Championship. He became one of the greatest threats to Bruno Sammartino's reign. Despite their animosity, Sammartino later expressed admiration for Kowalski's wrestling prowess.

THE REF PUT THE EAR IN HIS POCKET AND SAID, 'WHAT SHOULD I DO?' I SAID, 'RAISE MY ARM.'

That November, he formed one of WWE's most dominating teams with Gorilla Monsoon. The two monsters beat Skull Murphy and Brute Bernard to become United States Tag Team Champions. Kowalski also traveled to Japan and had a series of matches with Shoehi "Giant" Baba that were televised throughout the entire country.

When promoter Jim Barnett started a promotion in Australia in the mid-1960s, Kowalski was one of its biggest stars, holding the group's World Title three times, and Tag Team Championship twice—with old nemesis Skull Murphy.

Kowalski worked sporadically with the McMahon-led company over the following years, and in 1974, he concluded his battles against Sammartino in a Texas Death Match. In 1976, Kowalski and a young Big John Studd—one of the Killer's first students—donned masks to conceal their identities, competing as the Executioners.

In 1977, this legend retired from active competition and opened Killer Kowalski's School of Professional Wrestling. For the first time in decades, Kowalski was able to show people his passions outside the ring. He became a philanthropist working for children with special needs, as well as a renowned photographer. In 2001, he published a collection of his photos. Through his years as a teacher he trained Perry Saturn, John Kronus, Chyna, and future NXT coach, Matt "A-Train" Bloom.

In 1996, he was inducted by his most famous pupil, Triple H, into the WWE Hall of Fame. Kowalski was honored again in 2007 when he was inducted into the National Polish-American Sports Hall of Fame. On August 30, 2008, just two years after marrying for the first time, Kowalski passed away at 81.

Killer Kowalski was one of the true pioneers of sports-entertainment, and one of its first mainstream celebrities.

KIZARNY

| HT | 6'2" | WT | 236 lbs. | FROM | Wizard Beach |

There's strange, and then there's Kizarny.

The Superstar from Wizard Beach joined the carnival after running away from home as a child. It was there that he developed characteristics not typical of anybody, anywhere, ever. He became a fire-eater, befriended bearded ladies, developed a disturbing love for pain, and began speaking in carny, which is an antiquated secret language impossible for the normal population to understand.

Kizarny joined WWE in early 2009, defeating Montel Vontavious Porter in his debut match on *SmackDown*. The overly inked Superstar looked to have a limitless future, but following his elimination in a Battle Royal the following month on *SmackDown*, Kizarny mysteriously disappeared from WWE, much to the delight of those petrified by the carnival freak's behavior.

KLONDIKE BILL

| HT | 6'0" | WT | 365 lbs. | FROM | Kodiak Island, Alaska |
| SIGNATURE MOVE | Bear Hug | | | | |

After a successful amateur wrestling career, Bill Solowekyo turned to Stu Hart's legendary Dungeon to prepare him for a career in sports-entertainment. After amazing the hard-to-impress Hart with his toughness, Solowekyo donned a pair of worn blue jeans, wrapped a tattered rope around his waist, and adopted the name Klondike Bill. The rest is Canadian sports-entertainment history.

Billed from Kodiak Island, Alaska, Klondike Bill amazed Canadian crowds with his superhuman strength and firm bear hug. He was a threat to nearly every Champion; shockingly, however, Bill only captured one championship while in Canada.

Klondike Bill also brought his abilities to the United States, where he was equally feared. While in America, he enjoyed two NWA Tag Team Championship reigns with partners Nelson Royal and Luke Brown.

KLOUDY

Following Sunny's unpleasant departure as the Bodydonnas' manager, the duo sprung for a complete change in direction for her replacement. Enter Kloudy. Clad in the same attire as Sunny, Kloudy's figure stuffed inside form-fitting spandex did not radiate with quite the same beauty as her Hall of Fame predecessor, mostly because she was a dude.

With a blonde wig that fooled absolutely no one, Kloudy led the team to a victory at *King of the Ring 1996* over the New Rockers. Despite this strong start, the tattooed brute fell out of favor after just a few appearances. The overcast that was the Kloudy era lifted when Skip and Zip cut ties with him at *In Your House 9: International Incident*.

THE KLIQ

| MEMBERS | Shawn Michaels, Diesel, Razor Ramon, Triple H, & X-Pac |

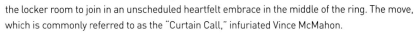

Though never acknowledged as a legitimate on-air faction, The Kliq was perhaps one of the most powerful WWE forces during the mid-1990s. Comprised of Shawn Michaels, Diesel, Razor Ramon, Triple H, and X-Pac (as 1-2-3 Kid), the rebellious group used their popularity and power in the locker room to make demands from WWE's top decision makers. As a result, they regularly found themselves gaining enviable opportunities, but also made many enemies along the way.

The Kliq's most infamous public appearance came at Madison Square Garden in 1996. With Diesel and Ramon about to leave WWE for rival WCW, members of the faction came to the ring from the locker room to join in an unscheduled heartfelt embrace in the middle of the ring. The move, which is commonly referred to as the "Curtain Call," infuriated Vince McMahon.

Years later, The Kliq's "Curtain Call" remains one of sports-entertainment's most powerful and controversial moments. Proving once again that anything can happen in WWE, a second "Curtain Call" took place almost fifteen years later during the closing moments of Shawn Michaels's WWE Hall of Fame induction.

KOFI KINGSTON

HT	6'0"	WT	212 lbs.	FROM	Ghana, West Africa
SIGNATURE MOVE		**Trouble in Paradise**			

Kofi Kingston has been beaming with positivity long before reinventing himself as a member of New Day. One of WWE's longest tenured Superstars, Kingston leaped onto the scene in 2008 with an ear-to-ear smile plastered across his face. Kofi's warm demeanor and instant likeability did not take away from his ferocity between the ropes. Sporting a vertical leap and agility that must be seen in high definition to believe, the Dreadlocked Dynamo could ratchet up the intensity at a moment's notice. In 2009, Kofi took a crowbar to Randy Orton's prized NASCAR, then dropped a majestic Boom Drop onto The Viper from the Madison Square Garden balcony.

The WWE Universe gravitated toward the athletic Superstar along with Championship gold. His first Title in WWE was the Intercontinental Championship, an accolade he claimed in 2008 from one of the most celebrated Intercontinental Champions of all time, Chris Jericho. Kofi has also defeated The Miz, Dolph Ziggler, and Drew McIntyre for the Intercontinental prize. He is also a three-time United States Champion and has captured Tag Team gold with four different partners—CM Punk, Evan Bourne, R-Truth, and New Day.

Instant replay was invented for Kofi Kingston. Despite never winning a Royal Rumble, he is one of the match's all-time greatest performers for the creative and near superhuman feats he performs to stave off elimination. He has also made jaws drop in several Money in the Bank Ladder Matches.

For years, fans "thunder clapped" with Kingston as he spelled trouble in paradise for evildoers. However, in 2014, the dawning of a New Day made the WWE Universe reluctant to clap along for the first time in Kofi's career.

Kofi, Big E, and Xavier Woods banded together to pull themselves out of a rut. Despite their understandable agenda, spectators were not feeling New Day's exuberance or the rallying cry of "NEW...Day rocks." While lesser men would have pulled the plug, New Day turned the dial up to eleven, going so far as to rock plastic unicorn horns on their heads. With unabashed enthusiasm, the trio has been unstoppable, collecting two Championship reigns and tooting their horn, quite literally, in the face of scorn.

Eventually, New Day's refusal to compromise (or perhaps a collective helping of Booty-O's) had audiences changing their tune. With the WWE Universe no longer sour on New Day, Kofi is back in a familiar position as a fan-favorite.

KOKO B. WARE

HT	5'7"	WT	228 lbs.	FROM	Union City, Tennessee
SIGNATURE MOVE		**Ghostbuster**			

Starting in 1986, competitors in WWE were dazzled by the high-flying attacks of Koko B. Ware. With the help of his macaw, Frankie, he taught fans all over the world how to do the "Birdman" dance. In the ring, Koko B. Ware

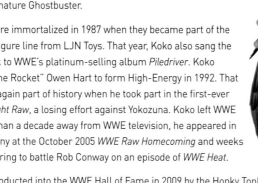

dazed opponents with his unmatched flying dropkick, and then finished off matches with his signature Ghostbuster.

Koko and Frankie were immortalized in 1987 when they became part of the famed WWE action-figure line from LJN Toys. That year, Koko also sang the lead on the title track to WWE's platinum-selling album *Piledriver*. Koko joined forces with "The Rocket" Owen Hart to form High-Energy in 1992. That next year, Koko was again part of history when he took part in the first-ever match on *Monday Night Raw*, a losing effort against Yokozuna. Koko left WWE in 1994. After more than a decade away from WWE television, he appeared in the Legends Ceremony at the October 2005 *WWE Raw Homecoming* and weeks later returned to the ring to battle Rob Conway on an episode of *WWE Heat*.

The "Birdman" was inducted into the WWE Hall of Fame in 2009 by the Honky Tonk Man. He has remained fairly active, still appearing at various independent wrestling events.

"KRIPPLER" KARL KOVACS

HT	6'2"	WT	290 lbs.
FROM	Minneapolis, Minnesota		

Given his brief stay in WWE during the early 1970s, many of today's fans don't recognize the name "Krippler" Karl Kovacs. The name Stan "The Big K" Kowalski, however, had a rich past. But when he came to WWE, The Big K changed his name to "Krippler" Karl Kovacs, presumably to avoid confusion with the great Walter "Killer" Kowalski, with whom Kovacs periodically teamed.

As Stan Kowalski, the Minnesota native has the distinction of winning the first-ever AWA World Tag Team Championship with his partner, Tiny Mills in 1960. He later teamed with Bob Geigel to capture his second AWA World Tag Team Championship, at the expense of Larry "The Axe" Hennig and Duke Hoffman.

KRISTAL MARSHALL

FROM	Los Angeles, California

After an eye-opening appearance in the 2005 *Raw Diva Search*, Kristal Marshall was welcomed into WWE as a member of the *SmackDown* broadcast team. While she shined in her role as an interviewer, it quickly became clear that the fiery Diva needed to be in the ring.

Upon making her in-ring debut in early 2006, Kristal engaged in bitter rivalries with Jillian Hall and Ashley. The three Divas squared off in several contests over the course of the year, including a Bra and Panties Match at *The Great American Bash*, which also featured Michelle McCool.

In 2007, Kristal began a torrid love affair with the considerably older Theodore Long. Those watching from afar assumed Kristal was merely after the *SmackDown* General Manager's power. But Long failed to see it that way and eventually asked for Kristal's hand in marriage.

The odd pairing planned a beautiful ceremony for the September 21, 2007, edition of *SmackDown*. Unfortunately, however, tragedy struck when a Theodore Long heart attack cut the ceremony short. Kristal was released from WWE shortly after.

KRONIK

MEMBERS	Brian Adams & Bryan Clark	COMBINED WT	573 lbs.

When Steven Richards verbally assaulted Undertaker in September 2001, fans everywhere assumed the former Right To Censor leader had lost his mind. In reality, however, he was simply luring in the legendary Superstar so his newest acquisition, Kronik, could attack from behind.

Shortly after their debut, Kronik, which consisted of former WCW Tag Team Champions Brian Adams and Bryan Clark, targeted the American Bad Ass. They made their focus clear as they cost Undertaker and Kane the World Tag Team Championship on a September 2001 edition of *Raw*. Later that same month, the Brothers of Destruction gained revenge when they decisively defeated Kronik at *Unforgiven*. A few days later, Adams and Clark were released from WWE. In all, their WWE tenure lasted less than one month.

KURT ANGLE

HT	6'0"	WT	250 lbs.	FROM	Pittsburgh, Pennsylvania
SIGNATURE MOVE	Ankle Lock, Angle Slam				

Oh, it's true! It's true!

Over seven Championship-winning years in WWE, Kurt Angle proved to be nothing short of a wrestling machine. One of the most highly touted WWE signees of all time (by both pundits and Angle himself), the 1996 Olympic gold medalist lived up to the hype. He debuted in WWE in late 1999 preaching his "3 I's,"—Intensity, Integrity, and Intelligence—and soon had WWE's best tapping to his dreaded Ankle Lock.

With an American flag-themed singlet and his cherished gold medal around his neck, Angle held on to his amateur roots but had no trouble adjusting to WWE-style competition. In his first year of sports-entertainment, Angle became a hybrid "Euro-continental Champion," a King of the Ring, and, most notably, a WWE Champion. Angle capped off the year 2000 with one of the most impressive Title defenses in history, retaining the WWE Championship by surviving a six-man Hell in a Cell at *Armageddon*.

Angle became a fixture in WWE's fight for survival against The WCW/ECW Alliance. After outlasting WCW owner Shane McMahon in an unsettling Street Fight, he turned his attention to Alliance turncoat, Stone Cold Steve Austin. In a memorable moment, Angle drove a milk truck to the ring and doused The Rattlesnake with milk. Angle later won another WWE Title from Austin himself. Still, his arrogance grated on the WWE Universe, who oftentimes chanted "You suck," along to the tune of his entrance music for the remainder of his WWE tenure.

Of course, no one really thought he sucked. How could they? In 2003, he overcame neck surgery after just fourteen weeks and defeated Brock Lesnar to gain his fourth WWE Championship. Whether facing a Beast or a high-flyer like Rey Mysterio, Angle was up to the task. When facing a man with similar traits, Shawn Michaels, at *WrestleMania 21*, the result was pure magic with Angle defeating HBK by submission.

Angle won a Battle Royal in January 2006 on *SmackDown* to claim his first World Heavyweight Championship. Later that year, Angle was brought to *ECW* to take his wrestling acumen to the extreme. He departed the company shortly after, closing the book on a decorated WWE career.

KWANG

HT	5'11"	WT	248 lbs.	FROM	Japan
SIGNATURE MOVE	Super Spin Kick

In 1994, WWE was infiltrated by a martial arts expert named Kwang. Managed by Harvey Whippleman, Kwang was known for his disregard for rules, and for using a mysterious Asian mist that often blinded opponents.

During his time in WWE, Kwang battled the likes of Undertaker, Lex Luger, Tatanka, 1-2-3 Kid, and Bret "Hit Man" Hart. At one point Kwang formed a dangerous alliance with another Superstar well-versed in several martial-arts styles, Hakushi. By the middle of 1995, Kwang left WWE and has not been seen on television since.

KYLE EDWARDS

His diverse assignments have included doing a retrospective on the long forgotten AWA "Turkey on a Pole" match between Colonel DeBeers and Jake "The Milkman" Milliman. When he interviewed Erick Rowan, the red-bearded Superstar refused to remove his sheep mask—or even speak, for that matter. During Seth Rollins' WWE World Heavyweight Championship reign, the Titlist went out of his way to pointedly avoid him.

Nonetheless, Kyle Edwards worked his dream job, covering the organization he followed passionately since childhood. The Ontario native covered many different sports and other live events in his native Canada, but gained a following while reporting on WWE happenings on The Score Television Network, alongside former referee Jimmy Korderas and future colleague Renee Young. He also promoted independent wrestling shows, bringing charity events to the remote Canadian Arctic.

Signed to WWE in 2014, Edwards hosted programs tailored to Europe, South America, and Asia, appeared on WWE's YouTube channel, and the WWE Network.

KYO DAI

MEMBERS	Tajiri, Akio, & Sakoda

When listing sports-entertainment's greatest factions, there's a good chance Kyo Dai would get overlooked. That's because, unlike the Four Horsemen or D-Generation X, Kyo Dai failed to leave any lasting impact from their short run together.

During Tajiri's Cruiserweight Championship defense against Rey Mysterio at No Mercy 2003, the "Japanese Buzzsaw" received some surprising support from Akio and Sakoda, who jumped the guardrail to help their new associate. Over the next few weeks, Tajiri, Akio, and Sakoda worked together to ensure their superiority over SmackDown's other cruiserweights. But after less than a year, Tajiri stepped away from the trio, leaving Akio and Sakoda to compete on their own. The Akio-Sakoda union eventually fizzled as well when Sakoda was released from WWE in the summer of 2004.

LA FAMILIA

MEMBERS	Edge, Vickie Guerrero, Zack Ryder, Curt Hawkins, Bam Neely, & Chavo Guerrero

Few things in life are more intoxicating than power, as evidenced by the torrid love affair between Vickie Guerrero and Edge. After all, it wasn't long after Guerrero assumed control over SmackDown that the Rated-R Superstar expressed his love for the considerably-older General Manager.

Vickie's nephew, Chavo Guerrero, first expressed great displeasure with the unconventional romance but came around after Edge helped him capture the ECW Championship. Soon, Bam Neely and "Edgehead's" Zack Ryder and Curt Hawkins rounded out the powerful sextet known as La Familia. The faction used Vickie's stroke to claim the WWE, World Heavyweight, ECW, and WWE Tag Team Championships. However, when the rigors of the job compelled Vickie to resign from her role as GM, Edge quickly dumped her and La Familia severed their ties.

LA RESISTANCE

	MEMBERS	Sylvain Grenier, Rene Dupree, & Robert Conway
	COMBINED WT	727 lbs.	FROM	Quebec, Canada

For just over two years, the arrogant French-Canadian combination dubbed La Resistance dominated the WWE tag team scene.

Original members Sylvain Grenier and Rene Dupree immediately opened the eyes of the WWE Universe when they attacked Scott Steiner in their April 2003 debut. Less than two months later, they seized the World Tag Team Championships. Using a whiplash side slam finisher known as Au Revoir, La Resistance turned back all challengers. However, they needed a little help from an American to get past the Dudley Boyz. At SummerSlam 2003, the faction's newest member, American turncoat Robert Conway, attacked D-Von and Bubba Ray, allowing La Resistance to pick up the win.

The three-man faction utilized their numbers advantage to succeed in WWE's competitive tag team ranks until Dupree was unexpectedly drafted to SmackDown in March 2004. Many insiders predicted doom for La Resistance. However, with Grenier and Conway holding down the fort, the new La Resistance proved more successful than the original. The team earned three more Championship reigns, waving their fleur-de-lis flag in defiance until they dissolved in 2005.

LANA

HT	5'7"	FROM	Moscow

Combining equal amounts of brains and beauty, Lana has proven to be one of history's most ruthless Divas. After debuting at the 2014 Royal Rumble, the Ravishing Russian has used her looks and cunning to catapult Rusev to the top with little regard for the waste she leaves in her wake.

Originally revealed as Rusev's social ambassador, Lana quickly proved to be so much more than a diplomat. As the Bulgarian Brute tore through WWE, it became evident that the leggy Diva held considerable power, as Rusev rarely released his dreaded Accolade without first being instructed to do so by Lana.

With Lana leading the way, Rusev defeated such top names as Big Show, Mark Henry, and Big E before dethroning Sheamus for the United States Championship in November 2014. The Bulgarian Brute held the Title for nearly five months before falling to John Cena at WrestleMania 31, thanks in part to a Lana miscue.

The WrestleMania loss marked the beginning of a public breakup between Lana and Rusev. Once the couple officially split, the Ravishing Russian began a relationship with Dolph Ziggler. And over the next several months, Lana and Ziggler engaged in a bitter rivalry with Rusev and his new lady, Summer Rae.

Amazingly, in October 2015, TMZ reported that Lana and Rusev had put their differences aside and agreed to get married. Together again, the powerful couple has picked up where they left off, intimidating the WWE roster.

LANCE CADE

HT	6'5"	WT	262 lbs.
FROM	Nashville, Tennessee		

A student of the Shawn Michaels Wrestling Academy, Lance Cade's career was catapulted in September 2005 by his allegiance with fellow redneck, Trevor Murdoch. The duo needed only a few weeks to capture the World Tag Team Championship. The rugged Southerners held the Titles for nearly two months before losing to the imposing team of Big Show and Kane. After the loss, Cade and Murdoch bucked sports-entertainment norms by splitting amicably.

On his own, Cade struggled to find his way for six long months, eventually leading to a reunion with Murdoch. This decision proved advantageous, as two more Tag Team Championship reigns soon followed. After an uncharacteristic losing streak plagued the team in 2008, Cade took out his frustrations on Murdoch, this time breaking up the old fashioned way.

Motivated to grab the spotlight for himself, Cade became a close associate of Chris Jericho and attacked the likes of John Cena, Batista, Shawn Michaels, and Triple H. Sadly, Lance Cade passed away in August 2010.

LANCE CADE AND TREVOR MURDOCH

MEMBERS	Lance Cade & Trevor Murdoch
COMBINED WT	501 lbs.

Trevor Murdoch, a cowpoke and truck-driving tough guy, used a blend of down-home fightin' and power to quickly make an impact in WWE. With Cade trained by Shawn Michaels and Murdoch trained by Harley Race, the rough and tumble twosome could not have been better prepared for the big stage.

Within two weeks of their *Raw* debut, Cade and Murdoch won the World Tag Team Championship from The Hurricane and Rosey at *Unforgiven 2005*. Shortly after their Title loss to Big Show and Kane at *Taboo Tuesday* they parted ways to focus on singles careers. The separation did not last long, however, and by 2007, the reformed duo was not only challenging WWE's top teams, they were doing so with a new regard for sportsmanship. "Playing by the rules" paid off, as they went on to hold two more Tag Team Titles facing teams like the Hardys, Paul London and Brian Kendrick, and Hardcore Holly and Cody Rhodes. Their relationship slowly unraveled, ultimately leading to Lance Cade turning on his longtime partner in early 2008.

LANCE CASSIDY

HT	6'1"	WT	232 lbs.	FROM	Texas
SIGNATURE MOVE	Top Rope Clothesline				

Sports-entertainment's storied history is rich with cowboys that have made the difficult transition from the ranch to the ring. Dick Murdoch, Blackjack Mulligan, and Terry Funk are among the most notable examples to have done so with great success.

Lance Cassidy tried to add his name to the list of successful cowboy competitors when he debuted in WWE in late 1992. Behind the power of his patented top-rope clothesline, he picked up early wins over Terry Taylor, Brooklyn Brawler, and The Berzerker, among others. Unfortunately for Cassidy, however, that's where the success stopped. By 1993, only a few months into his WWE career, his failures had gotten the best of Cassidy, who soon left the rigors of the ring to presumably return to his ranch.

LANCE STORM

HT	6'0"	WT	228 lbs.	FROM	Calgary, Alberta, Canada
SIGNATURE MOVE	Canadian Crab				

A graduate of Stu Hart's "Dungeon," Lance Storm first made waves in Canada, Japan, Germany, and the Middle East before he arrived in Smoky Mountain Wrestling, where he teamed with Chris Jericho as the Thrillseekers. He soon moved to ECW and formed the Impact Players with Justin Credible. He didn't claim to be the whole show, just the best part of it. In June of 2000, Storm went to World Championship Wrestling, where he acquired multiple Titles. Fans were treated to a preview of what was to come in WWE after Storm renamed each Title to suit a Canadian Champion.

Storm landed in WWE in 2001, first as part of the Alliance of former WCW and ECW stars hoping to dominate the company. When that effort fell short, he joined the hated Un-Americans group with Christian, Test, and William Regal. Storm enjoyed a few Tag Team Championship runs with his Un-American partners, but ultimately the group split after a string of losses.

He also wore the Intercontinental Championship, and inspired fellow athletes with his versatility and ethic. His last WWE match took place at the first *One Night Stand* against former partner Chris Jericho. He semi-retired from active ring competition in 2007. Today, this technically gifted athlete trains prospects for a career in the ring at the Storm Wrestling Academy.

LANNY POFFO

| HT | 6'0" | WT | 236 lbs. | FROM | Downers Grove, Illinois |
| SIGNATURE MOVE | Honor Roll |

Lanny Poffo has the unique distinction of being one of history's most-admired Superstars, as well as one of the most despised. Affectionately known as "Leaping" Lanny, Poffo amazed audiences with his high-flying offensive arsenal. In fact, many credit him for introducing the moonsault to the WWE Universe in the mid-1980s. Additionally, Poffo's aerial attacks featured a breathtaking top-rope backflip, which some consider a precursor to today's Swanton Bomb.

Poffo complemented his remarkable wrestling talent with an aptitude for writing poetry. Prior to each match, he would recite a witty limerick before throwing Frisbees to the crowd. Poffo's rhymes made him one of the most-beloved Superstars of his time.

In 1989, Poffo's poetry began to take a hurtful twist. The once fun-loving Superstar started to use his words to verbally attack the fans and their favorites, such as Hulk Hogan. Claiming to possess superior intellect, Poffo renamed himself The Genius. With his newfound conceit, he went on to become one of the most hated Superstars of his time.

LARRY "THE AXE" HENNIG

| HT | 6'1" | WT | 275 lbs. | FROM | Robbinsdale, Minnesota |
| SIGNATURE MOVE | The Axe |

More recent WWE fans might only recognize Larry "The Axe" Hennig as the father of Mr. Perfect and grandfather of Curtis Axel. Longtime fans know him as one of the toughest Superstars of the 1960s and 1970s.

During a 1963 tour of Texas, he formed a historic union with the legendary Harley Race. The duo won their first of three AWA World Tag Team Titles in 1965.

In 1973, the rugged Minnesotan entered WWE, leveling foes with his "Axe," or running forearm, and challenging Pedro Morales and then Bruno Sammartino for the WWE World Heavyweight Championship.

He's also known for defeating a young Roddy Piper in the Rowdy Scot's first match, and forming a successful tandem with Hall of Famer son, Mr. Perfect.

LARRY SHARPE

| FROM | New Jersey |

Larry Sharpe joined WWE in 1974 after a successful amateur wrestling career, in which he was inducted into the New Jersey College Hall of Fame. Despite his previous success, Sharpe was unable to reclaim the magic he created on the amateur level. Sharpe then went on to look for success in other wrestling promotions, including Stampede Wrestling. While a member of Stu Hart's Stampede promotion, Sharpe captured the International Tag Team Championship with his partner Ripper Collins.

Despite moderate success in the ring, Sharpe is most known for his role in training many of the sport's top names, including Big Show, Bam Bam Bigelow, and Kevin Von Erich.

LARRY ZBYSZKO

| HT | 5'9" | WT | 233 lbs. | FROM | Pittsburgh, Pennsylvania |
| SIGNATURE MOVE | Piledriver |

A longtime fan of Bruno Sammartino, Larry Zbyszko's dream came true when he became the legendary competitor's protégé in 1972. With Sammartino's support, Zbyszko became an instant fan favorite, wowing audiences with his technical skills and unmatched sportsmanship.

In November 1978, Zbyszko teamed with Tony Garea to defeat the Yukon Lumberjacks for the World Tag Team Championship. They held the Titles until March of the following year when they lost to the Valiant Brothers.

Toward the end of the decade, Zbyszko's frustration over being primarily known as Sammartino's pupil began to boil. He ultimately attacked his teacher during a technical exhibition. The attack led to the now-famous Steel Cage Match at the 1980 *Showdown at Shea*, in which Sammartino was victorious.

Zbyszko left WWE soon after the loss, but excelled at every subsequent stop he made, from the AWA to WCW. After retiring from competition, he became an announcer for WCW until the company closed its doors in 2001.

Zbyszko's greatness was recognized in 2015 when his mentor, Bruno Sammartino, inducted him into the WWE Hall of Fame.

LAUREN MAYHEW

| FROM | Tampa, Florida |

Lauren Mayhew is no stranger to the spotlight. She began her entertainment career in 1998, first appearing on the hit daytime soap opera, *Guiding Light*. She was also cast on several other television series including *Law & Order* and *CSI*.

As a singer, Mayhew was part of the all-girl quartet PYT (Prove Yourself True) until 2002. She appeared live on the *Super Bowl XXXV* pregame show and toured with Britney Spears, Destiny's Child, and 'N Sync.

In October 2009, Mayhew took her talents to WWE to become a ring announcer for *ECW*. She also sang both "The Star Spangled Banner" at events and "God Save the Queen" for UK audiences. Though talented, Mayhew's stay with WWE was brief, lasting only weeks.

LAYLA

HT	5'3"
FROM	Miami, Florida

As a WWE Diva, Layla was exactly how she described herself—flawless! That is why it was no surprise when the former Miami Heat dancer proved to be a shoe-in for WWE during the 2006 Diva Search. After winning the competition, Layla joined Kelly Kelly and Brooke on *ECW* to form the tantalizing Extreme Exposé.

Layla focused on managing in 2008 and gravitated toward fellow Brit, William Regal. However, it was when she joined forces with Michelle McCool in 2009 that Layla found her greatest success. Known as Team Lay-Cool, the mean-spirited duo terrorized other Divas, such as Mickie James and Beth Phoenix. When Layla pinned the Women's Champion, Phoenix, in a Handicap Match, she and McCool referred to themselves as the "co-Women's Champions." The two besties ultimately jigsawed the Title in half, infuriating *SmackDown* GM Teddy Long. Lay-Cool appeared inseparable until Michelle turned on Layla in 2011. Layla gained revenge by winning a match at *Extreme Rules* to force her former ally into retirement.

After a long year of rehabbing an unfortunate knee injury, Layla made a surprise return at *Extreme Rules 2012*. She upended Nikki Bella to win her first Diva's Championship and held the Title for 140 days.

In 2014, Layla unveiled a seductive side when she wooed Fandango away from his dance partner, Summer Rae. Their romance was short-lived, however, as an emotional Layla soon announced her retirement from WWE.

LEE WONG

FROM	Hong Kong

Lee Wong from Hong Kong was on the wrong side of nearly every match in which he competed. He began his WWE career in the early 1970s, where he regularly fattened the wallets of his victorious opponents, including future WWE Hall of Famers Killer Kowalski, George "The Animal" Steele, and Mr. Fuji. Though, Wong did manage to once defeat Johnny Rodz in May 1970.

After WWE, Wong travelled down the East Coast. Competitors from each territory along the way welcomed him with open arms. He eventually reached Florida, where he made the Sunshine State's stars look good before turning around and returning to WWE.

Wong's second tour of duty with WWE was much like his first —unsuccessful. By this time, Wong appeared to have beefed up his martial arts repertoire, but his karate chops rarely succeeded in eliciting fear from his foes. Instead, Blackjack Mulligan, Pedro Morales, "The Russian Bear" Ivan Koloff, and the rest of the WWE locker room simply saw Wong as another easy victory on their resumé.

LEGACY

MEMBERS	Randy Orton, Cody Rhodes, & Ted DiBiase

Only one generation ago, "Cowboy" Bob Orton, Dusty Rhodes, and Million Dollar Man Ted DiBiase travelled the globe, earning their reputations as some of the toughest men to ever lace up a pair of boots. Fast forward a few decades and their sons, Randy Orton, Cody Rhodes, and Ted DiBiase, collectively known as Legacy, carried on their parent's WWE Hall of Fame heritage.

But on the off-chance that the WWE Universe forgot that fact, Legacy was always happy to remind everyone of their natural abilities. With an open disregard for the rules and unmatched level of arrogance, the trio become one of the least-liked groups in WWE.

Unfortunately for their detractors, Legacy's success in the ring could not be questioned. During their year-plus together, the trio racked up a near spotless win-loss record as their leader, Randy Orton, claimed three WWE Championship reigns.

In early 2010, a series of miscues by Rhodes and DiBiase cost Orton some high-profile matches, causing the once-powerful faction to crumble. Finally at *WrestleMania XXVI*, all three Legacy members squared off in a Triple Threat Match, with Orton emerging victorious.

Legion of Doom

HoF **T T**

MEMBERS	Hawk, Animal, & Paul Ellering
COMBINED WT	530 lbs.

The Legion of Doom snacked on danger and dined on death for nearly two decades. Along the way, the face-painted Superstars earned a reputation as history's most influential tag team, winning Championships in nearly every major promotion all over the globe.

Hawk and Animal were originally paired by "Precious" Paul Ellering in the early-1980s. With their massive frames, unorthodox hairstyles, and spiked leather collars, the powerful duo tore through Georgia, upending the territory's top teams, including Ole and Arn Anderson, and Jack and Jerry Brisco. Within months of their debut, Hawk and Animal captured the NWA National Tag Team Championship, solidifying themselves as one of the nation's top teams.

A Top Team

The Legion of Doom jumped to the AWA in 1984. As they had done before in Georgia, the duo immediately made their presence felt when they defeated Baron Von Raschke and The Crusher for the AWA World Tag Team Championship within only weeks of their arrival. For the next four-hundred days, Hawk and Animal successfully turned back AWA's top teams, including The Fabulous Ones, and Curt and Larry Hennig. They also defeated Michael Hayes and Jimmy Garvin in a Steel Cage Match at *WrestleRock* in April 1986.

Following their *WrestleRock* victory, Hawk and Animal ventured to Jim Crockett Promotions, where they continued to cement their legacy as one of sports-entertainment's top tag teams. Along the way, they competed in some of Jim Crockett Promotions' most memorable matches, including the *Starrcade* 1986 Scaffold Match, as well as the inaugural WarGames Match at *The Great American Bash 1987*.

Hawk and Animal proved they were the top team in Jim Crockett Promotions when they defeated The Midnight Express to become the NWA World Tag Team Champions in October 1988. The victory added to their already-impressive resume, which also included the 1986 Jim Crockett Sr. Memorial Cup and ultimately, three NWA World Six-Man Tag Team Championship reigns.

Doom Comes to WWE

By 1990, The Legion of Doom had dominated nearly every territory in the sports-entertainment industry. The only locale they had yet to prove themselves was the biggest stage of them all, WWE. But that all changed when Hawk and Animal made their highly-anticipated WWE debut during the summer of 1990.

"OHHHHH, WHAT A RUSH!"

Upon their arrival, Hawk and Animal helped the Hart Foundation capture the World Tag Team Championships from Demolition. The Legion of Doom then spent the next several months proving their superiority over the supposed L.O.D. rip-offs when they teamed with Ultimate Warrior to continually defeat Ax, Smash, and Crush in arenas across the country.

Following impressive victories over such teams as Power and Glory and The Orient Express, Hawk and Animal finally found themselves in line to compete for the one prize that had eluded them over the course of their illustrious careers, the World Tag Team Championship. They got their opportunity at *SummerSlam 1991* and proceeded to take full advantage when they turned back the Nasty Boys to gain their first taste of WWE gold.

Hawk and Animal quietly left WWE in 1992, only to make a shocking return five years later. Many feared the 1997 version of L.O.D. were too long in the tooth to compete with the promotion's younger teams, but Hawk and Animal quickly put those fears to rest. They quickly defeated The Godwinns to reclaim the World Tag Team Championship in October. They held the Titles for nearly two months before losing to the up-and-coming New Age Outlaws.

Following the loss, Hawk and Animal slightly reinvented themselves as L.O.D. 2000. Led by the lovely Sunny, the recharged duo picked up their final major victory when they won the *WrestleMania XIV* Tag Team Battle Royal.

Sadly, Michael "Hawk" Hegstrand passed away in October 2003. With his passing came the end of one of the greatest tag team in sports-entertainment history. In 2011, on the eve of *WrestleMania XXVII*, The Legion of Doom's excellence was recognized as they were inducted into the WWE Hall of Fame, a fitting honor for one of the most feared and successful tag teams of all time.

LEILANI KAI

HT	5'7"	FROM	Hawaii
SIGNATURE MOVE		Aloha Splash	

Competitors don't come much tougher than this woman from Hawaii. Trained by the Fabulous Moolah, Leilani Kai learned the game in various regional promotions in the mid-1970s. In 1977, she joined WWE and became an instant contender for the Championship held by her teacher.

In 1985, she beat Wendi Richter at *The War To Settle The Score* special on MTV for the WWE Women's Championship. Shortly after her loss to Richter at *WrestleMania I*, Kai formed a team with another Moolah protégé, Judy Martin. Known as the Glamour Girls, Kai and Martin defeated Velvet McIntyre and Desiree Peterson in a wild Championship match in Cairo, Egypt. When they returned to North America, they found a new manager in "Mouth of the South" Jimmy Hart. The Girls traded Title reigns with the Jumping Bomb Angels until retiring as the Champions in 1989.

Leilani left WWE, but returned briefly in 1994 to challenge Alundra Blayze for the Women's Championship at *WrestleMania X*. She competed in WCW until the late 1990s and then became a women's trainer.

LENA YADA

HT	5'4"	FROM	Honolulu, Hawaii

Lena Yada was a 2007 Diva Search contestant whose talents led her to becoming a backstage interviewer on *ECW*. She especially turned heads in January 2008 when she hosted a Diva Dance Off and proclaimed herself the winner.

The self-proclaimed "Asian Sensation" lived life in the public eye before her career in sports-entertainment. In addition to competing as a professional surfer, Lena assembled an impressive acting resume with movie credits that included a role in the box-office hit *I Now Pronounce You Chuck & Larry*. She also appeared on the popular *Baywatch* parody, *Son of the Beach*. A fitness fanatic, Lena has also used her toned frame to open eyes in many swimsuit competitions. Although her WWE tenure was short, she made a lasting impression on the WWE Universe.

LES THORNTON

HT	5'9"	WT	225 lbs.	FROM	Manchester, England

A former boxer in the British Navy and a professional rugby player, Les Thornton made his sports-entertainment debut in the late 1950s. He quickly earned the respect of fans all over the globe, dominating such territories as Beirut, New Zealand, Germany, and Australia before moving on to North America.

When Thornton arrived in Canada, he began competing for Stu Hart's Stampede Wrestling. While there, he captured the North American Heavyweight Championship twice. Despite his worldwide success, Thornton didn't compete for WWE until the latter days of his career. During the infancy of WWE's global dominance, the organization recognized Thornton as a Superstar with great international influence, strategically making him a focal point of its overseas tours of the mid-1980s.

LEX LUGER

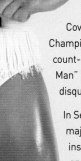

HT	6'6"	WT	275 lbs.	FROM	Chicago, Illinois
SIGNATURE MOVE		Running Forearm, Human Torture Rack			

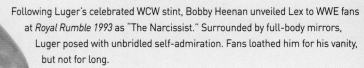

In 1987, NWA Superstars and fans learned in an instant that Lex Luger was indeed the "Total Package." As the replacement for Ole Anderson in the legendary Four Horsemen, the tanned, chiseled newcomer thrived. Luger won his first of five United States Titles with the Horsemen, while also providing added muscle for the popular faction, before ultimately choosing to fight his own battles. In fact, a number of these came against his former Horsemen running mates, including a showdown with Barry Windham at *The Great American Bash 1991*, in which Luger captured his first WCW Championship.

Following Luger's celebrated WCW stint, Bobby Heenan unveiled Lex to WWE fans at *Royal Rumble 1993* as "The Narcissist." Surrounded by full-body mirrors, Luger posed with unbridled self-admiration. Fans loathed him for his vanity, but not for long.

That summer, Luger shocked the world on America's birthday. After numerous WWE Superstars and professional athletes failed to slam then-WWE Champion Yokozuna, Luger arrived via helicopter on the deck of the *USS Intrepid* to answer the call. In a Herculean display of strength, Luger lifted and slammed the 600-plus pound Champion. As the WWE Universe rejoiced, "The Narcissist" was gone and WWE's "American Original" had arrived.

Covered in patriotic decor, Luger embarked on the "Lex Express," a nationwide bus tour during which he campaigned for a shot at the WWE Championship. Lex ultimately received his opportunity for Yokozuna's Title at *SummerSlam 1993*. While he emerged victorious, it was due to a count-out, which meant the WWE Championship would remain with the giant sumo. As co-winners of the 1994 Royal Rumble, Luger and Bret "Hit Man" Hart both earned a chance to unseat Yokozuna at *WrestleMania X*. Unfortunately for Lex, the WWE Title wasn't in the cards as Luger was disqualified in his match against Yokozuna, while Bret Hart ultimately emerged victorious in his later match as the new WWE Champion

In September 1995, Lex suddenly left WWE, making a shocking appearance on the premiere episode of *WCW Monday Nitro*, one of the first major salvos of the Monday Night War. The "Total Package" collected more WCW gold and stood with fellow WCW stalwarts against the nWo's insurgence. He would, however, complete another defection in 1998 when he joined the nWo splinter faction, The Wolfpac. This controversial and decorated competitor remained in WCW until it closed in 2001.

LIGHT HEAVYWEIGHT CHAMPIONSHIP

The WWE Light Heavyweight Championship was first primarily defended in the New Japan promotion, as well as the old UWA in Mexico after Perro Aguayo defeated El Gran Hamada in a tournament to crown the first Champion in 1981.

Designed to recognize the abilities of competitors 220 pounds or less, the Light Heavyweight Championship was held by such notables as Hamada, Fishman, Villano III, The Great Sasuke, and "Gentleman" Chris Adams. In 1997, the Title was vacated.

Later that year though, Taka Michinoku defeated Brian Christopher on a WWE card to revive the Title. From that point forward, it was only defended in WWE. For the next several years, the Light Heavyweight Championship was worn by some of the most eclectic and gifted athletes of that era, including Jerry Lynn, Tajiri, Dean Malenko, and X-Pac.

However, in some ways, the Title was a victim of WWE's expansion. In 2001, after WWE acquired WCW, numerous Championships were either combined or eliminated. It was during this period that the Light Heavyweight Championship was discontinued.

LILIAN GARCIA

As the longtime ring announcer of WWE, Lilian Garcia has become recognized as the voice that has introduced many of sports-entertainment's most historic moments.

In addition to announcing, Lilian is an accomplished vocalist. Prior to many WWE shows, the beautiful Diva has performed stirring renditions of "The Star-Spangled Banner." She has also opened up for many professional sports teams, including the New York Jets and Phoenix Suns. The popularity of her amazing voice eventually led to the release of her 2007 album, *!Quiero Vivir!*.

Given her beauty, it was only a matter of time before Lilian caught the eye of a WWE Superstar. In May 2005, the inevitable happened when Viscera proclaimed his love. On the surface, Lilian and Big Vis didn't look like a typical couple, but inside they shared a deep connection. Or so Lilian thought. The relationship eventually crumbled when Viscera chose The Godfather's ladies over her.

After a two-year hiatus, Lilian returned to WWE in December 2011. Since then, her angelic voice has remained synonymous with WWE's biggest moments.

LINDA MCMAHON
see page 206

LITA

HT	5'6"	FROM	Sanford, North Carolina
SIGNATURE MOVE		Litacanrana	

One of the most recognizable WWE Superstars of all time, Lita had fiery red hair and a punk rock presence, but she was known for her daredevil demeanor. Lita never met a challenge she wouldn't take to the extreme. Whether flying off a ladder or sinking to seductive new levels of sinister, Lita's next move was anyone's guess.

Lita joined WWE in 2000 and quickly made a name for herself, managing Essa Rios. When the pair split, she quickly aligned herself with the Hardy Boyz. As Team Xtreme, the threesome dazzled crowds with their acrobatic offense for nearly five years. During this period, Lita also developed a romantic relationship with Matt Hardy.

As a competitor, Lita enjoyed four reigns as Women's Champion. Her first came at the expense of Stephanie McMahon-Helmsley in August 2000. The match was the first *Raw* main event to feature two female competitors. Lita would later repeat this feat against her archrival, Trish Stratus. Her hallmark victory in her career-long rivalry with Trish came during a *Raw* main event in December 2004. During the match, the notorious daredevil put her high-risk aerial attacks on full display.

In 2004, Lita became the object of Kane's sadistic desires. Kane tormented her boyfriend, Matt Hardy, in an attempt to force Lita to cave in to his demands. While Lita found herself tempted by Kane, this was just the first of two indiscretions she hoped Matt would never discover.

The following year, Lita became romantic with Edge while she was still involved with Matt. The ugly love triangle became public as a broken-hearted Matt looked for revenge. Lita and Edge flaunted their love for the entire world to see. Their gratuitous PDA's included a controversial in-ring celebration following Edge's WWE Championship victory in January 2006.

Lita left WWE following a loss to Mickie James at *Survivor Series 2006*, seeking to once again keep her private life private. Eventually, time led to forgiveness, as Lita has been greeted warmly by the WWE Universe each time she has surprised them with a return. In 2014, her rival-turned-close-friend, Trish Stratus gave Lita a much-deserved induction into the WWE Hall of Fame. Now among the ranks of WWE immortals, it was only natural for this groundbreaking competitor to unveil the new WWE Women's Championship prior to *WrestleMania 32*, symbolizing a new era for the talented women of WWE.

LINDA McMAHON

FROM Greenwich, Connecticut

On the national stage, Linda McMahon is known for her two US Senate runs, her dedication to literacy and women's leadership, and her involvement with various charities and higher education. But she also helped develop WWE into the international juggernaut it is today, doing everything from spearheading merchandising efforts to editing the company's publications to lending a compassionate ear behind the scenes to both employees and WWE Superstars.

Born in New Bern, North Carolina, Linda Marie Edwards was a member of the Girl Scouts of America, athlete, honor student, and a member of her church choir. One day after service, a teenage Linda met a young Vince McMahon, and romance quickly blossomed.

Linda graduated from East Carolina University and, in 1979, she had her husband relocated to Massachusetts and created TitanSports. After purchasing the Cape Cod Coliseum, they promoted various events, from wrestling to rock concerts and professional hockey. In 1980, they incorporated Titan Sports and, in 1982, bought Capitol Wrestling Corporation from Vince's father. Together, Linda and Vince enabled WWE to be seen beyond the geographic region of the northeast and marketed as a premier form of entertainment.

Their revolutionary approach helped cultivate WWE's broader appeal, which led to syndication and later national and international television contracts. The McMahons ran these activities concurrently with new branding and trademarking initiatives that put World Wrestling Entertainment in a class by itself.

Linda negotiated and implemented WWE's first-ever licensing contract with then-industry leading toy company LJN to produce the WWE Superstar action figures. Today, that product line is considered a classic within the toy business and is sought-after by collectors. She also managed the development of WWE publications, and in the beginning, wrote a majority of the articles. This foresight, drive, and success were harbingers of the multi-million dollar revenue streams that Linda would go on to create for the company. In 1993, she became President of WWE and in 1997, was made its Chief Executive Officer. Under Linda's leadership, the company continued to prosper. In October 1999, WWE undertook a successful initial public offering and today trades on the New York Stock Exchange.

I REMEMBER WHEN WE LEASED A TYPEWRITER FOR $12 A MONTH AND I HAD TO ASSESS IF WE WERE BETTER OFF BUYING THE TYPEWRITER.

A SUBSTANTIAL LEGACY

She also spearheaded the creation of WWE's Get R.E.A.L. educational programs, as well as the company's nationwide WrestleMania Reading Challenge. She also led the development of WWE's SmackDown Your Vote! with partners including the League of Women Voters, the National Association of Secretaries of State, and the Harvard Institute of Politics.

In recognition for work over the past 20 years to support children, The Make-A-Wish Foundation awarded WWE its highest honor, the Chris Grecius Award in 2004. In honor of the company's efforts for over two decades, Linda was appointed to The Make-A-Wish Foundation of America National Advisory Council in 2005.

She also became an enthusiastic supporter of The Starlight Foundation Research Foundation and the USO. In addition, Linda served as the Honorary Corporate Chair of the Multiple Myeloma Research Foundation and on the Governor's Council for the World Special Olympics.

In 2007, she was named one of Multichannel News' Wonder Woman award recipients due to her accomplishments with WWE and as a leader in the U.S. cable television industry. Linda also guided the strategic direction of WWE's content and products that were distributed on a global basis via broadcast, syndication and cable television, publications, mobile phones, and the Internet. Other key businesses areas included licensing, merchandising, home video, e-commerce, and catalog sales.

For over three decades, the work of Linda McMahon was a critical component to the success of a company that was once run out of a basement with a staff of two. Now, it is an integrated, multi-billion dollar, publicly traded media giant. While the McMahon family shares a sense of pride in WWE, Linda McMahon was, in some ways, the power behind the throne until Fall 2009. It was then that she announced that she was leaving WWE in the capable hands of its executive team to follow another life-long passion, public service. Since then, Linda has dedicated herself to improving the overall quality of life both in her home state of Connecticut and around the United States.

In 2012, a building was named in her honor at Connecticut's Sacred Heart University.

LITTLE BEAVER

HT	4'4"	WT	60 lbs.	FROM	Quebec, Canada
SIGNATURE MOVE	Dropkick				

With his full-length headdress, signature Mohawk, and comedic approach to competing, the 4-foot-4 Little Beaver was as much a star as his larger counterparts for four decades, starting in the 1950s.

Beaver's earliest WWE days saw him team with Pancho Lopez to regularly battle Sky Low Low and Fuzzy Cupid in 1963. Years later, he and Little Louie defeated Sonny Boy Hayes and Pee Wee Adams at the first-ever *Showdown At Shea* in 1972.

Unfortunately for Little Beaver, the highest point of his career may have also been the lowest. While competing at *WrestleMania III*, Beaver found himself on the receiving end of a flattening elbow from King Kong Bundy. The impact was so great that Little Beaver was forced into retirement soon after.

LITTLE BOOGEYMAN

FROM	The Bottomless Pit	SIGNATURE MOVE	Pump Handle Slam

This little worm eater appeared in WWE alongside his larger counterpart in 2007 during the Boogeyman's rivalry with Finlay. "Little Boogey" was brought to the world of sports-entertainment to counter the presence of Hornswoggle. As the two beings from the Bottomless Pit battled Ireland's toughest sons, the shorter version showed he was just as disgusting and just as dangerous in the ring.

History has shown that the Superstars of WWE are never safe as long as the Boogeyman is around. Where he dwells, this frightening miniature sidekick is somewhere close.

LITTLE BRUTUS

Little Brutus competed in WWE's Northeast territory during miniature wrestling's surge in popularity in the 1960s. During this time, Little Brutus competed mainly as a tag team competitor, alongside Sky Low Low, Billy the Kid, and Butch Cassidy.

Brutus grew up in Quebec with an average-sized twin brother. When he first saw miniature wrestling on television, Brutus' career choice was made.

Chief rival, Jamaica Kid, normally upended the bearded Brutus during their encounters. In October 1969, Brutus gained the ultimate revenge when he defeated Jamaica Kid in one-on-one action in Boston.

After his in-ring career came to a close, Little Brutus worked as a police dispatcher, and trained future miniature wrestlers. His most noted pupil was Dink the Clown.

LITTLE TOKYO

HT	4'7"	WT	45 lbs.
SIGNATURE MOVE	Flying Chop		

One of the most well-known miniature stars of the 1970s and 1980s, Little Tokyo made a name for himself in WWE competing against the likes of Sonny Boy Hayes, Tiny Tom, and Little Louie.

Perhaps Little Tokyo's most intense rivalry came against Cowboy Lang. For years, the two competitors battled over who was the world's best miniature competitor. Unfortunately for Tokyo, Lang oftentimes walked away with the win.

As sports-entertainment grew, Little Tokyo maintained his presence as an elite competitor in his division. He even famously ventured outside division when he teamed with King Kong Bundy and Lord Littlebrook to square off against Hillbilly Jim, Little Beaver, and Haiti Kid at *WrestleMania III*.

LO DOWN

MEMBERS	D-Lo Brown & Chaz	COMBINED WT	511 lbs.

Prior to 2000, both D-Lo Brown and Chaz enjoyed championship-caliber WWE careers. When they decided to unite as Lo Down in July 2000, fans everywhere assumed the same level of success would follow the talented tandem. It didn't.

Many argue that Lo Down's biggest mistake was employing the managerial services of Tiger Ali Singh. Upon uniting, the duo inexplicably began to dress like their manager, complete with turbans. Their win-loss record also resembled that of Singh's, which wasn't very impressive. But it wasn't all bad. Lo Down did defeat Kaientai to earn a spot in the . Unfortunately, however, neither Superstar made it into the match. Comedian Drew Carey took their spot instead.

LORD ALFRED HAYES

HT	5'9"	WT	238 lbs.	FROM	Windermere, England
SIGNATURE MOVE	London Bridge				

Lord Alfred Hayes spent decades as one of the top figures in sports-entertainment, whether it was in the ring or behind the microphone.

Boasting a martial arts background, "Judo" Al Hayes was known throughout Europe and Japan. When he came to the United States, he took on the demeanor of a haughty "Lord," but remained the same dangerous grappler.

WWE audiences first saw Hayes in 1984 as host Vince McMahon's sidekick on the hit talk show *Tuesday Night Titans*. From there, Alfred's pleasant demeanor was regularly seen on WWE programming, as he served as a backstage interview correspondent, introductory announcer, and color commentator.

Hayes continued his exemplary work into the 1990s, and appeared on early episodes of *Monday Night Raw*. In 1995, Alfred and WWE parted ways after a successful partnership that lasted over a decade.

He retired from sports-entertainment and quietly enjoyed the fruits of his labor in his adopted state of Texas. Sadly, in July 2005, this WWE legend passed away at home.

LORD LITTLEBROOK

HT	4'4"	WT	108 lbs.	FROM	London, England

Hailing from London, England, Lord Littlebrook possessed many of the same noble qualities today's fans see in William Regal. Complete with his monocle and plaid jacket, the miniature wrestler looked every bit the part of a proper Englishman.

While competing in the United States, Littlebrook managed to capture the NWA World Midget Championship in 1966. He also garnered much attention during his days in the AWA. However, it was his *WrestleMania III* match that will always remain Littlebrook's ultimate highlight. Teaming with Little Tokyo and King Kong Bundy, he took on Hillbilly Jim and his mini friends, Haiti Kid and Little Beaver. In the end, Littlebrook's team lost via disqualification when Bundy inexplicably attacked Beaver.

LOS BORICUAS

MEMBERS	Savio Vega, Miguel Perez, Jose Estrada Jr., & Jesús Castillo

After being exiled from the Nation of Domination in 1997, Savio Vega aligned himself with fellow Puerto Rican Superstars Miguel Perez, Jose Estrada Jr., and Jesús Castillo to form Los Boricuas. Upon formation, the four-man gang immediately found conflict with The Nation, as well as The Disciples of Apocalypse, who Los Boricuas defeated at *SummerSlam 1997*.

Continuing to prove Los Boricuas' worth, Vega went on to defeat Faarooq, of The Nation, and Crush, of DOA, in a Triple Threat Match at *In Your House: Ground Zero* in September 1997. Unfortunately for Los Boricuas, *Ground Zero* is where the faction's momentum seemingly peaked, as DOA finally began to overcome the Puerto Rican quartet in subsequent matches, including *In Your House: Badd Blood* in October 1997.

Los Boricuas ultimately went their separate ways in the summer of 1998. Following the breakup, Vega regained his status as a singles star, while Perez, Estrada, and Castillo regularly competed on *Super Astros*.

LOS CONQUISTADORS

Men underneath gold masks entered WWE in 1987. They were conquerors of the ring in other parts of the world, but traveled to WWE to face the premier tag teams. Their disregard for the rules did not win them any fans and, in most instances, it did not help win matches either. But their win-loss record was not a true indicator of their abilities in the ring, and they were always considered a dangerous tag team.

The Conquistadors gave a glimpse of their old world form at the inaugural *Survivor Series* when they were the last team fighting for victory. Though they went down in a losing effort, that impressive showing kept them in the WWE Tag Team Title hunt.

Although they departed from WWE in the late 1980s, the masked men made sporadic appearances for decades. Both fans and Superstars alike questioned whether they were watching the originals or other Superstars assuming the golden identities for nefarious purposes.

LOS GUERREROS

MEMBERS	Eddie Guerrero & Chavo Guerrero		
COMBINED WT	441 lbs	FROM	El Paso, Texas

They lied, they cheated, and they stole. But despite their immoral qualities, Los Guerreros were one of the most popular tag teams of their time.

Eddie Guerrero began teaming with his nephew, Chavo, during the summer of 2002. After cheating their way to victory over many of *SmackDown*'s top teams, Los Guerreros were entered into a tournament to crown the first-ever WWE Tag Team Champions. Unfortunately for them, they fell short in the semifinals.

Eddie and Chavo rebounded from the defeat well. Only one month later, they found themselves on top of the tag team division when they won a Triple Threat Match to capture the Titles at *Survivor Series 2002*. They went on to hold the gold for three months before losing to The World's Greatest Tag Team, Shelton Benjamin and Charlie Haas.

The dastardly uncle-nephew combination enjoyed one more reign atop the tag division before Chavo brutally attacked Eddie in January 2004, signifying the end of the adored Los Guerreros. After the breakup, both Guerreros went on to lie, cheat, and steal their way to great singles success.

LOS MATADORES

MEMBERS	Fernando & Diego		
COMBINED WT	435 lbs.	FROM	Plaza de Toros

In a sport where so many have paid the ultimate price in an attempt to tame the seemingly untamable, Fernando and Diego have established themselves as true legends. Collectively known as Los Matadores, the duo's unmatched levels of bravery, speed, and fearlessness have left many to assume they have the blood of the bull flowing through their veins.

Drawing from their days in the bullfighting ring, Fernando and Diego, along with their legendary bull El Torito, transitioned to WWE rings in September 2013. After defeating Heath Slater and Jinder Mahal in their debut, the masked tandem went on to turn back such teams as The Real Americans and Hunico and Camacho.

Los Matadores' success led them to WWE Tag Team Championship opportunities in the Kickoff Shows of both *WrestleMania 30* and *WrestleMania 31*. They also challenged for the Titles at *SummerSlam 2015*. Each time, however, Fernando and Diego came up short. Frustrated by continually losing, Los Matadores eventually attacked longtime cohort El Torito. The disgusting act proved that Fernando and Diego should never be trusted.

LOU ALBANO

HoF TT USA

HT	5'10"
WT	350 lbs.
FROM	Carmel, New York

Capt. Lou Albano was a short, round man with limited ability, but that didn't stop him from becoming one of the greatest entertainers sports-entertainment has ever seen. After a brilliant five decades in the business, the eccentric Albano will forever be recognized as the manager of an unprecedented number of Champions, who also possessed an amazing speaking ability and an unusual penchant for attaching rubber bands to his face.

Albano originally hoped to make a name for himself as a boxer, but after promoter Willy Gilzenberg refused to use him due to his short stature, the New York native turned his efforts toward sports-entertainment. After being trained by the legendary Arnold Skaaland and Soldier Barry, Albano began his professional career competing in front of miniscule audiences in and around his home state. He eventually worked up to more prestigious promotions in Canada and Chicago. While in the Windy City, Albano began teaming with fellow Italian, Tony Altomare. Collectively known as The Sicilians, Albano and Altomare attracted great controversy due to their mafia innuendos.

A MANAGERIAL MOVE

In 1967, The Sicilians jumped to WWE where they immediately claimed the United States Tag Team Championship from Spiros Arion and Arnold Skaaland. Despite his success in the tag ranks, it was clear that Albano's skills were not going to carry him to further success. So rather than settle for a career of potential mediocrity, Albano made the decision to jump into the managerial ranks. The move proved to be a wise one, as Albano spent the next quarter-century cementing his legacy as one of the greatest managers in sports-entertainment history.

Albano's first client was the powerhouse Crusher Verdu. Like Albano, Verdu never seemed destined for greatness, but with Albano leading the way, he eventually earned an opportunity at Bruno Sammartino's coveted WWE Championship. Unfortunately, Verdu failed in his attempts to unseat Sammartino, but glory was right around the corner for Albano.

In January 1971, Albano's protégé, Ivan Koloff, ended one of history's greatest Title reigns when he defeated Sammartino for the WWE Championship inside New York's famed Madison Square Garden. The win ended Sammartino's nearly eight-year run at the top and catapulted Albano straight to the pinnacle of the managerial ranks.

OFTEN IMITATED, BUT NEVER DUPLICATED.

THE GOLDEN TOUCH

In the years that followed, Albano also led many of WWE's most reviled Superstars to the Intercontinental Championship. Pat Patterson, Don Muraco, and Greg Valentine all employed the services of Albano en route to claiming the Intercontinental Title.

Despite all his success guiding Superstars to singles Titles, Albano's greatest managerial accomplishments may have taken place in the tag team ranks. Over the course of his career, Albano's tandems captured an amazing seventeen Tag Team Title reigns. No other manager in sports-entertainment history can boast more. Albano's list of Championship duos includes such legendary teams as the Valiant Brothers, the Blackjacks, the Wild Samoans, and the British Bulldogs.

Albano also helped launch the "Rock 'n' Wrestling Connection" that took America by storm in the mid-1980s. His famed friendship with rocker, Cyndi Lauper, landed him in the "Girls Just Want to Have Fun" music video. In turn, Lauper appeared on several WWE televised events, including the first-ever *WrestleMania*. The on-air chemistry between Albano and Lauper made national news and eventually played a role in propelling WWE into the mainstream.

Albano's contributions to sports-entertainment were recognized in 1996 when he was inducted into the WWE Hall of Fame. The induction capped an amazing career for a man who was, as he would say, "often imitated, never duplicated."

Sadly, the world lost one of its most influential performers on October 14, 2009, when Albano passed away at the age of 76. He's survived by his loving family, friends, and a performance portfolio that's unmatched within the world of sports-entertainment.

LOU THESZ

HT	6'2"
WT	225 lbs.
FROM	St. Louis, Missouri

SIGNATURE MOVE
Lou Thesz Press

Perhaps no other competitor ever took sports-entertainment as seriously, and devoted as much of his life to it. He debuted in 1932 and wrestled his last match an incredible 58 years later. That means that Thesz wrestled in seven separate decades. During that time, he held six World Championships, all of them linked to the NWA lineage, including the NWA World Heavyweight Championship itself on three separate occasions.

By his estimation, he traveled 16-million miles and wrestled in 6,000 contests, breaking 200 bones along the way. Between 1948 and 1955, he compiled a winning streak of 936 matches. Among the in-ring maneuvers that bear his signature are the original powerbomb, STF, German suplex, and aptly-named Thesz Press.

SON OF A SHOEMAKER

Thesz was born in Michigan, but moved to St. Louis as a child. There, his father Martin, a Hungarian-born shoemaker and amateur wrestler in Europe, taught him the fine points of Greco Roman competition.

As a teen, he was trained by "catch" wrestling master Ad Santel and three-time Olympian George "Hercules" Tragos. In addition to schooling Thesz on the fundamentals, they taught him about torturous, and sometimes illegal, submission and nerve holds called "hooks." After Thesz made his professional debut at age 16, this education continued under the guidance of the legendary Ed "Strangler" Lewis.

Five years after his debut, in 1937, Thesz managed to beat Everett Marshall for the National Wrestling Association Title, a world Championship then on par with the emerging National Wrestling Alliance. At age 21, he was the youngest Champion ever.

UNIFYING THE TITLE

In 1948, a group of promoters gathered in Waterloo, Iowa, to unify the various world Titles under the National Wrestling Alliance, or NWA, banner. Although the first official Champion was Orville Brown, a unification match was planned with Thesz. However, weeks before the clash, Brown was in a career-ending car accident and Thesz was awarded the Championship. For the next several years, he conquered virtually every other world Title claimant in North America.

Because of Thesz' background as a premier "hooker," promoters were immensely happy with him as the NWA Champion, secure that he could handle any type of confrontation and protect their investment in the organization.

Still, there were controversies. In 1957, he was injured in a two-out-of-three fall match with Édouard Carpentier, and could not compete in the final round. Although Carpentier's hand was raised, the NWA decreed that Thesz was still the Champion. This did not prevent Carpentier from journeying to a number of promotions with his version of the Title, creating a muddled Championship picture.

Around the same time, Thesz became the first American Champion to defend his Title in Japan, engaging in a series of draws with the country's foremost mat hero, Rikidozan, that created a sensation in Asia. Many promoters were bewildered that he'd chosen to compete so far from home. But Thesz had become an international ambassador.

Later, after he'd lost the gold to three-time NCAA champion Dick Hutton, Thesz returned to Japan and toured Europe with a new Title, the NWA International Championship. To this day, the Title is defended on the All Japan promotion's cards.

In 1963, in Toronto, Thesz reclaimed the NWA World Heavyweight Championship from "Nature Boy" Buddy Rogers in one fall. But northeastern promoters Vincent J. McMahon and Toots Mondt did not acknowledge the decision, claiming that the rules at the time stipulated that Championships had to be decided in two-out-of-three fall contests. Breaking away from the NWA, the pair started the company that became WWE with Rogers as its inaugural champion.

AGELESS

Thesz held the NWA honors until 1966. But as late as 1978, Thesz was still a major name in the industry, becoming the first Champion of Mexico's Universal Wrestling Alliance at age 62.

Although he retired the next year, he made occasional comebacks, including his 1990 match, at age 74, with former student Masahiro Chono in Japan. He lost after his artificial hip buckled.

"I was old enough to know not to do it," Thesz explained, "but I did it anyway."

In 2002, 86-year-old Thesz passed away. In 2016 he took his rightful place among other legends when he was inducted into the WWE Hall of Fame.

I AM A WRESTLER, NOT A RASSLER, NOT A CLOWN, A WRESTLER

LOUIE SPICOLLI

HT	5'11"	WT	258 lbs.	FROM	Los Angeles, California
SIGNATURE MOVE	Spicolli Driver				

Because of his boyish features, Louie Spicolli was in the habit of calling himself "Cutie Pie." But, despite his lighthearted wit, he developed a serious following in Mexico and Japan, as well as independent promotions throughout the United States. In 1988, a teenaged Spicolli made his WWE debut, where he continued to appear intermittently in WWE through the mid-1990s.

In 1996, he debuted in Extreme Championship Wrestling and butted heads with the "Innovator of Violence" and ECW Original, Tommy Dreamer. After leaving ECW in 1997, he appeared in World Championship Wrestling and was an associate of the New World Order. He also entertained fans with his occasional commentary during broadcasts. Sadly, this gifted Superstar passed away in 1998.

LOUIS CERDAN

HT	5'10"	WT	240 lbs.	FROM	Montreal, Quebec, Canada
SIGNATURE MOVE	Figure-Four Leglock				

This French-Canadian began his WWE career in 1966 and was a close friend to then-World Champion Bruno Sammartino. For three years, Cerdan showed his fire in the ring, but in 1969 Cerdan left WWE and returned to Canada.

In 1974, Cerdan made a glorious return to WWE, teaming with close friend Tony Parisi. In November 1975, the duo defeated the Blackjacks to become World Tag Team Champions. They defended the Titles for six months until they crossed paths with the dangerous Executioners in May 1976. Following the loss to the masked tandem, Cerdan left WWE and returned to the rings of the Great White North, where he retired after a stellar 25-year career.

THE LUCHA DRAGONS

MEMBERS	Sin Cara & Kalisto
COMBINED WT	368 lbs.

Although Sin Cara and Kalisto have each compiled a number of single's accomplishments, forming the Lucha Dragons provided a way for the Mexican tandem to showcase the electrifying aerial maneuvers of their home country, as well as their pride in the lucha libre traditions that define them.

Sin Cara already had *WrestleMania* credentials, having appeared in the Andre the Giant Memorial Battle Royal at *WrestleMania 30*, when he arrived in NXT in 2014.

The alliance with fellow masked luchador, Kalisto, worked seamlessly. The Lucha Dragons won a tournament to become number one contenders for the NXT Tag Team Championship, capturing the gold from the Ascension.

After losing the Titles to Blake and Murphy, the pair rocketed onto the WWE main roster, making their premiere *Raw* appearance the night after *WrestleMania 31*. At *TLC: Tables, Ladders and Chairs* in December 2015, they engaged in a three-way thriller with The Usos and The New Day, a contest compared to the storied confrontations involving the Dudleys, Hardy Boyz, and Edge and Christian during WWE's "Attitude" era.

LUDVIG BORGA

HT	6'3"	WT	275 lbs.	FROM	Helsinki, Finland
SIGNATURE MOVE	Human Torture Rack				

This Finnish powerhouse burst on the WWE scene in 1993. The monster Borga squashed his opponents and showed little respect for the rulebook. Fans quickly came to despise this individual and his spread of anti-American sentiment, which resulted in him butting heads with "All-American" Lex Luger.

Borga withstood the attacks made by many opponents. After picking up a win at *SummerSlam* against Marty Jannetty, he ended the two-year undefeated streak of Tatanka, pinning him with one finger.

In early 1994, Borga left WWE to travel to Japan. He embarked on a successful professional boxing career, fighting both in the United States and Europe before briefly entering the political arena in his homeland in Finland.

LUKE GALLOWS

HT	6'8"	WT	304 lbs.
SIGNATURE MOVE	Gallows Pole		

Festus walked around WWE in a near-comatose state for almost two years. Most found his unresponsiveness to be somewhat entertaining. But not CM Punk. The "Straight Edge Superstar" saw a man struggling with torturous addictions.

In November 2009, Punk revealed that he helped Festus overcome his dark past. No longer off kilter, Festus transformed into a menacing force known as Luke Gallows. As Gallows, the reformed competitor found a new beginning as the muscle behind Punk's Straight Edge Society. Gallows's victims included some of WWE's brightest stars, such as Rey Mysterio and Matt Hardy.

Eventually Punk cast Gallows out of the Straight Edge Society following an embarrassing loss in September 2010. Leaderless, Gallows disappeared from WWE soon after. Nearly six years later, after reinventing and reinvigorating his career overseas, Gallows returned beside his partner Karl Anderson.

LUKE GRAHAM

HT	6'1"	WT	219 lbs.
FROM	Charlotte, North Carolina		

"Crazy" Luke Graham was just one of a long line of Grahams who thrived inside the ring. Counting brothers Dr. Jerry Graham, "Superstar" Billy Graham, and Eddie Graham, as well as the five sons that followed, the multi-generational Graham clan can claim a total of nine competitors.

Graham began teaming with his brother, Jerry, in Canada in 1963. It was during this time that fans began to recognize him as slightly deranged. Despite his efforts to convince them otherwise, Graham was constantly being called "crazy" by the fans. Infuriated by the chants, the bleached-blond Superstar would oftentimes hold his hands over his ears to drown out the sound, but that only made the crowds chant louder.

Graham's greatest singles success came in 1965 when he won the prestigious WWA Heavyweight Championship from Pedro Morales. The victory proved to be a bright point in Graham's career, but paled in comparison to the groundbreaking win he would earn six years later as a tag team competitor in WWE.

In June 1971, with Tarzan Tyler as his partner, Graham turned back The Sheik and Dick the Bruiser to become one-half of WWE's first-ever World Tag Team Champions. The historic duo held the gold proudly for six months, paving the way for all the great teams that followed, including the Road Warriors, Hart Foundation, and Edge and Christian.

LUKE HARPER

		HT	6'5"	WT	275 lbs.
		SIGNATURE MOVE			The Way

One doesn't need to look into the eyes of Luke Harper for very long to tell he's not like everybody else. As a faithful follower of the eerie Bray Wyatt, Harper's presumably unnerving mind is a mystery. But his dominance in the ring is undeniable.

The creepy Harper first made his presence felt in July 2013, when he, Erick Rowan, and Bray Wyatt, known as The Wyatt Family, attacked an unsuspecting Kane on *Raw*. In the months that followed, the strange duo of Harper and Rowan terrorized many of WWE's top tandems, including the Prime Time Players and The Usos.

With the new year came the inevitable showdown against WWE's other top faction, The Shield. Throughout the early portion of the year, the warring factions competed in arguably the most exciting six-man tag team matches seen in years, including at *Elimination Chamber*, where The Wyatt Family successfully eliminated The Shield.

Bray Wyatt set Harper free toward the end of the year. The result was the unleashing of one of the most unpredictable forces in recent memory. Few could figure Harper out, including Dolph Ziggler, who lost the Intercontinental Championship to the erratic Superstar in November, and Dean Ambrose, who was sent crashing through a ladder at the hands of Harper at *WrestleMania*.

Harper returned home to The Wyatt Family in 2015. Together again, the disturbing family picked up where they left off, terrorizing WWE Superstars, including the Brothers of Destruction, The Undertaker and Kane.

LUNA VACHON

HT	5'6"	FROM	Montreal, Quebec, Canada
FROM	Luna Eclipse		

Standing out in the world of sports-entertainment is not an easy task, especially when the family that precedes you includes the legendary Butcher, Mad Dog, and Vivian Vachon. But over the course of her twenty-plus year career, the colorful Luna Vachon managed to put her own indelible mark in sports-entertainment, striking fear in fans and foes alike along the way.

Following training from her aunt Vivian and Fabulous Moolah, Vachon made her debut in Florida in 1986. Her early days saw her battle the likes of Lady Maxine and Madusa Miceli. She later competed internationally in Japan and Puerto Rico, as well as domestically in the AWA, where she participated in the Lingerie Battle Royal at *SuperClash III* in December 1988.

In 1993, Vachon brought her unique style to WWE, joining forces first with Shawn Michaels, and later Bam Bam Bigelow. During this time, she famously teamed with the "Beast from the East" to defeat Doink and his sidekick, Dink, in a Mixed Tag Team Match at *WrestleMania X*.

In subsequent years, Vachon would appear briefly in both ECW and WCW before returning to WWE in 1997. Upon her return, she managed Goldust, Gangrel, and The Oddities, before leaving WWE in 2000.

Sadly, Luna Vachon passed away in August 2010. Though gone, she will forever be remembered as one of the most eccentric women to ever grace sports-entertainment.

LUTHER REIGNS

HT	6'5"	**WT**	295 lbs.	**FROM** Phoenix, Arizona
SIGNATURE MOVE	Reign of Terror			

In April 2004, *SmackDown* General Manager Kurt Angle hired Luther Reigns to serve as his assistant. But at nearly 300 pounds, it was only a matter of time before Reigns ditched his business suit for ring gear.

Reigns decimated Funaki in his debut and then did the same to Charlie Haas at *The Great American Bash*. He soon formed a tag team with Mark Jindrak. Still loyal to Angle, the duo distracted Big Show long enough for Angle to chop him down with a tranquilizer dart. While unconscious, the trio of Superstars celebrated by shaving Big Show's head bald.

Prior to his WWE release in May 2005, Reigns stood across the ring from some of the greatest, including Eddie Guerrero, Undertaker, and John Cena.

MABEL

HT	6'6"	**WT**	487 lbs.	**FROM** Harlem, New York
SIGNATURE MOVE	Big Splash			

The massive Mabel made his WWE debut in 1993 as a member of the rapping tag team Men on a Mission. Managed by Oscar, Mabel and his partner, Mo, hoped their success would serve as a positive influence for inner-city youths.

For most of their first year, the duo easily destroyed smaller competition. Their enormous success eventually earned them an opportunity at The Quebecers' WWE Tag Titles at *WrestleMania X*. The rapping tandem fell short at *WrestleMania* but defeated The Quebecers days later in England.

After losing the gold, Men on a Mission struggled for more than a year. They developed an unpopular mean streak, which alienated fans but turned things around for Mabel. He won the 1995 *King of the Ring* tournament, defeating Savio Vega in the finals. The colossal King soon found himself carried to the ring by peasants and competing in main events. He even challenged Diesel for the WWE Championship at *SummerSlam*.

After being abducted by Undertaker's Ministry in 1999, Mabel was reborn as Viscera.

THE MACHINES

MEMBERS	Giant Machine, Super Machine, & Big Machine
COMBINED WT	1,129 lbs.

Following the controversial 1986 suspension of Andre the Giant, rumors began to swirl that an equally-imposing masked competitor from Japan would soon be joining WWE. In an attempt to uncover the truth, "Mean" Gene Okerlund flew to the Land of the Rising Sun in search of the mysterious mammoth. When he got there, he found Giant Machine and Big Machine, who were both fluent in English and received double master's degrees from the University of Tokyo in Education and Business Administration.

With Super Machine rounding out the trio, The Machines weighed in at a whopping 1,129 pounds. Upon seeing them and fearing for his clients' safety, Bobby Heenan began a relentless campaign to prove that Giant Machine was actually the suspended Andre the Giant. But "The Brain" was never able to convince WWE officials of his theory.

The Machines disappeared from WWE by the end of 1986. Coincidentally, Andre the Giant's suspension was lifted around the same time.

MAD DOG VACHON

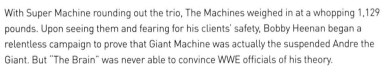

HT	5'7"	**WT**	230 lbs.	**FROM** Montreal, Quebec, Canada
SIGNATURE MOVE	Piledriver			

At only 5'7", Mad Dog Vachon was seemingly at a disadvantage nearly every time he stepped in the ring. But what he lacked in size, he more than made up for in determination and pure barbarism. Vachon was such a savage, in fact, that he could oftentimes be seen gnawing on his opponent, a tactic that made him one of the most despised villains of his time.

Regularly recognized as the leader of the Vachon family, the rabid Mad Dog found his greatest success in the AWA. While competing in the Minnesota-based company, Vachon accumulated five AWA World Heavyweight Championship reigns. Only Verne Gagne, whom Vachon beat for the Title twice, held it more times.

Vachon also achieved great tag team success, capturing the AWA World Tag Team Championship twice (once with Paul Vachon and once with Verne Gagne), as well as the AWA Midwest Tag Team Championship three times (twice with Bob Orton and once with Paul Vachon).

Aside from a few appearances in the early-to-mid 1970s, Vachon didn't compete for WWE until 1984. Though his best years were behind him, he regularly defeated the likes of The Missing Link, Tiger Chung Lee, and Rene Goulet.

Shortly after his 1986 retirement from the ring, Vachon was involved in a hit-and-run accident that resulted in the amputation of his right leg. Nearly one decade after the accident, WWE honored Vachon at *In Your House: Good Friends, Better Enemies*. During the event, Diesel remorselessly tore Vachon's prosthetic leg from his body in an attempt to use it as a weapon in his match against Shawn Michaels. The act remains one of the most infamous moments in WWE history, and it resulted in announcer, Vince McMahon, proclaiming, "That's the lowest thing I've ever seen in my life."

After nearly forty years in the ring, Mad Dog Vachon's legendary career was honored when he was inducted into the WWE Hall of Fame in March 2010.

MAD MAXINE

HT 6'4"

Though she only competed in a handful of WWE matches, Mad Maxine will forever be remembered as one of the most frightening females to ever lace a pair of boots. Standing at an astonishing 6'4" (6'7" if you include her bright green Mohawk) and sporting demonic eye makeup, Maxine instilled instant fear into her competition.

Brought into WWE by Fabulous Moolah in 1985, Maxine's sole responsibility was to strip Wendi Richter of the Women's Championship. In preparation for the task, Maxine decimated both Susan Star and Desiree Petersen in less than three minutes each. With the impressive victories under her belt, Maxine appeared primed to battle Richter. But before the highly-anticipated encounter could ever take place, Maxine mysteriously left WWE.

MAGNIFICENT MAURICE

Strutting about the ring in a cape and dark glasses, Magnificent Maurice was an effete, arrogant presence. His interviews were slow and pompous, and generally antagonized the fans at home into coming to the arena to jeer him.

Yet, the former amateur bodybuilder exuded flamboyant charisma second to none, utilizing outrageous antics to get inside opponents' heads.

Managed by the equally flashy Grand Wizard (then known as J. Wellington Radcliffe), Maurice and partner "Handsome" Johnny Barend antagonized audiences from the Midwest to Hawaii. As a single's competitor, he battled stars like Bobo Brazil, Pedro Morales, and Bruno Sammartino. Tragically, Magnificent Maurice's life was cut short when he was killed in an airplane crash while working as an actor in 1974.

MAN MOUNTAIN MIKE

HT 6'4" **WT** 600 lbs. **SIGNATURE MOVE** Big Splash

Perhaps no Superstar was more appropriately named than Man Mountain Mike. At an amazing 600 pounds, he was a true mountain of a man. After making his debut in 1968, Man Mountain Mike formed a feared tag team with fellow big man Haystacks Calhoun. Together, the pair tipped the scales at more than half a ton.

With so much weight tacked on to his enormous frame, Man Mountain Mike was nearly impossible to toss over the top rope, which is why he was called, "The Acknowledged King of Battle Royals."

After holding Tag Team Titles with Butcher Brannigan in Los Angeles, Man Mountain Mike competed for WWE briefly during the mid-1970s. His stay is most remembered for his teaming with fellow big man, Jerry "Crusher" Blackwell.

MAN MOUNTAIN ROCK

HT 6'6" **WT** 350 lbs.
SIGNATURE MOVE Front-Face Suplex

A former All-American wrestler, Man Mountain Rock ripped into WWE in 1995. He played his six-string electric guitar before bouts and rocked the crowd with his hard licks and opponents with his mix of power and surprising agility.

The man with tie-dye ring attire unleashed his force on villains like Brooklyn Brawler, Kwang, Jean-Pierre LaFitte, Tatanka, Mantaur, Dean Douglas, and Bob Backlund. By October 1995, Man Mountain Rock left WWE. Later, he would become involved in television and motion pictures, but WWE fans will always remember him as the tie-dye Superstar who rocked the house wherever he appeared.

MAE YOUNG

FROM Sand Springs, Oklahoma

Mae Young was an influential force in sports-entertainment for seventy years. Yes, you read that right. Seventy years!

A former member of her high school's boys' wrestling team, Young made her professional debut in 1939. Although she was only fifteen years old at the time, Young proved herself as a tough-as-nails competitor. In the decades that followed, her efforts helped pave the way for future female Superstars, such as The Fabulous Moolah and Judy Grable. Her success eventually led her to becoming the first United States Women's Champion.

In addition to achieving great in-ring success, Young is known as one of the most influential trainers of both male and female Superstars. Her most noted pupil was perhaps the greatest women's wrestler of all time, The Fabulous Moolah. She also helped mold the early career of Ric "The Equalizer" Drasin, the former lead guitarist of The Hollywood Vines.

More recently, Young became known as the fearless senior citizen who always seemed to attract controversy. Her most exposing moment occurred at the 2000 *Royal Rumble* when she flashed a packed Madison Square Garden crowd. The risqué act proved that Young was always up for a good time, something one-time boyfriend Mark Henry experienced firsthand.

Despite her advanced age, Young was never afraid to mix it up in the ring. Unfortunately, her attempts at physicality usually landed her in enormous amounts of trouble. It was not

uncommon to see Young flattened by competitors less than half her age. She was even sent off the stage and through a table at the hands of Bubba Ray Dudley.

In 2008, Young's contributions to sports-entertainment were recognized when she was inducted into the WWE Hall of Fame, alongside other great females The Fabulous Moolah and Sherri Martel.

Mae Young passed away in January 2014, leaving behind an amazing legacy that spanned nine different decades. Along the way, she proved to be an indestructible Diva who lived life to the absolute fullest.

MANTAUR

HT 6'0"　**WT** 401 lbs.　**FROM** The Isle of Crete

Mantaur is widely considered one of the most unorthodox competitors in WWE history. With his life-sized bull carcass costume and animalistic characteristics, the mighty Superstar was impossible to control, even by his own manager, Jim Cornette.

Upon his January 1995 debut, Mantaur made quick work of several lesser-known Superstars, including Leroy Howard and Jason Ahrndt. But as the weeks passed, the WWE locker room began to outsmart the animal. It wasn't long before the likes of Razor Ramon, Duke "The Dumpster" Droese, and Man Mountain Rock were pinning the peculiar Superstar's shoulders to the mat. Eventually, the ring proved too wild for Mantaur, who left WWE by year's end.

MANU

HT 6'2"　**WT** 290 lbs.
FROM Lehigh Valley, Pennsylvania
SIGNATURE MOVE Lights Out

In his native Samoan language, Manu means "animal," which is an appropriate name for the son of Afa, one of the original Wild Samoans. Manu's incredible strength, speed, and toughness were on display in WWE following his September 2008 debut. He aligned himself with other second-generation Superstars, Cody Rhodes and Ted DiBiase, in battles with CM Punk, Kofi Kingston, and others. Manu laid out opponents with his remarkable Lights Out finishing maneuver.

Manu proclaimed to be the last piece of the puzzle in the famed lineage of his family. He vied for membership in the Randy Orton-led Legacy. However, after a loss to Matt Hardy, Orton shunned him from the multi-generational group. Though his time with WWE was brief, this beast from the renowned Anoa'i bloodline displayed the power of Samoa.

MANUEL SOTO

HT 5'9"　**WT** 230 lbs.　**FROM** Puerto Rico

Manuel Soto was a no-nonsense competitor widely recognized for his superior technical ability. He competed mainly on the West Coast, as well as in Georgia (as Cyclone Soto). While in Los Angeles, the Puerto Rican star teamed with Porkchop Cash to wrest away the NWA Americas Tag Team Championship from Goliath and Black Gordman in July 1974.

In August 1974, Soto defeated Mr. California for the Beat the Champ Television Title. He only held the gold for one week before being defeated. Some historical records refuse to recognize the reign.

Soto had a short stay in WWE during the mid-1970s. While there, he became a favorite of the large Puerto Rican Northeast fan base. Perhaps his greatest victories came over future Hall of Famer Johnny Rodz in 1976.

MAPLE LEAF WRESTLING

Throughout the time when the sports-entertainment industry was divided into regions, Toronto's Maple Leaf Wrestling presented some of the most diverse shows in North America. Occasionally, the WWE, NWA, and AWA Championships were defended on the same Maple Leaf Gardens show, and all three promotions recognized the Canadian Heavyweight Champion.

In 1939, John and Frank Tunney took over promotional duties at Maple Leaf Gardens from their predecessor, Jack Corcoran. John died several months later, and Frank continued to promote for four decades, building cards around Whipper Billy Watson, Angelo Mosca, Sweet Daddy Siki, Bulldog Brower, Tiger Jeet Singh, The Sheik, and others.

Lou Thesz' controversial 1963 NWA Title win over Buddy Rogers in 1963 prompted WWE's formation. In 1978, Maple Leaf Gardens began specifically featuring talent from Jim Crockett's Mid-Atlantic promotion. But after Frank Tunney's death in 1983, his nephew, Jack, signed a deal with WWE. Jack Tunney was WWE president from 1984 to 1995.

MARC MERO

 **HT** 6'1"　**WT** 235 lbs.　**FROM** Macon, Georgia
SIGNATURE MOVE Merosault

Few WWE Superstars have made their debut at sports-entertainment's greatest spectacle. At *WrestleMania XII*, Marc Mero showed what he was all about when he came to the aid of Sable, who was being berated by Hunter Hearst-Helmsley.

Following his debut, an appreciative Sable led Mero to the ring as he fought WWE's most infamous Superstars. Taking on the nickname "Wildman," it was clear that Mero was no stranger to intense competition, having been an accomplished boxer and former WCW Television Champion. Within a year of his WWE debut, he defeated Faarooq in a tournament final to become Intercontinental Champion.

After recovering from a severe knee injury in 1997, Mero returned with a newfound arrogance, claiming he was "Marvelous." With Sable on her way to mega-stardom, Mero grew jealous of the attention. The two parted ways and Mero made it his vindictive mission to humiliate his former valet. During the remainder of his WWE career, Mero and his new ally, Jacqueline, were at odds with Sable until Mero left WWE in 1999. Today, Mero works as a motivational speaker.

MARCUS COR VON

HT 6'1" **WT** 265 lbs. **FROM** Detroit, Michigan **SIGNATURE MOVE** Pounce

Marcus Cor Von made his WWE debut in January 2007 as a member of the ECW roster. Shortly after his debut, "The Alpha Male" joined forces with fellow upstarts Elijah Burke, Matt Striker, and Kevin Thorn. Collectively known as the New Breed, the young stable took exception to the veteran presence of ECW Originals Rob Van Dam, Tommy Dreamer, Sandman, and Sabu.

At *WrestleMania 23*, Cor Von and his fellow New Breed teammates came up short against the Originals in an Eight-Man Tag Team Match. Following the loss, Cor Von spent the majority of the next few months looking to avenge the *WrestleMania* defeat. Unfortunately, he failed to appear on *ECW* after June and left WWE a few months later.

MARCUS LOUIS

HT 6'2" **WT** 245 lbs. **FROM** Bordeaux, France
SIGNATURE MOVE The French Revolution

Using the French tri-color as his inspiration, Marcus Louis joined NXT in 2013, hoping to attain the same level of glory as fellow countrymen Édouard Carpentier and Andre the Giant.

A former rugby player and veteran of the European mat scene, Louis formed a team with the like-minded Sylvester Lefort. The pair dubbed themselves the Legionnaires, in homage to both the French Foreign Legion and the 1970s team of the same name, Sgt. Jacques Goulet and Private Don Fargo.

After a strong start, the team struggled, and Louis and Lefort ended up competing against each other. "The French Paradox" then tried other partners, and engaged in single's competition until leaving WWE in 2016.

MARIA

HT 5'7" **FROM** Chicago, Illinois

WWE audiences were first wowed by Maria when she participated in the 2004 *Raw* Diva Search. Over time, this bubbly "WWE Kiss Cam" host and backstage correspondent proved she was not just another pretty face.

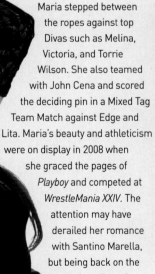

Maria stepped between the ropes against top Divas such as Melina, Victoria, and Torrie Wilson. She also teamed with John Cena and scored the deciding pin in a Mixed Tag Team Match against Edge and Lita. Maria's beauty and athleticism were on display in 2008 when she graced the pages of *Playboy* and competed at *WrestleMania XXIV*. The attention may have derailed her romance with Santino Marella, but being back on the market allowed none other than Snoop Dogg to plant a kiss on her following her match.

The former beauty queen added another highlight to her sports-entertainment career in 2009 when she was voted WWE Diva of the Year. Maria made a lasting impression on the sports-entertainment industry. She has since been active with several other entertainment ventures, including her own music album. She also received the first ever WWE Talent Scholarship in 2014.

MARIANNA

As Chaz's beautiful blonde girlfriend, Marianna was often seen at ringside supporting her man in his matches during the summer of 1999. Eventually, Marianna's beauty became too much to handle for Chaz, who broke up with his girlfriend after other Superstars began to make advances toward her.

The breakup didn't sit well with Marianna. In an attempt to get back at her former boyfriend, she showed up on *Raw* with a black eye, claiming she was the victim of domestic violence. With the help of GTV, though, it was revealed that Marianna's black eye was actually just makeup. The charade forced authorities to take her into custody. Marianna's career never rebounded.

MARIO MANCINI

HT 5'10" **WT** 236 lbs. **FROM** Milford, Connecticut

In the world of sports-entertainment, it's generally believed that in order to be successful a Superstar must possess at least some sort of charisma and/or muscle. Mario Mancini displayed neither. But he was recognized as one of the most resilient Superstars of all time. Despite losing nearly every match, Mancini always kept coming back for more.

Still a teenager, Mancini debuted in WWE in 1984. Looking back, he probably could've used some more seasoning, as he quickly became fodder for the likes of Greg Valentine, Kamala, and Don Muraco.

Unfortunately for Mancini, more experience didn't necessarily mean more wins. Instead, as the decade wore on, he helped a new crop of Superstars excel, including Bad News Brown, Ted DiBiase, and the Honky Tonk Man.

MARIO MILANO

| HT | 6'5" | WT | 265 lbs. | FROM | Trieste, Italy |
| SIGNATURE MOVE | Atomic Drop |

Because of his towering height, Mario Milano may have had the most punishing atomic drop in sports-entertainment. During a 1970 run with WWE, opponents like Crusher Verdu, George "The Animal" Steele, Ernie Ladd, and Professor Toru Tanaka learned this the hard way, while teammates were relieved to have him on their side.

Born in Italy, Milano was raised in Venezuela which enabled him to communicate in Italian and Spanish, attracting a variety of fans. After competing in South America, he wrestled in Tennessee, winning tag titles with Danny Hodge, Len Rossi, and Jackie Fargo.

In 1967, he relocated to Australia, where he became a national hero, tagging with Bruno Sammartino during the WWE Champion's Down Under visits. After retirement, Milano bought an Australian café.

MARK HENRY

| HT | 6'4" | WT | 399 lbs. | FROM | Silsbee, Texas |
| SIGNATURE MOVE | World's Strongest Slam |

For the past twenty years, hundreds of freakishly powerful men have passed through the WWE locker room, but none possessing the type of superhuman power as WWE's stalwart strongman Mark Henry. The mountainous Henry first captured the world's attention at the 1992 Olympic Games, then at the 1995 Pan-American Games. WWE took notice of his weightlifting prowess and signed him in 1996. Two decades later, his "Hall of Pain" keeps expanding.

Henry first displayed his mean streak in 1998 when he sided with Faarooq, The Rock, and others in the Nation of Domination. When the dangerous Nation disbanded, Henry showed he could be a lover as well as a fighter. Thankfully, his infatuation with the ladies did not derail his dominance in the ring.

In 2006, Henry overcame several injury-related setbacks and returned to the ring more determined than ever. He took aim at WWE's top names and even challenged the legendary Undertaker to a Casket Match at *WrestleMania 22*. In 2008, The World's Strongest Man seized his first Title in nearly a decade after he defeated Kane and Big Show at *Night of Champions* to capture the ECW Championship. Shortly after the victory, Henry aligned himself with Tony Atlas. With another historic powerhouse in his corner, Henry appeared more unstoppable than ever.

The WWE Universe began to appreciate Mark Henry and their cheers led him to form a popular tag team with MVP. Still, frustration from a World Championship drought drove Henry once again toward a vicious path of destruction. This path culminated in a victory over Randy Orton at 2011's *Night of Champions* for a long-awaited World Heavyweight Championship. For three months, he unleashed his pent up fury as Champion. At *Vengeance 2011*, a thunderous superplex to Big Show caused the entire ring to collapse under the weight of the two behemoths.

Another behemoth, Ryback, felt the brunt of Henry's force at *WrestleMania 29*. Shortly after picking up the win on the grandest stage, Henry appeared set to retire. His heartfelt speech moved spectators to tears, but it was all a ruse to set up John Cena for a punishing attack. Since then, Henry has continued to display his steel-bending strength and explosive temper against Roman Reigns, Rusev, and other rising stars.

MARK JINDRAK

| HT | 6'7" | WT | 305 lbs. | FROM | Atlanta, Georgia |
| SIGNATURE MOVE | Mark of Excellence |

Trained in WCW's Power Plant by Paul Orndorff, Mark Jindrak began his career in WCW as part of the Natural Born Thrillers. When WWE purchased WCW, he became part of The Alliance.

After the invasion fizzled, Jindrak stayed in WWE. In 2004, he teamed with Garrison Cade and saw action against several top teams. Soon he became so enamored with his own physique that he dubbed himself "The Reflection of Perfection." Even Teddy Long was impressed and briefly managed the egotistical star. Shortly after, he aligned with Luther Reigns and Kurt Angle. As the gold medalist's hired goon, Jindrak helped with dirty deeds such as forcefully shaving Big Show's head. In July 2005, Jindrak left WWE but still competed in Japan and Mexico.

MARK LEWIN

| HT | 6'2" | WT | 251 lbs. | FROM | Buffalo, New York |
| SIGNATURE MOVE | Sleeper Hold |

In his autobiography, Mark Lewin described himself as a man of multiple personalities, "sometimes all of them at the same time."

In the late 1950s, he was the handsome matinee idol, teaming with Don Curtis in Madison Square Garden and holding the United States Tag Team Championship. Later, he was sometimes billed as "Maniac" Mark Lewin, a reputation earned from bloody battles with men like The Sheik, Terry Funk, and King Curtis Iaukea. In the 1980s, Lewin became the "Purple Haze" in Kevin Sullivan's "Army of Darkness" in the Florida territory.

Few realized his pedigree. Lewin was the brother of fellow wrestlers, Donn and Ted, and brother-in-law of "Dangerous" Danny McShain. In addition to North America, Lewin also headlined in Malaysia, New Zealand, and other countries.

MARK YOUNG

| HT | 5'10" | WT | 236 lbs. | FROM | Milford, Connecticut |

Well-schooled in the grappling arts, Mark Young debuted in WWE in 1986. Over the next four years, he faced the most dangerous rule-breakers, including Dino Bravo, Boris Zhukov, and Earthquake. Unfortunately for Young, he rarely walked away victorious.

Young also tried his hand at tag team competition, but the change in scenery failed to change the results. He oftentimes wound up on the losing end against the likes of the Fabulous Rougeau Brothers, Brain Busters, and Orient Express.

By September 1990, Young left WWE to tour Asia, where his string of bad luck continued. His career ended a few years later; and while he never gained great success, he's remembered as a competitor who was willing to take on anybody at any time.

MARTY JANNETTY

| HT | 5'11" | WT | 234 lbs. | FROM | Columbus, Georgia |
| SIGNATURE MOVE | Rocker Dropper |

Marty Jannetty made his in-ring debut in 1984 in the Central States territory, where he challenged Ric Flair for the NWA Heavyweight Championship and met another future star, Shawn Michaels. The two formed a popular duo known as The Midnight Rockers, and then exploded onto the tag team scene in the AWA.

In June 1988, the pair, now abbreviating their name to The Rockers, skyrocketed to fame in WWE. With incredible speed, agility, quickness, and continuity, Jannetty and Michaels were considered by many as uncrowned World Tag Team Champions. Inseparable for years, Jannetty and Michaels began to drift apart. Audiences witnessed a violent split in 1992 when Michaels threw Jannetty through a window during an interview segment.

Jannetty recovered, and the former friends traded the Intercontinental Championship back and forth. In 1994, Jannetty teamed with 1-2-3 Kid to capture the World Tag Team Championship.

By 1997, Jannetty left WWE, but made regular comebacks, including several reunions with Michaels. Recently, he's gained a following among people who've seen his old matches on the WWE Network.

MARYSE

| HT | 5'8" | FROM | Montreal, Quebec, Canada |
| SIGNATURE MOVE | French Kiss |

This French-Canadian Superstar was first seen as a finalist in the 2006 *Raw* Superstar Search. Though she was eliminated from the competition, Maryse would not be denied, a trait that would make her a successful WWE Superstar. Maryse showcased her seductive methods in May 2008 when she stole Deuce and Domino away from their manager, Cherry. Once she entered active competition, she used the French Kiss, her devastating version of the DDT, to put down her competition. On December 26, 2008 she became the second Divas Champion in WWE history and ruled the division for eight months.

In 2010, Maryse enjoyed a second stint as Divas Champion defeating Gail Kim. Later, her appreciation for precious metals and rare stones led her to the side of Million Dollar Champion, Ted DiBiase. This glamorous material girl and "sexiest of the sexy" also served as co-host of NXT being lavished with gifts from the always charming Hornswoggle.

After nearly five years away, Maryse returned to WWE the night after *WrestleMania 32*. Her shocking arrival provided the distraction needed for her husband, The Miz, to defeat Zack Ryder for the Intercontinental Championship.

MASCARITA SAGRADA

| FROM | Mexico |
| SIGNATURE MOVE | Missile Dropkick |

A legend in Mexico, this masked Lucha Libre star was known in Mexico and WCW before his debut in WWE on the first episode of *Shotgun Saturday Night* in 1997. The daredevil occasionally battled his old rival from Mexico, Espectrito, and went undefeated in his first tour of duty with WWE.

In 2005, he returned to WWE as part of the newly-launched Juniors Division. Sagrada picked up where he left off and dominated his opponents. Though he left WWE in March 2006, he is one of few Superstars to go undefeated during his tenure with WWE.

THE MASKED SUPERSTAR

| HT | 6'3" | WT | 291 lbs | FROM | New York, New York |
| SIGNATURE MOVE | Swinging Neckbreaker |

The Masked Superstar was as mean as he was mysterious. Hiding behind a star-covered mask, the oversized competitor broke nearly every rule in the book to earn several high-profile encounters during his brief WWE stay.

The man behind the mask received his first opportunity at WWE immortality in 1983 when he challenged Bob Backlund for the WWE Championship at Madison Square Garden. On this night, The Masked Superstar accomplished what few were able to do when he defeated Backlund via countout. Unfortunately for The Masked Superstar, WWE Titles cannot change hands via countout.

Still searching for that elusive Title, The Masked Superstar earned another opportunity when he challenged the newly-crowned WWE Champion Hulk Hogan in early 1984. Again, he was unable to walk away with the Title after being disqualified for using a foreign object.

While Championship glory escaped The Masked Superstar during his WWE career, he did gain great success in his previous years. Among his many accolades, The Masked Superstar was a four-time Georgia Championship Wrestling Heavyweight Champion.

MASON RYAN

HT	6'5"	WT	289 lbs.	FROM	Cardiff, Wales
SIGNATURE MOVE	Swinging Side Slam				

When CM Punk was looking for muscle to add to the New Nexus, he turned to the nearly 300-pound powerhouse Mason Ryan.

The physically-imposing Ryan made an immediate impact when he defeated R-Truth via submission in his February 2011 debut match. After the final bell, however, it was quickly learned that Ryan didn't care about wins and losses. Instead, he was out to maim people. With R-Truth still suffering from the loss, Ryan continued his punishing assault. The attack forced the referee to reverse his decision and award the match to Truth via disqualification.

Ryan continued to plow through the *Raw* roster until an injury sidelined him later that summer. After months away, the monster from Wales returned in September 2011 to apparently help Vickie Guerrero's clients, Jack Swagger and Dolph Ziggler. But instead of aiding the arrogant duo, Ryan actually turned on them, much to the delight of the WWE Universe.

Ryan slowly faded from the scene following his return. He was eventually released from WWE in April 2014.

MATT BORNE

HT	6'0"	WT	241 lbs.	FROM	Portland, Oregon

Second-generation Superstar Matt Borne grew up watching his father, "Tough" Tony Borne, dominate the Pacific Northwest tag team scene during the 1960s. In the early 1980s, Matt followed in his dad's footsteps, capturing the territory's Tag Titles on four separate occasions (twice with "Mr. Electricity" Steve Regal and twice with Rip Oliver).

In 1985, Borne competed in the biggest match of his career when he battled Ricky "The Dragon" Steamboat at Madison Square Garden at the first-ever *WrestleMania*. Borne failed to pick up a victory against the legendary Steamboat, but he will forever be linked to the historic start of sports-entertainment's crown jewel.

MATT MORGAN

HT	6'10"	WT	328 lbs.	FROM	Fairfield, Connecticut
SIGNATURE MOVE	Vertical Suplex Side Slam				

When Paul Heyman formed Team Lesnar in 2003, it was with the hope of creating one of the most physically-imposing factions of all time. And he certainly succeeded. Led by Brock Lesnar, the group consisted of Nathan Jones, Big Show, A-Train, and newcomer Matt Morgan.

The monstrous Morgan spent the remainder of the year protecting Lesnar, as well as flattening the likes of Funaki and Shannon Moore in the ring. But when the calendar turned to 2004, injury forced Morgan out of action for several months.

When Morgan returned, it was learned that he had acquired a stutter. The oversized Superstar also struggled to regain his earlier momentum. After a brief run as Carlito's bodyguard, Morgan was released from WWE in July 2005.

MATT HARDY

HT	6'2"	WT	236 lbs.	FROM	Cameron, North Carolina
SIGNATURE MOVE	Twist of Fate				

At the time of his debut, Matt Hardy was seen as nothing more than a scrawny kid that WWE's top Superstars could prove their worth against. Refusing to be held down, however, Matt, alongside his brother, Jeff, soon proved himself as a legitimate force in the tag team ranks. In fact, many of today's critics credit The Hardy Boyz for revolutionizing the art of tag team competition.

During his climb to the top, Hardy fell madly in love with WWE Diva Lita. The two shared a long relationship until it was revealed that the fiery redhead was cheating on him with his friend, Edge. Hardy was released from his WWE contract shortly after, and many assumed the final chapter of his career had been written. Hardy, on the other hand, saw things a bit differently.

Hardy actually showed up on WWE television and attacked Edge. The popularity of the rebellious act forced WWE to re-sign Matt and exact revenge on his former best friend. Over the next several years, the resilient Hardy achieved great success when he captured the United States Championship, and the prestigious ECW Championship.

Hardy then stunned the WWE Universe when he turned on his brother and cost him the World Heavyweight Championship at the 2009 *Royal Rumble*. The brothers met in a variety of matches, including an Extreme Rules Match at *WrestleMania 25*. Thankfully, the rift was temporary and a classic Hardy air show followed at the Money In The Bank Match at *WrestleMania XXVI*. Matt also spent time mentoring Justin Gabriel on *NXT* before parting with WWE in 2010.

MATT STRIKER

| HT | 5'10" | WT | 224 lbs. | FROM | Bayside, New York |

While Matt Striker molded the minds of New York City's youth, he couldn't help but dream about one day transitioning into a career in sports-entertainment. Tired of daydreaming about a life in the ring, the teacher eventually turned to Johnny Rodz, who showed Striker the ropes at the famed Gleason's Gym.

In the beginning, Striker juggled both his teaching and sports-entertainment careers. That is until he participated in the Angle Invitational on *Raw* the same night he called in sick from school. After being recognized on TV, Striker was forced to resign, sparking a national media frenzy.

After being expelled from school, Striker began competing for WWE fulltime, where he earned early victories over the likes of Tajiri and Johnny Parisi. Later, Striker joined ECW's New Breed in their mission to rid sports-entertainment of the ECW Originals. They were largely unsuccessful, losing to the Originals at *WrestleMania 23*.

Striker transitioned to the announce table in 2008. He called the action for *Raw*, *SmackDown*, and *ECW* until leaving WWE in June 2013.

MAVEN

| HT | 6'2" | WT | 220 lbs. | FROM | Chantilly, Virginia |
| SIGNATURE MOVE | Halo DDT |

Originally a schoolteacher, Maven received the opportunity of a lifetime when he was chosen to participate on *Tough Enough*. After being crowned the first-ever male Champion in the show's history, he was awarded a contract and immediately began his professional career. Unfortunately for the newcomer, his lack of experience cost him, as he lost several of his early matches against more seasoned competitors such as Tazz and Chris Jericho.

Despite coming up short in his early days, Maven persevered. And by 2002, he was beaming with confidence. He used his newfound self-assurance to eliminate the legendary Undertaker from the 2002 Royal Rumble Match. A few weeks later, he defeated The Deadman for the Hardcore Championship.

In November 2004, Maven parlayed an impressive *Survivor Series* appearance into a World Heavyweight Championship opportunity against Triple H. Unfortunately for the youngster, he was unsuccessful in his bid to uncrown "The Game." Shortly after the loss, fans turned against Maven when he attacked the endearing Eugene. The former *Tough Enough* Champion left WWE later that year.

MAURO RANALLO

More than any other modern announcer, Mauro Ranallo is a throwback to sage commentators like Gordon Solie in Florida and Georgia, Lance Russell in Memphis, Kent Walton in the UK, and Dr. Alfonso Morales in Mexico.

When he made his *SmackDown* debut in 2016, calling the action alongside Jerry "The King" Lawler and Byron Saxton, praise flowed in from no less than WWE Hall of Fame announcer Jim Ross and ECW icon Joey Styles.

Despite his youthful appearance, Ranallo is a veteran who made his announcing and managing debut at age 16 in the old Vancouver territory, and later worked in Calgary.

"The voice of *SmackDown*" has also covered Canadian football, hockey, boxing, and MMA, where he worked alongside the legendary Bas Rutten.

MAX MINI

| HT | 3'7" | WT | 83 lbs. | FROM | Mexico |

Billed as "The World's Smallest Athlete," Max Mini first caught fans' imaginations in 1997. Despite his diminutive stature, he wasn't afraid to mix it up. And with his high-flying, have-no-fear attitude, he proved to be eighty-three pounds of pure excitement.

Mini's popularity led to a string of high-profile matches. At *Ground Zero 1997*, he defeated El Torito in singles action. He then teamed with Nova to top Tarantula and Mosaic at *Badd Blood*. And at the 1998 *Royal Rumble*, Mini was part of a team that defeated Battalion, El Torito, and Tarantula.

When he wasn't wowing in the ring, Mini became the obsession of El Tigre, the host of *WWE.com*'s *Code Rojo*. During each show, El Tigre could be seen inexplicably chasing Mini throughout arenas.

MAX MOON

| HT | 5'10" | WT | 240 lbs. | FROM | Outer Space |
| SIGNATURE MOVE | Spinning Flying Body Press |

WWE was invaded by a space traveler wearing a blue-armored suit in 1992. Max Moon defeated Superstars like the Brooklyn Brawler, Terry Taylor, Skinner, and Repo Man. But his short-lived in-ring success was overshadowed by the futuristic jetpack that propelled him from the floor to the ring and his gleaming spacesuit complete with pyro cannons.

The interstellar enigma continued to impress crowds and became a contender to the Intercontinental Championship, held at that time by "The Heartbreak Kid" Shawn Michaels. He etched his name into WWE history by challenging HBK during the first-ever *Raw* episode for the Title in a losing effort.

Though he will forever be an answer to a trivia question, this cyborg has not been seen in WWE since.

MAXINE

HT 5'4" **FROM** Tampa, Florida

According to Maxine, being sexy can only get you so far, which is why the power-obsessed Floridian also employed characteristics of cockiness, confidence, and intelligence.

With Alicia Fox serving as her Pro, Maxine debuted as a Rookie on the third season of *NXT*. Despite having a well-qualified Diva showing her the ropes, the former model failed to impress the judges. After just nine weeks, she was eliminated from competition.

Maxine's quest to be on top in WWE didn't end with *NXT* season three. In August 2011, the exiled Diva-wannabe returned to *NXT* season five as the love interest of Rookie Derrick Bateman. While the love affair appeared torrid, Maxine left WWE the following summer.

MEAN STREET POSSE

MEMBERS Pete Gas, Rodney, & Joey Abs
COMBINED WT Greenwich, Connecticut

Hailing from the "mean streets" of ritzy Greenwich, Connecticut, Pete Gas, Rodney, and Joey Abs may very well be the only people in the history of the world to claim their toughness while wearing argyle sweater vests. But luckily for them, they had childhood friend Shane McMahon open the door for them in WWE.

Prior to ever stepping foot in a WWE ring, the Mean Street Posse told tall tales of ruling the affluent streets of their hometown. Unfortunately for the Posse, their supposed toughness did not equate to success in WWE. Despite their inability to back up their boasts, all three Mean Street Posse members managed to permanently etch their names into the WWE record books when they briefly held (and quickly lost) the Hardcore Championship at *WrestleMania 2000*.

The Mean Street Posse faded from WWE in 2001, but rest assured that patrons of Papyrus stationary store on Greenwich Avenue are shaking in their loafers at the thought of Pete Gas, Rodney, and Joey Abs taking back the neighborhood.

MEAT/SHAWN STASIAK

HT 6'4" **WT** 250 lbs. **SIGNATURE MOVE** Meat Grinder

Meat made his debut as the masculine companion of Terri Runnels and Jacqueline of Pretty Mean Sisters in 1999. A natural athlete with an incredible physique, the man known as Meat displayed his abilities against Test, Ken Shamrock, Road Dogg, Val Venis, Kurt Angle, Billy Gunn, and The Godfather.

Pleasing Terri and Jacqueline took both a physical and mental toll on him. After ending his association with both Divas, Meat began using his real name, Shawn Stasiak. He left WWE by the end of 1999 and debuted in World Championship Wrestling shortly afterward.

In 2001, this son of former WWE Champion Stan Stasiak returned as part of The Alliance. Once the WCW/ECW invasion was squashed, Stasiak went on to win multiple Hardcore Titles before departing WWE in 2002.

THE MEGA MANIACS

MEMBERS Hulk Hogan & Brutus Beefcake **COMBINED WT** 573 lbs.

In the ultimate example of life imitating art, Hulk Hogan's *No Holds Barred* co-star, Zeus, followed him to WWE in 1989 in an attempt to finish what he started in the movie. And with Randy "Macho Man" Savage by his side, Zeus's chances looked pretty good. Luckily for the Hulkster, longtime friend Brutus "The Barber" Beefcake stepped up to even the sides.

Collectively known as The Mega Maniacs, Hogan and Beefcake proved their dominance by defeating Zeus and Savage at *SummerSlam 1989*. However, the devious duo simply would not go away, leaving the two teams to finally settle the score in December 1989. In a unique pay-per-view event that also saw the airing of the *No Holds Barred* movie, The Mega Maniacs once again toppled Zeus and Savage, this time in a steel cage.

Several years later, The Mega Maniacs reunited to challenge Money, Inc., for the WWE Tag Team Championship at *WrestleMania IX*. They were unable to claim the Titles after being disqualified for using Beefcake's titanium mask as a weapon.

THE MEGA POWERS

| MEMBERS | Randy Savage & Hulk Hogan | COMBINED WT | 548 lbs. |

Randy Savage and Hulk Hogan were inarguably the two biggest Superstars of the late 1980s, so when they aligned to form The Mega Powers, it was no surprise to see them dominate WWE.

One of The Mega Powers' biggest moments came at *WrestleMania IV*, where The Hulkster helped Macho Man defeat Ted DiBiase to become WWE Champion. Seeking retribution, DiBiase and Andre the Giant later double-teamed Savage, which set the stage for a tag team match at *SummerSlam 1988*.

In a match billed as "The Mega Powers vs. The Mega Bucks," Savage and Hogan defeated DiBiase and Andre after Elizabeth removed her skirt to distract the opposition. Everything seemed to be going great for The Mega Powers, but Savage soon developed an intense jealously over Elizabeth's friendship with Hogan, resulting in the end of the team.

With the WWE Championship on the line, the former friends collided at *WrestleMania V*. In the end, Hogan dropped his signature Leg Drop across the throat of Savage to claim his second WWE Championship.

MELINA

| HT | 5'4" | FROM | Los Angeles, California |
| SIGNATURE MOVE | Primal Scream |

A former fitness model, Melina first made a name for herself in WWE when she guided fellow socialites, Johnny Nitro and Joey Mercury, to the WWE Tag Team Championship in April 2005. During their reign, MNM annoyed nearly everybody with their namedropping of such people as Paris Hilton and Kevin Federline.

Melina's managerial credits also include leading Nitro to the Intercontinental Championship. But it was her in-ring prowess that Melina will be remembered for most. In early 2007, she dedicated herself to becoming a champion. And within weeks, she was on top of the division, defeating Mickie James for the Women's Championship, a Title she would go on to hold on three separate occasions.

In October 2009, Melina defeated Jillian to capture the Divas Championship and become one of the elite few to hold both the Women's and Divas Titles. She later became a two-time Divas Champion when she defeated Alicia Fox for the gold at *SummerSlam 2010*.

Melina's illustrious WWE career came to an end when she was released by WWE in the summer of 2011.

MEN ON A MISSION

| MEMBERS | Mo, Oscar, & Mabel |
| COMBINED WT | 770 lbs. |

At nearly 800 pounds, Men on a Mission oftentimes outweighed their opposition by hundreds of pounds. But despite their massive size, Mo and Mabel were also incredibly light on their feet, making them a complete threat in the ring.

Managed by the rapping Oscar, Men on a Mission made their WWE debut in 1993 and instantly wowed audiences with their flawless teamwork. Within months, they were featured in a major pay-per-view match when they painted their faces and competed as one-half of the Four Doinks *Survivor Series* team.

Men on a Mission proved their greatness when they defeated The Quebecers to capture the WWE Tag Team Championship in March 1994. Unfortunately for Mo and Mabel, they only held the Titles a few days before losing them back to Jacques and Pierre.

The following year, the normally fun-loving Men on a Mission began showing a more dark side. With the shift came great success, particularly for Mabel, who went on to become the 1995 King of the Ring and challenge Diesel for the WWE Championship at *SummerSlam*.

THE MEXICOOLS

| MEMBERS | Juventud Guerrera, Psicosis, & Super Crazy |

In 2005, these three crossed the border on their tricked-out John Deere tractors and rolled right into *SmackDown*. Their inspirational leader, Juventud, declared they were true Mexican luchadores and superior to their countrymen. They were not Mexicans—they were Mexicools. The angry trio constantly interfered in matches on *SmackDown* and faced other factions such as the bWo and the Full Blooded Italians.

Along the way, Juventud won the Cruiserweight Championship and gave the group instant credibility in WWE. In addition, Psicosis and Super Crazy were contenders for the WWE Tag Team Championship. Guerrera lost his Cruiserweight Title and eventually left WWE in January 2006. Psicosis and Super Crazy continued to team but several disagreements caused them to disband. Psicosis left WWE later that year.

MICHAEL BOLLEA

HT	6'2"	WT	255 lbs.
FROM	Tampa, Florida		
SIGNATURE MOVE	Full Nelson Slam		

Powerful, agile, and tough as nails, Michael Bollea was a promising up-and-coming star of the early '90s. His earliest days were spent competing in several Japanese promotions, most notably New Japan Pro Wrestling.

While in Japan, Bollea's intimidating and rugged demeanor impressed WWE officials, earning a contract with WWE in 1993. Unfortunately for Bollea, his success failed to follow him to the States. Superstars such as Virgil, Jim Powers, and Jim Brunzell regularly defeated Bollea, who competed in WWE as "The Predator."

Bollea's luck changed when he debuted in WCW in 1998 as Horace Hogan. While there, he became a member of both Raven's Flock and the nWo.

MICHAEL COLE

"And I quote..."

At times, this multi-time Slammy Award winner and "Voice of WWE" has gotten on the nerves of the WWE Universe. Like him or not, his contributions to WWE over a near twenty year tenure give him the right to be a little bit pompous.

Vintage Michael Cole hosted such programs as *Livewire* and *Shotgun Saturday Night*. He debuted in 1997 and became *SmackDown*'s lead announcer by 1999. For the next nine years, Cole provided the soundtrack for the blue brand.

In June 2008, Cole was surprisingly drafted to *Raw*. No stranger to taking abuse from Superstars, he soon sustained an attack by Kane. While calling the action on Monday nights, Cole also became the commentator for WWE's new program, *NXT*. During the show's inaugural season, he showed his unpleasant side by taunting then-WWE rookie, Daniel Bryan. On *Raw*, he smugly accepted the unpopular role of official spokesperson for the Anonymous *Raw* General Manager.

That fall, after he incurred Jerry Lawler's wrath, Cole shielded himself inside a protective glass booth, which he called the Cole Mine. Michael stooped to such hateful and personal levels that millions of fans were ready to see The King pummel him at *WrestleMania XXVII*. Fans got their wish, but despite having his orange-clad keister whipped from pillar to post, Cole emerged with a highly questionable disqualification victory.

Cole trumpeted his spotless *WrestleMania* record as if he were the next Undertaker, but he was soon humbled. At *Over the Limit 2011*, he was forced to kiss Lawler's feet with help from Eve and Jim Ross. He apologized to Jerry, but his mouth would get him into trouble again. In June 2012, his diatribes earned him an AA from John Cena.

In recent years, Cole has adapted a more even-keeled approach and has come to be appreciated by the WWE Universe. Outside of announcing, he has co-hosted *The JBL & Cole Show* on WWE.com and YouTube and conducted several tense, revealing interviews with WWE COO Triple H. Behind the scenes, he coaches WWE's younger announcers hoping to cultivate the next Voice of WWE.

"What a maneuver!"

MICHAEL TARVER

HT	6'3"	WT	250 lbs.	FROM	Akron, Ohio	SIGNATURE MOVE	Tarver's Lightning

"With a single strike, I can knock out any man in 1.9 seconds," claimed Michael Tarver heading into season one of the original *NXT*. Luckily for the other competitors, Tarver proved to be more bark than bite.

Tarver was cut from *NXT* after sporting a less-than-impressive record and refusing to participate in challenges. The dismissal, however, did not spell the end for the aspiring Superstar. Shortly after the *NXT* season ended, all eight competitors, including Tarver, united to form The Nexus. Together, they targeted John Cena, who Tarver and company battled in an Elimination Tag Team Match at *SummerSlam 2010*. The contest featured more than thirty minutes of action, but Tarver's participation lasted less than four minutes; he was quickly eliminated by John Morrison.

MICHELLE MCCOOL

 | **HT** 5'10" | **FROM** Palatka, Florida
SIGNATURE MOVE | Faith Breaker

As a former schoolteacher, Michelle McCool taught science. But anyone who knows her story agrees that the real lesson to learn from this Diva is one of perseverance. Michelle McCool pursued her lifelong dream by entering the 2004 Diva Search. Though she did not win, she showed enough fortitude to earn a WWE contract. However, four years would pass before this incredible opportunity would translate into a chance to excel in the ring.

After several managerial stints, Michelle began carving her own path. In July 2008, her resolve paid off when she defeated Natalya at *The Great American Bash* to become the first-ever Divas Champion. Her reign lasted five months. In that time, her mindset changed. She was still as determined as ever but gone was the fun-loving sweetheart, replaced by a malicious vixen.

The following year at *The Bash*, Michelle made history again when she became the first competitor to win both the Divas and Women's Championships. Soon, fellow mean girl Layla gravitated to her side. Dubbed "Lay-Cool," the two "besties" were as inseparable as they were insufferable. They belittled other Divas with adolescent antics and manipulated their way to becoming "co-Champions." Michelle then unified the Women's and Divas Championships at *Night of Champions 2010*.

Ironically, Layla would become Michelle McCool's undoing. When their friendship faltered in 2011, they faced each other in a Loser Leaves WWE Match at *Extreme Rules*. Layla won, driving this once unstoppable Diva from the company.

MICK FOLEY

see page 226

MICKIE JAMES

  | **HT** 5'4" | **FROM** Richmond, Virginia
SIGNATURE MOVE | Mick Kick, Implant DDT

Idolizing Trish Stratus is only natural for an aspiring WWE Diva. That is what Mickie James claimed to be up to when she first came to WWE in October 2005. The spunky newcomer stopped at nothing to get close to her hero, often too close for comfort. Trish felt smothered by Mickie's admiration and cut the friendship off. Then Mickie's real lunacy boiled to the surface. Unhinged by the rejection, the jilted James defeated Trish for her first Women's Championship at *WrestleMania 22*.

Mickie enjoyed Women's and Divas gold five more times collectively in her career. After Trish left WWE, Mickie's demented side went dormant and fans appreciated her in-ring ability. Melina emerged as Mickie's chief nemesis. The two Divas spent the first four months of 2007 competing over the Women's Championship, a Title they traded three times during this period. Soon after, Mickie tangled with a longstanding foe, Beth Phoenix.

In July 2009, Mickie defeated Maryse for her first Divas Championship. Following this Title reign, James found herself in a hurtful war of words with Lay-Cool. Mickie got her revenge on *SmackDown*'s mean girls at *Royal Rumble 2010*, defeating Michelle McCool in thirty seconds to seize the Women's Championship. These personal battles brought an unlikely ally, Beth Phoenix, to her side.

Mickie left WWE in April 2010. She went on to release her own country music album and still brings her fighting spirit to rings all over the world.

MID-ATLANTIC CHAMPIONSHIP WRESTLING/JIM CROCKETT PROMOTIONS

Of all the myriad wrestling territories, perhaps none was more competitive with WWE than Charlotte-based Mid-Atlantic Championship Wrestling—also known as Jim Crockett Promotions (JCP).

Jim Crockett, Sr.—a.k.a. "Big Jim"—opened JCP in 1931. In 1963, he began promoting in New York, in opposition to WWE. But the effort failed.

When Big Jim died in 1973, his son, Jim Crockett, Jr., showed the same type of ambition. Previously, JCP had been renowned for its tag teams like Rip Hawk and Swede Hanson, and Gene and Ole Anderson. Crockett focused on younger, dynamic performers, including Ric Flair, Ricky Steamboat, and Greg Valentine.

In 1983, Crockett created the first *Starrcade*. Although the show emanated from Greensboro, North Carolina, fans in other southern locales could watch closed circuit telecasts in theaters.

Crockett soon began spending large sums to absorb promotions in Georgia, Florida, Missouri, and Oklahoma, and relocated to Dallas. In 1987, he moved *Starrcade* to Chicago, alienating his southern base. Facing financial turmoil, his company was purchased by Ted Turner in 1988.

MIDEON

HT	6'3"
WT	288 lbs.

In January 1999, a grim ceremony transformed a former hillbilly into Mideon, a member of Undertaker's Ministry of Darkness. During his time with the Ministry of Darkness, Mideon often teamed up with the gigantic Viscera.

No other Superstar in WWE history had an easier time acquiring a Championship in WWE than Mideon. In June 1999 Mideon asked Shane McMahon if he could have the European Championship. When Shane O' Mac told him he could do what he wanted, Mideon took the prize but lost it a month later to D-Lo Brown. After a brief hiatus from the ring, he returned in 2000 as Naked Mideon, wearing only a thong and fanny pack. Fans at live events attended by Mideon during this time likely saw more of the Superstar than they really wanted.

MID-SOUTH CHAMPIONSHIP WRESTLING
see page 228

MIGHTY IGOR

FROM	Dearborn, Michigan	SIGNATURE MOVE	Bearhug

Prior to entering the world of sports-entertainment, Mighty Igor gained fame as an accomplished body builder. His immense size made him a force in the ring, but it was his pre-match antics that oftentimes gave him the psychological advantage—Mighty Igor was known to show off by having cinder blocks broken over his head with a sledgehammer.

Appropriately referred to as the "World's Strongest Wrestler," Mighty Igor's greatest accomplishment came when he overpowered the great Mad Dog Vachon for the AWA Championship. He only held the Title for one week before losing it back to Vachon, but he will forever be remembered alongside such great former AWA Champions as Verne Gagne, Nick Bockwinkel, and Larry Zbyszko.

Utilizing a Bearhug that sucked the life from his foes, Mighty Igor crossed paths with many of sports-entertainment's finest over the course of his thirty-year career. Some of his most notable rivalries include The Sheik, The Masked Superstar, and Jos LeDuc.

MIGUEL PEREZ

HT	6'1"	WT	238 lbs.	FROM	Puerto Rico
SIGNATURE MOVE	Sunset Flip				

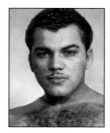

Miguel Perez shot to stardom in the late-1950s as one-half of one of the most successful tag teams in sports-entertainment history. Along with Antonino Rocca, the two Superstars were main event attractions throughout the east coast for Vincent J. McMahon's Capitol Wrestling Corporation. Perez and Rocca were heroes everywhere they went, as fans admired their heart, desire, and fire in the ring.

Perez stayed with McMahon when Capitol Wrestling continued to evolve. He later battled "Nature Boy" Buddy Rogers for the WWE Championship. In 1968, Perez left for Puerto Rico, where he reunited with Rocca before ultimately retiring from action in 1979. Decades later, Miguel Perez is still considered one of the greatest Superstars to ever emerge from Puerto Rico.

MIKE ADAMLE

Mike Adamle's broadcasting career has seen many highlights, including *American Gladiators* and the Summer Olympics. Unfortunately for Adamle, that same career has also seen one very high-profile lowlight: his time with WWE.

When Adamle debuted in 2008, many anticipated he'd become a respected member of the announce team. But when he inadvertently referred to Jeff Hardy as "Jeff Harvey," things went south in a hurry.

After weeks of continued mistakes, a frustrated Adamle inexplicably got up and walked out in the middle of an *ECW* broadcast. Amazingly, the act of defiance failed to derail his career. In fact, in July 2008, he was promoted to *Raw* General Manager.

Adamle eventually resigned from his post in November 2008 and was out of WWE shortly thereafter.

MIKE AWESOME

HT	6'6"	WT	292 lbs.	FROM	Tampa, Florida
SIGNATURE MOVE	Awesome Bomb				

Mike Awesome had the strength to powerbomb virtually any opponent and the agility to clear the top rope while nailing opponents with a plancha. A dominant Champion in ECW and Japan, Awesome sparked controversy in the beginning of the new millennium when he jumped to WCW while still reigning as ECW Champion. This resulted in Awesome, under contract with WCW, meeting Tazz, under contract with WWE, for the ECW Title at an ECW live event.

Awesome remained with WCW until the company was purchased by WWE in March 2001. In June, Awesome made his WWE debut and defeated Rhyno for the Hardcore Championship, making him the first WCW Superstar to win a Championship in WWE.

After time in independent promotions and Japan, Awesome competed at *ECW One Night Stand 2005*. The roof of the Hammerstein Ballroom almost blew off as Awesome warred with old nemesis Masato Tanaka. Tragically, in February 2007, Mike Awesome passed away. This dynamic competitor will always be regarded as one of the most agile big men the world has ever seen.

MICK FOLEY

HT	6'2"
WT	287 lbs.
FROM	Long Island, New York

SIGNATURE MOVE	
Mandible Claw, Double Arm DDT	

The story of Mick Foley is one of true genius coupled with complete insanity. Along the way, he used flashes of schizophrenia to introduce the world to three entirely different personas: Mankind, Dude Love, and Cactus Jack. Collectively, the Three Faces of Foley told the story of a man who was put on this earth for no other reason than to become a hardcore legend.

Foley's passion for sports-entertainment developed at a young age and grew to an obsession after he hitchhiked to Madison Square Garden in 1983. From the third row, Foley watched as Jimmy Snuka flew from the top of a steel cage onto Don Muraco. "It was a defining moment in my life," wrote Foley in his 1999 autobiography, *Have a Nice Day!* "It was the day I knew without a doubt what I wanted to do with my life."

After making the inspired decision to pursue a sports-entertainment career, Foley turned to the legendary Dominic DeNucci for training. While learning the game from the former WWE Superstar, Foley earned spare cash competing for independent promotions, along with a few WWE appearances in 1986, as Jack Foley.

THE BIRTH OF A HARDCORE LEGEND

Foley spent the next several years bouncing from promotion to promotion, including stints in the now-defunct Universal Wrestling Federation and World Class Championship Wrestling. During this time, he began to develop a cult following, largely due to his complete disregard for his own wellbeing. The more chances Foley took, the more fans cheered him. It wasn't long before his hardcore style caught the attention of World Championship Wrestling.

As Cactus Jack, Foley made his WCW debut in late-1991 and was instantly catapulted into high-profile rivalries against Sting, Ron Simmons, and most notably, Big Van Vader. The two Superstars competed in some of WCW's most brutal battles. Their March 17, 1994, encounter was so vicious that, after getting his head tangled between the ring ropes, Foley's ear tore off his head as he struggled to escape.

After leaving WCW, Foley split time between Extreme Championship Wrestling and Japan. His brutal ECW encounters against Sandman and Terry Funk are the stuff of legend, while his Japan exploits bordered on illegal.

MANKIND COMES TO WWE

Foley made his move to WWE in early-1996, but rather than competing as Cactus Jack, he debuted under the name Mankind. As Mankind, Foley appeared even more deranged. He was often seen sitting in dark boiler rooms, talking to his pet rat, George, about the internal pain he was suffering.

Using his dreaded Mandible Claw, Mankind made short work of his early competition. The victories put him in perfect position to move up the WWE ladder. To prove his worth, Mankind soon targeted one of WWE's most successful Superstars, Undertaker. The two men spent a year competing in revolutionary encounters such as the Boiler Room Brawl and a Buried Alive Match.

By mid-1997, Mankind was a bonafide main eventer. His in-ring conquests carried him to WWE Championship opportunities against Shawn Michaels, Sycho Sid, and Undertaker. He even fought to the finals of the 1997 *King of the Ring* tournament. Despite all his successes, he had difficulty garnering the admiration of fans. That all changed when Jim Ross began a series of probing interviews with the deranged Mankind.

THE THIRD FACE OF FOLEY

Ross' questioning revealed that a young Foley produced home videos of himself as a character called Dude Love. Fans became instantly enthralled by Foley's hippy alter-ego, and were pleasantly shocked when he debuted as Stone Cold Steve Austin's partner in July 1997. The tie-dye-clad Dude Love and Stone Cold went on to defeat Owen Hart and British Bulldog for the World Tag Team Championship, Foley's first WWE Title.

For the next several months, Foley kept his opponents on their toes, as they were never sure which persona they were going to face. Foley took the confusion a step further in September 1997 when a vignette aired featuring Mankind and Dude Love talking to each other about who should face Triple H. In the end, they decided neither persona should battle "The Game." Instead, they chose Foley's third face, Cactus Jack, to do the honors. The match marked the WWE debut of Foley's popular hardcore character.

In January 1998, Foley made history by competing in the *Royal Rumble Match* as all three personas. At *WrestleMania XIV*, Foley, as Cactus Jack, teamed with Terry Funk, who competed as Chainsaw Charlie, to win the WWE Tag Team Titles from the New Age Outlaws in a Dumpster Match.

HELL IN A CELL

Foley's popularity reached iconic status in June 1998 when, as Mankind, he faced Undertaker in a Hell in a Cell Match. In one of sports-entertainment's most shocking moments, Mankind was tossed off the top of the demonic structure down to the arena floor. The blood-curdling sight caused announcer Jim Ross to scream the now-famous words, "Good God Almighty! They've killed him! With God as my witness, he is broken in half!" Despite gaining medical attention, Mankind refused to leave in a gurney and made his way back atop the Cell. And as if the sixteen-foot fall wasn't enough, Mankind was then Chokeslammed through the top of the cell, all the way down to the ring. A steel chair followed his descent, hitting Foley in the face upon impact, causing his tooth to pierce through his lip.

In typical Foley fashion, the hardcore Superstar continued to evolve his in-ring personalities. In late 1998, Mankind went through significant changes and became a sensation with the fans, especially after debuting his sock puppet, Mr. Socko. Unfortunately for Mankind, he was as gullible as he was goofy. After accepting the newly-created Hardcore Championship from Mr. McMahon in November 1998, Mankind looked up to the WWE Chairman as a father figure. The diabolical McMahon took full advantage of this, luring the naïve Mankind close to him, and then screwing him over in the finals of the WWE Championship tournament at *Survivor Series*.

WWE CHAMPION

Within weeks of his heartbreaking *Survivor Series* loss, Mankind gained the ultimate revenge when he upended The Rock to capture the WWE Championship on January 4, 1999. The victory saw "Mrs. Foley's baby boy" realize a boyhood dream that many assumed impossible. The Mankind-Rock rivalry resulted in a series of brutal matches. Perhaps their most unsightly encounter occurred at the *Royal Rumble* where The Rock smashed Mankind with seemingly countless swings that eventually rendered Mankind unconscious. Mankind reclaimed the Title one week later during halftime of *Super Bowl XXXIII*.

Despite being nearly comatose at the hands of The Rock, Mankind found it within himself to forgive his foe and form a popular tag team known as The Rock 'n' Sock Connection. The duo defeated Undertaker and Big Show for the World Tag Team Championship in August 1999, the first of three reigns for the combination. Mankind later presented his partner with a "This is Your Life" walk down memory lane, one of the most memorable and popular segments in *Raw* history.

Foley captured his third and final WWE Championship when he defeated Triple H and Stone Cold at *SummerSlam* 1999. His reign lasted only twenty-four hours, but his rivalry with Triple H was merely beginning. The two battled for the WWE Championship in the main event of the 2000 *Royal Rumble*, and Foley put his career on the line for a final Title opportunity at *No Way Out*. He lost in a brutal Hell in a Cell encounter with "The Game," but was granted a spot in the main event of *WrestleMania 2000*. The contest, which was the culmination of a fifteen-year dream for Foley, saw the hardcore Superstar compete in a Fatal Four Way Elimination Match against Triple H, The Rock, and Big Show.

With his in-ring days nestled away in the history books, Foley focused much of his attention on his budding writing career. He is largely recognized for his best-selling autobiographical efforts *Have a Nice Day!*, *Foley is Good*, and *The Hardcore Diaries*, but he has also penned many children's books, as well as adult fiction. Foley also periodically assumed several roles on WWE television, most notably that of commissioner, referee, and announcer. He even made a few rare returns to the ring, including a Rock 'n' Sock reunion at *WrestleMania XX* and a brutal Hardcore Match against The Rated-R Superstar, Edge, at *WrestleMania 22*.

Foley's decades of excellence were eventually recognized when he was inducted into the WWE Hall of Fame in April 2013. Fittingly, the ceremony took place in MSG, the same arena where Foley initially realized an in-ring career was his ultimate calling.

MID-SOUTH WRESTLING

While most wrestling fans were monitoring events in New York, Atlanta and Tampa, the town of Bixby, Oklahoma was largely overlooked. But for the period that Bill Watts was promoting Mid-South Wrestling from his home there, it may have been the most creative location in the industry. Mid-South matches and television programs possessed an intensity akin to ECW. A young Jim Ross called the matches. Stars included Killer Karl Kox, Ernie Ladd, Bob Roop, Dick Slater, and "Hacksaw" Jim Duggan. The Midnight Express, Rock 'n' Roll Express, Fantastics, Sheepherders, and Freebirds were among the notable tag teams, as well as Eddie Gilbert's Hot Stuff International, Inc., a unit that featured Rick Steiner, Sting, and Blade Runner Rock (aka the Ultimate Warrior).

Former junior heavyweight Champion Leroy McGuirk had been promoting the Tri-State territory in Oklahoma, Louisiana, and Mississippi since 1950. Watts purchased the promotion in 1979 and renamed it Mid-South, adding venues in Arkansas and Texas, and cultivating several future WWE Hall of Famers.

The charismatic Junkyard Dog became Mid-South's most celebrated headliner, bridging racial divides and transforming New Orleans' Municipal Auditorium into "The Dog's Yard." In 1980, 31,000 fans jammed the Superdome to see JYD defeat Michael Hayes in a dog collar match in a steel cage. Five years later, Ted DiBiase, known as "The Big Cheese" in Mid-South, was scheduled to wrestle Ric Flair for the NWA Title on Mid-South television, but was attacked and bloodied by Dick Murdoch beforehand. Defying doctor's orders, a bandaged DiBiase wrestled anyway—only to have Murdoch deliver a brain buster to the challenger on the concrete floor.

The highly emotional series of DiBiase-Murdoch matches that followed saw fans cheer vigorously for the future "Million Dollar Man."

In 1986, Watts cut ties with the NWA and attempted to go national, rebranding the promotion the Universal Wrestling Federation (UWF). The UWF Title passed from Terry Gordy to One Man Gang, to Big Bubba Rogers, and to Steve "Dr. Death" Williams before promoter Jim Crockett purchased the group a year later. For a period, Williams defended the Championship in the NWA, but, by 1988, the Title was retired.

THE FANTASTICS

MEMBERS	Tommy Rogers & Bobby Fulton
COMBINED WT	445 lbs.

Because of their wholesome looks, the Fantastics were occasionally taken lightly by opponents who dismissed Tommy Rogers and Bobby Fulton as "pretty boys." That attitude changed the moment that the bell rang and their rivals discovered that they were in the fight of their lives. While renowned for flips, dual dropkicks, and other synchronized maneuvers, Rogers and Fulton were not beyond engaging adversaries in vicious bloodbaths, generally emerging with arms raised.

The tandem was formed in 1984 in Mid-South, where they launched into a rivalry with manager Jim Cornette's Midnight Express that continued as both teams moved to World Class, Memphis, Mid-Atlantic, Smoky Mountain, and other territories. They also had a brutal conflict with the Sheepherders, who were later known as the Bushwhackers in WWE. Rogers died in 2015.

THE BLADE RUNNERS

MEMBERS	Rock & Sting
COMBINED WT	530 lbs.

When Mid-South fans watched the Blade Runners in the ring, no one could have predicted how far each would go.

The Blade Runners were originally part of a four-man combination called Powerteam USA, trained by Rick Bassman and the legendary Red Bastien. In Memphis, the hulking pair rechristened themselves the Freedom Fighters, Justice and Flash. In 1986, they landed in Mid-South as the Blade Runners. Flash became Sting, a name he'd keep for the remainder of his career, while Justice became Rock. Managed by "Hot Stuff" Eddie Gilbert, the duo battled the tough team of Ted DiBiase and Steve "Dr. Death" Williams.

The pair soon split up. Sting went on to win NWA and WCW gold, while Rock became WWE Champion as the Ultimate Warrior.

SEE ALSO:

BILL WATTS

EDDIE GILBERT

"MILLION DOLLAR MAN" TED DIBIASE

"HACKSAW" JIM DUGGAN

JUNKYARD DOG

STEVE "DR. DEATH" WILLIAMS

MIKE KNOX

HT	6'6"	**WT**	293 lbs.	**FROM**	Phoenix, Arizona
SIGNATURE MOVE		Spinning Reverse STO			

Proving you only get one chance to make a good first impression, Mike Knox's extreme unpopularity can be traced back to his initial appearance, which saw him prevent then-girlfriend Kelly Kelly from disrobing for the ECW fans. From that moment on, Knox had a tough time gaining any fans, but that never seemed to bother the near 300-pound monster, as he became more focused on inflicting pain than making friends.

After dumping his exhibitionist other half, Knox earned several victories over some of ECW's longtime favorites, including Tommy Dreamer, Stevie Richards, and Balls Mahoney. In 2008, he reemerged with a more primal appearance and stronger thirst for brutality. He blindsided Rey Mysterio and pummeled the masked marvel for no reason in particular. The yeti-like Superstar earned entry into an Elimination Chamber Match for the World Heavyweight Championship at *No Way Out*. Claiming to harbor an in-depth knowledge of various methods for inflicting pain, Knox took part in the 26-Man Over-The-Top Battle Royal at *WrestleMania XXVI*. He parted ways with WWE in April 2010.

MIKE McGUIRK

Years before Lilian Garcia became a WWE staple, the lovely Mike McGuirk introduced audiences to such WWE Superstars as Hulk Hogan, Mr. Perfect, and Brutus Beefcake.

As a female ring announcer in the late 1980s, McGuirk oftentimes had difficulty fitting into the male-dominated industry. On more than one occasion, the blonde voice of WWE became the target of Bobby Heenan's verbal barbs, but it was Harvey Wippleman and Big Bully Busick who frightened McGuirk the most. On an episode of *Wrestling Challenge*, Wippleman and The Bully verbally harassed McGuirk to the point of tears. Luckily, Sid Justice ran to the ring to fend off the frightened female's offenders.

In addition to her ring announcing duties, McGuirk also worked as a commentator on WWE's *All-American Wrestling*.

MIL MASCARAS

HT	5'11"	**WT**	245 lbs.	**FROM**	Mexico City, Mexico
SIGNATURE MOVE		Plancha			

Mil Mascaras is arguably history's most admired masked competitor. Despite his immense popularity, he is difficult to identify upon appearance alone, as Mascaras rarely wears the same mask twice. Once the bell rings, however, "The Man of 1,000 Masks" has a style that is unmistakable.

Shortly after debuting in the mid-1960s, Mascaras began utilizing a high-flying style not normally associated with men of his size. His expansive repertoire of planchas and flying bodyblocks made him an instant success in Mexico. After becoming a national sensation in his homeland, Mascaras took his game internationally, where he continued to excel.

Mascaras' reputation followed him to WWE, resulting in him being propelled into main event status upon debuting. In addition to a memorable rivalry with Ernie Ladd, Mascaras challenged "Superstar" Billy Graham for the WWE Championship in 1977.

Mascaras' final in-ring WWE appearance came at the 1997 Royal Rumble Match. The masked man's unfamiliarity with the rules of the Rumble ultimately cost him, as he eliminated himself after leaping off the top rope to the outside.

MILLION DOLLAR CHAMPIONSHIP

Perhaps the most controversial Championship in the history of sports-entertainment, the Million Dollar Championship was conceived by "Million Dollar Man" Ted DiBiase when he could neither buy the WWE Championship nor defeat then-Champion, Hulk Hogan. This Championship was never officially acknowledged by the WWE.

1989

March 4 • Binghamton, NY

"**Million Dollar Man**" **Ted DiBiase** crowned himself Champion during an episode of *The Brother Love Show*.

1991

August 26 • New York, NY

Vigril def. "**Million Dollar Man**" **Ted DiBiase**.

November 24 • Utica, NY

"**Million Dollar Man**" **Ted DiBiase** def. **Virgil** via Pinfall.

From February 7, 1992, until January 8, 1996, The Million Dollar Championship was dormant.

1996

January 8 • Newark, DE

"**Million Dollar Man**" **Ted DiBiase** awarded the Million Dollar Championship to his protégé, **The Ringmaster**.

May 28 • North Charleston, SC

The Ringmaster lost a Caribbean Strap Match to **Savio Vega**. As a result, "**Million Dollar Man**" **Ted DiBiase** had to leave WWE.

2010

April 5 • Moline, IL

The heir to the "**Million Dollar Man's**" fortune, **Ted DiBiase** was handed the Championship. He gave up the Title on November 15 and it hasn't been seen since.

MILLION DOLLAR CORPORATION

MEMBERS	Nikolai Volkoff, Irwin R. Schyster, King Kong Bundy, Bam Bam Bigelow, Tatanka, 1-2-3 Kid, Sycho Sid, & Xanta Klaus

When "Million Dollar Man" Ted DiBiase became a manager in 1994, he was determined to acquire Superstars like he acquired assets in the business world. When DiBiase wanted a Superstar, he often persuaded them to join by interfering in their matches on their behalf and luring them with large sums of money. His first recruits were former tag team partner I.R.S. and Nikolai Volkoff.

If a recruited Superstar did not join the Million Dollar Corporation, they were considered an enemy of the Million Dollar Corporation. The group disbanded in 1994 after "The Ringmaster" Steve Austin lost to Savio Vega, thus eliminating the "Million Dollar Man" from WWE.

"MILLION DOLLAR MAN" TED DIBIASE

HT	6'1"
WT	260 lbs.
FROM	Palm Beach, Florida

SIGNATURE MOVE
Million Dollar Dream

Ted DiBiase used his never-ending bankroll to acquire the world's most lavish possessions. He had mansions, fur coats, limousines, and private jets. He even used his funds to nearly purchase the WWE Championship. In short, his spending was the stuff of legend, the legend of the "Million Dollar Man."

Prior to flaunting his wealth in WWE arenas, DiBiase proved himself as a legitimate in-ring force while competing in Bill Watts' Mid-South territory. During this time, he captured the Mid-South North American Heavyweight Championship an amazing five times. Only Watts himself held the Title more times. Along the way, DiBiase engaged in many memorable battles with future WWE Superstars, most notably Ric Flair and Junkyard Dog. He also nearly unseated Harley Race as NWA World Heavyweight Champion, but the match was eventually called off after DiBiase suffered a throat injury.

Though DiBiase's most acknowledged WWE run kicked off in the mid-to-late 1980s, he did enjoy a brief, yet historically significant, stay with the promotion in 1979. After being crowned WWE's first-ever North American Heavyweight Champion, DiBiase became embroiled in a bitter rivalry with Pat Patterson, who eventually claimed the Title in June 1979. Patterson later went on to unify the North American and South American versions of the Title to become the first-ever Intercontinental Champion. Decades later, historians still credit DiBiase for his part in helping create the Intercontinental Championship.

MILLION DOLLAR MAN

Claiming everybody has a price, the obnoxiously rich DiBiase returned to WWE in 1987. With bodyguard Virgil by his side, the "Million Dollar Man" often gave fans large sums of money to perform demeaning tasks such as barking like a dog and kissing his feet.

In one of the most infamous moments in WWE history, DiBiase funded a complex ploy designed to put the WWE Championship around his waist. Prior to Andre the Giant's WWE Championship Match against Hulk Hogan in February 1988, the "Million Dollar Man" paid Andre to hand over the Championship if he won. To better Andre's chances, DiBiase abducted the match's referee and replaced him with a man he paid to have plastic surgery to look like the referee. The substitute referee made several questionable calls, including the decisive pin, which resulted in Andre winning the Title.

After the match, Andre handed the WWE Championship over to DiBiase as planned. The devious scheme worked perfectly, with the exception of one thing: The always-reputable President Jack Tunney refused to recognize the Title change.

Unable to purchase the WWE Championship, DiBiase was put into a tournament designed to crown a new Champion at *WrestleMania IV*. Relying heavily on his in-ring acumen, as opposed to his incredible finances, DiBiase defeated Jim Duggan and Don Muraco before ultimately falling to Randy Savage in the finals.

After failing to claim the WWE Championship, DiBiase used his impressive bank account to create his own Title. In 1989, he debuted the Million Dollar Championship, a multi-million dollar prize covered in diamonds. DiBiase wore the Title proudly, despite WWE refusing to recognize it as an official Championship.

Often lost in all the talk of money is the fact that DiBiase was also an accomplished tag team competitor. Alongside Irwin R. Schyster, DiBiase claimed three World Tag Team Championships. Collectively known as Money, Inc., the duo's first reign came at the expense of the Legion of Doom in February 1992. Subsequent reigns came via victories over the Natural Disasters and the Steiner Brothers.

Toward the end of his career, DiBiase used his wealth to finance a powerful stable of competitors. His legendary reputation as a free spender helped him lure many of the game's top names, including Sycho Sid and Steve Austin. He also managed Bam Bam Bigelow to the main event of *WrestleMania XI* against Lawrence Taylor.

DiBiase's years of excellence in the sports-entertainment industry were recognized in 2010 when he was inducted into the WWE Hall of Fame on the eve of *WrestleMania XXVI*. Hours later, his in-ring legacy lived on through his son, Ted, who competed on the grandest stage against Randy Orton and Cody Rhodes.

EVERYBODY'S GOT A PRICE FOR THE MILLION DOLLAR MAN.

MINISTRY OF DARKNESS

MEMBERS Undertaker, The Acolytes, Mideon, Edge, Christian, Gangrel, Viscera, & Paul Bearer

After more than two years apart, Undertaker and Paul Bearer reconciled in 1999 to form the most sinister faction in WWE history. Known as The Ministry of Darkness, the group claimed to take orders from a "higher power," who ordered them to emotionally cripple Mr. McMahon.

The Ministry knew no boundaries when it came to their war against McMahon. They even took their devious assault to the WWE owner's private estate, where they left a burning Undertaker symbol in the yard. However, their most offensive attack came when The Deadman abducted Mr. McMahon's daughter, Stephanie McMahon. With Stephanie in custody, Undertaker threatened to join her in unholy matrimony if Mr. McMahon failed to hand over control of WWE. Luckily for Stephanie, Stone Cold Steve Austin saved her from the darkness.

In April 1999, The Ministry became even more powerful when they joined forces with The Corporation. The merger proved to be a shock, but the biggest surprise was yet to come. In June, The Ministry finally revealed that Mr. McMahon was, in fact, the "higher power" all along.

MISSING LINK

HT	6'2"	WT	250 lbs.
FROM	Parts Unknown		
SIGNATURE MOVE	Diving Headbutt		

One of the original oddities of sports-entertainment, Missing Link first appeared in WWE in May 1985. Upon arriving, he opened eyes with his incredible power and amazing speed, which was attributed to his days of hunting and consuming wild animals.

Managed by Bobby Heenan and later Jimmy Hart, Missing Link was almost impossible to control. It is assumed that not even Missing Link truly knew what he was doing, which was a theory he supported when he would regularly and inexplicably grab the back of his hair.

Missing Link left WWE in late-1985. He went on to compete in World Class Championship Wrestling and the Universal Wrestling Federation before vanishing a few years later. In 2004, Missing Link briefly reemerged to compete in other organizations.

MITSU ARAKAWA

	HT	5'10"	WT	240 lbs.	FROM	Japan
TT	SIGNATURE MOVE	Iron Claw				

Mitsu Arakawa wasn't very well liked by his fellow Superstars. Whether it was a result of his consistent illegal use of salt or his dreaded Iron Claw, Arakawa's colleagues practically refused to get in the ring with him. The fans weren't too fond of him either. In fact, many consider Arakawa to be one of the most despised villains of the 1960s.

In an attempt to avoid battling him, many actually aligned themselves with Arakawa instead. Eventually, he became one of the most sought after tag team partners in sports-entertainment His pairings resulted in ten tag team championship reigns over fifteen years. He even teamed with Prof. Toru Tanaka to capture the WWE International Tag Team Championship in June 1969.

MISS KITTY

HT	5'3"	FROM	Memphis, Tennessee
SIGNATURE MOVE	Stinkface		

This sweet femme debuted in August 1999 on an episode of *Monday Night Raw* as an assistant to Debra, manager of Jeff Jarrett. Audiences then saw her become the sidekick to Chyna. Before the end of the year, she stripped Ivory out of her gown and became Women's Champion in a Swimming Pool Evening Gown Match at *Armageddon 1999*. After her win, she spread the word that she would now be known as "The Kat."

In January 2000, The Kat became the first Women's Champion to lose her Title to a man, when a disguised Harvey Wippleman defeated her. Despite the controversial loss, she appeared at *WrestleMania 2000* and participated in a Stink Face Match at *SummerSlam*. In 2001, she took exception to the group known as Right to Censor, and created the Right to Nudity group to oppose it. Unfortunately, after her team lost a match at *No Way Out*, The Kat was forced to join the Right to Censor. After a single appearance with Right to Censor, Kat parted ways with WWE.

THE MIZ

HT	6'1"	WT	221 lbs.	FROM	Hollywood, California
SIGNATURE MOVE		Skull-Crushing Finale, Figure-Four Leglock			

When The Miz first arrived in WWE as a *Tough Enough* contestant in 2004, most assumed he was nothing more than a reality-television star looking to score another 15 minutes of fame. Those people were dead wrong. Today, The Miz is a must-see Superstar, unleashing his arrogant brand of awesome all over WWE.

Miz first proved his naysayers wrong when he teamed with John Morrison to capture the WWE Tag Team Titles in November 2007. As Champions, not only did Miz and Morrison rule the tag division for eight long months, they also debuted "The Dirt Sheet," a WWE.com segment used to ridicule other Superstars. Despite the team's dominance, however, singles success was right around the corner for the Cleveland native.

In 2009, the smug Superstar developed a more aggressive style in the ring. The change helped catapult him to multiple singles accomplishments, starting with the United States Championship in October 2009. In July 2010, he moved one step closer to realizing his ultimate goal of becoming WWE Champion when he turned back seven other Superstars to claim the Money in the Bank briefcase.

Over the next four months, The Miz patiently assessed the championship scene, until November 2010, when he picked off a weakened Randy Orton on *Raw* to capture the coveted WWE Championship. As Champion, Miz let his previous doubters hear it as he ruled WWE for five-plus months. His crowning achievement came at *WrestleMania XXVII*, where he defeated John Cena in the main event. Not bad for a kid who grew up impersonating The Rock in front of a mirror.

After becoming Intercontinental Champion at *Raw 1000*, Miz unveiled "The Most Must-See Talk Show in WWE History," *Miz TV*. Despite a litany of prestigious guests, Miz mostly uses the platform to extoll his own awesomeness. Today, with starring credits in *The Marine 3* and *4*, *Santa's Little Helper*, *Christmas Bounty*, and more, he relishes every second of airtime he gets to flaunt his grinning "moneymaker." One guest he did listen to, however, was "Nature Boy" Ric Flair. The 16-Time World Champion encouraged Miz to use his iconic Figure-Four Leglock, which he did to great success.

In 2014, the Hollywood star hired Damien Sandow as his stunt double. With matching shades and overpriced wardrobes, the duo won the WWE Tag Team Championships in November 2014. The renamed "Mizdow" was the fourth and most outlandish partner to claim tandem gold with Miz. Of course, that did not stop the egotistical Superstar from firing Sandow in 2015.

One night after WrestleMania 32, Miz received assistance from a most stunning source, his wife and former Divas Champion Maryse. The blonde bombshell provided a key distraction to help Miz pin Zack Ryder with a Skull Crushing Finale. The victory marked his fifth Intercontinental Championship.

So long as The Miz has a microphone, anyone with eardrums will hear his boasting as he continues to build on a decorated career.

MNM

MEMBERS	Joey Mercury, Johnny Nitro, & Melina
SIGNATURE MOVE	Snapshot

Unlike many newcomers, the bright lights of WWE failed to intimidate the self-proclaimed A-List celebrities MNM. With paparazzi commonplace in their everyday lives, "the 'it' team on the scene" made an instant impact upon their debut. In fact, Mercury and Nitro captured the WWE Tag Team Championship in their first match in April 2005.

Over the next year, the duo claimed the tag Titles three times, the gold matching well with their flowing fur coats and gaudy sunglasses. Mercury and Nitro's athleticism coupled with Melina's conniving tactics seemed unstoppable. They ended two of Rey Mysterio's tag Title reigns and also upended the modern day LOD. Unfortunately, things went sour for the red-carpet trio in May 2006 when Melina and Nitro viciously attacked Mercury following a loss. Melina continued to support Nitro as they both pursued solo success.

In true Hollywood fashion, MNM premiered their thrilling sequel in November 2006 when they reunited to challenge The Hardys. Unfortunately, they were unable to duplicate the greatness of their first blockbuster and went their separate ways soon after.

MOJO RAWLEY

HT	6'4"	WT	290 lbs.	FROM	Alexandria, Virginia
SIGNATURE MOVE		Hyperdrive			

Pulsating with energy and determination, Mojo Rawley has earned a reputation for "staying hyped."

Before entering sports-entertainment, Rawley played every defensive position on the NFL's Green Bay Packers and Arizona Cardinals. After making his NXT debut in 2013, he went on a high-voltage win streak, upending such rivals as Sylvester Lefort, Oliver Gray, and CJ Parker.

In 2015, "Long Island Ice Tea" Zack Ryder migrated to NXT and adopted Rawley's outlook. As the Hype Brothers, the two battled foes like Dash Wilder and Scott Dawson, Blake and Murphy, and American Alpha, and even joined with NXT Women's Champion Bayley in a memorable intergender encounter.

MOLLY HOLLY

HT	5'4"	FROM	Forrest Lake, Minnesota
SIGNATURE MOVE			Molly Go-Round

In 2000, Molly Holly joined her older cousins, Crash and Hardcore, in WWE. Molly started off battling Trish Stratus, but a relationship with Spike Dudley captured her attention for a time. Molly later became "Mighty Molly" alongside resident superhero The Hurricane, but she dissolved the partnership when she had the opportunity to take his Hardcore Championship. Molly was the first female to hold the tattered Title.

Molly soon separated herself from the rest of the Divas, claiming that she was pure, wholesome, and better than any of them. Molly backed up her claim in 2002 at *King of the Ring* when she defeated Trish Stratus for the Women's Championship. After losing the Title at *Unforgiven* in the same year, she managed to capture the Title again in 2003. Her most memorable WWE moment was one she would like to forget. After losing a Hair vs. Title Match against Victoria at *WrestleMania XX*, Molly was shaved bald. Molly left WWE in 2005 but is still remembered as a tough, no-frills competitor and proud Champion.

MONEY, INC.

MEMBERS	Ted DiBiase & Irwin R. Schyster
COMBINED WT	508 lbs.

Following successful singles careers, Ted DiBiase and Irwin R. Schyster began competing as a unit in February 1992. With Jimmy Hart as their manager, the money-hungry duo known as Money, Inc. gained instant success, capturing the World Tag Team Championship from the Legion of Doom shortly after their formation. The win ruffled the feathers of another team managed by Hart, the Natural Disasters, who believed their manager should have placed them into the Championship match instead. The contention set off a fiery rivalry between the two teams.

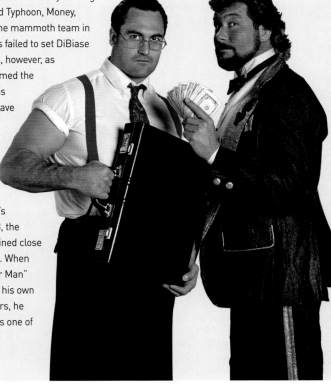

After five months of successfully fending off Earthquake and Typhoon, Money, Inc. finally fell to the mammoth team in July 1992. The loss failed to set DiBiase and Schyster back, however, as they quickly reclaimed the Titles a few months later. The victory gave them their second of three World Tag Team Championship reigns.

Following DiBiase's retirement in 1993, the affluent duo remained close business partners. When the "Million-Dollar Man" set out to manage his own stable of Superstars, he pinpointed I.R.S. as one of his crown jewels.

THE MONGOLIAN STOMPER

HT	6'1"	WT	260 lbs.	FROM	Mongolia

While most WWE fans may not be overly familiar with the Mongolian Stomper, his résumé boasts more than fifty Championship reigns from promotions all over North America. The chiseled Superstar from Mongolia achieved his greatest notoriety while competing for Stu Hart's Stampede Wrestling in Calgary, Alberta, Canada. While there, he engaged in heated rivalries with Bad News Allen (known as Bad News Brown to WWE fans) and a very young Bret Hart.

Between reigns atop Stampede Wrestling, the Mongolian Stomper achieved great success in the United States. On several occasions during the 1960s and 70s, he nearly defeated Lou Thesz, Gene Kiniski, and Harley Race for the NWA Championship.

THE MONGOLS

MEMBERS	Bepo, Geto, & Bolo

These beasts from Outer Mongolia were introduced in Stu Hart's Stampede Wrestling territory and journeyed to WWE in 1968. After being managed by Tony Angelo, Bepo and Geto Mongol became Captain Lou Albano's first protégés.

In June, 1970 the pair capped their Madison Square Garden debut by defeating Tony Marino and Victor Rivera for the International Tag Team Championship. But a year later, Bepo and Geto left WWE with the Titles. Also in 1971, "Crazy" Luke Graham and Tarzan Tyler became the inaugural WWE World Tag Team Champions in a tournament. To prove the legitimacy of the fledgling Title, they beat the Mongols.

In 1975, after Bepo left the team, Geto and a new partner, Bolo, competed in the IWA, a short-lived renegade promotion.

MOONDOG MAYNE

HT	6'0"	WT	275 lbs.
FROM	Crabtree, Oregon		
SIGNATURE MOVE			The Bone Smash

"Moondog" Lonnie Mayne was a crazed competitor who was unpredictable in and out of the ring, known for howling and chomping on pieces of broken glass during his interviews. His unorthodox means of dissecting opponents included biting them and raking their eyes. He even took beverages from those sitting in the audience to dump them in adversaries' faces.

Moondog debuted in WWE in 1972 and quickly set to eradicate the company's top Superstars. Mayne's "dog-eat-dog" mentality also led to many victories in Battle Royals before he left the company in late 1973. He took his brawling ways to the west coast of the United States, becoming a threat everywhere he appeared. Tragically, in August 1978, Moondog Mayne was killed in an automobile accident.

THE MOONDOGS

MEMBERS	Rex, Spot, & King
FROM	Parts Unknown

Although unorthodox in appearance, the Moondogs were one of the most skilled tag teams of the early 1980s. Managed by Capt. Lou Albano, the barrel-chested combination was known for its shaggy hair, ripped jeans, and affinity for gnawing on large animal bones.

Rex and King proved their bite was just as big as their bark when they beat Tony Garea and Rick Martel for the World Tag Team Championship in March 1981 in Allentown, Pennsylvania. A few months into their reign, however, King established himself as the runt of the litter when he ran away from WWE, presumably to return to Parts Unknown. Rex then filled the vacancy with an equally eccentric Moondog, Spot, and the duo went on to successfully defend the tag Titles for two more months.

After losing the World Tag Team Championship back to Garea and Martel in July 1981, Rex and Spot struggled to regain their momentum. The wild duo eventually moved on to moderately successful singles careers.

MORDECAI

HT	6'3"	WT	270 lbs.	SIGNATURE MOVE	Crucifix Powerbomb

According to Mordecai, sin eats away at the soul of society like a ravenous cancer, devouring it until there's nothing left but a black hole of despair. And from that hole, the mysterious Superstar emerged.

Clad in pure white, Mordecai made his debut at *Judgment Day 2004*, soundly defeating Scotty 2 Hotty. From there, he punished Billy Kidman and Akio before defeating veteran Hardcore Holly at *The Great American Bash*. With a perfect record, Mordecai went into battle against Rey Mysterio in July 2004. Given his impressive start, many assumed the newcomer could beat the then-Cruiserweight Champion. But it wasn't to be. Mysterio defeated Mordecai and the mysterious Superstar was never heard from again.

THE MOUNTIE

HT	6'1"	WT	257 lbs.	FROM	Montreal, Quebec, Canada
SIGNATURE MOVE	Carotid Control Technique				

A former member of the Royal Canadian Mounted Police, this Superstar debuted in WWE in 1991. Despite claims that the world was his jurisdiction and that he upheld international law and order, The Mountie often broke the rules to earn his victories. To add insult to injury, he often handcuffed fallen opponents to the ring ropes and tasered them with his shock stick.

Big Boss Man took exception to The Mountie's methods and the two former law enforcers battled for months, culminating in a Jailhouse Match at *SummerSlam 1991*. The stipulation was that the loser would spend the night in a New York City jail. The Mountie lost the match and was taken away by New York's Finest.

In January 1992, The Mountie caught Bret Hart on an off night and captured the Intercontinental Championship. Though memorable, his Title reign lasted a fleeting two days before Roddy Piper defeated him. By the end of 1992, The Mountie was gone from WWE, but fans will always remember him and his vow to always get his man!

MR. FUJI

HT	5'10"	WT	270 lbs.	FROM	Osaka, Japan
SIGNATURE MOVE	Cobra Hold				

In 1972, the inscrutable Mr. Fuji arrived to WWE, managed by the Grand Wizard. He quickly became known for secretly hiding bags of ceremonial Japanese salt on his person, and throwing the pellets into the eyes of opponents. He allied himself with the dreaded Professor Toru Tanaka, and on June 27, 1972, they began their first of three WWE Tag Team Championship reigns. After losing the Titles for the second time, Fuji and Tanaka left WWE and stormed into the NWA, where they won numerous regional tag team Championships.

In 1977, they returned with "Classy" Freddie Blassie as their new manager. Though their final Championship reign ended on March 14, 1978, they remained one of sports-entertainment's most feared teams until they separated in 1979.

Fuji reappeared in WWE in 1981 with a new partner, Mr. Saito. Managed by Captain Lou Albano, they enjoyed two reigns as WWE Tag Team Champions. Either alone or with a partner, Mr. Fuji was regarded as one of the world's most dangerous men, and one who could not be trusted under any circumstances.

In 1985, Fuji started to dress in a black tuxedo and black bowler hat, as he embarked on his managerial career. At *WrestleMania IV*, he led Demolition to the WWE Tag Team Titles for his first championship as a manager.

After managing multiple teams to great success, Fuji introduced the intimidating Yokozuna to WWE in 1992, and guided him straight to the top of sports-entertainment. At *WrestleMania IX*, Yokozuna, with Mr. Fuji in his corner, defeated Bret Hart for the WWE Championship. Despite losing the Title in a challenge to Hulk Hogan moments later, Yokozuna regained the prize at the *King of the Ring*. The devious one left WWE in 1995, but reappeared for the last time at *WrestleMania XII* with Yokozuna.

On the eve of *WrestleMania 23*, Mr. Fuji joined the WWE Hall of Fame. Mr. Fuji is one of the rare legendary figures of WWE that had as much success as a manager as he did a competitor.

MR. HUGHES

HT	6'6"	WT	330 lbs.	FROM	Kansas City, Missouri

SIGNATURE MOVE	Powerslam

Though he never stuck around for very long, Mr. Hughes proved to be a dangerous force during his three brief WWE stints. Alongside manager Harvey Wippleman, Hughes debuted in 1993 and made an immediate impact by stealing Undertaker's urn. He then spent the next several weeks tearing through many lesser-known Superstars. Surprisingly, however, Hughes made a quick exit in the summer of 1993.

Four years after mysteriously leaving, Hughes returned as Hunter Hearst-Helmsley's bodyguard. But he again disappeared just as quickly as he came. In 1999, a more svelte Hughes reemerged as Chris Jericho's bodyguard. The no-nonsense Superstar instantly earned his money, helping Y2J defeat Ken Shamrock. In typical Hughes fashion, the big man once again disappeared approximately one month later.

MR. KENNEDY

HT	6'2"	WT	235 lbs.	FROM	Green Bay, Wisconsin

SIGNATURE MOVE	Mic Check

Most *SmackDown* Superstars in 2005 were content with Tony Chimel's ring announcing. Not Mr. Kennedy...Kennedy!

This self-assured loudmouth had the chutzpah to demand that he introduce himself. With the arena lights dimmed and a microphone that could have been Buddy Holly's dangling from the rafters, Kennedy's voice cannoned through the speakers as he bellowed his name. Twice.

Not lacking in confidence, the former U.S. military member backed up his boastfulness in the ring. His pesky style frustrated the likes of Undertaker, Rey Mysterio, Batista, and Shawn Michaels. In September 2006, he won the United States Championship in a Triple Threat Match against Finlay and Bobby Lashley.

Kennedy kept rolling and became "Mr. Money in the Bank" at *WrestleMania 23*. The Green Bay native seemed like a shoe-in to bring a World Championship back to "Titletown" until Edge defeated him with the briefcase on the line on *Raw*. The next year Kennedy became a fan favorite and made his Hollywood debut in *Behind Enemy Lines: Colombia*. That spring, Kennedy and WWE parted ways.

MR. PERFECT

see page 236

MR. SAITO

HT	5'11"	WT	265 lbs.	FROM	Tokyo, Japan

SIGNATURE MOVE	Saito Suplex

A former Japanese Olympian, Mr. Saito was admired within amateur wrestling circles for his superior technical skills. When it came to his professional career, he refused to rest solely on his previous laurels. Instead, Saito developed a punishing high-impact offense, coupled with a complete disregard for the rules, which helped round out his impressive repertoire.

A noted tag team competitor, Mr. Saito captured gold in the NWA with partners Ivan Koloff, Mr. Sato, and Gene Kiniski, among others. However, it wasn't until 1981 that he reached the pinnacle of tag team competition when he teamed with Mr. Fuji to capture the World Tag Team Championship from Tony Garea and Rick Martel. Sans a few weeks in the summer of 1982, the devious tandem held the Titles for more than one year. Following his stay in WWE, Mr. Saito took his talents to Japan, where he proved himself as a force in both the tag team and singles ranks.

MR. T

HT	5'10"	WT	236 lbs.	FROM	Chicago, Illinois

Mr. T's sports-entertainment career only consisted of a handful of appearances, but don't be fooled. This former *The A-Team* star is connected to some of the biggest moments in WWE history.

In 1985, Mr. T teamed with friend Hulk Hogan to help usher in *WrestleMania*. The duo's main event clash with rivals "Rowdy" Roddy Piper and "Mr. Wonderful" Paul Orndorff helped propel WWE to an international sensation.

The following year, Mr. T used the fame he gained as Clubber Lang in *Rocky III* to secure a Boxing Match against Piper at *WrestleMania 2*. Mr. T's boxing prowess prevailed, as he defeated "Hot Rod" via disqualification.

Nearly a decade later, Mr. T served as the Special Guest Referee in a WCW Championship Match between Hogan and Ric Flair. He also defeated Kevin Sullivan at *Starrcade 1994*.

This 80s icon's role in catapulting sports-entertainment to the mainstream was honored in 2014 with induction into the WWE Hall of Fame. The following night at *WrestleMania 30*, Mr. T and Piper shared a tense handshake, finally agreeing to squash their thirty-year-old grudge.

MR. PERFECT

HT	6'3"
WT	257 lbs.
FROM	Robbinsdale, Minnesota

SIGNATURE MOVE
Perfectplex

Athletically, there wasn't anything Curt Hennig couldn't do. He could hit a home run, sink a forty-foot putt, and even catch his own Hail Mary football pass. Basically, he was perfect in every way. He was Mr. Perfect.

Hennig's flawlessness was evident early on. After making his 1980 debut in the American Wrestling Association, he spent much of the decade proving his dominance over the promotion's top stars, including Larry Zbyszko, Buddy Rose, and Colonel DeBeers.

Hennig captured his first piece of AWA Gold when he teamed with Scott Hall to defeat Jimmy Garvin and Steve Regal for the AWA World Tag Team Championship in January 1986. The Hennig-Hall pairing held the Titles for four months while also giving fans a glimpse into the future of sports-entertainment. In the years that followed, both Hennig and Hall went on to become among the most elite competitors the industry has ever seen.

Hennig captured the AWA World Heavyweight Championship in May 1987 when he defeated Nick Bockwinkel at *SuperClash II*. His 373-day reign proved to be one of the most successful in the promotion's history. Only Verne Gagne, Rick Martel, and Bockwinkel had longer runs with the gold.

PERFECTION

Following his successful stint in the AWA, Hennig made the jump to WWE in 1988. Upon his arrival, he fittingly became known as Mr. Perfect, a name that would become synonymous with Hennig throughout the remainder of his legendary career.

Convincing victories over The Red Rooster, Jim Brunzell, and Koko B. Ware, among others, highlighted Perfect's first year with WWE. And by April 1990, his superior technical ability earned him a spot in a tournament designed to crown a new Intercontinental Champion. In the finals, the master of the Perfectplex turned back Tito Santana to capture his first of two Intercontinental Championships. His second reign came at the expense of The Texas Tornado in November 1990.

In all, Perfect held the Title for more than 400 days. And while others have held the gold longer, many consider Mr. Perfect to be the greatest Intercontinental Champion of all time.

Injuries unfortunately sidelined Mr. Perfect through much of his prime, but he didn't let that stop him from gaining a prominent role within WWE. In addition to working as color commentator for many WWE television programs, he also served as Ric Flair's advisor during the Nature Boy's initial stint with the company.

Hennig dropped his Mr. Perfect persona in 1997 to embark on a three-year run with World Championship Wrestling. While in WCW, he returned to Championship glory when he defeated Steve McMichael for the United States Title in September 1997. Hennig also teamed with Barry Windham to capture the WCW World Tag Team Championship in February 1999.

Recognizing his greatness, many of Hennig's WCW peers attempted to lure him into their fold. During his stay in the Atlanta-based promotion, Hennig became a member of two of the most influential factions of all time, The Four Horsemen and New World Order. He was also a member of the West Texas Rednecks before leaving WCW in the summer of 2000.

Mr. Perfect returned to WWE in 2002 when he competed in a Royal Rumble Match. Looking like the Mr. Perfect of old, he impressed many as one of the final four participants in the match before ultimately being eliminated by eventual winner, Triple H. After the Rumble, Perfect stayed with WWE for several months, competing against the likes of Stone Cold Steve Austin, Edge, and Rob Van Dam.

Sadly, Curt Hennig passed away on February 10, 2003. Four years later, he took his rightful place alongside sports-entertainment's greats when he was posthumously inducted into the WWE Hall of Fame. Though gone, his amazing legacy lives on today in his son, WWE Superstar, Curtis Axel.

YOU ARE LOOKING AT THE MAN WHO WAS BORN WITH THE SIGN OF PERFECTION THAT HANGS OVER HIM.

MR. WRESTLING II

HT	5'11"	WT	236 lbs.	FROM	Atlanta, Georgia

SIGNATURE MOVE	Running High Knee

Mr. Wrestling II was one of the most popular Superstars of the Southern territories during the 1970s and early 1980s. President Jimmy Carter apparently considered Mr. Wrestling II his favorite ring gladiator. Spending the majority of his time in Georgia and Florida, the mysterious masked Superstar solidified himself as a force in both the singles and tag team ranks.

As a solo competitor, Mr. Wrestling II used his signature Running High Knee to claim an astonishing ten NWA Georgia Heavyweight Championships. He also won the NWA Florida Heavyweight Championship twice. A World Championship reign escaped Mr. Wrestling II during his illustrious career, but he did manage to battle NWA Champion Jack Brisco to several breathtaking draws during the 1970s.

Mr. Wrestling II was no stranger to tag team gold either, capturing Titles with such partners as Mr. Wrestling I, Tony Atlas, and "Cowboy" Bob Orton. Mr. Wrestling II's impressive career began to wind down toward the mid-1980s. In 1993, he was honored with induction into the short-lived WCW Hall of Fame.

MUFFY MOWER

Muffy Mower learned the hard way that insulting fans and co-workers is not the path to job security.

After debuting as Stephanie McMahon-Helmsley's personal trainer in 2000, Mower began spreading her health tips to anybody she came across, even if they didn't ask for them. She told the audience they needed to come to terms with the fact that they were fat and out of shape. She would then urge them to get on their feet for an arena-wide aerobic workout. The irritated crowds rarely cooperated.

To give Mower credit, she clearly knew what was needed to create a healthy body. She displayed washboard abs and nearly no body fat but her shenanigans quickly grew tired. After a handful of appearances, she faded from WWE.

MUHAMMAD HASSAN

HT	6'2"	WT	245 lbs.	FROM	Detroit, Michigan

SIGNATURE MOVE	Camel Clutch

In 2004, Muhammad Hassan entered WWE alongside his spokesperson, Daivari. He often interrupted the interview segments of others and verbally accosted Jim Ross and Jerry "The King" Lawler over their characterizations of him. Hassan's initial success led to several Title opportunities, most notably a chance to win John Cena's WWE Championship. After Cena rebuffed his attempt in a one-sided match, Hassan was drafted to *SmackDown*.

Hassan was last seen at the 2005 *Great American Bash* when he was powerbombed through the stage by Undertaker. Though his time in WWE was short, Muhammad Hassan will go down in WWE history books as one of the most controversial figures to appear in the company.

MVP

HT	6'3"	WT	259 lbs.	FROM	Miami, Florida

SIGNATURE MOVE	Playmaker

After MVP signed the most lucrative deal in *SmackDown* history in 2006, fans naturally had high expectations for the Miami native. And it didn't take long for him to prove he was the real deal, capturing the United States Championship in May 2007. As Champion, MVP practiced some unorthodox tactics to ensure the Title remain around his waist, including befriending potential threats.

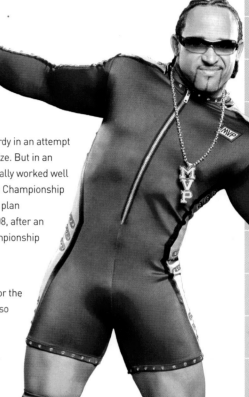

In August 2007, MVP teamed with Matt Hardy in an attempt to keep his foe from challenging for the prize. But in an unusual development, the odd couple actually worked well together and even won the WWE Tag Team Championship in August 2007. Unfortunately for MVP, his plan eventually proved to be flawed. In April 2008, after an ugly split, MVP lost the United States Championship to Hardy.

After a year on *Raw*, MVP returned to *SmackDown* in 2010, where he competed for the Intercontinental Championship and was also part of the victorious Team Mysterio at the 2010 *Survivor Series*. The following month, MVP was released from his WWE contract.

MYSTERY MAN

In July 1991, Mystery Man appeared in the ring, but exited as quickly as he entered. Dressed in black with his face covered, no one has learned how this individual came to WWE or why he was there. Ominous symbols were seen on his ring attire and fur covered his hands, arms, head, and back.

Mystery Man is one of the Superstars in WWE's storied history whose name was a literal description of his persona. Could he have returned to WWE with a new name? Did he leave sports-entertainment and establish himself in another profession? Is he a fan sitting next to you at a WWE event? Is he the man giving you a haircut? The answer may never be known.

NAILZ

HT	6'5"	WT	302 lbs.	FROM	Department of Corrections

After serving hard time in a Cobb County jail, Nailz made a beeline for WWE, where he immediately attacked his former prison guard, Big Boss Man. The ex-convict was so intent on exacting revenge from Boss Man, in fact, that he didn't even bother to change out of his orange prison jumpsuit. Instead, he wore the state-issued garb throughout the entirety of his brief WWE career.

The hardened criminal made short work of Virgil at *SummerSlam 1992*. Three months later, he finally had the opportunity to gain the upper hand from his former prison guard when the two Superstars battled in a Nightstick Match at *Survivor Series*. Boss Man ultimately proved his dominance that night and Nailz disappeared from WWE shortly after.

NAOMI

HT	5'5"
WT	Orlando, Florida
FROM	Rear View

Once known for a smile brighter than her neon shoes, Naomi has since shelved her colorful personality in favor of a more brooding attitude. As part of her makeover, Naomi joined forces with the equally-imposing Sasha Banks and Tamina. Collectively known as Team B.A.D., the threesome's athleticism has played a major role in WWE's Divas Revolution.

Prior to establishing herself as a beautiful and dangerous Diva, Naomi was a dancer for the NBA's Orlando Magic. She also danced with various hip-hop acts, including Flo Rida. Despite her success, Naomi wanted more. She wanted to be a WWE Diva.

Naomi parlayed her dance background into a WWE career when she debuted alongside Cameron as one of Brodus Clay's Funkadactyls in early 2012. As the dancing Diva, Naomi became so popular that she eventually appeared as one of the stars of *Total Divas* on E!

Following The Funkadactyls' 2014 breakup, Naomi began accompanying Jey and husband Jimmy Uso to the ring. With Naomi's support, The Usos went on to capture the WWE Tag Team Championship in December 2014.

NATHAN JONES

HT	6'10"	WT	305 lbs.	FROM	Australia
SIGNATURE MOVE		Gutwrench Suplex			

Formerly one of Australia's most wanted fugitives, Nathan Jones spent ten years in prison for his part in eight armed robberies. When he was released, the "Colossus of Boggo Road" attempted to find an outlet for his aggression in the WWE ring.

The untamed Jones was scheduled to make his WWE debut alongside Undertaker at *WrestleMania XIX*. But when Big Show and A-Train attacked the big man prior to the match, the American Bad Ass was forced to compete solo and Jones' debut was pushed back.

When he finally did compete in April 2003, he appeared unstoppable. An ankle injury laid him out for several months. He returned in October 2003, but just one month later, was gone from WWE.

THE NASTY BOYS

MEMBERS	Brian Knobbs & Jerry Saggs	COMBINED WT	546 lbs.
SIGNATURE MOVE		Pit Stop, Trip to Nastyville	

When you take a trip to Nastyville, you're travelling to one of the toughest places on Earth. Sporting black trench coats, wraparound shades, and perpetual sneers, these Mohawked punks of Nastyville left a trail of broken bodies in each of their many sports-entertainment stops, beginning with the AWA. After Knobbs and Saggs graduated from Verne Gagne's wrestling school in Minneapolis, the two ruffians joined Gagne's promotion, looking to brawl with the best tag teams in the world. They found the fight they were looking for when they met The Midnight Rockers. Mixing it up with a young Shawn Michaels and Marty Jennetty, the Nasty Boys bruising style put the sports-entertainment world on notice. Soon, they were collecting gold and bashing bodies in Memphis, Championship Wrestling from Florida, and WCW.

In 1991, WWE got "Nastisized" as the Boys made their debut with "Mouth of the South" Jimmy Hart as their manager. They quickly rose up the ranks by beating such legendary teams as the Road Warriors, Demolition, and their familiar foes The Rockers. In their *WrestleMania* debut, they defeated the Hart Foundation for the World Tag Team Championship. Shortly after losing their Titles to the Legion of Doom, the Nasty Boys did not take kindly to Jimmy Hart's shady business dealings with his new team, Money, Inc. They showed their underhanded manager the door, but not before giving him an up close and personal whiff of Knobb's hairy armpit.

In the fall of 1993, the Nasty Boys returned to WCW. With an offense as pretty as their sweaty, scowling mugs, they collected three reigns as WCW Tag Team Champions. Despite their ornery behavior, WCW fans eventually rallied to their side during battles with Harlem Heat and the nWo. In 1996, Saggs was forced out of the action for a number of years due to a serious neck injury. However, the Nasty Boys reunited in 2001 as a part of the short-lived XWF organization. Through the course of their careers, the Nasty Boys reached the top of the AWA, WCW, and WWE. Their hard-hitting style became legendary as the duo lived up to their Nasty name.

NATALYA

HT	5'5"	FROM	Calgary, Alberta, Canada	SIGNATURE MOVE	Sharpshooter

A member of the famed Hart family, Natalya has sports-entertainment royalty running through her veins. And like those before her, she has successfully created a legacy that will never be forgotten.

Natalya debuted in April 2008, when she came through the crowd to help Victoria fend off Michelle McCool and Cherry. Over the next few months, the third-generation star studied under the established Diva. But it was only a matter of time before Natalya would break off to help carry on the Hart name.

Natalya teamed with cousin, David Hart Smith, and future-husband, Tyson Kidd, to form The Hart Dynasty in 2009. Together they reestablished the Harts as a tag team powerhouse when Smith and Kidd captured the WWE Tag Team Championship in April 2010.

Seeking gold of her own, Natalya challenged Michelle McCool and Layla for the Divas Championship at *Survivor Series 2010*. Despite being outnumbered, she was able to topple Lay-Cool and achieve her childhood dream of being WWE's top female competitor. Weeks later at *TLC 2010*, Natalya continued to make Lay-Cool's life miserable. In the first-ever Divas Tag Team Tables Match, she and partner, Beth Phoenix, sent their rivals crashing through the timber.

Natalya's success inside the ring has led to great fame outside the ring. As one of the stars of E!'s *Total Divas*, she and Kidd allow cameras to capture the relationship drama that goes along with being a high-profile couple.

In 2013, jealous Divas lashed out at "Nattie" and her cast mates leading to an Elimination Match at *Survivor Series*. In the end, Natalya silenced the mouthpiece of the anti-Total Divas crew, AJ Lee, by forcing her to submit to the Sharpshooter. This trademark Hart maneuver sealed the win for her team.

Most recently, Natalya's undeniable athleticism has helped force her way into the renowned Divas Revolution, where she has educated the newcomers on what it truly means to be a WWE Diva.

NATION OF DOMINATION

MEMBERS	Faarooq, The Rock, Kama/The Godfather, D-Lo Brown, Owen Hart, Crush, Savio Vega, Ahmed Johnson, Mark Henry, Clarence Mason, & PG-13 (J.C. Ice & Wolfie D)

Led by Faarooq, The Nation of Domination was a militant group assembled to fight for rights that they felt were unfairly held back from them. The controversial faction set out to gain equality "by any means necessary."

The earliest version of the group contained Crush, Savio Vega, D-Lo Brown, PG-13, and Clarence Mason. When they failed to help Faarooq defeat Undertaker for the WWE Championship, the leader fired all of them, with the exception of D-Lo Brown. The new-look Nation was filled with Superstars that shared Faarooq's twisted visions: Kama, The Rock, and Mark Henry.

The Nation claimed its first piece of gold in December 1997 when The Rock was awarded the Intercontinental Championship after Stone Cold Steve Austin refused to defend the Title. As the faction's only Titleholder, The Rock slowly began to extract leadership responsibilities from Faarooq, before finally kicking him out of the Nation altogether in early 1998.

Under The Rock's leadership, the Nation developed a more hip quality. No longer mad at the world, various members were allowed to show their true personalities. The most notable change saw Kama transform into the fun-loving pimp, The Godfather.

By the end of 1998, The Godfather left the Nation to pursue his budding pimping career. Shortly after that, The Rock's ego grew to epic proportions, forcing Brown and Henry to attack their leader, thus ending the Nation's existence.

NATIONAL WRESTLING FEDERATION/INTERNATIONAL WRESTLING ASSOCIATION

For a time in the 1970s, the National Wrestling Federation (NWF) and, subsequently, the International Wrestling Association (IWA) attempted to compete as major league organizations.

The NWF was started by promoter, Pedro Martinez, in 1970. By 1972, the territory included Buffalo, Cleveland, and Pittsburgh. That same year, the promotion staged its "Superbowl of Wrestling" in Cleveland's Municipal Stadium. On the show, NWF Champion Johnny Powers defended his Title against Johnny Valentine; Ernie Ladd and Abdullah the Butcher fought to a wild double-disqualification.

In 1974, competition with WWE forced the NWF to fold. Even so, Powers took the NWF Title to Japan, and lost it to Antonio Inoki, who was instructed to stop listing himself as a "World" Champion.

In 1975, Martinez partnered with sports entrepreneur, Eddie Einhorn, to form the International Wrestling Association, which crowned Mil Mascaras as Champion and attempted to become a national organization. Other stars included Ivan Koloff, Thunderbolt Patterson, and Bulldog Brower. This group lasted until 1978. Afterwards, both Mascaras and Powers occasionally billed themselves as Champion on international tours.

NATURAL DISASTERS

MEMBERS	Earthquake & Typhoon
COMBINED WT	846 lbs.

At a time when most WWE tag teams topped out at 500 pounds, Earthquake and Typhoon joined forces to create a near half-ton of total destruction. Appropriately named, the Natural Disasters, the colossal duo stormed through their competition with the greatest of ease.

Prior to the Natural Disasters' formation, Typhoon spent many years competing as the hugely popular, Tugboat. In 1991, he revealed a darker side when he turned on his friends, the Bushwhackers, to align himself with the despised Earthquake. Together, the Natural Disasters left such destruction in their wake that a wrecking ball would cringe.

In January 1992, Earthquake and Typhoon scored a major count-out victory over the World Tag Team Champions, the Legion of Doom. By all accounts, the win should have put the Natural Disasters in line for another opportunity at the Titles, but their manager Jimmy Hart put Money, Inc. in the ring with the Champs instead. The move infuriated the oversized tag team, who immediately fired "The Mouth of the South." The bold move made Earthquake and Typhoon instant fan favorites and also propelled them into a heated rivalry with the new Champs, DiBiase and Schyster.

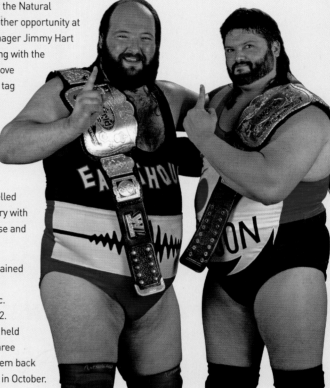

The Natural Disasters gained a level of revenge when they defeated Money, Inc. for the Titles in July 1992. Unfortunately, they only held the Championship for three months before losing them back to DiBiase and Schyster in October.

NEVILLE

HT	5'8"	WT	194 lbs.	FROM	Newcastle upon Tyne, England
SIGNATURE MOVE		Red Arrow			

Gravity may have forgotten Neville, but after watching the British-born Superstar compete just once, there's no way fans ever could.

After spending nearly a decade perfecting his craft worldwide, Neville signed a WWE developmental deal in 2012. He immediately wowed the NXT Universe with his amazing aerial assault and lightning-fast feet. As expected, it wasn't long before Neville captured Championship gold. In February 2013, he teamed with Oliver Grey to defeat The Wyatt Family for the NXT Tag Team Titles.

Neville would win the tag Titles one more time before focusing his attention on the NXT Championship, which he won by defeating Bo Dallas in a Ladder Match at *NXT arRIVAL* in February 2014. Neville held the Title for a record 287 days before losing to Sami Zayn in December. Despite the loss, things were about to look up for "The Man That Gravity Forgot."

Neville made his main roster debut the night after *WrestleMania 31*, when he defeated Curtis Axel on *Raw*. The win's momentum propelled Neville to the finals of the King of the Ring tournament, where he came up short against Bad News Barrett.

Undeterred by the King of the Ring loss, Neville gained a level of retribution when he teamed with Stephen Amell from the hit TV show *Arrow* to defeat Barrett and Stardust at *SummerSlam*. With the victory, Neville established himself as a real-life superhero with an amazing future in WWE.

NEW AGE OUTLAWS

MEMBERS	"Road Dogg" Jesse James & "Bad Ass" Billy Gunn
COMBINED WT	548 lbs.

"Oh...you didn't know?" This famous introduction brought capacity crowds around the world to their feet. In a case of good enemies/better friends, the two former rivals became a team in 1997. When Billy laid out his then-manager, the Honky Tonk Man, with a guitar, the spirit of the New Age Outlaws was born and tag team competition was about to change forever.

The New Age Outlaws became known for their abilities and antics both in and out of the ring. They quickly took aim at the top and stole the World Tag Team Championship from the legendary Legion of Doom. The Outlaws then showed their mean streak when they locked Cactus Jack and Terry Funk in a dumpster and pushed the dumpster off the *Raw* stage. Their handiwork caught the interest of Shawn Michaels and Hunter Hearst-Helmsley prior to their Title defense at *WrestleMania XIV*. Though they lost to Cactus Jack and Chainsaw Charlie, they regained the Titles the next night in a steel cage with a little help from their new friends.

This collaboration marked the second incarnation of D-Generation X, and the Outlaws helped build the group's legacy. Though differences caused them to split in 1999, "Road Dogg" and Billy reformed to show they were still the best against the Rock 'N' Sock Connection, Edge and Christian, and many others. The Outlaws rode together until February 2000 when they went their separate ways.

One of the Attitude Era's major attractions, fans remembered their signature entrance word-for-word when the two renegades returned in 2012 after ten years away from WWE. While their reunion with DX at *Raw 1000* seemed like a one-night-only attraction, Gunn and James weren't done. They returned to compete full time in January 2014 and defeated Cody Rhodes and Goldust at *Royal Rumble* to claim their sixth Tag Team Title. At *WrestleMania 31*, Billy and Dogg rushed to the aid of former DX cohort Triple H during his successful battle with Sting. This shocking late-career surge proved these old dogs still pack the same bite.

THE NEW BLACKJACKS

MEMBERS	Blackjack Windham & Blackjack Bradshaw	COMBINED WT	565 lbs.

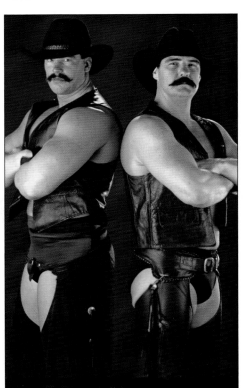

The tag team division in WWE was given a loud wake-up call in 1997. With classic rough-house tactics matched with innovative power moves, the cowboys in black became serious contenders for the WWE World Tag Team Championship.

The New Blackjacks attempted to revive the proud legacy of the original Blackjacks, Blackjack Mulligan and Blackjack Lanza. Barry Windham—a member of the Four Horsemen in the NWA, and a former tag team co-Titlist in WWE—was Mulligan's son. Lanza considered Bradshaw "kin."

The New Blackjacks had showdowns with the Godwinns, Faarooq and Kama, and the New Age Outlaws. This iteration of the classic duo did not last long. Blackjack Windham turned on Bradshaw in early 1998 to join Jim Cornette's collection of stars attempting to revive the NWA in WWE rings.

Even though the team lasted a short period of time, Windham and Bradshaw brought traditional Texas brutality back to the ring. Their stint as the New Blackjacks paid homage to the originals and celebrated the team's legacy in sports-entertainment.

THE NEW DAY

MEMBERS	Big E, Kofi Kingston, & Xavier Woods
COMBINED WT	702 lbs.

"It's a New Day, yes it is."

That slogan, uttered at the start of the celebrated trio's theme song, sounds like a boast. But since their debut on *Raw* in 2014, Big E, Kofi Kingston, and Xavier Woods have changed the perception of successful tag team wrestling.

Abundantly talented and profusely eccentric, the three motivate each other by repeatedly chanting, "New Day Rocks." Although cynical at first, fans eventually came around, embracing the threesome's unicorn imagery and gestures, as well as their taunting buzzword, "Booty." In fact, New Day even claims to have its own breakfast cereal, Booty-Os. And then, there's the beloved trombone Woods calls "Francesca."

During their Tag Team Championship reigns, New Day has employed the "Freebird rule," allowing any two members to defend the gold. Among their opponents are the Lucha Dragons, Usos, and Prime Time Players.

At *WrestleMania 32*, the trio clashed with Alberto Del Rio, Sheamus, Rusev, and Bad News Barrett. Although they lost the four-on-three confrontation, the New Day continued venturing where no team had treaded before.

NEW DREAM TEAM

| MEMBERS | Greg Valentine & Dino Bravo | COMBINED WT | 491 lbs. |

Contrary to popular belief, new doesn't always mean improved. Following a *WrestleMania III* argument between original Dream Team members Brutus Beefcake and Greg Valentine, Beefcake was unceremoniously ousted from the unit and replaced with Dino Bravo. The new union, however, failed to reach the same level of success as the original duo, who once ruled WWE as World Tag Team Champions.

Managed by "Luscious" Johnny Valiant, the New Dream Team saw its greatest success early on. After several impressive showings against the Islanders, Valentine and Bravo were granted an opportunity at the Hart Foundation's World Tag Team Titles. The new combination failed to capture the gold, however, and quickly slipped into obscurity. Shortly after the loss, Valentine and Bravo agreed to go their separate ways.

THE NEW FOUNDATION

| MEMBERS | Owen Hart & Jim "The Anvil" Neidhart | COMBINED WT | 508 lbs. |

When Bret Hart left the Hart Foundation to pursue singles success, Jim Neidhart didn't have to look very far to find a replacement. He simply turned to Bret's brother, Owen Hart.

With tag Title reigns alongside partners Yokozuna, British Bulldog, and Jeff Jarrett, Hart's body of work as a tag team competitor is legendary. Similarly, The Anvil will forever be remembered as one-half of one of history's greatest teams. Together, however, the New Foundation failed to catch on.

Luckily for both Superstars, their amazing success at other points in their respective careers far overshadows the team's checkerboard ring gear and unimpressive record. Years after the New Foundation crumbled, Neidhart stood by Owen's side as the young Hart claimed the 1994 King of the Ring crown.

THE NEW MIDNIGHT EXPRESS

| MEMBERS | Bob Holly & Bart Gunn | COMBINED WT | 493 lbs. |

Led by manager James E. Cornette, The Midnight Express became one of the NWA's most successful tag teams of the 1980s. A decade later, Cornette attempted to recreate the magic when he reformed the egotistical team in WWE. This time, he replaced its aging members with the considerably younger Bob Holly and Bart Gunn.

Known as The New Midnight Express, Holly and Gunn adopted nicknames fitting of the 1980s squad. Holly became "Bodacious" Bob, while Gunn went by "Bombastic" Bart. Together, they quickly climbed atop the NWA tag team scene when they defeated The Headbangers for the NWA World Tag Team Championship in March 1998.

Despite their success in the NWA tag ranks, the duo failed to make any real waves in WWE. Their highest-profile encounter came at *WrestleMania XV*, where they competed in the Tag Team Battle Royal, which was ultimately won by LOD 2000.

By the end of 1998, less than one year into their existence, The New Midnight Express went their separate ways.

THE NEW ROCKERS

| MEMBERS | Marty Jannetty & Leif Cassidy | COMBINED WT | 468 lbs. |

The familiar rock 'n' roll theme that echoed in arenas all over the world during the late 1980s and early 1990s played again in 1996. WWE saw the thrilling tag team duo of the original Rocker, Marty Jannetty and newcomer Leif Cassidy take on all of the WWE's top duos including the Godwinns, the Bodydonnas, the Smokin' Gunns, and the Bushwhackers.

Marty and Leif stayed true to the Rocker tradition of excellent continuity and double-team moves, and a finishing move that is still regarded as one of the most dangerous in WWE history. Despite only a brief time together, the New Rockers added another element to the legacy of the famed tandem and proved that they were in charge whenever they stepped in the ring.

NEXUS

| MEMBERS | Wade Barrett, CM Punk, Justin Gabriel, Heath Slater, David Otunga, Skip Sheffield, Daniel Bryan, Michael Tarver, Darren Young, Michael McGillicutty, Husky Harris, Mason Ryan, & John Cena |

During NXT's first season, eight Rookies battled relentlessly for the right to be called WWE's next breakout star. But once it was over, those eight men united to form Nexus, one of the most destructive forces in WWE history.

Led by Wade Barrett, Nexus shocked the sports-entertainment world when they invaded a June 2010 *Raw* main event between John Cena and CM Punk. The result of the invasion was pure devastation, as every soul in their wake was left a beaten and battered mess. They even destroyed the announce table, ring, and anything else in their way.

Over the next few months, Nexus performed some of the most detestable acts imaginable, including viciously attacking Ricky Steamboat, Bret Hart, and Mr. McMahon. Through it all, however, their main target was Cena. In October of 2010, Cena was forced into reluctant membership of Nexus, a power play designed with the goal of helping Barrett become WWE Champion.

Cena's virtue prevailed. Then in December 2010, Punk seized power of Nexus from Barrett, shifting leadership but still keeping a bull's-eye on Cena's back. In July 2011, Punk scored the keynote victory in the Nexus-versus-Cena rivalry when he defeated his nemesis for the WWE Championship.

NIA JAX

HT	6'0"	FROM	San Diego, California
SIGNATURE MOVE		Leg Drop	

Nia Jax's inspiration for entering the sport of kings occurred while watching her cousin, The Rock, tangle with John Cena at *WrestleMania XXVIII*.

Already accomplished as a college basketball standout and plus-sized model, Jax was quickly mastering moves that would play to her immense power, like the Samoan drop, backbreaker, and running body avalanche at NXT's Performance Center.

She made her first appearance on the NXT roster in 2015, first intimidating, then bulldozing through opponents. But she also learned that the women of NXT are a tough breed after encountering such stars as Bayley and Asuka.

She found an ally in flame-haired Eva Marie. As the Power Alliance, they proved to be as formidable in tag competition as Jax is as a single's competitor.

NICOLE BASS

HT	6'2"	FROM	New York, New York

Following a brief stint in ECW, Nicole Bass made her WWE debut in March 1999, helping Sable successfully defend the Women's Championship against Tori at *WrestleMania XV*. From there, the massive Diva went on to manhandle nearly every female on the WWE roster, including Ivory, Debra, and Jacqueline.

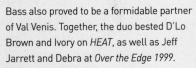

Bass also proved to be a formidable partner of Val Venis. Together, the duo bested D'Lo Brown and Ivory on *HEAT*, as well as Jeff Jarrett and Debra at *Over the Edge 1999*.

Despite her early success and intimidating presence, Bass abruptly disappeared from the WWE scene in the summer of 1999. During her short WWE career, she proved to be a legitimate force that struck fear into both the Divas and Superstars of WWE.

NIDIA

HT	5'6"	FROM	Mayaguez, Puerto Rico

A co-winner of *Tough Enough* season one, this former Diva debuted in 2002 and was revealed as the person sending letters to The Hurricane. Nidia began as Jamie Noble's trailer-park-dwelling better half. The backwoods couple went from rags to riches when Noble received a massive inheritance. However, when Noble started diverting his eyes and newfound money toward other Divas, Nidia walked out.

In time, Nidia proved she was just fine without Noble and that her win on *Tough Enough* was no fluke. She matched muscle in the ring with Torrie Wilson, Gail Kim, Dawn Marie, and Jazz. Before leaving WWE in November 2004, Nidia became a top contender for the Women's Championship and also showed her sexy side in the video release *Divas: Desert Heat*.

NIKKI BELLA

HT	5'6"	FROM	San Diego, California
SIGNATURE MOVE		Bella Buster, Rack Attack	

In August 2008, Nikki Bella joined Big Show and Hornswoggle in the elite fraternity of Superstars to debut in WWE from underneath the ring. The troublesome tactic of replacing her identical sister, Brie, mid-match became known as "Twin Magic." While Nikki was instrumental in Brie's first Divas Championship, the Fearless Diva would later cement her own status as one of the definitive female Titlists in WWE history.

Nikki claimed her first Championship in April 2012 by topping "The Glamazon" Beth Phoenix. Her maiden voyage with the butterfly Title was short-lived, but Bella's best was yet to come. After a hiatus from WWE, Nikki and Brie returned with a purpose. With *Total Divas* cameras tracking their every move, the twins became co-Divas of the Year in 2013.

At *SummerSlam 2014*, the Bella's sisterly bond was fractured when Nikki cost Brie her match against Stephanie McMahon. The betrayal led to Nikki further degrading Brie as her personal assistant for thirty days. Still, the sisters could not stay enemies. Their patched-up relationship was revealed when Brie helped Nikki dethrone AJ Lee for her second Divas Championship.

With Superstars such as AJ, Paige, Naomi, and others posing constant threats, Nikki Bella's second reign proved historic. For 301 days, no one could find the answer to her "fearless" arsenal. She surpassed AJ Lee to become the longest-reigning Divas Champion in history. Although Charlotte eventually defeated her, Nikki proved herself as one of the preeminent figures of the Divas Revolution in WWE.

During her acceptance speech as the 2015 Diva of the Year, Nikki dedicated her Slammy Award to women everywhere, from the locker room to the WWE Universe, all of whom have benefited from being part of Nikki Bella's career. Though put on hold due to surgery in late 2015, this Superstar is sure to inspire as her journey continues to unfold.

NIKOLAI VOLKOFF

see page 243

NORTH AMERICAN HEAVYWEIGHT CHAMPIONSHIP

Despite being its short history, many historians view the North American Heavyweight Championship as an important prize. In March 1979, after weeks of deliberation, the WWE Championship Committee awarded Ted DiBiase the North American Heavyweight Championship.

The reign did not last as long as the future "Million Dollar Man" hoped. On June 19, 1979, Pat Patterson dethroned DiBiase. But other factors conspired against the future of the North American Title. On September 1, 1979, Patterson unified the North American and South American Heavyweight Championships into the Intercontinental Title at a tournament in Rio de Janiero, Brazil.

Even so, the North American Championship did not die peacefully. In November 1979, Seiji Sakaguchi resurrected the Title in Japan, defending the gold until it was officially retired in April 1981.

NIKOLAI VOLKOFF

HT	6'4"
WT	313 lbs.
FROM	The Soviet Union

SIGNATURE MOVE
The Russian Backbreaker

During his days behind the Iron Curtain, Nikolai Volkoff was a world-class amateur wrestler and bodybuilder. While attending a 1968 weightlifting competition in Vienna, Austria, Nikolai risked his life and said goodbye to everything he knew when he defected from the Soviet Union. He traveled to Calgary, Alberta, Canada and was trained for a life in the ring by legend Stu Hart. In 1970, Volkoff came to America with fifty dollars in his pocket and one suit.

By the mid-1970s, Volkoff was a huge draw. He was "Classy" Freddie Blassie's first protégé after the Hollywood Fashion Plate ended his in-ring career. A match against Bruno Sammartino broke the live gate attendance record at Madison Square Garden.

Later, the hated Volkoff was involved in a near riot when fans discovered that he was part of the masked Executioners tag team—along with Killer Kowalski and Big John Studd—the Champions at the time. After the deceptive trio was stripped of the Titles, Volkoff split time between WWE, Japan, and the regional territories of the NWA.

Volkoff first played the Soviet National Anthem while wrestling in the Mid-South territory. The recording would be blasted after his victories, like in the Olympics. One night, he forgot to bring the tape and sang the tune instead. It was a habit that he'd continue after Blassie lured him back to WWE.

THE COLD WAR GETS HOT

In 1984, the manager paired Volkoff with another anti-American rule-breaker, Iron Sheik. As the duo spread panic throughout the United States, they became top contenders for the World Tag Team Championship. During the first Championship match of the first *WrestleMania*, they defeated the U.S. Express, Barry Windham and Mike Rotundo, and left New York City as Champions. Their success continued to grow and, on May 10, 1985, they appeared on the very first episode of NBC's *Saturday Night's Main Event*.

Following the loss of the Championship Titles in June 1985, Nikolai focused on a return to single's action. On the October 3, 1985 episode of *Saturday Night's Main Event*, two Cold War Superpowers clashed when Nikolai challenged Hulk Hogan to a Flag Match for the WWE Championship. Volkoff then sparked a rivalry against former United States Armed Forces member Corporal Kirschner in a series of Flag Matches. After the retirement of Blassie, the contractual rights for Volkoff and the Sheik were sold to WWE newcomer, Slick.

After the "Doctor of Style" led them to a reunion at *WrestleMania III* against the Killer Bees, Nikolai and his Iranian ally parted ways.

Volkoff then aligned himself with another Russian monster, Boris Zhukov. With Slick in their corner, the two referred to themselves as the Bolsheviks. They were top tag Title contenders and appeared at the first two *Survivor Series*. The Russians had a violent split at *WrestleMania VI* after a humiliating 19-second loss to the Hart Foundation. As the former comrades battled, WWE fans witnessed the birth of a patriot.

A CHANGED MAN

During an episode of *The Brother Love Show*, a WWE interview segment, newfound-friend "Hacksaw" Jim Duggan adopted Nikolai as a brother, and they formed a team with the stars and stripes of the USA as their inspiration. Nikolai was then awarded a Medal of Honor from the National Boy Scouts for his contribution to world peace. It was during this period that Volkoff began asking to be announced from the newly independent Lithuania rather than the old Soviet Union.

Their winning ways continued as they toppled The Orient Express at *SummerSlam 1990*. Nikolai became a member of Duggan's victorious Alliance team at that November's *Survivor Series*. The two then took aim at Sgt. Slaughter when he turned his back on his country and became an Iraqi sympathizer during the first Gulf War. Shortly afterward, Volkoff entered semi-retirement.

OLD HABITS

In 1995, Nikolai returned to WWE and broke the hearts of fans when he joined Ted DiBiase's Million Dollar Corporation as a low-level henchman. But when Volkoff appeared at *WrestleMania X-Seven*'s Gimmick Battle Royal, he was largely cheered.

In 2005, Nikolai's remarkable five-decade career was celebrated when he was inducted into the WWE Hall of Fame alongside several of his contemporaries, including former partner, Iron Sheik.

THERE'S NOT ALIVE AN AMERICAN IN THE WHOLE WORLD THAT CAN SCARE ME.

NORTHLAND WRESTLING ENTERPRISES

From 1946 to 1980, Northland Wrestling Enterprises was one of the industry's "hidden territories," stretching hundreds of miles across Northern and Eastern Ontario.

Operating out of North Bay, the circuit included Pembroke, Sudbury, and Sault Ste. Marie, and closed up in the inhospitable winter, when promoter Larry Kasaboski would wrestle around the United States and Canada—under the names Larry Kash and Larry Raymond, respectively—picking talent for Northland's summer shows.

Cards were filled with young competitors eager for experience, performers at the ends of their careers, and wrestlers who enjoyed rural Ontario's hunting and fishing. Along with Kasaboski himself, wrestlers included George Temple—brother of actress Shirley Temple—Roy Shire, Dory Funk, Sr., Skull Murphy, the Swedish Angel, Mad Dog Vachon, Ricki Starr, "Tough" Tony Borne, "Rubberman" Johnny Walker, Bull Curry, the Elephant Boy, Terry and Ronnie Garvin, Primo Carnera and Jacques Rougeau, Sr.

Although crowds rarely exceeded 1,000, the company remained in business until 1980, when Kasaboski retired to his farm.

NUNZIO

HT	5'7"	WT	170 lbs.
FROM	Rockland County, New York		
SIGNATURE MOVE	The Sicilian Slice		

To sports-entertainment fans of the extreme, this former Superstar looks familiar because in the mid-1990s he was Little Guido of the Full Blooded Italians in the original ECW. Though the cultural make-up of the faction changed over time, he remained a constant and was a two-time ECW World Tag Team Champion with partners Tracy Smothers and Tony Mamaluke.

The fierce Nunzio debuted in WWE in 2002 and established himself as one of its most dangerous cruiserweights. After a brief reformation of the FBI, he continued to challenge for cruiserweight gold, including an appearance in the Cruiserweight Open at *WrestleMania XX*. Nunzio had a reunion with the original FBI at 2005's *ECW One Night Stand*. On August 6, 2005 he defeated Paul London for his first Cruiserweight Championship. After an alliance with Vito went south in 2006, Nunzio went to the new ECW. Over time, attempts to pump new life into the FBI met little success and in August 2008 Nunzio left WWE, although he briefly resurfaced as a referee in 2011.

NWA

see page 246

NWA HEART OF AMERICA SPORTS/CENTRAL STATES WRESTLING

One cannot discuss the history of the NWA without including the Heart of America territory, which promoted in Missouri, Kansas, Iowa, Nebraska, and Illinois.

It was Iowa promoter Pinkie George who hosted the gathering that created the NWA in 1948, while Kansas City promoter Orville Brown was the first recognized Champion.

In 1963, after the name of the territory was changed to Central States Wrestling, Bob Geigel became the promoter. His partners included two NWA champions: Pat O'Conner and Harley Race. Geigel served three terms as NWA president.

Kansas City's Memorial Hall was the site of two NWA Title changes: Race's win over Dory Funk, Jr. in 1973 and Ric Flair's 1981 victory over Dusty Rhodes.

Other stars of the territory included Rufus R. Jones, Mike George, Roger "Rip" Kirby, Colonel Buck Robley, "Hangman" Bobby Jaggers, and the Batten Twins. "Bulldog" Bob Brown held the Central States Championship 16 times.

In 1986, Charlotte's Jim Crockett, Jr. took over the territory. Geigel reclaimed the promotion the next year, but closed down in 1988.

NWA HOLLYWOOD

From the time that it opened in 1925, the Olympic Auditorium in Los Angeles was a magical place. Over the years, Los Angeles promoters included Ray Fabiani, Jack Pfeffer, and Johnny Doyle. By the 1950s, Aileen Eaton and her husband, Cal, were the city's boxing and wrestling impresarios. Aileen's son, Mike LeBell, became a promoter, assisted by his brother, sometime-wrestler "Judo" Gene LeBell.

In 1961, the company broke off from the NWA, creating the Worldwide Wrestling Associates (WWA) Championship. The Title was defended throughout southern California, as well as Japan. Champions included Freddie Blassie, Pedro Morales, the Destroyer, and Bobo Brazil, along with Japanese icon Rikidozan.

In 1968, the company rejoined the NWA and renamed itself NWA Hollywood Wrestling, fascinating fans as far as New York, where Spanish-language broadcasts were shown, with its annual battle royal, and a roster featuring Blassie, John Tolos, and Mexican stars like Mil Mascaras, Rey Mendoza, Black Gordman, and Great Goliath. Before its closure in 1982, the territory's standouts were in-ring enemies Chavo Guerrero, Sr. and Roddy Piper.

NWA MID-AMERICA/ CONTINENTAL WRESTLING ASSOCIATION

Although wrestlers often referred to NWA Mid-America as the "Memphis territory," at various times the company stretched through Tennessee, Kentucky, Louisiana, Mississippi, Arkansas, Ohio, West Virginia, North Carolina, and Georgia.

It was not uncommon for a combatant to appear on Memphis' high-rated television show on Saturday morning (hosted by legends Lance Russell and Dave Brown) and then drive five-and-a-half hours to wrestle on television in Chattanooga that afternoon.

In 1977, the territory split over Nashville promoter Nick Gulas' son, George, receiving a lopsided number of main events. In Memphis, promoter Jerry Jarrett centered cards around Jerry Lawler, selling out the Mid-South Coliseum weekly. In 1981, Gulas' Mid-America group closed, and most of the talent rejoined Jarrett's Continental Wrestling Association (CWA).

Many of the rivalries pitted Lawler against manager Jimmy Hart's "Army," featuring, at different times, Hulk Hogan, Jesse Ventura, Iron Sheik, comedian Andy Kaufman, and Randy Savage—who'd previously taunted CWA performers while headlining his father Angelo Poffo's rival, independent league.

In 1988, Lawler thrilled CWA fans by winning the AWA Heavyweight Championship.

NXT
see page 252

THE ODDITIES

MEMBERS Giant Silva, Kurrgan, Golga, Insane Clown Posse, George "The Animal" Steele, Luna, & Sable

All too often, today's judgmental society shuns individuals who may be deemed a little different. In 1998, however, a band of misfits called The Oddities rallied together to make huge efforts towards reversing this unfortunate norm.

Each member of The Oddities suffered from their own social shortcomings: The intellectually unstable Golga was forced to wear a mask to hide his deformed face; Kurrgan scared young children with his tree-like height; and Giant Silva, who was even taller than Kurrgan, was plain inaudible when he spoke. Despite these perceived handicaps, The Oddities made it cool to cheer for a bunch of self-proclaimed sideshow freaks.

The fun-loving crew was all business after the bell rang. At *SummerSlam 1998*, they overmatched the smaller Kaientai faction and then proceeded to celebrate with their equally bizarre friends, Luna and the Insane Clown Posse.

In late 1998, the trio was joined by WWE's original oddity, George "The Animal" Steele. With the Hall of Famer by their side, The Oddities enjoyed their greatest success and popularity; however, the curious combination disappeared from WWE soon after.

ONE MAN GANG/AKEEM

HT	6'9"	WT	450 lbs.	FROM	Halsted Street, Chicago, Illinois
SIGNATURE MOVE	747 Splash				

In 1987, the "Dr. of Style" Slick introduced one of the largest monsters to enter WWE. His destructive work was already known nationwide, but One Man Gang had yet to display his dirty work for a global audience. The master of the 747 Splash was on a mission, and that mission was to destroy Hulkamania and all of those who supported it.

As One Man Gang pulled out all the stops in his matches, he began to show subtle changes in behavior. In 1988, "Mean" Gene Okerlund went on special assignment to get the inside scoop. Slick orchestrated a startling transformation and brought the spirit of Africa to WWE. The man once known as One Man Gang was reborn and became Akeem, "The African Dream." Despite the new name, his dedication to dismembering opponents never wavered.

Akeem soon joined Big Boss Man to form one of the largest teams in WWE history, the Twin Towers. The two giants became obsessed with ending the careers of The Mega-Powers. Their attempts proved futile and by the end of 1990, Akeem left WWE.

For the rest of the decade, One Man Gang competed in WCW, ECW, and in Japan. His last WWE appearance was in 2001 at the Gimmick Battle Royal during *WrestleMania X-7*. Whether he appeared as One Man Gang, or his soul brother #1 alter-ego Akeem, he was always an intimidating force in the ring.

NATIONAL WRESTLING ALLIANCE

Although the NWA traces its Championship to 1905, when European Greco-Roman titlist George Hackenschmidt defeated American claimant Tom Jenkins, the lineage is a bit more murky. Hackenschmidt dropped the Title to Frank Gotch, arguably the best American wrestler of the early 20th Century, in 1908. After Gotch retired in 1913, a number of organizations crowned competing World Champions. But in 1948, a conglomeration was formed to merge the various Titles.

From a core of five promoters (Pinkie George of Des Moines, Sam Muchnick of St. Louis, Orville Brown of Kansas City, Max Clayton of Omaha, and Tony Stecher of Minneapolis) the NWA was established to create a singular Champion who'd travel from territory to territory, defending the gold.

Brown, the Kansas City promoter, was the first Champion. In 1949, he planned to wrestle Lou Thesz, kingpin of the rival National Wrestling Association, in a unification contest. When Brown was injured in a car accident, Thesz was awarded the Championship.

At its peak, the NWA had more than 40 members in North America, Japan, Mexico, New Zealand, and Australia. Besides Thesz, celebrated Champions included Jack Brisco, Dory and Terry Funk, Gene Kiniski, Harley Race, and Ric Flair. The 1961 clash at Chicago's Comiskey Park that saw "Nature Boy" Buddy Rogers dethrone Pat O'Connor drew a then-record crowd of 38,622 fans. In 1963, northeastern promoters Vincent James McMahon and Toots Mondt splintered off from the NWA, starting the forerunner of WWE. Relations with the NWA remained cordial; McMahon even sat on the organization's board of directors.

There were several efforts to merge the Championships. Harley Race wrestled WWE Titlists Superstar Billy Graham and Bob Backlund. Flair collided with Backlund, too, but each clash had an inconclusive ending. In the 1980s, Charlotte promoter Jim Crockett absorbed several NWA territories in an attempt to compete nationally with WWE. After Crockett's promotion was purchased by Ted Turner (and became known as WCW) the affiliation with the NWA ended.

The NWA still exists, comprised of mainly small promotions. In 1998, NWA Champion Dan Severn regularly defended his Title in WWE.

JACK BRISCO

HT	6'0"	WT	231 lbs.	FROM	Blackwell, Oklahoma
SIGNATURE MOVE		Figure-Four Leglock			

No Champion exemplified the NWA standard more than Jack Brisco. The Oklahoman was an NCAA Titlist who could wrestle a 60-minute match in a different territory nightly, using a multitude of techniques—including the belly-to-back suplex, superplex, and figure four leglock—to reinforce his eminence on the mat.

Deeply proud of his Choctaw and Chickasaw ancestry, Brisco's goal as a child was to become the next Lou Thesz. Although the University of Oklahoma attempted to recruit him for its football squad, Oklahoma State snared Brisco when its wrestling coach Myron Roderick promised to introduce the teen to local promoter (and former NWA Junior Heavyweight Champion) Leroy McGuirk.

In 1965, Brisco became the first Native American to win the NCAA wrestling Championship. He was soon working for McGurik, winning the Oklahoma and Arkansas Championships.

Promoters everywhere were intrigued, but Brisco became a regular in Florida in 1969 after promoter Eddie Graham arranged a rigorous training session with noted stretch artists Hiro Matsuda and Don Curtis. Brisco swiftly planted both on the canvas and, by 1971, he and brother, Gerry, were Florida Tag Team Champions.

He also became the top contender for the NWA crown held by Dory Funk, Jr., commencing a rivalry that would continue for years.

In 1973, Brisco won the gold from Harley Race. He dropped it to Shohei "Giant" Baba in Japan the next year, but reclaimed it a mere four days later. In 1975, Terry Funk upended Brisco, who remained a threat to whoever held the Championship.

For most of his career, Brisco was cheered. But in 1983, the Brisco brothers drew the indignation of fans as they traded the NWA World Tag Team Championship with Rick Steamboat and Jay Youngblood, stealing fellow Native American Youngblood's headdress at one point.

In 1985, while the Briscos were contenders for the WWE Tag Team Championship, Jack decided to fly home during a snow storm, and never returned to the ring. He spent the rest of his life running the family body shop. In 2008, the Briscos were inducted into the WWE Hall of Fame. Jack died in 2010.

SAM MUCHNICK

If the NWA's success can be traced to one man, it's Sam Muchnick. During two lengthy reigns as NWA president (from 1950 to 1960 and 1963 to 1975) Muchnick mediated disputes between promoters, expanded internationally, and protected the integrity of the NWA World Heavyweight Championship.

A former sports reporter, Muchnick learned the business from St. Louis promoter Tom Packs before breaking off on his own in 1942. He was at the President Hotel in Waterloo, Iowa when the NWA was formed in 1948.

After early promotional differences, Muchnick and perennial titlist Lou Thesz were linked until the end of their lives.

As a promoter, Muchnick took presentation seriously, banning managers from ringside until 1969. His television show, *Wrestling at the Chase*, was broadcast from a hotel ballroom from 1953 to 1967 (and briefly in 1973) as observers ate dinner in evening ware.

After his retirement in 1982, WWE held a tournament in his honor in 1986. Former NWA Champion Harley Race took first place. Muchnick was 93 when he died in 1998.

WHIPPER BILLY WATSON

HT	5'10"	WT	237 lbs.	FROM	East York, Ontario, Canada
SIGNATURE MOVE		Canuck Commando Unconscious (Sleeper)			

Whipper Billy Watson's legacy in Canada transcends his triumphs on the mat. A true citizen of the Great White North, Watson raised millions of dollars for charity and has a school named after him in Keswick, Ontario.

After learning his craft in Canada, England, and Ireland, Watson became a headliner at Maple Leaf Gardens, winning the British Empire Title from Nanjo Singh in 1942.

In 1947, he defeated Wild Bill Longson for the old National Wrestling Association Championship—a year before the formation of the National Wrestling Alliance—only to drop it to Lou Thesz.

But Watson beat Thesz for the official NWA crown in 1956, and defended it against challengers like Yukon Eric, Fred Atkins, Mighty Ursus, Dick Hutton, and Gorgeous George. Thesz reclaimed the Championship eight months later.

In Canada, Watson was so popular that fans would mob airports to greet him and opponents had to fight their way back to the dressing room. Before retiring in 1971, he trained Rocky Johnson, father of The Rock. Watson died in 1990.

TOMMY RICH

HT	6'3"	WT	238 lbs.	FROM	Atlanta, Georgia
SIGNATURE MOVE		Thesz Press			

For five days in 1981, Tommy "Wildfire" Rich sat on top of the world. Although his reign as NWA World Heavyweight Champion was short, it transformed him from a heart throb in the American south to an international star.

On August 27, 1981, in Augusta, GA, he flattened NWA Champion Harley Race with a Thesz Press. As Race looked on in disbelief, Rich hugged the referee and they fell to the mat together. Then, Andre the Giant joined the celebration, hoisting up Wildfire for the exuberant crowd. In two Title defenses, Rich pinned Race again. Then, on May 1, 1981, Race won the Title back.

Rich is also known for his bloody rivalry with Buzz Sawyer, culminating in a 1983 clash in an enclosed cage called "The Last Battle of Atlanta." This match has been cited as the inspiration for WWE's Hell in a Cell.

In 1987 in Memphis, he turned on the fans, hiding underneath the ring all day in order to assault Jerry Lawler during a cage match. Rich later wrestled in ECW.

DANNY HODGE

HT	5'10"	WT	227 lbs.	FROM	Perry, Oklahoma
SIGNATURE MOVE		Oklahoma Roll			

During his seven NWA World Junior Heavyweight Championship reigns, Danny Hodge would travel anywhere to defend his Title. He'd even go out of his weight class, he said, in order to "show the people what wrestling was."

The 1956 Olympic silver medalist knew the topic well. Undefeated at the University of Oklahoma, Hodge won the NCAA Title three years in a row. After a brief career as a boxer (he had a flawless record as an amateur) he began chasing Angelo Savoldi for the NWA Junior Heavyweight crown. During one encounter, Savoldi's father rushed the ring and stabbed Hodge. Ultimately, Hodge snared the Title. He attributed his wrestling success to the double tendons in his hands. Hodge was so strong that he could crush an apple in one hand. He considered Mad Dog Vachon, a member of the 1948 Canadian Olympic squad, his toughest foe.

In 1976, Hodge was forced to relinquish the Championship after breaking his neck in a car accident. Maintaining his ties to the industry, he worked as a WWE talent scout.

PAT O'CONNOR

HT	6'0"	WT	230 lbs.	FROM	Wellington, New Zealand
SIGNATURE MOVE			Reverse Rolling Cradle		

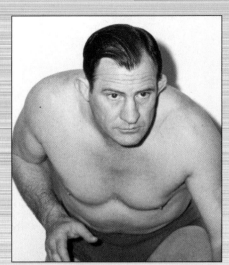

Pat O'Connor has the bizarre distinction of holding the NWA and AWA Heavyweight Championships simultaneously.

After beating Dick Hutton for the NWA Title in 1959, O'Connor was busy defending the crown against contenders like Cowboy Bob Ellis, Dr. Bill Miller, Don Leo Jonathan, and Johnny Valentine.

Meanwhile, in 1960, O'Connor was named the first Champion of the fledgling AWA and given 90 days to defend the Title. Unable to take time away from his NWA challenges, O'Connor was stripped of the prize.

In 1961, 38,622 fans saw O'Connor defend his NWA Championship against Buddy Rogers at Chicago's Comiskey Park. Rogers won the two-out-of-three fall contest after O'Conner missed a dropkick.

O'Connor, who'd competed for New Zealand in the Pan American and British Empire Games, wrestled his last match in his home country in 1982. The same year, he became a co-promoter in the St. Louis territory after Sam Muchnick's retirement.

In 1987, he was eliminated by Lou Thesz at the end of a WWE "old-timers'" battle royal. He died in 1990.

THE MIDNIGHT EXPRESS

MEMBERS	Dennis Condrey & Bobby Eaton	MEMBERS	Bobby Eaton & Stan Lane
COMBINED WT	485 lbs.	**COMBINED WT**	460 lbs.
OTHER MEMBERS	Randy Rose, Norvell Austin, "Bombastic" Bob Holly, & "Bodacious" Bart Gunn		

Like the nWo and Four Horsemen, the Midnight Express went through numerous personnel changes, but always remained at the center of the Championship picture.

Dennis Condrey and Randy Rose first teamed in Alabama-based Southwest Championship Wrestling in 1980. The next year, Norvell Austin joined the unit, now called the Midnight Express.

In 1983, Eaton and Condrey ventured to the Mid-South territory with manager Jim Cornette, and began warring with the Rock 'n' Roll Express. The hostilities continued after both teams joined Mid-Atlantic Wrestling, then the NWA's flagship promotion.

In 1987, Condrey was replaced by Stan Lane, but certain constants remained: moves like the Flapjack, Rocket Launcher, and Eaton's armbar, known as "Divorce Court."

When Rose and Condrey showed up with manager Paul E. Dangerously, aka Paul Heyman, in 1988 and labeled themselves "the Original" Midnight Express, both factions battled over the rightful use of the name.

In 1998, Cornette formed the New Midnight Express in WWE with Bob Holly and Bart Gunn. Although the team earned a version of the NWA Title, it provided few enduring memories.

ROCK 'N' ROLL EXPRESS

MEMBERS	Ricky Morton & Robert Gibson
COMBINED WT	460 lbs.

Entering the ring to pulsating rock music, and blasting foes with synchronized elbows and dropkicks, Ricky Morton and Robert Gibson were the sports-entertainment equivalent of an '80s hair band.

Formed in 1983 in Memphis, the Rock 'n' Roll Express induced shrieks of glee as they plucked opponents like guitar strings. After wrestling duos like Randy Savage and his brother Lanny Poffo, they moved to the Mid-South territory, where they battled Steve "Dr. Death" Williams and Ted DiBiase, and had the first of several scaffold matches with the Midnight Express.

Starting in the Mid-Atlantic territory in 1985, they held the NWA World Tag Team Championship four times, mixing it up with the Four Horsemen, Ivan and Nikita Koloff, and perennial rivals, the Midnights.

In the AWA in 1988, they fought Shawn Michaels and Marty Janetty, then called the Midnight Rockers. After breaking up in WCW in 1991, they reunited, competing against the Heavenly Bodies at the 1993 *Survivor Series*.

Despite their long association with the NWA, they also appeared in a 15-team battle royal at *WrestleMania XIV*.

JIM BARNETT

From the early days of television to the expansion of WWE, promoter Jim Barnett was part of every major wrestling breakthrough.

After assisting Chicago promoter Fred Kohler with his early broadcasts on the Dumont Television Network, Barnett is credited with creating the studio wrestling format in 1955 in Indianapolis. In 1964, he ignited a wrestling craze in Australia, using locals like George Barnes and Larry O'Dea, as well Killer Kowalski, Skull Murphy, Dominic DeNucci, and others.

The company's name, World Championship Wrestling (WCW), the same handle he'd use for the Georgia promotion he'd buy in 1973, became a show broadcast nationally on Ted Turner's cable network.

From 1983 to 1987, Barnett was WWE's senior vice president. He died in 2004.

BOB GEIGEL

HT	5'11"	WT	240 lbs.	FROM	Algona, Iowa
SIGNATURE MOVE	Knee Drop				

Although Bob Geigel had a respectable career inside the ring, he's best known for his work as a Kansas City-based promoter and two-term NWA president. As a competitor, Geigel engaged in a lengthy rivalry with Bulldog Bob Brown. He started promoting in the Heart of America, later known as Central States, territory in 1963. After Sam Muchnick's 1982 retirement, he co-promoted in St. Louis.

Geigel served as NWA president from 1978 to 1980, and from 1982 to 1987. In 1982, after Dusty Rhodes lost a "loser leaves Florida" match in Tampa, he returned as the masked Midnight Rider, and appeared to beat Ric Flair for the NWA Championship. The Rider had to hand back the Title after Geigel demanded that he unmask. He died in 2014.

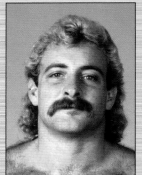

MAGNUM TA

| HT | 6'1" | WT | 245 lbs. | FROM | Virginia Beach, Virginia |
| SIGNATURE MOVE | Belly-to-Belly Suplex |

When a car accident curtailed his career, Magnum TA was en route to becoming one of the NWA's biggest names. He'd already battled the Four Horsemen, winning the United States Championship from Tully Blanchard, and was threatening "Nature Boy" Ric Flair for possession of the NWA crown.

Terry Allen had been given the name Magnum TA in the Mid-South territory because of his resemblance to handsome *Magnum P.I.* television star Tom Selleck. His closest ally in the NWA was Dusty Rhodes, who made Magnum godfather of his son, Cody.

Allen was in the midst of an epic rivalry with Nikita Koloff in 1986 when the crash occurred, paralyzing him for months. After recovering, he worked as a commentator in the NWA and WCW.

PAUL JONES

| HT | 6'0" | WT | 240 lbs. | FROM | Port Arthur, Texas |
| SIGNATURE MOVE | Indian Deathlock |

Even when fans booed Paul Jones, he happily signed autographs, handing out cards to remind them, "It's difficult to be humble when you're 'Number One.'"

Jones adopted his "Number One" nickname in 1972 in Florida, while embroiled in a rivalry with future NWA Champion Jack Brisco. He also rumbled with another Titlist, Terry Funk, becoming a top contender after beating Funk for the United States Championship in 1975.

Jones held the NWA World Tag Team Championship seven times with such partners as Ricky "The Dragon" Steamboat, Wahoo McDaniel, and Baron Von Raschke.

After retirement, Jones became a manager in the NWA. Former WWE Champions Ivan Koloff and Superstar Billy Graham, along with Abdullah the Butcher and the Assassins, were among those in "Paul Jones' Army."

TULLY BLANCHARD

| HT | 5'10" | WT | 238 lbs. | FROM | San Antonio, Texas |
| SIGNATURE MOVE | Slingshot Suplex |

Even before his WWE Hall of Fame run with the Four Horsemen, Tully Blanchard was making an impact.

The son of San Antonio promoter Joe Blanchard, Tully played football at West Texas State alongside fellow Hall of Famers Tito Santana and Ted DiBiase. After forming tandems with Gino Hernandez and Chris Adams in different territories, he battled Dusty Rhodes, Magnum TA, and Carlos Colon in the NWA, often with the help of hulking valet, Baby Doll.

As Horsemen, Tully and Arn Anderson won NWA Tag Team gold in 1987, before entering WWE the next year as the Brain Busters, managed by Bobby "The Brain" Heenan. He wrestled in the AWA, WCW, and ECW before becoming a preacher and working for WWE behind the scenes.

NIKITA KOLOFF

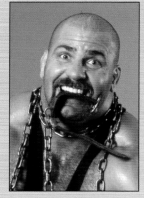

| HT | 6'3" | WT | 270 lbs. | FROM | Moscow, Russia |
| SIGNATURE MOVE | Russian Sickle |

Nikita Koloff and Dusty Rhodes were the bitterest of enemies, and then the closest of allies, tearing down the walls between East and West.

Koloff was brought into the NWA by his uncle, Ivan Koloff, in 1984, when the Soviet Union was commonly called "The Evil Empire." After warring with the Road Warriors, the two won NWA Tag Team gold by dethroning Rhodes and Manny Fernandez. A third member of the clan, Krusher Khruschev, sometimes substituted for one of the Koloffs in battle.

Nikita was engaged in a long conflict with Magnum TA, but when Magnum fought paralysis after a 1986 car wreck, Nikita admired his courage and ingratiated himself to fans. After retiring, he started a ministry, and appeared on the reality show, *Preacher's Daughters.*

JIMMY VALIANT

| HT | 6'3" | WT | 235 lbs. | FROM | New York, New York |
| SIGNATURE MOVE | Boogie Woogie Elbow Drop |

Jimmy Valiant is one of a handful of gladiators to have stepped through the ropes in five separate decades. During that period, he went from being despised in WWE to adored in the NWA.

Debuting in 1964, Valiant went to WWE in 1971, but enraged fans by betraying tag partner Chief Jay Strongbow. Unperturbed, Jimmy won the WWE World Tag Team Championship with brother Johnny in 1974 and another sibling, Jerry, in 1979. In the 1980s, though, he became the "Boogie Woogie Man" in the NWA, hugging fans before matches with Ivan Koloff, Baron Von Raschke, Paul Jones, and others. In Valiant's words, spectators viewed him as "a regular cat."

As his career wound down, the 1996 WWE Hall of Famer opened a Virginia training school.

MINNESOTA WRECKING CREW

MEMBERS	Gene, Lars, Ole, & Arn Anderson

Blowing into the NWA like a blizzard from the North Country, the Minnesota Wrecking Crew created hazardous, whiteout conditions for opponents, winning ten NWA World Tag Team Championships with combinations of four different members.

Formed by brothers Gene and Luscious Lars Anderson in 1966, the strength of the Minnesota Wrecking Crew lay in the ability to always summon another rampaging relative. In 1970, Ole Anderson replaced Lars. Although the Andersons counted Ric Flair as a cousin, that didn't stop them from targeting the Nature Boy. To balance the odds, Flair called on partners like Greg Valentine and Blackjack Mulligan. By 1985, the Andersons and Flair had made peace. In fact, Gene and Ole, as the Minnesota Wrecking Crew, were charter members of the Four Horsemen.

GORDON SOLIE

"So long from the Sunshine State." With that signature phrase, delivered in an even, credible tone, Gordon Solie, as much as anyone else on the Florida territory's broadcast, enticed viewers to return the following week.

Speaking calmly, concisely, and with conviction, Solie displayed a wide knowledge of technical wrestling and the impact of each hold. As a result, he was viewed as wrestling's Walter Cronkite, the CBS news anchor then considered the most trustworthy man in America.

A former disc jockey and ring announcer, Solie eventually expanded his tasks to the nationally-viewed Georgia promotion, where he described "Pier Six brawls" and faces covered by a "crimson mask."

He was inducted into the WWE Hall of Fame in 2008, eight years after his death from cancer.

THE ASSASSINS

MEMBERS	Assassins #1 & #2
COMBINED WT	465 lbs.

With their black and gold masks and full-body suits, the Assassins created an air of mystery that seemed to add a psychological edge to their arsenal, as they won more than a dozen Championships in Georgia, Florida, Vancouver, and other territories. They were also Champions in Australia's World Championship Wrestling group before promoter Jim Barnett exported the name to the United States.

The Assassins formed in Georgia in 1961, and then powered through other NWA territories before returning to the Peach State in 1968 and maintaining a base there until 1974. In 1984, Assassin #2 was forced to unmask after losing to Jimmy Valiant, and was exposed as Hercules Hernandez. A decade later, Assassin #1 managed "Pretty Wonderful," Paul Roma and Paul Orndorff, in WCW.

RUFUS R. JONES

HT	6'5"	WT	275 lbs.	FROM	Dillon, South Carolina
SIGNATURE MOVE	Headbutt				

Rufus R. Jones always said that the "R" in the middle of his name stood for "guts." The line was a joke; his spirit in the ring was not.

One of the most likeable performers in and out of the ring, Jones spent most of his career in the Kansas City and Charlotte-based territories, winning tag team Championships with partners like Bob Geigel, Wahoo McDaniel, and Bulldog Bob Brown. His cousin, Burrhead Jones, was another favorite teammate.

Known as the Freight Train (for his potent shoulder blocks), Jones, a former Golden Gloves boxer, thrilled fans in 1976 when he wrestled NWA World Heavyweight Champion Terry Funk to a draw, then beat him via disqualification.

In 1993, he succumbed to a heart attack while deer hunting.

SEE ALSO:

DORY FUNK, JR.

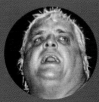

DUSTY RHODES

GENE KINISKI

HARLEY RACE

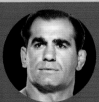

LOU THESZ

RIC FLAIR

THE FOUR HORSEMEN

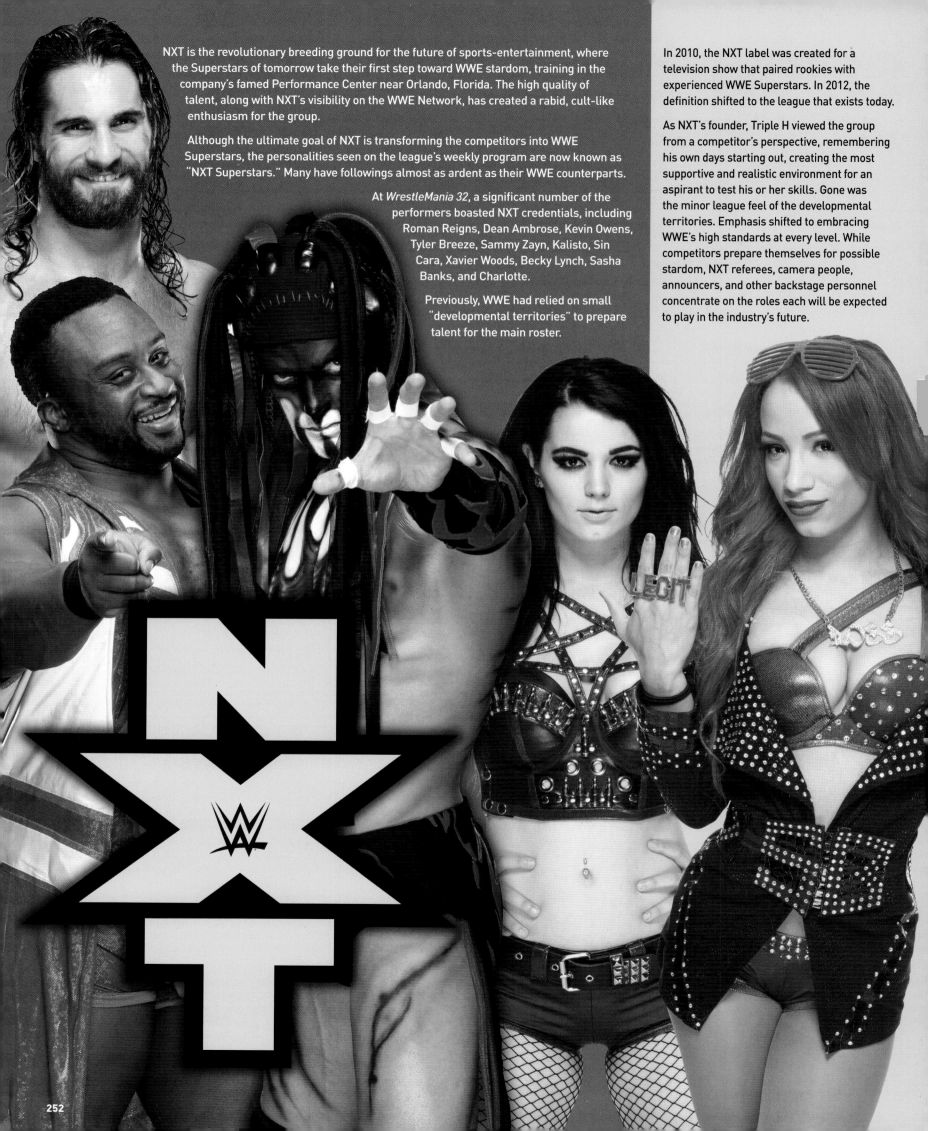

NXT is the revolutionary breeding ground for the future of sports-entertainment, where the Superstars of tomorrow take their first step toward WWE stardom, training in the company's famed Performance Center near Orlando, Florida. The high quality of talent, along with NXT's visibility on the WWE Network, has created a rabid, cult-like enthusiasm for the group.

Although the ultimate goal of NXT is transforming the competitors into WWE Superstars, the personalities seen on the league's weekly program are now known as "NXT Superstars." Many have followings almost as ardent as their WWE counterparts.

At *WrestleMania 32*, a significant number of the performers boasted NXT credentials, including Roman Reigns, Dean Ambrose, Kevin Owens, Tyler Breeze, Sammy Zayn, Kalisto, Sin Cara, Xavier Woods, Becky Lynch, Sasha Banks, and Charlotte.

Previously, WWE had relied on small "developmental territories" to prepare talent for the main roster.

In 2010, the NXT label was created for a television show that paired rookies with experienced WWE Superstars. In 2012, the definition shifted to the league that exists today.

As NXT's founder, Triple H viewed the group from a competitor's perspective, remembering his own days starting out, creating the most supportive and realistic environment for an aspirant to test his or her skills. Gone was the minor league feel of the developmental territories. Emphasis shifted to embracing WWE's high standards at every level. While competitors prepare themselves for possible stardom, NXT referees, camera people, announcers, and other backstage personnel concentrate on the roles each will be expected to play in the industry's future.

Athletes come from a variety of backgrounds: the independent sports-entertainment circuit, Japanese and Mexican rings, MMA, the NFL, even obscure sports like kushti and kabbadi, full contact disciplines from South Asia. WWE scouts have held tryouts everywhere from India to Dubai, Brazil, China, and Australia.

Once potential Superstars are selected, they train at WWE's elite Performance Center, modeled after the best Olympic facilities in the world. Coaches have included Norman Smiley, whose resume includes WCW, ECW, and a world championship reign in Mexico, former WWE Superstars Billy Gunn and Matt "A Train" Bloom, Terry Taylor, a veteran of sports-entertainment's territory days, England's Robbie Brookside, and Sara Del Rey, one of the world's most respected grapplers.

Before his death in 2015, WWE Hall of Famer Dusty Rhodes was the pillar of the Performance Center, using his vast experience to teach the competitors he called his "NXT kids" ring psychology and interview skills.

Among the NXT gladiators, the end goal is the same: WWE glory. But there are only so many open positions on the WWE roster, hence, the intensity of the clashes in NXT.

The creation of the WWE Network in 2014 gave NXT a degree of exposure that no developmental league had ever previously enjoyed. In addition to an hour-long, weekly show on the Network, there are live, two-hour specials.

The first, *NXT Arrival*, aired on February 27, 2014, and featured a ladder match between Bo Dallas, the NXT Champion at the time, and Neville. The event's name was deliberately chosen to announce that a new chapter in sports-entertainment was being written, and fans immediately responded, creating a kinetic excitement about the burgeoning product in social media posts.

As with the old ECW Arena, many of the same spectators can be seen week after week in the NXT television audience at Full Sail University in Florida, vociferously expressing their enthusiasm for the league. When NXT is presented at other venues, fans wait outside after the shows, still chanting "NXT! NXT!" two hours after the final bell. In fact, NXT chants can also be heard on WWE shows, particularly when NXT veterans are putting on a top caliber match.

For more than a year after its first WWE Network broadcast, NXT was confined to Florida. But as popularity rose, the company decided to sporadically present shows elsewhere. As part of *WrestleMania 31*'s fan Axxess activities in 2015, Hideo Itami won a NXT tournament to secure a spot in the big event's Andre the Giant Memorial Battle Royal. Although some organizers were uncertain if a developmental league could draw a large crowd, the moment that tickets went on sale for the tournament, all 5,000 seats immediately sold out.

Then, on July 4, 2015, the WWE Network featured a live broadcast of the *Beast in the East* card from Tokyo. As positive as the response was to the overall show, a sizeable number of fans said that their favorite match, by far, was the gripping collision that saw Finn Bálor capture the NXT Championship from Kevin Owens. The message was clear. When the timing was right, NXT could hold its own in any major arena.

On the night before *SummerSlam 2015*, Bálor and Owens continued their rivalry with a ladder match at *NXT TakeOver: Brooklyn*, one of a series of the live *TakeOver* specials that had begun on the WWE Network the year before. The card took place at the Barclay's Center in Brooklyn, New York, in front of more than 15,000 fans. It was the largest crowd that had ever attended an NXT event, and no one left disappointed.

In the most emotional moment of the night, Bayley dethroned Sasha Banks for the NXT Women's Championship.

That Bayley was perceived as an underdog who'd flourished through perseverance was only part of the contest's appeal.

An even greater factor was that the match symbolized the rise of female competitors as true main eventers. Because of Bayley, Banks, Charlotte, Becky Lynch, Paige, and others, the "Divas Revolution" that began in NXT has had a ripple effect in WWE. In other words, not only has NXT talent transformed WWE, but the development league is now setting trends that will be felt for generations.

In October, 2015, another tradition started when Finn Bálor and Samoa Joe won the finals of a tournament named for NXT's most beloved trainer, the Dusty Rhodes Tag Team Classic. When the relationship between the victors disintegrated, there was little question about the type of forums where the conflict might be resolved. Bálor and Joe battled each other in main events at both *NXT TakeOver: London* in December, 2015, and *NXT TakeOver: Dallas*, during *WrestleMania 32* weekend in 2016.

With the eyes of the world watching, Joe and Bálor tore up the arena in Texas. Just seconds into the match, the former partners butted heads, causing a large gash near Joe's eye. As blood poured down his face, medical officials rushed to the ring to administer care, but Joe waved them away. He knew that spectators had come to see a fight, and the rivals were united in their determination to deliver.

The end came when Joe clamped on a Kokina Clutch and Bálor began to fade. But at the final moment, he managed to kick off the ropes and tie Joe up for the pin, retaining the NXT Championship.

The card was also noteworthy because of the debut of two future WWE Superstars. Both Austin Aries and Shinsuke Nakamura had international reputations, but some were uncertain about how they'd fare under the WWE umbrella. Each used the special event to prove their cynics wrong. Aries defeated Baron Corbin, while Nakamura scored a win after a vicious war with Sami Zayn, introducing the NXT Universe to the "strong style" of submissions and striking blows he'd utilized in Japan.

Fans also witnessed two dramatic title changes. In the opening match, American Alpha, the team of Jason Jordan and Chad Gable, became NXT Tag Team Champions with a win over The Revival. And the mystical Asuka became the NXT Women's Champion after trapping the sentimental favorite, Bayley, in the Asuka lock.

Because of shows like this, WWE Superstars have begun feeling the "NXT Effect," the pressure to put on performances comparable to the exhilarating confrontations that have become part of the NXT brand.

ORIENT EXPRESS

MEMBERS Sato, Tanaka, & Kato

In 1990, Mr. Fuji handpicked the most deadly assassins from his homeland to spread terror among the world's greatest tag teams. Sato and Tanaka debuted on *Superstars of Wrestling* and mixed under-handed tactics with martial arts expertise. The duo met The Rockers at *WrestleMania VI* and stole a count-out victory with assistance from their ceremonial salt. The Orient Express also took on Demolition, "Hacksaw" Jim Duggan and Nikolai Volkoff, the Hart Foundation, and the Legion of Doom. At *Survivor Series* they were hired by Sgt. Slaughter for his team of "Mercenaries."

Shortly after Sato returned to Japan, a third member was brought to the United States, Kato. This masked man brought power and speed to complement Tanaka's skills. The Express had a classic match with the Rockers at the 1991 Royal Rumble, but came out on the short end of the stick. By early 1992 the Orient Express returned to Japan. That was a day that WWE fans and Superstars rejoiced, as they were finally safe from Fuji-orchestrated attacks at the hands of his ruthless tandem.

ORLANDO JORDAN

HT	6'4"	**WT**	257 lbs.	**FROM**	Miami, Florida	
SIGNATURE MOVE	Black Out					

For a brief period of time, Orlando Jordan was one of the most powerful Superstars on *SmackDown*. After aligning himself with JBL in August 2004, the Miami native quickly began to reap the benefits of making company with the WWE Champion. Serving in JBL's Cabinet as the Chief of Staff, Jordan and Secretaries of Defense, The Bashams, protected JBL's Title reign for nearly a year. As a by-product of his loyalty, Jordan also found himself thrust into many high-profile matches.

In March 2005, Jordan picked up the biggest win of his career when he toppled John Cena on *SmackDown* to capture the coveted United States Championship. He went on to successfully defend the gold against *SmackDown*'s greatest for more than five months.

Jordan's United States Championship reign came to an end at *SummerSlam 2005* in a historically short 25-second match. Shortly after, his alliance with JBL also fizzled. With the self-proclaimed "Wrestling God" no longer watching his back, Jordan struggled to find his way. By mid-2006, Jordan was gone from WWE completely.

OTTO VON HELLER

WT	260 lbs.	**FROM**	Germany

Wrestling's rulebook is filled with hundreds of rules. And Otto Von Heller broke them all. Known for his villainous tactics, the big German made a name for himself within WWE as one of the most dangerous men of the 1970s. He certainly looked the part. His bald head, dark goatee, cold eyes, and black cape always gave Von Heller the psychological advantage well before the bell even rang.

During his WWE tenure, Von Heller crossed paths with some of his era's best, including Bruno Sammartino, Haystacks Calhoun, and Pedro Morales. His post-WWE days were highlighted by a successful pairing with fellow countryman Karl Von Steiger. Together, Von Heller and Von Steiger captured many Titles, including the NWA Mid-America Tag Team Championship and NWA Mid-America United States Tag Team Championship.

OUTBACK JACK

HT	6'5"	**WT**	300 lbs.	**FROM**	Humpty Doo, Australia
SIGNATURE MOVE	The Boomerang				

In 1987, WWE welcomed a bushman from Australia's Northern Territory. Thanks to the survival skills learned after years with the Aborigines, Outback Jack feared nothing—not even a saltwater croc! To prepare fans for his arrival, video segments showed Jack in the Australian outback, training for his much anticipated debut.

When it came time to step through the ropes, Outback Jack did not disappoint. The Boomerang, a modified version of the dangerous Enzui Lariat, put all Superstars on notice. Australia's favorite son battled against the likes of Barry Horowitz, "Iron" Mike Sharpe, Jim "The Anvil" Neidhart, "Million Dollar Man" Ted DiBiase, and "Ravishing" Rick Rude. He left WWE in 1988.

"OUTLAW" RON BASS

HT	6'4"	**WT**	289 lbs.	**FROM**	Houston, Texas
SIGNATURE MOVE	Kneeling Facebuster				

During the 1970s, Bass debuted in the National Wrestling Alliance and quickly became known as one of the toughest men around. In the 1980s he competed mainly in Florida and formed a successful team with fellow future WWE Superstar, Black Bart. In early 1987, Bass brought his Texas toughness to WWE and threatened to end Hulkamania. Bass took on the likes of "Leapin'" Lanny Poffo, Corporal Kirschner, SD "Special Delivery" Jones, Koko B. Ware, Outback Jack, and Blackjack Mulligan.

The "Outlaw" thrived on dishing out pain and often lifted beaten opponents during the referees count to further the onslaught. His cold-blooded tenure in WWE is most remembered by his barbarous attack on Brutus "the Barber" Beefcake. Bass jumped Brutus from behind and choked him before he raked the spur from his boot across Beefcake's forehead. The attack and resulting injury left Beefcake out of action for weeks, and cost him a shot at the Intercontinental Championship at *SummerSlam 1988*. Bass left WWE in 1989 and retired from the ring in 1991.

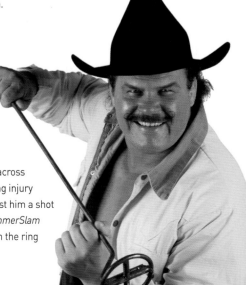

OWEN HART

see page 256

OWEN HART & YOKOZUNA

MEMBERS	Owen Hart & Yokozuna
COMBINED WT	827 lbs.

Owen Hart announced Yokozuna as his mystery partner just moments before challenging the Smokin' Gunns for the World Tag Team Championship at *WrestleMania XI*. Though they had no experience working together as a team, Hart and Yokozuna used their size advantage to unseat the longtime partners. Over the next five months, the pair turned back all challengers.

When Owen Hart was supposedly unable to compete at *In Your House III*, Davey Boy Smith stepped in as Yokozuna's partner against Diesel and Shawn Michaels. However, when Hart interjected himself into the match, Diesel pinned him and his team was awarded the Championships.

The next night, Hart and Yokozuna's lawyer Clarence Mason claimed the Titles could not change hands because Hart was not a legal participant in the match. The persuasive Mason eventually got his way. However, the emotional rollercoaster took its toll on the team, as they lost the Titles to the Smokin' Gunns approximately one hour later. Following the loss, Yokozuna focused his attention on a singles career, while Hart formed a successful team with Davey Boy Smith.

OX BAKER

HT	6'5"	WT	311 lbs.	FROM	Iowa
SIGNATURE MOVE	Heart Punch				

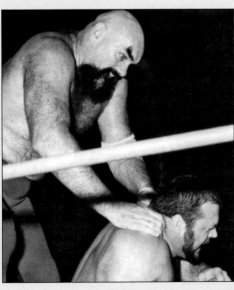

Ox Baker was unorthodox in every way, from his insatiable thirst to hurt people right down to his appearance, which featured a shaven head, long, curly eyebrows, and an even longer mustache. Behind the power of his dreaded heart punch—sometimes called the "Hurt Punch"—Baker immobilized some of sports-entertainment's greatest names, including Bruiser Brody, Harley Race, and a young Hulk Hogan.

Along the way, he compiled an impressive list of Championships. While competing in Puerto Rico, he turned back the native hero Carlos Colon to claim both the WWC Universal Heavyweight and Puerto Rico Heavyweight Championships. He also topped The Sheik for Detroit's United States Championship in September 1977.

Tag team success was not foreign to the oversized Ox Baker. Teaming with such greats as "Superstar" Billy Graham and Ole Anderson, he captured eight tag Titles over the course of his career.

While not quite a crossover celebrity, Baker did appear in the movies *Escape from New York*, *Blood Circus*, and *I Like to Hurt People*. He died in 2014.

PACIFIC NORTHWEST WRESTLING

Popularly referred to as "Portland Wrestling," the Pacific Northwest territory was represented around Oregon, as well as Washington, Idaho, Montana, British Columbia, and parts of California and Alaska.

Promoter Don Owen was the son of boxing and wrestling promoter Herb Owen. In 1925, the younger Owen began promoting his own shows—and didn't sell the operation until 1992.

Fans remember Owen as a man who favored bright suits and made ring introductions at the old bowling alley he turned into the Portland Sports Arena. Wrestlers recall him as a fair, well-paying promoter.

Portland Wrestling was a television staple since 1952. Some of the stars who passed through the territory included Curt and Larry Hennig, Jesse Ventura, Bull Ramos, Matt Borne, Moondog Mayne, and Jimmy Snuka. Memorable rivalries included Dutch Savage vs. the Iron Sheik, Billy Jack Haynes vs. Rip Oliver, and Roddy Piper vs. Buddy Rose. Piper and Rose even returned to battle at Don Owen's 60th anniversary show in 1985.

After Owen's retirement, several attempts were made to revive Portland Wrestling.

PAIGE

HT	5'8"	FROM	Norwich, England
SIGNATURE MOVE	Paige-Turner, Ram-Paige, PTO		

Perhaps no Diva in history has made as immediate an impact as Paige. After nearly one year of representing NXT as their first-ever Women's Champion, the determined Diva debuted on *Raw* in April 2014, and the results were historic. Competing in her first WWE match, Paige toppled AJ Lee to capture the Divas Championship.

With the victory, Paige became the youngest to ever hold the Divas Championship, while also being the first to claim the Title in her first-ever *Raw* match. Additionally, Paige will forever be recognized as the first competitor to hold both the NXT Women's and WWE Divas Championships simultaneously.

More recently, Paige proved to be an important player in the Divas Revolution when she teamed with Charlotte and Becky Lynch to form Team PCB. While initially successful, the partnership eventually disintegrated when Paige claimed Charlotte was only successful because she's Ric Flair's daughter.

Known as the Diva of Tomorrow, Paige certainly has a bright future. And along the way, you can bet she won't be shy about reminding other Divas whose house they're in.

PALMER CANON

By August 2005, Theodore Long had more than one full year under his belt as *SmackDown* General Manager. Despite his successes at the helm, network executives felt it necessary to send one of their own, Palmer Canon, to *SmackDown* to ensure the show ran smoothly.

Though Canon quickly proved to have minimal knowledge of sports-entertainment, the arrogant executive continued to undermine Long's authority. He cancelled a Lingerie Pillow Fight between Christy Hemme and Stacy Keibler, infuriating fans. Later on, he launched a failed New Talent Initiative, unveiling such underwhelming talents as The Dicks and The Juniors.

After only a few months, Canon finally realized he was in over his head. The Network executive backed off, allowing Long to do his job on his own.

OWEN HART

HT	5'10"
WT	227 lbs.
FROM	Calgary, Alberta, Canada

SIGNATURE MOVE
Sharpshooter

A Foundation for Success

Growing up in the famed Hart wrestling family, Owen Hart could have relied on the clan's storied reputation to open doors for him. Rather than ride his family's name to the top, he paved his own path to greatness. Owen competed in England, Japan, and his father Stu Hart's Stampede Wresting prior to joining WWE, developing one of the most technically sound offensive arsenals of all time.

After his brother, Bret, decided to focus on singles competition, Owen filled the void in the Hart Foundation by teaming with Jim "The Anvil" Neidhart. When Neidhart left WWE, Owen became part of a flashy and up-tempo tandem High Energy with the colorful Koko B. Ware.

King of Harts

Owen earned the nickname "The Rocket," but his career did not truly blast off until 1994 when he turned on his brother, Bret. Though it infuriated fans, the move served as a launching pad for the younger Hart to finally break free from his sibling's overwhelming shadow. Owen accomplished his goal when he defeated Bret in their classic *WrestleMania X* showdown, though his resentment toward Bret only deepened when Bret captured the WWE Championship later that night.

Owen's hot streak continued when he won the King of the Ring crown in June 1994. This newfound royalty inspired the new nickname "King of Harts," and strengthened Owen's resolve to dethrone Bret as the superior sibling. At *SummerSlam 1994*, Bret bested him in an incredible Steel Cage Match for the WWE Championship. Though defeated, Owen continued to torment Bret until he allied with the massive Yokozuna to win the Tag Team Championship. Their alliance, revealed at *WrestleMania XI*, gave birth to the villainous Camp Cornette faction.

The Blue Blazer

In August 1988, the Blue Blazer lit up rings with a never-before-seen blend of aerial assaults, speed, and expert grappling techniques. The masked superhero moved as if he was from another galaxy and immediately brought fans to their feet before each match as he landed in the ring via a top rope Moonsault.

At *Survivor Series 1988* he was part of the winning team captained by the Ultimate Warrior. At *WrestleMania V*, Blue Blazer had a thrilling match with Mr. Perfect. He vanished from the WWE in 1989, but returned in the 1990s to remind fans to train, say their prayers, and drink their milk.

IT'S KIND OF AN ART GOING OUT AND PERFORMING. I'D LIKE FANS TO REMEMBER ME AS A GUY WHO WOULD GO OUT AND ENTERTAIN THEM.

High Demand

Despite his maddening in-ring trickery, Owen developed a respectable reputation among his fellow Superstars. After Yokozuna, Owen found Championship chemistry with both his brother-in-law British Bulldog and Jeff Jarrett. With Jarrett, Owen struggled with an identity crisis of sorts, occasionally donning his Blue Blazer mask and taking on the visage of a superhero. But with the bosomy Debra by their side, the crafty duo toppled many top teams during their four-month Title reign.

Along the way, Owen became part of two of the most notorious entities of the late 1990s: The New Hart Foundation and the Nation of Domination. By 1997, Owen and his brother Bret were finally on the same page, as were both brothers-in-law, Neidhart and Bulldog, and Brian Pillman. The revitalized foundation became equally beloved in their native Canada and reviled in the United States. During this time, Owen grabbed that elusive singles Title, winning the Intercontinental Championship twice.

As the calendar flipped to 1998, Owen emerged a brasher, revenge-driven lone wolf that came to be known as "The Black Hart." He focused his newfound fury on D-Generation X. Months later, Owen's frustration boiled over after a loss to Hunter Hearst-Helmsley for the European Championship. More vicious than ever, Owen turned on ally Ken Shamrock and became a co-leader of the Nation. These actions shed light on his emotional outburst, "Enough is enough and it's time for a change!"

With the Nation, Owen's rivalry with DX only intensified. However, the gang warfare was halted when a vengeful Ken Shamrock returned. Not intimidated, Owen squared off in a Lions' Den Match against the dangerous MMA legend.

A Tragic End

A tragic accident claimed the life of Owen Hart on May 23, 1999. The loss of such a great man left a void that can never be filled. The memory of Owen's technical brilliance inside the ring and his kind, jovial nature outside of it will endure in the hearts and minds of WWE fans everywhere. In December 2015, WWE honored Owen's incredible legacy in a documentary appropriately titled *Hart of Gold*.

PAMPERO FIRPO

HT	5'9"	WT	225 lbs.	FROM	Buenos Aires, Argentina
SIGNATURE MOVE	El Garfio				

Pampero Firpo was one of the original horrors of sports-entertainment. The mighty madman from the Pampas of Argentina first appeared on the scene in the early 1950s. As if he was summoned from the Stone Age, Firpo's body was covered in his natural fur, while a bushy beard and wild hair obscured his head.

In 1960, he appeared in Capitol Wrestling Company and became known as a loathsome figure who was more concerned with hurting an opponent than winning a match. The wild bull vanished from the Northeast territory and traveled throughout the National Wrestling Alliance. The peculiar Pampero re-appeared in WWE in 1972, and once again took aim at fan-favorites.

Firpo often screamed during his matches and became the first figure to coin the phrase "Oh yeah!" during his fits of rage in and out of the ring.

His last match of public record was in October 1986 for Carlos Colon's WWC promotion in Puerto Rico. Today, words like "extreme" and "hardcore" would be used to describe Firpo's ring style and behavior.

PAPA SHANGO

HT	6'6"	WT	330 lbs.	FROM	Parts Unknown
SIGNATURE MOVE	Shoulder Breaker				

A master of voodoo, Papa Shango first began casting his mysterious spells in 1992. With a menacing skull painted over his entire face and a terrifying threat of black magic, the bizarre Superstar quickly became one of the most feared men on the WWE roster.

Though Papa Shango's time in WWE only lasted a little more than a year, he will forever be remembered for the reign of terror he unleashed on several top stars, especially Ultimate Warrior. Showing no fear of the former WWE Champion, Shango unleashed several supernatural spells that forced Ultimate Warrior to mysteriously double over in pain and excrete an ominous black liquid from his skull.

Despite standing 6'6" and possessing a devastating shoulder breaker, Shango's dark voodoo rarely translated into wins. Tito Santana, Bob Backlund, and Bret "Hit Man" Hart all picked up victories over Shango during his tenure. In April 1993, Papa Shango strangely disappeared from WWE. While nobody is certain of his whereabouts, it's safe to say the entire locker room was happy to see him go.

PAT PATTERSON

see page 258

THE PATRIOT

HT	6'5"	WT	275 lbs.	FROM	Columbia, South Carolina
SIGNATURE MOVE	Patriot Missile				

Donning a star spangled mask, he defended the honor of America in every match. The Patriot rose through the ranks quickly and won a 20-man over-the-top-rope battle royal.

The highlight of his WWE career was when he pinned Bret "Hit Man" Hart on the July 28th episode of *Raw*. Unfortunately later that year he suffered an injury that forced him to retire from the ring. Though his time in the spotlight was brief, The Patriot fought for all that was good about the American way. The WWE Universe will never forget how he inspired everyone to be the best American they can be.

PAUL BEARER

(HoF) | HT | 5'10" |

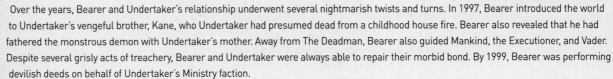

Vince McMahon once declared, "Paul Bearer is the most unique manager in the history of the business." That's exactly what fans discovered as this creepy individual came to WWE in 1991. Taking over the managerial duties of Undertaker from Brother Love, this licensed mortician was the keeper of the urn from which The Deadman drew a mysterious power. Bearer often led his client through the curtain as the frightening chords of Undertaker's music haunted venues around the world.

Bearer and Undertaker embarked on a campaign of destruction in WWE. Paul also issued his own cryptic predictions on his talk segment, "The Funeral Parlor," and became a key architect for WWE's scariest type of encounter, the Casket Match.

Over the years, Bearer and Undertaker's relationship underwent several nightmarish twists and turns. In 1997, Bearer introduced the world to Undertaker's vengeful brother, Kane, who Undertaker had presumed dead from a childhood house fire. Bearer also revealed that he had fathered the monstrous demon with Undertaker's mother. Away from The Deadman, Bearer also guided Mankind, the Executioner, and Vader. Despite several grisly acts of treachery, Bearer and Undertaker were always able to repair their morbid bond. By 1999, Bearer was performing devilish deeds on behalf of Undertaker's Ministry faction.

Bearer made a historic return to WWE at *WrestleMania XX* to help to resurrect The Deadman and exact revenge on Kane. Months later at *The Great American Bash*, this reunion came to a disturbing end when Undertaker was left with no choice but to encase his longtime manager in a crypt full of cement. The keeper of the urn vanished for years but made a shocking appearance in September 2010. Once again the mortician was on Undertaker's side as he battled his brother—or so it seemed. Amidst the chaos of Hell in a Cell, Bearer entered the cage and blinded Undertaker with a beam of light from the urn.

In March 2013, Paul Bearer passed away, leaving behind a legacy as one of the most unique and beloved characters in WWE history. Weeks later at *WrestleMania 29*, his memory inspired Undertaker as he extended his iconic win streak to 21-0. In 2014, Bearer was honored with posthumous induction into the WWE Hall of Fame.

PAT PATTERSON

HT	6'1"
WT	237 lbs.
FROM	Montreal, Quebec, Canada

SIGNATURE MOVE
Atomic Drop

With every phase of his career, Pat Patterson broke new ground. In the San Francisco territory, he won the famed battle royal held annually at Cow Palace on two separate occasions, and formed an iconic tag team with Ray Stevens. As a competitor in WWE, Patterson was the first Intercontinental Champion. Behind the scenes, he's credited with creating the concept of the Royal Rumble.

Patterson debuted in his native Montreal in 1958, calling himself "Pretty Boy" Pat Patterson, wearing pink tights and lipstick, and carrying a poodle to the ring. The youngster pretended to be above the rest of the roster, but even his rivals respected him for his innate toughness.

SAN FRANCISCO TREAT

Finding a home in the San Francisco territory, the flaxen-haired competitor became a true Superstar. In order to give himself an edge, he occasionally donned a mask, slipping a foreign object into the material to headbutt foes. Despite his questionable execution, his methods worked.

Patterson won the United States Championship six times, and tag team gold with The Rock's father, Rocky Johnson, and the charismatic Ray Stevens. Known as the Blond Bombers, Patterson and Stevens also journeyed to the AWA, where they became tag Titlists in 1978. Their relationship was an unsteady one, though, and they periodically battled each other before reconciling.

In 1979, Patterson was brought to WWE by the future Hall of Fame manager, the Grand Wizard, challenging Bob Backlund for the WWE World Heavyweight Championship. Although Patterson was unable to procure the promotion's biggest prize, he did topple a young Ted DiBiase for the old WWE North American Championship, aided by a pair of brass knuckles.

INTERCONTINENTAL GLORY

Later that same year, he traveled to Rio de Janiero, Brazil to participate in a tournament to merge the North American and South American Titles, returning with the newly-created Intercontinental Championship. Some believe that this feat alone all but guaranteed Patterson's later induction into the WWE Hall of Fame.

During his early days in WWE, Patterson was primarily booed. But when the Wizard attempted to sell his contract to fellow manager, Captain Lou Albano, Patterson rebelled, winning over a large share of the WWE Universe. Even after he lost the Intercontinental Championship to former Olympian Ken Patera in 1980, the fans remained in Patterson's corner.

Photo by Bob Cartago.

At the time, Sgt. Slaughter was one of the most detested men in WWE, and he and Patterson engaged in a bloody series of Boot Camp Matches, as well as an Alley Fight at New York's Madison Square Garden.

In 1981, as the San Francisco territory was closing, Patterson made a special appearance to win the group's final battle royal.

As his in-ring career was winding down, Patterson became a television commentator, sitting beside lead announcer Vince McMahon on English-language broadcasts, and offering perspective in French on other programs. When speaking his native tongue, Patterson was not beyond reverting to old habits. On an interview segment called "Le Brunch," he'd respectfully ask fellow combatants questions in English, then immediately ridicule them in his French translation.

RESPECTED AND ACCEPTED

With WWE building up to its inaugural *WrestleMania* in 1985, he assumed a larger role backstage. Although Muhammad Ali was chosen to referee the *WrestleMania I* main event, there was concern that the former boxing champion might get lost attempting to navigate the struggle between Hulk Hogan and Mr. T and their adversaries, Roddy Piper and Paul Orndorff. As a result, Patterson helped officiate.

As WWE's success expanded, so did Patterson's influence. In 1988, he may have contributed his most enduring idea to the company when he recommended a new kind of match called a Royal Rumble.

Although his role was generally hidden from the public, in 1997, he and Gerry Brisco were revealed as McMahon's backstage "stooges," willing to engage in any type of subterfuge for him. The two were not beyond getting physical and, in 2000, Patterson became the oldest competitor to win the Hardcore Title.

In 2014, WWE Network watchers saw a more personal side of the Hall of Famer when he bravely discussed his homosexuality on the *WWE Legends House* reality series. Patterson's inspirational life story was immortalized in print when he crafted his memoir *Accepted: How The First Gay Superstar Changed WWE* in 2016.

PAUL BURCHILL

HT	6'4"	WT	247 lbs.	FROM	Chelsea, England
SIGNATURE MOVE	Reverse Swinging Neckbreaker				

This Superstar was introduced to WWE in 2005 by his mentor, William Regal. Regal trained the British bruiser to be well versed in numerous fighting styles. However, when Burchill revealed his intentions to adapt the swashbuckling style of a theatrical pirate, he and Regal parted ways. Though his time swinging to the stage in full Jack Sparrow-esque regalia was short, it remains the lasting memory of Burchill's career among many fans.

Burchill reemerged in 2008 alongside his sister, the beautiful and sadistic Katie Lea. The fury he displayed in matches soon earned him the moniker "The Ripper." By year's end, he found himself on ECW against Gregory Helms, butting heads over the backstage interviewer's true identity. In the winter of 2010, Burchill was released from WWE.

PAUL ELLERING

Despite a brief WWE tenure, Paul Ellering will be remembered by sports-entertainment fans around the world as the loud-mouthed manager of arguably the greatest tag team of all time, Legion of Doom.

Ellering introduced himself to WWE fans in 1992 when he reunited with Hawk and Animal following a brief separation. Unfortunately, the reunion didn't go quite as planned. Ellering failed to gain fans after showing up at ringside with a ventriloquist dummy named Rocco.

Six years later, he began managing LOD's chief rivals, the Disciples of Apocalypse. A few months later, however, Hawk and Animal teamed with Droz to get their revenge when they defeated Ellering and DOA at *Judgment Day*. Unfortunately, Ellering's time in WWE failed to mirror the amazing success he achieved elsewhere as LOD's manager. Still, Ellering's unmatched intellect and guidance of Hawk and Animal in the 1980s was honored the night before *WrestleMania XXVII*. In an emotional induction ceremony, the LOD accepted their final accolade, taking their places in the WWE Hall of Fame.

PAUL HEYMAN

see page 260

PAUL LONDON

HT	5'10"	WT	195 lbs.	FROM	Austin, Texas
SIGNATURE MOVE	450 Splash				

This eccentric high-flyer is as innovative in the ring as it gets. Since his October 2003 debut, London has captivated audiences with imaginative moves like the "Dropsault" (a Moonsault and a Drop-Kick), "Mushroom Stomp" (where he leaps from the middle rope and presses his feet over a charging opponent's back), and the 450 Splash.

In July 2004, he and Billy Kidman defeated the Dudley Boyz to become WWE Tag Team Champions. They held the Titles for two months before London set his sights on the singles ranks. In March 2005, he won an 8-Man Cruiserweight Battle Royal for the Cruiserweight Championship. London then formed one of the most electric teams in WWE history with fellow high-flyer Brian Kendrick. The two captured the WWE Tag Team Titles in May 2006. Their Championship reign lasted a record 334 days. London and Kendrick were eventually split as a result of the WWE Draft in 2008. London continued to amaze WWE audiences with his high-risk offense until he parted from the company in November 2008.

PAUL LONDON & BRIAN KENDRICK

MEMBERS	Paul London & Brian Kendrick
COMBINED WT	380 lbs.

London and Kendrick briefly worked together in 2003, but it wasn't until they reunited in 2005 that the high-flying tandem began to realize their true potential. Sporting theatrical masks, the eccentric duo made short work of many tag teams on *SmackDown*.

Starting in February 2006, London and Kendrick tore off five straight non-Title victories over WWE Tag Team Champions MNM. Finally, at *Judgment Day 2006*, they upended the Champs when it counted, giving London his second reign with the Titles and Kendrick his first. They went on to hold the gold for nearly one year, longer than any other *SmackDown* team in history.

Drafted to *Raw* in June 2007, London and Kendrick picked up where they left off when they captured the World Tag Team Championship while on tour in South Africa. Despite a brief Title reign, the two remained one of the top tag teams in the world. Despite a rough patch that saw Kendrick walk out on his longtime partner, the duo resolved their differences and continued to bring the WWE Universe to its feet until the WWE Draft forced them apart in June 2008.

PAUL ORNDORFF

HT	6'0"	WT	252 lbs.	FROM	Brandon, Florida
SIGNATURE MOVE	Piledriver				

"Mr. Wonderful" was an amazing athlete even before he trained for a career in sports-entertainment. A student of Hiro Matsuda, Orndorff applied what he learned in the NWA and was quickly noticed for his intensity, skill, and devastating piledriver.

The former professional football player starred in territories around the American south, exciting audiences in Georgia, Texas, Alabama, Tennessee, Louisiana, and Oklahoma. He clashed with Ernie Ladd, Dusty Rhodes, Ted DiBiase, Ric Flair, and others.

Orndorff made his WWE debut in 1984. It was a time when WWE was expanding internationally, and the company needed a man of Mr. Wonderful's reputation and skills. He associated with the likes of "Dr. D" David Schultz, "Rowdy" Roddy Piper, and "Cowboy" Bob Orton. In fact, Orndorff was selected as Piper's partner in the main event of the original *WrestleMania*, tangling with Hulk Hogan and Mr. T.

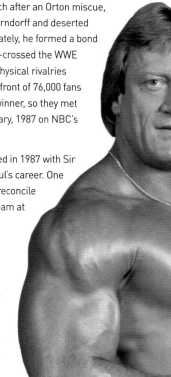

His team would lose the match after an Orton miscue, but Piper and Orton blamed Orndorff and deserted him in the ring. Almost immediately, he formed a bond with the Hulkster, but eventually double-crossed the WWE Champion and ignited one of the most physical rivalries WWE has ever seen. Their encounter in front of 76,000 fans at Toronto's CNE Stadium left no clear winner, so they met inside a 15-foot high Steel Cage in January, 1987 on NBC's *Saturday Night's Main Event*.

Taking a hiatus from the ring, he returned in 1987 with Sir Oliver Humperdink guiding Mr. Wonderful's career. One of the first things that Orndorff did was reconcile with Hogan, and was a member of his team at the first-ever *Survivor Series*.

In 1990, he appeared in World Championship Wrestling, but a serious neck injury forced Orndorff to retire in 1996. He then became a lead trainer at WCW's Power Plant before retiring in 2000. The night before *WrestleMania 21*, the three-decade career of "Mr. Wonderful" was honored, as he was inducted into the WWE Hall of Fame. "Mr. Wonderful" returned for a brief cameo at *WrestleMania 30* when he starred in a backstage segment with the participants from the main event of the first *WrestleMania*.

PAUL HEYMAN

He's been called the "Mad Scientist," "Messiah of a New Breed Unleashed," and "Rabbi of the Revolution." Certainly, few personalities in sports-entertainment have been as polarizing as Paul Heyman. While some extol him as the man who rejuvenated the industry, others accuse the brash New Yorker of causing most of its ills. But Heyman's success is undeniable.

As the creative force behind ECW, Heyman takes credit for influencing WWE and propagating the "Attitude Era." But his reach extends much further. Over the years, he's managed four WWE Champions, including Brock Lesnar, Big Show, CM Punk, and Kurt Angle. And before exploding as the "Texas Rattlesnake" in WWE, Stone Cold Steve Austin was managed by Heyman in WCW.

Heyman vowed to enter the sports-entertainment industry when he was a child, watching then-announcer Vince McMahon interview Superstar Billy Graham. At age 13, Heyman became a photographer. He also founded his own newspaper, called *The Wrestling Times*, and wrote for wrestling magazines. This enabled him to acquire a backstage pass, at 14 years old, for WWE shows at Madison Square Garden. There, he befriended the trilogy of managers involved with the promotion—the Grand Wizard, Captain Lou Albano, and "Classy" Freddie Blassie.

After managing on the independent circuit, Heyman began working in the Florida territory in 1987, dubbing himself Paul E. Dangerously—due to his resemblance to Michael Keaton in the movie *Johnny Dangerously*. He then moved to Memphis, where he managed Austin Idol in a now-notorious Hair vs. Hair Cage Match against Jerry Lawler. What no one knew was that Heyman had arranged for Tommy Rich to hide under the ring early in the day, allowing him to interfere in the match and cost "The King" his hair. The incident nearly caused a riot in the Mid-South Coliseum.

Shock value was always part of the Heyman ethic. In 1988, he appeared in WCW and issued a challenge to the Midnight Express, Bobby Eaton and Stan Lane. His charges were the original members of the Midnight Express, Dennis Condrey and Randy Rose. Heyman also started his "Dangerous Alliance" in WCW, which consisted of Austin, Rick Rude, Arn Anderson, and Eaton, who joined Heyman after the battle of the rival Midnight Express factions ended.

Eventually, Heyman ended up helping backstage at a new company called Eastern Championship Wrestling and engineered yet another astonishing antic. In 1994, ECW wrestler Shane Douglas won a tournament to crown a Champion of what remained of the once vibrant NWA. With Heyman's encouragement, Douglas threw down the belt and proclaimed the NWA was a "dead organization." The ECW Title was the one that mattered, he said. Within days, it was announced that the group was now changing its name to *Extreme* Championship Wrestling. Soon, Heyman became ECW's owner, and encouraged outrageous, uncensored behavior from both the wrestlers and fans, while also presenting some of the best technical matches ever seen.

From time to time, the company and WWE traded talent. But Heyman did not have the financial means to continue ECW. Instead, in 2001, after working as a *Raw* commentator, he helped spark an invasion of former WCW and ECW performers attempting to wrest control of WWE.

When the coup failed, Heyman looked around WWE and saw gold in the form of former NCAA Champion Brock Lesnar. Dubbing Lesnar "the next big thing," Heyman began advising the Beast Incarnate, leading him to the WWE World Heavyweight Championship. Although Heyman later turned on Lesnar in favor of Big Show, the two eventually reconciled.

Never content to stand in one place, Heyman became *SmackDown* General Manager, and then special ECW Representative when the company was relaunched in 2006 under the WWE banner. In 2012, he began advising Lesnar again, and took on CM Punk as a client. For 434 days, Punk ruled as Champion.

In time, Heyman and Punk had a violent falling out. Two other protégés, Curtis Axel and Cesaro, were gone quickly. But Heyman and Lesnar remained a team. Heyman is credited with helping Lesnar not only win the gold again, but leading him to his finest career moment—ending the Undertaker's 21-0 *WrestleMania* streak in 2014.

WHY BE SECOND BEST AT ANYTHING?

PAUL ROMA

HT 5'11" **WT** 235 lbs. **FROM** Kensington, New York
SIGNATURE MOVE Flying Cross Body

This Superstar was first seen by WWE audiences in 1984, and his impressive physique and good looks quickly brought him a great deal of attention. He also became known for throwing one of the best dropkicks in all of sports-entertainment. In 1987, Roma became one-half of an exciting duo known as the Young Stallions with partner Jim Powers.

The team disbanded in 1990 when Roma changed his ways and formed Power and Glory with Hercules, but that team split in late 1991. In 1993, Roma shocked the wrestling world when he debuted in WCW as the fourth member of the legendary stable, the Four Horsemen. After a brief WWE return in 1997, Roma retired. He now trains ring hopefuls at his Connecticut wrestling school.

PEDRO MORALES

HT 5'10" **WT** 235 lbs.
FROM Culebra, Puerto Rico

While rarely mentioned in the same breath as Bruno Sammartino, Hulk Hogan, or John Cena, Pedro Morales' accomplishments are the equal of any Superstar to ever lace a pair of boots. Over the course of his nearly thirty years in the ring, the Puerto Rican legend captured the WWE, World Tag Team, and Intercontinental Championships, making him the first-ever Triple Crown Champion.

Morales made his professional debut in 1959. While still a teenager, he spent much of his time competing on smaller cards around the northeast. It wasn't until 1963 that he appeared in Madison Square Garden, teaming with his boyhood hero Miguel Perez.

After working for other promotions, he competed on the same 1971 card that saw WWE kingpin Bruno Sammartino's nearly eight-year reign come to an end. A mere three weeks later, Morales defeated Ivan Koloff to claim the WWE Championship, an honor he held for nearly three years. Only Sammartino, Hogan, and Bob Backlund held the Title longer.

In August, 1980, he gave his passionate fan base even more reason to celebrate when he teamed with Bob Backlund to capture the Tag Team Championship. Later that year, he completed the trifecta when he won his first of two Intercontinental Championships.

In 1995, Morales was honored as one of WWE's all-time elite when he was inducted into the WWE Hall of Fame by fellow Puerto Rican Superstar Savio Vega.

PEPPER GOMEZ

HT 5'9" **WT** 225 lbs. **FROM** San Francisco, California
SIGNATURE MOVE Cannonball Leap

A former Mr. California, Pepper Gomez called himself the "Man with the Cast Iron Stomach," and was willing to accept any challenge to prove it. He once allowed a Volkswagen to drive over his abdominals. Killer Kowalski could not apply his stomach claw while competing against Pepper and, in 1962, Gomez dared Ray Stevens to leap on his mid-section from a ladder. Instead, Stevens executed his "Bombs Away" finisher on Gomez's neck, forcing him to spit blood and triggering one of the San Francisco territory's most emotional rivalries.

Gomez was trained by Mexican legend Blackie Guzman. In addition to facing names like Gene Kiniski, Buddy Rogers, and Fritz Von Erich, Pepper held tag team gold with Rocky Johnson, Pat Patterson, and others. He died in 2004.

PERCY WATSON

HT 6'6" **WT** 245 lbs. **FROM** South Beach, Miami, Florida
SIGNATURE MOVE The Percycution

"Showtime" Percy Watson paired with WWE Pro MVP for season two of the original *NXT*. With the former United States Champion guiding the way, the eccentric Rookie showed signs of being one of the season's top contenders, but was eliminated midway through the competition. Watson later resurfaced as the tag team partner of Titus O'Neil on *NXT Redemption*.

When he wasn't competing in the ring, Watson could often be found living it up on the Miami club scene. The self-professed "South Beach Party Boy" loved to feature the moves he learned on the dance floor in the ring. Unfortunately for Watson, though, he now has plenty of time to party following his release from WWE in the spring of 2013.

PERRY SATURN

HT 5'10" **WT** 241 lbs. **FROM** Boston, Massachusetts
SIGNATURE MOVE Death Valley Driver, Rings of Saturn

Perry Saturn's elevator didn't go to the top floor. Whether he realized it or not, that's exactly why WWE fans loved him. It didn't matter if he was declaring his love for a mop or uttering the term "you're welcome" for no apparent reason, audiences couldn't wait to see what he would do next.

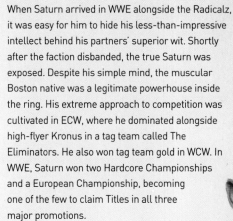

When Saturn arrived in WWE alongside the Radicalz, it was easy for him to hide his less-than-impressive intellect behind his partners' superior wit. Shortly after the faction disbanded, the true Saturn was exposed. Despite his simple mind, the muscular Boston native was a legitimate powerhouse inside the ring. His extreme approach to competition was cultivated in ECW, where he dominated alongside high-flyer Kronus in a tag team called The Eliminators. He also won tag team gold in WCW. In WWE, Saturn won two Hardcore Championships and a European Championship, becoming one of the few to claim Titles in all three major promotions.

Despite these lofty in-ring heights, it was his love affair with a cleaning tool that fans will forever remember. In the summer of 2000, the tattooed Superstar dumped his beautiful girlfriend Terri in favor of pursuing a romantic relationship with, believe it or not, a mop. Saturn was broken hearted when an upset Terri abducted "Moppy" and threw it into a wood chipper. He was never able to rebound from the loss and left WWE the following year.

PAY-PER-VIEWS & SPECIAL EVENTS

For over thirty years, WWE has kept itself on the cutting edge of primetime entertainment. Early forays into pay-per-view such as *The Wrestling Classic*, *Su[...] Series*, and, of course, *WrestleMania*, established Vince McMahon's company as one of the industry's leading pioneers. As its Superstars continued to shine [...] spotlight, WWE's offerings grew. For the past several years, the biggest rivalries in entertainment have reached a crescendo nearly once a month, with W[...] four" events acting as the pillars of the WWE calendar.

With the advent of the WWE Network, the term "pay-per-view" has been rendered a misnomer, as the subscription-based service delivers each monthly s[...] as part of its overall package for the measly cost of $9.99 per month. But while the business model has been turned on its ear, the action has only intensifi[...] are the marque events that have thrilled spectators throughout WWE's fascinating evolution.

1970

Showdown At Shea
1972, 1976, 1980

1980

The Brawl to End It All
1984

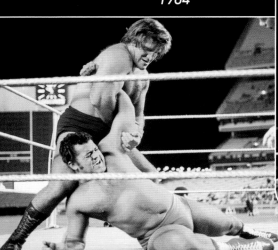

War to Settle the Score
1985

WrestleMania
1985-

The Wrestling Classic
1985

King of the Ring
1985 to 1989, 1991,
1993-2002, 2006, 2008, 2010, 2015

The Main Event/
Saturday Night's Main Event
1985-1992, 2006-2008

The Big Event
1986

Slammy Awards
1986-1987, 1994, 1996-1997, 2008-

Survivor Series
1987-

Royal Rumble
1988

SummerSlam
1988-

Great American Bash/ The Bash
1988-2000, 2004-2009

1990

SWS / WWE Tokyo Dom[...]
Super Show
1990-1991

This Tuesday In Texas
1991

In Your House
1995-1999

Bad Blood
1997, 2003-2004

Capital Carnage
1998

Judgment Day
1998, 2000-2009

No Way Out
1998, 2000-2009, 2012

Fully Loaded
1998-2000

No Mercy
1998-2008

Unforgiven
1998-2008

Armageddon
1999- 2000, 2002-2008

Backlash
1999-2009

One Night Stand
2005-2008

December to Dismember
2006

Night of Champions
2007-2016

Breaking Point
2009

Extreme Rules
2009-2016

Hell in a Cell
2009-

Payback
2013-

NXT Takeover
2014-

Beast in the East
2015

Fastlane
2015

**WWE Live from
Madison Square Garden**
2015

WWE Roadblock
2016

2000

Insurrection
2000-2003

Invasion
2001

Vengeance
2001-2006, 2011

Cyber Sunday/Taboo Tuesday
2004-2008

Money in the Bank
2005-

New Years Revolution
2005-2007

TLC
2009-

Bragging Rights
2009-2010

2010

Fatal 4-Way
2010

Over the Limit
2010-

Elimination Chamber
2010-2015

Capitol Punishment
2011

Battleground
2013-

ARMAGEDDON

1999 – 2000, 2002 – 2008

"The end is here!" For several years, the last month on the WWE calendar meant Armageddon. With the Y2K craze gripping humanity in late 1999, WWE gave its final pay-per-view of the year this ominous theme. While the end of days didn't come with the new millennium, the tradition continued, save for one year, until 2008.

The inaugural *Armageddon 1999* saw the birth of the diabolical union between Triple H and Stephanie McMahon, as Steph spurned her father in his main event match against The Game. Over the years, the event has been host to Hell in a Cell, Last Ride, Inferno Matches, and more. But all the apocalyptic chaos did not stand in the way of a little wholesome holiday cheer as jolly old St. Nick made his presence felt.

More *Armageddon* moments:

◆ Rikishi takes a perilous fall from the top of the Hell in a Cell structure into the bed of a truck (2000).

◆ John Cena unveils the U.S. Championship spinning Title (2004).

◆ Evolution claims all available Championships (2003).

◆ Joey Mercury sustains severe facial injuries when he is inadvertently struck by a ladder (2006).

◆ Jeff Hardy wins his first WWE Championship (2008).

BACKLASH

1999 – 2009

For many of WWE's most barbaric rivalries, *WrestleMania* is only the beginning. Victory on the grandest stage often leads to backlash from those seeking revenge. For a decade, this pay-per-view was the first major event after *WrestleMania* and served as the scene for retribution.

WrestleMania rematches such as Triple H and Batista's battle in 2005 were a common sight, though exciting and chaotic stipulations were often added to the brutality. This type of chaos became the order of the day in 2010 when *Backlash* was replaced by *Extreme Rules*.

More *Backlash* moments:

◆ The Dudleys puts Trish Stratus through a table (2000).

◆ Big Shows tosses John Cena through a spotlight that explodes on impact, allowing Edge to win the Last Man Standing Match for the World Heavyweight Championship (2009).

◆ The Two-Man Power Trip (Stone Cold Steve Austin and Triple H) seizes control of all major Championships by defeating The Brothers of Destruction for the World Tag Team Titles (2001).

◆ Hulk Hogan wins the WWE Championship for the first time in nine years (2002).

◆ Mr. McMahon wins the ECW Championship (2007).

BAD BLOOD

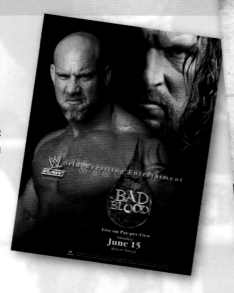

1997, 2003-2004

The first *Bad Blood* was an *In Your House* event that featured one of the most notorious matches of all time—the inaugural Hell in a Cell Match, featuring the debut of Kane in 1997. *Bad Blood* returned in 2003 and 2004. Both events served as home to "The Devil's Playground" with Triple H emerging victorious both years in Hell in a Cell matches against his former Kliq pals, Kevin Nash and Shawn Michaels, respectively.

WWE BATTLEGROUND

2013 –

Initially instituted in 2013 as a Fall pay-per-view, the first *Battleground* more than lived up to its name. The WWE Championship began and ended the night vacant after Big Show, coerced by The Authority, inserted his massive fist into Daniel Bryan and Randy Orton's WWE Championship Match for the vacated Title.

Along the way, the Rhodes brothers, Cody and Goldust, preserved their family's legacy and their jobs with a tag team victory over The Shield.

Battleground became a July event in 2014 and 2015. In its young history, it has been the setting for shocking events, such as The Miz's unpredictable victory in a 19-Man Battle Royal for the Intercontinental Championship in 2014 and 2015's surprise return of Undertaker to seek revenge on Brock Lesnar.

BEAST IN THE EAST

2015

WWE Network entered uncharted territory on July 4, 2015, when it held, for the first time ever, a live WWE broadcast from Japan. Emanating from inside a sold-out Ryougoko Sumo Hall, the event's promotion revolved around Brock Lesnar. Japanese fans were filled with excitement and anticipation for what The Beast would unleash on the other side of the world. Lesnar did not disappoint. Not only did he demolish Kofi Kingston with an F-5, he thrashed Kofi's New Day cohorts as well.

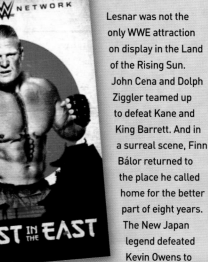

Lesnar was not the only WWE attraction on display in the Land of the Rising Sun. John Cena and Dolph Ziggler teamed up to defeat Kane and King Barrett. And in a surreal scene, Finn Bálor returned to the place he called home for the better part of eight years. The New Japan legend defeated Kevin Owens to capture the NXT Championship and have his hand raised by WWE Hall of Famer Tatsumi Fujinami.

1986

With a record 64,000 in attendance, *The Big Event* pitted Hulk Hogan against "Mr. Wonderful" Paul Orndorff, who lost the match after Bobby Heenan attacked Hogan with a stool.

With nearly a dozen matches on the day, many legendary names made appearances at the show, including Junkyard Dog, the Killer Bees, the Funks, and "King" Harley Race. There were two special matches at the event: a Snake Pit Match between Ricky Steamboat and Jake Roberts, and a Six-Man Tag Team Match that saw Big John Studd, King Kong Bundy, and Bobby Heenan facing Giant Machine, Super Machine, and Lou Albano.

2009 - 2010

During the era of WWE's brand extension, Superstars from *Raw* and *SmackDown* took tremendous pride in competing for the superior brand. In 2009, a pay-per-view was introduced that would give both red and blue a chance to prove their worth over the other.

The format of *Bragging Rights* was simple: matches pitted *Raw* vs. *SmackDown* and the winning brand for the night took home the *Bragging Rights* Trophy for the year. In its inaugural year, the winning brand was decided by the total number of matches won; however, in 2010, the victory went to the winner of a 7-on-7 Interpromotional Elimination Tag Team Match. Both years, it was the *SmackDown* brand that took home the trophy.

Despite the event's theme, individual rivalries were not completely put on the back burner. In 2009, John Cena and Randy Orton had one of their most grueling matches ever, a 60-Minute, "Anything Goes" Iron Man Match that Cena won 6-5. In 2010, Kane buried Undertaker alive with the help of Nexus.

1984

Nearly a year before the inaugural *WrestleMania* event, Madison Square Garden was the scene for *The Brawl to End it All*. Though Hulkamania was in full force by this time and The Hulkster himself defended his WWE Title against Greg "The Hammer" Valentine, the only match that was televised on MTV was the main event contested for the Women's Championship.

Historic as much for the in-ring result as it was for the entertainment forces it united under the WWE banner, the match featured Wendi Richter challenging the 28-year reign of the Fabulous Moolah. But what truly made this a revolutionary moment in WWE lore was the involvement of pop sensation Cyndi Lauper. Fresh off the success of her "Girls Just Want to Have Fun" video, the Big Apple native became embroiled in a dispute with the video's co-star, Captain Lou Albano. To settle things, the warring personalities chose sides in the Championship Match, with Lauper supporting Richter.

After countless competitors tried for nearly three decades, Wendi Richter etched her name as the one to end Moolah's insuperable reign. With this end came a new beginning, as the infusion of the day's hottest music idol into WWE laid the groundwork for the Rock 'n' Wrestling phenomenon that ultimately led to WWE's explosion of popularity.

BREAKINPOINT

2009

Breaking Point was an event with two twists: first, its name was chosen by the WWE Universe; second, many of the matches on the card could only be won via submission. *Breaking Point* matches included defenses of the Unified WWE Tag Team Championship, the United States Championship, and the ECW Championship.

Both the WWE and World Heavyweight Championships were on the line in the night's main events. First, WWE Champion Randy Orton faced John Cena in an "I Quit" Match and was unable to count on outside help after Mr. McMahon threatened to take his Title should anyone interfere on his behalf. In the end, John Cena forced "The Viper" to say "I quit" with a handcuff-aided STF. CM Punk left the host city of Montreal as World Heavyweight Champion after gaining victory in a controversy-filled match against Undertaker with a conclusion reminiscent of the notorious "Montreal Screwjob" at *Survivor Series 1997*.

Capital Carnage

1998

In December 1998, WWE stormed the capital for a star-studded event featuring a who's who of the Attitude Era, just not the capital American fans are thinking of. *Capital Carnage* was a rare UK only pay-per-view event that emanated from London, England. The Rock retained his WWE Championship with a disqualification victory over X-Pac. The New Age Outlaws also held onto their Tag Team Titles. In the night's main event, Stone Cold Steve Austin won a Fatal 4-Way Match and toasted the WWE Universe across the pond with a beer celebration that included soccer star Vinnie Jones.

2011

Themed after its host city of Washington D.C., the proceedings at *Capitol Punishment* were dominated by rivalries as intense as the age-old Capitol Hill rivalry between the Republicans and Democrats. Rey Mysterio faced off against CM Punk, Alex Riley scored revenge against his NXT mentor The Miz, and John Cena defended the WWE Championship against an unhinged R-Truth. While Randy Orton was able to keep his World Heavyweight Championship by defeating Christian, two other Titles did change hands during the night.

Ezekiel Jackson claimed the Intercontinental Championship when he forced his former Corre cohort, Wade Barrett, to submit to a backbreaker. Dolph Ziggler, with some help from Vickie Guerrero, put Kofi Kingston to sleep and left D.C. as the new United States Champion.

CYBER SUNDAY / TABOO TUESDAY

2004 - 2008

A precursor to the multi-platform, interactive experience that WWE is today, *Taboo Tuesday* gave fans the opportunity to call the shots. Votes were conducted on *WWE.com* to decide everything ranging from match stipulations, Divas' outfits, contenders for WWE's most coveted Championships, and much more.

After two editions, the annual event was moved to WWE's traditional pay-per-view timeslot and renamed *Cyber Sunday*.

Taboo Tuesday/Cyber Sunday moments:

◆ Eugene defeats Eric Bischoff and, as a consequence, gets to shave Bischoff's head (2004).

◆ Voted into a Steel Cage Match for the second consecutive year, Ric Flair defends the Intercontinental Championship and escapes to beat Triple H (2005).

◆ Teaming together in WWE for the first time ever, Ric Flair and Roddy Piper defeat the Spirit Squad for the World Tag Team Championship (2006).

◆ After several weeks of claiming he would top Honky Tonk Man's record Intercontinental Title reign, Santino Marella faces the cool, cocky, and bad one himself and wins (2008).

DECEMBER TO DISMEMBER

2006

December to Dismember was WWE's first and only pay-per-view dedicated to its ECW brand. The main attraction of the night was a brutal Extreme Elimination Chamber Match that locked ECW Champion Big Show in with ECW original Rob Van Dam, along with CM Punk, Test, Bobby Lashey, and Hardcore Holly. Lashley survived the extreme encounter (and Big Show's barbed wired bat!) to claim the ECW Title.

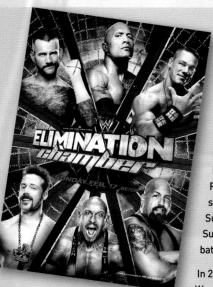

ELIMINATION CHAMBER

2010 - 2015

Created by *Raw* general manager Eric Bischoff in 2002, an Elimination Chamber Match combines elements from Royal Rumble, Survivor Series, and War Games matches into one steel structure. An Elimination Chamber Match starts with two Superstars in the ring. After a predetermined length of time, a new Superstar is released from a pod in the Chamber and enters the battle. The last Superstar standing is declared the winner.

Year	Winner(s)	Stakes
2010	JOHN CENA	WWE CHAMPIONSHIP
	CHRIS JERICHO	WORLD HEAVYWEIGHT CHAMPIONSHIP
2011	EDGE	WORLD HEAVYWEIGHT CHAMPIONSHIP
	JOHN CENA	#1 CONTENDER FOR WWE CHAMPIONSHIP
2012	DANIEL BRYAN	WORLD HEAVYWEIGHT CHAMPIONSHIP
	CM PUNK	WWE CHAMPIONSHIP
2013	JACK SWAGGER	#1 CONTENDER FOR WORLD HEAVYWEIGHT CHAMPIONSHIP
2014	RANDY ORTON	WWE WORLD HEAVYWEIGHT CHAMPIONSHIP
2015	RYBACK	INTERCONTINENTAL CHAMPIONSHIP
	NEW DAY	WWE TAG TEAM CHAMPIONSHIP

In 2010, *Elimination Chamber* became an annual pay-per-view event. Held in February, the callous chamber served as the final stop on the road to *WrestleMania* until 2015 when it was held in May.

EXTREME RULES

2009 -

WWE kicks its traditional rules to the curb each year at *Extreme Rules*. Since 2009, the lawless nature of this event has led to jaw-dropping highlights and incredible displays of courage and perseverance. From Stretcher Matches to Last Man Standing, Steel Cage, Ladder, and other lawless encounters, this event gives the perfect platform for Superstars to settle issues in an extreme manner.

Extreme Rules moments:

◆ John Cena uses duct tape to keep Batista down for the count in a Last Man Standing Match (2010).

◆ Michelle McCool is ousted by former best friend Layla in a "Loser Leaves WWE" Match (2011).

◆ Christian wins his first-ever World Heavyweight Championship in a Ladder Match (2011).

◆ Brock Lesnar brutalizes John Cena but is still defeated in his return match to WWE (2012).

◆ Ryback Spears John Cena through the set (2013).

◆ Seth Rollins leaps off the Izod Center balcony onto Evolution (2014).

FATAL 4-WAY

2010

This one-of-a-kind event featured contests where four Superstars battled at one time. By *Fatal 4-Way* rules, the first competitor to score a pinfall is declared the winner, meaning a Champion could lose his or her Title without being involved in the pinfall! The Divas Championship, World Heavyweight Championship, and WWE Championship were all on the line, and all three changed hands during the event.

In addition to the three Fatal 4-Way Matches during the night, the Intercontinental and United States Championships were put on the line, though the Titles were successfully defended by Kofi Kingston and The Miz, respectively.

FASTLANE

2015 -

With *WrestleMania* on the horizon, WWE action shifts into overdrive as the only lane leading to the Show of Shows is the *Fastlane*. In 2015, this new event was introduced as the final stop on the road to *WrestleMania*. In its brief but tumultuous history, *Fastlane* has belonged to the explosive Roman Reigns. Two years in a row, "The Big Dog" earned his spot in the main event of *WrestleMania* by prevailing at *Fastlane*—against Daniel Bryan in 2015 and against both Dean Ambrose and Brock Lesnar in 2016.

Also in 2016, The Phenomenal AJ Styles proved he could be a force in WWE. The international sensation topped Chris Jericho in his first Sunday, primetime one-on-one encounter, after his phenomenal debut in January 2016.

1988 - 2000 (WCW), 2004 - 2009 (WWE)

This patriotic event traces its roots back to the NWA in 1988. For several years, stars such as Ric Flair, Sting, Dusty Rhodes, and more clashed as July fireworks lit up the sky.

WWE revived this star spangled showdown in 2004, when American financial tycoon JBL highlighted the festivities by defeating Eddie Guerrero in a Bullrope Match to begin his historic WWE Title reign. In its final year, the event was given the more universal moniker, *The Bash*.

More *Great American Bash* moments:

◆ Sting pins Ric Flair to claim the NWA World Championship (1990).

◆ NWA Tag Team Champions Terry Gordy and Steve Williams go the distance in a tournament to retain their Titles (1992).

◆ Undertaker entombs Paul Bearer in a concrete crypt (2004).

◆ King Booker begins his imperial World Championship reign by beating Rey Mysterio (2006).

◆ Randy Orton outlasts Triple H in a 3 Stages of Hell Match (2009).

HELL IN A CELL

The career-altering match known as Hell in a Cell made its debut at *In Your House: Badd Blood* in October 1997. For years, no Superstar who entered ever emerged the same—especially Mankind, who Undertaker launched off the top of the cage through the Spanish announce table in 1998.

In September 2006, the 20-foot steel enclosure required a redesign. Hell in a Cell became 3,500 square feet of steel beams. In 2009, *Hell in a Cell* became a yearly pay-per-view that featured the namesake match as its main event. Not to be confined exclusively to one event, the unforgiving structure was also unleashed at *WrestleMania XXVIII* and *WrestleMania 32*.

More *Hell in a Cell* moments:

◆ D-Generation X defeats Legacy inside Hell in a Cell (2009).

◆ Alberto Del Rio wins the first-ever Triple Threat Hell in a Cell Match (2011).

◆ Shawn Michaels Superkicks his former trainee Daniel Bryan, costing him the WWE Championship (2013).

◆ Brock Lesnar defeats Undertaker to gain the upper hand in their bitter rivalry (2015).

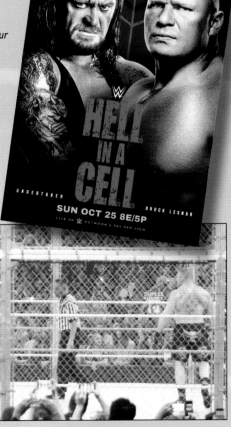

Fully Loaded

1998 - 2000

Fully Loaded was a short-lived annual pay-per-view that began as an *In Your House* event, but was eventually replaced by *Vengeance*. During its three-year existence, Stone Cold busted Undertaker open in a rare First Blood Match, Owen Hart and Ken Shamrock continued their hard-hitting rivalry in a Dungeon Match, and Perry Saturn beat fellow Radical Eddie Guerrero for the European Title.

1995 - 1999

During a five year span in the 1990s, *In Your House* was the setting for WWE's most pivotal clashes in the months sandwiched between its "big four" pay-per-view events. Twenty-eight shows were branded with its colorful logo of jumbled block letters and rooftop outline. *In Your House* will forever be linked to the WWE of the '90s, but its influence is still felt. Several match types the WWE Universe enjoys today were first unveiled during this timeless series.

More *In Your House* moments:

◆ Hunter Hearst-Helmsley wins a Hog Pen Match but is still tossed into the disgusting slop by Henry O. Godwinn, *Seasons Beatings* (1995).

◆ Diesel attempts to use Mad Dog Vachon's prosthetic leg to clock Shawn Michaels, *Good Friends, Better Enemies* (1996).

◆ The Buried Alive Match is invented. Trapped beneath six feet of dirt, Undertaker's unmistakable glove reaches up through the earth to announce that he will not rest in peace, *Buried Alive* (1996).

◆ The Hart family fills the ring to celebrate the Hart Foundation's victory on home soil, *Canadian Stampede* (1997).

◆ Big Show debuts in WWE by assaulting Stone Cold Steve Austin, *St. Valentine's Day Massacre* (1999).

2000 - 2003

For four straight years, WWE invaded the UK with an annual pay-per-view event known as *Insurrextion*. Produced exclusively for the UK audience, the British sector of the WWE Universe enjoyed high stakes encounters for the Tag Team, Intercontinental, Women's, and even the WWE Championship.

Triple H headlined all four events. For the final edition in 2003, The Game crossed the Atlantic with the World Heavyweight Championship and successfully defended the gold in a Street Fight with Kevin Nash.

INVASION

2001

For decades, sports-entertainment fans dreamed of what would happen if Superstars from their favorite promotion crossed over and battled competitors from a rival organization. In 2001, those dreams became a reality when WWE squared off against the WCW/ECW Alliance at the *Invasion* pay-per-view.

Team WWE (Stone Cold Steve Austin, Chris Jericho, Undertaker, Kane, and Kurt Angle) looked to be in control of the main event but in a shocking development, Stone Cold turned on his team late in the match, allowing the win to go to Team Alliance (Booker T, Diamond Dallas Page, the Dudley Boyz, and Rhyno). Other highlights included Rob Van Dam defeating Hardcore Champion Jeff Hardy, Tajiri beating Tazz, and Edge and Christian topping Lance Storm and Mike Awesome.

Judgment DAY

1998, 2000 - 2009

The first edition of *Judgment Day* was held in October 1998. Undertaker and his brother, Kane, battled for the vacant WWE Championship with Stone Cold Steve Austin acting as Guest Referee. After Austin failed to declare a winner with the result of the match a "no contest," Mr. McMahon fired him on the spot!

When *Judgment Day* was resumed in 2000, it became an annual May pay-per-view until 2009. From 2003 to 2006, competition was restricted to the *SmackDown* brand. *Judgment Day* has provided the final verdict on many important rivalries, but perhaps none as illustrious as John Cena's final showdown with JBL. In his first-ever WWE Championship defense, Cena proved worthy of the Champ moniker by outlasting the "Wrestling God" in an "I Quit" Match.

More *Judgment Day* moments:

◆ Triple H beats The Rock in an Iron Man Match to win the WWE Championship (2000).

◆ After losing to Edge in a Hair vs. Hair Match, Kurt Angle is showered with chants of "You're bald!" (2002).

◆ MVP wins a hard-fought Best 2-out-of-3 Falls Match to win the United States Championship (2007).

KING OF THE RING

1985 - 1989, 1991, 1993 - 2002, 2006, 2008, 2010, 2015

King of the Ring began as a one night, single-elimination tournament in 1985. Over the years, WWE's royal tradition has taken on many forms. In 1993, it became a yearly pay-per-view event. After it was revived in 2006, it evolved into a tournament that can occur over weeks or even months.

Some of WWE's all-time greats have used their ascension to the throne as a stepping-stone for greater success. Following his 1996 victory, Stone Cold Steve Austin spoke one of the most notorious lines in WWE history to usher in the era of Austin 3:16. Others such as Bad News Barrett, Booker T, Mabel, and Harley Race became consumed by their newfound majesty and adopted kingly personas.

As a pay-per-view, *King of the Ring* was used to settle other scores as well. In 2001, a personal grudge between Kurt Angle and Shane McMahon resulted in a Street Fight that is still notorious for the brutality that ensued.

Year	King of the Ring	Year	King of the Ring
1985	DON MURACO	1997	HUNTER HEARST-HELMSLEY
1986	HARLEY RACE	1998	KEN SHAMROCK
1987	RANDY SAVAGE	1999	BILLY GUNN
1988	MILLION DOLLAR MAN TED DIBIASE	2000	KURT ANGLE
1989	TITO SANTANA	2001	EDGE
1991	BRET HART	2002	BROCK LESNAR
1993	BRET HART	2006	BOOKER T
1994	OWEN HART	2008	WILLIAM REGAL
1995	MABEL	2010	SHEAMUS
1996	STONE COLD STEVE AUSTIN	2015	BAD NEWS BARRETT

MONEY IN THE BANK

2005 -

A revolutionary idea from Ladder Match extraordinaire Chris Jericho, *Money in the Bank* began as a special match at *WrestleMania 21*. Following *WrestleMania XXVI*, it became its own standalone event. In an otherwise standard Ladder Match, a briefcase is suspended over the ring. It contains a contract for a guaranteed World Championship Match any time the winner chooses. The matches have included anywhere from five to eight participants.

The original "Mr. Money in the Bank," Edge, laid the blueprint for cashing in the coveted Title opportunity when he invoked his contract on an exhausted John Cena. Few briefcase holders, namely Cena himself, have ended up taking the high road when cashing in their opportunity. Most have followed Edge's opportunistic example. In 2015, Seth Rollins became the first Superstar to cash in during the main event of *WrestleMania*.

	Money in the Bank Winner	World Championship Opportunity
WrestleMania 21, 2005	EDGE	ANY
WrestleMania 22, 2006	ROB VAN DAM	ANY
WrestleMania 23, 2007	MR. KENNEDY	ANY
WrestleMania XXIV, 2008	CM PUNK	ANY
WrestleMania 25, 2009	CM PUNK	ANY
WrestleMania XXVI, 2010	JACK SWAGGER	ANY
Money in the Bank 2010	KANE	WORLD HEAVYWEIGHT CHAMPIONSHIP
	THE MIZ	WWE CHAMPIONSHIP
Money in the Bank 2011	DANIEL BRYAN	WORLD HEAVYWEIGHT CHAMPIONSHIP
	ALBERTO DEL RIO	WWE CHAMPIONSHIP
Money in the Bank 2012	DOLPH ZIGGLER	WORLD HEAVYWEIGHT CHAMPIONSHIP
	JOHN CENA	WWE CHAMPIONSHIP
Money in the Bank 2013	DAMIEN SANDOW	WORLD HEAVYWEIGHT CHAMPIONSHIP
	RANDY ORTON	WWE CHAMPIONSHIP
Money in the Bank 2014	SETH ROLLINS	WWE WORLD HEAVYWEIGHT CHAMPIONSHIP
Money in the Bank 2015	SHEAMUS	WWE WORLD HEAVYWEIGHT CHAMPIONSHIP

NEW YEAR'S REVOLUTION

2005 - 2007

In January 2005, WWE unveiled *New Year's Revolution* as its first-ever pay-per-view event to take place in Puerto Rico. From the Coliseo de Puerto Rico in San Juan, Triple H overcame five other Superstars inside the Elimination Chamber to win back the World Heavyweight Championship.

The event came stateside the following year but the callous Chamber once again housed the main event. John Cena emerged with his lengthy WWE Title reign still intact. However, moments after the match, Money in the Bank holder Edge emerged to cash in and steal the gold. The final *Revolution* in 2007 was better for Cena. The Champ put the brakes on Umaga's undefeated record in WWE.

NO MERCY

1999 - 2008

This event was given a fitting start in 1999 when the main event showcased one of the most merciless Champions of all time, Triple H, defending his Title against Stone Cold Steve Austin. *No Mercy* was the highlight of WWE's October calendar for its entire ten year run.

More *No Mercy* moments:

◆ The Hardy Boyz win the managerial services of Terri in a thrilling Ladder Match against Edge and Christian (1999).

◆ Mr. McMahon competes in an "I Quit" Match against his own daughter Stephanie McMahon (2003).

◆ John Cena takes the rubber match of a Best-of-5 Series with Booker T to become United States Champion (2004).

◆ Randy Orton and his father, "Cowboy" Bob Orton, trap Undertaker inside a wooden casket and light it on fire! (2005).

◆ Triple H competes in three matches in one exhausting evening. The Game wins the World Heavyweight Title from Randy Orton in the opening match, later defeats Umaga, and then loses the Title back to Orton in the main event (2007).

◆ Chris Jericho loses a tooth, but not his World Heavyweight Championship, in a harrowing Ladder Match against Shawn Michaels (2008).

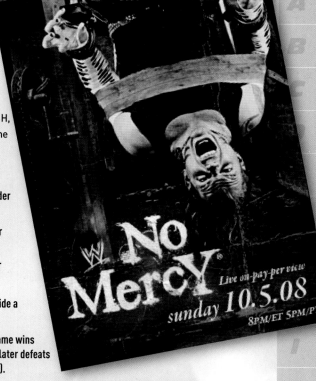

NIGHT OF CHAMPIONS

2007 -

In 2007, *Vengeance* was subtitled *Night of Champions* as every match at the event served up a Champion defending his or her Title against a top contender. For the inaugural event, sports-entertainment luminaries with deep ties to each respective Title were honored prior to those Titles being contested. Among those past Champions in attendance were Harley Race, Magnum TA, Ricky Steamboat, and Dean Malenko.

The following year, *Vengeance* was dropped from the event's name and *Night of Champions* became an annual tradition where every WWE titleholder must prove themselves worthy of the gold.

More *Night of Champions* moments:

◆ Cody Rhodes betrays his partner Hardcore Holly when he is revealed as the mystery partner for the debuting Ted DiBiase. The future Legacy members win the Tag Team Titles (2008).

◆ Team Hell No wins the WWE Tag Team Championships. Following the victory, both team members proclaim, "I am the Tag Team Champions!" (2012).

◆ AJ Lee ties Eve's record by winning her third Divas Championship (2014).

◆ WCW icon Sting challenges for the WWE World Heavyweight Championship for the only time in his illustrious career (2015).

NO WAY OUT

1998, 2000 - 2009, 2012

No Way Out began as an *In Your House* event that took place in 1998 and then became a regular pay-per-view event two years later. After consecutive years where the main events featured Elimination Chamber Matches, *No Way Out* was replaced by *Elimination Chamber* in 2010. In June 2012, with John Cena and Big Show set to determine the future of John Laurinaitis and Cena himself inside a Steel Cage, the *No Way Out* moniker was revived for one night only. Cena triumphed over Big Show to save his career. Mr. McMahon promptly fired Laurinaitis.

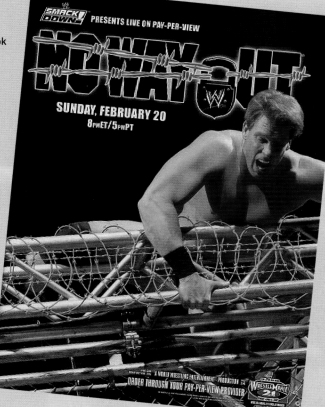

More *No Way Out* moments:

◆ After a disturbing scene in which Cactus Jack falls through the ceiling of the Hell in a Cell structure, Triple H pins Cactus to force him into retirement. (2000)

◆ The nWo appears in WWE for the first time, several years after its members left the company. (2002)

◆ Eddie Guerrero upsets Brock Lesnar and wins his first WWE Championship in an emotional scene. (2004)

◆ In a Barbed Wire Steel Cage Match, Big Show thinks he has won the WWE Championship when he Chokeslams a battered JBL through the ring canvas. However, JBL technically escapes by crawling out from under the ring to retain the Title. (2005)

◆ Big Show returns to WWE after an extended hiatus. He is confronted by boxing legend Floyd "Money" Mayweather, who bloodies his nose with several lighting-quick punches. (2008)

2014 –

As the popularity of the NXT brand skyrocketed, the WWE Network began producing regular, two-hour specials featuring the league's Superstars. Because every NXT competitor yearns for WWE fame, there's a hunger on the *NXT TakeOver* shows that cannot be duplicated elsewhere. Already, there's a stockpile of *NXT TakeOver* moments that have become part of history:

◆ Charlotte, accompanied by father Ric Flair, defeats Natalya, with her uncle Bret Hart, to snare the NXT Women's Championship (2014).

◆ Sami Zayn's NXT Championship victory party is broken up with a vicious attack from best friend, Kevin Owens (2014).

◆ Bayley becomes the queen of the burgeoning Diva's Revolution in Brooklyn. Her opponent, Sasha Banks, and rivals, Charlotte and Becky Lynch, briefly unite to embrace the new Champion (2015).

◆ The first *NXT TakeOver* outside the United States takes place in London, England (2015).

◆ A bloody Samoa Joe waves off doctors in a losing effort to NXT Champion Finn Bálor after they inadvertently bump heads in the opening seconds of their match (2016).

ONE NIGHT STAND

2005 – 2008

Over four years after Extreme Championship Wrestling folded, the outcry for its hardcore heroes to reunite inspired WWE to promote a one-time attraction called *One Night Stand* in 2005. The event, headlined by original ECW renegades The Sandman, Tommy Dreamer, and the Dudley Boyz, was so well received it became an annual tradition.

While rooted in ECW lore, the event took on a life of its own and in 2009 was replaced by *Extreme Rules*.

One Night Stand moments:

◆ ECW original Rob Van Dam rides an overwhelming home court advantage to beat John Cena for the WWE Championship. (2006)

◆ John Cena drops the seven-foot Great Khali off of a crane with an AA. (2007)

◆ Edge sends Undertaker plummeting through a stack of tables to win a TLC Match. (2008)

2010 – 2012

This high-octane event ran for three years in the May slot on WWE's pay-per-view calendar. John Cena headlined all three editions, the first two in his specialty, the "I Quit" Match. Both Batista and The Miz surrendered to The Champ by uttering WWE's most embarrassing two words. At his third *Over the Limit* go-round, Cena was the one humbled when Big Show's betrayal caused him to lose a match to John Laurinaitis.

PAYBACK

2013 –

"Payback should be hell."

Those were John Cena's words prior to the first edition of *Payback*, which pitted Ryback and Cena in a 3 Stages of Hell Match. The Champ prevailed after three falls by driving his opponent through the roof of an ambulance. CM Punk also scored a win over rival Chris Jericho that night in his hometown of Chicago.

WWE returned to the Windy City the following year, 2014. The rowdy WWE Universe witnessed a brazen Brie Bella slap Stephanie McMahon and, unbeknownst at the time, The Shield's final stand before Seth Rollins defected. Rollins headlined the 2015 *Payback* as WWE World Heavyweight Champion and won a Fatal 4-Way Match to retain the Title.

ROYAL RUMBLE

1988 –

As it approaches its 30th anniversary, the *Royal Rumble* remains one of WWE's most anticipated events. A brainchild from the imaginative mind of WWE Hall of Famer Pat Patterson, the first *Royal Rumble* was held in 1988 and featured twenty Superstars. In 1989, the field was increased to thirty where it has remained, with the exception of the 2011 event, which expanded to forty entrants.

With the WWE Championship vacated in 1992, "Nature Boy" Ric Flair made history by going the distance in the first Royal Rumble Match to be contested for the Title. The following year, it became tradition for the winner to earn the right to challenge for a World Championship at *WrestleMania*. That tradition was broken in 2016 when Roman Reigns became the first reigning Champion forced to defend the gold in the Royal Rumble Match.

The list of every Royal Rumble Match winner reads like a "Who's Who" of sports-entertainment, with thirty Superstars each year competing tooth-and-nail to become the next name in this prestigious lineage.

Year	Winner
1988	"HACKSAW" JIM DUGGAN
1989	BIG JOHN STUDD
1990	HULK HOGAN
1991	HULK HOGAN
1992	RIC FLAIR
1993	YOKOZUNA
1994	BRET HART / LEX LUGER
1995	SHAWN MICHAELS
1996	SHAWN MICHAELS
1997	STONE COLD STEVE AUSTIN
1998	STONE COLD STEVE AUSTIN
1999	MR. MCMAHON
2000	THE ROCK
2001	STONE COLD STEVE AUSTIN
2002	TRIPLE H
2003	BROCK LESNAR
2004	CHRIS BENOIT
2005	BATISTA
2006	REY MYSTERIO
2007	UNDERTAKER
2008	JOHN CENA
2009	RANDY ORTON
2010	EDGE
2011	ALBERTO DEL RIO
2012	SHEAMUS
2013	JOHN CENA
2014	BATISTA
2015	ROMAN REIGNS
2016	TRIPLE H

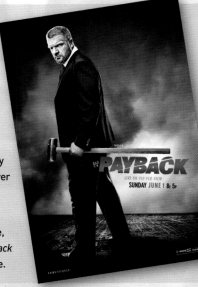

1985 - 1992, 2006 - 2008

After the entertainment world saw the incredible success generated by the WWE events *The Brawl To End It All* and *The War To Settle The Score* on MTV, television executives were eager to work with WWE. As sports-entertainment began to assault pop culture, NBC and WWE announced that WWE was returning to network television for the first time in decades.

The inaugural episode of *Saturday Night's Main Event* aired on May 11, 1985, from Nassau Coliseum in Uniondale, New York. That evening fans saw a lineup that included future WWE Hall of Famers George "The Animal" Steele, Iron Sheik, Nikolai Volkoff, Junkyard Dog, Fabulous Moolah, "Cowboy" Bob Orton, and Hulk Hogan. A new ratings record was set on the March 14, 1987, show that saw Hulk Hogan and Andre the Giant engaged in hostile contact for the first time in a 20-man over-the-top rope Battle Royal right before their monumental clash at *WrestleMania III*.

The success of the show was so great that in 1988 NBC began to air prime time broadcasts on Friday nights called *The Main Event*. That first event saw Andre The Giant end the Championship reign of Hulk Hogan in a rematch from *WrestleMania III*. WWE presented both *Saturday Night's Main Event* and *The Main Event* specials in 1992 before it left the airwaves after a historic eight-year run.

In March 2006, *Saturday Night's Main Event* made its amazing return. Audiences saw a beer drinking contest between Stone Cold Steve Austin and JBL, a Street Fight with Shane McMahon and Shawn Michaels, plus the battle of *WrestleMania* main eventers as John Cena and Triple H teamed against Kurt Angle, Rey Mysterio, and Randy Orton. In August 2008, WWE showed again what sports-entertainment is all about with main event caliber bouts featuring Edge, John Cena, Batista, JBL, and more, plus a special appearance by actress Jenny McCarthy.

In 2009, WWE Home Video released a special collector's DVD set on the history of this ground-breaking program.

1972, 1976, 1980

Showdown at Shea was a series of three supercards held at Shea Stadium, once home to the New York Mets in Flushing, Queens. Each event featured a star-studded line up from top to bottom. The first edition in 1972 saw WWE Champion Pedro Morales and Bruno Sammartino battle to a time limit draw. In 1976, two matches were held pitting "Wrestlers vs. Boxers," in which Andre the Giant defeated Chuck Wepner and Antonio Inoki battled Muhammad Ali to a draw.

The final *Showdown at Shea* in 1980 featured Hulk Hogan battling Andre the Giant seven years before their iconic *WrestleMania* clash. The main event of the night showcased Bruno Sammartino facing and defeating his former protégé, Larry Zbyszko, in a Steel Cage Match.

1986 - 1987, 1994, 1996 - 1997, 2008 -

Much like the television industry does with the popular Emmy Awards, WWE rewards excellence in sports-entertainment with their annual Slammy Awards. The prestigious awards ceremony, which was created by the Academy of Wrestling Arts and Science, can be traced all the way back to 1986. The inaugural ceremony focused largely on the musical efforts on *The Wrestling Album*.

The night's big winner was Junkyard Dog, who walked away with the award for Best Single Performer. The following year, the Slammys altered its categories to include the mat, as well as music. In the end, few remembered the winners and losers. Instead, the 1987 Slammy Awards are mainly remembered for Mr. McMahon's now-embarrassing rendition of "Stand Back." McMahon's musical act almost single-handedly sent the Slammys into a seven-year hiatus. When it finally returned in the mid 1990s, however, some of WWE's all-time greatest names walked away with golden statuettes, including Shawn Michaels, Bret Hart, Sunny, and WWE pioneers Freddie Blassie and Arnold Skaaland, who were honored with Lifetime Achievement Awards.

Following the 1997 ceremony, The Slammy Awards took another hiatus, but the prestigious honor returned in 2008. For the first time ever, the new millennium version of the Slammys included fan voting on *WWE.com*. In 2009, John Cena earned his Superstar of the Year Award by winning a tournament, besting Randy Orton in the finals.

Over the past decade, the Slammys have hit their stride as a time honored WWE tradition. Typically held on one of the final *Raw* episodes of each year, annual awards for Superstar, Diva, Tag Team, and Match of the Year have become coveted accolades for WWE's performers. Other areas of recognition such as the LOL Moment of the Year, Insult of the Year, or #Trending Now Moment of the Year may not pack the same prestige, but are fun to reflect on as WWE prepares to turn the page on its latest banner year.

1988 -

It has been touted as "The Biggest Party of the Summer," "The Summer's Biggest Blockbuster," and "WWE's Annual Summer Spectacular," none of which is hyperbole. One of WWE's longest running pay-per-view traditions, nothing exemplifies summer sizzle like *SummerSlam*.

In 1988, Hulk Hogan and Randy "Macho Man" Savage came together as The Mega Powers. Together, this juggernaut took on the evil, money-grubbing duo of Ted DiBiase and Andre the Giant, known as The Mega Bucks. The first *SummerSlam* at Madison Square Garden was the scene for the epic clash, where good ultimately triumphed over greed. Earlier in the night, Ultimate Warrior brought down the maddening Intercontinental Title reign of the Honky Tonk Man in under a minute.

Over the next three decades, *SummerSlam* grew into a mini-*WrestleMania*. No longer confined to three hours on a summer Sunday, WWE takes over the host town for an entire week with fan events, Superstar appearances, NXT specials and much more. From 2009 to 2014, Los Angeles played host for *SummerSlam* before the event moved east in 2015 to Brooklyn's Barclays Center.

More *SummerSlam* moments:

- ◆ Hulk Hogan turns back his *No Holds Barred* rival, Zeus, and Randy Savage with the help of Brutus Beefcake (1989).
- ◆ Ultimate Warrior silences Rick Rude in a Steel Cage Match for Warrior's WWE Championship (1990).
- ◆ Randy "Macho Man" Savage and Miss Elizabeth are married in a "Match Made in Heaven" Ceremony (1991).
- ◆ British Bulldog overtakes his brother-in-law, Bret Hart, in front of his rejoicing countrymen at Wembley Stadium in London (1992).
- ◆ The real Undertaker defeats his imposter (1994).
- ◆ Mankind beats Undertaker in a creepy Boiler Room Brawl (1996).
- ◆ Ken Shamrock and Owen Hart settle things in a Lions' Den Match (1998).
- ◆ Edge and Christian win the first-ever TLC Match (2000).
- ◆ Shawn Michaels returns to WWE for an Unsanctioned Street Fight against Triple H. HBK sticks around for eight more years (2002).
- ◆ Randy Orton becomes the youngest World Heavyweight Champion in history (2004).
- ◆ Rey Mysterio secures custody of his son, Dominick, by defeating Eddie Guerrero in a Ladder Match (2005).
- ◆ Undertaker Chokeslams Edge through the mat, which then erupts in flames (2008).
- ◆ DX reunites to take out Legacy (2009).
- ◆ Daniel Bryan overtakes John Cena for the WWE Championship, only for Randy Orton to cash in his Money in the Bank contract and derail the Yes! Man's moment (2013).
- ◆ Jon Stewart gives Seth Rollins the surprise assist in his victory over John Cena in a Title for Title Match (2015).

SURVIVOR SERIES

1987 -

Since Thanksgiving Day in 1987, *Survivor Series* has given the WWE Universe plenty to be thankful for. From a main course of tag team warfare with a side of scintillating controversy and historic innovations, this treasured event always satisfies the WWE Universe's appetite. For its first four years, *Survivor Series* remained on Thursday before shifting to Thanksgiving Eve and eventually the traditional Sunday slot, but has always been considered a Thanksgiving tradition.

Besides *WrestleMania*, no annual WWE tradition has stood the test of time longer, with *SummerSlam* and *Royal Rumble* following suit in 1988. First intended to shine a deserved spotlight on tag team competition, *Survivor Series* did not feature a one-on-one match until 1991, when Undertaker defeated Hulk Hogan to win his first WWE Championship. The traditional *Survivor Series* Elimination Match features two teams consisting of four or five Superstars. The match is contested under tag team rules, but unlike a standard tag team competition, the match does not end until all members of one side have been eliminated.

This type of gang warfare at the first *Survivor Series* intensified the rivalry between Hulk Hogan and Andre the Giant. Andre's villainous quintet outlasted the Hulkster and his crew in the night's main event, with Andre claiming bragging rights as the prestigious "Sole Survivor." Over the years, the team concept has brought several unlikely and curious combinations of allies and rivals together to fight for a common cause.

Of course, no discussion of *Survivor Series* is complete without highlighting two of the most monumental debuts (no, not the Gobbledy Gooker) in WWE history: Undertaker (1990) and The Rock (1996).

More *Survivor Series* moments:

◆ Dissention in the Mega Powers shows during victory celebration (1988).

◆ The Hart family prevails over Shawn Michaels and his Knights (1993).

◆ Chuck Norris serves as an outside enforcer for Undertaker and Yokozuna's Casket Match (1994).

◆ An incident known as "The Montreal Screwjob" costs Bret Hart the WWE Championship and is forever held in infamy (1997).

◆ The Rock becomes "The Corporate Champion" (1998).

◆ Big Show wins a 4-on-1 Handicap Elimination Match by himself, later defeats Triple H and The Rock to win the WWE Title (1999).

◆ Stone Cold Steve Austin drops a car from a crane with Triple H trapped inside (2000).

◆ Team WWE is victorious over Team Alliance, ending the WCW/ECW invasion (2001).

◆ The Elimination Chamber debuts (2002).

◆ Kane helps Vince McMahon bury Undertaker alive (2003).

◆ Team *SmackDown* tops Team *Raw* in a battle of the brands (2005).

◆ Team DX sweeps Team Rated RKO 5-0 (2006).

◆ John Cena returns to capture the World Heavyweight Championship for the first time (2008).

◆ The Rock competes in his first match in seven years as he teams with rival John Cena to beat The Awesome Truth (2011).

◆ The cast of *Total Divas* defends their honor by defeating a team of their biggest Diva detractors (2013).

◆ Sting arrives in a WWE ring for the first time to help John Cena's team upend The Authority's team, temporarily costing The Authority their jobs (2014).

◆ Undertaker's 25-year anniversary is celebrated and Sheamus cashes in Money in the Bank to win the WWE World Heavyweight Championship (2015).

SWS/WWE Tokyo Dome Supershow

1990 - 1991

In 1990 and 1991, WWE teamed up with Super World of Sports, a Japanese promotion, to hold a series of events that often saw WWE competitors facing an opponent from Japan. The first inter-promotional showcase, dubbed *Wrestling Summit*, featured Shohei "Giant" Baba teaming with Andre the Giant to defeat Demolition. One year later, the Tokyo Dome played host to *Wrestlefest*, where the Legion of Doom proved too much for Hulk Hogan and Genichiro Tenryu. At the final edition of the series, *Superwrestle*, Hogan and Tenryu battled each other, with the Hulkster picking up the victory.

1991

Following Undertaker's controversial WWE Championship victory over Hulk Hogan at *Survivor Series 1991*, WWE President Jack Tunney called for an immediate rematch. Unable to wait for January's *Royal Rumble*, he created the impromptu *This Tuesday in Texas* event, which was held in December 1991.

Just like at *Survivor Series*, the action quickly got out of hand. Though Tunney was seated at ringside to ensure order, he was inadvertently knocked out. Hogan blinded Undertaker with ashes from The Deadman's signature urn and went on to win the match, but Tunney later declared the WWE Championship vacant due to the turmoil.

This Tuesday in Texas also featured the emotional return of Randy "Macho Man" Savage, who had been forced to retire following his *WrestleMania VII* loss to Ultimate Warrior. In the record books, Savage earned a victory over rival Jake Roberts, but "The Snake" walked away with the psychological win when he delivered three DDTs to his opponent and menaced the lovely Elizabeth.

In other action, Intercontinental Champion Bret Hart successfully defended his Title against the undefeated Skinner, Ted DiBiase and Repo Man defeated Virgil and Tito Santana, and Davey Boy Smith beat The Warlord. WWE did not hold another Tuesday night event until the interactive *Taboo Tuesday* in 2004.

2009 -

A *TLC* Match takes three of WWE's most dangerous elements and combines them all together in one death-defying clash. Over the years, it has produced jaw-dropping highlights as competitors vie to be the first to scale a ladder and grab the object of desire dangling from the rafters.

In 2009, WWE took the *TLC* concept and applied it across an entire evening. Now an annual December tradition, Superstars compete in a series of matches with one or more of these dangerous equalizers added to the fray.

More *TLC* moments:

◆ DX (Triple H and Shawn Michaels) wins the Unified Tag Team Titles for the first time (2009).

◆ Natalya and Beth Phoenix put Lay-Cool through the lumber in the first-ever Divas Tag Team Tables Match (2010).

◆ Zack Ryder completes an improbable run to his first singles gold by winning the United States Championship (2011).

◆ Randy Orton becomes the inaugural WWE World Heavyweight Champion (2013).

◆ Stairs are added to the chaos as Big Show beats Erick Rowan in the first-ever Steel Stairs Match (2014).

◆ The Wyatt Family stand tall over four ECW originals in an 8-Man Tables Match (2015).

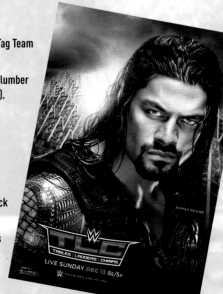

UNFORGIVEN

1998 - 2008

From grudges still simmering from *SummerSlam* to new and renewed hostilities over championships and more, sparks flew at *Unforgiven* for a solid decade. Originally an *In Your House* event, the first edition of *Unforgiven* set the tempo for the next ten years when Stone Cold Steve Austin defended the WWE Title against Dude Love, and Undertaker set his own brother, Kane, ablaze in an Inferno Match.

More *Unforgiven* moments:

◆ Al Snow defeated Big Bossman in a Kennel from Hell Match. The less said, the better (1999).

◆ Partners-turned-enemies, Christian and Edge, face each other for the Intercontinental Championship (2001.

◆ Shane McMahon leaps off the TitanTron (2003).

◆ John Cena AA's Edge off a ladder through two tables, Trish Stratus retires a seven-time Champion, and DX shoves Mr. McMahon's head into Big Show's backside (2006).

◆ Chris Jericho wins the World Heavyweight Championship as a last minute replacement in a Championship Scramble Match (2008).

2001-2007, 2011

In WWE, vengeance is best served cold, callous, merciless, and everything in between.

The first *Vengeance* event in 2001 featured a tournament to unify the WWE Championship and the WCW Championship, which arrived in WWE earlier in the year when WWE acquired WCW. It was a night that will forever live in infamy, as it was the night Chris Jericho became the first-ever undisputed champion by beating The Rock and Stone Cold in back-to-back matches.

In 2007, the event became *Vengeance: Night of Champions* (see *Night of Champions*) then the "Vengeance" was dropped. In 2011, *Vengeance* made its one-time return as a pay-per-view event.

More *Vengeance* moments:

◆ JBL cleans house in a Bar Room Brawl (2002).

◆ Batista overcomes Triple H inside Hell in a Cell (2005).

◆ The reunited DX sticks it to the Spirit Squad (2006).

◆ The force of Mark Henry's superplex to Big Show caves in the mat and collapses the ring posts. John Cena and Alberto Del Rio later compete for the WWE Championship inside the destroyed ring (2011).

1985

In hindsight, *The War to Settle the Score* was one of the great misnomers in sports-entertainment history. By night's end, all that was settled was that Roddy Piper and his cohorts were the antithesis to Hulk Hogan and his Rock 'n' Wrestling brigade. The one televised match, shown on MTV, pitted the bitter rivals against each other in a one-on-one match with Hogan's WWE Championship at stake. However, with Piper's resident goon, "Cowboy" Bob Orton, in his corner and Hogan's buddy Mr. T in the building, a fair fight with a clean conclusion was just not going to be an option.

Piper had long been the most vocal detractor to WWE's growing infusion of mainstream personalities into the mix. So disgusted was Piper that when he saw Captain Lou Albano embrace the idea and accept an award from pop sensation Cyndi Lauper, the ornery Scot stormed in and smashed the award over Albano's head. Lauper was knocked to the mat in the scrum, angering Hulk Hogan, who rushed in to clean house.

After a ten-match undercard that saw Lauper's friend Wendi Richter lose her Women's Championship to Leilani Kai, the pop star was back at ringside to support the Hulkster in his Title defense. During the main event clash, Paul Orndorff emerged and interfered on Piper's behalf along with Orton. This caused the match to end in disqualification and inspired Mr. T to jump the barrier to even the odds for the Hulkster in the post-match melee. To add further fuel to the fire, Cyndi Lauper sustained a kick in the fracas.

The score may have been far from settled, but *The War to Settle to Score* accomplished something far more important. It set the stage for Hogan and Mr T to team up against Piper and Orndorff in main event of the inaugural *WrestleMania*.

The Wrestling Classic

1985

The Wrestling Classic, also known as *WrestleVision*, was the first pay-per-view event WWE made available on a large scale (*WrestleMania* came first but was available in a limited number of markets). The event featured a 16-Superstar tournament including Adrian Adonis, Corporal Kirschner, Dynamite Kid, Nikolai Volkoff, Randy Savage, Ivan Putski, Ricky Steamboat, Davey Boy Smith, Junkyard Dog, Iron Sheik, Moondog Spot, Terry Funk, Tito Santana, the Magnificent Muraco, Paul Orndorff, and "Cowboy" Bob Orton. Junkyard Dog emerged victorious over Randy Savage at the end of the tournament with a hard-fought count-out victory.

The only match of the night that did not involve the tournament was a WWE Championship Match between Hulk Hogan and "Rowdy" Roddy Piper, who lost after being disqualified due to the interference of "Cowboy" Bob Orton.

2015

WWE Network aired an exclusive live show from historic Madison Square Garden in October 2015. The special event was hyped as part of Brock Lesnar's "Go to Hell" Tour and also served as a celebration of Chris Jericho's 25-year career in sports-entertainment.

Lesnar's opponent, Big Show, refused to be intimidated by the Beast Incarnate, but still ended up on the downtown express train to "Suplex City." Jericho's emotional night turned bittersweet when the brash Intercontinental Champion, Kevin Owens, pinned him to retain. Reigning United States Champion John Cena also retained his Title while paying the price for it in a brutal Steel Cage Match with Seth Rollins.

2016

Held just three weeks before *WrestleMania 32*, the first *WWE Roadblock* provided one final, unexpected barrier for those thought to be on the easy street to the Show of Shows. WWE World Heavyweight Champion Triple H accepted a challenge from Dean Ambrose, putting his spot in the *WrestleMania* main event in peril. Divas Champion Charlotte put her gold up for grabs as well against Natalya, who was sure to have her home Canadian crowd behind her. Brock Lesnar took on two members of the Wyatt Family and The New Day defended the WWE Tag Team Titles against the League of Nations.

All reigning Champions managed to escape the action-packed evening with their title reigns intact, setting the stage for a historic night at *WrestleMania 32*.

WRESTLEMANIA
see page 398

PETE DOHERTY

WT 232 lbs. **FROM** Dorchester, Massachusetts

Even in his heyday, the self-professed "Duke of Dorchester" owned one of the game's most unenviable losing streaks. In fact, during the mid-1980s, Pete Doherty competed in more than 300 WWE matches without a single win. It wasn't until 1987 that Doherty, empowered by the cheers of his hometown fans in Boston, finally defeated Lanny Poffo.

Unfortunately for "The Duke," his win failed to ignite a white-hot winning streak. Yet, despite his lackluster record, Doherty always maintained a big smile, sans several teeth.

Never lacking in personality, Doherty gave announcing a try after his days as a full-time wrestler ended, and he made occasional appearances on the Northeast's independent wrestling scene. In 2013, the New York Fringe Festival presented a play on Doherty's life.

PETE SANCHEZ

HT 6'0" **WT** 279 lbs. **FROM** San Juan, Puerto Rico
SIGNATURE MOVE Cannonball

A popular figure from the early days of WWE, Pete Sanchez was known throughout the northeast as a fiery competitor prominent in both singles and tag team competition. Through the 1960s and 1970s, Sanchez took on the likes of Crusher Verdu, the Mongols, Pampero Firpo, Stan "The Man" Stasiak, Gorilla Monsoon, Blackjack Mulligan, and "Superstar" Billy Graham. He even locked-up with Ric Flair in the "Nature Boy's" WWE and Madison Square Garden debut in 1976.

Sanchez was often on the losing side of the confrontation, but the disproportionate losses never diminished his determination. At one stage, he and Manuel Soto compiled a number of wins together.

Pete Sanchez continued to appear on WWE events until 1992, and remained one of the most respected journeymen to compete in the ring. Along with his opponents, Sanchez helped build the foundation of what today is the greatest sports-entertainment company in the world. With a career that spanned nearly three decades, Pete Sanchez's longevity in WWE is an accomplishment matched by few Superstars.

PETER MAIVIA

HT 5'9" **WT** 275 lbs. **FROM** The Isle of Samoa
SIGNATURE MOVE Samoan Stump Puller

Sports-entertainment has several influential families that have produced great competitors. Perhaps none is greater than the dynasty of High Chief Peter Maivia, whose wrestling family includes the famed Anoa'i clan, his son-in-law Rocky Johnson, and his grandson, The Rock.

In early 1960, Peter moved to New Zealand to train under Steve Rickard. Maivia's charisma, toughness, power, and speed led him to many Championships throughout the South Pacific. Maivia also made time for Hollywood as he appeared in the 1967 James Bond film, *You Only Live Twice*. He arrived on the American mainland in 1970 and held different versions of the NWA World Tag Team Titles with Chief Billy White Wolf, Ray Stevens, and Pat Patterson.

After a brief stop in Texas, Maivia debuted in WWE in 1977. Fans were drawn to his ring presence and his ancient Samoan tribal tattoos. Maivia was a genuine Samoan High Chief and fought for the pride of his people every time that he entered the ring. In 1978 Maivia broke the hearts of people everywhere when he turned on friends Chief Jay Strongbow and Bob Backlund. Managed by "Classy" Freddie Blassie, Maivia became one of the most despised men in all of sports-entertainment. He later became a promoter in Hawaii.

Sadly, Maivia was diagnosed with cancer in 1981, and passed away in June 1982 at the age of 45.

PEZ WHATLEY

HT 5'10" **WT** 245 lbs. **FROM** Chattanooga, Tennessee
SIGNATURE MOVE The Flying Headbutt

This Superstar and "Pistol" was the first-ever African American amateur wrestler at the University of Tennessee at Chattanooga. After competing in a number of territories, Whatley made his WWE debut in 1990 and brought the fight to Superstars like "Ravishing" Rick Rude, "Million Dollar Man" Ted DiBiase, Tito Santana, "Rowdy" Roddy Piper, and Mr. Perfect.

Pez left WWE in March of 1991, and returned to the ring in Japan and American independents before landing in WCW. He retired from active competition in 1995 and became a trainer at WCW's Power Plant.

Sadly, in January 2005, Pez passed away following complications from a heart attack. Pez Whatley will always be regarded as one of the toughest and most entertaining individuals in all of sports-entertainment history.

PG-13

MEMBERS J.C. Ice & Wolfie D **COMBINED WT** 410 lbs.

As members of the Nation of Domination, J.C. Ice and Wolfie D had one job—recite threatening rap lyrics while Faarooq, D-Lo Brown, and the rest of the Nation made their way to the ring.

On rare occasions, PG-13 would put their microphones down long enough to actually compete. But at a total combined weight of approximately 400 pounds, they proved to be a less-than-formidable duo.

Outside of WWE, J.C. Ice and Wolfie D were able to attain great success as a tag team, particularly in the Memphis-based United States Wrestling Association. From 1993 to 1997, the undersized rappers claimed the organization's tag Titles fifteen times.

PG-13 also made a few appearances in WCW during the promotion's waning days, competing mainly on *Thunder*.

PHANTASIO

| HT | 6'3" | WT | 235 lbs. |

A master illusionist, Phantasio made his WWE debut on *Wrestling Challenge* in July 1995. Following a few awe-inspiring magic tricks, including turning a candle into a walking stick, the WWE newcomer made short work of his opposition, Tony DeVito. After the match, the magic continued when Phantasio mysteriously removed the referee's striped underwear, despite the fact that the official was still wearing his pants.

With a perfect 1-0 professional record to his credit, Phantasio strangely disappeared from WWE, never to be seen again. While nobody knows for sure, legend claims he was the victim of an elaborate magic trick gone bad.

THE PITBULLS

| MEMBERS | Kid Kash & Jamie Noble | COMBINED WT | 402 lbs. |

In June 2006, two former Cruiserweight Champions joined forces to ambush the tag team division on *SmackDown*. Wearing dog collars, barking and attacking anything that moved, these Pitbulls were vicious and hungry for meat. While being aggressive and showing no regard for the rules of the ring, Kash and Noble also displayed great speed and teamwork.

They battled the Mexicools and then-WWE Tag Team Champions Brian Kendrick and Paul London, and appeared to be Title contenders. However, Kid Kash left WWE that September. While some fans were disappointed that the team never realized their full potential, tag teams throughout WWE were relieved they no longer had to worry about the bite of the Pitbulls.

PJ WALKER

| HT | 6'0" | WT | 229 lbs. | FROM | New York, New York |
| SIGNATURE MOVE | Superkick |

Identified as a top prospect in the early 1990s, PJ Walker was seen on *Monday Night Raw* and *Wrestling Challenge*. Walker was an accomplished grappler with speed, grit, and superior ring technique thanks to his training in Stu Hart's Dungeon.

As fans chanted his name, PJ took on anyone who had an open contract including Diesel, Yokozuna, Jeff Jarrett, Bam Bam Bigelow, and Undertaker. The highlight of his WWE tenure was when he beat Irwin R. Schyster on *Raw*. However, Walker's tenure was short-lived as he left WWE in early 1994 to pursue other professional endeavors.

POWER AND GLORY

| MEMBERS | Hercules & Paul Roma | COMBINED WT | 519 lbs. |

The "Doctor of Style," Slick brought a new era to tag team competition in July, 1990 when the mighty Hercules merged with Roma. It was Hercules who represented power, while the handsome Roma signified glory. Breaking the rules, the pair told off fans and former friends and lived by the motto, "nice guys finish last."

Hercules and Roma were devastating together in the ring, as they battled for supremacy and the WWE World Tag Team Championship. They clashed with the likes of the Rockers, the Hart Foundation, and the Legion of Doom. Power and Glory often teamed in six-man action with another Slick client, the Warlord. After disappointing losses and mounting frustration, the pair split in 1991.

POWERS OF PAIN

| MEMBERS | Warlord & Barbarian | COMBINED WT | 618 lbs. |

The story of the Powers of Pain is puzzling. They had the look. They had the size. They even had the speed. But despite all this, they never had WWE gold.

Warlord and Barbarian joined WWE in 1988, following a very successful year in NWA's Mid-Atlantic territory. Managed by the Baron, they became favorites with the fans, who were enamored by their immense size and colorful face paint. The team's popularity propelled them into a lengthy rivalry with the World Tag Team Champions, Demolition.

Following several unsuccessful attempts to wrest the gold from Ax and Smash, the Powers of Pain lured Mr. Fuji to their side. Bringing the devious manager into their camp proved unpopular with fans, but Warlord and Barbarian saw it as an opportunity to capture the elusive tag Titles. Unfortunately, however, not even Fuji could lead the Powers of Pain to gold.

In 1990, after failing to achieve success with Warlord and Barbarian, Fuji sold them separately to Slick and Bobby Heenan respectively. The sale marked the end of the Powers of Pain.

PMS

| MEMBERS | Terri, Jacqueline, & Ryan Shamrock |

Fresh off unsuccessful romances with Marc Mero and Goldust respectively, Jacqueline and Terri joined forces in November 1998 to exact revenge on WWE's male Superstars. Calling themselves Pretty Mean Sisters, they used their sensuality as a weapon and their sex appeal to get what they wanted from male Superstars.

The duo's first victim, Val Venis, was told he had impregnated Terri, which caused the former adult film star to run for the hills. PMS, however, was not done milking the pregnancy for all it was worth. Shortly after Terri announced she was with child, D'Lo Brown accidentally knocked the mother-to-be off the ring apron, causing her to apparently miscarry (it was later revealed that she was never pregnant in the first place). As payback, PMS forced Brown to be their servant.

The following year, Ryan Shamrock joined the sexually-charged faction. Together, the threesome adopted Meat as their boy toy. They worked the young Superstar so hard that he was too exhausted when it came time to compete, which might explain his lackluster win-loss record.

PRIME TIME PLAYERS

MEMBERS	Darren Young & Titus O'Neil
COMBINED WT	509 lbs.

When John Laurinaitis signed Darren Young and Titus O'Neil to *SmackDown* in April 2012, few knew what to expect from the arrogant newcomers claiming to be worth "millions of dollars." But after defeating The Usos in their debut match, the Prime Time Players proved they were among WWE's most elite tag teams.

It wasn't until mid-May that Young and O'Neil suffered their first loss, which failed to derail the confident duo, who went on to earn multiple Championship opportunities.

Despite the numerous chances, the Prime Time Players were unable to capture the Titles, which began to frustrate O'Neil. Finally in January 2014, O'Neil's frustrations led to him viciously attacking Young, marking the end of the Prime Time Players.

After a brief rivalry, O'Neil and Young went their separate ways. But they would eventually reunite in 2015 when O'Neil saved Young from an attack at the hands of The Ascension.

Together again, the Prime Time Players went on to achieve great success, including capturing the WWE Tag Team Championship when they defeated The New Day in June 2015.

PRIMO

HT	5'10"	WT	218 lbs.
FROM	San Juan, Puerto Rico		

As the younger brother of former WWE Superstar Carlito and son of Puerto Rican wrestling legend Carlos Colon, Primo entered WWE in 2008 with great expectations, and he didn't disappoint.

Only one month after making his successful debut against Charlie Haas, the agile Puerto Rican Superstar teamed with his brother to capture the WWE Tag Team Championship from Zack Ryder and Curt Hawkins. In the wake of losing the Titles in the summer of 2009, however, Primo found himself the victim of an inexplicable attack from his older brother. Despite the ugly assault, Primo later decided to rejoin Carlito, much to the fans' displeasure.

Proving that familial roots run deep, Primo began teaming with cousin Epico in 2011. With Rosa Mendes as their manager, the duo defeated Air Boom to claim the WWE Tag Team Championship in January 2012. Early the following year, Primo and Epico mysteriously disappeared from WWE. They reemerged, however, in 2016 as The Shining Stars.

PRINCESS VICTORIA

HT	5'8"
FROM	Canada

Even the greatest of Champions lose their Titles eventually. Unless, of course, you're Princess Victoria.

With partner Velvet McIntyre, Victoria proudly represented WWE as one-half of the first-ever Women's Tag Team Champions. But in September 1984, the popular trailblazer suffered a broken neck, effectively ending her promising career and forcing her to vacate her half of the Tag Titles. She was later replaced by Desiree Peterson.

Prior to WWE, Victoria and McIntyre were recognized by the NWA as the promotion's Women's Tag Team Champions. They defeated Joyce Grable and Wendi Richter for the Titles in 1983. Victoria held the same Titles with Sabrina one year earlier. That victory also came at the expense of Grable and Richter.

PROFESSOR TORU TANAKA

HT	5'11"	WT	280 lbs.
FROM	Hiroshima, Japan		

Famed manager Wild Red Berry lured Japanese powerhouse Toru Tanaka to the United States in the late 1960s. The barrel-chested Superstar from the Land of the Rising Sun reveled in his role as the evil foreigner. In fact, Tanaka often incited fans by using ceremonial Japanese salt as a blinding weapon.

Tanaka achieved most of his notoriety competing in the tag team ranks. With Mr. Fuji as his partner, Tanaka became a three-time World Tag Team Champion. The duo's first and lengthiest reign came after defeating Chief Jay Strongbow and Sonny King in June 1972. The pair went on to hold the Titles for nearly a full year.

As a singles competitor, Tanaka earned opportunities against WWE Champions Bruno Sammartino, Pedro Morales, and Bob Backlund. After retiring from the ring in the early 1980s, the Superstar parlayed his natural charisma into a successful movie career, appearing in *Pee Wee's Big Adventure*, *The Running Man*, and *The Last Action Hero*.

Professor Tanaka died in 2000.

PUBLIC ENEMY

| MEMBERS | Johnny Grunge & Flyboy Rocco | FROM | South Philly | COMBINED WT | 487 lbs. |

Johnny Grunge and Flyboy Rocco lived by one simple philosophy—if it ain't broke, break it! Collectively known as Public Enemy, Grunge and Rocco had an affinity for destruction, particularly when it came to tables. In fact, the duo from South Philly commonly carried tables to the ring with the sole intention of sending their opposition through the wooden furniture.

Upon arriving in WWE in 1999, Public Enemy earned an early disqualification victory over The Brood on *Raw*. Unfortunately for Grunge and Rocco, that's where the winning stopped. They soon found themselves on the wrong end of matches against the Hardys, Owen Hart and Jeff Jarrett, and APA, who boast they ran Public Enemy out of WWE only a few months after their debut.

Prior to WWE, Grunge and Rocco made a name for themselves obliterating the competition in ECW. Four ECW Tag Team Championship reigns later, they jumped to WCW, where they claimed the WCW Tag Team Titles from Harlem Heat in September 1996.

"THE PUG" ALEX PORTEAU

| HT | 5'10" | WT | 226 lbs. | FROM | New Orleans, Louisiana |
| SIGNATURE MOVE | The Pugbomb |

From The Big Easy, Alex Porteau started his career in the late 1980s in Fritz Von Erich's World Class Championship Wrestling. After a short tenure in World Championship Wrestling he spent the early 1990s in the GWF and Carlos Colon's World Wrestling Council. Porteau's power and technical skills earned him the opportunity to grapple with the best sports-entertainment had to offer.

In 1996 "The Pug" debuted in WWE and was a quick hit with fans everywhere. Alex battled all comers including Goldust, Mankind, Faarooq, Justin Bradshaw, the Sultan, Aldo Montoya, and Vader. He was a top contender for the Intercontinental Championship until he left WWE in early 1997. Since, then he has appeared on wrestling cards in United States, Puerto Rico, and Japan.

THE QUEBECERS

| MEMBERS | Jacques & Pierre |
| COMBINED WT | 479 lbs. |

Managed by the obnoxious Johnny Polo, the Quebecers joined the WWE ranks in 1993. They quickly became Tag Team Title contenders known for their rule-breaking ways, their manager interfering in matches, and their abilities in the ring.

On an episode of *Monday Night Raw* they challenged the Steiner Brothers for the World Tag Team Championship under Province of Quebec Rules, which meant that the Titles could change hands even on a disqualification. That minor change resulted in a victory when Scott Steiner lost his cool and nailed Johnny Polo with a hockey stick.

The Quebecers held the Titles until January 1994, and would hold them two more times before splitting in 1994 after a disappointing loss to the Headshrinkers. In the following two-year span, both men left WWE. They returned in 1998 where they competed in the Tag Team Battle Royal at *WrestleMania XIV*.

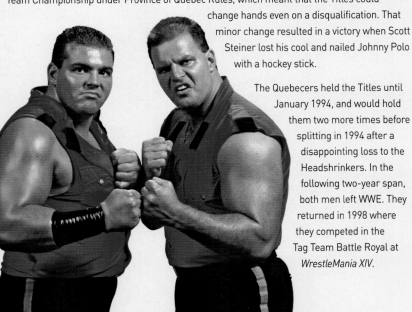

"QUICKDRAW" RICK MCGRAW

| HT | 5'7" | WT | 235 lbs. | FROM | Charlotte, North Carolina |

After a career as a stand-out talent in the Florida and Mid-South territories during the 1970's, Rick McGraw debuted in WWE in May, 1980. His explosive style and power made him an instant hit with the fans. Weeks later he debuted at Madison Square Garden and that energy carried him to the August *Showdown at Shea*, where he locked-up with Greg Gagne.

McGraw often teamed with Steve Travis and with Andre the Giant on two occasions, against the Moondogs and the Wild Samoans. On his own, "Quickdraw" faced the likes of Ken Patera, Bulldog Brower, Tor Kamata, Killer Kahn, Johnny Rodz, Baron Mikel Scicluna, and Harley Race.

Tragically, as McGraw's star was on the rise, he passed away in November, 1985.

RAD RADFORD

| HT | 5'11" | WT | 264 lbs. | FROM | Seattle, Washington |
| SIGNATURE MOVE | Northern Lights Suplex |

Rad Radford left his home in Seattle to become a WWE Superstar in 1995. A fan of grunge music, the flannel-clad Superstar certainly danced to the beat of his own drum. But inside the ring, he was just as sound as the most accomplished Superstar on the roster.

Armed with a devastating Northern Lights Suplex finisher, Radford picked up many wins early in his WWE stay, including victories over Jeff Hardy and Jerry Lynn. While impressive, Radford wanted to be known for more than just in-ring success; he also desired an amazing physique. That's when he turned to Skip and Sunny of the Bodydonnas. The fitness gurus agreed to take Radford on as a Bodydonna-in-training, but eventually fired the rotund Superstar after he failed to make any progress. Radford left WWE soon after.

THE RADICALZ

| MEMBERS | Chris Benoit, Eddie Guerrero, Dean Malenko, & Perry Saturn |

In one of the most noted talent jumps in history, Eddie Guerrero, Chris Benoit, Dean Malenko, and Perry Saturn moved en masse from WCW to WWE. Collectively known as The Radicalz, the foursome was displeased with WCW's lackluster direction in 2000. Despite Benoit being recognized as the WCW World Heavyweight Champion, the group opted to jump ship. WWE cameras soon caught them sitting in the front row at WWE events and it wasn't long before they jumped the barrier to the ring with dreams of superstardom.

Each member of the Radicalz enjoyed decorated careers. Together, however, their success was fleeting. The group only lasted a few months and would reunite on occasion. At *Survivor Series 2000*, they turned back the team of Road Dogg, Billy Gunn, K-Kwik and Chyna.

RANDY ORTON

HT	6'5"
WT	250 lbs.
FROM	St. Louis, Missouri

SIGNATURE MOVE
RKO

At birth, Randy Orton was bestowed with the natural gifts needed to do it all in sports-entertainment—and he has. Still going strong after well over a decade, this third-generation competitor boasts twelve World Championships, *WrestleMania* main events, a Royal Rumble victory, and countless other accolades.

The son of "Cowboy" Bob Orton and grandson of "The Big O" Bob Orton, Randy grew up rubbing elbows with some of WWE's most legendary figures. He knew he was destined for greatness and set out to prove it when he debuted in WWE in April 2002. It did not take long for his Hall of Fame bloodline and undeniable talents to have some of WWE's most influential minds taking notice.

EVOLUTION

Triple H recruited Randy to his Evolution faction. The third-generation Superstar represented the future of WWE alongside Batista. Under Triple H's wing, Orton won the Intercontinental Championship from Rob Van Dam in December 2003. His first Title reign lasted an impressive seven months and fanned the flames of his already cocky demeanor. He earned the nickname "Legend Killer" for his disturbing obsession with exterminating the greats of WWE's past.

Orton took a giant step toward becoming an all-time great himself at *SummerSlam 2004* when he captured the World Heavyweight Championship. At just 24 years of age, he was the youngest Superstar to ever hold the gold. This overachieving earned him a callous dismissal from Evolution by an envious Triple H.

VIPER

At *No Mercy 2005*, Orton and his father locked Undertaker inside a wooden casket and set it ablaze. This shocking act is just one example of the sordid depths to which Randy would stoop to eradicate all who stood in the way of his destiny. It was no surprise that he found a common bond with Edge. The likeminded Superstars struck tag team gold as the diabolical Rated RKO before resuming their World Title pursuits. Like Edge, Randy's most consistent obstacle to WWE's apex was John Cena. Orton put Cena out of action in October 2007 with a sickening RKO atop an announcer's table.

With Cena out of the way, Randy renewed hostilities with Triple H. Riding a rollercoaster of emotions at *No Mercy 2007*, Orton and The Game traded victories for the WWE Championship with Orton standing tall after the nightcap, slinging the Title over his tattooed shoulder. This crazy night ushered in the "Age of Orton," as The Viper ran roughshod over a litany of challengers. Over the next few years, he and Triple H continued their war over the WWE Championship, including main event matches at *WrestleMania XXIV* and *WrestleMania 25*.

By 2009, Randy's merciless disposition reached disturbing new depths. He chalked up his reptilian deeds, such as punting the entire McMahon family, to a bout of Intermittent Explosive Disorder. He won the Royal Rumble that year and though he fell short at *WrestleMania*, he had only begun committing atrocities. During a brutal series of WWE Championship Matches against John Cena, his vicious tactics were enough to dethrone his rival inside Hell in a Cell.

LEGACY

Along the way, Orton forged a partnership with fellow multi-generational Superstars Cody Rhodes and Ted DiBiase. Collectively known as Legacy, the Orton-led alliance dominated WWE, picking up wins over Triple H, Batista, and Shane McMahon, among others.

Part of the secret to Legacy's success was Rhodes and DiBiase's willingness to sacrifice themselves for Orton's greater good. But when the young duo's interference became more of a hindrance to Orton, Legacy began to crumble. In the end, Orton proved his superiority over his former allies, defeating them in a Triple Threat Match at *WrestleMania XXVI*.

On his own, Orton continued to shine as one of WWE's brightest stars. He pinned Sheamus to claim his sixth WWE Championship in September 2010. And later, he defeated CM Punk at *WrestleMania XXVII*, but not before punting nearly every member of Punk's Nexus to the sidelines.

Orton's amazing momentum continued into May 2011, when he defeated Christian to capture his second World Heavyweight Championship. A few months later at *SummerSlam*, he topped Christian again for the same Title.

FACE OF WWE

Orton lost the gold to Mark Henry at *Night of Champions 2011*, initiating a period that, by his lofty standards, represented a rut. He was thrown down a flight of stairs by Wade Barrett to close 2011.

IT'S NOT ARROGANCE. IT'S JUST DESTINY.

During the eighteen months that followed, he was defeated by Kane at *WrestleMania XXVIII* and was on the downside of a Six-Man Tag Team Match against The Shield at *WrestleMania 29*. Randy had his moments but saw the World Heavyweight Championship scene dominated by Big Show, Daniel Bryan, and Sheamus.

Determined to reignite the "Age of Orton," Randy climbed past five Superstars at *Money in the Bank 2013* to earn WWE's most coveted Title opportunity. One month later at *SummerSlam*, The Apex Predator received a shocking assist from WWE COO Triple H, who Pedigreed a celebrating Daniel Bryan to allow Orton to slither to the ring and claim his tenth World Championship.

Handpicked as the "Face of WWE" by one of his most longstanding foes Orton became The Authority's golden child. With corporate powers endorsing him as the industry's ideal representative, Orton proved his worth in a historic showdown at *TLC 2013*. Facing John Cena in a TLC Match, the two arch nemeses put their respective World Championships on the line. With each man carrying a century's worth of Championship legacies on his back, it was Orton who prevailed. The landmark victory unified the revered Titles and made Randy the inaugural WWE World Heavyweight Champion.

Orton's newfound bond with Triple H led to the reformation of Evolution in 2014. Back together after nearly ten years, the insidious group waged war with The Shield until Seth Rollins sold out to join Orton on the side of The Authority.

Soon it became clear that both Orton and Rollins could not coexist in the same unit. The writing was on the wall that Rollins was being groomed as Randy's replacement. After a bitter divorce from The Authority, Randy gave the bosses reason to second-guess themselves when he topped Rollins in an intense match at *WrestleMania 31*. He fell short in a rematch with Rollins at *Extreme Rules 2015* when The Authority banned his RKO maneuver.

As he continues to build on his monumental legacy, no one can predict Randy Orton's next move. He is still as cold-blooded as ever, leaving every Superstar in WWE leery of an "RKO outta nowhere."

RANDY SAVAGE

see page 280

RANJIN SINGH

The Great Khali is as incoherent to the WWE Universe as he is monstrous. Fortunately, Ranjin Singh arrived in 2007 to articulate every dangerous message from the menacing "Punjabi Nightmare."

As Khali's spokesperson, Singh took pleasure in delivering ominous warnings, as if his words packed the same pulverizing power as his 7-foot client. Singh managed Khali to a World Title reign in July 2007 and guided Khali to another WWE Championship opportunity at *SummerSlam 2008*, where he lost a hard-fought battle against Triple H.

Soon after, Singh premiered the "Khali Kiss Cam," unveiling the giant's endless supply of affection. Seeing Khali smooching with Divas and female spectators softened former perceptions of the big man, earning Khali the new moniker of "The Punjabi Playboy."

On a 2009 *SmackDown*, Kane held Singh hostage backstage where the terrified manager revealed he was actually Khali's brother. Although the meddlesome Jinder Mahal caused a strain in their relationship in 2011, the siblings were able to patch things up. Ranjin Singh's legacy lives on as the "Punjabi John Stamos" is always ready to make a return to the Squared Circle.

RAVEN

| HT | 6'1" | WT | 235 lbs. | FROM | The Bowery |
| SIGNATURE MOVE | | | Evenflow DDT | | |

Despite a privileged childhood, Raven grew to be a very troubled adult. Suffering from deep mental anguish, he used the memories of what he believed was a turbulent past as the inspiration to create a disturbing career in sports-entertainment.

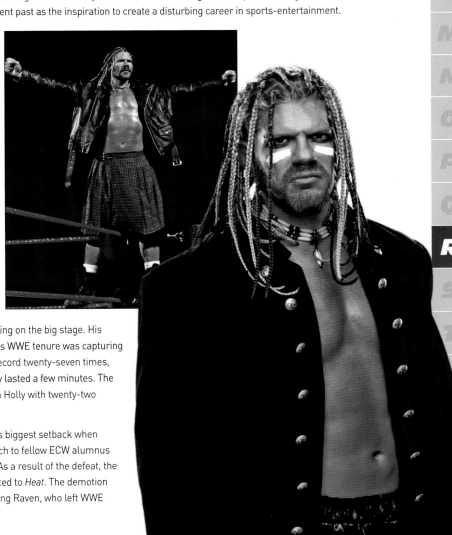

During the mid-to-late 1990s, Raven was recognized as one of the industry's up-and-coming stars. His dark persona intrigued fans, while his in-ring ability carried him to many prestigious accolades, including the ECW Championship and WCW United States Championship. His successes eventually caught the eye of WWE officials, who lured him into their fold in 2000.

As a WWE Superstar, big things were expected from Raven. Unfortunately, however, he was only able to achieve mediocre success while competing on the big stage. His greatest claim to fame during his WWE tenure was capturing the Hardcore Championship a record twenty-seven times, although many of his reigns only lasted a few minutes. The next closest to Raven was Crash Holly with twenty-two Hardcore Championship reigns.

Raven's WWE career suffered its biggest setback when he lost a Loser Leaves *Raw* Match to fellow ECW alumnus Tommy Dreamer in June 2002. As a result of the defeat, the troubled Superstars was relegated to *Heat*. The demotion did little to motivate the struggling Raven, who left WWE completely shortly after.

RANDY "MACHO MAN" SAVAGE

HT	6'2"
WT	237 lbs.
FROM	Sarasota, Florida

SIGNATURE MOVE
Flying Elbow Drop

Known for his unmistakable raspy voice and twitchy mannerisms, Randy "Macho Man" Savage was endowed with a primal magnetism that forced both supporters and detractors to watch his every move. In the course of his 32 years in the ring, he held a total of 20 Titles, including the WWE World Heavyweight Championship twice and WCW crown on four separate occasions.

Randy inherited both his toughness and savvy about the inner workings of the business from his father, Angelo Poffo, who set a world record for doing 6,033 sit-ups in 1945, and at one point was managed by Bobby "The Brain" Heenan. Still, Savage first aspired to be a baseball player, hitting .254 during four minor league seasons in the St. Louis Cardinals, Cincinnati Reds, and Chicago White Sox organizations. At one point, he painstakingly learned to throw left-handed. When asked why, he answered, "Making myself more valuable."

In 1973, Savage began wrestling, but opted to hide his identity from baseball executives. Coming to the ring in a white mask, Savage called himself The Spider. He was relatively lanky at the time, but drew attention by frantically bouncing off the ropes before the bell even rang.

When his minor league career ended, he made a clean break, destroying his bats and dedicating himself completely to sports-entertainment. After seeing him compete in the Georgia territory, competitor Ole Anderson told him that he wrestled "like a savage." Randy decided to use the term as a surname, and added "Macho Man" to his moniker after his mother, Judy, read an article that listed the expression as a new, popular term.

Along with brother, Lanny Poffo—also known as "The Genius"—Savage main evented for his father's renegade International Championship Wrestling (ICW) group. After a number of confrontations with wrestlers from the rival Memphis territory, Randy and Lanny staged an invasion of the established promotion. During one memorable conflict with the Rock 'n' Roll Express, Savage injured Ricky Morton by piledriving him through the announcer's table. But after losing a "Loser Leaves Town" conflict to Jerry Lawler, Savage, along with his brother, ventured to WWE.

Managers "Classy" Freddie Blassie, Bobby "The Brain" Heenan, "Mouth of the South" Jimmy Hart, Captain Lou Albano, and Mr. Fuji immediately stepped forward with offers to advise the industry's most coveted free agent. Shocking the world, Savage instead chose the demurely beautiful but unknown Miss Elizabeth.

Savage came to the ring to the song "Pomp and Circumstance," dressed in extravagant sequined robes, headbands, and wrap-around sunglasses.

The "Macho Man" served notice to all that he was an elite talent when he reached the finals of the company's first post-*WrestleMania* pay-per-view, *The Wrestling Classic*.

On February 8, 1986, he used a foreign object to defeat Tito Santana for the Intercontinental Championship. The "Macho Man" did everything imaginable to keep his Championship, even if it meant putting Miss Elizabeth in front of him. Savage's next opponent was more interested in his gorgeous manager than defeating him in the ring. At one stage, George "The Animal" Steele picked up Elizabeth and attempted to take her "into protective custody." But Savage vanquished Steele at *WrestleMania 2*.

In November 1986, "Macho Madness" took a dangerous turn when he crushed the larynx of Ricky Steamboat with the timekeeper's bell and put Steamboat out of commission for months. Upon Steamboat's return, a Championship rematch was signed for *WrestleMania III*. Despite the fact that Savage lost, this contest is regarded as one of the greatest matches in sports-entertainment history.

Months after this epic battle, Savage was the victim of an attack by The Honky Tonk Man and The Hart Foundation. One of the most thrilling moments in WWE history followed as Elizabeth rushed backstage looking for help and appeared with Hulk Hogan.

"Macho Madness" and Hulkamania now joined forces. As Randy mowed through the WWE Championship tournament at *WrestleMania IV*, the Hulkster was ringside for the final to watch Savage's back. With a capacity crowd on its feet, "Macho Man" dropped his famous elbow on "Million Dollar Man" Ted DiBiase and became the WWE Champion.

Miscommunication and misunderstandings led to Savage attacking Hulk Hogan in the locker room after a match against The Twin Towers, Akeem and Big Boss Man. This resulted in the Mega Powers exploding on each other at *WrestleMania V*. In one of the more hotly anticipated matches in *WrestleMania* history, Hogan defeated Savage for the Title.

MACHO ROYALTY

Savage began the new decade with a new valet, Sensational Sherri. The two became royalty when he beat Hacksaw "King" Duggan and became the "Macho King." After a series of matches against Dusty Rhodes, Savage turned his attention to Ultimate Warrior. The two met in a Retirement Match at *WrestleMania VII*, which Savage lost. Frustrated, Sherri attacked her fallen client, but was chased off by a returning Miss Elizabeth. The two reunited in a wash of emotion and married in what was dubbed a "Match Made in Heaven" at *SummerSlam 1991*. The heartfelt ceremony turned frightful when Jake Roberts presented a wrapped gift that contained a deadly king cobra, which bit Savage. After being reinstated by WWE President Jack Tunney, Savage defeated Roberts on NBC's *Saturday Night's Main Event*.

Savage was once again tested as Ric Flair made scandalous remarks about a one-time relationship with Miss Elizabeth. At *WrestleMania VIII*, "Macho Man" not only cleared the name of his wife, but he defeated Flair to become WWE Champion for the second time.

Randy then made the move to the broadcast booth for WWE programs, including the very first episode of *Monday Night Raw* in 1993 and *WrestleMania IX*. At *WrestleMania X*, he defeated former pupil Crush in a "Falls Count Anywhere" Match.

In 1994, Savage—frustrated that he was spending more time at the announcer's table and less in the ring—signed with WCW. He immediately continued his war with Ric Flair, a situation that worsened when the "Nature Boy" attacked Angelo Poffo. Nevertheless, success came quickly to the Macho Man. He won the 60-Man Battle Royal at the 1995 pay-per-view, *World War 3*, for the vacant WCW Title. This would be the first of his four Championships in the promotion.

Savage then briefly united with Miss Elizabeth, but she betrayed him for Flair, who claimed that the manager regaled him with money she received in her divorce settlement from Savage. After first battling the nWo, Savage joined the faction. As the group became larger, Savage and others splintered off to form the nWo Wolfpac. Before leaving the company in 1999, Savage and three female valets started a unit called Team Madness.

IMMORTALIZED

Following the end of WCW, Randy made his Hollywood debut as "Bonesaw McGraw" in the 2002 blockbuster *Spider-Man*. In 2003, he released his rap album *Be a Man*. In 2010, "Macho Man" was included as a part of Mattel's WWE Legends Series, his first WWE figure in over 15 years.

Randy "Macho Man" Savage is revered as one of the greatest figures in all of sports-entertainment and a true legend in the ring. Sadly, on May 20, 2011, he was driving with his second wife, Lynn, in Seminole, Florida when he crashed into a tree. Doctors determined that the 58-year-old legend had suffered a fatal heart attack.

People in the wrestling, baseball, and entertainment communities paid tribute to the Macho Man. But fans were bewildered that he hadn't been chosen for the WWE Hall of Fame. Although Randy's family had been approached about an induction, there was one holdup. Before his death, Savage had specified that his brother and father be included with him. As the demand for immortalization increased, Savage's brother agreed that Savage should be inducted alone, saying the honor was not just for "the Macho Man, but the Macho Fan."

In an emotional ceremony in 2015, Lanny Poffo accepted his brother's WWE Hall of Fame plaque, paying homage not only to Randy's in-ring accomplishments, but his relatively unpublicized charity work, particularly Savage's devotion to the Special Olympics athletes he'd grown to love.

"RAVISHING" RICK RUDE

HT	6'3"	WT	252 lbs.	FROM	Robbinsdale, Minnesota
SIGNATURE MOVE		The Rude Awakening			

"Cut the music!"

Rick Rude demanded silence from what he observed as "sweat hogs" in attendance while he disrobed and unveiled his rippling physique. Whether fans booed, blushed, or did both at the same time, no one could resist feasting their eyes on this impressive, albeit arrogant Superstar.

Before arriving in WWE, Rude was a noted arm wrestler who developed his professional wrestling skills in various regional promotions. In 1985, he traveled to World Class Championship Wrestling where he became the promotion's first World Champion after it withdrew from the NWA.

In 1987, the self-proclaimed "Sexiest Man Alive" debuted in WWE as a member of the Heenan Family and began demeaning fans and flaunting his masculinity on a nightly basis. After victories courtesy of the "Rude Awakening" neckbreaker, Rick selected a woman from the crowd and administered his other version of this maneuver, a kiss that often left the ladies breathless on the mat. This routine infuriated Jake Roberts when Rude unwittingly targeted Jake's wife. Not to be deterred, Rude took it a step further by having the lovely Cheryl's image airbrushed onto his tights.

As his unrelenting vanity rolled through WWE, he won the Jesse "The Body" award at that year's Slammy's. Rude held the Intercontinental Championship for four months in 1989 after defeating Ultimate Warrior. Shortly after challenging Warrior inside a Steel Cage at *SummerSlam 1990* for the WWE Championship, Rude left WWE.

In the years that followed, Rude displayed a penchant for doing the unexpected. First, he arrived in *ECW* in 1996 during Jerry "The King" Lawler's crusade against the renegade promotion. In 1997, he re-emerged in WWE as the insurance policy for DX but made history that November when he appeared on *Raw* and *WCW Monday Nitro* in the same evening!

Sadly, this true WWE legend passed away in 1999. "Ravishing" Rick Rude was one of the most infamous villains of all-time. With an incredible physique and the unparalleled athleticism needed to use it, he broke hearts wherever he went in the world. To those who knew him and to those who watched him, Rick Rude was simply "Ravishing."

RAY MORGAN

Sitting at ringside, sometimes with a cigarette in hand, Ray Morgan conducted his chores as announcer for WWE's early matches from Washington, DC's National Arena with the seriousness of a news commentator.

Previously, Morgan read live commercials on stage during broadcasts of Ed Sullivan's celebrated variety show. Aided by ring announcers "Friendly" Bob Freed and "Smiling" Sam Mason, Morgan was a welcome on-air presence, as he ran down the matchups for the evening, critically assessed the action, and reminded viewers to "make defensive driving a habit."

Morgan is credited with labeling Johnny Valentine's finisher the "Atomic Skull Crusher." Confrontations with loud tormentors like Killer Kowalski and manager Bobby Davis were handled with distinction. Morgan stayed with WWE until 1971, when the Washington broadcasts ended.

RAY STEVENS
see page 283

RAZOR RAMON/SCOTT HALL
see page 284

THE REAL AMERICANS

MEMBERS	Jack Swagger & Cesaro	**COMBINED WT**	507 lbs.

Looking to resuscitate his career in late 2012, Jack Swagger turned to the radical ideals of Zeb Colter. With Zeb's controversial viewpoints drilled into his head, a more aggressive Swagger took his nationalistic vision of a "Real American" to WWE rings.

Old Zeb came across as xenophobic to some, which made it surprising when Colter brought the Swiss Superstar Cesaro into his fold in June 2013. As "The Real Americans," Cesaro and Swagger waved a Gadsden flag as a symbol of their campaign to revolutionize WWE. For nearly nine months, they took on all threats, both foreign and domestic, but never won tag team gold. The night after a loss at *WrestleMania 30*, Cesaro declared independence from their union to become a "Paul Heyman guy."

REBECCA DIPIETRO

Following an eye-opening appearance in the 2006 *Raw* Diva Search, Rebecca DiPietro returned to WWE as a backstage interviewer for ECW. She only held the position briefly before being released by WWE; but during her time, she managed to ask the tough questions to such top ECW Superstars as Bobby Lashley, Big Show, and Rob Van Dam.

Rebecca enjoyed a successful modeling career prior to entering sports-entertainment. She has appeared in the pages of *Maxim* and *Stuff* magazines, among others. She also landed on the small screen as part of the *Wild On...* series on E! and gained notoriety as the 2005 Miss Hawaiian Tropic USA. After leaving WWE, Rebecca won the Miss MET-RX Model Search in 2008.

RAY "THE CRIPPLER" STEVENS

HT 5'8" **WT** 235 lbs. **FROM** San Francisco, California
SIGNATURE MOVE Bombs Away Knee-Drop

The man who first became known as "The Blonde Bomber" began his career as a teenager in 1950. Stevens' early dastardly acts made him one of the most loathed men in the business.

In 1961, San Francisco promoter Roy Shire began building his budding territory around Stevens, with bountiful results. Talking out of the side of his mouth, Stevens acted like a movie gangster, deriding the cosmopolitan city as a provincial backwater. In one memorable incident, popular Pepper Gomez boasted that his stomach muscles were so strong that he could endure virtually any blow to his abdomen. When Stevens disputed the claim, a ladder was set up so Stevens could leap onto Gomez's "cast iron" abs. But instead of aiming at the stomach, Stevens delivered his "Bombs Away" Knee-Drop to Pepper's neck. After Gomez recovered, the two engaged in a series of matches that smashed attendance records.

By the mid-1960s, Stevens teamed with Pat Patterson to form one of the most revered tag teams in history, the Blond Bombers. The pair won both the NWA and AWA World Tag Team Titles.

In 1967, Bruno Sammartino journeyed to San Francisco to put up his WWE World Heavyweight Championship against Stevens' United States Title. After a Bombs Away, Sammartino was counted out of the match. Stevens claimed that he won the WWE Championship, even though the rules stipulated that a Title could not change hands on a count-out.

In 1980, "The Crippler" headed to WWE. Ray had the distinction of having co-managers in Lou Albano and "Classy" Freddie Blassie. He showed how he got his nickname when he viciously attacked Jimmy "Superfly" Snuka and administered two piledrivers on the concrete floor.

Stevens soon returned to the AWA as a competitor and broadcaster until he retired in 1992. On April 5, 1995, Stevens' impact was recognized when the mayors of San Francisco and Oakland jointly declared it "Ray Stevens Day." In May 1996, one of sports-entertainment's true pioneers passed away at his California home.

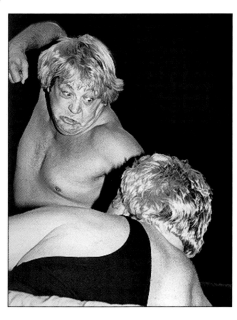

RED BASTIEN

HT 6'0" **WT** 190 lbs.
FROM Bottineau, North Dakota

While competing in California, Oregon, Texas, Florida, and British Columbia, Red Bastien was recognized as one of the game's toughest men. He combined his rugged persona with lightning-fast speed, which he acquired while training with noted Mexican speed merchant Manuel Barintez.

Although he was a savvy and versatile single's competitor, he gained his greatest fame in the tag team ranks. In WWE, he and Bruno Sammartino competed as a tandem. In Australia, Red and Mario Milano wore the gold three times, beating duos like the Von Stroheim brothers and Killer Kowalski and Skull Murphy.

Teaming with his brother, Lou, he enjoyed five tag team title reigns, toppling such storied pairs as the Golden Grahams and Fabulous Kangaroos. In later years, he went on to form championship combinations with several other Superstars, including Hercules Cortez, with whom he won the AWA Tag Team Championship in May, 1971.

After retirement, Bastien became one of sports-entertainment's most respected ambassadors, and is credited with discovering Sting and the Ultimate Warrior. He died in 2012.

RENE DUPREE

HT 6'3" **WT** 260 lbs. **FROM** Paris, France
SIGNATURE MOVE Dupree Bomb

Nobody loved Rene Dupree more than, well, Rene Dupree. The cocky Superstar believed himself to be an all-time WWE great and his earliest efforts began backing his boasts. In June 2003, a little more than a month after his in-ring debut, Dupree and Sylvain Grenier defeated Kane and Rob Van Dam to capture the World Tag Team Championship. The victory proved historic, as it put Dupree in the record books as the youngest Tag champ in WWE history (at 19 years old). Collectively known as La Resistance, Dupree and Grenier dominated the *Raw* tag team division until he was drafted to *SmackDown* in March 2004.

Dupree continued his tag team excellence with a new partner, Kenzo Suzuki. The multinational duo defeated Billy Kidman and Paul London for the WWE Tag Team Championship in September 2004. They held the Titles for three months before losing to Rey Mysterio and RVD. Following the loss, Dupree struggled to get back on track. After a brief reunion with Sylvain on *ECW*, he was released from WWE in July 2007.

RAZOR RAMON/ SCOTT HALL

HT	6'7"
WT	287 lbs.
FROM	Miami, Florida

SIGNATURE MOVE
Razor's Edge

One of history's most controversial Superstars, Scott Hall spent more than two decades doing things his way. He's certainly managed to ruffle a few feathers, but, in the end, history will prove that Hall's provocative approach to sports-entertainment resulted in one of the most successful careers the industry has ever seen.

Hall's earliest days were spent in the Florida and Carolina territories before jumping to the AWA, where he became a mainstay in the mid-to-late 1980s. While there, he teamed with Curt Hennig to defeat Jimmy Garvin and Steve Regal for the AWA World Tag Team Championship in January 1986. Together, Hall and Hennig held the Titles for four months before eventually losing to Doug Somers and Buddy Rose.

Following the loss, Hall set out on his own and was pegged by many insiders as a future AWA World Heavyweight Champion. But before the prophecy could become reality, Hall left the AWA and would eventually surface in WCW. Competing as The Diamond Studd, Hall found himself in several high-profile matches, including the infamous Chamber of Horrors Match at *Halloween Havoc* 1991.

THE BAD GUY

Hall jumped to WWE in 1992 where he would become better known as Razor Ramon. Claiming to be the only real man in WWE, "The Bad Guy" was initially hated for his arrogance, while also being respected for his superior abilities in the ring.

Upon his arrival, Ramon was immediately thrust into the main event picture, battling the likes of fan favorites Bret Hart, Bob Backlund, and Randy Savage. With each passing victory, Ramon's ego continued to inflate while fans' perceptions of him grew even uglier. Eventually, though, that would all change. After losing to the underdog 1-2-3 Kid in May 1993, Ramon uncharacteristically showed reverence for the upstart's efforts. With that, fans began to look at Ramon with great admiration.

With the fans now firmly in his corner, Ramon went on to establish himself as one of the greatest Intercontinental Champions of all time. His first of four reigns began in September 1993 when he defeated Rick Martel to claim the vacant Title. Ramon then maintained a firm grasp on the gold over the next six months. Along the way, he fended off the likes of Irwin R. Schyster, Ludvig Borga, and Crush. He also defeated Shawn Michaels in the groundbreaking *WrestleMania X* Ladder Match.

THE OUTSIDERS

Despite his popularity and success in WWE, Hall left in 1996 to sign with rival WCW. The departure left WWE reeling, as his buck-the-system attitude as a part of the New World Order caused regular *Monday Night Raw* viewers to switch to *Monday Nitro* by the millions. Alongside Kevin Nash and Hulk Hogan, Hall played a major roll in WCW, beating WWE in the Monday Night War for more than eighty straight weeks.

While in WCW, Hall became a Television Champion, two-time United States Champion, and seven-time World Tag Team Champion. He also won the 1997 *World War 3* Battle Royal. Unfortunately for WCW, however, not even Hall's popularity and success could save the deteriorating company, and the two split ways prior to the promotion's 2001 demise.

THE BAD GUY'S BACK

Alongside original nWo members Nash and Hogan, Hall returned to WWE in early 2002. His homecoming was highlighted by a *WrestleMania X8* encounter with Stone Cold Steve Austin. He also battled The Rock, Rikishi, and Bradshaw, among others, before temporarily parting ways with the company in the spring.

Hall's place in history was cemented in 2014 when he was inducted into the WWE Hall of Fame. After his acceptance speech, he famously reunited on stage with longtime friends Nash, Michaels, X-Pac, and Triple H.

Always a member of the WWE family, Hall still makes occasional appearances, most notably in March 2015 when the nWo showed up at *WrestleMania 31* to help Sting combat Triple H and D-Generation X.

SAY HELLO TO THE BAD GUY.

RENE GOULET

| HT | 6'0" | WT | 236 lbs. | FROM | Nice, France |

| SIGNATURE MOVE | Claw |

By the time WWE's mainstream boom of the 1980s came along, Rene Goulet's glory days were behind him. The self-proclaimed "number one Frenchman" spent much of the Hulkamania era falling to up-and-coming fan favorites, such as "Leaping" Lanny Poffo and Hillbilly Jim. But longtime WWE fans remember Goulet as a serious threat to all titleholders during the 1970s.

Goulet formed a formidable tandem with fellow European Karl Gotch of Belgium in 1971. In December, they defeated Luke Graham and Tarzan Tyler to become the second-ever WWE World Tag Team Champions.

Fans and insiders alike predicted a lengthy reign for Goulet and Gotch. Surprisingly, however, they were unseated by Baron Mikel Scicluna and King Curtis only two months later.

After the loss, Goulet left WWE to tour the globe. He competed in Japan, Australia, and Germany before returning to WWE in the early 1980s. Unfortunately by this time, the aged "Master of the Claw" rarely had the opportunity to apply his feared finisher—even though, he still wore a glove to apply the dreaded hold.

RENEE YOUNG

| HT | 5'5" | FROM | Toronto, Ontario, Canada |

The WWE Universe may have first been introduced to Renee Young in March 2013, but the talented announcer actually has sports-entertainment roots that go well beyond her debut on the big stage. Prior to joining WWE, Young worked at The Score television network in Canada where she co-hosted *WWE Aftermath* with future WWE announcer Kyle Edwards and former referee Jimmy Korderas.

Following her 2013 debut, Young went on to become a respected backstage interviewer, contributor on the Slammy Award winning *JBL and Cole Show*, color commentator on *NXT*, as well as WWE's first full-time female commentator in more than a decade when she called *WWE Superstars* alongside Tom Phillips.

Young later parlayed her success as an announcer into her own show on the WWE Network. Called *WWE Unfiltered with Renee Young*, she gives viewers a glimpse of WWE Superstars outside the ring, as well as speaking with celebrities about their WWE fandom.

A multi-talented personality, Young has already made a lasting imprint on WWE, which is quite impressive considering she's just getting started.

RENO RIGGINS

| HT | 5'10" | WT | 226 lbs. | FROM | Las Vegas, Nevada |

Reno Riggins won countless matches over the course of his career. Unfortunately, however, few of them were in WWE. As a WWE Superstar during the late-1980s and early-1990s, Riggins regularly fell short against the likes of Randy Savage, Earthquake, and Repo Man.

Riggins had considerably better success competing outside WWE. While in Tennessee, the Nevada native engaged in bitter rivalries with Wolfie D, Flash Flanagan, and Brian Christopher, who he defeated for the USWA Southern Heavyweight Championship in August 1992.

Riggins briefly retired in 1995, only to return later in the decade. When he came back, Riggins formed a tag team with Steve Dunn. Together, they claimed three NWA North American Tag Team Title reigns and one run with the NWA World Tag Team Championship.

REPO MAN

| HT | 6'2" | WT | 290 lbs. | FROM | The Crowbar |

In 1991, this Superstar was introduced to WWE audiences in vignettes that showed him repossessing cars from garages and parking lots. His services were retained by "Million Dollar Man" Ted DiBiase to acquire the Million Dollar Championship from DiBiase's former bodyguard, Virgil.

The man with his black mask and bull rope terrorized Superstars like Big Boss Man, British Bulldog, "Hacksaw" Jim Duggan, Sgt. Slaughter, "Rowdy" Roddy Piper, and Randy "Macho Man" Savage. On *Raw*'s second episode, he absconded with Savage's hat, only to lose the possession back to "Macho Man" the following week.

Repo Man left WWE in the Spring of 1993. He resurfaced in 2001 for the Gimmick Battle Royal at *WrestleMania X-Seven* and again in December 2007 for the *Raw 15th Anniversary* special. He was eliminated from both contests. Despite being absent for many years, many fans feel he is always lurking around the corner and it's just a matter of time before we see him again. The imprint he left on WWE is as permanent as the tire tracks on his ring attire.

THE REVIVAL

| MEMBERS | Dash Wilder & Scott Dawson |
| COMBINED WT | 446 lbs. |

In 2014, Dash Wilder debuted in NXT and joined forces with Scott Dawson. Like any good tag team, the pair seemed able to read each other's thoughts, resulting in well-synchronized maneuvers. However, it took some time to develop a rhythm.

The two earned their first televised win in 2015 against Enzo Amore and Colin Cassady, and ascended from there, making it to the semi-finals of the *Dusty Rhodes Tag Team Classic*, where they were bested by the eventual winners, Finn Bálor and Samoa Joe.

In November 2015, they dethroned The Vaudevillians for the NXT Tag Team Championship, holding the gold for five months until a loss to American Alpha at *NXT TakeOver: Brooklyn*, securing their position as one of the premier tandems of the future.

REY MYSTERIO

HT	5'6"
WT	175 lbs.
FROM	San Diego, California

SIGNATURE MOVE
619, West Coast Pop

At 5'6" and 175 pounds, Rey Mysterio was undoubtedly WWE's ultimate underdog. But despite his size disadvantage, it was not uncommon to see the masked marvel chop his opposition down to size at a dizzying pace. Utilizing a repertoire that featured a unique combination of high flying and heavy impact moves, Mysterio successfully established himself as one of sports-entertainment's premier Superstars.

Mysterio's earliest years were spent perfecting his Lucha Libre style on cards across Mexico. After more than five years battling the likes of Juventud Guerrera and Psicosis, the young high-flyer finally caught the eye of ECW's Paul Heyman, who introduced North American fans to Mysterio in 1995.

Word of Mysterio's innovative offense began to stretch past ECW's Philadelphia footprint; it wasn't long before the San Diego native was scooped up by national powerhouse WCW. Within weeks of his June 1996 debut, Mysterio picked off Dean Malenko to capture the coveted Cruiserweight Championship. The win marked Mysterio's first of a record eight reigns with the Title (WCW and WWE combined).

Mysterio made his WWE debut in July 2002 and, as expected, he cemented himself as a top threat in the cruiserweight division. He also started to show signs of becoming a main-event star. Shortly after his debut, the Master of the 619 captured the WWE Tag Team Championship with Edge. As time went on, he partnered with other main eventers to claim gold, including Rob Van Dam, Batista, and longtime friend, Eddie Guerrero.

Following Guerrero's tragic passing in 2005, Mysterio focused his efforts on honoring his friend; and what better way than to win the World Championship. He took the first step toward realizing his goal when he last eliminated Randy Orton to win the 2006 Royal Rumble Match.

At *WrestleMania 22*, Mysterio accomplished the unthinkable when he defeated Kurt Angle and Orton to win the World Championship. Following the match, Mysterio celebrated his victory with Guerrero's family. The image of him embracing Chavo and Vickie Guerrero on the *WrestleMania* stage remains one of the most emotional scenes in WWE history.

Ironically, Chavo Guerrero would cost Mysterio his World Championship three months later. Fueled by jealousy, Guerrero turned on Mysterio at *The Great American Bash*, allowing King Booker to walk away with the gold. Over the course of the next year-plus, Mysterio repeatedly gained retribution from his former friend, including at *No Mercy 2006* and *SummerSlam 2007*.

Mysterio joined elite company in April 2009, when he added another prestigious accolade to his resume. This latest *WrestleMania* moment came at the expense of John Bradshaw Layfield, who Mysterio trounced in a matter of seconds to claim the Intercontinental Title. A few months later, Mysterio became a two-time Intercontinental Champion when he defeated Chris Jericho to regain the gold in a Mask vs. Title Match.

In June 2010, Mysterio outlasted *SmackDown*'s best when he won a Battle Royal for the right to challenge for the World Championship. Mysterio was given his opportunity at *Fatal 4-Way*, where he turned back CM Punk, Big Show, and defending champ Jack Swagger to win the World Title for a second time. He held the gold for four weeks before Kane cashed in his Money in the Bank contract to defeat a weakened Mysterio for the Title.

The longtime *SmackDown* Superstar moved to *Raw* in April 2011, courtesy of the annual WWE Draft. As a member of the Monday night brand, Mysterio continued to prove himself as an elite Superstar. Just months into his stay, the Master of the 619 defeated The Miz in a tournament finals match to capture his first-ever WWE Championship. As a result of the victory, Mysterio became one of the elite few to have held both the World and WWE Titles.

Mysterio left WWE in February 2015. While no longer exciting the WWE Universe, Mysterio's lasting impact is undeniable. With multiple World Championship reigns, amazing *WrestleMania* moments and a Royal Rumble Match victory to his credit, the ultimate underdog will forever be remembered as WWE's "Biggest Little Man."

WHO'S THAT JUMPIN' OUT THE SKY? REY MYSTERIO. HERE WE GO!

RHYNO

HT	5'10"	WT	295 lbs.
FROM	Detroit, Michigan		
SIGNATURE MOVE	Gore		

Billed as half man/half beast, Rhyno entered WWE in 2001 with the distinction of being the original ECW's final Champion. With that accolade forever attached to him, fans demanded Rhyno live up to his hardcore reputation. Luckily for them, he refused to disappoint, defeating Kane for the Hardcore Championship just weeks after debuting. The Man Beast went on to win the Title two more times, once from Chris Jericho and once from Test.

In July 2001, Rhyno reverted back to his ECW roots when he joined forces with The Alliance, where he became Stephanie McMahon's pet, largely because he refused to allow Y2J to verbally berate her. The rivalry led to a *SummerSlam* showdown between the two Superstars. Despite coming out on the losing end, the match is widely regarded as a highlight of Rhyno's WWE career. Undeterred by the loss, The Man Beast defeated Tajiri for the United States Championship the following month at *Unforgiven*.

Proving he will always be tied to the original ECW, Rhyno battled Sabu in a thrilling throwback to his hardcore days at *One Night Stand* in 2005. Following the event, many assumed Rhyno's WWE days were over. But The Man Beast surprised the sports-entertainment world when he showed up at NXT in February 2015. Since his arrival, Rhyno has been teaching up-and-coming Superstars what it means to be extreme.

RHYTHM AND BLUES

MEMBERS	Honky Tonk Man & Greg Valentine
COMBINED WT	514 lbs.

Former Intercontinental Champions Honky Tonk Man and Greg Valentine joined forces in 1989 to help manager Jimmy Hart in his battle against his former protégés, Bret Hart and Jim Neidhart. Though not officially recognized as Rhythm and Blues yet, the duo battled the Hart Foundation at *WrestleMania V*.

A few months later, Valentine began his transformation from a no-nonsense professional to Elvis look-alike. He dyed his hair jet black, donned oversized sunglasses, and began carrying around a classic guitar. With the makeover complete, Valentine officially joined forces with Honky Tonk Man, and Rhythm and Blues was born.

The tone-deaf duo appeared to care more about their fledgling music careers than they did about competing in the ring. As a result, Rhythm and Blues failed to score any major hits in the tag ranks. They did, however, manage to debut their single "Hunka, Hunka, Honky Love" at *WrestleMania VI*. Unfortunately for Honky Tonk Man and Valentine, The Bushwhackers crashed the performance, destroying their guitars.

RIC FLAIR

see page 288

RICARDO RODRIGUEZ

HT	6'0"	WT	225 lbs.

Alberto Del Rio came to WWE in 2010, flaunting his many envied possessions. Among the cars, estates, and designer suits, the most valuable of all his excessive riches was arguably his personal ring announcer, Ricardo Rodriguez. Clad in a black tuxedo and sporting a perfectly parted head of hair, Ricardo gave an added punch to his boss's intro, rolling the Rs in "Rio" and enunciating with a guttural roar that infuriated crowds.

Rather than take a break between bells, Rodriguez was also busy during Del Rio's matches. With the referee's back turned, the crafty Rodriguez had a knack for interfering on his boss's behalf. He also proved a capable athlete, occasionally seeing success when thrust into competition himself. Despite Ricardo's invaluable support, Del Rio turned on him in 2013.

After recovering from Alberto's brutal attack, Rodriguez began to support his ex-employer's rival, Rob Van Dam. He also earned an upset victory over Del Rio in October 2013. This versatile performer finally served on WWE's Spanish commentary team prior to leaving the company in 2014.

RIC FLAIR

HT	6'1"
WT	243 lbs.
FROM	Charlotte, North Carolina

SIGNATURE MOVE
Figure-Four Leglock

Over the course of his 35 years inside the ring, Ric Flair orchestrated arguably the greatest career in the history of sports-entertainment. With an unprecedented 16 World Championships to his credit, the man known as the "Nature Boy" truly epitomized what it meant to be a champion between the ropes. Flair also lived like a champion outside the ring, earning an unparalleled reputation as a "kiss-stealing, wheeling dealing, jet-flying, limousine-riding son-of-a-gun."

As a youngster growing up in Minneapolis, Flair became so unruly that his parents were forced to send him to boarding school. While there, Flair was an amateur wrestling champion and star football player, and interacted with some of the area's most affluent kids, which he claims helped contribute to the lavish lifestyle he later embraced. After boarding school and a stint at the University of Minnesota, he had the opportunity to meet his friend's father, Verne Gagne, who was also the promoter of the American Wrestling Association (AWA). With no promises of a future career, Gagne agreed to let the gifted athlete take part in his training camp.

In late 1972, Flair enrolled in Gagne's ten-week wrestling school, but quit after only one day when the cardiovascular exercises proved to be too much. Luckily, Flair later reconsidered his decision and returned to the camp, which also produced such greats as The Iron Sheik, Greg Gagne, and Ken Patera.

After completing his training, Flair earned an opportunity to compete in Gagne's AWA. In his first-ever match, he battled George "Scrap Iron" Gadaski to a ten-minute draw at the Minneapolis Auditorium. The inexperienced Flair managed to form relationships that would eventually benefit him greatly, especially the close friendship he developed with the great Wahoo McDaniel.

When McDaniel moved south to compete in the Mid-Atlantic territory, he recommended that the promotion take a close look at his young friend. In April, 1974, Flair was on his way to North Carolina, a place that would eventually adopt the moniker "Flair Country" as a tribute to the man who cemented his amazing legacy in the Tar Heel State.

While competing for Mid-Atlantic, Flair finally started to make a name for himself. He defeated Paul Jones for the Television Championship in February, 1975. With the Title around his waist, Flair's future couldn't have looked brighter. However, tragedy struck one Sunday afternoon when the plane Flair was traveling on crashed. The accident claimed the life of the pilot and seriously injured competitors Johnny Valentine and Bob Bruggers, as well as announcer David Crockett.

Flair broke his back in three places, causing doctors to worry that he might never walk again, let alone compete. Unable to accept a life without wrestling, Flair persevered and was back in the ring six months and ten days later.

THE NATURE BOY

Flair adopted a new style upon returning to the ring. Following the advice of Mid-Atlantic executive George Scott, he patterned his persona after the legendary Buddy Rogers. He even adopted Rogers' nickname, "Nature Boy." As the "Nature Boy," Flair demonstrated an unquenchable thirst for the best the world had to offer.

Life was also good for Flair inside the ring. After capturing numerous titles, including the prestigious United States Championship, Flair reached the sports-entertainment pinnacle when he defeated Dusty Rhodes for the National Wrestling Alliance (NWA) Championship on September 17, 1981. The victory put Flair on the map as one of the most accomplished competitors at the time. However, after touring the globe and competing against such legends as Harley Race, Kerry Von Erich, and Ricky Steamboat every single night, Flair proved himself as one of the greatest Superstars in the world.

THE FOUR HORSEMEN

In 1986, Flair made a decision that would forever alter the face of sports-entertainment when he aligned himself with Tully Blanchard, Arn Anderson, Ole Anderson, and J.J.Dillon. Collectively known as The Four Horsemen, the well-dressed faction of bullies controlled the gold in the Mid-Atlantic territory. Blanchard held the United States Championship; the Andersons controlled the NWA Tag Team Championship, while Flair maintained a stranglehold on the NWA Championship. The unstoppable unit plowed through their competition, laying the groundwork for future great factions, such as the New World Order and D-Generation X.

By decade's end, Flair had become a multiple-time NWA Champion. If he had decided to retire then, he would have walked away as one of the finest to ever step foot in a ring. However, there was plenty more for the "Nature Boy" to accomplish. Surprisingly, however, he was forced to find a new place of employment for the next chapter of his legendary story.

The "Real World Heavyweight Champion"

After Ted Turner purchased Jim Crockett Promotions and renamed it World Championship Wrestling, the billionaire made a series of questionable decisions that rubbed some of the performers the wrong way, including hiring Jim Herd to run the operation. Unable to accept Herd's decisions and perceived disrespect of the industry, Flair left WCW.

The WWE Universe was sent into a frenzy when Bobby Heenan announced that a great champion was on his way to WWE and then displayed the WCW Championship, shocking millions of viewers. Flair soon debuted on WWE television with the WCW Title, claiming to be the "real World Champion." Flair displayed the Title proudly, while fans and Superstars alike looked on in utter disbelief.

For years, spectators had wondered how a match between Flair and Hulk Hogan, the two greatest competitors of their era, would play out. Fans would savor pondering a question that looked like it would never be answered. With Flair in WWE, however, the fantasy became a reality.

A mere three months after making his WWE debut, Flair put any doubt surrounding his championship claims to rest when he captured the WWE Championship by winning the 1992 Royal Rumble. Flair's victory put him in elite company, as he joined another "Nature Boy," Buddy Rogers, as the only men to capture both the NWA and WWE Championships. Flair enjoyed a second WWE Championship reign before finally falling to former confidant Mr. Perfect in a Loser Leaves WWE Match in January, 1993.

Back in World Championship Wrestling

Following the loss, Flair returned to WCW and picked up right where he left off. He defeated Vader at *Starrcade 1993* to reclaim the WCW Championship, a feat followed by an impressive win over Sting months later. Hulk Hogan and Flair renewed their epic rivalry at the 1994 *Bash at the Beach*. Though the result was not in Flair's favor, the star-studded encounter, which featured Shaquille O'Neal in Hogan's corner, will forever be remembered as one of sports-entertainment's most historic matches.

Despite going on to reclaim his WCW Championship and eventually reunite the Four Horsemen, internal politics caused Flair to become disenchanted with WCW. He spent the final years of the promotion's existence extremely unhappy. By the time WCW closed its doors, Flair's heart had already left the great sport he spent decades loving.

New Life in WWE

When WWE purchased WCW, Flair's passion for competition quickly resurfaced. Now over 50 years old, the "Nature Boy" miraculously located the fountain of youth and sipped from it for the following seven years.

Perhaps Flair's greatest accomplishment during his second WWE run was his union with Triple H, Batista, and Randy Orton. Collectively known as Evolution, the faction was built using ideologies borrowed from The Four Horsemen. During their successful time together, the well-dressed stable controlled WWE's championship scene. Years later, both Batista and Orton credited Flair's guidance with helping them achieve World Championship status.

Flair's unprecedented in-ring career came to an end on March 30, 2008. One day after being inducted into the WWE Hall of Fame, Shawn Michaels defeated the "Nature Boy" at *WrestleMania XXIV*. The historic match officially signified the end of an era that can never be duplicated.

Flair made a second trip to the Hall of Fame in 2012 when he was inducted as a member of The Four Horsemen.

Then, on September 20, 2015, Flair's daughter, Charlotte, won the WWE Divas Title. Soon, Flair was accompanying his immensely talented daughter to the ring. While initially appearing to be a proud father offering sage advice, Flair gradually persuaded Charlotte to adopt a philosophy similar to the one he espoused in the Horsemen. Because of this, two generations of Flairs have been able to boast about wearing the gold, and being "the dirtiest player in the game."

RICK MARTEL

HT	6'0"	WT	230 lbs.
FROM	Montreal, Quebec, Canada		

Although remembered for his cocky behavior, Martel was a fan favorite until later in his career. By that time, however, he had much to brag about, after appearing at the top of cards everywhere, and enhancing his ring style with each new encounter. In fact, his long-time followers choose to think of Martel as a modest warrior who allowed his skills to do the talking.

The earliest days of Martel's career saw the Canadian-born Superstar honing his craft all over the world, including Puerto Rico and New Zealand. It wasn't until 1980 that he joined WWE. Within months of his debut, Martel reunited with Tony Garea, a former partner from his days in New Zealand, to capture the WWE World Tag Team Championship from the Wild Samoans in Philadelphia. It was the first of two Championship reigns for the tandem.

Shortly after losing the Titles for the final time, Martel left WWE in favor of a singles career in the American Wrestling Association (AWA). Following an amazing 19-month reign as AWA Champion, Martel made his return to WWE and top level tag team competition in 1987. After a brief union with Tom Zenk, he settled in alongside Tito Santana as one-half of Strike Force. The new duo found immediate success, capturing the World Tag Team Championship from The Hart Foundation in October. It was Martel's third run with the prestigious Titles.

Strike Force's success was unexpectedly derailed when Martel accused Santana of riding his coattails. The accusation was uncharacteristic for Martel and helped pave the way for the arrogant Superstar he would soon become.

On his own, Martel began to display an obnoxious side never before seen by WWE fans. It wasn't long before the smug Superstar began to call himself "The Model." Perhaps Martel's most notorious moment as "The Model" came in 1990 when he temporarily blinded Jake Roberts after spraying him with his signature cologne, Arrogance. The incident eventually led to the famous *WrestleMania VII* Blindfold Match, which Roberts won.

Martel retired in 1997 after sustaining several injuries in WCW.

RICKI STARR

HT	5"10"	WT	205 lbs.	FROM	St. Louis, Missouri
SIGNATURE MOVE	Standing Moonsault				

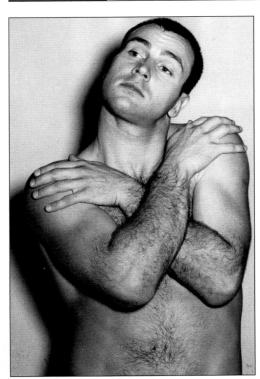

Tossing miniature ballet slippers to fans, Ricki Starr pirouetted across the ring, surprising cynical opponents with a graceful, acrobatic assault.

Raised in St. Louis, Starr capitalized on his training in both boxing and ballet. Because of his theatrical mannerisms, he was taken lightly by foes who quickly fell victim to his headscissors, ballet kicks, swift punches, and standing moonsault. After his 1953 debut, his fame quickly spread and, in 1957, he was working for the forerunner of WWE, Capitol Wrestling, drawing crowds for matches against Skull Murphy, Karl Von Hess, Dick the Bruiser, and Dr. Jerry Graham. He teamed with Antonino Rocca, then set a record by wrestling him in Washington, DC.

In 1962, he appeared on the television show, *Mr. Ed*. But a year later, at the height of his fame, he inexplicably left for England. With the exception of an American tour in 1973 and 1974, he competed exclusively in Europe.

Ever eccentric, he cut himself off from his wrestling contacts after retirement, living in relative obscurity until his death in 2014.

RICKY ORTIZ

HT	6'3"	WT	246 lbs.
FROM	Paradise Valley, Arizona		
SIGNATURE MOVE	The Big O		

A standout four-sport athlete, Ricky Ortiz grew up dreaming of being a WWE Superstar. Those dreams became a reality when ECW General Manager Theodore Long launched his "New Superstar Initiative" and welcomed Ortiz to the Land of Extreme in July 2008.

After a debut victory over Armando Estrada, Ortiz went on to impress against the likes of Carlito and Chavo Guerrero. In April 2009, the WWE Supplemental Draft shipped Ortiz to *SmackDown*, where he was viewed as one of the brand's promising young Superstars. But after an impressive string of matches, Ortiz came up on the losing end of a lopsided match against The Great Khali. The loss sent Ortiz reeling, and he left WWE soon after.

RICKY "THE DRAGON" STEAMBOAT

HT	5'10"
WT	235 lbs.
FROM	Honolulu, Hawaii

SIGNATURE MOVE
High Crossbody Block

Ricky Steamboat had a unique career that saw him switch promotions regularly during the period when competition between WWE and WCW was at its most fierce. Yet, fans of both promotions followed the athletic Hawaiian on his journeys. Wherever he appeared, Steamboat often had the best match on the card. His battles with Ric Flair and his *WrestleMania III* classic match with Randy "Macho Man" Savage produced some of the most memorable action of all-time.

Billed as the son of Hawaiian mat hero Sammy Steamboat, "The Dragon" was a bodybuilder and amateur wrestling champion who was socially acquainted with AWA promoter and multiple Heavyweight Champion Verne Gagne's daughter, and was invited to the group's rigorous training camp. Gagne, a onetime Olympic alternate, favored pure athletes, and Steamboat's high arm drags, dropkicks, and headscissors suggested that he had Superstar potential.

After wrestling in the AWA and Florida, Steamboat journeyed to the Mid-Atlantic wrestling territory in 1977 and ran directly into another graduate of Gagne's training academy, Ric Flair. Both men shared a passion for their vocation, but in drastically different ways. While Steamboat exuded humility, Flair was flashy and braggadocios. During one memorable encounter, Flair attacked Steamboat at a television taping, rubbing his face on the studio floor. The next week, Steamboat gained revenge, tearing the Nature Boy's pricey suit to pieces and leaving him, humiliated, in his underwear. The two became headliners all over the Mid-Atlantic territory, igniting the promotion.

For the next several years, Steamboat held the United States Title on three separate occasions, and the NWA Tag Team Championship with partners Paul Jones and Jay Youngblood, battling teams like Sgt. Slaughter and Don Kernodle and the Brisco Brothers.

In 1985, "The Dragon" arrived in WWE. Within months, he earned a spot on the inaugural *WrestleMania* card, defeating Matt Borne. Following *WrestleMania I*, Steamboat successfully proved his worth against Jake "The Snake" Roberts and fellow Hawaiian Don Muraco.

WWE's championship committee finally took note of Steamboat's success and afforded him an opportunity to challenge Savage for the Intercontinental Championship in late 1986.

Unfortunately for Steamboat, the "Macho Man" staved off the threat by viciously crushing the challenger's larynx with the ring bell from the top rope. The heinous act not only kept Steamboat from competing for months, but also threatened his chances of ever speaking again.

Luckily, "The Dragon" made a full recovery. With vengeance occupying his every thought, Steamboat challenged Savage for the Intercontinental Championship at *WrestleMania III*. It was a thrilling match remembered for its breathless combat and near-falls. In the end, Steamboat gained the ultimate measure of retribution, defeating "Macho Man" for the Title in a clash many considered the greatest match ever.

The following year, Steamboat returned to the NWA, where he again faced Flair in one of the most exciting series of matches ever witnessed, and enjoyed a three-month reign as NWA Champion. Steamboat briefly rejoined WWE in 1991. While he failed to recreate the same in-ring success as his initial WWE run, "The Dragon" did manage to amaze crowds with his fire-breathing pre-match rituals.

In 1991, he was back in his old territory, now renamed WCW, winning tag team gold with Dustin Rhodes, rekindling the conflict with Flair, and battling with a young, brash Steve Austin for the United States Championship. Unfortunately, the years of all-out competing had taken their physical toll and "The Dragon" retired in 1994.

THE LEGACY CONTINUES

But among the next generation of Superstars, Steamboat was revered. He now settled into a backstage producer role with WWE. "The Dragon's" three-decade career was commemorated when he entered the WWE Hall of Fame in 2009. The next day, he returned to action on the grandest stage of them all, *WrestleMania XXV*, alongside Roddy Piper and Jimmy Snuka to face Chris Jericho. Meanwhile, he continued to impart his knowledge as a NXT coach, leaving his imprint on sports-entertainment through the Superstars he trained.

TALK TO SOME OF MY OPPONENTS...WHEN THIS DRAGON GETS ON FIRE, HIS OPPONENTS BURN.

RICO

HT	6'0"	WT	238 lbs.	FROM	Las Vegas, Nevada
SIGNATURE MOVE		Spinning Roundhouse Kick			

In an industry overflowing with masculinity, Rico oozed femininity—and it worked for him. Clad in leopard print and sporting perfectly coiffed hair, Rico made his WWE debut in early 2002 as Billy and Chuck's overly-effeminate stylist. But simply making the then-World Tag Team Champions look good wasn't his only job responsibility. When needed, the surreptitiously tough Superstar also interfered to ensure the gold stayed with his guys.

At *Judgment Day 2002*, Rico became the reluctant tag team partner of Rikishi. Together, they actually defeated the stylist's clients for the World Tag Team Championship. Being the good friend that he was, however, Rico later helped Billy and Chuck regain the gold from him and Rikishi.

In late 2002, Rico briefly managed the destructive 3-Minute Warning. He would later get another chance to accessorize his flashy attire with gold. With the lovely Miss Jackie as an ally, he defeated Scotty 2 Hotty and Rikishi for the WWE Tag Team Championship with partner Charlie Haas. After WWE, this sneaky-tough Superstar and former policeman returned to his law enforcement career in Nevada.

RIGHT TO CENSOR

MEMBERS	Steven Richards, Val Venis, The Goodfather, Bull Buchanan, & Ivory

In the summer of 2000, WWE was raided by a self-righteous collection of transformed Superstars that had more conviction for censorship than all politicians put together. Spearheaded by Steven Richards, this faction brainwashed those who once loved the pageantry and glitz of sports-entertainment into believing life was about a tireless campaign to cover up Divas and scrub away much of the glorious grime that made the Attitude Era popular.

Despite Right to Censor's unpopular acts, they did achieve success in the ring, as Ivory became Women's Champion in November 2000. Days later, Bull Buchanan and The Goodfather became World Tag Team Champions. However, everyone started to tire of the squealing alarm sound that signaled their arrival and the pontification that followed. Each member was defeated at *WrestleMania X-Seven*. Soon after Undertaker performed a Last Ride on Richards, Right to Censor disappeared from WWE.

Fans will never agree that Right To Censor's actions were "for their own good," but perhaps the self-proclaimed moralists of society learned to take a long look at themselves before proclaiming how everyone else should live.

RIKISHI

HT	6'1"	WT	425 lbs.	FROM	Isle of Samoa
SIGNATURE MOVE		Stinkface			

This member of the famed Anoa'i family was known by several personas during his lengthy career. But his love affair with the WWE Universe will always stem back to his days as the bleached blond, fun-loving Rikishi.

With dangling black tassels and perpetual wedgie accentuating his massive hindquarters, Rikishi boogied onto the scene in 1999. Alongside Too Cool, his contagious dance moves brought audiences to their feet. Rikishi's infamous Stinkface finishing move, where he engulfs a helpless opponent's head between his rear end became one of the era's most feared maneuvers. Rikishi won an Intercontinental Championship in June 2000 and also enjoyed three Tag Team Titles in his career.

Rikishi's approval rating took a huge hit in late 2000 when it was revealed that he ran over Stone Cold Steve Austin with a car. This startling revelation earned the fans' scorn but also helped catapult him to greater heights. Over the next few months, Rikishi found himself battling many of WWE's all-time greats, including The Rock, Undertaker, and Stone Cold Steve Austin.

By December 2001, Rikishi had won back the fans' trust. All was forgiven when he unleashed a gag-inducing Stinkface to the WWE Chairman, Mr. McMahon. In 2010, Rikishi's sons Jimmy and Jey Uso broke into WWE, making it possible for the proud papa to occasionally dust off his dance moves together with his boys on *Raw*. In 2015, The Usos inducted their legendary dad into the WWE Hall of Fame.

"ROAD DOGG" JESSE JAMES

HT	6'1"	WT	241 lbs.	FROM	Marietta, Georgia
SIGNATURE MOVE		Shake, Rattle, and Roll			

A member of the famed Armstrong wrestling family, Road Dogg was pegged for success from the very beginning. But despite eventually becoming a tag team legend and an Attitude Era hallmark, Dogg's ascent to the top wasn't an easy one.

As Jeff Jarrett's personal roadie, Road Dogg did everything in his power to make his boss look good, including sing for him. In 1995, Jarrett began serenading WWE audiences with his single "With My Baby Tonight." However, it was later learned that Double J was lip-syncing the song that was actually performed by Road Dogg.

Once credit to the song went to Road Dogg, the young upstart's career began to skyrocket. In 1997, he shed the roadie persona and reinvented himself as a cocky loudmouth alongside Bully Gunn. Collectively known as the New Age Outlaws, Dogg and Gunn went on to become one of the most successful tag teams in WWE history, capturing the World Tag Team Championship on five separate occasions. Along the way, as members of the iconic D-Generation X faction, the Outlaws also established themselves among the most rebellious duos of all time.

Road Dogg proved to be just as rabid when he broke out on his own as a singles competitor. In addition to being the third in a long line of Superstars to hold the Hardcore Championship, he also topped Val Venis in March 1999 to become Intercontinental Champion.

After a decade-long hiatus, the "D-O-double G" returned in 2011 to induct his father, "Bullet" Bob Armstrong, into the WWE Hall of Fame. He then went on to become a trusted producer behind the scenes.

While excelling in his producer role, you never know when Road Dogg is going lace up the boots and get back into the action, as evidenced by a 2014 WWE Tag Team Championship reign alongside longtime partner Billy Gunn.

ROAD WARRIORS

see Legion of Doom page 203

ROADKILL

HT	6'0"	WT	323 lbs.	FROM	Lancaster, Pennsylvania

Roadkill can count his number of WWE televised appearances on one hand. Outside of a few losing efforts on *Velocity* and the reborn ECW in 2006, the "Angry Amish Warrior" doesn't have much WWE experience. He can, however, certainly look back at his efforts in the original ECW with great fondness.

While competing in the original ECW, Roadkill formed an unlikely, yet successful, tandem with Danny Doring. In December 2000, Roadkill and Doring bested Tony Mamaluke and Little Guido for the ECW Tag Team Championship. The duo remained Champions until the promotion closed its doors in the spring of 2001.

ROB BARTLETT

Vince McMahon, Randy "Macho Man" Savage, and comedian Rob Bartlett will forever be linked as the first-ever announce team for the longest running weekly episodic television show in history, *Monday Night Raw*.

In his very first statement on WWE TV, Bartlett unknowingly misidentified the legendary Yokozuna as "Yokozuma," then claimed the future WWE Champion was "the guy who's got that diaper." It was all downhill from there.

Bartlett was gone from WWE three months after his January 1993 debut. Following his departure, the comedian continued his standup act and also began a career as a stage actor. His Broadway credits include *More to Love* and *Little Shop of Horrors*. Bartlett is also known for his semi-regular appearances on his longtime friend Don Imus' radio programs.

ROB VAN DAM

see page 294

ROBERT CONWAY

	HT	6'2"	WT	230 lbs.	FROM	Atlantic City, New Jersey
	SIGNATURE MOVE		Neckbreaker			

Conway first made his presence felt in WWE in August 2003 when he disguised himself as a US serviceman and attacked the Dudley Boyz to reveal himself as the third member of La Resistance. Conway turned on his native USA and was introduced as being from the Province of Quebec. He formed a dangerous tag team with Sylvain Grenier and won the World Tag Team Championship three times. The two rule-breakers parted ways in 2005 when they couldn't keep their egos in check.

Conway later became part of the anti-ECW crusade. The narcissistic competitor started to refer to himself as "Con Man," but his fast talk got him in hot water during the WWE Homecoming. After interrupting a Legends ceremony, Conway felt the effects of the Von Erich Claw followed by a "Superfly" Splash.

Conway spent much of 2006 mired in a horrid losing streak. In January 2007, he proclaimed he would quit if he didn't defeat Jeff Hardy. After a disappointing twelve-second loss, WWE Chairman Mr. McMahon appeared and fired Conway on the spot.

ROB VAN DAM

HT	6'0"	WT	235 lbs.	FROM	Battle Creek, Michigan
SIGNATURE MOVE		Five-Star Frog Splash			

Considered by many to be sports-entertainment's ultimate risk taker, Rob Van Dam has utilized a lethal combination of acrobatic offense and martial arts to mold a WWE career that is truly "one of a kind."

A standout in ECW, RVD made his highly-anticipated WWE debut in 2001. Although a member of The Alliance, he managed to gain the

admiration of fans through his awe-inspiring aerial assault, which was highlighted by moves like the Van Terminator, Rolling Thunder, and Five-Star Frog Splash.

It wasn't long before Van Dam's innovative offense was driving him to Championship opportunities. RVD won his first major piece of WWE hardware at *WrestleMania X8* when he beat William Regal for the Intercontinental Title. Subsequent victories saw him claim nearly every other singles Championship in WWE, including the now-defunct Hardcore and European Championships. RVD also proved to be a force in the tag team ranks, winning Championships with Kane, Booker T, and Rey Mysterio.

In 2006, RVD's career took a major step forward when he won the Money in the Bank Ladder Match at *WrestleMania 22*. As "Mr. Money in the Bank," RVD was afforded the opportunity to challenge for a World Championship at the time and location of his choosing. He chose wisely.

In front of ECW's faithful at *One Night Stand*, RVD challenged the normally popular John Cena for the WWE Championship. The ECW contingent nearly booed Cena out of the arena, but not before Van Dam could defeat him for the WWE Title first. A few days later, Paul Heyman also awarded the rechristened ECW Championship to RVD, making him the first Superstar to hold both Titles simultaneously.

RVD quietly left WWE in the summer of 2007, only to return six years later to compete in the WWE Championship Money in the Bank Ladder Match in July 2013. While he didn't win the match, RVD later went on to challenge Alberto Del Rio for the World Heavyweight Championship.

Since his 2013 return, RVD has continued to make sporadic appearances, including at the 2014 Slammys where he presented the award for Extreme Moment of the Year.

ROCK 'N' SOCK CONNECTION

MEMBERS	The Rock & Mankind
COMBINED WT	562 lbs.

Know your role, and have a nice day.

What do you get when you combine a third-generation Superstar and a Hardcore Legend? The Rock 'N' Sock Connection. These two gifted performers and former adversaries were brought together by chance in August 1999 after Undertaker and Big Show attacked The Rock. As success helped bring the unlikely pair closer, Mankind wanted to surprise his new friend that September. On what would be a ratings record-setting segment on *Monday Night Raw*, Mankind treated The Rock to a special "This is Your Life." The segment, which produced a staggering 8.4 rating, saw Mankind reunite Rock with his high school coach, his old girlfriend, and other blasts from his past.

While The Rock grew tired of the team and accused Mankind of stealing his catchphrases and signature moves, there was always something about the odd couple that brought a smile to his face. Even after Mankind wrongfully accused "The Great One" of throwing his New York Times best-seller, *Have A Nice Day*, in the trash and letting him defend the World Tag Team Championship on his own, they were always able to get back on the same page. The popular tandem reunited from time-to-time as called for up until Mick Foley's brief retirement from the ring in 2000.

When all hope was lost for Foley, who was outnumbered in his fight against Evolution, the three-time World Tag Team Champions reformed for the last time on sports-entertainment's most famed stage at *WrestleMania XX*. The packed Madison Square Garden crowd saw the Rock 'N' Sock Connection battle "Nature Boy" Ric Flair, Batista and Randy Orton in a Handicap Match.

This duo ignited WWE and continuously showed that no matter the odds, the Rock 'N' Sock Connection could come together at any given time and take care of business. To this day, audiences fondly recall their thrilling matches and entertaining interviews.

THE ROCK

see page 296

THE ROCKERS

MEMBERS Shawn Michaels & Marty Jannetty **COMBINED WT** 455 lbs.

The Rockers are seen by many as the greatest tag team never to win the WWE Tag Team Titles. While this is an astonishing fact, it's even harder to grasp the idea that Shawn Michaels and Marty Jannetty almost never had an opportunity to prove themselves in WWE.

After opening eyes while competing as the Midnight Rockers in the AWA, Michaels and Jannetty made the move to WWE in 1987. The spandex-clad tandem had dreams of dominating the stacked tag division. WWE, however, believed the pair lacked backstage etiquette and fired the youngsters after only two weeks.

Feeling humbled, Michaels and Jannetty fretted over never getting another opportunity at greatness. The high-flying duo continued to work on their game for the better part of a year before WWE officials agreed to give them another look. By the summer of 1988, Michaels and Jannetty re-debuted as The Rockers, and the rest is sports-entertainment history.

The Rockers achieved early success, turning back such highly celebrated duos as the Brain Busters and the Rougeau Brothers. By 1990, their incredible teamwork earned them the reputation of tag team specialists. However, despite all their wins, they were never given a serious opportunity to claim the World Tag Team Championship.

In October 1990, The Rockers were finally granted a high-profile championship opportunity against The Hart Foundation on NBC's *Saturday Night's Main Event*. The match proved to be a controversial encounter, as The Rockers actually left the arena that night with the Titles. The Championship switch, however, was later stricken from the record after the match was ruled unsafe, due to a ring rope breaking during the bout.

That was the closest The Rockers ever came to claiming the World Tag Team Championship. By 1992, Michaels believed he had outgrown his role in The Rockers. To prove his point, he kicked his longtime partner through the window of the Barber Shop, thus signifying the end of one of the most popular tag teams in WWE history. In the coming decades, the duo would occasionally reunite, giving fans a glimpse at what made The Rockers such a groundbreaking and memorable tandem.

ROCKIN' ROBIN

 HT 5'7" **FROM** Charlotte, North Carolina
SIGNATURE MOVE Bulldog

Trained by former NWA Junior Heavyweight Champion Nelson Royal, Rockin' Robin made her WWE debut on one of the biggest stages possible when she joined the Fabulous Moolah's stable to turn back Sensational Sherri and her team of Divas at the 1987 *Survivor Series*.

The athletic brunette spent the next several months utilizing her devastating bulldog finisher to open the eyes of WWE officials. After racking up an impressive win-loss record, Robin finally earned an opportunity at the WWE Women's Championship. Capitalizing on her big break, she upended Sherri for the gold in France in October, 1988.

Proving her championship victory was no fluke, Robin handily defeated challenger Judy Martin at the 1989 *Royal Rumble*. A few months later, she established herself as a multi-talented Diva when she opened *WrestleMania V* with a stirring rendition of "America the Beautiful."

Robin remained Women's Champion until she left WWE in 1990. As a result of her departure, WWE deemed the Title inactive until 1993.

ROCKY JOHNSON

see page 299

RODNEY MACK

HT 6'2" **WT** 276 lbs. **FROM** Lafayette, Louisiana
SIGNATURE MOVE The Blackout

Claiming "the man" was holding him down, Rodney Mack made his *Raw* debut in February 2003, alongside manager Theodore Long. With Long leading the way, Mack ran over veteran Al Snow like a truck in his first-ever match.

Mack soon instituted an open challenge that guaranteed he could defeat any Caucasian competitor in under five minutes. He made good on his promise for several weeks against considerably weaker competition. Then in June 2003, Mack was finally met with a "white boy" worthy of the challenge—Goldberg. A mere 26 seconds into the match, Mack had fallen victim to the Jackhammer, en route to his first loss. Following the defeat, Mack went on to compete mainly as a tag-team competitor with partners Mark Henry and Christopher Nowinski.

THE ROCK

HT	6'5"
WT	260 lbs.
FROM	Miami, Florida
SIGNATURE MOVE	
The People's Elbow, Rock Bottom	

If there is any facet of the entertainment industry that Dwayne "The Rock" Johnson has yet to electrify, he will find it. The most successful crossover Superstar in WWE history, his limitless charisma and drive have propelled him to unimaginable celebrity with new, iconic roles seemingly added to his resume faster than IMDB can refresh itself. And it all started with the burning desire to continue a family tradition inside the rings of WWE.

HALL OF FAME BLOODLINE

Dwayne Johnson is the son of WWE Hall of Famer Rocky Johnson and grandson of WWE Hall of Famer High Chief Peter Maivia. Each branch of the expansive Maivia family tree features a who's who of sports-entertainment, but the High Chief was its patriarch. Revered for his toughness, Maivia also appeared in the 1967 James Bond classic, *You Only Live Twice*.

Because he idolized his father, grandfather, and their peers, it was only natural Dwayne thought about a life in both sports and entertainment. He became an All-American on the gridiron at Freedom High School in Bethlehem, Pennsylvania, and then was a central part of the Miami Hurricanes 1991 NCAA Championship team. After a brief career in the Canadian Football League, Johnson entered the industry that flowed through his veins. Trained by his father, along with Pat Patterson, Dwayne exceeded all expectations. Word reached WWE that the third-generation grappler was a potential megastar.

A ROCKY START

At *Survivor Series 1996*, Rocky Maivia debuted in front of a capacity Madison Square Garden crowd. The moniker was a tribute to his grandfather and father. As the next Maivia emerged the sole survivor, this Superstar was set to take WWE by storm. Within three months of his debut, Rocky captured the Intercontinental Championship from Hunter Hearst-Helmsley.

As the tone of sports-entertainment changed, fans rejected the blue chipper with chants of "Rocky Sucks" and "Die Rocky Die." Shortening his name to "The Rock" and referring to himself in the third person, he became a member of The Nation of Domination and fed off the fans' scorn. As his undiluted arrogance enraged crowds, The Rock dubbed himself "The People's Champion" and vowed to reach the top of WWE by any means necessary. The Rock soon overthrew Faarooq as Nation leader and became the self-appointed ruler of The Nation of Domination, citing the term "leader" was beneath him. In the summer of 1998, The Nation began a fierce rivalry against D-Generation X to decide which was the dominant faction in WWE. The two leaders met in the King of the Ring tournament. After The Rock pinned rival Triple H, both crews threw fists of fury as pure bedlam flooded the ring.

The Rock's career gained momentum and he left The Nation to construct his own path to glory. He invited all Superstars to "Go One-on-One with The Great One," and in the process attracted Mr. McMahon's intense scrutiny. "The People's Champion" made the final at the *Survivor Series* 14-man tournament for the WWE Championship, showing the perseverance and poise of a seasoned veteran. After he locked-in the Sharpshooter on Mankind, the bell unexpectedly rang and his collusion with the Chairman became known. The McMahons courted The Rock and made "The People's Champion" "The Corporate Champion." This event led to a string of classic clashes between The Rock and Mankind that brought out an even more barbarous "Brahma Bull." After several sadistic bouts, "The Most Electrifying Man in Sports-Entertainment" put his problems with Mankind behind and focused on a new enemy.

At *WrestleMania XV*, The Rock took on the rebellious Stone Cold Steve Austin for the WWE Championship. The carnage in Philadelphia proved to be the beginning of one of the greatest rivalries in WWE history. Despite a loss to the "Texas Rattlesnake," The Rock truly became "The People's Champion" when he left The Corporation and went his own way. As his mystique grew, audiences marveled at his undeniable charisma and wildly entertaining interview segments. Later in 1999, he resumed warring with a familiar foe, Triple H. When former enemy Mankind was looking for a friend, he treated The Rock to a parade of his past on an episode of "Rock, This is Your Life." In the process, the two joined forces as The Rock 'n' Sock Connection and surprised everyone with their chemistry as a Championship caliber tandem.

THE GREAT ONE AT #1

After he won the 2000 Royal Rumble Match, The Rock's popularity rose to new heights each week. The Rock wrote his autobiography, *The Rock Says*, which reached No. 1 on the prestigious New York Times Bestseller List. He hosted *Saturday Night Live* and appeared in Wyclef Jean's famous hip-hop video, "It Doesn't Matter." By 2001, The Rock was considered a multimedia superstar as he appeared in the feature film, *The Mummy Returns* and later starred in its highly successful prequel, *The Scorpion King*.

Of course, The Rock didn't sever his ties with WWE during this time. He secured the fate of WWE at *Survivor Series 2001* as he captained Team WWE and destroyed The Alliance. This defense of his first love became indisputable in February 2002, when Mr. McMahon injected the lethal poison of "Hollywood" Hulk Hogan and the nWo into WWE. At *WrestleMania X8*, he defeated Hogan in an epic fantasy-turned-reality Icon vs. Icon Match. In 2003, The Rock's Hollywood stock continued to rise, but he may have saved his greatest act for *WrestleMania XIX*, when he defeated his long-time nemesis Stone Cold Steve Austin, ending their historic three-match *WrestleMania* trilogy.

The Rock returned to Hollywood for *The Rundown* with Christopher Walken, but returned to WWE in 2004 to reform the Rock 'n' Sock Connection, and battle Evolution at *WrestleMania XX*. The Rock's international following grew and he continued to electrify movie screens as the main draw in multiple Hollywood blockbusters.

Across seven years away from WWE, The Rock appeared sparingly on taped segments. In 2008, he inducted his father, Rocky Johnson, and late grandfather, High Chief Peter Maivia, into the WWE Hall of Fame. As he continued to stockpile film credits, WWE fans could only fantasize about a return to the ring.

FINALLY, THE ROCK HAS COME BACK!

Fantasy became reality in February 2011 when the most electrifying man in all of entertainment was announced as the host of *WrestleMania XXVII*. The Brahma Bull also made it known he planned to bring it to John Cena. At *WrestleMania XXVII*, the Jabroni beating, pie eating, trailblazing, eyebrow raising Team Bring It captain electrified the event and aided in John Cena's defeat.

The next night on *Raw*, John Cena challenged The Rock to a match at *WrestleMania XXVIII* in The Rock's hometown of Miami.

For the rest of 2011, The Rock and John Cena traded verbal jabs, even when forced to team up at *Survivor Series*. While the duo rarely saw eye-to-eye, they put aside their differences long enough to defeat The Miz and R-Truth.

On Sunday April 1, 2012 The Rock returned home to Miami and battled John Cena in the main event of *WrestleMania XXVIII*. Over 78,000 people witnessed thirty grueling minutes of back-and-forth action between two Superstars who each defined their era of WWE history. In the end, The Rock emerged triumphant in the "Once in a Lifetime" confrontation, then basked in the adulation of his hometown fans.

For anyone else, "Once in a Lifetime" would have been the grand finale, but if you thought The Rock was done there, well, it doesn't matter what you think! It had been ten years since The Rock last held the WWE Championship and he had decided that was long enough. At *Royal Rumble 2013*, the Great One fulfilled his promise to grab the gold for the eighth time. With his mom seated in the front row of a ravenous crowd, Rock bottomed out CM Punk's historic 434-day reign.

The Rock's storybook win put him in line for a rematch with John Cena at *WrestleMania 29*. This time, Cena got the best of his electrifying foil. With their generational rivalry knotted at 1-1, the proud competitors showed mutual respect and admiration as the lights dimmed on the Grandest Stage. That same year, The Rock was named *Forbes* highest grossing actor, reeling in $1.3 billion dollars at the box office for multiple films including *Pain & Gain* and *G.I. Joe: Retaliation*. As fast as Hollywood can roll out red carpets, he continues laying the smackdown on the silver screen with starring roles in *Hercules, San Andreas*, the *Fast and Furious* franchise, and many more.

Despite his A-list status, The Rock never forgets where it all began. He emerged at *WrestleMania 30* to share a toast in the ring with Hulk Hogan and Stone Cold Steve Austin in an iconic *WrestleMania* moment. In 2015, he supported his cousin Roman Reigns during Roman's Royal Rumble Match victory and delighted the *WrestleMania 31* crowd by interrupting The Authority.

At *WrestleMania 32*, The Rock became tied to two historic WWE records, first doing the honors of announcing WWE's record-shattering attendance, then dropping Erick Rowan with a Rock Bottom to win an impromptu match in six seconds, the shortest *WrestleMania* match ever.

The WWE Universe eagerly awaits his next arrival while getting their fix in theaters across the globe. When that music hits, one thing is for sure, they will all smell what The Rock is cookin'!

WAKE UP DETERMINED. GO TO BED SATISFIED.

ROMAN REIGNS

HT 6'3"	**WT** 265 lbs.	**FROM** Pensacola, Florida

SIGNATURE MOVE Spear, Superman Punch

The Roman Empire is upon us. And its leader, Roman Reigns, sits atop his throne as the forbidding force hell-bent on conquering WWE and proving his detractors wrong.

Reigns' climb to the top began in November 2012 when Seth Rollins, Dean Ambrose, and he made their impactful debut, interfering in the *Survivor Series* main event. Collectively known as The Shield, the trio of newcomers went on to unleash a truly unique brand of justice onto the WWE roster. Along the way, Reigns and Rollins also teamed up to capture the WWE Tag Team Championship from Team Hell No at *Extreme Rules 2013*.

Though The Shield dominated WWE like no other group, they eventually splintered when Rollins shockingly attacked Reigns and Ambrose in June 2014. The assault marked the end of one of WWE's most popular factions, while also serving as the launching pad for Reigns' meteoric rise.

Reigns cemented himself as a main event Superstar in January 2015 when he last eliminated Rusev to win the *Royal Rumble* Match. With the victory, The Big Dog was awarded an opportunity at Brock Lesnar's WWE World Heavyweight Championship in the main event of *WrestleMania 31*. Despite successfully withstanding unbelievable punishment from Lesnar, Reigns was unable to claim the Title, as Rollins eventually swooped in to cash in his Money in the Bank contract and win the Title.

Losing at *WrestleMania* failed to derail Reigns; rather it further fueled his desire to one day become Champion. And in November 2015, he finally achieved his goal when he defeated Ambrose in a tournament finals match to capture the Title.

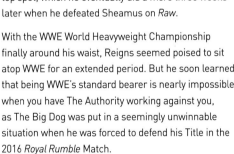

Unfortunately for Reigns, however, what should have been a triumphant occasion quickly turned catastrophic when Sheamus emerged to successfully cash in his Money in the Bank contract. The loss marked the second time Money in the Bank prevented Reigns from sitting atop WWE. In typical Reigns fashion, it also motivated him even more to reclaim his top spot, which he eventually did a mere three weeks later when he defeated Sheamus on *Raw*.

With the WWE World Heavyweight Championship finally around his waist, Reigns seemed poised to sit atop WWE for an extended period. But he soon learned that being WWE's standard bearer is nearly impossible when you have The Authority working against you, as The Big Dog was put in a seemingly unwinnable situation when he was forced to defend his Title in the 2016 *Royal Rumble* Match.

Despite a valiant effort, Reigns lost his Championship when he was eliminated by eventual winner Triple H. Roman got his ultimate revenge on The Game by defeating Triple H for the WWE World Heavyweight Championship at *WrestleMania 32*.

RON SHAW

WT 265 lbs.	**FROM** Philadelphia, Pennsylvania

Ivan Putski. Ricky Steamboat. Hillbilly Jim. Tito Santana. Ron Shaw wrestled them all, and lost each and every time. He was even defeated by Salvatore Bellomo.

Despite his lackluster record, Shaw continued to compete, hoping his luck would eventually change. And it did...once. While squaring off against David Sammartino, Shaw mustered up enough confidence to bodyslam the second-generation Superstar fifteen times before forcing him to submit via a bear hug.

Luck nearly found its way to Shaw again in July 1984, when he took part in a Battle Royal at *The Brawl to End It All*. Shaw outlasted seventeen other Superstars to become one of the final three combatants, but was eventually eliminated by Rene Goulet. Antonio Inoki was later declared the victor.

ROCKY JOHNSON

HT	6'2"	WT	243 lbs.	FROM	Toronto, Ontario, Canada
SIGNATURE MOVE	The Dropkick				

The "Soul Man" started out as a boxer and decided to enter professional wrestling during the mid-1960s. He made his debut in the Toronto area, where he was mentored by former NWA World Heavyweight Champion, Whipper Billy Watson.

But Johnson quickly emerged from Watson's shadow, and was soon acquiring titles all over North America. In Los Angeles, he scored the NWA Americas Tag Team Championship with Earl Maynard, and defeated Freddie Blassie for the single's Title. He also won tag team gold with both Pat Patterson and Gerry Brisco in San Francisco, and Pedro Morales in Florida, among other prizes .

In 1983, he journeyed to WWE. From his first match, audiences knew he was a special performer. Professional wrestling's first "Rock" was one of the most popular members of the roster. Fans admired his style combining speed, acrobatics, power, and mat wrestling.

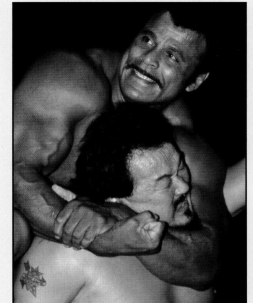

Rocky was also admired by the daughter of High Chief Peter Maivia, one of his tag team partners. The two were married, and had a son, Dwayne "The Rock" Johnson, in 1972.

Johnson matched up against the likes of "Superstar" Billy Graham, Mr. Fuji, Baron Mikel Scicluna, George "The Animal" Steele, and Big John Studd. On several occasions, he came within an eyelash of wresting the WWE Intercontinental Title from The Magnificent Muraco. On November 15, 1983, Johnson and "Mr. USA" Tony Atlas made history in Allentown, Pennsylvania, when they defeated the Wild Samoans to become the first-ever World Tag Team Champions of African descent.

After leaving the WWE in 1985, Rocky Johnson, along with Pat Patterson, trained his son for a career in sports-entertainment. During his son's debut as Rocky Maivia, things got heated and Mr. Johnson was not afraid to get into the mix and help the youngster fend off foes.

The night before *WrestleMania XXIV*, the career that was fueled by courage and desire was immortalized when Rocky Johnson was inducted into the WWE Hall of Fame by his son, now known as The Rock.

RON SIMMONS/FAAROOQ

HT	6'2"	WT	260 lbs.
FROM	Warner Robins, Georgia		

Following a Hall of Fame football career at Florida State University, Ron Simmons made the jump to the ring in 1986. What followed was a groundbreaking career that saw the rugged Superstar break down all color barriers to reach the pinnacle.

Simmons first made a name for himself competing in WCW during the late 1980s and early 1990s. As a member of the intimidating tag team Doom, alongside Butch Reed, he was recognized as one-half of the promotion's first-ever World Tag Team Champions. Led by manager Theodore Long, Doom held the titles for nine months before losing to the Fabulous Freebirds in February 1991.

In August 1992, Simmons made history when he defeated Vader for the WCW Championship. The landmark victory made Simmons the first African-American World Champion of any major promotion. He held the title for five months before dropping it back to Vader.

Following his time in WCW, Simmons dove into the chaotic waters of ECW, challenging Shane Douglas for the ECW World Heavyweight Championship.

Simmons underwent an identity change in 1996 when he debuted in WWE under the name Faarooq. With his new moniker, Simmons gained great fame, first as the leader of The Nation of Domination. Faarooq truly came into his own as a member of The Acolytes with Bradshaw, later known as John "Bradshaw" Layfield. Eventually, the two bruisers became bounty hunters of sorts, forming the Acolytes Protection Agency, or APA, collecting commissions from various Superstars who wished to see their rivals manhandled.

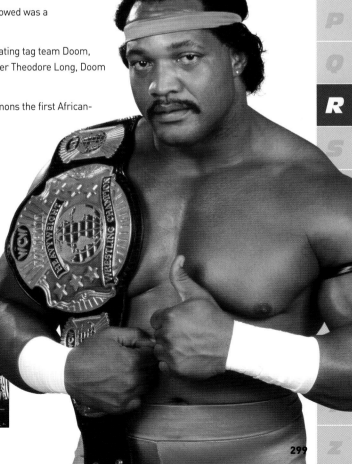

Outside the ring, Simmons and JBL were as close as brothers, a bond strengthened by their three WWE World Tag Team Championship reigns. Faarooq also became a backstage leader to younger Superstars, admired for his experience, toughness, and pride in the industry.

Even after he stepped away from full-time competition in 2004, Simmons remained part of the WWE scene, gaining a reputation for popping up at the most opportune times to utter his signature catchphrase, "Damn!"

In 2012, JBL proudly inducted his friend into the WWE Hall of Fame.

RONNIE GARVIN

HT	5'10"	WT	242 lbs.	FROM	Charlotte, North Carolina
SIGNATURE MOVE		**Figure-Four Leglock**			

Before ever stepping foot in a WWE ring, "Rugged" Ronnie Garvin spent more than two decades proving himself as one of the game's toughest competitors. At just 5'10", Garvin was forced to work overtime to gain success against larger rivals such as Dusty Rhodes and the Road Warriors. In the end, however, his dedication to his craft paid off, as Garvin claimed more than 30 titles over the course of his career, including the prestigious NWA Championship.

Garvin made his WWE debut in 1988 to much fanfare. Almost immediately after entering the promotion, he found himself in a bitter rivalry with the similarly styled Greg Valentine. For nearly one year, the two Superstars battled over which had the greater Figure Four Leglock. Garvin eventually proved his superiority when he defeated Valentine in a Submission Match at the 1990 *Royal Rumble*.

Garvin went into semi-retirement shortly afterward and eventually became a pilot. Despite his exit from the game, fans will forever remember the thunderous thump his "hands of stone" left on an opponent's chest.

ROSEY

HT	6'7"	WT	420 lbs.	FROM	San Francisco, California
SIGNATURE MOVE		**Super-Hero Slam**			

This former Superstar began his WWE career, along with his brother Jamal, as a hired gun for Eric Bischoff's 3-Minute Warning squad. After this short-lived act expired, WWE's resident super-hero, The Hurricane, gave the Samoan Superstar his special brand of training to enhance his natural abilities.

In the summer of 2004, Rosey had a new outlook on life, new ring attire and a new purpose. Together with The Hurricane they were the super-heroes the world needed. At *Backlash 2005*, their combined forces pushed them past La Resistance to become World Tag Team Champions. Unfortunately, the once indomitable team was unable to recover once their Title reign ended. The Hurricane ditched both Rosey and the crime-fighting gig. Rosey departed from WWE soon after, in March 2006.

"ROWDY" RODDY PIPER

see page 302

R-TRUTH

HT	6'2"	WT	220 lbs.	FROM	Charlotte, North Carolina
SIGNATURE MOVE		**Lie Detector**			

R-Truth first appeared in WWE in 1999 alongside Road Dogg as K-Kwik. After six years away, he returned to WWE in 2008 rapping his way to the ring with infectious enthusiasm and a crowd-pleasing catch phrase, "What's up?" His unparalleled agility inside the ring made him an instant fan favorite and legitimate championship threat. In the spring of 2010, R-Truth showed everyone what's up when he won the United States Championship and became a contender for the WWE Championship.

After being within heartbeats of claiming sports-entertainment's richest prize, R-Truth became unhinged. He accused WWE, its Superstars, and the "Little Jimmys" in the audience of conspiring against him. He turned on John Morrison and formed a team with another frustrated Superstar, The Miz, known as Awesome Truth.

Truth eventually returned to his fan-friendly ways, not only embracing "Little Jimmy," but also adopting the imaginary pint-sized pal as a ringside ally. Though Truth was clearly losing his marbles, he regained the trust of the fans and some reliable allies. In April 2012, he and another free-spirited high-flyer, Kofi Kingston, teamed up to win the WWE Tag Team Championship. The exciting duo held the gold for five months.

Since parting ways with Kofi, the sixteen-year ring veteran has proven to be a valuable mentor to Xavier Woods and other young Superstars, even if his kooky nature is a double-edged sword. Truth is unfazed by scaling a 15-foot ladder, but doing so in the 2016 Royal Rumble Match proved counterproductive to say the least! Despite these occasional mental gaffs, Truth keeps himself in the hunt for the Intercontinental and United States Championships. "The truth will set you free!"

ROSA MENDES

HT	5'9"	FROM	San Mateo, California

In 2008, Rosa Mendes' obsession with Beth Phoenix could have turned ugly, but rather than shun her crazed fan, the "Glamazon" made the unorthodox decision to hire her as an intern. The Costa Rican beauty quickly received a first-hand education in competing in the Divas division.

After a torrid relationship with Zack Ryder, Mendes was shipped from ECW to *SmackDown* in the spring of 2010. Determined to get in tip-top shape, Mendes' tireless work with a Shake-Weight actually earned her a 2010 Slammy Award.

The following year, Mendes managed Primo and Epico and guided the two cousins to a three-month WWE Tag Team Championship reign. Always a dependable ally, she has also helped Superstars such as Fandango and Adam Rose rediscover their spark.

In 2013, Mendes joined several other Divas in an ongoing crusade against the *Total Divas* cast. However, the following year she changed her tune, joining the reality show and allowing fans an inside look into her life away from the ring.

RUE DEBONA

The WWE Universe remembers Rue DeBona as the host of the weekly syndicated Show *After Burn* in 2003 and 2004. As a part of the WWE broadcast team, DeBona was seen by millions of fans worldwide, which was something she became accustomed to prior to pursuing a career in sports-entertainment.

As a member of the all-girl group, Boy Krazy, DeBona scored a hit single with "That's What Love Can Do" in 1993. That same year, she also appeared on Disney Channel's *The All New Mickey Mouse Club*, which also featured future A-list celebrities Ryan Gosling, Justin Timberlake, and Britney Spears, among others.

DeBona has appeared in several films following her brief WWE career. She is most known for her role as Emily in Steven Seagal's 2008 action movie, *Pistol Whipped*. She was also the face of the now-defunct television network VOOM.

Despite having a fleeting WWE career, DeBona's peppy personality and natural beauty left an impression on the WWE Universe that will not soon be forgotten.

RUSEV

HT 6'0" **WT** 304 lbs. **FROM** Bulgaria
SIGNATURE MOVE The Accolade

At more than three-hundred pounds, Rusev might be considered by many as the classic powerhouse. But The Bulgarian Brute effectively combines his great strength with an agility and speed not normally found in competitors his size to create one of the most well-rounded Superstars in recent memory.

Rusev made his WWE debut in the 2014 Royal Rumble Match. After witnessing his superior skills firsthand, the Superstars of the WWE quickly realized they would need to band together if they were to eliminate The Super Athlete. In the end, it took four Superstars to toss Rusev over the top rope.

Rusev's April 2014 *Raw* debut proved equally successful. With the lovely Lana by his side, The Bulgarian Brute decimated Zack Ryder before forcing him to submit to The Accolade. Afterward, an emotionless Rusev maintained his grip on The Accolade until Lana ordered him to release.

In the weeks that followed, Rusev made short work of several top names. His success eventually led to a United States Championship opportunity. Seen exclusively on the WWE Network, Rusev captured the Title when he forced Sheamus to lose consciousness via The Accolade.

Rusev's dominance continued into 2015 where he used his Accolade to defeat John Cena at *WWE Fastlane*. Going into *WrestleMania 31*, Rusev's shoulders weren't pinned to the mat. In a rematch at *WrestleMania 31*, however, The Super Athlete's luck finally ran out. After a Rusev-Lana miscommunication, Cena landed his Attitude Adjustment to hand The Bulgarian Brute his first pinfall loss.

Following *WrestleMania*, the relationship between Rusev and Lana began to crumble, eventually leading to a very public breakup. Though neither would remain single for long. Rusev eventually found love in Summer Rae, while Lana romanced Dolph Ziggler.

The two couples engaged in a months-long rivalry, highlighted by a match between Rusev and Ziggler at *SummerSlam*. The contest ended in a double countout, leading many to believe the ongoing battle would continue. But several weeks later, it was learned that Rusev and Lana had shockingly reconciled.

With The Ravishing Russian back by his side, Rusev has regained the ferocity he seemingly lost with Summer Rae. He has also aligned himself with Alberto Del Rio, Sheamus, and King Barrett. Collectively known as the League of Nations, the foreign foursome has put a target on all American Superstars.

RYAN BRADDOCK

HT 6'4" **WT** 262 lbs. **FROM** Chicago, Illinois
SIGNATURE MOVE Lariat

Rough, tough, and ready for anything, Ryan Braddock showed a fearless side when he squared off against the giant Big Show in his first WWE match in August 2008. Though he came up short, Braddock proved he had confidence to go up against even the largest of competition.

Unfortunately for Braddock, that confidence didn't equate to success in the ring. The Chicago native soon found himself losing to the likes of Ricky Ortiz and Super Crazy.

The ultimate embarrassment came in September 2008 when Jesse and Festus used duct tape to wrap Braddock in bubble wrap. That was one of the last times the WWE Universe ever saw Ryan Braddock.

RYAN SHAMROCK

HT 5'6" **FROM** Sacramento, California

With her quiet demeanor and innocent smile, Ryan Shamrock certainly played the part of a demure woman. In reality, though, Ken Shamrock's sister was anything but pure.

Just weeks after making her debut, Ryan co-starred in Val Venis' controversial *Sister Act*. Proving her act of indiscretion was not a momentary lapse of judgment, the leggy blonde later intentionally left the blinds to her SkyDome hotel room open so *Raw* fans could witness the couple in their most intimate moments.

Venis eventually kicked Ryan to the curb. Refusing to be a victim, the jilted Diva later joined forces with Terri and Jacqueline in the male-bashing faction Pretty Mean Sisters. As a member of PMS, Ryan used her sexuality to toy with the male WWE Superstars.

"ROWDY" RODDY PIPER

HT	6'2"
WT	230 lbs.
FROM	Glasgow, Scotland

SIGNATURE MOVE
Sleeper

A Superstar like Rowdy Roddy Piper comes along once or twice in a generation. Fueled by angst and bravado, Piper was naturally endowed as both an athlete and entertainer, enabling him to take center stage during that crucial period when WWE transitioned from a northeastern promotion to an international juggernaut.

Much of the torment Piper projected on camera came from a troubled background. Never one to follow orders, he was cast out of both his school and home, occasionally sleeping in the street. But he excelled at both boxing and judo, and celebrated his Scottish heritage by playing the bagpipes.

A skinny but determined Piper debuted at the Winnipeg Arena as the youngest competitor on the card. Ten seconds after the bell rang, though, he was defeated by legend Larry "The Ax" Hennig, grandfather of Curtis Axel. That night, Roddy began his initiation into the sacred fraternity of the ring.

Starting in 1973, Piper bounced around North America, losing more than winning in the AWA, Central States, Maritimes, Houston, and Dallas territories. Then, in 1975, he made his debut at the Olympic Auditorium in East Los Angeles for the NWA Hollywood promotion.

By now, the company's glory days had passed. But Piper was unlike anyone the largely Mexican audience at the Olympic had ever seen. Whipping himself into a shrieking frenzy during interviews and gaining the upper hand in matches with eye pokes and sucker punches, Piper engaged in an unforgettable battle with Chavo Guerrero, Sr. and his father, the great Gory Guerrero, winning the promotion's Americas Heavyweight Championship. After falling to Chavo in a "Loser Leaves Town" match, Piper returned under a mask, reclaiming the Title and creating havoc until another Guerrero, Hector, revealed the Scotsman's true identity.

Piper next exported his madness to the Pacific Northwest territory, entering into a rivalry with Buddy Rose that was exacerbated when Rose stole The Rowdy One's kilt. More significantly, Piper became an indelible part of the Portland Wrestling community, maintaining a loyalty to promoter Don Owen even after WWE stardom.

After a number of other stops, Piper was in Georgia Championship Wrestling in 1982, broadcasting the promotion's show alongside future WWE Hall of Famer Gordon Solie. At first, fans jeered Piper. But when the sagacious announcer was terrorized by Don Muraco, Roddy came to the aid of his fellow commentator, knocking out both Muraco and cohort Ole Anderson.

Piper then landed in the Charlotte territory, battling "Nature Boy" Ric Flair, Sgt. Slaughter, and Buzz Sawyer. He also engaged in a dog collar match with Greg "The Hammer" Valentine at the premier *Starrcade* in 1983 that was so ferocious that Roddy lost some of his hearing.

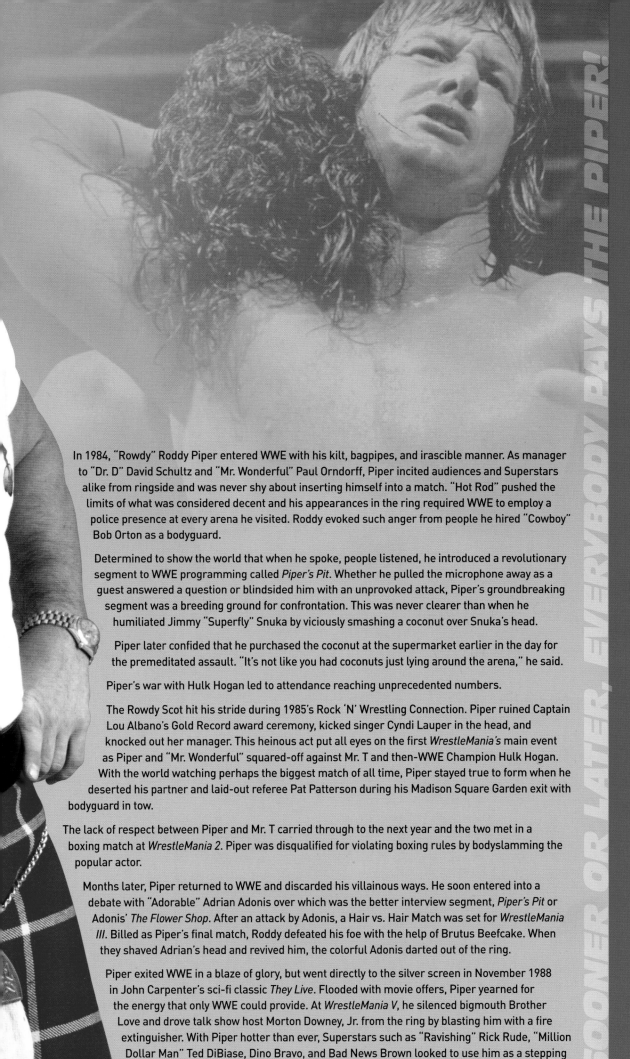

In 1984, "Rowdy" Roddy Piper entered WWE with his kilt, bagpipes, and irascible manner. As manager to "Dr. D" David Schultz and "Mr. Wonderful" Paul Orndorff, Piper incited audiences and Superstars alike from ringside and was never shy about inserting himself into a match. "Hot Rod" pushed the limits of what was considered decent and his appearances in the ring required WWE to employ a police presence at every arena he visited. Roddy evoked such anger from people he hired "Cowboy" Bob Orton as a bodyguard.

Determined to show the world that when he spoke, people listened, he introduced a revolutionary segment to WWE programming called *Piper's Pit*. Whether he pulled the microphone away as a guest answered a question or blindsided him with an unprovoked attack, Piper's groundbreaking segment was a breeding ground for confrontation. This was never clearer than when he humiliated Jimmy "Superfly" Snuka by viciously smashing a coconut over Snuka's head.

Piper later confided that he purchased the coconut at the supermarket earlier in the day for the premeditated assault. "It's not like you had coconuts just lying around the arena," he said.

Piper's war with Hulk Hogan led to attendance reaching unprecedented numbers.

The Rowdy Scot hit his stride during 1985's Rock 'N' Wrestling Connection. Piper ruined Captain Lou Albano's Gold Record award ceremony, kicked singer Cyndi Lauper in the head, and knocked out her manager. This heinous act put all eyes on the first *WrestleMania's* main event as Piper and "Mr. Wonderful" squared-off against Mr. T and then-WWE Champion Hulk Hogan. With the world watching perhaps the biggest match of all time, Piper stayed true to form when he deserted his partner and laid-out referee Pat Patterson during his Madison Square Garden exit with bodyguard in tow.

The lack of respect between Piper and Mr. T carried through to the next year and the two met in a boxing match at *WrestleMania 2*. Piper was disqualified for violating boxing rules by bodyslamming the popular actor.

Months later, Piper returned to WWE and discarded his villainous ways. He soon entered into a debate with "Adorable" Adrian Adonis over which was the better interview segment, *Piper's Pit* or Adonis' *The Flower Shop*. After an attack by Adonis, a Hair vs. Hair Match was set for *WrestleMania III*. Billed as Piper's final match, Roddy defeated his foe with the help of Brutus Beefcake. When they shaved Adrian's head and revived him, the colorful Adonis darted out of the ring.

Piper exited WWE in a blaze of glory, but went directly to the silver screen in November 1988 in John Carpenter's sci-fi classic *They Live*. Flooded with movie offers, Piper yearned for the energy that only WWE could provide. At *WrestleMania V*, he silenced bigmouth Brother Love and drove talk show host Morton Downey, Jr. from the ring by blasting him with a fire extinguisher. With Piper hotter than ever, Superstars such as "Ravishing" Rick Rude, "Million Dollar Man" Ted DiBiase, Dino Bravo, and Bad News Brown looked to use him as a stepping stone to stardom.

Piper's conflict with Brown culminated at *WrestleMania VI*. Still an expert psychologist, Piper raced through the SkyDome to the ring with half of his body painted black as a symbol of interracial harmony.

In 1991, Roddy brought his brand of mayhem to the broadcast position on WWE's *Prime Time Wrestling* show and pay-per-view events. On January 19, 1992, he won his first major Title in WWE by defeating the Mountie for the Intercontinental Championship at the 1992 Royal Rumble. He lost the Title to Bret "Hit Man" Hart a few months later at *WrestleMania VIII* in an emotional contest based on their shared history training with Bret's father, Stu Hart.

By the mid-1990s, Roddy was a bona fide leading man in Hollywood and one of WWE's most popular Superstars. Whether he was a surprise Special Guest Referee at *WrestleMania X*, or involved in a Backlot Brawl with Goldust at *WrestleMania XII,* "Hot Rod" brought audiences to their feet.

A TRIUMPHANT RETURN

After a seven-year absence, Piper stunned WWE audiences in 2003 when he returned at *WrestleMania XIX* during the Street Fight between Hulk Hogan and Mr. McMahon. On April 2, 2005, he was enshrined into the WWE Hall of Fame. The next night, at *WrestleMania 21*, he hosted a special *Piper's Pit* with guest, Stone Cold Steve Austin.

Then, on November 5, 2006, the Hall of Famer captured the World Tag Team Championship with Ric Flair. Three years later Piper was part of the team that taught Chris Jericho a wrestling lesson after he blatantly disrespected the legends of sports-entertainment. In 2010, Roddy inducted his sometime Rock 'n' Wrestling connection nemesis, Wendi Richter, into the WWE Hall of Fame.

During the next few years, Piper stayed busy, interviewing Superstars on periodic episodes of *Piper's Pit*, appearing in the WWE Network series *Legends House*, and making an effort to revive the Portland Wrestling territory. MMA champion Ronda Rousey added "Rowdy" to her name in tribute to Piper.

On July 31, 2015, the man who blew through the wrestling and entertainment worlds like a tornado, died in his sleep. Along with his many accomplishments, Piper is fondly remembered for his aggressive in-ring style and his no-holds-barred interviews on *Piper's Pit*.

RYBACK

| **HT** | 6'3" | **WT** | 291 lbs. | **FROM** | Las Vegas, Nevada |
| **SIGNATURE MOVE** | Shell Shocked | | | | |

Never before has the WWE Universe witnessed such a disastrous combination of size, strength, and intensity than that which is found in Ryback. Fueled by an insatiable appetite for destruction, the nearly 300-pound brute has annihilated almost every foe in his path, en route to establishing himself as a Human Wrecking Ball.

When Ryback first appeared on the scene in April 2012, The Big Guy crushed opponents at a record rate, sometimes two or three at a time. It wasn't long before his impressive win-loss record propelled him to main events where he challenged CM Punk for the WWE Championship. At *Hell in a Cell*, Ryback looked well on his way to dethroning Punk as Champion, but interference by rogue referee Brad Maddox dashed those dreams.

The following month at *Survivor Series 2012*, Ryback's championship aspirations were crushed again when the Triple Threat WWE Title Match he was competing in was marred by controversy, thanks to the debuting Shield. In the following months, The Shield continually targeted Ryback, making it impossible for him to capture the WWE Championship.

Enraged by the attacks from The Shield, Ryback eventually took his frustration out on John Cena, claiming Cena should've been there for him when the trio struck. The assault on the Cenation leader forced the fans to jeer Ryback. But he didn't care; he only had eyes for one thing—The WWE Championship.

Ryback challenged Cena for the WWE Title in mid-2013, most notably in a Three Stages of Hell Match at *Payback*, but was unable to pry the gold away. He then shifted his attention to tag team competition, teaming with Curtis Axel as one-half of RybAxel.

Ryback faded from the scene in the summer of 2014, only to return in October as popular as ever. With the crowd in his corner, The Big Guy captured his first championship by outlasting R-Truth, Mark Henry, Sheamus, King Barrett, and Dolph Ziggler in an Elimination Chamber Match for the Intercontinental Title.

Given Ryback's undying desire to be the best, it's probably pretty safe to assume that his Intercontinental Championship victory was the first in a long line of championships for The Big Guy.

RYUMA GO

| **FROM** | Japan |

While competing for New Japan Pro Wrestling in the late 1970s, Ryuma Go experienced a whirlwind two days that will forever link him to WWE. On October 2, 1979, the powerful Go ended Tatsumi Fujinami's amazing 600-plus day reign with the WWE Junior Heavyweight Championship when he defeated the legend in Osaka, Japan. Go enjoyed the now-defunct Title for two quick days before losing it back to Fujinami in a match contested in Tokyo, Japan.

In addition to his NJPW days, Go travelled the globe, competing mainly in Canada, Germany, and the United States. He captured the NWA Beat the Champ Television Title, the NWA Americas Tag Team Championship twice, and held the short-lived CWIA International Tag Team Championship.

SABA SIMBA

| **HT** | 6'2" | **WT** | 250 lbs. | **FROM** | Africa |

In the early 1990s, a mountain of a man emerged on the WWE scene under the moniker of Saba Simba. Clad in a giant feather headdress and leopard print tights, Saba Simba was billed as an African tribal warrior. He struggled to pick up wins and was gone from WWE, but not before he was able to compete in the 1991 *Royal Rumble Match*.

SABLE

HT	5'6"	FROM	Jacksonville, Florida
SIGNATURE MOVE			Sable Bomb

Sable is undoubtedly one of the greatest pioneers the Divas division has ever seen. Never before had one woman combined such athleticism and sex appeal to become a major force both in and out of the ring.

Sable's earliest days were spent by the side of Hunter Hearst-Helmsley. But when the haughty Superstar mistreated the fair-haired Diva, Marc Mero ran to her aid. For the better part of the next two years, the couple shared a strong bond both on and off the air.

By 1998, the spotlight began to shine brightest on Sable, leaving Mero's star to fade. Jealous of her popularity, Mero tried everything to dim her bright career. But there was no holding Sable back and she eventually broke free from his grasp.

On her own, Sable went on to achieve never-before-seen success. Her first step toward greatness was capturing the Women's Championship from Mero's new lady, Jacqueline, at *Survivor Series 1998*. The new champ then rode her popularity all the way to Hollywood, landing roles on several television programs, including *Pacific Blue* and *First Wave*.

Sable's surge into mainstream media continued when she landed the cover of *Playboy* in April 1999. The overwhelming success of her spread led to two more covers, and helped pave the way for future Divas such as Maria and Candice.

Sable began a nearly four-year hiatus in 1999. Upon returning, she cozied up to Mr. McMahon, which infuriated Stephanie McMahon. The two women engaged in a months-long rivalry, which saw Sable defeat Stephanie at *Vengeance 2003*. Sable was also in Mr. McMahon's corner when he defeated Stephanie in an "I Quit" Match at *No Mercy 2003*.

Sable returned to the pages of *Playboy* in March 2004, this time with the equally-beautiful Torrie Wilson posing alongside her. Sable and Torrie's success eventually caused a rift among the Divas, leading to the two *Playboy* models taking on Miss Jackie and Stacy Keibler at *WrestleMania XX*.

Sable left WWE in the summer of 2004. Though no longer an active competitor, the legacy she left behind can be seen in the smart, beautiful, and powerful Divas of today.

SABU

HT	6'0"	WT	235 lbs.	FROM	Bombay, Michigan
SIGNATURE MOVE		Arabian Facebuster			

Trained by his Hall of Fame uncle, the Sheik, Sabu knew no fear inside the ring. Possessing a complete disregard for his own well-being, the maniacal Superstar gained a cult-like following while competing in ECW in the mid-to-late 1990s.

Over the course of his lengthy ECW career, Sabu captured every piece of hardware the promotion offered, including three reigns with the prestigious ECW Championship. Despite his golden resumé, Sabu is best remembered for the abundance of injuries he suffered. Sliced open by barbed wire and shards of broken tables, his scarred body proudly displays permanent memories of his vicious battles.

Sabu competed at *ECW One Night Stand* in June, 2006. Battling Rey Mysterio for the WWE World Heavyweight Championship, he used his extreme style of competition to take the masked Superstar to the limit. In the end, the match was declared a no-contest after both men crashed through a table, rendering them unable to compete.

Following the success of his *One Night Stand* appearance, Sabu entered WWE's revived version of ECW. He used the brand's premiere episode to reintroduce himself as one of ECW's supreme Superstars, winning an Extreme Battle Royal to earn the right to challenge John Cena for the WWE Championship at *Vengeance*. He ultimately lost to Cena, but successfully reminded fans that he was the "Suicidal, Homicidal, Genocidal, Death-Defying Maniac."

"SAILOR" ART THOMAS

HT	6'6"	WT	265 lbs.	FROM	Fitchburg, Wisconsin
SIGNATURE MOVE		Bearhug			

A chiseled giant of the ring with 20-inch biceps, "Sailor" Art Thomas was a member of the United States Navy before he began his sports-entertainment career in 1943. During the 1950s, Thomas became one of the most beloved performers in the world and one of the first Superstars of African descent.

In the early 1960s, Thomas contended for the NWA Heavyweight Championship held at the time by "Nature Boy" Buddy Rogers. On more than a dozen occasions, Thomas came close to wresting away the gold from the cocky blond.

In 1963, he made his WWE debut, dazzling the fans in the northeast with his physique, power, and quickness. For the next seven years, "Sailor" appeared for WWE in singles competition and formed thrilling tandems with Bruno Sammartino and Bobo Brazil.

He continued his sports-entertainment career until his retirement early in the 1980s. Sadly, this cultural icon and legend of the ring passed away in 2003. "Sailor" Art Thomas was a hero to all and touched fans throughout the world over the course of his career.

SAKAMOTO

Sakamoto was loyal, perhaps to a fault.

As a worshiper of Tensai, Sakamoto accompanied the mighty Superstar to ringside upon his debut in the spring of 2012. At first, Sakamoto's presence was welcomed by Tensai, who picked up impressive wins over such names as CM Punk and Alex Riley. But once Tensai's luck began to run out, Sakamoto started to become the focus of the losing Superstar's frustrations.

Despite Tensai's less-than-favorable attitude toward his worshiper, Sakamoto continued to accompany the heavily-tattooed Superstar to the ring. Eventually, though, the losing became too much for Tensai to handle. In June 2012, the frustrated Superstar viciously attacked his loyal follower. Sakamoto left WWE shortly after the brutal assault at the hands of Tensai.

SALVATORE BELLOMO

HT	6'2"	WT	290 lbs.	FROM	Italy
SIGNATURE MOVE	Running Splash				

Known as the "Wildman," Italian Superstar Salvatore Bellomo gained moderate WWE success upon his arrival in the early 1980s. During this time, his greatest claim to fame was filling in for his injured friend, Junkyard Dog, on an in-ring edition of *Piper's Pit*. As a guest of "Rowdy" Roddy Piper, Bellomo was the target of severe verbal barbs from both Piper and his confederate, "Mr. Wonderful" Paul Orndorff. Finally, after the verbal attack turned physical, the injured JYD dragged himself to the ring to fend off Bellomo's adversaries.

After his WWE days came to a close, Bellomo brought his signature running splash finisher to ECW. With his in-ring days behind him, Bellomo began working in Belgium as a trainer to Superstars of tomorrow.

SALVATORE SINCERE

HT	6'3"	WT	262 lbs.	FROM	Philadelphia, Pennsylvania
SIGNATURE MOVE	Sincerely Yours				

Arrogant, charismatic and with a bodybuilder's physique, Salvatore Sincere entered WWE in 1996. Sincere battled Superstars such as Barry Horowitz, Savio Vega, Rocky Maivia, Jake "The Snake" Roberts, Shawn Michaels, and Undertaker. While fighting over the services of Sable, Marc Mero revealed Salvatore's real name was Tom Brandi, which lead to Salvatore often using that name while competing until he left WWE in April 1998.

Whichever name was announced to audiences, whether a villain or fan favorite, this rugged soldier brought the same grit and fight to the ring.

SAM HOUSTON

HT	6'1"	WT	227 lbs.	FROM	Waco, Texas
SIGNATURE MOVE	Bulldog				

Sam Houston liked to dance just as much as he liked to wrestle. While others were partial to metal or hip hop, Houston was a country boy. Coming to the ring in a cowboy hat and fringes, Houston wrestled in the Florida and Charlotte territories, picking up advice from veterans like Dusty Rhodes, Magnum TA, and Nelson Royal.

Houston's WWE career began in 1987 and was highlighted by decisive victories over Barry Horowitz and Danny Davis. He also competed in the first-ever Royal Rumble in 1988, and was a member of Ultimate Warrior's *Survivor Series* team later that year.

After WWE, he performed in WCW, among other promotions, and enjoyed a lengthy career, primarily on the independent circuit.

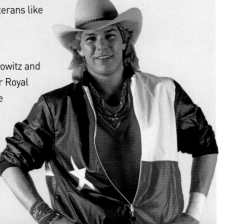

SAMI ZAYN

HT	6'1"	WT	205 lbs.
SIGNATURE MOVE	Helluva kick		

After competing in 29 separate countries, Sami Zayn was prepared for anything when he signed with WWE. Because he could adjust to so many styles, Zayn was able to bounce between NXT and the main roster, winning respect in both.

One of his most satisfying victories occurred in his hometown of Montreal, when he defeated Cesaro in 2013. Two years later, he took John Cena to the limit in the same arena. In between, he captured the NXT Championship from Neville. But his biggest rivalry, in both NXT and WWE, was with former buddy, Kevin Owens.

Time and again, Zayn has proven that he can withstand enormous punishment. And fans continue rallying behind "the underdog from the underground," convinced that he can do it all.

SAMOA JOE

HT	6'2"	WT	282 lbs.	FROM	Huntington Beach, California
SIGNATURE MOVE	Muscle Buster				

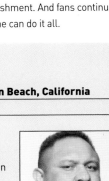

During the years when he was proving his worth in arenas in Japan, Mexico, and around North America, Samoa Joe was keeping a close watch on WWE, knowing that he'd already encountered men like John Cena, Daniel Bryan, Sami Zayn, Seth Rollins, and Kevin Owens while working for other promotions.

By the time he appeared in NXT in 2015, he was ready to renew old rivalries and cultivate new ones, relying on his repertoire of agonizing submissions and punishing kicks perfected while training at Muay Thai and Brazilian jiu-jitsu. A lone wolf averse to forming lasting allegiances, he warred with Owens and Zayn, as well as Baron Corbin, Finn Bálor, and Rhyno within months of his NXT debut.

On April 21, 2016, Samoa Joe captured the NXT Championship from Finn Bálor.

SAMU

HT	6'4"	WT	260 lbs.
FROM	Isle of Samoa		

Hailing from a long line of Samoan greats, Samu counts among his family the Wild Samoans (Afa and Sika), Peter Maivia, The Rock, Roman Reigns, Yokozuna, Rikishi, and the Usos.

At the young age of 20, Samu (then known as Samula) was thrust into the WWE spotlight. With his Uncle Sika sidelined by injury, Samula teamed with his father, Afa, to help defend the WWE World Tag Team Championship. He also earned success as a single's Superstar before taking a sabbatical from WWE in 1985.

Along with his cousin, Fatu, Samu formed the Samoan Swat Team, or SST, appearing in Puerto Rico, World Class Championship Wrestling, and WCW, where they were managed by Paul E. Dangerously and "Big Kahuna" Oliver Humperdink. In 1992, the pair entered WWE as The Headshrinkers. Managed by Afa and later Lou Albano, they won the WWE World Tag Team Championship in 1994. Soon after their Title run, Samu left the company. While wrestling in his family's independent promotion, Samu helped train the next generation of Samoan Superstars.

THE SANDMAN

HT	6'4"	WT	240 lbs.	FROM	Philadelphia, Pennsylvania
SIGNATURE MOVE	The White Russian Legsweep				

This Singapore Cane swingin', cigarette smokin', beer-chuggin' maniac was one of the primary reasons the "E" stood for Extreme in ECW. From its genesis in 1992 to its demise in 2001, nobody embodied the spirit of Paul Heyman's renegade promotion more than The Sandman, as evidenced by his record five ECW Championships.

The Sandman's entrance alone was an event, featuring Metallica's iconic track blaring as Sandman flattened a beer can over his head. In the ring, his rivalries with Tommy Dreamer, Shane Douglas, Raven, and other hardcore icons were not for the faint of heart. In 1996, Sandman witnessed his own wife and son become brainwashed into joining Raven's brooding followers, The Nest. In an emotional scene, he regained both his family and the ECW Championship by defeating Nest members Stevie Richards and Brian Lee.

After appearing at *ECW One Night Stand* in 2005 and 2006, he joined WWE's resurrection of ECW. With fellow ECW Originals, Sandman stood victorious in the ring at *WrestleMania 23* after defeating the New Breed. Sandman ultimately left WWE in September 2007.

SAPPHIRE

In 1989, longtime fan Sapphire bought a ticket to a WWE live event that changed her life forever. While sitting ringside, the superfan was spotted by WWE Superstar Dusty Rhodes. Admiring the woman's enthusiasm, the "American Dream" pulled Sapphire from her seat and took her on as his valet.

As Rhodes' second, Sapphire escorted her man to the ring and stood in his corner while he climbed the WWE ladder. As a sign of loyalty to Rhodes, she even wore matching yellow polka dots. As time went on, Sapphire's involvement increased. It wasn't long before the onetime fan soon became an in-ring competitor. At *WrestleMania VI*, Sapphire teamed with Rhodes to defeat Randy Savage and Sensational Sherri in WWE's first-ever Mixed Tag Team Match.

In the summer of 1990, Sapphire began to receive extravagant gifts from an unknown source. At *SummerSlam 1990*, Sapphire proved that everybody has a price when she turned her back on Rhodes to join forces with "Million Dollar Man" Ted DiBiase.

SANTINO MARELLA

HT	6'0"	WT	233 lbs.	FROM	Calabria, Italy
SIGNATURE MOVE	The Cobra				

Jumping the barrier at a WWE event is never advisable, but it's a good thing no one told that to Santino Marella. In what was dubbed "the Milan Miracle," Santino answered and won an Open Challenge for Umaga's Intercontinental Championship during *Raw*'s first ever broadcast in Italy on April 16, 2007. In the years that followed, this fan-turned-Superstar gave WWE the perfect, savory pinch of Italian seasoning for any situation.

Short on grammar but never on wisecracks, Santino's endearing wit charmed both the WWE Universe and his fair share of Divas. Even Beth Phoenix softened her intense glare at the sight of this affable goofball. As one half of "Glamarella," Santino won the Intercontinental Championship and then boldly took aim at the Honky Tonk Man's record reign. Though he fell short of his goal, he soon found his way into the record books by receiving the fastest ever elimination from the Royal Rumble (1.9 seconds). The Marella name was redeemed months later when his "twin sister" Santina became "Miss WrestleMania" at *WrestleMania 25*.

All hijinks aside, Santino gave his opponents more agita than a spicy fra diavolo. He nearly won the only 40-man Royal Rumble in history in 2011, and has also been a United States and WWE Tag Team Champion. His Championship tandem with Vladimir Kozlov was one of the most unlikely and entertaining in recent history. Most memorably, the two polar opposites hosted a tea party in front of WWE's UK audience. Soon after, Santino began using his dreaded Cobra sock puppet to flatten his foes in the ring.

In 2014, Santino appeared smitten with rookie Diva Emma. Though the Australian beauty did not return Santino's romantic vibes the inter-gender duo still had fun racking up wins together on *Raw* and *SmackDown*. That summer, Santino retired from active competition. Though his unibrow, shimmying powerwalk, and imaginary brass band are now part of WWE lore, the lovable Italian remains a loyal friend. He returns occasionally wielding a microphone and the same irrepressible sense of humor that has always brought a smile to faces of the the WWE Universe.

SASHA BANKS

HT 5'5" **FROM** Boston, Massachusetts
SIGNATURE MOVE Bank Statement

It's not uncommon for WWE Superstars to employ a bit of hyperbole in an attempt to put themselves in the best possible light. But in the case of Sasha Banks, she is every bit The Boss she claims to be, as evidenced by her incredible in-ring abilities.

Upon making her NXT debut in December 2012, it was clear that Sasha was special. And it wasn't long before the Boston native was getting the better of the likes of Emma and Bayley. Sasha's momentum eventually carried her into a months-long rivalry with NXT Women's Champion Charlotte, whom The Boss dethroned by winning a Fatal 4-Way Match in February 2015 that also included Becky Lynch and Bayley.

Later that year, Sasha and Bayley battled in what many believe is one of the greatest women's matches in sports entertainment history at *NXT Takeover: Brooklyn*. Sasha and Bayley again made history when they main evented *NXT Takeover: Respect* in the first-ever women's WWE Iron Man Match. Though she came up short, her effort went a long way in proving she was about to become a major force on the WWE main roster.

Banks' earliest days as a WWE Superstar saw her compete alongside Naomi and Tamina in Team B.A.D. Together, the three Superstars set out to destroy Team PCB and Team Bella, en route to establishing themselves as the dominant force in the bourgeoning Divas Revolution. Eventually, however, Sasha's desire to be the best drove a spike through Team B.A.D.

Now on her own, Sasha continues to prove she is The Boss, while arenas all over the globe affectionately chant, "We want Sasha!"

At *WrestleMania 32*, Banks etched her name as a preeminent figure in the Divas Revolution by competing in the historic Triple Threat Match for the inaugural WWE Women's Championship.

SAVANNAH

Savannah made her WWE debut in September 2009 as a part of the ECW broadcast team. As a backstage interviewer, she was tasked with asking the tough questions to ECW Superstars Zack Ryder, Vance Archer, and Christian, among others.

In November 2009, Lauren Mayhew's departure from *ECW* opened the door for Savannah to step in as the brand's official ring announcer, a job also previously held by Justin Roberts and Tony Chimel. When *ECW on Syfy* made way for the debut of WWE's groundbreaking show *NXT*, Savannah became the new show's ring announcer.

Savannah was released from her WWE contract in June 2010. Outside of WWE, Savannah has flaunted her stunning good looks as a model, cheerleader, and contestant on *Let's Make A Deal*.

SAVIO VEGA

HT 5'11" **WT** 260 lbs. **FROM** South Bronx, New York
SIGNATURE MOVE Spinning Heel Kick

Had it not been for Savio Vega, Razor Ramon might not have had the amazing career he eventually had. Ramon found himself on the receiving end of a vicious beat down at the hands of Jeff Jarrett and The Roadie in May 1995. The attack was so severe that many feared Ramon would never be the same. Luckily, a debuting Vega ran to Ramon's aid before permanent damage could be inflicted.

Afterward, Vega and Ramon formed a brief union. Together, they battled the likes of Men on a Mission and Owen Hart and Yokozuna. On his own, Vega earned early victories over Irwin R. Schyster, Hakushi, and Rad Radford, among others.

Vega joined the Nation of Domination in 1997, though the partnership was brief, as Faarooq expelled him from the group just months after joining. Vega then created a faction of his own with Miguel Perez, Jose Estrada Jr., and Jesús Castillo. Known as Los Boricuas, they waged war on the Nation and Disciples of Apocalypse.

Vega left WWE and returned to his homeland of Puerto Rico in 1999.

SCOTT CASEY

HT 6'0" **WT** 230 lbs. **FROM** Amarillo, Texas
SIGNATURE MOVE Bulldog

As a trainee of legendary Dory Funk Sr., Scott Casey understood both the art of mat wrestling and how to give and take in a Texas style brawl. After headlining in Southwest Championship Wrestling, Casey entered WWE in 1987.

Casey's greatest WWE highlight saw him team with "Hacksaw" Jim Duggan, Jake "The Snake" Roberts, Tito Santana, and Ken Patera at the 1988 *Survivor Series*. After a brutal thirty-minute battle, Casey's team succumbed to the mighty combination of Andre the Giant, "Ravishing" Rick Rude, Mr. Perfect, Dino Bravo, and Harley Race.

Following his retirement from WWE in 1990, Casey began working as a trainer to future Superstars. He is credited for helping shape the career of a young Booker T.

SCOTT PUTSKI

HT 5'9" **WT** 275 lbs. **FROM** Austin, Texas
SIGNATURE MOVE Polish Hammer

Scott Putski grew up in the sports-entertainment world of his father "Polish Power" Ivan Putski. In the early 1990s, Scott began his professional career and even toured Japan. In 1997, Scott Putski debuted in WWE on *Monday Night Raw* and had fans on their feet once his name was announced. His rivalry against Brian Christopher escalated to a father and son affair. On an episode of *Raw*, the father and son team of Scott Putski and "Polish Power" Ivan Putski clashed against Christopher and Jerry "The King" Lawler. The paternal Putski scored the winning pinfall in the historic match.

Scott soon left WWE and appeared in WCW in 1998 before returning to the North American independent scene.

SERENA

| HT | 5'4" | FROM | Fairfax, Virginia |

Prior to meeting CM Punk, Serena claimed that years of pill addiction had her questioning her worth. That all changed in January 2010, when the troubled beauty shed her self-destructive lifestyle (not to mention, her gorgeous hair) by pledging allegiance to Punk's Straight Edge Society.

After accepting CM Punk as her savior, a reborn Serena regularly sacrificed her own safety for the betterment of the Straight Edge Society. She became one of Punk's most trusted allies. Then in July 2010, Serena was spotted drinking alcohol. The relapse brought her spot within the controversial faction into question.

Punk ultimately forgave Serena for her wrongdoing, but fellow Straight Edge Society member Luke Gallows did not. After the incident, much hostility followed Serena until her release from WWE in August 2010.

SGT. SLAUGHTER

see page 312

SHAD GASPARD

| HT | 6'7" | WT | 295 lbs. | FROM | Brooklyn, New York |

Shad Gaspard and JTG were great friends and an even better tag team when they were united as Cryme Tyme. But after a frustrating loss in April 2010, Gaspard blasted his longtime friend with a big boot. According to Gaspard, it was time for him take what he deserved. To do so, he believed he needed to eliminate JTG.

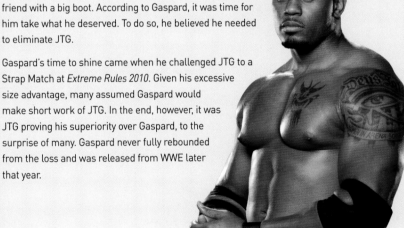

Gaspard's time to shine came when he challenged JTG to a Strap Match at *Extreme Rules 2010*. Given his excessive size advantage, many assumed Gaspard would make short work of JTG. In the end, however, it was JTG proving his superiority over Gaspard, to the surprise of many. Gaspard never fully rebounded from the loss and was released from WWE later that year.

THE SHADOW

As Vincent J. McMahon and "Toots" Mondt transformed Capitol Wrestling Corporation into WWE, grapplers from all over the world vied for employment in the fledgling company. Many of the hopefuls shared common characteristics, but there was one intriguing competitor who surfaced with an unknown origin, identity, and past. He was known only as The Shadow.

This stealth-like individual proved to be a hazard to opposing Superstars such as Bruno Sammartino, Pedro Morales, and Gorilla Monsoon. He was also a force as a tag team competitor, alongside partners Dr. Jerry Graham and Hans Mortier.

By the end of 1963, The Shadow disappeared into thin air never to be seen again.

SETH ROLLINS

| HT | 6'1" | WT | 217 lbs. | FROM | Davenport, Iowa |
| SIGNATURE MOVE | Pedigree |

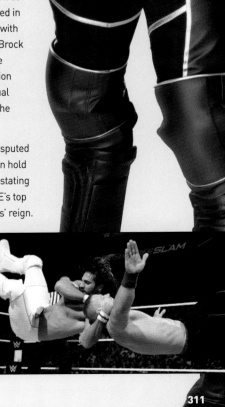

The chaos The Shield caused was merely a glimpse of what Seth Rollins is truly capable of.

At *Survivor Series 2012*, the former NXT Champion debuted in WWE alongside Dean Ambrose and Roman Reigns. Claiming to be a "shield from injustice," the trio wreaked havoc looking to sway the balance of power in WWE. The aerial artistry of Rollins provided perfect balance with the powerful Reigns and unpredictable Ambrose. The "brothers in arms" shined the most as a unit, going 2-0 at *WrestleMania* and stopping Evolution's comeback in its tracks. The Shield appeared poised to conquer WWE, but Rollins had other ideas.

The Aerialist betrayed his comrades on a June 2014 episode of *Raw*, aligning himself with the corrupt corporate powers he once fought against, The Authority. An unapologetic Rollins deflected chants of "you sold out" from the WWE Universe. Claiming to be "The Architect" of The Shield, Rollins made the cold, calculated business decision to tear down his creation in exchange for deeper pockets. The maneuver bore its first fruit weeks later when Rollins became Mr. Money in the Bank.

Seth Rollins lost to Randy Orton at *WrestleMania 31*, but that would not be his lasting memory of the night. In the waning moments of the main event, Seth's master plan came full circle when he cashed in his Title opportunity to create an impromptu Triple Threat Match. He pinned Roman Reigns to unseat Brock Lesnar as WWE World Heavyweight Champion.

With his own security team and an unending arsenal between the ropes, "The Architect" was dominant as a first-time World Champion. His reign was tested in a Steel Cage Match with Orton, a Ladder Match with Ambrose, and a trial-by-fire against a vengeful Brock Lesnar. Each time, Rollins escaped with his Title reign intact. He even beat United States Champion John Cena at *SummerSlam 2015* to become a dual Title-holder, then turned back WCW icon Sting the following month.

Seth Rollins was staking his claim as "The Undisputed Future" of WWE. However, that future was put on hold in November 2015 when Rollins suffered a devastating knee injury. After nearly eight months with WWE's top prize, only his own misfortune could stop Rollins' reign. Watching others carry the gold from afar was all the motivation the avid Crossfitter needed to work through his rigorous road to recovery. He announced his return at *Extreme Rules 2016* by blindsiding and brutalizing the current titleholder Roman Reigns. The attack sent a statement that a rebuilt, reenergized Rollins might be more dangerous than ever.

SGT. SLAUGHTER ⓗ Ⓦ ▣

HT	6'6"
WT	305 lbs.
FROM	Paris Island, South Carolina

SIGNATURE MOVE
Cobra Clutch

To the millions of fans who watched him compete over his 30-year career, Sgt. Slaughter remains a champion and pop-culture icon. After serving in the Marine Corps, Sgt. Slaughter worked as a roofer in Minnesota. During this time, a chance meeting with American Wrestling Association (AWA) promoter Verne Gagne changed his life. Impressed by his size and strength, Gagne convinced the roofer to take up wrestling.

At Gagne's spartan training camp, Slaughter first encountered an earlier graduate, Iron Sheik, who'd competed in numerous international competitions for his native Iran. While the pair tied each other up on the mats, neither realized that their future encounters would be bloody affairs that would sell out some of the largest arenas in the country.

Upon his debut in 1974, Slaughter labored in the AWA before attempting to establish his name elsewhere. In the Kansas City territory, he held the Central States Heavyweight Championship numerous times, trading it with foes like Bulldog Bob Brown and Ted Oates. As the masked Executioner, he and Pak Song became Georgia Tag Team Champions in 1977, upending Tony Atlas and Tommy Rich.

The next year, he returned to the AWA, again donning a mask, now as Super Destroyer II, managed by future WWE commentator Lord Alfred Hayes. But Super Destroyer II eventually grew tired of Hayes' condescension and publicly fired him, sparking a war with both the manager and former tag team partner, Super Destroyer III.

By the dawn of the next decade, Sgt. Slaughter fell back on his time serving in the Marine Corps. He wore military fatigues, a whistle, and sunglasses. In 1980, Vincent J. McMahon called to offer him a spot with WWE. Slaughter jumped at the opportunity and went on to have one of the most spectacular debuts in wrestling history. Prior to making his entrance in the arena, Slaughter asked McMahon to play the Marine Corps Hymn over the loudspeakers. The song garnered a huge reaction from the fans in attendance, as the use of entrance music was rare at the time.

BIG NAME COMPETITION

Impressed by Sarge's ability to excite audiences, McMahon watched the newcomer rocket straight to the top of the card. It wasn't long before he challenged Bob Backlund for the WWE Championship. Slaughter was even given the distinction of competing against Bruno Sammartino in the legend's final Madison Square Garden match.

Under the guidance of famed manager the Grand Wizard, Slaughter engaged in a brutal and bloody rivalry with Pat Patterson. In truly revolutionary fashion, the two Superstars battled for bragging rights in an infamous Alley Fight at Madison Square Garden that did not feature a referee. The match came to a stunning conclusion when the Grand Wizard, fearing the worst for his battered protégé, threw in the towel.

Taking a break from WWE, Slaughter entered the Mid-Atlantic territory in 1981, winning the vacant United States Championship in a tournament, and then the NWA World Tag Team Titles with Don Kernodle. He also dethroned Angelo "King Kong" Mosca for the NWA Canadian Heavyweight Championship in 1983.

In early 1984, he was back in WWE, where fans began to recognize Slaughter as a hero when he stood up to Iron Sheik and his manager "Ayatollah" Freddie Blassie. The Sarge's patriotic change of heart marked the end of an epic love-hate relationship between Slaughter and the fans. It also sparked the beginning of an amazing rivalry with the Sheik that packed spectators to the rafters.

I BLED FOR MY COUNTRY. I BLED FOR EACH ONE OF YOU... I'LL DIE FOR MY COUNTRY. GOD BLESS AMERICA!

A REAL AMERICAN HERO?

Shortly after his rivalry with Iron Sheik, Slaughter left WWE for the AWA, where he continued to wave the red, white, and blue in skirmishes with Boris Zukhov, Kamala, and Col. DeBeers. The decision to return to the Minnesota-based promotion caused Slaughter to miss out on the nationwide phenomenon WWE became in the mid-1980s. Ironically, the Sarge gained national exposure of his own when he became the spokesperson for the G.I. Joe line of toys. The new role saw the Sarge become a household name while being featured in cartoons, comic books, and as multiple action figures. During the administration of President Ronald Reagan, Slaughter was even invited to the White House, and challenged the commander in chief to give him ten pushups. Secret Service agents stepped in, as Reagan bent to comply.

Slaughter made his return to WWE in 1990. When news of his comeback began to circulate, fans couldn't wait to once again cheer their hero. Unfortunately, Slaughter soon broke their hearts, as he denounced his country to become an Iraqi sympathizer. The move shocked WWE fans, who needed a hero during the tumultuous times of the first Persian Gulf War.

Matters became worse for American fans when Slaughter defeated Ultimate Warrior for the coveted WWE Championship at the *Royal Rumble* in 1991—with an outside assist from Randy Savage. The victory resulted in Slaughter becoming even more hated than he was during his earlier days. It wasn't long before his family was receiving death threats.

Luckily, American hero Hulk Hogan saved the day when he defeated Slaughter for the WWE Championship at *WrestleMania VII*. Following the loss, Slaughter begged for his country back. The fans ultimately forgave the Marine Corps drill sergeant, who was given the opportunity to finish his competitive career with the support of his fans.

After retirement, Slaughter assumed several prominent roles within WWE, including Commissioner and road producer. In 2004, he was recognized with induction into the WWE Hall of Fame, a fitting honor for a man who was both a WWE great and real American hero.

After his induction into the Hall of Fame, the Sarge remained active behind the scenes in WWE, and on occasion, stepped through the ropes to lock disrespectful maggots in the Cobra Clutch. He appeared alongside "Nature Boy" Ric Flair, Ron Simmons, and "The American Dream" Dusty Rhodes at *Survivor Series* in 2006, saw action versus Alberto Del Rio in 2010, and laced up his boots for encounters with Cesaro in 2012 and Rusev in 2014.

Never forgetting his roots, Slaughter takes particular joy in visiting with American troops, reminiscing about his days defending liberty between the ropes, and leading them in the Pledge of Allegiance.

SHANE DOUGLAS

| HT | 6'1" | WT | 240 lbs. | FROM | Pittsburgh, Pennsylvania |
| SIGNATURE MOVE | Pittsburgh Plunge |

Oftentimes, the muddled history of sports-entertainment makes it impossible to pinpoint when a movement was born. With the birth of "Extreme," this is not the case. August 27, 1994, was the date; Shane Douglas was the competitor. After winning a tournament to crown a new Champion for the deteriorating NWA, Douglas threw down his newly won Championship in defiance. As the Title once held by Lou Thesz and Harley Race lay desecrated on the mat, Douglas proclaimed himself The Franchise of the upstart ECW promotion. The Franchise's refusal to run with an extinguished torch in turn ignited a new flame. The "E" in ECW became "Extreme" and the renegade promotion began to change the face of sports-entertainment with Douglas as its Champion.

Before he found his brash voice, Douglas first made a name for himself in the Universal Wrestling Federation. Trained by Dominic DeNucci, he showcased an exciting, high-flying style with a tough as nails, never say die attitude that made him popular.

Douglas made multiple stops in both WWE and WCW. His resiliency was on display during the 1991 Royal Rumble when he lasted almost 30 minutes before being eliminated. In 1995, he was awarded the Intercontinental Championship as the forgettable Dean Douglas persona. But he's most widely regarded for his time in ECW. He picked up additional ECW Titles against Terry Funk and Bam Bam Bigelow while never losing his unfiltered demeanor, even to this day.

SHANE MCMAHON
see page 314

SHANIQUA

After winning the second season of *WWE Tough Enough*, Linda Miles went through a surprising transformation that took many sports-entertainment insiders aback. Proving bright and cheery wasn't for her, the *Tough Enough* champ unleashed a dark and masochistic side as the manager of the Basham Brothers.

Miles' 2003 union with Danny and Doug Basham was accompanied by a name change. Known simply as Shaniqua, the amazon-like Diva began to dress in leather and carry a whip, which let everybody know, particularly the Bashams, that she wasn't afraid to get rough in or out of the ring.

Later that year, a Clothesline From Hell at the hands of JBL temporarily sidelined Shaniqua. When she returned, her low-cut leather ring gear revealed that the clothesline resulted in extreme and permanent swelling in her chest region. But she didn't seem to mind, and neither did the Bashams, who couldn't keep their eyes off her supposedly-injured area.

Shaniqua was released from WWE in early 2004.

SHANE McMAHON

HT	6'2"
WT	236 lbs.
FROM	Greenwich, Connecticut

SIGNATURE MOVE
Coast-To-Coast

Shane McMahon dreamed of one day following in the extraordinary path walked by his father, grandfather, and great grandfather in sports-entertainment. His childhood experiences were unique as he carried the bags of Superstars from the locker room. As an adolescent, Shane spent vacations stocking the company warehouse, and was later a member of the ring crew, referee, and ring announcer.

The fourth generation McMahon needed to work harder than everyone else and studied the intricacies of television production, sales, marketing, and international business development. In 1998, he was a driving force in the company's new exploration into the world of digital media and led the team that launched *WWE.com*, which, combined with the WWE App, exceeds 20.5 million monthly unique visitors worldwide.

While he was building an impressive résumé among the top professionals in the industry, he also began to entertain audiences in the ring. As the rivalry between his father and Stone Cold Steve Austin defined the Attitude Era, Shane was often involved in defending the McMahon name and adopted the moniker, Shane-O-Mac.

He made history on the February 15, 1999 episode of *Monday Night Raw* when he became the first McMahon to capture a WWE championship by covering X-Pac for the European Title.

Although he held the European Championship for almost two months, he retired it on an episode of *Sunday Night Heat*. While he continued to appear in the corners of his associates and as a special guest referee, Shane mixed it up in the ring with the likes of Triple H, Mankind, Ken Shamrock, and Test.

WCW UNDER NEW OWNERSHIP

In 2001, Shane rocked the foundation of sports-entertainment when he announced that he purchased the shares of the rival World Championship Wrestling (WCW). The brash McMahon rode that momentum into the granddaddy of them all and beat his father at *WrestleMania X-7* in a Street Fight. Shortly after, Shane led the invasion of WWE and came extremely close to ruling the world of sports-entertainment.

It was during this period that he established his reputation as perhaps the most daring performer in WWE. During a "Last Man Standing" match with the Big Show at *Backlash 2001*, Shane scaled the massive set and launched himself from the top onto his gargantuan foe.

In 2003 he returned to the public eye in the wake of his father's match with Hulk Hogan at *WrestleMania XIX*.

That July, he began his tenure as Executive Vice President of WWE Global Media, overseeing international TV distribution, live event bookings, digital media, consumer products, and publishing. Shane once again performed multiple tasks, as he brawled with Eric Bischoff at *SummerSlam*, and tangled with Chris Jericho.

While honoring the legacies of those before him, Shane was dedicated to blazing his own trail into the annals of sports-entertainment. With the additional responsibilities behind the scenes, Shane was rarely seen on television, but he found the time to help his family when The Legacy caused problems for the McMahons throughout 2008 and 2009.

In 2010, Shane left WWE to pursue other business opportunities. Then, in 2016, he reappeared, claiming that he didn't approve of the direction that his sister, Stephanie, and husband, Triple H, were taking the company, and demanding changes. His father told Shane he could take possession of *Raw* with one caveat: he had to beat Undertaker at *WrestleMania 32*.

Undertaker warned Vince McMahon that he was responsible for whatever befell his son. But Shane was not as overmatched as some assumed. Relying on pure daring, he bashed a trash can on The Phenom's chest in the corner, raced across the ring, and came soaring back, landing on Undertaker with a stunning Coast to Coast. He used bolt cutters to break the locks on the cage, then drove Undertaker through it. After hitting "The Deadman" with a toolbox and sprawling him on the German announcers' table, Shane scaled the 20-foot enclosure and came sailing off the top. If Undertaker hadn't moved at the last moment, Shane would have likely scored the victory.

But Undertaker did move, and Shane crashed through the table, enabling his opponent to beat him with a Tombstone. Nonetheless, even in losing, Shane reinforced both his bravery, and place among the immortals.

THIS ISN'T ABOUT MONEY. THIS IS ABOUT LEGACY.

SHANNON MOORE

HT 5'9"	**WT** 207 lbs.	**FROM**	Whispering Pines, North Carolina
SIGNATURE MOVE	The Halo		

A childhood friend of the Hardys, this former WWE Superstar appeared in their North Carolina-based OMEGA promotion. His first major exposure came in WCW as part of a trio called Three Count, a spoof of the late-'90s boy band craze.

Moore debuted in WWE in 2002 and reunited with Matt Hardy. As a devout "Mattitude" follower (aka an "MF'er") Moore bought in to Hardy's eccentric way of life and soon found a subordinate of his own, who was known as a "Moore-On."

After going solo, Moore participated in the Cruiserweight Open at *WrestleMania XX*. In 2005, he unearthed his punk rock persona with a new Mohawk haircut, elaborate body art, and piercings. After a hiatus, the high-flying nonconformist returned to WWE in 2006 as part of *ECW*. As "The Reject," he urged the WWE Universe to question the system and "fight the power." After being drafted to *SmackDown*, he befriended another outlandish Superstar, Jimmy Wang Yang. Moore was a stand out in Cruiserweight and tag team competition before leaving WWE in August 2008.

SHARMELL

Formerly a member of WCW's Nitro Girls dance team, Sharmell made her WWE debut in 2005 as a supportive presence for her husband, Booker T. While not known for her in-ring prowess, Sharmell did land a match on the grandest possible stage. At *WrestleMania 22*, she and Booker battled Boogeyman in a Handicap Match. The loving couple not only took the loss, but Sharmell also left the event with a lingering taste of worms in her mouth!

Sharmell quickly rebounded as she led Booker to victory in the King of the Ring tournament. Now WWE royalty, the elegant Queen Sharmell demanded all in attendance to "hail King Booker" as her man went on to win the World Heavyweight Championship at *The Great American Bash*. The imperial couple ruled *SmackDown* with an iron fist during the latter portion of 2006.

SHAWN MICHAELS
see page 316

SHEAMUS

HT 6'4"	**WT** 267 lbs.	**FROM**	Dublin, Ireland
SIGNATURE MOVE	Brogue Kick, Cloverleaf, Irish Curse Backbreaker, White Noise		

Cross this fella at your own risk. Since a rookie campaign that ranks among the greatest in WWE history, Sheamus has made his Celtic Warrior ancestors proud. With his barbaric offensive barrage and white-hot temper, he is among the most decorated and feared competitors in WWE today.

Sheamus began his career in 2009 by annihilating *ECW*'s locker room and quickly jumping to *Raw*. He won a Battle Royal to earn an opportunity at John Cena's WWE Championship at *TLC*. In a Tables Match, the Great White sent Cena sailing through a table to become the first-ever Irish-born WWE Champion. The fiery-haired Superstar claimed the gold again in June 2010. In a Fatal Four Way Match, he turned back Cena, Edge, and Randy Orton to become a two-time Titlist.

The Celtic Warrior's conquering ways continued when he defeated John Morrison in the finals of a 16-Superstar tournament to become the 2010 King of the Ring. As WWE royalty, Sheamus struggled. Looking to turn things around in March 2011, he put his career on the line against Daniel Bryan's U.S. Championship and won. Soon after, he evolved into a fan-favorite.

At the 2012 Royal Rumble, Sheamus outlasted 29 other competitors to add yet another milestone to his ever-expanding career résumé. The win lined him up once again to face Daniel Bryan, this time at *WrestleMania XXVIII* for the World Heavyweight Championship. Unlike their prior back-and-forth struggles, this bout ended in eighteen seconds, the result of an abrupt and unexpected Brogue Kick from Sheamus. For 211 days, Sheamus pulverized his competition as Champion before losing to Big Show at *Hell in a Cell 2012*. It was the longest World Heavyweight Championship reign in over six years but Sheamus was far from satisfied.

In May 2014, Sheamus did what he does best—emerge from a crowded scrum victorious. This time, the Irish bruiser bested nineteen others in a Battle Royal for the United States Championship.

After a hiatus from WWE, the sports-entertainment world was abuzz for the return of Sheamus in 2015. The night after *WrestleMania 31*, he reemerged with his fiery red hair shaved into a threatening Mohawk and a rekindled thirst for barbarity. Resembling the Celtic Warriors of yore, Sheamus issued savage beatings to Superstars he believed undeserving of his spotlight. At *Money in the Bank 2015*, he ascended past six Superstars, joining another prestigious list of names to hold the coveted briefcase.

For months, fans tried to get under Sheamus's milky white skin by mocking his new appearance. However, it was his naysayers who looked stupid at *Survivor Series 2015* when Sheamus cashed in his Title opportunity and flattened Roman Reigns to become WWE World Heavyweight Champion. As Champion, he formed the League of Nations with Alberto Del Rio, Rusev, and King Barrett. This dangerous collection of foreign-born Superstars went on to top The New Day at *WrestleMania 32*. That summer, Sheamus displayed his acting chops as the rampaging rhino Rocksteady in *Teenage Mutant Ninja Turtles: Out of the Shadows*.

With ruthless allies, an eclectic in-ring arsenal of brutality and a complete absence of mercy, there is no telling where or whom Sheamus will strike next.

SHAWN MICHAELS

HT	6'1"
WT	225 lbs.
FROM	San Antonio, Texas

SIGNATURE MOVE
Sweet Chin Music

In an industry where nicknames oftentimes get thrown around fairly liberally, Shawn Michaels has earned many monikers that can never be disputed: "The Showstopper," "The Headliner," "The Main Event," "The Icon," and "Mr. WrestleMania."

Shawn Michaels and his tag team partner, Marty Jannetty, first appeared in WWE in 1987. Known as the Midnight Rockers, the high-flying duo had grand visions of taking over WWE's tag team scene. WWE, however, saw things a bit differently, as they fired the team after only two weeks.

Michaels and Jannetty retreated to the AWA, but never gave up on their dream of competing for WWE. The following year, they were given another opportunity. This time, they took advantage of the situation. After dropping "Midnight" from their name, the Rockers took WWE by storm, proving themselves as true tag team specialists. They even captured the World Tag Team Championship from the Hart Foundation in October 1990. Though the Rockers were later forced to relinquish the Titles back to Bret "Hit Man" Hart and Jim "The Anvil" Neidhart when the championship committee ruled the gold couldn't change hands due to the ring becoming faulty during the match.

BARBER SHOP BREAK UP

By 1992, Michaels believed his union with Jannetty was holding him back from true greatness. So he severed their relationship in one of the most memorable scenes in WWE history. While guests on Brutus Beefcake's *Barber Shop*, Michaels superkicked Jannetty straight through a window. The kick marked the end of the popular tag team and the beginning of a truly iconic singles career.

On his own, the egotistical Michaels adopted the nickname "The Heartbreak Kid." With Sensational Sherri by his side stroking his ego, HBK went on an unbelievable tear that saw him capture his first WWE title when he defeated British Bulldog for the Intercontinental Championship on *Saturday Night's Main Event* in October 1992. The win over Bulldog marked the first of three Intercontinental Championship reigns for Michaels (subsequent victories came at the expense of Jannetty and Jeff Jarrett). Over the course of these reigns, HBK competed in some of WWE's most athletic and dangerous encounters, including the landmark *WrestleMania X* Ladder Match against Razor Ramon. With each passing match, it became more obvious that Michaels was destined for greatness.

A CHILDHOOD DREAM REALIZED

In January 1996, Michaels last eliminated Diesel to win the *Royal Rumble* Match for the second consecutive year.

The victory put HBK back in the main event of *WrestleMania* and gave him the opportunity to accomplish his boyhood dream of becoming WWE Champion. At *WrestleMania XII*, he faced Bret Hart in a grueling sixty-minute WWE Iron Man Match that required sudden-death overtime to deliver a conclusive winner. In the end, Michaels scored the victory after landing Sweet Chin Music to become WWE Champion.

In 1997, Michaels teamed with longtime friend Triple H to form the most controversial faction in WWE history, D-Generation X. Together, HBK and Triple H spat in the face of authority while their unparalleled popularity set the bar for all future factions.

As a member of DX, HBK captured the European Championship from British Bulldog at *One Night Only 1997*, making him the first-ever Grand Slam Champion in WWE history (he held the WWE, Intercontinental, World Tag Team, and European Titles during his career).

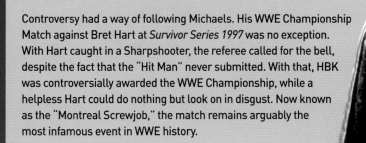

Controversy had a way of following Michaels. His WWE Championship Match against Bret Hart at *Survivor Series 1997* was no exception. With Hart caught in a Sharpshooter, the referee called for the bell, despite the fact that the "Hit Man" never submitted. With that, HBK was controversially awarded the WWE Championship, while a helpless Hart could do nothing but look on in disgust. Now known as the "Montreal Screwjob," the match remains arguably the most infamous event in WWE history.

RETIREMENT? NO, REJUVENATION!

Michaels' injured back forced him into early retirement following his main event match against Stone Cold Steve Austin at *WrestleMania XIV*. During this time, he became a spiritual person, which helped him overcome his personal demons. He also used this time to rest his battered back. By 2002, a reinvigorated HBK had the itch to compete again.

When he returned, Michaels found himself embedded in a brutal rivalry with former friend Triple H. Amazingly, HBK showed no sign of ring rust, defeating "The Game" in an unsanctioned Street Fight at *SummerSlam 2002*. A few months later at *Survivor Series*, Michaels last eliminated Triple H in an unforgiving Elimination Chamber Match that saw HBK claim the World Heavyweight Championship.

Over the next several years, the renewed Michaels worked effortlessly to recreate the magic of his earlier years. In typical HBK fashion, he found himself in the spotlight of WWE's biggest matches, including his contest at *WrestleMania XXIV* where he sent Ric Flair into retirement. Michaels spent the rest of 2008 battling Flair's former protégé, Batista, then engaging Chris Jericho in an incredibly personal rivalry that saw Michaels thrown through the Jeritron 6000. HBK ended the year in a financial hole and was forced to work for JBL until he defeated the former World Champion in an All or Nothing Match at *No Way Out 2009*.

CEMENTING THE SHOWSTOPPER'S LEGACY

As 2009 approached, Michaels looked back on his historic career and pondered his future before realizing only one thing remained for him to do—defeat Undertaker at *WrestleMania*. Hoping to be the first to topple Undertaker on the grandest stage, HBK battled "The Deadman" in a spectacular contest at *WrestleMania XXV*. Unfortunately for HBK, he failed to end Undertaker's *WrestleMania* undefeated streak. Years later, the match is still regularly regarded by many as the greatest match of all time.

Michaels took some time away from WWE after the loss. But when longtime friend and D-Generation X cohort Triple H needed a partner to take on The Legacy at *SummerSlam*, HBK was there for him. The reformed D-Generation X stayed together through the summer and fall, and managed to capture the Unified Tag Team Championship from Chris Jericho and Big Show. During his time as Tag Team Champion, Michaels reconciled with Bret Hart, healing a wound ripped open nearly fifteen years earlier in Montreal.

After D-Generation X lost the Unified Tag Team Titles, Michaels demanded a rematch with Undertaker at *WrestleMania XXVI*. In order to secure the match, Michaels put his legendary career on the line. With no disqualifications and no count-outs, the battle lines were drawn for a "Streak vs. Career" Match. Once again, however, Michaels was unable to solve "The Deadman," who buried HBK and his career after three spine-jarring Tombstones. Less than twenty-four hours later, a retired HBK gave a touching farewell on *Raw*.

On the eve of *WrestleMania XXVII*, in front of a capacity crowd, Shawn Michaels' brilliant quarter-century career was recognized with induction into the WWE Hall of Fame. Always the "Showstopper," Michaels used his acceptance speech as an opportunity to reunite the Kliq, welcoming Triple H, Kevin Nash, and X-Pac onto the stage with him.

While his competitive days are firmly behind him, Michaels still makes occasional appearances on WWE programming. One of his most noteworthy appearances took place at *WrestleMania XXVIII* when he served as special guest referee in the "End of an Era" Hell in a Cell Match between Triple H and Undertaker. He was also in The Game's corner at *WrestleMania 31* when he took on Sting.

In recent years, Michaels has proven to be a success outside the sports-entertainment world, as well. He can regularly be seen starring in *Shawn Michaels' MacMillan River Adventures* on the Outdoor Channel.

I WILL GIVE YOU A SHOW LIKE YOU HAVE NEVER SEEN BEFORE. WHY? BECAUSE I CAN.

THE SHEIK

HT	5'11"	WT	250 lbs.	FROM	The Syrian Desert
SIGNATURE MOVE		Camel Clutch			

A true pioneer of hardcore wrestling, The Sheik left a legacy that fans are reminded of every time a Superstar breaks a table or swings a flaming baseball bat. Considered by many as the father of extreme, many believe there never would have been an ECW without his vicious vision.

Using anything he could get his hands on as a weapon, The Sheik made a name for himself competing in Detroit, Toronto, and Japan. While wrestling in the Midwest, The Sheik began a bitter rivalry with Bobo Brazil, which lasted more than thirty years. Over the course of their bloody rivalry, The Sheik captured the now-defunct U.S.A. Heavyweight Championship twice.

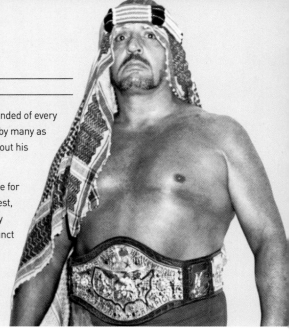

Amazingly, The Sheik managed to wrestle into the 1990s, despite having celebrated his seventieth birthday. The twilight of his career saw him compete in numerous ECW encounters against Kevin Sullivan and Tazz, who would later go on to become a heated rival of Sabu, The Sheik's nephew. In 2007, four years after his death, The Sheik's hardcore innovations earned him induction in the WWE Hall of Fame.

SHELTON BENJAMIN

HT	6'2"	WT	248 lbs.	FROM	Orangeburg, South Carolina
SIGNATURE MOVE		T-Bone Suplex			

Shelton Benjamin claims to be sports-entertainment's "Gold Standard." And by looking at his in-ring exploits, it's hard to argue against the lofty claim.

After successfully dodging his hometown's dangerous drug scene, Benjamin attended the University of Minnesota, where he became a national amateur wrestling powerhouse. Following graduation, he parlayed his college success into a WWE contract, thus fulfilling a lifelong dream of becoming a WWE Superstar.

Alongside partner Charlie Haas, Benjamin debuted in December 2002 as a part of the powerful Team Angle faction. In less than two months, Benjamin and Haas proved their dominance, defeating Los Guerreros for the WWE Tag Team Championship. Dubbed the "The World's Greatest Tag Team," they would go on to capture the Titles once more before the WWE Draft sent Benjamin to *Raw* and forced the athletic tandem to split.

With a shocking victory over Triple H in his debut match, Benjamin's *Raw* career had an electric start. The victory put the newcomer on the map as one of the brand's top stars. It also opened the eyes of the WWE Universe, who voted Benjamin into *Taboo Tuesday*'s Intercontinental Championship Match. Taking full advantage of the opportunity, Benjamin defeated Chris Jericho to capture his first WWE singles Title.

Following an impressive run on *Raw*, Benjamin jumped to ECW in November 2007. He used his time in the Land of the Extreme to cement his status as one of his era's most athletic competitors, as evidenced by his breathtaking efforts in the *WrestleMania XXIV* Money in the Bank Ladder Match.

Just when it seemed Benjamin was hitting his ECW stride, the 2008 WWE Draft once against sent the Superstar packing. In typical Shelton Benjamin fashion, however, he refused to be deterred by the move. Within one month of his *SmackDown* debut, Benjamin defeated Matt Hardy to claim the United States Championship.

Benjamin held the U.S. Title for eight months before losing it to MVP on *SmackDown*'s 500th episode. Following the loss, Benjamin was shipped back to ECW, where he challenged for the ECW Championship. Benjamin was released from his WWE contract in April 2010.

SHERRI MARTEL

HT	5'7"	FROM	New Orleans, Louisiana
SIGNATURE MOVE		**Sleeper**	

WWE turned "Sensational" when Sherri Martel debuted on July 24, 1987, and pinned her mentor, the Fabulous Moolah, for the WWE Women's Championship. Interestingly, Sherri had never lost her previous crown, the AWA Women's Championship, and simultaneously had possession of both Titles.

As champion, Sherri successfully defended her WWE Women's Championship for over 15 months against challengers such as Velvet McIntyre, Desiree Peterson, and Debbie Combs. Sherri also continued to battle Moolah, and the two captained opposing teams at the first *Survivor Series*. She was finally dethroned in October 1988 in Paris by Rockin' Robin.

Sherri transitioned to managing some of WWE's most infamous rule-breakers in the early 1990s. Her first client was Randy "Macho Man" Savage. When he pinned "King Hacksaw" Jim Duggan, Savage became a King, and Sherri his Queen. In 1991, "Million Dollar Man" Ted DiBiase enlisted her expert services and later a new bad boy, "The Heartbreak Kid" Shawn Michaels, signed her. In 1993, Sherri left WWE.

Later in the year and into 1994, she toured the independent circuit. That spring, she signed a contract with WCW and became "Sensuous" Sherri at the side of "Nature Boy" Ric Flair in his war against Sting and Hulk Hogan. Later, she became "Sister" Sherri and guided Harlem Heat to an amazing seven WCW World Tag Team Championship reigns before leaving the company in 1997.

On April 1, 2006, the 30 year career of the girl whose dream began with a ring of a bell in a barn was celebrated as she was inducted into the WWE Hall of Fame by DiBiase.

Sadly, Sherri passed away in June, 2007 while visiting her mother in Alabama. This pioneer was as tough as nails, but those around her remember Sherri for her big heart. Sensational Sherri is the only woman to ever hold both AWA and WWE Women's titles and was a legitimate force in and out of the ring. She was the forerunner to the women of WWE today and her legacy lives on through them. As DiBiase once described her, all who knew Sherri remember her as "truly priceless."

THE SHIELD

MEMBERS	Roman Reigns, Seth Rollins, & Dean Ambrose
COMBINED WT	**707 lbs.**

If you did not "believe in The Shield" at the outset of their WWE careers in 2012, you do now. Today, Seth Rollins, Roman Reigns, and Dean Ambrose have all achieved stardom as individuals. As a cohesive pack, they were one of the most destructive forces in WWE history.

Claiming to fight injustice in WWE, the trio disrupted the system while living completely outside of it. They wore riot gear, emerged from various portals of the arena, and communicated to the WWE Universe from undisclosed, darkened corners of the building.

After a series of heinous sneak attacks, The Shield backed up their words in the ring. They went unbeaten in 3-on-3 competition for several months, even winning their first *WrestleMania* match against three former WWE Champions. At one point, all three members held gold—Rollins and Reigns as a tag team and Ambrose as the United States Champion.

The winning ways continued into 2014 as an intense turf battle with the Wyatt Family brought the WWE Universe to their feet. A rebellion against The Authority further rallied the masses to their cause. Little did anyone know, Seth Rollins had his own agenda. The Aerialist double-crossed his "brothers," choosing the allure of The Authority's deep pockets and internal clout. This shocking betrayal marked the end for The Shield.

SHINSUKE NAKAMURA

HT	6'1"	WT	220 lbs.	FROM	Kyoto, Japan
SIGNATURE MOVE		**Kin-shasa**			

Trained by WWE Hall of Famer Antonio Inoki, Shinsuke Nakamura has labeled himself the "King of Strong Style," the combination of submissions, martial arts strikes, and kicks popular in Japan.

At 23, he became the youngest competitor to win Japan's prestigious IWGP Heavyweight Championship. Still, he harbored dreams of competing in WWE, and signed in 2016.

Watching Nakamura walk around the ring is a spectacle in itself. He moves as if dancing, wiggling his fingers, closing one eye and contorting his face, leaning against the ropes and twisting back the leg of his red leather pants. But there's nothing funny about his arsenal, particularly the kin-shasha, or knee strike, he used to defeat Sami Zayn while debuting in NXT during the *WrestleMania 32* weekend.

SHOHEI "GIANT" BABA

| HT | 6'10" | WT | 310 lbs. | FROM | Sanjo, Nigata, Japan |
| SIGNATURE MOVE | Running Yakuza Kick |

When a shoulder injury ended his baseball career, Giant Baba looked to make a name for himself in the ring. In 1959, he trained alongside Antonio Inoki with the founding father of puroresu, Rikidozan. Both future legends debuted in September 1959, and dominated the Japanese scene for the next thirty years. Baba debuted in WWE in 1964, challenging Champion Bruno Sammartino for the Heavyweight Championship. The two met again on several occasions in Japan in 1968.

Over the next decade, Baba competed against the biggest names in sports-entertainment. In December 1974, Baba defeated Jack Brisco to become the first-ever Japanese NWA Heavyweight Champion.

In January 1990 Vince McMahon appeared at an All-Japan event at Korauken Hall and announced a Wrestling Summit at Tokyo's Egg Dome, featuring WWE and the biggest names in Japan. Baba was instrumental in co-promoting shows with WWE in Japan and teamed with Andre The Giant to defeat Demolition.

On January 31, 1999, this legend passed away days after his 61st birthday, sparking a period of national mourning in Japan.

SIM SNUKA

| HT | 6'1" | WT | 234 lbs. | FROM | The Fiji Islands |

Following a tag team stint with partner Domino, Deuce revealed that he was the son of Jimmy "Superfly" Snuka and demanded that he be recognized by his real name, Sim Snuka. The second-generation competitor yearned to join forces with other multi-generational Superstars as a member of Legacy. However, the leader of the elite faction, Randy Orton, imposed a series of tests in order for new members to gain entry.

Snuka ultimately failed to pass Orton's tests and as a result, was denied a spot in Legacy. A frustrated Snuka attempted to exact revenge on Orton but was thwarted by Legacy members Cody Rhodes and Ted DiBiase.

Snuka's presence in WWE diminished greatly following his bid to join Legacy and in June 2009, he was released.

SID JUSTICE/ SYCHO SID

| HT | 6'9" | WT | 317 lbs. | FROM | West Memphis, Arkansas |
| SIGNATURE MOVE | Powerbomb |

An early master of the Chokeslam and powerbomb, this monster first appeared as Sid Vicious in WCW. He and partner Dan Spivey towered over WCW's tag team ranks. Soon, Sid became a member of the famed Four Horsemen stable and challenged longtime Horsemen nemesis Sting for the WCW Title. When he joined WWE in 1991 as Sid Justice, he appeared to have taken a more virtuous path similar to that of Hulk Hogan. He kept law and order in Hulk's match at SummerSlam and saved Randy Savage and Elizabeth from a Jake Roberts attack.

Shortly after the 1992 Royal Rumble, however, Sid revealed his true colors. After being passed over for a WWE Title opportunity, Sid turned his back on Hogan, his supposed friend, who took the spot Sid coveted. Sid's treacherous actions led to double main event at WrestleMania VIII. Sid failed to end Hulkamania during the encounter but fans got a glimpse of the "Sycho" side that would propel him to his greatest run of dominance years later.

After a second stint in WCW, he resurfaced in WWE in 1995. Now known as Sycho Sid, Shawn Michaels hired him as a bodyguard. After a mishap cost his boss the WWE Championship, Sid attacked Michaels the next night on Raw when he was told his services were no longer needed. After his tenure with Ted DiBiase's Million Dollar Corporation, Sid was not seen in WWE again until June 1996. He teamed with HBK and Ahmed Johnson against Camp Cornette. But while the hatchet with HBK was buried, the handle was still sticking out. By November, they were bitter enemies once again with Sid defeating Michaels for the WWE Championship. Sid captured the WWE Championship again in February 1997 but his second reign ended at the hands of Undertaker at WrestleMania 13.

Sid departed WWE in 1996. After a brief 1998 stop in ECW he returned to WCW, where he claimed World Championship gold twice before a horrific injury halted his career. Sid made a one night return to Raw in 2012 and brought back his vintage Powerbomb to silence Heath Slater.

SIMON DEAN

HT	5'10"	WT	210 lbs.	FROM	Clearwater, Florida
SIGNATURE MOVE	Simonizer				

Fitness guru Simon Dean first began shilling his Simon System to WWE viewers in late 2004. Decked out in bright purple, the annoying salesman claimed his "patented" system could transform any couch potato into a lean, mean, fighting machine.

Despite purchasing valuable advertising time on WWE television, sales for the system steadily sank along with Dean's career. It wasn't long before the unsuccessful salesman began losing to nearly every Superstar he faced, including Gunnar Scott, Tatanka, and the dress-wearing Vito.

Realizing his in-ring career wasn't taking off like he hoped, Dean turned to managing in 2006. Unfortunately his protégés, the Gymini, were just as unsuccessful in the ring as he was. Dean finally walked away from the ring completely later that year.

SIN CARA

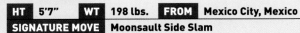

HT	5'7"	WT	198 lbs.	FROM	Mexico City, Mexico
SIGNATURE MOVE	Moonsault Side Slam				

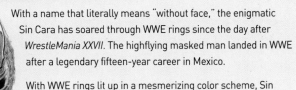

With a name that literally means "without face," the enigmatic Sin Cara has soared through WWE rings since the day after *WrestleMania XXVII*. The highflying masked man landed in WWE after a legendary fifteen-year career in Mexico.

With WWE rings lit up in a mesmerizing color scheme, Sin Cara and his flipping sambo suplex drew collective gasps from spectators and baffled many top Superstars. Despite his success, Sin Cara mysteriously became more aggressive. As weeks passed, it became clear why—there was an imposter!

Claiming the blue Sin Cara (Azul) stole his past identity, the evildoing black Sin Cara (Negro) sought to reclaim his name at *Hell in a Cell 2011*. In a tense encounter, Blue prevailed over his troublesome twin to keep his name intact.

In 2014, Sin Cara took flight in NXT where he found instant chemistry with Kalisto. As the Lucha Dragons, this sensational tandem ended The Ascension's record NXT Tag Team Championship reign at *NXT Takover: Fatal 4-Way*. By March 2015, the Lucha Dragons were dazzling crowds on *Raw* and *SmackDown*, where they continue to terrorize New Day and other high profile teams. Sin Cara produced several highlight reel moments flying solo in a 7-Man Ladder Match to open *WrestleMania 32*.

SIVI AFI

HT	5'11"	WT	248 lbs.	FROM	The Isle of Samoa
SIGNATURE MOVE	High Cross Body				

Sivi Afi made his debut appearance on WWE television in January 1986. Like fellow Polynesian Jimmy Snuka, Afi competed barefoot and employed a dizzying style of high-flying offense. In the months following his debut, Afi successfully turned back such Superstars as Rene Goulet, Moondog Spot, and Paul Roma.

Afi became recognized as a Samoan High Chief in 1988. With the acknowledgement came the traditional tribal tattoos indicative of such lofty status, as well as a new attitude. With Bobby "The Brain" Heenan serving as his manager, High Chief Afi briefly joined Tama and Haku as a member of the hated Islanders.

Following his WWE career, Afi worked as a Hollywood stuntman and celebrity bodyguard.

SKANDOR AKBAR

HT	6'2"	WT	242 lbs.	SIGNATURE MOVE	Camel Clutch

General Skandor Akbar competed professionally for nearly 15 years, including a brief WWE run in the late 1970s, but will forever be remembered for his decades of managerial service to some of the greatest names to ever run through the South.

Akbar's blatant disregard for the rules propelled him to become one of the most hated personalities in World Class Championship and Mid-South Wrestling, and the World Wrestling Council in Puerto Rico. He didn't care. His rebellious style, which included the dangerous use of fireballs, resulted in wins for his stable of Superstars, known as Devastation, Inc. It also resulted in threats on his life, which required the detested manager to often wear a bullet-proof vest while accompanying his Superstars to the ring.

Over the course of his managerial career, Akbar handled some of history's top draws, including WWE Hall of Famers Ted DiBiase and Abdullah the Butcher, along with King Kong Bundy, "Dr. Death" Steve Williams, Cactus Jack, and others. He died in 2010.

SIR OLIVER HUMPERDINK

With his long red beard, bright flowing hair, and outrageously colored suits, Sir Oliver Humperdink became one of the game's most easily recognized managers. Prior to entering WWE, he managed the Hollywood Blonds, Buddy Roberts, and Jerry Brown in Quebec and Florida. In the Charlotte territory, he formed a stable called the House of Humperdink.

While his WWE timeline only spanned a year, he was largely cheered when he appeared with Bam Bam Bigelow and future Hall of Famer "Mr. Wonderful" Paul Orndorff. In November, 1987, Humperdink led his duo into action in the first-ever *Survivor Series* pay-per-view main event, as they teamed with Hulk Hogan, Don Muraco, and Ken Patera to take on a squad headed by Andre the Giant.

By 1988, Humperdink had left WWE in favor of a managerial career in WCW, where he guided the Fabulous Freebirds—then consisting of Michael Hayes and Jimmy Garvin—among others, and was referred to as Big Daddy Dink.

In 2011, he died after a battle with cancer.

SKINNER

HT	6'0"	**WT**	215 lbs.	**FROM**	The Everglades
SIGNATURE MOVE	Gatorbreaker				

Skinner emerged from the sawgrass prairies of one of the world's most diverse eco-regions. Having survived close encounters with the most dangerous predators that inhabit the Everglades, the hardened Southerner was about as pleasant as the gators he tangled with before his mud-soaked boots began their path to WWE.

Skinner entered WWE in 1991 intent on treating its Superstars just like he did those alligators back in Florida. Audiences witnessed Skinner brawl with Undertaker, Tatanka, Crush, Sid, Ultimate Warrior, and Mr. Perfect. Although Skinner was a contender for both the Intercontinental and WWE Championships, he was not interested in material prizes. His trophy was taking something from a fallen opponent and keeping it to show his superior fighting skill.

In 1993, Skinner returned to the Everglades and his familiar wild surroundings. He reappeared in October 2005 for *WWE Raw Homecoming* and then again in 2007 for the *Raw 15th Anniversary*. Skinner remains one of WWE's most unusual Superstars nearly two decades after his debut.

SKULL MURPHY

HT	6'1"	**WT**	265 lbs	**FROM**	Hamilton, Ontario, Canada
SIGNATURE MOVE	Heart Punch				

Long before Stone Cold Steve Austin made the bald head a widely recognized fashion of the ring, John Joseph Murphy proudly sported the hairless cranium. The Canadian Superstar, however, didn't have much of a choice, as a childhood disease left him permanently hairless. Murphy chose to embrace the unique trait, though; he even adopted the moniker "Skull."

As Skull Murphy, the bald Superstar became one of the ring's most hated personalities during the 1950s and 1960s. Utilizing a devastating heart punch, Murphy was able to claim many NWA singles titles, but it was in the tag team ranks that he gained his greatest notoriety.

As a 14-time tag team Titlist, Murphy was accustomed to wearing gold around his waist. His most prestigious victory came in May, 1963 when he teamed with Brute Bernard to defeat Buddy Austin and The Great Scott for the United States Tag Team Championship. They held the titles for six months before being unseated by Killer Kowalski and Gorilla Monsoon.

Murphy died in 1970.

SKY LOW LOW

HT	3'7"	**WT**	86 lbs.	**FROM**	Montreal, Quebec, Canada
SIGNATURE MOVE	Hanging Vertical Suplex				

Always in impeccable physical condition, Sky Low Low was revered as "The Little Atlas of the Wrestling World." His performances became legendary; he fought in front of Queen Elizabeth of the United Kingdom and King Farouk of Egypt. Sky Low Low amazed fans by standing on top of his head without using his hands for balance.

In 1949, he captured the first-ever NWA Midget World Championship. He made his WWE debut in 1963, where he battled the likes of Little Beaver, Farmer Pete, Tiny Tim, Pancho Lopez, The Jamaica Kid, Irish Jackie, and Cowboy Bradley.

His career continued into the Hulkamania era, when he appeared in the classic Mixed-Tag Match at *WrestleMania III*. Sadly, in November 1998 this sports-entertainment pioneer passed away.

SLAM MASTER J

HT	5'9"	**WT**	210 lbs.	**FROM**	The ATL

Representing the ATL, or Atlanta to most people, Slam Master J spent the majority of his brief *SmackDown* career trying to impress Cryme Tyme. Hoping he would get to roll with JTG and Shad, Slam Master set out on a crusade to prove he was street tough. His antics included vandalizing Theodore Long's office, stealing DVDs, and generally speaking in an urban vernacular incomprehensible to anybody within earshot.

Despite a win in his 2009 in-ring debut against Charlie Haas, he was unable to keep the momentum going. Hoping his family's history of tag-team success would rub off (his father is Terry Gordy of the Fabulous Freebirds), Slam Master formed a partnership with Jimmy Wang Yang. The odd pairing, however, failed to mirror the Freebirds' success. Slam Master J was gone from WWE soon after.

SLATER-GATOR

MEMBERS	Heath Slater & Titus O'Neil	**COMBINED WT**	486 lbs.

Both Heath Slater and Titus O'Neil have achieved great success in the tag team division. Just not with each other.

Collectively known as Slater-Gator, Slater and O'Neil began teaming in July 2014, and after picking up wins against the likes of Gold and Stardust and Los Matadores, the duo appeared to have championship chemistry. Then the wheels came off.

Unable to capitalize on their early success, Slater-Gator began coming up short against nearly every team they faced, regardless of size or species. In fact, in August 2014, they lost to the pairing of El Torito and Hornswoggle, who collectively weigh less than O'Neil. The following month, Slater-Gator fell to the pairing of Adam Rose and The Bunny. Slater and O'Neil wisely disbanded shortly after.

SLICK

While his academic record may dispute it, Slick arrived in WWE in 1986 claiming to be a doctor. A "Doctor of Style," that is.

The impeccably dressed manager had previously been in the NWA's Central States territory, where protégés included "Hacksaw" Butch Reed and "Bulldog" Bob Brown. In WWE, he introduced himself by dipping into his "pockets of green" to purchase half interest in the legendary "Classy" Freddie Blassie's stable of Superstars. The innovative merger gave the newcomer instant credibility, as he was thrust into the spotlight alongside such greats as Iron Sheik and Nikolai Volkoff. He eventually added old charge Reed to his list of clients before finally assuming full ownership of Blassie's crop. Within months, the "Doctor of Style" assembled one of the most dominant forces in WWE.

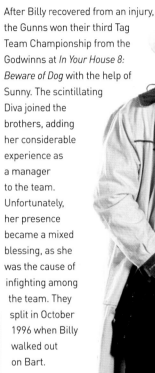

Always looking to make a buck, Slick became a popular recording artist in 1987. With his hit single, "Jive Soul Bro," Slick attempted to convince everyone that he was an honest man. His claims fell on deaf ears in the WWE Universe.

In the early 1990s, Slick took an unexpected leave of absence from WWE. When he returned, the normally fast-talking manager was barely recognizable. Instead of his traditional claims of greatness, the manager presented a more reserved personality. Renamed Reverend Slick, he preached the importance of good over evil. Today, he lives this philosophy, working as a minister in Texas.

SMASHER SLOAN

| HT | 6'0" | WT | 275 lbs. | FROM | Butte, Montana |
| SIGNATURE MOVE | Backbreaker | | | | |

Son of wrestler Whitey Whitler, Smasher Sloan made his WWE debut in 1964, taking on foes like WWE World Heavyweight Champion Bruno Sammartino and "Golden Boy" Arnold Skaaland. Shortly after becoming a pro, the second generation Superstar teamed with Baron Mikel Scicluna to defeat Johnny Valentine and Antonio Pugliese in controversial fashion to claim the United States Tag Team Championship. They held the Titles for two months before losing the gold back to Pugliese and his new tag team partner, Spiros Arion.

After dropping the Titles, Sloan left WWE to compete in other promotions, forming a successful tag team with "Spoiler" Don Jardine in Texas. When he was unable to recreate the success he found in WWE, he began to compete under a mask using several different monikers, including The Beast.

Sloan made a brief and unsuccessful return to WWE in 1972, managed by The Grand Wizard. When Sammartino began taking regular matches after losing his first World Championship, he wrestled Sloan in Boston and New York.

The Smasher died in 2001.

THE SMOKIN' GUNNS

| MEMBERS | Billy Gunn & Bart Gunn |
| COMBINED WT | 534 lbs. |

These cowboys arrived in WWE in 1993 and were an instant sensation. At that year's *King of the Ring* they joined the Steiner Brothers to defeat the Headshrinkers and Money, Inc. The Smokin' Gunns came out guns-a-blazin' as they climbed the tag team championship ladder. At the 1994 *Survivor Series* they joined Lex Luger's "Guts & Glory" team to battle Ted DiBiase's Million Dollar Corporation.

In January 1995 Billy and Bart defeated Bob "Spark Plug" Holly and 1-2-3 Kid to become World Tag Team Champions. They lost the Titles at *WrestleMania XI* but regained them in September by defeating Owen Hart and Yokozuna.

After Billy recovered from an injury, the Gunns won their third Tag Team Championship from the Godwinns at *In Your House 8: Beware of Dog* with the help of Sunny. The scintillating Diva joined the brothers, adding her considerable experience as a manager to the team. Unfortunately, her presence became a mixed blessing, as she was the cause of infighting among the team. They split in October 1996 when Billy walked out on Bart.

SMOKY MOUNTAIN WRESTLING

At the beginning of each Smoky Mountain Wrestling (SMW) broadcast, announcer Bob Caudle would describe it as "professional wrestling the way it used to be, and the way you like it."

That was the philosophy of Jim Cornette, who started the group in 1991 with Tim Horner, Sandy Scott, and Stan Lane—with financial assistance from music pioneer, Rick Rubin.

As WWE and WCW staged glitzy pay-per-views, SMW entertained fans at small venues in Kentucky, Tennessee, the Carolinas, Virginia, and West Virginia, offering a hard-working lineup that included Terry Funk, Bob Armstrong, Chris Jericho, Al Snow, and New Jack.

The 1993 *Survivor Series* featured a SMW match in which the Heavenly Bodies (Tom Prichard and Jimmy Del Ray) upended the Rock 'n' Roll Express for the group's tag team titles.

In 1994, SMW competitor Chris Candido won a tournament to become champion of the now-struggling NWA. But when Candido lost to Dan Severn, the new kingpin was often too busy to visit the territory.

The territory closed the next year when Cornette began working full-time in WWE.

SNITSKY

| HT | 6'8" | WT | 307 lbs. | FROM | Nesquehoning, Pennsylvania |
| SIGNATURE MOVE | Pump Handle Slam |

This deranged lunatic committed a lifetime's worth of atrocities in his four-year WWE career, even if some were not his fault. Snitsky showed no remorse after his inauspicious WWE debut sent Lita to the hospital. He did, however, promise that the destruction that he caused from that point forward would indeed be all his fault.

Snitsky gave audiences the creeps as he battled Superstars such as Kane, Big Show, and John Cena. In 2007, Snitsky became even more grotesque when he was introduced to the reborn ECW brand with disgusting yellow teeth. With this menacing look and unsettling demeanor, Snitsky enjoyed a hot streak but was never able to sink his rotting choppers into WWE gold prior to being released in 2008.

SOLOMON CROWE

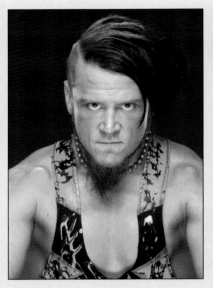

| HT | 5'10" | WT | 207 lbs. | FROM | Anonymous, Ohio |
| SIGNATURE MOVE | Pendulum Splash |

A veteran of the indie circuit, Solomon Crowe spent the early years of his career colliding with such legends as the Great Muta and future icons like Dean Ambrose.

In 2013, he arrived in NXT with a unique strategy. Rather than simply relying on his experience and physical prowess, Crowe attempted to disable rivals through psychological warfare. Using his skills as a computer hacker, he caused technical mishaps in the arena, once commandeering the house lights to confuse Kalisto and leave him vulnerable to an assault. Always provocative, his NXT opponents included Sylvester Lefort, Bull Dempsey, CJ Parker, and Brian Kendrick.

In late 2015, he parted ways with NXT to return to the independent battlegrounds.

SONNY BOY HAYES

| HT | 4'6" | WT | 76 lbs. |

The doubly tough Sonny Boy Hayes began his WWE career in 1967. Competing mainly in tag team action, Hayes regularly paired with Joey Russell or The Jamaica Kid to battle fellow diminutive wrestlers Little Brutus and Sky Low Low.

Perhaps Hayes' biggest match took place at the inaugural *Showdown at Shea* in September 1972, when he teamed with Pee Wee Adams in a losing effort against Little Beaver and Little Louie. However, the animosity between Hayes and Louie proved brief, as the two later teamed together to wrest the NWA Midget World Tag Team Championship from Bobo Johnson and Wee Willie Wilson in April 1975.

SONNY KING

Sonny King arrived in WWE in 1971 and showed from the start that he was ready for anything. During the early portion of 1972, he teamed up with Chief Jay Strongbow. By May 1972, the duo won the World Tag Team Championships at Madison Square Garden.

King and Strongbow defended the Titles for one month until they were defeated by Professor Toru Tanaka and Mr. Fuji. By Spring 1973, King left the company, but quickly became a force in the National Wrestling Alliance. In the early 1980s, he transitioned into a career as a manager, sharing his methods of success with up-and-coming competitors. The WWE Universe will always remember him as a great singles contender and part of one of the most popular teams of the 1970s.

SOUTHEASTERN CHAMPIONSHIP WRESTLING

Knoxville had seen a number of wrestling promotions since the 1930s. Throughout the 1960s, longtime promoter John Cazana traded talent with Nick Gulas' Nashville-based Mid-America territory. Then, in 1974, Cazana sold his company to Ron Fuller, who intended to establish Southeastern Championship Wrestling as one of the premier operations in the United States.

Fuller was a natural promoter. His father was Buddy Fuller and grandfather was Roy Welch, both founders of the Gulf Coast territory. Under Ron's leadership, the company outgrew smaller buildings for the Knoxville Civic Coliseum.

A multi-faceted talent, Fuller was often in the main events, sometimes brawling with Ron Wright, the "King of Kingsport," Tennessee. Wright was so hated that fans once reportedly burned his private plane at the airport.

In 1978, Fuller purchased Gulf Coast and added it to the Southeastern empire. But two years later, he sold the Knoxville wing of his operation. The promotion changed hands several times, owned at one point by both Ric Flair and Blackjack Mulligan.

Eventually, Knoxville was merged into the Continental Championship Wrestling, which closed in 1989.

SOUTHWEST CHAMPIONSHIP WRESTLING

In 1978, Joe Blanchard stopped promoting in San Antonio for Fritz Von Erich's Dallas territory and attempted to start his own league. Invigorated by cable television exposure, he hoped to create an "undisputed world heavyweight champion."

Not surprisingly, the promoter's son, Tully Blanchard—a future member of the Four Horsemen—was one of Southwest Championship Wrestling's biggest stars. Other top names included Wahoo McDaniel, the Funk Brothers, Tito Santana, Bruiser Brody, and the Sheepherders.

In 1982, the promotion's show became the first weekly wrestling telecast on the USA Network. The next year, the group held a one-night tournament to crown the first Southwest Championship Wrestling World Heavyweight Champion. Commissioner Lou Thesz ultimately awarded one of his old titles to the winner, Adrian Adonis.

But the company failed to pick up momentum from there. USA objected to SCW's content, particularly a bloody match between Tully and "Bruiser" Bob Sweetan, and an incident in which Scott Casey dumped pig manure on "Hangman" Bobby Jaggers. In September 1983, WWE claimed Southwest's spot on USA Network.

Joe Blanchard divested himself of the promotion in 1985, eventually becoming AWA president.

SPANISH ANNOUNCE TEAM

MEMBERS Carlos Cabrera & Marcelo Rodriguez

The story of the Spanish announce table is worthy of its own book. In the heat of battle, WWE Superstars have a tendency to turn their attention to the inanimate object, delivering DDTs and suplexes, among other perilous maneuvers, on the hard, uneven surface.

But what about the men seated behind the table? To Latin viewers, they're the trusted faces who help bring the action into homes throughout the WWE Universe.

In 1985, former WWE World Heavyweight Champion Pedro Morales and Miguel Alonso, formerly a broadcaster in the old Los Angeles territory, became WWE's Spanish language commentators. In 1994, former Colombian newscaster Carlos Cabrera and Ecuadorian-born Hugo Savinovich, a colorful former wrestler and manager in Puerto Rico, became a team. At one point, the duo was joined by future Hall of Famer Tito Santana.

After Savinovich's departure in 2011, Venezuelan actor and director Marcelo Rodriguez joined Carbrera. Rodriguez formerly commentated on WWE's short-lived *Super Astros* show, featuring Mexican Superstars, and is known for taking controversial positions that often contrast with Cabrera's steady observations.

SPIKE DUDLEY

HT	5'8"	**WT**	150 lbs.	**FROM**	New York City, New York
SIGNATURE MOVE		Dudley Dog			

As the runt of the Dudley litter, Spike Dudley entered WWE to very low expectations, but over the course of his career, the half-brother of Bubba Ray and D-Von Dudley proved to the WWE Universe that size doesn't matter.

Spike made an immediate impact when he helped his brothers defeat Edge and Christian for the World Tag Team Championship in March 2001. Unfortunately, the brotherly love didn't last long, as he eventually turned his back on his brothers and the ECW-WCW Alliance to stay by the side of his girlfriend, Molly Holly. His decision to follow his heart resulted in a bitter rivalry between brothers. Teaming with Tazz, Spike eventually gained the ultimate retribution over his bullying brothers when he pinned Bubba Ray to gain his brothers' cherished World Tag Team Championship.

In addition to his success in the tag team division, Spike also achieved notoriety as a singles competitor. Not only did he capture both the European and Hardcore Championships, he also defeated Rey Mysterio for the Cruiserweight Championship in July 2004.

SPIKE HUBER

HT	5'9"	**WT**	235 lbs.	**FROM**	Indianapolis, Indiana

Spike Huber was a scientifically-minded wrestler who plied his trade the world over. But Huber is best known for his time spent competing in the Indianapolis-based World Wrestling Association, which was owned and operated by his father-in-law, the legendary Dick The Bruiser.

While in WWA, Huber earned a reputation as a tag-team specialist. He won the organization's World Tag Team Championship five times with three different partners (Dick The Bruiser, Wilbur Snyder, and Steve Regal). He also defeated Bobby Colt to capture the WWA World Heavyweight Championship in January 1984.

Huber joined WWE during the promotion's national expansion of the mid-1980s. He had early success over the likes of Dennis Stamp, Max Blue, and Billy Travis. He eventually formed a short-lived tag team with Brian Blair, who later became one-half of the popular Killer Bees duo.

SPIRIT SQUAD

 MEMBERS Kenny, Johnny, Nicky, Mikey, & Mitch

This all-male cheerleading quintet first began antagonizing the WWE Universe with their uncoordinated routines in January 2006. What the group lacked in self-awareness, they made up tenfold with their talents in the ring. Within months of their debut, the high-flyers surprised Kane and Big Show to take their World Tag Team Championships.

In May 2006, the normally comical quintet showed a callous side, nearly crippling Shawn Michaels with a vicious attack, sparking a bitter rivalry with the revived D-Generation X. Later that year, the annoying faction hit the skids. Mired in a losing streak, the group lost their Tag Team Titles to Ric Flair and Roddy Piper at *Cyber Sunday*. Shortly after the loss, longtime rivals DX packed Spirit Squad into a shipping crate and sent them off to WWE's developmental territory, OVW in Louisville, Kentucky.

SPIROS ARION

	HT	6'5"	**WT**	260 lbs.	**FROM**	Athens, Greece
	SIGNATURE MOVE		Atomic Drop			

The man known throughout the world as "the Iron Greek" first appeared in WWE rings in 1966. Spiros Arion's fiery Mediterranean nature quickly made him one of the most popular Superstars in the Northeast as he squared off against Angelo Savoldi, Tony Nero, Smasher Sloan, and Tank Morgan. In December 1966, he won his first Title in WWE when he and Antonio Pugliese teamed up to win the United States Tag Team Championship. In 1967, Arion's close friendship with Bruno Sammartino led to another United States Tag Team reign.

Over the next few years, Arion traveled the globe, returning to WWE in 1974 to team with his friend and mentor, Chief Jay Strongbow. Sadly, Spiros eventually turned on Strongbow and fell under the sinister influence of "Classy" Freddie Blassie. Filled with hate, the once heroic Greek gladiator became a treacherous and crafty villain. In one memorable incident, he tied Strongbow in the ropes, destroying the proud warrior's feather headdress.

He last appeared in WWE in 1978, teaming with another fallen hero, Victor Rivera. In 1979, Arion journeyed to England for Joint Promotions, ending his career there.

THE SPOILER

HT	6'4"	WT	293 lbs.	FROM	Parts Unknown
SIGNATURE MOVE	Iron Claw				

Don Jardine made his in-ring debut at the young age of 15. He spent more than ten years competing under his given name, as well such aliases as The Butcher and Sonny Cooper. Then in 1967, famed promoter Fritz Von Erich gave him the name "The Spoiler." From there, Jardine went on to become one of the best-known masked Superstars of all time.

The Spoiler was a double threat in the ring. At 6'4" and nearly 300 pounds, he possessed immense strength. But Jardine was also very athletic for a man of his size, and displayed uncanny balance.

As a member of WWE, The Spoiler used his feared Iron Claw to earn an opportunity at Pedro Morales' World Heavyweight Championship in New York. He was unable to unseat the Champ, but the match holds historical significance, since state regulations forced The Spoiler to compete without his trademark mask.

Yet, his most significant contribution was teaching Undertaker his signature walk across the top rope.

He died in 2006.

ST. LOUIS WRESTLING CLUB

Regarded as the NWA's flagship promotion, the St. Louis Wrestling Club attracted the world's best competitors and aspired to the highest standards.

Promoter Sam Muchnick, a two-time NWA president between 1950 and 1975, was strict about the way his shows were presented, insisting that matches be confined to the ring and forbidding outside interference. The company's television show was taped in a banquet room, where spectators dined in formal ware.

Muchnick was so devoted to the NWA that he didn't expand his territory outside St. Louis, although the Central States territory was regarded as a sister promotion. His Missouri State title was considered a stepping stone to a world championship, with Bob Backlund, Harley Race, Jack Brisco, Dory Funk, Jr., Kerry Von Erich, and Ted DiBiase among those holding the prize.

When Muchnick retired in 1982, Bob Geigel and Race became promoters, while several former associates shifted allegiance to WWE. In 1985, Jim Crockett purchased the St. Louis office and absorbed it into the company that became WCW.

STACY KEIBLER

HT	5'11"	FROM	Baltimore, Maryland	SIGNATURE MOVE	Roundhouse Kick

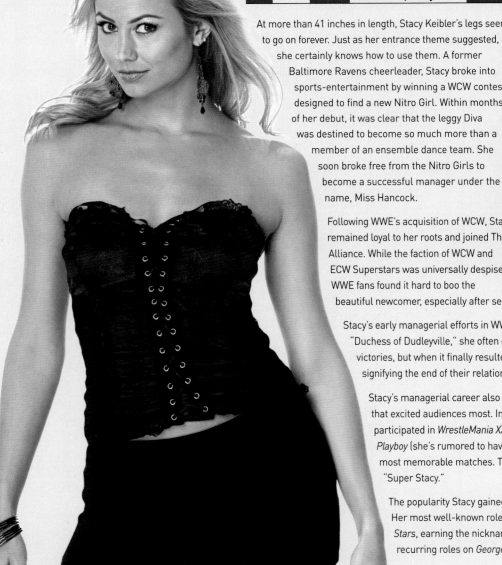

At more than 41 inches in length, Stacy Keibler's legs seem to go on forever. Just as her entrance theme suggested, she certainly knows how to use them. A former Baltimore Ravens cheerleader, Stacy broke into sports-entertainment by winning a WCW contest designed to find a new Nitro Girl. Within months of her debut, it was clear that the leggy Diva was destined to become so much more than a member of an ensemble dance team. She soon broke free from the Nitro Girls to become a successful manager under the name, Miss Hancock.

Following WWE's acquisition of WCW, Stacy remained loyal to her roots and joined The Alliance. While the faction of WCW and ECW Superstars was universally despised, WWE fans found it hard to boo the beautiful newcomer, especially after seeing her compete in a Bra and Panties Match during the *Invasion* pay-per-view.

Stacy's early managerial efforts in WWE saw her guide the careers of Bubba Ray and D-Von Dudley. Known as the "Duchess of Dudleyville," she often distracted her team's opposition. The sexy ploy carried the Dudleys to numerous victories, but when it finally resulted in a loss for Bubba Ray and D-Von, the team drove the Diva through a table, signifying the end of their relationship.

Stacy's managerial career also landed her by the sides of Scott Steiner and Test, but it was her in-ring action that excited audiences most. In March 2004, she competed in the biggest match of her career when she participated in *WrestleMania XX*'s Playboy Evening Gown Match. Despite never having graced the pages of *Playboy* (she's rumored to have declined numerous invitations), Stacy's participation made it one of the event's most memorable matches. The following year, Stacy joined the crime fighting team of Hurricane and Rosey as "Super Stacy."

The popularity Stacy gained while competing in WWE rings eventually led her to a career in Hollywood. Her most well-known role saw the Diva dance all the way to the finals of ABC's hit series, *Dancing with the Stars*, earning the nickname "The Weapon of Mass Seduction" from judge Bruno Tonioli. She also landed recurring roles on *George Lopez* and *What About Brian*.

THE STALKER

HT	6'6"	WT	274 lbs.	FROM	The Environment
SIGNATURE MOVE	Superplex				

In August 1996 WWE began to air videos showing a man who could see you, but go unseen. Wearing camouflage, the Stalker hunted Superstars such as Goldust, Faarooq, Justin Bradshaw, Hunter Hearst-Helmsley, Stone Cold Steve Austin, the Goon, and Jerry "The King" Lawler.

Shortly after his pay-per-view debut at the 1996 Survivor Series he disappeared from WWE. Anything could happen when he was in the ring and for all anyone knows he could be watching you right now, waiting for the right moment to strike.

STAMPEDE WRESTLING

see page 328

STAN HANSEN

HT	6'4"	WT	321 lbs.	FROM	Borger, Texas
SIGNATURE MOVE	The Lariat				

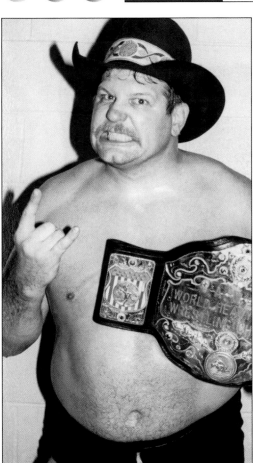

Stan Hansen began his sports-entertainment career in the early 1970s in Amarillo. In 1976, manager Freddie Blassie brought the double-tough roughneck to WWE. He quickly proved his reputation when on April 26, 1976, in the main event at Madison Square Garden, he broke Champion Bruno Sammartino's neck after connecting with his Lariat clothesline.

After this brutal attack, Hansen gained a reputation as a vicious bounty hunter. Although Bruno settled the score during the 1976 Showdown at Shea, Hansen continued with more despicable attacks against the likes of Ivan Putski, Andre The Giant, and Gorilla Monsoon.

Hansen returned to WWE in 1981 and hunted the WWE and Intercontinental Titles, calling out respective Champions Bob Backlund and Pedro Morales. He left WWE in 1982 and spent time in Georgia and Japan, where he regularly main evented.

In late 1985, Hansen captured the AWA World Heavyweight Championship from Rick Martel. But after a disagreement with promoter Verne Gagne, he ran over the title with his truck, sending the remnants back to Gagne. In 2010, he inducted longtime adversary turned friend, Antonio Inoki, into the WWE Hall of Fame. In 2016, this controversial and enduring figure was inducted into Hall of Fame as well.

STAN LANE

HT	6'1"	WT	230 lbs.	FROM	Pensacola, Florida

Members of the WWE Universe might only recognize Stan Lane for his brief run as an announcer on WWE Superstars during the mid-1990s. But in the two decades preceding his time behind the microphone, "Sweet" Stan excelled as one-half of three of the greatest tag teams around: The Fabulous Ones, The Midnight Express, and The Heavenly Bodies.

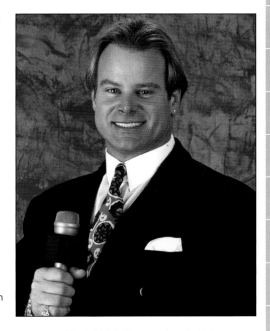

Trained by Ric Flair, Lane debuted in 1974 as a singles competitor, but didn't truly break out until he teamed with Steve Keirn to form The Fabulous Ones. Together, they captured more than 20 tag titles from promotions across North America, including the AWA Southern Tag Team Championship 15 times.

Lane later teamed with Bobby Eaton as a member of The Midnight Express. Among their accomplishments was a reign with the prestigious NWA World Tag Team Championship in late 1988.

In the 1990s, Lane teamed with Tom Prichard to create The Heavenly Bodies. The duo earned the distinction of being the first-ever Smoky Mountain Wrestling Tag Team Champions in April 1992. They went on to win the gold four more times.

STAN STASIAK

HT	6'4"	WT	270 lbs.	FROM	Buzzard Creek, Oregon
SIGNATURE MOVE	Heart Punch				

Stan Stasiak's nine-day stint with the prestigious WWE Championship served as a historic bridge between Pedro Morales and Bruno Sammartino's lengthy runs with the Title.

Stasiak made his professional debut in Quebec in 1958. Known for his long sideburns and rugged offensive approach, he bounced back and forth between territories in Canada and the United States' Pacific Northwest. During this time, Stasiak became known for his paralyzing heart punch, but it wasn't until he took his game to the Northeast that he truly became immortal.

In December 1973, Stan "The Man" forever cemented his name in sports-entertainment when he defeated Pedro Morales for the WWE Championship in Philadelphia, Pennsylvania. The victory made him the fifth Champion in WWE history.

While Stasiak's reign lasted little more than a week, until his death in 1997, he was regularly recognized as one of the few Superstars lucky enough to have reached the sport's zenith. During the reign of Superstar Billy Graham in 1977, he again challenged for the Title, but, unfortunately for Stasiak, lightning only struck once.

STAMPEDE WRESTLING

Established in 1948, Stampede Wrestling was considered the "missing link" between North American wrestling and the styles popularized in Asia, Europe, and Latin America.

Promoter Stu Hart, father of future WWE Superstars Bret and Owen Hart, imported talent from around the world, and often challenged visiting competitors to spar in the "Dungeon" beneath the family's Calgary mansion. While many would describe their experience in the Dungeon as brutal, the Alumni were generally proud of the hard lessons they learned in Stu's basement.

Stampede's stars risked long rides on icy roads, traveling through Alberta, British Columbia, Saskatchewan, and Montana. These stars included Fritz Von Erich, Superstar Billy Graham, Jim Neidhart, Roddy Piper, Lance Storm, Chris Benoit, Edge, Chris Jericho, Bad News Brown, Brian Pillman, the British Bulldogs, and Junkyard Dog, among others.

In Calgary, Stampede Wrestling was a true institution. Its performers would often compete and appear in the parade at the annual Calgary Stampede. Stu was also awarded the prestigious Order of Canada.

In 1984, WWE purchased Stampede. But the next year, the company was sold back. Bruce Hart, one of Stu's 12 children, oversaw the promotion until 1990.

STARDUST

    HT 6'2" **WT** 220 lbs. **FROM** The Fifth Dimension
SIGNATURE MOVE The Queen's Crossbow

For Cody Rhodes, living in the shadows of his father, Dusty Rhodes, and the so-called embarrassment of his brother, Goldust, is a lot to shoulder. In fact, Cody would say it's a disaster...a beautiful disaster that caused him to self-destruct and become the super galactic Superstar he is today—Stardust!

While Stardust's familial fallout is well-documented, his earliest days were actually spent alongside his brother. The inter-dimensional oddity debuted as Goldust's partner in June 2014, and within months, the face-painted pairing went on to become WWE Tag Team Champions.

Despite their early successes, Gold and Stardust began to struggle in 2015. Weeks of tensions eventually caused the team to implode after Goldust called his brother "Cody." Claiming Cody was dead, an upset Stardust later attacked Goldust, marking the official end of the pairing.

A darker and even more mystifying Stardust turned his attention toward *Arrow* actor Stephen Amell in the summer of 2015. After attacking an unsuspecting Neville on *Raw*, The Prince of Dark Matter inexplicably went after Amell. The actions eventually led to a high-profile encounter at *SummerSlam*, where Amell teamed with Neville to defeat Stardust and King Barrett.

Following the loss, Stardust continued his obsession with Amell, most notably by invading the actor's appearance at the 2016 Dallas Comic Con. Stardust also began associating with The Ascension. Collectively known as The Cosmic Wasteland, Stardust, Konnor, and Viktor are on a continued quest to terminate superheroes everywhere.

STEINER BROTHERS

 MEMBERS Rick Steiner & Scott Steiner
COMBINED WT 510 lbs.

These superior athletes and All-Americans from the University of Michigan began teaming professionally in the National Wrestling Alliance in 1989. After some early success as solo competitors, the brothers achieved almost instant success as a tag team. Only months after joining forces, they knocked off the legendary Fabulous Freebirds in November for their first of seven WCW Tag Team Titles. This was only the beginning and for the next three years, Rick and Scott ruled WCW's tag team scene. The duo collected wins at several of the promotion's most prestigious events including *Starrcade*, *Clash of the Champions*, and *The Great American Bash*.

In late 1992, the Steiners made their debut in WWE, where they showcased their unmatched teamwork and technical prowess. In 1993, they appeared on the debut episode of *Monday Night Raw*, beat the Beverly Brothers at *Royal Rumble* and defeated the Headshrinkers at *WrestleMania IX*. Their year hit its peak in June when they defeated Money, Inc., for the World Tag Team Championships. After trading the Titles with Money Inc., and ultimately losing them to the Quebecers in a bizarre "Province of Quebec" Rules Match, the Steiners left WWE.

The brothers appeared in ECW in 1995 before returning to WCW. Though it had been over four years since the Steiners first departed the Atlanta-based organization, its top tag teams would have probably preferred they stayed away. Their second stint with WCW was just as dominant. This time around, they clashed with teams like the Nasty Boys and Public Enemy. By 1998, they had regained the WCW Tag Team Titles at the

expense of Harlem Heat, The Outsiders, and others. However, at *SuperBrawl VIII* in February 1998, their brotherly bond met a shocking end. During a WCW Tag Team Title defense, Scott turned his back on Rick and joined the dominant faction in WCW, nWo. In recent years, the Steiner Brothers have gotten back on the same page and sometimes appear together in promotions around the world—a good sign for a team that will go down as one of the most prevailing and talented units in sports entertainment history.

STEPHANIE MCMAHON

see page 330

STEPHANIE WIAND

Stephanie Wiand is best known as the super-hyper cohost of *WWE Mania* during the mid-1990s. Alongside Todd Pettengill, she regularly recapped the week in WWE. Heading into the first-ever *In Your House*, Wiand proved ahead of her time when she toured a house which would be given away to a lucky fan. Years later, networks such as HGTV and MTV would also begin touring houses, using the same template laid out by Wiand.

Wiand remained in entertainment following her brief WWE run. In 1998, she appeared in two episodes of *The Bold and the Beautiful*. She later appeared in the series *Afterworld*. And most recently, she wrote, produced, and appeared in *Revenge of the Bimbot Zombie Killers*. Despite her myriad experience in Hollywood, though she will always be remembered fondly as Pettengill's over-caffeinated sidekick.

STEVE BLACKMAN

HT	6'2"	WT	245 lbs.
FROM	Annville, Pennsylvania		

When Steve Blackman walked to the ring with his patented eskrima and Kendo sticks in hand, it was clear that danger lurked ahead. But despite being heavily armed, it was Blackman's bare hands and mastery of martial arts that earned him the nickname "The Lethal Weapon."

Blackman's no-nonsense approach to competition made him a natural fit for WWE's hardcore division. There were few Superstars that could match his intensity and training with martial arts weaponry. One thing Blackman couldn't combat, however, was being out-manned. In August 2000, "The Lethal Weapon" lost his Hardcore Championship to Shane McMahon when the Chairman's son enlisted the help of several other Superstars to help him become the WWE Hardcore Champion. Later that month at *SummerSlam*, Blackman regained the Title in a brutal contest after knocking McMahon off the top of the TitanTron onto the arena floor approximately fifty feet below. Blackman followed suit by jumping off the structure onto McMahon's limp body, covering him for the win. The image of "The Lethal Weapon" flying through the air remains one of Blackman's greatest career highlights.

STEVE "DR. DEATH" WILLIAMS

HT	6'1"	WT	285 lbs.	FROM	Norman, Oklahoma
SIGNATURE MOVE	Oklahoma Stampede				

Steve Williams initially came to prominence as an All-American in amateur wrestling and football at the University of Oklahoma. After training under "Cowboy" Bill Watts, Dr. Death transitioned to a career in sports-entertainment, becoming famous all over North America and Japan, winning titles at virtually every stop he made. His natural athleticism, combined with an innate toughness, had many experts predicting that Williams might soon capture a major world Title.

In 1998, Williams arrived in sports-entertainment's most competitive landscape, WWE. He was an early favorite to win the *Brawl For All* Tournament, but he suffered a severe hamstring tear. He returned in 1999, but soon left for WCW and Japan. In 2006, Williams made surprise appearances for WWE after a heroic fight against throat cancer.

In 2007, he penned his inspirational autobiography, *How Dr. Death Became Dr. Life*. Sadly, on December 29, 2009, this legendary athlete's life was cut short after the cancer he valiantly battled for years returned. Steve Williams' influence on the gridiron and inside the ring will be surpassed only by his love of life, family, and friends.

STEVIE RICHARDS

HT	6'2"	WT	230 lbs.	FROM	Philadelphia, Pennsylvania
SIGNATURE MOVE	Stevie Kick				

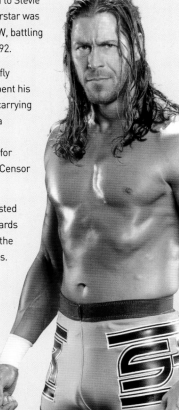

While ECW announcer Joey Styles often referred to Stevie Richards as a "clueless putz," the talented Superstar was partially responsible for the early success of ECW, battling in the outlaw promotion's inaugural match in 1992.

Following an eventful ECW career, Richards briefly competed in WCW before landing in WWE. He spent his earliest WWE days mocking fellow Superstars, carrying forward the tradition of his popular bWo persona from ECW. But Richards soon made a shocking transformation, trading in his cutoff jean shorts for more formal attire, becoming leader of Right to Censor in order to protest WWE's risqué content.

Luckily for the WWE Universe, the movement lasted less than a year. After the faction broke up, Richards defeated fellow ECW alum Tommy Dreamer for the Hardcore Championship, the first of his 21 reigns.

After the retirement of the Hardcore Championship, WWE audiences saw Richards return to his extreme roots during the rebirth of ECW as a WWE brand. After leaving WWE in 2008, he became a certified DDP Yoga instructor and competed on the independent scene.

STEPHANIE McMAHON

FROM Greenwich, Connecticut

Over a lifetime of soaking up the infinite knowledge of her father, WWE Chairman Vince McMahon, one lesson Stephanie McMahon never absorbed was the notion that WWE is a man's world. Since a childhood that involved modeling t-shirts for the WWEShop catalogue and a friendship with Andre the Giant, she has eradicated this myth. Now a Principle Owner of WWE and the company's Chief Brand Officer, Stephanie wields enough power to swing the fate of suited executives and WWE Superstars alike.

Proving the apple doesn't fall far from the tree, Stephanie demands nothing short of excellence inside the ring and out. For five years running, CableFax named her one of "The Most Powerful Women in Cable" for her various roles behind the WWE scenes. In front of the camera, she is one half of the ruthless power couple known as The Authority, along with her husband Triple H. As a woman in charge, her expectation for the WWE Superstars is quite simple—fall in line...or get out of her ring.

Stephanie was introduced to the WWE Universe in early 1999 when the sadistic Undertaker abducted her as a means to get to her father. Fortunately, an unlikely hero made the save when noted McMahon nemesis, Stone Cold Steve Austin, ran to the ring to prevent The Deadman from locking Steph in the bonds of unholy matrimony. This traumatic experience was the first of several onscreen roles that have seen Stephanie evolve into a confident leader, calculated decision maker, and even a formidable competitor.

THE GAME OF LOVE

Stephanie's first genuine love interest came in the form of WWE Superstar Test, much to the chagrin of her protective older brother, Shane. Despite Shane's best efforts to put a stop to the romance, Stephanie and Test wound up standing at the altar, set to be wed on a November 1999 episode of *Raw*. Just before the couple could exchange vows, one Superstar made a very revealing objection. Armed with video evidence, Triple H exposed the shocking truth that Stephanie was already a married woman.

In an attempt to salvage his daughter's good name, an irate Mr. McMahon battled Triple H at *Armageddon 1999*. Late in the match, The Chairman was shocked even further when Stephanie helped her husband defeat him, then jumped into Triple H's arms, proving they had been in cahoots all along.

The power-hungry couple usurped control over WWE. In what was dubbed the McMahon-Helmsley Era, the husband-and-wife team abused their power to their own benefit. As a result, Triple H regained the WWE Championship while Stephanie claimed the Women's Championship from Jacqueline in March 2000.

In July 2001, Stephanie broke her father's heart again when she revealed herself as the new owner of ECW. Merged with her brother's WCW, The Alliance aimed to put her father and WWE out of business forever. Though several top Superstars, including a traitorous Stone Cold Steve Austin, aided in their cause, The Alliance was forced to disband when Team WWE defeated them at *Survivor Series 2001*. Stephanie was forced out of sports-entertainment, but not for long. She connived her way back in through a hoax pregnancy that drove a wedge in her marriage and led to the "Billion Dollar Princess" supporting Chris Jericho in his match against Triple H at *WrestleMania X8*.

A LEADER ON THE RISE

Stephanie resurfaced in July 2002 when her father appointed her General Manager of *SmackDown*. Though she displayed an aggressive and innovative leadership style, Mr. McMahon eventually forced her out of power in the most brutal way possible, defeating her in an "I Quit" Match at *No Mercy*.

For the next several years, Stephanie assumed various executive roles behind the scenes, including a prominent position heading up the WWE Creative team. She appeared sparingly on programming, each time making her commanding presence felt. In 2009, Stephanie was caught in the crossfire of her husband's emotional rivalry with Randy Orton. The painful incident did not dissuade her from sticking by The Game's side in subsequent battles, and by the summer of 2013, the happy couple was ready to rule WWE with a heavier hand than ever before.

THE AUTHORITY

After Triple H helped Randy Orton squash Daniel Bryan's triumphant moment at *SummerSlam 2013*, the era of The Authority was born. Hand in hand, Triple H and Stephanie worked to mold WWE into their ideal image, often belittling popular Superstars and exerting their considerable influence on the outcomes of matches. Stephanie notoriously coined the phrase "B+ player" in reference to Daniel Bryan. For the better part of a year, the corporate higher-ups spared no resources imposing a glass ceiling over the "Yes!" Man, favoring the more archetypal Champion, Orton.

The Authority's vendetta against Bryan even extended to his wife, Brie Bella. Brie's defiant slap to Stephanie ignited a summer-long game of one-upmanship that at one point saw Stephanie led away from *Raw* in handcuffs. At *SummerSlam 2014*, in her first match in over ten years, Stephanie scored the ultimate revenge when Brie's own sister, Nikki Bella, turned on her. Nikki's betrayal opened the door for Stephanie to plant Brie on the mat with Triple H's signature Pedigree for the win.

QUEEN OF WWE

Stephanie McMahon was named to the WWE Board of Directors in 2015, and away from her onscreen role, has carved a real-life legacy of business acumen. Her corporate responsibilities extend across all areas of business within WWE, as she works closely with top-level executives to champion key growth initiatives for the company. As WWE's global brand ambassador, Stephanie provides an invaluable link between the organization and its wide-ranging scope of constituencies including government bodies, investors, business partners and media. She tackles these enormous responsibilities while maintaining a recurring role on worldwide TV and raising three young daughters at home.

As WWE continues to expand its footprint, Stephanie never loses sight of what is truly important. She believes passionately in the power of community and is the head of WWE's vast array of charitable initiatives. Under her guidance, WWE supports such efforts as the Special Olympics, Susan G. Komen, WWE's anti-bullying program Be a STAR, and countless others. Inspired by the memory of eight-year old Connor "The Crusher" Michalek, she and Triple H established Connor's Cure in 2014, a fund dedicated to further advances in pediatric cancer research.

Stephanie also has a seat at the Board for two separate organizations, has completed the Eisenhower Fellowship Leadership Program, trains like a WWE Women's Champion and every so often, she sleeps. Perhaps no one in entertainment history has logged so much tireless work, only to get booed vociferously by her core consumer base each and every week. It is a thankless job, but Stephanie wouldn't have it any other way. After all, it is what's best for business.

Thanks to the actions of Sting, The Authority was ousted from power at *Survivor Series 2014*, but not for long. The callous power brokers orchestrated an attack on Edge that forced John Cena to reinstate them. Back in control, they proceeded to make life hell for all who had rebelled against their imperial reign.

At *WrestleMania 31*, Stephanie proclaimed, "The Authority always wins." More often than not, that statement has proven to be true. When Roman Reigns refused to play ball with them, they eventually forced him to defend the WWE World Heavyweight Championship in the Royal Rumble Match, all but assuring a new Titleholder. Mr. McMahon showed his pride for his daughter's merciless leadership in February 2016 by presenting her with the Vincent J. McMahon Legacy of Excellence Award, in honor of her grandfather. However, Stephanie's returning brother Shane interrupted the ceremony, igniting a bitter power struggle between the imminent heirs to the McMahon family legacy.

"BOW DOWN TO THE KING AND BOW DOWN TO YOUR QUEEN...ME!"

STING...

HT	6'2"
WT	250 lbs.
FROM	Venice Beach, California

SIGNATURE MOVE
Scorpion Deathlock, Stinger Splash, Scorpion Death Drop

"Against an army of shadows, lies the dark warrior.

The prevailer of good.

With a voice of silence

And a mission of justice

This is Sting."

For decades, this brooding, ghostly defender of righteousness lurked in the minds of the WWE Universe but never emerged into the light of a WWE ring. That all changed in November 2014. At *Survivor Series*, the white painted face of "The Vigilante" materialized out of the darkness.

Sting's signature stare, silent and expressionless, was a welcome sight for many fans who long considered him the greatest competitor to never step foot in a WWE arena. A six-time WCW World Champion, Sting was considered "The Franchise" for WWE's most formidable competitor from the late 1980s until the day it closed its doors in 2001. Over a decade later, WWE would be the setting for the final chapter in what was already a surefire Hall of Fame career.

THE BLADE RUNNERS

Long before striking fear into the blackest hearts in sports-entertainment, Steve Borden was an exceptional athlete in his native Southern California. He played football and dominated on the hardwood as a member of the Hart High School basketball team. His natural size led him to begin a career in bodybuilding but he soon became inspired to pursue what would be his true calling.

In the mid-1980s, Borden joined a local California-based wrestling promotion as part of a muscle bound quartet called Power Team USA. Though hard to imagine today, his original in-ring moniker was Flash Borden. Soon, Borden broke off from the group along with the man who would one day rise to immortality in WWE as Ultimate Warrior. Together, Borden and the future Warrior worked in Mid-Southern territories as the Freedom Fighters and then later, the Blade Runners.

After joining the Universal Wrestling Federation and adopting their new name, The Blade Runners began to see their first real success. Borden adopted his now-iconic name Sting, and the two face-painted hulks became a force in UWF's tag team division. Though Warrior left the promotion in 1986, Sting captured the UFW Tag Team Titles partnering with both Eddie Gilbert and Rick Steiner before embarking on his NWA career.

A MAJOR SPLASH

NWA officials knew they had acquired something special when Sting arrived in 1987. He had a tanned, sculpted physique and radiated charisma from head to toe. With bleached blonde hair shaved into a flattop, vibrant face paint and neon colored ring gear, the newcomer had all makings of a budding megastar. Sting was thrust into the spotlight without hesitation, entrusted with a spot in the opening match of the organization's first pay-per-view, *Starrcade 1987*. When the NWA unveiled the first *Clash of the Champions* the following year, Sting was the main attraction when he challenged "Nature Boy" Ric Flair for the NWA World Title.

Sting fought valiantly in the forty-five minute, time limit draw with Flair, proving he belonged among the NWA's upper-echelon. Following the Championship bout, Sting continued to battle Flair and other members of the notorious Four Horsemen. He found an ally in the stable's most longstanding rival, Dusty Rhodes. Together, Rhodes and Sting took on Arn Anderson and Tully Blanchard at the second *Clash of the Champions* and at *Starrcade 1988*, locked up with the legendary Road Warriors.

For the remainder of the 1980s, Sting's popularity soared. On the surface, he was the epitome of cool. If not for his ever-changing face paint, one might have mistaken him for a laid-back surfer dude content with soaking in the SoCal sun. In the ring, he became a turbocharged warrior with a piercing war cry that rattled the eardrum and an electric offense highlighted by the majestic Stinger Splash. Even the Four Horsemen warmed up to him. In 1989, common enemies such as Terry Funk and the Great Muta brought The Stinger and Flair together. For a brief period, Sting actually joined the stable. However, when his rising stardom became a threat to Flair's pedestal, he was ostracized from the group.

THE FRANCHISE OF WCW

Sting got his revenge on the Horsemen at *The Great American Bash 1990* when he defeated Ric Flair to capture his first NWA World Title. His first reign lasted an impressive six months and served as a preview of the next decade in which he would tack six more WCW World Titles into his resume. His second came at *Superbrawl II* in 1992 against Lex Luger. By this time, Sting had been marked as WCW's "Franchise," a flattering label, but one that made him the target for WCW's most dangerous Superstars, including the 450-pound Vader.

Sting traded World Championship victories with "The Mastodon" as part of a brutal rivalry that spanned nearly eighteen months and included a grisly Strap Match. Following these battles, Sting became United States Champion and soon after, renewed his conflict with Flair. The two WCW stalwarts met on the first episode of *WCW Monday Nitro* and again at *World War 3*. In 1996, the foundation of WCW was turned upside down, and with the chaos, came Sting's shocking metamorphosis from beach brawler to dark vigilante.

OUT OF THE DARKNESS

With the New World Order laying waste to all that was sacred in WCW, Sting was one of the valiant Superstars leading the charge of resistance against the WWE insurgents. But when a peculiar sequence of events led his fellow comrades and fans to question his loyalty, a jilted Sting retreated into the shadows. When he returned, he wore a somber expression with ghoulish, black and white face paint. He donned a black trench coat and surveyed the action from the rafters above the arena, waiting to descend and inflict justice.

I AM THE FACE OF RETRIBUTION. I AM THE SILENCER OF INJUSTICE.

This new, gothic version of Sting did not speak, but made his intentions clear, attacking nWo members or simply warning them with the menacing point of his trusty black baseball bat. Sting got his wish at *Starrcade 1997* and capitalized by defeating the figurehead of the nWo, "Hollywood" Hulk Hogan for the WCW World Championship. After a controversy led him to be stripped of the gold, Sting bested Hogan again at *Superbrawl 1998*. This time, he gave "Hollywood" a taste of his own medicine by spray-painting "WCW" across his chest.

His virtue no longer in question, Sting later joined the nWo Wolfpac, an offshoot of the original faction, minus the villainy. With new red and black face paint, Sting was a force in tag team competition with allies such as Kevin Nash and Lex Luger. After some time off, Sting collected two more WCW World Titles in 1999, defeating Diamond Dallas Page and once again dethroning Hogan.

As the era of WCW wound to a close, only two men could possibly belong in the discussion of who should compete in the company's final match—Sting and his old nemesis, Ric Flair. *Nitro* ended the way it began, with WCW's unquestionable two cornerstones going face to face. Sting prevailed with a Scorpion Deathlock as his longtime home ceased to exist.

THE ONLY THING SURE ABOUT STING IS... NOTHING'S FOR SURE

For over a decade following WCW's demise, speculation ran rampant about the future of Sting. Would it ever be "show time" for The Vigilante in WWE? At *Survivor Series 2014*, this question was answered once and for all. Sting not only showed up but helped drive The Authority from power, albeit temporarily. His bold actions led to a dream match for the WWE Universe at *WrestleMania 31* against the Chief Operating Officer of WWE, Triple H. Though not victorious, Sting performed like he did in the thick of the Monday Night War.

The ageless icon earned an opportunity to challenge Seth Rollins for the WWE World Heavyweight Championship at *Night of Champions 2015*. During the lead up to the bout, Sting delighted the WWE Universe by sending a newly minted bronze statue of Rollins into the waiting jowls of a trash compactor. He fell short of trashing Seth's Title reign, but once again wowed spectators in his first and only WWE World Heavyweight Championship Match.

Sting's iconic career was honored in 2016 with induction into the WWE Hall of Fame. Over 30 years in sports-entertainment, he continues to provide intrigue and excitement as the WWE Universe anticipates his next move, always wondering if he is lurking in the rafters above.

STONE COLD
STEVE AUSTIN

HT	6'2"
WT	252 lbs.
FROM	Victoria, Texas

SIGNATURE MOVE
Stone Cold Stunner

Stone Cold Steve Austin never had the look of a typical Superstar. Dressed in simple black trunks and black boots, many thought he was missing the sizzle needed to become a success in WWE. Those critics were quickly silenced when Stone Cold hit the ring. His defiant, buck-the-system attitude led Austin to an amazing six WWE Championships, while making him one of the most popular competitors of all time.

A little more than one year after his professional debut, Austin made the gigantic leap to WCW. Though relatively inexperienced, the young Texan found instant success, defeating Bobby Eaton for the WCW Television Championship in June 1991. Over the next four years, Austin went on to capture the United States Championship and WCW Tag Team Championship with Brian Pillman. Despite Austin's success in the ring, WCW boss Eric Bischoff didn't see him as a marketable commodity and soon fired him.

FROM ECW TO WWE

Austin was without a home for only one day before Paul Heyman called Austin with an offer to join ECW, despite Austin being injured at the time. Unable to compete, Austin was given a microphone and a mandate to enthrall the ECW faithful with his words. What followed were some of the most emotionally charged promos sports-entertainment has ever seen. Austin's anti-WCW tirades entertained the ECW fans, but more importantly, served as a preview to his future in WWE, which soon came calling.

Competing as the Ringmaster, Austin made his WWE debut in January 1996, handily defeating a young Matt Hardy. With Ted DiBiase as his manager, the Ringmaster then began to butt heads with Savio Vega. The rivalry saw the Ringmaster defeat the Puerto Rican Superstar at *WrestleMania XII*, but resulted in DiBiase losing his job when Vega later won a Strap Match.

With his manager fired, Austin's career could've easily suffered another debilitating setback. But a determined Austin refused to be held back any longer, and soon turned the negative into a huge positive. With nobody at his side telling him what to do, Austin rid himself of the Ringmaster name and rebuilt his image on his own terms. The result was a rechristened "Stone Cold" Steve Austin.

PAY-PER-VIEW VICTORIES

It didn't take long for Stone Cold to prove he was WWE's "toughest S.O.B." Just one month after remaking his image, Austin defeated Jake Roberts to become the 1996 King of the Ring. After the match, Stone Cold made his now-famous Austin 3:16 speech that would forever change the face of sports-entertainment.

Within days, Austin 3:16 T-shirts were everywhere. Stone Cold fans soon started dressing like their hero, making it impossible to walk through a mall without seeing a bald-headed, goatee-wearing fan in jeans and a black T-shirt. Not since Hulkamania had WWE been taken over by such a phenomenon.

As a result of his King of the Ring victory, Stone Cold was afforded opportunities that were denied him in WCW, which led to friction between him and his polar opposite, the dutiful Bret Hart. After eliminating Hart to win the 1997 *Royal Rumble* Match, the Texas Rattlesnake squared off against his rival in a Submission Match at *WrestleMania 13*. While the result did not go in his favor, the sight of the resolute Stone Cold profusely bleeding to the point of losing consciousness proved to be one of WWE's most memorable images.

Several other members of the famed Hart family muscled their way into the historic rivalry, including Bret's brother Owen. While competing against the younger Hart at *SummerSlam 1997*, Stone Cold suffered a career-threatening injury when a piledriver delivered by Owen broke his neck. Miraculously, Austin was able to recover just enough to roll Owen up for the win and the Intercontinental Championship.

Unfortunately for Stone Cold, the severity of his injury forced him to relinquish the Title. Upon returning to the ring later that year, the Texas Rattlesnake gained retribution by defeating Owen to become a two-time Intercontinental Champion.

At the *D-Generation X* pay-per-view in December 1997, Stone Cold defeated The Rock to retain his Title. By all accounts, the victory should've silenced The Rock's quest to become Intercontinental Champion. However, the next night on *Raw*, Mr. McMahon demanded Stone Cold defend his Title against the same man he defeated only a day earlier. When a defiant Austin refused to give in to McMahon's demands, the Chairman stripped Stone Cold of the Intercontinental Championship. A fired-up Austin responded by knocking McMahon out of the ring, officially igniting one of the greatest rivalries in the history of WWE: Stone Cold vs. Mr. McMahon.

THE ATTITUDE ERA PERSONIFIED

After winning the 1998 *Royal Rumble* Match, Stone Cold challenged Shawn Michaels for the WWE Championship in the main event of *WrestleMania XIV*. With Mike Tyson serving as special enforcer, Austin turned HBK's signature Sweet Chin Music around and quickly floored the Champion with his signature Stone Cold Stunner. Three seconds later, Stone Cold was celebrating his first of six WWE Championship reigns in front of a capacity crowd in Boston's FleetCenter.

The victory infuriated Mr. McMahon, who found himself a beer-swilling, middle-finger-raising Superstar representing his company as Champion. Unable to stand by and allow Stone Cold to act in such a rebellious fashion, McMahon demanded that the new Titleholder act more like a "corporate champion." But the authority-defying Austin had other plans. In typical Stone Cold fashion, he delivered a Stunner to his boss and continued to drink beers while flipping the middle finger.

Stone Cold and Mr. McMahon continued their heated rivalry for the better part of the next three years. However, in April 2001, Austin did the unthinkable and joined forces with his ultimate rival. While competing against The Rock at *WrestleMania X-Seven*, Stone Cold used assistance from Mr. McMahon to defeat the Great One. Afterward, the former adversaries shook hands and shared a beer.

Stone Cold's shocking allegiance to Mr. McMahon was among the most heinous acts Austin fans could imagine. But unfortunately for them, just when it seemed things couldn't get any worse, Stone Cold dropped another bomb when he turned his back on the entire WWE locker room to join the WCW/ECW Alliance.

Stone Cold's defection from WWE ultimately proved to be an unsuccessful venture. After The Alliance was forced to disband, he found himself right back on the WWE roster. The fans were happy to see him back, but unsure about whether they could trust him again. Stone Cold quickly put all their misgivings to rest the best way he knew how, by attacking Mr. McMahon.

POST-WRESTLING CAREER

Chronic neck injuries began to take their toll on Stone Cold in 2002. After taking off the second half of the year, he returned to WWE in 2003 to battle The Rock at *WrestleMania XIX*. Despite a valiant effort, Austin came up short in what was ultimately his final official WWE match.

No longer an active competitor, Stone Cold still manages to leave his undeniable mark on WWE. Among his most notable appearances include *WrestleMania XX,* where he served as guest referee for the match between Goldberg and Brock Lesnar. He also donned the stripes for the famous Battle of the Billionaires Match at *WrestleMania 23* and helped kick off *WrestleMania 30* alongside The Rock and Hulk Hogan.

Outside the ring, Austin entertains WWE Network subscribers with his *Stone Cold Podcast*. His guest list reads like a who's who of sports-entertainment, as everyone from Mr. McMahon to Ric Flair to Triple H has appeared on the show, despite knowing that Stone Cold doesn't pull any punches when conducting interviews.

Over the course of his nearly-thirty years in sports entertainment, Stone Cold Steve Austin has established himself as perhaps the greatest attraction the industry has ever seen with an undeniable attitude inside and outside the ring. As a result of his greatness, the Texas Rattlesnake was recognized in 2009 when he assumed his rightful spot in the WWE Hall of Fame.

STRAIGHT EDGE SOCIETY

MEMBERS	CM Punk, Luke Gallows, Serena, & Joseph Mercury

CM Punk credits part of his success to his clean-living, never smoking, drinking, or doing drugs. But in late 2009, the "Second-City Savior" began obsessively preaching these lifestyle choices to the WWE Universe. Claiming that he was the role model the world needed, Punk began recruiting disciples to help him in his crusade against drugs and alcohol. His first convert was Luke Gallows, who Punk saved from a supposed prescription pain pill addiction. The prophetic leader then rescued fan Serena and Superstar Joey Mercury, who rechristened himself, "Joseph" Mercury.

Collectively known as the Straight Edge Society, the foursome spent the next several months promoting abstinence and discipline. Then in July, Serena was caught drinking and the foundation of the faction began to crack. Not long after that, Punk blamed Gallows for a loss to Big Show and nailed his disciple with a thunderous GTS, marking the end of the Straight Edge Society.

STRIKE FORCE

MEMBERS	Tito Santana & Rick Martel
COMBINED WT	460 lbs.

Tito Santana and Rick Martel first began teaming together in 1987 after Santana ran to the ring to save the Quebec native from a double-team attack at the hands of the Islanders. From that point on, the team of Santana and Martel became known as Strike Force, a good-looking tandem whose sound technical skills carried all the way to the top of the tag team division.

After defeating the Hart Foundation for the World Tag Team Championship in October 1987, Strike Force looked nearly unstoppable. But the impact of Mr. Fuji's cane caused the pair to lose their Titles to Demolition at *WrestleMania IV*. The loss proved to be a major setback for the popular tag team, as they struggled to regain their momentum.

After a brief hiatus, Strike Force reunited to battle the Brain Busters at *WrestleMania V*. However, in a shocking turn of events, Martel betrayed his partner during the match, marking the official end of Strike Force. Over the next several years, the two Superstars engaged in an emotional rivalry that never saw a clear-cut winner declared.

STRONG KOBAYASHI

HT	6'2"	WT	275 lbs.	FROM	Japan
SIGNATURE MOVE	Canadian Backbreaker				

For a period of time in the 1970s, the International Wrestling Alliance World Heavyweight Championship was considered to be the premiere title in all of Japan, thanks in large part to the tireless effort of one of its greatest titleholders, Strong Kobayashi.

Ironically, Kobayashi first staked claim to the title after beating Dr. Bill Miller in Minnesota in June 1971. He then brought the title back to Japan, trading it back and forth with Wahoo McDaniel.

In 1974, he vacated the title when he left the promotion. He later traveled to the United States to compete for WWE. His overseas success, however, failed to follow him stateside. He regularly lost to the likes of SD Jones, Tony Garea, and a very young Curt Hennig.

THE STRONGBOWS

MEMBERS	Chief Jay Strongbow & Jules Strongbow

In 1982, Chief Jay Strongbow initially asked his brother Jules for help to counteract the influence of WWE's rule-breakers. In the process, the two brought audiences to their feet. Their high-flying moves, ground-attacks, and double-team actions paved the road to Tag Team success. In June 1982, they defeated Mr. Fuji and Mr. Saito for the World Tag Team Championship.

Over the next few months, they traded title reigns with the Japanese duo. Their final title reign ended in March 1983 when they lost to the Wild Samoans. Shortly after the loss, the Chief retired from the ring and Jules left WWE to spend the rest of his career competing on the independent scene.

THE SULTAN

HT	6'3"	WT	295 lbs.	FROM	The Middle East
SIGNATURE MOVE	Camel Clutch				

When this former masked Superstar was first seen in 1997, some experts speculated that his face was deformed. After his impressive debut win against Jake "The Snake" Roberts, the focus turned from his mask to his dangerous array of maneuvers in the ring. Mentored by Iron Sheik and Mr. Bob Backlund, The Sultan was well versed in submission wrestling, mat techniques, and rule-breaking.

Although The Sultan met foes like Phineas Godwinn, Yokozuna, Goldust, Undertaker, and Bret Hart, the dangerous Superstar's greatest battle was with Rocky Maivia over the Intercontinental Championship. The two Superstars settled their score at *WrestleMania 13*. By early 1998 Sultan returned to the home of the one-time Persian Empire and has not appeared in WWE since.

SUMMER RAE

HT 5'10"   **FROM** Raleigh, North Carolina

When you're as stunning as Summer Rae, you expect men to fall at your feet. And since the blonde bombshell made her debut in 2013, that's exactly what many WWE Superstars have done.

Summer Rae first caught the eyes of the WWE Universe as the long-legged dance partner of Fandango. While in his corner, Summer helped the dangerous dancer in his battles against Chris Jericho, Wade Barrett, and Sheamus. Unfortunately, the pairing only lasted a year, as Fandango abruptly severed their relationship via Twitter in April 2014.

Following the breakup, Summer Rae entered into a curious rivalry-turned-alliance with Fandango's new love interest, Layla. At first, the two Divas couldn't stand the sight of one another. But eventually, they formed a surprising partnership based on their mutual goal of causing Fandango pain. They succeeded by costing him several matches.

Summer Rae then entered into a romantic relationship with Rusev. But just when it looked like the couple would take the next step of marriage, it was revealed that the Bulgarian Brute was engaged to Lana, marking the end of the Summer Rae-Rusev relationship. The beautiful blonde wasn't down long, as she quickly rebounded to find herself by the side of Tyler Breeze.

Outside the ring, Summer Rae has proven to be just as talented. In addition to appearing on *Total Divas*, Summer co-starred in the 2015 film *The Marine 4* alongside WWE Superstar, The Miz.

SUNNY

"My definition of a Diva is that all-around, well-rounded performer."

This statement perfectly sums up the career of the woman who is arguably WWE's original Diva, Sunny. In her incredible career, Sunny did it all: managing, competing, modeling, and everything in between.

A life-long fan, this trailblazing Diva began her sports-entertainment career in Smoky Mountain Wrestling in the early 1990s. In 1995, Sunny debuted in WWE as the manager of fellow Bodydonna, Skip. Audiences were captivated by her striking beauty, charisma, and energetic persona. As her career expanded, Sunny became a broadcast correspondent, a ring announcer, color commentator, and ambassador during her time with WWE. With no shortage of confidence, Sunny was happy to tout her many virtues and those of the various clients she managed to success. In 1996, Sunny brought Faarooq to WWE, was the most downloaded woman on America Online, and won two Slammy Awards.

Sunny guided The Bodydonnas to the Tag Team Titles at *WrestleMania XII*, but left the team behind following a loss a few months later. Sunny's stay with the Godwinns came to a sudden halt when she helped the Smokin' Gunns beat them for the World Tag Team Championships. Though she fully embraced the cowpoke persona, her affections eventually caused problems between the brothers.

In 1998, she rejuvenated the Legion of Doom as they won the Tag Team Battle Royal at *WrestleMania XIV*. Later that year, Sunny left WWE. Over the next few years she would resurface in ECW and WCW.

During the *Raw 15th Anniversary*, Sunny returned to WWE for the first time in almost a decade. Her theme song "I Know You Want Me" sent shivers down the spines of male fans around the world. The tingles returned when she appeared as part of the "Miss WrestleMania" 25-Diva Battle Royal at *WrestleMania 25*.

Two years later her ground-breaking career was recognized when, in an incredible show of respect, the innovative blonde was inducted into the WWE Hall of Fame by the entire Divas roster. Without this vivacious performer's beauty, intellect, and talent, the term "WWE Diva" might not exist today.

SUPER ASTROS

Super Astros was not so much a sports-entertainment territory as it was a Latin-flavored sub-division of WWE.

Some credit WCW as the inspiration for *Super Astros*. For all its faults, WWE's chief rival had an impressive cruiserweight division, which included among its ranks Mexican stars like Rey Mysterio, Psicosis, Hector Garza, and Juventud Guerrera.

In 1998, WWE created the *Super Astros* television show. Broadcasts were in Spanish and the hosts were Hugo Savinovich and Carlos Cabrera. Max Mini, a little person who electrified crowds with daring, high-flying maneuvers, conducted backstage interview segments that were often humorous.

The talent consisted of primarily lightweight headliners from not just Mexico, but other Latino locales. These competitors included El Hijo del Santo, Negro Casas, Apolo Dantes, Rey Bucanero, and Essa Rios. The roster was supplemented with Americans like Al Snow and Japanese stars like Funaki.

But fans didn't unanimously embrace *Super Astros*. It was the start of WWE's "Attitude" era so the WWE Universe's attentions were elsewhere. Plus, *Super Astros* matches were frequently taped before *Raw* and didn't feel special. In 1999, *Super Astros* was discontinued.

SUPER CRAZY

HT	5'8"	WT	200 lbs.	FROM	Tulancingo, Hidalgo, Mexico
SIGNATURE MOVE		Moonsault			

He's super. He's crazy. He's Super Crazy.

One of the most appropriately named Superstars of all time, Super Crazy began his career in Mexico. Throughout his native country's wild independent scene and its AAA promotion, he drove audiences loco before ultimately taking his lucha libre lunacy to ECW. From 1998 to 2001, "The Insane Luchador" battled other high-flyers such as Yoshihiro Tajiri and Little Guido until the extreme promotion closed its doors.

WWE inked Super Crazy to a contract after witnessing his insane moonsault off the Hammerstein Ballroom's second balcony at the ECW revival event, *One Night Stand*. Alongside Juventud and Psicosis, Super Crazy made his WWE debut as a member of the Mexicools faction. Despite being rule breakers, the Mexicools' high-flying style made them instant fan favorites.

By late 2006, the Mexicools had dissolved. Super Crazy went on to have an impressive stretch of singles competition as well as a short-lived pairing with the legendary "Hacksaw" Jim Duggan. Super Crazy returned to WWE's *ECW* brand in 2008 and battled the likes of The Miz, Chavo Guerrero, and John Morrison before parting ways with WWE by year's end.

SUPERSTAR BILLY GRAHAM

see page 339

SWEDE HANSON

HT	6'5"	WT	307 lbs.	FROM	Slaughter Creek, North Carolina
SIGNATURE MOVE		Bearhug			

A former Golden Gloves competitor, this giant was trained by the legendary George Tragos and debuted in Vincent J. McMahon's Capitol Wrestling in the late 1950s, often facing off against Bruno Sammartino. In the early 1960s, Swede ventured to the Charlotte territory, where he was part of one of its most famous tandems with Rip Hawk.

In 1979, the man known as "Big Swede" returned to WWE, managed by Freddy Blassie. He reignited his rivalry with Sammartino and warred with Ivan Putski, Chief Jay Strongbow, Gorilla Monsoon, Andre the Giant, Tito Santana, and Pedro Morales, but was ultimately unable to dethrone WWE Champion Bob Backlund.

Swede remained with WWE until 1985, and retired from the ring one year later. He passed away in 2002.

SWEET DADDY SIKI

HT	5'10"	WT	245 lbs.	FROM	Montgomery, Texas
SIGNATURE MOVE		Airplane Spin			

With a blond Afro towering over his bronzed skin, Sweet Daddy Siki was both a maverick and a trendsetter.

Born into poverty in Texas, Siki found his way to Los Angeles and discovered wrestling on television. Because of his flashy ring outfit and strut, he offended those who couldn't keep pace with history, and his life was threatened by the Ku Klux Klan. Settling in Toronto in 1961, he found both tolerance and acclaim. Any Canadian fan who grew up during this period remembers Sweet Daddy Siki.

He also had an influence on future performers. Rocky Johnson, father of The Rock, claims Siki encouraged him to stay in wrestling after some early disappointments. In Calgary, where Siki won the territory's North American Heavyweight Championship in 1970, Bret Hart became a lifetime fan. Meanwhile, Siki enjoyed a sideline as a country singer.

During the twilight of his career, Siki trained future competitors out of Sully's Gym in Toronto, including future WWE Champion, Edge. A Toronto treasure to this day, he hosts a popular karaoke gathering each weekend.

SYLVAIN GRENIER

HT	6'0"	WT	250 lbs.	FROM	Montreal, Quebec, Canada
SIGNATURE MOVE		3 Seconds of Fame			

After a chance meeting in Florida with Pat Patterson, Grenier changed from a supermodel to a sports entertainer. He first debuted in WWE as a referee but soon transitioned to competition as part of a French elitist group known as La Resistance with Rene Dupree. In June 2003, he and Dupree defeated Rob Van Dam and Kane to capture the World Tag Team Championship. Sylvain later reformed La Resistance with an American turncoat, Rob Conway, in March 2004. With Conway, the haughty Frenchman captured three more Tag Team Titles.

In August 2005, a move to *SmackDown* prompted Grenier to drop his partner, his last name and the "i" in "Sylvain." With a new techno theme song and appreciation for high fashion, he took aim at other Superstar's lack of style. Despite the glitzier persona, the newly-named "Sylvan" still harbored a superiority complex toward Americans. He became the Ambassador to Quebec, imploring the WWE Universe to visit the "Crown Jewel of North America." In February 2007, Grenier briefly reunited with Dupree before parting ways with WWE in August of the same year.

"SUPERSTAR" BILLY GRAHAM

HT	6'4"
WT	275 lbs.
FROM	Paradise Valley, Arizona

SIGNATURE MOVE
Bearhug

As a high-school track and field star, "Superstar" Billy Graham held national records for discus and shot-put events and seemed groomed for success in the 1964 Olympic Games. After he won the Teenage Mr. America contest, Graham landed in Santa Monica in 1968 and trained at the original Gold's Gym with future movie star, Governor of California, and WWE Hall of Famer, Arnold Schwarzenegger. After attempts at pro football left him uninspired, Graham traveled to Calgary to train with the legendary Stu Hart.

In 1975, "Superstar" Billy Graham debuted in WWE. Wearing a psychedelic kaleidoscope of tie-dyed outfits, feathered boas, sunglasses, and a sun-kissed tan, Graham was the finest physical specimen the world had ever seen. He possessed a physique chiseled from granite and a cornucopia of catchphrases that were so innovative, people wrote down his words to study and recite. Brought to the ring by The Grand Wizard, Graham hunted then-Champion Bruno Sammartino for wrestling's richest honor. On April 30, 1977, Graham met Sammartino for the WWE Championship in Baltimore. As Sammartino barraged Graham in the corner, the challenger swept Bruno's feet out from under him and pinned his shoulders to the mat. However, Graham was only able to unseat the multi-year reigning champion by illegally placing his feet on the ropes for leverage.

Sports entertainment changed overnight as "Superstar" held its most prestigious trophy and transcended pop culture.

Six months later, Graham had a series of Title matches against Dusty Rhodes that sold out Madison Square Garden and electrified the world of sports-entertainment. Graham ultimately retained his Title, cementing his place in the annals of WWE history. But on February 20, 1978, Graham lost the Title to Bob Backlund, despite the placement of Superstar's foot under the rope as the referee counted three.

Devastated in defeat, Billy took a sabbatical from competition, slowly becoming detached from reality.

In 1982, Graham returned to WWE as a martial arts expert with a new look, complete with shaved head, black mustache, and black karate pants. Once again managed by The Grand Wizard, Graham chased Backlund in unsuccessful attempts to regain the WWE Championship.

I AM THE MAN OF THE HOUR, THE MAN WITH THE POWER, TOO SWEET TO BE SOUR.

A dejected Graham left WWE again and briefly appeared in the NWA. While there, he brought back the popular Technicolor appearance and poetic flow with a new two-toned goatee.

In 1987, "Superstar" made his triumphant WWE return to swarms of adoring fans.

A HEAVY TOLL

Unfortunately, years of competition had taken its toll and Graham was in need of hip replacement surgery. With the desire to inspire, Graham transitioned from in-ring competition to manage fellow future WWE Hall of Famer Don Muraco and used his gift of gab in the broadcast booth.

Sadly, Graham's body continued to break down and he was no longer physically able to perform for the company in any capacity. Graham was forced to leave the profession he so dearly loved at age 45.

Soon, Graham was facing another obstacle, as he was in dire need of a liver replacement. Things looked so grim, he considered planning his own funeral in 2002, but luckily, a suitable donor was found. As he enjoyed a new lease on life, Graham was invigorated like never before and started his crusade for organ donor awareness. After being estranged from WWE for 14 years, Graham had a joyous reunion with Vince McMahon backstage at *SummerSlam 2003*. In March 2004, Graham finally found his rightful place in history alongside the immortals of sports-entertainment when he was inducted into the WWE Hall of Fame.

In January 2006, he penned his personal tale of torment and triumph in a brutally honest autobiography, *Tangled Ropes*.

There was never a finer physical specimen or as masterful a communicator than "Superstar" Billy Graham. He was the ultimate entertainer and an original like no other. Graham's unparalleled success and unique style touched generations, as evidenced by future WWE Hall of Famers Hulk Hogan and Jesse "The Body" Ventura, who both listed the Superstar as their inspiration.

SYLVESTER LEFORT

| HT | 5'11" | WT | 190 lbs. | FROM | Nice, France |

SIGNATURE MOVE Superkick

During a three year span, Sylvester Lefort tried to restore the once-mighty French Empire in NXT, working as both a manager and competitor.

Trained by former WWE Intercontinental Champion and World Tag Team Co-Titlist Lance Storm, Lefort wrestled for numerous French promotions, as well as cards in Spain, Italy, Mexico, Turkey, and Canada. On one Parisian show, he teamed with future WWE Champion Daniel Bryan.

In NXT, he used both brawn and brains to command attention, managing the team of Scott Dawson and Garrett Dylan, as well as Rusev. But Rusev eventually betrayed Lefort to take on Lana as an advisor. As the Legionnaires, Lefort and fellow Frenchman Marcus Louis started strong until personal differences obliterated the alliance. Lefort left NXT in 2016.

SYLVESTER TERKAY

| HT | 6'6" | WT | 320 lbs. | FROM | Big Bear, California |

This former college wrestler nearly won a Division 1 NCAA Championship in college but finished second to future Olympic gold medalist, Kurt Angle. After enjoying similar success in mixed martial arts, Sylvester Terkay made the jump to sports entertainment in July 2006. With corner man Elijah Burke backing him, the Superstar dubbed "the Man Bear" made quick work of *SmackDown* Superstars, including Matt Hardy and Tatanka.

In November 2006, Terkay began competing in *ECW*, where he struggled despite his size. Outside of a victory at *December to Dismember*, "the Man Bear" struggled to make waves as a member of the ECW roster. WWE finally released him in January 2007.

However, in 2013, Turkay got his rematch against Kurt Angle when they clashed in the film *Pro Wrestlers vs. Zombies*.

TAKA MICHINOKU

| HT | 5'8" | WT | 201 lbs. | FROM | Iwate, Japan |

SIGNATURE MOVE Michinoku Driver

Trained by the legendary Great Sasuke, Japanese Superstar Taka Michinoku first arrived in the United States by way of ECW February 1997. A master of martial arts, lucha libre, and grappling, he quickly amassed his fair share of admirers.

Michinoku made his WWE debut in July 1997 when he lost to his mentor, Sasuke, at *In Your House: Canadian Stampede*. The loss failed to derail Michinoku, though, who went on to become the first-ever WWE Light Heavyweight Champion, defeating Brian Christopher in a tournament final in December 1997. He held the Title for ten months before ultimately losing to Christian.

During his 1998 rivalry with Kaientai, Michinoku enlisted the help of Val Venis, who was allegedly having an affair with Yamaguchi-San's wife. In the end, Michinoku turned his allegiance to his fellow countrymen, betraying the Big Valboski in the process.

Michinoku maintained his status as a Kaientai member through the end of his WWE career, often teaming with Funaki. In 2002, Michinoku returned to Japan, where he remains one of the country's most popular competitors.

TAJIRI

| HT | 5'9" | WT | 205 lbs. | FROM | Japan |

SIGNATURE MOVE Tarantula

After training as a kickboxer, and learning the nuances of wrestling in both Japan and Mexico, Tajiri introduced his lightning quick offense to American audiences in 1997. He made several appearances in WWE to minimal fanfare before returning to Mexico, where he was spotted by ECW boss Paul Heyman.

Conscious of competing with the "big two," WWE and its chief rival at the time, WCW, Heyman relied on innovative talent to set his company apart; Tajiri more than met the criteria. As a member of ECW, he quickly reminded fans of fellow Japanese export Great Muta with his flying somersaults, roundhouse kicks, and mysterious mist, earning the grudging admiration of foes like Tazz, Super Crazy, and Tommy Dreamer.

When financial woes forced ECW's doors to close in 2001, Tajiri followed many of his colleagues in signing with WWE. Initially, he served as the comedic sidekick to WWE Commissioner William Regal. Despite never speaking English, Tajiri exhibited a hilarious sense of humor, but in sharp contrast, there was nothing funny about his in-ring skills.

His signature Tarantula and hand spring back elbow smash struck fear into the locker room. If the referee wasn't looking, the "Japanese Buzzsaw" was never above spitting a blinding green mist into the eyes of his competition. His combination of fierce talent and a little rule breaking propelled Tajiri to numerous singles titles, including four combined runs with the WWE Cruiserweight and Light Heavyweight Championships.

Over the course of his five-year stay with WWE, Tajiri was also considered a top tag team talent. In May 2003, he teamed with Eddie Guerrero to claim the WWE Tag Team Championship from Shelton Benjamin and Charlie Haas. A few years later, alongside longtime associate William Regal, he bested La Resistance for the World Tag Team Titles in his home country of Japan.

Tajiri last competed for WWE at *One Night Stand* in 2006 before returning to action in Japan. In 2008, he made an appearance at a WWE event in Tokyo. Since then, he's primarily competed for Japanese promotions and trained a new breed of Asian talent.

TAMINA

HT 5'9" **FROM** The Pacific Islands

Tamina boasts a unique blend of beauty and brawn that few of her rivals can match. The daughter of WWE Hall of Famer Jimmy "Superfly" Snuka, Tamina debuted alongside fellow second-generation Superstars, The Usos in May 2010. Over the next few months, Tamina and The Usos traded several victories with The Hart Dynasty in Six-Person Tag Team Matches.

Later in the year, Tamina's budding romance with Santino Marella led to her splitting time between The Usos and Marella. She even supported Santino when he captured the WWE Tag Team Championship with Vladimir Kozlov.

Since early 2011, Tamina's focus has been on the Divas/Women's division, where she has been an imposing presence. Aside from her own battles with rival Superstars, she served as a bodyguard for Divas Champion AJ Lee during her record setting reign. Recently, she has joined forces with Naomi and Sasha Banks to form Team B.A.D., and has claimed wins over Paige, The Bellas, and others. With such dangerous allies, this powerful and athletic Superstar always poses a threat to claim a Championship of her own.

TANK MORGAN

Fans who witnessed the beatings delivered by Tank Morgan may forever hold the images of his battered opponents in their minds. The wrestlers who took the beatings likely relive them in their worst nightmares. A detested villain, Morgan barreled into WWE in October 1966. He used power, agility, and cunning to further his ambitions to destroy his competition, and earned a series of title opportunities against Heavyweight Champion Bruno Sammartino.

As a tag team wrestler, Tank ruined lives alongside associates like "Crazy" Luke Graham, Bull Ortega, Smasher Sloan, Gorilla Monsoon, and Baron Mikel Scicluna.

Morgan left WWE in 1967 and toured the National Wrestling Alliance, developing a soft-spot in his blackheart for its Hawaiian territory. He died in 1991.

TARZAN TYLER

  HT 6'3" **WT** 270 lbs. **FROM** Miami Beach, Florida
SIGNATURE MOVE Big Boot

After nearly a decade competing in Canadian rings, Tarzan Tyler took his abilities to the United States during the 1960s. Clad in multi-colored trunks and sporting bleached blonde hair, Tyler incited the crowds by breaking every rule in the book. For years, fans suspected that he illegally loaded his boots, making them nearly lethal weapons. Referees, however, were unable to confirm the allegations.

As a singles star, Tyler was a regular world title contender. In the early 1960s, he challenged AWA Champion Verne Gagne. He also attempted to wrest the NWA Title from Lou Thesz and Dory Funk, Jr., and the WWE Championship from Bruno Sammartino and Pedro Morales. In 1971, under the tutelage of Captain Lou Albano, he and "Crazy" Luke Graham became WWE's first-ever World Tag Team Champions.

Following his retirement, Tyler worked as a manager in Quebec, advising King Tonga and the Masked Superstar. On Christmas Eve 1985, Tarzan Tyler and fellow sports entertainer, Pierre "Mad Dog" Lefebvre were sadly killed in an auto accident after a show.

TATANKA

HT 6'2" **WT** 285 lbs.
FROM Pembroke, North Carolina
SIGNATURE MOVE Indian Death Drop

This Native American warrior and trainee of the famed Larry Sharpe Monster Factory came to WWE in 1992. Marked by his Lumbee tribe war cry, his opponents knew that Tatanka's war dance marked the beginning of the end for them. He enjoyed a lengthy undefeated streak that only ended in September 1993 when Ludvig Borga slammed a foreign object on Tatanka's back as the referee was distracted.

Tatanka earned so much respect that Chief Jay Strongbow became his mentor, presenting him with a Lumbee tribe chief headdress. Unfortunately, something in Tatanka snapped at *SummerSlam 1994*. He turned on Lex Luger, accusing of him of joining the Million Dollar Corporation, before doing just the same himself. Tatanka spent nearly two years with the underhanded faction before departing WWE after a loss to Bret Hart in March 1996. After spending the next ten years on the independent scene, he made an amazing return to WWE in 2005. For the next two years Tatanka battled Kurt Angle, Booker T, Mr. Kennedy, and others.

At *WrestleMania 32*, nearly ten years removed from his last appearance in a WWE ring, Tatanka entered the Andre the Giant Memorial Battle Royal. His strong showing in the 20-man scrum reminded the WWE Universe of the warrior he always was.

TATSUMI FUJINAMI

HT	6'0"	WT	238 lbs.	FROM	Oita, Japan
SIGNATURE MOVE	Dragon Sleeper				

Tatsumi Fujinami's career started in 1971. His intensity and superior technical abilities quickly earned him the nickname "The Dragon." He developed revolutionary moves including the Dragon Sleeper, Dragon Suplex, and Dragon Backbreaker.

As a teen, he was one of the first members of the fledgling New Japan promotion. Hoping to expand his arsenal, Fujinami left Asia, competing in Mexico and Jim Crockett Promotions before his WWE arrival in 1976. He immediately made a name for himself as he defeated Jose Estrada in his debut to become WWE Light Heavyweight Champion.

Fujinami's fame brought him to the 1980 *Showdown At Shea*, where he defeated Lucha Libre legend Chavo Guerrero, Sr. In August 1982, Fujinami defeated Gino Brito to capture the prized International Heavyweight Championship, continuing a lineage dating back to Antonino "Argentina" Rocca. Three years later, Fujinami and partner Kengo Kimura won related International Tag Team honors.

Fujinami made headlines in 1991 when he opposed WCW World Heavyweight Champion "Nature Boy" Ric Flair in Japan. Japanese fans believed that Fujinami won the gold when Flair submitted, but WCW argued that Fujinami had been disqualified shortly beforehand for throwing Flair over the ropes.

In 1999, while still an active competitor, Fujinami became New Japan's president. Because of his impact on sports entertainment on both sides of the Pacific Ocean, Fujinami was inducted into the WWE Hall of Fame by his former rival, Ric Flair in 2015.

TEAM HELL NO

MEMBERS	Daniel Bryan & Kane
COMBINED WT	533 lbs.

Those who say anger management is nothing more than a hoax have probably never heard of Dr. Shelby. As the esteemed head of the Shelby Academy of Anger Management, Dr. Shelby not only successfully channeled the rage of Daniel Bryan and Kane, but he also helped shape them into one of the WWE's top tag teams.

When rivals Bryan and Kane battled at *SummerSlam 2012*, few thought the day would come where they could coexist. But following the match, then-*Raw*-General-Manager AJ Lee forced them to see Dr. Shelby. Less than a month later, Bryan and Kane were WWE Tag Team Champions.

Known as Team Hell No, the duo ruled the WWE Tag Team Division, holding the Titles for more than eight months. They finally lost the gold to Roman Reigns and Seth Rollins at *Extreme Rules 2013*.

Following the loss, Daniel Bryan, who took the deciding fall, became hell-bent on proving he was not the team's weak link. He went a long way in proving this when he defeated Kane in July 2013, followed by a WWE Championship victory at *SummerSlam* one month later.

TAZZ

HT	5'9"	WT	240 lbs.
FROM	Red Hook Section of Brooklyn		

During his days in the ring, Tazz was widely regarded as one of the most dangerous competitors of his time. Though undersized by most traditional standards, his offensive attack was pure dynamite.

Known as "the Human Suplex Machine," Tazz's rise to the top started in 1993 when he joined ECW. Over the next six years, he defined himself as a true ECW icon, winning every single ECW Championship. He even proudly carried his own FTW Championship, a title he created in 1998. He was known to challenge opponents to "Win if you can; survive if I let you."

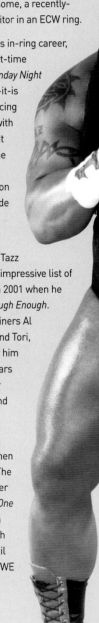

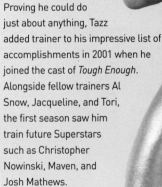

Tazz made his WWE debut at the 2000 *Royal Rumble* after a series of ominous vignettes, handily defeating the then-undefeated Kurt Angle. While he win started Tazz's WWE career on the right foot, little did anybody realize the extreme Superstar still had some ECW fight left in him. A few months after his WWE debut, Tazz returned to ECW and defeated Mike Awesome for the ECW Championship. The victory was truly historic as Tazz, under contract with WWE at the time, defeated Awesome, a recently-signed WCE competitor in an ECW ring.

Toward the end of his in-ring career, Tazz served as a part-time commentator on *Sunday Night Heat*. His tell-it-like-it-is approach to announcing made him popular with the WWE Universe. It wasn't long before he was the permanent color commentator on *SmackDown* alongside Michael Cole.

Proving he could do just about anything, Tazz added trainer to his impressive list of accomplishments in 2001 when he joined the cast of *Tough Enough*. Alongside fellow trainers Al Snow, Jacqueline, and Tori, the first season saw him train future Superstars such as Christopher Nowinski, Maven, and Josh Mathews.

Tazz returned to the ring in June 2006 when he defeated Jerry "The King" Lawler in under one minute at *ECW One Night Stand*. He then returned to the booth where he stayed until parting ways with WWE three years later.

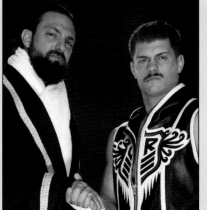

TEAM RHODES SCHOLARS

MEMBERS Cody Rhodes & Damien Sandow **COMBINED WT** 533 lbs.

Sporting equal levels of arrogance and inflated self-worth, Cody Rhodes and Damien Sandow were undoubtedly one of the most like-minded tag teams WWE has ever seen. Collectively known as Team Rhodes Scholars, the duo began teaming together in September 2012. And though they never accomplished their ultimate goal of capturing the WWE Tag Team Championship, they certainly acted as if they were superior to everybody else.

Rhodes and Sandow remained one of WWE's top teams until February 2013, when they amicably split to pursue singles success. Following the breakup, the two Superstars vowed to remain best friends, but eventually an opportunity at the World Heavyweight Championship put their friendship to the test.

During the 2013 World Heavyweight Championship Money in the Bank Ladder Match, Rhodes climbed toward the briefcase en route to what looked like certain victory. But out of nowhere came Sandow to knock his supposed friend off the ladder and claim the guaranteed championship opportunity for himself. With that, the one-time best friends became bitter rivals and Team Rhodes Scholars was nothing but a memory.

TED ARCIDI

HT 5'11" **WT** 285 lbs. **FROM** Boston, Massachusetts

The sports entertainment world has seen many Superstars claim to be the world's strongest man, but in 1985, Ted Arcidi proved his bold assertion when he became the first human being to ever bench press more than seven-hundred pounds. The awesome Arcidi put up 705 pounds, breaking the world record once held by legendary WWE Champion, Bruno Sammartino.

The record-breaking feat caught the eyes of WWE officials, who quickly signed Arcidi to a contract. He soon after engaged in rivalries with fellow tough men, Hercules and Big John Studd.

Arcidi's impressive strength earned him a spot in the WWE/NFL Battle Royal at *WrestleMania 2*. While he didn't win the competition, he impressed those watching, as it took the colossal combination of Hillbilly Jim, B. Brian Blair, and Danny Spivey to eliminate him.

TED DIBIASE

HT 6'3" **WT** 235 lbs. **FROM** Palm Springs, Florida
SIGNATURE MOVE Cobra Clutch Legsweep

Growing up, Ted DiBiase watched his father, the "Million Dollar Man" prove that everyone has a price. He dreamed of taking the DiBiase name into the next millennium. After graduating college in 2005, Ted took the first steps toward making that dream a reality, starting to train under Harley Race.

In 2008, he joined with Cody Rhodes to capture the WWE World Tag Team Championship. In addition to Cody, DiBiase aligned himself with other men of distinguished sports-entertainment lineages, including Manu and Randy Orton, calling themselves The Legacy. Proclaiming that they were "born better," the trio stalked some of WWE's most respected figures.

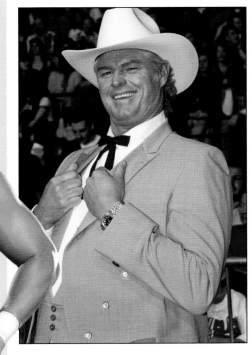

Flaunting his father's Million Dollar Championship, "The Fortunate Son" employed the elder DiBiase's former assistant, Virgil, but eventually replaced him with the dazzling Maryse.

DiBiase soon gave up the Million Dollar Championship and found himself in a strange position, a favorite of the WWE Universe. In 2011, he began to host "DiBiase Posse" tailgating parties before WWE events.

Unfortunately, DiBiase sustained a series of setbacks that contributed to his departure from the company in 2013.

TEKNO TEAM 2000

MEMBERS Travis & Troy **COMBINED WT** 480 lbs.

Following successful collegiate football careers with the University of Louisville, Travis and Troy reunited in 1995 to compete in WWE's heated tag team division. Dressed in shiny silver jackets and ultramodern elbow and knee pads, the agile duo claimed to be the tag team of the future. Their youth and style suggested that they might be correct. Unfortunately for Tekno Team 2000, their record said differently.

After picking up easy victories over combinations such as the Brooklyn Brawler and Barry Horowitz, Travis and Troy found it difficult to defeat the Smokin' Gunns and other top-notch tandems. In 1996, the futuristic tag team disappeared from WWE, leaving the next millennium to commence without them.

TENNESSEE LEE

When you're a star of the magnitude that Jeff Jarrett thought he was in 1998, you need to have a strong support system. For the country Superstar known as "Double J," the support team included Southern Justice, serving as his bodyguards, and Tennessee Lee, working as Jarrett's promoter and manager.

With his 10-gallon hat, cowboy boots, and distinct southern accent, Tennessee Lee was easily recognizable as the irritating figure behind Jarrett. Unlike most, however, Double J wasn't annoyed by Tennessee Lee, especially considering the manager oftentimes interfered to ensure his man would pick up the win.

In the summer of 1998, Tennessee Lee's interference started to become somewhat clumsy. Rather than helping Jarrett, the overzealous manager actually wound up costing him matches.

Finally, after Droz dropped Jarrett on an episode of *Sunday Night Heat*, Jarrett and Southern Justice delivered a vicious beatdown to Tennessee Lee, marking the end of their short-lived business agreement. A deflated Tennessee Lee disappeared from WWE shortly after.

TENSAI

| HT | 6'6" | WT | 360 lbs. | SIGNATURE MOVE | Claw |

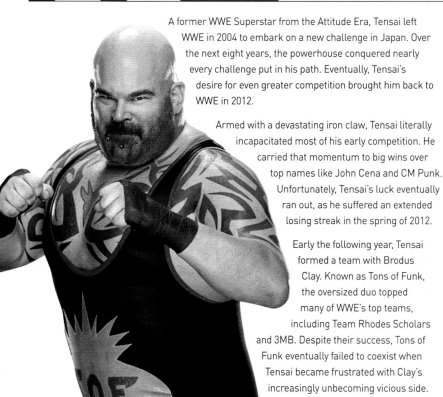

A former WWE Superstar from the Attitude Era, Tensai left WWE in 2004 to embark on a new challenge in Japan. Over the next eight years, the powerhouse conquered nearly every challenge put in his path. Eventually, Tensai's desire for even greater competition brought him back to WWE in 2012.

Armed with a devastating iron claw, Tensai literally incapacitated most of his early competition. He carried that momentum to big wins over top names like John Cena and CM Punk. Unfortunately, Tensai's luck eventually ran out, as he suffered an extended losing streak in the spring of 2012.

Early the following year, Tensai formed a team with Brodus Clay. Known as Tons of Funk, the oversized duo topped many of WWE's top teams, including Team Rhodes Scholars and 3MB. Despite their success, Tons of Funk eventually failed to coexist when Tensai became frustrated with Clay's increasingly unbecoming vicious side.

The partners engaged in a bitter rivalry, capped off by a Tensai victory in December 2012. Both competitors faded from the scene soon after.

TERRI RUNNELS

| HT | 5'0" | FROM | Gainesville, Florida |

Sitting in a director's chair watching her masterpiece unfold, Terri Runnels, known as "Marlena," debuted at the 1996 *Royal Rumble*, where her leading man, Goldust defeated Razor Ramon for the Intercontinental Championship.

In the months that followed, the bizarre duo pushed the limits of acceptable social behavior, including public displays of affection and posing in various states of undress for *Raw Magazine*. Unfortunately for Marlena, what she assumed to be a storybook romance revealed itself as horror in November 1997. While a stipulation forced Marlena to be by the side of Brian Pillman for thirty days, Goldust was out making magic with the exotic Luna. The affair crushed Marlena's spirit, but gave Terri Runnels new life.

With her "Marlena" persona a distant memory, Terri joined forces with Jacqueline and Ryan Shamrock to form Pretty Mean Sisters. Together, PMS used their sexuality to prey on WWE's male Superstars. Despite her petite frame, Terri also held her own in the ring, highlighted by her greatest victory at *WrestleMania 2000* when she defeated The Kat in one-on-one action.

TERRY DANIELS

| HT | 5'10" | WT | 225 lbs. | FROM | Amarillo, Texas |

As the first inductee into Sgt. Slaughter's elite Cobra Corps, a young Terry Daniels was immediately thrust into high-profile matches after making his 1984 WWE in-ring debut. With little ring experience under his belt, the former Marine private teamed with his Hall of Fame leader to challenge Dick Murdoch and Adrian Adonis for the WWE World Tag Team Championship at the historic *Brawl to End It All*, held at Madison Square Garden.

Unfortunately for Daniels, the *Brawl to End It All* is where the Texas native's WWE career peaked. For the remainder of the decade and into the early 1990s, Daniels regularly found himself on the wrong side of decisions against the likes of George "The Animal" Steele, Iron Sheik, and "Ravishing" Rick Rude.

TERRY FUNK

see page 345

TERRY GIBBS

| HT | 6'0" | WT | 240 lbs. | FROM | Tampa, Florida |
| SIGNATURE MOVE | | Inverted Atomic Drop | | | |

This tough customer wrestled his way through the Central States, and Pacific Northwest territories, along with Puerto Rico's World Wrestling Council and the Poffo family's renegade promotion before making his WWE debut in November 1984. Over the next four years, Terry Gibbs clashed with the premiere Superstars on programs like *Championship Wrestling*, *All-Star Wrestling*, and *Prime-Time Wrestling*.

Gibbs took on individuals like Mr. Wrestling II, Hillbilly Jim, SD Jones, Barry Windham, Ultimate Warrior, and Hulk Hogan. By the late 1980s, Gibbs had left WWE and returned to the independent scene.

Terry Gibbs was one of the fixtures of WWE programming during the early days of Hulkamania, and will always be remembered as a determined competitor who made the preliminary matches interesting.

TERRY TAYLOR

| HT | 6'1" | WT | 225 lbs. | FROM | Vero Beach, Florida |
| SIGNATURE MOVE | | Scorpion Death Lock | | | |

This Superstar began his career in 1979, honing his abilities in various territories, including the Mid-South, Mid-Atlantic, and World Class promotions.

In 1988, on his first night in WWE, he attacked partner Sam Houston after a loss to Los Conquistadors, earning the ire of the crowd. Soon, he became a member of manager Bobby "The Brain" Heenan's Family, and rebranded himself the "Red Rooster," moving his head forward and back like a barnyard critter. In clashes with the Brooklyn Brawler and Mr. Perfect, he won back the fans' support.

In 1992, after a period in WCW, he returned to WWE as "Terrific" Terry Taylor with a new signature move, the Gutwrench Sit-out Powerbomb. He also became an on-air commentator, a job he continued after he decided to go back to WCW.

During his time at the announcer's table, he closely studied the repertories of the combatants in the ring. In 2012, he channeled those astute observations into training the next crop of Superstars at NXT.

TERRY FUNK

HT	6'1"
WT	247 lbs.
FROM	The Double Cross Ranch, Amarillo, Texas

Terry Funk attempted to retire so many times that he lost count himself.

The first time the "Hardcore Legend" attempted to hang up the boots was in 1983, following a match pitting Terry and his brother, Dory Funk, Jr. against Stan Hansen and Terry Gordy. Nearing 40 years old, with offers to act in Hollywood, Funk believed that he could build a life for himself away from the arena. However, the lure of the ring was too strong, and he soon returned, brawling and bleeding from Orlando to Osaka.

Another retirement was announced in 1997, after Bret Hart put up his WWE World Heavyweight Championship against Funk in his hometown of Amarillo, Texas. Yet, within a year, Terry was delivering his distinct brand of "extreme" to the WWE Universe.

When Funk declared, at age 68, that he was finally serious about retiring, many believed that he had no choice. After nearly a half century of being battered with steel objects and slammed across the announcer's table, his career appeared to be over. But looks were deceiving.

Simply put, Terry needed more.

The fans haven't been the only beneficiaries of Funk's indecision. Hundreds of Superstars have learned from watching and tangling with the Hardcore Legend. In fact, multiple generations of rookies mentored by Terry have long since retired.

Raised in a wrestling family, Funk was determined to follow the career path of his famous father, Dory Funk, Sr., and brother, Dory, Jr. In 1965, Terry was regarded as one of the brightest stars in the NWA. He combined rough housing, mat skills, and a mean streak a mile wide to become an international legend. The 1971 series of brother-versus-brother skirmishes with the Funks taking on Jack and Gerry Brisco are still regarded as technical classics.

Although closely associated with the NWA, Terry and his father made several WWE appearances that year, battling the Fabulous Kangaroos, as well as King Curtis and "Crazy" Luke Graham.

In 1973, Jack Brisco won the NWA World Heavyweight Championship and was hotly pursued by Dory, Jr., a former NWA Champion himself. But in 1975, it was Terry who had the gold strapped around his waist after a 60-minute, two-out-of-three fall spectacle in Miami. The Funks are the only brothers to ever both win the prize.

Terry was a fighting Champion who was known for waging combat past the point of exhaustion. Even after he lost the Championship to Harley Race in 1977, he continued at the same pace. His 1981 empty arena brawl in Memphis against Jerry "The King" Lawler is remembered as one of wrestling's most unusual confrontations. Funk attempted to score the win by hammering a spike into Lawler.

But The King used Funk's momentum against him, and the weapon went into the former Champion's eye, as his painful cries echoed throughout the vacant building.

In 1985, Terry came to WWE, challenging WWE Champion Hulk Hogan, and threatening to brand the Junkyard Dog like the cattle on the Funk family's famed Double Cross Ranch. Later, his brother Dory joined Terry in WWE in several matches against JYD and Hogan.

In 1989, Terry was back in the NWA, staging a series of attacks against NWA Champion Ric Flair before falling to him in a classic "I Quit" Match.

After gaining a reputation for his violent "death matches" in Japan, Funk became the backbone of the upstart ECW promotion the following decade, leading the revolution in sports entertainment, as he fought names like Raven, Sabu, Tommy Dreamer, and the Sandman.

In 1998, Funk joined his friend Mick Foley in WWE, and captured the World Tag Team Championships under their demented alter-egos, Chainsaw Charlie and Cactus Jack.

As the years went on, this legend got tougher and crazier. In 2006, he returned to WWE for *One Night Stand* to join Tommy Dreamer and Beulah against Mick Foley, Edge, and Lita.

Unable to wait for an official retirement, WWE honored Funk in 2009 by inducting Terry and his brother, Dory, into the WWE Hall of Fame.

Some Superstars graduated from The School of Hard Knocks. Terry Funk—meaner than a Texas rattlesnake, tougher than shoe leather, and more dangerous than a hollow-eyed scorpion—built that institution brick-by-brick with his bare hands.

THE GREATEST THING IS TO DO YOUR JOB SO WELL THAT SOMEONE WANTS TO KILL YOU

TEST

HT	6'6"	WT	285 lbs.	FROM	Toronto, Ontario, Canada
SIGNATURE MOVE			Big Boot, Pumphandle Slam		

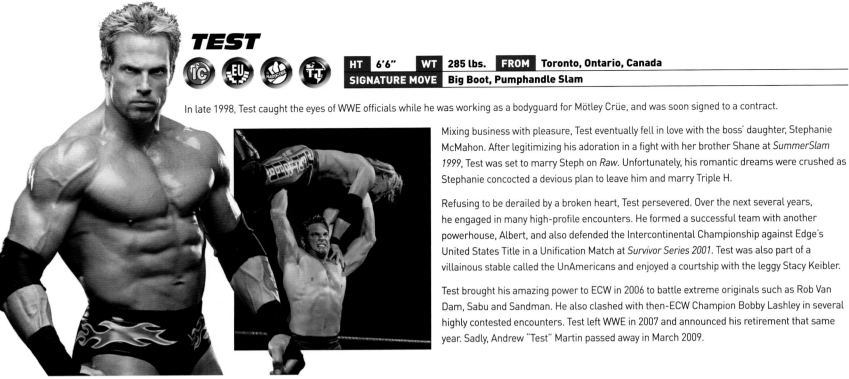

In late 1998, Test caught the eyes of WWE officials while he was working as a bodyguard for Mötley Crüe, and was soon signed to a contract.

Mixing business with pleasure, Test eventually fell in love with the boss' daughter, Stephanie McMahon. After legitimizing his adoration in a fight with her brother Shane at *SummerSlam 1999*, Test was set to marry Steph on *Raw*. Unfortunately, his romantic dreams were crushed as Stephanie concocted a devious plan to leave him and marry Triple H.

Refusing to be derailed by a broken heart, Test persevered. Over the next several years, he engaged in many high-profile encounters. He formed a successful team with another powerhouse, Albert, and also defended the Intercontinental Championship against Edge's United States Title in a Unification Match at *Survivor Series 2001*. Test was also part of a villainous stable called the UnAmericans and enjoyed a courtship with the leggy Stacy Keibler.

Test brought his amazing power to ECW in 2006 to battle extreme originals such as Rob Van Dam, Sabu and Sandman. He also clashed with then-ECW Champion Bobby Lashley in several highly contested encounters. Test left WWE in 2007 and announced his retirement that same year. Sadly, Andrew "Test" Martin passed away in March 2009.

THEODORE LONG

Theodore Long has practically done it all in sports-entertainment, from constructing the ring all the way up to being a respected General Manager.

After more than a decade in the NWA and WCW, Long appeared in WWE in 1998 as a referee. He called it down the middle for several years before leaving officiating to help guide the careers of such Superstars as Rodney Mack, Mark Henry, and Jazz.

In 2004, Long moved up the corporate ladder when he became *SmackDown* GM. As the blue brand's leader, Long is credited with such popular ideas as the New Talent Initiative and reviving the King of the Ring tournament. He also defended *SmackDown*'s honor when he defeated *Raw* GM Eric Bischoff at the 2005 *Survivor Series*.

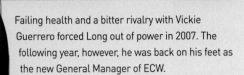

Failing health and a bitter rivalry with Vickie Guerrero forced Long out of power in 2007. The following year, however, he was back on his feet as the new General Manager of ECW.

Long's ECW success caught the attention of WWE brass, who lured him back to *SmackDown* in the spring of 2009. For the next three years, Long stewarded the *SmackDown* ship with great pride, and became known for creating thrilling tag team matches on the fly.

Unfortunately for Long, he lost his position to John Laurinaitis when Team Johnny defeated Team Teddy at *WrestleMania XXVIII*.

Long eventually faded from the scene in 2013, but there is no denying that the decades-long impact he had on sports-entertainment will be felt for generations.

TIFFANY

HT	5'6"	FROM	New Orleans, Louisiana

When Theodore Long was looking for an Executive Assistant during the summer of 2008, the ECW General Manager turned to the stunning Tiffany to do the job. Armed with incredible business acumen, strong marketing skills, and the ability to create and maintain quality relationships, Tiffany quickly became a valued member of Long's team.

Alongside Long, Tiffany learned the importance of taking calculated risks and being firm when making difficult decisions. When Long left ECW for *SmackDown* in April 2009, all the decision-making was left in Tiffany's hands, as she was named General Manager of The Land of the Extreme.

Tiffany called the shots for ECW all the way up until the brand closed its doors. Even afterward, the bright businesswoman helped transition her former Superstars' contracts to *Raw* and *SmackDown*.

After ECW, the dynamic executive hung up her business suit in favor of an in-ring career. Unfortunately for Tiffany, she failed to gain momentum as an active competitor and was eventually released from WWE in November 2010.

TIGER ALI SINGH

HT	6'5"	WT	275 lbs.	FROM	The Continent of Asia
SIGNATURE MOVE		**Reverse Neck Breaker**			

Considering his familial ties to the sports-entertainment industry, one would assume Tiger Ali Singh would understand the concept of respect. Unfortunately, the apple fell very far from the legendary Tiger Jeet Singh's tree because the only thing his son, Tiger Ali Singh, respected was his money.

Tiger Ali Singh succeeded in hiding his true persona during the early portion of his WWE career. But after winning WWE's second-annual Kuwaiti Cup Invitational in April 1997, the second-generation Superstar began to reveal his true colors. It wasn't long before he began bragging about his riches. With his servant, Babu, by his side, he would regularly offer piles of cash to any American fan willing to perform humiliating tasks.

In the ring, Tiger Ali Singh successfully turned back such Superstars as Al Snow and Gillberg before focusing his efforts on managing. In 2000, he briefly guided the careers of Lo Down (Chaz and D-Lo Brown) before being released from WWE in 2002.

TIGER JEET SINGH

HT	6'3"	WT	265 lbs.	FROM	Punjab, India
SIGNATURE MOVE		**Tiger Claw**			

Tiger Jeet Singh was a famous bodybuilder in his native India before immigrating to Canada in 1965. Over the next few years, he became one of the most feared men of the ring. His match in 1967 at the Maple Leaf Gardens in Toronto, Ontario against Bruno Sammartino was such a huge draw that thousands of fans were turned away after the arena reached its capacity.

For the next three decades, Tiger Jeet Singh continued to maul opponents all over the world while appearing alongside WWE Superstars. His popularity was greatest in Japan, where he fought in the IWA "King of the Death Match" tournament with fellow Superstars Terry Funk, Cactus Jack, and Terry "Bam Bam" Gordy.

Singh appeared in the crowd at *SummerSlam 1997* alongside his son, Tiger Ali Singh. Tiger Jeet managed his son into the Attitude Era before returning to terrorize foes overseas. Today, he remains one of the greatest figures in all of Japan, and an inspiration in Canada, where a Milton, Ontario, public school bears his name.

TIGER CHUNG LEE

HT	6'4"	WT	289 lbs.	FROM	Korea

A master of martial arts, Tiger Chung Lee made a name for himself early on in his career while competing in Japan. While there, he and tag team partner Kintaro Ohki traded the All Japan International Tag Team Championship twice with Giant Baba and Jumbo Tsuruta.

After losing the titles for the final time in May 1978, Tiger Chung Lee made his way to the United States where he briefly wrestled for the National Wrestling Alliance before landing in WWE.

Affectionately referred to as "the Chunger" by WWE Hall of Fame commentator Gorilla Monsoon, Tiger Chung Lee proved his toughness almost immediately when he broke solid bricks on live television using only his bare hands. Unfortunately, his toughness failed to translate into victories as Tiger Chung Lee oftentimes walked away from his WWE matches with the loser's share of the purse.

After leaving WWE, Tiger continued his career in Japan and Mexico, and acted in several movies.

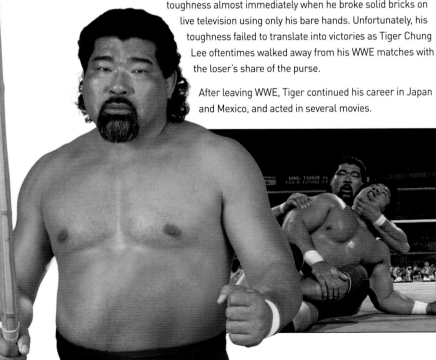

TIGER MASK

HT	5'8"	WT	198 lbs.	FROM	Japan
SIGNATURE MOVE		**Tiger Suplex**			

Originally a Japanese comic book superhero, Tiger Mask came to life in 1981 when he debuted in New Japan Pro Wrestling. With superior mat skills and high-flying aerial assaults, the furry masked Superstar was a legitimate double threat in the ring.

Tiger Mask's legendary rivalries with fellow technicians Bret Hart and Chris Adams made news all over the world, but it was his battles with Dynamite Kid that resonated most. In January, 1982, he defeated Dynamite Kid in Japan to capture the WWE Junior Heavyweight Championship. Over the next several years, the two Superstars engaged in a global battle for junior heavyweight supremacy. In all, Tiger Mask held the Title three times during the course of their epic rivalry.

By the mid-1980s, Tiger Mask lost his passion to compete. Still relatively young at the time, he left the ring at the height of his popularity. Over the next several years, other Japanese Superstars donned the furry mask, claiming to be the masked Superstar. However, true historians only recognize the original as the true Tiger Mask.

TIM HORNER

| HT | 5'10" | WT | 230 lbs. | FROM | Morristown, Tennessee |

As one half of the Lightning Express with partner Brad Armstrong, Tim Horner made a name for himself as a tag team specialist early in his career. After only a brief time together, the young duo topped Rip Rogers and Ted Oates to win the NWA National Tag Team Championship in November 1984. However, Lightning Express was forced to relinquish the gold later that month when an injury prevented Horner from defending their Championship. Years later, the Lighting Express would strike again when Horner and Armstrong defeated Sting and Rick Steiner for the UWF World Tag Team Championship.

As a singles competitor, Horner attempted to establish himself inside WWE and WCW rings with limited success. After retirement, he applied his knowledge by working backstage for WWE.

TITUS O'NEIL

| HT | 6'6" | WT | 270 lbs. | FROM | Live Oak, Florida |
| SIGNATURE MOVE | Clash of the Titus |

Physically gifted, O'Neil was a University of Florida football star who played several seasons in the Arena Football League before landing in WWE. In 2012, he formed an alliance with Prime Time Players partner Darren Young in NXT. Very quickly, the pair elevated themselves to the WWE roster.

Soon, fans were imitating the Prime Time Players' unique entrance, dancing in synch from side to side. Despite the attention, the two were thwarted in their repeated efforts to win the WWE World Tag Team Championship and began to take out their frustrations on each other, engaging in a series of matches in 2014.

For a period, O'Neil and Heath Slater formed a team, with less than stellar results. But in 2015, the Prime Time Players put their differences aside to reunite and defeat the New Day for the World Tag Team Titles. Although they only held the Championship for two months, O'Neil's confidence was back, and "The Real Deal" began flourishing as a single's competitor and WWE ambassador to groups focused on family and education.

TL HOPPER

| HT | 5'10" | WT | 235 lbs. |

This plumber-turned-performer first appeared in WWE in 1996. His appearances in the ring were heralded by the sound of a flushing toilet, and he never strayed far from Betsy, his beloved plunger. During his tenure with WWE, he battled the likes of the Stalker, Aldo Montoya, the Bushwhackers, Marc Mero, and the Godwinns. He was also involved in a match where he teamed up with Billy Gunn to face Bart Gunn and Freddie Joe Floyd after the Smokin' Gunns' tumultuous split. After less than a year competing in WWE, TL Hopper left the company to return to his former profession.

TITO SANTANA

| HT | 6'2" | WT | 234 lbs. | FROM | Tocula, Mexico |
| SIGNATURE MOVE | Flying Forearm |

A two-time Intercontinental and World Tag Team Champion, Tito Santana pieced together an impressive career that spanned decades. Along the way, he displayed class and a sound technical ability that made him one of sports-entertainment's elite.

While Santana is best recognized for the success he experienced during the 1980s, his first taste of WWE superstardom actually came in the late 1970s. During a brief stay in WWE, he teamed with Ivan Putski to claim the World Tag Team Championship from the Valiant Brothers. Santana and Putski held the Titles for nearly six months before losing to The Samoans. Following the loss, Santana departed for the AWA.

In 1983, Santana returned to WWE and immediately found himself back in the Title hunt. This time, Santana had his eyes on Don Muraco's Intercontinental Championship. After a few unsuccessful tries, Santana was finally able to end Muraco's lengthy reign in February 1984. The win gave Santana his first of two Intercontinental Championship reigns.

Between runs with the Intercontinental Championship, Santana made history when he defeated The Executioner in the first-ever *WrestleMania* match. He went on to earn a spot on the first nine *WrestleMania* cards (although his *WrestleMania IX* match was untelevised). Only the immortal Hulk Hogan can make the same claim.

Santana returned to his tag team roots in 1987, teaming with Rick Martel. Known as Strike Force, the duo defeated the Hart Foundation for the World Tag Team Championship in October. The popular tag team operated as a successful unit until April 1989, when Martel turned on Santana at *WrestleMania V*.

Following Strike Force's untimely demise, Santana adopted a bullfighting persona. Aptly named El Matador, Santana enjoyed a resurgence to his maturing career. El Matador's most notable encounter came at *WrestleMania VIII* where he fell to an up-and-coming Shawn Michaels. Interestingly, it was Michaels who inducted his rival into the WWE Hall of Fame in 2004.

Outside the ring, Santana also thrived. For a period, he was a WWE Spanish announcer. After saving his money wisely, he enjoyed a satisfying career as a business owner and teacher.

TODD GRISHAM

FROM Bay Minette, Alabama

A former sports reporter in Arizona, Todd Grisham developed his witty style of journalism while working closely with such organizations as the NFL, NBA, NHL, and MLS. When he had the chance to work for WWE in 2004, he jumped at the once-in-a-lifetime opportunity.

As a member of WWE's esteemed announce team, Grisham did it all. He was best known for his hard-hitting line of questioning as *Raw*'s backstage interviewer, but also served on the now-defunct *Heat* as play-by-play man and hosted WWE.com's webcast, *Byte This!*

Grisham's chance to become a lead announcer first came on the ECW brand. Soon, his popular broadcasting style landed him next to WWE Hall of Famer Jim Ross on *SmackDown*. Proving to be versatile with a microphone, Todd hosted WWE's 2009 Hall of Fame induction ceremony and later became lead announcer on *NXT*.

Grisham left WWE in August 2011 and pursued a career with ESPN. Today, he still serves as an anchor on *SportsCenter*, joining Jonathan Coachman and other WWE broadcasters in making a successful transition to mainstream sports.

TOM MAGEE

HT 6'5" **WT** 245 lbs. **FROM** Vancouver, British Columbia, Canada

Holding a black belt in karate, and world titles in competitive bodybuilding, Tom Magee trained for the ring with the incomparable Stu Hart. After appearing in Japan, Magee took his impressive physique and charisma to WWE in 1986.

The WWE Universe was initially excited. Magee, known by his nickname "Mega Man," had won the World Superheavyweight Powerlifting Championship in 1982, and big things were predicted for him in WWE.

Magee's opponents included Jimmy Jack Funk, Tiger Chung Lee, Ron Bass, Barry O, Iron Mike Sharpe, and Bret "Hit Man" Hart. Yet, he never won a WWE Title. In 1990, he left the company and pursued a career as an actor. Today, he lends his training expertise to bodybuilding hopefuls.

TOM PHILLIPS

HT 6' 0" **FROM** Philadelphia, Pennsylvania

Since high school, Tom Phillips has strived to become a major player in the world of broadcasting. The Penn State graduate came to WWE in 2012 possessing a lifelong enthusiasm for sports-entertainment. Having been a child of the Attitude Era and hailing from the city that gave birth to Extreme Championship Wrestling, Phillips felt right at home.

His first efforts in a WWE booth were seen on *NXT*. Alongside Alex Riley, Renee Young, and several others, Phillips became the brand's lead announcer. He called the groundbreaking event *NXT ArRIVAL* and soon found opportunity knocking on WWE's flagship shows, *Raw* and *SmackDown*. Whether calling the action or scoring exclusive interviews for the WWE App, Phillips has proven that his future as a broadcaster is a bright one.

TODD PETTENGILL

Todd Pettengill debuted in WWE in early 1993, and over the next several years, performed nearly every task imaginable to a sports-entertainment broadcaster and then some.

Some of Pettengill's more unorthodox job responsibilities included interviewing Superstars at *WrestleMania IX* while wearing a toga, providing fans with tips for all types of video games (not just WWE), even giving away a house to a lucky member of the WWE Universe. But perhaps his most memorable performance came at the prestigious 1996 Slammy Awards ceremony, where the always-smiley announcer sang the show's opening number. Much like Neil Patrick Harris, Ricky Gervais, or any other of today's award show hosts, Pettengill used his song to poke fun at WWE's most prominent Superstars, including Shawn Michaels, Ultimate Warrior, and Triple H.

Pettengill left WWE in 1997, but maintained his spot in the public eye as the co-host of WPLJ's hit morning radio show, which can be heard in the New York market.

TOMMY DREAMER

 HT 6'2" **WT** 265 lbs. **FROM** Yonkers, New York
SIGNATURE MOVE The Dreamer DDT

From the moment he saw Jimmy "Superfly" Snuka dive from the top of the cage at Madison Square Garden, all Tommy Dreamer, a kid from Yonkers, wanted to do was wrestle. After training under WWE Hall of Famer Johnny Rodz, Dreamer became one of the primary forces that changed the E in ECW from "Eastern" to "Extreme." Known as "the Innovator of Violence," Dreamer often turned the ring into a blood-stained battleground. He faithfully remained with the company until it closed in 2001.

He then joined the WWE roster and became a 14-time Hardcore Champion, and a central component in the two *One Night Stand* events, as well as the revived ECW, where he won the ECW World Heavyweight Championship in June 2009.

Tommy competed for the final time in an ECW ring in December 2009. But his relationship with WWE continued. After promoting a number of well-received indie shows, Dreamer appeared in *NXT*, tackling Baron Corbin in 2015, and soon merged with his former ECW companions, the Dudley Boyz and Rhyno as Team Extreme to take on the Wyatt Family at *Survivor Series* in 2015.

THE TONGA KID

HT 6'3" **WT** 225 lbs. **FROM** The Isle of Tonga **SIGNATURE MOVE** Flying Headbutt

This son of the Isle of Tonga flew into WWE in August 1983. Billed as the cousin of Jimmy "Superfly" Snuka, the Kid took to the air against Mr. Fuji, Iron Sheik, "Mr. Wonderful" Paul Orndorff, "Cowboy" Bob Orton, and "Rowdy" Roddy Piper.

The Kid also joined forces with his famous cousin and electrified audiences with their high-flying moves and exciting style. When Roddy Piper attacked Snuka with a coconut on *Piper's Pit*, it was The Tonga Kid who sought revenge.

In 1986, he rechristened himself Tama and formed the Islanders with multi-talented Haku. Initially cheered by the WWE Universe, the duo fell under the corrupt sway of manager Bobby "The Brain" Heenan.

TONS OF FUNK

MEMBERS Tensai & Brodus Clay **COMBINED WT** 735 lbs.

When Brodus Clay re-debuted as the fun-loving Funkasaurus in early 2012, the WWE Universe was awed by the big man's incredible dance moves. Never before had a Superstar his size shown such rhythm. One year later, the oversized dancing became twice as nice as Clay teamed with the equally imposing and rhythmically talented, Tensai to form Tons of Funk.

Alongside Funkadactyls Naomi and Cameron, Clay and Tensai brought arenas to their feet with their contagious dance moves. But once the music stopped and the tear-away pants came off, Tons of Funk were all business. Among the teams who felt the wrath of the enormous tandem include 3MB and Team Rhodes Scholars.

Unfortunately, the fun began to fade in late 2013 when Clay started to exhibit a dark rage. Wanting nothing to do with an evil Funkasaurus, Tensai walked away from the partnership. The former friends later engaged in a bitter rivalry, highlighted by a Tensai victory over Clay on *SmackDown*.

TONY ALTOMARE

HT 5'11" **WT** 265 lbs.
FROM Stamford, Connecticut

An Italian-American tough guy, Tony Altomare and partner Lou Albano competed as The Sicilians, spinning a convincing tale about their purported mob ties. They were so believable, in fact, that real mobsters hunted them down in the 1960s to warn the duo to give up the façade.

In July 1967, Altomare and Albano defeated Spiros Arion and Arnold Skaaland to capture the WWE United States Tag Team Championship. They held the Titles for only two weeks before losing to Arion and his new partner, Bruno Sammartino.

Shortly after the loss, Albano switched to managing, leaving the self-professed "Stamford Stomper" to fend for himself. In addition to wrestling, refereeing, and training, Altomare worked a lifeguard for 25 years before passing away in 2003.

TONY ATLAS

  HT 6'2" **WT** 250 lbs. **FROM** Roanoke, Virginia
SIGNATURE MOVE Gorilla Press Slam

A former bodybuilder, Tony Atlas possessed one of the most impressive physiques to ever grace a WWE ring. Known as "Mr. USA," he used his great strength to break through racial barriers and become a true WWE legend.

Atlas made his professional debut in 1974. Despite having little experience to draw upon, his early days were filled with numerous NWA regional championships. By the early 1980s, he had properly honed his skills, developed a powerful Gorilla Press Slam and moved up to WWE.

In November 1983, Atlas made sports-entertainment history when he teamed with Rocky Johnson to become the first African-Americans to capture the WWE World Tag Team Championship from the Wild Samoans. They held the Titles for five months before losing to Adrian Adonis and Dick Murdoch.

Following the loss, Atlas traveled to various territories, including the WWC in Puerto Rico, Dallas-based World Class Championship Wrestling, and the AWA.

Despite being inducted into the 2006 WWE Hall of Fame, Atlas refused to retreat into retirement. In 2008, he revealed himself as the manager of ECW Champion Mark Henry. For the first time in his WWE career, he found himself on the wrong side of the fans' admiration. While in The Land of Extreme, Atlas even returned to the ring on occasion.

Today, a younger generation of fans knows "Mr. USA" from his role on the WWE Network series, *Legends House*.

TONY CHIMEL

HT 6'1" **FROM** Cherry Hill, New Jersey

Tony Chimel is best recognized for his resonant voice as a longtime WWE ring announcer, but his sports-entertainment career started long before his first microphone duties. In the early 1980s, Chimel parlayed his friendship with Gorilla Monsoon's son into a job setting up wrestling rings. This weekend gig soon became a livelihood as Mr. McMahon made Chimel a full-time technician.

In 1999, Chimel permanently moved in front of the cameras when he defeated legendary ring announcer Howard Finkel in a Tuxedo Match to become the original *SmackDown* ring announcer. Chimel spent the next eight years on *SmackDown* before joining the ECW brand in September 2007. When ECW closed its doors, Chimel returned to the familiar surroundings of *SmackDown*. Tony's trademark energy and delivery got the WWE Universe ready to see their favorite WWE "*Suuuuperstars*" at events all over the world.

Since 2011, Chimel has served predominantly in a valuable role behind the scenes, but he always keeps his suit handy. He has announced several NXT events in recent years and made a rare appearance on *Raw* in December 2015.

TONY GAREA

 HT 6'2" **WT** 246 lbs. **FROM** Auckland, New Zealand
SIGNATURE MOVE The Octopus Hold

This sensational athlete debuted in WWE in 1972. His accomplishments within the ranks of tag team wrestling set him apart from every other Superstar before or since. In May 1973, the former rugby player teamed with giant Haystacks Calhoun and defeated Professor Toru Tanaka and Mr. Fuji.

Over the next eight years, Garea enlisted other gladiators like Dean Ho, Larry Zbyszko, and Rick Martel to help capture tag team gold against the likes of the Valiant Brothers, Yukon Lumberjacks, Wild Samoans, and Moondogs.

During the reign of Superstar Billy Graham, Garea was a regular contender for the WWE World Heavyweight Championship. He also wrestled in the San Francisco territory, holding the tag team title there with future WWE Hall of Famer Pat Patterson.

Garea continued his in-ring career until his retirement in 1986. During this time, he also dabbled as a commentator alongside Vince McMahon on episodes of WWE's syndicated shows. Garea soon made the transition to WWE's front office, and was often seen breaking apart violent brawls on WWE programming. Today, he is still a valued WWE employee, regularly known for scouting the next WWE Superstar.

During his in-ring career, Garea was a five-time WWE World Tag Team Champion. His abilities and heart made him a favorite among fans, and a difficult individual for opposing Superstars to beat.

TONY MAMALUKE

HT 5'10" **WT** 170 lbs. **FROM** Bensonhurst, Brooklyn
SIGNATURE MOVE Sicilian Stretch

After a brief stint in WCW, Tony Mamaluke made his mark in ECW as part of the Full Blooded Italians. He became ECW World Tag Team Champions with Little Guido and remained a star until ECW closed its doors in March 2001.

Tony spent the next few years competing at independent events. In 2005 he appeared with the FBI at *ECW One Night Stand*. The event was so popular that WWE brought it back the following year. Mamaluke used the opportunity to reunite with Little Guido to defeat Tajiri and Super Crazy. Following the victory he was seen on WWE's reincarnated *ECW* battling the likes of Sabu, Test, and Mike Knox. In January 2007 Mamaluke and WWE severed ties and he returned to the independent circuit.

TONY MARINO

 HT 5'10" **WT** 240 lbs. **FROM** New York
SIGNATURE MOVE Abdominal Stretch

Tony "Dino" Marino began his wrestling career in 1954 and made his WWE debut nine years later, appearing prominently during WWE's Pittsburgh events. It was during this period that he started to don a dark mask and call himself Battman, based on the popular superhero, Batman.

On two occasions, he won the WWE International Tag Team Championship, once with Bruno Sammartino, before departing the company. He found success in Detroit, where he won the territory's tag team championship with "Flyin'" Fred Curry and future WWE Hall of Famer Bobo Brazil.

In March, 1974, Marino won his only single's title, the Detroit version of the United States Championship from the legendary Sheik, losing it back to the Mid-Eastern madman two weeks later. He retired in 1987.

TONY PARISI

  HT 5'11" **WT** 241 lbs.
FROM Cozena, Italy

Early in his WWE career, Tony Parisi, then known as Antonio Pugliese, was billed as the cousin of the WWE kingpin Bruno Sammartino, making himself a target for enemies of the "Living Legend." Within weeks of his WWE debut in 1966, the proud Italian was co-holder of the United States Tag Team Championship with Johnny Valentine, beating Dan and Dr. Bill Miller.

In mid-1967, Parisi left WWE to compete in various territories throughout the United States and Australia. When he finally returned several years later, he periodically teamed with Sammartino before forming a championship combination with Louis Cerdan. The new pairing defeated the Blackjacks for the World Tag Team Championship in November, 1975. They held the Titles for six months before being upended by The Executioners.

In the 1980s, he wrestled in Montreal's Lutte Internationale promotion, winning tag team gold with Gino Brito and Dino Bravo. He also promoted shows in Niagara Falls.

He last competed in 1997, teaming with Brito against Greg Valentine and Terry Funk, three years before his death.

TONY SCHIAVONE

With 20 years behind the microphone, Tony Schiavone became one of the most recognizable sports-entertainment voices of the late 1980s and 1990s. Despite his years of tireless service, Schiavone will forever be remembered most for a poor choice of words during a pivotal moment of the WWE-WCW Monday Night War.

On January 4, 1999, while serving as the lead announcer of *Monday Nitro*, Schiavone spoiled the results of a pre-taped WWE Championship Match on *Raw*:

"Tonight, fans, Mick Foley, who wrestled here as Cactus Jack and now wrestles as Mankind, will win the WWE Title," said Schiavone before sarcastically proclaiming, "That'll put some butts in the seats."

The move backfired when a large portion of WCW's viewers switched over to see Foley win the WWE Championship. Reportedly, Schiavone —who'd previously worked for WWE—was simply following the orders of WCW boss Eric Bischoff. He later apologized to Foley. Regardless, it proved to be a turning point in the Monday Night War, as WWE won the ratings battle that night and never looked back.

After WCW, Schiavone became an announcer for the Atlanta Braves' AAA baseball affiliate.

TOO COOL

MEMBERS	Scotty 2 Hotty & Grand Master Sexay
COMBINED WT	433 lbs.

A pair of hip-hoppers who stood out from the crowd, Scotty 2 Hotty and Grand Master Sexay were a huge hit with the WWE Universe, who cheered as much for their wins as they did their post-match dances.

Collectively known as Too Cool, Scotty and Grand Master proved they were too good in May 2000 when they defeated Edge and Christian for the World Tag Team Championship. The duo held the Titles for nearly a month before losing them back to Edge and Christian at *King of the Ring*.

Despite no longer being Champions, Too Cool remained one of WWE's most popular pairings all the way up through Grand Master Sexay's release in 2001.

More than a decade later, Too Cool reunited with longtime friend Rikishi to defeat 3MB on *Raw* in January 2014. The following month, Scotty and Grand Master challenged The Ascension for the NXT Tag Team Championship at *NXT ArRIVAL*. Konnor and Viktor won the match, but Scotty and Grand Master successfully proved that you never know when Too Cool will pop up next to get the WWE Universe on their feet and dancing along.

TOR KAMATA

HT	6'3"	WT	350 lbs.	FROM	The South Pacific Islands
SIGNATURE MOVE	Big Splash				

Tor Kamata toured the globe many times over during the course of his 30-year career, but it was his time spent in Calgary's Stampede territory that fans remember most. While competing for Stampede Wrestling, the hated Kamata, who often used salt as a weapon to blind his foes, captured the prestigious North American Heavyweight Championship on three separate occasions. He also teamed with Sugi Siti to win the promotion's International Tag Team Championship in February 1972.

Kamata wrestled in the Florida, Central States, Mid-Atlantic, and other territories, and generally stood out from everyone else, unless Abdullah the Butcher was also on the roster. The WWE Hall of Famer and Kamata shared a similar look, and were alternately tag team partners and bitter enemies.

In 1976 and 1977 Kamata rampaged through WWE, managed by Freddie Blassie. Before Bob Backlund was granted a shot at the WWE World Heavyweight Championship held by Superstar Billy Graham, Backlund had to go through Kamata. Backlund barely passed the test, but went on to make wrestling history and capture the WWE Championship.

Kamata died in 2007.

TORI

HT	5'9"	FROM	Portland, Oregon
SIGNATURE MOVE	Tori-Plex		

This former bodybuilder burst into the sports-entertainment spotlight late in 1998. In her rookie year, Tori faced Sable for the Women's Championship at *WrestleMania XV*. She may have pulled off a miraculous victory if not for the meddling of the massive Nicole Bass. Following the defeat, Tori continued to face WWE's fiercest females and also showed her skills in Mixed Tag Matches with partners, Val Venis and Al Snow. After continued success, Tori attempted her luck at the Women's Championship and engaged in a ruthless rivalry with the Women's Champion, Ivory, that culminated in a rare Women's Hardcore Rules Match.

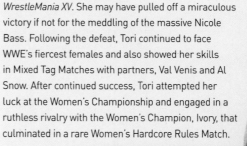

In late 1999, Tori became romantically involved with Kane but eventually left him for his tag team partner and D-Generation X member, X-Pac. Tori's in-ring savvy later served her well as she became a trainer on the first season of *Tough Enough*. Today she is a yoga guru and makes the occasional appearance on shows around the world.

TORRIE WILSON

HT	5' 7"	**FROM**	Boise, Idaho
SIGNATURE MOVE		Springboard Elbow	

Torrie Wilson grew up as a competitive athlete and dancer. She was passionate about nutrition and fitness and won the prestigious *Miss Galaxy* competition in 1998.

Torrie began her sports-entertainment career with WCW in 1999. She worked as a manager through late 2000, supporting the likes of Shane Douglas, the Filthy Animals, and others. The WWE Universe was happy to see Torrie appear on *SmackDown* in June 2001 with Mr. McMahon, though it would soon become apparent that she was part of the WCW/ECW Alliance. Her in-ring debut came at *Invasion* where she joined fellow Alliance member, Stacy Keibler, against Lita and Trish Stratus in a Bra and Panties Match.

Despite being a part of the enemy, this breathtaking blonde became an instant sensation with audiences all over the globe. She returned to managing when she aligned herself with "Japanese Buzzsaw" Tajiri. Torrie engaged in a serious family affair when her rival, Dawn Marie, became involved with Torrie's father. Torrie ultimately defeated Dawn, but the controversial events surrounding their clash left a lasting effect.

Torrie's fame continued to skyrocket during 2005 which led to a Playboy Pillow Fight against Candice Michelle at *WrestleMania 22*. Then in June 2006, she defeated Candice again in the first-ever Wet & Wild Match where the winner graced the cover of WWE's *Summer Special* magazine. Torrie went on to grace the cover of *FHM* magazine as well as *FHM*'s 2007 Calendar. Torrie entered the fashion world when she unveiled her own clothing line called, "Officially Jaded."

To the sadness of her fans worldwide, Torrie and WWE parted ways in May 2008. Torrie Wilson will forever be remembered for her charisma, athleticism, and dedication to sports-entertainment.

TRENT BARRETA

HT	6'2"	**WT**	195 lbs.	**FROM**	Mount Sinai, New York
SIGNATURE MOVE		Dudebuster DDT			

ECW's New Superstar Initiative brought the ever-exciting Trent Barreta to WWE in 2009. Alongside lifelong best friend and tag team partner, Caylen Croft, Barreta emerged victorious in the pair's debut match that December. Together, Barreta and Croft continued their hot streak until ECW closed in February 2010.

Following Croft's release from WWE in late 2010, Baretta competed mostly in singles action. Behind the force of his feared Dudebuster DDT, the New York native delivered "can't miss" matches and earned victories over the likes of Tyson Kidd and Curt Hawkins. He also eked out victories against former Intercontinental Champions Goldust and Drew McIntyre.

Trent Barreta became a regular on *NXT* in 2011 and 2012 before parting ways with WWE in January 2013.

TRINITY

FROM	Long Island, New York

You didn't have to look hard to see that Trinity was a dangerous Superstar. With peaking biceps and yellow police tape strapped across her sculpted chest, it was practically written all over her. The stuntwoman-turned-competitor made her debut in June 2006 as the manager of ECW's Full Blooded Italians. Before she could make her mark, an unfortunate knee injury sidelined her for close to three months. When Trinity finally returned, her signature caution tape earned her a fan-determined victory in an Extreme Halloween Costume Contest. However, further chances to assert herself in the ring were limited and Trinity was released from WWE in 2007.

TRIPLE H
see page 354

TRISH STRATUS
see page 356

THE TRUTH COMMISSION

MEMBERS	The Jackyl, Kurrgan the Interrogator, Recon, Sniper, Tank, & The Commandant

Introduced to WWE audiences by the Commandant in 1997, Recon, Sniper, Tank, and Kurrgan displayed a style of South African guerilla warfare that struck fear into the WWE locker room.

Shortly after their debut, however, the frightening faction went through a bit of restructuring when The Jackyl assumed leadership responsibilities from the Commandant, and Tank was relieved of his duties. The new-look Truth Commission proved to be equally as dangerous as the original.

Out of everyone, seven-foot tall Kurrgan was the monster solo Superstar of the group, while Recon and Sniper competed mainly as a tag team. The entire Commission managed to make a rare appearance as an entire unit at the 1997 *Survivor Series* when they defeated The Disciples of Apocalypse.

Despite their success at *Survivor Series*, the Truth Commission struggled in the early parts of 1998. Unhappy with his team's performance, The Jackyl frequently ordered the monstrous Kurrgan to attack Recon and Sniper. As a result of the infighting, the faction slowly crumbled.

TRIPLE H

HT	6'4"
WT	255 lbs.
FROM	Greenwich, Connecticut

SIGNATURE MOVE
Pedigree

Over the course of his twenty-plus year WWE career, Triple H has captured every major championship, headlined multiple *WrestleMania* cards, won the *Royal Rumble* Match, and even spearheaded two of sports-entertainment's most influential factions. But despite all the amazing in-ring accomplishments, The Game might just be scratching the surface when it comes to his legacy. As WWE's Chief Operating Officer and the mastermind behind NXT, Triple H is not only responsible for today's success, but is also concurrently putting his imprint on future generations of sports-entertainment.

Prior to becoming recognized as The King of Kings, Triple H first opened eyes in WWE as a snobbish Connecticut blueblood in the spring of 1995. Known as Hunter Hearst-Helmsley, his early days were spent making quick work of the likes of Bob Holly and Henry Godwinn en route to what would become one of history's most impressive careers.

Outside the ring, Helmsley formed close bonds with several Superstars, most notably Shawn Michaels, Kevin Nash, and Scott Hall. Collectively known as "The Kliq," the group competed in many memorable matches in front of the camera, while maintaining a close brotherhood behind it.

In May 1996, prior to Hall and Nash defecting to WCW, "The Kliq" shared a heartfelt in-ring embrace at Madison Square Garden. It was the first time the group publicly acknowledged their friendship and was also viewed as a highly-scandalous moment. As a result of the controversy, Vince McMahon punished Helmsley, relegating him to low profile matches.

Lesser Superstars never would've rebounded from McMahon's wrath. But Helmsley refused to stay down, using his in-ring talent to force his way back toward the top. And in less than six months, he defeated Marc Mero to become Intercontinental Champion.

By 1997, the successful Helmsley became targeted by many Superstars. To combat their attacks, he employed the services of a muscle-bound female bodyguard known as Chyna. With his new enforcer watching his back, Helmsley became an even greater force in the ring.

FORMING D-GENERATION X

As 1997 continued, Helmsley began to shed his pretentious persona in favor of a more rebellious attitude. He also began regularly hanging out with HBK in front of the cameras. Together, they continually pushed the envelope of acceptable behavior while becoming one of the most notorious factions of all time—D-Generation X.

THE GAME

Hoping to reach the top of WWE as a singles star, Triple H eventually left DX to pursue the WWE Championship. Given the faction's popularity, the move was seen by many as risky. But the risk eventually paid off in August 1999 when he defeated Mankind to claim his first-ever WWE Championship.

By year's end, Triple H managed to also advance his personal life when he married Mr. McMahon's daughter, Stephanie. Their union sickened The Chairman, especially after learning that the nuptials happened while Stephanie was seemingly in an altered state of mind.

Mr. McMahon nearly cleared his daughter's name when he battled Triple H at *Armageddon*. But before he could end The Game, Stephanie shockingly attacked her father to reveal she was in on the ruse all along. From there, the newlyweds went on one of the most blatant abuses of power ever seen. And in the ring, Triple H pieced together an impressive string of victories, including a *WrestleMania 2000* win over Big Show, The Rock, and Mick Foley.

GAME OVER?

Triple H's remarkable career nearly reached a premature conclusion in May 2001 when his left quadriceps tore completely off the bone. The injury's severity caused noted orthopedic surgeon Dr. James Andrews to predict the end of The Game's in-ring days. Triple H, however, refused to believe Andrews' prognosis and began an exhausting eight months of rehabilitation.

The Game made his highly-anticipated return to a thunderous ovation in January 2002. Three weeks later, Triple H put an exclamation point on his return when he won the *Royal Rumble* Match. He followed that by defeating Chris Jericho at *WrestleMania X8* to reclaim the WWE Championship.

THE EVOLUTION OF SPORTS-ENTERTAINMENT

Triple H accomplished a lifelong dream by joining forces with childhood hero Ric Flair to form Evolution in 2003. Also including Batista and Randy Orton, the well-dressed stable had the feel of a present-day Four Horsemen and was equally as dangerous. At *Armageddon 2003*, Evolution proved as such when all four members walked away with gold.

The following year, Triple H and Michaels reunited for DX's triumphant return. In typical DX fashion, the duo targeted anybody with authority, most notably Mr. McMahon.

Unfortunately, Triple H suffered another debilitating setback when he tore his right quadriceps in January 2007. With nothing left to prove, he could've easily walked away following the injury. Instead, after willing himself through another eight months of rehabilitation, The Cerebral Assassin returned to the ring to defeat King Booker at *SummerSlam*. And he didn't stop there. By mid-2009, Triple H had captured his then-record eighth WWE Championship.

THE LAST OUTLAW

The summer of 2009 saw Triple H and Michaels once again reform DX. Together, they defeated Legacy at *SummerSlam* before setting their attention on Chris Jericho and Big Show, whom they beat for the WWE Tag Team Championship in December. The victory marked the first time The Game and HBK held the Titles together.

In 2011, Triple H turned his attention to Undertaker, who retired Michaels the year prior. Hoping to be the first to blemish The Deadman's perfect record on The Grandest Stage of Them All, The Game battled Undertaker at *WrestleMania XXVII*. But like so many before him, The Cerebral Assassin fell to The Phenom, but not before delivering a beating so brutal that Undertaker had to be carted from ringside.

Convinced he had unfinished business with Triple H, Undertaker challenged The Game to another encounter at *WrestleMania XXVIII*. This time, however, it would be a Hell in a Cell Match. Several times throughout the encounter, it appeared Triple H would be the one to break Undertaker's streak. In the end, though, a Tombstone ended The Game's quest to conquer The Deadman.

THIS, UNTIL MY DYING BREATH, IS MY RELIGION, MY LAW AND MY CHURCH.

THE AUTHORITY

Heading into *SummerSlam 2013*, Triple H used his power as COO to anoint himself referee of the night's main event, which saw John Cena defend his WWE Championship against Daniel Bryan. Utilizing his patented running knee, Bryan dethroned Cena for the gold, though he would not be champion for long. While the WWE Universe showered the new champ with a "YES" chant, Triple H shockingly flattened Bryan with a Pedigree, allowing Randy Orton to swoop in, cash in his Money in the Bank contract, and capture the Title.

Triple H's heinous betrayal of Bryan caused the WWE Universe to turn on the COO. But he didn't mind; instead he and Stephanie, collectively known as The Authority, went on an egotistical power trip that incensed the fans. Claiming they were doing what was "best for business," The Authority made life hell for many of WWE's most popular Superstars, most notably Bryan.

After months of demoralizing Bryan with physical assaults and political machinations, Triple H finally fell victim to the supposed "B-plus player" at *WrestleMania 30*. Later that same night, Bryan went on to also defeat Orton and Batista to reclaim the WWE Championship.

Triple H fared far better the following year when he battled Sting at *WrestleMania 31*. In a match that saw involvement from both WCW stars as well as WWE Attitude Era stalwarts, The Game proved his dominance, downing Sting with a sledgehammer for the win.

Following his defeat of Sting, Triple H seemingly became content on focusing his attention on WWE's business affairs rather than competing. But when Roman Reigns challenged The Authority's dominance, The Game returned to action; and this time, he used his power to claim Reigns' WWE World Heavyweight Championship.

After announcing that Reigns' Title would be on the line in the 2016 *Royal Rumble* Match, Triple H not only put himself in the contest, but also dubiously drew number thirty. With the favorable spot, The Game was afforded a somewhat clear path to his fourteenth World Championship.

Following successful defenses against Dean Ambrose and Dolph Ziggler, Triple H faced off against Reigns at *WrestleMania 32*. The Cerebral Assassin was as vicious as ever in defending the gold, but on this night, there was no stopping Reigns, who upended Triple H to claim the Title.

Despite the loss, the legend of Triple H could not be questioned following *WrestleMania*. Few could run an international conglomerate at such a high level, nurture the development of NXT, and defend the WWE World Heavyweight Championship all at the same time. Though his methods may be controversial at times, even his victims concede that Triple H's longevity and consistent success in the ring, as well as the boardroom, qualify him as one of sports-entertainment's greatest figures.

TRISH STRATUS

HT	5' 5"
FROM	Toronto, Ontario, Canada
SIGNATURE MOVE	
Stratusfaction	

33% Beauty + 34% Brains + 33% Brawn = 100% Stratusfaction guaranteed!

With one simple formula, Trish Stratus revolutionized what it means to be a woman in sports-entertainment, carving an unmatched legacy as the quintessential female Superstar. A former fitness model, the Canadian bombshell arrived in March 2000 during the height of the Attitude Era. Starting as the manager of a team called T&A, it would have been easy for Trish to be dismissed as just that. Instead, she clawed her way to a record seven Women's Championships in a Hall of Fame career.

SLAP SHOT

Trish's mettle was on full display at *WrestleMania X-7*. Subject to humiliation for several weeks by Mr. McMahon, Stratus got her revenge by giving the Chairman a smack that echoed off the Houston Astrodome roof. This brazen act made Trish a fan favorite and emboldened her to set out for a career in the ring. Months later at *Survivor Series 2001*, she earned her first Women's Championship in impressive fashion, defeating five other competitors in a Six-Pack Challenge.

SHE'S HARDCORE!

As her career unfolded, her rivalries intensified. The powerful Jazz spoiled Trish's *WrestleMania X8* homecoming in her native Toronto. However, in May 2002, Trish won the now-defunct Hardcore Title, one of few women to do so. The following week, she met Jazz again North of the Border. In a physical match at the Air Canada Centre, Trish grabbed her second Women's Title. Soon, she became the target of Divas such as Molly Holly, Victoria, and Gail Kim.

In 2003, Trish ran her Championship tally to four and gained her first *WrestleMania* win at *WrestleMania XIX*. At *Raw 10th Anniversary*, she was named Diva of the Decade. Though she had obliterated any notions that she was merely "eye candy," her stunning looks still earned her perennial "Babe of the Year" honors and attracted several suitors.

Among the most eager were Chris Jericho and Christian. As both Superstars attempted to woo Trish, she led Jericho to believe their connection was real. However, at *WrestleMania XX*, she double-crossed Y2J and revealed a devilish side by sharing a sultry kiss with Christian.

TRISH AND LITA

Though they are now friends, Trish vs. Lita was one of WWE's fiercest rivalries. Over the years, the two Superstars proved to be each other's equal. In several hard-hitting matches, each earned bragging rights by winning Women's Championships over the other. At times, it was debatable what was more intense, the in-ring action or the insults exchanged on the microphone.

On a historic episode of *Raw* in December 2004, the bitter foes became the first women to main event WWE's flagship program. Lita prevailed with the Title on the line, only for Trish to reclaim the gold a month later. Even when Lita was out of action, she tried (unsuccessfully) to harm Trish by training Christie Hemme to face her at *WrestleMania 21*.

#1 FAN

By October 2005, Trish had millions of adoring fans but none quite like Mickie James. The spunky newcomer first seemed innocent in her admiration of Trish. This admiration, however, proved to be an unhealthy obsession. When Trish became unnerved by Mickie and tried to terminate the friendship, James became unhinged. At *WrestleMania 22*, the deranged Superstar upended Stratus for the Women's Title.

The two rivals battled for the better part of a year until September 11, 2006. In Trish's final match on *Raw*, she defeated Mickie and offered her a hug following the match. Maybe that was all she wanted all along!

RETIREMENT

Trish Stratus closed the book on her active career in the most appropriate way imaginable. In her native Toronto, she faced and defeated her nemesis, Lita, one last time. The storybook win afforded Trish the opportunity to retire while basking in the familiar Championship glow.

Today, Trish remains busy while keeping her WWE ties. At *WrestleMania XXVII*, she proved she hadn't lost a step by teaming with John Morrison and *Jersey Shore's* Nicole "Snooki" Polizzi for a victory. She also joined Stone Cold in 2011 as a trainer on *Tough Enough* and appeared at *Raw 1000* in 2012.

Prior to *WrestleMania 29*, the WWE Hall of Fame got a dose of Stratusfaction as Trish was inducted by WWE Principal Owner, Stephanie McMahon.

Booker T, Eddie Guerrero, Rey Mysterio and the incomparable Undertaker, *SmackDown* proved it was no "B-show." This healthy competition within WWE brought out the best in both brands and provided many Superstars the opportunity to carry the torch as the main attraction.

SmackDown celebrated its 15-year anniversary in October of 2014 and the following month, shifted back to its original Thursday timeslot after several years of airing on Friday nights. In 2016, it found a new home on the USA Network, putting both of WWE's signature shows on the same network for the first time ever. Since then, *SmackDown* viewers have enjoyed Superstars such as Roman Reigns, Dean Ambrose, Kevin Owens, Sasha Banks, and others eager to settle scores. In May 2016, it was announced that SmackDown would soon become a live, Tuesday night broadcast.

The giant metallic fist that first adorned its set may have been relegated to the WWE warehouse, but *SmackDown* is still going strong and will celebrate its milestone 900th episode in November 2016.

METAL

1999 - 2002

Airing Saturday afternoons in syndication, *Metal* featured in-ring WWE action. Kevin Kelly and Dr. Tom Prichard called the matches from ringside.

JAKKED

1999 - 2002

Airing Saturday nights in syndication, *Jakked* featured in-ring WWE action. Over the course of the show's history, matches were called by Michael Cole, Michael Hayes, and Jonathan Coachman.

2001 - 2002

Telecast live from WWE studios in Connecticut, *Excess* was touted as the premiere show for TNN's Slammin' Saturday Night lineup of programming. The show's format featured two hours of highlights and interviews, as well as the opportunity for fans to call in and talk to their favorite Superstars.

TOUGH ENOUGH

2001 - 2004;
2011 - 2015

Think you have what it takes to be a WWE Superstar? In June of 2001 fans of sports-entertainment had the opportunity to enter a competition based program with the goal of winning a WWE contract. In the inaugural season, 13 out of over 4000 that auditioned were invited to participate. Contestants were drilled relentlessly by an expert staff of WWE veterans. Over the years, *Tough Enough* raised the stakes and in 2004, offered a $1,000,000 contract to the winner.

After a seven-year hiatus, the show returned the night after *WrestleMania XXVII* with an ornery new host, Stone Cold Steve Austin. The Rattlesnake's presence made the rigors of training even more intense. In 2015, *Tough Enough* returned with Chris Jericho as its figurehead. Accomplished grapplers such as Daniel Bryan and Paige served as judges.

Season 1:
Maven Huffman & Nidia Guenard

Season 2:
Linda Miles & Jackie Gayda

Season 3:
John Hennigan & Matt Cappotelli

Season 4: Daniel Puder

Season 5: Andy Leavine

Season 6: Josh Bredle & Sara Lee

CONFIDENTIAL

2002 - 2004

Hosted by "Mean" Gene Okerlund, *Confidential* was known for pulling the curtain back to allow fans to see inside the sports-entertainment industry. The show touched on topics previously considered taboo, including the truth behind the Montreal Incident and Stone Cold Steve Austin's highly-publicized departure from WWE in 2002.

2002 - 2005

A weekend syndication show, *AfterBurn* highlighted the past week's high points from *SmackDown* and *Velocity*, including matches and interviews.

BOTTOM LINE

2002 - 2005

A weekly syndicated magazine show, *Bottom Line* looked back at the week that was on *Monday Night Raw* and *Heat*. Marc Loyd served as the show's main host; Jonathan Coachman and Todd Grisham also briefly held the honors.

VELOCITY
2002 - 2006

Much like *Heat* did for *Raw*, *Velocity* served as platform to highlight the recent action on *SmackDown*, as well as feature exclusive matches involving the brand's Superstars. In 2005, the show moved from television screens to computer monitors when it began streaming over WWE.com.

2003 - Present

A patriotic television event like no other, *Tribute To The Troops* is one of the ways WWE supports the U.S. Military and says "Thank you." This annual event has been broadcast from Iraq, Afghanistan and military bases across the United States. Featuring incredible matches, soldiers have also been treated to WWE Hall of Famer appearances, as well as star-studded guests from Hollywood, the world of music, and special video messages from U.S. Presidents George W. Bush and Barack Obama.

2004 - Present

Originally hosted by Todd Grisham and Ivory, *WWE Experience* began as a one-hour recap of the week that was in WWE. The show also took viewers behind the scenes to see Superstars' favorite activities outside the ring.

The show went off the air in the United States when *WWE A.M. Raw* made its debut but it continues to appear on television stations around the world. Josh Matthews, Jack Korpella and Matt Striker all served as hosts of *WWE Experience* before Renee Young assumed the current role in 2013.

2005 - 2014

A.M. Raw condensed the two most recent hours or Monday Night Raw into a fast-paced sixty minutes of action. The highlight show also featured a continuous ticker at the bottom of the screen where fans could catch up on the latest WWE news and test their knowledge with trivia and fun facts.

2006 - 2010 See page 102

WWE MADISON SQUARE GARDEN CLASSICS
2006 - 2009

Aired Wednesday nights on the MSG Network, Madison Square Garden Classics looked back at the greatest matches to ever take place in the "World's Most Famous Arena."

2008 - Present

Hosted by "Mean" Gene Okerlund, *Vintage Collection* is an overseas sensation and features classic matches from WWE's expansive library.

2009 - Present

A weekly show with lineage to the original Superstars of Wrestling, Superstars features competitors from all corners of WWE. A place where heated rivalries continue and are conceived, audiences never know when a new champion will be crowned and when new wars will be waged.

2010 - Present
See page 252

2012 - 2013

Aimed for a younger demographic, *Saturday Morning Slam* held a brief but memorable run on the CW network. Matches were contested with a more kid-friendly approach, yet still captivated older WWE Universe members who grew up watching sports-entertainment on Saturday mornings. WWE Hall of Famer Mick Foley served as General Manager, giving the "Hardcore Legend" a chance to display his jovial side.

TOTAL DIVAS

2013 -

The E! Network's smash hit reality show *Total Divas* has given fans an intimate look into the chaotic lives of WWE's top female performers for over five seasons. From locker room drama to relationships to trials and tribulations on both sides of the ropes, this eye-opening program has made household names out of its stars such as the Bella Twins, Natalya, Paige, Alicia Fox, and Eva Marie. In addition to raising the profile of the WWE Divas division to unprecedented heights, the show proved so successful that it earned a spinoff. *Total Bellas*, starring the title characters and their significant others, John Cena and Daniel Bryan, was announced to debut in the Fall of 2016.

WWE NETWORK

For WWE Network and its exciting slate of original programming, see page 404.

TYSON KIDD

HT 5'10" **WT** 195 lbs. **FROM** Calgary, Alberta, Canada

SIGNATURE MOVE Sharpshooter

The lineage of the historic Hart Family Dungeon can be traced all the way back to the 1940s. Over the course of its existence, the facility produced some of sports-entertainment's greatest names, including Bret Hart, Brian Pillman, and "Superstar" Billy Graham. Decades later, when the Dungeon finally closed its doors, it left the sports-entertainment world with one final graduate, Tyson Kidd.

With huge shoes to fill, Kidd made his WWE debut in early-2009. Upon arriving, he almost immediately joined forces with Hart family members David Hart Smith and Natalya. Collectively known as The Hart Dynasty, the trio set out to prove they were worthy of being in the same class as their legendary forefathers, which they accomplished by beating The Miz and Big Show for the Unified Tag Team Championship in April 2010.

More recently, Kidd enjoyed a successful stay at NXT, where he inexplicably developed a self-involved attitude. While not incredibly popular with the fans, Kidd's new arrogance catapulted him straight back to the main WWE roster where he formed a successful pairing with Cesaro. Together, Kidd and Cesaro defeated the Usos at *WWE Fastlane 2015* to claim the WWE Tag Team Championship.

Outside the ring, Kidd can be regularly seen alongside his wife, Natalya, on E's *Total Divas*. And when he's not be followed by reality television cameras, Kidd can be found posting photos of his beloved cats on social media.

TYSON TOMKO

HT 6'6" **WT** 275 lbs. **FROM** Jacksonville, Florida

SIGNATURE MOVE Big Boot

If there's a problem, Tyson Tomko could solve it. Introduced to WWE in April 2004, the behemoth was brought in as Christian's "Problem Solver" with the purpose of protecting "Captain Charisma" and his beautiful girlfriend, Trish Stratus, against Chris Jericho. A man of few words, Tomko used his unique appearance to intimidate fellow Superstars. In addition to sporting a bald skull and pointy goatee, his entire upper body was covered in tattoos. Coupled with his immense size, Tomko truly was an unmistakable figure.

In January 2005, Tomko and Christian challenged William Regal and Eugene for the World Tag Team Championship. A reign atop the tag scene was not to be, however, as Eugene pinned Tomko to retain the Titles. It was the closest the tattooed Superstar came to claiming a championship.

After Christian was drafted to *SmackDown* in June 2005, Tomko went on to gain moderate success on *Raw*. Using his big boot to flatten opponents, he racked up an impressive string of victories. Tomko formed a tag team with Snitsky before leaving WWE in the spring of 2006.

ULTIMATE WARRIOR

see page 361

ULTIMO DRAGON

HT 5'8" **WT** 185 lbs. **FROM** Nagoya, Japan

SIGNATURE MOVE Asai DDT

Said to be Bruce Lee's final student, Ultimo Dragon, which translates to "Last Dragon," coupled a dizzying martial arts repertoire with a high-flying, daredevil offense. It was this unforgettable pairing that made him extra dangerous.

Born Yoshihiro Asai, Ultimo Dragon became such an international superstar during his time in Japan and Mexico that the sports-entertainment world named the Asai moonsault after him. At one point, he even held ten championships at the same time.

His most successful North American run came as a member of WCW. While there, he defeated Eddie Guerrero and Dean Malenko to become a two-time Cruiserweight Champion. In 2003, the masked Superstar took his legacy with him to WWE, where he competed mainly in the cruiserweight division. In addition to teaming with Rey Mysterio, he clashed with Tajiri, who shared a similar background, Shannon Moore, and Eddie and Chavo Guerrero.

He then returned to Japan and Mexico, and trained students in the fighting disciplines prevalent in both countries. In 2014, he appeared on a rare show in North Korea.

ULTIMATE WARRIOR

HT	6'2"
WT	280 lbs.
FROM	Parts Unknown

With an unmatched energy, Ultimate Warrior exploded onto the scene in 1987. In record time, the face-painted Superstar became a household name and sports-entertainment icon. He had a natural charisma that was undeniable, which he combined with an energetic entrance and chiseled frame that made him an instant hit with fans. Within months of his debut, Warrior had turned back many of WWE's top names on his way to becoming one of the company's top draws.

Warrior claimed his first Championship when he ended Honky Tonk Man's record fifteen-month Intercontinental Championship reign at *SummerSlam 1988*. The now-famous match lasted a mere thirty seconds and went a long way in proving that nobody was safe from Warrior's intensity. With the Intercontinental Championship around his waist, Warrior became one of WWE's most marketable Superstars. It wasn't long before arenas were filled with Ultimate Warrior T-shirts.

Warrior's superhuman strength carried him to a nearly eight-month Intercontinental Championship reign. Along the way, he successfully defended against the likes of King Haku, Akeem, and Greg Valentine. It eventually took outside interference from Bobby Heenan for Rick Rude to pry the Title from Warrior at *WrestleMania V*.

Warrior later got his revenge on Rude when he defeated him at *SummerSlam 1989* to reclaim the Intercontinental Championship. His second stint with the Title proved to be even more popular with the fans, setting the stage for an inevitable showdown with WWE Champion Hulk Hogan. WWE's two most popular Superstars finally met at *WrestleMania VI* in an historic encounter dubbed, "The Ultimate Challenge." With both Titles on the line, Warrior defeated Hogan in front of more than 67,000 fans in Toronto's SkyDome. The victory was capped off by an amazing fireworks display, a precursor to the pyrotechnics seen on today's WWE programming.

As WWE Champion, Warrior successfully fended off Mr. Perfect, Randy Savage, and Ted DiBiase, among others, en route to what appeared to be a never-ending Title reign. But his whirlwind run at the top was eventually silenced when Sgt. Slaughter, with some help from Savage, defeated him for the Title at the 1991 *Royal Rumble*.

With retribution foremost on his mind, Warrior focused his attention on ending the career of the Macho Man, which he succeeded in doing when he defeated Savage in a Retirement Match at *WrestleMania VII*. The victory helped catapult Warrior back toward the top of the card. But before he could reestablish himself, the popular Superstar abruptly left WWE.

WARRIOR RETURNS

In the years that followed, Warrior made two brief returns to WWE. First in 1992, he shocked *WrestleMania VIII* viewers when he ran to the ring to aid The Hulkster from an attack at the hands of Sid Justice and Papa Shango. Warrior's return resulted in a memorable rivalry with Shango, who cast several spells on the popular Superstar, one which caused Warrior to vomit uncontrollably.

In 1996, Warrior returned at *WrestleMania XII* to defeat Triple H. He then went on to battle Jerry "The King" Lawler, Goldust, and Isaac Yankem before once again abruptly leaving WWE.

HALL OF FAME

After more than a decade of being at odds, Ultimate Warrior and WWE made amends in 2013 when the popular Superstar became a prominent figure in the *WWE 2K14* video game. The working relationship extended into the next year where Warrior was given the ultimate honor of being inducted into the WWE Hall of Fame.

The night after his induction, Warrior appeared on *Raw* to share some of the most prophetic words ever spoken on WWE television. "No WWE talent becomes a legend on their own," he said. "Every man's heart one day beats its final beat. His lungs breathe their final breath. And if what that man did in his life makes the blood pulse through the body of others and makes them believe deeper in something larger than life then his essence, his spirit will be immortalized."

Sadly, within hours of his memorable *Raw* appearance, Ultimate Warrior passed away at age 54. Though gone, his memory lives on with WWE's annual Warrior Award and, more importantly, through the lives of his daughters, Mattigan and Indiana, and widow, Dana.

I NEED NOT THE NORMALS TO PROTECT ME FROM WHAT I FIND MOST COMFORTING: THE CHARGE OF PAIN AND THE SMELL OF COMBAT!

UMAGA

HT 6'4" **WT** 350 lbs. **FROM** The Isle of Samoa
SIGNATURE MOVE Samoan Spike

The Samoan Bulldozer, Umaga, was a vicious giant whose raw power and incredible speed made him one of WWE's most feared Superstars. Introduced in 2006 by his slippery manager Armando Alejandro Estrada, Umaga immediately targeted the incomparable "Nature Boy" Ric Flair. After several months of dominance, he became the #1 contender for the WWE Championship.

On February 19, 2007, Umaga was named Mr. McMahon's representative in the Battle of the Billionaires at *WrestleMania 23*. That same night he crushed Jeff Hardy to become the Intercontinental Champion. At *Backlash*, Umaga teamed with Mr. McMahon again. This time the duo, along with Shane McMahon, defeated Bobby Lashley to make the WWE Chairman the new ECW Champion.

The Samoan Bulldozer continued to aim his dreaded Samoan Spike at WWE's most beloved heroes. He clashed with Batista at *WrestleMania XXIV* and challenged Triple H for the WWE Championship, showing animalistic ferocity and complete disregard for humanity in each encounter.

This monster from the legendary Anoa'i family soon left WWE and toured the globe on independent cards before his untimely passing in 2009.

THE UN-AMERICANS

MEMBERS Lance Storm, Christian, Test, & William Regal

Led by Lance Storm, this collection of resident malcontents formed in June 2002 on *SmackDown*. Citing unfounded claims of decades-long patterns of bias in WWE, this group spewed anti-American rhetoric wherever they traveled. Their antics were hammered home in the ring as they attempted, but failed, on several occasions to burn the American flag. The Un-Americans' plans were thwarted by the likes of Booker T, Goldust, Bradshaw, Kane, Rey Mysterio, Rikishi, Edge, Undertaker, and Hulk Hogan.

The group did see success as Christian and Lance Storm captured the World Tag Team Championships on July 21, 2002 from Edge and "Hollywood" Hogan. They held the Titles for two months, however, when they lost the Titles two months later the team eventually crumbled.

UNCLE CLETUS

FROM Bitters, Arkansas

According to Henry Godwinn, his Uncle Cletus was "one of the dirtiest, meanest S.O.B.'s around." And upon making his September 1997 debut, Cletus wasted no time proving his nephew correct when he whacked Mosh with a horseshoe, which helped give the Godwinns an all-important victory over the Headbangers.

In the weeks that followed, Cletus continued to stick his nose in his nephews' business, most notably at *Badd Blood 1997* where the Godwinns claimed the World Tag Team Championships from the Headbangers. Cletus' interference, however, didn't always lead to victory. In October 1997, Cletus inadvertently hit Henry with his horseshoe, allowing the Legion of Doom to defeat the farmers for the tag Titles. Afterward, the Godwinns attacked Cletus, making him pay for his mistake. Cletus was never seen again.

UNCLE ELMER

HT 6'10" **WT** 430 lbs. **FROM** Pascagoula, Mississippi
SIGNATURE MOVE Big Splash

Introduced to WWE audiences in 1985, Uncle Elmer proudly stood by the side of his nephew, Hillbilly Jim, and later, Cousin Luke and Cousin Junior. As far as technical skills were concerned, the big man didn't necessarily have any. Furthermore, he was as slow as a turtle, but he did possess a more than 400-pound frame that struck fear into his competition. His size was such a factor, in fact, that he once beat an opponent in just six seconds after dropping all his weight on him.

In a world where weddings rarely go as planned, Uncle Elmer actually pulled it off when he married his longtime girlfriend, Joyce, on *Saturday Night's Main Event* in October 1985. The nuptials featured some major star power, as Elmer's wedding party consisted of both Hulk Hogan and Andre the Giant. The following year, the newlywed competed in the biggest match of his career when he lost to Adrian Adonis at *WrestleMania 2*. Shortly afterward, he retreated back to his bride and farm in Mississippi.

UNCLE ZEBEKIAH

As identical twins, Jacob and Eli Blu were never above using their similar appearances to fool opponents and referees. And while their trickery was certainly dastardly, it paled in comparison to the rule breaking their manager, Uncle Zebekiah, often employed.

The bushy-bearded manager and his dirty tactics helped catapult the Blu Brothers toward the top of WWE's tag division, but the duo could never seem to win when it counted most. Jacob and Eli eventually left WWE shortly after losing to the Smokin' Gunns at *SummerSlam 1995*.

No longer at the side of the Blus, Zebekiah remained in WWE to manage the hard-hitting Justin "Hawk" Bradshaw. With Zebekiah leading the way, Bradshaw seemingly cared more about inflicting pain than earning victories, as evidenced by the big Texan getting intentionally disqualified for viciously attacking Sycho Sid with a bullrope in July 1996.

Unfortunately for Zebekiah, his partnership with Bradshaw soured after the manager inadvertently nailed his protégé with a branding iron. An upset Bradshaw attacked Zebekiah, who fled WWE shortly after.

UNDERTAKER
see page 364 see page 364

THE UNION

MEMBERS Mankind, Big Show, Ken Shamrock, & Test

Frustrated employees huddle in office corners worldwide to whisper about how unfairly they're treated. Rarely do they have the courage to voice their feelings aloud. When four WWE Superstars felt this way, however, they refused to sit back silently. Instead, they formed a union and waged war on their boss.

In May 1999 former Corporation members Mankind, Big Show, Ken Shamrock, and Test banded together to form the "Union of People You Oughta Respect, Son" or U.P.Y.O.U.R.S., which was a blatant sign of disrespect toward their former boss, Shane McMahon. Upon their debut, The Union was able to gain some of the respect they were looking for when they defeated McMahon's Corporate Ministry at *Over the Edge*. The stable silently disbanded shortly after the win.

UNITED STATES CHAMPIONSHIP
see page 368 see page 368

THE U.S. EXPRESS

| **MEMBERS** | Barry Windham & Mike Rotundo |
| **COMBINED WT** | 505 lbs. |

Blessed with boyish good looks, Barry Windham and Mike Rotundo teamed up in 1984 and quickly became America's sweethearts. Collectively referred to as the U.S. Express, the duo captured the World Tag Team Championship a mere three months after making their debut when they defeated Adrian Adonis and Dick Murdoch in Hartford, Connecticut.

Behind some outside interference from "Classy" Freddie Blassie, the U.S. Express lost their Titles to Iron Sheik and Nikolai Volkoff at the inaugural *WrestleMania*. Unable to stand by and allow the rule-breaking Iranian and Russian parade around America with the gold, Windham and Rotunda focused on exacting revenge, which they gained in June 1985 when they regained the Titles from their rivals.

Later that year, Windham left WWE to return to the Florida territories. But the U.S. Express would eventually reunite more than twenty years later when they signed on to battle Sheik and Volkoff in a *WrestleMania* rematch on *Raw*. Unfortunately, the match never got underway, as Jillian interrupted the proceedings to sing "Born in the U.S.A."

THE USOS

| **MEMBERS** | Jimmy Uso & Jey Uso | **COMBINED WT** | 479 lbs. |
| **FROM** | San Francisco, California | | |

As members of the famed Anoa'i family, Jimmy and Jey Uso have greatness flowing through their veins. Among the notable Superstars the twins share bloodlines with include father Rikishi, great uncles The Wild Samoans, and The Rock. And like the successful Samoans before them, The Usos are constructing an amazing legacy of excellence within WWE.

Jimmy and Jey followed in their ancestors' rich history of tag team success in March 2014 when they defeated the New Age Outlaws to claim their first taste of WWE Tag Team Championship glory. Carrying on the family tradition, The Usos went on to successfully defend the Titles for more than two-hundred days, turning back the likes of the Real Americans and RybAxel in the process.

The Usos were ultimately dethroned by Gold and Stardust in September, but weren't without the Titles for long. Just a few months later, Jimmy and Jey regained the gold when they defeated The Miz and Damien Mizdow in December. The victory went a long way in solidifying The Usos as WWE's premier tandem, which they were officially recognized as when they were named Tag Team of the Year at the 2014 Slammy Awards.

Proving 2014 was no fluke, The Usos went on to claim the Slammy for Tag Team of the Year again in 2015. Today, they continue to cement their legacy as one of the greatest tag teams of their generation.

UNDERTAKER

HT	6'10½"
WT	299 lbs.
FROM	Death Valley

SIGNATURE MOVE
Tombstone Piledriver, Chokeslam, Last
Ride, Old School, Hell's Gate, Snake Eyes

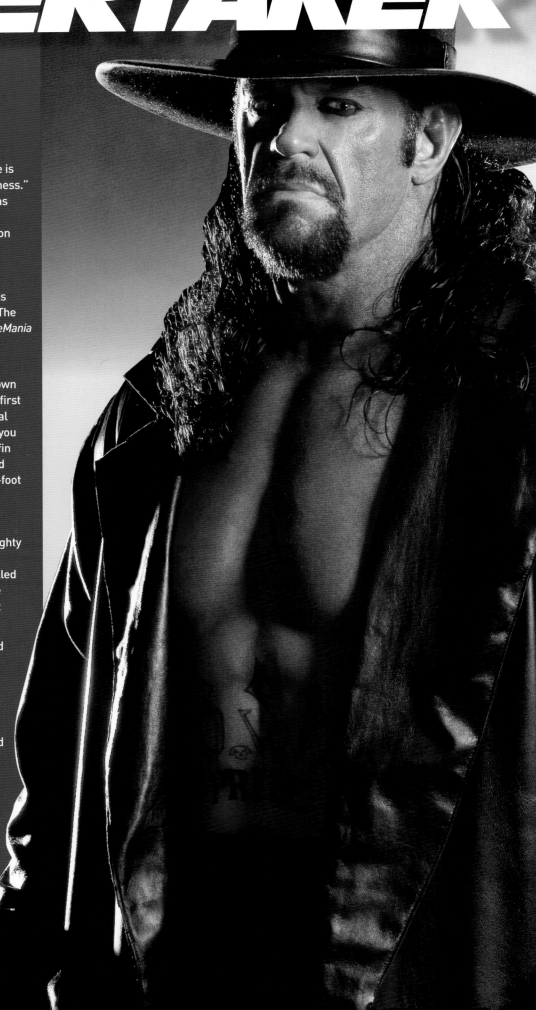

From darkness, he emerged to build a dynasty second to none. He is the "The Deadman." He is the "Phenom." He is the "Lord of Darkness." He is Undertaker. The mysterious Superstar from Death Valley was unveiled at the 1990 *Survivor Series*. Over the next 25 years, The Deadman would rule WWE and *WrestleMania* like a vengeful demon cast from the fiery pits of damnation.

DEADMAN WALKING

The first chapter in Undertaker's remarkable *WrestleMania* epic was penned in Los Angeles in 1991. Under the tutelage of Paul Bearer, The Phenom destroyed Jimmy "Superfly" Snuka. This emphatic *WrestleMania* win catapulted The Deadman straight to main-event status.

Undertaker spent the next several months using caskets and his mysteriously powerful urn to exploit his opponents' fear of their own mortality. At *Survivor Series 1991*, he defeated Hulk Hogan for his first WWE Championship, capping off a foreboding rookie year. Colossal competitors looking to rid WWE of Undertaker soon learned that you can't kill what is already dead. Undertaker won the first-ever Coffin Match at the 1992 *Survivor Series*, closing the lid on the 400-pound Kamala. The following year, The Phenom topped the nearly eight-foot Giant Gonzalez at *WrestleMania IX*.

TWO UNDERTAKERS!

Many believed Undertaker had finally met his match when the mighty Yokozuna and a posse of oversized Superstars teamed up to stuff him in a casket at *Royal Rumble 1994*. However, an eerie smoke filled the arena, followed by the familiar gong of Undertaker's entrance theme. The Deadman then issued an ominous warning, "I will not rest in peace."

In the summer of 1994, both "Million Dollar Man" Ted DiBiase and Paul Bearer claimed to have found Undertaker. At *SummerSlam*, Bearer's Undertaker proved to be the real thing, ousting the imposter with three Tombstone Piledrivers. His dark dominance continued throughout the mid-1990s. When the demented Mankind landed in WWE, an intense rivalry was born along with two revolutionary match types, the Boiler Room Brawl and Buried Alive Match. It also marked the shocking end to Undertaker's alliance with Paul Bearer, who his used his mystical urn against him at *SummerSlam 1996*.

Despite losing his manager to Mankind, Undertaker earned a WWE Championship opportunity against Sycho Sid at *WrestleMania 13*. Following a skull-crushing Tombstone, The Phenom reclaimed the Title he lost more than five years earlier. The victory catapulted Undertaker back to the top of the sports-entertainment scene.

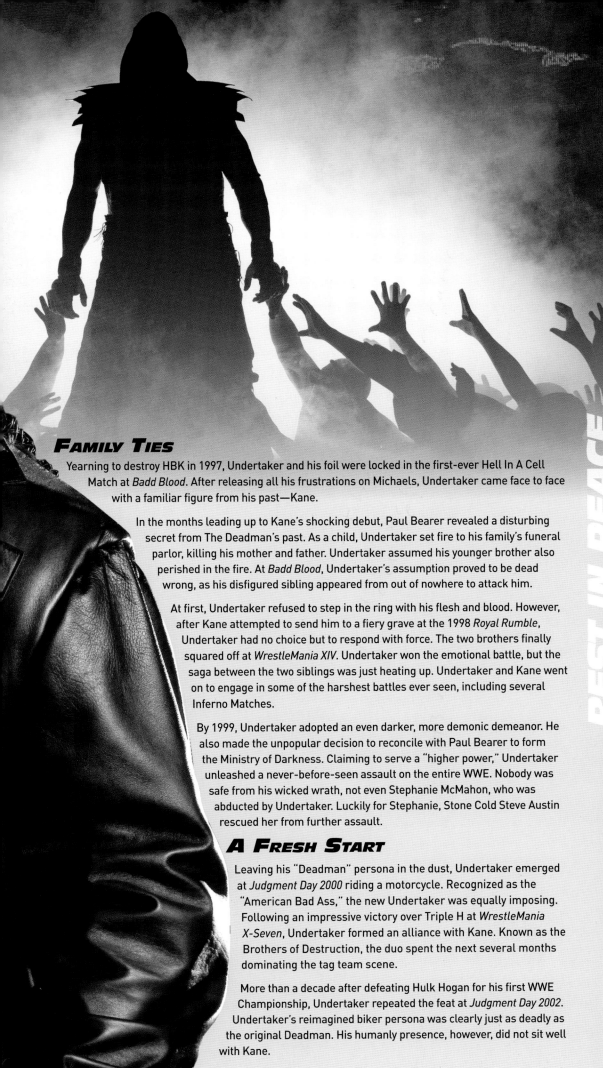

FAMILY TIES

Yearning to destroy HBK in 1997, Undertaker and his foil were locked in the first-ever Hell In A Cell Match at *Badd Blood*. After releasing all his frustrations on Michaels, Undertaker came face to face with a familiar figure from his past—Kane.

In the months leading up to Kane's shocking debut, Paul Bearer revealed a disturbing secret from The Deadman's past. As a child, Undertaker set fire to his family's funeral parlor, killing his mother and father. Undertaker assumed his younger brother also perished in the fire. At *Badd Blood*, Undertaker's assumption proved to be dead wrong, as his disfigured sibling appeared from out of nowhere to attack him.

At first, Undertaker refused to step in the ring with his flesh and blood. However, after Kane attempted to send him to a fiery grave at the 1998 *Royal Rumble*, Undertaker had no choice but to respond with force. The two brothers finally squared off at *WrestleMania XIV*. Undertaker won the emotional battle, but the saga between the two siblings was just heating up. Undertaker and Kane went on to engage in some of the harshest battles ever seen, including several Inferno Matches.

By 1999, Undertaker adopted an even darker, more demonic demeanor. He also made the unpopular decision to reconcile with Paul Bearer to form the Ministry of Darkness. Claiming to serve a "higher power," Undertaker unleashed a never-before-seen assault on the entire WWE. Nobody was safe from his wicked wrath, not even Stephanie McMahon, who was abducted by Undertaker. Luckily for Stephanie, Stone Cold Steve Austin rescued her from further assault.

A FRESH START

Leaving his "Deadman" persona in the dust, Undertaker emerged at *Judgment Day 2000* riding a motorcycle. Recognized as the "American Bad Ass," the new Undertaker was equally imposing. Following an impressive victory over Triple H at *WrestleMania X-Seven*, Undertaker formed an alliance with Kane. Known as the Brothers of Destruction, the duo spent the next several months dominating the tag team scene.

More than a decade after defeating Hulk Hogan for his first WWE Championship, Undertaker repeated the feat at *Judgment Day 2002*. Undertaker's reimagined biker persona was clearly just as deadly as the original Deadman. His humanly presence, however, did not sit well with Kane.

The fiery family hostility returned and Kane helped Mr. McMahon bury his brother alive at *Survivor Series 2003*. As mounds of dirt covered Undertaker's seemingly lifeless body, it appeared Kane had rid WWE of Undertaker.

THE DEADMAN RETURNS

Much to Kane's disbelief, Undertaker made his triumphant return at *WrestleMania XX*, once again assuming the ghoulish persona that first wreaked havoc over WWE in the 1990s. He defeated Kane to improve his *WrestleMania* record to an astonishing 12-0. The Phenom's iconic status made him the perfect target for the brash youngster Randy Orton. But the third-generation Superstar could not vanquish Undertaker's spotless *WrestleMania* record. Instead, "The Legend Killer" became unlucky victim number thirteen.

By 2007, there were two glaring holes on Undertaker's impressive résumé: he had never won a Royal Rumble or captured the World Heavyweight Championship. In January 2007, he filled one void when he last eliminated Shawn Michaels to win the Royal Rumble. Winning that match allowed him to meet Batista at *WrestleMania 23* for the World Heavyweight Championship, which he won after a Tombstone Piledriver. Undertaker duplicated his efforts the following year when he toppled Edge at *WrestleMania XXIV* to become a two-time World Heavyweight Champion.

Edge and his wife, Vickie Guerrero, worked in cahoots to force Undertaker out of WWE. Fortunately for the WWE Universe, Edge and Vickie had a bitter falling out, resulting in Vickie reinstituting Undertaker two months later. Undertaker made Edge pay by Chokeslamming him through the mat at *SummerSlam 2008*, then setting the ring ablaze.

THE STREAK PUT IN JEOPARDY

With his *WrestleMania* appearances now eclipsing legendary status, Shawn Michaels demanded a shot to end The Streak at *WrestleMania 25*. In what is widely considered one of the most epic matches in WWE history, Undertaker won the encounter to run his record to 17-0, then went on to claim the World Heavyweight Championship from CM Punk later in the year. Shawn Michaels, demanding a second chance at Undertaker's *WrestleMania* streak, cost him the Title by interfering in his match at *Elimination Chamber*. Undertaker laid out the terms for the *WrestleMania* rematch—if Shawn Michaels lost, he must retire. The "Streak versus Career" Match took place at *WrestleMania XXVI*. In the end, Undertaker sent Michaels into retirement with a Tombstone.

Shortly after his victory, Undertaker was put out of action by an unknown assailant who was later revealed to be Kane. The brothers rekindled their rivalry. In a Buried Alive Match at *Hell In A Cell*, Paul Bearer and Nexus helped Kane bury Undertaker, who then wasn't seen for months.

THE END OF AN ERA

Hints of Undertaker's return first appeared during the 2011 *Royal Rumble*. His return on February 21 was interrupted by Triple H, making his first appearance in nearly a year. Following in the footsteps of his friend, Shawn Michaels, The Game sought to end The Streak. The No-Holds Barred Match between WWE's two "Last Outlaws" at *WrestleMania XXVII* ended in a win for Undertaker, but he left the ring on a stretcher while Triple H walked out under his own power.

Undertaker vanished from WWE for the rest of 2011, returning in January 2012 to demand a rematch against an initially-reluctant Triple H. The two met at *WrestleMania XXVIII* in a Hell In A Cell Match refereed by Shawn Michaels. The brutal encounter left both men bloodied and battered, but in the end Undertaker claimed victory and pushed his streak to 20-0. Leaving the ring, the three proud warriors supported each other and walked into the night, together, symbolizing the "End of an Era."

THE DEATH OF THE STREAK

In 2013, as WWE and the WWE Universe mourned the loss of the great Paul Bearer, Undertaker defended the honor of his late manager by topping CM Punk at *WrestleMania 29*. The Paul Heyman-led Punk had incited The Deadman by disrespecting Bearer's memory. Undertaker made him and his slimy manager pay, running his celebrated streak to 21-0. Heyman never let go of his disappointment. The following year, he sent another one of his clients, Brock Lesnar, into battle for a chance to do what most observers had long deemed impossible.

Until *WrestleMania 30*, there were three guarantees in life: death, taxes, and The Streak. That all changed in one shocking night in New Orleans, when The Streak met The Beast. After three jarring F-5s to The Deadman, Lesnar achieved the unthinkable. As the referee's hand fell for the third time, disbelief flooded the Super Dome, millions of homes, and social media. 21-0 became 21-1.

RESURRECTED

The Streak may have been dead, but Undertaker's legacy can never be buried. Somewhere in Bray Wyatt's warped mind, he knew this. Yet the Sinister Sermonizer made it his mission to lure The Deadman back to WWE's Grandest Stage, taunting him with a series of cryptic messages. Wyatt is the New Face of Fear in WWE, but he should not have raised the dead. Resurrected and looking like the grim reaper of justice he always was, Undertaker reclaimed his yard, sealing Wyatt's fate with a hellish Tombstone.

Undertaker reaffirmed his status as the greatest warrior to ever grace a *WrestleMania* stage. Still, his one blemish and Lesnar's endless gloating ignited a thirst for revenge. At *Battleground 2015*, Undertaker made a shocking return to cost Lesnar the WWE World Heavyweight Championship. This led to two brutal and controversial showdowns that saw Undertaker the victor at *SummerSlam* and Lesnar grabbing the win at *Hell in a Cell*.

Following Undertaker's heroic effort inside the steel, Bray Wyatt came calling once again, this time with his reunited flock of followers to help do his bidding. The sadistic family's attacks brought the Brothers of Destruction together once again. At *Survivor Series 2015*, the devil's favorite sons took the Wyatt clan to hell and back. On a night when Undertaker's incomparable 25 years of destruction were celebrated, it was The Phenom providing the final death knell with a Tombstone.

Over a quarter century, Undertaker has established himself in many discerning minds as the greatest WWE Superstar of all time. So when Shane McMahon returned to WWE seeking control over his father's kingdom, Mr. McMahon decided to schedule his only son inside Hell in a Cell with The Phenom himself at *WrestleMania 32*. The Undertaker turned back Shane-O-Mac to go 23-1 at *WrestleMania*.

VADER

HT	6'5"	**WT**	450 lbs.	**FROM**	The Rocky Mountains
SIGNATURE MOVE		Vader Splash, Vader Bomb			

Before ever stepping foot in a WWE ring, the man they call Vader earned a worldwide reputation as a bona fide tough man. At well over four-hundred pounds, he possessed the power of a super heavyweight, while also owning the unbelievable ability to fly through the air like a cruiserweight.

Vader's earliest days were spent in the AWA, but it wasn't until he went to Japan in the late-1980s that the Colorado native began to become a true force. A three-time IWGP Heavyweight Champion, Vader's name is regularly mentioned alongside such Japanese legends as The Great Muta and Tatsumi Fujinami, who The Mastodon beat for the title in January 1991.

Recognizing his greatness, WCW lured Vader back to the United States in the early-1990s. As many predicted, his success easily translated to American rings, as Vader secured three WCW Championships, as well as a reign with the U.S. Title.

The Mastodon made his WWE debut at the 1996 *Royal Rumble*. While impressive, his momentum was almost immediately halted when he was suspended for attacking WWE President Gorilla Monsoon. When he finally returned, Vader created a scary path of destruction that claimed many of WWE's biggest names, including Yokozuna, Razor Ramon, and Sycho Sid.

Vader's impressive record eventually earned him a WWE Championship opportunity against Shawn Michaels at *SummerSlam*. In an odd turn of events, The Mastodon actually defeated HBK twice that night (by countout and disqualification) before ultimately falling to the champ via pinfall.

The following year, Vader traded in manager Jim Cornette for Paul Bearer. The move proved to be wise, as his new manager helped him gain a huge victory over Undertaker at the 1997 *Royal Rumble*. Bearer also paired Vader with Mankind in an attempt to claim tag team gold. The duo nearly dethroned Owen Hart and Davey Boy Smith at *WrestleMania 13*, but fell just short after the match was declared a double countout. Following losses to Edge and Bradshaw in late 1998, Vader disappeared from the WWE scene, but will long be remembered as one of the most dominant forces sports-entertainment has ever witnessed.

VAL VENIS

HT	6'3"	**WT**	244 lbs.	**FROM**	Las Vegas, Nevada
SIGNATURE MOVE		Money Shot			

"Hello Ladies!"

Val Venis emerged with a towel around his waist and performed gyrations before his matches that left female fans in a hypnotic trance. The Big Valbowski often made waves in WWE by seducing the wives and sisters of other Superstars and managers. His actions resulted in battles against Kaientai, Goldust, and Ken Shamrock. In the ring, this sinful Superstar proved that his skills extended beyond his lusty exploits.

At *St. Valentine's Day Massacre 1999*, Venis defeated Shamrock for the Intercontinental Title. At *Armageddon 1999*, he defeated British Bulldog and D-Lo Brown in a Triple Threat Match to become European Champion.

In 2000, Venis became the antithesis of his former self when he joined the Right To Censor. Later, he became Chief of Staff to *Raw* GM, Eric Bischoff. Not wanting the association with Bischoff to tarnish the name he cultivated earlier in his career, he operated under the name Chief Morley.

Working as an authority figure ultimately left Val unsatisfied, so he returned to his true calling, making the ladies swoon while showing off his impressive in-ring repertoire.

THE VALIANT BROTHERS

MEMBERS	Jimmy Valiant, Johnny Valiant, & Jerry Valiant
COMBINED WT	490 lbs.

"Handsome" Jimmy and "Luscious" Johnny Valiant were two of the most charismatic characters of the 1970s. With their bleached blond hair and outrageous ring attire, they possessed a collective magnetism that made them tough not to like, despite their villainous status.

Within days of their 1974 arrival in WWE, they defeated Dean Ho and Tony Garea for the World Tag Team Championship. They would go on to hold the Titles for more than one year, longer than any other tandem at that time. Demolition's reign of the late 1980s is the only one to top Jimmy and Johnny in length.

After a brief hiatus, The Valiants returned to WWE in 1978. This time, however, Jimmy stepped aside and brother "Gentleman" Jerry stepped in. With Jimmy serving as manager, Johnny and Jerry defeated Larry Zbyszko and Tony Garea for the World Tag Team Championship in March 1979.

Jimmy and Johnny Valiant took their rightful place alongside the all-time best when they were inducted into the WWE Hall of Fame in 1996.

UNITED STATES CHAMPIONSHIP

Today's fans recognize the United States Championship as the Title defended in WWE arenas by the likes of Rusev, Dean Ambrose, and Kalisto. However, what many might not realize is that the U.S. Championship had its start in the NWA in 1975.

Harley Race, Terry Funk, Magnum T. A., and a host of other legendary names drove the highways of the southern United States in the 1970s and 1980s, defending the Title in small arenas in Florida, North Carolina, and Virginia. When the Championship became exclusive to WCW in 1991, it was defended nationwide by Sting, Rick Rude, and Dustin Rhodes.

The U.S. Championship appeared in WWE with the purchase of WCW in 2001. Unfortunately, fans had less than one year to truly appreciate the Title, as it was unified with the Intercontinental Championship when Edge defeated Test in November 2001. But the prestigious Title was not gone for long. In July 2003, Stephanie McMahon restored the gold in a tournament that saw Eddie Guerrero emerge victorious. The U.S. Championship has been a staple in WWE ever since.

1975

January 1 • Tallahassee, FL
Harley Race def. **Johnny Weaver** in the finals of a tournament to crown a United States Champion

July 3 • Greensboro, NC
Johnny Valentine def. **Harley Race**
Injuries forced Johnny Valentine to vacate the United States Championship in October 1975.

November 9 • Greensboro, NC
Terry Funk def. **Paul Jones** in the finals of a tournament to crown a new United States Champion

November 27 • Greensboro, NC
Paul Jones def. **Terry Funk**

1976

March 13 • Greensboro, NC
Blackjack Mulligan def. **Paul Jones**

October 16 • Greensboro, NC
Paul Jones def. **Blackjack Mulligan**

December 15 • Greensboro, NC
Blackjack Mulligan def. **Paul Jones**

1977

July 7 • Norfolk, VA
Bobo Brazil def. **Blackjack Mulligan**

July 29 • Richmond, VA
Ric Flair def. **Bobo Brazil**

October 21 • Greensboro, NC
Ricky Steamboat def. **Ric Flair**

1978

January 1 • Greensboro, NC
Blackjack Mulligan def. **Ricky Steamboat**

March 19 • Greensboro, NC
Mr. Wrestling def. **Blackjack Mulligan**

April 9, Charlotte, NC
Ric Flair def. **Mr. Wrestling**

December 18 • Toronto, Ontario
Ricky Steamboat def. **Ric Flair**

1979

April 1 • Greensboro, NC
Ric Flair def. **Ricky Steamboat**
After winning the NWA World Tag Team Championship in August 1979, Ric Flair was forced to vacate the United States Championship.

September 1 • Charlotte, NC
Jimmy Snuka def. **Ricky Steamboat** in the finals of a tournament to crown a new United States Champion

1980

April 19 • Greensboro, NC
Ric Flair def. **Jimmy Snuka**

1981

January 27 • Raleigh, NC
Roddy Piper def. **Ric Flair**

August 8 • Greensboro, NC
Wahoo McDaniel def. **Roddy Piper**
Injury forced Wahoo McDaniel to vacate the United States Championship in September 1981.

October 4 • Charlotte, NC
Sgt. Slaughter def. **Ricky Steamboat** in the finals of a tournament to crown a new United States Champion

1982

May 21 • Richmond, VA
Wahoo McDaniel def. **Sgt. Slaughter**
Injury forced Wahoo McDaniel to vacate the United States Championship.

June 7 • Greensville, SC
Sgt. Slaughter is awarded United States Championship

August 22 • Charlotte, NC
Wahoo McDaniel def. **Sgt. Slaughter**

November 4 • Norfolk, VA
Greg Valentine def. **Wahoo McDaniel**

1983

April 16 • Greensboro, NC
Roddy Piper def. **Greg Valentine**

April 30 • Greensboro, NC
Greg Valentine def. **Roddy Piper**

December 14 • Shelby, NC
Dick Slater def. **Greg Valentine**

1984

April 21 • Greensboro, NC
Ricky Steamboat def. **Dick Slater**

June 24 • Greensboro, NC
Wahoo McDaniel def. **Ricky Steamboat**
Wahoo McDaniel was forced to vacate the United States Championship after Tully Blanchard interfered in McDaniel's match.

October 7 • Charlotte, NC
Wahoo McDaniel def. **Manny Fernandez** in the finals of a tournament to crown a new United States Champion

1985

March 23 • Charlotte, NC
Magnum T.A. def. **Wahoo McDaniel**

July 21 • Charlotte, NC
Tully Blanchard def. **Magnum T.A.**

November 28 • Greensboro, NC
Magnum T.A. def. **Tully Blanchard**
Magnum T.A. was stripped of the United States Championship in May 1985 after attacking NWA President Bob Geigel.

1986

August 17 • Charlotte, NC
Nikita Koloff def. **Magnum T.A.** in the finals of a tournament to crown a new United States Champion

1987

July 11 • Greensboro, NC
Lex Luger def. **Nikita Koloff**

November 26 • Chicago, IL
Dusty Rhodes def. **Lex Luger**
Dusty Rhodes was stripped of the United States Championship in April 1987 after attacking Jim Crockett.

1988

May 13 • Houston, TX
Barry Windham def. **Nikita Koloff** in the finals of a tournament to crown a new United States Champion

1989

February 20 • Chicago, IL
Lex Luger def. **Barry Windham**

May 7 • Nashville, TN
Michael Hayes def. **Lex Luger**

May 22 • Bluefield, WV
Lex Luger def. **Michael Hayes**

1990

October 27 • Chicago, IL
Stan Hansen def. **Lex Luger**

December 16 • St. Louis, MO
Lex Luger def. **Stan Hansen**
Lex Luger vacated the United States Championship on July 14 after winning the WCW Championship.

1991

August 25 • Atlanta, GA
Sting def. **Steve Austin** in the finals of a tournament to crown a new United States Champion

November 19 • Savannah, GA
Rick Rude def. **Sting**
Injury forced Rick Rude to vacate the United States Championship in December 1992.

1993

January 11 • Atlanta, GA
Dustin Rhodes def. **Ricky Steamboat**
Rhodes was forced to vacate the title in May 1993 after a title defense against Rick Rude ended in a double pinfall.

August 30 • Atlanta, GA
Dustin Rhodes def. **Rick Rude** in a match for the vacant United States Championship

December 27 • Charlotte, NC
Steve Austin def. **Dustin Rhodes**

1994

August 24 • Cedar Rapids, IA
Ricky Steamboat def. **Steve Austin**
Injury forced Ricky Steamboat to vacate the United States Championship.

September 18 • Roanoke, VA
Steve Austin is awarded the United States Championship

September 18 • Roanoke, VA
Jim Duggan def. **Steve Austin**

December 27 • Nashville, TN
Vader def. **Jim Duggan**
Vader defeated Jim Duggan, Vader was stripped of the United States Championship by WCW Commissioner Nick Bockwinkel in March 1995.

1995

June 18 • Dayton, OH
Sting def. **Meng** in the finals of a tournament to crown a new United States Champion

November 13 • Tokyo, Japan
Kensuke Sasaki def. **Sting**

December 27 • Nashville, TN
One Man Gang def. **Kensuke Sasaki**

1996

January 29 • Canton, OH
Konnan def. **One Man Gang**

July 7 • Daytona Beach, FL
Ric Flair def. **Konnan**
Injury forced Ric Flair to vacate the United States Championship in September 1996.

December 29 • Nashville, TN
Eddie Guerrero def. **Diamond Dallas Page** in the finals of a tournament to crown a new United States Champion

1997

March 16 • Charleston, SC
Dean Malenko def. **Eddie Guerrero**

June 9 • Boston, MA
Jeff Jarrett def. **Dean Malenko**

August 21 • Nashville, TN
Steve McMichael def. **Jeff Jarrett**

September 15 • Charlotte, NC
Curt Hennig def. **Steve McMichael**

December 28 • Washington, DC
Diamond Dallas Page def. **Curt Hennig**

1998

April 19 • Denver, CO
Raven def. **Diamond Dallas Page**

April 20 • Colorado Springs, CO
Goldberg def. **Raven**
Goldberg vacated the United States Championship on July 6 after winning the WCW Championship.

July 20 • Salt Lake City, UT
Bret Hart def. **Diamond Dallas Page** in a match to determine a new United States Champion

August 10 • Rapid City, SD
Lex Luger def. **Bret Hart**

August 13 • Fargo, ND
Bret Hart def. **Lex Luger**

October 26 • Phoenix, AZ
Diamond Dallas Page def. **Bret Hart**

November 30 • Chattanooga, TN
Bret Hart def. **Diamond Dallas Page**

1999

February 8 • Buffalo, NY
Roddy Piper def. **Bret Hart**

February 21 • Oakland, CA
Scott Hall def. **Roddy Piper**
WCW President Ric Flair stripped Scott Hall of the United States Championship on March 18.

April 11 • Tacoma, WA
Scott Steiner def. **Booker T** in the finals of a tournament to crown a new United States Champion
WCW President Ric Flair stripped Scott Steiner of the United States Championship on July 5.

July 5 • Atlanta, GA
David Flair is awarded the United States Championship

August 9 • Boise, ID
Chris Benoit def. **David Flair**

September 12 • Winston-Salem, NC
Sid Vicious def. **Chris Benoit**

October 24 • Las Vegas, NV
Goldberg def. **Sid Vicious**

October 25 • Phoenix, AZ
Bret Hart def. **Goldberg**

November 8 • Indianapolis, IN
Scott Hall def. **Bret Hart, Goldberg** and **Sid Vicious** in a Ladder Match
Injury forced Scott Hall to vacate the United States Championship on December 19.

December 19 • Washington, DC
Chris Benoit is awarded the United States Championship

December 20 • Baltimore, MD
Jeff Jarrett def. **Chris Benoit**
Injury forced Jeff Jarrett to vacate the United States Championship in January 2000.

2000

January 17 • Columbus, OH
Jeff Jarrett is awarded the United States Championship
Jeff Jarrett was stripped of the title on April 10, when WCW heads Vince Russo and Eric Bischoff vacated all titles.

April 16 • Chicago, IL
Scott Steiner def. **Sting** in the finals of a tournament to crown a new United States Champion
After using a banned maneuver in a match, Steiner was stripped of the title by WCW Commissioner Ernest Miller on July 9.

July 18 • Auburn Hills, MI
Lance Storm def. **Mike Awesome** in the finals of a tournament to crown a new United States Champion

September 22 • Amarillo, TX
Terry Funk def. **Lance Storm**

September 23 • Lubbock, TX
Lance Storm def. **Terry Funk**

October 29 • Las Vegas, NV
Gen. Rection def. **Jim Duggan** and **Lance Storm** in a Handicap Match

November 13 • London, England
Lance Storm def. **Gen. Rection**

November 26 • Milwaukee, WI
Gen. Rection def. **Lance Storm**

2001

January 14 • Indianapolis, IN
Shane Douglas def. **Gen. Rection**

February 5 • Tupelo, MS
Rick Steiner def. **Shane Douglas**

March 18 • Jacksonville, FL
Booker T def. **Rick Steiner**

July 26 • Pittsburgh, PA
Kanyon is awarded the United States Championship by then-champion **Booker T**

September 10 • San Antonio, TX
Tajiri def. **Kanyon**

September 23 • Pittsburgh, PA
Rhyno def. **Tajiri**

October 22 • Kansas City, MO
Kurt Angle def. **Rhyno**

November 12 • Boston, MA
Edge def. **Kurt Angle**
Edge unified the United States and Intercontinental Championships. The Title was declared inactive until July 2003.

2003

July 27 • Denver, CO
Eddie Guerrero def. **Chris Benoit** in the finals of a tournament to crown a new United States Champion

October 19 • Baltimore, MD
Big Show def. **Eddie Guerrero** 2004

March 14 • New York, NY
John Cena def. **Big Show**
John Cena was stripped of the United States Championship in July 2004.

July 29 • Cincinnati, OH
Booker T last eliminated **Rob Van Dam** in an 8-man Elimination Match that also included **Billy Gunn, Rene Dupree, Kenzo Suzuki, John Cena, Charlie Haas,** and **Luther Reigns**

October 3 • East Rutherford, NJ
John Cena def. **Booker T**

October 7 • Boston, MA
Carlito def. **John Cena**

November 18 • Dayton, OH
John Cena def. **Carlito**

2005

March 3 • Albany, NY
Orlando Jordan def. **John Cena**

August 21 • Washington, DC
Chris Benoit def. **Orlando Jordan**

October 21 • Reno, NV
Booker T def. **Chris Benoit**
Booker T was forced to vacate the United States Championship after a title defense against Chris Benoit ended with a double pinfall.

2006

January 13 • Philadelphia, PA
Booker T def. **Chris Benoit**
Substituting for Booker T, Randy Orton beat Chris Benoit. As a result, Booker T was named new United States Champion.

February 19 • Baltimore, MD
Chris Benoit def. **Booker T**

April 2 • Chicago, IL
JBL def. **Chris Benoit**

May 26 • Bakersfield, CA
Bobby Lashley def. **JBL**

July 14 • Minneapolis, MN
Finlay def. **Bobby Lashley**

September 1 • Reading, PA
Mr. Kennedy def. **Bobby Lashley** and **Finlay** in a Triple Threat Match

October 13 • Jacksonville, FL
Chris Benoit def. **Mr. Kennedy**

2007

May 20 • St. Louis, MO
Montel Vontavious Porter def. **Chris Benoit**

2008

April 27 • Baltimore, MD
Matt Hardy def. **Montel Vontavious Porter**

July 20 • Uniondale, NY
Shelton Benjamin def. **Matt Hardy**

2009

March 20 • Corpus Christi, TX
Montel Vontavious Porter def. **Shelton Benjamin**

June 1 • Birmingham, AL
Kofi Kingston def. **Montel Vontavious Porter**

October 5 • Wilkes-Barre, PA
The Miz def. **Kofi Kingston**

2010

May 17 • Toronto, Ontario
Bret Hart def. **The Miz**
Bret Hart vacated the title in May 2010.

May 24 • Toledo, OH
R-Truth def. **The Miz** in a match for the vacant United States Championship

June 14 • Charlotte, NC
The Miz def. **R-Truth**

September 19 • Chicago, IL
Daniel Bryan def. **The Miz**

2011

March 14 • St. Louis, MO
Sheamus def. **Daniel Bryan**

May 1 • Tampa, FL
Kofi Kingston def. **Sheamus**

June 19 • Washington, D.C
Dolph Ziggler def. **Kofi Kingston**

December 18 • Baltimore, MD
Zack Ryder def. **Dolph Ziggler**

2012

January 16 • Anaheim, CA
Jack Swagger def. **Zack Ryder**

March 5 •Boston, MA
Santino Marella def. **Jack Swagger**

2012

March 5 • Boston, MA
Santino Marella def. **Jack Swagger**

August 19 • Los Angeles, CA
Cesaro def. **Santino Marella**

2013

April 15 • Greenville, SC
Kofi Kingston def. **Cesaro**

May 19 • St. Louis, MO
Dean Ambrose def. **Kofi Kingston**

2014

May 5 • Albany, NY
Sheamus def. **Dean Ambrose**

November 3 • Buffalo, NY
Rusev def. **Sheamus**

2015

March 29 • Santa Clara, CA
John Cena def. **Rusev**

August 23 • Brooklyn, NY
Seth Rollins def. **John Cena**

September 20 • Houston, TX
John Cena def. **Seth Rollins**

October 25 • Los Angeles, CA
Alberto Del Rio def. **John Cena**

2016

January 11 • New Orleans, LA
Kalisto def. **Alberto Del Rio**

January 14 • Lafayette, LA
Alberto Del Rio def. **Kalisto**

January 24 • Orlando, FL
Kalisto def. **Alberto Del Rio**

May 22 • Newark, NJ
Rusev def. **Kalisto**

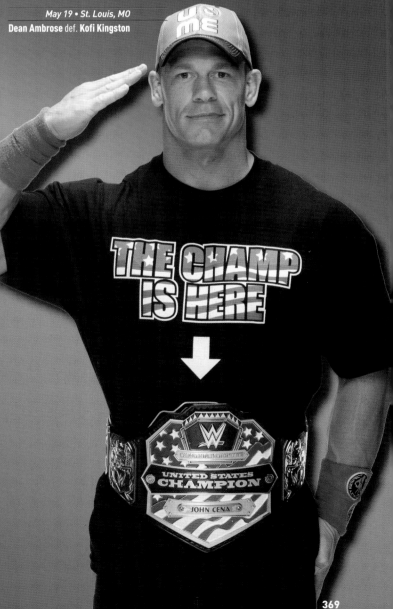

VANCE ARCHER

HT	6'9"	WT	272 lbs.	FROM	Dallas, Texas
SIGNATURE MOVE	Inverted DDT				

Introduced to the ECW brand in late 2009, Vance Archer debuted with one simple goal: make sure something bad happened to his opponents. If Archer was successful in achieving his goal, he could one day reach the top of ECW, while painting his self-proclaimed masterpiece of agony along the way.

Archer developed his penchant for pain growing up on the rough streets of Dallas. As a result, he was able to keep his focus on the abuse he inflicted in the ring. This ability led to impressive victories over such stars as Goldust and ECW Original Tommy Dreamer.

In 2010, Archer formed a tag team with Curt Hawkins on *SmackDown*. However, his intimidation factor began to wear off and he was released from WWE later that year.

THE VAUDEVILLAINS

MEMBERS	Aiden English & Simon Gotch

Aiden English and Simon Gotch have chosen to live in the past, and the decision has greatly benefitted them in the present.

The era of their choosing is the age of vaudeville, a type of live theater from the early 20th century that sometimes featured strongmen wearing the same types of handlebar mustaches English and Gotch favor. So committed are the duo to the time period that they've asked to be introduced by megaphone.

But there's little comedic about the way the two compete, sometimes winning matches with their Whirling Dervish, a double-team move culminating in a swinging neckbreaker.

In 2015, they used the maneuver to capture the NXT Tag Team crown from Blake and Murphy, with an assist from female star, Blue Pants.

VELVET MCINTYRE

HT	5'9"	WT	143 lbs.
FROM	County Cork, Ireland		

Over the course of her nearly-20-year career, Velvet McIntyre established herself as one of the most successful female competitors of all time.

With Princess Victoria as her partner, McIntyre entered WWE in 1984 and immediately became recognized as one-half of the promotion's first-ever Women's Tag Team Champions. Later that same year, a career-ending injury forced Princess Victoria aside, allowing Desiree Peterson to slide in as McIntyre's Championship partner. In all, McIntyre held the gold for more than one year before losing to The Glamour Girls in Egypt.

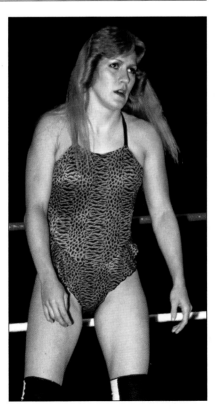

McIntyre's trophy case did not stay empty for long. The fiery, Irish-born Superstar finally claimed the gold from the Fabulous Moolah in July 1986. She held the Championship for six days before losing it back to the future WWE Hall of Famer during a tour of Australia.

McIntyre's impressive resume also includes a match at the first-ever *Survivor Series*, where she teamed with former nemesis, Moolah, to defeat the squad captained by Sherri Martel.

VICKIE GUERRERO

HT	5'4"	FROM	El Paso, Texas	SIGNATURE MOVE	Cougar Splash

First known as the widow of beloved WWE Hall of Famer Eddie Guerrero, few could have imagined Vickie Guerrero's ruthless rise to power in WWE. For nearly a decade, Vickie was greeted by thunderous jeers as her earsplitting voice reverberated off the rafters. As shrewd and conniving as any authority figure in history, Vickie provoked unanimous scorn with one simple phrase, "EXCUSE ME!!!"

Vickie first flashed her talons in 2006 when she sabotaged Rey Mysterio in his rivalry with her deceitful nephew, Chavo. Vickie soon manipulated herself into the position of *SmackDown* General Manager and later, *Raw* General Manager. As she savored her first taste of power, she revealed a romantic tryst with "The Rated-R Superstar," Edge, and used her newfound influence to seize the World Heavyweight Championship for her sleazy squeeze. Their courtship gave birth to "La Familia," an insidious faction designed to keep gold around Edge's waist. Infidelity and other issues eventually spelled the end for the power couple but Vickie's days of "cougaring" were far from over.

At *WrestleMania XXVI*, Vickie showed she was not just a screeching witch behind a microphone. She channeled her legendary husband and executed the winning Frog Splash in a 10-Diva Tag Team Match. Later in 2010, Vickie was back to her scandalous ways. She found a new boy toy, Dolph Ziggler, and eventually used her executive stroke to award her blonde beau the World Heavyweight Title and fire her ex-husband, Edge.

Vickie's egregious power abuse drew the inevitable ire of WWE's most insurmountable powerbroker, Mr. McMahon. The big cheese subjected Vickie to a public job evaluation, giving the WWE Universe the ultimate platform to voice their displeasure. Vickie was fired and though she was quickly hired back, she never escaped the crosshairs of the McMahon family. Her final undoing came in a career-threatening match in which Stephanie McMahon threw her into a pool of soupy brown muck. Vickie was fired as a result but gained revenge by hurling Stephanie into the stench and earning a fond sendoff from the WWE Universe. Her past treachery excused, Vickie penned a heartfelt thank you letter to the masses announcing her retirement in 2014.

VICTOR RIVERA

HT	6'2"	**WT**	240 lbs.	**FROM** Puerto Rico

SIGNATURE MOVE Cannonball

Victor Rivera arrived in WWE in 1964, and quickly attained hero status while warring with the Graham Brothers, Hans Mortier, and Gorilla Monsoon. Over the years, he worked with partners like Bruno Sammartino, Haystacks Calhoun, and Spiros Arion. In December 1969, Rivera claimed half the International Tag Team Championship with Tony Marino.

In March, 1975, Victor paired with Dominic DeNucci to defeat the Valiant Brothers for the WWE World Tag Team Championship. But Rivera exhibited something of a personality disorder. While wildly popular as a Tag Team Co-Titlist, he abruptly left WWE for the renegade IWA. Then, in 1978, he was back in WWE with a starkly different attitude. With Freddie Blassie as his manager, Rivera displayed his anti-social side, pursuing Bob Backlund for the WWE Championship.

After failing to wrest away the gold, he became a staple of the Los Angeles territory during its final days in the early 1980s, battling John Tolos, Bobo Brazil, Peter Maivia, and others.

He made his last WWE appearance in 1989.

VICTORIA

HT	5'8"	**FROM**	San Bernardino, California

SIGNATURE MOVE Widow's Peak

Victoria quickly gained notoriety in her 2002 debut match with Trish Stratus. The brutality she showed sent a message that she was not a lady to mess with. That November, she beat Trish for the Women's Championship and held the prize for almost five months, often with the help of Steven Richards.

Almost a year later, this dangerous black widow spun her web of pain in the first-ever Women's Steel Cage Match where she defeated Lita. Victoria's winning ways continued, including a second Title run that started in February 2004. That March, Victoria shaved Molly Holly's hair at *WrestleMania XX*.

Victoria remained a feared member of the Divas roster until she left WWE in January 2009. At one point, she became so brazen as to keep a checklist of her future "victims." She made a surprise one-night return for the "Miss WrestleMania" Divas Battle Royal at *WrestleMania 25*.

In the ring, Victoria earned a reputation for dishing out punishment. Today, she dishes out delicious pizza and burgers from her own themed restaurant called, "The Squared Circle," in Chicago.

VINCENT J. MCMAHON

see page 372

VINCENT K. MCMAHON

see page 374

VIRGIL

HT	5'11"	**WT**	250 lbs.	**FROM** Pittsburgh, Pennsylvania

SIGNATURE MOVE Million-Dollar Dream

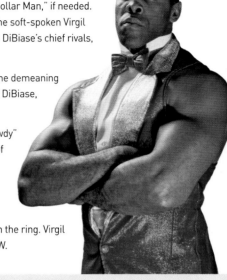

Despite possessing exceptional in-ring skills, Virgil's WWE career will best be remembered for his days outside the ring, rather than in it. As Ted DiBiase's personal bodyguard, his main purpose was to be at ringside to provide assistance to the "Million Dollar Man," if needed. This less-than-desirable position resulted in the soft-spoken Virgil taking the lion's share of the punishment from DiBiase's chief rivals, including Hulk Hogan and Randy Savage.

In January 1991, the bodyguard grew tired of the demeaning tasks imposed by his boss, and turned against DiBiase, becoming a fan favorite in the process.

Armed with the training he received from "Rowdy" Roddy Piper, Virgil earned the biggest victory of his career when he defeated DiBiase for the Million Dollar Championship at *SummerSlam 1991*. Following the win, Virgil managed to maintain his high level of popularity, but struggled to reach the same level of success in the ring. Virgil left WWE in 1994 before ultimately joining WCW.

VIRGIL THE KENTUCKY BUTCHER

HT	6'5"	**WT**	290 lbs.	**FROM** Hamilton, Ontario, Canada

Virgil the Kentucky Butcher brought an impressive Canadian win-loss record with him when he entered WWE in the mid-1960s. His reputation earned him instant respect in the United States, where he almost immediately moved to the top of the mountain. After turning back WWE Hall of Famer Arnold Skaaland several times, Virgil was awarded an opportunity at Bruno Sammartino's WWE Championship. He was unsuccessful in his quest to dethrone Sammartino, but did earn several rematches.

Before moving on to other promotions in North America and England, he clashed with Bobo Brazil, Victor Rivera, Sailor Art Thomas, and Tony "Battman" Marino, and teamed with Gorilla Monsoon, Bull Ramos, Baron Mikel Scicluna, and George "The Animal" Steele, among others.

VISCERA

HT	6'9"	**WT**	450 lbs.

SIGNATURE MOVE Viscera Drop

In 1998 this giant Superstar became an unwilling member of Undertaker's Ministry of Darkness. Viscera abused opponents with a methodical style that utilized his size and brute strength. He worked with The Acolytes to eliminate any individuals who tried to hinder Undertaker's work. After breaking free of Undertaker's control, Viscera vanished in 2000.

Upon his return a few years later, parts of his personality that were previously dormant bubbled to the surface and he soon became known as "The World's Biggest Love Machine." He pursued a few Divas, but focused his attention on Lilian Garcia. *Raw*'s glamorous announcer eventually warmed up to the big lug, but an untimely appearance by The Godfather derailed their blossoming love connection. Viscera teamed briefly with Val Venis, and later Charlie Haas, but ultimately both partnerships dissolved.

VINCENT J. McMAHON

FROM New York, New York

The global phenomenon known today as WWE would not exist had it not been for Vincent J. McMahon. The father of current WWE Chairman Vincent K. McMahon, the elder McMahon used his keen business acumen and passion for wrestling to lay the groundwork for what would become the world's most successful sports-entertainment company.

The son of Rose and Jess McMahon, Vincent J. was born on July 6, 1915, in Harlem. He spent much of his childhood roaming the backstage hallways of Madison Square Garden while his father, an accomplished boxing promoter, booked the famed arena.

In the early 1930s, Vince's father took an uncharacteristic step back from the boxing world to focus his attention on promoting wrestling events.

Vince had his first taste of working in the business in 1935 when he began promoting fights out of Hempstead, Long Island. But his career was put on hold when he joined the US Coast Guard. While serving in North Carolina, he married a woman named Vicki, who gave birth to two sons, Vincent and Rod.

Following his divorce, Vince was eager to get back into the wrestling business in a major way. However, successful promoter, Toots Mondt, controlled the New York territory, so Vince was forced to take his ambition elsewhere. He eventually settled on Washington, D.C.

CAPITOL WRESTLING CORPORATION

Upon arrival, Vince purchased a small dilapidated venue he later called Capitol Arena. On January 7, 1953, he put on the first-ever Capitol Wrestling Corporation event. Like most startups, Capitol Wrestling experienced its share of growing pains, but the company took its first real step toward greatness when Vince decided to embrace television, a new technology at the time. On January 5, 1956, Capitol Wrestling produced its first-ever television program. The show was an instant hit.

Proving that timing is everything, Vince miraculously was able to promote Capitol Wrestling shows at Madison Square Garden while Mondt had his promoter's license temporarily suspended.

FORGING AN ALLIANCE

Eventually, Vince welcomed former adversary Mondt into Capitol Wrestling as a partner. In what would prove to be one of the most important talent signings in sports-entertainment history, Capitol Wrestling assumed the booking rights to Buddy Rogers in 1960.

One year later, Rogers captured the National Wrestling Alliance (NWA) Championship. The victory provided an amazing opportunity for Vince to use Rogers' drawing power to sell out Madison Square Garden time after time.

Realizing he had a hot commodity on his hands, Vince only allowed Rogers to defend his title outside of the Northeast on rare occasions. This didn't sit well with the other NWA promoters, who eventually demanded Rogers cease his reign. The promoters got their wish when Lou Thesz defeated Rogers for the title in Toronto on January 24, 1963.

THE BEGINNING OF WWE

Vince and Mondt refused to recognize the title change, claiming a championship could not change hands during a one-fall match (championship matches were traditionally two-out-of-three falls at this time). To further show his dissatisfaction, Vince made the decision to withdraw Capitol Wrestling from the NWA and start his own independent wrestling promotion. Shortly thereafter, WWE was born, with Buddy Rogers as its first Champion.

After buying out Mondt in 1969, Vince and new partners Gorilla Monsoon, Arnold Skaaland, and Phil Zacko took WWE into the 1970s with main eventers like Bruno Sammartino, Andre the Giant, Pedro Morales, and "Superstar" Billy Graham.

After nearly 50 years in the business, Vince decided it was time to retire in 1982 and sold the promotion to his ambitious son, Vincent K. McMahon, who'd been astutely studying the industry while working as an on-air commentator.

On January 23, 1984, Vince walked the halls of his home away from home, Madison Square Garden, for the final time. In the main event of the evening, a youthful Hulk Hogan defeated Iron Sheik for the WWE Championship. A proud Vince watched as The Hulkster's victory ushered in his son's new vision of sports-entertainment.

On May 27, 1984, Vincent J. McMahon passed away after a battle with pancreatic cancer. He was 68. Were it not for his labor and foresight, the phenomenon known as WWE would not exist today.

> I JUST SAT AROUND, THINKING BACK. IT FELT EERIE, THINKING ABOUT THE THINGS I SAW.

"I just sat around, thinking back. It felt eerie, thinking about the things I saw."

—Vincent J. McMahon, on the closing of the old Madison Square Garden

VITO

HT	6'2"	WT	250 lbs.	FROM	Little Italy, Manhattan
SIGNATURE MOVE	Code of Silence

The hard-headed Italian handed out beatings in ECW and won Tag Team Championship gold in WCW, before debuting in WWE in August 2005. Trained by Johnny Rodz, Vito teamed with Nunzio and locked up with Charlie Haas, the Mexicools, Steven Richards, Bobby Lashley, Tatanka, Matt Hardy, and Funaki.

In June 2006, Vito began frequenting department stores and purchasing dresses. These lovely garments were not for his lady friends, but for himself. Not one to be upstaged by Divas doing pictorials, Vito appeared in the pages of *Playgirl* magazine in April 2007. Despite his controversial wardrobe choices, Vito remained a feared member of the *SmackDown* roster until he and WWE parted ways late in 2007.

VIVIAN VACHON

HT	5'4"	WT	160 lbs.	FROM	Montreal, Quebec, Canada
SIGNATURE MOVE	Body Press

Sports-entertainment flowed through Vivian Vachon's veins. As the 13th child of the storied Vachon family, Vivian could effortlessly bodyslam her brothers, Maurice "Mad Dog" and Paul "Butcher" Vachon. After training for her siblings' profession with the Fabulous Moolah, she gained her greatest accolade when she captured the AWA Women's Championship in November 1971.

Many consider Vivian to be one of the supreme female competitors of the 1970s, despite the fact that she retired midway through the decade. Vachon made a brief return to the ring in 1986 when she toured Japan with her brother, Mad Dog. Adding acting to her resume, Vivian also starred in the 1975 motion picture, *Wrestling Queen*.

Sadly, she died in 1991 when she was struck by a drunk driver.

VLADIMIR KOZLOV

HT	6'8"	WT	302 lbs.	FROM	Moscow, Russia
SIGNATURE MOVE	The Iron Curtain

Judo, Sambo, and kickboxing are just a few of the fighting styles Vladimir Kozlov perfected prior to his WWE debut in April 2008. This experience, coupled with his massive three hundred pound frame, earned him his "Moscow Mauler" moniker. Kozlov demanded better competition after spending the first few months of his WWE career decimating his opposition. Armed with his patented battering ram head butt, the mighty Russian targeted WWE's top stars.

With a fearless attitude and multiple offensive weapons, Kozlov ambushed anyone that held WWE gold and soon attacked ECW. After an unlikely string of events in 2010, he formed a team with Santino Marella. To the shock of most prognosticators, the stone-faced Russian and Italian goofball were the most entertaining duo in WWE. They even hosted a hilarious Monday night tea party for Sheamus and won the WWE Tag Team Championships that December.

Kozlov helped tackle The Corre at *WrestleMania XXVIII* and continued to be a popular Superstar. After he was a Pro on *NXT Redemption*, Vladimir suddenly disappeared from WWE after an attack by Mark Henry.

WADE BARRETT

see Bad News Barrett page 20

WAHOO MCDANIEL

HT	6'2"	WT	265 lbs.	FROM	Midland, Texas
SIGNATURE MOVE	Tomahawk Chop

Even as a football player with the New York Jets and Miami Dolphins, Wahoo McDaniel had appeal that seemed to be tailored for sports-entertainment. After hearing fans repeatedly chant his name, a number of promoters invited him to try his hand in the ring. When he did, the proud Chocktaw-Chickasaw warrior distinguished himself as one of the toughest men alive.

Trained by the legendary Dory Funk, Sr., "The Chief" competed in WWE while still active on the gridiron. After he became a full-time competitor, he largely left the Northeast to fellow Native American, Chief Jay Strongbow. In Houston, McDaniel engaged in a series of bloodbaths with Johnny Valentine, then settled into the Mid-Atlantic territory. There he became king of the Indian strap match and cut down foes with his often-imitated overhand chop. Ric Flair perfected his own chop while warring with Wahoo.

In August 1981, McDaniel defeated Roddy Piper for the first of five United States Championship reigns. He also competed in the AWA and WCW, among other places. Wahoo died in 2002.

WALDO VON ERICH

HT	6'0"	WT	260 lbs.	FROM	Germany
SIGNATURE MOVE	Blitzkrieg

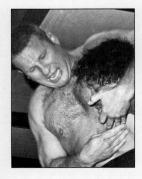

When this merciless remnant of the Third Reich entered WWE in 1963, audiences were horrified. The brother of Fritz Von Erich, Waldo operated with a controlled fury that threatened the careers of countless heroes. People watched in fear as Von Erich stalked Bruno Sammartino in sold-out arenas from Maine to Washington, DC.

In 1965, Waldo teamed with Gene Kiniski and defeated Dr. Jerry Graham and "Crazy" Luke Graham to capture the United States Tag Team Championship. Even after he lost the gold, Von Erich continued his forward march, recruiting "Classy" Freddie Blassie as his manager in battles against Chief Jay Strongbow and Andre the Giant.

He became a coach after his 1979 retirement, focusing on training, rather than politics, until his death in 2009.

VINCENT K. McMAHON

HT	6'2"
FROM	Greenwich, Connecticut
SIGNATURE MOVE	
Power Walk	

Vince McMahon did not meet his biological father until the age of 12, an event that would forever change the direction of his life. From that day, he became enamored with professional wrestling. However, the elder McMahon wanted his son to become either a physician or attorney and sent a protesting Vince to military school. As Vince grew up, major career influences continued to be the wrestling kind. He even patterned himself after the extravagant Superstar, Dr. Jerry Graham and at one point bleached his hair blond to duplicate the looks of the good doctor. After graduating from college, he married the love of his life and entrepreneurial muse Linda Marie Edwards. Vince's unwavering ambition propelled him to do everything he could to get into the business he prized above all else. His father did everything he could to keep him out. After a few years as a reluctant traveling salesman, Vince's dream finally came true.

In 1971, Vince McMahon had one chance to prove himself in the arena he longed to enter. Failure would put him out of the business forever; success meant a ticket to the main event. Thankfully, his effort in Bangor, Maine was a huge success, and Vince became the third generation McMahon promoter. As he learned the ropes of the business, another opportunity came his way in 1972. Right before a show was to go on the air, then-announcer Ray Morgan tried to hold up the McMahons for more money. The elder McMahon promptly showed Ray the way out. As the door closed for Mr. Morgan, it opened for the young Vince McMahon, and he became the new voice of WWE. As hundreds of thousands of fans watched every week on television, few people knew the major role Vince was playing behind the scenes. For the remainder of the 1970s he was a driving force behind the company's success, responsible for an almost quadruple increase in its television syndication. Vince's innovative implementation of his father's business formula prepared him to turn the corner, and catapult the company into the era of sports-entertainment.

TITAN SPORTS AND WRESTLEMANIA

In 1980, the entrepreneurial McMahon edged toward the pinnacle as he incorporated Titan Sports. In 1982, he and his wife, Linda, acquired Capital Wrestling Company shares, taking control of WWE, and ultimately changing the model of the professional wrestling business. Vince adopted the formula his father created for dominance in the Northeast section of the United States and began implementing key initiatives to expand the company's reach.

As he took the first steps toward expansion, Vince approached many of the members of the old wrestling territory fiefdoms and offered them buy-outs. Set in their ways and resting on past laurels, they laughed him out of their offices. In a classic example of "He who laughs last, laughs loudest," Vince flexed his entrepreneurial muscle and assembled a world-class roster of Superstars. His vision of global expansion was complete when he orchestrated the return of Hulk Hogan. With McMahon as the brains and Hogan providing the brawn, the unstoppable team steamrolled through the United States, breaking down the imaginary walls of the territory system.

In 1985, with Hulkamania running wild, the driven McMahon rolled the dice and bet it all on a one-time experiment called *WrestleMania*. This star-studded event garnered global attention as it featured Muhammad Ali, Liberace, The Rockettes, Billy Martin, and Mr. T. The happening became an annual phenomenon, and today *WrestleMania* is considered the greatest sports-entertainment spectacle on Earth. After the success of *WrestleMania*, McMahon brought WWE to network television with a bi-monthly showcase called *Saturday Night's Main Event*. Once a successful regional entity, WWE was now a global entertainment powerhouse. WWE exploded with television programs, pay-per-view events, a monthly magazine, home video, action figures, official Superstar merchandise, and interactive video game software. The era of sports-entertainment had arrived with an indescribable fervor.

In 1987, Vince achieved the unthinkable and packed 93,173 fans into the Pontiac Silverdome for *WrestleMania III*. As Hulk Hogan bodyslammed Andre the Giant in the night's main event, WWE solidified its position as the premiere sports-entertainment company in the world.

SPORTS-ENTERTAINMENT, LIVE ON TV!

As WWE marched into the 1990s setting records for live crowd attendance, pay-per-view revenue, cable television ratings, and licensed merchandise sales, McMahon once again changed the face of broadcast television. In January 1993, he launched *Monday Night Raw*. In 1995, media magnate Ted Turner chose to go head-to-head with Vince McMahon and broadcast his competing *WCW Monday Nitro* during the same time-slot on his own network, which lead to the Monday Night War.

After a number of duplicitous gambits and billions of dollars, WCW became a formidable opponent, and took the lead in the ratings battle. Fighting for his company and his livelihood, Vince reconfigured his creative game plan, adding a diabolical new character to the mix: himself.

After the controversial 1997 *Survivor Series*, Vince McMahon the broadcaster morphed into "Mr. McMahon," and an infamous, wicked character was born. During WWE's intrepid Attitude Era, the white-hot rivalry between Mr. McMahon and Stone Cold Steve Austin propelled WWE to fantastical heights. In 1999, WWE made history when it became a publicly traded company. Now that its fans could truly be part of the company's success, WWE proved that it ruled Wall Street and the world.

A NEW MILLENNIUM

In March 2001, Vince declared victory in the Monday Night War after acquiring WCW. In November 2001, riding this wave of success, Vince instituted the Vince McMahon Kiss My Ass Club, designed for individuals to kiss the Chairman's bare posterior or suffer the threat of suspension or termination. The Chairman's maniacal exploits continued through *WrestleMania XIX*, where a Street Fight 20 years in the making was held between he and Hulk Hogan. As the two historical figures annihilated each other, this battle showed once again that Mr. McMahon would do anything to entertain the fans. In September 2003, the entrepreneurial pioneer took his rightful place —next to his father—in the Madison Square Garden Walk of Fame, inducted by his children Shane and Stephanie. In March 2008, Vince joined entertainment immortals when he received a star on the Hollywood Walk of Fame.

The first months of 2009 were troubled times for the McMahon family, largely due to the reprehensible actions of Randy Orton. The night after *WrestleMania 25* the Chairman booked himself, son Shane, and Triple H in a six-man match against Orton and Legacy. The troubles continued when Vince McMahon sold *Monday Night Raw* to Donald Trump, though he bought it back—for twice as much—the following week.

In January 2010, the Chairman shocked the sports-entertainment world when Bret "Hit Man" Hart returned to WWE for the first time in over a decade. Hart was looking for closure with Mr. McMahon after the 1997 Montreal Incident. What he received was a surprise kick to the stomach from Mr. McMahon. The end result was a No Holds Barred Match at *WrestleMania XXVI*. After losing to the "Hit Man", Mr. McMahon retired from in-ring competition.

Vince McMahon still appears on WWE programming, and in recent years, has seen the next generation of McMahons begin to stake their claim in the family legacy. In 2011, he became embroiled in a corporate struggle with his son-in-law, Triple H, over who should oversee the day-to-day operations of *Raw*. The Chairman ultimately survived the coup. In subsequent years, he would subject all within his leadership structure to rigorous performance standards. John Laurinaitis, AJ Lee, Vickie Guerrero and Booker T all tried, with mixed reviews, to steer the course of WWE programming under Vince's watchful eye. Proving blood is always thicker, his daughter Stephanie and her husband Triple H returned to the corporate fold in the summer of 2013 as The Authority. Together, the power couple rules with an iron fist. However, the buck still stops with the Chairman, a fact he has made known on many occasions.

TITAN OF THE DIGITAL AGE

Vince McMahon remains on the cutting edge of entertainment. The company he created has grown into a global entity with offices in New York, Los Angeles, London, Mumbai, Istanbul, Shanghai, Singapore, Tokyo and more. He does not just evolve to keep up with the times; he marches ahead of the curve with an insatiable drive to assert his everlasting dominance over the entertainment spectrum. In 2011, WWE received Mashable Awards for "Digital Company of the Year" and "Must Follow Brand on Social Media." The following year, WWE launched its own YouTube channel and enhanced its viewing experience with the unveiling of the WWE App.

In 2014, the App became a key component in the delivery of one of Vince McMahon's grandest innovations yet, the WWE Network. Today, WWE Network is enjoyed by over one million subscribers.

As his forward-thinking approach continued to transform WWE, Vince decided his company needed to refresh its image for the future. Like a proud monarch, he stood atop WWE Headquarters in August 2014 and unveiled a sleek, new WWE logo. He touted the design as a beacon of sports-entertainment and a symbol of WWE's iconic brand.

In 2015, The Chairman became animated, as he voiced over his role as Vince McMagma in the crossover film *WWE & The Flintstones: Stone Age SmackDown*. That same year, at age sixty-nine, Vince graced the March cover of *Muscle & Fitness Magazine* flexing a ripped physique worthy of envy from men half his age.

Despite all his accolades, there is another side of the WWE Chairman: his boundless philanthropy and patriotism. Vince McMahon works with the Special Olympics. He has launched a non-partisan campaign to help Americans register to vote. He hosts a yearly show dedicated to the people serving in the armed forces and has held a prominent role in The Make-A-Wish Foundation for over a decade. For the WWE Chairman, it's not just about giving back. It's about leading by example.

THE WARLORD

HT	6'5"	WT	323 lbs.	FROM	Parts Unknown
SIGNATURE MOVE	Full Nelson

Few teams in history could match strength with the colossal duo of Warlord and Barbarian. Collectively known as The Powers of Pain, the muscular tandem amazed audiences with their incredible athleticism and frightening face paint.

After tangling with legendary tag teams, The Hart Foundation and Demolition, including a failed attempt at unseating Ax and Smash for the World Tag Team Championship at *WrestleMania V*, The Powers of Pain went their separate ways. With manager Slick guiding him, Warlord's singles career looked bright early on. He even defeated former Intercontinental Champion Tito Santana at *SummerSlam 1990*. Unfortunately, however, that's where the success stopped.

Over the next several years, Warlord found himself on the wrong end of rivalries with, "Texas Tornado" Kerry Von Erich, and fellow strongman, British Bulldog. Despite coming up short, however, Warlord did push Bulldog to the limit during their encounter at *WrestleMania VII*.

The Warlord left WWE in April 1992.

WAYLON MERCY

HT	6'7"	WT	290 lbs.	SIGNATURE MOVE	Sleeperhold

A man of few words but a variety of violent actions, Waylon Mercy came to WWE in 1995. He claimed to be a peaceful person and friend to all mankind. During his slow walk to the ring he shook hands with fans, ring announcers, referees, and opponents alike with an eerily calm demeanor. His interviews sent chills down people's spines as he stated, "Lives are gonna be in Waylon Mercy's hands."

When the bell rang Waylon became a man possessed and attacked opponents in a fit of rage. By October of that year, Waylon was forced to leave the ring after feeling the bone-crushing effects from Diesel's Jacknife Powerbomb. Waylon Mercy was not a man to be trusted, associated with, or challenged. He could snap at the slightest move or word and made people pay dearly for such offenses.

WCW

see page 378

WELL DUNN

MEMBERS	Timothy Well & Steve Dunn	COMBINED WT	470 lbs.

A well-known team in the southeastern United States, Timothy Well and Steven Dunn debuted in the big time in 1993. Well Dunn combined excellent tag team action with relentless rule-breaking tactics, along with their always-irritating manager, Harvey Wippleman.

The duo attacked the Smokin' Gunns, Men On A Mission, the Bushwhackers, the Headshrinkers, Allied Powers, and others. Despite being contenders for WWE tag team gold, they were never able to win the prizes and left WWE in the spring of 1995. As the duo soon went their separate ways, Dunn joined WCW and was in the ring the night Scott Hall made his historic debut on *Nitro*. Sadly, in 2009, Steve Doll (Dunn) passed away.

WENDI RICHTER

HT	5'8"	WT	150 lbs.	FROM	Dallas, Texas
SIGNATURE MOVE	Sitout DDT

Cowgirl Wendi Richter came to WWE in 1984 and was an exciting addition to the roster, boasting an impressive combination of size, agility, and power. Describing herself as "150 pounds of twisted steel and sex appeal," the former rodeo competitor took audiences on a thrilling ride when she joined forces with singer, Cyndi Lauper, and Hulk Hogan to form a ground-breaking alliance called, "the Rock 'N' Wrestling Connection." Exchanging her cowboy hat for a more alternative look, Wendi became a pop-culture phenomenon during WWE's growth into a global brand.

On July 23, 1984, Wendi ended the three-decade Championship reign of her former mentor, Fabulous Moolah on MTV's *The Brawl To End It All*. Despite losing to Leilani Kai, Richter remained a top attraction. Their rematch, won by Richter, took place at the first *WrestleMania*.

On November 25, 1985, Wendi walked into New York's Madison Square Garden to defend her Title against a new opponent. There was something familiar about the masked Spider, but Wendi had no time to analyze her foe. Yet, she noticed that, for every hold Richter executed, the Spider appeared to have a counter. As Wendi was pondering this situation, the Spider suddenly pinned the champion to the mat, removed her mask, and revealed herself to be Moolah.

Richter was so incensed by the treachery that she stormed out of the Garden, still in her ring gear, hailed a taxi cab and flew back home. It was the last time that she ever competed in WWE.

In the following years, Wendi toured North America, Japan, and Puerto Rico. She also briefly competed in the AWA, winning the promotion's championship from future Champion, Alundra Blayze, in 1988. But soon afterward, she stepped away from the ring.

With her high profile days behind her, Wendi earned a master's degree in occupational therapy, competed in dog shows, and worked as a real estate agent.

In 2010, audiences saw her on WWE television for the first time in more than 25 years when her sports-entertainment career was celebrated at the WWE Hall of Fame ceremonies.

WORLD CHAMPIONSHIP WRESTLING

When wrestling's territory system began to crumble, only two major promotions were left in North America, facing off against each other in what could only be characterized as a death match between WWE and WCW.

From 1995 to 2001, fans were left with two television choices on Monday nights, *Raw* and WCW's *Nitro*. Some chose to switch channels between the two, stopping when something caught their interest. Others were explicit in their preference. WCW supporters argued that their company's product was superior, based on the mix of former WWE headliners like Hulk Hogan, Randy "Macho Man" Savage, Ultimate Warrior, Rowdy Roddy Piper, Bret Hart, and others, NWA greats such as "Nature Boy" Ric Flair and Sting, homegrown stars like Goldberg, Diamond Dallas Page, Booker T, and The Giant (later known as the Big Show) and the militant influence of the nWo.

Before everything fell apart, WCW even boasted a roster of celebrity participants, including basketball bad boy Dennis Rodman, KISS, late night talk show host Jay Leno, and actor David Arquette—who briefly held the WCW World Heavyweight Championship.

Interestingly, the WCW name comes not from the American south, as most assume, but Australia, where promoter Jim Barnett ran his operation in the 1960s. By 1982, Barnett was in charge of the Georgia territory. When his television show received national exposure on Ted Turner's super-station, TBS, a decision was made to make the name sound less regional, and the program was dubbed World Championship Wrestling.

In time, Charlotte-based promoter Jim Crockett, Jr. procured the time slot. Like Vince McMahon, Crockett was raised in the industry, and had designs of expanding from his traditional base. As WWE began attracting some of the biggest names in sports-entertainment, Crockett absorbed promotions from Georgia, Missouri, Oklahoma, and other places, transforming his company into the embodiment of the NWA.

But it cost money to grow and, in 1988, Crockett needed a bailout. It came in the form of Turner, who made the group part of his media empire. Although the promotion was officially called WCW, for the first several years, it was still closely associated with the NWA.

For the first year, the company flourished, as Flair engaged in thrilling contests with Ricky "The Dragon" Steamboat and the ageless Terry Funk, while the rest of the roster was

supported by exciting performers like Flyin' Brian Pillman, Lex Luger, The Great Muta, and the Road Warriors.

During this period, the relationship with the NWA, now largely a collection of small promoters, was unsteady. In 1993, ties were permanently severed. The ultimate prize would now be the WCW World Heavyweight Championship.

Flair, who'd recently been in WWE, returned to great fanfare and, in a brutal and exhilarating match, vanquished Vader for the title at the 1993 *Starrcade*, an achievement that had many of fans in the Nature Boy's hometown of Charlotte openly crying.

Earlier in the year, WCW television announcer Eric Bischoff had assumed the reigns of the company. With Turner's financial and personal encouragement, Bischoff was permitted to vigorously compete with WWE in a way that no promotion had ever done.

It was Bischoff who convinced Hulk Hogan to switch allegiances to WCW after the golden symbol of the 1980s parted with WWE. Hogan's introduction to WCW began with a ticker tape parade through the Disney-MGM lot in Orlando, Florida, where many of the promotion's shows were taped. At the 1994 *Bash at the Beach* pay-per-view, he defeated Flair for the

Championship—satisfying fans who wished that they'd clashed at *WrestleMania* while both were in WWE.

Capitalizing on the Turner bankroll, Bischoff also lured away Randy Savage, who'd been working primarily as an announcer in WWE and believed that he was worthy of another championship run.

But the executive's most striking achievement was the launch of *Nitro*. The premier show, on September 4, 1995, featured a ring set up in the Mall of America in Minnesota, and such compelling matches as Pillman vs. Jushin "Thunder" Liger, and Flair vs. Sting. The most shocking moment occurred when Hogan was defending his WCW title against Big Bubba Rogers. Lex Luger, who'd competed in WWE the night before in Halifax, Nova Scotia, suddenly appeared and challenged the champion. This was something that no one anticipated. By the next morning, everybody in the industry, including those in WWE, was abuzz over the news.

This was the point when the Monday Night War officially began. In one night, Bischoff had established *Nitro* as television that couldn't be missed.

Understanding the impact that he'd caused, Bischoff continuously gloated about his desire to overtake WWE. Because some episodes of *Raw* were taped in advance, Bischoff would give away WWE match results on the air, a decision that worked against WCW when he mentioned that Mick Foley was about to beat The Rock for the WWE World Heavyweight Championship on *Raw*, and 600,000 fans changed channels. On another occasion, Bischoff challenged McMahon to a fight in a WCW ring; McMahon chose to ignore the dare rather than give credence to his rivals.

WWE hit back, doing skits about "Billionaire Ted" and his aging performers, and sending the members of DX to a WCW show to agitate security and provoke fans into belittling the product.

But no one denied that interesting things were happening in WCW. In 1996, the promotion established a cruiserweight championship, and would begin hiring fast-moving, internationally-seasoned athletes like Chris Jericho, Dean Malenko, Chavo Guerrero Jr., Billy Kidman, Eddie Guerrero, and Juventud Guerrera—all of whom would later showcase their talents in WWE.

On May 31, 1996, Scott Hall, who'd been competing as Razor Ramon in WWE, walked through the crowd, and disrupted a *Nitro* broadcast, asking, "You want a war?" Two weeks later, Kevin Nash, who'd held the WWE Championship as Diesel, joined Hall on TV. Both had recently signed WCW contracts, but many fans speculated that the pair, known at the time as "The Outsiders," might have been dispatched to the show by McMahon himself.

At the next *Bash at the Beach*, the two promised to produce a mystery partner. Fans watched, anticipating another WWE defection. Instead, Hogan revealed himself to be the newest member of the unit. As angry spectators tossed garbage in the ring, Hogan proclaimed that he was tired of being a hero, and his new group would henceforth be called the "New World Order," or nWo.

There were other surprises, too. In October 1997, "Ravishing" Rick Rude appeared on *Nitro* on the same night that he was featured on a taped episode of *Raw*. In the meantime, between 1996 and 1998, *Nitro* beat *Raw* in the ratings for 84 straight weeks.

The promotion also created a sensation around former football player Bill Goldberg's lengthy winning streak, not to mention his WCW Championship win over Hogan on *Nitro*.

WWE countered by using former WCW standouts Stone Cold Steve Austin, who'd been terminated via FedEx while recuperating from injuries at home, and Mick Foley to help spark the "Attitude Era," the organization's most daring period.

At a certain point, WCW's momentum began to dry up, and WWE pulled ahead. So many names were added to the nWo that satellite factions (nWo Hollywood, nWo Wolfpac, Latino World Order, etc.) started, and fan interest waned. Followers were irate when Nash, now the WCW champion, allowed Hogan to pin him following a finger poke to the chest. After Vince Russo replaced Bischoff in 2000, fans were equally upset when the WCW Championship was awarded to actor David Arquette, then Russo himself.

At one stage, Bischoff came back and tried to run WCW alongside Russo, but nothing appeared to work. On March 26, 2001, Vince McMahon appeared on *Nitro* to announce that the Monday Night War was over—WCW was being sold to WWE.

Flair reprised his match with Sting from the first *Nitro* on the final show. But the biggest surprise occurred during the final moments, simulcast on *Raw*, when Shane McMahon announced that he, not his father, was in charge of WCW.

For several months, Shane led a contingent of stars representing WCW and ECW, which had also been purchased by WWE. During this time, WCW titles were defended on WWE cards. At *Vengeance* in December 2001, Chris Jericho unified the WWE and WCW Championships.

Today, *Nitro* broadcasts can be viewed on the WWE Network.

JIM CROCKETT, JR.

Although Jim Crockett, Jr. was closely associated with the NWA in the days before Ted Turner purchased his company in 1988, he remained part of WCW during the early years and was president of the NWA until 1991.

Crockett grew up around the business, the son of Jim Crockett, Sr. (a.k.a. "Big Jim") who was 25 when he began promoting wrestling in Charlotte, North Carolina, in 1935. In addition to staging shows in the Carolinas and Virginia, Big Jim was also a concert promoter and theater owner. In 1963, he briefly attempted to run shows in New York, opposite WWE.

Insiders believed that Big Jim was grooming his son-in-law to take over the Charlotte-based territory, but when the elder Crockett died in 1973, his daughter had become estranged from her husband. As a result, 28-year-old Jim, Jr. gained control of the company that he'd call Mid-Atlantic Wrestling.

Crockett already had a formidable roster from his father's time, including Rip Hawk, Swede Hanson, Johnny Valentine, and Johnny Weaver. But now, Mid-Atlantic experienced an infusion of youth, with stars like Ric Flair, Ricky Steamboat, Greg Valentine, and Roddy Piper.

Behind the scenes, Crockett was also consolidating power, serving three terms as NWA president, starting in 1980.

As WWE transformed from a northeastern to an international operation, Crockett competed with exciting shows, eventually absorbing six territories and becoming the most powerful promoter in the NWA. To honor Big Jim, he hosted the Jim Crockett, Sr. Memorial Tag Team Tournament from 1986 to 1988. Like his father, he also dabbled in other ventures, including the Charlotte Orioles baseball club, the Baltimore Orioles' AA affiliate.

After a brief period when WWE matches were seen on the TBS Superstation, Crockett purchased the timeslot from Vince McMahon for $1-million. The WWE boss reportedly predicted, "You'll choke on that million."

Indeed, Crockett's promotion was in financial straits when Turner bought it. Still, what Crockett created provided the foundation for WCW. Even after Crockett left the company, two of his siblings remained integral parts of WCW, announcer David Crockett and another brother, Jackie, who was considered an indispensible cameraman.

THE GREAT MUTA

HT	6'2"	WT	230 lbs.	FROM	Yamanashi, Japan
SIGNATURE MOVE	Moonsault				

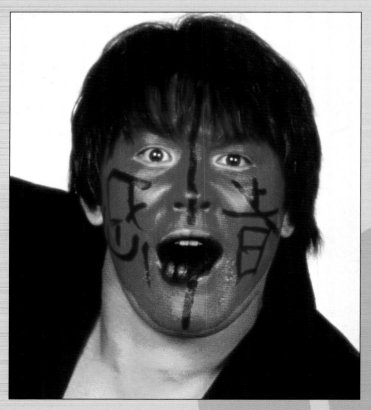

In a career spanning more than 30 years, The Great Muta became one of the most decorated warriors on both sides of the Pacific Ocean, winning more than 20 championships for a number of promotions in Japan and North America.

During a period when the relationship between WCW and the NWA was eroding, Muta won the NWA World Heavyweight Championship from countryman Masahiro Chono in 1993. Because WCW recognized its own titlist at the time, the accomplishment is often not viewed with the same veneration as the reigns of Lou Thesz, Harley Race, Ric Flair and other esteemed NWA champs.

But Muta's achievement should never be minimized. At the same time that he wore NWA gold, Muta also held the prestigious IWGP crown in Japan. Over the years, he also had an ownership stake in several Japanese promotions, including All Japan Pro Wrestling.

A former amateur wrestling and judo competitor, Muta competed under a number of aliases during his career, including his birth name, Keiji Mutoh.

In 1989, he was introduced to WCW fans as The Great Muta by manager Gary Hart. With his theatrical face paint, supernatural appearance and dazzling athleticism, Muta flattened foes with such moves as the cartwheel back elbow and shining wizard, a maneuver that involved running across the ring, then kicking a downed adversary in the head. Hart claimed that Muta was the son of another former protégé, the Great Kabuki. Like Kabuki, Muta possessed the ability to spew a toxic mist in opponents' faces.

WCW's best lined up to challenge him. Muta had gripping matches with Ric Flair and Lex Luger. But Sting, another brilliant athlete who came to the ring with his face painted, was his most memorable competitor. In 1994, after several trips to and from Japan, Muta locked up with Steve Austin.

After the formation of the nWo, Mutoh joined a Japanese faction of the renegade group, becoming its leader in 1998. Two years later, he made his final return to WCW as The Great Muta, teaming with Vampiro, among others.

KONNAN

HT	5'10"	WT	237 lbs.
FROM	Mexico City, Mexico		
SIGNATURE MOVE		Montezuma's Revenge	

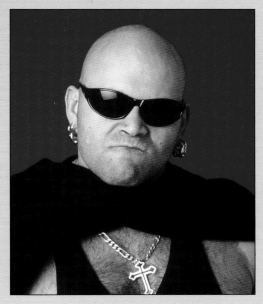

He was arguably the most popular superstar in Mexico. Yet, Konnan's main impact on WCW was paving the way for other luchadores to showcase their skills to an American audience.

In 1996, while continuing to compete and defend the AAA Heavyweight Championship , Konnan persuaded a number of Mexican stars to appear in WCW, among them, Juventud Guerrera, La Parka, Psicosis, and Rey Mysterio.

Just as significant was the faction he formed in 1999, the Filthy Animals. The majority of the members were frustrated because they weren't receiving main events in WCW. But Konnan knew how to cultivate talent. Along with Mysterio and Juventud, the Filthy Animals included Billy Kidman, Eddie Guerrero, and valet, Torrie Wilson, all of whom ended up in WWE, along with other personalities.

Konnan first appeared in WCW in 1990, teaming with his trainer, the original Rey Mysterio, uncle of the future WWE Champion. After several runs with other promotions, including ECW, Konnan became a WCW United States champion and, in 1997, a member of the nWo.

SCOTT NORTON

HT	6'3"	WT	360 lbs.
FROM	Minneapolis, Minnesota		
SIGNATURE MOVE		Release Powerbomb	

While competing as a four-time US National arm wrestling champion, Scott Norton earned the nickname "Flash" for his ability to swiftly slam an opponent's arm into the table. He gained a similar reputation once he started planting foes on the mat in Japan and WCW.

Norton grew up watching AWA stars like Mad Dog Vachon and Verne Gagne in Minnesota. A former schoolmate of "Ravishing" Rick Rude and Road Warrior Hawk, Norton also knew Golden State natives Mr. Perfect, Wayne Bloom, and the Berserker. Yet, he resisted entering the mat wars, acting in Sylvester Stallone's arm wrestling movie, *Over the Top*, and working as a bodyguard for Prince.

After being trained by former Olympian Brad Rheingans, Norton debuted in the AWA in 1989, and teamed with Rick Steiner and Hercules Hernandez in Japan.

In WCW, he battled Sting in 1993. In 1996, he joined the nWo, representing the US and Japanese divisions.

He is one of a handful of foreigners (others include Brock Lesnar and Vader) to hold Japan's vaunted IWGP Championship.

BOBBY EATON

HT	6'0"	WT	235 lbs.
FROM	Huntsville, Alabama		
SIGNATURE MOVE		Alabama Jammer	

The consummate tag team specialist, Bobby Eaton was a coveted partner because, more times than not, he was the most gifted competitor on the show.

Eaton is best remembered as a member of the Midnight Express (with Dennis Condrey and then Stan Lane) and their wars with teams like the Rock 'n' Roll Express and the Road Warriors.

A lifelong fan, he began putting up rings in his native Alabama and Tennessee, and, by 1978, was teaming with "Leaping" Lanny Poffo. He soon formed the Jet Set with George Gulas and New Wave with Koko B. Ware.

After the Midnight Express, Eaton was recruited into WCW's Dangerous Alliance by manager Paul E. Dangerously (a.k.a. Paul Heyman) in 1991 with Rick Rude, Larry Zbyszko, Arn Anderson, and Steve Austin.

In 1995 he and British competitors William Regal, then known as "Lord Steven," and "Squire" David Taylor became the Blue Bloods, an odd allegiance given Eaton's Alabama roots.

As a single's competitor, he once pinned WCW World Heavyweight Champion Ric Flair in the first fall of a two-out-of-three falls contest.

MISSY HYATT

Missy Hyatt liked getting her way, instigating battles between male admirers, bashing rivals with a loaded designer handbag, and becoming one of the most controversial managers in WCW and other groups.

Hyatt first became known when she entered WCCW in 1985 with boyfriend John Tatum. She quickly insinuated herself into everything, grappling with likeable valet, Sunshine, in a mudpit match at Texas Stadium, and getting spanked by Lance Von Erich, cousin of the famous clan.

After departing for Mid-South, she formed a managerial partnership with "Hot Stuff" Eddie Gilbert, dumping Tatum for him. Missy and Gilbert married in 1988.

In 1987, she auditioned with WWE to host an interview segment called "Missy's Manor."

Working as both a commentator and manager in WCW, Missy's protégés included the Steiner Brothers, Nasty Boys, Barbarian, and Ric Flair.

After Gilbert's death, Missy dated actor Jason Hervey. When manager Paul E. Dangerously (a.k.a. Paul Heyman) taunted the couple, Hyatt defeated him in an arm wrestling contest.

In 1996 she managed the Sandman in ECW, antagonizing his wife, Lori.

nWo

From the moment that Scott Hall swaggered onto a 1996 episode of *Nitro*, sports-entertainment was changed forever.

Hall had been competing in WWE as Razor Ramon and because of the way that he introduced himself to WCW—walking through the crowd, as opposed to down the aisle—there was the feeling that the company was being invaded. Two weeks later, when he was joined by Kevin Nash, the given name of former WWE World Heavyweight Champion Diesel, a movement was underway.

All the rules that came before were broken. WCW (and, for that matter, WWE) was condemned as monotonous and stale. The rebellious faction, then called The Outsiders, was going to tear the promotion apart and rebuild it as their own.

When Eric Bischoff, the company's president and announcer, expressed his displeasure, Nash Jackknife Powerbombed him off the entrance area. Fans knew that they were supposed to jeer this type of bedlam, but, instead, they were titillated by it. Longtime WCW stars vowed to extinguish the fire, but The Outsiders seemed unstoppable.

Then, at *Bash at the Beach*, the heroic Hulk Hogan joined the faction. Fans were shocked, then even some who'd cheered The Outsiders were furious, filling the ring with garbage, as Hogan rechristened himself "Hollywood" Hogan, and named the group the New World Order, or nWo.

"Well, the first thing you've got to realize, brother, is this right here is the future of wrestling," Hogan declared. Coming to the ring in their distinctive black and white colors, the nWo was as ruthless as any street gang, except they had the technical wherewithal to hijack WCW's signal to champion their subversive agenda. One by one, some of the biggest names in sports-entertainment became part of the pack.

"Million Dollar Man" Ted DiBiase was introduced as the group's financer. Randy "Macho Man" Savage and "Mr. Perfect" Curt Hennig announced their allegiance. The Giant, soon to be known as the Big Show, also joined. And then, Bischoff turned against WCW himself, becoming the tyrannical boss of the nWo, demanding that the entire locker room either sign up or suffer the consequences.

There was an exclusive nWo pay-per-view, *Souled Out*. Basketball bad boy Dennis Rodman donned the black and white. The nWo even expanded into the New Japan promotion across the Pacific.

The only hope for WCW appeared to be Sting. For the better part of a year, he lowered himself from the rafters, the colorful face paint of his past replaced by a grimmer design, bashing nWo members with a black baseball bat. At *Starrcade 1997*, he defeated Hogan for the WCW World Heavyweight Championship.

But relying on their characteristic, backstage manipulation—along with the assistance of an aligned referee, Nick Patrick—the nWo managed to have the decision overturned. In fact, they may have dominated indefinitely, if they hadn't destructed from within.

First, Kevin Nash splintered off and started his own faction, the red and black nWo Wolfpac. Other units followed—nWo Hollywood, Elite, and Black and White.

The one WCW bright spot was when Bill Goldberg vanquished Hogan for the title in 1998. But at the following *Starrcade*, Nash took the championship, with an assist from Hall. The new champion was scheduled to defend the gold against Hogan. The two had been estranged but, on this night, they united in shocking fashion when Nash intentionally fell to the mat after Hogan poked him in the chest.

The incident became known as the "fingerpoke of doom," and it did little for the nWo. and less for WCW. Feeling cheated, legions of fans began watching *Raw* on Monday nights instead of *Nitro*.

The group, nWo 2000, would appear in the new millennium, but never receive traction. The nWo was no longer a factor in WCW in 2001 when the company was absorbed by WWE.

But the legendary faction wasn't finished. Hogan, Nash, and Hall reunited in WWE for a short-term nWo run in 2002. Before they dispersed, a retired Shawn Michaels was welcomed, carving a place for himself in history as the only nWo member who'd never appeared in WCW.

HARLEM HEAT

MEMBERS Booker T, Stevie Ray   **COMBINED WT** 545 lbs.

Powerful and telegenic, Harlem Heat was a dominant presence in WCW for much of the 1990s, tangling with duos like Rick and Scott Steiner, Kevin Nash and Scott Hall, and Lex Luger and Sting, and holding the WCW World Tag Team Championship ten times.

After they were orphaned, Stevie Ray was a paternal influence on younger brother, Booker T. Together, they attended Ivan Putski's training school and debuted in WCW in 1993. Although they had several managers, Stevie and Booker formed their strongest bond with Sister Sherri.

After WCW was sold in 2001, the siblings' paths diverged, and Booker became a multiple-time Champion in WWE. Stevie inducted Booker into the Hall of Fame in 2013.

THE HOLLYWOOD BLONDS

MEMBERS "Stunning" Steve Austin & "Flyin'" Brian Pillman   **COMBINED WT** 479 lbs.

Before he became the Texas Rattlesnake, Steve Austin was a pretty boy, competing alongside Brian Pillman in the Hollywood Blonds. Other pairs had used the moniker before, but Austin and Pillman are remembered most.

In 1993 they toppled Rick Steamboat and Shane Douglas to win the tag titles, then recognized by both the NWA and WCW. Among their strongest challengers were the reformed Four Horsemen, consisting of Ric Flair, Ole and Arn Anderson, and Paul Roma. The Roma-Anderson combo eventually dethroned the Blonds when "Lord" Steven Regal, later known as William Regal in WWE, filled in for an injured Pillman. By the end of the year, the Blonds disintegrated when Austin, provoked by his new manager, Col. Rob Parker, turned against his partner.

DAVID CROCKETT

Best-known as an NWA announcer, David Crockett stayed with WCW until the bitter end, behind the microphone and behind the scenes. Crockett, the brother of NWA president Jim Crockett, was the consummate insider. In 1975, he was on a private plane that crashed, along with Ric Flair, Johnny Valentine, Tim "Mr. Wrestling" Woods, and Bob Bruggers. After hosting Mid-Atlantic broadcasts with Bob Caudle, he received national exposure doing play by play with Tony Schiavone from TBS Studios on Saturday nights.

When his family's promotion was purchased by Ted Turner in 1988, Crockett served as a producer in WCW. Before the final *Nitro* in 2001, he delivered an emotional, backstage speech about the Crockett legacy, and his hopes for the industry's future.

NORMAN SMILEY

HT 6'2"   **WT** 238 lbs.   **FROM** Miami, Florida
SIGNATURE MOVE Crossface Chickenwing

A comical figure in WCW, Norman Smiley was actually a submission specialist who'd learned the technical aspects of the sport from masters Professor Boris Malenko and Karl Gotch. Smiley became a fan in his native England, then moved to Florida, where he competed at power lifting and amateur wrestling, and cheered stars like Dusty Rhodes.

After winning Mexico's esteemed CMLL Heavyweight Championship, Smiley established himself in WCW by doing his "Big Wiggle," gyrating his hips to celebrate a rally, and spanking foes in the midst of the action. Faced with a dangerous opponent, Smiley would emit a loud shriek. He'd also show up for matches in hockey gear. But his fundamentals remained impeccable. After the dissolution of WCW, he became a trainer for WWE.

ELIX SKIPPER

HT 6'0"   **WT** 222 lbs.   **FROM** Atlanta, Georgia
SIGNATURE MOVE Double Underhood Suplex from the second rope

Perhaps no one represented WCW's cruiserweight division better than Elix Skipper. A graduate of WCW's training academy, the Power Plant, Skipper was a fleet-footed, high flyer who'd take down much larger foes with corkscrew planchas and springboard legdrops. Referring to himself as "Prime Time" Elix Skipper, he held both the WCW Cruiserweight Championship and Cruiserweight Tag Team title, procured when he and partner, Kid Romeo, bested Rey Mysterio and Billy Kidman in 2001. According to some critics, Skipper and his fellow cruiserweights were WCW's brightest spot at the end. Despite his American nationality, he was a member of Lance Storm's Team Canada faction. He briefly participated in an invasion of WWE consisting of WCW and ECW standouts, before continuing to build his reputation in Japan.

3 COUNT

MEMBERS Shane Helms, Evan Karagias, Shannon Moore, & Tank Abbot

The brainchild of former recording artist, manager Jimmy Hart, 3 Count was WCW's version of a boy band. As an overhead light cast green circles in the ring, members performed the Hart-penned tune, "Can't Get You Outta My Heart", before matches. Original members Helms, Karagias, and Moore were all superb cruiserweights. Because of some loophole in the WCW rule book, they were allowed to compete as a trio for the WCW Hardcore Championship, winning it from Brian Knobbs in 2000.

They were soon accompanied by brawny Tank Abbot, who claimed to be the group's "biggest fan." But they parted ways when Abbot wanted to take "center circle," while the others served as backup singers. It was the type of jealousy that eventually broke up the band.

JUSHIN "THUNDER" LIGER

HT 5'7"   **WT** 210 lbs.   **FROM** Tokyo, Japan
SIGNATURE MOVE Shooting Star Press, Liger Bomb

With a costume inspired by vibrant, Japanese anime superheroes and a move set to match, Jushin "Thunder" Liger" was a celebrated light heavyweight in Japan for nearly a decade before his 1991 arrival in WCW. Many credit Liger's breathtaking rivalry with Flyin' Brian Pillman for introducing the cruiserweight style that became prevalent in WCW years later. Liger remained a journeyman for the rest of his career, constantly traversing from WCW to smaller promotions. His impact is still felt today as WWE's more acrobatic Superstars study his tactics looking to bolster their in-ring arsenals. At *NXT TakeOver: Brooklyn* in 2015, Liger made his lone appearance in a WWE ring, defeating Tyler Breeze with a Liger Bomb.

VAN HAMMER

HT	6'6"	**WT**	289 lbs.	**FROM** New York, New York
SIGNATURE MOVE	Hammer Rocks			

While much of the world was transitioning to grunge and rap in 1991, Van Hammer represented the hair metal scene of the 1980s, throwing back his tresses while shaking his guitar en route to the ring.

Trained by Professor Boris Malenko and Danny Spivey, he made a spectacular debut at *Clash of the Champions XVI*, dismantling Terry Taylor in 39 seconds. His overall record, though, was mixed.

In 1997, after a hiatus from WCW, he returned and joined Raven's "Flock." But after he defeated Perry Saturn in a "Loser Leaves the Flock" match, the rest of the group attacked him.

He later reinvented himself as a hippie, then joined another faction, the Misfits in Action, renaming himself Major Stash, before leaving the promotion.

ALEX WRIGHT

HT	6'4"	**WT**	221 lbs.	**FROM** Nuremberg, Germany
SIGNATURE MOVE	German Suplex			

Entering the ring to a pounding techno beat, "Das Wunderkind" Alex Wright animated crowds, and impressed cynics with his in-ring acumen.

The son of British superstar, Steve Wright, Alex was born in Germany, where he competed in his first match at 16. He made his WCW debut in 1994 and stayed for seven years.

Because of their conflicting music tastes, Wright clashed with Disco Inferno, as well as Masahiro Chono, Eddie Guerrero, Bobby Eaton, and Dean Malenko.

In 1997, he beat Chris Jericho for the WCW Cruiserweight Championship. At one point, he changed his name to Berlyn, and morosely refused to speak English.

KISS DEMON

HT	6'7"	**WT**	285 lbs.	**FROM** Mountainside, New Jersey
SIGNATURE MOVE	Love Gun			

When WCW head, Eric Bischoff, made a deal with the group KISS in 1999, a decision was made to create a Superstar to represent the foursome.

Dale Torborg, the son of baseball manager Jeff Torborg, loved the band and was anxious to step into the role. Breathing fire and spitting blood seemed to come naturally to Torborg, and the effort was underway.

But when Bischoff had a falling out with the company, enthusiasm for the newcomer waned. Renamed simply The Demon, he collided with the hellish Vampiro, who locked him in a coffin and set it ablaze.

Still, The Demon has no regrets. He married his WCW valet, Asya, in 2000 and now works as a baseball strength and conditioning coach.

SONNY OONO

To his critics, Sonny Oono was the equivalent of the Japanese Imperial soldiers found in the jungle, refusing to accept their nation's defeat years after the end of World War II.

Starting in 1995, Oono managed a string of Japanese competitors, seemingly bent on embarrassing the USA. Among his charges were Jushin "Thunder" Liger, Masahiro Chono, Koji Kanemoto, Kensuke Sasaki, Masa Saito, The Great Muta, and Bull Nakano.

With Oono's guidance, Akira Hokuto became the WCW Women's Champion, and Ultimo Dragon snared the WCW Cruiserweight title.

Oono also handled the contracts of some of Mexico's finest luchadores, including La Parka and Psicosis. A decorated martial artist once considered the top bantamweight kickboxer in the world, Oono also managed karate expert, Ernest "The Cat" Miller.

VINCE RUSSO

HT	6'2"	**WT**	190 lbs.
FROM	New York, New York		

Evil genius or bungling madman? Visionary or fraud? Even today, Vince Russo remains one of sports-entertainment's most polarizing figures.

A prolific radio host and writer, Russo started in WWE, editing the company's magazines and encouraging the salaciousness that became the hallmark of the "Attitude Era."

In 1999, he was hired away by WCW, becoming one of the promotion's most divisive personalities. Under Russo's watch, actor David Arquette won WCW gold. In fact, Russo became the Champion himself, when Goldberg speared him through a cage, resulting in the wordsmith's victory. And it was Russo who encouraged David Flair to wage war on his father, Ric Flair.

After WCW's demise, Russo briefly worked for WWE again before parting ways with the company.

FILTHY ANIMALS

MEMBERS	Eddie Guerrero, Billy Kidman, Rey Mysterio, Konnan, Juventud Guerrera, & Disqo (Disco Inferno)
VALETS	Torrie Wilson & Tygress

They called themselves the Filthy Animals, a collection of pranksters targeting WCW mainstays as they refined their skills between the ropes. While the faction was often lost in the WCW shuffle, members like Rey Mysterio and Eddie Guerrero, launched themselves to stardom in WWE.

It was in the Filthy Animals that Guerrero developed the "lie, cheat and steal" philosophy that the WWE Universe would come to embrace, blasting an opponent with a chair behind the referee's back, then placing the object on the unconscious victim, and laying down himself. The Filthy Animals won WCW Tag Team gold twice, with Billy Kidman and Konnan beating Harlem Heat in 1999 and Mysterio and Juventud Guerrero toppling The Great Muta and Vampiro the next year.

SEE ALSO:

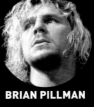

BIG SHOW (THE GIANT)   **BILLY KIDMAN**   **BOOKER T**   **BRET "HIT MAN" HART**   **BRIAN PILLMAN**   **CHRIS JERICHO**

HULK HOGAN   **LEX LUGER**   **NASTY BOYS**   **RANDY "MACHO MAN" SAVAGE**   **RAZOR RAMON/SCOTT HALL**   **REY MYSTERIO**

BUNKHOUSE BUCK

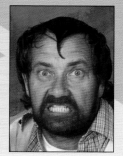

| HT | 6'5" | WT | 250 lbs. | FROM | Bucksnort, Tennessee |
| SIGNATURE MOVE | Piledriver |

He was called the "meanest man south of the Mason-Dixon line," and worked hard to live up to the phrase.

Bunkhouse Buck was the product of the old-fashioned bunkhouse, the barracks found on remote, southern ranches, where cowboys settled their differences in unrestricted brawls.

Lured to WCW in 1994 by manager Col. Robert Parker, Buck pummeled foes with a work glove-sheathed fist. Even after the final bell, he'd humiliate the victim, tying him up like a rodeo calf.

Buck won the WCW Tag Team Championship with rugged Dick Slater, and teamed with the legendary Terry Funk, who developed his taste for confrontation of his family's ranch. One on one, Buck had his most notable rivalry with a young Dustin Rhodes, later known as Goldust in WWE.

THE WEST TEXAS REDNECKS

| MEMBERS | Curt Hennig, Bobby Duncum Jr., Barry and Kendall Windham, & Curly Bill |

They were supposed to be among the most despised teams in WCW. Instead, the West Texas Rednecks became folk heroes.

Initially comprised of gifted, second generation Superstars—Curt Henning, son of Larry "The Axe" Hennig, Bobby Duncum, Jr., and Blackjack Mulligan's sons, Barry and Kendall Windham—the West Texas Rednecks sang, as well as competed. When they engaged in a rivalry with rapper Master P and his No-Limit Soldiers, their song, "Rap is Crap" even received airplay on southern radio stations.

The tune, about country girls, Willie Nelson, and NASCAR, spoke to fans who felt overlooked.

That Hennig was actually from Minnesota was of little consequence. Later, the unit was joined by a cowboy hat-wearing Curly Bill, better known as Virgil in WWE.

EVAN KARAGIAS

HT	5'11"	WT	205 lbs.
FROM	Gastonia, North Carolina
SIGNATURE MOVE	Victory Roll

Evan Karagias' career in WCW had a rough start: a record of 8-42 following his 1997 television debut. But within two years, his fortunes had turned, as he won the WCW Cruiserweight Championship and became the leader of one of the promotion's hottest trios.

Later, when the team, 3 Count, also consisting of Shannon Moore and Shane Helms, became the closest thing that WCW had to pop idols, followers noted that Karagias was a former actor, who'd appeared on the TV show, *All My Children*.

Unfortunately, Karagias sometimes suffered from an over-inflated sense of self, prompting his partners to oust him. But by the time of the final *Nitro* in 2001, 3 Count was reunited, and doing their synchronized moves before and after the bell.

KENDALL WINDHAM

| HT | 6'5" | WT | 242 lbs. | FROM | Sweetwater, Texas |
| SIGNATURE MOVE | Bulldog |

The son of WWE Hall of Famer, Blackjack Mulligan, and brother of former Four Horsemen member, Barry Windham, Kendall Windham's first notable tag team in WCW was the Texas Broncos, with fellow second generation star, Dustin Rhodes.

In 1989, both Windham brothers and Ric Flair became part of the Yamasaki Corporation, a stable headed by Hiro Matsuda. Other members included Butch Reed and Michael Hayes.

After a stint in ECW, Kendall formed the West Texas Rednecks in 1997 with Barry, Curt Hennig, and Bobby Duncum, Jr., representing country music in a rivalry with rapper, Master P, and his No Limit Soldiers. During this period, the Windhams became WCW World Tag Team Champions. Kendall and Hennig would later reunite as a tag team in Japan.

VAMPIRO

| HT | 6'2" | WT | 260 lbs. | FROM | Mexico City |
| SIGNATURE MOVE | Nail in the Coffin |

A gothic gladiator in dreadlocks and greasepaint, Vampiro went from superstardom in Mexico to the dark side in WCW in 1998, aligning himself with his favorite performing artists, the Insane Clown Posse, and Raven, in a morbid unit called the Dead Pool.

The former bodyguard was originally called Vampiro Canadiense (Canadian Vampire) in Mexico, where he became one of the country's biggest attractions. Oddly, in WCW, he'd target other Mexican icons, particularly Eddie Guerrero, Rey Mysterio, and Konnan, as well as the KISS Demon and Sting. Opponents often found themselves drenched in red liquid.

He also aligned himself with a contingent tied to punk rockers, The Misfits. In 2000, he and The Great Muta won WCW Tag Team gold. After WCW, Vampiro returned to Mexico.

STEVE "MONGO" MCMICHAEL

| HT | 6'2" | WT | 270 lbs. | FROM | Chicago, Illinois |
| SIGNATURE MOVE | Mongo Spike |

A former member of football's New England Patriots, Green Bay Packers, and Chicago Bears, Steve McMichael followed the tradition of going from the gridiron to the mat.

In 1995, Mongo accepted an offer to co-host *Nitro*, bringing along his small dog, Pepe, as a companion. His voluptuous wife, Debra, was often at ringside and, soon, both were involved in the WCW fireworks.

After McMichael and former linebacker, Kevin Greene, tagged together at the 1996 *Great American Bash*, Mongo accepted a lucrative offer to turn against his partner and join the Four Horsemen. The catalyst for the move was Debra. Eventually, she left McMichael for Jeff Jarrett, resulting in a 1997 match that saw Mongo capture the WCW United States title. He's now a sports broadcaster and indoor football coach.

DEAN MALENKO

DIAMOND DALLAS PAGE

DIESEL/KEVIN NASH

EDDIE GUERRERO

ERIC BISCHOFF

GOLDBERG

RIC FLAIR

SCOTT STEINER

STEINER BROTHERS

STING

THE FOUR HORSEMEN

VADER

WESTERN STATES SPORTS AMARILLO

For fans who loved a good, Texas-style brawl, there was no better territory than Amarillo-based Western States Sports. Well before the term "hardcore wrestling" existed, the Amarillo territory was offering brass knuckles, Russian Chain, and Texas Death Matches on a regular basis.

Although Dory Detton, Doc Sarpolis, and Sam Menacker had all promoted Amarillo, the territory will always be associated with the Funk family. Dory Funk Sr., purchased the promotion in 1967, and it was home base for his sons, Dory Jr., and Terry, during their NWA World Heavyweight Championship reigns.

The territory's cities included Colorado Springs, Albuquerque, Lubbock, and El Paso—where Gory Guerrero, father of future WWE Champion Eddie Guerrero, promoted for the Funks.

When Dory Sr., died in 1973, his sons kept the territory alive. But they had international commitments, and in 1978, Blackjack Mulligan and Dick Murdoch (whose father, Frank, often wrestled Dory Sr.) became owners. By then, attendance had declined and they closed the territory in 1980. Fritz Von Erich then made Amarillo a stop on his Dallas-based circuit.

WESTERN STATES WRESTLING ALLIANCE PHOENIX

There were few things that WWE, and the obscure Western States Wrestling Alliance, had in common. One of them was Madison Square Garden. The difference was that the mecca of Western States Wrestling happened to be in Phoenix.

In the 1930s, Dr. Joseph Lentz, the son of Madison Square Gardens' builder, was bringing sports-entertainment events to the arena. After his retirement in 1946, celebrated champion, Jim Londos, also promoted there. Other promoters included Ernie Muhammed, Monte LaDue, and Al Fenn, who ran the Western States territory during the Tito Montez era.

Montez, who appealed to the area's Hispanic community, arrived in Phoenix in 1956. Before his retirement in 1970, he held the Arizona Heavyweight Championship six times, colliding with foes like Don "Bulldog" Kent and Chris Colt.

Other Arizona territory stars included Cowboy Bob Yuma, Hercules Stevenson, Jody Arnold, John Ringer, and Billy Anderson. Former NFL players Ron Pritchard and Bob Lueck occasionally wrestled in "football gear" matches.

Eventually, Phoenix became an AWA city. But by 1985, fan loyalty had shifted to WWE.

WHO

WT Who Knows What   **FROM** Who Knows Where

With an anvil-shaped chest and impressive power game, Who began his brief and befuddling WWE career in 1996. During his time in the ring, the masked competitor regularly impressed onlookers with his strength, while greatly confusing broadcasters. Typical banter during a Who match:

Vince McMahon, "The question is, who is in the ring?"

Mr. Perfect, "Exactly, Who is in the ring."

Jim Ross, "Who's the referee for this match?"

Mr. Perfect, "No, Who's wrestling."

Luckily, the broadcast team didn't have to fumble over Who's identity for long. After coming up short against the likes of Savio Vega and Jake Roberts, Who realized he didn't have the heart to be a WWE Superstar. He soon left WWE and retreated back to his home in Who Knows Where.

WILD BULL CURRY

HT 6'0"   **WT** 220 lbs.   **FROM** Hartford, Connecticut
SIGNATURE MOVE Left Hook

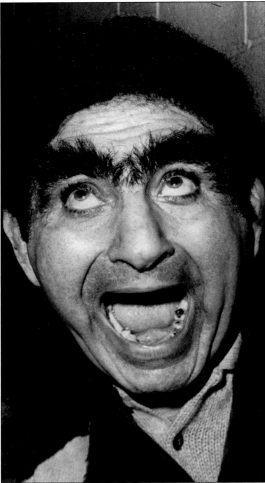

With his bulging eyes, menacing scowl and one bushy eyebrow protruding across his forehead, Wild Bull Curry would literally make fans faint while exchanging haymakers with blood-saturated opponents.

A descendent of Lebanese immigrants, Curry accepted spectator challenges in carnivals as a teen. Later, as a police officer in Hartford, Connecticut, he received a report of a steer that broke out of the stockyard. Facing off against the animal in the streets, he earned the "Wild Bull" nickname by subduing the steer after snatching it by its horns.

Curry's fondness for fisticuffs resulted in his being crowned Texas Brass Knuckles Champion in a 1953 tournament. Over the next 14 years, he held the title 20 times, battling such names as Killer Karl Kox, Brute Bernard, and Fritz and Waldo Von Erich.

In the Detroit territory, he exchanged hammering blows with The Sheik and Bobo Brazil, and formed a tag team with son, "Flyin'" Fred Curry. Curry loved fighting so much that he was nearly 70 when he retired. He died in 1985.

WILD RED BERRY

HT	5'8"	**WT**	200 lbs.
FROM	Pittsburg, Kansas		
SIGNATURE MOVE		Gilligan Twist	

Boxer-turned-sports-entertainer, Red Berry had a reputation for being a bit outrageous. In fact, it was his unorthodox style that eventually led to his nickname. After spending three days in a tree outside Memorial Hall in Kansas, the local newspaper dubbed Berry a "wild man." The description was perfect, and Wild Red Berry was born.

Standing only 5'8", Berry had to find creative ways to win his matches, which is why he oftentimes turned to rule breaking. His defiant in-ring actions made him one of the most reviled Superstars of the 1930s, 1940s, and 1950s. Berry didn't care, as his disregard for authority eventually led him to more than fifteen championship reigns over the course of his lengthy career.

Berry continued his deviant behavior long after his in-ring career came to a close. As manager to such top stars as Gorilla Monsoon, the Fabulous Kangaroos, and Bull Ramos, Berry was not above using his signature cane as a weapon.

After suffering a stroke that impaired his notable speaking skills, Berry died in 1973.

THE WILD SAMOANS

MEMBERS	Afa & Sika		
COMBINED WT	645 lbs.		

In the early 1970s, Wild Samoan Afa started training with his uncle, High Chief Peter Maivia, and Rocky Johnson. Afa took what he learned and trained his brother, Sika. From there the two began a 30 year reign of terror that may never be duplicated. They tore through Stu Hart's Stampede Wrestling as well as the territories of the NWA.

In the fall of 1979, the Samoans were brought to WWE by Capt. Lou Albano. Afa and Sika ripped apart opponents and were so dominant, both were individually contenders for the WWE Championship. On April 12, 1980, they defeated "Polish Power" Ivan Putski and Tito Santana for their first World Tag Team Championship.

The two held the Titles for five months until at the 1980 mega-event, *Showdown at Shea*, the dream team of WWE Champion Bob Backlund and Pedro Morales beat them in a 2-out-of-3 Falls Match.

The duo had to vacate the Titles because of a since-altered rule that didn't allow Backlund to hold two Championships simultaneously. A tournament was arranged to crown new Champs, and the Samoans defeated Tony Garea and Rene Goulet to recapture the World Tag Team Titles. After a loss to Garea and Rick Martel, they soon departed from WWE.

For the next two years, they dominated the Mid-South and Mid-Atlantic Wrestling scenes. However, after a call from Albano, the Wild Samoans were back in WWE frightening audiences, speaking in their ancient tongue, and consuming raw fish. Their third and final Title reign came at the expense of Jay and Jules Strongbow in March, 1983. By 1984, they'd left the company.

While Sika briefly came back as a singles competitor, Afa returned to co-manage The Headshrinkers with Captain Lou Albano, guiding them to the World Tag Team Championship. Shortly after he left WWE, Afa opened The Wild Samoan Training Center. Today, Sika is widely known as the father of Roman Reigns.

WrestleMania 23 saw the Wild Samoans take their rightful place among the immortals of sports-entertainment when they were inducted into the WWE Hall of Fame.

WILLIAM REGAL

HT	6'2"	**WT**	240 lbs.	**FROM**	Blackpool, England
SIGNATURE MOVE		Regal Stretch			

William Regal never went out of his way to appeal to the fans. "Do you know what my New Year's Resolution is going to be?" he asked while competing in WCW. "To wake up a half an hour earlier so I can hate you more."

Still, Regal was able to compensate for his arrogance with superior in-ring skills and a thorough understanding of the mat game. In addition to serving as WWE Commissioner and General Manager for the company's various brands, he became an encyclopedia of international styles, stepping through the ropes in some two dozen countries and holding a total of 60 titles.

Regal was 15 when he began testing his submission skills against all adversaries at a carnival in his native Blackpool. His fearsome reputation spread quickly, and soon, he was battling around the United Kingdom, forming a tandem with future NXT trainer Robbie Brookside, known as the Golden Boys.

In 1991, WCW toured England and Regal received a tryout. Officials were impressed, and he was summoned to the United States to appear on the promotion's roster.

At the time, he was known as Steve Regal (not to be confused with the former AWA Light Heavyweight Champion of the same name) or, more specifically, "Lord" Steven Regal, head of a pretentious unit called the Blue Bloods.

Although he'd competed in WWE before, he became a company staple in 2000. Despite a reputation for relying on a pair of brass knuckles to earn some victories, he compiled an impressive championship resume. In addition to runs with the now-defunct European and Hardcore Championships, he defeated Edge to capture the Intercontinental Championship at *Royal Rumble 2002*. With partners Lance Storm, Eugene, and Tajiri, he won Tag Team gold.

Regal joined the WWE incarnation of ECW in 2009 and was a top challenger for its title. In 2014 he became NXT General Manager and later, introduced fans to Japanese Superstar, Hideo Itami.

During his 2016 retirement speech, Daniel Bryan named Regal as a mentor.

WILLIE GILZENBERG

In the early 1960s, Vince McMahon Sr., and his partners were about to sever ties with the National Wrestling Alliance, and establish WWE as its own entity. McMahon needed a savvy administrator to deal with promoters, venue executives, the public, and Superstars, and Willie Gilzenberg was the man for the job.

Willie was a successful promoter based out of Newark, New Jersey. As McMahon's first President, Gilzenberg influenced the careers of some of the most pivotal figures in sports-entertainment such as Antonino Rocca, Buddy Rogers, Bruno Sammartino, and Swede Hanson.

Sadly, on November 15, 1978, this innovator of great attractions passed away. Willie Gilzenberg set the standard for the on-air positions of authority seen for decades on WWE programming.

THE WIZARD

His brutally scarred forehead served as a reminder of the barbarous battles he competed in during his days as an active competitor. But while the cavernous ditches in The Wizard's skull were certainly disturbing, it was his relationships with the wild Kamala and Sika that freaked fans out most.

For a brief period of time during the mid-1980s, the four-hundred-pound manager not only served as Kamala and Sika's representation, but more importantly their voices. While the untamed Superstars shouted indecipherable noises, The Wizard was there to translate their offensive words. The Wizard's words, however, were only slightly more intelligible than those of his charges. He could often be heard mysteriously going on about the mystical powers of the gigantic saber tooth he wore around his neck.

The Wizard claimed to draw inspiration from Hall of Fame manager, The Grand Wizard. But unlike the legendary leader who came before him, The Wizard failed to bring his protégés to great success. After a brief stint by the sides of Kamala and Sika, he disappeared from WWE in 1987.

THE WOLFMAN

HT	6'2"	WT	260 lbs.	FROM	The Wilds of Canada
SIGNATURE MOVE	Hanging Neckbreaker				

Ushered to the ring on a chain by Lou Albano, this Superstar debuted in 1970, and appeared to be half man and half beast. According to his manager, he was raised among the wolves of the Great White North. Once he was released from his chain, The Wolfman's animalistic tendencies were only controllable by Albano.

After many of his victories, television stations throughout the northeast demanded that WWE place a large X on the screen due to Wolfman's proclivity for chewing on fallen opponents.

In 1975, Freddie Blassie assumed managerial duties for The Wolfman shortly before the Superstar fled WWE and returned to the Canadian wilderness.

WORLD MARTIAL ARTS HEAVYWEIGHT CHAMPIONSHIP

Because of his background battling opponents from a number of fighting disciplines, including Muhammad Ali in a "boxer vs. wrestler" clash in 1976, future WWE Hall of Famer Antonio Inoki was awarded the World Martial Arts Championship in 1978.

The Title was periodically defended on both WWE shows in the United States and on the New Japan promotion's shows in Inoki's native country. During WWE's 1980 *Showdown at Shea* outdoor extravaganza and *Brawl to End It All* in 1984, pro wrestling rules were enforced. In Japan, traditional martial arts guidelines often applied.

Eventually, the Championship was only defended in New Japan. Inoki lost to former Soviet gold medalist, Shota Chochishvili, in 1989, but regained the gold later that year before the Title was discontinued.

WORLD WRESTLING ASSOCIATION

In 1964, Dick the Bruiser won the Worldwide Wrestling Associates title from Freddie Blassie in Los Angeles. Bruiser then returned to Indianapolis, and declared himself the champion of his new promotion, the World Wrestling Association, using the same acronym, WWA.

Previously, Bruiser and his promotional partner, Wilbur Snyder, had held the AWA Tag Team Championship on cards handled by the company's Indianapolis promoter, Balk Estes. The two now said that they were WWA Tag Team Champions.

The WWA entered talent sharing agreements with both the Los Angeles version of the WWA and AWA, as well as groups in Quebec, Ontario, and Pittsburgh. After first warring with Big Time Wrestling over Detroit, the two companies reached an accord.

In fact, promoters of both territories (Bruiser and the original Sheik) engaged in several memorable skirmishes. The WWA and AWA co-promoted cards at the Chicago Amphitheater.

Dominant WWA talents included the Blackjacks, Valiant Brothers, and their manager, "Pretty Boy" Bobby Heenan. The last of Bruiser's nine title reigns ended in 1985. The promotion closed six years later.

WORLD WRESTLING COUNCIL

In 1973, journeyman Carlos Colon started the World Wrestling Council (WWC) in his native Puerto Rico, promoting shows in San Juan, Ponce, Bayamon, Arecibo, Guaynabo, Caguas, and other spots around the island. His promotional partners included Gorilla Monsoon and Victor Jovica.

The fans immediately embraced the promotion and Colon, as he main evented emotional matches against the Funk Brothers, Harley Race, Stan Hansen, Bruiser Brody, and Dutch Mantell. He once estimated that he shed 80 percent of his blood in battles with Abdullah the Butcher. In addition to high profile visitors, WWC had a roster of such local stars as Hercules Ayala, Chicky Starr, and Los Invaders.

In 1983, WWC Champion Colon beat NWA World Heavyweight Champion Ric Flair in a unification match, but the NWA never recognized the stipulation.

All went well until 1988 when Brody was stabbed to death in a Bayamon dressing room, and many fans abandoned the promotion. Still, Colon held on, promoting a new generation of stars. In 2014, his efforts earned him a WWE Hall of Fame induction.

THE WORLD'S GREATEST TAG TEAM

MEMBERS	Shelton Benjamin & Charlie Haas
COMBINED WT	497 lbs.

In 2002, former Olympic gold medalist Kurt Angle presented the world with "Team Angle," the highly athletic duo of Shelton Benjamin and Charlie Haas. In addition to doing whatever they could to help Angle retain his WWE Championship, the pair managed to capture the WWE Tag Team Title from Los Guerreros in February 2003.

After losing the prize back to Eddie Guerrero and his new partner, Tajiri, in May 2003, Team Angle found themselves in an uncharacteristic slump. As a result, Angle fired them as his associates. On their own, Benjamin and Haas dubbed themselves The World's Greatest Tag Team, and quickly duplicated their earlier success, regaining the WWE Tag Team Championship from Guerrero and Tajiri.

But fate intervened. The tandem was forced to go their separate ways when Benjamin was sent to *Raw* via the WWE Draft in March 2004. They briefly reformed several times before parting ways with WWE in 2010. Afterward, they continued showcasing their vast talents across the world.

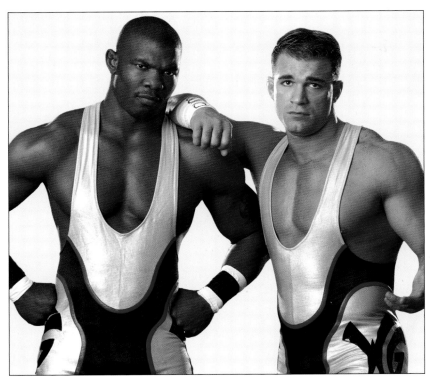

WRESTLEMANIA
see page 398

WWE HALL OF FAME
see page 400

WWE INTERNATIONAL HEAVYWEIGHT CHAMPIONSHIP

One of sports-entertainment's first prizes recognized globally, this Championship traces its history to the National Wrestling Alliance and Vince McMahon Sr.'s Capitol Wrestling. In 1959, a little over three years before WWE's official formation, WWE Hall of Famer Antonio "Argentina" Rocca became the first International Champion when he defeated future NWA World Heavyweight Champion "Nature Boy" Buddy Rogers.

In every way, Rocca was a "people's champion." The Italian-born and Argentinean-bred Superstar appealed to a variety of ethnicities and didn't need a title to draw a sellout crowd. When the WWE Championship was created in 1963, the International Heavyweight Championship was temporarily vacated.

But in 1982, the Championship was reintroduced. Tony Parisi and Gino Brito were Champions, followed by future Hall of Famer Tatsumi Fujinami. During this era, the prize was recognized in promotions in the United States, Canada, and Japan.

However, the various companies occasionally differed over whom to recognize as Champion. In 1984, Akira Maeda defeated Pierre "Mad Dog" Lefebvre for the disputed Title at Madison Square Garden before it was abandoned.

WWE INTERNATIONAL TAG TEAM CHAMPIONSHIP

This tag team Championship was the precursor to the most prestigious prize in all of tag team competition, the WWE World Tag Team Championship. In 1969, the Rising Suns (Mitsu Arakawa and Professor Toru Tanaka) came into WWE with the Titles, after winning the gold in a Japanese tournament. Later that year, Victor Rivera and Tony "Battman" Marino dethroned the Champions in New York, but the switch was not recognized in Pittsburgh, which started its own title lineage. In 1971, Geto Mongol and "Jumping" Johnny DeFazio were the last International champions recognized in Pittsburgh before the Championship was vacated.

For a brief period in 1985, the International Tag Team Championship was revived in the New Japan promotion before being deactivated again.

WWE NETWORK
see page 404

WWE US HEAVYWEIGHT CHAMPIONSHIP
see page 405

WWE US TAG TEAM CHAMPIONSHIP
see page 405

WWE TAG TEAM CHAMPIONSHIP
see page 406

WOMEN'S CHAMPIONSHIP

This prestigious prize was regarded as the pinnacle of women's wrestling for more than 50 years. The Championship's first title-holder, Fabulous Moolah, is considered the most successful, with an almost three decade Title reign. During its existence, incredible performers like Wendi Richter, Chyna, Trish Stratus, Lita, Maryse, and many other great names have enjoyed reigns atop the women's division. Stratus won the Title an amazing seven times in her Hall of Fame career, the seventh time serving as her Retirement Match. The Women's Championship was retired in 2010 after Michelle McCool defeated Melina to unify it with the Divas Championship.

1956

September 18 • Baltimore, MD
Fabulous Moolah def. **Judy Grable** in the finals of a tournament to crown a new Women's Champion

1984

July 23 • New York, NY
Wendi Richter def. **Fabulous Moolah**

1985

February 18 • New York, NY
Lelani Kai def. **Wendi Richter**

March 31 • New York, NY
Wendi Richter def. **Lelani Kai**

November 25 • New York, NY
Fabulous Moolah def. **Wendi Richter**

1986

July 3 • Brisbane, Australia
Velvet McIntyre def. **Fabulous Moolah**

July 9 • Sydney, Australia
Fabulous Moolah def. **Velvet McIntyre**

1987

July 24 • Houston, TX
Sherri Martel def. **Fabulous Moolah**

1988

October 7 • Paris, France
Rockin' Robin def. **Sheri Martel**
Rockin' Robin held the Women's Championship until 1990 when the Title was deemed inactive.

1993

December 13 • Poughkeepsie, NY
Alundra Blayze def. **Heidi Lee Morgan** in the finals of a tournament to crown a new Women's Champion

1994

November 27 • Tokyo, Japan
Bull Nakano def. **Alundra Blayze**

1995

April 3 • Poughkeepsie, NY
Alundra Blayze def. **Bull Nakano**

August 27 • Pittsburgh, PA
Bertha Faye def. **Alundra Blayze**

October 23 • Brandon, Manitoba
Alundra Blayze def. **Bertha Faye**
The Women's Championship was deemed inactive in December 1995 after Alundra Blayze left WWE.

1998

September 21 • Sacramento, CA
Jacqueline def. **Sable** in a match to crown a new Women's Champion

November 15 • St. Louis, MO
Sable def. **Jacqueline**

1999

May 10 • Orlando, FL
Debra def. **Sable**

June 14 • Worcester, MA
Ivory def. **Debra**

October 17 • Cleveland, OH
Fabulous Moolah def. **Ivory**

October 25 • Providence, RI
Ivory def. **Fabulous Moolah**

December 12 • Sunrise, FL
The Kat def. **Ivory, Jacqueline,** and **B.B.** in an Evening Gown in a Pool Match

2000

January 31 • Pittsburgh, PA
Hervina def. **The Kat**

February 3 • Detroit, MI
Jacqueline def. **Hervina**

March 30 • San Antonio, TX
Stephanie McMahon def. **Jacqueline**

August 21 • Lafayette, LA
Lita def. **Stephanie McMahon**

November 2 • Rochester, NY
Ivory def. **Lita, Trish Stratus,** and **Jacqueline** in a Fatal Four Way Match

June 13 • Columbus, OH
Trish Stratus def. **Lita, Gail Kim,** and **Victoria** in a Fatal Four Way Match

December 6 • Charlotte, NC
Lita def. **Trish Stratus**

2005

January 9 • Puerto Rico
Trish Stratus def. **Lita**

2006

April 2 • Chicago, IL
Mickie James def. **Trish Stratus**

August 14 • Charlottesville, VA
Lita def. **Mickie James**

September 17 • Toronto, Ontario
Trish Stratus def. **Lita**
Trish Stratus retired after the match, vacating the Women's Championship.

November 5 • Cincinnati, OH
Lita def. **Mickie James** in the finals of a tournament to crown a new Women's Champion

November 26 • Philadelphia, PA
Mickie James def. **Lita**

2007

February 19 • Bakersfield, CA
Melina def. **Mickie James**

April 24 • Paris, France
Mickie James def. **Melina** and **Victoria** in a Triple Threat Match

April 24 • Paris, France
Melina def. **Mickie James**

June 24 • Houston, TX
Candice def. **Melina**

October 7 • Chicago, IL
Beth Phoenix def. **Candice**

2008

April 14 • London, England
Mickie James def. **Beth Phoenix**

August 17 • Indianapolis, IN
Santino Marella & Beth Phoenix def. **Kofi Kingston & Mickie James** in an Intergender Winners-Take-All Match

2009

January 25 • Detroit, MI
Melina def. **Beth Phoenix**

June 28 • Sacramento, CA
Michelle McCool def. **Melina**

2010

January 31 • Atlanta, GA
Mickie James def. **Michelle McCool**

February 26 • Milwaukee, WI
Michelle McCool def. **Mickie James**

April 25 • Baltimore, MD
Beth Phoenix def. **Michelle McCool**

May 14 • Buffalo, NY
Layla def. **Beth Phoenix** in a Handicap Tornado Match that also included **Michelle McCool**

September 19 • Rosemont, IL
Michelle McCool def. **Melina**
Michelle McCool unified the Divas Championship and the Women's Championship at Night of Champions; the Women's Championship was declared inactive as a result.

WWE WOMEN'S CHAMPIONSHIP
see page 407

2001

April 1 • Houston, TX
Chyna def. **Ivory**
Chyna was stripped of the Women's Championship upon leaving WWE in November 2001.

November 18 • Greensboro, NC
Trish Stratus def. **Ivory, Jazz, Jacqueline, Molly Holly,** and **Lita** in a Six-Pack Challenge Match

2002

February 4 • Las Vegas, NV
Jazz def. **Trish Stratus**

May 13 • Toronto, Ontario
Trish Stratus & Bubba Ray Dudley def. **Jazz & Steven Richards** in a Mixed Gender Tag Team Match with the stipulation that if Trish Stratus pinned Jazz, then she would win the Women's Championship

June 23 • Columbus, OH
Molly Holly def. **Trish Stratus**

September 22 • Los Angeles, CA
Trish Stratus def. **Molly Holly**

November 17 • New York, NY
Victoria def. **Trish Stratus**

2003

March 30 • Seattle, WA
Trish Stratus def. **Victoria** and **Jazz** in a Triple Threat Match

April 27 • Worcester, MA
Jazz def. **Trish Stratus**

June 30 • Buffalo, NY
Gail Kim last eliminated **Victoria** in a 7-Diva Battle Royal that also included **Molly Holly, Trish Stratus, Ivory, Jacqueline,** and **Jazz**

July 28 • Colorado Springs, CO
Molly Holly def. **Gail Kim**

2004

February 23 • Omaha, NE
Victoria last eliminated **Lita** to become Women's Champion in a Fatal Four Way Elimination Match that also included **Jazz** and **Molly Holly**

WOMEN'S WORLD TAG TEAM CHAMPIONSHIP

The Women's World Tag Team Championship provided some of the greatest bouts in tag team history. WWE rings all over the world saw these femme fatales clash to capture tag team gold.

1983

May 1 • Calgary, Alberta
Velvet McIntyre & Princess Victoria are recognized as Champions
In late 1983 Princess Victoria gives her half of the Championship to Desiree Peterson.

1985

August 15 • Cairo, Egypt
The Glamour Girls def. **Velvet McIntyre & Desiree Peterson**

1988

January 24 • Hamilton, Ontario
The Jumping Bomb Angels def. **The Glamour Girls** in a Best 2-out-of-3 Falls Match

June 8 • Omiya, Japan
The Glamour Girls def. **The Jumping Bomb Angels**
The Women's Tag Team Championship was retired in 1989.

WCCW

In the early 1980s, Dallas-based WCCW erupted, due largely to the appeal of promoter Fritz Von Erich's charismatic sons. Popularity extended from Texas to Israel.

Von Erich became a partner in the territory, then called Big Time Wrestling, in 1966, assuming sole ownership in 1969. The debut of Fritz's oldest son, Kevin, in 1976, triggered a glory period. Brothers David, Kerry, Mike, and Chris followed, along with a youthful ensemble that included the Fabulous Freebirds, Gino Hernandez, Chris Adams, and Steve Austin. The Ultimate Warrior (then known as the Dingo Warrior) also appeared.

Sadly, WCCW is remembered for tragedy as well as triumph. David's untimely death in 1984 spawned a tribute show at Texas Stadium, featuring Kerry honoring his sibling by beating Ric Flair for the NWA title.

In 1986, WCCW left the NWA, recognizing Rick Rude as its inaugural champion.

But the 1987 death of Mike, along with growing competition, hurt morale. In 1988, WCCW partnered with Memphis-based CWA, renaming itself the United States Wrestling Association (USWA). By 1991, the USWA was running a limited Dallas schedule.

FRITZ VON ERICH

HT	6'4"	WT	270 lbs.
FROM	Lake Dallas, Texas		
SIGNATURE MOVE		Iron Claw	

Because of the excitement WCCW created, Fritz Von Erich is best remembered for his ownership of the promotion, and for his sons, Kevin, David, Kerry, Mike, and Chris. But he was also one of the biggest names in the industry, holding roughly 40 titles in seven territories, including the AWA crown. He served as NWA president from 1975 to 1976.

Trained by Doc Sarpolis and former champion Ed "Strangler" Lewis, Fritz lost his first 12 matches. In 1957, he migrated to Canada, where he began competing for Calgary promoter Stu Hart.

Claiming to be a Nazi sympathizer, Von Erich infuriated crowds, squeezing foes with his Iron Claw and kicking them with a size 15 boot, but adversity led to success. Back when the AWA was split into two regions, he won the Championship in both locations. He also competed in Japan, battling its top attractions, Shohei "Giant" Baba and Antonio Inoki.

In 1966, his attitude changed. He spoke fondly of the United States and purchased part of the Dallas territory with longtime promoter Ed McLemore. When McLemore died in 1969, Fritz became sole owner.

Rival Johnny Valentine claimed that Texas crowds were eager to cheer the man they'd previously booed. "If you're mean enough or tough enough," Valentine said, "they get to where they respect you."

At the Reunion Arena, as well as the "world famous Dallas Sportatorium," fans screamed for Fritz, as he brawled with The Sheik, Professor Toru Tanaka, Stan "The Man" Stasiak, and others—particularly manager Gary Hart's stable of evildoers.

By 1982, the Von Erichs were "the first family of Texas," with Kevin, Kerry, and David occasionally teaming with their father. That year, in a spectacle at Texas Stadium, Fritz competed in his retirement match, defeating King Kong Bundy. Although Fritz made periodic appearances later, the spotlight shifted to the next generation.

As WWE expanded, Fritz tried competing, launching a national tour and alliance with the AWA and other promotions. But in 1989, he sold his shares in WCCW.

Sadly, by the time Fritz died in 1997, all of his sons, except Kevin, had passed away.

GARY HART

"Playboy" Gary Hart possessed the cadence of a country preacher and the shrewdness of an underworld boss. Immaculately clad in handmade suits and alligator shoes, Hart changed the complexion of every territory he entered, but none more than WCCW.

The Chicago native was 18 when he made his debut at the Marigold Arena in 1960. But his life changed when Angelo Poffo, father of Randy "Macho Man" Savage, recruited Hart as an advisor. Clients eventually included a number of future WWE Hall of Famers, including Roddy Piper, the Funk Brothers, Larry Zbysko, and the Dingo Warrior—later known as the Ultimate Warrior.

In 1974, while managing Pak Song in the Florida territory, Hart gained infamy by using billboards to advertise a bounty on Dusty Rhodes.

Starting in 1976, he battled Fritz Von Erich and, later, Von Erich's sons in WCCW, recruiting disciples like The Spoiler and Abdullah the Butcher. After WCCW folded, he started a group called J-Tex Corporation in WCW, featuring Terry Funk and the Great Muta.

He died in 2008.

KEVIN VON ERICH

HT	6'2"	WT	235 lbs.
FROM	Lake Dallas, Texas		
SIGNATURE MOVE		Iron Claw	

When Kevin Von Erich became the first of his siblings to debut in WCCW in 1976, he viewed the endeavor as a "summer job." Instead, he ended up wrestling for 22 years, winning every major title in WCCW and mentoring future talent.

Kevin was a true matinee idol. When the "Golden Warrior" would walk to the ring, females of all ages surged forward to kiss him.

Early in his career, another competitor played a practical joke on Kevin by hiding his boots in the dressing room, forcing him to come to the ring barefoot. Between the ropes, Kevin felt unencumbered without his boots, and soon became known for wrestling barefoot, like onetime opponent, Jimmy "Superfly" Snuka. As with Snuka, Kevin began leaping on foes from the top rope.

Kevin battled everyone from King Kong Bundy to Ox Baker to Wild Bill Irwin. He called "Gentleman" Chris Adams his toughest opponent. A young Steve Austin considered Kevin a valuable advisor.

At the 2016 WWE Hall of Fame ceremony, The Fabulous Freebirds paid tribute to their old enemy.

DAVID VON ERICH

HT	6'7"	**WT**	240 lbs.
FROM	Denton County, Texas		
SIGNATURE MOVE			Iron Claw

Almost universally, wrestling experts agree that, had David Von Erich not died tragically young, he would have eventually won the NWA Championship.

Certainly, David appeared to be headed in that direction. In 1979, he defeated NWA Champion Harley Race in a non-title affair, after wrestling him to a draw two years earlier. He also beat Ric Flair for the Missouri Championship during a period when the "Nature Boy" was not the NWA kingpin.

In 1983, Jim Garvin and valet Sunshine were forced to perform menial tasks on David's ranch for the day after Garvin lost to the competitor fans lovingly called "The Yellow Rose of Texas."

David was 25 when he died during a Japan tour in 1984. he line of mourners extended five miles.

GINO HERNANDEZ

HT	6'3"	**WT**	240 lbs.
FROM	Highland Park, Texas		
SIGNATURE MOVE			Flying Elbow

Like WCCW itself, Gino Hernandez's time in the spotlight was brief and spectacular. Although fans generally jeered the "Handsome Half-Breed," so-named because of his mixed Latino and Italian heritage, even his adversaries were awed by his athletic skills and ability to contort events in his favor.

In WCCW, Hernandez made the Von Erichs his primary targets, teaming with a hulking woman, named Andrea the Lady Giant, in skirmishes against Mike Von Erich and valet Sunshine.

Hernandez also partnered with Jake Roberts and Chris Adams, who he convinced to turn on the Von Erichs. As the Dynamic Duo, the pair became known for clipping rivals' hair with a golden pair of scissors.

By the time of his 1986 death, Hernandez and Adams had become in-ring enemies.

"GENTLEMAN" CHRIS ADAMS

HT	6'1"	**WT**	237 lbs.
FROM	Stratford-upon-Avon, United Kingdom		
SIGNATURE MOVE			Superkick

At one time, Chris Adams was so close to the "First family of Texas" that he was called an "honorary Von Erich." When the relationship blew apart, fans condemned the Englishman as "Benedict Adams."

A 1976 British Olympian in judo, Adams arrived in WCCW in 1983, cutting down opponents with his martial arts-inspired Superkick. He utilized the finisher in battles alongside the Von Erichs against the Freebirds. But everything changed in 1984 when manager Gary Hart and partner Gino Hernandez convinced him to betray the Von Erichs. He regained fan favor when Hernandez temporarily blinded him.

Adams won the WCCW Heavyweight title from Rick Rude in 1986, and gained a reputation as a premier trainer, coaching Steve Austin and Scott Hall.

Adams died in 2001.

PERCIVAL PRINGLE III

A son of privilege, Percival Pringle III used his family funds to further the careers of clients like the Great Kabuki, Hollywood John Tatum, Blackjack Mulligan, and The Assassin.

The cousin of Gulf Coast territory superstar, "Marvelous" Marcel Pringle, Percival had a short career between the ropes, but was managing by 1978. In 1985, he began advising Rude in WCCW confrontations against Kevin Von Erich, "Gentleman" Chris Adams, and Iceman King Parsons.

For brief periods, the manager handled the Dingo Warrio—better known as the Ultimate Warrior—as well as a youthful Steve Austin.

In 1989, Pringle garnered cheers while supporting Eric Embry. But the fans' attitude soured during a conflict with Chris Von Erich that saw the portly manager again don the tights.

JIMMY GARVIN

HT	5'10"	**WT**	235 lbs.
FROM	Miami, Florida		
SIGNATURE MOVE			Brain Buster

When Jimmy Garvin started competing, he never imagined that a dog-washing incident would conjure up memories decades later.

Garvin provoked a rivalry with David Von Erich in 1983. When Garvin lost, he and his valet, Sunshine, were forced to spend a day performing lowly chores at Von Erich's horse ranch—]including washing the star's five dogs.

It was the first sign of discontent Sunshine exhibited with her boss. Eventually, she turned against Garvin and engaged in a series of matches with his new valet, Precious.

Yet, it was in WCCW that Garvin formed a deep bond with the Fabulous Freebirds, who came to regard him as a member.

Garvin became an airline pilot after retiring from the ring.

ERIC EMBRY

HT	5'10"	**WT**	250 lbs.
FROM	Phoenix, Arizona		
SIGNATURE MOVE			Piledriver

During WCCW's final days, "Flamboyant" Eric Embry made it his mission to represent the proud traditions of Dallas, becoming the promotion's last, true hero.

After performing in territories like Calgary, Vancouver, and San Antonio, he arrived in WCCW in 1987, warring with Jeff Jarrett. The two traded the WCCW Light Heavyweight Championship back and forth, with Embry scoring a victory at *SuperClash III*, a 1988 pay-per-view that also featured the stars of the AWA.

In 1989, General Skandor Akbar attempted to entice Embry into joining his devious "Army." Embry refused, and teamed with Jarrett and Chris Adams in struggles against Cactus Jack, Gary Young, Iceman King Parsons, and other Akbar charges.

His career was cut short by a 1992 car accident.

SEE ALSO:

THE VON ERICHS

THE FABULOUS FREEBIRDS

KERRY VON ERICH

World Class **CHAMPIONSHIP WRESTLING**

World Heavyweight Championship

For close to four decades, WWE recognized only one World Champion. But that all changed in 2002 when then-WWE Champion Brock Lesnar chose to become exclusive to *SmackDown*, leaving *Raw* without a top Superstar. General Manager Eric Bischoff quickly moved to rectify the situation by dusting off the old WCW Championship and awarding it to Triple H, making him the first-ever World Heavyweight Champion in WWE history.

Affectionately referred to by many as "the big gold belt," the World Heavyweight Championship entered WWE with decades of history. For more than ten years, the Championship was proudly worn by WCW's best, including Ric Flair, Sting, and Booker T. Before that, its lineage could be traced back to the NWA, where the likes of Dusty Rhodes and Ricky Steamboat represented the promotion as Champion.

Upon making its WWE debut, the World Heavyweight Championship remained *Raw*'s top prize until June 2005 when then-champ Batista was drafted to *SmackDown*. In subsequent years, after the *Raw-SmackDown* brand split ended, the Championship remained a prestigious Title within WWE, thanks in large part to the popularity of the Superstars who held it, most notably Daniel Bryan and John Cena.

The World Heavyweight Championship was unified in December 2013 when WWE Champion Randy Orton defeated World Heavyweight Champion John Cena, creating what is known today as the WWE World Heavyweight Championship.

2002

September 2 • Milwaukee, WI
Triple H was awarded the World Heavyweight Championship by *Raw* General Manager Eric Bischoff

November 11 • New York, NY
Shawn Michaels last eliminated **Triple H** to win the World Heavyweight Championship in an Elimination Chamber Match that also included **Chris Jericho**, **Kane**, **Booker T**, and **Rob Van Dam**

December 15 • Fort Lauderdale FL
Triple H def. **Shawn Michaels**

2003

September 21 • Hershey, PA
Goldberg def. **Triple H**

December 14 • Orlando, FL
Triple H def. **Goldberg** in a Triple Threat Match that also included **Kane**

2004

March 14 • New York, NY
Chris Benoit def. **Triple H** in a Triple Threat Match that also included **Shawn Michaels**

August 15 • Toronto, Ontario
Randy Orton def. **Chris Benoit**

September 12 • Portland, OR
Triple H def. **Randy Orton**
Eric Bischoff declared the World Heavyweight Championship vacant in December 2004 after a controversial ending to a Title defense.

2005

January 9 • Puerto Rico
Triple H last eliminated **Randy Orton** in an Elimination Chamber Match that also included **Edge**, **Chris Benoit**, **Chris Jericho,** and **Batista**

April 3 • Los Angeles, CA
Batista def. **Triple H**
Batista is forced to vacate the Championship due to injury.

2006

January 10 • Philadelphia, PA
Kurt Angle won a Battle Royal to become the World Heavyweight Champion

April 2 • Chicago, IL
Rey Mysterio def. **Randy Orton** in a Triple Threat Match that also included **Kurt Angle**

July 23 • Indianapolis, IN
King Booker def. **Rey Mysterio**

November 26 • Philadelphia, PA
Batista def. **King Booker**

2007

April 1 • Detroit, MI
Undertaker def. **Batista**

May 8 • Pittsburgh, PA
Edge def. **Undertaker**
An injury forced Edge to vacate the title in July, 2007.

July 17 • Laredo, TX
The Great Khali won a Battle Royal to become the World Heavyweight Champion

September 16 • Memphis, TN
Batista def. **The Great Khali** in a Triple Threat Match that also included **Rey Mysterio**

December 16 • Pittsburgh, PA
Edge def. **Batista** in a Triple Threat Match that also included **Undertaker**

2008

March 30 • Orlando, FL
Undertaker def. **Edge**
Vickie Guerrero stripped Undertaker of the World Heavyweight Championship in May, 2008.

June 1 • San Diego, CA
Edge def. **Undertaker** in a TLC Match

June 30 • Oklahoma City, OK
CM Punk def. **Edge**

September 7 • Cleveland, OH
Chris Jericho def. **Kane** in a Championship Scramble Match that also included **Batista**, **JBL** and **Rey Mysterio**

October 26 • Tampa, FL
Batista def. **Chris Jericho**

November 3 • Boston, MA
Chris Jericho def. **Batista**

November 23 • Boston, MA
John Cena def. **Chris Jericho**

2009

February 15 • Seattle, WA
Edge last eliminated **Rey Mysterio** in an Elimination Chamber match that also included WWE Champion **John Cena**, **Chris Jericho**, **Mike Knox**, and **Kane**

April 5 • Houston, TX
John Cena def. World Heavyweight Champion **Edge** and **Big Show** in a Triple Threat Match

April 26 • Providence, RI
Edge def. **John Cena**

June 7 • New Orleans, LA
Jeff Hardy def. **Edge**

June 7 • New Orleans, LA
CM Punk def. **Jeff Hardy**

July 26 • Philadelphia, PA
Jeff Hardy def. **CM Punk**

August 23 • Los Angeles, CA
CM Punk def. **Jeff Hardy**

October 4 • Newark, NJ
Undertaker def. **CM Punk**

2010

February 21 • St. Louis, MO
Chris Jericho def. **Undertaker**

April 2 • Las Vegas, NV
Jack Swagger def. **Chris Jericho**

June 20 • Uniondale, NY
Rey Mysterio def. **Jack Swagger**, **CM Punk**, and **Big Show** in a Fatal 4-Way Match

July 18 • Kansas City, MO
Kane def. **Rey Mysterio**

December 19 • Houston, TX
Edge def. **Kane**, **Rey Mysterio**, and **Alberto Del Rio** in a Tables, Ladders & Chairs Match
Edge was stripped of the Title in February, 2011 after using a move banned by SmackDown General Manager, Vickie Guerrero.

2011

February 18 • San Diego, CA
Dolph Ziggler was awarded the World Heavyweight Title

February 18 • San Diego, CA
Edge def. **Dolph Ziggler**
Edge gave up the Title when injuries forced him to retire in April, 2011.

May 1 • Tampa, FL
Christian def. **Alberto Del Rio**

May 6 • Orlando, FL
Randy Orton def. **Christian**

July 17 • Chicago, IL
Christian def. **Randy Orton**

August 14 • Los Angeles, CA
Randy Orton def. **Christian**

September 18 • Buffalo, NY
Mark Henry def. **Randy Orton**

December 18 • Baltimore, MD
Big Show def. **Mark Henry**

December 18 • Baltimore, MD
Daniel Bryan def. **Big Show**

2012

April 1 • Miami, FL
Sheamus def. **Daniel Bryan**

October 28 • Atlanta, GA
Big Show def. **Sheamus**

2013

January 8 • Miami, FL
Alberto Del Rio def. **Big Show**

April 8 • East Rutherford, NJ
Dolph Ziggler def. **Alberto Del Rio**

June 16 • Chicago, IL
Alberto Del Rio def. **Dolph Ziggler**

October 27 • Miami, FL
John Cena def. **Alberto Del Rio**

December 15 • Houston, TX
Randy Orton def. **John Cena**
Randy Orton became the inaugural WWE World Heavyweight Champion, merging the World Heavyweight and WWE Championships.

WORLD TAG TEAM CHAMPIONSHIP

The original tag team prize in WWE, the World Tag Team Championship was first awarded in 1971 and was later unified with the WWE Tag Team Championship at *WrestleMania 25*.

In its first decade of existence, Hall of Famers like The Blackjacks and The Valiants battled over the Championship before passing the torch to teams like Demolition and The Hart Foundation, who dominated the tag team scene in the 1980s. The memorable matches between these teams caught the attention of many young, aspiring Superstars. Teams like the Hardy Boyz, Edge and Christian, and the Dudley Boyz were living their lifelong dreams as World Tag Team Champions.

1971

June 3 • New Orleans, LA
Luke Graham & Tarzan Tyler def. **Dick the Bruiser & The Sheik** in the finals of a tournament to crown World Tag Team Champions

December 6 • New York, NY
Karl Gotch & Rene Goulet def. **Luke Graham & Tarzan Tyler**

1972

February 1 • Philadelphia, PA
Mikel Scicluna & King Curtis def. **Karl Gotch & Rene Goulet**

May 22 • New York, NY
Chief Jay Strongbow & Sonny King def. **Mikel Scicluna & King Curtis**

June 27 • Philadelphia, PA
Professor Tanaka & Mr. Fuji def. **Chief Jay Strongbow & Sonny King**

1973

May 30 • Hamburg, PA
Tony Garea & Haystacks Calhoun def. **Professor Tanaka & Mr. Fuji**

September 11 • Philadelphia, PA
Professor Tanaka & Mr. Fuji def. **Tony Garea & Haystacks Calhoun**

November 14 • Hamburg, PA
Tony Garea & Dean Ho def. **Professor Tanaka & Mr. Fuji**

1974

May 8 • Hamburg, PA
Jimmy & Johnny Valiant def. **Tony Garea & Dean Ho**

1975

May 13 • Philadelphia, PA
Victor Rivera & Dominic DeNucci def. **Jimmy & Johnny Valiant.**
Pat Barrett became Dominic DeNucci's partner when Victor Rivera left WWE in June 1975

August 26 • Philadelphia, PA
The Blackjacks def. **Dominic DeNucci & Pat Barrett**

November 8 • Philadelphia, PA
Tony Parisi & Louis Cerdan def. **The Blackjacks**

1976

May 11 • Philadelphia, PA
The Executioners def. **Tony Parisi & Louis Cerdan**
The Executioners were stripped of the World Tag Team Championship in December 1976 when they illegally used a third Executioner during a match.

December 7 • Philadelphia, PA
Chief Jay Strongbow & Billy White Wolf won a three-team tournament to capture the World Tag Team Championship
Injury forced Strongbow & White Wolf to vacate the Titles in August 1977.

1977

September 27 • Philadelphia, PA
Professor Tanaka & Mr. Fuji def. **Tony Garea & Larry Zbyszko** in the finals of a tournament to become new World Tag Team Champions

1978

March 14 • Philadelphia, PA
Dino Bravo & Dominic DeNucci def. **Professor Tanaka & Mr. Fuji**

June 26 • New York, NY
The Yukon Lumberjacks def. **Dino Bravo & Dominic DeNucci**

November 21 • Allentown, PA
Tony Garea & Larry Zbyszko def. **The Yukon Lumberjacks**

1979

March 6 • Allentown, PA
Johnny & Jerry Valiant def. **Tony Garea & Larry Zbyszko**

October 22 • New York, NY
Ivan Putski & Tito Santana def. **Johnny & Jerry Valiant**

1980

April 12 • Philadelphia, PA
The Samoans def. **Ivan Putski & Tito Santana**

August 9 • New York, NY
Bob Backlund & Pedro Morales def. **The Samoans.**
Shortly after winning the World Tag Team Championship, Bob Backlund & Pedro Morales were forced to vacate the Title due to Backlund already holding the WWE Championship.

September 9 • Allentown, PA
The Samoans def. **Tony Garea & Rene Goulet** in the finals of a tournament to crown new World Tag Team Champions

November 8 • Philadelphia, PA
Tony Garea & Rick Martel def. **The Samoans**

1981

March 17 • Allentown, PA
The Moondogs def. **Tony Garea & Rick Martel**

July 21 • Allentown, PA
Tony Garea & Rick Martel def. **The Moondogs**

October 13 • Allentown, PA
Mr. Fuji & Mr. Saito def. **Tony Garea & Rick Martel**

1982

June 28 • New York, NY
Jules & Chief Jay Strongbow def. **Mr. Fuji & Mr. Saito**

July 13 • Allentown, PA
Mr. Fuji & Mr. Saito def. **Jules & Chief Jay Strongbow**

October 26 • Allentown, PA
Jules & Chief Jay Strongbow def. **Mr. Fuji & Mr. Saito**

1983

March 8 • Allentown, PA
The Samoans def. **Jules & Chief Jay Strongbow**

November 15 • Allentown, PA
Tony Atlas & Rocky Johnson def. **The Samoans**

1984

April 17 • Hamburg, PA
Adrian Adonis & Dick Murdoch def. **Tony Atlas & Rocky Johnson**

1985

January 21 • Hartford, CT
Mike Rotundo & Barry Windham def. **Adrian Adonis & Dick Murdoch**

March 31 • New York, NY
Iron Sheik & Nikolai Volkoff def. **Mike Rotundo & Barry Windham**

June 17 • Poughkeepsie, NY
Mike Rotundo & Barry Windham def. **Iron Sheik & Nikolai Volkoff**

August 24 • Philadelphia, PA
Brutus Beefcake & Greg Valentine def. **Mike Rotundo & Barry Windham**

1986

April 7 • Rosemont, IL
The British Bulldogs def. **Brutus Beefcake & Greg Valentine**

1987

January 26 • Tampa, FL
The Hart Foundation def. **The British Bulldogs**

October 27 • Syracuse, NY
Strike Force def. **The Hart Foundation**

1988

March 27 • Atlantic City, NJ
Demolition def. **Strike Force**

1989

July 18 • Worcester, MA
Brain Busters def. **Demolition**

October 2 • Wheeling, WV
Demolition def. **Brain Busters**

December 13 • Huntsville, AL
Andre the Giant & Haku def. **Demolition**

1990

April 1 • Toronto, Ontario
Demolition def. **Andre the Giant & Haku**

August 27 • Philadelphia, PA
The Hart Foundation def. **Demolition**

1991

March 24 • Los Angeles, CA

The Nasty Boys def. **The Hart Foundation**

August 26 • New York, NY

The Legion of Doom def. **The Nasty Boys**

1992

February 7 • Denver, CO

Money, Inc. def. **The Legion of Doom**

July 20 • Worcester, MA

Natural Disasters def. **Money, Inc.**

October 13 • Regina, Saskatchewan

Money, Inc. def. **Natural Disasters**

1993

June 14 • Columbus, OH

The Steiners def. **Money, Inc.**

June 16 • Rockford, IL

Money, Inc. def. **The Steiners**

June 19 • St. Louis, MO

The Steiners def. **Money, Inc.**

September 13 • New York, NY

The Quebecers def. **The Steiners**

1994

January 10 • Richmond, VA

Marty Jannetty & 1-2-3 Kid def. **The Quebecers**

January 17 • New York, NY

The Quebecers def. **Marty Jannetty & 1-2-3 Kid**

March 29 • London, England

Men on a Mission def. **The Quebecers**

March 31 • Sheffield, England

The Quebecers def. **Men on a Mission**

April 26 • Burlington, VT

The Headshrinkers def. **The Quebecers**

August 28 • Indianapolis, IN

Diesel & Shawn Michaels def. **The Headshrinkers**

Diesel & Shawn Michaels were forced to vacate the World Tag Team Championship on November 23, 1994, after they were unable to co-exist as a team.

1995

January 22 • Tampa, FL

Bob Holly & 1-2-3 Kid def. **Bam Bam Bigelow & Tatanka** in the finals of a tournament to become new World Tag Team Champions

January 23 • Palmetto, FL

The Smokin' Gunns def. **Bob Holly & 1-2-3 Kid**

April 2 • Hartford, CT

Owen Hart & Yokozuna def. **The Smokin' Gunns**

January 23 • Palmetto, FL

The Smokin' Gunns def. **Bob Holly & 1-2-3 Kid**

April 2 • Hartford, CT

Owen Hart & Yokozuna def. **The Smokin' Gunns**

September 24 • Saginaw, MI

Diesel & Shawn Michaels def. **Owen Hart & Yokozuna**

The World Tag Team Championship was returned to Owen Hart & Yokozuna after their lawyer threatened legal action.

September 25 • Grand Rapids, MI

The Smokin' Gunns def. **Owen Hart & Yokozuna**

An injury to Billy Gunn's neck forced the Smokin' Gunns to vacate the World Tag Team Championship in February 1996.

1996

March 31 • Anaheim, CA

The Bodydonnas def. **The Godwinns** in the finals of a tournament to become new World Tag Team Champions

May 19 • New York, NY

The Godwinns def. **The Bodydonnas**

May 26 • Florence, SC

The Smokin' Gunns def. **The Godwinns**

September 22 • Philadelphia, PA

Owen Hart & Davey Boy Smith def. **The Smokin' Gunns**

1997

May 25 • Evansville, IN

Stone Cold Steve Austin & Shawn Michaels def. **Owen Hart & Davey Boy Smith**

An injury to Shawn Michaels forced Stone Cold Steve Austin & Shawn Michaels to vacate the World Tag Team Championship in July 1997.

July 14 • San Antonio, TX

Stone Cold Steve Austin & Dude Love def. **Owen Hart & Davey Boy Smith** in a match to determine new World Tag Team Champions

An injury to Austin's neck forced the duo to vacate the Titles in September 1997.

September 7 • Louisville, KY

Owen Hart & Davey Boy Smith won the World Tag Team Championship in a Fatal Four-Way Elimination Match that also included The Legion of Doom and The Godwinns

October 5 • St. Louis, MO

The Godwinns def. **The Headbangers**

October 7 • Topeka, KS

The Legion of Doom def. **The Godwinns**

November 24 • Fayetteville, NC

The New Age Outlaws def. **The Legion of Doom**

1998

March 29 • Boston, MA

Cactus Jack & Chainsaw Charlie def. **The New Age Outlaws**

Cactus Jack & Chainsaw Charlie were forced to vacate the World Tag Team Championship due to a controversial ending to their Title victory.

March 30 • Albany, NY

The New Age Outlaws def. **Cactus Jack & Chainsaw Charlie** in a Steel Cage Match

July 13 • East Rutherford, NJ

Kane & Mankind def. **New Age Outlaws**

July 26 • Fresno, CA

Stone Cold Steve Austin & Undertaker def. **Kane & Mankind**

August 10 • Omaha, NE

Kane & Mankind last eliminated **Stone Cold Steve Austin & Undertaker** to win the World Tag Team Championship in a Fatal Four-Way Match that also included the **New Age Outlaws** and **The Rock & D'Lo Brown**

August 30 • New York, NY

The New Age Outlaws def. **Mankind**

December 14 • Tacoma, WA

Big Boss Man & Ken Shamrock def. **The New Age Outlaws**

1999

January 25 • Phoenix, AZ

Owen Hart & Jeff Jarrett def. **Big Boss Man & Ken Shamrock**

March 30 • Uniondale, NY

Kane & X-Pac def. **Owen Hart & Jeff Jarrett**

May 31 • Moline, IL

The Acolytes def. **Kane & X-Pac**

July 5 • Fayetteville, NC

The Hardy Boyz def. **The Acolytes**

July 25 • Buffalo, NY

The Acolytes def. **The Hardy Boyz & Michael Hayes**

August 9 • Rosemont, IL

Kane & X-Pac def. **The Acolytes**

August 22 • Minneapolis, MN

Undertaker & Big Show def. **Kane & X-Pac**

August 30 • Boston, MA

Mankind & The Rock def. **Undertaker & Big Show**

September 9 • Albany, NY

Undertaker & Big Show def. **Mankind & The Rock**

September 20 • Houston, TX

Mankind & The Rock def. **Undertaker & Big Show**

September 23 • Dallas, TX

The New Age Outlaws def. **Mankind & The Rock**

October 14 • Birmingham, AL

Mankind & The Rock def. **The New Age Outlaws**

October 18 • Columbus, OH

Crash & Hardcore Holly def. **Mankind & The Rock**

November 4 • Philadelphia, PA

Mankind & Al Snow def. **Crash & Hardcore Holly**

November 8 • State College, PA

The New Age Outlaws def. **Mankind & Al Snow**

2000

February 27 • Hartford, CT

The Dudley Boyz def. **New Age Outlaws**

April 2 • Anaheim, CA

Edge & Christian def. **The Dudley Boyz & The Hardy Boyz** in a Triple Threat Ladder Match

May 29 • Vancouver, British Columbia

Too Cool def. **Edge & Christian**

June 25 • Boston, MA

Edge & Christian last eliminated **Too Cool** to win the World Tag Team Championship in Four Corners Elimination Match that also included **The Hardy Boyz** and **Test & Albert**

September 24 • Philadelphia, PA

The Hardy Boyz def. **Edge & Christian**

October 22 • Albany, NY

Edge & Christian def. **The Hardy Boyz**

October 23 • Hartford, CT

The Hardy Boyz def. **Edge & Christian**

December 10 • Birmingham, AL

Edge & Christian last eliminated **The Dudley Boyz** in a Four Corners Match that also included **Road Dogg & K-Kwik** and **Bull Buchanan & Goodfather**

December 18 • Greenville, SC

The Rock & Undertaker def. **Edge & Christian**

December 21 • Charlotte, NC

Edge & Christian def. **The Rock & Undertaker**

2007

January 29 • Dallas, TX

John Cena & Shawn Michaels def. **Edge & Randy Orton**

April 2 • Dayton, OH

The Hardy Boyz last eliminated **Lance Cade & Trevor Murdoch** in a 10-team Battle Royal that also included **Tommy Dreamer & Sandman, Brian Kendrick & Paul London, William Regal & Dave Taylor, Chavo Guerrero & Gregory Helms, Johnny Nitro & The Miz, Viscera & Val Venis, Kevin Thorn & Marcus Cor Von** and **John Cena & Shawn Michaels**

June 4 • Tampa, FL

Lance Cade & Trevor Murdoch def. **The Hardy Boyz**

Sep. 5 • Cape Town, South Africa

Paul London & Brian Kendrick def. **Lance Cade & Trevor Murdoch**

September 8 • Johannesburg, South Africa

Lance Cade & Trevor Murdoch def. **Paul London & Brian Kendrick**

December 10 • Bridgeport, CT

Cody Rhodes & Hardcore Holly def. **Lance Cade & Trevor Murdoch**

2008

June 29 • Dallas, TX

Cody Rhodes & Ted DiBiase def. **Hardcore Holly**

August 4 • Knoxville, TN

Batista & John Cena def. **Cody Rhodes & Ted DiBiase**

August 11 • Richmond, VA

Cody Rhodes & Ted DiBiase def. **Batista & John Cena**

October 27 • Tucson, AZ

CM Punk & Kofi Kingston def. **Cody Rhodes & Ted DiBiase**

December 13 • Hamilton, Ontario

The Miz & John Morrison def. **CM Punk & Kofi Kingston**

2009

April 5 • Houston, TX

Carlito & Primo def. **The Miz & John Morrison** to unify the World and WWE Tag Team Championships

June 28 • Sacramento, CA

Edge & Chris Jericho def. **Carlito & Primo**

July 26 • Philadelphia, PA

Big Show & Chris Jericho def. **Ted DiBiase & Cody Rhodes**

December 13 • San Antonio, TX

D-Generation X def. **Big Show & Chris Jericho**

2010

February 8 • Lafayette, LA

The Miz & Big Show def. **D-Generation X**

April 26 • Richmond, VA

The Hart Dynasty def. **The Miz & Big Show**
In August 2010, the new WWE Tag Team Titles were awarded to the Hart Dynasty and the World Tag Team Championship was retired.

2001

January 21 • New Orleans, LA

The Dudley Boyz def. **Edge & Christian**

March 5 • Washington, D.C.

The Hardy Boyz def. **The Dudley Boyz**

March 19 • Albany, NY

Edge & Christian def. **The Hardy Boyz**

March 19 • Albany, NY

The Dudley Boyz def. **Edge & Christian**

April 1 • Houston, TX

Edge & Christian def. **The Dudley Boyz & The Hardy Boyz** in a Tables, Ladders and Chairs Match

April 19 • Nashville, TN

Undertaker & Kane def. **Edge & Christian**

April 29 • Chicago, IL

Stone Cold Steve Austin & Triple H def. **Undertaker & Kane**

May 21 • San Jose, CA

Chris Benoit & Chris Jericho def. **Stone Cold Steve Austin & Triple H**

June 21 • Orlando, FL

The Dudley Boyz def. **Chris Benoit & Chris Jericho**

July 9 • Atlanta, GA

The APA def. **The Dudley Boyz**

August 9 • Los Angeles, CA

Kanyon & Diamond Dallas Page def. **The APA**

August 19 • San Jose, CA

Undertaker & Kane def. **Kanyon & Diamond Dallas Page**

September 17 • Nashville, TN

The Dudley Boyz def. **Undertaker & Kane**

October 22 • Kansas City, MO

The Rock & Chris Jericho def. **The Dudley Boyz**

November 1 • Cincinnati, OH

Booker T & Test def. **The Rock & Chris Jericho**

November 12 • Boston, MA

The Hardy Boyz def. **Booker T & Test**

November 18 • Greensboro, NC

The Dudley Boyz def. **The Hardy Boyz**
The Dudley Boyz beat the Hardy Boyz in a Steel Cage Match to unify the World and WCW Tag Team Championships.

2002

January 7 • New York, NY

Tazz & Spike Dudley def. **The Dudley Boyz**

February 21 • Rockford, IL

Billy & Chuck def. **Tazz & Spike Dudley**

May 19 • Nashville, TN

Rico & Rikishi def. **Billy & Chuck**

June 6 • Oklahoma City, OK

Billy & Chuck def. **Rico & Rikishi**

July 4 • Boston, MA

Hulk Hogan & Edge def. **Billy & Chuck**

July 21 • Detroit, MI

Christian & Lance Storm def. **Hulk Hogan & Edge**

September 23 • Anaheim, CA

Kane & the Hurricane def. **Christian & Lance Storm**

October 14 • Montreal, Quebec

Christian & Chris Jericho def. **Kane & the Hurricane**

December 15 • Fort Lauderdale, FL

Booker T & Goldust last eliminated **Christian & Chris Jericho** to win the World Tag Team Championship in a Fatal Four Way Elimination Match that also included **The Dudley Boyz** and **Lance Storm & William Regal**

2003

January 6 • Phoenix, AZ

William Regal & Lance Storm def. **Booker T & Goldust**

January 19 • Boston, MA

The Dudley Boyz def. **William Regal & Lance Storm**

January 20 • Providence, RI

William Regal & Lance Storm def. **The Dudley Boyz**
An injury to William Regal forced him to vacate the World Tag Team Championship on in March 2003.

March 24 • Sacramento, CA

Lance Storm & Chief Morley are awarded the World Tag Team Championship

March 31 • Seattle, WA

Kane & Rob Van Dam last eliminated **Lance Storm & Chief Morley** in an Elimination Match that also included **The Dudley Boyz**

June 15 • Houston, TX

Sylvain Grenier & Rene Dupree def. **Kane & Rob Van Dam**

September 21 • Hershey, PA

The Dudley Boyz def. **Sylvain Grenier, Rene Dupree & Rob Conway**

December 14 • Orlando, FL

Ric Flair & Batista last eliminated **The Dudley Boyz** to win the World Tag Team Championship in a Tag Team Turmoil Match that also included **The Hurricane & Rosey, Mark Jindrak & Garrison Cade, La Resistance, Val Venis & Lance Storm,** and **Scott Steiner & Test**

2004

February 16 • Bakersfield, CA

Booker T & Rob Van Dam def. **Ric Flair & Batista**

March 22 • Detroit, MI

Ric Flair & Batista def. **Booker T & Rob Van Dam**

April 19 • Calgary, Alberta

Chris Benoit & Edge def. **Ric Flair & Batista**

May 31 • Montreal, Quebec

Sylvain Grenier & Rob Conway def. **Chris Benoit & Edge**

October 19 • Milwaukee, WI

Chris Benoit & Edge def. **Sylvain Grenier & Rob Conway**

November 1 • Peoria, IL

Sylvain Grenier & Rob Conway def. **Chris Benoit**

November 15 • Indianapolis, IN

Eugene & William Regal beat **Sylvain Grenier & Rob Conway** to win the World Tag Team Championship in an Elimination Match that also included **Rhyno & Tajiri**

2005

January 16 • Winnipeg, Manitoba

Sylvain Grenier & Rob Conway def. **William Regal & Jonathan Coachman,** who was filling in for an injured Eugene

February 7 • Tokyo, Japan

Tajiri & William Regal def. **Sylvain Grenier & Rob Conway**

May 1 • Manchester, NH

The Hurricane & Rosey def. **Sylvain Grenier & Rob Conway** in a Tag Team Turmoil Match that also included **The Heart Throbs, Simon Dean & Maven** and **Tajiri & William Regal**

Sep.18 • Oklahoma City, OK

Lance Cade & Trevor Murdoch def. **The Hurricane & Rosey**

November 1 • San Diego, CA

Big Show & Kane def. **Lance Cade & Trevor Murdoch**

2006

April 3 • Chicago, IL

Spirit Squad def. **Big Show & Kane**

November 5 • Cincinnati, OH

Ric Flair & Roddy Piper def. **Spirit Squad**

November 13 • Manchester, England

Edge & Randy Orton def. **Ric Flair & Roddy Piper**

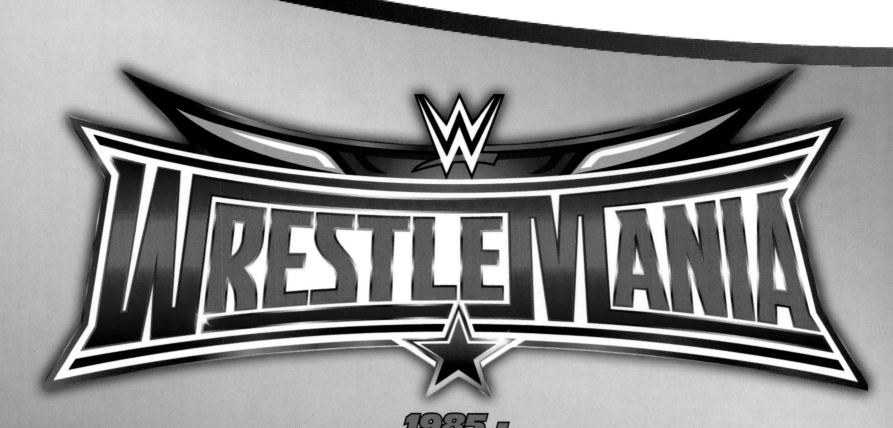

WRESTLEMANIA

1985 -

For over thirty years, it has been the Grandest Stage of Them All. Every year, *WrestleMania* produces moments that resound through generations, transform Superstars into legends and legends into immortals. It is the dream of every Superstar who steps into a WWE ring to one day compete in its main event. For the elite few that have, it is a surreal experience that has shaped and defined their legacies.

WWE's annual pop culture extravaganza was conceived in the mid-1980s based on the notion that WWE needed a yearly event that celebrates its unique brand of entertainment, much like any other sports or entertainment entity. During a period of national expansion for WWE, Vince McMahon opened his doors to celebrated luminaries from the mainstream. This infusion of star power paired with the growing phenomena of WWE became known as "Rock 'n' Wrestling." The formula proved successful and, as WWE's popularity grew, its roster became stockpiled with the most illustrious names in the industry, with top Superstars becoming increasingly eager to become part of the excitement. Vince and his inner brain trust sensed the time was right to put on one massive event, one that would be to WWE what the Oscars are to Hollywood and what the Super Bowl is to football. The event was held in the world famous Madison Square Garden on March 31, 1985, broadcast on closed circuit television (a concept as foreign as a rotary phone in modern times) and was dubbed *WrestleMania*.

Today, it is hard to appreciate the gravity of the situation. After thirty-two editions of the Show of Shows, the WWE Universe has grown accustomed to seeing attendance and viewership records shattered on an annual basis. In 1985, no one (except *maybe* Mr. McMahon) could have envisioned the exponential growth that would be witnessed in the decades to come. As eager fans began filing in through the Madison Square Garden concourse, tension mounted backstage. There was no guarantee that the event would be a success. Had it failed, WWE would likely have been out of business and not exist today.

As you've surely deduced, it did not fail. Not only was the inaugural *WrestleMania* a major triumph for WWE, it was the dawning of a new era in sports-entertainment. Two years later, 93,173 spectators flocked to the Pontiac Silverdome for *WrestleMania III*, setting an indoor attendance record. Records continued to fall like dominoes over the next thirty years as *WrestleMania* realized WWE's original vision and became a must-see attraction packed with pomp, grandeur, a celebrity influx, and the most monumental matches on the WWE calendar.

Over the years, the greatest Superstars have risen to the occasion under its bright lights, becoming synonymous with the event itself. Hulk Hogan's titanic slamming of Andre the Giant is but one of the lasting images in WWE history.

Shawn Michaels built a Hall of Fame career around his show-stopping performances at the Show of Shows, which earned him the moniker "Mr. WrestleMania." The rivalry between Stone Cold Steve Austin and The Rock reached a crescendo an amazing three times at *WrestleMania*, further cementing both men's place in WWE lore. Triple H has ascended to WWE royalty and in the process, competed in an astounding twenty matches on the Grandest Stage. And no *'Mania* would be complete without WWE's longtime cornerstone, John Cena, unveiling a grandiose entrance, taking his signature sprint down the extended ramp and coming through in another pressure-packed main event. Among all these WWE deities, however, no one has staked a claim to the annual spectacle as profound as Undertaker. For a mindboggling twenty-one straight contests, no one could upstage The Deadman. The Demon from Death Valley turned back a who's who of WWE legends during his two-decade reign of terror before Brock Lesnar finally snapped his celebrated Streak at *WrestleMania 30*. With a victory over Shane McMahon at *WrestleMania 32*, Undertaker ran his win-loss record to an unfathomable 23-1.

WWE returned to its home, Madison Square Garden, for the tenth and twentieth editions of the Show of Shows. Famed arenas such as the Los Angeles Staples Center, Chicago's Allstate Arena, and Boston's TD Garden have also played host. However, when *'Mania* returned to the Motor City for the twentieth anniversary of the "Slam Heard Round the World," it was clear the extravaganza was indeed "All Grown Up," as the theme for its 23rd showcase suggested. Since then, *WrestleMania* has been held exclusively in stadiums, allowing WWE to outdo itself each year and show off how far it has come since that fateful experiment in 1985. In 2016, WWE finally surpassed its twenty-nine-year-old attendance mark, packing the Dallas Cowboys' AT&T Stadium to the brim with 101,763 screaming members of the WWE Universe.

Beyond the main Sunday attraction, *WrestleMania* has also evolved into a weeklong celebration as fans pour in from all fifty states and as many as thirty-seven countries. WWE takes over the host city with its annual interactive fan event, Axxess, NXT specials, the WWE Hall of Fame induction ceremony, Superstar appearances, community events, and much more. The festivities have even extended to Monday, as the *Raw* episode following *'Mania* has become notorious for the boisterous atmosphere in the stands.

As "The Showcase of the Immortals" continues into its fourth decade, WWE's modern day Superstars look to claim their piece of history, leading many to believe that the best is yet to come.

HALL OF FAME

The WWE Hall of Fame honors not just the legends of WWE, but stars from throughout professional wrestling history, along with celebrities and other personalities who've contributed to the growth of sports-entertainment.

Among those notables: baseball's all-time hit leader, Pete Rose, who engaged in a series of conflicts with Kane; Mr. T, who teamed with Hulk Hogan at *WrestleMania I*; and Donald Trump, who shaved Vince McMahon's head at *WrestleMania 23*.

The WWE Hall of Fame ceremony takes place the night before *WrestleMania*, and provides memories inextricably tied to the big event. Today, Hall of Fame rites are held in a large arena, like the American Airlines Center in Dallas and Madison Square Garden in New York. But the first induction occurred on *Monday Night Raw* in 1993, when Andre the Giant was honored shortly after his death. For the next two years, ceremonies occurred in hotel ballrooms on the eve of the *King of the Ring*. In 1996, the ritual as held in conjunction with *Survivor Series*.

For the next eight years, no inductions took place, but in 2004, the Hall of Fame became a permanent attraction, presented on a wider scale and directly tied to *WrestleMania*. The next year, an abridged version of the event was televised, first on Spike TV and, from 2006, on the USA Network. In 2014, live telecasts started on the WWE Network, which also allows subscribers to view past Hall of Fame ceremonies.

Over time, these observances created to enshrine history have become part of history themselves. In 1994, Vince McMahon himself inducted a figure unknown to most fans, but whose contributions were groundbreaking for the industry. In addition to working for Vince's grandfather, Jess, as well as father, Vincent J. McMahon, James Dudley became the first African-American to manage a major American arena when he began overseeing operations at Turner's Arena in Washington, DC, during a time when much of the country was still segregated.

Two years later, the ceremony included another key moment for the McMahon family when an emotional Shane inducted his grandfather, Vincent J. McMahon, while future brother-in-law, Triple H enshrined the man who trained him for the sport of kings, Killer Kowalski.

Of every Hall of Fame speech, few were as amusing as the one delivered by manager Bobby "The Brain" Heenan in 2004. After talking about his battle with throat cancer and the

way former protégé Blackjack Lanza's black mustache would turn white when he attempted to sneak powder donuts, the man disparagingly called "The Weasel" described his days announcing alongside Gorilla Monsoon:

"When I came here, they had three Freebirds, they had the Junkyard Dog, two Bulldogs with (mascot) Matilda, another dog. You had two Killer Bees. You had a guy with a snake (Jake Roberts). You had a Hawaiian guy (Ricky Steamboat) with a lizard...I'm not done yet. And to top it all off, I'm the Weasel doing commentary with a Gorilla...*That's* wildlife!"

Equally entertaining was Iron Sheik's 2006 induction. On several occasions, he seemed to complete his speech, only to become possessed by another thought and veer off on a new tangent. Remembering the night he lost the WWE World Heavyweight Championship to Hulk Hogan in 1983, he revealed that Verne Gagne, promoter of the rival AWA at the time, asked him to deliberately snap The Hulkster's leg in the match. Then, the Sheik claimed, Gagne advised him to appear on the AWA's Minneapolis-based television show with the Title.

"Mr. Gagne told me, 'Break that Hollywood blond jabroni's leg, take the belt to Minnesota,'" the Iranian-born legend said in heavily accent English. "But I tell Mr. Gagne, 'I'm sorry. Maybe you think Hulk Hogan is a jabroni Hollywood blond. But my boss, (Vincent J.) McMahon is not jabroni. He is the real number one promoter in the world.'"

Both fans and Superstars rose to their feet, laughing and cheering. "God bless his soul," the Sheik proclaimed. "I love him forever!"

In 2005, Cowboy Bob Orton went from revered Hall of Fame inductee to hated provocateur in less than 24 hours, when he showed up at *WrestleMania XXI* and interfered in his son, Randy's match with Undertaker. It was a pointless effort, as The Viper became The Phenom's 13th consecutive *WrestleMania* victim.

Another interesting family dynamic occurred in 2012 when masked Mexican great Mil Mascaras was inducted by his nephew, Alberto Del Rio.

For years, many fans believed that there was a large void in the WWE Hall of Fame, since Bruno Sammartino, the man who, in many ways, symbolized the company for a sizeable chunk of the 1960s and 1970s, had yet to be inducted.

Some were uncertain if this would ever occur, due to Sammartino's longtime estrangement from the company. In 2013, those differences were resolved, and Bruno assumed his rightful place in the Hall of Fame. Making the moment even more poignant was the fact that the ceremony was held in Madison Square Garden, the site of Bruno's most notable triumphs.

The next year, WWE and another disenfranchised former WWE World Heavyweight Champion, Ultimate Warrior, reconciled their differences, as well. In this case, Warrior requested that Linda McMahon, the former WWE president and CEO who'd frequently hosted the former Titlist at her home, induct him.

During his speech, Warrior made it a point to "thank the Superstars that you never see...all the people behind the scenes here that work for WWE, some of them for years, 25, 30 years." He also reminded the fans, "You are legendary. I am here because of you." Sadly, within days of the ceremony, Ultimate Warrior passed away.

However, the Warrior's legacy continues to be felt at each ceremony. In 2015, Connor "The Crusher" Michalek, an eight-year-old fan who died from cancer the previous year, posthumously received the first Warrior Award for exhibiting "unwavering strength and perseverance, and (living) life with the courage and compassion that embodies the indomitable spirit of the Ultimate Warrior."

The next year's recipient, television anchor Joan Lunden, described her public battle with breast cancer, a fight she won, she claimed, because she possessed the same fortitude as Ultimate Warrior.

The 2016 Hall of Fame introduced a new, important element to the institution. Since only a limited number of honorees can be inducted at a time, many of the old-time greats had been missing from the WWE Hall of Fame. The situation was alleviated with the first "Legacy" enshrinements. The recipients included Frank Gotch, who became the first American to be recognized as a world champion in 1908; his primary rival, "Russian Lion" George Hackenschmidt; Lou Thesz, known as the "Babe Ruth of Wrestling;" Ed "Strangler" Lewis, a champion and promoter in the 1920s and 1930s credited with developing the sleeper hold; Mildred Burke, who became "Queen of the Ring" with her 1935 championship win; Pat O'Connor, the only competitor to hold the NWA and AWA Titles simultaneously, and "Sailor" Art Thomas, one of the first African-Americans to be allowed to regularly compete for world championships.

One year after competing against Triple H at *WrestleMania 31*, Sting used his 2016 induction to announce his retirement. As fans chanted, "Thank you, Sting," he slipped on a pair of dark sunglasses and swung the black baseball bat he'd wield against WCW villains, assuring his followers, "This isn't goodbye. It's just 'see you later.'"

Another touching moment occurred when the surviving members of the Fabulous Freebirds, Michael Hayes and Jimmy Garvin, united on stage with old enemy Kevin Von Erich, who emphasized that, even when they hurt each other, they were always united by the brotherhood that came from entertaining the fans who lived for the sport of kings.

WWE Hall of Fame Inductees

1993

- ★ ANDRE THE GIANT

1994

- ★ ARNOLD SKAALAND
- ★ BOBO BRAZIL
- ★ BUDDY ROGERS
- ★ CHIEF JAY STRONGBOW
- ★ "CLASSY" FREDDIE BLASSIE
- ★ GORILLA MONSOON
- ★ JAMES DUDLEY

1995

- ★ ANTONINO ROCCA
- ★ ERNIE LADD
- ★ FABULOUS MOOLAH
- ★ GEORGE "THE ANIMAL" STEELE
- ★ THE GRAND WIZARD
- ★ IVAN PUTSKI
- ★ PEDRO MORALES

1996

- ★ BARON MIKEL SCICLUNA
- ★ "CAPTAIN" LOU ALBANO
- ★ JIMMY "SUPERFLY" SNUKA
- ★ JOHNNY RODZ
- ★ KILLER KOWALSKI
- ★ PAT PATTERSON
- ★ THE VALIANT BROTHERS
- ★ VINCENT J. MCMAHON

2004

- ★ BIG JOHN STUDD
- ★ BOBBY "THE BRAIN" HEENAN
- ★ DON MURACO
- ★ GREG "THE HAMMER" VALENTINE
- ★ HARLEY RACE
- ★ JESSE "THE BODY" VENTURA
- ★ JUNKYARD DOG
- ★ PETE ROSE
- ★ SGT. SLAUGHTER
- ★ "SUPERSTAR" BILLY GRAHAM
- ★ TITO SANTANA

2005

- ★ "COWBOY" BOB ORTON
- ★ HULK HOGAN
- ★ IRON SHEIK
- ★ JIMMY HART
- ★ NIKOLAI VOLKOFF
- ★ PAUL ORNDORFF
- ★ "ROWDY" RODDY PIPER

2006

- ★ THE BLACKJACKS
- ★ BRET "HIT MAN" HART
- ★ EDDIE GUERRERO
- ★ "MEAN" GENE OKERLUND
- ★ "SENSATIONAL" SHERRI
- ★ TONY ATLAS
- ★ VERNE GAGNE
- ★ WILLIAM PERRY

2007

- ★ DUSTY RHODES
- ★ JERRY "THE KING" LAWLER
- ★ JIM ROSS
- ★ MR. FUJI
- ★ "MR. PERFECT" CURT HENNIG
- ★ NICK BOCKWINKEL
- ★ THE SHEIK
- ★ THE WILD SAMOANS

2008

- ★ THE BRISCO BROTHERS
- ★ EDDIE GRAHAM
- ★ GORDON SOLIE
- ★ "HIGH CHIEF" PETER MAIVIA
- ★ MAE YOUNG
- ★ RIC FLAIR
- ★ ROCKY JOHNSON

2009

- ★ BILL WATTS
- ★ THE FUNKS
- ★ HOWARD FINKEL
- ★ KOKO B. WARE
- ★ RICKY "THE DRAGON" STEAMBOAT
- ★ STONE COLD STEVE AUSTIN
- ★ THE VON ERICHS

2010

- ★ ANTONIO INOKI
- ★ BOB UECKER
- ★ GORGEOUS GEORGE
- ★ MAURICE "MAD DOG" VACHON
- ★ STU HART
- ★ "MILLION DOLLAR MAN" TED DIBIASE
- ★ WENDI RICHTER

2011

- ★ ABDULLAH THE BUTCHER
- ★ "BULLET" BOB ARMSTRONG
- ★ DREW CAREY
- ★ "HACKSAW" JIM DUGGAN
- ★ ROAD WARRIORS W/ PAUL ELLERING
- ★ SHAWN MICHAELS
- ★ SUNNY

2012

- ★ EDGE
- ★ FOUR HORSEMEN
- ★ MIKE TYSON
- ★ MIL MASCARAS
- ★ RON SIMMONS
- ★ YOKOZUNA

2013

- ★ BOB BACKLUND
- ★ BOOKER T
- ★ BRUNO SAMMARTINO
- ★ DONALD TRUMP
- ★ MICK FOLEY
- ★ TRISH STRATUS

2014

- ★ CARLOS COLÓN
- ★ JAKE "THE SNAKE" ROBERTS
- ★ LITA
- ★ MR. T
- ★ PAUL BEARER
- ★ RAZOR RAMON
- ★ THE ULTIMATE WARRIOR

2015

- ★ ALUNDRA BLAYZE
- ★ ARNOLD SCHWARZENEGGER
- ★ THE BUSHWHACKERS
- ★ CONNOR "THE CRUSHER" MICHALEK
- ★ KEVIN NASH
- ★ LARRY ZBYSZKO
- ★ "MACHO MAN" RANDY SAVAGE
- ★ RIKISHI
- ★ TATSUMI FUJINAMI

2016

- ★ BIG BOSS MAN
- ★ THE FABULOUS FREEBIRDS
- ★ THE GODFATHER
- ★ JACQUELINE
- ★ JOAN LUNDEN
- ★ SNOOP DOGG
- ★ STAN HANSEN
- ★ STING

LEGACY INDUCTEES

- ★ ED "STRANGLER" LEWIS
- ★ FRANK GOTCH
- ★ GEORGE HACKENSCHMIDT
- ★ LOU THESZ
- ★ MILDRED BURKE
- ★ PAT O' CONNOR
- ★ "SAILOR" ART THOMAS

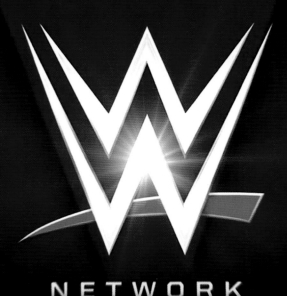

NETWORK

WWE Network is the first-ever, 24-hour-a-day direct to consumer network, offering fans selections culled from more than 100,000 hours of content in WWE's library, along with original programs and other features. Viewers can either watch WWE Network live or scroll through its menu and select any show previously broadcast. Subscribers also have the luxury of turning off a program, then resuming at the exact spot where they left off.

When WWE Network was introduced in the United States in 2014, the innovative service was compared to the company's pioneering efforts in the pay-per-view field three decades earlier. However, given the way consumers in the 21st Century will watch sports, news, and entertainment, the patterns set by the streaming service have already had far greater impact.

Shortly after the network's launch, the *New York Times* noted that WWE had "positioned themselves on the cutting edge of Internet television." Within nine months of the launch date, total subscribers increased a staggering 79 percent. The English-language version of WWE Network can now be watched in more than 180 countries, including Australia, New Zealand, the United Kingdom, Hong Kong, North Africa, and the Middle East. In Canada, WWE Network can be seen on television via a partnership between WWE and Rogers Communications.

Part of the popularity can be attributed to the fact that, along with shows created specifically for the network, documentaries, reality programs, and classic matches, fans automatically receive all 12 annual WWE pay-per-views, as well as one-time events like *The Beast in the East*, a WWE card emanating from Tokyo's Ryogoku Kokugikan (formerly Sumo Hall) on July 4, 2015, *NXT TakeOver: London* on December 16, 2015, and *WWE Roadblock* from Toronto's Ricoh Coliseum on March 12, 2016.

In other words, in the course of a day, a viewer can witness Roman Reigns, Bruno Sammartino, John Cena, and Ric Flair all defending WWE gold in different epochs.

Another appealing aspect of the network is the wide range of viewing possibilities. Along with watching on desktop computers and laptops through WWE.com, shows can be accessed via the WWE App on Amazon Fire TV and Kindle Fire Devices, Android devices like Samsung Galaxy, iOS devices like Apple

iPad and iPhone, Apple TV, Roku streaming devices, Sony PlayStation 3 and Sony PlayStation4, Xbox One and Xbox 360, Sony Internet connected televisions, Blu-ray Disc players and Blue-ray Home Theater systems, and Samsung Smart TV devices, among others.

Programs include old episodes of *Raw* and *SmackDown,* as well as every pay-per-view ever offered by WWE, WCW, and ECW. Among the other choices: the comedic *Tuesday Night Titans* show that aired at the height of the "Rock 'n' Wrestling" era, all the *WWE Tribute to the Troops* broadcasts, and each WWE Hall of Fame ceremony. As the caretakers of history, WWE provides old AWA, NWA Mid-South, Smoky Mountain, and World Class Championship Wrestling television programs too.

The first WWE Network show that drew a vociferously loyal audience was *WWE Legend's House,* a reality series featuring WWE Hall of Famers "Hacksaw" Jim Duggan, Tony Atlas, "Rowdy" Roddy Piper, Pat Patterson, Jimmy Hart, "Mean" Gene Okerlund, and others. This was quickly followed by a number of compelling series, including *The Monday Night War: WWE vs. WCW,* about the epic battle between the two companies in the 1990s and early 2000s, *WWE Slam City,* a children's program depicting WWE Superstars as animated characters, *Ride Along,* a true-life chronicle of WWE Superstars and Divas driving from city to city, the comedic *Edge and Christian Show That Totally Reeks of Awesomeness,* and no-holds-barred interview shows like *Live! With Chris Jericho,* and the Steve Austin-hosted *Stone Cold Podcast.* On a memorable episode of *WWE Rivalries,* Bret "Hit Man" Hart and Shawn Michaels sat in the same studio, describing their heated rivalry in and out of the arena. With the cameras rolling, the retired gladiators tearfully made peace, leaving the building as friends.

There are also expertly curated *Collections* programs centered on themes like the most exciting clashes in Canada, show stealing *WrestleMania* matches, and enthralling TLC collisions.

In addition to peering back into the past, WWE Network has looked into the future, presenting weekly NXT matches, a global cruiserweight tournament and a Diva search. With this wealth of programming, fans can always find great sports-entertainment on the WWE Network.

U.S. WWE HEAVYWEIGHT CHAMPIONSHIP

Shortly after "Nature Boy" Buddy Rogers became the first Champion of what would become WWE in 1963, the company created the United States Heavyweight Championship, a Title as important as the Intercontinental crown today. The prize is not connected to the United States Championship currently defended in WWE, a Title that traces its lineage to WCW and the old Mid-Atlantic territory. The Championship was discontinued in 1976.

1963
Bobo Brazil is recognized as the first United States Heavyweight Champion

1963
June 8 • Philadelphia, PA
Johnny Barend def. Bobo Brazil

July 9 • Philadelphia, PA
Bobo Brazil def. Johnny Barend

1967
June 18
Ray Stevens def. Bobo Brazil

August 24 • Trenton, NJ
Bobo Brazil def. Ray Stevens

September 22 • Salisbury, MD
The Sheik def. Bobo Brazil

1968
November 25 • Washington, D.C.
Bobo Brazil def. The Sheik

1969
January 20 • Boston, MA
The Sheik def. Bobo Brazil

February 10 • Washington, D.C.
Bobo Brazil def. The Shiek

1971
January • Los Angeles, CA
Pedro Morales def. Fred Blassie in the finals of a tournament
On February 8, 1971, Pedro Morales forfeited the title when he became the WWE Heavyweight Champion.

February 15
Bobo Brazil was recognized as Champion and would go on to hold the championship until it was retired from WWE.

U.S. WWE TAG TEAM CHAMPIONSHIP

The WWE United States Tag Team Championship predates the founding of WWE. The Title was introduced in 1958, after Mark Lewin and Don Curtis defeated Hans Schmidt and Dick the Bruiser in a tournament final, and defended it in the Capitol Wrestling territory run by Vincent J. McMahon and Toots Mondt. Initially, the Championship was associated with the NWA. But when WWE was formed in 1963, the Title was defended under the new company's banner.

1963
March 7 • Washington, D.C.
Buddy Austin & The Great Scott def. "Nature Boy" Buddy Rogers & Johnny Barend

May 16 • Washington, D.C.
Skull Murphy & Brute Bernard def. Buddy Austin & The Great Scott

November 14 • Washington, D.C.
Killer Kowalski & Gorilla Monsoon def. Skull Murphy & Brute Bernard

December 28 • Teaneck, N.J.
Chris & John Tolos def. Killer Kowalski & Gorilla Monsoon

1964
February 16 • New Haven, CT
Don McClarity & Vittorio Apollo def. Chris & John Tolos

June 6 • Washington, D.C.
Dr. Jerry & Luke Graham def. Don McClarity & Vittorio Apollo

1965
February 4 • Washington, D.C.
Gene Kiniski & Waldo Von Erich def. Dr. Jerry & Luke Graham

April 6 • Washington, D.C.
Gorilla Monsoon & Cowboy Bill Watts def. Gene Kiniski & Waldo Von Erich

August 7 • Washington, D.C.
Dr. Bill Miller & Dan Miller def. Gorilla Monsoon & Cowboy Bill Watts

1966
February 21 • New York, NY
Antonio Pugliese & Johnny Valentine def. Dr. Bill Miller & Dan Miller

September 22 • Washington, D.C.
Baron Mikel Scicluna & Smasher Sloan def. Antonio Pugliese & Johnny Valentine

December 8 • Washington, D.C.
Spiros Arion & Antonio Pugliese def. Baron Mikel Scicluna & Smasher Sloan
In June 1967, Antonio Pugliese abruptly left the United States; Sprios Arion selected Arnold Skaaland as his new tag team partner to defend the Championship.

1967
July 10 • Atlantic City, N.J.
The Sicilians def. Spiros Arion & Arnold Skaaland

July 24 • Atlantic City, N.J.
Bruno Sammartino & Spiros Arion def. The Sicilians
In late 1967, Bruno Sammartino vacated his half of the championship to concentrate on his WWE Champion title defenses; the United States Tag Team Champion would remain vacant and eventually vanish from WWE.

WWE's Superstars travel the world year-round and wherever they go, the WWE referees follow. From setting up the ring to enforcing the rules (albeit loosely) inside of it, their tireless and under-appreciated work is essential to the action the WWE Universe enjoys. For that reason, anything they say is the law between those ropes. Unless, of course, they are not looking!

CHAD PATTON

CHARLES ROBINSON

DANIEL ENGLER

DARRICK MOORE

JASON AYERS

JOHN CONE

MIKE CHIODA

ROD ZAPATA

RYAN TRAN

SCOTT ARMSTRONG

WWE TAG TEAM CHAMPIONSHIP

Once it was decided by WWE brass in 2002 that the World Tag Team Championship would be exclusive to *Raw*, *SmackDown* General Manager Stephanie McMahon created her own version of the Tag Team Championship. She stated that the first team to wear these prestigious Titles could only do so if they survived a brutal tournament. Since that historic tournament several outstanding tag teams have claimed this prominent Championship including the Dudley Boyz, Los Guerreros, John Morrison and The Miz, Team Hell No, The Usos, and New Day.

In April 2010, it became the only Tag Team Championship available in WWE, making every match contested for it a must-see attraction. Since then, the unlikely combo of Kane and Daniel Bryan (Team Hell No) boasts the longest reign.

2002

October 20 • Little Rock, AR
Kurt Angle & Chris Benoit def. **Edge & Rey Mysterio** in the finals of tournament to crown the first-ever WWE Tag Team Champions

November 7 • Manchester, NH
Edge & Rey Mysterio def. **Kurt Angle & Chris Benoit**

November 17 • New York, NY
Los Guerreros def. **Edge & Rey Mysterio**

2003

February 6 • Philadelphia, PA
The World's Greatest Tag Team def. **Los Guerreros**

May 18 • Charlotte, NC
Eddie Guerrero & Taijiri def. **The World's Greatest Tag Team**

July 3 • Rochester, NY
The World's Greatest Tag Team def. **Eddie Guerrero & Taijiri**

September 18 • Raleigh, NC
Los Guerreros def. **The World's Greatest Tag Team**

October 23 • Albany, NY
The Basham Brothers def. **Los Guerreros**

2004

February 5 • Cleveland, OH
Scotty 2 Hotty & Rikishi def. **The Basham Brothers**

April 22 • Kelowna, BC
Charlie Haas & Rico def. **Scotty 2 Hotty & Rikishi**

June 17 • Chicago, IL
The Dudley Boyz def. **Charlie Haas & Rico**

July 8 • Winnipeg, Manitoba
Billy Kidman & Paul London def. **The Dudley Boyz**

September 9 • Tulsa, OK
Kenzo Suzuki & Rene Dupree def. **Billy Kidman & Paul London**

December 9 • Greenville, SC
Rob Van Dam & Rey Mysterio def. **Kenzo Suzuki & Rene Dupree**

2005

January 13 • Tampa, FL
The Basham Brothers def. **Rob Van Dam & Rey Mysterio**

February 20 • Pittsburgh, PA
Rey Mysterio & Eddie Guerrero def. **The Basham Brothers**

April 21 • New York, NY
MNM def. **Rey Mysterio & Eddie Guerrero**

July 25 • Buffalo, NY
Road Warrior Animal & Heidenreich def. **MNM**

October 28 • San Francisco, CA
MNM def. **Road Warrior Animal & Heidenreich**

December 16 • Springfield, MA
Batista & Rey Mysterio def. **MNM**

December 30 • Uncasville, CT
MNM def. **Batista & Rey Mysterio**

2006

May 21 • Phoenix, AZ
Brian Kendrick & Paul London def. **MNM**

2007

April 20 • Milan, Italy
Deuce & Domino def. **Brian Kendrick & Paul London**

August 31 • Albany, NY
MVP & Matt Hardy def. **Deuce & Domino**

November 16 • Wichita, KS
John Morrison & The Miz def. **MVP & Matt Hardy**

2008

July 20 • Uniondale, NY
Curt Hawkins & Zack Ryder def. **Deuce & Domino**

September 26 • Columbus, OH
Carlito & Primo def. **Curt Hawkins & Zack Ryder**

2009

April 5 • Houston, TX
Carlito & Primo def. **The Miz & John Morrison**
Carlito & Primo unified the World and WWE Tag Team Championships into the Unified Tag Team Title.

June 28 • Sacramento, CA
Edge & Chris Jericho def. **Carlito & Primo**
Big Show teamed up with Chris Jericho when injury forced Edge to vacate his half of the gold.

July 26 • Philadelphia, PA
Chris Jericho & Big Show def. **Ted DiBiase & Cody Rhodes**

December 13 • San Antonio, TX
D-Generation X def. **Chris Jericho & Big Show**

2010

February 8 • Lafayette, LA
The Miz & Big Show def. **D-Generation X**

April 26 • Richmond, VA
The Hart Dynasty def. **Big Show & The Miz**
The Hart Dynasty is recognized as the final World Tag Team Championship team, as the Titles were retired during this reign. They continued to reign as WWE Tag Team Champions.

September 19 • Chicago, IL
Drew McIntrye & Cody Rhodes def. **The Hart Dynasty**

October 24 • Minneapolis, MN
John Cena & David Otunga def. **Drew McIntrye & Cody Rhodes**

October 25 • Green Bay, WI
Justin Gabriel & Heath Slater def. **John Cena & David Otunga**

December 6 • Louisville, KY
Santino Marella & Vladimir Kozlov def. **Justin Gabriel & Heath Slater**

2011

February 20 • Oakland, CA
Justin Gabriel & Heath Slater def. **Santino Marella & Vladimir Kozlov**

February 21 • Fresno, CA
John Cena & The Miz def. **Justin Gabriel & Heath Slater**

February 21 • Fresno, CA
Justin Gabriel & Heath Slater def. **John Cena & The Miz**

April 22 • London, England
Big Show & Kane def. **Justin Gabriel & Heath Slater**

May 23 • Portland, OR
David Otunga & Michael McGillicutty def. **Big Show & Kane**

August 22 • Edmonton, Alberta
Kofi Kingston & Evan Bourne def. **David Otunga & Michael McGillicutty**

2012

January 15 • Oakland, CA
Primo & Epico def. **Kofi Kingston & Evan Bourne**

April 30 • Dayton, OH
Kofi Kingston and R-Truth def. **Primo & Epico**

September 16 • Boston, MA
Team Hell No def. **Kofi Kingston & R-Truth**

2013

May 19 • St. Louis, MO
Seth Rollins and Roman Reigns def. **Team Hell No** in a Tornado Tag Team Match

October 14 • St. Louis, MO
Cody Rhodes and Goldust def. **Seth Rollins and Roman Reigns**

2014

January 26 • Pittsburgh, PA
The New Age Outlaws def. **Cody Rhodes and Goldust**

March 3 • Chicago, IL
The Usos def. **The New Age Outlaws**

September 21 • Nashville, TN
Gold and Stardust def. **The Usos**

November 23 • St. Louis, MO
The Miz & Damien Mizdow won a Fatal 4-Way Match

December 29 • Washington, D.C.
The Usos def. **The Miz and Damien Mizdow**

2015

February 22 • Memphis, TN
Tyson Kidd & Cesaro def. **The Usos**

April 26 • Chicago, IL
New Day def. **Tyson Kidd & Cesaro**

June 14 • Columbus, OH
The Prime Time Players def. **New Day**

August 23 • Brooklyn, NY
New Day won a Fatal 4-Way Match

WWE WOMEN'S CHAMPIONSHIP

Whether vying for the original Women's Championship that was retired in 2010 or the butterfly-themed Divas Championship that took its place, WWE's female competitors have always been among the most talented and dynamic in the world. As a Divas Revolution took WWE by storm, it became clear that current and future generations of women needed a new symbol of excellence to strive for, one befitting their status as athletes, role models, and Superstars.

During the *WrestleMania 32* pre-show, WWE Hall of Famer Lita announced that the night's Triple Threat Match would no longer be contested for the Divas Championship. Instead, the new WWE Women's Championship would be on the line. Lita unveiled the prestigious prize, which was adorned with a regal WWE logo faceplate similar to its male counterpart and greeted with approving cheers from the WWE Universe. It is considered the start of a new lineage of Champions and the catalyst of the fiercest competition between WWE's female Superstars.

2016

April 3, 2016 • Dallas, TX

Charlotte def. **Sasha Banks** and **Becky Lynch**

WWE WORLD HEAVYWEIGHT CHAMPIONSHIP
see page 408

THE WYATT FAMILY

MEMBERS	Bray Wyatt, Luke Harper, Erick Rowan, & Braun Strowman

Things may appear different than they really are, warns Bray Wyatt. In the case of The Wyatt Family, however, they are every bit as disturbing and dangerous as their peculiar appearance would suggest.

After weeks of warnings, The Wyatt Family made their WWE debut in July 2013 when Luke Harper and Erick Rowan attacked Kane, while a sinister Bray watched from his rocking chair. The merciless beating marked the beginning of a long nightmare from which WWE has yet to awaken.

The Wyatt Family unnervingly stalked Kane for weeks before finally laying waste to The Demon at *SummerSlam 2013* when Bray defeated Kane in a Ring of Fire Match.

The Wyatt Family's attention shifted to The Shield in early-2014, resulting in a thrilling series of tag matches. And while history will show The Shield was one of WWE's most impactful factions, The Wyatt Family successfully proved their dominance over them on several occasions, including *Elimination Chamber 2014*.

Also at *Elimination Chamber*, an interfering Bray Wyatt cost John Cena his chance at becoming WWE World Heavyweight Champion. The unwarranted act kicked off a months-long rivalry between Wyatt and Cena that resulted in The Eater of Worlds suffering his first singles loss at *WrestleMania 30*. Bray later gained a level of retribution when he used assistance from his followers, as well as a mysterious singing child, to defeat Cena in a Steel Cage Match at *Extreme Rules*.

Wyatt set his disciples free later that year. The separation was only temporary, as The Wyatt Family reunited in the summer of 2015. This time they welcomed a fourth member, Braun Strowman. Known as the "Black Sheep" and standing at a monstrous six-foot-eight, Strowman adds a frightening level of strength to the already fearsome Family.

After falling to Undertaker and Kane at *Survivor Series 2015*, The Wyatt Family reestablished themselves as true monsters in 2016. In addition to defeating the Dudleys, the Wyatt-led clan delivered savage beatings to Roman Reigns and Brock Lesnar. They even eliminated Lesnar from the 2016 Royal Rumble Match.

Hell-bent on delivering their twisted message, The Wyatt Family continually confound all with their eerie words, while also offering succinct and sage advice—Run!

WWE WORLD HEAVYWEIGHT CHAMPIONSHIP

Widely recognized as the top prize in all of sports-entertainment, the WWE World Heavyweight Championship's historic existence can be traced back to April 29, 1963, when Buddy Rogers defeated Antonino Rocca in the finals of a tournament to crown the first-ever Titleholder.

Many memorable reigns atop WWE followed Rogers' inaugural tour of duty, but none as lengthy as Bruno Sammartino's first Championship run. Sammartino defeated Rogers on May 17, 1963, and went on to hold the gold until January 18, 1971, when he was finally upended by Ivan Koloff. Sammartino's reign of nearly eight years is a record many sports-entertainment insiders believe will never be broken.

The Championship reached iconic levels in January 1984 when Hulk Hogan won it from the reviled Iron Sheik, initiating the era of Hulkamania and a golden period for WWE. In the years that followed, such great names as Ric Flair, Ultimate Warrior, Bret Hart, and Shawn Michaels achieved their dreams and ascended to WWE's most elite fraternity. In March 1998, the defiant Stone Cold Steve Austin captured the WWE Championship and brought the Title to heights once thought unimaginable.

Stone Cold's bitter rivalry with The Rock upheld the Title's remarkable reputation. The Rock, Triple H, and later, Randy Orton, became synonymous with the cherished prized. Each experienced eight separate reigns with its glistening presence draped over his shoulder. Then at *Royal Rumble 2016*, Triple H reached the mountaintop for the ninth time.

Among all these revered icons of WWE lore, however, only one man carries the nickname "The Champ." Since he first unseated JBL at *WrestleMania 21*, John Cena has etched his name on this prestigious list an incredible twelve times. In December of 2013, Cena held the classic World Heavyweight Championship, an NWA-born honor that had been carried forward in WWE. At *TLC 2013*, reigning WWE Champion Randy Orton defeated Cena in a monumental unification match. The result was the newly minted WWE World Heavyweight Championship. This Title, contested for by today's top Superstars, merges the legacies of sports-entertainment's two most time-honored Championships and carries forward the lineage first established by Buddy Rogers in 1963.

1963

April 25 • Rio de Janeiro
Buddy Rogers def. **Antonino Rocca** in the finals of a tournament to be crowned the first-ever WWE Champion

May 17 • New York, NY
Bruno Sammartino def. **Buddy Rogers**

1971

January 18 • New York, NY
Ivan Koloff def. **Bruno Sammartino**

February 8 • New York, NY
Pedro Morales def. **Ivan Koloff**

1973

December 1 • Philadelphia, PA
Stan Stasiak def. **Pedro Morales**

December 10 • New York, NY
Bruno Sammartino def. **Stan Stasiak**

1977

April 30 • Baltimore, MD
Superstar Billy Graham def. **Bruno Sammartino**

1978

February 20 • New York, NY
Bob Backlund def. **Superstar Billy Graham**

1983

December 26 • New York, NY
The Iron Sheik def. **Bob Backlund**

1984

January 23 • New York, NY
Hulk Hogan def. **The Iron Sheik**

1988

February 5 • Indianapolis, IN
Andre the Giant def. **Hulk Hogan**
WWE President Jack Tunney vacated the title after learning Ted DiBiase had paid a corrupt referee to have plastic surgery in order to look like the official referee assigned to the match.

March 27 • Atlantic City, NJ
Randy Savage def. **Ted DiBiase** in the finals of a 14-man tournament to crown a new WWE Champion

1989

April 2 • Atlantic City, NJ
Hulk Hogan def. **Randy Savage**

1990

April 1 • Toronto, Ontario
Ultimate Warrior def. **Hulk Hogan**

1991

January 19 • Miami, FL
Sgt. Slaughter def. **Ultimate Warrior**

March 24 • Los Angeles, CA
Hulk Hogan def. **Sgt. Slaughter**

November 27 • Detroit, MI
Undertaker def. **Hulk Hogan**

December 3 • San Antonio, TX
Hulk Hogan def. **Undertaker**
WWE President Jack Tunney vacated the title due to controversy surrounding Hulk Hogan's victory over Undertaker.

1992

January 19 • Albany, NY
Ric Flair last eliminated **Sid Justice** to win the Royal Rumble and the WWE Championship

April 5 • Indianapolis, IN
Randy Savage def. **Ric Flair**

September 1 • Hershey, PA
Ric Flair def. **Randy Savage**

October 12 • Saskatoon, Saskatchewan
Bret Hart def. **Ric Flair**

1993

April 4 • Las Vegas, NV
Yokozuna def. **Bret Hart**

April 4 • Las Vegas, NV
Hulk Hogan def. **Yokozuna**

June 13 • Dayton, OH
Yokozuna def. **Hulk Hogan**

1994

March 20 • New York, NY
Bret Hart def. **Yokozuna**

November 23 • San Antonio, TX
Bob Backlund def. **Bret Hart**

November 26 • New York, NY
Diesel def. **Bob Backlund**

November 19 • Landover, MD
Bret Hart def. **Diesel**

March 31 • Anaheim, CA
Shawn Michaels def. **Bret Hart**

November 17 • New York, NY
Sid def. **Shawn Michaels**

January 19 • San Antonio, TX
Shawn Michaels def. **Sid**
Injuries forced Shawn Michaels to vacate the title shortly after his victory.

February 16 • Chattanooga, TN
Bret Hart last eliminated **Undertaker** in a Fatal Four-Way Match that also included **Vader** and **Stone Cold Steve Austin**

February 17 • Nashville, TN
Sid def. **Bret Hart**

March 23 • Chicago, IL
Undertaker def. **Sid**

August 3 • East Rutherford, NJ
Bret Hart def. **Undertaker**

November 9 • Montreal, Quebec
Shawn Michaels def. **Bret Hart**

March 29 • Boston, MA
Stone Cold Steve Austin def. **Shawn Michaels**

June 28 • Pittsburgh, PA
Kane def. **Stone Cold Steve Austin**

June 29 • Cleveland, OH
Stone Cold Steve Austin def. **Kane**
Mr. McMahon vacated the title in September, 1998 after a controversial ending to a Triple Threat Match featuring Stone Cold Steve Austin, Undertaker, and Kane.

November 15 • St. Louis, MO
The Rock def. **Mankind** in the finals of a 14-man tournament to crown a new WWE Champion

January 4 • Worcester, MA
Mankind def. **The Rock**

January 24 • Anaheim, CA
The Rock def. **Mankind**

January 31 • Tucson, AZ
Mankind def. **The Rock**

February 15 • Birmingham, AL
The Rock def. **Mankind**

March 28 • Philadelphia, PA
Stone Cold Steve Austin def. **The Rock**

May 23 • Kansas City, MO
Undertaker def. **Stone Cold Steve Austin**

June 28 • Charlotte, NC
Stone Cold Steve Austin def. **Undertaker**

August 22 • Minneapolis, MN
Mankind def. **Stone Cold Steve Austin** in a Triple Threat Match that also included **Triple H**

August 23 • Ames, IA
Triple H def. **Mankind**

September 16 • Las Vegas, NV
Mr. McMahon def. **Triple H**
Mr. McMahon vacates the Title in September, 1999.

September 26 • Charlotte, NC
Triple H def. **The Rock** in a Six-Pack Challenge Match that also included **Mankind, British Bulldog, Big Show,** and **Kane**

November 14 • Detroit, MI
Big Show def. **Triple H** in a Triple Threat Match that also included **The Rock**

January 3 • Miami, FL
Triple H def. **Big Show**

April 30 • Washington, DC
The Rock def. **Triple H**

May 21 • Louisville, KY
Triple H def. **The Rock**

June 25 • Boston, MA
The Rock becomes WWE Champion
The Rock, Undertaker & Kane met Triple H, Shane McMahon & Mr. McMahon in a six-man tag team match with a pre-match stipulation which stated that if anybody on Triple H's team lost, he would lose the WWE Championship; The Rock pinned Mr. McMahon to win the Title.

October 22 • Albany, NY
Kurt Angle def. **The Rock**

February 25 • Las Vegas, NV
The Rock def. **Kurt Angle**

April 1 • Houston, TX
Stone Cold Steve Austin def. **The Rock**

September 23 • Pittsburgh, PA
Kurt Angle def. **Stone Cold Steve Austin**

October 8 • Indianapolis, IN
Stone Cold Steve Austin def. **Kurt Angle**

December 9 • San Diego, CA
Chris Jericho def. **Stone Cold Steve Austin**

March 17 • Toronto, Ontario
Triple H def. **Chris Jericho**

April 21 • Kansas City, MO
Hulk Hogan def. **Triple H**

May 19 • Nashville, TN
Undertaker def. **Hulk Hogan**

July 21 • Detroit, MI
The Rock def. **Kurt Angle** and **Undertaker** in a Triple Threat Match

August 25 • Uniondale, NY
Brock Lesnar def. **The Rock**

November 17 • New York, NY
Big Show def. **Brock Lesnar**

December 15 • Fort Lauderdale, FL
Kurt Angle def. **Big Show**

March 30 • Seattle, WA
Brock Lesnar def. **Kurt Angle**

July 27 • Denver, CO
Kurt Angle def. **Brock Lesnar** and **Big Show** in a Triple Threat Match

September 18 • Raleigh, NC
Brock Lesnar def. **Kurt Angle**

2004

February 15 • San Francisco, CA
Eddie Guerrero def. **Brock Lesnar**

June 27 • Norfolk, VA
JBL def. **Eddie Guerrero**

2005

April 3 • Los Angeles, CA
John Cena def. **JBL**

2006

January 8 • Albany, NY
Edge def. **John Cena**

January 29 • Miami, FL
John Cena def. **Edge**

June 11 • New York, NY
Rob Van Dam def. **John Cena**

July 3 • Philadelphia, PA
Edge def. **Rob Van Dam** and **John Cena** in a Triple Threat Match

September 17 • Toronto, Ontario
John Cena def. **Edge**
Injuries forced John Cena to vacate the Championship.

2007

October 7 • Chicago, IL
Randy Orton is awarded the WWE Championship

October 7 • Chicago, IL
Triple H def. **Randy Orton**

October 7 • Chicago, IL
Randy Orton def. **Triple H**

2008

April 27 • Baltimore, MD
Triple H def. **Randy Orton, John Cena** and **JBL** in a Fatal 4-Way Match

November 23 • Boston, MA
Edge def. **Triple H**

December 14 • Buffalo, NY
Jeff Hardy def. **Edge**

2009

January 25 • Detroit, MI
Edge def. **Jeff Hardy**

February 15 • Seattle, WA
Triple H last eliminated **Undertaker** in an Elimination Chamber Match that also included **Jeff Hardy, Big Show, Vladimir Kozlov,** def. **WWE Champion Edge**

April 26 • Providence, RI
Randy Orton def. **Triple H**

June 7 • New Orleans, LA
Batista def. **Randy Orton**
Injuries forced Batista to vacate the title shortly after winning it.

June 15 • Charlotte, NC
Randy Orton def. **Triple H, John Cena** and **Big Show** in a Fatal 4-Way Match

September 13 • Montreal, Quebec
John Cena def. **Randy Orton**

October 4 • Newark, NJ
Randy Orton def. **John Cena**

October 25 • Pittsburgh, PA
John Cena def. **Randy Orton**

December 13 • San Antonio, TX
Sheamus def. **John Cena**

2010

February 21 • St. Louis, MO
John Cena def. **Sheamus**

February 21 • St. Louis, MO
Batista def. **John Cena**

March 28 • Phoenix, AZ
John Cena def. **Batista**

June 20 • Uniondale, NY
Sheamus def. **John Cena, Randy Orton** and **Edge** in a Fatal 4-Way Match

September 19 • Chicago, IL
Randy Orton def. **Sheamus**

November 22 • Orlando, FL
The Miz def. **Randy Orton**

2011

May 1 • Tampa, FL
John Cena def. **The Miz**

July 17 • Chicago, IL
CM Punk def. **John Cena**
CM Punk's WWE contract expired shortly after winning the title, so a tournament was held to determine a new champion.

July 25 • Hampton, VA
Rey Mysterio def. **The Miz** in the finals of the tournament

July 25 • Hampton, VA
CM Punk def. **John Cena** in a WWE Championship Unification Match at SummerSlam on August 14, 2011

August 14 • Los Angeles, CA
Alberto Del Rio def. **CM Punk**

September 18 • Buffalo, NY
John Cena def. **Alberto Del Rio**

October 2 • New Orleans, LA
Alberto Del Rio def. **CM Punk** and **John Cena** in a Triple Threat Hell In A Cell Match

November 20 • New York, NY
CM Punk def. **Alberto Del Rio**

2013

January 27 • Phoenix, AZ
The Rock def. **CM Punk**

April 7 • East Rutherford, NJ
John Cena def. **The Rock**

August 18 • Los Angeles, CA
Daniel Bryan def. **John Cena**

August 18 • Los Angeles, CA
Randy Orton cashed in Money in the Bank to defeat **Daniel Bryan**

September 15 • Detroit, MI
Daniel Bryan def. **Randy Orton**. However, the Title was held in abeyance the following day amidst controversy.

October 27 • Miami, FL
Randy Orton def. **Daniel Bryan** in a Hell in a Cell Match
On December 15, Randy Orton became the inaugural WWE World Heavyweight Champion, merging the World Heavyweight and WWE Championships.

2014

April 6 • New Orleans, LA
Daniel Bryan def. **Randy Orton** and **Batista** in a Triple Threat Match

June 29 • Boston, MA
John Cena def. seven other Superstars in a Ladder Match to win the vacated Championship

August 17 • Los Angeles, CA
Brock Lesnar def. **John Cena**

2015

March 29 • Santa Clara, CA
Seth Rollins cashed in Money in the Bank to create and win a Triple Threat Match against **Brock Lesnar** and **Roman Reigns**

November 22 • Atlanta, GA
Roman Reigns def. **Dean Ambrose** in the finals of a 16-Man tournament to win the vacated Championship

November 22 • Atlanta, GA
Sheamus def. **Roman Reigns**

December 14 • Philadelphia, PA
Roman Reigns def. **Sheamus**

2016

January 24 • Orlando, FL
Triple H won the Royal Rumble Match over **Roman Reigns** and 28 other Superstars

April 3 • Dallas, TX
Roman Reigns def. **Triple H** to win the Championship

XANTA CLAUS

| HT | 6'2" | WT | 305 lbs. | FROM | The South Pole |
| SIGNATURE MOVE | Nutcracker Suite |

During the December 1995 *In Your House* pay-per-view it appeared that Santa Claus was giving gifts to young fans with the help of Savio Vega. The "Million Dollar Man" Ted DiBiase then appeared and disparaged both Santa and his helper. Just as his verbal exchange with Vega ended, the Million Dollar Man's twisted sense of holiday gift giving presented itself. Suddenly, Santa attacked Savio Vega in front of the capacity crowd.

Thanks to Jim Ross, audiences soon learned that this individual claimed to be Santa's twin brother "Xanta Claus." He hailed from the South Pole, stole presents from good children and used underhanded maneuvers to put away opponents. While Xanta Claus had a brief tenure in WWE history, his despicable actions made a lasting impression.

XAVIER WOODS

| HT | 5'11" | WT | 205 lbs. | FROM | Atlanta, Georgia |
| SIGNATURE MOVE | Honor Roll, Lost in the Woods |

Few competitors have as much fun being a WWE Superstar as Xavier Woods. Packed with positivity, the accomplished athlete oftentimes walks to the ring playing "Francesca," his signature trombone, which can't help but make partners Kofi Kingston and Big E smile. Heck, even the WWE Universe grins when Woods starts belting out his melodic tunes, even if they think, "New Day Sucks."

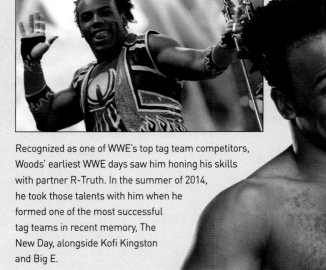

Recognized as one of WWE's top tag team competitors, Woods' earliest WWE days saw him honing his skills with partner R-Truth. In the summer of 2014, he took those talents with him when he formed one of the most successful tag teams in recent memory, The New Day, alongside Kofi Kingston and Big E.

The overly-positive trio proved their dominance by claiming the WWE Tag Team Championship from Tyson Kidd and Cesaro at *Extreme Rules 2014*. Proving the victory was no fluke, The New Day once again became Champs when they won a Fatal 4-Way Match at *SummerSlam* that same year. Competing under "Freebird Rules," Woods, Kingston, and Big E turned back some of the greatest tandems of all time, including The Dudleys.

Outside the ring, Woods is an accomplished video gamer. As host of his own video game channel on YouTube, "UpUpDownDown," Woods creates daily programming that focuses on the world of gaming. Along the way, he's joined by WWE Superstars, YouTube celebrities, and video game editors.

X-FACTOR

| MEMBERS | X-Pac, Albert, & Justin Credible | COMBINED WT | 775 lbs. |

X-Factor is a historically underrated faction that compiled an astonishing four championship reigns during its brief eight-month union.

The leader of the group, X-Pac, enjoyed two Light Heavyweight Championship reigns before unifying the Title with the Cruiserweight Championship in July 2001. Albert attained the group's greatest success when he used his patented Baldo Bomb to defeat Kane for the Intercontinental Championship in June 2001. Finally, the faction's most extreme Superstar, Justin Credible, was a perennial contender for the Hardcore Championship, which he eventually captured eight times after X-Factor split up.

Together, X-Factor's biggest victory came when they defeated Bubba Ray, D-Von, and Spike Dudley at *Backlash 2001*. The faction began to slowly crumble after Credible left X-Pac and Albert to join forces with the WCW/ECW Alliance.

X-PAC

see page 411

YOKOZUNA

see page 412

YOSHI TATSU

| HT | 6'1" | WT | 211 lbs. | FROM | Tokyo, Japan |
| SIGNATURE MOVE | Buzzsaw Kick |

Behind an arsenal of high-impact kicks, Yoshi Tatsu immediately became one of sports-entertainment's most exciting Superstars upon making his debut in ECW in June 2009. During his tenure in ECW, the man from the "Land of the Rising Sun" successfully turned back many of the brand's top stars, including Shelton Benjamin, Jack Swagger, and William Regal.

When ECW ceased operations in February 2010, the Japanese Superstar signed with *Raw*. He soon prevailed in the 26-Man Battle Royal to kick off *WrestleMania XXVI*.

Tatsu continued to use his educated feet to outsmart the likes of Zack Ryder and Primo. He later served as Byron Saxton's Pro on *NXT* season five. Under Tatsu's tutelage, Saxton lasted until Week 13 until finally being eliminated. Despite Saxton's ousting, Tatsu stuck around *NXT* to battle Tyson Kidd in a thrilling rivalry that culminated with a Necklace on a Pole Match, which Tatsu won.

At *WrestleMania 30*, Tatsu competed in the Andre the Giant Memorial Battle Royal but this time did not outlast his competition. Two months later, he left WWE.

X-PAC

HT	6'1"	WT	212 lbs.	FROM	Minneapolis, Minnesota
SIGNATURE MOVE		1-2-3 Kick			

When he made his WWE debut in 1993, the electrifying performer billed as "The Kid" seemed to come out of nowhere. In reality, he'd been trained by mat masters like Karl Gotch and Professor Boris Malenko and, as the Lightning Kid, had been setting the indie scene ablaze.

During his first match on *Raw*, The Kid shocked the world by beating the much larger and established Razor Ramon. Renamed the 1-2-3 Kid, he teamed with Marty Jannetty to win the WWE World Tag Team Championship. Sadly, WWE's shy hero soon took a new career direction as a member of Ted DiBiase's Million Dollar Corporation.

In late 1996 the 1-2-3 Kid left WWE and stunned audiences when he appeared in the front row of an episode of *WCW Monday Nitro*, calling himself Syxx. In March 1998, his contract was suddenly terminated, but he didn't idle for long. During an episode of *Raw*, Triple H introduced the latest recruit to DX, X-Pac. Though Triple H later turned on him, causing a split within DX, X-Pac would eventually rejoin the group.

Away from DX, X-Pac also had a vibrant WWE career, Partnering with Kane, he won the World Tag Team Championship. And in 2001, he formed the short-lived X-Factor with Justin Credible and Albert.

After the dissolution of WCW, some of its competitors came to WWE and defended their titles. During this period, X-Pac was the only Superstar to wear both the WCW Cruiserweight and WWE Light Heavyweight Championships at the same time.

After a long sabbatical, he made a surprising return to WWE in April 2011 at the end of Shawn Michaels' WWE Hall of Fame induction speech, along with other Kliq members Triple H and Kevin Nash. In 2014 the band came back together, this time as Michaels, Nash, and X-Pac gathered to support Razor Ramon's Hall of Fame induction. The next year, at *WrestleMania 31*, X-Pac was on the grandest stage of all, accompanying fellow DXers Billy Gunn and Road Dogg to back Triple H in his historic battle with Sting.

THE YOUNG STALLIONS

MEMBERS	Paul Roma & Jim Powers	COMBINED WT	481 lbs.

No strangers to WWE audiences, these two former single's competitors joined forces in the late 1980s. As a cohesive unit, Roma and Powers were an exciting and telegenic combination during one of the greatest eras of tag team competition. They battled the Hart Foundation over the rights to the theme song, "Crank It Up," when Jimmy Hart claimed that the tune was intended for his men.

The shining moment for the Young Stallions came at the 1987 *Survivor Series* when, along with the Killer Bees, they were the sole survivors in the tag team elimination match. They also appeared in the 20-Man Over the Top Rope Battle Royal at *WrestleMania IV* before taking on top teams like the Brain Busters, Fabulous Rougeaus, and Twin Towers.

Unfortunately for their fans, mounting losses turned frustration into fighting and the Stallions fell apart. Paul Roma became a member of Power and Glory, while Jim Powers returned to single's action.

THE YUKON LUMBERJACKS

MEMBERS	Eric & Pierre	
COMBINED WT	551 lbs.	FROM	The Yukon

Managed by Capt. Lou Albano, the Yukon Lumberjacks spent a brief, but successful, time competing in WWE. Eric and Pierre made their WWE debut in 1978. Shortly after their initial appearance, the bearded duo defeated the legendary Dominic DeNucci and Dino Bravo in New York City to capture the World Tag Team Championship. Behind Eric's devastating big boot and Pierre's Cobra Clutch, the Yukon Lumberjacks sawed through all challengers before finally losing the Titles to Tony Garea and Larry Zbyszko in November 1978.

The Yukon Lumberjacks split up shortly after losing the World Tag Team Championship. Eric went on to compete for various southern United States promotions, while Pierre achieved most of his notoriety competing in Canada.

ZACH GOWEN

HT	6'1"	WT	169 lbs.	FROM	Flint, Michigan
SIGNATURE MOVE		Unisault			

When Zach Gowen was eight years old he lost his left leg to cancer, but the lifelong WWE fan did not let this stop him from pursuing his dream. In May 2003, Zach appeared on *SmackDown* supporting Mr. America.

Zach spent a year in WWE fending off Big Show, Brock Lesnar, and the manipulative Mr. McMahon. Zach stood up to the diabolical Chairman on several occasions, even facing him in a match at *Vengeance 2003*. At *No Mercy 2003*, Zach scored his most high profile victory, defeating Matt Hardy with a moonsault. In early 2004, Zach and WWE parted ways, but his brief tenure remains an inspiration.

YOKOZUNA

HT	6'4"
WT	600 lbs.
FROM	The Land of the Rising Sun
SIGNATURE MOVE	
Bonzai Drop	

When Yokozuna first entered a WWE ring in October 1992, every Superstar was forced to take notice of the massive newcomer. A mountain of a man, he used his unbelievable size to compress his foes. To make matters worse, Yokozuna complemented his enormous frame with an amazing agility rarely found in big men.

He also had a genetic advantage. As a member of the Anoa'i clan, Yokozuna counted among his relatives Wild Samoans Afa and Sika, Rikishi, Samu, Rosey, Umaga, High Chief Peter Maivia, and his grandson, The Rock—not to mention future stars Jimmy and Jey Uso and Roman Reigns.

Despite his Polynesian heritage, Yokozuna was known in Japan for his sumo exploits. In fact, the term "Yokozuna" means sumo grand champion.

In WWE, his impact was immediate. Shortly after his debut, the Superstar muscled his way to main event status when he eliminated Randy Savage to win the 1993 *Royal Rumble*. The victory earned Yokozuna the opportunity at Bret "Hit Man" Hart's WWE World Heavyweight Championship at *WrestleMania IX*.

WEARING GOLD

The size differential notwithstanding, Yokozuna knew that he'd have to keep up with the man known as the "Excellence of Execution," and rose to the task. In the end, though, he needed his crafty manager Mr. Fuji's assistance to score the victory.

As Hart tied up Yokozuna's bulky legs in the Sharpshooter, Fuji tossed a handful of salt in the Champion's eyes. Unable to see, the Hit Man quickly fell victim to Yokozuna's perilous Bonzai Drop from the second rope.

Unfortunately for Yokozuna, his reign was one of the shortest of all time. Irate over the unsportsmanlike tactics, Hulk Hogan rushed to the ring to complain to the referee. Overcome with zeal, Fuji challenged the Hulkster to a Championship match on the spot. Once the bell rang, the manager tried the same strategy that worked with Hart, hurling salt at Hogan. But the Hulkster avoided the blitz and Yokozuna was blinded instead. As a result, it was Hogan who left *WrestleMania IX* with WWE gold.

Yokozuna was able to avenge his loss when he toppled "The Hulkster" to regain the WWE Championship at the *1993 King of the Ring*. This time, Yokozuna kept a firm grasp on the gold for an amazing 280 days.

In addition to his dominance as a single's competitor, Yokozuna also found success in the tag team ranks. With "The Rocket" Owen Hart as his partner, Yokozuna enjoyed two reigns atop the WWE tag team division.

A DIFFERENT YOKOZUNA

Prior to leaving WWE, the mighty Yokozuna was able to endear himself to the fans when he finally broke free from the chains of manager Jim Cornette. Serving as Yokozuna's American spokesperson, Cornette forbade the big man from speaking for himself. However, in early 1996 Yokozuna, communicating in English for the first time, declared he would no longer be held down by Cornette. The WWE Universe immediately began to show appreciation for the former WWE Champion. For the first time in his career, Yokozuna heard cheers from the crowd while delivering his Bonzai Drop.

Behind the scenes, Yokozuna was always a friendly presence, happy to be among his brothers, but in October 2000, he sadly passed away at 34.

Nearly twelve years later, Yokozuna was inducted into the WWE Hall of Fame in a touching ceremony involving his close-knit, extended family.

AMERICAN ATHLETES ARE JUST LIKE AMERICAN PRODUCTS. THEY ARE NO GOOD. BANZAI!

ZACK RYDER

HT	6'2"	WT	224 lbs.
FROM	Long Island, New York		
SIGNATURE MOVE	Rough Ryder		

In WWE, the spotlight will not seize you. You must seize it. No one knows this better than Zack Ryder. Overlooked for much of his career, the spiked-hair Superstar took to YouTube in 2011 to display his wildly charismatic side. In a matter of weeks, Ryder's *Z! True Long Island Story* web show caused an unforeseeable groundswell of support. It wasn't long before "We want Ryder" chants and pro-Ryder signs began to overwhelm arenas.

Thanks to his powerful grassroots efforts, the former Tag Team Champion became a breakout Superstar. The self-proclaimed WWE Internet Champion had fans fist-pumping along as he was thrust into more high stakes competition. He even had Hollywood heavyweight Hugh Jackman in his corner for a match. Ryder's work ethic earned him an endorsement from John Cena and a United States Championship opportunity. At *TLC 2011*, the 21st Century Superstar capitalized by beating Dolph Ziggler for his first singles Title.

Even *Sports Illustrated* took notice of WWE's resident "Broski," naming @ZackRyder one of the most influential Twitter accounts in all of sports in 2011. Though his Title reign lasted only a month, Ryder's ambitious and innovative journey is one of the most memorable in the history of the U.S gold.

In 2015, Ryder formed The Hype Bros. with NXT's Mojo Rawley. Together, the duo turned up the tempo in the NXT tag team ranks. Zack was considered a dark horse heading into a 7-Man Intercontinental Championship Ladder Match at *WrestleMania 32*. In front of the largest ever audience for a WWE event, Ryder climbed past the competition to grab the prize. Following the match, an emotional Zack proclaimed it the best night of his life.

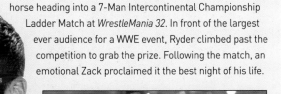

ZEB COLTER

HT	6'0"	WT	225 lbs.	FROM	Nashville, Tennessee

A proud Vietnam veteran, Zeb Colter arrived in WWE in February 2013 to help guide the career of Jack Swagger. Along the way, he has continually spewed his passionate views on such controversial issues as freedom of speech and immigration.

Among Colter's biggest targets was the supposed "illegal" Alberto Del Rio. In April 2013, Colter led Swagger into battle against then-World Heavyweight Champion Del Rio at *WrestleMania 29*. Unfortunately for Colter, Del Rio successfully defused any threats of "Jack Swagger's America" taking over.

Colter later paired Swagger with Cesaro to form the Real Americans tag team. Together, they bested such tandems as Cody Rhodes and Goldust and Los Matadores (or Los Illegals, as Colter called them).

After a nearly-yearlong hiatus, Colter shocked the WWE Universe when he returned alongside former foe Del Rio. Together, the duo claimed to create a proud MexAmerica, which is a far cry from Colter's original message, proving that you can never trust the manager's radical views.

ZEUS

HT	6'5"	WT	300 lbs.	FROM	Parts Unknown

During the filming of the movie, *No Holds Barred*, reports spread that tensions were high on the set between Hulk Hogan and the man known as "The Human Wrecking Machine," Zeus. In the spring of 1989, Zeus suddenly appeared in WWE with manager Slick, and attacked Hulk Hogan before his steel cage Match with Big Boss Man. Zeus claimed that he was the real star of *No Holds Barred*, and pledged to destroy Hulk Hogan.

Zeus continued to stalk Hogan in arenas around North America and joined forces with Randy Savage. At *SummerSlam 1989*, they challenged the team of Hogan and Brutus "The Barber" Beefcake. The battle didn't end there as the four men brought others into the fray at that November's *Survivor Series*. Zeus made his last appearance with WWE in December, 1989 in a clash called "No Holds Barred: The Match."

Months later, Zeus appeared in Puerto Rico, and later in WCW as Z-Gangsta. Today, the man once known as Zeus can be seen in movies and television programs.